PRAISE FOR PREVIOUS EDITIONS OF *A PRACTICAL GUIDE TO FEDORA™ AND RED HAT® ENTERPRISE LINUX®*

"Since I'm in an educational environment, I found the content of Sobell's book to be right on target and very helpful for anyone managing Linux in the enterprise. His style of writing is very clear. He builds up to the chapter exercises, which I find to be relevant to real-world scenarios a user or admin would encounter. An IT/IS student would find this book a valuable complement to their education. The vast amount of information is extremely well balanced and Sobell manages to present the content without complicated asides and meandering prose. This is a 'must have' for anyone managing Linux systems in a networked environment or anyone running a Linux server. I would also highly recommend it to an experienced computer user who is moving to the Linux platform."

> —*Mary Norbury*
> *IT Director*
> *Barbara Davis Center*
> *University of Colorado at Denver*
> *from a review posted on slashdot.org*

"I had the chance to use your UNIX books when I when was in college years ago at Cal Poly, San Luis Obispo, CA. I have to say that your books are among the best! They're quality books that teach the theoretical aspects and applications of the operating system."

> —*Benton Chan*
> *IS Engineer*

"The book has more than lived up to my expectations from the many reviews I read, even though it targets FC2. I have found something very rare with your book: It doesn't read like the standard technical text, it reads more like a story. It's a pleasure to read and hard to put down. Did I say that?! :-)"

> —*David Hopkins*
> *Business Process Architect*

"Thanks for your work and for the book you wrote. There are really few books that can help people to become more efficient administrators of different workstations. We hope (in Russia) that you will continue bringing us a new level of understanding of Linux/UNIX systems."

> —*Anton Petukhov*

PRAISE FOR OTHER BOOKS BY MARK G. SOBELL

"This book is a very useful tool for anyone who wants to 'look under the hood' so to speak, and really start putting the power of Linux to work. What I find particularly frustrating about man pages is that they never include examples. Sobell, on the other hand, outlines very clearly what the command does and then gives several common, easy-to-understand examples that make it a breeze to start shell programming on one's own. As with Sobell's other works, this is simple, straightforward, and easy to read. It's a great book and will stay on the shelf at easy arm's reach for a long time."

—Ray Bartlett
Travel Writer

"Overall I found this book to be quite excellent, and it has earned a spot on the very front of my bookshelf. It covers the real 'guts' of Linux— the command line and its utilities—and does so very well. Its strongest points are the outstanding use of examples, and the Command Reference section. Highly recommended for Linux users of all skill levels. Well done to Mark Sobell and Prentice Hall for this outstanding book!"

—Dan Clough
Electronics Engineer and
Slackware Linux User

"Totally unlike most Linux books, this book avoids discussing everything via GUI and jumps right into making the power of the command line your friend."

—Bjorn Tipling
Software Engineer
ask.com

"This book is the best distro-agnostic, foundational Linux reference I've ever seen, out of dozens of Linux-related books I've read. Finding this book was a real stroke of luck. If you want to really understand how to get things done at the command line, where the power and flexibility of free UNIX-like OSes really live, this book is among the best tools you'll find toward that end."

—Chad Perrin
Writer, TechRepublic

"I currently own one of your books, *A Practical Guide to Linux®*. I believe this book is one of the most comprehensive and, as the title says, practical guides to Linux I have ever read. I consider myself a novice and I come back to this book over and over again."

—*Albert J. Nguyen*

"Thank you for writing a book to help me get away from Windows XP and to never touch Windows Vista. The book is great; I am learning a lot of new concepts and commands. Linux is definitely getting easier to use."

—*James Moritz*

"I am so impressed by how Mark Sobell can approach a complex topic in such an understandable manner. His command examples are especially useful in providing a novice (or even an advanced) administrator with a cookbook on how to accomplish real-world tasks on Linux. He is truly an inspired technical writer!"

—*George Vish II*
Senior Education Consultant
Hewlett-Packard Company

"Overall, I think it's a great, comprehensive Ubuntu book that'll be a valuable resource for people of all technical levels."

—*John Dong*
Ubuntu Forum Council Member
Backports Team Leader

"The JumpStart sections really offer a quick way to get things up and running, allowing you to dig into the details of the book later."

—*Scott Mann*
Aztek Networks

"I would so love to be able to use this book to teach a class about not just Ubuntu or Linux but about computers in general. It is thorough and well written with good illustrations that explain important concepts for computer usage."

—*Nathan Eckenrode*
New York Local Community Team

"Ubuntu is gaining popularity at the rate alcohol did during Prohibition, and it's great to see a well-known author write a book on the latest and greatest version. Not only does it contain Ubuntu-specific information, but it also touches on general computer-related topics, which will help the average computer user to better understand what's going on in the background. Great work, Mark!"

—*Daniel R. Arfsten*
Pro/ENGINEER Drafter/Designer

"I read a lot of Linux technical information every day, but I'm rarely impressed by tech books. I usually prefer online information sources instead. Mark Sobell's books are a notable exception. They're clearly written, technically accurate, comprehensive, and actually enjoyable to read."

—*Matthew Miller*
Senior Systems Analyst/Administrator
BU Linux Project
Boston University Office
of Information Technology

"This is well written, clear, comprehensive information for the Linux user of any type, whether trying Ubuntu on for the first time and wanting to know a little about it, or using the book as a very good reference when doing something more complicated like setting up a server. This book's value goes well beyond its purchase price and it'll make a great addition to the Linux section of your bookshelf."

—*Linc Fessenden*
Host of The LinuxLink TechShow
tllts.org

"The author has done a very good job at clarifying such a detail-oriented operating system. I have extensive Unix and Windows experience and this text does an excellent job at bridging the gaps between Linux, Windows, and Unix. I highly recommend this book to both 'newbs' and experienced users. Great job!"

—*Mark Polczynski*
Information Technology Consultant

"When I first started working with Linux just a short 10 years or so ago, it was a little more difficult than now to get going. . . . Now, someone new to the community has a vast array of resources available on the web, or if they are inclined to begin with Ubuntu, they can literally find almost every single thing they will need in the single volume of Mark Sobell's *A Practical Guide to Ubuntu Linux®*.

"I'm sure this sounds a bit like hyperbole. Everything a person would need to know? Obviously not everything, but this book, weighing in at just under 1200 pages, covers so much so thoroughly that there won't be much left out. From install to admin, networking, security, shell scripting, package management, and a host of other topics, it is all there. GUI and command line tools are covered. There is not really any wasted space or fluff, just a huge amount of information. There are screen shots when appropriate but they do not take up an inordinate amount of space. This book is information-dense."

—*JR Peck*
Editor
GeekBook.org

"I have been wanting to make the jump to Linux but did not have the guts to do so—until I saw your familiarly titled *A Practical Guide to Red Hat® Linux®* at the bookstore. I picked up a copy and am eagerly looking forward to regaining my freedom."

—*Carmine Stoffo*
Machine and Process Designer
to pharmaceutical industry

"I am currently reading *A Practical Guide to Red Hat® Linux®* and am finally understanding the true power of the command line. I am new to Linux and your book is a treasure."

—*Juan Gonzalez*

"Overall, *A Practical Guide to Ubuntu Linux®* by Mark G. Sobell provides all of the information a beginner to intermediate user of Linux would need to be productive. The inclusion of the Live DVD of the Gutsy Gibbon release of Ubuntu makes it easy for the user to test-drive Linux without affecting his installed OS. I have no doubts that you will consider this book money well spent."

—*Ray Lodato*
Slashdot contributor
www.slashdot.org

A Practical Guide to Fedora™ and Red Hat® Enterprise Linux®

SIXTH EDITION

A Practical Guide to Fedora™ and Red Hat® Enterprise Linux®

SIXTH EDITION

Mark G. Sobell

PRENTICE
HALL

Upper Saddle River, NJ • Boston • Indianapolis • San Francisco
New York • Toronto • Montreal • London • Munich • Paris • Madrid
Capetown • Sydney • Tokyo • Singapore • Mexico City

Library of Congress Cataloging-in-Publication Data

Sobell, Mark G.
  A practical guide to Fedora and Red Hat Enterprise Linux / Mark G. Sobell.—6th ed.
      p.   cm.
  Includes index.
  ISBN 978-0-13-275727-0 (pbk. : alk. paper) 1. Linux. 2. Operating systems (Computers) I. Title.
  QA76.76.O63S5945 2012
  005.4'32—dc23

                                                          2011023929

ISBN-13: 978-0-13-275727-0
ISBN-10:   0-13-275727-3
Text printed in the United States on recycled paper at Edwards Brothers in Ann Arbor, Michigan.
First printing, August 2011

For my great-niece
Casey Rose.
Welcome to the world!

BRIEF CONTENTS

CONTENTS

PART II   GETTING STARTED WITH FEDORA/RHEL   87

CHAPTER 4: INTRODUCTION TO FEDORA AND RED HAT ENTERPRISE LINUX   89

CHAPTER 5: THE LINUX UTILITIES   145

CHAPTER 6: THE LINUX FILESYSTEM   185

CHAPTER 10: NETWORKING AND THE INTERNET   359

PART IV   SYSTEM ADMINISTRATION   405

CHAPTER 11: SYSTEM ADMINISTRATION: CORE CONCEPTS   407

CHAPTER 12: FILES, DIRECTORIES, AND FILESYSTEMS   501

CHAPTER 13: FINDING, DOWNLOADING, AND INSTALLING SOFTWARE 531

CHAPTER 14: PRINTING WITH CUPS 559

CHAPTER 17: CONFIGURING AND MONITORING A LAN   645

CHAPTER 20: sendmail: SETTING UP MAIL SERVERS, CLIENTS, AND MORE   729

CHAPTER 21: NIS AND LDAP   759

CHAPTER 22: NFS: SHARING DIRECTORY HIERARCHIES   791

CHAPTER 23: SAMBA: LINUX AND WINDOWS FILE AND PRINTER SHARING   817

CHAPTER 26: APACHE (httpd): SETTING UP A WEB SERVER   917

PART VI PROGRAMMING TOOLS 967

CHAPTER 27: PROGRAMMING THE BOURNE AGAIN SHELL 969

JumpStarts

JumpStarts get you off to a quick start when you need to use a client or set up a server. Once you have the client or server up and running, you can refine its configuration using the information presented in the sections following each JumpStart.

yum (Software Packages)

CUPS (Printing)

MySQL (Database)

OpenSSH (Secure Communication)

FTP (Download and Upload Files)

Email

NFS (Network Filesystem)

Samba (Linux/Windows File Sharing)

DNS (Domain Name Service)

system-config-firewall (Firewall)

Apache (HTTP)

PREFACE

The book Whether you are an end user, a system administrator, or a little of both, this book explains with step-by-step examples how to get the most out of a Fedora or RHEL (Red Hat Enterprise Linux) system. In 28 chapters, this book takes you from installing a Fedora/RHEL system, through understanding its inner workings, to setting up secure servers that run on the system.

The audience This book is designed for a wide range of readers. It does not require you to have programming experience, although having some experience using a general-purpose computer, such as a Windows, Macintosh, UNIX, or another Linux system is certainly helpful. This book is appropriate for

- **Students** who are taking a class in which they use Linux

- **Home users** who want to set up and/or run Linux

- **Professionals** who use Linux at work

- **System administrators** who need an understanding of Linux and the tools that are available to them, including the bash and Perl scripting languages

- **Computer science students** who are studying the Linux operating system

- **Technical executives** who want to get a grounding in Linux

Benefits *A Practical Guide to Fedora™ and Red Hat® Enterprise Linux®, Sixth Edition,* gives you a broad understanding of many facets of Linux, from installing Fedora/RHEL, through using and customizing it. No matter what your background, this book provides the knowledge you need to get on with your work. You will come away from this book understanding how to use Linux, and this book will remain a valuable reference for years to come.

Features in this edition This edition covers many topics to help you get your work done using Fedora/RHEL.

- A chapter on the Perl programming language (Chapter 28; page 1057)

- Seven chapters on system administration (Section IV; page 405)

- A chapter on writing programs using bash (Chapter 27; page 1057)

- Coverage of LDAP in Chapter 21 (page 776)

- Coverage of the MySQL relational database in Chapter 16 (page 635).

- A section on the Cacti network monitoring tool in Chapter 17 (page 657).

- New coverage of IPv6 in Chapter 10 (page 373).

- Updated chapters reflecting new features in Fedora 15 and RHEL 6

- Four indexes, making it easier to quickly find what you are looking for. These indexes locate tables (page numbers followed by the letter **t**), provide definitions (italic page numbers), and differentiate between light and comprehensive coverage (light and standard fonts).

  - The JumpStart index (page 1199) lists all JumpStart sections in this book. These sections help you set up servers and clients as quickly as possible.

  - The File Tree index (page 1201) lists, in hierarchical fashion, most files mentioned in this book. These files are also listed in the Main index.

  - The Utility index (page 1205) supplies the location of all utilities mentioned in this book. A page number in a light font indicates a brief mention of the utility, while the regular font indicates more substantial coverage. The Utility index also appears on the inside of the front and back covers of the print book.

  - The revised Main index (page 1211) is designed for ease of use.

Overlap If you have read *A Practical Guide to Linux® Commands, Editors, and Shell Programming, Second Edition,* you will notice some overlap between that book and the one you are reading now. The first chapter; the chapters on the utilities and the filesystem; the appendix on regular expressions; and the Glossary are very similar in the two books, as are the three chapters on the Bourne Again Shell (bash) and the chapter on Perl. Chapters that appear in this book but do not appear in *A Practical Guide to Linux® Commands, Editors, and Shell Programming, Second Edition,* include Chapters 2 and 3 (installation), Chapters 4 and 8 (Fedora/RHEL and the GUI), Chapter 10 (networking), all of the chapters in Part IV (system administration) and Part V (servers), and Appendix C (security).

Differences While this book explains how to use Linux from a graphical interface and from the command line (a textual interface), *A Practical Guide to Linux® Commands, Editors, and Shell Programming, Second Edition,* works exclusively with the command line and covers Mac OS X in addition to Linux. It includes full chapters on the vim and emacs editors, as well as chapters on the gawk pattern processing language, the sed stream editor, and the rsync secure copy utility. In addition, it has a command reference section that provides extensive examples of the use of 100 of the most important Linux and Mac OS X utilities. You can use these utilities to solve problems without resorting to programming in C.

THIS BOOK INCLUDES A FEDORA 15 (LOVELOCK) DVD

The print book includes an install DVD that holds Fedora 15 (Lovelock). You can use this DVD to install or upgrade to Fedora 15. Chapter 2 helps you get ready to install Fedora/RHEL. Chapter 3 provides step-by-step instructions for installing Fedora from this DVD as well as installing RHEL. This book guides you through learning about, using, and administrating a Fedora/RHEL system.

DVD features   The DVD includes many of the software packages supported by Fedora. You can use it to perform a graphical or textual (command line) installation of either a graphical or a textual Fedora system. If you do not have an Internet connection, you can use the DVD as a software repository: After you have installed Fedora, you can install supported software packages from the DVD.

FEATURES OF THIS BOOK

This book is designed and organized so you can get the most out of it in the least amount of time. You do not have to read this book straight through in page order. Instead, once you are comfortable using Linux, you can use this book as a reference: Look up a topic of interest in the table of contents or in an index and read about it. Or think of the book as a catalog of Linux topics: Flip through the pages until a topic catches your eye. The book includes many pointers to Web sites where you can obtain additional information: Consider the Internet to be an extension of this book.

A Practical Guide to Fedora™ and Red Hat® Enterprise Linux®, Sixth Edition, is structured with the following features:

- In this book, the term "Fedora/RHEL" refers to both **Fedora** and **Red Hat Enterprise Linux**. Features that apply to only one operating system or the other are marked as such using these indicators: (Fedora) or (RHEL).

- **Optional sections** enable you to read the book at different levels, returning to more difficult material when you are ready to delve into it.

- **Caution boxes** highlight procedures that can easily go wrong, giving you guidance *before* you run into trouble.

- **Tip boxes** highlight ways you can save time by doing something differently or situations when it may be useful or just interesting to have additional information.

- **Security boxes** point out places where you can make a system more secure. The **security appendix** presents a quick background in system security issues.

- Concepts are illustrated by **practical examples** throughout the book.

- Each chapter starts with a list of **Chapter objectives**—a list of important tasks you should be able to perform after reading the chapter.

- **Chapter summaries** review the important points covered in each chapter.

- **Review exercises** are included at the end of each chapter for readers who want to further hone their skills. Answers to even-numbered exercises are posted at www.sobell.com.

- The **Glossary** defines more than 500 commonly encountered terms.

- The chapters covering servers include **JumpStart** sections that get you off to a quick start using clients and setting up servers. Once a server is up and running, you can test and modify its configuration, as is explained in the rest of each of these chapters.

- This book provides resources for **finding software** on the Internet. It also explains how to **download** and **install** software using yum, the Add/Remove Software window, BitTorrent, and, for RHEL, Red Hat Network (RHN). It details controlling automatic updates using the Software Update Preferences window.

- This book describes in detail many important **GNU tools**, including the GNOME desktop, the Nautilus File Browser, the parted, palimpsest, and gparted partition editors; the gzip compression utility; and many command-line utilities that come from the GNU project.

- Pointers throughout the text provide help in obtaining **online documentation** from many sources, including the local system, the Fedora/RHEL Web sites, and other locations on the Internet.

- The multiple **comprehensive indexes** help you locate topics quickly and easily.

KEY TOPICS COVERED IN THIS BOOK

This section distills and summarizes the information covered by this book. In addition, "Details" (starting on page xlvii) describes what each chapter covers. Finally, the Table of Contents (starting on page xv) provides more detail. This book:

Installation
- Describes how to download Fedora ISO images from the Internet and burn the Fedora live CD or the Fedora install DVD.

- Helps you plan the layout of the system's hard disk. It includes a discussion of partitions, partition tables, and mount points, and assists you in using Disk Druid, the GNOME palimpsest disk utility, or the gparted graphical partition editor to examine and partition the hard disk.

- Explains how to set up a dual-boot system so you can install Fedora/RHEL on a Windows system and boot either operating system.

- Discusses booting into a live Fedora session and installing Fedora from that session.

- Describes in detail how to use **Anaconda**, Fedora/RHEL's installation program, to install Fedora/RHEL from an install DVD.

- Covers testing a Fedora/RHEL CD/DVD for defects, setting boot command-line parameters (boot options), and creating a RAID array.

- Explains how to use the Logical Volume Manager (LVM2) to set up, grow, and migrate logical volumes, which are similar in function to traditional disk partitions.

Working with Fedora/RHEL
- Introduces the GNOME desktop (GUI) and explains how to use desktop tools, including the panels, panel objects, the Main menu, object context menus, the Workspace Switcher, the Nautilus File Browser, and the GNOME terminal emulator.

- Covers the Bourne Again Shell (bash) in three chapters, including an entire chapter on shell programming, which includes many sample shell scripts. These chapters provide clear explanations and extensive examples of how bash works both from the command line in day-to-day work and as a programming language in which to write shell scripts.

- Explains the textual (command-line) interface and introduces more than 30 command-line utilities.

- Presents a tutorial on the vim textual editor.

- Covers types of networks, network protocols (including IPv6), and network utilities.

- Explains hostnames, IP addresses, and subnets, and explores how to use host and dig to look up domain names and IP addresses on the Internet.

- Covers distributed computing and the client/server model.

- Explains how to use ACLs (Access Control Lists) to fine-tune user access permissions.

CentOS
- Describes CentOS by virtue of that operating system's compatibility with RHEL. CentOS (www.centos.org) is a free Linux distribution that has more long-term stability than Fedora but has less support than RHEL.

System
administration

- Explains how to use the Fedora/RHEL graphical and textual (command-line) tools to configure the display, DNS, NFS, Samba, Apache, a firewall, a network interface, and more. You can also use these tools to add users and manage local and remote printers.

- Describes how to use su to work with **root** privileges (become Superuser), and the advantages and dangers of working with escalated privileges.

- Goes into detail about using sudo to allow specific users to work with **root** privileges and customizing the way sudo works by editing the **sudoers** configuration file.

- Describes how to use the following tools to download and install software to keep a system up-to-date and to install new software:

  - If you do not have an Internet connection, you can use the **Software Update Preferences** window to set up the DVD included with this book as a software repository. You can then install from this repository software packages that Fedora/RHEL supports.

  - Based on how you set up updates in the Software Update Preferences window, the **Software Update** window appears on the desktop to let you know when software updates are available. You can download and install updates from the Software Update window.

  - The **Add/Remove Software** window provides an easy way to select, download, and install a wide range of software packages.

  - The yum utility downloads and installs software packages from the Internet, keeping a system up-to-date and resolving dependencies as it processes the packages.

  - **BitTorrent** is a good choice for distributing large amounts of data such as the Fedora/RHEL installation DVD and CDs. The more people who use BitTorrent to download a file, the faster it works.

- Covers graphical system administration tools, including the many tools available from the GNOME Main menu.

- Explains system operation, including the boot process, init scripts, rescue (single-user) and multiuser modes, and steps to take if the system crashes.

- Details the workings of the new **systemd init daemon**, which replaces both the Upstart and System V **init** daemons (Fedora).

- Describes how to use and program the new **Upstart init daemon**, which replaces the System V **init** daemon (RHEL).

- Explains how to set up and use the **Cacti** network monitoring tool to graph system and network information over time, including installing and setting up the **LAMP** (Linux, Apache, MySQL, and PHP) stack.

- Provides instructions on installing and setting up a **MySQL** relational database.

- Describes files, directories, and filesystems, including types of files and filesystems, **fstab** (the filesystem table), and automatically mounted filesystems, and explains how to fine-tune and check the integrity of filesystems.

- Covers backup utilities, including tar and cpio.

- Describes compression/archive utilities, including gzip, bzip2, compress, and zip.

- Explains how to customize and build a Linux kernel.

Security
- Helps you manage basic system security issues using ssh (secure shell), **vsftpd** (secure FTP server), Apache (Web server), iptables (firewalls), and more.

- Describes how to use the graphical system-config-firewall utility to protect the system.

- Provides instructions on using iptables to share an Internet connection over a LAN and to build advanced firewalls.

- Presents a complete section on SELinux (Security-Enhanced Linux), including instructions for using system-config-selinux to configure SELinux.

- Describes how to set up a chroot jail to help protect a server system.

- Explains how to use TCP wrappers to control who can access a server.

Clients and servers
- Explains how to set up and use the most popular Linux servers, providing a chapter on each: Apache, Samba, OpenSSH, **sendmail**, DNS, NFS, FTP, system-config-firewall and iptables, and NIS/LDAP.

- Describes how to set up a CUPS printer server.

- Explains how to set up and use a MySQL relational database.

- Describes how to set up and use a DHCP server.

Programming
- Provides a chapter on the Perl programming language and a full chapter covering shell programming using bash, including many examples.

DETAILS

Chapter 1 **Chapter 1** presents a brief history of Linux and explains some of the features that make it a cutting-edge operating system. The "Conventions Used in This Book" section on page 18 details the typefaces and terminology used in this book.

Part I Part I, "Installing Fedora and Red Hat Enterprise Linux," discusses how to install Fedora/RHEL Linux. **Chapter 2** presents an overview of the process of installing Fedora/RHEL Linux, including hardware requirements, downloading and burning a CD or DVD, and planning the layout of the hard disk. **Chapter 3** is a step-by-step guide to installing Fedora and RHEL; it covers installing from a CD/DVD and from a live session (Fedora).

Part II Part II, "Getting Started with Fedora and Red Hat Enterprise Linux," familiarizes you with Fedora/RHEL, covering logging in, the GUI, utilities, the filesystem, and the shell. **Chapter 4** introduces desktop features, including the panels and the Main menu; explains how to use the Nautilus File Browser to manage files, run programs, and connect to FTP and HTTP servers; covers finding documentation, dealing with login problems, and using the window manager; and presents some suggestions on where to find documentation, including manuals, tutorials, software notes, and HOWTOs. **Chapter 5** introduces the shell command-line interface, describes more than 30 useful utilities, and presents a tutorial on the vim text editor. **Chapter 6** discusses the Linux hierarchical filesystem, covering files, filenames, pathnames, working with directories, access permissions, and hard and symbolic links. **Chapter 7** introduces the Bourne Again Shell (bash) and discusses command-line arguments and options, redirecting input to and output from commands, running programs in the background, and using the shell to generate and expand filenames.

Experienced users may want to skim Part II

tip If you have used a UNIX or Linux system before, you may want to skim or skip some or all of the chapters in Part II. Two sections that should *not* be skipped are: "Conventions Used in This Book" (page 18), which explains the typographic and layout conventions used in this book, and "Where to Find Documentation" (page 125), which points out both local and remote sources of Linux and Fedora/RHEL documentation.

Part III Part III, "Digging into Fedora and Red Hat Enterprise Linux," goes into more detail about working with the system. **Chapter 8** discusses the GUI (desktop) and includes a section about running a graphical program on a remote system and having the display appear locally. The section on GNOME describes several GNOME utilities and goes into more depth about the Nautilus File Browser. **Chapter 9** extends the bash coverage from Chapter 7, explaining how to redirect error output, avoid overwriting files, and work with job control, processes, startup files, important shell builtin commands, parameters, shell variables, and aliases. **Chapter 10** explains networks, network security, and the Internet, and discusses types of networks, subnets, protocols, addresses, hostnames, and various network utilities. A new section covers the all-important IPv6 protocol. The section on distributed computing describes the client/server model and some of the servers you can use on a network. (Details of setting up and using clients and servers are reserved until Part V.)

Part IV Part IV covers system administration. **Chapter 11** discusses core concepts, such as the use of su and sudo; working with **root** privileges; SELinux (Security-Enhanced Linux); system operation, including a discussion of the Upstart (RHEL) and systemd (Fedora) **init** daemons; chroot jails; TCP wrappers; general information about how to set up a server; DHCP; and PAM. **Chapter 12** explains the Linux filesystem, going into detail about types of files, including special and device files; the use of fsck to verify the integrity of and repair filesystems; and the use of tune2fs to change filesystem parameters. **Chapter 13** explains how to keep a system up-to-date by downloading software from the Internet and installing it, including examples that use yum to perform these tasks. It also covers the RPM software packaging system and the use of the rpm utility. Finally, it explains how to use BitTorrent from the command line to download files. **Chapter 14** explains how to set up the CUPS printing system so you can print on both local and remote systems. **Chapter 15** details customizing and building a Linux kernel. **Chapter 16** covers additional administration tasks, including setting up user accounts, backing up files, scheduling automated tasks, tracking disk usage, solving general problems, and setting up a MySQL relational database. **Chapter 17** explains how to set up a local area network (LAN), including both hardware (including wireless) and software configuration, and how to set up Cacti to monitor the network.

Part V   Part V goes into detail about setting up and running servers and connecting to them using clients. Where appropriate, these chapters include JumpStart sections, which get you off to a quick start in using clients and setting up servers. The chapters in Part V cover the following clients/servers:

- **OpenSSH**—Set up an OpenSSH server and use ssh, scp, and sftp to communicate securely over the Internet.
- **FTP**—Set up a **vsftpd** secure FTP server and use any of several FTP clients to exchange files with the server.
- **Email**—Configure **sendmail** and use Webmail, POP3, or IMAP to retrieve email; use SpamAssassin to combat spam.
- **NIS and LDAP**—Set up NIS to facilitate system administration of a LAN and LDAP to maintain databases.
- **NFS**—Share filesystems between systems on a network.
- **Samba**—Share filesystems and printers between Windows and Linux systems.
- **DNS/BIND**—Set up a domain nameserver to let other systems on the Internet know the names and IP addresses of local systems they may need to contact.
- system-config-firewall and iptables—Set up a firewall to protect local systems and share a single Internet connection between systems on a LAN.
- **Apache**—Set up an HTTP server that serves Web pages, which browsers can then display. This chapter includes many suggestions for increasing Apache security.

Part VI   Part VI covers two important programming tools that are used extensively in Fedora/RHEL system administration and general-purpose programming. **Chapter 27** continues where Chapter 9 left off, going into greater depth about shell programming using bash, with the discussion enhanced by extensive examples. **Chapter 28** introduces the popular, feature-rich Perl programming language, including coverage of regular expressions and file handling.

Part VII   Part VII includes appendixes on regular expressions, helpful Web sites, system security, and free software. This part also includes an extensive Glossary with more than 500 entries plus the JumpStart index, the File Tree index, the Utility index, and a comprehensive Main index.

SUPPLEMENTS

The author's home page (www.sobell.com) contains downloadable listings of the longer programs from this book, as well as pointers to many interesting and useful Linux sites on the World Wide Web, a list of corrections to the book, answers to even-numbered exercises, and a solicitation for corrections, comments, and suggestions.

THANKS

First and foremost, I want to thank Mark L. Taub, Editor-in-Chief, Prentice Hall, who provided encouragement and support through the hard parts of this project. Mark is unique in my 30 years of book writing experience: an editor who works with the tools I write about. Because Mark runs Linux on his home computer, we shared experiences as I wrote this book. Mark, your comments and direction are invaluable; this book would not exist without your help. Thank you, Mark T.

The production people at Prentice Hall are wonderful to work with: Julie Nahil, Full-Service Production Manager, worked with me day-by-day during production of this book providing help and keeping everything on track, while John Fuller, Managing Editor, kept the large view in focus. Thanks to Bob Campbell and Linda Seifert, Proofreaders, who made each page sparkle and found the mistakes the author left behind.

Thanks also to the folks at Prentice Hall who helped bring this book to life, especially Kim Boedigheimer, Editorial Assistant, who attended to the many details involved in publishing this book; Heather Fox, Publicist; Stephane Nakib, Marketing Manager; Dan Scherf, Media Developer; Cheryl Lenser, Senior Indexer; Sandra Schroeder, Design Manager; Chuti Prasertsith, Cover Designer; and everyone else who worked behind the scenes to make this book come into being.

Susan Lauber, Lauber System Solutions, Inc., had a big impact on this book. She reviewed drafts of many chapters, providing insights, tips, and corrections throughout. She also helped with the objectives and exercises. I was very impressed with the depth and breadth of her knowledge of Fedora/RHEL systems.

I am also indebted to Denis Howe, Editor of *The Free On-Line Dictionary of Computing* (FOLDOC). Denis has graciously permitted me to use entries from his compilation. Be sure to visit www.foldoc.org to look at this dictionary.

A big "thank you" to the folks who read through the drafts of the book and made comments that caused me to refocus parts of the book where things were not clear or were left out altogether: Doug Hughes, long-time system designer and administrator, who gave me a big hand with the system administration chapter; Richard Woodbury, Site Reliability Engineer, Google, whose knowledge of IPv6 proved invaluable; Max Sobell, Intrepidus Group; Lennart Poettering, Red Hat, Inc.; George Vish II, Senior Education Consultant, Hewlett-Packard; Matthew Miller, Senior Systems Analyst/Administrator, BU Linux Project, Boston University Office of Information Technology; Garth Snyder; Nathan Handler; Dick Seabrook, Emeritus Professor, Anne Arundel Community College; Chris Karr, Audacious Software; Scott McCrea, Instructor, ITT Technical Schools.

Thanks also to the following people who helped with my previous Linux books, which provided a foundation for this book: John Dong, Ubuntu Developer, Forums Council Member; Andy Lester, author of *Land the Tech Job You Love: Why Skill and Luck Are Not Enough*; Scott James Remnant, Ubuntu Development Manager and Desktop Team Leader; David Chisnall, Swansea University; Scott Mann, Aztek Networks; Thomas Achtemichuk, Mansueto Ventures; Daniel R. Arfsten, Pro/Engineer Drafter/Designer; Chris Cooper, Senior Education Consultant, Hewlett-Packard Education Services; Sameer Verma, Associate Professor of Information Systems, San Francisco State University; Valerie Chau, Palomar College and Programmers Guild; James Kratzer; Sean McAllister; Nathan Eckenrode, New York Ubuntu Local Community Team; Christer Edwards; Nicolas Merline; Michael Price; Mike Basinger, Ubuntu Community and Forums Council Member; Joe Barker, Ubuntu Forums Staff Member; James Stockford, Systemateka, Inc.; Stephanie Troeth, Book Oven; Doug Sheppard; Bryan Helvey, IT Director, OpenGeoSolutions; and Vann Scott, Baker College of Flint.

Also, thanks to Jesse Keating, Fedora Project; Carsten Pfeiffer, Software Engineer and KDE Developer; Aaron Weber, Ximian; Cristof Falk, Software Developer at CritterDesign; Steve Elgersma, Computer Science Department, Princeton University; Scott Dier, University of Minnesota; Robert Haskins, Computer Net Works; Lars Kellogg-Stedman, Harvard University; Jim A. Lola, Principal Systems Consultant, Privateer Systems; Eric S. Raymond, Cofounder, Open Source Initiative; Scott Mann; Randall Lechlitner, Independent Computer Consultant; Jason Wertz, Computer Science Instructor, Montgomery County Community College; Justin Howell, Solano Community College; Ed Sawicki, The Accelerated Learning Center; David Mercer; Jeffrey Bianchine, Advocate, Author, Journalist; John Kennedy; and Jim Dennis, Starshine Technical Services.

Thanks also to Dustin Puryear, Puryear Information Technology; Gabor Liptak, Independent Consultant; Bart Schaefer, Chief Technical Officer, iPost; Michael J. Jordan, Web Developer, Linux Online; Steven Gibson, Owner, SuperAnt.com; John Viega, Founder and Chief Scientist, Secure Software; K. Rachael Treu, Internet Security Analyst, Global Crossing; Kara Pritchard, K & S Pritchard Enterprises; Glen Wiley, Capital One Finances; Karel Baloun, Senior Software Engineer, Looksmart; Matthew Whitworth; Dameon D. Welch-Abernathy, Nokia Systems; Josh Simon, Consultant; Stan Isaacs; and Dr. Eric H. Herrin II, Vice President, Herrin Software Development.

More thanks go to consultants Lorraine Callahan and Steve Wampler; Ronald Hiller, Graburn Technology; Charles A. Plater, Wayne State University; Bob

Palowoda; Tom Bialaski, Sun Microsystems; Roger Hartmuller, TIS Labs at Network Associates; Kaowen Liu; Andy Spitzer; Rik Schneider; Jesse St. Laurent; Steve Bellenot; Ray W. Hiltbrand; Jennifer Witham; Gert-Jan Hagenaars; and Casper Dik.

A Practical Guide to Fedora™ and Red Hat® Enterprise Linux®, Sixth Edition, is based in part on two of my previous UNIX books: *UNIX System V: A Practical Guide* and *A Practical Guide to the UNIX System.* Many people helped me with those books, and thanks here go to Pat Parseghian; Dr. Kathleen Hemenway; Brian LaRose; Byron A. Jeff, Clark Atlanta University; Charles Stross; Jeff Gitlin, Lucent Technologies; Kurt Hockenbury; Maury Bach, Intel Israel; Peter H. Salus; Rahul Dave, University of Pennsylvania; Sean Walton, Intelligent Algorithmic Solutions; Tim Segall, Computer Sciences Corporation; Behrouz Forouzan, DeAnza College; Mike Keenan, Virginia Polytechnic Institute and State University; Mike Johnson, Oregon State University; Jandelyn Plane, University of Maryland; Arnold Robbins and Sathis Menon, Georgia Institute of Technology; Cliff Shaffer, Virginia Polytechnic Institute and State University; and Steven Stepanek, California State University, Northridge, for reviewing the book.

I continue to be grateful to the many people who helped with the early editions of my UNIX books. Special thanks are due to Roger Sippl, Laura King, and Roy Harrington for introducing me to the UNIX system. My mother, Dr. Helen Sobell, provided invaluable comments on the original manuscript at several junctures. Also, thanks go to Isaac Rabinovitch, Professor Raphael Finkel, Professor Randolph Bentson, Bob Greenberg, Professor Udo Pooch, Judy Ross, Dr. Robert Veroff, Dr. Mike Denny, Joe DiMartino, Dr. John Mashey, Diane Schulz, Robert Jung, Charles Whitaker, Don Cragun, Brian Dougherty, Dr. Robert Fish, Guy Harris, Ping Liao, Gary Lindgren, Dr. Jarrett Rosenberg, Dr. Peter Smith, Bill Weber, Mike Bianchi, Scooter Morris, Clarke Echols, Oliver Grillmeyer, Dr. David Korn, Dr. Scott Weikart, and Dr. Richard Curtis.

I take responsibility for any errors and omissions in this book. If you find one or just have a comment, let me know (mgs@sobell.com) and I will fix it in the next printing. My home page (www.sobell.com) contains a list of errors and credits those who found them. It also offers copies of the longer scripts from the book and pointers to interesting Linux pages on the Internet. You can follow me at twitter.com/marksobell.

Mark G. Sobell
San Francisco, California

WELCOME TO LINUX

OBJECTIVES

After reading this chapter you should be able to:

▸ Discuss the history of UNIX, Linux, and the GNU project

▸ Explain what is meant by "free software" and list characteristics of the GNU General Public License

▸ List characteristics of Linux and reasons the Linux operating system is so popular

An operating system is the low-level software that schedules tasks, allocates storage, and handles the interfaces to peripheral hardware, such as printers, disk drives, the screen, keyboard, and mouse. An operating system has two main parts: the *kernel* and the *system programs*. The kernel allocates machine resources—including memory, disk space, and *CPU* (page 1159) cycles—to all other programs that run on the computer. The system programs include device drivers, libraries, utility programs, shells (command interpreters), configuration scripts and files, application programs, servers, and documentation. They perform higher-level housekeeping tasks, often acting as servers in a client/server relationship. Many of the libraries, servers, and utility programs were written by the GNU Project, which is discussed shortly.

Linux kernel The Linux *kernel* was developed by Finnish undergraduate student Linus Torvalds, who used the Internet to make the source code immediately available to others for free. Torvalds released Linux version 0.01 in September 1991.

The new operating system came together through a lot of hard work. Programmers around the world were quick to extend the kernel and develop other tools, adding functionality to match that already found in both BSD UNIX and System V UNIX (SVR4) as well as new functionality. The name *Linux* is a combination of *Linus* and *UNIX*.

The Linux operating system, which was developed through the cooperation of numerous people around the world, is a *product of the Internet* and is a *free* operating system. In other words, all the source code is free. You are free to study it, redistribute it, and modify it. As a result, the code is available free of cost—no charge for the software, source, documentation, or support (via newsgroups, mailing lists, and other Internet resources). As the GNU Free Software Definition (reproduced in Appendix D) puts it:

Free beer "Free software" is a matter of liberty, not price. To understand the concept, you should think of "free" as in "free speech," not as in "free beer."

THE HISTORY OF UNIX AND GNU–LINUX

This section presents some background on the relationships between UNIX and Linux and between GNU and Linux.

THE HERITAGE OF LINUX: UNIX

The UNIX system was developed by researchers who needed a set of modern computing tools to help them with their projects. The system allowed a group of people working together on a project to share selected data and programs while keeping other information private.

Universities and colleges played a major role in furthering the popularity of the UNIX operating system through the "four-year effect." When the UNIX operating system became widely available in 1975, Bell Labs offered it to educational institutions at nominal cost. The schools, in turn, used it in their computer science programs, ensuring that computer science students became familiar with it. Because UNIX was such an advanced development system, the students became acclimated to a sophisticated programming environment. As these students graduated and went into industry, they expected to work in a similarly advanced environment. As more of them worked their way up the ladder in the commercial world, the UNIX operating system found its way into industry.

In addition to introducing students to the UNIX operating system, the Computer Systems Research Group (CSRG) at the University of California at Berkeley made significant additions and changes to it. In fact, it made so many popular changes that one version of the system is called the Berkeley Software Distribution (BSD) of the UNIX system (or just Berkeley UNIX). The other major version is UNIX System V (SVR4), which descended from versions developed and maintained by AT&T and UNIX System Laboratories.

Fade to 1983

Richard Stallman (www.stallman.org) announced[1] the GNU Project for creating an operating system, both kernel and system programs, and presented the GNU Manifesto,[2] which begins as follows:

> GNU, which stands for Gnu's Not UNIX, is the name for the complete UNIX-compatible software system which I am writing so that I can give it away free to everyone who can use it.

Some years later, Stallman added a footnote to the preceding sentence when he realized that it was creating confusion:

> The wording here was careless. The intention was that nobody would have to pay for *permission* to use the GNU system. But the words don't make this clear, and people often interpret them as saying that copies of GNU should always be distributed at little or no charge. That was never the intent; later on, the manifesto mentions the possibility of companies providing the service of distribution for a profit. Subsequently I have learned to distinguish carefully between "free" in the sense of freedom and "free" in the sense of price. Free software is software that users have the freedom to distribute and change. Some users may obtain copies at no charge, while others pay to obtain copies—and if the funds help support improving the software, so much the better. The important thing is that everyone who has a copy has the freedom to cooperate with others in using it.

---

1. www.gnu.org/gnu/initial-announcement.html
2. www.gnu.org/gnu/manifesto.html

In the manifesto, after explaining a little about the project and what has been accomplished so far, Stallman continues:

> **Why I Must Write GNU**
>
> I consider that the golden rule requires that if I like a program I must share it with other people who like it. Software sellers want to divide the users and conquer them, making each user agree not to share with others. I refuse to break solidarity with other users in this way. I cannot in good conscience sign a nondisclosure agreement or a software license agreement. For years I worked within the Artificial Intelligence Lab to resist such tendencies and other inhospitalities, but eventually they had gone too far: I could not remain in an institution where such things are done for me against my will.
>
> So that I can continue to use computers without dishonor, I have decided to put together a sufficient body of free software so that I will be able to get along without any software that is not free. I have resigned from the AI Lab to deny MIT any legal excuse to prevent me from giving GNU away.

NEXT SCENE, 1991

The GNU Project has moved well along toward its goal. Much of the GNU operating system, except for the kernel, is complete. Richard Stallman later writes:

> By the early '90s we had put together the whole system aside from the kernel (and we were also working on a kernel, the GNU Hurd,[3] which runs on top of Mach[4]). Developing this kernel has been a lot harder than we expected, and we are still working on finishing it.[5]
>
> ...[M]any believe that once Linus Torvalds finished writing the kernel, his friends looked around for other free software, and for no particular reason most everything necessary to make a UNIX-like system was already available.
>
> What they found was no accident—it was the GNU system. The available free software[6] added up to a complete system because the GNU Project had been working since 1984 to make one. The GNU Manifesto had set forth the goal of developing a free UNIX-like system, called GNU. The Initial Announcement of the GNU Project also outlines some of the original plans for the

---

3. www.gnu.org/software/hurd/hurd.html
4. www.gnu.org/software/hurd/gnumach.html
5. www.gnu.org/software/hurd/hurd-and-linux.html
6. See Appendix D or www.gnu.org/philosophy/free-sw.html.

GNU system. By the time Linux was written, the [GNU] system was almost finished.[7]

Today the GNU "operating system" runs on top of the FreeBSD (www.freebsd.org) and NetBSD (www.netbsd.org) kernels with complete Linux binary compatibility and on top of Hurd pre-releases and Darwin (developer.apple.com/opensource) without this compatibility.

THE CODE IS FREE

The tradition of free software dates back to the days when UNIX was released to universities at nominal cost, which contributed to its portability and success. This tradition eventually died as UNIX was commercialized and manufacturers came to regard the source code as proprietary, making it effectively unavailable. Another problem with the commercial versions of UNIX related to their complexity. As each manufacturer tuned UNIX for a specific architecture, the operating system became less portable and too unwieldy for teaching and experimentation.

MINIX Two professors created their own stripped-down UNIX look-alikes for educational purposes: Doug Comer created XINU, and Andrew Tanenbaum created MINIX. Linus Torvalds created Linux to counteract the shortcomings in MINIX. Every time there was a choice between code simplicity and efficiency/features, Tanenbaum chose simplicity (to make it easy to teach with MINIX), which meant this system lacked many features people wanted. Linux went in the opposite direction.

You can obtain Linux at no cost over the Internet (page 44). You can also obtain the GNU code via the U.S. mail at a modest cost for materials and shipping. You can support the Free Software Foundation (www.fsf.org) by buying the same (GNU) code in higher-priced packages, and you can buy commercial packaged releases of Linux (called *distributions*), such as Fedora/RHEL, that include installation instructions, software, and support.

GPL Linux and GNU software are distributed under the terms of the GNU General Public License (GPL, www.gnu.org/licenses/licenses.html). The GPL says you have the right to copy, modify, and redistribute the code covered by the agreement. When you redistribute the code, however, you must also distribute the same license with the code, thereby making the code and the license inseparable. If you get source code off the Internet for an accounting program that is under the GPL and then modify that code and redistribute an executable version of the program, you must also distribute the modified source code and the GPL agreement with it. Because this arrangement is the reverse of the way a normal copyright works (it *gives* rights instead of *limiting* them), it has been termed a *copyleft*. (This paragraph is not a legal interpretation of the GPL; it is intended merely to give you an idea of how it works. Refer to the GPL itself when you want to make use of it.)

---

7. www.gnu.org/gnu/linux-and-gnu.html

HAVE FUN!

Two key words for Linux are "Have Fun!" These words pop up in prompts and documentation. The UNIX—now Linux—culture is steeped in humor that can be seen throughout the system. For example, less is more—GNU has replaced the UNIX paging utility named more with an improved utility named less. The utility to view PostScript documents is named ghostscript, and one of several replacements for the vi editor is named elvis. While machines with Intel processors have "Intel Inside" logos on their outside, some Linux machines sport "Linux Inside" logos. And Torvalds himself has been seen wearing a T-shirt bearing a "Linus Inside" logo.

WHAT IS SO GOOD ABOUT LINUX?

In recent years Linux has emerged as a powerful and innovative UNIX work-alike. Its popularity has surpassed that of its UNIX predecessors. Although it mimics UNIX in many ways, the Linux operating system departs from UNIX in several significant ways: The Linux kernel is implemented independently of both BSD and System V, the continuing development of Linux is taking place through the combined efforts of many capable individuals throughout the world, and Linux puts the power of UNIX within easy reach of both business and personal computer users. Using the Internet, today's skilled programmers submit additions and improvements to the operating system to Linus Torvalds, GNU, or one of the other authors of Linux.

Standards   In 1985, individuals from companies throughout the computer industry joined together to develop the POSIX (Portable Operating System Interface for Computer Environments) standard, which is based largely on the UNIX System V Interface Definition (SVID) and other earlier standardization efforts. These efforts were spurred by the U.S. government, which needed a standard computing environment to minimize its training and procurement costs. Released in 1988, POSIX is a group of IEEE standards that define the API (application programming interface), shell, and utility interfaces for an operating system. Although aimed at UNIX-like systems, the standards can apply to any compatible operating system. Now that these standards have gained acceptance, software developers are able to develop applications that run on all conforming versions of UNIX, Linux, and other operating systems.

Applications   A rich selection of applications is available for Linux—both free and commercial—as well as a wide variety of tools: graphical, word processing, networking, security, administration, Web server, and many others. Large software companies have recently seen the benefit in supporting Linux and now have on-staff programmers whose job it is to design and code the Linux kernel, GNU, KDE, or other software that runs on Linux. For example, IBM (www.ibm.com/linux) is a major Linux supporter. Linux conforms increasingly more closely to POSIX standards, and some distributions and parts of others meet this standard. These developments indicate that Linux is becoming mainstream and is respected as an attractive alternative to other popular operating systems.

Peripherals Another aspect of Linux that appeals to users is the amazing range of peripherals that is supported and the speed with which support for new peripherals emerges. Linux often supports a peripheral or interface card before any company does. Unfortunately some types of peripherals—particularly proprietary graphics cards—lag in their support because the manufacturers do not release specifications or source code for drivers in a timely manner, if at all.

Software Also important to users is the amount of software that is available—not just source code (which needs to be compiled) but also prebuilt binaries that are easy to install and ready to run. These programs include more than free software. Netscape, for example, was available for Linux from the start and included Java support before it was available from many commercial vendors. Its sibling Mozilla/Thunderbird/ Firefox is now a viable browser, mail client, and newsreader, performing many other functions as well.

Platforms Linux is not just for Intel-based platforms (which now include Apple computers): It has been ported to and runs on the Power PC—including older Apple computers (ppclinux), Compaq's (née Digital Equipment Corporation) Alpha-based machines, MIPS-based machines, Motorola's 68K-based machines, various 64-bit systems, and IBM's S/390. Nor is Linux just for single-processor machines: As of version 2.0, it runs on multiple-processor machines (*SMPs;* page 1188). It also includes an O(1) scheduler, which dramatically increases scalability on SMP systems.

Emulators Linux supports programs, called *emulators,* that run code intended for other operating systems. By using emulators you can run some DOS, Windows, and Macintosh programs under Linux. For example, Wine (www.winehq.com) is an open-source implementation of the Windows API that runs on top of the X Window System and UNIX/Linux.

Virtual machines A virtual machine (VM or guest) appears to the user and to the software running on it as a complete physical machine. It is, however, one of potentially many such VMs running on a single physical machine (the host). The software that provides the virtualization is called a *virtual machine monitor* (VMM) or *hypervisor.* Each VM can run a different operating system from the other VMs. For example, on a single host you could have VMs running Windows 7, Ubuntu 10.10, Ubuntu 11.04, and Fedora 15.

A multitasking operating system allows you to run many programs on a single physical system. Similarly, a hypervisor allows you to run many operating systems (VMs) on a single physical system.

VMs provide many advantages over single, dedicated machines:

- **Isolation**—Each VM is isolated from the other VMs running on the same host: Thus, if one VM crashes or is compromised, the others are not affected.

- **Security**—When a single server system running several servers is compromised, all servers are compromised. If each server is running on its own VM, only the compromised server is affected; other servers remain secure.

- **Power consumption**—Using VMs, a single powerful machine can replace many less powerful machines, thereby cutting power consumption.

- **Development and support**—Multiple VMs, each running a different version of an operating system and/or different operating systems, can facilitate development and support of software designed to run in many environments. With this organization you can easily test a product in different environments before releasing it. Similarly, when a user submits a bug, you can reproduce the bug in the same environment it occurred in.

- **Servers**—In some cases, different servers require different versions of system libraries. In this instance, you can run each server on its own VM, all on a single piece of hardware.

- **Testing**—Using VMs, you can experiment with cutting-edge releases of operating systems and applications without concern for the base (stable) system, all on a single machine.

- **Networks**—You can set up and test networks of systems on a single machine.

- **Sandboxes**—A VM presents a sandbox—an area (system) that you can work in without regard for the results of your work or for the need to clean up.

- **Snapshots**—You can take snapshots of a VM and return the VM to the state it was in when you took the snapshot simply by reloading the VM from the snapshot.

Xen   Xen, which was created at the University of Cambridge and is now being developed in the open-source community, is an open-source virtual machine monitor (VMM). A VMM enables several virtual machines (VMs), each running an instance of a separate operating system, to run on a single computer. Xen isolates the VMs so that if one crashes it does not affect any of the others. In addition, Xen introduces minimal performance overhead when compared with running each of the operating systems natively.

Fedora 15 supports Xen 4.1. This book does not cover the installation Xen or the use of Xen. For more information on Xen, refer to the Xen home page at www.cl.cam.ac.uk/research/srg/netos/xen and wiki.xensource.com/xenwiki.

VMware   VMware, Inc. (www.vmware.com) offers VMware Server, a free, downloadable, proprietary product you can install and run as an application under Fedora/RHEL. VMware Server enables you to install several VMs, each running a different operating system, including Windows and Linux. VMware also offers a free VMware player that enables you to run VMs you create with the VMware Server.

KVM   The Kernel-based Virtual Machine (KVM; www.linux-kvm.org and libvirt.org) is an open-source VM and runs as part of the Linux kernel.

Qemu   Qemu (wiki.qemu.org), written by Fabrice Bellard, is an open-source VMM that runs as a user application with no CPU requirements. It can run code written for a different CPU than that of the host machine.

KVM/Qemu merge   Fedora/RHEL has merged KVM and Qemu. For more information visit the page at fedoraproject.org/wiki/Features/KVM_and_QEMU_merge.

VirtualBox   VirtualBox (www.virtualbox.org) is a VM developed by Sun Microsystems. If you want to run a virtual instance of Windows, you might want to investigate VirtualBox.

WHY LINUX IS POPULAR WITH HARDWARE COMPANIES AND DEVELOPERS

Two trends in the computer industry set the stage for the growing popularity of UNIX and Linux. First, advances in hardware technology created the need for an operating system that could take advantage of available hardware power. In the mid-1970s, minicomputers began challenging the large mainframe computers because, in many applications, minicomputers could perform the same functions less expensively. More recently, powerful 64-bit processor chips, plentiful and inexpensive memory, and lower-priced hard disk storage have allowed hardware companies to install multiuser operating systems on desktop computers.

Proprietary operating systems   Second, with the cost of hardware continually dropping, hardware manufacturers could no longer afford to develop and support proprietary operating systems. A *proprietary* operating system is one that is written and owned by the manufacturer of the hardware (for example, DEC/Compaq owns VMS). Today's manufacturers need a generic operating system they can easily adapt to their machines.

Generic operating systems   A *generic* operating system is written outside of the company manufacturing the hardware and is sold (UNIX, Windows) or given (Linux) to the manufacturer. Linux is a generic operating system because it runs on different types of hardware produced by different manufacturers. Of course, if manufacturers can pay only for development and avoid per-unit costs (which they have to pay to Microsoft for each copy of Windows they sell), they are much better off. In turn, software developers need to keep the prices of their products down; they cannot afford to create new versions of their products to run under many different proprietary operating systems. Like hardware manufacturers, software developers need a generic operating system.

Although the UNIX system once met the needs of hardware companies and researchers for a generic operating system, over time it has become more proprietary as manufacturers added support for their own specialized features and introduced new software libraries and utilities. Linux emerged to serve both needs: It is a generic operating system that takes advantage of available hardware power.

LINUX IS PORTABLE

A *portable* operating system is one that can run on many different machines. More than 95 percent of the Linux operating system is written in the C programming language, and C is portable because it is written in a higher-level, machine-independent language. (The C compiler is written in C.)

Because Linux is portable, it can be adapted (ported) to different machines and can meet special requirements. For example, Linux is used in embedded computers, such as the ones found in cellphones, PDAs, and the cable boxes on top of many TVs. The file structure takes full advantage of large, fast hard disks. Equally important, Linux was originally designed as a multiuser operating system—it was not modified to serve several users as an afterthought. Sharing the computer's power among many users and giving them the ability to share data and programs are central features of the system.

Because it is adaptable and takes advantage of available hardware, Linux runs on many different microprocessor-based systems as well as mainframes. The popularity of the microprocessor-based hardware drives Linux; these microcomputers are getting faster all the time at about the same price point. This widespread acceptance benefits both users, who do not like having to learn a new operating system for each vendor's hardware, and system administrators, who like having a consistent software environment.

The advent of a standard operating system has given a boost to the development of the software industry. Now software manufacturers can afford to make one version of a product available on machines from different manufacturers.

THE C PROGRAMMING LANGUAGE

Ken Thompson wrote the UNIX operating system in 1969 in PDP-7 assembly language. Assembly language is machine-dependent: Programs written in assembly language work on only one machine or, at best, on one family of machines. For this reason, the original UNIX operating system could not easily be transported to run on other machines: It was not portable.

To make UNIX portable, Thompson developed the B programming language, a machine-independent language, from the BCPL language. Dennis Ritchie developed the C programming language by modifying B and, with Thompson, rewrote UNIX in C in 1973. Originally, C was touted as a "portable assembler." The revised operating system could be transported more easily to run on other machines.

That development marked the start of C. Its roots reveal some of the reasons why it is such a powerful tool. C can be used to write machine-independent programs. A programmer who designs a program to be portable can easily move it to any computer that has a C compiler. C is also designed to compile into very efficient code. With the advent of C, a programmer no longer had to resort to assembly language to produce code that would run well (that is, quickly—although an assembler will always generate more efficient code than a high-level language).

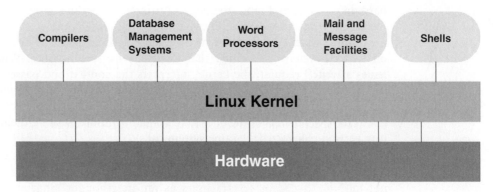

Figure 1-1   A layered view of the Linux operating system

C is a good systems language. You can write a compiler or an operating system in C. It is a highly structured but not necessarily a high-level language. C allows a programmer to manipulate bits and bytes, as is necessary when writing an operating system. At the same time, it has high-level constructs that allow for efficient, modular programming.

In the late 1980s the American National Standards Institute (ANSI) defined a standard version of the C language, commonly referred to as *ANSI C* or *C89* (for the year the standard was published). Ten years later the C99 standard was published; it is mostly supported by the GNU Project's C compiler (named gcc). The original version of the language is often referred to as *Kernighan & Ritchie* (or *K&R*) C, named for the authors of the book that first described the C language.

Another researcher at Bell Labs, Bjarne Stroustrup, created an object-oriented programming language named C++, which is built on the foundation of C. Because object-oriented programming is desired by many employers today, C++ is preferred over C in many environments. Another language of choice is Objective-C, which was used to write the first Web browser. The GNU Project's C compiler supports C, C++, and Objective-C.

OVERVIEW OF LINUX

The Linux operating system has many unique and powerful features. Like other operating systems, it is a control program for computers. But like UNIX, it is also a well-thought-out family of utility programs (Figure 1-1) and a set of tools that allow users to connect and use these utilities to build systems and applications.

LINUX HAS A KERNEL PROGRAMMING INTERFACE

The Linux kernel—the heart of the Linux operating system—is responsible for allocating the computer's resources and scheduling user jobs so each one gets its fair share of system resources, including access to the CPU; peripheral devices, such as hard disk, DVD, and tape storage; and printers. Programs interact with the kernel through *system calls,* special functions with well-known names. A programmer can use a single system call to interact with many kinds of devices. For example, there is one **write**() system call, rather than many device-specific ones. When a program issues a **write**() request, the kernel interprets the context and passes the request to the appropriate device. This flexibility allows old utilities to work with devices that did not exist when the utilities were written. It also makes it possible to move programs to new versions of the operating system without rewriting them (provided the new version recognizes the same system calls).

LINUX CAN SUPPORT MANY USERS

Depending on the hardware and the types of tasks the computer performs, a Linux system can support from 1 to more than 1,000 users, each concurrently running a different set of programs. The per-user cost of a computer that can be used by many people at the same time is less than that of a computer that can be used by only a single person at a time. It is less because one person cannot generally take advantage of all the resources a computer has to offer. That is, no one can keep all the printers going constantly, keep all the system memory in use, keep all the disks busy reading and writing, keep the Internet connection in use, and keep all the terminals busy at the same time. By contrast, a multiuser operating system allows many people to use all of the system resources almost simultaneously. The use of costly resources can be maximized, and the cost per user can be minimized—the primary objectives of a multiuser operating system.

LINUX CAN RUN MANY TASKS

Linux is a fully protected multitasking operating system, allowing each user to run more than one job at a time. Processes can communicate with one another but remain fully protected from one another, just as the kernel remains protected from all processes. You can run several jobs in the background while giving all your attention to the job being displayed on the screen, and you can switch back and forth between jobs. If you are running the X Window System (page 16), you can run different programs in different windows on the same screen and watch all of them. This capability helps users be more productive.

LINUX PROVIDES A SECURE HIERARCHICAL FILESYSTEM

A *file* is a collection of information, such as text for a memo or report, an accumulation of sales figures, an image, a song, or an executable program. Each file is stored under a unique identifier on a storage device, such as a hard disk. The Linux filesystem provides a structure whereby files are arranged under *directories,* which are like folders or boxes. Each directory has a name and can hold other files and

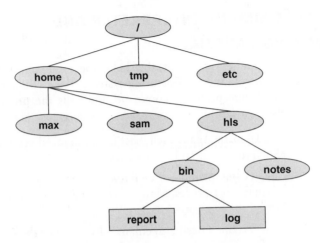

Figure 1-2 The Linux filesystem structure

directories. Directories, in turn, are arranged under other directories and so forth in a treelike organization. This structure helps users keep track of large numbers of files by grouping related files in directories. Each user has one primary directory and as many subdirectories as required (Figure 1-2).

Standards   With the idea of making life easier for system administrators and software developers, a group got together over the Internet and developed the Linux Filesystem Standard (FSSTND), which has since evolved into the Linux Filesystem Hierarchy Standard (FHS). Before this standard was adopted, key programs were located in different places in different Linux distributions. Today you can sit down at a Linux system and expect to find any given standard program at a consistent location (page 199).

Links   A *link* allows a given file to be accessed by means of two or more names. The alternative names can be located in the same directory as the original file or in another directory. Links can make the same file appear in several users' directories, enabling those users to share the file easily. Windows uses the term *shortcut* in place of *link* to describe this capability. Macintosh users will be more familiar with the term *alias*. Under Linux, an *alias* is different from a *link;* it is a command macro feature provided by the shell (page 334).

Security   Like most multiuser operating systems, Linux allows users to protect their data from access by other users. It also allows users to share selected data and programs with certain other users by means of a simple but effective protection scheme. This level of security is provided by file access permissions, which limit the users who can read from, write to, or execute a file. Linux also implements ACLs (Access Control Lists), which give users and administrators finer-grained control over file access permissions.

THE SHELL: COMMAND INTERPRETER AND PROGRAMMING LANGUAGE

In a textual environment, the shell—the command interpreter—acts as an interface between you and the operating system. When you enter a command on the screen, the shell interprets the command and calls the program you want. A number of shells are available for Linux. The four most popular shells are

- The Bourne Again Shell (bash), an enhanced version of the original Bourne Shell (the original UNIX shell).

- The Debian Almquist Shell (dash; page 281), a smaller version of bash with fewer features. Many startup shell scripts call dash in place of bash to speed the boot process.

- The TC Shell (tcsh), an enhanced version of the C Shell, developed as part of BSD UNIX.

- The Z Shell (zsh), which incorporates features from a number of shells, including the Korn Shell.

Because different users might prefer different shells, multiuser systems can have several different shells in use at any given time. The choice of shells demonstrates one of the advantages of the Linux operating system: the ability to provide a customized interface for each user.

Shell scripts Besides performing its function of interpreting commands from a keyboard and sending those commands to the operating system, the shell is a high-level programming language. Shell commands can be arranged in a file for later execution (Linux calls these files *shell scripts*; Windows calls them *batch files*). This flexibility allows users to perform complex operations with relative ease, often by issuing short commands, or to build with surprisingly little effort elaborate programs that perform highly complex operations.

FILENAME GENERATION

Wildcards and ambiguous file references When you type commands to be processed by the shell, you can construct patterns using characters that have special meanings to the shell. These characters are called *wildcard* characters. The patterns, which are called *ambiguous file references*, are a kind of shorthand: Rather than typing in complete filenames, you can type patterns; the shell expands these patterns into matching filenames. An ambiguous file reference can save you the effort of typing in a long filename or a long series of similar filenames. For example, the shell might expand the pattern **mak*** to **make-3.80.tar.gz**. Patterns can also be useful when you know only part of a filename or cannot remember the exact spelling of a filename.

COMPLETION

In conjunction with the Readline library, the shell performs command, filename, pathname, and variable completion: You type a prefix and press TAB, and the shell lists the items that begin with that prefix or completes the item if the prefix specifies a unique item.

DEVICE-INDEPENDENT INPUT AND OUTPUT

Redirection Devices (such as a printer or a terminal) and disk files appear as files to Linux programs. When you give a command to the Linux operating system, you can instruct it to send the output to any one of several devices or files. This diversion is called output *redirection*.

Device In a similar manner, a program's input, which normally comes from a keyboard, can
independence be redirected so that it comes from a disk file instead. Input and output are *device independent;* that is, they can be redirected to or from any appropriate device.

As an example, the cat utility normally displays the contents of a file on the screen. When you run a cat command, you can easily cause its output to go to a disk file instead of the screen.

SHELL FUNCTIONS

One of the most important features of the shell is that users can use it as a programming language. Because the shell is an interpreter, it does not compile programs written for it but rather interprets programs each time they are loaded from the disk. Loading and interpreting programs can be time-consuming.

Many shells, including the Bourne Again Shell, support shell functions that the shell holds in memory so it does not have to read them from the disk each time you execute them. The shell also keeps functions in an internal format so it does not have to spend as much time interpreting them.

JOB CONTROL

Job control is a shell feature that allows users to work on several jobs at once, switching back and forth between them as desired. When you start a job, it is frequently run in the foreground so it is connected to the terminal. Using job control, you can move the job you are working with to the background and continue running it there while working on or observing another job in the foreground. If a background job then needs your attention, you can move it to the foreground so it is once again attached to the terminal. The concept of job control originated with BSD UNIX, where it appeared in the C Shell.

A LARGE COLLECTION OF USEFUL UTILITIES

Linux includes a family of several hundred utility programs, often referred to as *commands*. These utilities perform functions that are universally required by users. The sort utility, for example, puts lists (or groups of lists) in alphabetical or numerical order and can be used to sort lists by part number, last name, city, ZIP code, telephone number, age, size, cost, and so forth. The sort utility is an important programming tool that is part of the standard Linux system. Other utilities allow users to create, display, print, copy, search, and delete files as well as to edit, format, and typeset text. The man (for manual) and info utilities provide online documentation for Linux.

INTERPROCESS COMMUNICATION

Pipes and filters   Linux enables users to establish both pipes and filters on the command line. A *pipe* sends the output of one program to another program as input. A *filter* is a special kind of pipe that processes a stream of input data to yield a stream of output data. A filter processes another program's output, altering it as a result. The filter's output then becomes input to another program.

Pipes and filters frequently join utilities to perform a specific task. For example, you can use a pipe to send the output of the sort utility to head (a filter that lists the first ten lines of its input); you can then use another pipe to send the output of head to a third utility, lpr, that sends the data to a printer. Thus, in one command line, you can use three utilities together to sort and print part of a file.

SYSTEM ADMINISTRATION

On a Linux system the system administrator is frequently the owner and only user of the system. This person has many responsibilities. The first responsibility might be to set up the system, install the software, and possibly edit configuration files. Once the system is up and running, the system administrator is responsible for downloading and installing software (including upgrading the operating system), backing up and restoring files, and managing such system facilities as printers, terminals, servers, and a local network. The system administrator is also responsible for setting up accounts for new users on a multiuser system, bringing the system up and down as needed, monitoring the system, and taking care of any problems that arise.

ADDITIONAL FEATURES OF LINUX

The developers of Linux included features from BSD, System V, and Sun Microsystems' Solaris, as well as new features, in their operating system. Although most of the tools found on UNIX exist for Linux, in some cases these tools have been replaced by more modern counterparts. This section describes some of the popular tools and features available under Linux.

GUIs: GRAPHICAL USER INTERFACES

The X Window System (also called X or X11) was developed in part by researchers at MIT (Massachusetts Institute of Technology) and provides the foundation for the GUIs available with Linux. Given a terminal or workstation screen that supports X, a user can interact with the computer through multiple windows on the screen, display graphical information, or use special-purpose applications to draw pictures, monitor processes, or preview formatted output. X is an across-the-network protocol that allows a user to open a window on a workstation or computer system that is remote from the CPU generating the window.

Desktop manager   Usually two layers run on top of X: a desktop manager and a window manager. A *desktop manager* is a picture-oriented user interface that enables you to interact with system programs by manipulating icons instead of typing the corresponding commands to a shell. Fedora/RHEL runs the GNOME desktop manager (www.gnome.org) by default, but it can also run KDE (www.kde.org) and a number of other desktop managers.

Window manager   A *window manager* is a program that runs under the desktop manager and allows you to open and close windows, run programs, and set up a mouse so it has different effects depending on how and where you click it. The window manager also gives the screen its personality. Whereas Microsoft Windows allows you to change the color of key elements in a window, a window manager under X allows you to customize the overall look and feel of the screen: You can change the way a window looks and works (by giving it different borders, buttons, and scrollbars), set up virtual desktops, create menus, and more.

Several popular window managers run under X and Linux. RHEL provides both Metacity (the default under GNOME 2) and kwin (the default under KDE). In addition to KDE, Fedora provides Mutter (the default under GNOME 3). *Mutter* is short for Metacity Clutter (the graphics library is named Clutter). Other window managers, such as Sawfish and WindowMaker, are also available. Chapters 4 and 8 present information on GUIs.

(INTER)NETWORKING UTILITIES

Linux network support includes many utilities that enable you to access remote systems over a variety of networks. In addition to sending email to users on other systems, you can access files on disks mounted on other computers as if they were located on the local system, make your files available to other systems in a similar manner, copy files back and forth, run programs on remote systems while displaying the results on the local system, and perform many other operations across local area networks (LANs) and wide area networks (WANs), including the Internet.

Layered on top of this network access is a wide range of application programs that extend the computer's resources around the globe. You can carry on conversations with people throughout the world, gather information on a wide variety of subjects, and download new software over the Internet quickly and reliably. Chapter 10 discusses networks, the Internet, and the Linux network facilities.

SOFTWARE DEVELOPMENT

One of Linux's most impressive strengths is its rich software development environment. Linux supports compilers and interpreters for many computer languages. Besides C and C++, languages available for Linux include Ada, Fortran, Java, Lisp, Pascal, Perl, and Python. The bison utility generates parsing code that makes it easier to write programs to build compilers (tools that parse files containing structured information). The flex utility generates scanners (code that recognizes lexical patterns in text). The make utility and the GNU Configure and Build System make it easier to manage complex development projects. Source code management systems, such as CVS, simplify version control. Several debuggers, including ups and gdb, can help you track down and repair software defects. The GNU C compiler (gcc) works with the gprof profiling utility to help programmers identify potential bottlenecks in a program's performance. The C compiler includes options to perform extensive checking of C code, thereby making the code more portable and reducing debugging time. Table 0-4 on page 1120 lists some sites you can download software from.

CONVENTIONS USED IN THIS BOOK

This book uses conventions to make its explanations shorter and clearer. The following paragraphs describe these conventions.

Widgets A widget is a simple graphical element that a user interacts with, such as a text box, radio button, or combo box. When referring to a widget, this book specifies the type of widget and its label. The term "tick" refers to the mark you put in a check box, sometimes called a check mark. For example, "put a tick in the check box labeled **Run in terminal**." See the glossary for definitions of various widgets.

Tabs and frames Tabs allow windows to display sets of related information, one set at a time. For example, Figure 4-21 on page 122 shows an Object Properties window with three tabs. A frame isolates a set of information within a window. See Figure 14-2 on page 563 for an example.

Menu selection path The menu selection path is the name of the menu or the location of the menu, followed by a colon, a SPACE, and the menu selections separated by ⇨ markers. The entire menu selection path appears in **bold** type. You can read **Main menu: Applications⇨ System Tools⇨Terminal** as "From the Main menu, select **Applications**; from **Applications**, select **System Tools**; and then select **Terminal**."

Text and examples The text is set in this type, whereas examples are shown in a `monospaced font` (also called a *fixed-width* font):

```
$ cat practice
This is a small file I created
with a text editor.
```

Items you enter Everything you enter at the keyboard is shown in a bold typeface. Within the text, **this bold typeface** is used; within examples and screens, **`this one`** is used. In the previous example, the dollar sign ($) on the first line is a prompt that Linux displays, so it is not bold; the remainder of the first line is entered by a user, so it is bold.

Utility names Names of utilities are printed in this sans serif typeface. This book references the emacs text editor and the ls utility or ls command (or just ls) but instructs you to enter **ls –a** on the command line. In this way the text distinguishes between utilities, which are programs, and the instructions you enter on the command line to invoke the utilities.

Filenames Filenames appear in a bold typeface. Examples are **memo5**, **letter.1283**, and **reports**. Filenames might include uppercase and lowercase letters; however, Linux is *case sensitive* (page 1155), so **memo5**, **MEMO5**, and **Memo5** name three different files.

Character strings Within the text, characters and character strings are marked by putting them in a bold typeface. This convention avoids the need for quotation marks or other delimiters before and after a string. An example is the following string, which is displayed by the passwd utility: **Sorry, passwords do not match.**

Buttons and labels Words appear in a bold typeface in the sections of the book that describe a GUI. This font indicates you can click a mouse button when the mouse pointer is over these words on the screen or over a button with this name: Click **Next**.

Keys and characters This book uses SMALL CAPS for three kinds of items:

- Keyboard keys, such as the SPACE bar and the RETURN,[8] ESCAPE, and TAB keys.

- The characters that keys generate, such as the SPACEs generated by the SPACE bar.

- Keyboard keys that you press with the CONTROL key, such as CONTROL-D. (Even though D is shown as an uppercase letter, you do not have to press the SHIFT key; enter CONTROL-D by holding the CONTROL key down and pressing **d**.)

Prompts and RETURNS Most examples include the *shell prompt*—the signal that Linux is waiting for a command—as a dollar sign (**$**), a hashmark (**#**), or sometimes a percent sign (**%**). The prompt does not appear in a bold typeface in this book because you do not enter it. Do not type the prompt on the keyboard when you are experimenting with examples from this book. If you do, the examples will not work.

Examples *omit* the RETURN keystroke that you must use to execute them. An example of a command line is

```
$ vim memo.1204
```

To use this example as a model for running the vim text editor, enter the command **vim memo.1204** and press the RETURN key. (Press ESCAPE **ZZ** to exit from vim; see page 172 for a vim tutorial.) This method of entering commands makes the examples in the book correspond to what appears on the screen.

Definitions All glossary entries marked with FOLDOC are courtesy of Denis Howe, editor of the Free Online Dictionary of Computing (foldoc.org), and are used with permission. This site is an ongoing work containing definitions, anecdotes, and trivia.

---

optional **OPTIONAL INFORMATION**

Passages marked as optional appear in a gray box. This material is not central to the ideas presented in the chapter but often involves more challenging concepts. A good strategy when reading a chapter is to skip the optional sections and then return to them when you are comfortable with the main ideas presented in the chapter. This is an optional paragraph.

---

8. Different keyboards use different keys to move the *cursor* (page 1160) to the beginning of the next line. This book always refers to the key that ends a line as the RETURN key. The keyboard you are using might have a RET, NEWLINE, ENTER, RETURN, or other key. Use the corresponding key on your keyboard each time this book asks you to press RETURN.

URLs (Web addresses) Web addresses, or URLs, have an implicit **http://** prefix, unless **ftp://** or **https://** is shown. You do not normally need to specify a prefix when the prefix is **http://**, but you must use a prefix from a browser when you specify an FTP or secure HTTP site. Thus you can specify a URL in a browser exactly as shown in this book.

ls output This book uses the output of **ls –l** commands as produced by including the option **--time-style=ISO**. This output produces shorter lines, making the examples more readable.

Tip, caution, and security boxes The following boxes highlight information that might be helpful while you are using or administrating a Linux system.

This is a tip box

tip A tip box might help you avoid repeating a common mistake or might point toward additional information.

This box warns you about something

caution A caution box warns you about a potential pitfall.

This box marks a security note

security A security box highlights a potential security issue. These notes are usually intended for system administrators, but some apply to all users.

CHAPTER SUMMARY

The Linux operating system grew out of the UNIX heritage to become a popular alternative to traditional systems (that is, Windows) available for microcomputer (PC) hardware. UNIX users will find a familiar environment in Linux. Distributions of Linux contain the expected complement of UNIX utilities, contributed by programmers around the world, including the set of tools developed as part of the GNU Project. The Linux community is committed to the continued development of this system. Support for new microcomputer devices and features is added soon after the hardware becomes available, and the tools available on Linux continue to be refined. Given the many commercial software packages available to run on Linux platforms and the many hardware manufacturers offering Linux on their systems, it is clear that the system has evolved well beyond its origin as an undergraduate project to become an operating system of choice for academic, commercial, professional, and personal use.

EXERCISES

1. What is free software? List three characteristics of free software.

2. Why is Linux popular? Why is it popular in academia?

3. What are multiuser systems? Why are they successful?

4. What is the Free Software Foundation/GNU? What is Linux? Which parts of the Linux operating system did each provide? Who else has helped build and refine this operating system?

5. In which language is Linux written? What does the language have to do with the success of Linux?

6. What is a utility program?

7. What is a shell? How does it work with the kernel? With the user?

8. How can you use utility programs and a shell to create your own applications?

9. Why is the Linux filesystem referred to as *hierarchical?*

10. What is the difference between a multiprocessor and a multiprocessing system?

11. Give an example of when you would want to use a multiprocessing system.

12. Approximately how many people wrote Linux? Why is this project unique?

13. What are the key terms of the GNU General Public License?

PART I

Installing Fedora/RHEL Linux

2

INSTALLATION OVERVIEW

OBJECTIVES

After reading this chapter you should be able to:

▸ Choose the best distribution and version to meet your needs

▸ Download the ISO image for the install DVD or the Live CD

▸ Burn the CD/DVD ISO images to physical media

▸ Use a live session to test hardware and check system requirements

▸ List considerations of disk partitioning

▸ Describe advantages and disadvantages of software RAID and LVM partitioning schemes

Installing Fedora/RHEL is the process of copying operating system files from a CD, DVD, or USB flash drive to hard disk(s) on a system and setting up configuration files so Linux runs properly on the hardware. Several types of installations are possible, including fresh installations, upgrades from older releases of Fedora/RHEL, and dual-boot installations.

This chapter discusses the installation process in general: planning, partitioning the hard disk, obtaining the files for the installation, burning a CD or a DVD, and collecting information about the hardware that might be helpful for installation and administration. Chapter 3 covers the process of installing Fedora/RHEL.

Anaconda is a user-friendly tool that installs Fedora/RHEL. To install Fedora/RHEL on standard hardware, you can typically insert a live CD or an install DVD and boot the system. After you answer a few questions, you are done. Of course, sometimes you might want to customize the system or you might be installing on nonstandard hardware: The installer presents you with these kinds of choices as the installation process unfolds. Fedora/RHEL also provides a textual installer that gives you more control over the installation. Refer to "Installing Fedora/RHEL" (page 54) and "Installation Tasks" (page 67) for information about installing and customizing Fedora/RHEL.

THE DESKTOP LIVE CD AND THE INSTALL DVD

Live CD   This book refers to the Fedora Desktop Live Media as a *live CD*. The live CD runs a *live session*: it runs Fedora without installing it on the hard disk. To boot from a live CD, make sure the computer is set up to boot from a CD; see "BIOS setup" and "CMOS" both on page 29 for more information. When you boot a live CD, it brings up a GNOME desktop: You are running a live session. When you exit from the live session, the system returns to the state it was in before you booted from the CD. If the system has a Linux swap partition (most Linux systems have one; see page 39), the live session uses it to improve its performance but does not otherwise write to the hard disk. You can also install Fedora from a live session. RHEL does not provide a live session.

Running a live session is a good way to test hardware and fix a system that will not boot from the hard disk. A live session is ideal for people who are new to Fedora or Linux and want to experiment with Fedora but are not ready to install it on their system.

Saving files during a live session

tip   You cannot save a file to a live/install CD/DVD as these are readonly media. During a live session, even though you might appear to save a file, it will not be there after you exit from the live session. To save data from a live session, save it to a network share or a USB flash drive, or mail it to yourself. Alternatively, you can boot from a Live USB flash drive with persistent storage; for more information see fedoraproject.org/wiki/FedoraLiveCD/USBHowTo.

Install DVD   This book refers to the Install Media, which is provided as a single DVD (included with this book), as an *install DVD*. An install DVD does not bring up a desktop before you install Fedora/RHEL. When you boot an install DVD, it brings up a menu that allows you to install Fedora/RHEL. An install DVD gives you more choices when you install Fedora than does a live CD. For example, an install DVD allows you to use the graphical installer or the textual installer (use the **text** parameter when booting; page 70) or to rescue an installed system (select **Rescue installed system** from the Welcome menu; page 57). You can also rescue an installed system using the first installation CD or the Net Install CD.

Net Install CD   The Net Install CD (previously called the Net Boot CD) boots a system and displays the same menu as an install DVD (previous). It does not hold the software packages needed to install Fedora/RHEL but does allow you to install a new system from a hard disk or over a network. See **askmethod** on page 69 for more information.

MORE INFORMATION

In addition to the following references, see "Where to Find Documentation" on page 125 and refer to Appendix B for additional resources.

Web   memtest86+: www.memtest.org
Partition HOWTO: tldp.org/HOWTO/Partition
LVM Resource Page (includes many links): sourceware.org/lvm2
LVM HOWTO: www.tldp.org/HOWTO/LVM-HOWTO
Transmission BitTorrent client: www.transmissionbt.com
X.org release information: wiki.x.org
Hardware compatibility: hardware.redhat.com
RHEL versions: www.redhat.com/rhel/compare
Upgrading: fedoraproject.org/wiki/YumUpgradeFaq
Boot command-line parameters: fedoraproject.org/wiki/Anaconda/Options and
        www.tldp.org/HOWTO/BootPrompt-HOWTO.html
Release notes: docs.fedoraproject.org/en-US/Fedora/15/html/Release_Notes
Swap space: docs.fedoraproject.org/en-US/Fedora/15/html/Installation_Guide/
        s2-diskpartrecommend-x86.html
Burning a CD/DVD:
        docs.fedoraproject.org/en-US/Fedora/15/html/Installation_Guide/
        sn-making-media.html#sn-making-disc-media
Installing from a USB flash drive: docs.fedoraproject.org/en-US/Fedora/15/html/
        Installation_Guide/Making_USB_Media.html
RAID: raid.wiki.kernel.org/index.php/Linux_Raid
PXE: www.kegel.com/linux/pxe.html

Download   Easiest download: fedoraproject.org/get-fedora
Fedora/RHEL   Downloads: fedoraproject.org/en/get-fedora-all
Torrents: torrent.fedoraproject.org
Fedora and RHEL Mirrors: mirrors.fedoraproject.org/publiclist
RHEL extra packages: fedoraproject.org/wiki/EPEL
Spins: spins.fedoraproject.org

PLANNING THE INSTALLATION

The major decision when planning an installation is determining how to divide the hard disk into partitions or, in the case of a dual-boot system, where to put the Linux partitions. Once you have installed Fedora/RHEL, you can decide which software packages you want to add to the base system (or whether you want to remove some). In addition to these topics, this section discusses hardware requirements for Fedora/RHEL and fresh installations versus upgrades.

CONSIDERATIONS

SELinux   SELinux (Security-Enhanced Linux) improves system security by implementing mandatory access control policies in the Fedora/RHEL kernel (page 459). By default, Fedora installs SELinux in Enforcing mode. If you do not plan to use SELinux, you can change it to Permissive mode once the system is installed. Because SELinux sets extended attributes on files, it can be a time-consuming process to enable SELinux on a system on which it has been turned off.

GUI   On most systems, except for servers, you probably want to install a graphical user interface (a desktop). Fedora/RHEL installs GNOME by default.

Software and services   As you install more software packages on a system, the number of updates and the interactions between the packages increase. Server packages that listen for network connections make the system more vulnerable by increasing the number of ways the system can be attacked. Including additional services can also slow the system down.

If you want a development system or a system to learn on, additional packages and services might be useful. For a more secure production system, it is best to install and maintain the minimum number of packages required and to enable only needed services. See page 426 for information on the systemd Fedora **init** daemon and page 436 for information on the RHEL Upstart **init** daemon, both of which start and stop system services.

REQUIREMENTS

Hardware   This chapter and Chapter 3 cover installing Fedora/RHEL on 32-bit Intel and compatible processor architectures (including AMD processors) as well as 64-bit processor architectures such as AMD64 processors and Intel processors with Intel EM64T technology. Within these processor architectures, Fedora/RHEL runs on much of the available hardware. You can view Fedora/RHEL's list of compatible and supported hardware at hardware.redhat.com. Although these lists pertain to RHEL, they serve as a good guide to what Fedora will run on. The release notes also provide hardware information (see the install DVD, the first install CD, or the Fedora/RHEL Web sites). Many Internet sites discuss Linux hardware; use Google (www.google.com) to search for **linux hardware**, **fedora hardware**, or **linux** and the specific hardware you want more information on (for example, **linux sata** or **linux a8n**). In addition, many HOWTOs cover specific hardware. The *Linux Hardware Compatibility HOWTO* is also available, although it might not be up-to-date at the time you read it. Fedora/RHEL usually runs on the same systems Windows runs on, unless the system includes a very new or unusual component.

The hardware required to run Fedora/RHEL depends on which kind of system you want to set up. A very minimal system that runs a textual (command-line) interface and has very few software packages installed requires very different hardware from a system that runs a GUI, an Apache Web server, and has many installed packages.

A network connection is invaluable for keeping Fedora/RHEL up-to-date. A sound card (or a sound chip on the motherboard) is nice to have for multimedia applications. If you are installing Fedora on old or minimal hardware and want to run a GUI, consider installing LXDE (spins.fedoraproject.org/lxde), as it provides a lightweight desktop that uses system resources more efficiently than GNOME does.

CPU (processor) At a minimum, Fedora requires an Intel Pentium Pro processor; it is optimized for i686 and later processors. Minimum recommended processor speed for a textual system is 200 megahertz and for a graphical system is 400 megahertz. See www.redhat.com/rhel/compare for information on RHEL systems.

RAM (memory) Memory requirements are the same for installing 32-bit and 64-bit Fedora systems. See the tip regarding gibibytes/mebibytes versus gigabytes/megabytes on page 38. At a minimum, a textual (command-line) system requires 256 mebibytes of RAM and a graphical (desktop) system requires 384–512 mebibytes of RAM. In some cases you can get by with less RAM for a very minimal textual installation. See www.redhat.com/rhel/compare for information on RHEL systems.

Running a live CD requires a minimum of 256 mebibytes of RAM.

Linux makes good use of extra memory: The more memory a system has, the faster it runs. Adding memory is one of the most cost-effective ways you can speed up a Linux system.

Hard disk space The amount of hard disk space Fedora/RHEL requires depends on which edition of Fedora/RHEL you install, which packages you install, how many languages you install, and how much space you need for user data (your files). The Fedora operating system typically requires 2–8 gibibytes, although a minimal system can make do with as little as 90 mebibytes. User data requires additional space. Leave at least five percent free space for proper filesystem operation. See www.redhat.com/rhel/compare for information on RHEL systems.

BIOS setup Modern computers can be set up to boot from a CD/DVD, hard disk, or USB flash drive. The BIOS determines the order in which the system tries to boot from each device. You might need to change this order: Make sure the BIOS is set up to try booting from the CD/DVD before it tries to boot from the hard disk. See page 595 for more information.

CMOS CMOS is the persistent memory that stores hardware configuration information. To change the BIOS setup, you need to edit the information stored in CMOS. When the system boots, it displays a brief message about how to enter System Setup or CMOS Setup mode. Usually you need to press DEL or F2 while the system is booting. Press the key that is called for and then move the cursor to the screen and line that deal with booting the system. Generally there is a list of three or four devices that the system tries to boot from; if the first attempt fails, the system tries the second device, and so on. Manipulate the list so the CD/DVD is the first choice, save the list, and reboot. Refer to the hardware/BIOS manual for more information.

PROCESSOR ARCHITECTURE

Fedora/RHEL CDs and DVDs hold programs compiled to run on a specific processor architecture (class of processors, or CPUs). The following list describes each of the architectures Fedora/RHEL is compiled for. See docs.fedoraproject.org/en-US/Fedora/15/html/Installation_Guide/ch-new-users.html#sn-which-arch for a detailed list of processors in each architecture. Because Linux source code is available to everyone, a knowledgeable user can compile Fedora/RHEL to run on other processor architectures.

Should I install 32-bit or 64-bit Fedora/RHEL on a 64-bit-capable processor?

tip   The following information might help you decide whether to install 32-bit or 64-bit Fedora/RHEL on a 64-bit-capable processor.

- EM64T/AMD64 processors can run either version of Fedora/RHEL equally well.

- A 64-bit distribution allows each process to address more than 4 gigabytes of RAM. Larger address space is the biggest advantage of a 64-bit distribution. It is typically useful only for certain engineering/scientific computational work and when you are running multiple virtual machines.

- A 64-bit processor is not faster than a 32-bit processor in general; most benchmarks show more or less similar performance. In some cases the performance is better and in some cases it is worse: There is no clear performance advantage for either type of processor.

- The memory model for 64-bit Linux makes pointers twice as big as those in 32-bit Linux. This size difference translates to a more than 5 percent RAM usage increase, depending on the application. If a system is low on RAM, this overhead might make performance worse.

- ASLR (Address Space Layout Randomization) works better with the larger address space provided by 64-bit Fedora/RHEL. ALSR can help improve system security. See en.wikipedia.org/wiki/Address_space_layout_randomization.

- Some multimedia encoders run 10–30 percent faster under 64-bit Fedora/RHEL.

- Because more people are using 32-bit Linux, bugs in 32-bit Linux tend to be discovered and fixed faster than those in 64-bit Linux.

- Fedora/RHEL can set up Flashplayer and Java with a single click on 64-bit systems just as it can on 32-bit systems. However, for some applications, such as Skype, you must apply ugly workarounds to run them on 64-bit systems.

- Some features of proprietary third-party applications are not available for 64-bit architecture.

- There is no simple way to go back and forth between 32-bit and 64-bit versions of Fedora/RHEL without reinstalling Fedora/RHEL.

- If you are not sure which distribution to use, install the 32-bit version of Fedora/RHEL.

i386/i686 (Intel x86)   Software on an Fedora/RHEL 32-bit PC CD/DVD is compiled to run on Intel x86-compatible processors, including most machines with Intel and AMD processors, almost all machines that run Microsoft Windows, and newer Apple Macintosh machines that use Intel processors. The N and Z Series Atom processors are also based on this architecture. If you are not sure which type of processor a machine has, assume it has this type of processor.

x86_64 (AMD64 and Intel EM64T)   Software on a Fedora/RHEL 64-bit PC CD/DVD is compiled to run on AMD64 processors, including the Athlon64, Opteron, and Intel 64-bit processors that incorporate EM64T technology, such as the EMT64 Xeon. The 230 and 330 Series Atom processors are also based on this architecture.

Mac PowerPC (ppc)   The Fedora/RHEL PPC release runs on the Apple Macintosh G3, G4, G5, PowerBook, and PPC-based Macintoshes.

INTERFACES: INSTALLER AND INSTALLED SYSTEM

When you install Fedora/RHEL, you have a choice of interfaces to use while you install it (to work with the installer). You also have a choice of interfaces to use to work with the installed system. This section describes the two basic interfaces: textual and graphical.

Textual (TUI/CLI)   A textual user interface (TUI), also called a command-line interface (CLI) or character-based interface, displays characters and some simple graphical symbols. It is line oriented; you give it instructions using a keyboard only.

Graphical (GUI)   A graphical user interface (GUI) typically displays a desktop (such as GNOME) and windows; you give it instructions using a mouse and keyboard. You can run a textual interface within a GUI by opening a terminal emulator window (page 117). A GUI uses more computer resources (CPU time and memory) than a textual interface does.

Pseudographical   A pseudographical interface is a textual interface that takes advantage of graphical elements on a text-based display device such as a terminal. It might also use color. This interface uses text elements, including simple graphical symbols, to draw rudimentary boxes that emulate GUI windows and buttons. Pressing the TAB key frequently moves the cursor from one element to the next and pressing the RETURN key selects the element the cursor is on.

Advantages   A GUI is user friendly, whereas the textual interface is compact, uses fewer system resources, and can work on a text-only terminal or over a text-only connection. Because it is more efficient, a textual interface is useful for older, slower systems and systems with minimal amounts of RAM. Server systems frequently use a textual interface because it allows the system to dedicate more resources to carrying out the job it is set up to do and fewer resources to pleasing the system administrator. Not running a GUI can also improve system security.

Even though it uses a graphical interface, Fedora/RHEL's live installer installs Fedora/RHEL faster than the textual installer. The live installer copies an installed system image to the hard disk and then sets up the system, whereas the textual installer uses yum and RPM to unpack hundreds of packages one by one.

Figure 2-1   Graphical (left) and textual (pseudographical, inset) installers

Installer interfaces   Fedora/RHEL provides a user-friendly installer named Anaconda that works in both graphical and pseudographical modes. Used in pseudographical mode, Anaconda offers more options and gives you greater control over the installation (Figure 2-1). Both interfaces accomplish the same task: They enable you to tell the installer how you want it to configure Fedora/RHEL.

WHICH ARE YOU INSTALLING: FEDORA OR RED HAT ENTERPRISE LINUX?

This book describes two products: Fedora and RHEL (Red Hat Enterprise Linux). This section briefly highlights the differences between these products.

Fedora   The Fedora Project is sponsored by Red Hat and supported by the open-source community. With releases, called Fedora, coming out about every six months, this Linux distribution incorporates cutting-edge code. It is *not* a supported Red Hat product and is *not* recommended for production environments where the set of software packages and features must remain constant over a longer period of time. Fedora aims to reflect the upstream projects it incorporates, including the kernel. It is widely regarded as the most stable "free" Linux distribution. In contrast, RHEL includes many changes introduced by Fedora.

RHEL   Red Hat Enterprise Linux is typically sold through an annual subscription that includes access to the Red Hat Network (RHN; page 554) and technical support. It is more stable but less cutting edge than Fedora. RHEL provides at least 7 years of updates; Fedora provides 13 months.

Red Hat Enterprise Linux comes in several configurations; for more information see www.redhat.com/wapps/store/catalog.html. See www.redhat.com/rhel/compare for more information on the various versions of RHEL.

CentOS   CentOS (www.centos.org) is a free, RHEL-compatible Linux distribution. It has more long-term stability than Fedora but has less support than RHEL. Because CentOS is RHEL compatible, this book also describes CentOS.

FEDORA/RHEL RELEASES

The Fedora Project distributes a new release of Fedora about every six months. Each release has both a number and a name. For example, Fedora 15 is named Lovelock and Fedora 16 is named Verne. Previous versions were named Constantine (12), Goddard (13), and Laughlin (14). See fedoraproject.org/wiki/Releases/Names for a description of how names are chosen.

Red Hat distributes a new release of RHEL every few years. For information on the RHEL life cycle see access.redhat.com/support/policy/updates/errata.

FEDORA STANDARD VERSIONS

Standard versions of Fedora are compiled for i686 and x86_64 architectures and are available via BitTorrent, direct download, and mirrors. To download a standard version visit fedoraproject.org/en/get-fedora-all.

Install media   Install media is available as an install DVD or a series of install CDs. From these media you can install a graphical or textual system using a graphical or textual installer. Installing from install media gives you many more options than installing from a live session (next). You can also use install media to boot a minimal textual system you can use to rescue an installed system.

Desktop live media   Desktop live media is available as a live CD. From this CD you can run a live session. From the live session you can install a basic Fedora system. Once installed, you can use an Internet connection to add more software packages to the system.

KDE live media   The KDE live media is the same as the desktop live media except it runs a KDE live session instead of a GNOME live session. When you install from KDE live media you install a KDE-based Fedora system.

FEDORA SPINS

In addition to the standard versions, Fedora releases many alternative versions called *spins*. Some of the most popular spins are

- KDE—A complete, modern desktop built using the KDE Plasma Desktop
- LXDE—A light, fast, less-resource hungry desktop environment
- XFCE—A complete, well-integrated Xfce desktop
- Security—Security analysis tools
- Games—Includes many games

See spins.fedoraproject.org for a complete list of spins.

INSTALLING A FRESH COPY OR UPGRADING AN EXISTING FEDORA/RHEL SYSTEM?

Clean install   An *installation,* sometimes referred to as a *clean install,* writes all fresh data to a disk. The installation program overwrites all system programs and data as well as the kernel. You can preserve some user data during an installation depending on where it is located and how you format/partition the hard disk. Alternatively, you can perform a clean install on an existing system without overwriting data by setting up a dual-boot system (page 82).

Upgrade   An *upgrade* replaces all installed software packages with the most recent version available on the new release. During an upgrade, the installation program preserves both system configuration and user data files. An upgrade brings utilities that are present in the old release up-to-date and installs new utilities. Before you upgrade a system, back up all files on the system. In general, all new features are provided by an upgrade.

SETTING UP THE HARD DISK

Free space   A hard disk must be prepared in several ways so Linux can write to and read from it. Low-level formatting is the first step in preparing a disk for use. You do not need to perform this task, as it is done at the factory where the hard disk is manufactured. The next steps in preparing a hard disk for use are to write a partition table to it and to create partitions on the disk. Finally, you need to create a filesystem on each partition. The area of a partitioned disk that is not occupied by partitions is called *free space.* A new disk has no partition table, no partitions, and no free space. Under DOS/Windows, the term *formatting* means creating a filesystem on a partition; see "Filesystems" below.

Partitions   A *partition,* or *slice,* is a logical section of a hard disk that has a device name, such as **/dev/sda1**, so you can refer to it separately from other sections. For normal use, you must create at least one partition on a hard disk. From a live session before you install Fedora/RHEL, you can use palimpsest, the GNOME Disk Utility (page 77), to view, resize, and create partitions on an existing system. During installation, you can use the Disk Druid partition editor (page 71) to create partitions. After installation, you can use palimpsest, parted (page 617), or fdisk to manipulate partitions. See **/dev** on page 503 for more information on device names.

Partition table   A partition table holds information about the partitions on a hard disk. Before the first partition can be created on a disk, the program creating the partition must set up an empty partition table on the disk. As partitions are added, removed, and modified, information about these changes is recorded in the partition table. If you remove the partition table, you can no longer access information on the disk except by extraordinary means.

LVM   By default, during installation Disk Druid sets up logical volumes (LVs) that function like partitions. With LVs, you can use the Logical Volume Manager (LVM; page 42) to change the sizes of volumes easily after the system is installed. Using LVM to manipulate LVs is more convenient than working with one of the tools that manipulates partitions.

Filesystems   Before most programs can write to a partition, a *data structure* (page 1160), called a *filesystem,* needs to be written to the partition. This data structure holds inodes (page 515) that map locations on the disk that store files to the names of the files. At the top of the data structure is a single unnamed directory. As will be explained shortly, this directory joins the system directory structure when the filesystem is mounted.

When the Fedora/RHEL installer creates a partition, it automatically writes a filesystem to the partition. You can use the mkfs (make filesystem; page 472) utility, which is similar to the DOS/Windows format utility, to manually create a filesystem on a partition. Table 12-1 on page 519 lists some common types of filesystems. Fedora/RHEL typically creates **ext4** filesystems for data; unless you have reason to use another filesystem type, use **ext4**. Windows uses FAT16, FAT32, and NTFS filesystems. Apple uses HFS (Hierarchical Filesystem) and HFS+. OS X uses either HFS+ or UFS. Different types of filesystems can coexist in different partitions on a single hard disk, including both Windows and Linux filesystems.

PRIMARY, EXTENDED, AND LOGICAL PARTITIONS

You can divide an IDE/ATA/SATA disk into a maximum of 63 partitions and a SCSI disk into a maximum of 15 partitions. You can use each partition independently for swap devices, filesystems, databases, other resources, and even other operating systems.

Primary and extended partitions   Unfortunately, disk partitions follow the template established for DOS machines a long time ago. At most, a disk can hold four *primary partitions*. You can divide one (and only one) of these primary partitions into multiple *logical partitions;* this divided primary partition is called an *extended partition*. If you want more than four partitions on a drive—and you frequently do—you must set up an extended partition.

A typical disk is divided into three primary partitions (frequently numbered 1, 2, and 3) and one extended partition (frequently numbered 4). The three primary partitions are the sizes you want the final partitions to be. The extended partition occupies the rest of the disk. Once you establish the extended partition, you can subdivide it into additional logical partitions (numbered 5 or greater), each of which is the size you want. You cannot use the extended partition (number 4)—only the logical partitions it holds. Figure 16-3 on page 619 illustrates the disk described in this paragraph. See the *Linux Partition HOWTO* (tldp.org/HOWTO/Partition) for more information.

The Linux Directory Hierarchy

Skip this section for a basic installation

tip This section briefly describes the Linux directory hierarchy so you might better understand some of the decisions you might need to make when you divide the hard disk into partitions while installing Linux. You do not have to read this section to install Linux. You can use default partitioning (page 62) to set up the disk and return to this section when and if you want to. See the beginning of Chapter 6 for a more thorough explanation of the Linux directory hierarchy.

Namespace A *namespace* is a set of names (identifiers) in which each name is unique.

Windows versus Linux As differentiated from a Windows machine, a Linux system presents a single namespace that holds all files, including directories, on the local system. The Linux system namespace is called the *directory hierarchy* or *directory tree*. Under Windows, **C:** is a separate namespace from **D:**. The directory hierarchy rooted at **C:** is separate from the directory hierarchy rooted at **D:** and there is no path or connection between them. Under Linux, the single system namespace is rooted at **/**, which is the *root directory*. Under the root directory are top-level subdirectories such as **bin**, **boot**, **etc**, **home**, and **usr**.

Absolute pathnames All files on a Linux system, including directories, have a unique identifier called an *absolute pathname*. An absolute pathname traces a path through the directory hierarchy starting at the root directory and ending at the file or directory identified by the pathname. Thus the absolute pathname of the top-level directory named **home** is **/home**. For more information refer to "Absolute Pathnames" on page 192.

Slashes (/) in pathnames Within a pathname, a slash (**/**) follows (appears to the right of) the name of a directory. Thus **/home/sam** specifies that the ordinary or directory file named **sam** is located in the directory named **home**, which is a subdirectory of the root directory (**/**). The pathname **/home/sam/** (with a trailing slash) explicitly specifies **sam** is a directory file. In most instances this distinction is not important. The root directory is implied when a slash appears at the left end of a pathname or when it stands alone.

Linux system namespace The Linux system namespace comprises the set of absolute pathnames of all files, including directories, in the directory hierarchy of a system.

Mount Points

A filesystem on a partition holds no information about where it will be mounted in the directory hierarchy (the top-level directory of a filesystem does not have a name). When you use the installer to create most partitions, you specify the type of filesystem to be written to the partition and the name of a directory that Fedora/RHEL associates with the partition.

Mounting a filesystem associates the filesystem with a directory in the directory hierarchy. You can mount a filesystem on any directory in the directory hierarchy. The directory that you mount a filesystem on is called a *mount point*. The directory you specify when you use the installer to create a partition is the mount point for the partition. Most mount points are top-level subdirectories, with a few exceptions (such as **/usr/local**, which is frequently used as a mount point).

Do not create files on mount points before mounting a filesystem

caution Do not put any files in a directory that is a mount point while a filesystem is not mounted on that mount point. Any files in a directory that is used as a mount point are covered up while the filesystem is mounted on that directory; you will not be able to access them. They reappear when the filesystem is unmounted.

For example, suppose the second partition on the first hard disk has the device name **/dev/sda2**. To create an **ext4** filesystem that you want to appear as **/home** in the directory hierarchy, you must instruct Linux to mount the **/dev/sda2** partition on **/home** when the system boots. With this filesystem mounted on its normal mount point, you can access it as the **/home** directory.

Filesystem independence The state of one filesystem does not affect other filesystems: One filesystem on a drive might be corrupt and unreadable, while other filesystems function normally. One filesystem might be full so you cannot write to it, while others have plenty of room for more data.

/etc/fstab The file that holds the information relating partitions to mount points is **/etc/fstab** (filesystem table; page 524). The associations stored in the **fstab** file are the normal ones for the system, but you can easily override them. When you work in recovery mode, you might mount a filesystem on the **/target** directory so you can repair the filesystem. For example, if you mount on **/target** the partition holding the filesystem normally mounted on **/home**, the directory you would normally find at **/home/sam** will be located at **/target/sam**.

Naming partitions and filesystems A partition and any filesystem it holds have no name or identification other than a device name (and a related UUID value—see page 524). Instead, the partition and the filesystem are frequently referred to by the name of the partition's normal mount point. Thus "the **/home** partition" and "the **/home** filesystem" refer to the partition that holds the filesystem normally mounted on the **/home** directory. See page 520 for more information on mounting filesystems.

PARTITIONING A DISK

During installation, the installer calls the Disk Druid partition editor to set up disk partitions. This section discusses how to plan partition sizes. Although this section uses the term *partition*, planning and sizing LVs (logical volumes; page 42) works the same way. For more information refer to page 71 and to the *Linux Partition HOWTO* at www.tldp.org/HOWTO/Partition.

DEFAULT PARTITIONING

It can be difficult to plan partition sizes appropriately if you are not familiar with Linux. During installation, Fedora/RHEL provides *default partitioning*. Without asking any questions, default partitioning divides the portion of the disk allotted to Fedora/RHEL into three or four partitions. One partition is a small **/boot** partition, and one is the swap partition which can be any size from 512 megabytes to 2 or more gigabytes. Another partition is designated as **/** (root) and occupies up to about 50 gigabytes. If enough disk space is available, default partitioning creates a partition designated as **/home**. This partition takes up the remainder of the disk space. The next section discusses the advantages of manual partitioning.

GiB versus GB

tip Historically a *gigabyte* (GB) meant either 2^{30} (1,073,741,824) or 10^9 (1,000,000,000) bytes. Recently the term *gibibyte* (giga binary byte; abbreviated as GiB) has been used to mean 2^{30} bytes; in turn, *gigabyte* is used more frequently to mean 10^9 bytes. Similarly, a *mebibyte* (MiB) is 2^{20} (1,048,576) bytes. The Fedora/RHEL partitioner still uses megabytes and gigabytes for specifying the size of partitions.

MANUAL PARTITIONING: PLANNING PARTITIONS

This section discusses additional partitions you might want to create. Consider setting up LVM (page 42) *before* you create partitions; LVM allows you to change partition sizes easily after the system is installed. Under Fedora/RHEL, default partitioning sets up LVM. If you decide to manually partition the hard disk and set up partitions other than a root partition (**/**), a swap partition, and possible a **/home** partition, first consider which kinds of activities will occur under each top-level subdirectory. Then decide whether it is appropriate to isolate that subdirectory by creating a filesystem in a partition and mounting it on its own mount point. Advantages of creating additional filesystems include the following points:

- Separating data that changes frequently (e.g., **/var** and **/home**) from data that rarely changes (e.g., **/usr** and **/boot**) can reduce fragmentation on the less frequently changing filesystems, helping to maintain optimal system performance.

- Isolating filesystems (e.g., **/home**) can preserve data when you reinstall Linux.

- Additional filesystems can simplify backing up data on a system.

- If all directories are part of a single filesystem, and if a program then runs amok or the system is the target of a *DoS attack* (page 1162), the entire disk can fill up. System accounting and logging information, which might contain data that can tell you what went wrong, might be lost. On a system with multiple filesystems, such problems typically fill a single filesystem and do not affect other filesystems. Data that might help determine what went wrong will likely be preserved and the system is less likely to crash.

/ (root) The following paragraphs discuss the advantages of making each of the major top-level subdirectories a separate, mountable filesystem. Any directories you do not create filesystems for automatically become part of the root (/) filesystem. For example, if you do not create a **/home** filesystem, **/home** is part of the root (/) filesystem.

(swap) Linux temporarily stores programs and data on a swap partition when it does not have enough RAM to hold all the information it is processing. The swap partition is also used when a system hibernates (is suspended to disk). The size of the swap partition should be 2 gigabytes for systems with up to 4 gigabytes of RAM, 4 gigabytes for 4–16 gigabytes of RAM, and 8 gigabytes for 16–64 gigabytes of RAM. The worst-case hibernation requires a swap size that is one and a half times the size of RAM. For example, a system with 1 gigabyte of RAM should have a 2-gigabyte swap partition. Although a swap partition is not required, most systems perform better when one is present. On a system with more than one drive, having swap partitions on each drive can improve performance even further. A swap partition is not mounted, so it is not associated with a mount point. See **swap** on page 513 for more information.

/boot The **/boot** partition holds the kernel and other data the system needs when it boots. This partition is typically approximately 500 megabytes, although the amount of space required depends on how many kernel images you want to keep on hand. It can be as small as 100 megabytes.

Although you can omit the **/boot** partition, it is useful in many cases. Many administrators put an **ext2** filesystem on this partition because the data on it does not change frequently enough to justify the overhead of the **ext4** journal. Systems that use software RAID (page 41) or LVM (page 42) require a separate **/boot** partition. Some BIOSs, even on newer machines, require the **/boot** partition [or the **/** (root) partition if there is no **/boot** partition] to appear near the beginning of the disk (page 595).

Where to put the /boot partition

caution On some systems, the **/boot** partition must reside *completely below cylinder 1023* of the hard disk. An easy way to ensure compliance with this restriction is to make the **/boot** partition one of the first partitions on the disk. When a system has more than one hard disk, the **/boot** partition must also reside on a drive in the following locations:

- Multiple IDE or EIDE drives: the primary controller
- Multiple SCSI drives: ID 0 or ID 1
- Multiple IDE and SCSI drives: the primary IDE controller or SCSI ID 0

/var The name **var** is short for *variable:* The data in this partition changes frequently. Because it holds the bulk of system logs, package information, and accounting data, making **/var** a separate partition is a good idea. Then, if a user runs a job that consumes all of the users' disk space, system log files in **/var/log** will not be affected. The **/var** partition can occupy from 500 megabytes to as much as several gigabytes for extremely active systems with many verbose daemons and a lot of printer and mail activity (the print queues reside in **/var/spool/cups** and incoming mail is stored in **/var/mail**). For example, software license servers are often extremely active systems. By default, Apache content (the Web pages it serves) is stored on **/var** under Fedora/RHEL; you might want to change the location Apache uses.

Although such a scenario is unlikely, many files or a few large files might be created under the **/var** directory. Creating a separate filesystem to hold the files in **/var** will prevent these files from overrunning the entire directory structure, bringing the system to a halt, and possibly creating a recovery problem.

/var/log   Some administrators choose to put the log directory in a separate partition to isolate system logs from other files in the **/var** directory.

/home   It is a common strategy to put user home directories on their own filesystem. Such a filesystem is usually mounted on **/home**. Having **/home** as a separate filesystem allows you to perform a clean install without risking damage to or loss of user files. Also, having a separate **/home** filesystem prevents a user from filling the directory structure with her data; at most she can fill the **/home** filesystem, which will affect other users but not bring the system down.

Set up partitions to aid in making backups

tip   Plan partitions based on which data you want to back up and how often you want to back it up. One very large partition can be more difficult to back up than several smaller ones.

/usr   Separating the **/usr** partition can be useful if you plan to export **/usr** to another system and want the security that a separate partition can give. Many administrators put an **ext2** filesystem on this partition because the data on it does not change frequently enough to justify the overhead of the **ext4** journal. The size of **/usr** depends on the number of packages you install. On a default system, it is typically 2–4 gigabytes.

/usr/local
and /opt   Both **/usr/local** and **/opt** are candidates for separation. If you plan to install many packages in addition to Fedora/RHEL, such as on an enterprise system, you might want to keep them on a separate partition. If you install the additional software in the same partition as the users' home directories, for example, it might encroach on the users' disk space. Many sites keep all **/usr/local** or **/opt** software on one server; from there, they export the software to other systems. If you choose to create a **/usr/local** or **/opt** partition, its size should be appropriate to the software you plan to install.

Table 2-1 gives guidelines for minimum sizes for partitions used by Linux. Set the sizes of other partitions, such as those for **/home, /opt,** and **/usr/local,** according to need and the size of the hard disk. If you are not sure how you will use additional disk space, you can create extra partitions using whatever names you like (for example, **/b01, /b02,** and so on). Of course, you do not have to partition the entire drive when you install Linux; you can wait until later to divide the additional space into partitions.

Table 2-1 Example minimum partition sizes[a]

Partition	Example size
/boot	100–500 megabytes
/ (root)	1 gigabyte
(swap)	2–8 gigabytes (page 39)
/home	As large as necessary; depends on the number of users and the type of work they do
/tmp	Minimum of 500 megabytes
/usr	Minimum of 2–16 gigabytes; depends on which and how many software packages you install
/var	Minimum of 500 megabytes—much larger if you are running a server

a. The sizes in this table assume you create all partitions separately. For example, if you create a 1-gigabyte / (root) partition and do not create a **/usr** partition, in most cases you will not have enough room to store all of the system programs.

RAID

RAID (Redundant Array of Inexpensive/Independent Disks) employs two or more hard disk drives or partitions in combination to improve fault tolerance and/or performance. Applications and utilities see these multiple drives/partitions as a single logical device. RAID, which can be implemented in hardware or software (Fedora/RHEL gives you this option), spreads data across multiple disks. Depending on which level you choose, RAID can provide data redundancy to protect data in the case of hardware failure. Although it can improve disk performance by increasing read/write speed, software RAID uses quite a bit of CPU time, which might be a consideration. True hardware RAID requires hardware designed to implement RAID and is not covered in this book (but see "Fake RAID" on the next page).

RAID does not replace backups

caution   The purposes of RAID are to improve performance and/or to minimize downtime in the case of a disk failure. RAID does not replace backups.

Do not use RAID as a replacement for regular backups. If the system experiences a catastrophic failure, RAID is useless. Earthquake, fire, theft, and other disasters might leave the entire system inaccessible (if the hard disks are destroyed or missing). RAID also does not take care of the simple case of replacing a file when a user deletes it by accident. In these situations, a backup on a removable medium (which has been removed) is the only way you will be able to restore a filesystem.

RAID can be an effective *addition* to a backup. Fedora/RHEL offers RAID software that you can install either when you install a Fedora/RHEL system or as an afterthought. The Linux kernel automatically detects RAID arrays (sets of partitions) at boot time if the partition ID is set to **0xfd** (**raid autodetect**).

Software RAID, as implemented in the kernel, is much cheaper than hardware RAID. Not only does this approach avoid the need for specialized RAID disk controllers, but it also works with the less expensive ATA disks as well as SCSI disks.

Fake RAID   Fedora/RHEL does not officially support motherboard-based RAID (known as *fake RAID*) but accepts it through the **dmraid** driver set. Linux software RAID is almost always better than fake RAID. Visit help.ubuntu.com/community/FakeRaidHowto for background information on fake RAID.

The partition editor gives you the choice of implementing RAID level 0, 1, or 5, 6, or 10. For levels 1 and 5, be sure to put member partitions on different drives. That way, if one drive fails, the data will be preserved.

- **RAID level 0 (striping)**—Improves performance but offers no redundancy. The storage capacity of the RAID device is equal to that of the member partitions or disks.

- **RAID level 1 (mirroring)**—Provides simple redundancy, improving data reliability, and can improve the performance of read-intensive applications. The storage capacity of the RAID device is equal to one of the member partitions or disks.

- **RAID level 5 (disk striping with parity)**—Provides redundancy and improves performance (most notably, read performance). The storage capacity of the RAID device is equal to that of the member partitions or disks, minus one of the partitions or disks (assuming they are all the same size).

- **RAID level 6 (disk striping with double parity)**—Improves upon level 5 RAID by protecting data when two disks fail at once. Level 6 RAID is inefficient with a small number of drives.

- **RAID level 10 (mirroring and striping)**—A combination of RAID 1 and RAID 0 (also called RAID 1+0), RAID 10 uses mirroring to improve fault tolerance and striping to improve performance. Multiple RAID 1 arrays (mirroring) are overlaid with a RAID 0 array (striping). The storage capacity of the RAID device is equal to one-half that of the member partitions or disks. You must use at least four partitions or disks.

For more information see raid.wiki.kernel.org/index.php/Linux_Raid.

LVM: LOGICAL VOLUME MANAGER

The Logical Volume Manager (LVM2, which this book refers to as LVM) allows you to change the size of *logical volumes* (LVs, the LVM equivalent of partitions) on the fly. With LVM, if you make a mistake in setting up LVs or if your needs change, you can make LVs either smaller or larger without affecting user data. You must choose to use LVM at the time you install the system or add a hard disk; you cannot

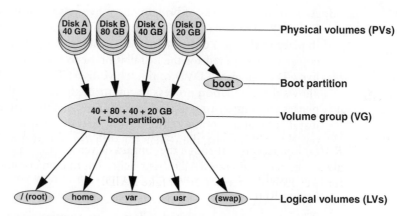

Figure 2-2   LVM: Logical Volume Manager

retroactively apply it to a disk full of data. LVM supports IDE and SCSI drives as well as multiple devices such as those found in RAID arrays.

LVM groups disk components (partitions, hard disks, or storage device arrays), called *physical volumes* (PVs), into a storage pool, or virtual disk, called a *volume group* (VG). See Figure 2-2. You allocate a portion of a VG to create a *logical volume* (LV).

An LV is similar in function to a traditional disk partition in that you can create a filesystem on an LV. It is much easier, however, to change and move LVs than partitions: When you run out of space on a filesystem on an LV, you can grow (expand) the LV and its filesystem into empty or new disk space, or you can move the filesystem to a larger LV. For example, you can add a hard disk to a system and incorporate it into an LV to expand the capacity of that LV. LVM's disk space manipulation is transparent to users; service is not interrupted.

LVM also eases the burden of storage migration. When you outgrow the PVs or need to upgrade them, LVM can move data to new PVs. To read more about LVM, refer to the resources listed on page 27.

THE INSTALLATION PROCESS

The following steps outline the process of installing Fedora/RHEL from the install DVD. Installation from other media follows similar steps. See Chapter 3 for specifics.

1. Make sure the BIOS is set to boot from a CD/DVD (page 29). Insert the install DVD in and reset the computer. The computer boots from the DVD and displays the install DVD Welcome menu (Figure 3-5, page 57).

2. You can make a selection from the Welcome menu, press the TAB key to display the boot command line (which you can modify), and begin installing Fedora/RHEL when you are ready. One of the menu items checks the installation medium. If you do nothing, the Fedora install DVD starts installing the system after 60 seconds

3. As part of the process of bringing up a live session or installing Fedora/RHEL, Fedora/RHEL creates *RAM disks* (page 1184) that it uses in place of the hard disk used for a normal boot operation. The installer copies tools required for the installation or to bring up a system from a live CD or an install DVD to the RAM disks. The use of RAM disks allows the installation process to run through the specification and design phases without writing to the hard disk and enables you to opt out of the installation at any point before the last step of the installation. If you opt out before this point, the system is left in its original state. The RAM disks also allow a live session to leave the hard disk untouched.

4. The installer prompts you with questions about how you want to configure Fedora/RHEL.

5. When the installer is finished collecting information, it writes the operating system files to the hard disk.

6. When you reboot the system, Firstboot asks questions that are required to complete the installation (page 65).

7. The Fedora/RHEL system is ready for you to log in and use.

DOWNLOADING AND BURNING A CD/DVD

There are several ways to obtain an Fedora/RHEL CD/DVD. Fedora/RHEL makes available releases of Linux as CD and DVD *ISO image* files (named after the ISO 9660 standard that defines the CD filesystem). This section describes how to download one of these images and burn a CD/DVD. You can also purchase a CD/DVD from a Web site. If you cannot obtain Fedora/RHEL by any other means, you can point a browser at fedoraproject.org/wiki/Distribution/FreeMedia to display a Web page with links that enable you to request a free Fedora CD.

THE EASY WAY TO DOWNLOAD A CD/DVD ISO IMAGE FILE

This section explains the easiest way to download a CD/DVD ISO image file. This technique works in most situations; it is straightforward but limited. For example, it does not allow you to use BitTorrent to download the file.

To begin, point a browser at fedoraproject.org and click **Download Now!**. The download should start shortly. If the browser gives you a choice of what to do with the file, save it to the hard disk. The browser saves the ISO image file to the hard disk. Continue reading at "Burning the CD/DVD" on page 48.

You can find ISO images for all supported architectures here

tip   If you cannot find an ISO image for a CD that supports the type of hardware you want to install Fedora on, visit mirrors.fedoraproject.org/publiclist. For RHEL visit access.redhat.com and select **Downloads** and then **Evaluations and Demos**.

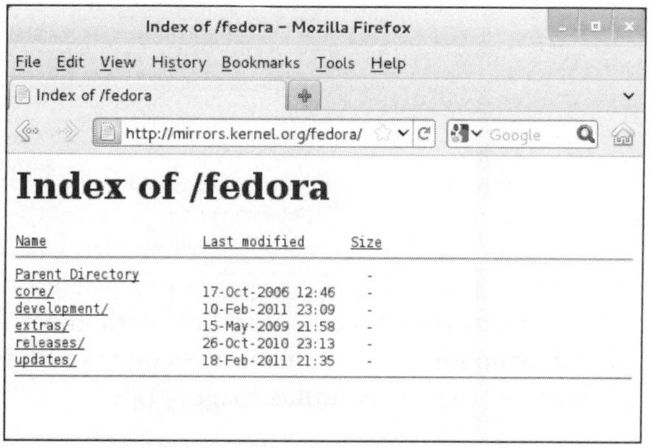

Figure 2-4   A Fedora mirror site

The list on the newly displayed Web page is in country code order. For example, FR is France and US is the United States. To conserve network bandwidth, scroll to and download from a mirror site close to you. Look at the Content, Bandwidth, and Comments columns. Pick the row of an appropriate site and click the protocol you want to use in the Content column. From a browser there is little difference between the FTP and HTTP protocols, although accessing a site using FTP might be a bit faster.

When you click a protocol, the browser displays a page similar to the one shown in Figure 2-4. Follow these steps to download the ISO image file you want:

1. Click **releases**. The browser displays a list of Fedora releases. All sites have the current release. Most sites keep at least one or two older releases while some keep many older releases.

2. Click the number of the release of Fedora you want to download. The browser displays a list that includes **Fedora** and **Live**.

3. Click **Live** if you want to download a live CD and **Fedora** if you want to download an install DVD. Make sure you have room for the file on the hard disk: A DVD ISO image file occupies almost 4 gigabytes.

4. Click the architecture (page 30) you want to install Fedora on: **i386** or **i686** for 32-bit systems and **x86_64** for 64-bit systems.

5. If you are downloading an install ISO image, click **iso**. If you are downloading a live CD, go to the next step.

6. Download the **CHECKSUM** file.

7. Click the name of the ISO image file you want to download and choose to download (not install) the image. **Live** gives you the choice of a **Fedora-15-i686-Live-Desktop.iso**, which runs and installs a Fedora/GNOME desktop and **Fedora-15-i686-Live-KDE.iso**, which runs and installs a KDE desktop. **Fedora** gives you the choice of downloading the Install DVD ISO image file, the Install CD ISO image files, or the Net Install CD ISO image file.

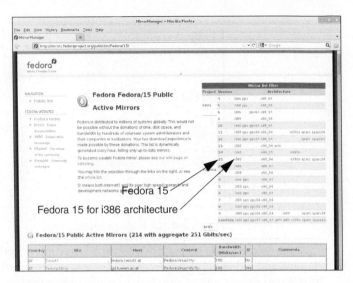

Figure 2-3   The mirrors.fedoraproject.org Web page

OTHER WAYS TO DOWNLOAD A CD/DVD ISO IMAGE FILE

This section explains how to download a DVD image or a release that is not downloaded automatically, and how to download a torrent that enables you to use BitTorrent to download an ISO image file. See "Download Fedora/RHEL" on page 27 for other locations you can download Fedora/RHEL from.

Browser   When you use a Web browser to download a file, the browser contacts a Web (HTTP) or FTP server and downloads the file from that server. If too many people download files from a server at the same time, the downloads become slower.

BitTorrent   BitTorrent efficiently distributes large amounts of static data, such as ISO image files. Unlike using a browser to download a file from a single server, BitTorrent distributes the functions of a server over its clients. As each client downloads a file, it becomes a server for the parts of the file it has downloaded. To use BitTorrent, you must download a small file called a *torrent* (or have a Web browser do it for you). This file, which holds information that allows clients to communicate with one another, has a filename extension of **.torrent**. As more people use a torrent to download a file at the same time, the downloads become faster. Downloading an ISO image file using BitTorrent is covered later in this section.

Mirrors   Many sites mirror (hold copies of) the Fedora ISO image files and BitTorrent torrent files. Some mirrors use HTTP, while others use FTP; you can use a browser to download files from either type of site. FTP and HTTP sites appear slightly different.

Locate a mirror site by pointing a browser at mirrors.fedoraproject.org. Below the heading information, the page displays Public Active Mirrors. Narrow your choices by clicking a selection in the Mirror list filter at the upper-right corner of the page (Figure 2-3). For example, click **15** to list sites from which you can download Fedora 15 or click **i386** in the row that starts with 15 to list sites from which you can download the i386 version of Fedora 15.

Using BitTorrent   As mentioned earlier, you can use BitTorrent to obtain an ISO image file. BitTorrent is especially effective for downloading an ISO image file shortly after a new release of Fedora/RHEL is made available.

To download a torrent, point a browser at fedoraproject.org/en/get-fedora-all or torrent.fedoraproject.org and click the filename of the torrent. You can identify a torrent file by its filename extension of **.torrent**. A BitTorrent client should start automatically and ask where to put the downloaded file. You can also download the torrent manually. Once you have a BitTorrent client such as Transmission (www.transmissionbt.com; installed with most Fedora/RHEL editions), you can start downloading the file from the command line (page 546) or by clicking it in a file browser such as Nautilus (page 102).

You can download and burn the CD/DVD on any operating system

tip   You can download and burn the CD/DVD on any computer that is connected to the Internet, has a browser, has enough space on the hard disk to hold the ISO image file (about 700 megabytes for a CD and 4 gigabytes for a DVD), and can burn a CD/DVD. You can often use ftp (page 704) or, on a Linux system, **Nautilus menubar: File⇨Places⇨Connect to Server** (page 270) in place of a browser to download the file.

VERIFYING AN ISO IMAGE FILE

This section assumes you have an ISO image file and a **CHECKSUM** file saved on the hard disk and explains how to verify the ISO IMAGE file is correct. The **CHECKSUM** file contains the *SHA2* (page 1187) sums for each of the available ISO image files. When you process a file using the sha256sum utility, sha256sum generates a number based on the file. If that number matches the corresponding number in the **CHECKSUM** file, the downloaded file is correct. With the –c option and the name of the CHECKSUM file, sha256sum checks each of the files listed in the CHECKSUM file. The following example shows the Live Desktop ISO image file is OK and the Live KDE ISO image file is not present:

```
$ sha256sum -c *-CHECKSUM
Fedora-15-i686-Live-Desktop.iso: OK
sha256sum: Fedora-15-i686-Live-KDE.iso: No such file or directory
Fedora-15-i686-Live-KDE.iso: FAILED open or read
...
```

Computing an SHA2 sum for a large file can take a while. If sha256sum does not report the file is OK, you must download the file again.

Make sure the software is set up to burn an ISO image

tip   Burning an ISO image is not the same as copying files to a CD/DVD. Make sure the CD/DVD burning software is set up to burn an ISO image. If you simply copy the ISO file to a CD/DVD, it will not work when you try to install Fedora/RHEL.

BURNING THE CD/DVD

An ISO image file is an exact image of what needs to be on the CD/DVD. Putting that image on a CD/DVD involves a different process than copying files to a CD/DVD. For that reason, CD/DVD burning software has a special selection for burning an ISO image, which bears a label similar to **Record CD from CD Image** or **Burn CD Image**. Refer to the instructions for the software you are using for information on how to burn an ISO image file to a CD/DVD.

The CD-RW blank must be large enough to hold the ISO file

tip   When you burn a Fedora/RHEL CD from an ISO image, you might need to use a 700-megabyte blank; in some cases a 650-megabyte blank is not large enough.

GATHERING INFORMATION ABOUT THE SYSTEM

It is not difficult to install and bring up an Fedora/RHEL system. Nevertheless, the more you know about the process before you start, the easier it will be. The installation software collects information about the system and can help you make decisions during the installation process. However, the system will work better when you know how you want to partition the hard disk rather than letting the installation program create partitions without your input. There are many details, and the more details you take control of, the more pleased you are likely to be with the finished product. Finding the information this section asks for will help ensure you end up with a system you understand and know how to change when necessary. To an increasing extent, the installation software probes the hardware and figures out what it is. Newer equipment is more likely to report on itself than older equipment is.

Test the ISO image file and test the CD/DVD

tip   It is a good idea to test the ISO image file and the burned CD/DVD before you use it to install Fedora/RHEL. When you boot the system from the CD/DVD, Fedora/RHEL gives you the option of checking the CD/DVD for defects (see the tip on page 58). A bad file on a CD might not show up until you finish installing Fedora/RHEL and have it running. At that point, it might be difficult and time-consuming to figure out where the problem lies. Testing the file and CD/DVD takes a few minutes but can save you hours of trouble if something is not right. If you decide to perform one test only, test the CD/DVD.

It is critical to have certain pieces of information before you start. One thing Linux can never figure out is all the relevant names and IP addresses (unless you are using DHCP, in which case the addresses are set up for you).

Following is a list of items you might need information about. Gather as much information about each item as you can: manufacturer, model number, size (megabytes, gigabytes, and so forth), number of buttons, chipset (for cards), and so on. Some items, such as the network interface card and the sound card, might be built into the motherboard.

- Hard disks
- Memory. You don't need it for installation, but it is good to know.
- SCSI interface card
- Network interface card (NIC)
- Video interface card (including the amount of video RAM/memory)
- Sound card and compatibility with standards, such as SoundBlaster
- Mouse (PS/2, USB, AT, and number of buttons)
- Monitor (size and maximum resolution)
- IP addresses and names, unless you are using DHCP (page 489; most routers are set up as DHCP servers), in which case the IP addresses are automatically assigned to the system. Most of this information comes from the system administrator or ISP.
  - System hostname (anything you like)
  - System address
  - Network mask (netmask)
  - Gateway address (the connecting point to the network or Internet) or a phone number when you use a dial-up connection
  - Addresses for nameservers, also called DNS addresses
  - Domain name (not required)

CHAPTER SUMMARY

A live CD can run a live Fedora session without installing Fedora on the system. You can install Fedora from a live session. Running a live session is a good way to test hardware and fix a system that will not boot from the hard disk.

When you install Fedora/RHEL, you copy operating system files from a CD or DVD to hard disk(s) on a system and set up configuration files so that Linux runs properly on the hardware. Operating system files are stored on a CD or DVD as ISO image files. You can use a Web browser, FTP, or BitTorrent to download an ISO image file. It is a good idea to test the ISO image file when it is downloaded and the burned CD/DVD before you use it to install Fedora/RHEL.

When you install Fedora/RHEL, you can let the installer decide how to partition the hard disk (default partitioning) or you can manually specify how you want to partition it.

The Fedora Project is sponsored by Red Hat and supported by the open-source community. Fedora is a Linux release that contains cutting-edge code; it is not recommended for production environments. RHEL (Red Hat Enterprise Linux) is more stable than Fedora.

EXERCISES

1. Briefly, what does the process of installing an operating system such as Fedora/RHEL involve?

2. What is an installer?

3. Would you set up a GUI on a server system? Why or why not?

4. A system boots from the hard disk. To install Linux, you need it to boot from a CD/DVD. How can you make the system boot from a CD/DVD?

5. What is free space on a hard disk? What is a filesystem?

6. What is an ISO image? How do you burn an ISO image to a CD/DVD?

ADVANCED EXERCISES

7. Give two reasons why RAID cannot replace backups.

8. What are RAM disks? How are they used during installation?

9. What is SHA2? How does it work to ensure that an ISO image file you download is correct?

3

STEP-BY-STEP
INSTALLATION

OBJECTIVES

After reading this chapter you should be able to:

▸ Run a live session and use palimpsest to view and
change disk partitioning

▸ Install Fedora from a Live session

▸ Install or upgrade Fedora/RHEL using the
Fedora/RHEL install DVD

▸ Modify system behavior with boot time parameters

▸ Modify partitions during installation

▸ Select software during installation

▸ Perform initial configuration with Firstboot

▸ List the requirement and considerations for a
dual-boot configuration

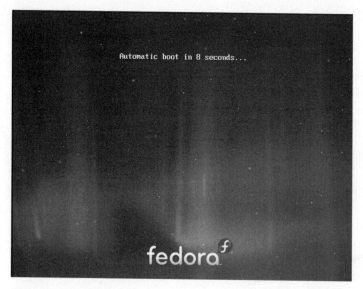

Figure 3-1   Live session, automatic boot screen

Chapter 2 covered planning the installation of Fedora/RHEL: determining the requirements; performing an upgrade versus a clean installation; planning the layout of the hard disk; obtaining the files you need for the installation, including how to download and burn CD/DVD ISO images; and collecting information about the system. This chapter focuses on installing Fedora/RHEL. Frequently the installation is quite simple, especially if you have done a good job of planning. Sometimes you might run into a problem or have a special circumstance; this chapter gives you tools to use in these cases. Read as much of this chapter as you need to; once you have installed Fedora/RHEL, continue with Chapter 4, which covers getting started using the Fedora/RHEL desktop. If you install a textual (command line) system, refer to Chapter 5.

RUNNING A FEDORA LIVE SESSION

As discussed in Chapter 2, a live session is a Linux session you run on a computer without installing Linux on the computer. When you reboot after a live session, the computer is untouched. If you are running Windows, after a live session Windows boots the way it did before the live session. If you choose, you can install Fedora from a live session. Red Hat Enterprise Linux does not offer a live session.

A live session gives you a chance to preview Fedora without installing it. Boot from the live CD to begin a live session and work with Fedora as explained in Chapter 4. When you are finished, remove the CD and reboot the system. The system will then boot as it did before the live session took place.

Because a live session does not write to the hard disk (other than using a swap partition, if one is available), none of the work you save will be available once you reboot. You can use a USB flash drive, Webmail, or another method to transfer files you want to preserve to another system.

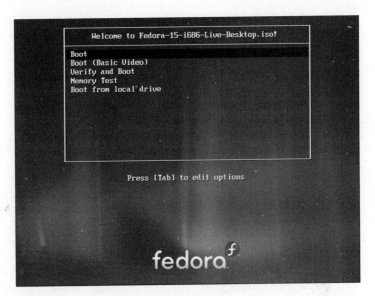

Figure 3-2 The Fedora Live Welcome menu

BOOTING THE SYSTEM

Before Fedora can display the desktop of a live session or install itself on a hard disk, the Linux operating system must be read into memory (booted). This process can take a few minutes on older, slower systems and systems with minimal RAM (memory).

In most cases, you can boot Fedora to run a live session that displays a desktop without doing anything after you boot from a live CD. To begin, insert the live CD (the standard GNOME **Fedora Desktop Live Media**) into the CD drive and turn on or reset the system. Refer to "BIOS setup" on page 29 if the system does not boot from the CD. Refer to "Modifying Boot Parameters (Options)" on page 67 if Fedora does not boot or displays an error message.

A few moments after you start the system, Fedora displays a screen that says **Automatic boot in 10 seconds** and counts down from 10 to 1 (Figure 3-1). Next the system displays a graphical screen showing a shaded blue progress bar.

Checking the CD   The first time you use a CD, it is a good idea to check it for defects. To do so, interrupt the automatic boot by pressing a key such as the SPACE bar while Fedora is counting down. Fedora displays the Welcome menu (Figure 3-2). Use the DOWN ARROW key to highlight the **Verify and Boot** line and press RETURN (the mouse will not work yet). Fedora displays a shaded blue progress bar as it verifies the contents of the CD; nothing happens for a while. If the CD is good, the system boots.

Memory test   Selecting **Memory Test** from the Welcome menu runs memtest86+, a GPL-licensed, stand-alone memory test utility for x86-based computers. Press C to configure the test; press ESCAPE to exit and reboot. See www.memtest.org for more information.

GNOME   If you are booting from Fedora Desktop Live Media (what this book refers to as the *live CD*), the system will run the GNOME desktop manager. When you boot from this CD, Fedora automatically logs in as the user named **liveuser** and displays the GNOME desktop (Figure 3-3).

KDE   If you are booting from Fedora KDE Live Media, the system will run the KDE desktop manager. When you boot from this disk, Fedora next displays a KDE startup screen and then the KDE desktop—there is no need to log in.

optional **SEEING WHAT IS GOING ON**

If you are curious and want to see what Fedora is doing as it boots from a live CD, remove **quiet**, which controls kernel messages, and **rhgb** (Red Hat graphical boot), which controls messages from the graphical installer, from the boot parameters. See Figure 3-13 on page 68; the list of parameters on the screen will be different from those in the figure. With the Fedora Live Welcome menu displayed (Figure 3-2), press TAB to display the boot command-line parameters. Use the LEFT ARROW key to back up over—but not remove—any words to the right of **quiet**. Press BACKSPACE or DEL to back up over and erase **quiet** and **rhgb** from the boot command line. Press RETURN. Now as Fedora boots, it displays information about what it is doing. Text scrolls on the screen, although sometimes too rapidly to read. When you boot Fedora from a DVD and when you boot RHEL, this information is displayed by default: You do not have to change the command line.

INSTALLING FEDORA/RHEL

You can install Fedora from a live session (preceding) or install Fedora/RHEL from the install DVD. Installing from a live session is simpler but does not give you the flexibility installing from the install DVD does. For example, you cannot select the language the installer uses, nor can you choose which software packages you want to install when you install from a live session.

Check to see what is on the hard disk before installing Fedora/RHEL

caution   Unless you are certain the hard disk you are installing Fedora/RHEL on has nothing on it (it is a new disk) or you are sure the disk holds no information of value, it is a good idea to examine the contents of the disk before you start the installation. You can use the **palimpsest** GNOME Disk Utility (page 77) from a live session for this purpose.

The install DVD holds many of the software packages that Fedora/RHEL supports. You can install whichever packages you like from this DVD without connecting to the Internet. However, without an Internet connection, you will not be able to update the software on the system.

The live CD holds a limited set of software packages. Once you install from this CD, you must connect to the Internet to update the software on the system and to download and install additional packages.

To begin most installations, insert the live CD or the install DVD into the CD/DVD drive and turn on or reset the system. For hard disk and network-based installations, you can use the Net Install CD, the install DVD, or a USB flash drive.

Figure 3-3   A full GNOME 3 Live desktop; install to hard drive

INSTALLING FROM A LIVE SESSION (FEDORA)

Bring up a live GNOME session as explained on page 52. GNOME will display either

- A full GNOME 3 desktop that has the word **Activities** in the upper-left corner of the screen or

- A window with the words **GNOME 3 Failed to Load.** When you click **Close** on that window, GNOME displays a desktop running in Fallback mode with the words **Applications** and **Places** in the upper-left corner of the screen.

GNOME 3 desktop   From a full GNOME 3 desktop, click **Activities**; GNOME displays buttons labeled **Windows** and **Applications** with the button labeled **Windows** highlighted (Figure 3-3). At the bottom of the icons on the left side of the window is an icon depicting a hard drive with a green tick above it. Left-click this icon to begin installing Fedora.

Figure 3-4 A GNOME Fallback Live desktop; install to hard drive

Fallback mode
desktop

To begin installing Fedora from a desktop running in Fallback mode, select **Main menu: Applications⇨System Tools⇨Install to Hard Drive** (Figure 3-4) by (left-) clicking **Applications** at the upper-left corner of the screen, clicking **System Tools**, and finally clicking **Install to Hard Drive**.

Continue reading at "Using Anaconda" on page 59.

INSTALLING/UPGRADING FROM THE INSTALL DVD

To install/upgrade Fedora/RHEL from the install DVD, insert the DVD into the DVD drive and turn on or reset the system. After a few moments, the system displays the Welcome to Fedora/RHEL menu (Figure 3-5) and a message that says **Automatic boot in 60 seconds**.

Press a key, such as the SPACE bar, within 60 seconds to stop the countdown and display the message **Press [TAB] to edit options** as shown in Figure 3-5. If you do not press a key, after 60 seconds Fedora/RHEL begins a graphical install/upgrade. Refer to "BIOS setup" on page 29 if the system does not boot from the DVD. Refer to "Modifying Boot Parameters (Options)" on page 67 if Fedora/RHEL does not boot or displays an error message.

The Welcome menu has the following selections:

Install a new system
or upgrade an
existing system

Installs a graphical Fedora/RHEL system using the graphical installer.

Install system with
basic video driver

Installs a graphical Fedora/RHEL system using the graphical installer. Fedora/RHEL does not attempt to determine the type of display attached to the system; it uses a

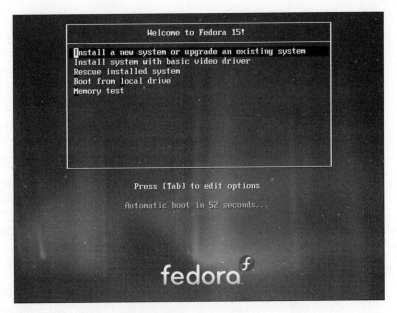

Figure 3-5 The install DVD Welcome menu

basic video driver that works with most displays. Choose this selection if the previous selection fails just after the Disc Found screen (below).

Rescue installed system Brings up a minimal Fedora/RHEL system but does not install it. After detecting the system's disks and partitions, the system enters single-user/rescue mode and allows you to mount an existing Linux filesystem. For more information refer to "Rescue Installed System" on page 457.

Boot from local drive Boots the system from the hard disk. This selection frequently has the same effect as booting the system without the CD/DVD (depending on how the BIOS [page 29] is set up).

Memory test Runs the memory test described on page 53 (Fedora).

STARTING THE INSTALLATION

Make a selection from the Welcome menu and press RETURN to boot the system. Text scrolls by as the system boots.

THE DISC FOUND SCREEN

The first screen the DVD installation process displays is the pseudographical Disc Found screen. Because it is not a true graphical screen, the mouse does not work. Instead, you must use the TAB or ARROW keys to highlight different choices and then press RETURN to select the highlighted choice. This screen allows you to test as many installation CD/DVDs as you like. Choose **OK** to test the media or **Skip** to bypass the test. See the caution box on the next page.

Test the install DVD

caution It is possible for data to become corrupted while fetching an ISO image; it is also possible for a transient error to occur while writing an image to recordable media. When you boot Fedora/RHEL from an install DVD, Anaconda displays the Disc Found screen before starting the installation. From this screen, you can verify that the install DVD does not contain any errors. Testing the DVD takes a few minutes but can save you hours of aggravation if the installation fails due to bad media.

A DVD might fail the media test if the software that was used to burn the disk did not include padding. If a DVD fails the media test, try booting with the **nodma** parameter. See page 67 for information on adding parameters to the boot command line.

If the DVD passes the media test when you boot the system with the **nodma** parameter, the DVD is good; reboot the system without this parameter before installing Fedora/RHEL. If you install Linux after having booted with this parameter, the kernel will be set up to always use this parameter. As a consequence, the installation and operation of the system can be slow.

THE ANACONDA INSTALLER

Anaconda, which is written in Python and C, identifies the hardware, builds the filesystems, and installs or upgrades the Fedora/RHEL operating system. Anaconda can run in textual or graphical (default) interactive mode or in batch mode (see "Using the Kickstart Configurator" on page 81).

Exactly which screens Anaconda displays depends on whether you are installing Fedora from a live session or from the install DVD, whether you are installing RHEL, and which parameters you specify on the boot command line. With some exceptions—most notably if you are running a textual installation—Anaconda probes the video card and monitor, and starts a native X server.

While it is running, Anaconda opens the virtual consoles (page 138) shown in Table 3-1. You can display a virtual console by pressing CONTROL-ALT-F*x*, where *x* is the virtual console number and F*x* is the function key that corresponds to the virtual console number.

Table 3-1   Virtual console assignments during installation

Virtual console	Information displayed during installation	
	Install DVD	**Live CD**
1	Installation dialog	Installation dialog
2	Shell	Login prompt (log in as **liveuser**)
3	Installation log	Installation log
4	System messages	Login prompt (log in as **liveuser**)
5	X server output	Login prompt (log in as **liveuser**)
6	GUI interactive installation screen[a]	Login prompt (log in as **liveuser**)
7	GUI interactive installation screen[a]	GUI interactive installation

a. The GUI appears on virtual console 6 or 7.

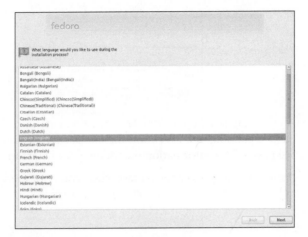

Figure 3-6   The language screen

At any time during the installation, you can switch to virtual console 2 (press CONTROL-ALT-F2) and give commands to see what is going on. Do not give any commands that change any part of the installation process. To switch back to the graphical installation screen, press CONTROL-ALT-F6 or CONTROL-ALT-F7.

USING ANACONDA

Anaconda displays a button labeled **Next** at the lower-right corner of each installation screen and a button labeled **Back** next to it on most screens. When you have completed the entries on an installation screen, click **Next** or press F12; from a textual installation, press the TAB key until the **Next** button is highlighted and then press RETURN. Select **Back** to return to the previous screen.

ANACONDA SCREENS

Anaconda displays different screens depending on which commands you give and which choices you make. During a graphical installation, Anaconda starts, loads drivers, and probes for the devices it will use during installation. After probing, it starts the X server. This section describes the screens Anaconda displays during a default installation and explains the choices you can make on each of them.

Language   Anaconda displays the language screen (Figure 3-6) after it obtains enough information to start the X Window System. Installing from a live session does not display this screen. RHEL displays a welcome screen before it displays the language screen. Select the language you want to use for the installation. This language is not necessarily the same language the installed system will display. Click **Next**.

Keyboard   Select the type of keyboard attached to the system.

Error processing drive   Anaconda displays this warning if the hard disk has not been used before. The dialog box says the drive might need to be initialized. When you initialize a drive, all data on the drive is lost. Click **Re-initialize drive** if it is a new drive or if you do not need the data on the drive. Anaconda initializes the hard disk immediately.

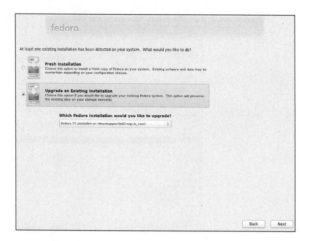

Figure 3-7   The Install or Upgrade screen

Devices   This screen asks you to specify the type of devices you are installing Linux on. In most cases click the radio button labeled **Basic Storage Devices**. If you are installing on an enterprise device, such as a SAN (Storage Area Network), click the radio button labeled **Specialized Storage Devices**.

Warning   If Anaconda does not detect information on the hard drive you are installing Linux on, it displays the Storage Device Warning window. If you are sure there is no data you want to keep on the hard drive you are installing Linux on, put a tick in the check box labeled **Apply my choice to all devices with undetected partitions or filesystems** and click **Yes, discard my data** (Fedora) or click **Re-initialize** all (RHEL).

Hostname   Specify the name of the system on this screen. If the system will not use DHCP to configure its network connection, click Configure Network at the lower-left corner of the screen to display the Network Connections window; see page 651 for more information. Click **Next**.

Time zone   The time zone screen allows you to specify the time zone where the system is located (Figure 2-1, page 32). Use the scroll wheel on the mouse or the slider to the left of the map to zoom in or out on the selected portion of the map, drag the horizontal and vertical *thumbs* (page 1193) to position the map in the window, and then click a city in the local system's time zone. Alternatively, you can scroll through the list and highlight the appropriate selection. Remove the tick from the check box labeled **System clock uses** UTC if the system clock is not set to *UTC* (page 1195). Click **Next**.

Root password   Enter and confirm the password for the **root** user (Superuser). See page 409 for more information on **root** privileges. If you enter a password that is not very secure, Anaconda displays a dialog box with the words **Weak password**; click **Cancel** or **Use Anyway**, as appropriate. Click **Next**.

Install or Upgrade   (This choice is not available from the live CD.) Anaconda displays the Install or Upgrade screen (Figure 3-7) only if it detects a version of Fedora/RHEL it can upgrade on the hard disk. Anaconda gives you the choice of upgrading the existing installation or overwriting the existing installation with a new one. Refer to

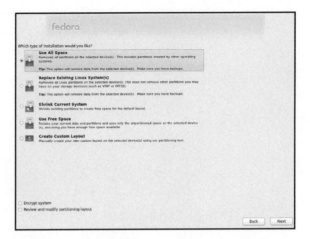

Figure 3-8   The Type of Installation screen

"Installing a Fresh Copy or Upgrading an Existing Fedora/RHEL System?" on page 34 for help in making this selection. Select one of the entries and click **Next**.

Type of Installation   The Type of Installation screen (Figure 3-8) allows you to specify partition information, encrypt the filesystem, and review partition information. Anaconda presents the following choices in the upper part of the screen:

- **Use All Space**—Deletes all data on the hard disk and creates a default layout on the entire hard disk, as though you were working with a new hard disk.

- **Replace Existing Linux System(s)**—Removes all Linux partitions, deleting the data on those partitions and creating a default layout in place of one or more of the removed partitions. If there is only a Linux system on the hard disk, this choice is the same as the previous one.

- **Shrink Current System**—Shrinks the partitions that are in use by the operating system that is already installed on the hard disk. This choice creates a default layout in the space it has recovered from the installed operating system.

- **Use Free Space**—Installs Fedora/RHEL in the *free space* (page 34) on the disk. This choice does not work if there is not enough free space.

- **Create Custom Layout**—Does not alter hard disk partitions. This choice causes Anaconda to run Disk Druid (page 71) so you can preserve those partitions you want to keep and overwrite other partitions. It is a good choice for installing Fedora/RHEL over an existing system where you want to keep **/home**, for example, but want a clean installation and not an upgrade.

Click the radio button adjacent to the choice you want and click **Next**.

Encrypt system   To encrypt the filesystems you are creating, put a tick in the check box labeled **Encrypt system**. If you choose to encrypt the filesystems, Anaconda will ask for a passphrase. You will need this passphrase to log in on the system.

Figure 3-9   The Boot Loader Configuration screen

Default layout   The default layout the first four choices create includes two or three logical volumes (swap, root [/], and if the hard disk is big enough, **/home**) and one standard partition (**/boot**). With this setup, most of the space on the disk is assigned to the **/home** partition, or if there is no **/home** partition, to the root partition. For information on the Logical Volume Manager, see page 42.

Disk Druid   Anaconda runs Disk Druid only if you put a tick in the check box labeled **Review and modify partitioning layout** or if you select **Create custom layout** from the list described earlier. You can use Disk Druid to verify and modify the layout before it is written to the hard disk. For more information refer to "Using Disk Druid to Partition the Disk" on page 71.

Warning   Anaconda displays a warning if you are removing or formatting partitions. Click **Yes, Format,** or **Write changes to disk** to proceed.

Two hard drives   If the machine you are installing Fedora/RHEL on has two or more hard drives, Anaconda displays a screen that allows you to specify which drives are data storage devices and which are install target devices. Disk Druid sets up data storage devices to be mounted on the installed system; they are not formatted. Install target devices are the devices the system is installed on. Some or all of the partitions on these devices will be formatted, destroying any data on them. This screen also allows you to specify which of the install target devices is to hold the boot loader.

Boot Loader Configuration   Anaconda displays the Boot Loader Configuration screen (Figure 3-9) only when you put a tick in the check box labeled **Review and modify partitioning layout** or select **Create custom layout** from the list in the Type of Installation screen. By default, Anaconda installs the grub boot loader (page 595). If you do not want to install a boot loader, remove the tick from the check box labeled **Install boot loader on /dev/xxx**. To change the device the boot loader is installed on, click **Change device**. When you install Fedora/RHEL on a machine that already runs another operating system, Anaconda frequently recognizes the other operating system and sets up grub so you can boot from either operating system. Refer to "Setting Up a Dual-Boot System" on page 82. To manually add other operating systems to grub's

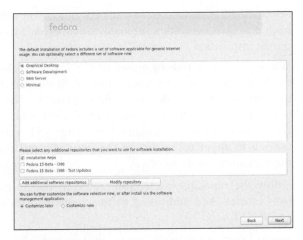

Figure 3-10   The Software Selection screen

list of bootable systems, click **Add** and specify a label and device to boot from. For a more secure system, specify a boot loader password.

Select Network Interface   This window is displayed at this time by the Net Install CD only. See "Select Network Interface" on page 64.

Installing from a live CD   If you are installing from a live CD you are done with the first part of the installation. Click **Close** and then reboot the system by first clicking **Live System User** at the upper-right corner of the screen to display a drop-down menu. If **Suspend** appears at the bottom of this menu, you are running full GNOME 3; press and hold the ALT key to cause **Suspend** to change to **Power Off**. Click **Power Off** and then click **Restart** from the resulting window. If **Shut Down** appears at the bottom of the drop-down menu you are running in Fallback mode (page 92); click **Shut Down** and then click **Restart** from the resulting window. Anaconda ejects the CD as the system shuts down. Continue with "Firstboot: When You Reboot" on page 65.

Software Selection   As the Software Selection screen explains, by default Anaconda installs a basic system, including software that allows you to use the Internet. See Figure 3-10. Near the top of the screen are four check boxes that you can put ticks in to select categories of software to install: **Graphical Desktop** (selected by default), **Software Development**, **Web Server**, and **Minimal** (Fedora; RHEL selections differ slightly).

Fedora/RHEL software is kept in repositories (page 533). When you install Fedora, middle of the screen holds check boxes you can put ticks in to select repositories that hold the following items:

- **Installation Repo**—Indicates Anaconda is to install from the repository included on the installation medium.

- **Fedora 15 – *xxx***—Indicates Anaconda is to use the online Fedora 15 repository. The *xxx* indicates the system architecture (e.g., i386).

- **Fedora 15 – *xxx* – Updates**—Indicates Anaconda is to use the online Fedora 15 Updates repository. The *xxx* indicates the system architecture (e.g., i386).

Selecting either of the last two choices gives you more software packages to choose from later in the installation process if you decide to customize the software selection during installation.

Select Network Interface When you put a tick in either of the last two check boxes, Anaconda displays the Select Network Interface window. Select the interface you want to use from this window. Click **OK**; Anaconda opens the Network Connections window. If the system is configured using DHCP click **Close**. Otherwise configure the network connection as explained on page 651 and then click **Close**. Anaconda takes a moment to configure the network and then retrieves information from the repository you specified.

Below the repository selection frame in the Software Selection screen are buttons labeled **Add additional software repositories** and **Modify repository** (Fedora and RHEL).

Toward the bottom of the screen are two radio buttons:

- **Customize later**—Installs the default packages plus those required to perform the tasks selected from the list at the top of the screen.

- **Customize now**—Displays the package selection screen (next) after you click **Next** on this screen so you can select specific categories of software and package groups you want to install. If you want to set up servers as described in Part V of this book, select **Customize now** and install them in the next step.

In most cases it is a good idea to customize the software selection before installation. Regardless of which software groups and packages you select now, you can change which software groups and packages are installed on a system any time after the system is up and running (as long as the system can connect to the Internet).

Package selection If you selected **Customize now**, Anaconda displays a package selection screen that contains two side-by-side frames near the top of the screen (Figure 3-11). If you added repositories in addition to the Installation repository or if you are installing RHEL, this screen will display more choices. Select a software category from the frame on the left and package groups from the frame on the right. Each package group comprises many software packages, some mandatory (the base packages) and some optional.

For example, to install KDE, which is not installed by default, click **Desktop Environments** in the left frame. Anaconda highlights your selection and displays a list of desktop environments you can install in the right frame. Put a tick in the check box labeled **KDE Software Compilation**; Anaconda highlights KDE, displays information about KDE in the frame toward the bottom of the window, displays the number of optional packages that are selected, and activates the button labeled **Optional packages**. Click this button to select which optional

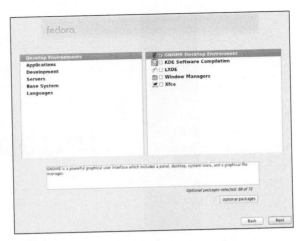

Figure 3-11 The package selection screen

packages you want to install in addition to the base packages. If you install KDE and you do not want to install GNOME too, you must remove the tick from the check box labeled **GNOME Desktop Environment**. To get started, accept the default optional packages. If you will be running servers on the system, click **Servers** on the left and select the servers you want to install from the list on the right. Select other package categories in the same manner. When you are done, click **Next**; Anaconda begins writing to the hard disk.

BEGINNING INSTALLATION

After going through some preliminary steps, Anaconda installs Fedora/RHEL based on your choices in the preceding screens, placing a Kickstart file (page 81) in **/root/anaconda-ks.cfg**. To change the way you set up Fedora/RHEL, you can press CONTROL-ALT-DEL to reboot the system and start over. If you reboot the system, you will lose all the work you did up to this point.

Installing Fedora/RHEL can take a while. The amount of time depends on the hardware you are installing the operating system on and the number of software packages you are installing.

Installation Complete   When Anaconda is finished, it tells you the installation is complete. An installation from a live CD ejects the CD. If you are using another installation technique, you must remove the CD/DVD or other installation medium. Click **Reboot**.

FIRSTBOOT: WHEN YOU REBOOT

When the system reboots, it is running Fedora/RHEL. The first time it boots, Fedora/RHEL runs Firstboot, which asks a few questions before allowing you to log in.

Figure 3-12   The Welcome screen

Welcome   There is nothing to do on the Welcome screen (Figure 3-12). Click **Forward**.

License Information   After the Welcome screen, Firstboot displays the License Information screen. If you understand the license information, click **Forward**.

Software Updates (RHEL)   When installing RHEL, the next screen asks you to set up software updates by registering with RHN (Red Hat Network; page 554).

Create User   The next screen allows you to set up a user account. For more information refer to "Configuring User and Group Accounts" on page 602.

Putting a tick in check box labeled **Add to Administrators group** (Fedora) adds the user to the **wheel** group. The user can then gain **root** privileges by running sudo and providing her password (not the **root** password). See page 415 for more information on using sudo and page 422 for more information on the **wheel** group. Click the button labeled **Use Network Login** to set up a network login using Kerberos, LDAP, or NIS.

Click **Advanced** to display the User Manager window (page 602).

Date and Time   The next screen allows you to set the system date and time. Running the Network Time Protocol (NTP) causes the system clock to reset itself periodically from a clock on the Internet. If the system is connected to the Internet, you can enable NTP by putting a tick in the check box labeled **Synchronize date and time over the network**. Click **Forward**.

Kdump (RHEL)   Kdump captures and preserves kernel dump information. When installing RHEL, put a tick in the box labeled **Enable kdump** to enable Kdump.

Hardware Profile (Fedora)   When you are installing Fedora, the next screen allows the system to share its profile with the Fedora Project. The information is shared anonymously and helps build an up-to-date Linux hardware database that includes distribution information. You can use this database to help you choose components when you buy or build a Linux system.

Click the radio button labeled **Send Profile** to cause the smolt hardware profiler to send monthly updates of the system's hardware profile to smolts.org. Select the radio button labeled **Do not send profile** if you do not want to share the system's profile. Click **Finish**.

When the Hardware Profile (Fedora) or Kdump (RHEL) screen closes, the installation is complete. You can now use the system and set it up as you desire. For example, you might want to customize the desktop (as explained in Chapters 4 and 8) or set up servers (as discussed in Part V of this book).

INITIALIZING DATABASES AND UPDATING THE SYSTEM

Updating the **mandb** (Fedora) or **makewhatis** (RHEL) database ensures the whatis (page 128) and apropos (page 127) utilities will work properly. Similarly, updating the **locate** database ensures that locate will work properly. (The locate utility indexes and allows you to search for files on the system quickly and securely.) Instead of updating these databases when you install the system, you can wait for **crond** (page 611) to run them, but be aware that whatis, apropos, and locate will not work for a while. The best way to update these databases is via the cron scripts that run daily. Working with **root** privileges (page 409), give the following commands:

```
# /etc/cron.daily/man-db.cron        (Fedora)
# /etc/cron.daily/makewhatis.cron    (RHEL)
# /etc/cron.daily/mlocate.cron       (Fedora/RHEL)
```

These utilities run for several minutes and might complain about not being able to find a file or two. When the system displays a prompt, the **mandb/makewhatis** and **locate** databases are up-to-date.

INSTALLATION TASKS

This section details some common tasks you might need to perform during or after installation. It covers modifying the boot parameters, using Disk Druid to partition the disk during installation, using palimpsest to view and modify partitions, using logical volumes (LVs) to facilitate disk partitioning, using Kickstart to automate installation, and setting up a system that will boot either Windows or Linux (a dual-boot system).

MODIFYING BOOT PARAMETERS (OPTIONS)

To modify boot parameters, you must interrupt the automatic boot process by pressing a key such as the SPACE bar while Fedora/RHEL is counting down when you first boot from a live CD (page 53) or install DVD (page 56). When you press a key, Fedora displays the Welcome menu (Figure 3-2 on page 53 or Figure 3-5 on page 57). Use the ARROW keys to highlight the selection you want

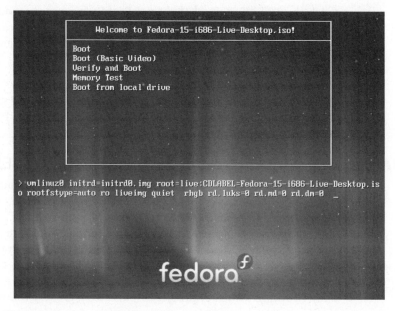

Figure 3-13   The Welcome screen displaying boot parameters (options)

before proceeding. With the desired selection highlighted, press the TAB key to display the boot command-line parameters (Figure 3-13).

Type a SPACE before you enter any parameters. You can specify multiple parameters separated by SPACEs. Press RETURN to boot the system. For more information on boot parameters, refer to www.kernel.org/doc/Documentation/kernel-parameters.txt, www.kernel.org/pub/linux/kernel/people/gregkh/lkn/lkn_pdf/ch09.pdf, or the Web page at fedoraproject.org/wiki/Anaconda/Options. Alternatively, you can use Google to search for **linux boot parameters**.

What to do if the installation does not work

tip   On some hardware, the installation might pause for as long as ten minutes. Before experimenting with other fixes, try waiting for a while. If the installation hangs, try booting with one or more of the boot parameters described in this section. Try running the installer in pseudographical (textual) mode.

Following are some of the parameters you can add to the boot command line. If you encounter problems with the display during installation, supply the **nofb** parameter, which turns off video memory. If you are installing from a medium other than a DVD— that is, if you are installing from files on the local hard disk or from files on another system using FTP, NFS, or HTTP—supply the **askmethod** or **method** parameter.

Many of these parameters can be combined. For example, to install Linux in text mode using a terminal running at 115,200 baud, no parity, 8 bits, connected to the first serial device, supply the following parameters (the **,115200n8** is optional).

```
text console=ttyS0,115200n8
```

The next set of parameters installs Fedora/RHEL on a monitor with a resolution of 1024 × 768, without probing for any devices. The installation program asks you to specify the source of the installation data (CD, DVD, FTP site, or other) and requests a video driver.

```
resolution=1024x768 noprobe askmethod
```

noacpi Disables ACPI (Advanced Configuration and Power Interface). This parameter is useful for systems that do not support ACPI or that have problems with their ACPI implementation. The default is to enable ACPI. Specifying **acpi=off** has the same effect.

noapic Disables APIC (Advanced Programmable Interrupt Controller). The default is to enable APIC.

noapm Disables APM (Advanced Power Management). The default is to enable APM. Specifying **apm=off** has the same effect.

askmethod Displays the Installation Method screen, which presents a choice of installation sources: Local CD/DVD, Hard drive, NFS directory, and URL (first installation CD, Net Install CD, and install DVD only).

- **Local CD/DVD**—Displays the Disc Found screen, which allows you to test the installation media (the same as if you had not entered any boot parameters).

- **Hard drive**—Prompts for the partition and directory that contain the installation tree or the ISO image of the install DVD. Do not include the name of the mount point when you specify the name of the directory. For example, if the ISO images are in the **/home/sam/FC15** directory and **/dev/sda6** holds the partition that is normally mounted on **/home**, you would specify the partition as **/dev/sda6** and the directory as **sam/FC15** (no leading slash).

- The next two selections attempt to use NetworkManager (page 651) to set up a DHCP connection automatically. Manual configuration requires you to enter the system's IP address and netmask as well as the IP addresses of the default gateway and primary nameserver.

  - **NFS directory**—Displays the NFS Setup screen, which allows you to enter the NFS server name, the name of the directory that contains the installation tree or the ISO image of the install DVD, and optionally NFS mount options (page 797). Enter the server's IP address and the *name* of the exported directory, not its device name. The remote (server) system must export (page 805) the directory hierarchy that holds the installation tree or the ISO image of the install DVD.

  - **URL**—Displays the URL Setup screen, which allows you to enter the URL of the directory that contains the installation tree or the ISO image of the install DVD, and optionally the URL of a proxy server, a username, and a password.

nodma Turns off direct memory access (DMA) for all disk controllers. This parameter might make buggy controllers (or controllers with buggy drivers) more reliable, but also causes them to perform very slowly because the connected devices have to run in PIO mode instead of DMA mode. It can facilitate testing CD/DVDs that were not written correctly. For more information refer to "The Disc Found Screen" on page 57.

nofb (**no framebuffer**) Turns off the framebuffer (video memory). This option is useful if problems arise when the graphical phase of the installation starts.

irqpoll Changes the way the kernel handles interrupts.

ks=*URI* Specifies the location of a Kickstart (page 81) file to use to control the installation process. The *URI* is the pathname or network location of the Kickstart file.

nolapic Disables local APIC. The default is to enable local APIC.

lowres Runs the installation program at a resolution of 640 × 480 pixels. See also **resolution** (below).

mem=*xxx*M Overrides the detected memory size. Replace *xxx* with the number of megabytes of RAM in the computer.

repo=*URI* Specifies an installation method and location without prompting as **askmethod** does. For example, you can use the following parameter to start installing from the specified server:

```
repo=ftp://fedora.mirrors.pair.com/fedora/linux/releases/15/Fedora/i386/os
```

noprobe Disables hardware probing for all devices, including network interface cards (NICs), graphics cards, and the monitor. This option forces you to select devices from a list. You must know exactly which cards or chips the system uses when you use this parameter. Use **noprobe** when probing causes the installation to hang or otherwise fail. This parameter allows you to supply arguments for each device driver you specify.

rescue Sets the system up to rescue an installed system; see page 457 for details.

resolution=*WxH* Specifies the resolution of the monitor you are using for a graphical installation. For example, **resolution=1024x768** specifies a monitor with a resolution of 1024 × 768 pixels.

text Installs Linux in pseudographical (page 31) mode. Although the images on the screen appear to be graphical, they are composed entirely of text characters.

vnc Installs Linux via a VNC (virtual network computing) remote desktop session. After providing an IP address, you can control the installation remotely using a VNC client from a remote computer. You can download a free VNC client that runs on several platforms from www.realvnc.com. Use **yum** (page 534) to install the **vnc** software package to run a VNC client on a Fedora/RHEL system.

vncpassword=*passwd* Enables a password for a VNC connection. This option requires you also use the **vnc** option.

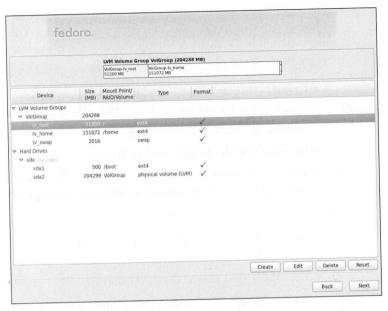

Figure 3-14   Disk Druid: main screen, default layout

USING DISK DRUID TO PARTITION THE DISK

See page 34 for a discussion of the setup of the hard disk and partitions.

Disk Druid, a graphical disk-partitioning program that can add, delete, and modify partitions on a hard disk, is part of the Fedora/RHEL installation system. You can use Disk Druid only while you are installing a system; it cannot be run on its own. You can use palimpsest (page 77), parted (page 617), or fdisk to manipulate partitions and system-config-lvm to work with LVs after you install Fedora/RHEL. As explained earlier, if you want a basic set of partitions, you can allow Anaconda to partition the hard disk automatically. See page 42 for a discussion of LVM (Logical Volume Manager) including PVs, VGs, and LVs.

Anaconda runs Disk Druid when you put a tick in the check box labeled **Review and modify partitioning layout** or when you select **Create custom layout** in the Type of Installation screen (Figure 3-8, page 61).

Default layout   Figure 3-14 shows the Disk Druid main screen as it appears when you have chosen the default layout for the hard disk (see "Type of Installation" on page 61). The middle of the screen holds a table listing hard drives and LVM Volume Groups and the partitions or LVs each holds, one per line.

Fedora names the Volume Group after the hostname you specified earlier in the installation. If you specified **tiger** as the hostname, the Volume Group name would be **vg_tiger**. If you accept the default hostname of **localhost.localdomain**, Fedora names the Volume Group **VolGroup** as in the examples in this section.

The highlighted logical volume, **lv_root**, is in the Volume Group named **VolGroup**, which is depicted graphically at the top of the screen. The **lv_swap** logical volume is very small; it is the sliver at the right end of the graphical representation.

The following buttons appear near the bottom of the screen:

- **Create**—Displays the Create Storage window (next) that allows you to create a partition or set up software RAID or LVM LVs
- **Edit**—Edits the highlighted device (next page)
- **Delete**—Deletes the highlighted device
- **Reset**—Cancels the changes you have made and causes the Disk Druid table to revert so it matches the layout of the disk

The Disk Druid table contains the following columns:

- **Device**—The name of the device in the **/dev** directory (for example, **/dev/sda1**) or the name of the LV
- **Size (MB)**—The size of the partition or LV in megabytes
- **Mount Point/RAID/Volume**—Specifies where the partition will be mounted when the system is brought up (for example, **/usr**); it is also used to specify the RAID device or LVM volume the partition/LV is part of
- **Type**—The type of the partition, such as **ext4**, **swap**, or **physical volume (LVM)**
- **Format**—A tick in this column indicates the partition will be formatted as part of the installation process; all data on the partition will be lost

THE CREATE STORAGE WINDOW

Clicking Create on the Disk Druid main screen displays the Create Storage window (Figure 3-15). This window has three sections, each of which has one or more selections:

- Create Partition (pages 34 and 74)
  - ◆ Standard Partition—Create a partition
- Create Software RAID (pages 41 and 77)
  - ◆ RAID Partition—Create a software RAID partition
  - ◆ RAID Device—Join two or more RAID partitions into a RAID device
- Create LVM (pages 42 and 73)
  - ◆ LVM Volume Group—(VG) Specify PVs that make up a VG; also allows you to specify LVs that are in the VG

Figure 3-15   The Create Storage window

- ◆ LVM Logical Volume—(LV) Specify LVs that are in a VG
- ◆ LVM Physical Volume—(PV) Specify PVs that make up a VG

Make a selection by clicking the adjacent radio button. Click **Information** to display information about the adjacent section.

WORKING WITH LVs (LOGICAL VOLUMES)

When you instruct Anaconda to partition the hard disk with a default layout (see "Type of Installation" on page 61), it uses LVM (page 42) to set up most of the hard disk, creating LVs (logical volumes) instead of partitions. It places **/boot** on the first partition on the drive, not under the control of LVM. LVM creates a VG (volume group) named **VolGroup** that occupies the rest of the disk space. Within this VG it creates two or three LVs: root (**/**, **lv_root**), swap (**lv_swap**), and if there is room, **/home** (**lv_home**). The swap LV occupies up to a few gigabytes; the root LV takes up to about 50 gigabytes. If there is room for a **/home** LV, it occupies the rest of **VolGroup**. This section explains how to make the **/home** LV smaller so you can add an additional LV to **VolGroup**. If the hard drive on the machine you are working with is small and Anaconda does not create a **/home** LV, you can follow this example by making the root LV smaller instead.

If you highlight **VolGroup** and click **Create**, Disk Druid displays a Create Storage window in which **Create LVM/LVM Logical Volume** is grayed out. You cannot add a logical volume because there is no free space in **VolGroup**.

To make the **/home** LV smaller and make room for additional partitions, first highlight the **/home** LV (**lv_home**) and click **Edit**. Disk Druid displays the Edit

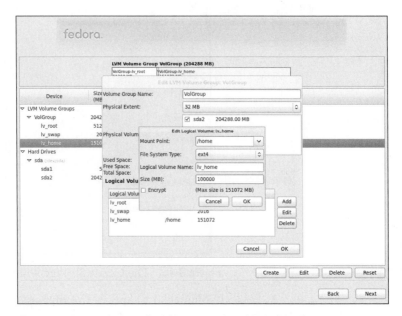

Figure 3-16   Disk Druid: Edit Logical Volume window

LVM Volume Group window with the Edit Logical Volume window on top of it (Figure 3-16). Initially, the size of **lv_home** is the same as its maximum size.

Replace the numbers in the text box labeled **Size (MB)** with the number of megabytes you want to assign to the **lv_home** LV. Figure 3-16 shows the size of the **lv_home** LV being changed to 100 gigabytes (100,000 megabytes). Click **OK**.

Once you decrease the size of the **lv_home** LV, the Disk Druid main screen shows a device named Free in **VolGroup** indicating **VolGroup** has free space. You can now add another LV to **VolGroup**. Click **Create** to display the Create Storage window (Figure 3-15 on the previous page), which no longer has **Create LVM/LVM Logical Volume** grayed out. Click the radio button labeled **LVM Logical Volume**; Disk Druid puts the name of the only possible VG in the adjacent spin box: **VolGroup**. Click **Create**. Disk Druid displays the Make Logical Volume window (Figure 3-17). Select/specify a mount point, filesystem type, and size for the LV. You can change the LV name if you like, although Disk Druid assigns logical, sequential names that are easy to use. Figure 3-17 shows a mount point of **/extra** with a name of **lv_extra** and a filesystem type of **ext4** being created with a size of 20 gigabytes. Click **OK** when the LV is set up the way you want.

Figure 3-18 shows the modified Disk Druid main screen with the new **/extra** LV.

WORKING WITH PARTITIONS

Create a new partition | To create a new partition on a hard disk, *the hard disk must have enough free space to accommodate the partition*; see "Resizing a partition" on page 77. Click

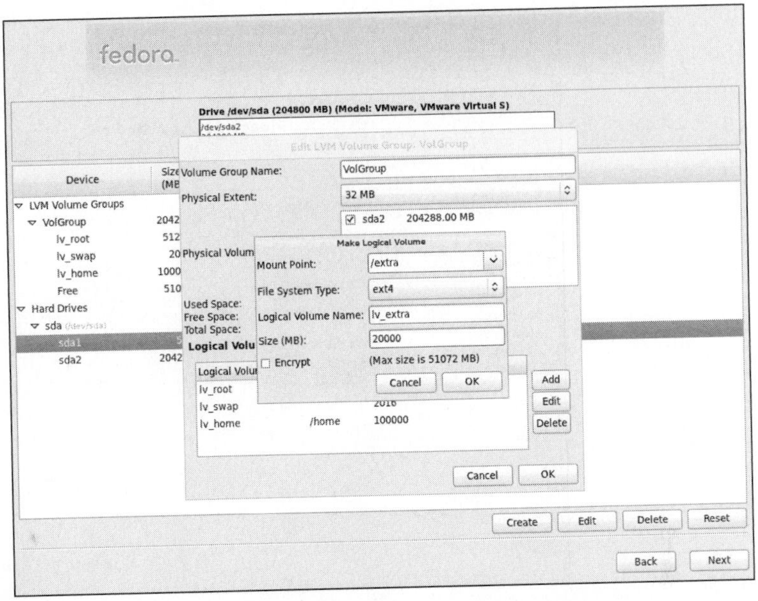

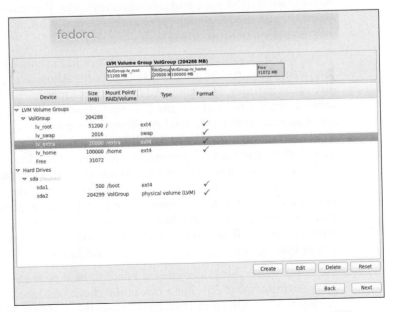

Figure 3-17   Disk Druid: Make Logical Volume window

the **Create** button to add a partition. In response, Disk Druid displays the Create Storage window (Figure 3-15, page 73). Click the radio button labeled **Create**

Figure 3-18   Disk Druid: main screen with the new **/extra** LV

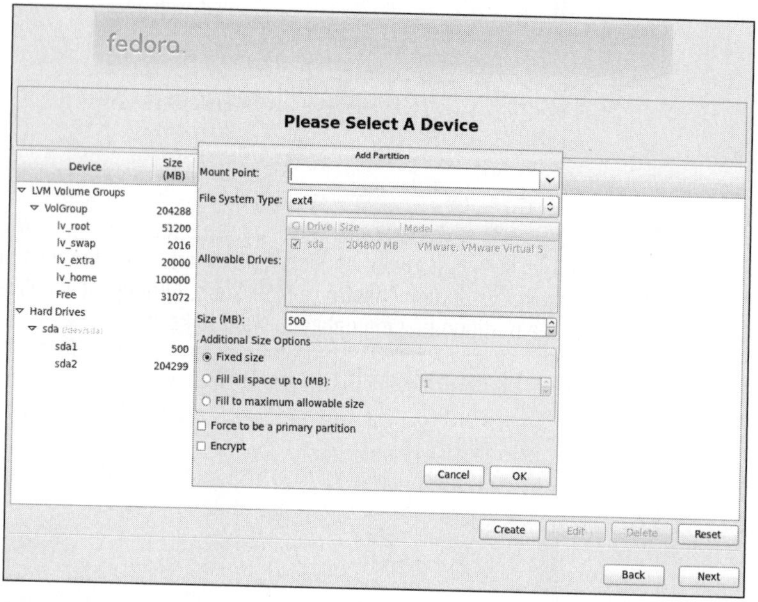

Figure 3-19 Disk Druid: Add Partition window, **ext4** filesystem

Partition/Standard Partition and then click Create (in the Create Storage window). Disk Druid displays the Add Partition window (Figure 3-19). Specify the mount point (the name of the directory the partition will be mounted on; page 36) and the filesystem type; use the arrow buttons at the right ends of these boxes to display drop-down lists.

If more than one drive is available, put a tick in the check box adjacent to the drive you want the partition to be created on in the Allowable Drives frame. Specify the size of the partition and, in the Additional Size Options frame, click the radio button labeled **Fixed size** to create the partition close to the size you specify. Because of block-size constraints, the final partitions are not usually exactly the size you specify. Click the radio button labeled **Fill all space up to (MB)** and fill in the maximum size you want the partition to be to create a partition that takes up the existing free space, up to the maximum size you specify. In other words, Disk Druid will not complain if it cannot create the partition as large as you would like. Click the radio button labeled **Fill to maximum allowable size** to cause the partition to occupy all of the remaining free space on the disk, regardless of size. (If you create another partition after creating a **Fill to maximum allowable size** partition, the new partition will pull blocks from the existing maximum size partition.)

Put a tick in the check box labeled **Force to be a primary partition** to create a primary partition (page 35). Put a tick in the check box labeled **Encrypt** to encrypt the partition. Click **OK**, and Disk Druid adds the partition to its table (but does not write the changes to the hard disk).

Edit an existing partition   To modify an existing partition, highlight the partition in the Disk Druid table or the graphical representation of the hard disk and click **Edit**; Disk Druid displays the Edit Partition window. Using this window, you can change the mount point or size of a partition, or format the partition as another type (e.g., **ext3**, **vfat**, **swap**, etc.).

Always back up the data on a hard disk

caution   If you are installing Fedora/RHEL on a disk that holds data that is important to you, always back up the data before you start the installation process. Things can and do go wrong. The power might go out in the middle of an installation, corrupting the data on the hard disk. A bug in the partitioning software might destroy a filesystem. Although it is unlikely, you might make a mistake and format a partition holding data you want to keep.

Resizing a partition   When you are working with a hard disk with a single partition that occupies the entire disk, such as when you are setting up a dual-boot system by adding Fedora/RHEL to a Windows system (page 82), you might be able to resize the partition to install Fedora/RHEL. The process of resizing a partition is the same regardless of the type of partition: You can use the following technique to resize Windows, Linux, or other types of partitions.

To install Fedora/RHEL on this system, you must resize (shrink) the partition to make room for Fedora/RHEL. Before you resize a Windows partition, you must boot Windows and defragment the partition using the Windows defragmenter; see the tip on page 83. To resize the partition, highlight the partition in the Disk Druid table or the graphical representation of the hard disk and click **Edit**; Disk Druid displays the Edit Partition window.

In the Edit Partition window, put a tick in the check box labeled **Resize**. Then enter the size, in megabytes, you want to shrink the filesystem to. Make sure that the size you specify is larger than the amount of space the data on the filesystem occupies. When you click **OK**, Disk Druid shrinks the partition.

SETTING UP A RAID DEVICE

To set up a RAID array (page 41), you must first create two or more partitions of the same size. Usually these partitions will be on different hard disks. You create RAID partitions by pressing the button labeled **Create** to display the Create Storage window (Figure 3-15, page 73), selecting **Create Software RAID/RAID Partition**, and specifying the partition. Typically a RAID device comprises partitions of the same size. Once you have created two or more RAID partitions, click **Create**, select **Create Software RAID/RAID Device** from the Create Storage window, and specify the RAID partitions that make up the RAID device and the mount point for the RAID device.

palimpsest: THE GNOME DISK UTILITY

The palimpsest graphical disk utility can create, remove, and modify partitions and filesystems on many types of media, including internal and external hard disks,

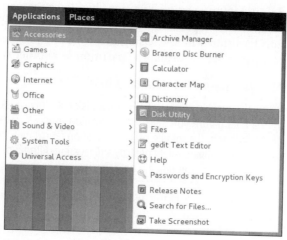

Figure 3-20 Selecting the palimpsest disk utility from the Main menu

CD/DVDs, and USB flash drives. It can encrypt partitions and change passwords on already encrypted partitions.

Unless you are certain the hard disk on which you are installing Fedora/RHEL has nothing on it (it is a new disk) or you are sure the disk holds no information of value, it is a good idea to examine the contents of the disk before you start the installation. The palimpsest disk utility is a good tool for this job. It is part of the **gnome-disk-utility** package.

Open the Palimpsest Disk Utility window by selecting **Main menu: Applications⇨ Accessories⇨Disk Utility** (Fedora; Figure 3-20; if **Applications** is not visible see "Configuring Fallback Mode" on page 92) or **Main menu: Applications⇨System Tools⇨Disk Utility** (RHEL). Alternatively, you can give the command **palimpsest** from a terminal emulator (page 117) or Run Application window (ALT-F2).

With a hard disk selected, the palimpsest Disk Utility window is divided into three sections (Figure 3-21): **Storage Devices** holds a list of CD/DVD drives, hard disks, and other devices; **Drive** holds information about the hard disk that is highlighted in the list of storage devices; and **Volumes** displays information about the partition highlighted in the graphical representation of the hard drive.

When you select a hard disk in the Storage Devices section, palimpsest displays information about that disk in the Drive section of the window. Click one of the partitions in the graphical representation of the hard disk, and palimpsest displays information about that partition in the Volumes section.

From this window you can view, create, and delete partitions. Although you can create partitions using palimpsest, you cannot specify the mount point (page 36) for a partition—this step must wait until you are installing Fedora/RHEL and using the Disk Druid partition editor. You can save time if you use palimpsest to examine a hard disk and Disk Druid to set up the partitions you install Fedora/RHEL on.

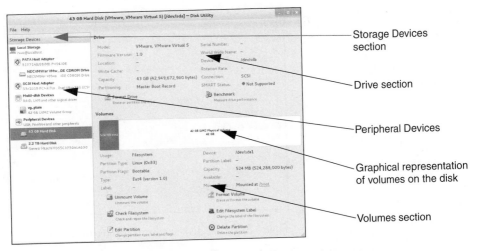

Figure 3-21   The palimpsest Disk Utility window

DISPLAYING THE CONTENTS OF A FILESYSTEM

To display the contents of a filesystem, select the partition holding the filesystem as described on the previous page and click **Mount Volume** in the Volumes section of the Disk Utility window. Figure 3-21 shows **Unmount Volume** because the partition is already mounted. When you click the mount point (the link following **Mount Point: mounted at**) in the Volumes section, Nautilus displays the filesystem in a Nautilus window (Figure 3-22; more about Nautilus on page 102). When you have finished examining the contents of the filesystem, click **Unmount Volume** to unmount the filesystem.

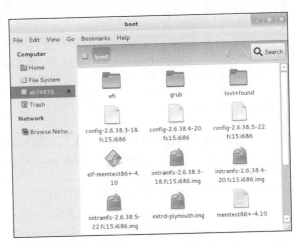

Figure 3-22   Browsing a partition using palimpsest

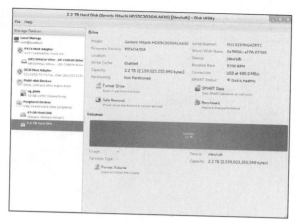

Figure 3-23   A disk without a partition table

Writing a Partition Table

A new disk does not have a partition table (page 34) and looks similar to the disk high-lighted in Figure 3-23. In the Drive section of a Disk Utility window, **Not Partitioned** follows the **Partitioning** label, the graphical representation of the disk is marked **Unknown** or **Unrecognized**, and Usage is blank. If the disk you are working with already has a partition table, skip to the next section.

To partition a hard disk, click **Format Drive** in the Drive section of the Disk Utility window: palimpsest opens a Format window holding a drop-down list labeled **Scheme**. Select a scheme. In most cases you will want to accept the default scheme of **Master Boot Record**. Click **Format**. After checking that you really want to format the drive, palimpsest creates the partition table. Now **Master Boot Record** follows the **Partitioning** label, the graphical representation of the disk is marked **Free** (free space; page 34), and **Unallocated Space** follows the **Usage** label.

If you want to create a single filesystem that occupies the entire disk drive, instead of following the instructions in the preceding paragraph, click **Format Volume** in the Volumes section of the Disk Utility window: palimpsest opens a Format whole-disk volume window. To create a filesystem, follow the instructions for the Create partition window in the next section.

Creating a Partition and a Filesystem

Once you have created a partition table, you will be able to create a partition that holds a filesystem in the free space (page 34; labeled **Free**). When you click **Create Partition**, palimpsest opens a Create partition window (Figure 3-24).

In this window, use the slider labeled **Size** or the adjacent spin box to specify the size of the new partition. Next specify a filesystem type; **ext4** filesystems are the most common. You can optionally enter a disk label in the text box labeled **Name**. This name is not the mount point for the disk. Typically you will want to own the filesystem, so allow the tick to remain in the check box labeled **Take**

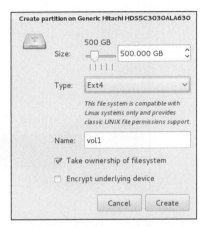

Figure 3-24   The palimpsest Create partition window

ownership of file system. If you want the filesystem to be encrypted, put a tick in the check box labeled **Encrypt underlying device.** Click **Create.** After checking with you, palimpsest creates the filesystem. Now the graphical representation of the disk is divided to represent the division of the hard disk, and **Usage** corresponds to the highlighted section of the graphical representation (Filesystem or Unallocated Space). If you did not use all the free space, you can create additional partitions and filesystems in the same manner.

DELETING A PARTITION

Before deleting a partition, make sure it does not contain any data you need. To use the palimpsest utility to delete a partition, highlight the partition you want to delete in the graphical representation of the hard disk and click **Delete Partition.** After checking with you, palimpsest deletes the partition.

USING SMART TO DISPLAY DISK PERFORMANCE INFORMATION

SMART (Self-Monitoring, Analysis, and Reporting Technology) monitors hard disks and attempts to predict hard disk failures. To see a SMART report for a disk on the system, highlight the disk in the Storage Devices section and click **Smart Data** in the Drive section; palimpsest displays a window similar to the one shown in Figure 3-25 on the next page. From this window you can run various self-tests and scroll through the information at the bottom of the window.

USING THE KICKSTART CONFIGURATOR

Kickstart is a Fedora/RHEL program that completely or partially automates the same installation and post-installation configuration on one or more machines. To use Kickstart, you create a single file that answers all the questions that are normally asked during an installation. Anaconda then refers to this file instead of asking you questions during installation. See the **ks** boot parameter on page 70.

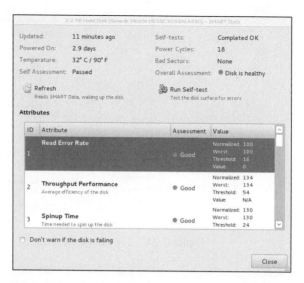

Figure 3-25 SMART data as displayed by palimpsest

Using Kickstart, you can automate language selection, network configuration, keyboard selection, boot loader installation, disk partitioning, X Window System configuration, and more.

The system-config-kickstart utility displays the Kickstart Configurator window (Figure 3-26), which creates a Kickstart installation script. This utility is part of the **system-config-kickstart** software package but is not installed by default. You can install this package using yum; see page 534. To run this utility, enter **system-config-kickstart** on a command line or select **Main menu: Applications⇨System Tools⇨ Kickstart**.

Figure 3-26 shows the first window the Kickstart Configurator displays. To generate a Kickstart file (**ks.cfg** by default), go through each section of this window (the items along the left side) and fill in the answers and put ticks in the appropriate check boxes. It might be helpful to start with the Kickstart installation script that Anaconda generated when you installed the system (**/root/anaconda-ks.cfg**). Click **Help** on the menubar for instructions on completing these tasks. When you are finished, click **File⇨Save**. The Kickstart Configurator gives you a chance to review the generated script before it saves the file.

SETTING UP A DUAL-BOOT SYSTEM

A *dual-boot* system is one that can boot one of two (or more) operating systems. This section describes how to add Fedora/RHEL to a system that can boot Windows, thereby creating a system that can boot Windows or Linux. You can use the same technique for adding Fedora/RHEL to a system that runs a different version or distribution of Linux.

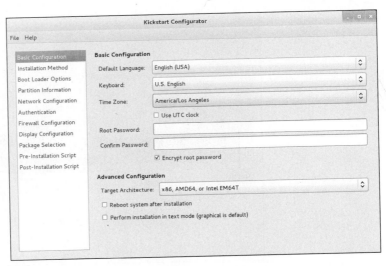

Figure 3-26   The Kickstart Configurator window

Before you start setting up a dual-boot system, you need to find disk space for the new Fedora/RHEL system. The next section discusses several ways to create the needed space.

CREATING FREE SPACE ON A WINDOWS SYSTEM

Typically you install Fedora/RHEL in free space on a hard disk. To add Fedora/RHEL to a Windows system, you must have enough free space on a hard disk that already holds Windows. There are several ways to provide or create this free space. The following paragraphs discuss these options in order from easiest to most difficult.

Add a new hard disk. Add another hard disk to the system and install Linux on the new disk, which contains only free space. This technique is very easy and clean but requires a new hard disk.

Use existing free space. If there is sufficient free space on the Windows disk, you can install Linux there. This technique is the optimal choice, but there is rarely enough free space on an installed hard disk.

Always defragment before resizing

caution You must boot Windows and defragment a Windows partition before you resize it. Sometimes you might need to run the Windows defragmenter several times to consolidate most file fragments. Not only will defragmenting give you more space for a Linux partition, but it might also keep the process of setting up a dual-boot system from failing.

Resize Windows partitions. Windows partitions often occupy the entire disk, which explains why resizing a Windows partition is the technique most commonly used to free

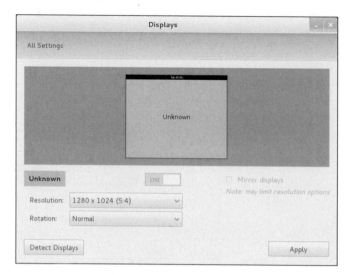

Figure 3-27   The Displays window

up space. Windows systems typically use NTFS, FAT32, and/or FAT16 filesystems. You can resize an existing Windows partition when you install Fedora/RHEL. Alternatively, you can use the palimpsest utility from a live session to examine and resize a partition to open up free space in which to install Linux (page 77).

Remove a Windows partition. If you can delete a big enough Windows partition, you can install Linux in its place. To delete a Windows partition, you must have multiple partitions under Windows and be willing to lose the data in the partition you delete. In many cases, you can save this data by moving it from the partition you will delete to another Windows partition.

Once you are sure a partition contains no useful information, you can delete it when you install Fedora/RHEL. Alternatively, you can use palimpsest from a live session to delete it (page 81). After deleting the partition, you can install Fedora/RHEL in the free space formerly occupied by the partition you deleted.

INSTALLING FEDORA/RHEL AS THE SECOND OPERATING SYSTEM

After you have created enough free space on a Windows system, you can begin installing Fedora/RHEL. When you get to the Type of Installation screen (Figure 3-8, page 61), choose **Use free space** to have Anaconda partition the free space on the hard disk automatically. If you need to delete a Windows partition, you must choose **Create custom layout**; this selection calls Disk Druid (page 71) so you can delete the appropriate Windows partition and create Linux partitions in the free space. When you boot the system, you will be able to choose which operating system you want to run.

gnome-control-center/Displays: Configures the Display

Most of the time the monitor attached to the system just works: Fedora/RHEL probes the monitor and autoconfigures X.org to work properly. This section explains how to configure the display in case you need to.

Under Fedora you can use the Displays window (Figure 3-27) to configure the monitor. To display this window, select **Main menu: Applications⇨System Tools⇨System Settings** (if **Applications** is not visible see "Configuring Fallback Mode" on page 92) or give the command **gnome-control-center** from a terminal emulator or Run Application window (ALT-F2) and click **Displays** in the Hardware section. Check the specifications for the monitor and select the appropriate resolution value from the drop-down list. RHEL uses the Display Preferences window for the same purpose. To display this window, select **Main menu: System⇨Preferences⇨Display** or give the command **gnome-display-properties** from a terminal emulator or Run Application window (ALT-F2).

Chapter Summary

Most installations of Fedora/RHEL begin by booting from the live CD or the install DVD. When the system boots from the CD/DVD, it displays a message saying when it will boot automatically. During the time it displays this message, you can give various commands and then have the system continue booting.

The program that installs Fedora/RHEL is named Anaconda. Anaconda calls tools that identify the hardware, build the necessary filesystems, and install or upgrade the Fedora/RHEL operating system. Anaconda can run in textual or graphical (default) interactive mode or in batch mode using Kickstart.

The Disk Druid graphical disk-partitioning program can add, delete, and modify partitions and logical volumes (LVs) on a hard disk during installation. The palimpsest utility reports on and manipulates hard disk partitions before or after installation. The system-config-lvm utility works with logical volumes after installation.

A dual-boot system can boot one of two or more operating systems, frequently Windows and Linux. The biggest task in setting up a dual-boot system, assuming you want to add Linux to a Windows system, is finding enough disk space to hold Linux.

Fedora/RHEL uses the X.org X Window System. Fedora/RHEL uses the GNOME display manager (gdm) to provide a graphical login.

EXERCISES

1. What is a live system? What advantages does it have over an installed system?

2. Which boot parameter would you use to begin an FTP installation?

3. Describe the Anaconda installer.

4. Where on the disk should you put your **/boot** partition or the root (**/**) partition if you do not use a **/boot** partition?

5. If the graphical installer does not work, what three steps should you try?

6. When might you specify an **ext2** filesystem instead of **ext4**?

7. Describe Disk Druid.

ADVANCED EXERCISES

8. When does a Fedora/RHEL system start X by default?

9. If you do not install grub on the master boot record of the hard disk, how can you boot Linux?

10. Why would you place **/var** at the beginning of the disk?

11. How does Anaconda set up a hard disk by default?

PART II

Getting Started with Fedora/RHEL

4

INTRODUCTION TO FEDORA AND RED HAT ENTERPRISE LINUX

OBJECTIVES

After reading this chapter you should be able to:

- ▶ Log in on the Fedora desktop
- ▶ Understand **root** privileges
- ▶ Configure GNOME to run in Fallback mode
- ▶ Change the desktop background
- ▶ Install and work with gnome-tweak-tool
- ▶ Change the number of workspaces on the desktop
- ▶ Use Nautilus to work with files
- ▶ Explain what you can do using a window titlebar
- ▶ Update and install software
- ▶ Find documentation
- ▶ Open a terminal emulator and launch programs from the command line

One way or another you are sitting in front of a computer that is running Fedora or RHEL (Red Hat Enterprise Linux). After describing **root** (Superuser) privileges, this chapter takes you on a tour of the system to give you some ideas about what you can do with it. The tour does not go into depth about choices, options, menus, and so on; that is left for you to experiment with and to explore in greater detail in Chapter 8 and throughout later chapters of this book. Instead, this chapter presents a cook's tour of the Linux kitchen: As you read it, you will have a chance to sample the dishes that you will enjoy more fully as you read the rest of this book.

Following the tour is a section that describes where to find Linux documentation (page 125). The next section offers more about logging in on the system, including information about passwords (page 134).

Be sure to read the warning about the dangers of misusing the powers of **root** (Superuser) in the next section. While heeding that warning, feel free to experiment with the system: Give commands, create files, click objects, choose items from menus, follow the examples in this book, and have fun.

CURBING YOUR POWER (SUPERUSER/root PRIVILEGES)

While you are logged in as the user named **root**, you are referred to as *Superuser* or *administrator;* you are working with **root** privileges and have extraordinary systemwide powers. Running the su or sudo utility can give you similar privileges. When working with **root** privileges, you can read from or write to almost any file on the system, execute programs that ordinary users cannot, and more. On a multiuser system you might not be permitted to know the **root** password and so might not be able to run certain programs. Nevertheless, someone—the *system administrator*—knows the **root** password, and that person maintains the system. When you are running Linux on your own computer, you will assign a password to **root** when you install Linux. Refer to "Running Commands with **root** Privileges" on page 409 for more information.

Do not experiment while you are working with root privileges

caution   Feel free to experiment when you are *not* working with **root** privileges. When you *are* working with **root** privileges, do only what you have to do and make sure you know exactly what you are doing. After you have completed the task at hand, revert to working as yourself. When working with **root** privileges, you can damage the system to such an extent that you will need to reinstall Linux to get it working again.

A TOUR OF THE FEDORA/RHEL DESKTOP

This section presents new words (for some readers) in a context that explains the terms well enough to get you started using the Linux desktop. If you would like exact definitions as you read this section, refer to "GNOME Desktop Terminology"

Figure 4-1   The Fedora GNOME Login screen

on page 112 and to the Glossary. The Glossary also describes the data entry *widgets* (page 1197), such as the *combo box* (page 1157), *drop-down list* (page 1163), *list box* (page 1173), and *text box* (page 1192).

GNOME   GNOME (www.gnome.org), a product of the GNU project (page 5), is the user-friendly default desktop manager under Fedora/RHEL. KDE, the K Desktop Environment, is a powerful desktop manager and complete set of tools you can use in place of GNOME (www.kde.org/community/whatiskde). Use the Fedora KDE live media or the Fedora KDE spin to install KDE.

This tour describes GNOME, a full-featured, mature desktop environment that boasts a rich assortment of configurable tools. After discussing logging in, this section covers desktop features—including panels, objects, and workspaces—and explains how to move easily from one workspace to another. It describes several ways to launch objects (run programs) from the desktop, how to set up the desktop to meet your needs and please your senses, and how to manipulate windows. As the tour continues, it explains how to work with files and folders using the Nautilus File Browser window, one of the most important GNOME tools. The tour concludes with a discussion of the Software Update window, the tool that allows you to keep a system up-to-date with the click of a button; getting help; and logging out.

LOGGING IN ON THE SYSTEM

When you boot a standard Fedora/RHEL system, GDM (GNOME display manager) displays a Login screen (Figure 4-1) on the system console. In the middle of the screen is a window that holds a list of names. When you click a name, Fedora/RHEL displays a text box labeled **Password**. In addition, at the upper-right corner of the Fedora login screen and the lower-right corner of the RHEL login screen is an icon that allows you to restart or shut down the system. For more information refer to "The Login Screen" on page 134.

Figure 4-2   The System Settings window

To log in, click your name. A text box labeled **Password** appears. Enter your password and press RETURN. If Fedora/RHEL displays an error message, try clicking your name and entering your password again. Make sure the CAPS LOCK key is not on (Fedora/RHEL displays a message if it is) because the routine that verifies your entries is case sensitive. See page 135 if you need help with logging in and page 137 if you want to change your password. The system takes a moment to set things up and then displays a workspace.

CONFIGURING FALLBACK MODE (FEDORA)

Fedora 15 introduced GNOME 3, the GNOME shell, and the Mutter window manager. (*Mutter* is short for Metacity Clutter; the graphics library is named Clutter). RHEL uses GNOME 2 and the Metacity window manager. GNOME 3 is radically different from GNOME 2, following the trend toward simpler, more graphical desktops that have more icons and fewer menus.

This book uses the Linux textual interface for most tasks, including setting up servers and programming in bash and Perl. Where this book does refer to the graphical interface (GUI), it refers to a desktop running in Fallback mode, which appears similar to GNOME 2/Metacity. Most modern graphics cards support the full GNOME 3 desktop. When you log in on a Fedora system that has a graphics card that cannot support GNOME 3, GNOME displays a window with the message **GNOME 3 Failed to Load**. When you click **Close** on that window, GNOME displays a desktop running in Fallback mode. Figure 3-3 on page 55 shows part of a full GNOME 3 desktop, and Figure 3-4 on page 56 shows menus on a desktop running in Fallback mode.

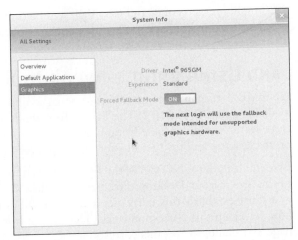

Figure 4-3   The System Info window showing Graphics settings

To follow the examples in this book, you must run GNOME in Fallback mode

tip   The following instructions explain how to force Fedora to run in Fallback mode.

To follow the examples in this book while running Fedora, you must run GNOME in Fallback Mode. No action is needed if you are running RHEL. The following instructions explain how to force Fedora to run GNOME in Fallback mode:

1. With GNOME running the full GNOME 3 desktop, it displays the word **Activities** at the upper-left corner of the screen, and your name (if you are logged in on an installed system) or **Live System User** (if you are running a live session) at the upper-right corner of the screen. Click your name or **Live System User**; GNOME displays a menu.

2. Click **System Settings** on the menu; GNOME displays the System Settings window (Figure 4-2).

3. Click **System Info** in the section labeled **System** at the bottom of the window; GNOME displays the System Info window (Figure 4-3).

4. Click Graphics at the right of the window; GNOME displays a switch labeled **Forced Fallback Mode** on the right side of the window.

5. To run in Fallback mode, the switch labeled **Forced Fallback Mode** must display **ON**. If it displays **OFF**, click the switch so it displays **ON**; GNOME displays **The next login will use the fallback mode ...** below the switch.

6. Click the **x** at the upper-right corner of the window to close the window.

7. Log off by clicking your name or **Live System User** at the upper-right corner of the screen, click **Log Out** from the menu GNOME displays, and then click the button labeled **Log Out** from the small window GNOME displays.

8. Log in on the system and GNOME will be running in Fallback mode. The desktop is in Fallback mode if the words **Applications** and **Places** appear at the upper-left corner of the screen.

Installing and Using gnome-tweak-tool (Fedora)

GNOME 3 turns off many desktop manager and file manager features that were available under GNOME 2. The Tweak Tool window enables you to turn on some of these features. One of these features is the correspondence between the files displayed on the desktop and the files in your **Desktop** directory.

By default under GNOME 3, the files displayed on the desktop *do not* correspond to the files in your **Desktop** directory. To follow some of the examples in this book you must establish this correspondence. See the following tip for instructions on how to set up this correspondence. The section titled "The **Desktop** Directory" on page 105 demonstrates this correspondence.

Before you can display and work with the Tweak Tool window, you must install the **gnome-tweak-tool** software package. To do so, open a terminal emulator window by selecting **Main menu: Applications⇨System Tools⇨Terminal** as shown in Figure 4-5 on page 96. (If **Applications** does not appear on the Main menu, set GNOME to run in Fallback mode as explained in the previous section.) Then give the following command:

```
$ su -c 'yum install gnome-tweak-tool'
```

The su utility will prompt for the **root** password. Once you enter the **root** password and press RETURN, yum will ask for your confirmation and then install the **gnome-tweak-tool** package. For more information on using yum to install packages see page 534.

The Tweak Tool window (Figure 4-4) enables you to set up the Nautilus file manager to handle the desktop and to configure other aspects of the desktop and file manager. To display this window, select **Main menu: Applications⇨Accessories⇨ Tweak Advanced Settings** or give the command **gnome-tweak-tool** from a terminal emulator or Run Application window (ALT-F2).

To follow the examples in this book, you must have the file manager handle the desktop

tip   By default, the files displayed on the desktop *do not* correspond to the files in your **Desktop** directory. To follow some of the examples in this book you must establish this correspondence. To do so, install **gnome-tweak-tool** and open the Tweak Tool window as explained in this section. Then click **File Manager** at the left of the Tweak Tool window (Figure 4-4); GNOME displays a switch labeled **Have file manager handle the desktop** at the right of the window. Click the switch so it displays **ON** and close the window. Now the files on the desktop will (mostly; see the optional section on page 105 for exceptions) correspond to those in your **Desktop** directory. You might have to take an action, such as selecting **Main menu: Places⇨Desktop** before icons appear on the desktop.

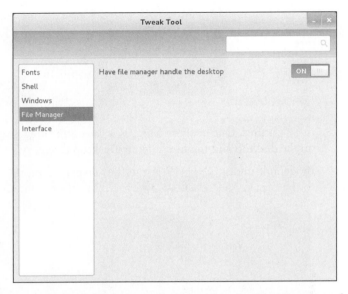

Figure 4-4   The Tweak Tool window showing the File Manager selection

The left side of the Tweak Tool window displays the following selections. Click a selection to change the display on the right side of the window. Click **x** at the upper-right corner of the window to close the window.

- **Fonts**—Changes and resizes the fonts used on the desktop
- **Shell**—Controls what the system does when you close the lid on a laptop, which buttons appear on window titlebars, and more
- **Windows**—Selects the window theme and controls how windows respond to various mouse clicks
- **File Manger**—Controls whether the files on the desktop correspond to the files in your **Desktop** directory (page 105) and activates the desktop right-click menu (page 117)
- **Interface**—Selects the desktop, icon, and cursor themes

Introduction to the Desktop

You can use the desktop as is or you can customize it until it looks and functions nothing like the initial desktop. If you have a computer of your own, you might want to add a user (page 602) and work as that user while you experiment with the desktop. When you figure out which features you like, you can log in as yourself and implement those features. That way you need not concern yourself with "ruining" your desktop and not being able to get it back to a satisfactory configuration.

Panels and objects   When you log in, GNOME displays a workspace that includes Top and Bottom panels (bars) that are essential to getting your work done easily and efficiently

Figure 4-5   The initial workspace showing **Main menu: Applications⇨ System Tools⇨Terminal**

(Figure 4-5). Each of the panels holds several icons and words called objects. (Buttons, applets, and menus, for example, are all types of objects.) When you click an object, something happens. A panel does not allow you to do anything you could not do otherwise, but rather collects objects in one place and makes your work with the system easier.

Workspaces and the desktop   What you see displayed on the screen is a *workspace*. Initially Fedora/RHEL configures GNOME with two workspaces. The desktop, which is not displayed all at once, is the collection of all workspaces. "Switching Workspaces" on page 98 describes some of the things you can do with workspaces.

LAUNCHING PROGRAMS FROM THE DESKTOP

This section describes three of the many ways you can start a program running from the desktop.

Click an object   The effect of clicking an object depends on what the object is designed to do. Clicking an object might, for example, start a program, display a menu or a folder, or open a file, a window, or a dialog box.

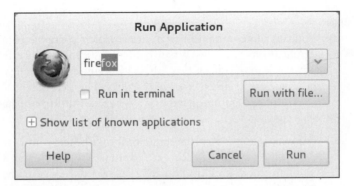

Figure 4-6   The Run Application window

For example, to display the volume control, (left-) click the sound object on the Top panel (Figure 4-5). GNOME opens the volume control. When you are done using the volume control, click anywhere on the desktop (but not on the volume control) to close it.

When you (left-) click the date and time on the Top panel, the Clock applet displays a calendar for the current month. Click the date and time again to close the calendar.

Click and right-click

tip   This book uses the term **click** when you need to click the *left* mouse button. It uses the term **right-click** when you need to click the *right* mouse button. See page 101 for instructions on adapting the mouse for left-handed use.

Select from the Main menu   The second way to start a program is by selecting it from a menu. The Main menu is the object at the left end of the Top panel that includes the words **Applications** and **Places**. Click one of these words to display the corresponding menu. Each menu selection that holds a submenu displays an open triangle (pointing to the right) to the right of the name of the menu (Figure 4-5). When you move the mouse pointer over one of these selections and leave it there for a moment (this action is called *hovering*), the menu displays the submenu. When you allow the mouse cursor to hover over one of the submenu selections, GNOME displays a *tooltip* (page 112).

Experiment with the Main menu. Start Solitaire (**Main menu: Applications⇨ Games⇨AisleRiot Solitaire** [Fedora; RHEL does not include games by default]), a terminal emulator (**Main menu: Applications⇨System Tools⇨Terminal**, and other programs from the Applications menu. The Places menu is discussed on page 114.

Use the Run Application window   You can also start a program by pressing ALT-F2 to display the Run Application window (Figure 4-6). As you start to type **firefox** in the text box at the top of the window, for example, the window recognizes what you are typing and displays the Firefox logo and the rest of the word **firefox**. Click **Run** to start Firefox.

optional

Running textual applications

You can run command-line utilities, which are textual (not graphical), from the Run Applications window. When you run a textual utility from this window, you must put a tick in the check box labeled **Run in terminal** (click the check box to put a tick in it; click it again to remove the tick). The tick tells GNOME to run the command in a terminal emulator window. When the utility finishes running, GNOME closes the window.

For example, type **vi** (the name of a text-based editor) in the text box, put a tick in the check box labeled **Run in terminal**, and click **Run**. GNOME opens a Terminal (emulator) window and runs the vim text editor in that window. When you exit from vim (press ESCAPE:**q!**RETURN sequentially to do so), GNOME closes the Terminal window.

You can run a command-line utility that only displays output and then terminates. Because the window closes as soon as the utility is finished running and because most utilities run quickly, you will probably not see the output. Type the following command in the text box to run the **df** (disk free; page 794) utility and keep the window open until you press RETURN (remember to put a tick in the check box labeled **Run in terminal**):

```
bash -c "df -h ; read"
```

This command starts a bash shell (Chapter 7) that executes the command line following the **–c** option. The command line holds two commands separated by a semicolon. The second command, read (page 1019), waits for you to press RETURN before terminating. Thus the output from the **df –h** command remains on the screen until you press RETURN. Replace **read** with **sleep 10** to have the window remain open for ten seconds.

SWITCHING WORKSPACES

Workspace Switcher

Each rectangle in the *Workspace Switcher applet* (or just *Switcher*)—the group of rectangles near the right end of the Bottom panel—represents a workspace (Figure 4-5, page 96). When you click a rectangle, the Switcher displays the corresponding workspace and highlights the rectangle to indicate which workspace is displayed. You can also press CONTROL-ALT-RIGHT ARROW to display the workspace to the right of the current workspace; pressing CONTROL-ALT-LEFT ARROW works in the opposite direction.

Click the rightmost rectangle in the Switcher and then select **Main menu: Applications**⇨**System Tools**⇨**System Settings** and select **Hardware/Mouse and Touchpad** (Fedora) or **Main menu: System**⇨**Preferences**⇨**Mouse** (RHEL). GNOME opens the Mouse and Touchpad window. The Switcher rectangle that corresponds to the workspace you are working in displays a small rectangle. This rectangle corresponds in size and location within the Switcher rectangle to the window within the workspace. Click and hold the left mouse button with the mouse pointer on the titlebar at the top of the window and drag the window to the edge of the desktop. The small rectangle within the Switcher moves to the corresponding location within the Switcher rectangle.

Figure 4-7   The Workspace Switcher Preferences window

Now click a different rectangle in the Switcher and open another application—for example, the Desktop Help window (select **Main menu: Applications➪Accessories➪Help** [Fedora] or **Main menu: System➪Help** [RHEL]). With the Desktop Help window in one workspace and the Mouse Preferences window in another, you can click the corresponding rectangles in the Switcher to switch back and forth between the workspaces (and applications).

You can move a window from one workspace to another by right-clicking the Window List applet (page 113) on the Bottom panel and selecting one of the choices that starts with **Move**.

Right-click to display an Object context menu

tip A *context menu* is one that is appropriate to its context. When you right-click an object, it displays an Object context menu. Each object displays its own context menu, although similar objects have similar context menus. Most Object context menus have either a Preferences or Properties selection. See the following section, "Setting Personal Preferences," and page 119 for more information on Object context menus.

SETTING PERSONAL PREFERENCES

You can set preferences for many objects on the desktop; you can also change the desktop background.

Workspace Switcher   To display the Workspace Switcher Preferences window (Figure 4-7), first *right*-click anywhere on the Switcher to display the Switcher menu and then select **Preferences** (the only entry in this menu). Specify the number of workspaces you want in the spin

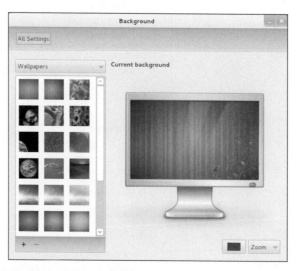

Figure 4-8   The Background window

box labeled **Number of workspaces**. The number of workspaces the Switcher displays changes as you change the number in the spin box—you can see the result of your actions before you close the Preferences window. Four workspaces is typically a good number to start with. Click **Close**.

Clock applet   The Clock applet has an interesting Preferences window. Right-click the Clock applet (Figure 4-5, page 96) and select **Preferences**. GNOME displays the General tab of the Clock Preferences window. This tab enables you to customize the date and time displayed on the Top panel. The clock immediately reflects the changes you make in this window. Click the **Locations** tab and then the **Add** button and enter the name of the city you are in or near to cause the Clock applet to display weather information. Click the **Weather** tab to specify temperature and wind speed units.

Different objects display different Preferences windows. In contrast, objects that launch programs display Properties windows and do not have Preferences windows. Experiment with different Preferences and Properties windows and see what happens.

Desktop   The Background window (Figure 4-8) enables you to change the desktop back-
background   ground. To display this window, select **Main menu: Applications⇨System Tools⇨System Settings** or give the command **gnome-control-center** from a terminal emulator or Run Application window (ALT-F2). Then click **Personal/Background**. Or, under RHEL or with the file manager handling the desktop (page 94) under Fedora, right-click on an empty space on the desktop and select Change Desktop Background.

Click the drop-down list near the upper-left corner of the window to select from Wallpapers, Pictures Folder, and Colors & Gradients. Click the drop-down list at

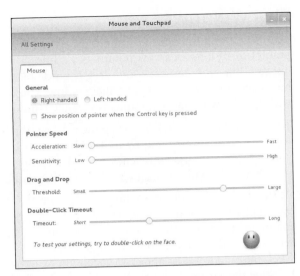

Figure 4-9   The Mouse and Touchpad window

the lower-right corner of the window to select how you want the image displayed on the desktop (e.g., zoom, center, tile). Click the colored button to the left of this drop-down list to select a color for the desktop from the Pick a Color window (page 274).

MOUSE PREFERENCES

The Mouse and Touchpad window (Figure 4-9) enables you to change the characteristics of the mouse to suit your needs. To display this window, select **Main menu: Applications⇨System Tools⇨System Settings** or give the command **gnome-control-center** from a terminal emulator or Run Application window (ALT-F2). Then click **Hardware/Mouse and Touchpad**.

Left-handed mouse To change the orientation of the mouse buttons for use by a left-handed person, click the radio button labeled **Left-handed**. If you change the setup of the mouse buttons, remember to reinterpret the descriptions in this book accordingly. That is, when this book asks you to click the left button or does not specify a button to click, click the right button, and vice versa. See "Remapping Mouse Buttons" on page 264 for information on changing the orientation of the mouse buttons from the command line.

Double-click timeout Use the Double-Click Timeout slider to change the speed with which you must double-click a mouse button to have the system recognize your action as a double-click rather than as two single clicks. You can also control the acceleration and sensitivity of the mouse. The Drag and Drop Threshold specifies how far you must drag an object before the system considers the action to be the drag part of a drag-and-drop operation.

Working with Windows

To resize a window, position the mouse pointer over an edge of the window; the pointer turns into an arrow pointing to a line. When the pointer is an arrow pointing to a line, you can click and drag the side of a window. When you position the mouse pointer over a corner of the window, you can resize both the height and the width of the window simultaneously. Some windows are not resizeable.

To move a window, click and drag the titlebar (the bar across the top of the window with the name of the window in it). Alternatively, when you hold the ALT key down you can move a window by clicking and dragging any part of the window. For fun, try moving the window past either side of the workspace. What happens?

Titlebar   At the right of the titlebar are up to three icons that control the window (Figure 4-18, page 115). Clicking the line, which usually appears at the left end of the set of icons, minimizes (iconifies) the window so the only indication of the window is the object with the window's name in it on the Bottom panel (a Window List applet; page 113). Click the Window List applet to toggle the window between visible and minimized. Clicking the square icon, which usually appears in the middle of the three icons, maximizes the window (displays the window at its maximum size). Clicking the rectangle again returns the window to its normal size. Double-clicking the titlebar toggles the window between its normal and maximum size. The Shell selection of the Tweak Tool window (page 94) controls which buttons appear on titlebars.

Terminating a   Clicking the x closes the window and usually terminates the program running in the
program   window. In some cases you might need to click several times. Some programs, such as Rhythmbox Music Player, do not terminate but rather continue to run in the background. When in this state, the program displays an icon on the Top panel. Right click the icon and select **Quit** from the drop-down list to terminate the program.

Using Nautilus to Work with Files

Nautilus, the GNOME file manager, is a simple, powerful file manager. You can use it to create, open, view, move, and copy files and folders as well as to execute programs and scripts. One of its most basic and important functions is to create and manage the desktop. This section introduces Nautilus and demonstrates the correspondence between Nautilus and the desktop. See page 266 for more detailed information on Nautilus.

Set up desktop Fallback mode and file manager control of the desktop

tip   To follow the examples in this section, you must run the desktop in Fallback mode: See "Configuring Fallback Mode" on page 92.

The examples also require you to install **gnome-tweak-tool** and configure the file manager to handle the desktop: See page 94.

Terms: folder and   Nautilus displays the File Browser window, which displays the contents of a folder.
directory   The terms *folder* and *directory* are synonymous; "folder" is frequently used in graphical contexts, whereas "directory" might be used in textual or command-line contexts. This book uses these terms interchangeably.

Figure 4-10   The Nautilus Spatial view (left) and File Browser window (right)

Term: File Browser This book sometimes uses the terms *File Browser window* and *File Browser* when referring to the Nautilus File Browser window.

Opening Nautilus Select **Main menu: Places⇨Home Folder** to open a Nautilus File Browser window that shows the files in your home folder.

Double-clicking an object in a File Browser window has the same effect as double-clicking an object on the desktop: Nautilus takes an action appropriate to the object. For example, when you double-click a text file, Nautilus opens the file with a text editor. When you double-click an LibreOffice document, Nautilus opens the file with LibreOffice. If the file is executable, Nautilus runs it. If the file is a folder, Nautilus opens the folder and displays its contents in place of what had previously appeared in the window.

From within a Nautilus File Browser window, you can open a folder in a new tab. To do so, middle-click the folder or right-click the folder and select **Open in New Tab** from the drop-down list; Nautilus displays a new tab named for the folder you clicked. Click the tab to display contents of the directory.

To follow examples under RHEL, turn off Nautilus Spatial view, turn on File Browser windows

tip By default, RHEL display the Nautilus Spatial view. The examples in this book show Nautilus displaying File Browser windows. To make the Nautilus windows on your desktop correspond to the windows in the figures in this book, turn on Nautilus File Browser windows by following the instructions under the next section, "The Two Faces of Nautilus."

THE TWO FACES OF NAUTILUS (RHEL)

Under RHEL, the appearance of Nautilus differs depending on how it is set up: It can display a *Spatial view* or a *File Browser window*. Figure 4-10 shows an example of each type of display. By default, RHEL is set up to display the Spatial view. Because the Spatial view is less conventional, this book uses the Nautilus File Browser window in examples. The following steps make File Browser windows the Nautilus default and ensure that Nautilus windows on the screen look similar to those in this book. See page 272 for information on the Spatial view.

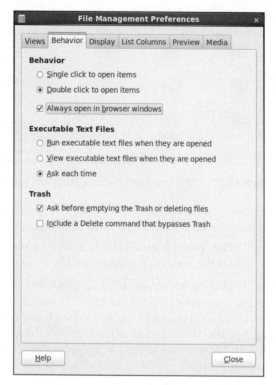

Figure 4-11 The File Management Preferences window, Behavior tab

To turn off the Nautilus Spatial view and turn on File Browser windows under RHEL:

1. Select **Main menu: Places⇨Home folder.** Nautilus opens a window that displays a Spatial view of the contents of your home folder (also called your home directory; page 191). It appears similar to the left side of Figure 4-10 (previous page).

2. From the menubar of the new window, select **Edit⇨Preferences.** Nautilus displays the File Management Preferences window.

3. Click the tab labeled **Behavior.** See Figure 4-11.

4. Click the check box labeled **Always open in browser windows.** A tick will appear in the check box.

5. Click the button labeled **Close** at the lower-right corner of the File Management Preferences window to close the window.

6. Click the **x** at the upper-right corner of the home folder window to close the window.

After following these steps, Nautilus will always display File Browser windows as shown in this book.

Figure 4-12   Part of a workspace with a Nautilus File Browser window

THE Desktop DIRECTORY

Before you start reading this section ...

tip   The examples in this section do not work with the default Fedora/RHEL settings. Before continuing:

Fedora: If you are running Fedora, set up the desktop to run in Fallback mode (page 92) and use **gnome-tweak-tool** to set up the Nautilus file manager to handle the desktop (page 94).

RHEL: If you are running RHEL, turn off the Nautilus Spatial view (page 103).

The files on the desktop are held in a directory that has a pathname (page 191) of **/home/*username*/Desktop**, where *username* is your login name or, if you are logged in on a live session, **Live System User**. The simple directory name is **Desktop**. When you select **Main menu: Places⇨Desktop**, GNOME opens a File Browser window showing the files on the desktop (Figure 4-12). Nautilus does not show the Computer, home directory, and Trash directory in the browser window; see the following optional section for an explanation. The buttons below the toolbar and to the right of **Computer** or **Devices** show the pathname of the directory Nautilus is displaying (**Home Desktop** in the Figure 4-12).

optional   Although icons for the Computer, home directory, and Trash directory appear on the desktop, these files are not stored in the **/home/*username*/Desktop** directory. Because they are not in the **Desktop** directory, they do not appear in a Nautilus window that displays the contents of the **Desktop** directory. These icons appear on the desktop because of the way the GNOME configuration files are set up. The

GNOME configuration files are *XML* (page 1198) files that reside in the directory hierarchy with its root at **/home/*username*/.gconf**. Although it is not recommended, you can edit these files with gconf-editor. You might need to install the **gconf-editor** package to use this editor. See projects.gnome.org/gconf for more information.

To see the correspondence between the graphical desktop and the **Desktop** directory, right-click anywhere within the large clear area of the Desktop File Browser window. Select **Create New Document⇨Empty Document**. Nautilus creates a new file on the desktop and displays its object in this window. When you create this file, GNOME highlights the name **Untitled Document** under the file: You can type any name you like at this point. Press RETURN when you are finished entering the name. If you double-click the new file, Nautilus assumes it is a text file and opens the file in a gedit window. (The gedit utility is a simple text editor.) Type some text and click **Save** on the toolbar. Close the window either by selecting **Quit** from the File menu or by clicking the **x** at the left end of the titlebar. You have created a text document on the desktop. You can now double-click the document object on the desktop or in the File Browser window to open and edit it.

Next, create a folder by right-clicking the root window (any empty part of the workspace) and selecting **Create New Folder.** You can name this folder in the same way you named the file you created previously. The folder object appears on the desktop and within the Desktop File Browser window.

On the desktop, drag the file until it is over the folder; the folder opens. Release the mouse button to drop the file into the folder; GNOME moves the file to the folder. Again on the desktop, double-click the folder you just moved the file to. GNOME opens another File Browser window, this one displaying the contents of the folder. The file you moved to the folder appears in the new window. Now drag the file from the window to the previously opened Desktop File Browser window. The file is back on the desktop, although it might be hidden by one of the File Browser windows.

Next, open a word processing document by selecting **Main menu: Applications⇨ Office⇨LibreOffice Writer**. If that program is not available, select **Main menu: Applications⇨Accessories⇨gedit Text Editor**. Type some text and click the Save icon (the floppy disk) or select **menubar: File⇨Save** to save the document. The editor displays a Save window (Figure 4-13). Type the name you want to save the document as (use **memo** for now) in the text box labeled **Name**. You can specify the directory in which you want to save the document in one of two ways: by using the drop-down list labeled **Save in folder** or by using the **Browse for other folders** section of the Save window.

Click the triangle to the left of **Browse for other folders** to open this section of the window. When you open this section, the arrow changes orientation; click the arrow again to close this section. Figure 4-13 shows the Save window with this

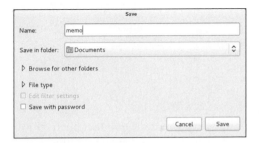

Figure 4-13   The Save window

section closed. With the **Browse for other folders** section closed, you can select a directory from the drop-down list labeled **Save in folder**. This technique is quick and easy but presents a limited number of choices of folders. By default, it saves the document in **Documents (/home/*username*/Documents)**. If you want to save the document to the desktop, select **Desktop** from this drop-down list and then click **Save**. LibreOffice saves the document with a filename extension of **.odt**, which indicates it is an LibreOffice word processing document. The object for this type of file has some text and a stripe or picture in it.

optional

Browse/Save window

With the **Browse for other folders** section opened (click the triangle to the left of **Browse for other folders**), the Save window grays out the drop-down list labeled **Save in folder** and expands the **Browse for other folders** section, as shown in Figure 4-14 on the next page. This expanded section holds two large side-by-side list boxes: Places and Name. The list box labeled **Places** displays directories and locations on the system, including File System. The list box labeled **Name** lists the files within the directory named in the highlighted button above the Places list box.

The **Browse for other folders** section of the Save window allows you to look through the filesystem and select a directory or file. GNOME utilities and many applications use this window, although sometimes applications call it a Browse window. In this example, the word processor calls it a Save window and uses it to locate the directory in which it will save the document.

Assume you want to save a file in the **/tmp** directory. Click **File System** in the list box on the left. The list box on the right displays the files and directories in the root directory (represented by **/**; see "Absolute Pathnames" on page 192 for more information). Next, double-click **tmp** in the list box on the right. The buttons above the list box on the left change to reflect the directory displayed in the list box on the right. Click **Save**.

The buttons above the left-side list box represent directories. The right-side list box displays the directories found within the directory named in the highlighted (darker)

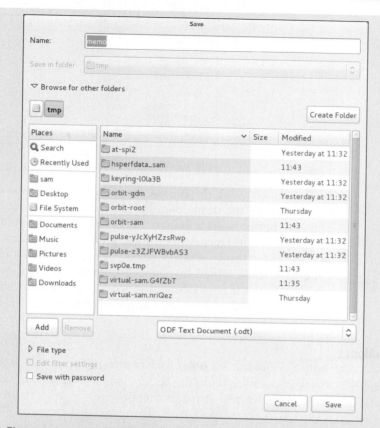

Figure 4-14   The Save window with Browse for other folders open

button. This directory is the one you would save the file to if you clicked **Save** at this point. Click one of these buttons to display the corresponding directory in the list box on the right and then click **Save** to save the file in that directory.

When you have finished editing the document, close the window. If you have made changes since you last saved it, the word processor asks if you want to save the document. If you choose to save it, the word processor saves the revised version over (in the same file as) the version you saved previously. Now the **memo.odt** object appears on the desktop and in the Desktop File Browser window. Double-click either object to open it.

The Desktop directory is special   In summary, the **Desktop** directory is like any other directory, except GNOME displays its contents on every workspace of the desktop (but only when you have set up the file manager to handle the desktop as explained on page 94). It is as though the desktop were a large, plain Desktop File Browser window. You can work with the **Desktop** directory because it is always displayed. Within the GUI, you must use a utility, such as Nautilus, to display and work with the contents of any other directory.

Selecting Objects

The same techniques can be used to select one or more objects in a File Browser window or on the desktop. Select an object by clicking it once; GNOME highlights the object. Select additional objects by holding down the CONTROL key while you click each object. To select a group of adjacent objects, highlight the first object and then, while holding down the SHIFT key, click the last object; GNOME highlights all objects between the two objects you clicked. Alternatively, you can use the mouse pointer to drag a box around a group of objects.

To experiment with these techniques, open a File Browser window displaying your home folder. Select a few objects, right-click, and select **Copy**. Now move the mouse pointer over an empty part of the desktop, right-click, and select **Paste**. You have copied the selected objects from your home folder to the desktop. You can drag and drop objects to move them, although you cannot move the **Desktop** folder on top of itself.

Trash

Selecting **File Browser menubar: Edit⇨Move to Trash** moves the selected (high-lighted) object to the **Trash** directory. Because files in the trash take up space on the hard disk (just as any files do), it is a good idea to remove them periodically. To view the files in the trash, double-click the Trash icon on the desktop (visible if you have the file manager handling the desktop [page 94]) or click the word **Trash** on the left side of a File Browser window; Nautilus displays the Trash File Browser window.

Emptying the trash Select **Empty Trash** from the Trash icon right-click (context) menu to permanently remove all files from the trash. (This selection does not appear if there are no files in the trash.) You can also select **Empty Trash** from the context menu Nautilus displays when you right-click the word **Trash** on the left side of a File Browser window. Alternatively, you can right-click an object in the Trash File Browser window and select **Delete Permanently** to remove only that object (file), or you can select **Restore** to move the file back to its original location. You can drag and drop files to and from the trash just as you can with any other folder.

Updating Software

On systems connected to the Internet, Fedora/RHEL is initially set up to search for daily and notify you when software updates are available. GNOME displays the message **Important software updates are available** in a popup notification window and places a notification indicator (an envelope icon) toward the right end of the Top panel when updates are available. Clicking this object opens the

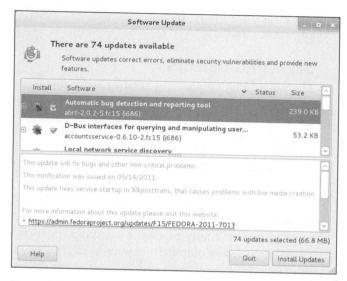

Figure 4-15 The Software Update window

Software Update window (Figure 4-15). You can open this window manually by selecting **Main menu: Applications⇨System Tools⇨Software Update** (Fedora) or **Main menu: System⇨Administration⇨Software Update** (RHEL) or by giving the command **gpk-update-viewer** from a terminal emulator or Run Application window (ALT-F2).

Software Update window   When the Software Update window opens, it displays the message **Checking for updates**; after it finishes checking it displays the number of available updates. If no updates are available, the window displays the message **All software is up to date**.

If updates are available, click **Install Updates**. As it downloads and installs the software packages, the Software Update window displays messages and a progress bar. When it is finished, the Software Update window closes. If the updates require you to reboot the system or log out, the Software Update window prompts you to do so. For more information refer to "Updating, Installing, and Removing Software Packages" on page 122.

Session Management

A session starts when you log in and ends when you log out or reset the session. With fully GNOME-compliant applications, GNOME can manage sessions so the desktop looks the same when you log in as it did when you logged out: The same windows will be positioned as they were on the same workspaces, and programs will be as you left them.

The Startup Applications Preferences window allows you to select which applications you want to run each time you log in. It also allows you to save automatically those applications that were running and those windows that were open when you log out;

they will start running when you log on again. To open the Startup Applications Preferences window give the command **gnome-session-properties** from a terminal emulator or Run Application window (ALT-F2). You must give this command while logged in as yourself (not while working with **root** privileges).

To save your sessions automatically when you log out, click the **Options** tab in the Startup Applications Preferences window and put a tick in the check box labeled **Automatically remember running applications when logging out**.

GETTING HELP

Fedora/RHEL provides help in many forms. Selecting **Main menu: Applications⇨ Accessories⇨Help** displays the Desktop Help browser, which provides information on the desktop. To display other information, click a topic in this window. You can also enter text to search for in the text box at the top of the window and then press RETURN. In addition, most windows provide a Help object or menu. See "Where to Find Documentation" on page 125 for more resources.

FEEL FREE TO EXPERIMENT

Try selecting different items from the Main menu and see what you discover. Following are some applications you might want to explore:

- The gedit text editor is a simple text editor. Select **Main menu: Applications⇨ Accessories⇨gedit Text Editor** to start it.

- LibreOffice's Writer is a full-featured word processor that can import and export Microsoft Word documents. Select **Main menu: Applications⇨ Office⇨LibreOffice Writer**. If this application is not available on the system, install the **libreoffice-writer** software package as explained on page 534. The **Office** menu also offers a drawing program, presentation manager, and spreadsheet.

- Firefox is a powerful, full-featured Web browser. Select **Main menu: Applications⇨Internet⇨Firefox**.

- Empathy is a graphical IM (instant messaging) client that allows you to chat on the Internet with people who are using IM clients such as AOL, MSN, and Yahoo! To start Empathy, select **Main menu: Applications⇨ Internet⇨Empathy Internet Messaging**.

  The first time you start Empathy, it opens a window that says **Welcome to Empathy**. Follow the instructions to access an existing IM account or open a new one. Visit live.gnome.org/Empathy for more information.

LOGGING OUT

Log off by clicking your name or **Live System User** at the upper-right corner of the screen, click **Log Out** from the menu GNOME displays, and then click the button labeled **Log Out** from the small window GNOME displays. Select **Shut down** to shut down or restart the system, among other options. From a textual environment, press CONTROL-D or give the command **exit** in response to the shell prompt.

GETTING THE MOST OUT OF THE DESKTOP

The GNOME desktop is a powerful tool with many features. This section covers many aspects of its panels, the Main menu, windows, terminal emulation, and ways to update, install, and remove software. Chapter 8 continues where this chapter leaves off, discussing the X Window System, covering Nautilus in more detail, and describing a few of the GNOME utilities.

GNOME DESKTOP TERMINOLOGY

The following terminology, which is taken from the GNOME Users Guide, establishes a foundation for discussing the GNOME desktop. Figure 4-5 on page 96 shows the initial Fedora GNOME desktop.

Desktop The *desktop* comprises all aspects of the GNOME GUI. While you are working with GNOME, you are working on the desktop. There is always exactly one desktop.

Panels Panels are bars that appear on the desktop and hold (panel) objects. There are two panels: one along the top of the screen (the Top Edge panel, or just Top panel) and one along the bottom (the Bottom Edge panel, or just Bottom panel). See the next page for more information on panels.

Panel objects Panel objects appear as words or icons on panels. You can click these objects to display menus, run applets, or launch programs. The four types of panel objects are applets, launchers, buttons, and menus. See the next page for more information on panel objects.

Windows A graphical application typically displays a window and runs within that window. At the top of most windows is a titlebar you can use to move, resize, and close the window. The *root window* is the unoccupied area of the workspace and is frequently obscured. The desktop can have no windows, one window, or many windows. Although most windows have decorations (page 118), some, such as the Logout window, do not.

Workspaces Workspaces divide the desktop into one or more areas, with one such area filling the screen at any given time. Initially there are two workspaces. Because panels and objects on the desktop are features of the desktop, all workspaces display the same panels and objects. By default, a window appears in a single workspace. The Switcher (page 98) enables you to display any one of several workspaces.

Tooltips Tooltips (Figure 4-5, page 96) is a minicontext help system that you activate by moving the mouse pointer over a button, icon, window border, or applet (such as those on a panel) and allowing it to hover there. When the mouse pointer hovers over an object, GNOME displays a brief explanation of the object called a tooltip.

Figure 4-16   Window List applets

OPENING FILES

By default, you double-click an object to open it; alternatively, you can right-click the object and select **Open** from the drop-down list. When you open a file, GNOME figures out the appropriate tool to use by determining the file's *MIME* (page 1176) type. GNOME associates each filename extension with a MIME type and each MIME type with a program. Initially GNOME uses the filename extension to try to determine a file's MIME type. If it does not recognize the filename extension, it examines the file's *magic number* (page 1174).

For example, when you open a file with a filename extension of **ps**, GNOME calls the Evince document viewer, which displays the PostScript file in a readable format. When you open a text file, GNOME uses gedit to display and allow you to edit the file. When you open a directory, GNOME displays its contents in a File Browser window. When you open an executable file such as Firefox, GNOME runs the executable. When GNOME uses the wrong tool to open a file, the tool generally issues an error message. See "Open With" on page 121 for information on how to use a tool other than the default tool to open a file.

PANELS

As explained earlier, panels are the bars that initially appear at the top and bottom of the desktop. They are part of the desktop, so they remain consistent across workspaces.

PANEL OBJECTS

The icons and words on a panel, called *panel objects,* display menus, launch programs, and present information. The panel object with the speaker icon, for example, displays the volume control.

The envelope icon tells you a notification is waiting for you, and you can click your name on the Top panel to log off or shut down the system. You can start almost any utility or program on the system using a panel object. This section describes the various types of panel objects.

Applets An applet is a small program that displays its user interface on or adjacent to the panel. You interact with the applet using its Applet panel object. The Clock (date and time) and Workspace Switcher (both shown in Figure 4-5 on page 96) are applets.

Window List applet Although not a distinct type of object, the Window List applet is a unique and important tool. One Window List applet (Figure 4-16) appears on the Bottom panel for each open or iconified window on the displayed workspace. Left-clicking this object minimizes its window or restores the window if it is minimized. Right-click this object

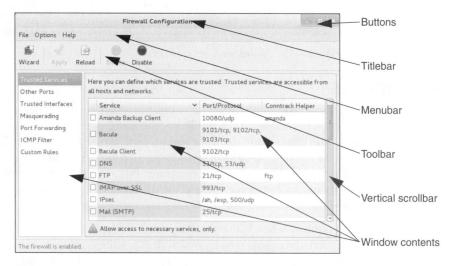

Figure 4-17   A typical window

to display the Window Operations menu (page 115). If a window is buried under other windows, click its Window List applet to make it visible.

Launchers   When you open a launcher, it can execute a command, start an application, display the contents of a folder or file, open a URI in a Web browser, and so on. In addition to appearing on panels, launchers can appear on the desktop. Under **Main menu: Applications**, you can find launchers that start other applications. Under **Main menu: Places**, the Home Folder, Documents, Desktop, and Computer objects are launchers that open File Browser windows that display folders.

Buttons   A button performs a single, simple action. The Sound button (Figure 4-5, page 96) displays a volume control.

Menus   A menu displays a list of selections you can choose from. Some of the selections can be submenus with more selections. All other selections are launchers. The next section discusses the Main menu.

The Main Menu

The Main menu appears at the left end of the Top panel and includes Applications and Places. Click one of these words to display the corresponding menu.

Applications   The Applications menu holds several submenus, each named for a category of applications (e.g., Games, Graphics, Internet, Office—the list varies depending on the software installed on the system). Selections from the submenus launch applications—peruse these selections, hovering over those you are unsure of to display the associated tooltips.

Places   The Places menu holds a variety of launchers, most of which open a File Browser window. The Home Folder, Desktop, and Documents objects display your directories with corresponding names. The Computer, CD/DVD Creator, and Network objects

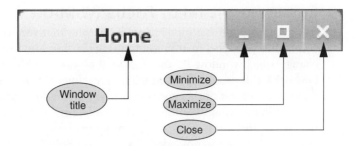

Figure 4-18 A window titlebar

display special locations. Each of these locations enables you to access file manager functions. For example, the CD/DVD Creator selection enables you to burn a CD or DVD. The Connect to Server selection opens a window that allows you to connect to various types of servers, including SSH and FTP servers (see "File" on page 270). The Search for Files selection enables you to search for files (page 274).

WINDOWS

In a workspace, a *window* is a region that runs, or is controlled by, a particular program (Figure 4-17). Because you can control the look and feel of windows— even the buttons they display—your windows might not look like the ones shown in this book. Each window in a workspace has a Window List applet (page 113) on the Bottom panel.

Titlebar A titlebar (Figures 4-17 and 4-18) appears at the top of most windows and controls the window it is attached to. You can change the appearance and function of a titlebar, but it will usually have at least the functionality of the buttons shown in Figure 4-18. You can use gnome-tweak-tool (page 94) to change titlebars.

The minimize (iconify) button collapses the window so the only indication of its presence is its Window List applet on the Bottom panel; click this applet to restore the window. Click the maximize button to expand the window so that it occupies the whole workspace; click the same button to restore the window to its former size. You can also double-click the titlebar to maximize and restore a window. Clicking the close button closes the window and usually terminates the program running in it. To reposition the window, left-click the titlebar and drag the window to the desired location.

Window Operations menu The Window Operations menu contains operations you can perform on any window. Right-click either the titlebar or the Window List applet (page 113) to display this menu. You can use this menu to move a window to another workspace, keep the window on top of or below other windows, and cause the window to always be visible on the displayed workspace.

Toolbar A *toolbar* (Figure 4-17) usually appears near the top of a window and contains icons, text, applets, menus, and more. Many kinds of toolbars exist. The titlebar is not a toolbar; rather, it is part of the window decorations placed there by the window manager (page 118).

CHANGING THE INPUT FOCUS (WINDOW CYCLING)

The window with the input focus is the one that receives keyboard characters and commands you type. In addition to using the Window List applet (page 113), you can change which window on the displayed workspace has the input focus by using the keyboard; this process is called *window cycling*. When you press ALT-TAB, GNOME displays in the center of the workspace a box that holds icons representing the programs running in the windows in the workspace. It also shifts the input focus to the window that was active just before the currently active window, making it easy to switch back and forth between two windows. When you hold ALT and press TAB multiple times, the focus moves from window to window. Holding ALT and SHIFT and repeatedly pressing TAB cycles in the other direction.

CUTTING AND PASTING OBJECTS USING THE CLIPBOARD

There are two similar ways to cut/copy and paste objects and text on the desktop and both within and between windows. In the first method, you use the clipboard, technically called the *copy buffer*, to copy or move objects or text. To do so, you explicitly copy an object or text to the buffer and then paste it somewhere else. Applications that follow the user interface guidelines use CONTROL-X to cut, CONTROL-C to copy, and CONTROL-V to paste. Application context menus frequently provide these same options.

You might not be familiar with the second method to copy and paste text—using the *selection* or *primary* buffer, which always contains the text you most recently selected (highlighted). You cannot use this method to copy objects. Clicking the middle mouse button (click the scroll wheel on a mouse that has one) pastes the contents of the selection buffer at the location of the mouse pointer. If you are using a two-button mouse, click both buttons at the same time to simulate clicking the middle button.

With both these techniques, start by highlighting an object or text to select it. You can drag a box around multiple objects to select them or drag the mouse pointer over text to select it. Double-click to select a word or triple-click to select a line or a paragraph.

Next, to use the clipboard, explicitly copy (CONTROL-C) or cut (CONTROL-X) the objects or text. If you want to use the selection buffer, skip this step.

To paste the selected objects or text, position the mouse pointer where you want to put it and then either press CONTROL-V (clipboard method) or press the middle mouse button (selection buffer method).

Use SHIFT-CONTROL-C and SHIFT-CONTROL-V within a terminal emulator

tip   The CONTROL-C, CONTROL-X, and CONTROL-V characters do not work in a terminal emulator window because the shell running in the window intercepts them before the terminal emulator can receive them. However, you can use SHIFT-CONTROL-C and SHIFT-CONTROL-V in place of CONTROL-C and CONTROL-V, respectively. There is no keyboard shortcut for CONTROL-X. You can also use the selection buffer in this environment or use copy/paste from the **Edit** selection on the menubar or from the context menu (right-click).

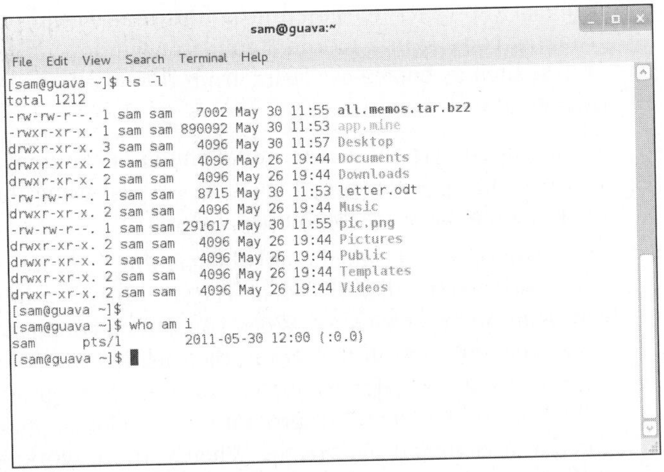

```
                              sam@guava:~

 File   Edit   View   Search   Terminal   Help
[sam@guava ~]$ ls -l
total 1212
-rw-rw-r--. 1 sam sam   7002 May 30 11:55 all.memos.tar.bz2
-rwxr-xr-x. 1 sam sam 890092 May 30 11:53 app.mine
drwxr-xr-x. 3 sam sam   4096 May 30 11:57 Desktop
drwxr-xr-x. 2 sam sam   4096 May 26 19:44 Documents
drwxr-xr-x. 2 sam sam   4096 May 26 19:44 Downloads
-rw-rw-r--. 1 sam sam   8715 May 30 11:53 letter.odt
drwxr-xr-x. 2 sam sam   4096 May 26 19:44 Music
-rw-rw-r--. 1 sam sam 291617 May 30 11:55 pic.png
drwxr-xr-x. 2 sam sam   4096 May 26 19:44 Pictures
drwxr-xr-x. 2 sam sam   4096 May 26 19:44 Public
drwxr-xr-x. 2 sam sam   4096 May 26 19:44 Templates
drwxr-xr-x. 2 sam sam   4096 May 26 19:44 Videos
[sam@guava ~]$
[sam@guava ~]$ who am i
sam        pts/1         2011-05-30 12:00 (:0.0)
[sam@guava ~]$ ▮
```

Figure 4-19   A Terminal (emulator) window

When using the clipboard, you can give as many commands as you like between the CONTROL-C or CONTROL-X and CONTROL-V, as long as you do not press CONTROL-C or CONTROL-X again. When using the selection buffer, you can give other commands after selecting text and before pasting it, as long as you do not select (highlight) other text.

USING THE ROOT WINDOW

The *root window* is any part of a workspace that is not occupied by a window, panel, or object. It is the part of the workspace where you can see the background.

Desktop menu   Right-click the root window to display the Desktop menu which enables you to create a folder, launcher, or document. The Change Desktop Background selection opens the Background window (page 100). You must set up the file manager to handle the desktop (page 94) before GNOME will display the Desktop menu.

RUNNING COMMANDS FROM A TERMINAL EMULATOR/SHELL

A *terminal emulator* is a window that presents a command-line interface (CLI); it functions as a textual (character-based) terminal and is displayed in a graphical environment.

To display the GNOME terminal emulator named Terminal (Figure 4-19), select **Main menu: Applications⇨System Tools⇨Terminal** or enter the command **gnome-terminal** from a Run Application window (ALT-F2). Because you are already logged in and are creating a subshell in a desktop environment, you do not need to log in again. Once you have opened a terminal emulator window, try giving the command **man man** to read about the man utility (page 126), which displays Linux manual pages. Chapter 5 describes utilities you can run from a terminal emulator.

You can run character-based programs that would normally run on a terminal or from the console in a terminal emulator window. You can also start graphical programs, such as gnome-calculator, from this window. A graphical program opens its own window.

When you are typing in a terminal emulator window, several characters, including *, ?, |, [, and], have special meanings. Avoid using these characters until you have read "Special Characters" on page 146.

The shell Once you open a terminal emulator window, you are communicating with the command interpreter called the *shell*. The shell plays an important part in much of your communication with Linux. When you enter a command at the keyboard in response to the shell prompt on the screen, the shell interprets the command and initiates the appropriate action—for example, executing a program; calling a compiler, a Linux utility, or another standard program; or displaying an error message indicating you entered a command incorrectly. When you are working on a GUI, you bypass the shell and execute a program by clicking an object or a name. Refer to Chapter 7 for more information on the shell

THE WINDOW MANAGER

A *window manager*—the program that controls the look and feel of the basic GUI—runs under a desktop manager (such as GNOME or KDE) and controls all aspects of the windows in the X Window System environment. The window manager defines the appearance of the windows on the desktop and controls how you operate and position them: open, close, move, resize, minimize, and so on. It might also handle some session management functions, such as how a session is paused, resumed, restarted, or ended (page 110).

Window managers Mutter, Metacity, and Compiz—the default window managers for GNOME— provide window management and start many components through GNOME panel objects. They also communicate with and facilitate access to other components in the environment.

Using the standard X libraries, programmers have created other window managers, including **blackbox, fluxbox,** and **WindowMaker.** You can use yum (page 534) to install any of these packages.

Window decorations A window manager controls *window decorations*—that is, the titlebar and border of a window. Aside from the aesthetic aspects of changing window decorations, you can alter their functionality by modifying the number and placement of buttons on the titlebar. You can use gnome-tweak-tool (Fedora; page 94) to alter the look and functionality of window decorations.

The window manager takes care of window manipulation so client programs do not need to do so. This setup is very different from that of many other operating systems, and the way that GNOME deals with window managers is different from how other desktop environments work. Window managers do more than simply

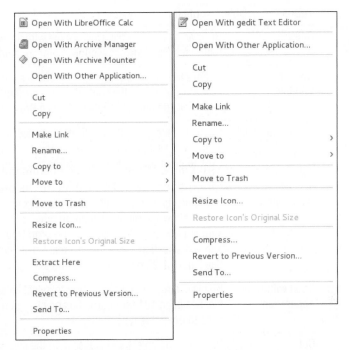

Figure 4-20   The Object context menus for a spreadsheet (left) and a text file (right)

manage windows—they provide a useful, good-looking, graphical shell where you can work. Their open design allows users to define their own policies, down to the fine details.

Theoretically GNOME is not dependent on any particular window manager and can work with any of several window managers. Because of their flexibility, you would not see major parts of the desktop environment change if you were to switch from one window manager to another. A desktop manager collaborates with the window manager to make your work environment intuitive and easy to use. Although the desktop manager does not control window placement, it does get information from the window manager about window placement.

THE OBJECT CONTEXT MENU

When you right-click an object or group of objects either on the desktop or in a File Browser window, GNOME displays an Object context menu. Different types of objects display different context menus, but most context menus share common selections. Figure 4-20 shows context menus for an LibreOffice spreadsheet file and for a plain text file. Table 4-1 on the next page lists some common Object context menu selections.

Table 4-1   Object context menu selections

Open	Runs an executable file. Opens a file with an appropriate application. Opens a folder in a File Browser window. Same as double-clicking the object.
Open in New Window	(From a File Browser window only.) Opens a folder in a new File Browser window instead of replacing the contents of the current window. Same as holding down SHIFT while double-clicking a folder in a Browser window.
Open with "*App*"	Opens the file using the application named *App*. When this selection appears as the first selection in the menu, *App* is the default application that GNOME uses to open this type of file. See page 121 for information on changing this default.
Open with ➤	A triangle appearing to the right of a selection indicates the selection is a menu. Allow the mouse pointer to hover over the selection to display the submenu. Each submenu selection is an Open with "*App*" selection (above). The last selection in the submenu is Open with Other Application (below). See Figure 4-22 on page 123 for an example.
Open with Other Application	Displays a menu that allows you to select an application to open this type of file. See page 121 for information on changing the default application GNOME uses to open this type of file.
Cut	Removes the object and places it on the clipboard (page 116).
Copy	Copies the object to the clipboard (page 116).
Extract Here	Extracts the contents of an archive and some other types of files, such as some documents, to a directory with the same name as the original file plus **_FILES**. If you do not have permission to write to the working directory (page 190), this menu selection appears as **Extract To**.
Extract To	Extracts the contents of an archive and some other types of files, such as some documents, to a directory you select using the Browse/Save window (page 107). This selection appears only if you do not have permission to write to the working directory (page 190). Otherwise, this menu selection appears as **Extract Here**.
Make Link	Creates a symbolic link to the object in the same directory as the object. You can then move the link to a different directory where it might be more useful. For more information refer to "Symbolic Links" on page 216.
Move to Trash	Moves the object to the trash (page 109).
Send to	Opens a Send To window that allows you to send the object using various techniques including email.
Compress	Opens the Compress window, which allows you to specify a format and a name for an archive containing one or more objects (page 270).
Properties	Displays the Object Properties window (next).

THE OBJECT PROPERTIES WINDOW

The Object Properties window displays information about a file, such as its owner, permissions, size, location, MIME type, ways to work with it, and so on. This window is titled *filename* **Properties**, where *filename* is the name of the file you clicked to open the window. To display this window, right-click an object and select **Properties** from the drop-down list. The Properties window initially displays some basic information. Click the tabs at the top of the window to display additional information. Different sets of tabs appear for different types of files. You can modify the settings in this window only if you have permission to do so. This section describes the three tabs most commonly found in Object Properties windows.

Basic   The Basic tab displays information about the file, including its *MIME* (page 1176) type, and enables you to select a custom icon for the file and change its name. To change the name of the file, replace the name in the text box labeled **Name**. If the filename is not listed in a text box, you do not have permission to change it. An easy way to change the icon is to open a File Browser window at **/usr/share/icons**. Work your way down through the directories until you find an icon you like, and then drag and drop it on the icon to the left of **Name** in the Basic tab of the Object Properties window.

Permissions   The Permissions tab (Figure 4-21 on the next page) allows the owner of a file to change the file's permissions (page 202) and to change the group (see **/etc/group** on page 506) the file is associated with to any group the owner is associated with. When running with **root** privileges, you can also change the owner of the file. The command **su** –RETURN followed by the command **nautilus**, when given from a terminal emulator window, opens a File Browser window running with **root** privileges (but read the caution on page 90). Nautilus grays out items you are not allowed to change.

Using the drop-down lists, you can give the owner (called *user* elsewhere; see the tip about chmod on page 204), group, and others read or read and write permission for a file. Alternatively, you can prohibit the group and others from accessing the file by specifying permissions as **None**. Put a tick in the check box labeled **Execute** to give all users permission to execute the file. This tab does not give you as fine-grained control over assigning permissions as chmod (page 203) does.

Permissions for a directory work as explained on page 207. Owner, group, and others can be allowed to list files in a directory, access (read and—with the proper permissions—execute) files, or create and delete files. Group and others permissions can also be set to **None**. A tick in the check box labeled **Execute** allows the directory to be searched. Click **Apply Permissions to Enclosed Files** to apply the permissions in the Permissions tab to all files in the directory.

Open With   When you ask GNOME to open a file that is not executable (by double-clicking its icon or right-clicking and selecting the first **Open with** selection), GNOME determines which application or utility it will use to open the file. GNOME uses several techniques to determine the *MIME* (page 1176) type of a file and selects the default application based on that determination.

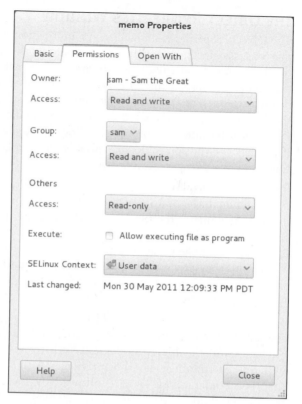

Figure 4-21   The Object Properties window, Permissions tab

The Open With tab (Figure 4-22) enables you to change which applications GNOME can use to open the file and other files of the same MIME type (typically files with the same filename extension). Click the **Add** button to add to the list of applications. Highlight an application and click **Remove** to remove an application from the list. You cannot remove the default application.

When you add an application, GNOME adds that application to the Open With list but does not change the default application it uses to open that type of file. Highlight the application and click **Set as default** to cause that application to become the default application GNOME uses to open this type of file.

When a file has fewer than four applications in the Open With tab, the Object context menu displays all applications in that menu. With four or more applications, the Object context menu provides an Open With submenu (Figure 4-22).

UPDATING, INSTALLING, AND REMOVING SOFTWARE PACKAGES

Fedora/RHEL software comes in packages that include all necessary files, instructions so a program can automatically install and remove the software, and a list of

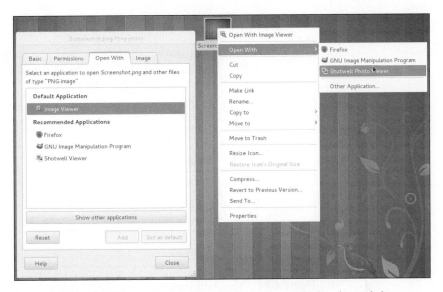

Figure 4-22   The Object Properties window, Open With tab, and the
Object context menu, Open With submenu for the same file

other packages the package depends on. There are many ways to search for and
install software packages. The notification indicator (an envelope icon on the Top
panel; page 109) prompts you each time updates are available for software on the
system. The Add/Remove Software window (discussed on the next page) is an easy
way to install popular software. Chapter 13 explains how to work with software
packages from the command line.

UPDATES

The the Software Update Preferences window (Figure 4-23) allows you to choose
how often you want the system to check for updates and which updates you want
the system to automatically install (it prompts you to install other updates). Open
this window by selecting **Main menu: Applications⇨Other⇨Software Updates**
(Fedora) or **Main menu: System⇨Preferences⇨Software Updates** (RHEL).

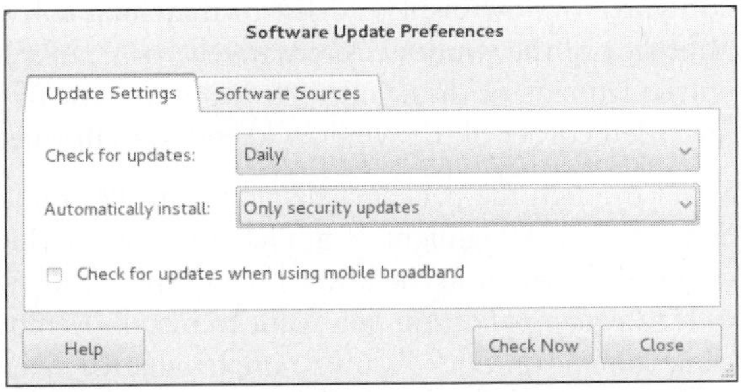

Figure 4-23   The Software Update Preferences window

Figure 4-24　The Add/Remove Software window

ADD/REMOVE SOFTWARE

The Add/Remove Software window (Figure 4-24) adds and removes applications from the system. Open this window by selecting **Main menu: Applications⇨System Tools⇨Add/Remove Software** (Fedora), **Main menu: System⇨Administration⇨Add/Remove Software** (RHEL), or by giving the command **gpk-application** from a terminal emulator or Run Application window (ALT-F2). Maximizing this window might make it easier to use. Under RHEL it might be easier to use RHN (page 554) to add and remove software.

The text box at the upper-left corner of the Add/Remove Software window (adjacent to the grayed-out button labeled **Find**) is the key to finding the package you want to add or remove. Initially, the icon at the left of this text box is a pencil and paper, indicating you will search for software packages by description. Click this icon to select other types of searches from a drop-down list.

Enter the name or part of the name of an application in the text box at the upper-left corner of the window and click **Find** to search for an application. The Add/Remove Software window displays a list of matching software packages in the frame on the right side of the window. Alternatively, you can select one of the entries from the list on the left side of the window to display a list of packages. An icon and text at the lower-left corner of the window keeps you informed of the utility's progress.

Scroll through the packages displayed in the frame on the right side of the window. When you click/highlight an application, the window displays a summary of the application in the frame at the lower-right corner of the window. Put a tick in the check box next to each application you want to install. Remove ticks from any applications you want to remove. Click **Apply** to implement the changes you have marked. If a package you want to install depends on other packages that are not installed, the utility will ask for permission to install the dependent packages. Because you need to work with **root**

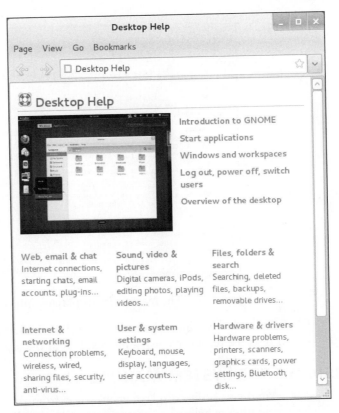

Figure 4-25   The Desktop Help window

privileges to install and remove software, the utility might ask for the **root** password. When it is finished, the utility might ask if you want to run the new application. Close the Add/Remove Software window when you are finished. Packages you installed might be available on the Main menu.

WHERE TO FIND DOCUMENTATION

Distributions of Linux, including Fedora/RHEL, typically do not come with hardcopy reference manuals. However, its online documentation has always been one of Linux's strengths. The man (or manual) and info pages have been available via the man and info utilities since early releases of the operating system. The GNOME desktop provides a graphical Desktop Help browser. Not surprisingly, with the ongoing growth of Linux and the Internet, the sources of documentation have expanded as well. This section discusses some of the places you can look for information on Linux in general and on Fedora/RHEL in particular. See also Appendix B.

GNOME DESKTOP HELP WINDOW

To display the GNOME Desktop Help window (Figure 4-25), select **Main menu: Applications⇒Accessories⇒Help** (Fedora) or **Main menu: System⇒Help** (REHL).

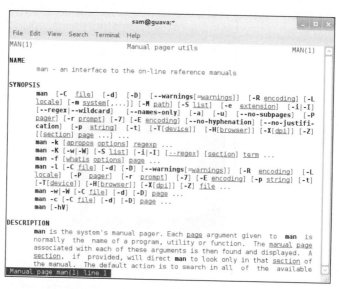

Figure 4-26   The man utility displaying information about itself

Click topics in this window until you find the information you are looking for. You can also search for a topic using the text box at the top of the window.

man: DISPLAYS THE SYSTEM MANUAL

The textual man utility displays (man) pages from the system documentation. This documentation is helpful when you know which utility you want to use but have forgotten exactly how to use it. You can also refer to the man pages to get more information about specific topics or to determine which features are available with Linux. Because the descriptions in the system documentation are often terse, they are most helpful if you already understand the basic functions of a utility.

Because man is a character-based utility, you need to open a terminal emulator window (page 117) to run it. You can also log in on a virtual terminal (page 138) and run man from there.

To find out more about a utility, give the command **man**, followed by the name of the utility. Figure 4-26 shows man displaying information about itself; the user entered a **man man** command.

less (pager)   The man utility sends its output through a *pager*—usually less (page 149), which displays one screen of information at a time. When you display a manual page using man, less displays a prompt [e.g., **Manual page man(1) line 1**] at the bottom of the screen after it displays each screen of text and waits for you to request another screen of text by pressing the SPACE bar. You can also use the PAGE UP, PAGE DOWN, UP ARROW, and DOWN ARROW keys to navigate the text. Pressing **h** (help) displays a list of less commands. Pressing **q** (quit) stops less and causes the shell to display a prompt. You can search for topics covered by man pages using the apropos utility (next).

Manual sections Based on the FHS (Filesystem Hierarchy Standard; page 199), the Linux system manual and the man pages are divided into ten sections, where each section describes related tools:

1. User Commands
2. System Calls
3. Subroutines
4. Devices
5. File Formats
6. Games
7. Miscellaneous
8. System Administration
9. Kernel
10. New

This layout closely mimics the way the set of UNIX manuals has always been divided. Unless you specify a manual section, man displays the earliest occurrence in the manual of the word you specify on the command line. Most users find the information they need in sections 1, 6, and 7; programmers and system administrators frequently need to consult the other sections.

In some cases the manual contains entries for different tools with the same name. For example, the following command displays the man page for the passwd utility from section 1 of the system manual:

```
$ man passwd
```

To see the man page for the **passwd** file from section 5, enter this command:

```
$ man 5 passwd
```

The preceding command instructs man to look only in section 5 for the man page. In documentation you might see this man page referred to as **passwd(5)**. Use the –a option (see the adjacent tip) to view all man pages for a given subject (press qRETURN to display each subsequent man page). For example, give the command **man –a passwd** to view all man pages for **passwd**.

Options

tip An option modifies the way a utility or command works. Options are usually specified as one or more letters that are preceded by one or two hyphens. An option typically appears following the name of the utility you are calling and a SPACE. Other *arguments* (page 1151) to the command follow the option and a SPACE. For more information refer to "Options" on page 227.

apropos: SEARCHES FOR A KEYWORD

When you do not know the name of the command required to carry out a particular task, you can use apropos with a keyword to search for it. This utility searches for the keyword in the short description line of all man pages and displays those that contain a match. The man utility, when called with the **–k** (keyword) option, provides the same output as apropos.

The database apropos uses, named **mandb** (Fedora) and **makewhatis** (RHEL), is not available on Fedora/RHEL systems when they are first installed, but is built automatically by **crond** (page 611). If apropos does not produce any output, see "Initializing Databases and Updating the System" on page 67.

The following example shows the output of apropos when you call it with the **who** keyword. The output includes the name of each command, the section of the manual that contains it, and the short description from the man page. This list includes the utility you need (who) and identifies other, related tools you might find useful:

```
$ apropos who
at.allow (5)            - determine who can submit jobs via at or batch
jwhois (1)              - client for the whois service
w (1)                   - Show who is logged on and what they are doing.
who (1)                 - show who is logged on
who (1p)                - display who is on the system
whoami (1)              - print effective userid
whois (1)               - client for the whois service
whois.jwhois (1)        - client for the whois service
```

whatis   The whatis utility is similar to apropos but finds only complete word matches for the name of the utility:

```
$ whatis who
who (1p)                - display who is on the system
who (1)                 - show who is logged on
```

info: DISPLAYS INFORMATION ABOUT UTILITIES

The textual info utility (www.gnu.org/software/texinfo/manual/info) is a menu-based hypertext system developed by the GNU project (page 3) and distributed with Fedora/RHEL. It includes a tutorial on itself (give the command **info info**) and documentation on many Linux shells, utilities, and programs developed by the GNU project. Figure 4-27 shows the screen that info displays when you give the command **info coreutils** (the **coreutils** software package holds the Linux core utilities).

man **and** info **display different information**

tip   The info utility displays more complete and up-to-date information on GNU utilities than does man. When a man page displays abbreviated information on a utility that is covered by info, the man page refers to info. The man utility frequently displays the only information available on non-GNU utilities. When info displays information on non-GNU utilities, it is frequently a copy of the man page.

Because the information on this screen is drawn from an editable file, your display might differ from the screens shown in this section. You can press any of the following keys while the initial info screen is displayed:

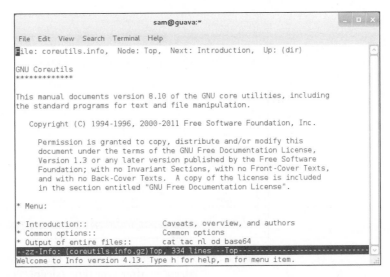

Figure 4-27   The initial screen displayed by the command **info coreutils**

- **h** or **?** to list info commands
- SPACE to scroll through the display
- **m** followed by the name of the menu you want to display or a SPACE to display a list of menus
- **q** or CONTROL-C to quit

The notation info uses to describe keyboard keys might not be familiar to you. The notation **C-h** is the same as CONTROL-H. Similarly, **M-x** means hold down the META or ALT key and press **x**. (On some systems you need to press ESCAPE and then **x** to duplicate the function of META-X.)

After giving the command **info coreutils**, press the SPACE bar a few times to scroll through the display. Type **/sleep**RETURN to search for the string **sleep**. When you type **/**, the cursor moves to the bottom line of the window and displays **Regexp search [*string*]:**, where *string* is the last string you searched for. Press RETURN to search for *string* or enter the string you want to search for. Typing **sleep** displays **sleep** on that line, and pressing RETURN displays the next occurrence of **sleep**.

You might find pinfo **easier to use than** info

tip   The pinfo utility is similar to info but is more intuitive if you are not familiar with the emacs editor. This utility runs in a textual environment, as does info. When it is available, pinfo uses color to make its interface easier to use. If pinfo is not installed on the system, use the Add/Remove Software window (page 124) to install the **pinfo** package. Run pinfo from a terminal emulator or Run Application window (ALT-F2) and select **Run in terminal**.

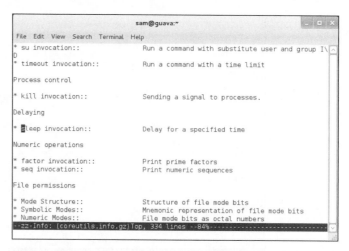

Figure 4-28   The screen displayed by the command **info coreutils** after you type **/sleep**RETURN twice

Now type **/**RETURN (or **/sleep**RETURN) to search for the next occurrence of **sleep** as shown in Figure 4-28. The asterisk at the left end of the line indicates that this entry is a menu item. Following the asterisk is the name of the menu item and a description of the item.

Each menu item is a link to the info page that describes the item. To jump to that page, search for or use the ARROW keys to move the cursor to the line containing the menu item and press RETURN. With the cursor positioned as it is in Figure 4-28, press RETURN to display information on **sleep**. Alternatively, you can type the name of the menu item in a menu command to view the information: To display information on **sleep**, for example, you can give the command **m sleep**, followed by RETURN. When you type **m** (for *menu*), the cursor moves to the bottom line of the window (as it did when you typed **/**) and displays **Menu item:**. Typing **sleep** displays **sleep** on that line, and pressing RETURN displays information about the menu item you have specified.

Figure 4-29 shows the *top node* of information on **sleep**. A node groups a set of information you can scroll through by pressing the SPACE bar. To display the next node, press **n**. Press **p** to display the previous node.

As you read through this book and learn about new utilities, you can use man or info to find out more about those utilities. If you can print PostScript documents, you can print a manual page by using the man utility with the **–t** option. For example, **man –t cat | lpr** prints information about the cat utility. You can also use a Web browser to display the documentation at docs.fedoraproject.org, www.redhat.com/docs, or www.tldp.org, and then print the desired information from the browser.

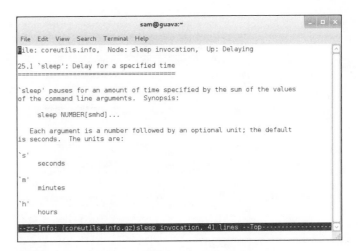

Figure 4-29   The info page on the sleep utility

THE --help OPTION

Another tool you can use in a textual environment is the **--help** option. Most GNU utilities provide a **--help** option that displays information about the utility. Non-GNU utilities might use a **–h** or **–help** option to display help information.

```
$ cat --help
Usage: cat [OPTION] [FILE]...
Concatenate FILE(s), or standard input, to standard output.

  -A, --show-all           equivalent to -vET
  -b, --number-nonblank    number nonempty output lines, overrides -n
  -e                       equivalent to -vE
  -E, --show-ends          display $ at end of each line
  ...
```

If the information that **--help** displays runs off the screen, send the output through the less pager (page 126) using a pipe (page 156):

```
$ ls --help | less
```

HOWTOs: FINDING OUT HOW THINGS WORK

A HOWTO document explains in detail how to do something related to Linux—from setting up a specialized piece of hardware to performing a system administration task to setting up specific networking software. Mini-HOWTOs offer shorter explanations. As with Linux software, one person or a few people generally are responsible for writing and maintaining a HOWTO document, but many people might contribute to it.

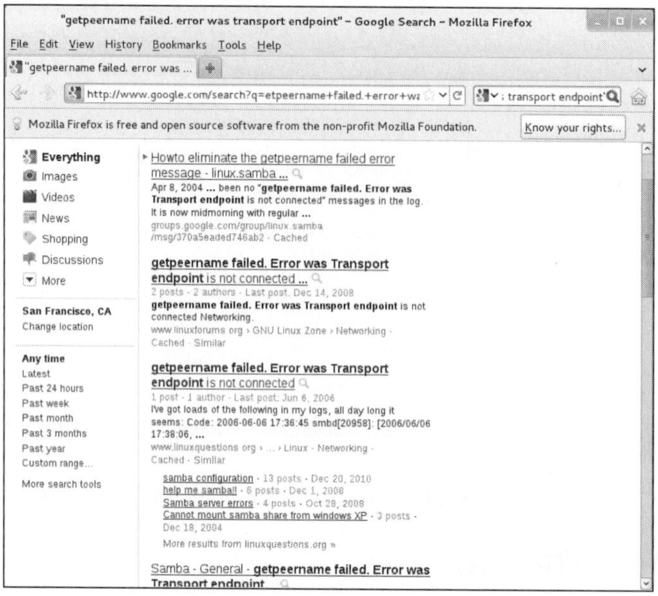

Figure 4-30   Google reporting on an error message

The Linux Documentation Project (LDP; page 133) site houses most HOWTO and mini-HOWTO documents. Use a Web browser to visit www.tldp.org, click **HOWTOs**, and pick the index you want to use to find a HOWTO or mini-HOWTO. You can also use the LDP search feature on its home page to find HOWTOs and other documents.

Getting Help

GNOME provides tooltips (page 112), a context-sensitive Help system, and the Desktop Help window, discussed on page 125.

Finding Help Locally

/usr/share/doc   The **/usr/src/linux/Documentation** (present only if you install the kernel source code, as explained in Chapter 15) and **/usr/share/doc** directories often contain more detailed and different information about a utility than either man or info provides. Frequently this information is meant for people who will be compiling and modifying the utility, not just using it. These directories hold thousands of files, each containing information on a separate topic.

Using the Internet to Get Help

The Internet provides many helpful sites related to Linux. Aside from sites that offer various forms of documentation, you can enter an error message from a program you are having a problem with in a search engine such as Google (www.google.com, or its Linux-specific version at www.google.com/linux). Enclose the error message within double quotation marks to improve the quality of the results. The search will likely yield a post concerning your problem and suggestions about how to solve it. See Figure 4-30.

Fedora/Red Hat Web sites The Red Hat and Fedora Web sites are rich sources of information. The following list identifies locations that may be of interest:

- Fedora documentation is available at docs.fedoraproject.org.

- Manuals and other documentation for RHEL are available at docs.redhat.com and access.redhat.com.

- Various types of support documents and support are available at www.redhat.com/apps/support (requires free registration).

- You can query the Red Hat Knowledgebase at kbase.redhat.com (requires free registration).

- The home pages for Fedora (fedoraproject.org) and RHEL (www.redhat.com) have a wealth of information.

- Fedora/RHEL support forums are online discussions about any Red Hat–related issues that people want to raise. One forum is dedicated to new users; others to Apache, the X Window System, and so on. Visit www.redhat.com/mailman/listinfo to browse the lists. Another (nonauthoritative) site that has similar, useful information is fedoraforum.org.

- The Fedora/RHEL bugs database is available at bugzilla.redhat.com. Anyone can search the database. To submit new bugs or append to existing bugs, you need to sign up for a free account.

- Fedora weekly news is available at fedoraproject.org/wiki/FWN.

- RHEL hardware help is available from the Red Hat hardware catalog at hardware.redhat.com. The hardware that Fedora supports is mostly a superset of that supported by RHEL.

GNU GNU manuals are available at www.gnu.org/manual. In addition, you can visit the GNU home page (www.gnu.org) to obtain other documentation and GNU resources. Many of the GNU pages and resources are available in a variety of languages.

The Linux Documentation Project The Linux Documentation Project (www.tldp.org; Figure 4-31 on the next page), which has been around for almost as long as Linux, houses a complete collection of guides, HOWTOs, FAQs, man pages, and Linux magazines. The home page is available in English, Portuguese, Spanish, Italian, Korean, and French. It is easy to use and supports local text searches. It also provides a complete set of links you can use to find almost anything you want related to Linux (click **Links** in the Search box or go to www.tldp.org/links). The links page includes sections on general information, events, getting started, user groups, mailing lists, and newsgroups, with each section containing many subsections.

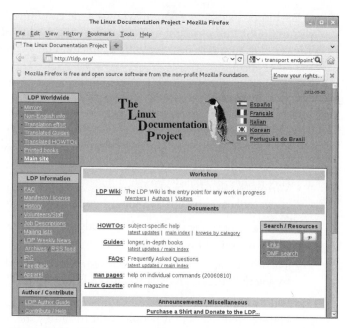

Figure 4-31   The Linux Documentation Project home page

MORE ABOUT LOGGING IN

Refer to "Logging In on the System" on page 91 for information about logging in. This section covers options you can choose from the Login screen and solutions to common login problems. It also describes how to log in from a terminal and from a remote system.

Always use a password

security   Unless you are the only user of a system; the system is not connected to any other systems, the Internet, or a modem; and you are the only one with physical access to the system, it is poor practice to maintain a user account without a password.

THE LOGIN SCREEN

The Login screen (Figure 4-1, page 91) presents a list of users who are allowed to log in on the system. At the right end of the panel at the top of the screen is a terminal icon. Click this icon to suspend, restart, or shut down the system. Click your name from the list of users to log in.

Once you have clicked your name, the login screen displays a text box labeled **Password**. Enter your password in the text box and click the button labeled **Log In** or press RETURN to log in.

Sessions   After you click your name, the Login screen displays a drop-down list to the left of the button labeled **Cancel**. Select the desktop manager you want to use for the upcoming and future sessions from this list, enter your password, and then click **Log In**.

What to Do if You Cannot Log In

If you enter either your username or your password incorrectly, the system displays an error message after you enter *both* your username *and* your password. This message indicates you have entered either the username or the password incorrectly or that they are not valid. It does not differentiate between an unacceptable username and an unacceptable password—a strategy meant to discourage unauthorized people from guessing names and passwords to gain access to the system.

Following are some common reasons why logins fail:

- **The username and password are case sensitive.** Make sure the CAPS LOCK key is off and enter your username and password exactly as specified or as you set them up.

- **You are not logging in on the right machine.** The login/password combination might not be valid if you are trying to log in on the wrong machine. On a larger, networked system, you might have to specify the machine you want to connect to before you can log in.

- **Your username is not valid.** The login/password combination might not be valid if you have not been set up as a user. If you are the system administrator, refer to "Configuring User and Group Accounts" on page 602. Otherwise, check with the system administrator.

- **A filesystem is full.** When a filesystem critical to the login process is full, it might appear as though you have logged in successfully, but after a moment the Login screen reappears. You must boot the system in rescue (page 449) and delete some files.

- **The account is disabled.** The **root** account is disabled from a GUI login by default. An administrator might disable other accounts. Often the **root** account is not allowed to log in over a network. Use su (page 413) if you need to work with root privileges from a remote system.

Refer to "Changing Your Password" on page 137 if you want to change your password.

Logging In Remotely: Terminal Emulators, ssh, and Dial-Up Connections

When you are not using a console, terminal, or other device connected directly to the Linux system you are logging in on, you are probably connected to the Linux system using terminal emulation software on another system. Running on the local system, this software connects to the remote Linux system via a network (Ethernet, asynchronous phone line, PPP, or other type) and allows you to log in.

Make sure **TERM** is set correctly

tip No matter how you connect, make sure you have the **TERM** variable set to the type of terminal your emulator is emulating. For more information refer to "Specifying a Terminal" on page 1122.

When you log in via a dial-up line, the connection is straightforward: You instruct the local emulator program to contact the remote Linux system, it dials the phone, and the remote system displays a login prompt. When you log in via a directly connected network, you either use ssh (secure; page 681) or telnet (not secure; page 383) to connect to the remote system. The ssh program has been implemented on many operating systems, not just Linux. Many user interfaces to ssh include a terminal emulator. From an Apple, Windows, or UNIX machine, open the program that runs ssh and give it the name or IP address (refer to "Host Address" on page 376) of the system you want to log in on. For examples and more details on working with a terminal emulator, refer to "Running Commands from a Terminal Emulator/Shell" on page 117. The next section provides more information about logging in from a terminal emulator.

LOGGING IN FROM A TERMINAL (EMULATOR)

Before you log in on a terminal, terminal emulator, or other textual device, the system displays a message called *issue* (stored in the **/etc/issue** file) that identifies the version of Fedora/RHEL running on the system. A sample issue message follows:

```
Fedora release 15 (Lovelock)
Kernel 2.6.38.6-27.fc15.i686.PAE on an i686 (tty2)
```

This message is followed by a prompt to log in. Enter your username and password in response to the system prompts. If you are using a *terminal* (page 1192) and the screen does not display the **login:** prompt, check whether the terminal is plugged in and turned on, and then press the RETURN key a few times. If **login:** still does not appear, try pressing CONTROL-Q (Xoff). If you are using a *workstation* (page 1197), run ssh (page 681), telnet (page 383), or whatever communications/emulation software you use to log in on the system.

Did you log in last?

security When you log in to a textual environment, after you enter your username and password, the system might display information about the last login on this account, showing when it took place and where it originated. You can use this information to determine whether anyone has accessed the account since you last used it. If someone has, perhaps an unauthorized user has learned your password and logged in as you. In the interest of maintaining security, advise the system administrator of any circumstances that make you suspicious—and change your password.

Once the *shell prompt* (or just *prompt*) appears, you have successfully logged in; this prompt shows the system is ready for you to give a command. The first shell prompt line might be preceded by a short message called the *message of the day*, or **motd** (page 508), which is stored in the **/etc/motd** file. Fedora/RHEL establishes a prompt of *[user@host directory]$*, where **user** is your username, *host* is the name of the system, and **directory** is the name of the directory you are working in. A tilde (~) represents your home directory. For information on how to change the prompt, refer to page 310.

CHANGING YOUR PASSWORD

If someone else assigned you a password, it is a good idea to give yourself a new one. For security reasons, none of the passwords you enter is displayed by any utility.

Protect your password

security   Do not allow someone to find out your password: *Do not* put your password in a file that is not encrypted, allow someone to watch you type your password, or give your password to someone you do not know (a system administrator never needs to know your password). You can always write your password down and keep it in a safe, private place.

Choose a password that is difficult to guess

security   Do not use phone numbers, names of pets or kids, birthdays, words from a dictionary (not even a foreign language), and so forth. Do not use permutations of these items or a l33t-speak variation of a word: Modern dictionary crackers might also try these permutations.

Include nonalphanumeric characters in your password

security   Automated password cracking tools first try using alphabetic and numeric characters when they try to guess your password. Including at least one character such as @ or # in a password makes it take longer for one of these tools to crack your password.

Differentiate between important and less important passwords

security   It is a good idea to differentiate between important and less important passwords. For example, Web site passwords for blogs or download access are not very important; it is acceptable to use the same password for these types of sites. However, your login, mail server, and bank account Web site passwords are critical: Never use these passwords for an unimportant Web site.

To change your password, select **Main menu: Applications⇨System Tools⇨System Settings** and select **System/User Accounts** (Fedora) or **Main menu: System⇨ Preferences⇨About Me** and click **Change Password** (RHEL). From a command line, give the command **passwd**.

Under Fedora, click the text box labeled **Password** in the User Accounts window. The first item the system asks for is your current (old) password. This password is verified to ensure that an unauthorized user is not trying to alter your password. Then the system requests a new password.

To be relatively secure, a password should contain a combination of numbers, uppercase and lowercase letters, and punctuation characters. It should also meet the following criteria:

- Must be at least six characters long (or longer if the system administrator sets it up that way). Seven or eight characters is a good compromise between length and security.

- Should not be a word in a dictionary of any language, no matter how seemingly obscure.

- Should not be the name of a person, place, pet, or other thing that might be discovered easily.

- Should contain at least two letters and one digit or punctuation character.

- Should not be your username, the reverse of your username, or your username shifted by one or more characters.

Only the first item is mandatory. Avoid using control characters (such as CONTROL-H) because they might have a special meaning to the system, making it impossible for you to log in. If you are changing your password, the new password should differ from the old one by at least three characters. Changing the case of a character does not make it count as a different character. Refer to "Keeping the System Secure" on page 630 for more information about choosing a password.

pwgen **helps you pick a password**

security   The pwgen utility (install the **pwgen** package) generates a list of almost random passwords. With a little imagination, you can pronounce, and therefore remember, some of these passwords.

After you enter your new password, the system asks you to retype it to ensure you did not make a mistake when you entered it the first time. If the new password is the same both times you enter it, your password is changed. If the passwords differ, you made an error in one of them. In this situation the system displays an error message or does not allow you to click the **OK** button. If the password you enter is not long enough, the system displays a message similar to **The password is too short**.

When you successfully change your password, you change the way you log in. If you forget your password, a user running with **root** privileges can change it and tell you the new password.

USING VIRTUAL CONSOLES

When running Linux on a personal computer, you will frequently work with the display and keyboard attached to the computer. Using this physical console, you can access as many as 63 *virtual consoles* (also called *virtual terminals*). Some are set up to allow logins; others act as graphical displays. To switch between virtual consoles, hold the CONTROL and ALT keys down and press the function key that corresponds to the console you want to view. For example, CONTROL-ALT-F5 displays the fifth virtual console.

By default, five or six virtual consoles are active and have textual login sessions running. When you want to use both textual and graphical interfaces, you can set up a textual session on one virtual console and a graphical session on another. By default, under Fedora/RHEL a graphical session runs on virtual console number 1.

WORKING FROM THE COMMAND LINE

Before the introduction of the graphical user interface (GUI), UNIX and then Linux provided only a command-line (textual) interface (CLI). Today, a CLI is available when you log in from a terminal, a terminal emulator, or a textual virtual console, or when you use ssh (secure; page 677) or telnet (not secure; page 383) to log in on a system.

This section introduces the Linux CLI. Chapter 5 describes some of the more important utilities you can use from the command line. Most of the examples in Parts IV and V of this book use the CLI, adding examples of graphical tools where available.

Advantages of the CLI
Although the concept might seem antiquated, the CLI has a place in modern computing. In some cases an administrator might use a command-line tool either because a graphical equivalent does not exist or because the graphical tool is not as powerful or flexible as the textual one. Frequently, on a server system, a graphical interface might not even be installed. The first reason for this omission is that a GUI consumes a lot of system resources; on a server, those resources are better dedicated to the main task of the server. Additionally, security considerations mandate that a server system run as few tasks as possible because each additional task can make the system more vulnerable to attack.

You can also write scripts using the CLI. Using scripts, you can easily reproduce tasks on multiple systems, enabling you to scale the tasks to larger environments. When you are the administrator of only a single system, using a GUI is often the easiest way to configure the system. When you act as administrator for many systems, all of which need the same configuration installed or updated, a script can make the task go more quickly. Writing a script using command-line tools is frequently easy, whereas the same task can be difficult to impossible using graphical tools.

Pseudographical interface
Before the introduction of GUIs, resourceful programmers created textual interfaces that included graphical elements such as boxes, borders outlining rudimentary windows, highlights, and, more recently, color. These textual interfaces, called pseudographical interfaces, bridge the gap between textual and graphical interfaces.

CORRECTING MISTAKES

This section explains how to correct typographical and other errors you might make while you are logged in on a textual display. Because the shell and most other utilities do not interpret the command line or other text until after you press RETURN, you can readily correct your typing mistakes before you press RETURN.

You can correct such mistakes in several ways: erase one character at a time, back up a word at a time, or back up to the beginning of the command line in one step. After you press RETURN, it is too late to correct a mistake: At that point, you must either wait for the command to run to completion or abort execution of the program (next page).

ERASING A CHARACTER

While entering characters from the keyboard, you can back up and erase a mistake by pressing the *erase key* once for each character you want to delete. The erase key backs over as many characters as you wish. It does not, in general, back up past the beginning of the line.

The default erase key is BACKSPACE. If this key does not work, try pressing DEL or CONTROL-H. If these keys do not work, give the following stty[1] command to set the erase and line kill (see "Deleting a Line") keys to their default values:

```
$ stty ek
```

DELETING A WORD

You can delete a word you entered by pressing CONTROL-W. A *word* is any sequence of characters that does not contain a SPACE or TAB. When you press CONTROL-W, the cursor moves left to the beginning of the current word (as you are entering a word) or the previous word (when you have just entered a SPACE or TAB), removing the word.

CONTROL-Z **suspends a program**

tip Although it is not a way of correcting a mistake, you might press the suspend key (typically CONTROL-Z) by mistake and wonder what happened. If you see a message containing the word **Stopped**, you have just stopped your job using job control (page 243). If you give the command **fg** to continue your job in the foreground, you should return to where you were before you pressed the suspend key. For more information refer to "bg: Sends a Job to the Background" on page 297.

DELETING A LINE

Any time before you press RETURN, you can delete the line you are entering by pressing the (*line*) *kill key*. When you press this key, the cursor moves to the left, erasing characters as it goes, back to the beginning of the line. The default line kill key is CONTROL-U. If this key does not work, try CONTROL-X. If these keys do not work, give the stty command described under "Erasing a Character."

ABORTING EXECUTION

Sometimes you might want to terminate a running program. For example, you might want to stop a program that is performing a lengthy task such as displaying the contents of a file that is several hundred pages long or copying a large file that is not the one you meant to copy.

To terminate a program from a textual display, press the *interrupt key* (CONTROL-C or sometimes DELETE or DEL). When you press this key, the Linux operating system sends a termination signal to the program you are running and to the shell. Exactly what effect this signal has depends on the program. Some programs stop execution

---

1. The command stty is an abbreviation for *set teletypewriter,* the first terminal UNIX ran on. Today stty is commonly thought of as meaning *set terminal.*

immediately, some ignore the signal, and some take other actions. When the shell receives a termination signal, it displays a prompt and waits for another command.

If these methods do not terminate the program, try sending the program a quit signal (CONTROL-\). If all else fails, try pressing the suspend key (typically CONTROL-Z), giving a **jobs** command to verify the number of the job running the program, and using kill to abort the job. The job number is the number within the brackets at the left end of the line displayed by **jobs** ([1]). In the next example, the **kill** command (page 470) uses **–TERM** to send a termination signal[2] to the job specified by the job number, which is preceded by a percent sign (**%1**). You can omit **–TERM** from the command, as kill sends a termination signal by default.

```
$ bigjob
^Z
[1]+  Stopped                 bigjob
$ jobs
[1]+  Stopped                 bigjob
$ kill -TERM %1
[1]+  Killed                  bigjob
```

The **kill** command returns a prompt; you might need to press RETURN again to see the confirmation message. For more information refer to "Running a Command in the Background" on page 242.

REPEATING/EDITING COMMAND LINES

To repeat a previous command, press the UP ARROW key. Each time you press this key, the shell displays an earlier command line. To re-execute the displayed command line, press RETURN. Press the DOWN ARROW key to browse through the command lines in the other direction.

You can also repeat the previous command using **!!**. This technique is useful if you forgot to use su (page 413) before a command. In this case, if you type **su –c "!!"**, the shell will run the previous command with **root** privileges.

The command **^old^new^** reruns the previous command, substituting the first occurrence of **old** with **new**. Also, on a command line, the shell replaces the characters **!$** with the last argument (word) of the previous command. The following example shows the user correcting the filename **meno** to **memo** using **^n^m^** and then printing the file named **memo** by giving the command **lpr !$**. The shell replaces **!$** with **memo**, the last argument of the previous command.

```
$ cat meno
cat: meno: No such file or directory
$ ^n^m^
cat memo
This is the memo file.
$ lpr !$
lpr memo
```

---

2. When the termination signal does not work, use the kill signal (**–KILL**). A running program cannot ignore a kill signal; it is sure to abort the program (page 470).

The RIGHT and LEFT ARROW keys move the cursor back and forth along the displayed command line. At any point along the command line, you can add characters by typing them. Use the erase key to remove characters from the command line.

For information about more complex command-line editing, see page 320.

CHAPTER SUMMARY

As with many operating systems, your access to a Linux system is authorized when you log in. To do so, you enter your username and password on the Login screen. You can change your password at any time while you are logged in. Choose a password that is difficult to guess and that conforms to the criteria imposed by the utility that changes your password.

The system administrator is responsible for maintaining the system. On a single-user system, you are the system administrator. On a small, multiuser system, you or another user might act as the system administrator, or this job might be shared. On a large, multiuser system or a network of systems, there is frequently a full-time system administrator. When extra privileges are required to perform certain system tasks, the system administrator logs in as the **root** user by entering the username **root** and the **root** password; this user is called Superuser or administrator. On a multiuser system, several trusted users might be given the **root** password.

Do not work with **root** privileges (as Superuser) as a matter of course. When you have to do something that requires **root** privileges, work with **root** privileges for only as long as absolutely necessary; revert to working as yourself as soon as possible.

Understanding the desktop and its components is essential to getting the most out of the Fedora/RHEL GUI. Its panels offer a convenient way to launch applications, either by clicking objects or by using the Main menu. The Main menu is a multilevel menu you can work with to start many commonly used applications. A window is the graphical manifestation of an application. You can control its size, location, and appearance by clicking buttons on the window's titlebar. A terminal emulator allows you to use the Linux command-line interface from a graphical environment. You can use a terminal emulator to launch both textual and graphical programs.

Panels and menus enable you to select an object (which can be just about anything on the system). On a panel, you generally click an object; on a menu, you typically click text in a list.

The GNOME environment provides users with a variety of interests and experience levels—the casual user, the office worker, the power user, and the programmer/system designer—with a space to work in and a set of tools to work with. GNOME also provides off-the-shelf productivity and many ways to customize its look, feel, and response.

Nautilus is GNOME's simple, yet powerful file manager. It can create, open, display, move, and copy files and directories as well as execute programs and scripts. One of its most basic and important functions is to create and manage the desktop.

The man utility provides online documentation for system utilities. This utility is helpful both to new Linux users and to experienced users, who must often delve into system documentation for information on the finer points of a utility's behavior. The info utility also helps the beginner and the expert alike. It provides a tutorial on its use and documentation on many Linux utilities.

The textual or command-line interface (CLI) continues to have a place in modern computing. For example, sometimes a graphical tool does not exist or might not be as powerful or flexible as its textual counterpart. Security concerns on a server system mandate that the system run as few tasks as possible. Because each additional task can make a server more vulnerable to attack, frequently these systems do not have GUIs installed.

EXERCISES

1. The system displays the following message when you attempt to log in with an incorrect username *or* an incorrect password:

   ```
   Login incorrect
   ```

   a. This message does not indicate whether your username, your password, or both are invalid. Why does it not reveal this information?

   b. Why does the system wait for a couple of seconds to respond after you supply an incorrect username or password?

2. Give three examples of poor password choices. What is wrong with each?

3. Is **fido** an acceptable password? Give several reasons why or why not.

4. What is a context menu? How does a context menu differ from other menus?

5. What appears when you right-click the root window? How can you use this object?

6. How would you swap the effects of the right and left buttons on a mouse? What is the drag-and-drop threshold? How would you change it?

7. What are the primary functions of the Main menu?

8. Describe three ways to

   a. Change the size of a window.

   b. Delete a window.

9. What are the functions of a Window Operations menu? How do you display this menu?

10. What is a panel? Name a few objects on the panels and explain what you can use them for. What do the Workspace Switcher applet and the Window List applet do?

11. What are tooltips? How are they useful?

ADVANCED EXERCISES

12. How does the mouse pointer change when you move it to the edge of a window? What happens when you left-click and drag the mouse pointer when it looks like this? Repeat this experiment with the mouse pointer at the corner of a window.

13. Assume you have started a window manager without a desktop manager. What would be missing from the screen? Describe what a window manager does. How does a desktop manager make it easier to work with a GUI?

14. When the characters you type do not appear on the screen, what might be wrong? How can you fix this problem?

15. What happens when you run vi from the Run Application window without specifying that it be run in a terminal? Where does the output go?

16. The example on page 127 shows that the man pages for passwd appear in sections 1 and 5 of the system manual. Explain how you can use man to determine which sections of the system manual contain a manual page with a given name.

17. How many man pages are in the Devices subsection of the system manual? (*Hint:* Devices is a subsection of Special Files.)

5

The Linux Utilities

Chapter Objectives

After reading this chapter you should be able to:

▶ List special characters and methods of preventing interpretation of these characters

▶ Use basic utilities to list files and display text files

▶ Copy, move, and remove files

▶ Search, sort, print, and compare text files

▶ String commands together using a pipe

▶ Compress, decompress, and archive files

▶ Locate utilities on the system

▶ Display information about users

▶ Communicate with other users

When Linus Torvalds introduced Linux and for a long time thereafter, Linux did not have a graphical user interface (GUI): It ran on character-based terminals only, using a command-line interface (CLI), also referred to as a textual interface. All the tools ran from a command line. Today the Linux GUI is important, but many people—especially system administrators—run many command-line utilities. Command-line utilities are often faster, more powerful, or more complete than their GUI counterparts. Sometimes there is no GUI counterpart to a textual utility, and some people just prefer the hands-on feeling of the command line.

When you work with a command-line interface, you are working with a shell (Chapters 7, 9, and 27). Before you start working with a shell, it is important that you understand something about the characters that are special to the shell, so this chapter starts with a discussion of special characters. The chapter then describes five basic utilities: ls, cat, rm, less, and hostname. It continues by describing several other file manipulation utilities as well as utilities that compress and decompress files, pack and unpack archive files, locate utilities, display system information, communicate with other users, and print files. It concludes with a tutorial on the vim text editor.

SPECIAL CHARACTERS

Special characters, which have a special meaning to the shell, are discussed in "Filename Generation/Pathname Expansion" on page 244. These characters are mentioned here so you can avoid accidentally using them as regular characters until you understand how the shell interprets them. For example, it is best to avoid using any of the following characters in a filename (even though emacs and some other programs do) because they make the file harder to reference on the command line:

    & ; | * ? ' " ` [ ] ( ) $ < > { } # / \ ! ~

Whitespace
Although not considered special characters, RETURN, SPACE, and TAB have special meanings to the shell. RETURN usually ends a command line and initiates execution of a command. The SPACE and TAB characters separate elements on the command line and are collectively known as *whitespace* or *blanks*.

Quoting special characters
If you need to use a character that has a special meaning to the shell as a regular character, you can *quote* (or *escape*) it. When you quote a special character, you keep the shell from giving it special meaning. The shell treats a quoted special character as a regular character. However, a slash (/) is always a separator in a pathname, even when you quote it.

Backslash
To quote a character, precede it with a backslash (\). When two or more special characters appear together, you must precede each with a backslash (for example, you would enter ** as **). You can quote a backslash just as you would quote any other special character—by preceding it with a backslash (\\).

Single quotation marks
Another way of quoting special characters is to enclose them between single quotation marks: '**'. You can quote many special and regular characters between a pair

of single quotation marks: **'This is a special character: >'**. The regular characters are interpreted as usual, and the shell also interprets the special characters as regular characters.

The only way to quote the erase character (CONTROL-H), the line kill character (CONTROL-U), and other control characters (try CONTROL-M) is by preceding each with a CONTROL-V. Single quotation marks and backslashes do not work. Try the following:

```
$ echo 'xxxxxxCONTROL-U'
$ echo xxxxxxCONTROL-V CONTROL-U
```

optional   Although you cannot see the CONTROL-U displayed by the second of the preceding pair of commands, it is there. The following command sends the output of echo (page 157) through a pipe (page 156) to od (octal display, see the od man page) to display CONTROL-U as octal 25 (025):

```
$ echo xxxxxxCONTROL-V CONTROL-U | od -c
0000000   x   x   x   x   x   x 025  \n
0000010
```

The \n is the NEWLINE character that echo sends at the end of its output.

BASIC UTILITIES

One of the important advantages of Linux is that it comes with thousands of utilities that perform myriad functions. You will use utilities whenever you work with Linux, whether you use them directly by name from the command line or indirectly from a menu or icon. The following sections discuss some of the most basic and important utilities; these utilities are available from a CLI. Some of the more important utilities are also available from a GUI; others are available only from a GUI.

Run these utilities from a command line

tip   This chapter describes command-line, or textual, utilities. You can experiment with these utilities from a terminal, a terminal emulator within a GUI (page 117), or a virtual console (page 138).

Folder/directory   The term *directory* is used extensively in the next sections. A directory is a resource that can hold files. On other operating systems, including Windows and Macintosh, and frequently when speaking about a Linux GUI, a directory is referred to as a *folder*. That is a good analogy: A traditional manila folder holds files just as a directory does.

In this chapter you work in your home directory

tip   When you log in on the system, you are working in your *home directory*. In this chapter that is the only directory you use: All the files you create in this chapter are in your home directory. Chapter 6 goes into more detail about directories.

```
$ ls
practice
$ cat practice
This is a small file that I created
with a text editor.
$ rm practice
$ ls
$ cat practice
cat: practice: No such file or directory
$
```

Figure 5-1   Using ls, cat, and rm on the file named **practice**

ls: LISTS THE NAMES OF FILES

Using the editor of your choice, create a small file named **practice**. (A tutorial on the vim editor appears on page 172.) After exiting from the editor, you can use the ls (list) utility to display a list of the names of the files in your home directory. In the first command in Figure 5-1, ls lists the name of the **practice** file. (You might also see files that the system or a program created automatically.) Subsequent commands in Figure 5-1 display the contents of the file and remove the file. These commands are described next.

cat: DISPLAYS A TEXT FILE

The cat utility displays the contents of a text file. The name of the command is derived from *catenate,* which means to join together, one after the other. (Figure 7-8 on page 235 shows how to use cat to string together the contents of three files.)

A convenient way to display the contents of a file on the screen is by giving the command **cat**, followed by a SPACE and the name of the file. Figure 5-1 shows cat displaying the contents of **practice**. This figure shows the difference between the ls and cat utilities: The ls utility displays the *name* of a file, whereas cat displays the *contents* of a file.

rm: DELETES A FILE

The rm (remove) utility deletes a file. Figure 5-1 shows rm deleting the file named **practice**. After rm deletes the file, ls and cat show that **practice** is no longer in the directory. The ls utility does not list its filename, and cat says that no such file exists. Use rm carefully.

A safer way of removing files

tip   You can use the interactive form of rm to make sure you delete only the file(s) you intend to delete. When you follow rm with the **–i** option (see page 127 for a tip on options) and the name of the file you want to delete, rm prompts with the name of the file and waits for you to respond with **y** (yes) before it deletes the file. It does not delete the file if you respond with a string that begins with a character other than **y**. The **–i** option is set up by default for the **root** user under Fedora/RHEL:

```
$ rm -i toollist
rm: remove regular file 'toollist'? y
```

Optional: You can create an alias (page 334) for **rm –i** and put it in your startup file (page 191) so rm always runs in interactive mode.

less Is more: DISPLAY A TEXT FILE ONE SCREEN AT A TIME

Pagers When you want to view a file that is longer than one screen, you can use either the less utility or the more utility. Each of these utilities pauses after displaying a screen of text; press the SPACE bar to display the next screen of text. Because these utilities show one page at a time, they are called *pagers*. Although less and more are very similar, they have subtle differences. At the end of the file, for example, less displays an **END** message and waits for you to press **q** before returning you to the shell. In contrast, more returns you directly to the shell. While using both utilities you can press **h** to display a Help screen that lists commands you can use while paging through a file. Give the commands **less practice** and **more practice** in place of the **cat** command in Figure 5-1 to see how these commands work. Use the command **less /etc/services** instead if you want to experiment with a longer file. Refer to the less and more man pages for more information.

hostname: DISPLAYS THE SYSTEM NAME

The hostname utility displays the name of the system you are working on. Use this utility if you are not sure that you are logged in on the correct machine.

```
$ hostname
guava
```

WORKING WITH FILES

This section describes utilities that copy, move, print, search through, display, sort, compare, and identify files.

Filename completion

tip After you enter one or more letters of a filename (following a command) on a command line, press TAB, and the Bourne Again Shell will complete as much of the filename as it can. When only one filename starts with the characters you entered, the shell completes the filename and places a SPACE after it. You can keep typing or you can press RETURN to execute the command at this point. When the characters you entered do not uniquely identify a filename, the shell completes what it can and waits for more input. If pressing TAB does not change the display, press TAB again to display a list of possible completions. For more information refer to "Pathname Completion" on page 331.

cp: COPIES A FILE

The cp (copy) utility (Figure 5-2) makes a copy of a file. This utility can copy any file, including text and executable program (binary) files. You can use cp to make a backup copy of a file or a copy to experiment with.

```
$ ls
memo
$ cp memo memo.copy
$ ls
memo memo.copy
```

Figure 5-2 cp copies a file

The cp command line uses the following syntax to specify source and destination files:

cp source-file destination-file

The *source-file* is the name of the file that cp will copy. The *destination-file* is the name cp assigns to the resulting (new) copy of the file.

The cp command line in Figure 5-2 copies the file named **memo** to **memo.copy**. The period is part of the filename—just another character. The initial ls command shows that **memo** is the only file in the directory. After the cp command, a second ls shows two files in the directory, **memo** and **memo.copy**.

Sometimes it is useful to incorporate the date into the name of a copy of a file. The following example includes the date January 30 (0130) in the copied file:

```
$ cp memo memo.0130
```

Although it has no significance to Linux, the date can help you find a version of a file you created on a certain date. Including the date can also help you avoid overwriting existing files by providing a unique filename each day. For more information refer to "Filenames" on page 188.

Use scp (page 677) or ftp (page 701) when you need to copy a file from one system to another on a common network.

cp **can destroy a file**

caution   If the ***destination-file*** exists *before* you give a cp command, cp overwrites it. Because cp overwrites (and destroys the contents of) an existing ***destination-file*** without warning, you must take care not to cause cp to overwrite a file that you need. The cp **–i** (interactive) option prompts you before it overwrites a file. See page 127 for a tip on options.

The following example assumes the file named **orange.2** exists before you give the cp command. The user answers **y** to overwrite the file:

```
$ cp -i orange orange.2
cp: overwrite 'orange.2'? y
```

mv: CHANGES THE NAME OF A FILE

The mv (move) utility can rename a file without making a copy of it. The mv command line specifies an existing file and a new filename using the same syntax as cp:

mv existing-filename new-filename

The command line in Figure 5-3 changes the name of the file **memo** to **memo.0130**. The initial ls command shows that **memo** is the only file in the directory. After you give the mv command, **memo.0130** is the only file in the directory. Compare this result to that of the cp example in Figure 5-2.

```
$ ls
memo
$ mv memo memo.0130
$ ls
memo.0130
```

Figure 5-3   mv renames a file

The mv utility can be used for more than changing the name of a file. Refer to "mv, cp: Move or Copy Files" on page 198. See the mv info page for more information.

mv **can destroy a file**

caution   Just as cp can destroy a file, so can mv. Also like cp, mv has a **–i** (interactive) option. See the caution box labeled "cp can destroy a file."

lpr: PRINTS A FILE

The lpr (line printer) utility places one or more files in a print queue for printing. Linux provides print queues so only one job is printed on a given printer at a time. A queue allows several people or jobs to send output simultaneously to a single printer with the expected results. For systems that have access to more than one printer, you can use **lpstat –p** to display a list of available printers. Use the **–P** option to instruct lpr to place the file in the queue for a specific printer—even one that is connected to another system on the network. The following command prints the file named **report**:

```
$ lpr report
```

Because this command does not specify a printer, the output goes to the default printer, which is *the* printer when you have only one printer.

The next command line prints the same file on the printer named **mailroom**:

```
$ lpr -P mailroom report
```

You can see which jobs are in the print queue by giving an **lpstat –o** command or by using the lpq utility:

```
$ lpq
lp is ready and printing
Rank  Owner   Job Files              Total Size
active max        86 (standard input)     954061 bytes
```

In this example, Max has one job that is being printed; no other jobs are in the queue. You can use the job number (86 in this case) with the lprm utility to remove the job from the print queue and stop it from printing:

```
$ lprm 86
```

```
$ cat memo

Helen:

In our meeting on June 6 we
discussed the issue of credit.
Have you had any further thoughts
about it?

              Max

$ grep 'credit' memo
discussed the issue of credit.
```

Figure 5-4   grep searches for a string

You can send more than one file to the printer with a single command. The following command line prints three files on the printer named **laser1**:

```
$ lpr -P laser1 05.txt 108.txt 12.txt
```

Refer to Chapter 14 for information on setting up a printer and defining the default printer.

grep: SEARCHES FOR A STRING

The grep[1] utility searches through one or more files to see whether any contain a specified string of characters. This utility does not change the file it searches but simply displays each line that contains the string.

The grep command in Figure 5-4 searches through the **memo** file for lines that contain the string **credit** and displays the single line that meets this criterion. If **memo** contained such words as **discredit, creditor,** or **accreditation**, grep would have displayed those lines as well because they contain the string it was searching for. The **–w** (words) option causes grep to match only whole words. Although you do not need to enclose the string you are searching for in single quotation marks, doing so allows you to put SPACES and special characters in the search string.

The grep utility can do much more than search for a simple string in a single file. Refer to the grep info page and Appendix A, "Regular Expressions," for more information.

head: DISPLAYS THE BEGINNING OF A FILE

By default the head utility displays the first ten lines of a file. You can use head to help you remember what a particular file contains. For example, if you have a file

---

1. Originally the name grep was a play on an ed—an original UNIX editor, available on Fedora/RHEL—command: g/re/p. In this command g stands for global, **re** is a regular expression delimited by slashes, and **p** means print.

```
$ head months
Jan
Feb
Mar
Apr
May
Jun
Jul
Aug
Sep
Oct

$ tail -5 months
Aug
Sep
Oct
Nov
Dec
```

Figure 5-5   head displays the first ten lines of a file

named **months** that lists the 12 months of the year in calendar order, one to a line, then head displays **Jan** through **Oct** (Figure 5-5).

This utility can display any number of lines, so you can use it to look at only the first line of a file, at a full screen, or even more. To specify the number of lines displayed, include a hyphen followed by the number of lines you want head to display. For example, the following command displays only the first line of **months**:

```
$ head -1 months
Jan
```

The head utility can also display parts of a file based on a count of blocks or characters rather than lines. Refer to the head info page for more information.

tail: DISPLAYS THE END OF A FILE

The tail utility is similar to head but by default displays the *last* ten lines of a file. Depending on how you invoke it, this utility can display fewer or more than ten lines, use a count of blocks or characters rather than lines to display parts of a file, and display lines being added to a file that is changing. The tail command in Figure 5-5 displays the last five lines (**Aug** through **Dec**) of the **months** file.

You can monitor lines as they are added to the end of the growing file named **logfile** with the following command:

```
$ tail -f logfile
```

Press the interrupt key (usually CONTROL-C) to stop tail and display the shell prompt. Refer to the tail info page for more information.

```
$ cat days
Monday
Tuesday
Wednesday
Thursday
Friday
Saturday
Sunday

$ sort days
Friday
Monday
Saturday
Sunday
Thursday
Tuesday
Wednesday
```

Figure 5-6   sort displays the lines of a file in order

sort: DISPLAYS A FILE IN ORDER

The sort utility displays the contents of a file in order by lines; it does not change the original file.

Figure 5-6 shows cat displaying the file named **days,** which contains the name of each day of the week on a separate line in calendar order. The sort utility then displays the file in alphabetical order.

The sort utility is useful for putting lists in order. The **–u** option generates a sorted list in which each line is unique (no duplicates). The **–n** option puts a list of numbers in numerical order. Refer to the sort info page for more information.

uniq: REMOVES DUPLICATE LINES FROM A FILE

The uniq (unique) utility displays a file, skipping adjacent duplicate lines; it does not change the original file. If a file contains a list of names and has two successive entries for the same person, uniq skips the extra line (Figure 5-7).

If a file is sorted before it is processed by uniq, this utility ensures that no two lines in the file are the same. (Of course, sort can do that all by itself with the **–u** option.) Refer to the uniq info page for more information.

diff: COMPARES TWO FILES

The diff (difference) utility compares two files and displays a list of the differences between them. This utility does not change either file; it is useful when you want to compare two versions of a letter or a report or two versions of the source code for a program.

The diff utility with the **–u** (unified output format) option first displays two lines indicating which of the files you are comparing will be denoted by a plus sign (**+**)

```
$ cat dups
Cathy
Fred
Joe
John
Mary
Mary
Paula

$ uniq dups
Cathy
Fred
Joe
John
Mary
Paula
```

Figure 5-7 uniq removes duplicate lines

and which by a minus sign (–). In Figure 5-8, a minus sign indicates the **colors.1** file; a plus sign indicates the **colors.2** file.

The **diff –u** command breaks long, multiline text into *hunks*. Each hunk is preceded by a line starting and ending with two at signs (**@@**). This hunk identifier indicates the starting line number and the number of lines from each file for this hunk. In Figure 5-8, the hunk covers the section of the **colors.1** file (indicated by a minus sign) from the first line through the sixth line. The **+1,5** then indicates the hunk covers **colors.2** from the first line through the fifth line.

Following these header lines, **diff –u** displays each line of text with a leading minus sign, a leading plus sign, or a SPACE. A leading minus sign indicates that the line occurs only in the file denoted by the minus sign. A leading plus sign indicates the line occurs only in the file denoted by the plus sign. A line that begins with a SPACE (neither a plus sign nor a minus sign) occurs in both files in the same location. Refer to the diff info page for more information.

```
$ diff -u colors.1 colors.2
--- colors.1    2011-04-05 10:12:12.322528610 -0700
+++ colors.2    2011-04-05 10:12:18.420531033 -0700
@@ -1,6 +1,5 @@
 red
+blue
 green
 yellow
-pink
-purple
 orange
```

Figure 5-8 diff displaying the unified output format

file: IDENTIFIES THE CONTENTS OF A FILE

You can use the file utility to learn about the contents of any file on a Linux system without having to open and examine the file yourself. In the following example, file reports that **letter_e.bz2** contains data that was compressed by the bzip2 utility (page 160):

```
$ file letter_e.bz2
letter_e.bz2: bzip2 compressed data, block size = 900k
```

Next file reports on two more files:

```
$ file memo zach.jpg
memo:      ASCII text
zach.jpg: JPEG image data, ... resolution (DPI), 72 x 72
```

Refer to the file man page for more information.

| (PIPE): COMMUNICATES BETWEEN PROCESSES

Because pipes are integral to the functioning of a Linux system, this chapter introduces them for use in examples. Pipes are covered in detail beginning on page 239.

A *process* is the execution of a command by Linux (page 316). Communication between processes is one of the hallmarks of both UNIX and Linux. A *pipe* (written as a vertical bar [|] on the command line and appearing as a solid or broken vertical line on a keyboard) provides the simplest form of this kind of communication. A pipe takes the output of one utility and sends that output as input to another utility. More accurately, a pipe takes standard output of one process and redirects it to become standard input of another process. See page 232 for more information on standard output and standard input.

Some utilities, such as head, can accept input from a file named on the command line or, via a pipe, from standard input. In the following command line, sort processes the **months** file (Figure 5-5, page 153); using a pipe, the shell sends the output from sort to the input of head, which displays the first four months of the sorted list:

```
$ sort months | head -4
Apr
Aug
Dec
Feb
```

The next command line displays the number of files in a directory. The wc (word count) utility with the **–w** (words) option displays the number of words in its standard input or in a file you specify on the command line:

```
$ ls | wc -w
14
```

```
$ ls
memo  memo.0714  practice
$ echo Hi
Hi
$ echo This is a sentence.
This is a sentence.
$ echo star: *
star: memo memo.0714 practice
$
```

Figure 5-9   echo copies the command line (but not the word **echo**) to the screen

You can also use a pipe to send output of a program to the printer:

```
$ tail months | lpr
```

FOUR MORE UTILITIES

The echo and date utilities are two of the most frequently used members of the large collection of Linux utilities. The script utility records part of a session in a file, and unix2dos makes a copy of a text file that can be read on either a Windows or a Macintosh machine.

echo: DISPLAYS TEXT

The echo utility copies the characters you type on the command line after **echo** to the screen. Figure 5-9 shows some echo commands. The last command shows what the shell does with an unquoted asterisk (✻) on the command line: It expands the asterisk into a list of filenames in the directory.

The echo utility is a good tool for learning about the shell and other Linux utilities. Some examples on page 246 use echo to illustrate how special characters, such as the asterisk, work. Throughout Chapters 7, 9, and 27, echo helps explain how shell variables work and how you can send messages from shell scripts to the screen. Refer to the **coreutils** info page, echo section, for more information.

optional   You can use echo to create a simple file by redirecting its output to a file:

```
$ echo 'My new file.' > myfile
$ cat myfile
My new file.
```

The greater than (>) sign tells the shell to send the output of echo to the file named **myfile** instead of to the screen. For more information refer to "Redirecting Standard Output" on page 234.

date: Displays the Time and Date

The date utility displays the current date and time:

```
$ date
Tue Apr  5 10:14:41 PDT 2011
```

The following example shows how you can specify the format and contents of the output of date:

```
$ date +"%A %B %d"
Tuesday April 05
```

Refer to the date info page for more information.

script: Records a Shell Session

The script utility records all or part of a login session, including your input and the system's responses. This utility is useful only from character-based devices, such as a terminal or a terminal emulator. It does capture a session with vim; however, because vim uses control characters to position the cursor and display different type-faces, such as bold, the output will be difficult to read and might not be useful. When you cat a file that has captured a vim session, the session quickly passes before your eyes.

By default script captures the session in a file named **typescript**. To specify a different filename, follow the script command with a SPACE and the filename. To append to a file, use the **–a** option after **script** but before the filename; otherwise script overwrites an existing file. Following is a session being recorded by script:

```
$ script
Script started, file is typescript
$ ls -l /bin | head -5
total 7804
-rwxr-xr-x. 1 root root      123 02-07 17:32 alsaunmute
-rwxr-xr-x. 1 root root    25948 02-08 03:46 arch
lrwxrwxrwx. 1 root root        4 02-25 16:52 awk -> gawk
-rwxr-xr-x. 1 root root    25088 02-08 03:46 basename
$ exit
exit
Script done, file is typescript
```

Use the exit command to terminate a script session. You can then view the file you created using cat, less, more, or an editor. Following is the file created by the preceding script command:

```
$ cat typescript
Script started on Tue 05 Apr 2011 10:16:36 AM PDT
$ ls -l /bin | head -5
total 7804
-rwxr-xr-x. 1 root root      123 02-07 17:32 alsaunmute
-rwxr-xr-x. 1 root root    25948 02-08 03:46 arch
lrwxrwxrwx. 1 root root        4 02-25 16:52 awk -> gawk
```

```
-rwxr-xr-x. 1 root root   25088 02-08 03:46 basename
$ exit
exit

Script done on Tue 05 Apr 2011 10:16:50 AM PDT
```

If you will be editing the file with vim, emacs, or another editor, you can use dos2unix (next) to eliminate from the **typescript** file the ^M characters that appear at the ends of the lines. Refer to the script man page for more information.

unix2dos: CONVERTS LINUX AND MACINTOSH FILES TO WINDOWS FORMAT

unix2dos, unix2mac — If you want to share a text file you created on a Linux system with someone on a Windows or Macintosh system, you need to convert the file for the person on the other system to read it easily. The unix2dos utility converts a Linux text file so it can be read on a Windows machine; use unix2mac to convert for a Macintosh system. This utility is part of the **dos2unix** software package; give the command **su –c "yum install dos2unix"** to install this package. Then enter the following command to convert a file named **memo.txt** (created with a text editor) to a DOS-format file (use unix2mac to convert to a Macintosh-format file):

```
$ unix2dos memo.txt
```

You can now email the file as an attachment to someone on a Windows or Macintosh system. This utility overwrites the original file.

dos2unix, dos2mac — The dos2unix utility converts Windows files so they can be read on a Linux system (use dos2mac to convert from a Macintosh system):

```
$ dos2unix memo.txt
```

See the dos2unix man page for more information.

tr — You can also use tr (translate) to change a Windows or Macintosh text file into a Linux text file. In the following example, the **–d** (delete) option causes tr to remove RETURNs (represented by \r) as it makes a copy of the file:

```
$ cat memo | tr -d '\r' > memo.txt
```

The greater than (>) symbol redirects the standard output of tr to the file named **memo.txt**. For more information refer to "Redirecting Standard Output" on page 234. Converting a file the other way without using unix2dos is not as easy.

COMPRESSING AND ARCHIVING FILES

Large files use a lot of disk space and take longer than smaller files to transfer from one system to another over a network. If you do not need to look at the contents of a large file often, you might want to save it on a USB flash drive, DVD, or another medium and remove it from the hard disk. If you have a continuing need for the file, retrieving a copy from another medium might be inconvenient. To reduce the amount of disk space you use without removing the file entirely, you can compress the file without losing any of the information it holds. Similarly a single archive of several files packed into a larger file is easier to manipulate, upload, download, and email than multiple files. You might frequently download compressed, archived files from the Internet. The utilities described in this section compress and decompress files and pack and unpack archives.

bzip2: COMPRESSES A FILE

The bzip2 utility compresses a file by analyzing it and recoding it more efficiently. The new version of the file looks completely different. In fact, because the new file contains many nonprinting characters, you cannot view it directly. The bzip2 utility works particularly well on files that contain a lot of repeated information, such as text and image data, although most image data is already in a compressed format.

The following example shows a boring file. Each of the 8,000 lines of the **letter_e** file contains 72 e's and a NEWLINE character that marks the end of the line. The file occupies more than half a megabyte of disk storage.

```
$ ls -l
-rw-rw-r--. 1 sam pubs 584000 03-01 22:31 letter_e
```

The **–l** (long) option causes ls to display more information about a file. Here it shows that **letter_e** is 584,000 bytes long. The **–v** (verbose) option causes bzip2 to report how much it was able to reduce the size of the file. In this case, it shrank the file by 99.99 percent:

```
$ bzip2 -v letter_e
letter_e: 11680.00:1, 0.001 bits/byte, 99.99% saved, 584000 in, 50 out.
$ ls -l
-rw-rw-r--. 1 sam pubs 50 03-01 22:31 letter_e.bz2
```

.bz2 filename extension Now the file is only 50 bytes long. The bzip2 utility also renamed the file, appending **.bz2** to its name. This naming convention reminds you that the file is compressed; you would not want to display or print it, for example, without first decompressing it. The bzip2 utility does not change the modification date associated with the file, even though it completely changes the file's contents.

Keep the original file by using the –k option

tip The bzip2 utility (and its counterpart, bunzip2) remove the original file when they compress or decompress a file. Use the **–k** (keep) option to keep the original file.

In the following, more realistic example, the file **zach.jpg** contains a computer graphics image:

```
$ ls -l
-rw-r--r--. 1 sam pubs 33287 03-01 22:40 zach.jpg
```

The bzip2 utility can reduce the size of the file by only 28 percent because the image is already in a compressed format:

```
$ bzip2 -v zach.jpg
zach.jpg:  1.391:1,  5.749 bits/byte, 28.13% saved, 33287 in, 23922 out.

$ ls -l
-rw-r--r--. 1 sam pubs 23922 03-01 22:40 zach.jpg.bz2
```

Refer to the bzip2 man page, www.bzip.org, and the *Bzip2 mini-HOWTO* (see page 131 for instructions on obtaining this document) for more information.

bzcat AND bunzip2: DECOMPRESS A FILE

bzcat The bzcat utility displays a file that has been compressed with bzip2. The equivalent of cat for **.bz2** files, bzcat decompresses the compressed data and displays the decompressed data. Like cat, bzcat does not change the source file. The pipe in the following example redirects the output of bzcat so instead of being displayed on the screen it becomes the input to head, which displays the first two lines of the file:

```
$ bzcat letter_e.bz2 | head -2
eeeeeeeeeeeeeeeeeeeeeeeeeeeeeeeeeeeeeeeeeeeeeeeeeeeeeeeeeeeeeeeeeeeeee
eeeeeeeeeeeeeeeeeeeeeeeeeeeeeeeeeeeeeeeeeeeeeeeeeeeeeeeeeeeeeeeeeeeeee
```

After bzcat is run, the contents of **letter_e.bz** is unchanged; the file is still stored on the disk in compressed form.

bunzip The bunzip2 utility restores a file that has been compressed with bzip2:

```
$ bunzip2 letter_e.bz2
$ ls -l
-rw-rw-r--. 1 sam pubs 584000 03-01 22:31 letter_e
$ bunzip2 zach.jpg.bz2
$ ls -l
-rw-r--r--. 1 sam pubs 33287 03-01 22:40 zach.jpg
```

bzip2recover The bzip2recover utility supports limited data recovery from media errors. Give the command **bzip2recover** followed by the name of the compressed, corrupted file from which you want to try to recover data.

gzip: COMPRESSES A FILE

gunzip and zcat The gzip (GNU zip) utility is older and less efficient than bzip2. Its flags and operation are very similar to those of bzip2. A file compressed by gzip is marked with a **.gz** filename extension. Linux stores manual pages in gzip format to save disk space; likewise, files you download from the Internet are frequently in gzip format. Use gzip, gunzip, and zcat just as you would use bzip2, bunzip2, and bzcat, respectively. Refer to the gzip info page for more information.

compress The compress utility can also compress files, albeit not as well as gzip. This utility marks a file it has compressed by adding **.Z** to its name.

gzip **versus** zip

tip Do not confuse gzip and gunzip with the zip and unzip utilities. These last two are used to pack and unpack zip archives containing several files compressed into a single file that has been imported from or is being exported to a Windows system. The zip utility constructs a zip archive, whereas unzip unpacks zip archives. The zip and unzip utilities are compatible with PKZIP, a Windows program that compresses and archives files.

tar: PACKS AND UNPACKS ARCHIVES

The tar utility performs many functions. Its name is short for *tape archive,* as its original function was to create and read archive and backup tapes. Today it is used to create a single file (called a *tar file, archive,* or *tarball*) from multiple files or directory hierarchies and to extract files from a tar file. The cpio utility (page 609) performs a similar function.

In the following example, the first ls shows the sizes of the files **g, b,** and **d.** Next tar uses the −c (create), −v (verbose), and −f (write to or read from a file) options to create an archive named **all.tar** from these files. Each line of output displays the name of the file tar is appending to the archive it is creating.

The tar utility adds overhead when it creates an archive. The next command shows that the archive file **all.tar** occupies about 9,700 bytes, whereas the sum of the sizes of the three files is about 6,000 bytes. This overhead is more appreciable on smaller files, such as the ones in this example:

```
$ ls -l g b d
-rw-r--r--. 1 zach other 1178 08-20 14:16 b
-rw-r--r--. 1 zach zach  3783 08-20 14:17 d
-rw-r--r--. 1 zach zach  1302 08-20 14:16 g

$ tar -cvf all.tar g b d
g
b
d

$ ls -l all.tar
-rw-r--r--. 1 zach zach 9728 08-20 14:17 all.tar

$ tar -tvf all.tar
-rw-r--r-- zach /zach    1302 2011-08-20 14:16 g
-rw-r--r-- zach /other   1178 2011-08-20 14:16 b
-rw-r--r-- zach /zach    3783 2011-08-20 14:17 d
```

The final command in the preceding example uses the −t option to display a table of contents for the archive. Use −x instead of −t to extract files from a tar archive. Omit the −v option if you want tar to do its work silently.[2]

You can use bzip2, compress, or gzip to compress tar files, making them easier to store and handle. Many files you download from the Internet will already be in one of these formats. Files that have been processed by tar and compressed by bzip2 frequently have a filename extension of **.tar.bz2** or **.tbz.** Those processed by tar and gzip have an extension of **.tar.gz** or **.tz,** whereas files processed by tar and compress use **.tar.Z** as the extension.

---

2. Although the original UNIX tar did not use a leading hyphen to indicate an option on the command line, the GNU/Linux version accepts hyphens but works as well without them. This book precedes tar options with a hyphen for consistency with most other utilities.

You can unpack a tarred and gzipped file in two steps. (Follow the same procedure if the file was compressed by bzip2, but use bunzip2 instead of gunzip.) The next example shows how to unpack the GNU make utility after it has been downloaded (ftp.gnu.org/pub/gnu/make/make-3.82.tar.gz):

```
$ ls -l mak*
-rw-r--r--. 1 sam pubs 1712747 04-05 10:43 make-3.82.tar.gz

$ gunzip mak*
$ ls -l mak*
-rw-r--r--. 1 sam pubs 6338560 04-05 10:43 make-3.82.tar

$ tar -xvf mak*
make-3.82/
make-3.82/vmsfunctions.c
make-3.82/getopt.h
make-3.82/make.1
...
make-3.82/README.OS2
make-3.82/remote-cstms.c
```

The first command lists the downloaded tarred and gzipped file: **make-3.82.tar.gz** (about 1.7 megabytes). The asterisk (∗) in the filename matches any characters in any filenames (page 246), so ls displays a list of files whose names begin with **mak**; in this case there is only one. Using an asterisk saves typing and can improve accuracy with long filenames. The gunzip command decompresses the file and yields **make-3.82.tar** (no **.gz** extension), which is about 6.3 megabytes. The tar command creates the **make-3.82** directory in the working directory and unpacks the files into it.

```
$ ls -ld mak*
drwxr-xr-x. 8 sam pubs    4096 2010-07-27  make-3.82
-rw-r--r--. 1 sam pubs 6338560 04-05 10:43 make-3.82.tar

$ ls -l make-3.82
total 2020
-rw-r--r--. 1 sam pubs 53838 2010-07-27  ABOUT-NLS
-rw-r--r--. 1 sam pubs  4783 2010-07-12  acinclude.m4
-rw-r--r--. 1 sam pubs 36990 2010-07-27  aclocal.m4
-rw-r--r--. 1 sam pubs 14231 2002-10-14  alloca.c
...
-rw-r--r--. 1 sam pubs 18391 2010-07-12  vmsjobs.c
-rw-r--r--. 1 sam pubs 17905 2010-07-19  vpath.c
drwxr-xr-x. 6 sam pubs  4096 2010-07-27  w32
```

After tar extracts the files from the archive, the working directory contains two files whose names start with **mak: make-3.82.tar** and **make-3.82**. The **–d** (directory) option causes ls to display only file and directory names, not the contents of directories as it normally does. The final ls command shows the files and directories in the **make-3.82** directory. Refer to the tar info page for more information.

tar: the –x option might extract a lot of files

caution   Some tar archives contain many files. To list the files in the archive without unpacking them, run tar with the **–tf** options followed by the name of the tar file. In some cases you might want to create a new directory (mkdir [page 194]), move the tar file into that directory, and expand it there. That way the unpacked files will not mingle with existing files, and no confusion will occur. This strategy also makes it easier to delete the extracted files. Depending on how they were created, some tar files automatically create a new directory and put the files into it; the **–t** option indicates where tar will place the files you extract.

tar: the –x option can overwrite files

caution   The **–x** option to tar overwrites a file that has the same filename as a file you are extracting. Follow the suggestion in the preceding caution box to avoid overwriting files.

optional   You can combine the gunzip and tar commands on one command line with a pipe (|), which redirects the output of gunzip so it becomes the input to tar:

```
$ gunzip -c make-3.82.tar.gz | tar -xvf -
```

The –c option causes gunzip to send its output through the pipe instead of creating a file. The final hyphen (–) causes tar to read from standard input. Refer to "Pipes" (page 239) and gzip (page 161) for more information about how this command line works.

A simpler solution is to use the –z option to tar. This option causes tar to call gunzip (or gzip when you are creating an archive) directly and simplifies the preceding command line to

```
$ tar -xvzf make-3.82.tar.gz
```

In a similar manner, the –j option calls bzip2 or bunzip2.

LOCATING UTILITIES

The whereis and locate utilities can help you find a command whose name you have forgotten or whose location you do not know. When multiple copies of a utility or program are present, which tells you which copy you will run. The locate utility searches for files on the local system.

which AND whereis: LOCATE A UTILITY

When you give Linux a command, the shell searches a list of directories for a program with that name. This list of directories is called a *search path*. For information on how to change the search path, refer to "PATH: Where the Shell Looks for Programs" on page 308. If you do not change the search path, the shell searches only a standard set of directories and then stops searching. However, other directories on the system might also contain useful utilities.

which   The which utility locates utilities by displaying the full pathname of the file for the utility. (Chapter 6 contains more information on pathnames and the structure of the

Linux filesystem.) The local system might include several utilities that have the same name. When you type the name of a utility, the shell searches for the utility in your search path and runs the first one it finds. You can find out which copy of the utility the shell will run by using which. In the following example, which reports the location of the tar utility:

```
$ which tar
/bin/tar
```

The which utility can be helpful when a utility seems to be working in unexpected ways. By running which, you might discover that you are running a nonstandard version of a tool or a different one from the one you expected. ("Important Standard Directories and Files" on page 199 provides a list of standard locations for executable files.) For example, if tar is not working properly and you find that you are running **/usr/local/bin/tar** instead of **/bin/tar**, you might suspect the local version is broken.

whereis   The whereis utility searches for files related to a utility by looking in standard locations instead of using your search path. For example, you can find the locations for files related to tar:

```
$ whereis tar
tar: /bin/tar /usr/share/man/man1/tar.1.gz
```

In this example whereis finds two references to tar: the tar utility file and the tar man page.

which **versus** whereis

tip   Given the name of a utility, which looks through the directories in your *search path* (page 308) in order and locates the utility. If your search path includes more than one utility with the specified name, which displays the name of only the first one (the one you would run).

The whereis utility looks through a list of *standard directories* and works independently of your search path. Use whereis to locate a binary (executable) file, any manual pages, and source code for a program you specify; whereis displays all the files it finds.

which, whereis, **and builtin commands**

caution   Both the which and whereis utilities report only the names for utilities as they are found on the disk; they do not report shell builtins (utilities that are built into a shell; page 249). When you use whereis to try to find where the echo command (which exists as both a utility program and a shell builtin) is kept, you get the following result:

```
$ whereis echo
echo: /bin/echo /usr/share/man/man1/echo.1.gz
```

The whereis utility does not display the echo builtin. Even the which utility reports the wrong information:

```
$ which echo
/bin/echo
```

Under bash you can use the type builtin (page 1019) to determine whether a command is a builtin:

```
$ type echo
echo is a shell builtin
```

locate: Searches for a File

The locate utility (**locate** package) searches for files on the local system:

```
$ locate init
/boot/initramfs-2.6.38-0.rc5.git1.1.fc15.i686.img
/boot/initrd-plymouth.img
/etc/gdbinit
/etc/gdbinit.d
/etc/init
/etc/init.d
...
```

Before you can use locate, the updatedb utility must build or update the locate database. Typically the database is updated once a day by a cron script (page 611).

If you are not on a network, skip to the vim tutorial

tip   If you are the only user on a system that is not connected to a network, you might want to skip to the tutorial on the vim editor on page 172. If you are not on a network but are set up to send and receive email, read "Email" on page 171.

Displaying User and System Information

This section covers utilities that provide information about who is using the system, what those users are doing, and how the system is running.

To find out who is using the local system, you can employ one of several utilities that vary in the details they provide and the options they support. The oldest utility, who, produces a list of users who are logged in on the local system, the device each person is using, and the time each person logged in.

The w and finger utilities show more detail, such as each user's full name and the command line each user is running. The finger utility can retrieve information about users on remote systems. Table 5-1 on page 169 summarizes the output of these utilities.

who: Lists Users on the System

The who utility displays a list of users who are logged in on the local system. In Figure 5-10 the first column who displays shows that Sam, Max, and Zach are logged in. (Max is logged in from two locations.) The second column shows the device that each user's terminal, workstation, or terminal emulator is connected to. The third column shows the date and time the user logged in. An optional fourth column shows (in parentheses) the name of the system a remote user logged in from.

The information who displays is useful when you want to communicate with a user on the local system. When the user is logged in, you can use write (page 170) to establish communication immediately. If who does not list the user or if you do not need to communicate immediately, you can send email to that person (page 171).

```
$ who
sam       tty4        2011-07-25 17:18
max       tty2        2011-07-25 16:42
zach      tty1        2011-07-25 16:39
max       pts/4       2011-07-25 17:27 (guava)
```

Figure 5-10   who lists who is logged in

If the output of who scrolls off the screen, you can redirect the output through a pipe (l, page 156) so it becomes the input to less, which displays the output one screen at a time. You can also use a pipe to redirect the output through grep to look for a specific name.

If you need to find out which terminal you are using or what time you logged in, you can use the command **who am i**:

```
$ who am i
max       pts/4          2011-07-25 17:27 (guava)
```

finger: Lists Users on the System

The finger utility displays a list of users who are logged in on the local system and in some cases, information about remote systems and users (page 381). In addition to usernames, finger supplies each user's full name along with information about which device the user's terminal is connected to, how recently the user typed something on the keyboard, when the user logged in, and what contact information is available. If the user has logged in over the network, the name of the remote system is shown as the user's office. For example, in Figure 5-11 Max is logged in from the remote system named **guava**. The asterisks (✱) in front of the device names in the **Tty** column indicate the user has blocked messages sent directly to his terminal (refer to "mesg: Denies or Accepts Messages" on page 170).

finger **can be a security risk**

security   On systems where security is a concern, the system administrator might disable finger because it can reveal information that can help a malicious user break into a system.

You can also use finger to learn more about an individual by specifying a username on the command line. In Figure 5-12 on the next page, finger displays detailed information about Max: He is logged in and actively using one of his terminals (**tty2**), and he has not used his other terminal (**pts/4**) for 3 minutes and 7 seconds. You also learn from finger that if you want to set up a meeting with Max, you should contact Sam at extension 1693.

```
$ finger
Login     Name           Tty      Idle  Login Time   Office ...
max       Max Wild       *tty2          Jul 25 16:42
max       Max Wild       pts/4     3    Jul 25 17:27 (guava)
sam       Sam the Great  *tty4     29   Jul 25 17:18
zach      Zach Brill     *tty1     1:07 Jul 25 16:39
```

Figure 5-11   finger I: lists who is logged in

```
$ finger max
Login: max                                    Name: Max Wild
Directory: /home/max                          Shell: /bin/bash
On since Fri Jul 25 16:42 (PDT) on tty2 (messages off)
On since Fri Jul 25 17:27 (PDT) on pts/4 from guava
    3 minutes 7 seconds idle
New mail received Fri Jul 25 17:16 2010 (PDT)
    Unread since Fri Jul 25 16:44 2010 (PDT)
Plan:
I will be at a conference in Hawaii next week.
If you need to see me, contact Sam, x1693.
```

Figure 5-12   finger II: lists details about one user

.plan and .project   Most of the information in Figure 5-12 was collected by finger from system files. The information shown after the heading **Plan:**, however, was supplied by Max. The finger utility searched for a file named **.plan** in Max's home directory and displayed its contents. (Filenames that begin with a period, such as **.plan**, are not normally listed by ls and are called hidden filenames [page 190].)

You might find it helpful to create a **.plan** file for yourself; it can contain any information you choose, such as your schedule, interests, phone number, or address. In a similar manner, finger displays the contents of the **.project** and **.pgpkey** files in your home directory. If Max had not been logged in, finger would have reported only his user information, the last time he logged in, the last time he read his email, and his plan.

You can also use finger to display a user's username. For example, on a system with a user named Helen Simpson, you might know that Helen's last name is Simpson but might not guess her username is **hls**. The finger utility, which is not case sensitive, can search for information on Helen using her first or last name. The following commands find the information you seek as well as information on other users whose names are Helen or Simpson:

```
$ finger HELEN
Login: hls                                    Name: Helen Simpson.
...
$ finger simpson
Login: hls                                    Name: Helen Simpson.
...
```

w: LISTS USERS ON THE SYSTEM

The w utility displays a list of the users who are logged in. As discussed in the section on who, the information that w displays is useful when you want to communicate with someone at your installation.

The first column in Figure 5-13 shows that Max, Zach, and Sam are logged in. The second column shows the name of the device file each user's terminal is connected to. The

```
$ w
 17:47:35 up 1 day,  8:10,  6 users,  load average: 0.34, 0.23, 0.26
 USER     TTY     FROM          LOGIN@   IDLE   JCPU   PCPU WHAT
 sam      tty4    -             17:18   29:14m  0.20s  0.00s vi memo
 max      tty2    -             16:42    0.00s  0.20s  0.07s w
 zach     tty1    -             16:39    1:07    0.05s  0.00s run_bdgt
 max      pts/4   guava         17:27    3:10m  0.24s  0.24s -bash
```

Figure 5-13   The w utility

third column shows the system that a remote user is logged in from. The fourth column shows the time each user logged in. The fifth column indicates how long each user has been idle (how much time has elapsed since the user pressed a key on the keyboard). The next two columns identify how much computer processor time each user has used during this login session and on the task that user is running. The last column shows the command each user is running.

The first line that the w utility displays includes the time of day, the period of time the computer has been running (in days, hours, and minutes), the number of users logged in, and the load average (how busy the system is). The three load average numbers represent the number of jobs waiting to run, averaged over the past 1, 5, and 15 minutes. Use the uptime utility to display just this line. Table 5-1 compares the w, who, and finger utilities.

Table 5-1   Comparison of w, who, and finger

Information displayed	w	who	finger
Username	X	X	X
Terminal-line identification (tty)	X	X	X
Login time (and day for old logins)	X		
Login date and time		X	X
Idle time	X		X
Program the user is executing	X		
Location the user logged in from			X
CPU time used	X		
Full name (or other information from **/etc/passwd**)			X
User-supplied vanity information			X
System uptime and load average	X		

COMMUNICATING WITH OTHER USERS

The utilities discussed in this section enable you to exchange messages and files with other users either interactively or through email.

write: SENDS A MESSAGE

The write utility sends a message to another user who is logged in. When you and another user use write to send messages to each other, you establish two-way communication. Initially a write command (Figure 5-14) displays a banner on the other user's terminal, saying that you are about to send a message.

The syntax of a write command line is

write username [terminal]

The **username** is the username of the user you want to communicate with. The **terminal** is an optional device name that is useful if the user is logged in more than once. You can display the usernames and device names of all users who are logged in on the local system by using who, w, or finger.

To establish two-way communication with another user, you and the other user must each execute write, specifying the other's username as the **username**. The write utility then copies text, line by line, from one keyboard/display to the other (Figure 5-15). Sometimes it helps to establish a convention, such as typing o (for "over") when you are ready for the other person to type and typing oo (for "over and out") when you are ready to end the conversation. When you want to stop communicating with the other user, press CONTROL-D at the beginning of a line. Pressing CONTROL-D tells write to quit, displays **EOF** (end of file) on the other user's terminal, and returns you to the shell. The other user must do the same.

If the **Message from** banner appears on your screen and obscures something you are working on, press CONTROL-L or CONTROL-R to refresh the screen and remove the banner. Then you can clean up, exit from your work, and respond to the person who is writing to you. You have to remember who is writing to you, however, because the banner will no longer appear on the screen.

mesg: DENIES OR ACCEPTS MESSAGES

By default, messages to your screen are blocked. Give the following mesg command to allow other users to send you messages:

```
$ mesg y
```

```
$ write max
Hi Max, are you there? o
```

Figure 5-14   The write utility I

```
$ write max
Hi Max, are you there? o

Message from max@guava on pts/4 at 16:23 ...
Yes Zach, I'm here. o
```

Figure 5-15   The write utility II

If Max had not given this command before Zach tried to send him a message, Zach might have seen the following message:

```
$ write max
write: max has messages disabled
```

You can block messages by entering **mesg n**. Give the command **mesg** by itself to display **is y** (for "yes, messages are allowed") or **is n** (for "no, messages are not allowed").

If you have messages blocked and you write to another user, write displays the following message because even if you are allowed to write to another user, the user will not be able to respond to you:

```
$ write max
write: you have write permission turned off.
```

EMAIL

Email enables you to communicate with users on the local system as well as those on the network. If you are connected to the Internet, you can communicate electronically with users around the world.

Email utilities differ from write in that they can send a message when the recipient is not logged in. In this case the email is stored until the recipient reads it. These utilities can also send the same message to more than one user at a time.

Many email programs are available for Linux, including the original character-based mail program, Mozilla/Thunderbird, pine, mail through emacs, KMail, and evolution. Another popular graphical email program is sylpheed (sylpheed.sraoss.jp/en).

Two programs are available that can make any email program easier to use and more secure. The procmail program (www.procmail.org) creates and maintains email servers and mailing lists; preprocesses email by sorting it into appropriate files and directories; starts various programs depending on the characteristics of incoming email; forwards email; and so on. The GNU Privacy Guard (GPG or GNUpg, page 1130) encrypts and decrypts email and makes it almost impossible for an unauthorized person to read.

Refer to Chapter 20 for more information on setting email clients and servers.

Network addresses   If the local system is part of a LAN, you can generally send email to and receive email from users on other systems on the LAN by using their usernames. Someone sending Max email on the Internet would need to specify his *domain name* (page 1162) along with his username. Use this address to send email to the author of this book: **mgs@sobell.com**.

TUTORIAL: USING vim TO CREATE AND EDIT A FILE

This section explains how to start vim, enter text, move the cursor, correct text, save the file to the disk, and exit from vim. The tutorial discusses three of the modes of operation of vim and explains how to switch from one mode to another.

vimtutor   In addition to working with this tutorial, you might want to try vim's instructional program, vimtutor. Enter its name as a command to run it.

vimtutor and vim help files are not installed by default

tip   To run vimtutor and to get help as described on page 176, you must install the **vim-enhanced** package; give the command **su –c 'yum install vim-enhanced'** to install this package.

Specifying a terminal   Because vim takes advantage of features that are specific to various kinds of terminals, you must tell it what type of terminal or terminal emulator you are using. On many systems, and usually when you work on a terminal emulator, your terminal type is set automatically. If you need to specify your terminal type explicitly, refer to "Specifying a Terminal" on page 1122.

STARTING vim

Start vim with the following command to create and edit a file named **practice** (use **vi** in place of **vim** if you have not installed the **vim-enhanced** package):

```
$ vim practice
```

When you press RETURN, the command line disappears, and the screen looks similar to the one shown in Figure 5-16.

vim is not installed by default: use vi

tip   The full version of the vim editor is not installed by default. Instead, a small version of vim, named vi, is installed. You can either replace each **vim** command in this section with **vi**, or you can install the full vim editor by giving the command **su –c 'yum install vim-enhanced'** and then use the **vim** command as shown in this section.

The tildes (~) at the left of the screen indicate the file is empty. They disappear as you add lines of text to the file. If your screen looks like a distorted version of the

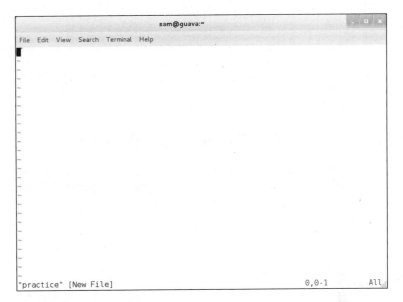

Figure 5-16   Starting vim

one shown in Figure 5-16, your terminal type is probably not set correctly (see "Problem," next).

The **practice** file is new so contains no text. The vim editor displays a message similar to the one shown in Figure 5-16 on the status (bottom) line of the terminal to indicate you are creating and editing a new file. When you edit an existing file, vim displays the first few lines of the file and gives status information about the file on the status line.

Problem If you start vim with a terminal type that is not in the **terminfo** database, vim displays an error message and waits for you to press RETURN:

```
$ vim
E437: terminal capability "cm" required
Press ENTER or type command to continue
```

Emergency exit To reset the terminal type, press ESCAPE and then give the following command to exit from vim and display the shell prompt:

```
:q!
```

When you enter the colon (:), vim moves the cursor to the bottom line of the screen. The characters **q!** tell vim to quit without saving your work. (You will not ordinarily exit from vim this way because you typically want to save your work.) You must press RETURN after you give this command. When the shell displays its prompt, refer to "Specifying a Terminal" on page 1122 and start vim again.

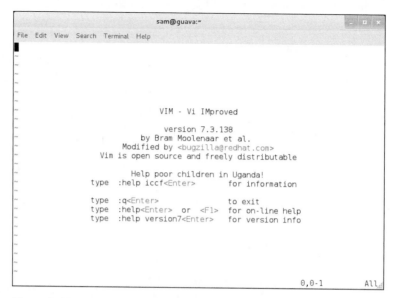

Figure 5-17   Starting vim without a filename

If you start vim without a filename, it displays information about itself (Figure 5-17).

COMMAND AND INPUT MODES

Two of vim's modes of operation are *Command mode* (also called *Normal mode*) and *Input mode* (Figure 5-18). While vim is in Command mode, you can give vim commands. For example, you can delete text or exit from vim. You can also command vim to enter Input mode. In Input mode, vim accepts anything you enter as text and displays it on the screen. Press ESCAPE to return vim to Command mode. By default the vim editor keeps you informed about which mode it is in: It displays **INSERT** at the lower-left corner of the screen while it is in Insert mode.

The following command causes vim to display line numbers next to the text you are editing:

   :set number RETURN

Last Line mode   The colon (:) in the preceding command puts vim into another mode, *Last Line mode*. While in this mode, vim keeps the cursor on the bottom line of the screen. When you finish entering the command by pressing RETURN, vim restores the cursor to its place in the text. Give the command **:set nonumber** RETURN to turn off line numbering.

vim is case sensitive   When you give vim a command, remember that the editor is case sensitive. In other words, vim interprets the same letter as two different commands, depending on

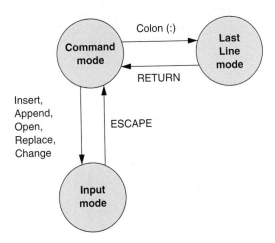

Figure 5-18 Modes in vim

whether you enter an uppercase or lowercase character. Beware of the CAPS LOCK (SHIFT-LOCK) key. If you set this key to enter uppercase text while you are in Input mode and then exit to Command mode, vim interprets your commands as uppercase letters. It can be confusing when this happens because vim does not appear to be executing the commands you are entering.

ENTERING TEXT

i/a (Input mode) When you start vim, you must put it in Input mode before you can enter text. To put vim in Input mode, press the **i** (insert before cursor) key or the **a** (append after cursor) key.

If you are not sure whether vim is in Input mode, press the ESCAPE key; vim returns to Command mode if it is in Input mode or beeps, flashes, or does nothing if it is already in Command mode. You can put vim back in Input mode by pressing the **i** or **a** key again.

While vim is in Input mode, you can enter text by typing on the keyboard. If the text does not appear on the screen as you type, vim is not in Input mode.

To continue with this tutorial, enter the sample paragraph shown in Figure 5-19 on the next page, pressing the RETURN key at the end of each line. If you do not press RETURN before the cursor reaches the right side of the screen or window, vim wraps the text so that it appears to start a new line. Physical lines will not correspond to programmatic (logical) lines in this situation, so editing will be more difficult. While you are using vim, you can correct typing mistakes. If you notice a mistake on the line you are entering, you can correct it before you continue (page 176). You can correct other mistakes later. When you finish entering the paragraph, press ESCAPE to return vim to Command mode.

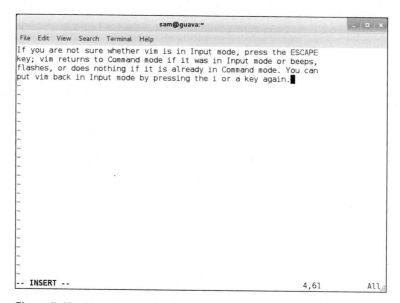

Figure 5-19 Entering text with vim

Getting Help

You must have the **vim-runtime** package installed to use vim's help system; see the tip on page 172.

To get help while you are using vim, enter the command **:help** [*feature*] followed by RETURN. The editor must be in Command mode when you enter this command. The colon moves the cursor to the last line of the screen. If you type **:help**, vim displays an introduction to vim Help (Figure 5-20). Each dark band near the bottom of the screen names the file that is displayed above it. (Each area of the screen that displays a file, such as the two areas shown in Figure 5-20, is a vim "window.") The **help.txt** file occupies most of the screen (the upper window) in Figure 5-20. The file that is being edited (**practice**) occupies a few lines in the lower portion of the screen (the lower window).

Read through the introduction to Help by scrolling the text as you read. Press **j** or the DOWN ARROW key to move the cursor down one line at a time; press CONTROL-D or CONTROL-U to scroll the cursor down or up half a window at a time. Give the command **:q** to close the Help window.

You can display information about the insert commands by giving the command **:help insert** while vim is in Command mode (Figure 5-21).

Correcting Text as You Insert It

The keys that back up and correct a shell command line serve the same functions when vim is in Input mode. These keys include the erase, line kill, and word kill keys (usually CONTROL-H, CONTROL-U, and CONTROL-W, respectively). Although vim might not remove deleted text from the screen as you back up over it using one of these keys, the editor does remove it when you type over the text or press RETURN.

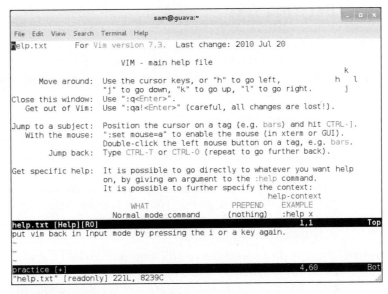

Figure 5-20   The main vim Help screen

MOVING THE CURSOR

You need to be able to move the cursor on the screen so you can delete, insert, and correct text. While vim is in Command mode, the RETURN key, the SPACE bar, and the ARROW keys move the cursor. If you prefer to keep your hand closer to the center of the keyboard, if your terminal does not have ARROW keys, or if the emulator you are using does not support them, you can use the **h, j, k,** and l (lowercase "l") keys to move the cursor left, down, up, and right, respectively.

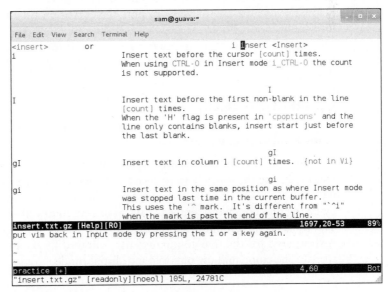

Figure 5-21   Help with insert commands

DELETING TEXT

x (Delete character)
dw (Delete word)
dd (Delete line)

You can delete a single character by moving the cursor until it is over the character you want to delete and then giving the command **x**. You can delete a word by positioning the cursor on the first letter of the word and then giving the command **dw** (Delete word). You can delete a line of text by moving the cursor until it is anywhere on the line and then giving the command **dd**.

UNDOING MISTAKES

u (Undo)

If you delete a character, line, or word by mistake or give any command you want to reverse, give the command **u** (Undo) immediately after the command you want to undo. The vim editor will restore the text to the way it was before you gave the last command. If you give the **u** command again, vim will undo the command you gave before the one it just undid. You can use this technique to back up over many of your actions. With the **compatible** parameter (page 179) set, however, vim can undo only the most recent change.

:redo (Redo)

If you undo a command you did not mean to undo, give a Redo command: CONTROL-R or **:redo** (followed by a RETURN). The vim editor will redo the undone command. As with the Undo command, you can give the Redo command many times in a row.

ENTERING ADDITIONAL TEXT

i (Insert)
a (Append)

When you want to insert new text within existing text, move the cursor so it is on the character that follows the new text you plan to enter. Then give the **i** (Insert) command to put vim in Input mode, enter the new text, and press ESCAPE to return vim to Command mode. Alternatively, you can position the cursor on the character that precedes the new text and use the **a** (Append) command.

o/O (Open)

To enter one or more lines, position the cursor on the line above where you want the new text to go. Give the command **o** (Open). The vim editor opens a blank line below the line the cursor was on, puts the cursor on the new, empty line, and goes into Input mode. Enter the new text, ending each line with a RETURN. When you are finished entering text, press ESCAPE to return vim to Command mode. The **O** command works in the same way **o** works, except it opens a blank line *above* the line the cursor is on.

CORRECTING TEXT

To correct text, use **dd**, **dw**, or **x** to remove the incorrect text. Then use **i**, **a**, **o**, or **O** to insert the correct text.

For example, to change the word **pressing** to **hitting** in Figure 5-19 on page 176, you might use the ARROW keys to move the cursor until it is on top of the **p** in **pressing**. Then give the command **dw** to delete the word **pressing**. Put vim in Input mode by giving an **i** command, enter the word **hitting** followed by a SPACE, and press ESCAPE. The word is changed, and vim is in Command mode, waiting for another command. A shorthand for the two commands **dw** followed by the **i** command is **cw** (Change word). The command **cw** puts vim into Input mode.

Page breaks for the printer

tip   CONTROL-L tells the printer to skip to the top of the next page. You can enter this character anywhere in a document by pressing CONTROL-L while you are in Input mode. If **^L** does not appear, press CONTROL-V before CONTROL-L.

ENDING THE EDITING SESSION

While you are editing, vim keeps the edited text in an area named the *Work buffer*. When you finish editing, you must write out the contents of the Work buffer to a disk file so the edited text is saved and available when you next want it.

Make sure vim is in Command mode and use the **ZZ** command (you must use uppercase Zs) to write the newly entered text to the disk and end the editing session. After you give the **ZZ** command, vim returns control to the shell. You can exit with **:q!** if you do not want to save your work.

Do not confuse ZZ with CONTROL-Z

caution   When you exit from vim with **ZZ**, make sure that you type **ZZ** and not CONTROL-Z (typically the suspend key). When you press CONTROL-Z, vim disappears from your screen, almost as though you had exited from it. In fact, vim will continue running in the background with your work unsaved. Refer to "Job Control" on page 296. If you try to start editing the same file with a new **vim** command, vim displays a message about a swap file.

THE compatible PARAMETER

The **compatible** parameter makes vim more compatible with vi. By default this parameter is not set. While you are running vim, give the command **:set compatible** RETURN to set the **compatible** parameter; use **nocompatible** to unset this parameter. To get started with vim, you can ignore this parameter.

Setting the **compatible** parameter changes many aspects of how vim works. For example, when the **compatible** parameter is set, the Undo command (page 178) can undo only the most recent change; in contrast, with the **compatible** parameter unset, you can call Undo repeatedly to undo many changes. To obtain more details on the **compatible** parameter, give the command **:help compatible** RETURN. To display a complete list of vim's differences from the original vi, use **:help vi-diff** RETURN. See page 176 for a discussion of the **help** command.

CHAPTER SUMMARY

The utilities introduced in this chapter are a small but powerful subset of the many utilities available on a Fedora/RHEL system. Because you will use them frequently and because they are integral to the following chapters, it is important that you become comfortable using them.

The utilities listed in Table 5-2 manipulate, display, compare, and print files.

Table 5-2   File utilities

Utility	Function
cp	Copies one or more files (page 149)
diff	Displays the differences between two files (page 154)
file	Displays information about the contents of a file (page 156)
grep	Searches file(s) for a string (page 152)
head	Displays the lines at the beginning of a file (page 152)
lpq	Displays a list of jobs in the print queue (page 151)
lpr	Places file(s) in the print queue (page 151)
lprm	Removes a job from the print queue (page 151)
mv	Renames a file or moves file(s) to another directory (page 150)
sort	Puts a file in order by lines (page 154)
tail	Displays the lines at the end of a file (page 153)
uniq	Displays the contents of a file, skipping adjacent duplicate lines (page 154)

To reduce the amount of disk space a file occupies, you can compress it using the bzip2 utility. Compression works especially well on files that contain patterns, as do most text files, but reduces the size of almost all files. The inverse of bzip2—bunzip2—restores a file to its original, decompressed form. Table 5-3 lists utilities that compress and decompress files. The bzip2 utility is the most efficient of these.

Table 5-3   (De)compression utilities

Utility	Function
bunzip2	Returns a file compressed with bzip2 to its original size and format (page 161)
bzcat	Displays a file compressed with bzip2 (page 161)
bzip2	Compresses a file (page 160)
compress	Compresses a file (not as well as bzip2 or gzip; page 161)
gunzip	Returns a file compressed with gzip or compress to its original size and format (page 161)
gzip	Compresses a file (not as well as bzip2; page 161)
unzip	Unpacks zip archives, which are compatible with Windows PKZIP

Table 5-3 (De)compression utilities (continued)

zcat	Displays a file compressed with gzip (page 161)
zip	Constructs zip archives, which are compatible with Windows PKZIP

An archive is a file, frequently compressed, that contains a group of files. The tar utility (Table 5-4) packs and unpacks archives. The filename extensions **.tar.bz2**, **.tar.gz**, and **.tgz** identify compressed tar archive files and are often seen on software packages obtained over the Internet.

Table 5-4 Archive utility

Utility	Function
tar	Creates or extracts files from an archive file (page 162)

The utilities listed in Table 5-5 determine the location of a utility on the local system. For example, they can display the pathname of a utility or a list of C++ compilers available on the local system.

Table 5-5 Location utilities

Utility	Function
locate	Searches for files on the local system (page 166)
whereis	Displays the full pathnames of a utility, source code, or man page (page 164)
which	Displays the full pathname of a command you can run (page 164)

Table 5-6 lists utilities that display information about the local system and other users. You can easily learn a user's full name, login status, login shell, and other items of information maintained by the system.

Table 5-6 User and system information utilities

Utility	Function
finger	Displays detailed information about users, including their full names (page 167)
hostname	Displays the name of the local system (page 149)
w	Displays detailed information about users who are logged in on the local system (page 168)
who	Displays information about users who are logged in on the local system (page 166)

The utilities shown in Table 5-7 can help you stay in touch with other users on the local network.

Table 5-7 User communication utilities

Utility	Function
mesg	Permits or denies messages sent by write (page 170)
write	Sends a message to another user who is logged in (page 170)

Table 5-8 lists miscellaneous utilities.

Table 5-8 Miscellaneous utilities

Utility	Function
date	Displays the current date and time (page 158)
echo	Copies its *arguments* (page 1151) to the screen (page 157)
vim	Edits text (page 172)

EXERCISES

1. Which commands can you use to determine who is logged in on a specific terminal?

2. How can you keep other users from using write to communicate with you? Why would you want to?

3. What happens when you give the following commands if the file named **done** already exists?

   ```
   $ cp to_do done
   $ mv to_do done
   ```

4. How can you find out which utilities are available on your system for editing files? Which utilities are available for editing on your system?

5. How can you find the phone number for **Ace Electronics** in a file named **phone** that contains a list of names and phone numbers? Which command can you use to display the entire file in alphabetical order? How can you display the file without any adjacent duplicate lines? How can you display the file without any duplicate lines?

6. What happens when you use diff to compare two binary files that are not identical? (You can use gzip to create the binary files.) Explain why the diff output for binary files is different from the diff output for ASCII files.

7. Create a **.plan** file in your home directory. Does finger display the contents of your **.plan** file?

8. What is the result of giving the which utility the name of a command that resides in a directory that is *not* in your search path?

9. Are any of the utilities discussed in this chapter located in more than one directory on the local system? If so, which ones?

10. Experiment by calling the file utility with the names of files in **/usr/bin**. How many different types of files are there?

11. Which command can you use to look at the first few lines of a file named **status.report**? Which command can you use to look at the end of the file?

ADVANCED EXERCISES

12. Re-create the **colors.1** and **colors.2** files used in Figure 5-8 on page 155. Test your files by running **diff –u** on them. Do you get the same results as in the figure?

13. Try giving these two commands:

    ```
    $ echo cat
    $ cat echo
    ```

    Explain the differences between the output of each command.

14. Repeat exercise 5 using the file **phone.gz**, a compressed version of the list of names and phone numbers. Consider more than one approach to answer each question and explain how you made your choices.

15. Find or create files that

    a. gzip compresses by more than 80 percent.

    b. gzip compresses by less than 10 percent.

    c. Get larger when compressed with gzip.

    d. Use **ls –l** to determine the sizes of the files in question. Can you characterize the files in a, b, and c?

16. Older email programs were not able to handle binary files. Suppose you are emailing a file that has been compressed with gzip, which produces a binary file, and the recipient is using an old email program. Refer to the man page on uuencode, which converts a binary file to ASCII. Learn about the utility and how to use it.

    a. Convert a compressed file to ASCII using uuencode. Is the encoded file larger or smaller than the compressed file? Explain. (If uuencode is not on the local system, you can install it using yum [page 534]; it is part of the **sharutils** package.)

b. Would it ever make sense to use uuencode on a file before compressing it? Explain.

6

THE LINUX FILESYSTEM

OBJECTIVES

After reading this chapter you should be able to:

▶ Define hierarchical filesystem, ordinary files, directory files, home directory, working directory, and parent directory

▶ List best practices for filenames

▶ Determine the name of the working directory

▶ Explain the difference between absolute and relative pathnames

▶ Create and remove directories

▶ List files in a directory, remove files from a directory, and copy and move files between directories

▶ List and describe the uses of standard Linux directories and files

▶ View and interpret file and directory ownership and permissions

▶ Modify file and directory permissions

▶ Expand access control using ACLs

▶ Describe the uses, differences, and methods of creating hard links and symbolic links

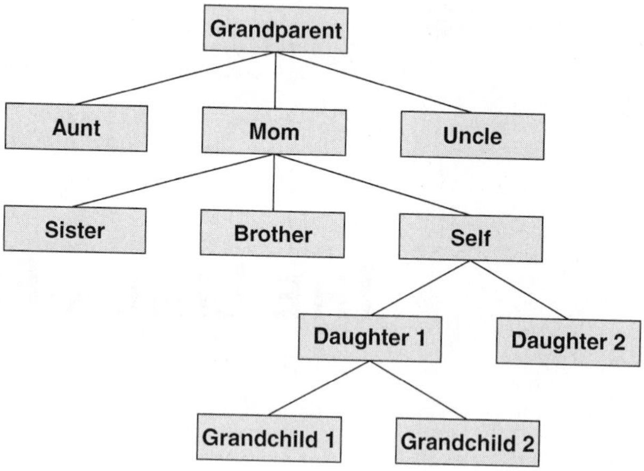

Figure 6-1   A family tree

A *filesystem* is a set of *data structures* (page 1160) that usually resides on part of a disk and that holds directories of files. Filesystems store user and system data that are the basis of users' work on the system and the system's existence. This chapter discusses the organization and terminology of the Linux filesystem, defines ordinary and directory files, and explains the rules for naming them. It also shows how to create and delete directories, move through the filesystem, and use absolute and relative pathnames to access files in various directories. It includes a discussion of important files and directories as well as file access permissions and ACLs (Access Control Lists), which allow you to share selected files with specified users. It concludes with a discussion of hard and symbolic links, which can make a single file appear in more than one directory.

In addition to reading this chapter, you can refer to the df info page and to the fsck, mkfs, and tune2fs man pages for more information on filesystems. For information on additional important Linux files, see "Important Files and Directories" on page 502.

THE HIERARCHICAL FILESYSTEM

Family tree   A *hierarchical* (page 1168) structure frequently takes the shape of a pyramid. One example of this type of structure is found by tracing a family's lineage: A couple has a child, who might in turn have several children, each of whom might have more children. This hierarchical structure is called a *family tree* (Figure 6-1).

Directory tree   Like the family tree it resembles, the Linux filesystem is called a *tree*. It consists of a set of connected files. This structure allows you to organize files so you can easily find any particular one. On a standard Linux system, each user starts with one

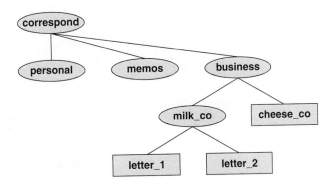

Figure 6-2   A secretary's directories

directory, to which the user can add subdirectories to any desired level. By creating multiple levels of subdirectories, a user can expand the structure as needed.

Subdirectories   Typically each subdirectory is dedicated to a single subject, such as a person, project, or event. The subject dictates whether a subdirectory should be subdivided further. For example, Figure 6-2 shows a secretary's subdirectory named **correspond**. This directory contains three subdirectories: **business**, **memos**, and **personal**. The **business** directory contains files that store each letter the secretary types. If you expect many letters to go to one client, as is the case with **milk_co**, you can dedicate a subdirectory to that client.

One major strength of the Linux filesystem is its ability to adapt to users' needs. You can take advantage of this strength by strategically organizing your files so they are most convenient and useful for you.

DIRECTORY FILES AND ORDINARY FILES

Like a family tree, the tree representing the filesystem is usually pictured upside down with its *root* at the top. Figures 6-2 and 6-3 (on the next page) show that the tree "grows" downward from the root with paths connecting the root to each of the other files. At the end of each path is either an ordinary file or a directory file. Special files, which can also appear at the ends of paths, are described on page 515. *Ordinary files*, or simply *files*, appear at the ends of paths that cannot support other paths. *Directory files*, also referred to as *directories* or *folders*, are the points that other paths can branch off from. (Figures 6-2 and 6-3 show some empty directories.) When you refer to the tree, *up* is toward the root and *down* is away from the root. Directories directly connected by a path are called *parents* (closer to the root) and *children* (farther from the root). A *pathname* is a series of names that trace a path along branches from one file to another. See page 191 for more information about pathnames.

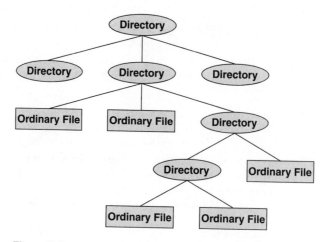

Figure 6-3   Directories and ordinary files

FILENAMES

Every file has a *filename*. The maximum length of a filename varies with the type of filesystem; Linux supports several types of filesystems. Although most of today's filesystems allow files with names up to 255 characters long, some filesystems restrict filenames to fewer characters. Although you can use almost any character in a filename, you will avoid confusion if you choose characters from the following list:

- Uppercase letters (A–Z)
- Lowercase letters (a–z)
- Numbers (0–9)
- Underscore (_)
- Period (.)
- Comma (,)

Like the children of one parent, no two files in the same directory can have the same name. (Parents give their children different names because it makes good sense, but Linux requires it.) Files in different directories, like the children of different parents, can have the same name.

The filenames you choose should mean something. Too often a directory is filled with important files with such unhelpful names as **hold1, wombat,** and **junk,** not to mention **foo** and **foobar.** Such names are poor choices because they do not help you recall what you stored in a file. The following filenames conform to the suggested syntax *and* convey information about the contents of the file:

- **correspond**
- **january**

- davis
- reports
- 2001
- acct_payable

Filename length When you share your files with users on other systems, you might need to make long filenames differ within the first few characters. Systems running DOS or older versions of Windows have an 8-character filename body length limit and a 3-character filename extension length limit. Some UNIX systems have a 14-character limit, and older Macintosh systems have a 31-character limit. If you keep filenames short, they are easy to type; later you can add extensions to them without exceeding the shorter limits imposed by some filesystems. The disadvantage of short filenames is that they are typically less descriptive than long filenames. See "stat: Displays Information About a File or Filesystem" on page 473 for a way to determine the maximum length of a filename on the local system.

Long filenames enable you to assign descriptive names to files. To help you select among files without typing entire filenames, shells support filename completion. For more information about this feature, see the "Filename completion" tip on page 149.

Case sensitivity You can use uppercase and/or lowercase letters within filenames. Linux is case sensitive, so files named **JANUARY**, **January**, and **january** represent three distinct files.

Do not use SPACEs within filenames

caution Although Linux allows you to use SPACEs within filenames, it is a poor idea. Because a SPACE is a special character, you must quote it on a command line. Quoting a character on a command line can be difficult for a novice user and cumbersome for an experienced user. Use periods or underscores instead of SPACEs: **joe.05.04.26**, **new_stuff**.

If you are working with a filename that includes a SPACE, such as a file from another operating system, you must quote the SPACE on the command line by preceding it with a backslash or by placing quotation marks on either side of the filename. The two following commands send the file named **my file** to the printer.

```
$ lpr my\ file
$ lpr "my file"
```

FILENAME EXTENSIONS

A *filename extension* is the part of the filename that follows an embedded period. In the filenames listed in Table 6-1 on the next page, filename extensions help describe the contents of the file. Some programs, such as the C programming language compiler, default to specific filename extensions; in most cases, however, filename extensions are optional. Use extensions freely to make filenames easy to understand. If you like, you can use several periods within the same filename—for example, **notes.4.10.54** or **files.tar.gz**.

Table 6-1   Filename extensions

Filename with extension	Meaning of extension
compute.c	A C programming language source file
compute.o	The object code file for **compute.c**
compute	The executable file for **compute.c**
memo.0410.txt	A text file
memo.pdf	A PDF file; view with xpdf or kpdf under a GUI
memo.ps	A PostScript file; view with ghostscript or kpdf under a GUI
memo.Z	A file compressed with compress (page 161); use uncompress or gunzip (page 161) to decompress
memo.gz	A file compressed with gzip (page 161); view with zcat or decompress with gunzip (both on page 161)
memo.tgz or **memo.tar.gz**	A tar (page 162) archive of files compressed with gzip (page 161)
memo.bz2	A file compressed with bzip2 (page 160); view with bzcat or decompress with bunzip2 (both on page 161)
memo.html	A file meant to be viewed using a Web browser, such as Firefox
photo.gif, **photo.jpg**, **photo.jpeg**, **photo.bmp**, **photo.tif**, or **photo.tiff**	A file containing graphical information, such as a picture

HIDDEN FILENAMES

A filename that begins with a period is called a *hidden filename* (or a *hidden file* or sometimes an *invisible file*) because ls does not normally display it. The command ls –a displays *all* filenames, even hidden ones. Names of startup files (next page) usually begin with a period so that they are hidden and do not clutter a directory listing. The .plan file (page 168) is also hidden. Two special hidden entries—single and double periods (. and ..)—appear in every directory (page 196).

THE WORKING DIRECTORY

pwd   While you are logged in on a character-based interface to a Linux system, you are always associated with a directory. The directory you are associated with is called the *working directory* or *current directory*. Sometimes this association is referred to in a physical sense: "You are *in* (or *working in*) the **zach** directory." The pwd (print working directory) builtin displays the pathname of the working directory.

```
login: max
Password:
Last login: Wed Oct 20 11:14:21 from 172.16.192.150
$ pwd
/home/max
```

Figure 6-4   Logging in and displaying the pathname of your home directory

YOUR HOME DIRECTORY

When you first log in on a Linux system or start a terminal emulator window, the working directory is your *home directory*. To display the pathname of your home directory, use pwd just after you log in (Figure 6-4).

When used without any arguments, the ls utility displays a list of the files in the working directory. Because your home directory has been the only working directory you have used so far, ls has always displayed a list of files in your home directory. (All the files you have created up to this point were created in your home directory.)

STARTUP FILES

Startup files, which appear in your home directory, give the shell and other programs information about you and your preferences. Frequently one of these files tells the shell what kind of terminal you are using (page 1122) and executes the stty (set terminal) utility to establish the erase (page 140) and line kill (page 140) keys.

Either you or the system administrator can put a shell startup file containing shell commands in your home directory. The shell executes the commands in this file each time you log in. Because the startup files have hidden filenames (filenames that begin with a period; page 190), you must use the ls –a command to see whether one is in your home directory. A GUI has many startup files. Usually you do not need to work with these files directly but can control startup sequences using icons on the desktop. See page 282 for more information about startup files.

PATHNAMES

Every file has a *pathname,* which is a trail from a directory through part of the directory hierarchy to an ordinary file or a directory. Within a pathname, a slash (/) following (to the right of) a filename indicates that the file is a directory file. The file following (to the right of) the slash can be an ordinary file or a directory file. The simplest pathname is a simple filename, which points to a file in the working directory. This section discusses absolute and relative pathnames and explains how to use each.

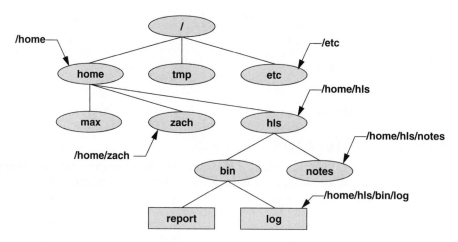

Figure 6-5   Absolute pathnames

ABSOLUTE PATHNAMES

/ (root)   The root directory of the filesystem hierarchy does not have a name; it is referred to as the *root directory* and is represented by a slash (**/**) standing alone or at the left end of a pathname.

An *absolute pathname* starts with a slash (**/**), which represents the root directory. The slash is followed by the name of a file located in the root directory. An absolute pathname can continue, tracing a path through all intermediate directories, to the file identified by the pathname. String all the filenames in the path together, following each directory with a slash (**/**). This string of filenames is called an absolute pathname because it locates a file absolutely by tracing a path from the root directory to the file. Typically the absolute pathname of a directory does not include the trailing slash, although that format can be used to emphasize that the pathname specifies a directory (e.g., **/home/zach/**). The part of a pathname following the final slash is called a *simple filename, filename,* or *basename.* Figure 6-5 shows the absolute pathnames of directories and ordinary files in part of a filesystem hierarchy.

Using an absolute pathname, you can list or otherwise work with any file on the local system, assuming you have permission to do so, regardless of the working directory at the time you give the command. For example, Sam can give the following command while working in his home directory to list the files in the **/etc/ssh** directory:

```
$ pwd
/home/sam
$ ls /etc/ssh
moduli        ssh_host_dsa_key      ssh_host_key.pub
ssh_config    ssh_host_dsa_key.pub  ssh_host_rsa_key
sshd_config   ssh_host_key          ssh_host_rsa_key.pub
```

~ (TILDE) IN PATHNAMES

In another form of absolute pathname, the shell expands the characters ~/ (a tilde followed by a slash) at the start of a pathname into the pathname of your home directory. Using this shortcut, you can display your **.bashrc** startup file (page 283) with the following command no matter which directory is the working directory:

```
$ less ~/.bashrc
```

A tilde quickly references paths that start with your or someone else's home directory. The shell expands a tilde followed by a username at the beginning of a pathname into the pathname of that user's home directory. For example, assuming he has permission to do so, Max can examine Sam's **.bashrc** file with the following command:

```
$ less ~sam/.bashrc
```

Refer to "Tilde Expansion" on page 348 for more information.

RELATIVE PATHNAMES

A *relative pathname* traces a path from the working directory to a file. The pathname is *relative* to the working directory. Any pathname that does not begin with the root directory (represented by /) or a tilde (~) is a relative pathname. Like absolute pathnames, relative pathnames can trace a path through many directories. The simplest relative pathname is a simple filename, which identifies a file in the working directory. The examples in the next sections use absolute and relative pathnames.

SIGNIFICANCE OF THE WORKING DIRECTORY

To access any file in the working directory, you need only a simple filename. To access a file in another directory, you *must* use a pathname. Typing a long pathname is tedious and increases the chance of making a mistake. This possibility is less likely under a GUI, where you click filenames or icons. You can choose a working directory for any particular task to reduce the need for long pathnames. Your choice of a working directory does not allow you to do anything you could not do otherwise—it just makes some operations easier.

When using a relative pathname, know which directory is the working directory

caution   The location of the file you are accessing with a relative pathname is dependent on (is relative to) the working directory. Always make sure you know which directory is the working directory before you use a relative pathname. Use pwd to verify the directory. If you are creating a file using vim and you are not where you think you are in the file hierarchy, the new file will end up in an unexpected location.

It does not matter which directory is the working directory when you use an absolute pathname. Thus, the following command always edits a file named **goals** in your home directory:

```
$ vim ~/goals
```

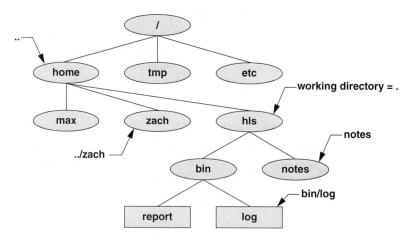

Figure 6-6 Relative pathnames

Refer to Figure 6-6 as you read this paragraph. Files that are children of the working directory can be referenced by simple filenames. Grandchildren of the working directory can be referenced by short relative pathnames: two filenames separated by a slash. When you manipulate files in a large directory structure, using short relative pathnames can save you time and aggravation. If you choose a working directory that contains the files used most often for a particular task, you need use fewer long, cumbersome pathnames.

WORKING WITH DIRECTORIES

This section discusses how to create directories (mkdir), switch between directories (cd), remove directories (rmdir), use pathnames to make your work easier, and move and copy files and directories between directories. It concludes with brief descriptions of important standard directories and files in the Linux filesystem.

mkdir: CREATES A DIRECTORY

The mkdir utility creates a directory. The *argument* (page 1151) to mkdir is the pathname of the new directory. The following examples develop the directory structure shown in Figure 6-7. In the figure, the directories that are added appear in a lighter shade than the others and are connected by dashes.

In Figure 6-8, pwd shows that Max is working in his home directory (**/home/max**), and ls shows the names of the files in his home directory: **demo**, **names**, and **temp**. Using mkdir, Max creates a directory named **literature** as a child of his home directory. He uses a relative pathname (a simple filename) because he wants the **literature** directory to be a child of the working directory. Max could have used an absolute pathname to create the same directory: **mkdir /home/max/literature**, **mkdir ~max/literature**, or **mkdir ~/literature**.

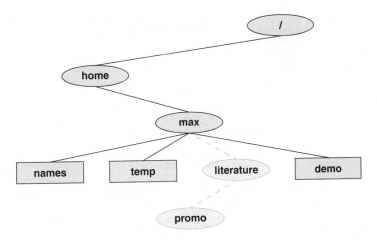

Figure 6-7   The file structure developed in the examples

The second **ls** in Figure 6-8 verifies the presence of the new directory. The **–F** option to **ls** displays a slash after the name of each directory and an asterisk after each executable file (shell script, utility, or application). When you call it with an argument that is the name of a directory, **ls** lists the contents of that directory. The final **ls** displays nothing because there are no files in the **literature** directory.

The following commands show two ways for Max to create the **promo** directory as a child of the newly created **literature** directory. The first way checks that **/home/max** is the working directory and uses a relative pathname:

```
$ pwd
/home/max
$ mkdir literature/promo
```

The second way uses an absolute pathname:

```
$ mkdir /home/max/literature/promo
```

```
$ pwd
/home/max
$ ls
demo   names   temp
$ mkdir literature
$ ls
demo   literature   names   temp
$ ls -F
demo   literature/   names   temp
$ ls literature
$
```

Figure 6-8   The mkdir utility

```
$ cd /home/max/literature
$ pwd
/home/max/literature
$ cd
$ pwd
/home/max
$ cd literature
$ pwd
/home/max/literature
```

Figure 6-9   cd changes the working directory

Use the **–p** (parents) option to mkdir to create both the **literature** and **promo** directories with one command:

```
$ pwd
/home/max
$ ls
demo  names  temp
$ mkdir -p literature/promo
```

or

```
$ mkdir -p /home/max/literature/promo
```

cd: CHANGES TO ANOTHER WORKING DIRECTORY

The cd (change directory) utility makes another directory the working directory; it does not *change* the contents of the working directory. Figure 6-9 shows two ways to make the **/home/max/literature** directory the working directory, as verified by pwd. First Max uses cd with an absolute pathname to make **literature** his working directory—it does not matter which is the working directory when you give a command with an absolute pathname.

A pwd command confirms the change Max made. When used without an argument, cd makes your home directory the working directory, as it was when you logged in. The second cd command in Figure 6-9 does not have an argument, so it makes Max's home directory the working directory. Finally, knowing that he is working in his home directory, Max uses a simple filename to make the **literature** directory his working directory (**cd literature**) and confirms the change using pwd.

THE . AND .. DIRECTORY ENTRIES

The mkdir utility automatically puts two entries in each directory it creates: a single period (.) and a double period (..). The . is synonymous with the pathname of the working directory and can be used in its place; the .. is synonymous with the pathname of the parent of the working directory. These entries are hidden because their filenames begin with a period.

With the **literature** directory as the working directory, the following example uses ..
three times: first to list the contents of the parent directory (**/home/max**), second to

copy the **memoA** file to the parent directory, and third to list the contents of the parent directory again.

```
$ pwd
/home/max/literature
$ ls ..
demo   literature   names   temp
$ cp memoA ..
$ ls ..
demo   literature   memoA   names   temp
```

After using cd to make **promo** (a subdirectory of **literature**) his working directory, Max can use a relative pathname to call vim to edit a file in his home directory.

```
$ cd promo
$ vim ../../names
```

You can use an absolute or relative pathname or a simple filename virtually anywhere a utility or program requires a filename or pathname. This usage holds true for ls, vim, mkdir, rm, and most other Linux utilities.

The working directory versus your home directory

tip   The working directory is not the same as your home directory. Your home directory remains the same for the duration of your session and usually from session to session. Immediately after you log in, you are always working in the same directory: your home directory.

Unlike your home directory, the working directory can change as often as you like. You have no set working directory, which explains why some people refer to it as the *current directory*. When you log in and until you change directories using cd, your home directory is the working directory. If you were to change directories to Sam's home directory, then Sam's home directory would be the working directory.

rmdir: DELETES A DIRECTORY

The rmdir (remove directory) utility deletes a directory. You cannot delete the working directory or a directory that contains files other than the . and .. entries. If you need to delete a directory that has files in it, first use rm to delete the files and then delete the directory. You do not have to (nor can you) delete the . and .. entries; rmdir removes them automatically. The following command deletes the **promo** directory:

```
$ rmdir /home/max/literature/promo
```

The rm utility has a –r option (**rm –r** *filename*) that recursively deletes files, including directories, within a directory and also deletes the directory itself.

Use rm –r carefully, if at all

caution   Although **rm –r** is a handy command, you must use it carefully. Do not use it with an ambiguous file reference such as ∗. It is frighteningly easy to wipe out your entire home directory with a single short command.

USING PATHNAMES

touch   Use a text editor to create a file named **letter** if you want to experiment with the examples that follow. Alternatively you can use touch to create an empty file:

```
$ cd
$ pwd
/home/max
$ touch letter
```

With **/home/max** as the working directory, the following example uses cp with a relative pathname to copy the file **letter** to the **/home/max/literature/promo** directory. (You will need to create **promo** again if you deleted it earlier.) The copy of the file has the simple filename **letter.0210**:

```
$ cp letter literature/promo/letter.0210
```

If Max does not change to another directory, he can use vim as shown to edit the copy of the file he just made:

```
$ vim literature/promo/letter.0210
```

If Max does not want to use a long pathname to specify the file, he can use cd to make **promo** the working directory before using vim:

```
$ cd literature/promo
$ pwd
/home/max/literature/promo
$ vim letter.0210
```

To make the parent of the working directory (named **/home/max/literature**) the new working directory, Max can give the following command, which takes advantage of the .. directory entry:

```
$ cd ..
$ pwd
/home/max/literature
```

mv, cp: MOVE OR COPY FILES

Chapter 5 discussed the use of mv to rename files. However, mv works even more generally: You can use this utility to move files from one directory to another (change the pathname of a file) as well as to change a simple filename. When used to move one or more files to a new directory, the mv command has this syntax:

mv existing-file-list directory

If the working directory is **/home/max**, Max can use the following command to move the files **names** and **temp** from the working directory to the **literature** directory:

```
$ mv names temp literature
```

This command changes the absolute pathnames of the **names** and **temp** files from **/home/max/names** and **/home/max/temp** to **/home/max/literature/names** and

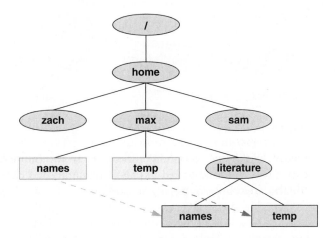

Figure 6-10   Using mv to move **names** and **temp**

/home/max/literature/temp, respectively (Figure 6-10). Like most Linux commands, mv accepts either absolute or relative pathnames.

As you work with Linux and create more files, you will need to create new directories using mkdir to keep the files organized. The mv utility is a useful tool for moving files from one directory to another as you extend your directory hierarchy.

The cp utility works in the same way mv does, except that it makes copies of the *existing-file-list* in the specified *directory*.

mv: MOVES A DIRECTORY

Just as it moves ordinary files from one directory to another, so mv can move directories. The syntax is similar except you specify one or more directories, not ordinary files, to move:

> *mv existing-directory-list new-directory*

If *new-directory* does not exist, the *existing-directory-list* must contain just one directory name, which mv changes to *new-directory* (mv renames the directory). Although you can rename directories using mv, you cannot copy their contents with cp unless you use the **−r** (recursive) option. Refer to the tar and cpio man pages for other ways to copy and move directories.

IMPORTANT STANDARD DIRECTORIES AND FILES

Originally files on a Linux system were not located in standard places within the directory hierarchy. The scattered files made it difficult to document and maintain a Linux system and just about impossible for someone to release a software package that would compile and run on all Linux systems. The first standard for the Linux filesystem, the FSSTND (Linux Filesystem Standard), was released early in 1994. In early 1995 work was started on a broader standard covering many UNIX-like systems: FHS

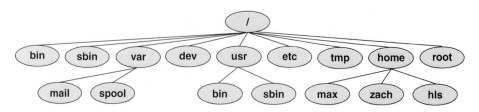

Figure 6-11   A typical FHS-based Linux filesystem structure

(Linux Filesystem Hierarchy Standard; proton.pathname.com/fhs). More recently FHS has been incorporated in LSB (Linux Standard Base; www.linuxfoundation.org/collaborate/workgroups/lsb), a workgroup of FSG (Free Standards Group). Finally, FSG combined with Open Source Development Labs (OSDL) to form the Linux Foundation (www.linuxfoundation.org). Figure 6-11 shows the locations of some important directories and files as specified by FHS. The significance of many of these directories will become clear as you continue reading.

The following list describes the directories shown in Figure 6-11, some of the directories specified by FHS, and some other directories. Fedora/RHEL, however, does not use all the directories specified by FHS. Be aware that you cannot always determine the function of a directory by its name. For example, although **/opt** stores add-on software, **/etc/opt** stores configuration files for the software in **/opt**. See also "Important Files and Directories" on page 502.

   /   **Root** The root directory, present in all Linux filesystem structures, is the ancestor of all files in the filesystem. It does not have a name and is represented by a slash (**/**) standing alone or at the left end of a pathname.

  /bin **Essential command binaries** Holds the files needed to bring the system up and run it when it first comes up in single-user mode (page 450).

 /boot **Static files of the boot loader** Contains all the files needed to boot the system.

  /dev **Device files** Contains all files that represent peripheral devices, such as disk drives, terminals, and printers. Previously this directory was filled with all possible devices. The udev utility (page 516) provides a dynamic device directory that enables **/dev** to contain only devices that are present on the system.

  /etc **Machine–local system configuration files** Holds administrative, configuration, and other system files.

/etc/opt **Configuration files for add-on software packages kept in /opt**

/etc/X11 **Machine–local configuration files for the X Window System**

/home **User home directories** Each user's home directory is typically one of many subdirectories of the **/home** directory. As an example, assuming that users' directories are under **/home**, the absolute pathname of Zach's home directory is **/home/zach**. On some systems the users' directories might not be found under **/home** but instead might be spread among other directories such as **/inhouse** and **/clients**.

  /lib **Shared libraries**

/lib/modules	Loadable kernel modules
/mnt	Mount point for temporarily mounting filesystems
/opt	Add-on (optional) software packages
/proc	Kernel and process information virtual filesystem
/root	Home directory for the root account
/run	**Runtime data** A **tmpfs** filesystem (mounted, but stored in RAM) that holds startup files previously hidden in **/dev** and other directories. For more information see lists.fedoraproject.org/pipermail/devel/2011-March/150031.html.
/sbin	**Essential system binaries** Utilities used for system administration are stored in **/sbin** and **/usr/sbin**. The **/sbin** directory includes utilities needed during the booting process, and **/usr/sbin** holds utilities used after the system is up and running.
/sys	**Device pseudofilesystem** See udev on page 516 for more information.
/tmp	**Temporary files**
/usr	**Second major hierarchy** Traditionally includes subdirectories that contain information used by the system. Files in **/usr** subdirectories do not change often and can be shared by several systems.
/usr/bin	**Most user commands** Contains the standard Linux utility programs—that is, binaries that are not needed in single-user mode (page 450).
/usr/games	Games and educational programs
/usr/include	Header files included by C programs
/usr/lib	Libraries
/usr/local	**Local hierarchy** Holds locally important files and directories that are added to the system. Subdirectories can include **bin, games, include, lib, sbin, share,** and **src.**
/usr/sbin	Nonvital system administration binaries See /sbin.
/usr/share	**Architecture-independent data** Subdirectories can include **dict, doc, games, info, locale, man, misc, terminfo,** and **zoneinfo.**
/usr/share/doc	Documentation
/usr/share/info	GNU info system's primary directory
/usr/share/man	Online manuals
/usr/src	Source code
/var	**Variable data** Files with contents that vary as the system runs are kept in subdirectories under **/var.** The most common examples are temporary files, system log files, spooled files, and user mailbox files. Subdirectories can include **cache, lib, lock, log, mail, opt, run, spool, tmp,** and **yp.**
/var/log	**Log files** Contains **lastlog** (a record of the last login by each user), **messages** (system messages from **syslogd**), and **wtmp** (a record of all logins/logouts), among other log files.
/var/spool	**Spooled application data** Contains **anacron, at, cron, lpd, mail, mqueue, samba,** and other directories. The file **/var/mail** is typically a link to **/var/spool/mail.**

ACCESS PERMISSIONS

In addition to the controls imposed by SELinux (page 459), Fedora/RHEL supports two methods of controlling who can access a file and how they can access it: traditional Linux access permissions and ACLs (Access Control Lists). This section describes traditional Linux access permissions. See page 208 for a discussion of ACLs, which provide finer-grained control of access permissions than do traditional access permissions.

Three types of users can access a file: the owner of the file (*owner*), a member of a group that the file is associated with (*group;* see page 506 for more information on groups), and everyone else (*other*). A user can attempt to access an ordinary file in three ways: by trying to *read from, write to,* or *execute* it.

ls –l: DISPLAYS PERMISSIONS

When you call ls with the **–l** option and the name of one or more ordinary files, ls displays a line of information about the file(s). See "ls output" on page 20 for information about the format of the display this book uses. The following example displays information for two files. The file **letter.0210** contains the text of a letter, and **check_spell** contains a shell script, a program written in a high-level shell programming language:

```
$ ls -l check_spell letter.0210
-rwxr-xr-x. 1 sam pubs  766 03-21 14:02 check_spell
-rw-r--r--. 1 sam pubs 6193 02-10 14:22 letter.0210
```

From left to right, the lines that an ls –l command displays contain the following information (refer to Figure 6-12):

- The type of file (first character)
- The file's access permissions (the next nine characters)
- The ACL flag (present if the file has an ACL, page 208)
- The number of links to the file (page 213)
- The name of the owner of the file (usually the person who created the file)

Figure 6-12   The columns displayed by the ls –l command

- The name of the group the file is associated with

- The size of the file in characters (bytes)

- The date and time the file was created or last modified

- The name of the file

The type of file (first column) for **letter.0210** is a hyphen (–) because it is an ordinary file (directory files have a **d** in this column).

The next three characters specify the access permissions for the *owner* of the file: **r** indicates read permission, **w** indicates write permission, and **x** indicates execute permission. A – in a column indicates that the owner does *not* have the permission that could have appeared in that position.

In a similar manner the next three characters represent permissions for the *group,* and the final three characters represent permissions for *other* (everyone else). In the preceding example, the owner of **letter.0210** can read from and write to the file, whereas the group and others can only read from the file, and no one is allowed to execute it. Although execute permission can be allowed for any file, it does not make sense to assign execute permission to a file that contains a document such as a letter. The **check_spell** file is an executable shell script, so execute permission is appropriate for it. (The owner, group, and others have execute permission.)

chmod: CHANGES ACCESS PERMISSIONS

The Linux file access permission scheme lets you give other users access to the files you want to share yet keep your private files confidential. You can allow other users to read from *and* write to a file (handy if you are one of several people working on a joint project). You can allow others only to read from a file (perhaps a project specification you are proposing). Or you can allow others only to write to a file (similar to an inbox or mailbox, where you want others to be able to send you mail but do not want them to read your mail). Similarly you can protect entire directories from being scanned (covered shortly).

A user with **root** privileges can access any file on the system

security   There is an exception to the access permissions described in this section. Anyone who can gain **root** privileges has full access to *all* files, regardless of the file's owner or access permissions. Of course, if the file is encrypted, read access does not mean the person reading the file can understand what is in the file.

The owner of a file controls which users have permission to access the file and how those users can access it. When you own a file, you can use the chmod (change mode) utility to change access permissions for that file. You can specify symbolic (relative) or numeric (absolute) arguments to chmod.

SYMBOLIC ARGUMENTS TO chmod

The following example, which uses symbolic arguments to chmod, adds (**+**) read and write permissions (**rw**) for all (**a**) users:

```
$ ls -l letter.0210
-rw-r-----. 1 sam pubs 6193 02-10 14:22 letter.0210
$ chmod a+rw letter.0210
$ ls -l letter.0210
-rw-rw-rw-. 1 sam pubs 6193 02-10 14:22 letter.0210
```

You must have read permission to execute a shell script

tip   Because a shell needs to read a shell script (a text file containing shell commands) before it can execute the commands within that script, you must have read permission for the file containing the script to execute it. You also need execute permission to execute a shell script directly from the command line. In contrast, binary (program) files do not need to be read; they are executed directly. You need only execute permission to run a binary program.

Using symbolic arguments with chmod modifies existing permissions; the change a given argument makes depends on (is relative to) the existing permissions. In the next example, chmod removes (**–**) read (**r**) and execute (**x**) permissions for other (**o**) users. The owner and group permissions are not affected.

```
$ ls -l check_spell
-rwxr-xr-x. 1 sam pubs 766 03-21 14:02 check_spell
$ chmod o-rx check_spell
$ ls -l check_spell
-rwxr-x---. 1 sam pubs 766 03-21 14:02 check_spell
```

In addition to **a** (all) and **o** (other), you can use **g** (group) and **u** (user, although *user* refers to the *owner* of the file who might or might not be the user of the file at any given time) in the argument to chmod. For example, **chmod a+x** adds execute permission for all users (other, group, and owner), and **chmod go–rwx** removes all permissions for all but the owner of the file.

chmod: **o** for other, **u** for owner

tip   When using chmod, many people assume that the **o** stands for *owner;* it does not. The **o** stands for *other,* whereas **u** stands for *owner (user).* The acronym UGO (user-group-other) might help you remember how permissions are named.

NUMERIC ARGUMENTS TO chmod

You can also use numeric arguments to specify permissions with chmod. In place of the letters and symbols specifying permissions used in the previous examples, numeric arguments comprise three octal digits. (A fourth, leading digit controls setuid and setgid permissions and is discussed next.) The first digit specifies permissions for the owner, the second for the group, and the third for other users. A **1** gives the specified user(s) execute permission, a **2** gives write permission, and a **4** gives read permission. Construct the digit representing the permissions for the owner, group, or others by ORing (adding) the appropriate values as shown in the following examples. Using numeric arguments sets file permissions absolutely; it does not modify existing permissions as symbolic arguments do.

In the following example, chmod changes permissions so only the owner of the file can read from and write to the file, regardless of how permissions were previously set. The **6** in the first position gives the owner read (**4**) and write (**2**) permissions. The 0s remove all permissions for the group and other users.

```
$ chmod 600 letter.0210
$ ls -l letter.0210
-rw-------. 1 sam pubs 6193 02-10 14:22 letter.0210
```

Next, **7** (**4** + **2** + **1**) gives the owner read, write, and execute permissions. The **5** (**4** + **1**) gives the group and other users read and execute permissions:

```
$ chmod 755 check_spell
$ ls -l check_spell
-rwxr-xr-x. 1 sam pubs 766 03-21 14:02 check_spell
```

Refer to Table 6-2 for more examples of numeric permissions.

Table 6-2   Examples of numeric permission specifications

Mode	Meaning
777	Owner, group, and others can read, write, and execute file
755	Owner can read, write, and execute file; group and others can read and execute file
711	Owner can read, write, and execute file; group and others can execute file
644	Owner can read and write file; group and others can read file
640	Owner can read and write file, group can read file, and others cannot access file

Refer to page 288 for more information on using chmod to make a file executable and to the chmod man page for more information on absolute arguments and chmod in general. Refer to page 506 for more information on groups.

SETUID AND SETGID PERMISSIONS

When you execute a file that has setuid (set user ID) permission, the process executing the file takes on the privileges of the file's owner. For example, if you run a setuid program that removes all files in a directory, you can remove files in any of the file owner's directories, even if you do not normally have permission to do so. In a similar manner, setgid (set group ID) permission gives the process executing the file the privileges of the group the file is associated with.

Minimize use of setuid and setgid programs owned by root

security   Executable files that are setuid and owned by **root** have **root** privileges when they run, even if they are not run by **root**. This type of program is very powerful because it can do anything that **root** can do (and that the program is designed to do). Similarly executable files that are setgid and belong to the group **root** have extensive privileges.

Because of the power they hold and their potential for destruction, it is wise to avoid indiscriminately creating and using setuid programs owned by **root** and setgid programs belonging to the group **root**. Because of their inherent dangers, many sites minimize the use of these programs on their systems. One necessary setuid program is passwd. See page 412 for a tip on setuid files owned by **root** and page 459 for a command that lists setuid files on the local system.

Because of this danger, Fedora/RHEL will be removing most setuid files in a future release. See fedoraproject.org/wiki/Features/RemoveSETUID for more information.

The following example shows a user working with **root** privileges and using symbolic arguments to chmod to give one program setuid privileges and another program setgid privileges. The **ls –l** output (page 202) shows setuid permission by displaying an **s** in the owner's executable position and setgid permission by displaying an **s** in the group's executable position:

```
# ls -l myprog*
-rwxr-xr-x. 1 root pubs 362804 03-21 15:38 myprog1
-rwxr-xr-x. 1 root pubs 189960 03-21 15:38 myprog2

# chmod u+s myprog1
# chmod g+s myprog2

# ls -l myprog*
-rwsr-xr-x. 1 root pubs 362804 03-21 15:38 myprog1
-rwxr-sr-x. 1 root pubs 189960 03-21 15:38 myprog2
```

The next example uses numeric arguments to chmod to make the same changes. When you use four digits to specify permissions, setting the first digit to **1** sets the *sticky bit* (page 1190), setting it to **2** specifies setgid permissions, and setting it to **4** specifies setuid permissions:

```
# ls -l myprog*
-rwxr-xr-x. 1 root pubs 362804 03-21 15:38 myprog1
-rwxr-xr-x. 1 root pubs 189960 03-21 15:38 myprog2

# chmod 4755 myprog1
# chmod 2755 myprog2

# ls -l myprog*
-rwsr-xr-x. 1 root pubs 362804 03-21 15:38 myprog1
-rwxr-sr-x. 1 root pubs 189960 03-21 15:38 myprog2
```

Do not write setuid shell scripts

security   Never give shell scripts setuid permission. Several techniques for subverting them are well known.

DIRECTORY ACCESS PERMISSIONS

Access permissions have slightly different meanings when they are applied to directories. Although the three types of users can read from or write to a directory, the directory cannot be executed. Execute permission is redefined for a directory: It means that you can cd into the directory and/or examine files that you have permission to read from in the directory. It has nothing to do with executing a file.

When you have only execute permission for a directory, you can use ls to list a file in the directory if you know its name. You cannot use ls to list the entire contents of the directory. In the following exchange, Zach first verifies that he is logged in as himself. He then checks the permissions on Max's **info** directory. You can view the access permissions associated with a directory by running ls with the **–d** (directory) and **–l** (long) options:

```
$ who am i
zach       pts/7   Aug 21 10:02
$ ls -ld /home/max/info
drwx-----x. 2 max pubs 4096 08-21 09:31 /home/max/info
$ ls -l /home/max/info
ls: /home/max/info: Permission denied
```

The **d** at the left end of the line that ls displays indicates **/home/max/info** is a directory. Max has read, write, and execute permissions; members of the pubs group have no access permissions; and other users have execute permission only, indicated by the **x** at the right end of the permissions. Because Zach does not have read permission for the directory, the **ls –l** command returns an error.

When Zach specifies the names of the files he wants information about, he is not reading new directory information but rather searching for specific information, which he is allowed to do with execute access to the directory. He has read permission for **notes** so he has no problem using cat to display the file. He cannot display **financial** because he does not have read permission for it:

```
$ ls -l /home/max/info/financial /home/max/info/notes
-rw-------. 1 max pubs 34 08-21 09:31 /home/max/info/financial
-rw-r--r--. 1 max pubs 30 08-21 09:32 /home/max/info/notes
$ cat /home/max/info/notes
This is the file named notes.
$ cat /home/max/info/financial
cat: /home/max/info/financial: Permission denied
```

Next Max gives others read access to his **info** directory:

```
$ chmod o+r /home/max/info
```

When Zach checks his access permissions on **info**, he finds he has both read and execute access to the directory. Now **ls –ld** displays the contents f the **info** directory, but he still cannot read **financial**. (This restriction is an issue of file permissions, not directory permissions.) Finally, Zach tries to create a file named **newfile** using touch.

If Max were to give him write permission to the **info** directory, Zach would be able to create new files in it:

```
$ ls -ld /home/max/info
drwx---r-x. 2 max pubs 4096 08-21 09:31 /home/max/info
$ ls -l /home/max/info
total 8
-rw-------. 1 max pubs 34 08-21 09:31 financial
-rw-r--r--. 1 max pubs 30 08-21 09:32 notes
$ cat /home/max/info/financial
cat: financial: Permission denied
$ touch /home/max/info/newfile
touch: cannot touch '/home/max/info/newfile': Permission denied
```

ACLs: Access Control Lists

ACLs (Access Control Lists) provide finer-grained control over which users can access specific directories and files than do traditional Linux permissions (page 202). Using ACLs you can specify the ways in which each of several users can access a directory or file. Because ACLs can reduce performance, do not enable them on filesystems that hold system files, where the traditional Linux permissions are sufficient. Also, be careful when moving, copying, or archiving files: Not all utilities preserve ACLs. In addition, you cannot copy ACLs to filesystems that do not support ACLs.

An ACL comprises a set of rules. A rule specifies how a specific user or group can access the file that the ACL is associated with. There are two kinds of rules: *access rules* and *default rules*. (The documentation refers to *access ACLs* and *default ACLs*, even though there is only one type of ACL: There is one type of list [ACL] and there are two types of rules that an ACL can contain.)

An access rule specifies access information for a single file or directory. A default ACL pertains to a directory only; it specifies default access information (an ACL) for any file in the directory that is not given an explicit ACL.

Most utilities do not preserve ACLs

caution   When used with the **–p** (preserve) or **–a** (archive) option, cp preserves ACLs when it copies files. The mv utility also preserves ACLs. When you use cp with the **–p** or **–a** option and it is not able to copy ACLs, and in the case where mv is unable to preserve ACLs, the utility performs the operation and issues an error message:

```
$ mv report /tmp
mv: preserving permissions for '/tmp/report': Operation not supported
```

Other utilities, such as tar, cpio, and dump, do not support ACLs. You can use cp with the **–a** option to copy directory hierarchies, including ACLs.

You can never copy ACLs to a filesystem that does not support ACLs or to a filesystem that does not have ACL support turned on.

ENABLING ACLs

The **acl** package must be installed before you can use ACLs. Fedora/RHEL officially supports ACLs on **ext2**, **ext3**, and **ext4** filesystems only, although informal support for ACLs is available on other filesystems. To use ACLs on an **ext2/ext3/ext4** filesystem, you must mount the device with the **acl** option (**no_acl** is the default). For example, if you want to mount the device represented by **/home** so that you can use ACLs on files in **/home**, you can add **acl** to its options list in **/etc/fstab**:

```
$ grep home /etc/fstab
LABEL=/home              /home          ext4    defaults,acl        1 2
```

remount option After changing **fstab**, you need to remount **/home** before you can use ACLs. If no one else is using the system, you can unmount it and mount it again (working with **root** privileges) as long as the working directory is not in the **/home** hierarchy. Alternatively you can use the **remount** option to mount to remount **/home** while the device is in use:

```
# mount -v -o remount /home
/dev/sda3 on /home type ext4 (rw,acl)
```

See page 524 for information on **fstab** and page 520 for information on mount.

WORKING WITH ACCESS RULES

The setfacl utility modifies a file's ACL and getfacl displays a file's ACL. When you use getfacl to obtain information about a file that does not have an ACL, it displays some of the same information as an **ls –l** command, albeit in a different format:

```
$ ls -l report
-rw-r--r--. 1 max pubs 9537 01-12 23:17 report

$ getfacl report
# file: report
# owner: max
# group: pubs
user::rw-
group::r--
other::r--
```

The first three lines of the getfacl output comprise the header; they specify the name of the file, the owner of the file, and the group the file is associated with. For more information refer to "**ls –l**: Displays Permissions" on page 202. The **--omit-header** (or just **--omit**) option causes getfacl not to display the header:

```
$ getfacl --omit-header report
user::rw-
group::r--
other::r--
```

In the line that starts with **user,** the two colons (**::**) with no name between them indicate that the line specifies the permissions for the owner of the file. Similarly, the two colons in the **group** line indicate that the line specifies permissions for the group the file is associated with. The two colons following **other** are there for consistency: No name can be associated with **other**.

The setfacl **--modify** (or **-m**) option adds or modifies one or more rules in a file's ACL using the following format:

> setfacl --modify *ugo:name:permissions file-list*

where *ugo* can be either **u**, **g**, or **o** to indicate that the command sets file permissions for a user, a group, or all other users, respectively; *name* is the name of the user or group that permissions are being set for; *permissions* is the permissions in either symbolic or absolute format; and *file-list* is the list of files the permissions are to be applied to. You must omit *name* when you specify permissions for other users (**o**). Symbolic permissions use letters to represent file permissions (**rwx**, **r-x**, and so on), whereas absolute permissions use an octal number. While chmod uses three sets of permissions or three octal numbers (one each for the owner, group, and other users), setfacl uses a single set of permissions or a single octal number to represent the permissions being granted to the user or group represented by *ugo* and *name*. See the discussion of chmod on page 203 for more information about symbolic and absolute representations of file permissions.

For example, both of the following commands add a rule to the ACL for the **report** file that gives Sam read and write permission to that file:

```
$ setfacl --modify u:sam:rw- report
```

or

```
$ setfacl --modify u:sam:6 report
```

```
$ getfacl report
# file: report
# owner: max
# group: pubs
user::rw-
user:sam:rw-
group::r--
mask::rw-
other::r--
```

The line containing **user:sam:rw-** shows that the user named **sam** has read and write access (**rw-**) to the file. See page 202 for an explanation of how to read access permissions. See the following optional section for a description of the line that starts with **mask**.

When a file has an ACL, ls **-l** displays a plus sign (**+**) following the permissions, even if the ACL is empty:

```
$ ls -l report
-rw-rw-r--+ 1 max pubs 9537 01-12 23:17 report
```

optional   EFFECTIVE RIGHTS MASK

The line in the output of getfacl that starts with **mask** specifies the *effective rights mask*. This mask limits the effective permissions granted to ACL groups and users. It does not affect the owner of the file or the group the file is associated with. In other words, it does not affect traditional Linux permissions. However, because setfacl always sets the effective rights mask to the least restrictive ACL permissions for the file, the mask has no effect unless you set it explicitly after you set up an ACL for the file. You can set the mask by specifying **mask** in place of *ugo* and by not specifying a *name* in a setfacl command.

The following example sets the effective rights mask to **read** for the **report** file:

```
$ setfacl -m mask::r-- report
```

The **mask** line in the following getfacl output shows the effective rights mask set to read (**r--**). The line that displays Sam's file access permissions shows them still set to read and write. However, the comment at the right end of the line shows that his effective permission is read.

```
$ getfacl report
# file: report
# owner: max
# group: pubs
user::rw-
user:sam:rw-                          #effective:r--
group::r--
mask::r--
other::r--
```

As the next example shows, setfacl can modify ACL rules and can set more than one ACL rule at a time:

```
$ setfacl -m u:sam:r--,u:zach:rw- report

$ getfacl --omit-header report
user::rw-
user:sam:r--
user:zach:rw-
group::r--
mask::rw-
other::r--
```

The **–x** option removes ACL rules for a user or a group. It has no effect on permissions for the owner of the file or the group that the file is associated with. The next example shows setfacl removing the rule that gives Sam permission to access the file:

```
$ setfacl -x u:sam report

$ getfacl --omit-header report
user::rw-
user:zach:rw-
group::r--
mask::rw-
other::r--
```

You must not specify *permissions* when you use the **–x** option. Instead, specify only the *ugo* and *name*. The **–b** option, followed by a filename only, removes all ACL rules and the ACL itself from the file or directory you specify.

Both setfacl and getfacl have many options. Use the **––help** option to display brief lists of options or refer to the man pages for details.

SETTING DEFAULT RULES FOR A DIRECTORY

The following example shows that the **dir** directory initially has no ACL. The setfacl command uses the **–d** (default) option to add two default rules to the ACL for **dir**. These rules apply to all files in the **dir** directory that do not have explicit ACLs. The rules give members of the **pubs** group read and execute permissions and give members of the **adm** group read, write, and execute permissions.

```
$ ls -ld dir
drwx------. 2 max pubs 4096 02-12 23:15 dir
$ getfacl dir
# file: dir
# owner: max
# group: pubs
user::rwx
group::---
other::---

$ setfacl -d -m g:pubs:r-x,g:adm:rwx dir
```

The following ls command shows that the **dir** directory now has an ACL, as indicated by the **+** to the right of the permissions. Each of the default rules that getfacl displays starts with **default:**. The first two default rules and the last default rule specify the permissions for the owner of the file, the group that the file is associated with, and all other users. These three rules specify the traditional Linux permissions and take precedence over other ACL rules. The third and fourth rules specify the permissions for the **pubs** and **adm** groups. Next is the default effective rights mask.

```
$ ls -ld dir
drwx------+ 2 max pubs 4096 02-12 23:15 dir
$ getfacl dir
# file: dir
# owner: max
# group: pubs
user::rwx
group::---
other::---
default:user::rwx
default:group::---
default:group:pubs:r-x
default:group:adm:rwx
default:mask::rwx
default:other::---
```

Remember that the default rules pertain to files held in the directory that are not assigned ACLs explicitly. You can also specify access rules for the directory itself.

When you create a file within a directory that has default rules in its ACL, the effective rights mask for that file is created based on the file's permissions. In some cases the mask can override default ACL rules.

In the next example, touch creates a file named **new** in the **dir** directory. The ls command shows this file has an ACL. Based on the value of umask (page 473), both the owner and the group that the file is associated with have read and write permissions for the file. The effective rights mask is set to read and write so that the effective permission for **pubs** is read and the effective permissions for **adm** are read and write. Neither group has execute permission.

```
$ cd dir
$ touch new
$ ls -l new
-rw-rw----+ 1 max pubs 0 02-13 00:39 new
$ getfacl --omit new
user::rw-
group::---
group:pubs:r-x                    #effective:r--
group:adm:rwx                     #effective:rw-
mask::rw-
other::---
```

If you change the file's traditional permissions to read, write, and execute for the owner and the group, the effective rights mask changes to read, write, and execute, and the groups specified by the default rules gain execute access to the file.

```
$ chmod 770 new
$ ls -l new
-rwxrwx---+ 1 max pubs 0 02-13 00:39 new
$ getfacl --omit new
user::rwx
group::---
group:pubs:r-x
group:adm:rwx
mask::rwx
other::---
```

LINKS

A *link* is a pointer to a file. Each time you create a file using vim, touch, cp, or by some other means, you are putting a pointer in a directory. This pointer associates a filename with a place on the disk. When you specify a filename in a command, you are indirectly pointing to the place on the disk that holds the information you want.

Sharing files can be useful when two or more people are working on the same project and need to share some information. You can make it easy for other users to access one of your files by creating additional links to the file.

To share a file with another user, first give the user permission to read from and write to the file (page 203). You might also have to change the access permissions of the parent directory of the file to give the user read, write, or execute permission (page 207). When the permissions are appropriately set, the user can create a link to the file so each of you can access the file from your separate directory hierarchies.

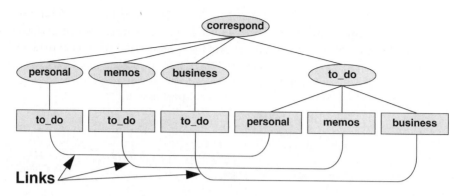

Figure 6-13   Using links to cross-classify files

A link can also be useful to a single user with a large directory hierarchy. You can create links to cross-classify files in your directory hierarchy, using different classifications for different tasks. For example, if you have the file layout depicted in Figure 6-2 on page 187, a file named **to_do** might appear in each subdirectory of the **correspond** directory—that is, in **personal, memos,** and **business**. If you find it difficult to keep track of everything you need to do, you can create a separate directory named **to_do** in the **correspond** directory. You can then link each subdirectory's to-do list into that directory. For example, you could link the file named **to_do** in the **memos** directory to a file named **memos** in the **to_do** directory. This set of links is shown in Figure 6-13.

Although it might sound complicated, this technique keeps all your to-do lists conveniently in one place. The appropriate list is easily accessible in the task-related directory when you are busy composing letters, writing memos, or handling personal business.

About the discussion of hard links

tip   Two kinds of links exist: hard links and symbolic (soft) links. Hard links are older and becoming outdated. The section on hard links is marked as optional; you can skip it, although it discusses inodes and gives you insight into the structure of the filesystem.

optional
HARD LINKS

A hard link to a file appears as another file. If the file appears in the same directory as the linked-to file, the links must have different filenames because two files in the same directory cannot have the same name. You can create a hard link to a file only from within the filesystem that holds the file.

ln: CREATES A HARD LINK

The ln (link) utility (without the **–s** or **––symbolic** option) creates a hard link to an existing file using the following syntax:

ln existing-file new-link

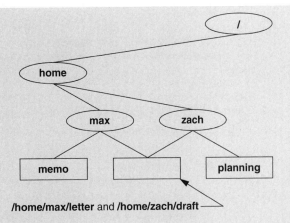

/home/max/letter and /home/zach/draft ———

Figure 6-14   Two links to the same file: **/home/max/letter** and **/home/zach/draft**

The next command shows Zach making the link shown in Figure 6-14 by creating a new link named **/home/max/letter** to an existing file named **draft** in Zach's home directory:

```
$ pwd
/home/zach
$ ln draft /home/max/letter
```

The new link appears in the **/home/max** directory with the filename **letter**. In practice, Max might need to change directory permissions so Zach will be able to create the link. Even though **/home/max/letter** appears in Max's directory, Zach is the owner of the file because he created it.

The ln utility creates an additional pointer to an existing file, but it does *not* make another copy of the file. Because there is only one file, the file status information—such as access permissions, owner, and the time the file was last modified—is the same for all links; only the filenames differ. When Zach modifies **/home/zach/draft**, for example, Max sees the changes in **/home/max/letter**.

cp VERSUS ln

The following commands verify that ln does not make an additional copy of a file. Create a file, use ln to make an additional link to the file, change the contents of the file through one link, and verify the change through the other link:

```
$ cat file_a
This is file A.
$ ln file_a file_b
$ cat file_b
This is file A.
$ vim file_b
...
$ cat file_b
This is file B after the change.
$ cat file_a
This is file B after the change.
```

If you try the same experiment using cp instead of ln and change a *copy* of the file, the difference between the two utilities will become clearer. After you change a *copy* of a file, the two files are different:

```
$ cat file_c
This is file C.
$ cp file_c file_d
$ cat file_d
This is file C.
$ vim file_d
...
$ cat file_d
This is file D after the change.
$ cat file_c
This is file C.
```

ls and link counts   You can use ls with the –l option, followed by the names of the files you want to compare, to confirm that the status information is the same for two links to the same file and is different for files that are not linked. In the following example, the 2 in the links field (just to the left of **max**) shows there are two links to **file_a** and **file_b** (from the previous example):

```
$ ls -l file_a file_b file_c file_d
-rw-r--r--. 2 max pubs 33 05-24 10:52 file_a
-rw-r--r--. 2 max pubs 33 05-24 10:52 file_b
-rw-r--r--. 1 max pubs 16 05-24 10:55 file_c
-rw-r--r--. 1 max pubs 33 05-24 10:57 file_d
```

Although it is easy to guess which files are linked to one another in this example, ls does not explicitly tell you.

ls and inodes   Use ls with the –i option to determine without a doubt which files are linked. The –i option lists the *inode* (page 1169) number for each file. An inode is the control structure for a file. If the two filenames have the same inode number, they share the same control structure and are links to the same file. Conversely, when two filenames have different inode numbers, they are different files. The following example shows that **file_a** and **file_b** have the same inode number and that **file_c** and **file_d** have different inode numbers:

```
$ ls -i file_a file_b file_c file_d
3534 file_a  3534 file_b  5800 file_c  7328 file_d
```

All links to a file are of equal value: The operating system cannot distinguish the order in which multiple links were created. When a file has two links, you can remove either one and still access the file through the remaining link. You can remove the link used to create the file, for example, and as long as one link remains, still access the file through that link.

SYMBOLIC LINKS

In addition to hard links, Linux supports *symbolic links*, also called *soft links* or *symlinks*. A hard link is a pointer to a file (the directory entry points to the inode), whereas a symbolic link is an *indirect* pointer to a file (the directory entry contains the pathname of the pointed-to file—a pointer to the hard link to the file).

Advantages of symbolic links Symbolic links were developed because of the limitations inherent in hard links. You cannot create a hard link to a directory, but you can create a symbolic link to a directory.

In many cases the Linux file hierarchy encompasses several filesystems. Because each filesystem keeps separate control information (that is, separate inode tables or filesystem structures) for the files it holds, it is not possible to create hard links between files in different filesystems. A symbolic link can point to any file, regardless of where it is located in the file structure, but a hard link to a file must be in the same filesystem as the other hard link(s) to the file. When you create links only among files in your home directory, you will not notice this limitation.

A major advantage of a symbolic link is that it can point to a non-existent file. This ability is useful if you need a link to a file that is periodically removed and re-created. A hard link keeps pointing to a "removed" file, which the link keeps alive even after a new file is created. In contrast, a symbolic link always points to the newly created file and does not interfere when you delete the old file. For example, a symbolic link could point to a file that gets checked in and out under a source code control system, a .o file that is re-created by the C compiler each time you run make, or a log file that is repeatedly archived.

Although they are more general than hard links, symbolic links have some disadvantages. Whereas all hard links to a file have equal status, symbolic links do not have the same status as hard links. When a file has multiple hard links, it is analogous to a person having multiple full legal names, as many married women do. In contrast, symbolic links are analogous to nicknames. Anyone can have one or more nicknames, but these nicknames have a lesser status than legal names. The following sections describe some of the peculiarities of symbolic links.

ln: CREATES SYMBOLIC LINKS

The ln utility with the --symbolic (or -s) option creates a symbolic link. The following example creates a symbolic link /tmp/s3 to the file **sum** in Max's home directory. When you use an ls -l command to look at the symbolic link, ls displays the name of the link and the name of the file it points to. The first character of the listing is l (for link).

```
$ ln --symbolic /home/max/sum /tmp/s3
$ ls -l /home/max/sum /tmp/s3
-rw-rw-r--. 1 max pubs 38 06-12 09:51 /home/max/sum
lrwxrwxrwx. 1 max pubs 14 06-12 09:52 /tmp/s3 -> /home/max/sum
$ cat /tmp/s3
This is sum.
```

The sizes and times of the last modifications of the two files are different. Unlike a hard link, a symbolic link to a file does not have the same status information as the file itself.

You can also use ln to create a symbolic link to a directory. When you use the --symbolic option, ln works as expected whether the file you are creating a link to is an ordinary file or a directory.

Use absolute pathnames with symbolic links

caution   Symbolic links are literal and are not aware of directories. A link that points to a relative pathname, which includes simple filenames, assumes the relative pathname is relative to the directory that the link was created *in* (not the directory the link was created *from*). In the following example, the link points to the file named **sum** in the **/tmp** directory. Because no such file exists, cat gives an error message:

```
$ pwd
/home/max
$ ln --symbolic sum /tmp/s4
$ ls -l sum /tmp/s4
lrwxrwxrwx. 1 max pubs 3 06-12 10:13 /tmp/s4 -> sum
-rw-rw-r--. 1 max pubs 38 06-12 09:51 sum
$ cat /tmp/s4
cat: /tmp/s4: No such file or directory
```

optional   cd and Symbolic Links

When you use a symbolic link as an argument to cd to change directories, the results can be confusing, particularly if you did not realize that you were using a symbolic link.

If you use cd to change to a directory that is represented by a symbolic link, the pwd shell builtin (page 249) lists the name of the symbolic link. The pwd utility (**/bin/pwd**) lists the name of the linked-to directory, not the link, regardless of how you got there.

```
$ ln -s /home/max/grades /tmp/grades.old
$ pwd
/home/max
$ cd /tmp/grades.old
$ pwd
/tmp/grades.old
$ /bin/pwd
/home/max/grades
```

When you change directories back to the parent, you end up in the directory holding the symbolic link:

```
$ cd ..
$ pwd
/tmp
$ /bin/pwd
/tmp
```

rm: Removes a Link

When you create a file, there is one hard link to it. You can then delete the file or, using Linux terminology, remove the link with the rm utility. When you remove the last hard link to a file, you can no longer access the information stored there, and the operating system releases the space the file occupied on the disk for use by other files. This space is released even if symbolic links to the file remain. When there is more than one hard link to a file, you can remove a hard link and still access the file from any remaining link. Unlike DOS and Windows, Linux does not provide an easy way to undelete a file once you have removed it. A skilled hacker, however, can sometimes piece the file together with time and effort.

When you remove all hard links to a file, you will not be able to access the file through a symbolic link. In the following example, cat reports that the file **total** does not exist because it is a symbolic link to a file that has been removed:

```
$ ls -l sum
-rw-r--r--. 1 max pubs 981 05-24 11:05 sum
$ ln -s sum total
$ rm sum
$ cat total
cat: total: No such file or directory
$ ls -l total
lrwxrwxrwx. 1 max pubs 6 05-24 11:09 total -> sum
```

When you remove a file, be sure to remove all symbolic links to it. Remove a symbolic link in the same way you remove other files:

```
$ rm total
```

CHAPTER SUMMARY

Linux has a hierarchical, or treelike, file structure that makes it possible to organize files so you can find them quickly and easily. The file structure contains directory files and ordinary files. Directories contain other files, including other directories; ordinary files generally contain text, programs, or images. The ancestor of all files is the root directory and is represented by / standing alone or at the left end of a pathname.

Most Linux filesystems support 255-character filenames. Nonetheless, it is a good idea to keep filenames simple and intuitive. Filename extensions can help make filenames more meaningful.

When you are logged in, you are always associated with a working directory. Your home directory is the working directory from the time you log in until you use cd to change directories.

An absolute pathname starts with the root directory and contains all the filenames that trace a path to a given file. The pathname starts with a slash, representing the root directory, and contains additional slashes following each of the directories in the path, except for the last directory in the case of a path that points to a directory file.

A relative pathname is similar to an absolute pathname but traces the path starting from the working directory. A simple filename is the last element of a pathname and is a form of a relative pathname; it represents a file in the working directory.

A Linux filesystem contains many important directories, including **/usr/bin**, which stores most of the Linux utilities, and **/dev**, which stores device files, many of which represent physical pieces of hardware. An important standard file is **/etc/passwd**; it contains information about users, such as a user's ID and full name.

Among the attributes associated with each file are access permissions. They determine who can access the file and how the file may be accessed. Three groups of users can potentially access the file: the owner, the members of a group, and all other users. An ordinary file can be accessed in three ways: read, write, and execute. The ls utility with the –l option displays these permissions. For directories, execute access is redefined to mean that the directory can be searched.

The owner of a file or a user working with **root** privileges can use the chmod utility to change the access permissions of a file. This utility specifies read, write, and execute permissions for the file's owner, the group, and all other users on the system.

ACLs (Access Control Lists) provide finer-grained control over which users can access specific directories and files than do traditional Linux permissions. Using ACLs you can specify the ways in which each of several users can access a directory or file. Few utilities preserve ACLs when working with files.

An ordinary file stores user data, such as textual information, programs, or images. A directory is a standard-format disk file that stores information, including names, about ordinary files and other directory files. An inode is a data structure, stored on disk, that defines a file's existence and is identified by an inode number. A directory relates each of the filenames it stores to an inode.

A link is a pointer to a file. You can have several links to a file so you can share the file with other users or have the file appear in more than one directory. Because only one copy of a file with multiple links exists, changing the file through any one link causes the changes to appear in all the links. Hard links cannot link directories or span filesystems, whereas symbolic links can.

Table 6-3 summarizes the utilities introduced in this chapter.

Table 6-3   Utilities introduced in Chapter 6

Utility	Function
cd	Associates you with another working directory (page 196)
chmod	Changes access permissions on a file (page 203)
getfacl	Displays a file's ACL (page 209)
ln	Makes a link to an existing file (page 214)
mkdir	Creates a directory (page 194)
pwd	Displays the pathname of the working directory (page 190)
rmdir	Deletes a directory (page 197)
setfacl	Modifies a file's ACL (page 209)

EXERCISES

1. Is each of the following an absolute pathname, a relative pathname, or a simple filename?

   a. **milk_co**

   b. **correspond/business/milk_co**

   c. **/home/max**

   d. **/home/max/literature/promo**

   e. **..**

   f. **letter.0210**

2. List the commands you can use to perform these operations:

   a. Make your home directory the working directory

   b. Identify the working directory

3. If the working directory is **/home/max** with a subdirectory named **literature**, give three sets of commands you can use to create a subdirectory named **classics** under **literature**. Also give several sets of commands you can use to remove the **classics** directory and its contents.

4. The df utility displays all mounted filesystems along with information about each. Use the df utility with the **–h** (human-readable) option to answer the following questions.

   a. How many filesystems are mounted on your Linux system?

   b. Which filesystem stores your home directory?

   c. Assuming your answer to exercise 4a is two or more, attempt to create a hard link to a file on another filesystem. What error message do you get? What happens when you attempt to create a symbolic link to the file instead?

5. Suppose you have a file that is linked to a file owned by another user. How can you ensure that changes to the file are no longer shared?

6. You should have read permission for the **/etc/passwd** file. To answer the following questions, use cat or less to display **/etc/passwd**. Look at the fields of information in **/etc/passwd** for the users on the local system.

   a. Which character is used to separate fields in **/etc/passwd**?

   b. How many fields are used to describe each user?

   c. How many users are on the local system?

   d. How many different login shells are in use on your system? (*Hint:* Look at the last field.)

e. The second field of **/etc/passwd** stores user passwords in encoded form. If the password field contains an **x,** your system uses shadow passwords and stores the encoded passwords elsewhere. Does your system use shadow passwords?

7. If **/home/zach/draft** and **/home/max/letter** are links to the same file and the following sequence of events occurs, what will be the date in the opening of the letter?

a. Max gives the command **vim letter.**

b. Zach gives the command **vim draft.**

c. Zach changes the date in the opening of the letter to January 31, writes the file, and exits from vim.

d. Max changes the date to February 1, writes the file, and exits from vim.

8. Suppose a user belongs to a group that has all permissions on a file named **jobs_list,** but the user, as the owner of the file, has no permissions. Describe which operations, if any, the user/owner can perform on **jobs_list.** Which command can the user/owner give that will grant the user/owner all permissions on the file?

9. Does the root directory have any subdirectories you cannot search as an ordinary user? Does the root directory have any subdirectories you cannot read as a regular user? Explain.

10. Assume you are given the directory structure shown in Figure 6-2 on page 187 and the following directory permissions:

```
d--x--x---   3 zach pubs 512 2010-03-10 15:16 business
drwxr-xr-x   2 zach pubs 512 2010-03-10 15:16 business/milk_co
```

For each category of permissions—owner, group, and other—what happens when you run each of the following commands? Assume the working directory is the parent of **correspond** and that the file **cheese_co** is readable by everyone.

a. **cd correspond/business/milk_co**

b. **ls –l correspond/business**

c. **cat correspond/business/cheese_co**

ADVANCED EXERCISES

11. What is an inode? What happens to the inode when you move a file within a filesystem?

12. What does the **..** entry in a directory point to? What does this entry point to in the root (**/**) directory?

13. How can you create a file named –i? Which techniques do not work, and why do they not work? How can you remove the file named –i?

14. Suppose the working directory contains a single file named **andor**. What error message do you get when you run the following command line?

    $ mv andor and\/or

    Under what circumstances is it possible to run the command without producing an error?

15. The **ls –i** command displays a filename preceded by the inode number of the file (page 216). Write a command to output inode/filename pairs for the files in the working directory, sorted by inode number. (*Hint:* Use a pipe.)

16. Do you think the system administrator has access to a program that can decode user passwords? Why or why not? (See exercise 6.)

17. Is it possible to distinguish a file from a hard link to a file? That is, given a filename, can you tell whether it was created using an **ln** command? Explain.

18. Explain the error messages displayed in the following sequence of commands:

    ```
    $ ls -l
    total 1
    drwxrwxr-x. 2 max pubs 1024 03-02 17:57 dirtmp
    $ ls dirtmp
    $ rmdir dirtmp
    rmdir: dirtmp: Directory not empty
    $ rm dirtmp/*
    rm: No match.
    ```

7

THE SHELL

OBJECTIVES

After reading this chapter you should be able to:

▶ Understand command line syntax and run commands with options and arguments

▶ Explain how the shell interprets the command line syntax

▶ Understand the purpose of the **PATH** variable

▶ Redirect, overwriting or appending, output of a command to a file

▶ Obtain input for a command from a file

▶ Connect commands using a pipe

▶ Run commands in the background

▶ Use special characters as wildcards to generate filenames

▶ Explain the difference between an executable file and a shell builtin command

225

This chapter takes a close look at the shell and explains how to use some of its features. For example, it discusses command-line syntax and describes how the shell processes a command line and initiates execution of a program. This chapter also explains how to redirect input to and output from a command, construct pipes and filters on the command line, and run a command in the background. The final section covers filename expansion and explains how you can use this feature in your everyday work.

The exact wording of the shell output differs from shell to shell: What the shell you are using displays might differ slightly from what appears in this book. Refer to Chapter 9 for more information on bash (the default shell under Fedora/RHEL) and to Chapter 27 for information on writing and executing bash shell scripts.

THE COMMAND LINE

The shell executes a program when you enter a command in response to its prompt. For example, when you give the ls command, the shell executes the utility program named ls. You can cause the shell to execute other types of programs—such as shell scripts, application programs, and programs you have written—in the same way. The line that contains the command, including any arguments, is called the *command line*.

Command   This book uses the term *command* to refer to both the characters you type on the command line and the program that action invokes.

SYNTAX

Command-line syntax dictates the ordering and separation of the elements on a command line. When you press the RETURN key after entering a command, the shell scans the command line for proper syntax. The syntax for a basic command line is

> *command [arg1] [arg2] ... [argn]* RETURN

One or more SPACEs must separate elements on the command line. The *command* is the name of the command, *arg1* through *argn* are arguments, and RETURN is the keystroke that terminates all command lines. The brackets in the command-line syntax indicate that the arguments they enclose are optional. Not all commands require arguments: Some commands do not allow arguments; other commands allow a variable number of arguments; and still others require a specific number of arguments. Options, a special kind of argument, are usually preceded by one or two hyphens (also called a dash or minus sign: –).

COMMAND NAME

Usage message   Some useful Linux command lines consist of only the name of the command without any arguments. For example, ls by itself lists the contents of the working directory. Commands that require arguments typically give a short error message, called a *usage message,* when you use them without arguments, with incorrect arguments, or with the wrong number of arguments.

For example, the mkdir (make directory) utility requires an argument that specifies the name of the directory you want it to create. Without this argument, it displays a usage message (*operand* is another term for argument):

```
$ ls
hold    mark   names   oldstuff  temp  zach
house   max    office  personal  test
$ ls -r
zach  temp       oldstuff  names  mark   hold
test  personal   office    max    house
$ ls -x
hold       house      mark  max   names  office
oldstuff   personal   temp  test  zach
$ ls -rx
zach    test   temp  personal  oldstuff  office
names   max    mark  house     hold
```

Figure 7-1 Using options

```
$ mkdir
mkdir: missing operand
Try 'mkdir --help' for more information.
```

ARGUMENTS

Token   On the command line each sequence of nonblank characters is called a *token* or *word*. An *argument* is a token, such as a filename, string of text, number, or other object that a command acts on. For example, the argument to a vim or emacs command is the name of the file you want to edit.

The following command line uses cp to copy the file named **temp** to **tempcopy**:

```
$ cp temp tempcopy
```

Arguments are numbered starting with the command itself, which is argument zero. In this example, **cp** is argument zero, **temp** is argument one, and **tempcopy** is argument two. The cp utility requires at least two arguments on the command line. Argument one is the name of an existing file. Argument two is the name of the file that cp is creating or overwriting. Here the arguments are not optional; both arguments must be present for the command to work. When you do not supply the right number or kind of arguments, cp displays a usage message. Try typing **cp** and then pressing RETURN.

OPTIONS

An *option* is an argument that modifies the effects of a command. You can frequently specify more than one option, modifying the command in several different ways. Options are specific to and interpreted by the program that the command line calls, not by the shell.

By convention options are separate arguments that follow the name of the command and usually precede other arguments, such as filenames. Many utilities require options to be prefixed with a single hyphen. However, this requirement is specific to the utility and not the shell. GNU program options are frequently prefixed with two hyphens. For example, **--help** generates a (sometimes extensive) usage message.

Figure 7-1 first shows the output of an ls command without any options. By default ls lists the contents of the working directory in alphabetical order, vertically sorted in columns. Next the –r (reverse order; because this is a GNU utility, you can also specify ––reverse) option causes the ls utility to display the list of files in reverse alphabetical order, still sorted in columns. The –x option causes ls to display the list of files in horizontally sorted rows.

Combining options   When you need to use several options, you can usually group multiple single-letter options into one argument that starts with a single hyphen; do not put SPACEs between the options. You cannot combine options that are preceded by two hyphens in this way. Specific rules for combining options depend on the program you are running. Figure 7-1 shows both the –r and –x options with the ls utility. Together these options generate a list of filenames in horizontally sorted columns in reverse alphabetical order. Most utilities allow you to list options in any order; thus ls –xr produces the same results as ls –rx. The command ls –x –r also generates the same list.

Option arguments   Some utilities have options that themselves require arguments. For example, the gcc utility (C compiler) has a –o (output) option that must be followed by the name you want to give the executable file that gcc generates. Typically an argument to an option is separated from its option letter by a SPACE:

```
$ gcc -o prog prog.c
```

Displaying readable file sizes: the –h option

tip   Most utilities that report on file sizes specify the size of a file in bytes. Bytes work well when you are dealing with smaller files, but the numbers can be difficult to read when you are working with file sizes that are measured in megabytes or gigabytes. Use the **–h** (or **––human-readable**) option to display file sizes in kilo-, mega-, and gigabytes. Experiment with the **df –h** (disk free) and **ls –lh** commands.

Arguments that start with a hyphen   Another convention allows utilities to work with arguments, such as filenames, that start with a hyphen. If a file's name is –l, the following command is ambiguous:

```
$ ls -l
```

This command could be a request to display a long listing of all files in the working directory (–l option) or a request for a listing of the file named –l. The ls utility interprets it as the former. Avoid creating files whose names begin with hyphens. If you do create them, many utilities follow the convention that a –– argument (two consecutive hyphens) indicates the end of the options (and the beginning of the arguments). To disambiguate the command, you can type

```
$ ls -- -l
```

Using two consecutive hyphens to indicate the end of the options is a convention, not a hard-and-fast rule, and a number of utilities do not follow it (e.g., find). Following this convention makes it easier for users to work with your program. When you write shell programs that require options, follow this convention.

For utilities that do not follow this convention, there are other ways to specify a filename that begins with a hyphen. You can use a period to refer to the working directory and a slash to indicate that the following filename refers to a file in the working directory:

```
$ ls ./-l
```

You can also specify the absolute pathname of the file:

```
$ ls /home/max/-l
```

PROCESSING THE COMMAND LINE

As you enter a command line, the Linux tty device driver (part of the Linux kernel) examines each character to see whether it must take immediate action. When you press CONTROL-H (to erase a character) or CONTROL-U (to kill a line), the device driver immediately adjusts the command line as required; the shell never sees the character(s) you erased or the line you killed. Often a similar adjustment occurs when you press CONTROL-W (to erase a word). When the character you entered does not require immediate action, the device driver stores the character in a buffer and waits for additional characters. When you press RETURN, the device driver passes the command line to the shell for processing.

The --help option

tip   Many utilities display a (sometimes extensive) help message when you call them with an argument of **--help**. All utilities developed by the GNU Project (page 3) accept this option. Following is the help message displayed by the bzip2 compression utility (page 160).

```
$ bzip2 --help
bzip2, a block-sorting file compressor.  Version 1.0.6, 6-Sept-2010.

   usage: bunzip2 [flags and input files in any order]

   -h --help           print this message
   -d --decompress     force decompression
   -z --compress       force compression
   -k --keep           keep (don't delete) input files
   -f --force          overwrite existing output files
...
   If invoked as 'bzip2', default action is to compress.
             as 'bunzip2',  default action is to decompress.
             as 'bzcat', default action is to decompress to stdout.
...
```

Parsing the command line   When the shell processes a command line, it looks at the line as a whole and *parses* (breaks) it into its component parts (Figure 7-2, next page). Next the shell looks for the name of the command. Usually the name of the command is the first item on the command line after the prompt (argument zero). The shell takes the first characters on the command line up to the first blank (TAB or SPACE) and then looks for a command with that name. The command name (the first token) can be specified on the command line either as a simple filename or as a pathname. For example, you can call the ls command in either of the following ways:

```
$ ls
```

```
$ /bin/ls
```

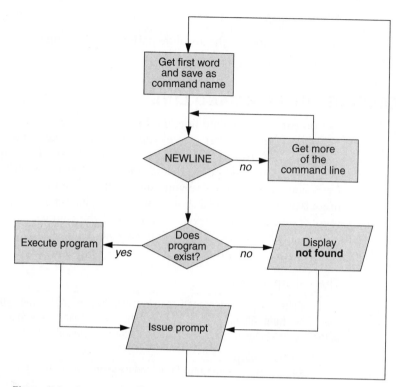

Figure 7-2   Processing the command line

optional   The shell does not require the name of the program to appear first on the command line. Thus you can structure a command line as follows:

```
$ >bb <aa cat
```

This command runs cat with standard input coming from the file named **aa** and standard output going to the file named **bb**. When the shell recognizes the redirect symbols (page 234), it recognizes and processes them and their arguments before finding the name of the program that the command line is calling. This is a properly structured—albeit rarely encountered and possibly confusing—command line.

Absolute versus relative pathnames   From the command line, you can specify the name of a file you want the shell to execute in three ways: as an absolute pathname (starts with a slash [/]; page 192), as a relative pathname (includes a slash but does not start with a slash; page 193), or as a simple filename (no slash). When you specify the name of a file for the shell to execute in either of the first two ways (the pathname includes a slash), the shell looks in the specified directory for a file with the specified name that you have permission to execute. When you specify a simple filename (no slash), the shell searches through a list of directories for a filename that matches the specified name and for which you have execute permission. The shell does not look through all directories but only the ones specified by the variable named **PATH**. Refer to page 308 for more information on **PATH**. Also refer to the discussion of the which and whereis utilities on page 164.

When it cannot find the file, bash displays the following message:

```
$ abc
bash: abc: command not found...
```

One reason the shell might not be able to find the executable file is that it is not in a directory listed in the **PATH** variable. Under bash the following command temporarily adds the working directory (.) to **PATH**:

```
$ PATH=$PATH:.
```

For security reasons, it is poor practice to add the working directory to **PATH** permanently; see the following tip and the one on page 309.

When the shell finds the file but cannot execute it (i.e., because you do not have execute permission for the file), it displays a message similar to

```
$ def
bash: ./def: Permission denied
```

See "ls –l: Displays Permissions" on page 202 for information on displaying access permissions for a file and "chmod: Changes Access Permissions" on page 203 for instructions on how to change file access permissions.

Try giving a command as *./command*

tip You can always execute an executable file in the working directory by prepending ./ to the name of the file. For example, if **myprog** is an executable file in the working directory, you can execute it with the following command, regardless of how **PATH** is set:

```
$ ./myprog
```

EXECUTING A COMMAND

Process If it finds an executable file with the name specified on the command line, the shell starts a new process. A *process* is the execution of a command by Linux (page 316). The shell makes each command-line argument, including options and the name of the command, available to the called program. While the command is executing, the shell waits for the process to finish. At this point the shell is in an inactive state called *sleep*. When the program finishes execution, it passes its exit status (page 1012) to the shell. The shell then returns to an active state (wakes up), issues a prompt, and waits for another command.

The shell does not process arguments Because the shell does not process command-line arguments but merely passes them to the called program, the shell has no way of knowing whether a particular option or other argument is valid for a given program. Any error or usage messages about options or arguments come from the program itself. Some utilities ignore bad options.

EDITING THE COMMAND LINE

You can repeat and edit previous commands and edit the current command line. See pages 141 and 320 for more information.

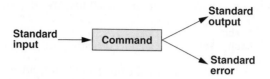

Figure 7-3 The command does not know where standard input comes from or where standard output and standard error go

STANDARD INPUT AND STANDARD OUTPUT

Standard output is a place to which a program can send information (e.g., text). The program never "knows" where the information it sends to standard output is going (Figure 7-3). The information can go to a printer, an ordinary file, or the screen. The following sections show that by default the shell directs standard output from a command to the screen[1] and describe how you can cause the shell to redirect this output to another file.

Standard input is a place a program gets information from; by default, the shell directs standard input from the keyboard. As with standard output the program never "knows" where the information comes from. The following sections explain how to redirect standard input to a command so that it comes from an ordinary file instead of from the keyboard.

In addition to standard input and standard output, a running program has a place to send error messages: *standard error*. By default, the shell directs standard error to the screen. Refer to page 285 for more information on redirecting standard error.

THE SCREEN AS A FILE

Device file   Chapter 6 introduced ordinary files, directory files, and hard and soft links. Linux has an additional type of file: a *device file*. A device file resides in the Linux file structure, usually in the **/dev** directory, and represents a peripheral device, such as a screen, printer, or disk drive.

The device name the who utility displays after a username is the filename of the screen that user is working on. For example, when who displays the device name **pts/4**, the pathname of the screen is **/dev/pts/4**. When you work with multiple windows, each window has its own device name. You can also use the tty utility to display the name of the device that you give the command from. Although you would not normally have occasion to do so, you can read from and write to this file as though it were a text file. Reading from the device file that represents the screen you

---

1. This book uses the term *screen* to refer to a screen, terminal emulator window, or workstation—in other words, to the device that the shell displays its prompt and messages on.

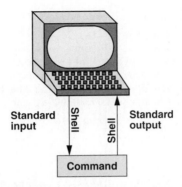

Figure 7-4 By default, standard input comes from the keyboard, and standard output goes to the screen

are using reads what you enter on the keyboard; writing to it displays what you write on the screen.

THE KEYBOARD AND SCREEN AS STANDARD INPUT AND STANDARD OUTPUT

When you log in, the shell directs standard output of commands you enter to the device file that represents the screen (Figure 7-4). Directing output in this manner causes it to appear on the screen. The shell also directs standard input to come from the same file, so commands receive as input anything you type on the keyboard.

cat   The cat utility provides a good example of the way the keyboard and screen function as standard input and standard output, respectively. When you run cat, it copies a file to standard output. Because the shell directs standard output to the screen, cat displays the file on the screen.

Up to this point cat has taken its input from the filename (argument) you specify on the command line. When you do not give cat an argument (that is, when you give the command cat followed immediately by RETURN), cat takes its input from standard input. Thus, when called without an argument, cat copies standard input to standard output, one line at a time.

To see how cat works, type **cat** and press RETURN in response to the shell prompt. Nothing happens. Enter a line of text and press RETURN. The same line appears just under the one you entered. The cat utility is working. Because the shell associates cat's standard input with the keyboard and cat's standard output with the screen, when you type a line of text cat copies the text from standard input (the keyboard) to standard output (the screen). Figure 7-5 on the next page shows this exchange.

CONTROL-D   The cat utility keeps copying text until you enter CONTROL-D on a line by itself. Pressing
signals EOF   CONTROL-D sends an EOF (end of file) signal to cat. This signal indicates to cat that it has reached the end of standard input and there is no more text for it to copy. The cat utility then finishes execution and returns control to the shell, which displays a prompt.

```
$ cat
This is a line of text.
This is a line of text.
Cat keeps copying lines of text
Cat keeps copying lines of text
until you press CONTROL-D at the beginning
until you press CONTROL-D at the beginning
of a line.
of a line.
CONTROL-D
$
```

Figure 7-5   The cat utility copies standard input to standard output

REDIRECTION

The term *redirection* encompasses the various ways you can cause the shell to alter where standard input of a command comes from and where standard output goes to. By default the shell associates standard input and standard output of a command with the keyboard and the screen. You can cause the shell to redirect standard input or standard output of any command by associating the input or output with a command or file other than the device file representing the keyboard or the screen. This section demonstrates how to redirect input from and output to ordinary text files and utilities.

REDIRECTING STANDARD OUTPUT

The *redirect output symbol* (>) instructs the shell to redirect the output of a command to the specified file instead of to the screen (Figure 7-6). The format of a command line that redirects output is

> *command [arguments] > filename*

where ***command*** is any executable program (such as an application program or a utility), ***arguments*** are optional arguments, and ***filename*** is the name of the ordinary file the shell redirects the output to.

Figure 7-7 uses cat to demonstrate output redirection. This figure contrasts with Figure 7-5, where standard input *and* standard output are associated with the

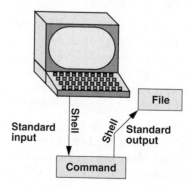

Figure 7-6   Redirecting standard output

```
$ cat > sample.txt
This text is being entered at the keyboard and
cat is copying it to a file.
Press CONTROL-D to indicate the
end of file.
CONTROL-D
$
```

Figure 7-7   cat with its output redirected

keyboard and screen. The input in Figure 7-7 comes from the keyboard. The redirect output symbol on the command line causes the shell to associate cat's standard output with the **sample.txt** file specified following this symbol.

Redirecting output can destroy a file I

caution   Use caution when you redirect output to a file. If the file exists, the shell will overwrite it and destroy its contents. For more information see the tip "Redirecting output can destroy a file II" on page 237.

After giving the command and typing the text shown in Figure 7-7, the **sample.txt** file contains the text you entered. You can use cat with an argument of **sample.txt** to display this file. The next section shows another way to use cat to display the file.

Figure 7-7 shows that redirecting standard output from cat is a handy way to create a file without using an editor. The drawback is that once you enter a line and press RETURN, you cannot edit the text. While you are entering a line, the erase and kill keys work to delete text on that line. This procedure is useful for creating short, simple files.

Figure 7-8 shows how to run cat and use the redirect output symbol to *catenate* (join one after the other—the derivation of the name of the cat utility) several files into one larger file. The first three commands display the contents of three files: **stationery**, **tape**, and **pens**. The next command shows cat with three filenames as arguments. When you call it with more than one filename, cat copies the files, one at a time, to

```
$ cat stationery
2,000 sheets letterhead ordered:     October 7
$ cat tape
1 box masking tape ordered:          October 14
5 boxes filament tape ordered:       October 28
$ cat pens
12 doz. black pens ordered:          October 4

$ cat stationery tape pens > supply_orders

$ cat supply_orders
2,000 sheets letterhead ordered:     October 7
1 box masking tape ordered:          October 14
5 boxes filament tape ordered:       October 28
12 doz. black pens ordered:          October 4
$
```

Figure 7-8   Using cat to catenate files

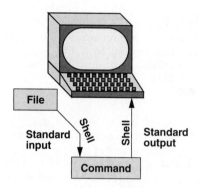

Figure 7-9   Redirecting standard input

standard output. This command redirects standard output to the file **supply_orders**. The final cat command shows that **supply_orders** contains the contents of the three of the original files.

REDIRECTING STANDARD INPUT

Just as you can redirect standard output, so you can redirect standard input. The *redirect input symbol* (<) instructs the shell to redirect a command's input to come from the specified file instead of from the keyboard (Figure 7-9). The format of a command line that redirects input is

  command [arguments] < filename

where *command* is any executable program (such as an application program or a utility), *arguments* are optional arguments, and *filename* is the name of the ordinary file the shell redirects the input from.

Figure 7-10 shows cat with its input redirected from the **supply_orders** file created in Figure 7-8 and standard output going to the screen. This setup causes cat to display the **supply_orders** file on the screen. The system automatically supplies an EOF signal at the end of an ordinary file.

Utilities that take input from a file or standard input   Giving a cat command with input redirected from a file yields the same result as giving a cat command with the filename as an argument. The cat utility is a member of a class of Linux utilities that function in this manner. Other members of this class of utilities include lpr, sort, grep, and Perl. These utilities first examine the command line that called them. If the command line includes a filename as an argument, the utility takes its input from the specified file. If no filename argument is present, the utility takes its input from standard input. It is the utility or program—not the shell or operating system—that functions in this manner.

```
$ cat < supply_orders
2,000 sheets letterhead ordered:    October 7
1 box masking tape ordered:         October 14
5 boxes filament tape ordered:      October 28
12 doz. black pens ordered:         October 4
```

Figure 7-10   cat with its input redirected

Redirecting output can destroy a file II

caution Depending on which shell you are using and how the environment is set up, a command such as the following can yield undesired results:

```
$ cat orange pear > orange
cat: orange: input file is output file
```

Although cat displays an error message, the shell destroys the contents of the existing **orange** file. The new **orange** file will have the same contents as **pear** because the first action the shell takes when it sees the redirection symbol (**>**) is to remove the contents of the original **orange** file. If you want to catenate two files into one, use cat to put the two files into a temporary file and then use mv to rename the **temp** file:

```
$ cat orange pear > temp
$ mv temp orange
```

What happens in the next example can be even worse. The user giving the command wants to search through files **a**, **b**, and **c** for the word **apple** and redirect the output from grep (page 152) to the file **a.output**. Unfortunately the user enters the filename as **a output**, omitting the period and inserting a SPACE in its place:

```
$ grep apple a b c > a output
grep: output: No such file or directory
```

The shell obediently removes the contents of **a** and then calls grep. The error message could take a moment to appear, giving you a sense that the command is running correctly. Even after you see the error message, it might take a while to realize that you have destroyed the contents of **a**.

noclobber: AVOIDS OVERWRITING FILES

The shell provides the **noclobber** feature that prevents overwriting a file using redirection. Enable this feature by setting **noclobber** using the command **set –o noclobber**. The same command with **+o** unsets **noclobber**. With **noclobber** set, if you redirect output to an existing file, the shell displays an error message and does not execute the command. The following example creates a file using touch, sets **noclobber**, attempts to redirect the output from echo to the newly created file, unsets **noclobber**, and performs the same redirection:

```
$ touch tmp
$ set -o noclobber
$ echo "hi there" > tmp
-bash: tmp: cannot overwrite existing file
$ set +o noclobber
$ echo "hi there" > tmp
```

You can override **noclobber** by putting a pipe symbol after the redirect symbol (**>|**). In the following example, the user creates a file by redirecting the output of date. Next the user sets the **noclobber** variable and redirects output to the same file again. The shell displays an error message. Then the user places a pipe symbol after the redirect symbol, and the shell allows the user to overwrite the file.

```
$ date > tmp2
$ set -o noclobber
$ date > tmp2
-bash: tmp2: cannot overwrite existing file
$ date >| tmp2
```

APPENDING STANDARD OUTPUT TO A FILE

The *append output symbol* (>>) causes the shell to add new information to the end of a file, leaving existing information intact. This symbol provides a convenient way of catenating two files into one. The following commands demonstrate the action of the append output symbol. The second command accomplishes the catenation described in the preceding caution box:

```
$ cat orange
this is orange
$ cat pear >> orange
$ cat orange
this is orange
this is pear
```

The first command displays the contents of the **orange** file. The second command appends the contents of the **pear** file to the **orange** file. The final command displays the result.

Do not trust noclobber

caution   Appending output is simpler than the two-step procedure described in the preceding caution box, but you must be careful to include both greater than signs. If you accidentally use only one greater than sign and the **noclobber** feature is not set, the shell will overwrite the **orange** file. Even if you have the **noclobber** feature turned on, it is a good idea to keep backup copies of the files you are manipulating in case you make a mistake.

Although it protects you from overwriting a file using redirection, **noclobber** does not stop you from overwriting a file using cp or mv. These utilities include the **–i** (interactive) option that helps protect you from this type of mistake by verifying your intentions when you try to overwrite a file. For more information see the tip "cp can destroy a file" on page 150.

Figure 7-11 shows how to create a file that contains the date and time (the output from date), followed by a list of who is logged in (the output from who). The first command in the example redirects the output from date to the file named **whoson**. Then cat displays the file. The next command appends the output from who to the **whoson** file. Finally cat displays the file containing the output of both utilities.

```
$ date > whoson
$ cat whoson
Sun Mar 27 14:31:18 PST 2011
$ who >> whoson
$ cat whoson
Sun Mar 27 14:31:18 PST 2011
sam        tty1         2011-03-27 05:00(:0)
max        pts/4        2011-03-27 12:23(:0.0)
max        pts/5        2011-03-27 12:33(:0.0)
zach       pts/7        2011-03-26 08:45 (172.16.192.1)
```

Figure 7-11   Redirecting and appending output

/dev/null: MAKING DATA DISAPPEAR

The **/dev/null** device is a *data sink*, commonly referred to as a *bit bucket*. You can redirect output you do not want to keep or see to **/dev/null**, and the output will disappear without a trace:

```
$ echo "hi there" > /dev/null
$
```

When you read from **/dev/null**, you get a null string. The following command truncates the file named **messages** to zero length while preserving the ownership and permissions of the file:

```
$ ls -lh messages
-rw-rw-r--. 1 sam pubs 125K 03-16 14:30 messages
$ cat /dev/null > messages
$ ls -lh messages
-rw-rw-r--. 1 sam pubs 0 03-16 14:32 messages
```

See also page 503.

PIPES

The shell uses a *pipe* to connect standard output of one command to standard input of another command. A pipe (sometimes referred to as a *pipeline*) has the same effect as redirecting standard output of one command to a file and then using that file as standard input to another command. A pipe does away with separate commands and the intermediate file. The symbol for a pipe is a vertical bar (|). The syntax of a command line using a pipe is

command_a [arguments] | command_b [arguments]

The preceding command line uses a pipe on a single command line to generate the same result as the following three command lines:

command_a [arguments] > temp
command_b [arguments] < temp
rm temp

In the preceding sequence of commands, the first line redirects standard output from *command_a* to an intermediate file named *temp*. The second line redirects standard input for *command_b* to come from *temp*. The final line deletes *temp*. The command using a pipe is not only easier to type but is generally more efficient because it does not create a temporary file.

tr   You can use a pipe with any of the Linux utilities that accept input either from a file specified on the command line or from standard input. You can also use pipes with commands that accept input only from standard input. For example, the tr (translate) utility takes its input from standard input only. In its simplest usage tr has the following format:

tr string1 string2

```
$ ls > temp
$ lpr temp
$ rm temp

or

$ ls | lpr
```

Figure 7-12   A pipe

The tr utility accepts input from standard input and looks for characters that match one of the characters in *string1*. Upon finding a match, it translates the matched character in *string1* to the corresponding character in *string2*. (The first character in *string1* translates into the first character in *string2*, and so forth.) The tr utility sends its output to standard output. In both of the following examples, tr displays the contents of the **abstract** file with the letters **a**, **b**, and **c** translated into **A**, **B**, and **C**, respectively:

```
$ cat abstract | tr abc ABC
$ tr abc ABC < abstract
```

The tr utility does not change the contents of the original file; it cannot change the original file because it does not "know" the source of its input.

lpr   The lpr (line printer) utility also accepts input from either a file or standard input. When you type the name of a file following lpr on the command line, it places that file in the print queue. When you do not specify a filename on the command line, lpr takes input from standard input. This feature enables you to use a pipe to redirect input to lpr. The first set of commands in Figure 7-12 shows how you can use ls and lpr with an intermediate file (**temp**) to send a list of the files in the working directory to the printer. If the **temp** file exists, the first command overwrites its contents. The second set of commands uses a pipe to send the same list (with the exception of **temp**) to the printer.

sort   The commands in Figure 7-13 redirect the output from the who utility to **temp** and then display this file in sorted order. The sort utility (page 154) takes its input from the file specified on the command line or, when a file is not specified, from standard input; it sends its output to standard output. The sort command line in Figure 7-13 takes its input from standard input, which is redirected (<) to come from **temp**. The output that sort sends to the screen lists the users in sorted (alphabetical) order.

Because sort can take its input from standard input or from a filename on the command line, omitting the < symbol from Figure 7-13 yields the same result.

Figure 7-14 achieves the same result without creating the **temp** file. Using a pipe, the shell redirects the output from who to the input of sort. The sort utility takes input from standard input because no filename follows it on the command line.

grep   When many people are using the system and you want information about only one of them, you can send the output from who to grep (page 152) using a pipe.

```
$ who > temp
$ sort < temp
max        pts/4        2011-03-24 12:23
max        pts/5        2011-03-24 12:33
sam        tty1         2011-03-24 05:00
zach       pts/7        2011-03-23 08:45
$ rm temp
```

Figure 7-13   Using a temporary file to store intermediate results

The grep utility displays the line containing the string you specify—**sam** in the following example:

```
$ who | grep 'sam'
sam        tty1         2011-03-24 05:00
```

less and more   Another way of handling output that is too long to fit on the screen, such as a list of files in a crowded directory, is to use a pipe to send the output through less or more (both on page 149).

```
$ ls | less
```

The less utility displays text one screen at a time. To view another screen, press the SPACE bar. To view one more line, press RETURN. Press **h** for help and **q** to quit.

Some utilities change the format of their output when you redirect it. Compare the output of ls by itself and when you send it through a pipe to less.

FILTERS

A *filter* is a command that processes an input stream of data to produce an output stream of data. A command line that includes a filter uses a pipe to connect standard output of one command to the filter's standard input. Another pipe connects the filter's standard output to standard input of another command. Not all utilities can be used as filters.

In the following example, sort is a filter, taking standard input from standard output of who and using a pipe to redirect standard output to standard input of lpr. This command line sends the sorted output of who to the printer:

```
$ who | sort | lpr
```

The preceding example demonstrates the power of the shell combined with the versatility of Linux utilities. The three utilities who, sort, and lpr were not specifically

```
$ who | sort
max        pts/4        2011-03-24 12:23
max        pts/5        2011-03-24 12:33
sam        tty1         2011-03-24 05:00
zach       pts/7        2011-03-23 08:45
```

Figure 7-14   A pipe doing the work of a temporary file

```
$ who | tee who.out | grep sam
sam          tty1          2011-03-24 05:00
$ cat who.out
sam          tty1          2011-03-24 05:00
max          pts/4         2011-03-24 12:23
max          pts/5         2011-03-24 12:33
zach         pts/7         2011-03-23 08:45
```

Figure 7-15   tee sends its output to a file and to standard output

designed to work with each other, but they all use standard input and standard output in the conventional way. By using the shell to handle input and output, you can piece standard utilities together on the command line to achieve the results you want.

tee: SENDS OUTPUT IN TWO DIRECTIONS

The tee utility copies its standard input both to a file and to standard output. This utility is aptly named: It takes a single stream of input and sends the output in two directions. In Figure 7-15 the output of who is sent via a pipe to standard input of tee. The tee utility saves a copy of standard input in a file named **who.out** and also sends a copy to standard output. Standard output of tee goes via a pipe to standard input of grep, which displays only those lines containing the string **sam**. Use the **–a** (append) option to cause tee to append to a file instead of overwriting it.

RUNNING A COMMAND IN THE BACKGROUND

Foreground   All commands up to this point have been run in the foreground. When you run a command in the *foreground,* the shell waits for it to finish before displaying another prompt and allowing you to continue. When you run a command in the *background,* you do not have to wait for the command to finish before running another command.

Jobs   A *job* is a series of one or more commands that can be connected by pipes. You can have only one foreground job in a window or on a screen, but you can have many background jobs. By running more than one job at a time, you are using one of Linux's important features: multitasking. Running a command in the background can be useful when the command will run for a long time and does not need supervision. It leaves the screen free so you can use it for other work. Alternatively, when you are using a GUI, you can open another window to run another job.

Job number,   To run a command in the background, type an ampersand (**&**) just before the RETURN
PID number   that ends the command line. The shell assigns a small number to the job and displays this *job number* between brackets. Following the job number, the shell displays the *process identification (PID) number*—a larger number assigned by the operating system. Each of these numbers identifies the command running in the background. The shell then displays another prompt, and you can enter another command. When the

background job finishes, the shell displays a message giving both the job number and the command line used to run the command.

The next example runs in the background; it sends the output of ls through a pipe to lpr, which sends it to the printer.

```
$ ls -l | lpr &
[1] 22092
$
```

The [1] following the command line indicates that the shell has assigned job number 1 to this job. The **22092** is the PID number of the first command in the job. When this background job completes execution, you see the message

```
[1]+ Done            ls -l | lpr
```

(In place of ls –l, the shell might display something similar to ls ––color=auto –l. This difference is due to the fact that ls is aliased [page 334] to ls ––color=auto.)

MOVING A JOB FROM THE FOREGROUND TO THE BACKGROUND

CONTROL-Z and bg — You can suspend a foreground job (stop it from running) by pressing the suspend key, usually CONTROL-Z. The shell then stops the process and disconnects standard input from the keyboard. You can put a suspended job in the background and restart it by using the bg command followed by the job number. You do not need to specify the job number when there is only one suspended job.

fg — Only the foreground job can take input from the keyboard. To connect the keyboard to a program running in the background, you must bring it to the foreground. To do so, type **fg** without any arguments when only one job is in the background. When more than one job is in the background, type **fg**, or a percent sign (%), followed by the number of the job you want to bring into the foreground. The shell displays the command you used to start the job (**promptme** in the following example), and you can enter any input the program requires to continue:

```
bash $ fg 1
promptme
```

Redirect the output of a job you run in the background to keep it from interfering with whatever you are working on in the foreground (on the screen). Refer to "Separating and Grouping Commands" on page 292 for more detail about background tasks.

kill: ABORTING A BACKGROUND JOB

The interrupt key (usually CONTROL-C) cannot abort a background process; you must use kill (page 470) for this purpose. Follow **kill** on the command line with either the PID number of the process you want to abort or a percent sign (%) followed by the job number.

Determining the PID of a process using ps

If you forget a PID number, you can use the ps (process status) utility (page 317) to display it. The following example runs a **tail –f outfile** command (the **–f** [follow] option causes tail to watch **outfile** and display new lines as they are written to the file) as a background job, uses ps to display the PID number of the process, and aborts the job with kill:

```
$ tail -f outfile &
[1] 18228
$ ps | grep tail
18228 pts/4    00:00:00 tail
$ kill 18228
[1]+  Terminated              tail -f outfile
$
```

Determining the number of a job using jobs

If you forget a job number, you can use the jobs command to display a list of job numbers. The next example is similar to the previous one except it uses the job number instead of the PID number to identify the job to be killed. Sometimes the message saying the job is terminated does not appear until you press RETURN after the RETURN that executes the kill command.

```
$ tail -f outfile &
[1] 18236
$ bigjob &
[2] 18237
$ jobs
[1]-  Running                 tail -f outfile &
[2]+  Running                 bigjob &
$ kill %1
$ RETURN
[1]-  Terminated              tail -f outfile
$
```

FILENAME GENERATION/PATHNAME EXPANSION

Wildcards, globbing

When you give the shell abbreviated filenames that contain *special characters*, also called *metacharacters*, the shell can generate filenames that match the names of existing files. These special characters are also referred to as *wildcards* because they act much as the jokers do in a deck of cards. When one of these characters appears in an argument on the command line, the shell expands that argument in sorted order into a list of filenames and passes the list to the program called by the command line. Filenames that contain these special characters are called *ambiguous file references* because they do not refer to one specific file. The process that the shell performs on these filenames is called *pathname expansion* or *globbing*.

Ambiguous file references refer to a group of files with similar names quickly, saving the effort of typing the names individually. They can also help find a file whose name you do not remember in its entirety. If no filename matches the ambiguous file reference, the shell generally passes the unexpanded reference—special characters and all—to the command.

THE ? SPECIAL CHARACTER

The question mark (?) is a special character that causes the shell to generate filenames. It matches any single character in the name of an existing file. The following command uses this special character in an argument to the lpr utility:

```
$ lpr memo?
```

The shell expands the **memo?** argument and generates a list of files in the working directory that have names composed of **memo** followed by any single character. The shell then passes this list to lpr. The lpr utility never "knows" the shell generated the filenames it was called with. If no filename matches the ambiguous file reference, the shell passes the string itself (**memo?**) to lpr or, if it is set up to do so, passes a null string (see **nullglob** on page 343).

The following example uses ls first to display the names of all files in the working directory and then to display the filenames that **memo?** matches:

```
$ ls
mem    memo12  memo9  memomax  newmemo5
memo   memo5   memoa  memos

$ ls memo?
memo5   memo9   memoa   memos
```

The **memo?** ambiguous file reference does not match **mem, memo, memo12, memomax,** or **newmemo5.** You can also use a question mark in the middle of an ambiguous file reference:

```
$ ls
7may4report  may4report     mayqreport  may_report
may14report  may4report.79  mayreport   may.report

$ ls may?report
may4report   mayqreport   may_report   may.report
```

echo   You can use echo and ls to practice generating filenames. The echo utility displays the arguments that the shell passes to it:

```
$ echo may?report
may4report mayqreport may_report may.report
```

The shell first expands the ambiguous file reference into a list of all files in the working directory that match the string **may?report**. It then passes this list to echo, just as though you had entered the list of filenames as arguments to echo. The echo utility displays the list of filenames.

A question mark does not match a leading period (one that indicates a hidden filename; see page 190). When you want to match filenames that begin with a period, you must explicitly include the period in the ambiguous file reference.

THE * SPECIAL CHARACTER

The asterisk (*) performs a function similar to that of the question mark but matches any number of characters, *including zero characters,* in a filename. The following example first shows all files in the working directory and then shows commands that display all the filenames that begin with the string **memo**, end with the string **mo**, and contain the string **alx**:

```
$ ls
amemo    memalx   memo.0612   memoalx.0620   memorandum   sallymemo
mem      memo     memoa       memoalx.keep   memosally    user.memo

$ echo memo*
memo memo.0612 memoa memoalx.0620 memoalx.keep memorandum memosally

$ echo *mo
amemo memo sallymemo user.memo

$ echo *alx*
memalx memoalx.0620 memoalx.keep
```

The ambiguous file reference **memo*** does not match **amemo, mem, sallymemo,** or **user.memo**. Like the question mark, an asterisk does *not* match a leading period in a filename.

The –a option causes ls to display hidden filenames. The command **echo *** does not display . (the working directory), .. (the parent of the working directory), **.aaa**, or **.profile**. In contrast, the command **echo .*** displays only those four names:

```
$ ls
aaa  memo.0612  memo.sally  report  sally.0612  saturday  thurs

$ ls -a
.    aaa    memo.0612    .profile  sally.0612  thurs
..   .aaa   memo.sally   report    saturday

$ echo *
aaa memo.0612 memo.sally report sally.0612 saturday thurs

$ echo .*
. .. .aaa .profile
```

In the following example, **.p*** does not match **memo.0612, private, reminder,** or **report**. The ls **.*** command causes ls to list **.private** and **.profile** in addition to the contents of the . directory (the working directory) and the .. directory (the parent of the working directory). When called with the same argument, echo displays the names of files (including directories) in the working directory that begin with a dot (.) but not the contents of directories.

```
$ ls -a
.  ..  memo.0612  private  .private  .profile  reminder  report
```

```
$ echo .p*
.private .profile

$ ls .*
.private .profile
.:
memo.0612   private      reminder    report
..:
...

$ echo .*
. .. .private .profile
```

You can plan to take advantage of ambiguous file references when you establish conventions for naming files. For example, when you end the names of all text files with **.txt**, you can reference that group of files with ***.txt**. The next command uses this convention to send all text files in the working directory to the printer. The ampersand causes lpr to run in the background.

```
$ lpr *.txt &
```

THE [ ] SPECIAL CHARACTERS

A pair of brackets surrounding a list of characters causes the shell to match filenames containing the individual characters. Whereas **memo?** matches **memo** followed by any character, **memo[17a]** is more restrictive: It matches only **memo1**, **memo7**, and **memoa**. The brackets define a *character class* that includes all the characters within the brackets. (GNU calls this a *character list*; a GNU *character class* is something different.) The shell expands an argument that includes a character-class definition by substituting each member of the character class, *one at a time*, in place of the brackets and their contents. The shell then passes the list of matching filenames to the program it is calling.

Each character-class definition can replace only a single character within a filename. The brackets and their contents are like a question mark that substitutes only the members of the character class.

The first of the following commands lists the names of all files in the working directory that begin with **a**, **e**, **i**, **o**, or **u**. The second command displays the contents of the files named **page2.txt**, **page4.txt**, **page6.txt**, and **page8.txt**.

```
$ echo [aeiou]*
...

$ less page[2468].txt
...
```

A hyphen within brackets defines a range of characters within a character-class definition. For example, [6–9] represents [6789], [a–z] represents all lowercase letters in English, and [a–zA–Z] represents all letters, both uppercase and lowercase, in English.

The following command lines show three ways to print the files named **part0**, **part1**, **part2**, **part3**, and **part5**. Each of these command lines causes the shell to call lpr with five filenames:

```
$ lpr part0 part1 part2 part3 part5
```

```
$ lpr part[01235]
```

```
$ lpr part[0-35]
```

The first command line explicitly specifies the five filenames. The second and third command lines use ambiguous file references, incorporating character-class definitions. The shell expands the argument on the second command line to include all files that have names beginning with **part** and ending with any of the characters in the character class. The character class is explicitly defined as 0, 1, 2, 3, and 5. The third command line also uses a character-class definition but defines the character class to be all characters in the range 0–3 plus 5.

The following command line prints 39 files, **part0** through **part38**:

```
$ lpr part[0-9] part[12][0-9] part3[0-8]
```

The first of the following commands lists the files in the working directory whose names start with **a** through **m**. The second lists files whose names end with **x**, **y**, or **z**.

```
$ echo [a-m]*
...
```

```
$ echo *[x-z]
...
```

optional When an exclamation point (!) or a caret (^) immediately follows the opening bracket ([) that defines a character class, the string enclosed by the brackets matches any character *not* between the brackets. Thus [^tsq]* matches any filename that does *not* begin with t, s, or q.

The following examples show that *[^ab] matches filenames that do not end with the letters a or b and that [^b-d]* matches filenames that do not begin with b, c, or d.

```
$ ls
aa  ab  ac  ad  ba  bb  bc  bd  cc  dd
```

```
$ ls *[^ab]
ac  ad  bc  bd  cc  dd
```

```
$ ls [^b-d]*
aa  ab  ac  ad
```

You can cause a character class to match a hyphen (–) or a closing bracket (]) by placing it immediately before the final closing bracket.

The next example demonstrates that the ls utility cannot interpret ambiguous file references. First ls is called with an argument of **?old**. The shell expands **?old** into a matching filename, **hold**, and passes that name to ls. The second command is the same as the first, except the **?** is quoted (by preceding it with a backslash [\]; refer to "Special Characters" on page 146). Because the **?** is quoted, the shell does not recognize it as a special character and passes it to ls. The ls utility generates an error message saying that it cannot find a file named **?old** (because there is no file named **?old**).

```
$ ls ?old
hold

$ ls \?old
ls: ?old: No such file or directory
```

Like most utilities and programs, ls cannot interpret ambiguous file references; that work is left to the shell.

The shell expands ambiguous file references

tip *The shell does the expansion* when it processes an ambiguous file reference, not the program that the shell runs. In the examples in this section, *the utilities* (ls, cat, echo, lpr) *never see the ambiguous file references.* The shell expands the ambiguous file references and passes a list of ordinary filenames to the utility. In the previous examples, echo demonstrates this fact because it simply displays its arguments; it never displays the ambiguous file reference.

BUILTINS

A *builtin* is a utility (also called a *command*) that is built into a shell. Each of the shells has its own set of builtins. When it runs a builtin, the shell does not fork a new process. Consequently builtins run more quickly and can affect the environment of the current shell. Because builtins are used in the same way as utilities, you will not typically be aware of whether a utility is built into the shell or is a stand-alone utility.

The echo utility, for example, is a shell builtin. The shell always executes a shell builtin before trying to find a command or utility with the same name. See page 1018 for an in-depth discussion of builtin commands and page 1031 for a list of bash builtins.

Listing bash builtins
To display a list of bash builtins, give the command **info bash shell builtin**. To display a page with information on each builtin, move the cursor to **Bash Builtins** line and press RETURN. Because bash was written by GNU, the info page has better information than does the man page. If you want to read about builtins in the man page, give the command **man bash** and search for the section on builtins with the command **/^SHELL BUILT** (search for a line that begins with **SHELL BUILT**).

CHAPTER SUMMARY

The shell is the Linux command interpreter. It scans the command line for proper syntax, picking out the command name and any arguments. The first argument is argument one, the second is argument two, and so on. The name of the command itself is argument zero. Many programs use options to modify the effects of a command. Most Linux utilities identify an option by its leading one or two hyphens.

When you give it a command, the shell tries to find an executable program with the same name as the command. When it does, the shell executes the program. When it does not, the shell tells you it cannot find or execute the program. If the command is a simple filename, the shell searches the directories listed in the **PATH** variable to locate the command.

When it executes a command, the shell assigns one file or device to the command's standard input and another file to its standard output. By default the shell causes a command's standard input to come from the keyboard and its standard output to go to the screen. You can instruct the shell to redirect a command's standard input from or standard output to any file or device. You can also connect standard output of one command to standard input of another command using a pipe. A filter is a command that reads its standard input from standard output of one command and writes its standard output to standard input of another command.

When a command runs in the foreground, the shell waits for it to finish before it displays a prompt and allows you to continue. When you put an ampersand (&) at the end of a command line, the shell executes the command in the background and displays another prompt immediately. Run slow commands in the background when you want to enter other commands at the shell prompt. The jobs builtin displays a list of suspended jobs and jobs running in the background and includes the job number of each.

The shell interprets special characters on a command line to generate filenames. A question mark represents any single character, and an asterisk represents zero or more characters. A single character might also be represented by a character class: a list of characters within brackets. A reference that uses special characters (wildcards) to abbreviate a list of one or more filenames is called an ambiguous file reference.

A builtin is a utility that is built into a shell. Each shell has its own set of builtins. When it runs a builtin, the shell does not fork a new process. Consequently builtins run more quickly and can affect the environment of the current shell.

UTILITIES AND BUILTINS INTRODUCED IN THIS CHAPTER

Table 7-1 lists the utilities introduced in this chapter.

Table 7-1   New utilities

Utility	Function
tr	Maps one string of characters to another (page 239)
tee	Sends standard input to both a file and standard output (page 242)
bg	Moves a process to the background (page 243)
fg	Moves a process to the foreground (page 243)
jobs	Displays a list of suspended jobs and jobs running in the background (page 244)

Exercises

1. What does the shell ordinarily do while a command is executing? What should you do if you do not want to wait for a command to finish before running another command?

2. Using sort as a filter, rewrite the following sequence of commands:

```
$ sort list > temp
$ lpr temp
$ rm temp
```

3. What is a PID number? Why are these numbers useful when you run processes in the background? Which utility displays the PID numbers of the commands you are running?

4. Assume that the following files are in the working directory:

```
$ ls
intro      notesb     ref2       section1     section3     section4b
notesa     ref1       ref3       section2     section4a    sentrev
```

Give commands for each of the following, using wildcards to express filenames with as few characters as possible.

a. List all files that begin with section.

b. List the section1, section2, and section3 files only.

c. List the intro file only.

d. List the section1, section3, ref1, and ref3 files.

5. Refer to the info or man pages to determine which command will

   a. Display the number of lines in the standard input that contain the *word* a or **A**.

   b. Display only the names of the files in the working directory that contain the pattern **$(**.

   c. List the files in the working directory in reverse alphabetical order.

   d. Send a list of files in the working directory to the printer, sorted by size.

6. Give a command to

   a. Redirect standard output from a sort command to a file named **phone_list**. Assume the input file is named **numbers**.

   b. Translate all occurrences of the characters [and { to the character (, and all occurrences of the characters] and } to the character) in the file **permdemos.c**. (*Hint:* Refer to the tr man page.)

   c. Create a file named **book** that contains the contents of two other files: **part1** and **part2**.

7. The lpr and sort utilities accept input either from a file named on the command line or from standard input.

   a. Name two other utilities that function in a similar manner.

   b. Name a utility that accepts its input only from standard input.

8. Give an example of a command that uses grep

   a. With both input and output redirected.

   b. With only input redirected.

   c. With only output redirected.

   d. Within a pipe.

   In which of the preceding cases is grep used as a filter?

9. Explain the following error message. Which filenames would a subsequent ls display?

   ```
   $ ls
   abc  abd  abe  abf  abg  abh
   $ rm abc ab*
   rm: cannot remove 'abc': No such file or directory
   ```

ADVANCED EXERCISES

10. When you use the redirect output symbol (>) with a command, the shell creates the output file immediately, before the command is executed. Demonstrate that this is true.

11. In experimenting with shell variables, Max accidentally deletes his **PATH** variable. He decides he does not need the **PATH** variable. Discuss some of the problems he could soon encounter and explain the reasons for these problems. How could he *easily* return **PATH** to its original value?

12. Assume permissions on a file allow you to write to the file but not to delete it.

    a. Give a command to empty the file without invoking an editor.

    b. Explain how you might have permission to modify a file that you cannot delete.

13. If you accidentally create a filename that contains a nonprinting character, such as a CONTROL character, how can you remove the file?

14. Why does the **noclobber** variable *not* protect you from overwriting an existing file with cp or mv?

15. Why do command names and filenames usually not have embedded SPACEs? How would you create a filename containing a SPACE? How would you remove it? (This is a thought exercise, not recommended practice. If you want to experiment, create and work in a directory that contains only your experimental file.)

16. Create a file named **answer** and give the following command:

    ```
    $ > answers.0102 < answer cat
    ```

    Explain what the command does and why. What is a more conventional way of expressing this command?

PART III
Digging into Fedora/RHEL

8

LINUX GUIs: X AND GNOME

OBJECTIVES

After reading this chapter you should be able to:

▶ Describe the history of the X Window System

▶ Start X from a character-based display

▶ Use X remotely across a network

▶ Customize the mouse buttons in the X Window System using the command line

▶ Explain the similarities, differences, and history of GNOME and KDE desktops

▶ Use the Nautilus File Browser

▶ Start a terminal emulator and run a graphical program from the emulator

▶ Search for files using the Search for Files window

This chapter covers the Linux graphical user interface (GUI). It continues where Chapter 4 left off, going into more detail about the X Window System, the basis for the Linux GUI. It presents a brief history of GNOME and KDE and discusses some of the problems and benefits of having two major Linux desktop environments. The section on the Nautilus File Browser covers the View pane, Sidebar, Main toolbar, menubar, and Spatial view. The final section explores some GNOME utilities, including Terminal, the GNOME terminal emulator.

X WINDOW SYSTEM

History of X   The X Window System (www.x.org) was created in 1984 at the Massachusetts Institute of Technology (MIT) by researchers working on a distributed computing project and a campuswide distributed environment, called Project Athena. This system was not the first windowing software to run on a UNIX system, but it was the first to become widely available and accepted. In 1985, MIT released X (version 9) to the public, for use without a license. Three years later, a group of vendors formed the X Consortium to support the continued development of X, under the leadership of MIT. By 1998, the X Consortium had become part of the Open Group. In 2001, the Open Group released X version 11, release 6.6 (X11R6.6).

The X Window System was inspired by the ideas and features found in earlier proprietary window systems but is written to be portable and flexible. X is designed to run on a workstation, typically attached to a LAN. The designers built X with the network in mind. If you can communicate with a remote computer over a network, running an X application on that computer and sending the results to a local display is straightforward.

Although the X protocol has remained stable for a long time, additions to it in the form of extensions are quite common. One of the most interesting—albeit one that has not yet made its way into production—is the Media Application Server, which aims to provide the same level of network transparency for sound and video that X does for simple windowing applications.

XFree86 and X.org   Many distributions of Linux used the XFree86 X server, which inherited its license from the original MIT X server, through release 4.3. In early 2004, just before the release of XFree86 4.4, the XFree86 license was changed to one that is more restrictive and not compatible with the GPL (page 5). In the wake of this change, a number of distributions abandoned XFree86 and replaced it with an X.org X server that is based on a pre-release version of XFree86 4.4, which predates the change in the XFree86 license. Fedora/RHEL uses the X.org X server, named Xorg; it is functionally equivalent to the one distributed by XFree86 because most of the code is the same. Thus modules designed to work with one server work with the other.

The X stack   The Linux GUI is built in layers (Figure 8-1). The bottom layer is the kernel, which provides the basic interfaces to the hardware. On top of the kernel is the X server, which is responsible for managing windows and drawing basic graphical primitives such as lines and bitmaps. Rather than directly generating X commands, most programs use Xlib, the next layer, which is a standard library for interfacing with an X

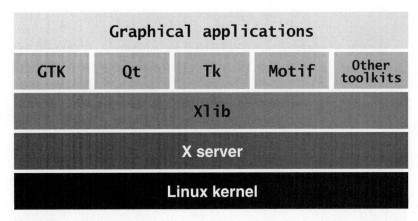

Figure 8-1 The X stack

server. Xlib is complicated and does not provide high-level abstractions, such as buttons and text boxes. Rather than using Xlib directly, most programs rely on a toolkit that provides high-level abstractions. Using a library not only makes programming easier, but also brings consistency to applications.

In recent years, the popularity of X has grown outside the UNIX community and extended beyond the workstation class of computers it was originally conceived for. Today X is available for Macintosh computers as well as for PCs running Windows.

Client/server environment Computer networks are central to the design of X. It is possible to run an application on one computer and display the results on a screen attached to a different computer; the ease with which this can be done distinguishes X from other window systems available today. Thanks to this capability, a scientist can run and manipulate a program on a powerful supercomputer in another building or another country and view the results on a personal workstation or laptop computer. For more information refer to "Remote Computing and Local Displays" on page 260.

When you start an X Window System session, you set up a *client/server environment*. One process, called the *X server*, displays a desktop and windows under X. Each application program and utility that makes a request of the X server is a *client* of that server. Examples of X clients include xterm, Compiz, gnome-calculator, and such general applications as word processing and spreadsheet programs. A typical request from a client is to display an image or open a window.

The roles of X client and server might be counterintuitive

tip The terms *client* and *server,* when referring to X, have the opposite meanings of how you might think of them intuitively: The server runs the mouse, keyboard, and display; the application program is the client.

This disparity becomes even more apparent when you run an application program on a remote system. You might think of the system running the program as the server and the system providing the display as the client, but in fact it is the other way around. With X, the system providing the display is the server, and the system running the program is the client.

Events The server also monitors keyboard and mouse actions (*events*) and passes them to the appropriate clients. For example, when you click the border of a window, the server sends this event to the window manager (client). Characters you type into a terminal emulation window are sent to that terminal emulator (client). The client takes appropriate action when it receives an event—for example, making a window active or displaying the typed character on the server.

Separating the physical control of the display (the server) from the processes needing access to the display (the client) makes it possible to run the server on one computer and the client on another computer. Most of the time, this book discusses running the X server and client applications on a single system. "Remote Computing and Local Displays" describes using X in a distributed environment.

optional You can run xev (X event) by giving the command **xev** from a terminal emulator window and then watch the information flow from the client to the server and back again. This utility opens the Event Tester window, which has a box in it, and asks the X server to send it events each time anything happens, such as moving the mouse pointer, clicking a mouse button, moving the mouse pointer into the box, typing, or resizing the window. The xev utility displays information about each event in the window you opened it from. You can use xev as an educational tool: Start it and see how much information is processed each time you move the mouse. Close the Event Tester window to exit from xev.

USING X

This section provides basic information about starting and configuring X from the command line. For more information see the Xserver man page and the man pages listed at the bottom of the Xserver man page.

STARTING X FROM A CHARACTER-BASED DISPLAY

Once you have logged in on a virtual console (page 138), you can start an X Window System server by using startx. See "Setting the Persistent Runlevel" on page 432 for instructions on setting Fedora to boot to single-user/rescue mode (specify a target of **rescue.target**) where it displays a textual interface. See "rcS task and **inittab**" on page 442 for information on changing the **initdefault** entry in the /etc/inittab file under RHEL that causes Linux to boot into single-user mode, where it displays a textual interface. When you run startx, the X server displays an X screen, using the first available virtual console. The following command causes startx to run in the background so you can switch back to this virtual console and give other commands:

```
$ startx &
```

REMOTE COMPUTING AND LOCAL DISPLAYS

Typically the X server and the X client run on the same machine. To identify a remote X server (display) an X client (application) is to use, you can either set a global shell variable or use a command-line option. Before you can connect to a remote X server, you must turn off two security features: You must turn off the Xorg –nolisten tcp option on the server and you must run xhost on the server to give the client permission to connect to the X server. You also need to disable the firewall or open TCP port 6000 (page 893). Unless you have a reason to leave these features off, turn them back on when you finish with the examples in this section—leaving them off weakens system security. These tasks must be performed on the X server because the features protect the server. You do not have to prepare the client. The examples in this section assume the server is named **tiny** and the client is named **dog**.

Security and the Xorg **–nolisten tcp option**

security In a production environment, if you need to place an X server and the clients on different systems, it is best to forward (tunnel) X over ssh. This setup provides a secure, encrypted connection. The method described in this section is useful on local, secure networks and for understanding how X works. See "Forwarding X11" on page 696 for information on setting up ssh so it forwards X.

THE X –nolisten tcp OPTION

As Fedora/RHEL is installed, the X server starts with the **–nolisten tcp** option, which protects the X server by preventing TCP connections to the X server. To connect to a remote X server, you must turn this option off on the server. To turn it off, while working with **root** privileges edit the file named **/etc/gdm/custom.conf** and add the following lines:

```
max@tiny:~$ cat /etc/gdm/custom.conf
[security]
DisallowTCP=false
```

Reboot the system to restart the X server and gdm (gdm-binary) to effect this change. Use the command **ps –ef | grep Xorg** to display the options the X server is running with. See library.gnome.org/admin/gdm/3.0/configuration.html.en#daemonconfig for more information.

xhost GRANTS ACCESS TO A DISPLAY

As installed, xhost protects each user's X server. A user who wants to grant access to his X server needs to run xhost. Assume Max is logged in on the system named **tiny** and wants to allow a user on **dog** to use his display (X server). Max runs this command:

```
max@tiny:~$ xhost +dog
dog being added to access control list
max@tiny:~$ xhost
access control enabled, only authorized clients can connect
INET:dog
...
```

Without any arguments, xhost describes its state. In the preceding example, **INET** indicates an IPv4 connection. If Max wants to allow all systems to access his display, he can give the following command:

```
$ xhost +
access control disabled, clients can connect from any host
```

If you frequently work with other users via a network, you might find it convenient to add an xhost line to your **.bash_profile** file (page 282)—but see the following tip regarding security and xhost. Be selective in granting access to your X display with xhost; if another system has access to your display, you might find your work frequently interrupted.

Security and xhost

security   Giving a remote system access to your display using xhost means any user on the remote system can watch everything you type in a terminal emulation window, including passwords. For this reason, some software packages, such as the Tcl/Tk development system (www.tcl.tk), restrict their own capabilities when xhost permits remote access to the X server. If you are concerned about security or want to take full advantage of systems such as Tcl/Tk, you should use a safer means of granting remote access to your X session. See the xauth man page for information about a more secure replacement for xhost.

THE DISPLAY VARIABLE

The most common method of identifying a display is to use the **DISPLAY** shell environment variable to hold the X server ID string. This locally unique identification string is automatically set up when the X server starts. The **DISPLAY** variable holds the screen number of a display:

```
$ echo $DISPLAY
:0.0
```

The format of the complete (globally unique) ID string for a display is

[hostname]:display-number[.screen-number]

where *hostname* is the name of the system running the X server, *display-number* is the number of the logical (physical) display (0 unless multiple monitors or graphical terminals are attached to the system, or if you are running X over ssh), and *screen-number* is the logical number of the (virtual) terminal (0 unless you are running multiple instances of X). When you are working with a single physical screen, you can shorten the identification string. For example, you can use **tiny:0.0** or **tiny:0** to identify the only physical display on the system named **tiny**. When the X server and the X clients are running on the same system, you can shorten this identification string even further to :0.0 or :0. An ssh connection shows **DISPLAY** as **localhost:10.0**. You might have to use **ssh –X** to see this value. See "X11 forwarding" on page 675 for information on setting up ssh so it forwards X.

If **DISPLAY** is empty or not set, the screen you are working from is not running X. An application (the X client) uses the value of the **DISPLAY** variable to determine which display, keyboard, and mouse (collectively, the X server) to use. One way to run an X application, such as gnome-calculator, on the local system but have it use the X display on a remote system is to change the value of the **DISPLAY** variable on the client system so it identifies the remote X server.

```
sam@dog:~$ export DISPLAY=tiny:0.0
sam@dog:~$ gnome-calculator &
```

The preceding example shows Sam running gnome-calculator with the default X server running on the system named **tiny**. After setting the **DISPLAY** variable to the ID of the **tiny** server, all X programs (clients) Sam starts use **tiny** as their server (i.e., output appears on **tiny**'s display and input comes from **tiny**'s keyboard and mouse). Try running xterm in place of gnome-calculator and see which keyboard it accepts input from. If this example generates an error, refer to the two preceding sections, which explain how to set up the server to allow a remote system to connect to it.

When you change the value of DISPLAY

tip When you change the value of the **DISPLAY** variable, all X programs send their output to the new display named by **DISPLAY**.

THE –display OPTION

For a single command, you can usually specify the X server on the command line:

```
sam@dog:~$ gnome-calculator -display tiny:0.0
```

Many X programs accept the **–display** option. Those that do not accept this option send their output to the display specified by the **DISPLAY** variable.

RUNNING MULTIPLE X SERVERS

You can run multiple X servers on a single system. The most common reason for running a second X server is to use a second display that allocates a different number of bits to each screen pixel (uses a different *color depth* [page 1157]). The possible values are 8, 16, 24, and 32 bits per pixel. Most X servers available for Linux default to 24 or 32 bits per pixel, permitting the use of millions of colors simultaneously. Starting an X server with 8 bits per pixel permits the use of any combination of 256 colors at the same time. The maximum number of bits per pixel allowed depends on the computer graphics hardware and X server. With fewer bits per pixel, the system has to transfer less data, possibly making it more responsive. In addition, many games work with only 256 colors.

When you start multiple X servers, each must have a different ID string. The following command starts a second X server:

```
$ startx -- :1
```

The –– option marks the end of the startx options and arguments. The startx script uses the arguments to the left of this option and passes arguments to the right of this option to the X server. When you give the preceding command in a graphical environment, such as from a terminal emulator, you must work with **root** privileges; you will initiate a privileged X session. The following command starts a second X server running at 16 bits per pixel:

```
$ startx -- :1 -depth 16 &
```

"Using Virtual Consoles" on page 138 describes how to switch to a virtual console to start a second server where you do not have to work with **root** privileges.

Switch User   To allow another user to log on while you remain logged in as yourself, click your name at the upper-right corner of the screen and click **Switch User** from the menu GNOME displays (Fedora) or select **Main menu: System**⇨**Log Out** *username...* and click **Switch User** (RHEL). GNOME displays a login screen and another user can log on. When appropriate, that user can log off or switch users to allow you to log on and resume your session.

X over ssh   See "Tunneling/Port Forwarding" on page 696 for information about running X over an ssh connection.

STOPPING THE X SERVER

How you terminate a window manager depends on which window manager is running and how it is configured. If X stops responding, switch to a virtual terminal, log in from another terminal or a remote system, or use ssh to access the system. Then kill (page 470) the process running Xorg.

REMAPPING MOUSE BUTTONS

Throughout this book, each description of a mouse click refers to the button by its position (left, middle, or right, with left implied when no button is specified) because the position of a mouse button is more intuitive than an arbitrary name or number. X numbers buttons starting at the left and continuing with the mouse wheel. The buttons on a three-button mouse are numbered 1 (left), 2 (middle), and 3 (right). A mouse wheel, if present, is numbered 4 (rolling it up) and 5 (rolling it down). Clicking the wheel is equivalent to clicking the middle mouse button. The buttons on a two-button mouse are 1 (left) and 2 (right).

If you are right-handed, you can conveniently press the left mouse button with your index finger; X programs take advantage of this fact by relying on button 1 for the most common operations. If you are left-handed, your index finger rests most conveniently on button 2 or 3 (the right button on a two- or three-button mouse).

"Mouse Preferences" on page 101 describes how to use a GUI to change a mouse between right-handed and left-handed. You can also change how X interprets the mouse buttons using xmodmap. If you are left-handed and using a three-button mouse with a wheel, the following command causes X to interpret the right button as button 1 and the left button as button 3:

```
$ xmodmap -e 'pointer = 3 2 1 4 5'
```

Omit the 4 and 5 if the mouse does not have a wheel. The following command works for a two-button mouse without a wheel:

```
$ xmodmap -e 'pointer = 2 1'
```

If xmodmap displays a message complaining about the number of buttons, use the xmodmap –pp option to display the number of buttons X has defined for the mouse:

```
$ xmodmap -pp
There are 9 pointer buttons defined.
```

Physical Button	Button Code
1	1
2	2
3	3
4	4
5	5
6	6
7	7
8	8
9	9

Then expand the previous command, adding numbers to complete the list. If the **–pp** option shows nine buttons, give the following command:

```
$ xmodmap -e 'pointer = 3 2 1 4 5 6 7 8 9'
```

Changing the order of the first three buttons is critical to making the mouse suitable for a left-handed user. When you remap the mouse buttons, remember to reinterpret the descriptions in this book accordingly. When this book asks you to click the left button or does not specify which button to click, use the right button, and vice versa.

DESKTOP ENVIRONMENTS/MANAGERS

Conceptually X is very simple. As a consequence, it does not provide some of the more common features found in GUIs, such as the ability to drag windows. The UNIX/Linux philosophy is one of modularity: X relies on a window manager, such as Mutter, Metacity, or Compiz, to draw window borders and handle moving and resizing operations.

Unlike a window manager, which has a clearly defined task, a desktop environment (manager) does many things. In general, a desktop environment, such as GNOME or KDE, provides a means of launching applications and utilities, such as a file manager, that work with a window manager.

GNOME AND KDE

The KDE project began in 1996, with the aim of creating a consistent, user-friendly desktop environment for free UNIX-like operating systems. KDE is based on the Qt toolkit made by Trolltech. When KDE development began, the Qt license was not compatible with the GPL (page 5). For this reason the Free Software Foundation decided to support a different project, the GNU Network Object Model Environment (GNOME). More recently Qt has been released under the terms of the GPL, eliminating part of the rationale for GNOME's existence.

GNOME   GNOME is the default desktop environment for Fedora/RHEL. It provides a simple, coherent user interface that is suitable for corporate use. GNOME uses GTK for drawing widgets. GTK, developed for the GNU Image Manipulation Program (gimp), is written in C, although bindings for C++ and other languages are available.

GNOME does not take much advantage of its component architecture. Instead, it continues to support the traditional UNIX philosophy of relying on many small programs, each of which is good at doing a specific task.

KDE　KDE is written in C++ on top of the Qt framework. KDE tries to use existing technology, if it can be reused, but creates its own if nothing else is available or if a superior solution is needed. For example, KDE implemented an HTML rendering engine long before the Mozilla project was born. Similarly, work on KOffice began a long time before StarOffice became the open-source OpenOffice.org (which is now LibreOffice). In contrast, the GNOME office applications are stand-alone programs that originated outside the GNOME project. KDE's portability is demonstrated by the use of most of its core components, including Konqueror and KOffice, under Mac OS X.

Interoperability　Since the release of version 2, the GNOME project has focused on simplifying the user interface, removing options where they are deemed unnecessary, and aiming for a set of default settings that the end user will not wish to change. Fedora 15 introduced GNOME 3, which is radically different from GNOME 2, following the trend towards simpler, more graphical desktops that have more icons and fewer menus. KDE has moved in the opposite direction, emphasizing configurability.

The freedesktop.org group (freedesktop.org), whose members are drawn from the GNOME and KDE projects, is improving interoperability and aims to produce standards that will allow the two environments to work together. One standard released by freedesktop.org allows applications to use the notification area of either the GNOME or KDE panel without being aware of which desktop environment they are running in.

GNUStep

The GNUStep project (www.gnustep.org), which began before both the KDE and GNOME projects, is creating an open-source implementation of the OPENSTEP API and desktop environment. The result is a very clean and fast user interface.

The default look of WindowMaker, the GNUStep window manager, is somewhat dated, but it supports themes so you can customize its appearance. The user interface is widely regarded as one of the most intuitive found on a UNIX platform. Because GNUStep has less overhead than GNOME and KDE, it runs better on older hardware. If you are running Linux on hardware that struggles with GNOME and KDE or if you would prefer a user interface that does not attempt to mimic Windows, try GNUStep. WindowMaker is provided in the **WindowMaker** package.

THE NAUTILUS FILE BROWSER WINDOW

"Using Nautilus to Work with Files" on page 102 presented an introduction to using Nautilus. This section discusses the Nautilus File Browser window in more depth.

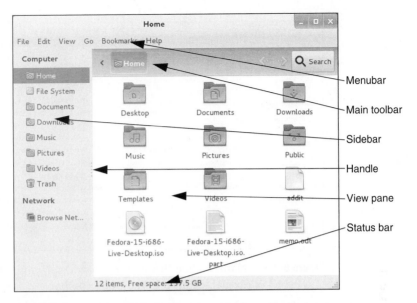

Figure 8-2   A Nautilus File Browser window displaying icons

RHEL: turn off Spatial view; turn on File Browser windows

tip   Under RHEL, to make the Nautilus windows on the desktop you are working on correspond to the figures in this book, you must turn off Spatial view (page 272) and turn on File Browser windows. For more information refer to "The Two Faces of Nautilus" on page 103.

Figure 8-2 shows a File Browser window with a Sidebar, View pane, menubar, Main toolbar, and status bar. To display your home folder in a File Browser window, select **Main menu: Places⇨Home Folder.**

THE VIEW PANE

The View pane displays icons or a list of filenames. Select the view you prefer from the bottom of the **File Browser menubar: View** menu. Figure 8-2 shows an Icon view and Figure 8-3 on the next page shows a List view. A Compact view is also available. Objects in the View pane behave exactly as objects on the desktop do. See the sections starting on page 95 for information on working with objects.

You can cut/copy and paste objects within a single View pane, between View panes, or between a View pane and the desktop. The Object context menu (right-click) has cut, copy, and paste selections. Alternatively, you can use the clipboard (page 116) to cut/copy and paste objects.

THE SIDEBAR

The Sidebar augments the information Nautilus displays in the View pane. You can close or display the Sidebar by pressing F9 or by selecting **File Browser menubar: View⇨Sidebar⇨Show Sidebar.** To change the horizontal size of the Sidebar, drag the handle (Figure 8-2) on its right side. The **File Browser menubar:**

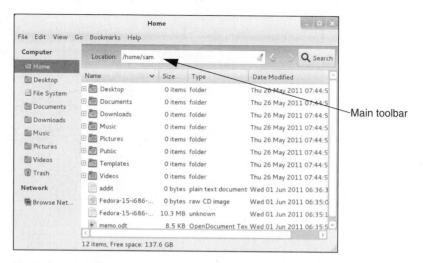

Figure 8-3 A Nautilus File Browser window displaying a List view and a textual location in the Main toolbar

View⇨Sidebar menu controls whether the Sidebar displays places or a file tree as described following.

Places Places lists folders, bookmarks, devices, and network locations. Double-click one of these places to display that place in the View pane. You can open a place in a new File Browser tab or window by right-clicking the directory in the Sidebar and selecting **Open in New Tab** or **Open in New Window**, respectively.

Add a bookmark by displaying the directory you want to bookmark in the View pane and pressing CONTROL-D or by selecting **File Browser menubar: Bookmarks⇨Add Bookmark**. Remove a bookmark by selecting **File Browser menubar: Bookmarks⇨ Edit Bookmarks** or by right-clicking the bookmark in the Sidebar and selecting **Remove**.

Tree Tree presents an expandable tree view of your home folder and each mounted filesystem. Each directory in the tree has a plus (**+**) or minus (**–**) sign to its left. Click a plus sign to expand a directory; click a minus sign to close a directory. Click a directory in the tree to display that directory in the View pane. Double-click a directory to expand or close it in the Sidebar and display it in the View pane.

Nautilus can open a terminal emulator

tip When you install the **nautilus-open-terminal** package (see page 534 for instructions) and log out and log back in, Nautilus presents an Open in Terminal selection in context menus where appropriate. For example, with this package installed, when you right-click a folder (directory) object and select **Open in Terminal**, Nautilus opens a terminal emulator with that directory as the working directory (page 190).

CONTROL BARS

This section discusses the three of the control bars that can appear in a File Browser window: the status bar, menubar, and Main toolbar (Figure 8-2, page 267). From **File Browser menubar: View,** you can choose which of these bars to display—except for the menubar, which Nautilus always displays.

Menubar The menubar appears at the top of the File Browser window and displays a menu when you click one of its selections. Which menu selections Nautilus displays depends on what the View pane is displaying and which objects are selected. The next section describes the menubar in detail.

Main toolbar The Main toolbar appears below the menubar and holds navigation tool icons: Location, Back, Forward, and Search. The Location buttons display the name of the directory that appears in the View pane. By default, Nautilus displays Location in iconic format. Press CONTROL-L to change the Location to textual format. If the Main toolbar is too short to hold all icons, Nautilus displays a button with a triangle pointing down at the right end of the toolbar. Click this button to display a dropdown list of the remaining icons. Display or remove the Main toolbar by selecting **File Browser menubar: View⇨Main toolbar.**

In iconic format, each button represents a directory in a pathname (page 191). The View pane displays the directory of the depressed (darker) button. Click one of these buttons to display that directory. If the leftmost button holds a triangle that points to the left, Nautilus is not displaying buttons for all the directories in the absolute (full) pathname; click the button with a triangle in it to display more directory buttons.

In textual format, the text box displays the absolute pathname of the displayed directory. Nautilus displays another directory when you enter the pathname of the directory and press RETURN.

Status bar If no items are selected, the status bar, at the bottom of the window, indicates how many items are displayed in the View pane. If the directory you are viewing is on the local system, it also tells you how much free space is available on the device that holds the directory displayed by the View pane. If an item is selected, the status bar displays the name of the item and its size. Display or remove the status bar by selecting **File Browser menubar: View⇨Statusbar.**

MENUBAR

The Nautilus File Browser menubar controls which information the File Browser displays and how it displays that information. Many of the menu selections duplicate controls found elsewhere in the File Browser window. This section highlights some of the selections on the menubar; click **Help** on the menubar and select **Contents** for more information. The menus the menubar holds are described next.

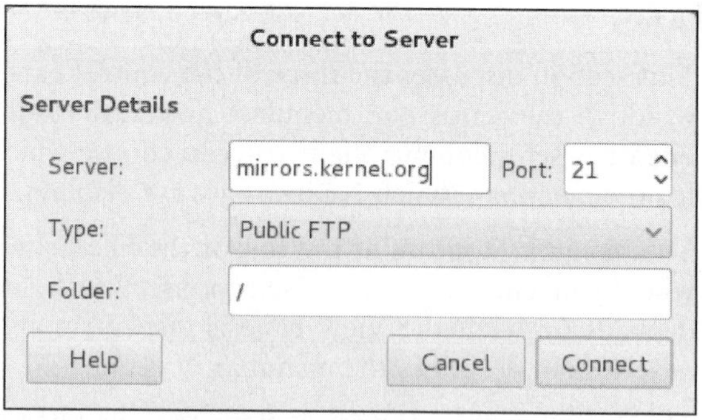

Connect to Server
Server Details
Server:
mirrors.kernel.org
Port:
21
Type:
Public FTP
Folder:
/
Help
Cancel
Connect

Figure 8-4 The Connect to Server window

File The several Open selections and the Property selection of File work with the highlighted object(s) in the View pane. If no objects are highlighted, these selections are grayed out or absent. Selecting **Connect to Server** (also available from **Main menu: Places**) displays the Connect to Server window (Figure 8-4). This window presents a **Type** drop-down list that allows you to select FTP, SSH, Windows, or other types of servers. Enter the URL of the server in the text box labeled **Server**. For an FTP connection, do not enter the **ftp://** part of the URL. Fill in the optional information as appropriate. Click **Connect**. If the server requires authentication, Nautilus displays a window in which you can enter a username and password. Nautilus opens a window displaying a directory on the server and an object, named for the URL you specified, on the desktop. After you close the window, you can open the object to connect to and display a directory on the server.

Edit Many of the Edit selections work with highlighted object(s) in the View pane; if no objects are highlighted, these selections are grayed out or absent. This section discusses two selections from Edit: Compress and Preferences.

The **Edit⇨Compress** selection creates a single archive file comprising the selected objects. This selection opens a Compress window (Figure 8-5) that allows you to specify the name and location of the archive. The drop-down list to the right of the text box labeled **Filename** allows you to specify a filename extension that determines the type of archive this tool creates. For example, **.tar.gz** creates a tar (page 162) file compressed by gzip (page 161) and **.tar.bz2** creates a tar file compressed by bzip2 (page 160). Click the plus sign to the left of Other Objects to specify a password for and/or to encrypt the archive (available only with certain types of archives). You can also split the archive into several files (volumes).

Compress
Filename:
Pictures
.tar.bz2
Location:
sam
Other Options
Help
Cancel
Create

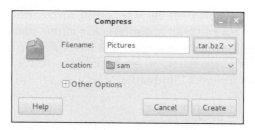

Figure 8-5 The Compress window

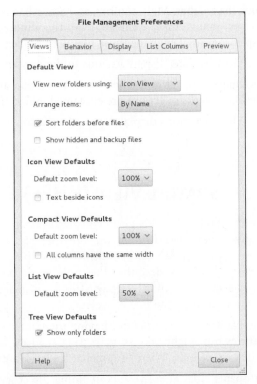

Figure 8-6 The File Management Preferences window, Views tab

The **Edit⇨Preferences** selection displays the File Management Preferences window (Figure 8-6). This window has five tabs that control the appearance and behavior of File Browser windows.

The **Views** tab sets several defaults, including which view the File Browser displays (Icon, List, or Compact view), the arrangement of the objects, the default zoom level, and default settings for the Compact view.

The **Behavior** tab controls how many clicks it takes to open an object and what Nautilus does when it opens an executable text object (script). For more confident users, this tab has an option that includes a Delete selection in addition to the Move to Trash selection on several menus. The Delete selection immediately removes the selected object instead of moving it to the **Trash** folder.

The **Display** tab specifies which information Nautilus includes in object (icon) captions. The three drop-down lists specify the order in which Nautilus displays information as you increase the zoom level of the View pane. This tab also specifies the date format Nautilus uses.

The **List Columns** tab specifies which columns Nautilus displays, and in what order it displays them, in the View pane when you select **List View**.

The **Preview** tab controls when Nautilus displays or plays previews of files (by size and Always, Local Files Only, Never).

View   Click the **Sidebar, Main toolbar,** and **Statusbar** selections in the View submenu to display or remove these elements from the window. The **Show Hidden Files** selection displays in the View pane those files with hidden filenames (page 190).

Go   The Go selections display various folders in the View pane.

Bookmarks   Bookmarks appear at the bottom of this menu and in the Sidebar under Bookmarks. The Bookmarks selections are explained under "Places" on page 268.

Help   The Help selections display local information about Nautilus.

optional

THE NAUTILUS SPATIAL VIEW (RHEL)

Under RHEL, Nautilus gives you two ways to work with files: the traditional File Browser view described in the previous section and the innovative Spatial view shown in Figure 8-7. By default, RHEL displays the Spatial view. Other than in this section, this book describes the more traditional File Browser window. See "The Two Faces of Nautilus" on page 103 for instructions on how to turn off the Spatial view and turn on the File Browser.

The Nautilus Spatial (as in "having the nature of space") view has many powerful features but might take some getting used to. It always provides one window per folder. By default, when you open a folder, Nautilus displays a new window.

To open a Spatial view of your home directory, Select **Main menu: Home Folder** and experiment as you read this section. If you double-click the Desktop icon in the Spatial view, Nautilus opens a new window that displays the **Desktop** folder.

A Spatial view can display icons, a list of filenames, or a compact view. To select your preferred format, click **View** on the menubar and choose **Icons, List,** or **Compact.** To create files to experiment with, right-click in the window (not on an icon) to display the Nautilus context menu and select **Create Folder** or **Create Document.**

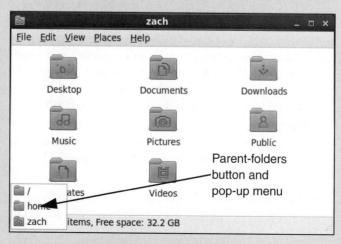

Figure 8-7   The Nautilus Spatial view

Use SHIFT **to close the current window as you open another window**

tip   If you hold the SHIFT key down when you double-click to open a new window, Nautilus closes the current window as it opens the new one. This behavior might be more familiar and can help keep the desktop from becoming cluttered. If you do not want to use the keyboard, you can achieve the same result by double-clicking the middle mouse button.

Window memory   Move the window by dragging the titlebar. The Spatial view has *window memory*— that is, the next time you open that folder, Nautilus opens it at the same size and in the same location. Even the scrollbar will be in the same position.

Parent-folders button   The key to closing the current window and returning to the window of the parent directory is the **Parent-folders** button (Figure 8-7). Click this button to display the Parent-folders pop-up menu. Select the directory you want to open from this menu. Nautilus then displays in a Spatial view the directory you specified.

From a Spatial view, you can open a folder in a traditional view by right-clicking the folder and selecting **Browse Folder**.

GNOME UTILITIES

GNOME comes with numerous utilities that can make your work with the desktop easier and more productive. This section covers several tools that are integral to the use of GNOME.

PICK A FONT WINDOW

The Pick a Font window (Figure 8-8) appears when you select **Fonts** from the Tweak Tool window (page 94) and click one of the font buttons on the right side of the window. From the Pick a Font window you can select a font family, a style, and a size. A preview of your choice appears in the Preview frame in the lower part of the window. Click **OK** when you are satisfied with your choice.

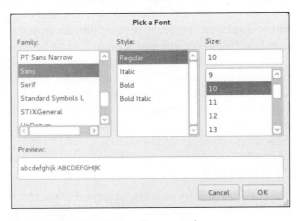

Figure 8-8   The Pick a Font window

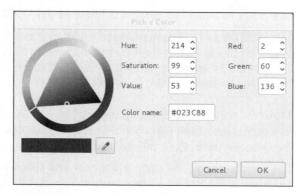

Figure 8-9   The Pick a Color window

PICK A COLOR WINDOW

The Pick a Color window (Figure 8-9) appears when you need to specify a color, such as when you click the colored button near the lower-right corner of the Background window (Figure 4-8, page 100).

When the Pick a Color window opens, the bar below the color circle displays the current color. Click the desired color on the color ring, and click/drag the lightness of that color in the triangle. As you change the color, the right end of the bar below the color circle previews the color you are selecting, while the left end continues to display the current color. You can also use the eyedropper to pick up a color from the workspace: Click the eyedropper and then click the resulting eyedropper mouse pointer on the color you want to select. The color you choose appears in the bar. Click **OK** when you are satisfied with the color you have specified.

RUN APPLICATION WINDOW

The Run Application window (Figure 4-6, page 97) enables you to run a program as though you had initiated it from a command line. To display the Run Application window, press ALT-F2. Enter a command in the text box. As soon as GNOME can uniquely identify the command you are entering, it completes the command and might display an object that identifies the application. Keep typing if the displayed command is not the one you want to run. Otherwise, press RETURN to run the command or TAB to accept the command in the text box. You can then continue entering information in the window. Click **Run with file** to specify a file to use as an argument to the command in the text box. Put a tick in the check box labeled **Run in terminal** to run a textual application, such as vi, in a terminal emulator window. As explained under "Running textual applications" on page 98, GNOME closes the resulting window when the program terminates.

SEARCHING FOR FILES

The Search for Files window (Figure 8-10) can help you find files whose locations or names you do not know or have forgotten. To open this window, select **Main menu: Places⇨Search for Files** or enter **gnome-search-tool** on a command line from

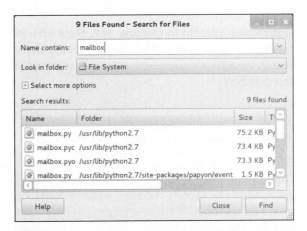

Figure 8-10   The Search for Files window

a terminal emulator or Run Application window (ALT-F2). To search by filename or partial filename, enter the (partial) filename in the combo box labeled **Name contains** and then select the folder you want to search in from the drop-down list labeled **Look in folder**. When GNOME searches in a folder, it searches subfolders to any level (it searches the directory hierarchy). To search all directories in all mounted filesystems, select **File System** from the drop-down list labeled **Look in folder**. Select **Other** to search a folder not included in the drop-down list; GNOME opens a Browse/Save window (page 107). Once you have entered the search criteria, click **Find**. GNOME displays the list of files matching the criteria in the list box labeled **Search results**. Double-click a file in this list box to open it.

To refine the search, you can enter more search criteria. Click the plus sign to the left of **Select more options** to expand the window and display more search criteria. GNOME initially displays one search criterion and a line for adding another criterion as shown in Figure 8-11. With this part of the window expanded, GNOME incorporates all visible search criteria when you click **Find**.

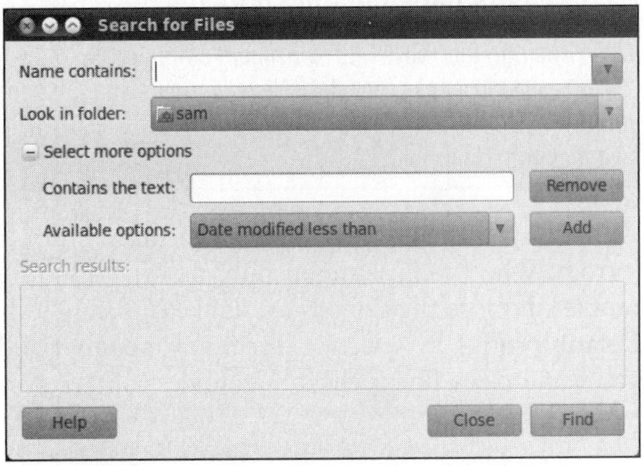

Figure 8-11   The Search for Files window with Select more options expanded

The first line below **Select more options** holds a text box labeled **Contains the text.** If nothing is entered in this text box, the search matches all files. You can leave this text box as is or remove the line by clicking **Remove** at the right end of the line. To search for a file that contains a specific string of characters (text), enter the string in this text box.

To add search criteria, make a selection from the list box labeled **Available options** and click **Add** to the right of the drop-down list. To remove criteria, click **Remove** at the right end of the line that holds the criterion you want to remove.

To select files that were modified fewer than a specified number of days ago, select **Date modified less than** from the drop-down list labeled **Available options** and click **Add**. The Search for Files window adds a line with a spin box labeled **Date modified less than.** With this spin box showing 0 (zero), as it does initially, no file matches the search criteria. Change this number as desired and click **Find** to begin the search.

GNOME TERMINAL EMULATOR/SHELL

The GNOME terminal emulator displays a window that mimics a character-based terminal (page 117). To display a terminal emulator window, select **Main menu: Applications⇨System Tools⇨Terminal** or enter **gnome-terminal** on a command line or from a Run Application window (ALT-F2). When the GNOME terminal emulator is already displayed, select **Terminal menubar: File⇨Open Terminal** or right-click within the Terminal window and select **Open Terminal** to display a new terminal emulator window.

To open an additional terminal session within the same Terminal window, select **Terminal menubar: File⇨Open Tab** or right-click the window and select **Open Tab** from the context menu. A row of tabs appears below the menubar as gnome-terminal opens another terminal session on top of the existing one. Add as many terminal sessions as you like; click the tabs to switch between sessions.

GNOME terminal emulator shortcuts

tip   While using the GNOME terminal emulator, CONTROL-SHIFT-N opens a new window and CONTROL-SHIFT-T opens a new tab. New windows and tabs open to the working directory. In addition, you can use CONTROL-PAGE UP and CONTROL-PAGE DOWN to switch between tabs. In addition, CONTROL-*x* switches to tab number *x*.

A session you add from the context menu uses the same profile as the session you open it from. When you use the menubar to open a session, GNOME gives you a choice of profiles, if more than one is available. You can add and modify profiles, including the Default profile, by selecting **Terminal menubar: Edit⇨Profiles.** Highlight the profile you want to modify or click **New** to design a new profile.

CHAPTER SUMMARY

The X Window System GUI is portable and flexible and makes it easy to write applications that work on many different types of systems without having to know low-level details for the individual systems. This GUI can operate in a networked environment, allowing a user to run a program on a remote system and send the results to a local display. The client/server concept is integral to the operation of the X Window System, in which the X server is responsible for fulfilling requests made of X Window System applications or clients. Hundreds of clients are available that can run under X. Programmers can also write their own clients, using tools such as the GTK+ and GTK+2 GNOME libraries to write GNOME programs and the Qt and KDE libraries to write KDE programs.

The window managers, and virtually all X applications, are designed to help users tailor their work environments in simple or complex ways. You can designate applications that start automatically, set such attributes as colors and fonts, and even alter the way keyboard strokes and mouse clicks are interpreted.

Built on top of the X Window System, the GNOME desktop manager can be used as is or customized to better suit your needs. It is a graphical user interface to system services (commands), the filesystem, applications, and more. Although not part of GNOME, the Metacity, Mutter, and Compiz window managers work closely with GNOME and are the default window managers for GNOME under Fedora. A window manager controls all aspects of the windows, including placement, decoration, grouping, minimizing and maximizing, sizing, and moving.

The Nautilus File Browser window is a critical part of GNOME; the desktop is a modified File Browser window. The File Browser View pane displays icons or a list of filenames you can work with. The Sidebar, which can display two types of information, augments the information Nautilus displays in the View pane.

GNOME also provides many graphical utilities you can use to customize and work with the desktop. It supports MIME types; thus, when you double-click an object, GNOME generally knows which tool to use to display the data represented by the object. In sum, GNOME is a powerful desktop manager that can make your job both easier and more fun.

EXERCISES

1. a. What is Nautilus?

   b. List four things you can do with Nautilus.

   c. How do you use Nautilus to search for a file?

2. What is a terminal emulator? What does it allow you to do from a GUI that you would not be able to do without one?

3. How would you search the entire filesystem for a file named **today.odt**?

4. a. List two ways you can open a file using Nautilus.

   b. How does Nautilus "know" which program to use to open different types of files?

   c. What are the three common Nautilus control bars? Which kinds of tools do you find on each?

   d. Discuss the use of the Nautilus location bar in textual mode.

ADVANCED EXERCISES

5. Assume you are using a mouse with nine pointer buttons defined. How would you reverse the effects of using the mouse wheel?

6. How would you use Nautilus to connect to the FTP server at mirrors.kernel.org/fedora?

7. Discuss the client/server environment set up by the X Window System. How does the X server work? List three X clients. Where is the client and where is the server when you log in on a local system? What is an advantage of this setup?

8. Run xwininfo from a terminal emulator window and answer these questions:

   a. What does xwininfo do?

   b. What does xwininfo give as the name of the window you clicked? Does that agree with the name in the window's titlebar?

   c. What is the size of the window? In which units does xwininfo display this size? What is the depth of a window?

   d. How can you get xwininfo to display the same information without having to click the window?

9. Find and install xeyes (not tuxeyes). Write an xeyes command to display a window that is 600 pixels wide and 400 pixels tall, is located 200 pixels from the right edge of the screen and 300 pixels from the top of the screen, and contains orange eyes outlined in blue with red pupils. (*Hint:* Refer to the xeyes man page.)

9

THE BOURNE AGAIN SHELL

OBJECTIVES

After reading this chapter you should be able to:

▸ Describe the purpose and history of the Bourne Again Shell

▸ List the startup files bash runs

▸ Use three different methods to run a shell script

▸ Manage multiple processes with job control

▸ Redirect error messages to a file

▸ Use special characters to separate and group commands

▸ Create variables and display the values of variables and parameters

▸ List and describe common variables found on the system

▸ Reference, repeat, and modify previous commands using history

▸ Use control characters to edit the command line

▸ Create, display, and remove aliases and functions

▸ Customize the bsh environment using set and shopt builtins

▸ List the order of command line expansion

This chapter picks up where Chapter 7 left off. Chapter 27 expands on this chapter, exploring control flow commands and more advanced aspects of programming the Bourne Again Shell (bash). The bash home page is at www.gnu.org/software/bash. The bash info page is a complete Bourne Again Shell reference.

The Bourne Again Shell is a command interpreter and high-level programming language. As a command interpreter, it processes commands you enter on the command line in response to a prompt. When you use the shell as a programming language, it processes commands stored in files called *shell scripts*. Like other languages, shells have variables and control flow commands (e.g., **for** loops and **if** statements).

When you use a shell as a command interpreter, you can customize the environment you work in. You can make your prompt display the name of the working directory, create a function or an alias for cp that keeps it from overwriting certain kinds of files, take advantage of keyword variables to change aspects of how the shell works, and so on. You can also write shell scripts that do your bidding—anything from a one-line script that stores a long, complex command to a longer script that runs a set of reports, prints them, and mails you a reminder when the job is done. More complex shell scripts are themselves programs; they do not just run other programs. Chapter 27 has some examples of these types of scripts.

Most system shell scripts are written to run under bash (or dash; next page). If you will ever work in single-user mode—when you boot the system or perform system maintenance, administration, or repair work, for example—it is a good idea to become familiar with this shell.

This chapter expands on the interactive features of the shell described in Chapter 7, explains how to create and run simple shell scripts, discusses job control, introduces the basic aspects of shell programming, talks about history and aliases, and describes command-line expansion. Chapter 27 presents some more challenging shell programming problems.

BACKGROUND

The Bourne Again Shell is based on the Bourne Shell (the early UNIX shell; this book refers to it as the *original Bourne Shell* to avoid confusion), which was written by Steve Bourne of AT&T's Bell Laboratories. Over the years the original Bourne Shell has been expanded, but it remains the basic shell provided with many commercial versions of UNIX.

sh Shell   Because of its long and successful history, the original Bourne Shell has been used to write many of the shell scripts that help manage UNIX systems. Some of these scripts appear in Linux as Bourne Again Shell scripts. Although the Bourne Again Shell includes many extensions and features not found in the original Bourne Shell, bash maintains compatibility with the original Bourne Shell so you can run Bourne Shell scripts under bash. On UNIX systems the original Bourne Shell is named sh.

On Fedora/RHEL systems sh is a symbolic link to bash ensuring that scripts that require the presence of the Bourne Shell still run. When called as sh, bash does its best to emulate the original Bourne Shell.

dash Shell   The bash executable file is almost 900 kilobytes, has many features, and is well suited as a user login shell. The dash (Debian Almquist) shell is about 100 kilobytes, offers Bourne Shell compatibility for shell scripts (noninteractive use), and because of its size, can load and execute shell scripts much more quickly than bash.

Korn Shell   System V UNIX introduced the Korn Shell (ksh), written by David Korn. This shell extended many features of the original Bourne Shell and added many new features. Some features of the Bourne Again Shell, such as command aliases and command-line editing, are based on similar features from the Korn Shell.

POSIX   The POSIX (Portable Operating System Interface) family of related standards is being developed by PASC (IEEE's Portable Application Standards Committee; www.pasc.org/plato). A comprehensive FAQ on POSIX, including many links, appears at www.opengroup.org/austin/papers/posix_faq.html.

POSIX standard 1003.2 describes shell functionality. The Bourne Again Shell provides the features that match the requirements of this standard. Efforts are under way to make the Bourne Again Shell fully comply with the POSIX standard. In the meantime, if you invoke bash with the --posix option, the behavior of the Bourne Again Shell will closely match the POSIX requirements.

SHELL BASICS

This section covers writing and using startup files, redirecting standard error, writing and executing simple shell scripts, separating and grouping commands, implementing job control, and manipulating the directory stack.

chsh: changes your login shell

tip   The person who sets up your account determines which shell you use when you first log in on the system or when you open a terminal emulator window in a GUI environment. Under Fedora/RHEL, bash is the default shell. You can run any shell you like after you are logged in. Enter the name of the shell you want to use (bash, tcsh, or another shell) and press RETURN; the next prompt will be that of the new shell. Give an **exit** command to return to the previous shell. Because shells you call in this manner are nested (one runs on top of the other), you will be able to log out only from your original shell. When you have nested several shells, keep giving **exit** commands until you reach your original shell. You will then be able to log out.

Use the chsh utility to change your login shell permanently. First give the command **chsh**. In response to the prompts, enter your password and the absolute pathname of the shell you want to use (**/bin/bash**, **/bin/tcsh**, or the pathname of another shell). When you change your login shell in this manner using a terminal emulator (page 117) under a GUI, subsequent terminal emulator windows will not reflect the change until you log out of the system and log back in. See page 469 for an example of how to use chsh.

STARTUP FILES

When a shell starts, it runs startup files to initialize itself. Which files the shell runs depends on whether it is a login shell, an interactive shell that is not a login shell (such as you get by giving the command **bash**), or a noninteractive shell (one used to execute a shell script). You must have read access to a startup file to execute the commands in it. Fedora/RHEL puts appropriate commands in some of these files. This section covers bash startup files.

LOGIN SHELLS

A *login shell* is the first shell that displays a prompt when you log in on a system from the system console or a virtual console (page 138), remotely using ssh or another program (page 135), or by another means. When you are running a GUI and open a terminal emulator such as gnome-terminal (page 276), you are not logging in on the system (you do not provide your username and password), so the shell the emulator displays is not a login shell; it is an interactive nonlogin shell (next). Login shells are, by their nature, interactive.

This section describes the startup files that are executed by login shells and shells that you start with the bash --**login** option.

/etc/profile The shell first executes the commands in **/etc/profile**, establishing systemwide default characteristics for users running bash. In addition to executing the commands it holds, **profile** executes the commands within each of the files with a **.sh** filename extension in the **/etc/profile.d** directory. This setup allows a user working with **root** privileges to modify the commands **profile** runs without changing the **profile** file itself. Because profile can be replaced when the system is updated, making changes to files in the **profile.d** directory ensures the changes will remain when the system is updated.

Set global variables for all users in a ✷.sh file in /etc/profile.d

tip Setting and exporting a variable in a file with a **.sh** filename extension in the **/etc/profile.d** directory makes that variable available to every user's login shell. Because the variable is exported, it is also available to all interactive and noninteractive subshells of the login shell.

.bash_profile Next the shell looks for ~/**.bash_profile**, ~/**.bash_login**, or ~/**.profile** (~/ is short-
.bash_login hand for your home directory), in that order, executing the commands in the first of
.profile these files it finds. You can put commands in one of these files to override the defaults set in **/etc/profile**.

By default, Fedora/RHEL sets up new accounts with ~/**.bash_profile** and ~/**.bashrc** files. The default ~/**.bash_profile** file calls ~/**.bashrc**, which calls **/etc/bashrc** (next).

.bash_logout When you log out, bash executes commands in the ~/**.bash_logout** file. This file often holds commands that clean up after a session, such as those that remove temporary files.

INTERACTIVE NONLOGIN SHELLS

The commands in the preceding startup files are not executed by interactive, non-login shells. However, these shells inherit values from the login shell variables that are set by these startup files.

.bashrc   An interactive nonlogin shell executes commands in the ~/.bashrc file. The default ~/.bashrc file calls /etc/bashrc.

/etc/bashrc   Although not called by bash directly, the Fedora/RHEL ~/.bashrc file calls /etc/bashrc.

NONINTERACTIVE SHELLS

The commands in the previously described startup files are not executed by noninteractive shells, such as those that runs shell scripts. However, these shells inherit login shell variables that are set by these startup files.

BASH_ENV   Noninteractive shells look for the environment variable **BASH_ENV** (or **ENV** if the shell is called as sh) and execute commands in the file named by this variable.

SETTING UP STARTUP FILES

Although many startup files and types of shells exist, usually all you need are the **.bash_profile** and **.bashrc** files in your home directory. Commands similar to the following in **.bash_profile** run commands from **.bashrc** for login shells (when **.bashrc** exists). With this setup, the commands in **.bashrc** are executed by login and nonlogin shells.

```
if [ -f ~/.bashrc ]; then . ~/.bashrc; fi
```

The [**–f ~/.bashrc**] tests whether the file named **.bashrc** in your home directory exists. See pages 971 and 974 for more information on test and its synonym [ ]. See page 284 for information on the . (dot) builtin.

Set PATH in .bash_profile

tip   Because commands in **.bashrc** might be executed many times, and because subshells inherit exported variables, it is a good idea to put commands that add to existing variables in the **.bash_profile** file. For example, the following command adds the **bin** subdirectory of the **home** directory to **PATH** (page 308) and should go in **.bash_profile**:

```
PATH=$PATH:$HOME/bin
```

When you put this command in **.bash_profile** and not in **.bashrc**, the string is added to the **PATH** variable only once, when you log in.

Modifying a variable in **.bash_profile** causes changes you make in an interactive session to propagate to subshells. In contrast, modifying a variable in **.bashrc** overrides changes inherited from a parent shell.

Sample **.bash_profile** and **.bashrc** files follow. Some commands used in these files are not covered until later in this chapter. In any startup file, you must export variables and functions that you want to be available to child processes. For more information refer to "Locality of Variables" on page 1008.

```
$ cat ~/.bash_profile
if [ -f ~/.bashrc ]; then
    . ~/.bashrc                      # Read local startup file if it exists
fi
PATH=$PATH:/usr/local/bin            # Add /usr/local/bin to PATH
export PS1='[\h \W \!]\$ '           # Set prompt
```

The first command in the preceding **.bash_profile** file executes the commands in the user's **.bashrc** file if it exists. The next command adds to the **PATH** variable (page 308). Typically **PATH** is set and exported in **/etc/profile**, so it does not need to be exported in a user's startup file. The final command sets and exports **PS1** (page 310), which controls the user's prompt.

A sample **.bashrc** file is shown below. The first command executes the commands in the **/etc/bashrc** file if it exists. Next the file sets and exports the **LANG** (page 314) and **VIMINIT** (for vim initialization) variables and defines several aliases. The final command defines a function (page 338) that swaps the names of two files.

```
$ cat ~/.bashrc
if [ -f /etc/bashrc ]; then
    source /etc/bashrc               # read global startup file if it exists
fi

set -o noclobber                     # prevent overwriting files
unset MAILCHECK                      # turn off "you have new mail" notice
export LANG=C                        # set LANG variable
export VIMINIT='set ai aw'           # set vim options
alias df='df -h'                     # set up aliases
alias rm='rm -i'                     # always do interactive rm's
alias lt='ls -ltrh | tail'
alias h='history | tail'
alias ch='chmod 755 '

function switch()                    # a function to exchange the names
{                                    # of two files
    local tmp=$$switch
    mv "$1" $tmp
    mv "$2" "$1"
    mv $tmp "$2"
}
```

. (DOT) OR source: RUNS A STARTUP FILE IN THE CURRENT SHELL

After you edit a startup file such as **.bashrc**, you do not have to log out and log in again to put the changes into effect. Instead, you can run the startup file using the **.** (dot) or **source** builtin (they are the same command). As with all other commands, the . must be followed by a SPACE on the command line. Using . or source is similar to running a shell script, except these commands run the script as part of the current process. Consequently, when you use . or source to run a script, changes you make to variables from within the script affect the shell you run the script from. If you ran a startup file as a regular shell script and did not use the . or source builtin, the variables created in the startup file would remain in effect only in the subshell running the script—not in the shell you ran the script from. You can use the . or source command to run any shell script—not just a startup file—but undesirable side effects (such as changes in the values of shell variables you rely on) might occur. For more information refer to "Locality of Variables" on page 1008.

In the following example, **.bashrc** sets several variables and sets **PS1**, the bash prompt, to the name of the host. The . builtin puts the new values into effect.

```
$ cat ~/.bashrc
export TERM=xterm                     # set the terminal type
export PS1="$(hostname -f): "         # set the prompt string
export CDPATH=:$HOME                  # add HOME to CDPATH string
stty kill '^u'                        # set kill line to control-u

$ . ~/.bashrc
guava:
```

COMMANDS THAT ARE SYMBOLS

The Bourne Again Shell uses the symbols (,), [,], and $ in a variety of ways. To minimize confusion, Table 9-1 lists the most common use of each of these symbols and the page on which it is discussed.

Table 9-1   Builtin commands that are symbols

Symbol	Command
( )	Subshell (page 295)
$( )	Command substitution (page 351)
(( ))	Arithmetic evaluation; a synonym for let (use when the enclosed value contains an equal sign; page 1032)
$(( ))	Arithmetic expansion (not for use with an enclosed equal sign; page 349)
[ ]	The test command (pages 971 and 974)
[[ ]]	Conditional expression; similar to [ ] but adds string comparisons (page 1033)

REDIRECTING STANDARD ERROR

Chapter 7 covered the concept of standard output and explained how to redirect standard output of a command. In addition to standard output, commands can send output to *standard error*. A command can send error messages to standard error to keep them from getting mixed up with the information it sends to standard output.

Just as it does with standard output, by default the shell directs standard error to the screen. Unless you redirect one or the other, you might not know the difference between the output a command sends to standard output and the output it sends to standard error. This section describes the syntax used by the Bourne Again Shell to redirect standard error and to distinguish between standard output and standard error.

File descriptors   A *file descriptor* is the place a program sends its output to and gets its input from. When you execute a program, Linux opens three file descriptors for the program: 0 (standard input), 1 (standard output), and 2 (standard error). The redirect output symbol (> [page 234]) is shorthand for 1>, which tells the shell to redirect standard output. Similarly < (page 236) is short for 0<, which redirects standard input. The symbols 2> redirect standard error. For more information refer to "File Descriptors" on page 1003.

The following examples demonstrate how to redirect standard output and standard error to different files and to the same file. When you run the cat utility with the name of a file that does not exist and the name of a file that does exist, cat sends an error message to standard error and copies the file that does exist to standard output. Unless you redirect them, both messages appear on the screen.

```
$ cat y
This is y.
$ cat x
cat: x: No such file or directory

$ cat x y
cat: x: No such file or directory
This is y.
```

When you redirect standard output of a command, output sent to standard error is not affected and still appears on the screen.

```
$ cat x y > hold
cat: x: No such file or directory
$ cat hold
This is y.
```

Similarly, when you send standard output through a pipe, standard error is not affected. The following example sends standard output of cat through a pipe to tr, which in this example converts lowercase characters to uppercase. (See the tr info page for more information.) The text that cat sends to standard error is not translated because it goes directly to the screen rather than through the pipe.

```
$ cat x y | tr "[a-z]" "[A-Z]"
cat: x: No such file or directory
THIS IS Y.
```

The following example redirects standard output and standard error to different files. The filename following 2> tells the shell where to redirect standard error (file descriptor 2). The filename following **1>** tells the shell where to redirect standard output (file descriptor 1). You can use **>** in place of **1>**.

```
$ cat x y 1> hold1 2> hold2
$ cat hold1
This is y.
$ cat hold2
cat: x: No such file or directory
```

Combining standard output and standard error — In the next example, the **&>** token redirects standard output and standard error to a single file:

```
$ cat x y &> hold
$ cat hold
cat: x: No such file or directory
This is y.
```

Duplicating a file descriptor — In the next example, first **1>** redirects standard output to **hold**, and then **2>&1** declares file descriptor 2 to be a duplicate of file descriptor 1. As a result, both standard output and standard error are redirected to **hold**.

```
$ cat x y 1> hold 2>&1
$ cat hold
cat: x: No such file or directory
This is y.
```

In this case, **1> hold** precedes **2>&1**. If they had been listed in the opposite order, standard error would have been made a duplicate of standard output before standard output was redirected to **hold**. Only standard output would have been redirected to **hold** in that case.

The next example declares file descriptor 2 to be a duplicate of file descriptor 1 and sends the output for file descriptor 1 through a pipe to the tr command.

```
$ cat x y 2>&1 | tr "[a-z]" "[A-Z]"
CAT: X: NO SUCH FILE OR DIRECTORY
THIS IS Y.
```

Sending errors to standard error — You can use **1>&2** to redirect standard output of a command to standard error. Shell scripts use this technique to send the output of echo to standard error. In the following script, standard output of the first echo is redirected to standard error:

```
$ cat message_demo
echo This is an error message. 1>&2
echo This is not an error message.
```

If you redirect standard output of **message_demo**, error messages such as the one produced by the first echo appear on the screen because you have not redirected standard error. Because standard output of a shell script is frequently redirected to another file, you can use this technique to display on the screen any error messages generated by the script. The **lnks** script (page 979) uses this technique. You can also use the exec builtin to create additional file descriptors and to redirect standard input, standard output, and standard error of a shell script from within the script (page 1023).

The Bourne Again Shell supports the redirection operators shown in Table 9-2.

Table 9-2   Redirection operators

Operator	Meaning
< *filename*	Redirects standard input from *filename*.
> *filename*	Redirects standard output to *filename* unless *filename* exists and **noclobber** (page 237) is set. If **noclobber** is not set, this redirection creates *filename* if it does not exist and overwrites it if it does exist.
>| *filename*	Redirects standard output to *filename*, even if the file exists and **noclobber** (page 237) is set.
>> *filename*	Redirects and appends standard output to *filename*; creates *filename* if it does not exist.
&> *filename*	Redirects standard output and standard error to *filename*.
<&*m*	Duplicates standard input from file descriptor *m* (page 1004).
[*n*]>&*m*	Duplicates standard output or file descriptor *n* if specified from file descriptor *m* (page 1004).
[*n*]<&–	Closes standard input or file descriptor *n* if specified (page 1004).
[*n*]>&–	Closes standard output or file descriptor *n* if specified.

WRITING A SIMPLE SHELL SCRIPT

A *shell script* is a file that holds commands that the shell can execute. The commands in a shell script can be any commands you can enter in response to a shell prompt. For example, a command in a shell script might run a Linux utility, a compiled program, or another shell script. Like the commands you give on the command line, a command in a shell script can use ambiguous file references and can have its input or output redirected from or to a file or sent through a pipe. You can also use pipes and redirection with the input and output of the script itself.

In addition to the commands you would ordinarily use on the command line, *control flow* commands (also called *control structures*) find most of their use in shell scripts. This group of commands enables you to alter the order of execution of commands in a script in the same way you would alter the order of execution of statements using a structured programming language. Refer to "Control Structures" on page 971 for specifics.

The shell interprets and executes the commands in a shell script, one after another. Thus a shell script enables you to simply and quickly initiate a complex series of tasks or a repetitive procedure.

chmod: MAKES A FILE EXECUTABLE

To execute a shell script by giving its name as a command, you must have permission to read and execute the file that contains the script (refer to "Access Permissions" on page 202). Read permission enables you to read the file that holds the script. Execute

```
$ ls -l whoson
-rw-rw-r--. 1 max pubs 40 05-24 11:30 whoson

$ chmod u+x whoson
$ ls -l whoson
-rwx-rw-r--. 1 max pubs 40 05-24 11:30 whoson

$ ./whoson
Wed May 25 11:40:49 PDT 2011
Users Currently Logged In
zach     pts/7     2011-05-23 18:17
hls      pts/1     2011-05-24 09:59
sam      pts/12    2011-05-24 06:29 (guava)
max      pts/4     2011-05-24 09:08
```

Figure 9-1   Using chmod to make a shell script executable

permission tells the shell and the system that the owner, group, and/or public has permission to execute the file; it implies that the content of the file is executable.

When you create a shell script using an editor, the file does not typically have its execute permission set. The following example shows a file named **whoson** that contains a shell script:

```
$ cat whoson
date
echo "Users Currently Logged In"
who

$ ./whoson
bash: ./whoson: Permission denied
```

You cannot execute **whoson** by giving its name as a command because you do not have execute permission for the file. The shell does not recognize **whoson** as an executable file and issues the error message **Permission denied** when you try to execute it. (See the tip on the next page if you get a **command not found** error message.) When you give the filename as an argument to bash (**bash whoson**), bash takes the argument to be a shell script and executes it. In this case bash is executable, and **whoson** is an argument that bash executes, so you do not need execute permission to **whoson**. You must have read permission.

The chmod utility changes the access privileges associated with a file. Figure 9-1 shows ls with the –l option displaying the access privileges of **whoson** before and after chmod gives execute permission to the file's owner.

The first ls displays a hyphen (–) as the fourth character, indicating the owner does not have permission to execute the file. Next chmod gives the owner execute permission: **u+x** causes chmod to add (**+**) execute permission (**x**) for the owner (**u**). (The **u** stands for *user,* although it means the owner of the file.) The second argument is the name of the file. The second ls shows an **x** in the fourth position, indicating the owner has execute permission.

Command not found?

If you give the name of a shell script as a command without including the leading ./, the shell typically displays the following error message:

```
$ whoson
bash: whoson: command not found
```

This message indicates the shell is not set up to search for executable files in the working directory. Enter this command instead:

```
$ ./whoson
```

The ./ tells the shell explicitly to look for an executable file in the working directory. Although not recommended for security reasons, you can change the environment so the shell searches the working directory automatically; see the section about **PATH** on page 308.

If other users will execute the file, you must also change group and/or public access permissions for the file. Any user must have execute access to use the file's name as a command. If the file is a shell script, the user trying to execute the file must have read access to the file as well. You do not need read access to execute a binary executable (compiled program).

The final command in Figure 9-1 shows the shell executing the file when its name is given as a command. For more information refer to "Access Permissions" on page 202 as well as the discussions of ls (page 202) and chmod (page 203).

#! Specifies a Shell

You can put a special sequence of characters on the first line of a shell script to tell the operating system which shell (or other program) should execute the file. Because the operating system checks the initial characters of a program before attempting to execute it using **exec**, these characters save the system from making an unsuccessful attempt. If **#!** are the first two characters of a script, the system interprets the characters that follow as the absolute pathname of the program that should execute the script. This pathname can point to any program, not just a shell, and can be useful if you have a script you want to run with a shell other than the shell you are running the script from. The following example specifies that bash should run the script:

```
$ cat bash_script
#!/bin/bash
echo "This is a Bourne Again Shell script."
```

The next example runs under Perl and can be run directly from the shell without explicitly calling Perl on the command line:

```
$ cat ./perl_script.pl
#!/usr/bin/perl -w
print "This is a Perl script.\n";

$ ./perl_script.pl
This is a Perl script.
```

The next example shows a script that should be executed by tcsh (tcsh package):

```
$ cat tcsh_script
#!/bin/tcsh
echo "This is a tcsh script."
set person = zach
echo "person is $person"
```

Because of the **#!** line, the operating system ensures that tcsh executes the script no matter which shell you run it from.

You can use **ps –f** within a shell script to display the name of the program that is executing the script. The three lines that ps displays in the following example show the process running the parent bash shell, the process running the tcsh script, and the process running the ps command:

```
$ cat tcsh_script2
#!/bin/tcsh
ps -f

$ ./tcsh_script2
UID        PID  PPID  C STIME TTY          TIME CMD
max       3031  3030  0 Nov16 pts/4    00:00:00 -bash
max       9358  3031  0 21:13 pts/4    00:00:00 /bin/tcsh ./tcsh_script2
max       9375  9358  0 21:13 pts/4    00:00:00 ps -f
```

If you do not follow **#!** with the name of an executable program, the shell reports it cannot find the program you asked it to run. You can optionally follow **#!** with SPACEs. If you omit the **#!** line and try to run, for example, a tcsh script from bash, the script will run under bash and might generate error messages or not run properly.

BEGINS A COMMENT

Comments make shell scripts and all code easier to read and maintain by you and others. If a hashmark (#) in the first character position of the first line of a script is not immediately followed by an exclamation point (!) or if a hashmark occurs in any other location in a script, the shell interprets it as the beginning of a comment. The shell then ignores everything between the hashmark and the end of the line (the next NEWLINE character).

EXECUTING A SHELL SCRIPT

fork and **exec** system calls   As discussed earlier, you can execute commands in a shell script file that you do not have execute permission for by using a bash command to **exec** a shell that runs the script directly. In the following example, bash creates a new shell that takes its input from the file named **whoson**:

```
$ bash whoson
```

Because the bash command expects to read a file containing commands, you do not need execute permission for **whoson**. (You do need read permission.) Even though bash reads and executes the commands in **whoson**, standard input, standard output, and standard error remain directed from/to the terminal.

Although you can use bash to execute a shell script, this technique causes the script to run more slowly than giving yourself execute permission and directly invoking the script. Users typically prefer to make the file executable and run the script by typing its name on the command line. It is also easier to type the name, and this practice is consistent with the way other kinds of programs are invoked (so you do not need to know whether you are running a shell script or an executable file). However, if bash is not your interactive shell or if you want to see how the script runs with different shells, you might want to run a script as an argument to bash or tcsh.

sh does not call the original Bourne Shell

caution   The original Bourne Shell was invoked with the command **sh**. Although you can call bash with an **sh** command, it is not the original Bourne Shell. The **sh** command (**/bin/sh**) is a symbolic link to **/bin/bash**, so it is simply another name for the **bash** command. When you call bash using the command **sh**, bash tries to mimic the behavior of the original Bourne Shell as closely as possible. It does not always succeed.

SEPARATING AND GROUPING COMMANDS

Whether you give the shell commands interactively or write a shell script, you must separate commands from one another. This section reviews the ways to separate commands that were covered in Chapter 7 and introduces a few new ones.

; AND NEWLINE SEPARATE COMMANDS

The NEWLINE character is a unique command separator because it initiates execution of the command preceding it. You have seen this behavior throughout this book each time you press the RETURN key at the end of a command line.

The semicolon (;) is a command separator that *does not* initiate execution of a command and *does not* change any aspect of how the command functions. You can execute a series of commands sequentially by entering them on a single command line and separating each from the next with a semicolon (;). You initiate execution of the sequence of commands by pressing RETURN:

```
$ x ; y ; z
```

If x, y, and z are commands, the preceding command line yields the same results as the next three commands. The difference is that in the next example the shell issues a prompt after each of the commands (x, y, and z) finishes executing, whereas the preceding command line causes the shell to issue a prompt only after z is complete:

```
$ x
$ y
$ z
```

Whitespace   Although the whitespace around the semicolons in the earlier example makes the command line easier to read, it is not necessary. None of the command separators needs to be surrounded by SPACEs or TABs.

\ Continues a Command

When you enter a long command line and the cursor reaches the right side of the screen, you can use a backslash (\) character to continue the command on the next line. The backslash quotes, or escapes, the NEWLINE character that follows it so the shell does not treat the NEWLINE as a command terminator. Enclosing a backslash within single quotation marks or preceding it with another backslash turns off the power of a backslash to quote special characters such as NEWLINE. Enclosing a backslash within double quotation marks has no effect on the power of the backslash.

Although you can break a line in the middle of a word (token), it is typically simpler to break a line immediately before or after whitespace.

optional You can enter a RETURN in the middle of a quoted string on a command line without using a backslash. The NEWLINE (RETURN) you enter will then be part of the string:

```
$ echo "Please enter the three values
> required to complete the transaction."
Please enter the three values
required to complete the transaction.
```

In the three examples in this section, the shell does not interpret RETURN as a command terminator because it occurs within a quoted string. The greater than (>) sign is a secondary prompt (**PS2**; page 311) indicating the shell is waiting for you to continue the unfinished command. In the next example, the first RETURN is quoted (escaped) so the shell treats it as a separator and does not interpret it literally.

```
$ echo "Please enter the three values \
> required to complete the transaction."
Please enter the three values required to complete the transaction.
```

Single quotation marks cause the shell to interpret a backslash literally:

```
$ echo 'Please enter the three values \
> required to complete the transaction.'
Please enter the three values \
required to complete the transaction.
```

| AND & Separate Commands and Do Something Else

The pipe symbol (|) and the background task symbol (&) are also command separators. They *do not* start execution of a command but *do* change some aspect of how the command functions. The pipe symbol alters the source of standard input or the destination of standard output. The background task symbol causes the shell to execute the task in the background and display a prompt immediately; you can continue working on other tasks.

Each of the following command lines initiates a single job comprising three tasks:

```
$ x | y | z
$ ls -l | grep tmp | less
```

In the first job, the shell redirects standard output of task **x** to standard input of task **y** and redirects **y**'s standard output to **z**'s standard input. Because it runs the entire job in the foreground, the shell does not display a prompt until task **z** runs to completion: Task **z** does not finish until task **y** finishes, and task **y** does not finish until task **x** finishes. In the second job, task **x** is an **ls –l** command, task **y** is **grep tmp**, and task **z** is the pager **less**. The shell displays a long (wide) listing of the files in the working directory that contain the string **tmp**, piped through **less**.

The next command line executes tasks **d** and **e** in the background and task **f** in the foreground:

```
$ d & e & f
[1] 14271
[2] 14272
```

The shell displays the job number between brackets and the PID number for each process running in the background. It displays a prompt as soon as **f** finishes, which might be before **d** or **e** finishes.

Before displaying a prompt for a new command, the shell checks whether any background jobs have completed. For each completed job, the shell displays its job number, the word **Done**, and the command line that invoked the job; the shell then displays a prompt. When the job numbers are listed, the number of the last job started is followed by a **+** character, and the job number of the previous job is followed by a **–** character. Other jobs are followed by a SPACE character. After running the last command, the shell displays the following lines before issuing a prompt:

```
[1]-  Done                    d
[2]+  Done                    e
```

The next command line executes all three tasks as background jobs. The shell displays a shell prompt immediately:

```
$ d & e & f &
[1] 14290
[2] 14291
[3] 14292
```

You can use a pipe to send the output from one command to the next command and an ampersand (**&**) to run the entire job in the background. Again the shell displays the prompt immediately. The shell commands joined by a pipe form a single job. That is, it treats all pipes as single jobs, no matter how many commands are connected with the pipe (|) symbol or how complex they are. The Bourne Again Shell reports only one process in the background (although there are three):

```
$ d | e | f &
[1] 14295
```

optional ## () GROUPS COMMANDS

You can use parentheses to group commands. The shell creates a copy of itself, called a *subshell*, for each group. It treats each group of commands as a job and creates a new process to execute each command (refer to "Process Structure" on page 316 for more information on creating subshells). Each subshell (job) has its own environment, meaning it has its own set of variables whose values can differ from those in other subshells.

The following command line executes commands **a** and **b** sequentially in the background while executing **c** in the background. The shell displays a prompt immediately.

```
$ (a ; b) & c &
[1] 15520
[2] 15521
```

The preceding example differs from the earlier example **d** & **e** & **f** & in that tasks **a** and **b** are initiated sequentially, not concurrently.

Similarly the following command line executes **a** and **b** sequentially in the background and, at the same time, executes **c** and **d** sequentially in the background. The subshell running **a** and **b** and the subshell running **c** and **d** run concurrently. The shell displays a prompt immediately.

```
$ (a ; b) & (c ; d) &
[1] 15528
[2] 15529
```

The next script copies one directory to another. The second pair of parentheses creates a subshell to run the commands following the pipe. Because of these parentheses, the output of the first tar command is available for the second tar command, despite the intervening cd command. Without the parentheses, the output of the first tar command would be sent to cd and lost because cd does not process standard input. The shell variables **$1** and **$2** hold the first and second command-line arguments (page 1013), respectively. The first pair of parentheses, which creates a subshell to run the first two commands, allows users to call **cpdir** with relative pathnames. Without them, the first cd command would change the working directory of the script (and consequently the working directory of the second cd command). With them, only the working directory of the subshell is changed.

```
$ cat cpdir
(cd $1 ; tar -cf - . ) | (cd $2 ; tar -xvf - )
$ ./cpdir /home/max/sources /home/max/memo/biblio
```

The **cpdir** command line copies the files and directories in the **/home/max/sources** directory to the directory named **/home/max/memo/biblio**. This shell script is almost the same as using cp with the **–r** option. Refer to the cp and tar man pages for more information.

JOB CONTROL

A *job* is a command pipeline. You run a simple job whenever you give the shell a command. For example, if you type **date** on the command line and press RETURN, you have run a job. You can also create several jobs with multiple commands on a single command line:

```
$ find . -print | sort | lpr & grep -l max /tmp/* > maxfiles &
[1] 18839
[2] 18876
```

The portion of the command line up to the first & is one job consisting of three processes connected by pipes: find, sort (page 154), and lpr (page 151). The second job is a single process running grep. The trailing & characters put each job in the background, so bash does not wait for them to complete before displaying a prompt.

Using job control you can move commands from the foreground to the background and vice versa, stop commands temporarily, and list all commands that are running in the background or stopped.

jobs: LISTS JOBS

The jobs builtin lists all background jobs. Following, the sleep command runs in the background and creates a background job that jobs reports on:

```
$ sleep 60 &
[1] 7809
$ jobs
[1] + Running                 sleep 60 &
```

fg: BRINGS A JOB TO THE FOREGROUND

The shell assigns a job number to each command you run in the background. For each job run in the background, the shell lists the job number and PID number immediately, just before it issues a prompt:

```
$ gnome-calculator &
[1] 1246
$ date &
[2] 1247
$ Tue Dec 7 11:44:40 PST 2010
[2]+ Done          date
$ find /usr -name ace -print > findout &
[2] 1269
$ jobs
[1]- Running           gnome-calculator &
[2]+ Running           find /usr -name ace -print > findout &
```

Job numbers, which are discarded when a job is finished, can be reused. When you start or put a job in the background, the shell assigns a job number that is one more than the highest job number in use.

In the preceding example, the jobs command lists the first job, gnome-calculator, as job 1. The date command does not appear in the jobs list because it finished before jobs was run. Because the date command was completed before find was run, the find command became job 2.

To move a background job to the foreground, use the fg builtin followed by the job number. Alternatively, you can give a percent sign (%) followed by the job number as a command. Either of the following commands moves job 2 to the foreground. When you move a job to the foreground, the shell displays the command it is now executing in the foreground.

```
$ fg 2
find /usr -name ace -print > findout
```

or

```
$ %2
find /usr -name ace -print > findout
```

You can also refer to a job by following the percent sign with a string that uniquely identifies the beginning of the command line used to start the job. Instead of the preceding command, you could have used either **fg %find** or **fg %f** because both uniquely identify job 2. If you follow the percent sign with a question mark and a string, the string can match any part of the command line. In the preceding example, **fg %?ace** also brings job 2 to the foreground.

Often the job you wish to bring to the foreground is the only job running in the background or is the job that jobs lists with a plus (**+**). In these cases fg without an argument brings the job to the foreground.

SUSPENDING A JOB

Pressing the suspend key (usually CONTROL-Z) immediately suspends (temporarily stops) the job in the foreground and displays a message that includes the word **Stopped**.

```
CONTROL-Z
[2]+  Stopped                    find /usr -name ace -print > findout
```

For more information refer to "Moving a Job from the Foreground to the Background" on page 243.

bg: SENDS A JOB TO THE BACKGROUND

To move the foreground job to the background, you must first suspend the job (previous). You can then use the bg builtin to resume execution of the job in the background.

```
$ bg
[2]+ find /usr -name ace -print > findout &
```

If a background job attempts to read from the terminal, the shell stops the program and displays a message saying the job has been stopped. You must then move the job to the foreground so it can read from the terminal.

```
$ (sleep 5; cat > mytext) &
[1] 1343
$ date
Wed Dec  7 11:58:20 PST 2011
[1]+ Stopped                    ( sleep 5; cat >mytext )
$ fg
( sleep 5; cat >mytext )
Remember to let the cat out!
CONTROL-D
$
```

In the preceding example, the shell displays the job number and PID number of the background job as soon as it starts, followed by a prompt. Demonstrating that you can give a command at this point, the user gives the command date, and its output appears on the screen. The shell waits until just before it issues a prompt (after date has finished) to notify you that job 1 is stopped. When you give an **fg** command, the shell puts the job in the foreground, and you can enter the data the command is waiting for. In this case the input needs to be terminated with CONTROL-D, which sends an EOF (end of file) signal to cat. The shell then displays another prompt.

The shell keeps you informed about changes in the status of a job, notifying you when a background job starts, completes, or stops, perhaps because it is waiting for input from the terminal. The shell also lets you know when a foreground job is suspended. Because notices about a job being run in the background can disrupt your work, the shell delays displaying these notices until just before it displays a prompt. You can set **notify** (page 343) to cause the shell to display these notices without delay.

If you try to exit from a nonlogin shell while jobs are stopped, the shell issues a warning and does not allow you to exit. If you then use jobs to review the list of jobs or you immediately try to exit from the shell again, the shell allows you to exit. If **huponexit** (page 343) is not set (the default), stopped jobs remain stopped and background jobs keep running in the background. If it is set, the shell terminates these jobs.

MANIPULATING THE DIRECTORY STACK

The Bourne Again Shell allows you to store a list of directories you are working with, enabling you to move easily among them. This list is referred to as a *stack*. It is analogous to a stack of dinner plates: You typically add plates to and remove plates from the top of the stack, so this type of stack is named a LIFO (last in, first out) stack.

dirs: DISPLAYS THE STACK

The dirs builtin displays the contents of the directory stack. If you call dirs when the directory stack is empty, it displays the name of the working directory:

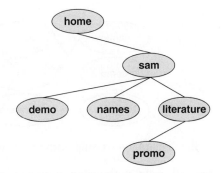

Figure 9-2 The directory structure in the examples

```
$ dirs
~/literature
```

The dirs builtin uses a tilde (~) to represent the name of a user's home directory. The examples in the next several sections assume you are referring to the directory structure shown in Figure 9-2.

pushd: PUSHES A DIRECTORY ON THE STACK

When you supply the pushd (push directory) builtin with one argument, it pushes the directory specified by the argument on the stack, changes directories to the specified directory, and displays the stack. The following example is illustrated in Figure 9-3:

```
$ pushd ../demo
~/demo ~/literature
$ pwd
/home/sam/demo
$ pushd ../names
~/names ~/demo ~/literature
$ pwd
/home/sam/names
```

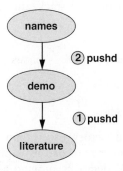

Figure 9-3 Creating a directory stack

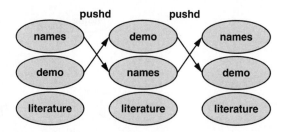

Figure 9-4   Using pushd to change working directories

When you call pushd without an argument, it swaps the top two directories on the stack, makes the new top directory (which was the second directory) the new working directory, and displays the stack (Figure 9-4):

```
$ pushd
~/demo ~/names ~/literature
$ pwd
/home/sam/demo
```

Using pushd in this way, you can easily move back and forth between two directories. You can also use **cd –** to change to the previous directory, whether or not you have explicitly created a directory stack. To access another directory in the stack, call pushd with a numeric argument preceded by a plus sign. The directories in the stack are numbered starting with the top directory, which is number 0. The following pushd command continues with the previous example, changing the working directory to **literature** and moving **literature** to the top of the stack:

```
$ pushd +2
~/literature ~/demo ~/names
$ pwd
/home/sam/literature
```

popd: POPS A DIRECTORY OFF THE STACK

To remove a directory from the stack, use the popd (pop directory) builtin. As the following example and Figure 9-5 show, without an argument, popd removes the top directory from the stack and changes the working directory to the new top directory:

```
$ dirs
~/literature ~/demo ~/names
$ popd
~/demo ~/names
$ pwd
/home/sam/demo
```

To remove a directory other than the top one from the stack, use popd with a numeric argument preceded by a plus sign. The following example removes directory number 1, **demo**. Removing a directory other than directory number 0 does not change the working directory.

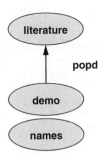

Figure 9-5   Using popd to remove a directory from the stack

```
$ dirs
~/literature ~/demo ~/names
$ popd +1
~/literature ~/names
```

PARAMETERS AND VARIABLES

Variables   Within a shell, a *shell parameter* is associated with a value that is accessible to the user. There are several kinds of shell parameters. Parameters whose names consist of letters, digits, and underscores are often referred to as *shell variables,* or simply *variables.* A variable name must start with a letter or underscore, not with a number. Thus **A76, MY_CAT,** and **___X___** are valid variable names, whereas **69TH_STREET** (starts with a digit) and **MY-NAME** (contains a hyphen) are not.

User-created variables   Shell variables that you name and assign values to are *user-created variables.* You can change the values of user-created variables at any time, or you can make them *readonly* so that their values cannot be changed. You can also make user-created variables *global.* A global variable (also called an *environment variable*) is available to all shells and other programs you fork from the shell in which it was created. One naming convention is to use only uppercase letters for global variables and to use mixed-case or lowercase letters for other variables. Refer to "Locality of Variables" on page 1008 for more information on global variables.

To assign a value to a variable in the Bourne Again Shell, use the following syntax:

VARIABLE=value

There can be no whitespace on either side of the equal sign (=). An example assignment follows:

```
$ myvar=abc
```

The Bourne Again Shell permits you to put variable assignments on a command line. This type of assignment creates a variable that is local to the command shell—that is, the variable is accessible only from the program the command runs. The **my_script** shell script displays the value of **TEMPDIR**. The following command runs **my_script** with **TEMPDIR** set to **/home/sam/temp**. The echo builtin shows that the interactive shell has no value for **TEMPDIR** after running **my_script**. If **TEMPDIR** had been set in the interactive shell, running **my_script** in this manner would have had no effect on its value.

```
$ cat my_script
echo $TEMPDIR
$ TEMPDIR=/home/sam/temp ./my_script
/home/sam/temp
$ echo $TEMPDIR

$
```

Keyword variables   *Keyword shell variables* (or simply *keyword variables*) have special meaning to the shell and usually have short, mnemonic names. When you start a shell (by logging in, for example), the shell inherits several keyword variables from the environment. Among these variables are **HOME**, which identifies your home directory, and **PATH**, which determines which directories the shell searches and in what order to locate commands that you give the shell. The shell creates and initializes (with default values) other keyword variables when you start it. Still other variables do not exist until you set them.

You can change the values of most keyword shell variables. It is usually not necessary to change the values of keyword variables initialized in the **/etc/profile** or **/etc/csh.cshrc** systemwide startup files. If you need to change the value of a bash keyword variable, do so in one of your startup files (page 282). Just as you can make user-created variables global, so you can make keyword variables global—a task usually done automatically in startup files. You can also make a keyword variable readonly.

Positional and special parameters   The names of positional and special parameters do not resemble variable names. Most of these parameters have one-character names (for example, **1**, **?**, and **#**) and are referenced (as are all variables) by preceding the name with a dollar sign (**$1**, **$?**, and **$#**). The values of these parameters reflect different aspects of your ongoing interaction with the shell.

Whenever you run a command, each argument on the command line becomes the value of a *positional parameter* (page 1012). Positional parameters enable you to access command-line arguments, a capability you will often require when you write shell scripts. The set builtin (page 1014) enables you to assign values to positional parameters.

Other frequently needed shell script values, such as the name of the last command executed, the number of command-line arguments, and the status of the most recently executed command, are available as *special parameters* (page 1010). You cannot assign values to special parameters.

USER-CREATED VARIABLES

The first line in the following example declares the variable named **person** and initializes it with the value **max**:

```
$ person=max
$ echo person
person
$ echo $person
max
```

Parameter
substitution

Because the echo builtin copies its arguments to standard output, you can use it to display the values of variables. The second line of the preceding example shows that **person** does not represent **max**. Instead, the string **person** is echoed as **person**. The shell substitutes the value of a variable only when you precede the name of the variable with a dollar sign ($). Thus the command **echo $person** displays the value of the variable **person**; it does not display **$person** because the shell does not pass **$person** to echo as an argument. Because of the leading $, the shell recognizes that **$person** is the name of a variable, *substitutes* the value of the variable, and passes that value to echo. The echo builtin displays the value of the variable—not its name—never "knowing" you called it with a variable.

Quoting the $

You can prevent the shell from substituting the value of a variable by quoting the leading $. Double quotation marks do not prevent the substitution; single quotation marks or a backslash (\) do.

```
$ echo $person
max
$ echo "$person"
max
$ echo '$person'
$person
$ echo \$person
$person
```

SPACES

Because they do not prevent variable substitution but do turn off the special meanings of most other characters, double quotation marks are useful when you assign values to variables and when you use those values. To assign a value that contains SPACEs or TABs to a variable, use double quotation marks around the value. Although double quotation marks are not required in all cases, using them is a good habit.

```
$ person="max and zach"
$ echo $person
max and zach
$ person=max and zach
bash: and: command not found
```

When you reference a variable whose value contains TABs or multiple adjacent SPACEs, you must use quotation marks to preserve the spacing. If you do not quote the variable, the shell collapses each string of blank characters into a single SPACE before passing the variable to the utility:

```
$ person="max    and    zach"
$ echo $person
max and zach
$ echo "$person"
max    and    zach
```

Pathname
expansion in
assignments
When you execute a command with a variable as an argument, the shell replaces the name of the variable with the value of the variable and passes that value to the program being executed. If the value of the variable contains a special character, such as * or ?, the shell *might* expand that variable.

The first line in the following sequence of commands assigns the string **max*** to the variable **memo**. The Bourne Again Shell does *not expand the string* because bash does not perform pathname expansion (page 244) when it assigns a value to a variable. All shells process a command line in a specific order. Within this order bash expands variables before it interprets commands. In the following echo command line, the double quotation marks quote the asterisk (*****) in the expanded value of **$memo** and prevent bash from performing pathname expansion on the expanded **memo** variable before passing its value to the echo command:

```
$ memo=max*
$ echo "$memo"
max*
```

All shells interpret special characters as special when you reference a variable that contains an unquoted special character. In the following example, the shell expands the value of the **memo** variable because it is not quoted:

```
$ ls
max.report
max.summary
$ echo $memo
max.report max.summary
```

Here the shell expands the **$memo** variable to **max***, expands **max*** to **max.report** and **max.summary**, and passes these two values to echo.

optional

Braces
The *$VARIABLE* syntax is a special case of the more general syntax *${VARIABLE}*, in which the variable name is enclosed by ${}. The braces insulate the variable name from adjacent characters. Braces are necessary when catenating a variable value with a string:

```
$ PREF=counter
$ WAY=$PREFclockwise
$ FAKE=$PREFfeit
$ echo $WAY $FAKE

$
```

The preceding example does not work as expected. Only a blank line is output because although the symbols **PREFclockwise** and **PREFfeit** are valid variable names, they are not set. By default bash evaluates an unset variable as an empty (null) string and displays this value. To achieve the intent of these statements, refer to the **PREF** variable using braces:

```
$ PREF=counter
$ WAY=${PREF}clockwise
$ FAKE=${PREF}feit
$ echo $WAY $FAKE
counterclockwise counterfeit
```

The Bourne Again Shell refers to the arguments on its command line by position, using the special variables **$1**, **$2**, **$3**, and so forth up to **$9**. If you wish to refer to arguments past the ninth argument, you must use braces: **${10}**. The name of the command is held in **$0** (page 1013).

unset: REMOVES A VARIABLE

Unless you remove a variable, it exists as long as the shell in which it was created exists. To remove the *value* of a variable but not the variable itself, assign a null value to the variable:

```
$ person=
$ echo $person

$
```

You can remove a variable using the unset builtin. The following command removes the variable **person**:

```
$ unset person
```

VARIABLE ATTRIBUTES

This section discusses attributes and explains how to assign them to variables.

readonly: MAKES THE VALUE OF A VARIABLE PERMANENT

You can use the readonly builtin to ensure that the value of a variable cannot be changed. The next example declares the variable **person** to be readonly. You must assign a value to a variable *before* you declare it to be readonly; you cannot change its value after the declaration. When you attempt to unset or change the value of a readonly variable, the shell displays an error message:

```
$ person=zach
$ echo $person
zach
$ readonly person
$ person=helen
bash: person: readonly variable
```

If you use the readonly builtin without an argument, it displays a list of all readonly shell variables. This list includes keyword variables that are automatically set as readonly as well as keyword or user-created variables that you have declared as readonly. See page 306 for an example (**readonly** and **declare –r** produce the same output).

declare AND typeset: ASSIGN ATTRIBUTES TO VARIABLES

The declare and typeset builtins (two names for the same command) set attributes and values for shell variables. Table 9-3 lists five of these attributes.

Table 9-3   Variable attributes (typeset or declare)

Attribute	Meaning
−a	Declares a variable as an array (page 1006)
−f	Declares a variable to be a function name (page 338)
−i	Declares a variable to be of type integer (page 307)
−r	Makes a variable readonly; also readonly (page 305)
−x	Exports a variable (makes it global); also export (page 1008)

The following commands declare several variables and set some attributes. The first line declares **person1** and assigns it a value of **max**. This command has the same effect with or without the word **declare**.

```
$ declare person1=max
$ declare -r person2=zach
$ declare -rx person3=helen
$ declare -x person4
```

The readonly and export builtins are synonyms for the commands **declare −r** and **declare −x**, respectively. You can declare a variable without assigning a value to it, as the preceding declaration of the variable **person4** illustrates. This declaration makes **person4** available to all subshells (i.e., makes it global). Until an assignment is made to the variable, it has a null value.

You can list the options to declare separately in any order. The following is equivalent to the preceding declaration of **person3**:

```
$ declare -x -r person3=helen
```

Use the + character in place of − when you want to remove an attribute from a variable. You cannot remove the readonly attribute. After the following command is given, the variable **person3** is no longer exported, but it is still readonly.

```
$ declare +x person3
```

You can use typeset in place of declare.

Listing variable attributes   Without any arguments or options, declare lists all shell variables. The same list is output when you run set (page 1014) without any arguments.

If you use a declare builtin with options but no variable names as arguments, the command lists all shell variables that have the indicated attributes set. For example, the command **declare −r** displays a list of all readonly shell variables. This list is the same as that produced by the **readonly** command without any arguments. After the declarations in the preceding example have been given, the results are as follows:

```
$ declare -r
declare -r BASHOPTS="checkwinsize:cmdhist:expand_aliases: ... "
declare -ir BASHPID
declare -ar BASH_VERSINFO='([0]="4" [1]="2" [2]="8" [3]="1" ... '
declare -ir EUID="500"
declare -ir PPID="1936"
declare -r SHELLOPTS="braceexpand:emacs:hashall:histexpand: ... "
declare -ir UID="500"
declare -r person2="zach"
declare -rx person3="helen"
```

The first seven entries are keyword variables that are automatically declared as readonly. Some of these variables are stored as integers (–i). The –a option indicates that **BASH_VERSINFO** is an array variable; the value of each element of the array is listed to the right of an equal sign.

Integer By default the values of variables are stored as strings. When you perform arithmetic on a string variable, the shell converts the variable into a number, manipulates it, and then converts it back to a string. A variable with the integer attribute is stored as an integer. Assign the integer attribute as follows:

```
$ declare -i COUNT
```

KEYWORD VARIABLES

Keyword variables are either inherited or declared and initialized by the shell when it starts. You can assign values to these variables from the command line or from a startup file. Typically you want these variables to apply to all subshells you start as well as to your login shell. For those variables not automatically exported by the shell, you must use export (page 1008) to make them available to child shells.

HOME: YOUR HOME DIRECTORY

By default your home directory is the working directory when you log in. Your home directory is established when your account is set up; its name is stored in the **/etc/passwd** file.

```
$ grep sam /etc/passwd
sam:x:500:500:Sam the Great:/home/sam:/bin/bash
```

When you log in, the shell inherits the pathname of your home directory and assigns it to the variable **HOME**. When you give a **cd** command without an argument, **cd** makes the directory whose name is stored in **HOME** the working directory:

```
$ pwd
/home/max/laptop
$ echo $HOME
/home/max
$ cd
$ pwd
/home/max
```

This example shows the value of the **HOME** variable and the effect of the cd builtin. After you execute cd without an argument, the pathname of the working directory is the same as the value of **HOME**: your home directory.

Tilde (~) The shell uses the value of **HOME** to expand pathnames that use the shorthand tilde (~) notation (page 193) to denote a user's home directory. The following example uses echo to display the value of this shortcut and then uses ls to list the files in Max's **laptop** directory, which is a subdirectory of his home directory:

```
$ echo ~
/home/max
$ ls ~/laptop
tester      count      lineup
```

PATH: WHERE THE SHELL LOOKS FOR PROGRAMS

When you give the shell an absolute or relative pathname rather than a simple file-name as a command, it looks in the specified directory for an executable file with the specified filename. If the file with the pathname you specified does not exist, the shell reports **command not found**. If the file exists as specified but you do not have execute permission for it, or in the case of a shell script you do not have read and execute permission for, the shell reports **Permission denied.**

If you give a simple filename as a command, the shell searches through certain directories (your search path) for the program you want to execute. It looks in several directories for a file that has the same name as the command and that you have execute permission for (a compiled program) or read and execute permission for (a shell script). The **PATH** shell variable controls this search.

The default value of **PATH** is determined when bash is compiled. It is not set in a startup file, although it might be modified there. Normally the default specifies that the shell search several system directories used to hold common commands. These system directories include **/bin** and **/usr/bin** and other directories appropriate to the local system. When you give a command, if the shell does not find the execut-able—and, in the case of a shell script, readable—file named by the command in any of the directories listed in **PATH**, the shell generates one of the aforementioned error messages.

Working directory The **PATH** variable specifies the directories in the order the shell should search them. Each directory must be separated from the next by a colon. The following command sets **PATH** so a search for an executable file starts with the **/usr/local/bin** directory. If it does not find the file in this directory, the shell looks next in **/bin** and then in **/usr/bin**. If the search fails in those directories, the shell looks in the **~/bin** directory, a subdirectory of the user's home directory. Finally the shell looks in the working directory. Exporting **PATH** makes its value accessible to subshells:

```
$ export PATH=/usr/local/bin:/bin:/usr/bin:~/bin:
```

A null value in the string indicates the working directory. In the preceding example, a null value (nothing between the colon and the end of the line) appears as the last element of the string. The working directory is represented by a leading colon (not recommended; see the following security tip), a trailing colon (as in the example), or two colons next to each other anywhere in the string. You can also represent the working directory explicitly with a period (.).

Because Linux stores many executable files in directories named **bin** (*binary*), users typically put their executable files in their own **~/bin** directories. If you put your own **bin** directory at the end of your **PATH**, as in the preceding example, the shell looks there for any commands that it cannot find in directories listed earlier in **PATH**.

PATH and security

security Do not put the working directory first in **PATH** when security is a concern. If you are working as **root**, you should *never* put the working directory first in **PATH**. It is common for **root**'s **PATH** to omit the working directory entirely. You can always execute a file in the working directory by prepending ./ to the name: **./myprog**.

Putting the working directory first in **PATH** can create a security hole. Most people type **ls** as the first command when entering a directory. If the owner of a directory places an executable file named **ls** in the directory, and the working directory appears first in a user's **PATH**, the user giving an **ls** command from the directory executes the ls program in the working directory instead of the system ls utility, possibly with undesirable results.

If you want to add directories to **PATH**, you can reference the old value of the **PATH** variable in setting **PATH** to a new value (but see the preceding security tip). The following command adds **/usr/local/bin** to the beginning of the current **PATH** and the **bin** directory in the user's home directory (**~/bin**) to the end:

```
$ PATH=/usr/local/bin:$PATH:~/bin
```

MAIL: WHERE YOUR MAIL IS KEPT

The **MAIL** variable contains the pathname of the file that holds your mail (your *mailbox*, usually **/var/mail/***name*, where ***name*** is your username). If **MAIL** is set and **MAILPATH** (next) is not set, the shell informs you when mail arrives in the file specified by **MAIL**. In a graphical environment you can unset **MAIL** so the shell does not display mail reminders in a terminal emulator window (assuming you are using a graphical mail program).

The **MAILPATH** variable contains a list of filenames separated by colons. If this variable is set, the shell informs you when any one of the files is modified (for example, when mail arrives). You can follow any of the filenames in the list with a question mark (?) and a message. The message replaces the **you have mail** message when you receive mail while you are logged in.

The **MAILCHECK** variable specifies how often, in seconds, the shell checks for new mail. The default is 60 seconds. If you set this variable to zero, the shell checks before each prompt.

PS1: USER PROMPT (PRIMARY)

The default Bourne Again Shell prompt is a dollar sign ($). When you run bash with **root** privileges, bash typically displays a hashmark (#) prompt. The **PS1** variable holds the prompt string the shell uses to let you know it is waiting for a command. When you change the value of **PS1**, you change the appearance of your prompt.

You can customize the prompt displayed by **PS1**. For example, the assignment

```
$ PS1="[\u@\h \W \!]$ "
```

displays the following prompt:

[user@host directory event]$

where *user* is the username, *host* is the hostname up to the first period, *directory* is the basename of the working directory, and *event* is the event number (page 320) of the current command.

If you are working on more than one system, it can be helpful to incorporate the system name into your prompt. For example, you might change the prompt to the name of the system you are using, followed by a colon and a SPACE (a SPACE at the end of the prompt makes the commands you enter after the prompt easier to read). This command uses command substitution (page 351) in the string assigned to **PS1**:

```
$ PS1="$(hostname): "
guava: echo test
test
guava:
```

The first example that follows changes the prompt to the name of the local host, a SPACE, and a dollar sign (or, if the user is running with **root** privileges, a hashmark). The second example changes the prompt to the time followed by the name of the user. The third example changes the prompt to the one used in this book (a hashmark for a user running with **root** privileges and a dollar sign otherwise):

```
$ PS1='\h \$ '
guava $

$ PS1='\@ \u $ '
09:44 PM max $

$ PS1='\$ '
$
```

Table 9-4 describes some of the symbols you can use in **PS1**. For a complete list of special characters you can use in the prompt strings, open the bash man page and search for the third occurrence of **PROMPTING** (enter the command **/PROMPTING** and then press **n** two times).

Table 9-4   **PS1** symbols

Symbol	Display in prompt
\$	# if the user is running with **root** privileges; otherwise, **$**
\w	Pathname of the working directory
\W	Basename of the working directory
\!	Current event (history) number (page 324)
\d	Date in Weekday Month Date format
\h	Machine hostname, without the domain
\H	Full machine hostname, including the domain
\u	Username of the current user
\@	Current time of day in 12-hour, AM/PM format
\T	Current time of day in 12-hour HH:MM:SS format
\A	Current time of day in 24-hour HH:MM format
\t	Current time of day in 24-hour HH:MM:SS format

PS2: USER PROMPT (SECONDARY)

The **PS2** variable holds the secondary prompt. On the first line of the next example, an unclosed quoted string follows echo. The shell assumes the command is not finished and on the second line gives the default secondary prompt (>). This prompt indicates the shell is waiting for the user to continue the command line. The shell waits until it receives the quotation mark that closes the string and then executes the command:

```
$ echo "demonstration of prompt string
> 2"
demonstration of prompt string
2
$ PS2="secondary prompt: "
$ echo "this demonstrates
secondary prompt: prompt string 2"
this demonstrates
prompt string 2
```

The second command changes the secondary prompt to **secondary prompt:** followed by a SPACE. A multiline echo demonstrates the new prompt.

PS3: MENU PROMPT

The **PS3** variable holds the menu prompt for the **select** control structure (page 1000).

PS4: DEBUGGING PROMPT

The PS4 variable holds the bash debugging symbol (page 982).

IFS: SEPARATES INPUT FIELDS (WORD SPLITTING)

The **IFS** (Internal Field Separator) shell variable specifies the characters you can use to separate arguments on a command line. It has the default value of SPACE TAB NEWLINE. Regardless of the value of **IFS**, you can always use one or more SPACE or TAB characters to separate arguments on the command line, provided these characters are not quoted or escaped. When you assign **IFS** character values, these characters can also separate fields—but only if they undergo expansion. This type of interpretation of the command line is called *word splitting*.

Be careful when changing IFS

Changing **IFS** has a variety of side effects, so work cautiously. You might find it useful to save the value of **IFS** before changing it. Then you can easily restore the original value if you get unexpected results. Alternatively, you can fork a new shell using a **bash** command before experimenting with **IFS**; if you get into trouble, you can **exit** back to the old shell, where **IFS** is working properly.

The following example demonstrates how setting IFS can affect the interpretation of a command line:

```
$ a=w:x:y:z

$ cat $a
cat: w:x:y:z: No such file or directory
$ IFS=":"

$ cat $a
cat: w: No such file or directory
cat: x: No such file or directory
cat: y: No such file or directory
cat: z: No such file or directory
```

The first time cat is called, the shell expands the variable **a**, interpreting the string **w:x:y:z** as a single word to be used as the argument to cat. The cat utility cannot find a file named **w:x:y:z** and reports an error for that filename. After **IFS** is set to a colon (:), the shell expands the variable **a** into four words, each of which is an argument to cat. Now cat reports errors for four files: **w**, **x**, **y**, and **z**. Word splitting based on the colon (:) takes place only *after* the variable **a** is expanded.

The shell splits all *expanded* words on a command line according to the separating characters found in **IFS**. When there is no expansion, there is no splitting. Consider the following commands:

```
$ IFS="p"
$ export VAR
```

Although IFS is set to **p**, the **p** on the **export** command line is not expanded, so the word **export** is not split.

The following example uses variable expansion in an attempt to produce an **export** command:

```
$ IFS="p"
$ aa=export
$ echo $aa
ex ort
```

This time expansion occurs, so the **p** in the token **export** is interpreted as a separator (as the echo command shows). Now when you try to use the value of the **aa** variable to export the **VAR** variable, the shell parses the $aa VAR command line as **ex ort VAR**. The effect is that the command line starts the **ex** editor with two filenames: **ort** and **VAR**.

```
$ $aa VAR
2 files to edit
"ort" [New File]
Entering Ex mode.  Type "visual" to go to Normal mode.
:q
E173: 1 more file to edit
:q
$
```

If you unset **IFS**, only SPACEs and TABs work as field separators.

Multiple separator characters

tip   Although the shell treats sequences of multiple SPACE or TAB characters as a single separator, it treats *each occurrence* of another field-separator character as a separator.

CDPATH: BROADENS THE SCOPE OF cd

The **CDPATH** variable allows you to use a simple filename as an argument to the cd builtin to change the working directory to a directory other than a child of the working directory. If you have several directories you typically work in, this variable can speed things up and save you the tedium of using cd with longer pathnames to switch among them.

When **CDPATH** is not set and you specify a simple filename as an argument to cd, cd searches the working directory for a subdirectory with the same name as the argument. If the subdirectory does not exist, cd displays an error message. When **CDPATH** is set, cd searches for an appropriately named subdirectory in the directories in the **CDPATH** list. If it finds one, that directory becomes the working directory. With **CDPATH** set, you can use cd and a simple filename to change the working directory to a child of any of the directories listed in **CDPATH**.

The **CDPATH** variable takes on the value of a colon-separated list of directory pathnames (similar to the **PATH** variable). It is usually set in the ~/.bash_profile startup file with a command line such as the following:

```
export CDPATH=$HOME:$HOME/literature
```

This command causes cd to search your home directory, the **literature** directory, and then the working directory when you give a cd command. If you do not include the working directory in **CDPATH**, cd searches the working directory if the search of all the other directories in **CDPATH** fails. If you want cd to search the working directory first, include a null string, represented by two colons (::), as the first entry in **CDPATH**:

```
export CDPATH=::$HOME:$HOME/literature
```

If the argument to the cd builtin is anything other than a simple filename—one that contains a slash (/)—the shell does not consult **CDPATH**.

KEYWORD VARIABLES: A SUMMARY

Table 9-5 presents a list of bash keyword variables.

Table 9-5   bash keyword variables

Variable	Value
BASH_ENV	The pathname of the startup file for noninteractive shells (page 283)
CDPATH	The cd search path (page 313)
COLUMNS	The width of the display used by **select** (page 999)
FCEDIT	The name of the editor that fc uses by default (page 322)
HISTFILE	The pathname of the file that holds the history list (default: **~/.bash_history**; page 319)
HISTFILESIZE	The maximum number of entries saved in **HISTFILE** (default: 1000; page 319)
HISTSIZE	The maximum number of entries saved in the history list (default: 1000; page 319)
HOME	The pathname of the user's home directory (page 307); used as the default argument for cd and in tilde expansion (page 193)
IFS	Internal Field Separator (page 312); used for word splitting (page 352)
INPUTRC	The pathname of the Readline startup file (default: **~/.inputrc**; page 332)
LANG	The locale category when that category is not specifically set with an **LC_*** variable
LC_*	A group of variables that specify locale categories including **LC_COLLATE**, **LC_CTYPE**, **LC_MESSAGES**, and **LC_NUMERIC**; use the locale builtin to display a complete list with values
LINES	The height of the display used by **select** (page 999)
MAIL	The pathname of the file that holds a user's mail (page 309)
MAILCHECK	How often, in seconds, bash checks for mail (default 60; page 309)

Table 9-5   bash keyword variables (continued)

Variable	Value
MAILPATH	A colon-separated list of file pathnames that bash checks for mail in (page 309)
PATH	A colon-separated list of directory pathnames that bash looks for commands in (page 308)
PROMPT_COMMAND	A command that bash executes just before it displays the primary prompt
PS1	Prompt String 1; the primary prompt (page 310)
PS2	Prompt String 2; the secondary prompt (default: > ; page 311)
PS3	The prompt issued by **select** (page 999)
PS4	The bash debugging symbol (page 982)
REPLY	Holds the line that read accepts (page 1020); also used by **select** (page 999)

SPECIAL CHARACTERS

Table 9-6 lists most of the characters that are special to the bash shell.

Table 9-6   Shell special characters

Character	Use
NEWLINE	Initiates execution of a command (page 292)
;	Separates commands (page 292)
( )	Groups commands (page 295) for execution by a subshell or identifies a function (page 338)
(( ))	Expands an arithmetic expression (page 349)
&	Executes a command in the background (pages 242 and 293)
|	Sends standard output of the preceding command to standard input of the following command (pipe; page 293)
>	Redirects standard output (page 234)
>>	Appends standard output (page 238)
<	Redirects standard input (page 236)
<<	Here document (page 1001)
*	Any string of zero or more characters in an ambiguous file reference (page 246)

Table 9-6   Shell special characters (continued)

Character	Use
?	Any single character in an ambiguous file reference (page 245)
\	Quotes the following character (page 146)
'	Quotes a string, preventing all substitution (page 146)
"	Quotes a string, allowing only variable and command substitution (pages 146 and 303)
`...`	Performs command substitution [deprecated, see **$()**]
[ ]	Character class in an ambiguous file reference (page 247)
$	References a variable (page 301)
. (dot builtin)	Executes a command (page 284)
#	Begins a comment (page 291)
{ }	Surrounds the contents of a function (page 338)
: (null builtin)	Returns *true* (page 1027)
&& (Boolean AND)	Executes command on right only if command on left succeeds (returns a zero exit status; page 1038)
‖ (Boolean OR)	Executes command on right only if command on left fails (returns a nonzero exit status; page 1038)
! (Boolean NOT)	Reverses exit status of a command
$()	Performs command substitution (preferred form; page 351)
[]	Evaluates an arithmetic expression (page 349)

PROCESSES

A *process* is the execution of a command by the Linux kernel. The shell that starts when you log in is a command, or a process, like any other. When you give the name of a Linux utility on the command line, you initiate a process. When you run a shell script, another shell process is started, and additional processes are created for each command in the script. Depending on how you invoke the shell script, the script is run either by the current shell or, more typically, by a subshell (child) of the current shell. Running a shell builtin, such as cd, does not start a process.

PROCESS STRUCTURE

fork system call   Like the file structure, the process structure is hierarchical, with parents, children, and even a *root*. A parent process *forks* a child process, which in turn can fork other processes. (The term *fork* indicates that, as with a fork in the road, one process turns into two. Initially the two forks are identical except that one is identified as the parent and one as the child. You can also use the term *spawn;* the words are interchangeable.) The operating system routine, or *system call,* that creates a new process is named **fork**().

init daemon   When Linux begins execution as a system is started, it starts the **init** daemon, a single process called a *spontaneous process,* with PID number 1. This process holds the same position in the process structure as the root directory does in the file structure: It is the ancestor of all processes the system and users work with. When a command-line system is in multiuser mode, init runs getty or mingetty processes, which display **login:** prompts on terminals and virtual consoles. When a user responds to the prompt and presses RETURN, getty or mingetty passes control to a utility named login, which checks the username and password combination. After the user logs in, the login process becomes the user's shell process.

When you enter the name of a program on the command line, the shell **forks** a new process, creating a duplicate of the shell process (a subshell). The new process attempts to **exec** (execute) the program. Like **fork,** the **exec** routine is executed by the operating system (a system call). If the program is a binary executable, such as a compiled C program, **exec** succeeds, and the system overlays the newly created subshell with the executable program. If the command is a shell script, **exec** fails. When **exec** fails, the program is assumed to be a shell script, and the subshell runs the commands in the script. Unlike a login shell, which expects input from the command line, the subshell takes its input from a file—namely, the shell script.

PROCESS IDENTIFICATION

PID numbers   Linux assigns a unique PID (process identification) number at the inception of each process. As long as a process exists, it keeps the same PID number. During one session the same process is always executing the *login shell* (page 1174). When you fork a new process—for example, when you use an editor—the PID number of the new (child) process is different from that of its parent process. When you return to the login shell, it is still being executed by the same process and has the same PID number as when you logged in.

The following example shows that the process running the shell forked (is the parent of) the process running ps. When you call it with the **–f** option, ps displays a full listing of information about each process. The line of the ps display with **bash** in the **CMD** column refers to the process running the shell. The column headed by **PID** identifies the PID number. The column headed by **PPID** identifies the PID number of the *parent* of the process. From the PID and PPID columns you can see that the process running the shell (PID 21341) is the parent of the process running sleep (PID 22789). The parent PID number of sleep is the same as the PID number of ps (21341).

```
$ sleep 10 &
[1] 22789
$ ps -f
UID        PID  PPID  C STIME TTY          TIME CMD
max      21341 21340  0 10:42 pts/16   00:00:00 bash
max      22789 21341  0 17:30 pts/16   00:00:00 sleep 10
max      22790 21341  0 17:30 pts/16   00:00:00 ps -f
```

Refer to the ps man page for more information on ps and the columns it displays with the –f option. A second pair of **sleep** and **ps –f** commands shows that the shell is still being run by the same process but that it forked another process to run sleep:

```
$ sleep 10 &
[1] 22791
$ ps -f
UID         PID  PPID  C STIME TTY        TIME CMD
max       21341 21340  0 10:42 pts/16  00:00:00 bash
max       22791 21341  0 17:31 pts/16  00:00:00 sleep 10
max       22792 21341  0 17:31 pts/16  00:00:00 ps -f
```

You can also use pstree (or **ps ––forest**, with or without the –e option) to see the parent–child relationship of processes. The next example shows the –p option to pstree, which causes it to display PID numbers:

```
$ pstree -p
systemd(1)-+-NetworkManager(655)---{NetworkManager}(702)
           |-abrtd(657)---abrt-dump-oops(696)
           |-accounts-daemon(1204)---{accounts-daemo}(1206)
           |-agetty(979)
  ...
           |-login(984)---bash(2071)-+-pstree(2095)
           |                         `-sleep(2094)
  ...
```

The preceding output is abbreviated. The first line shows the PID 1 (**systemd init**) and a few of the processes it is running. The line that starts with **–login** shows a textual user running sleep in the background and running pstree in the foreground. The tree for a user running a GUI is much more complex. Refer to "$$: PID Number" on page 1011 for a description of how to instruct the shell to report on PID numbers.

EXECUTING A COMMAND

fork and sleep When you give the shell a command, it usually forks [spawns using the **fork**() system call] a child process to execute the command. While the child process is executing the command, the parent process *sleeps* [implemented as the **sleep**() system call]. While a process is sleeping, it does not use any computer time; it remains inactive, waiting to wake up. When the child process finishes executing the command, it tells its parent of its success or failure via its exit status and then dies. The parent process (which is running the shell) wakes up and prompts for another command.

Background process When you run a process in the background by ending a command with an ampersand (&), the shell forks a child process without going to sleep and without waiting for the child process to run to completion. The parent process, which is executing the shell, reports the job number and PID number of the child process and prompts for another command. The child process runs in the background, independent of its parent.

Builtins Although the shell forks a process to run most of the commands you give it, some commands are built into the shell. The shell does not need to fork a process to run builtins. For more information refer to "Builtins" on page 249.

Variables   Within a given process, such as your login shell or a subshell, you can declare, initialize, read, and change variables. By default, however, a variable is local to a process. When a process forks a child process, the parent does not pass the value of a variable to the child. You can make the value of a variable available to child processes (global) by using the export builtin (page 1008).

HISTORY

The history mechanism, a feature adapted from the C Shell, maintains a list of recently issued command lines, also called *events*, that provides a quick way to re-execute any of the events in the list. This mechanism also enables you to execute variations of previous commands and to reuse arguments from them. You can use the history list to replicate complicated commands and arguments that you used earlier in this login session or in a previous one and enter a series of commands that differ from one another in minor ways. The history list also serves as a record of what you have done. It can prove helpful when you have made a mistake and are not sure what you did or when you want to keep a record of a procedure that involved a series of commands.

history **can help track down mistakes**

tip   When you have made a mistake on a command line (not an error within a script or program) and are not sure what you did wrong, look at the history list to review your recent commands. Sometimes this list can help you figure out what went wrong and how to fix things.

The history builtin displays the history list. If it does not, read the next section, which describes the variables you need to set.

VARIABLES THAT CONTROL HISTORY

The value of the **HISTSIZE** variable determines the number of events preserved in the history list during a session. A value in the range of 100 to 1,000 is normal.

When you exit from the shell, the most recently executed commands are saved in the file whose name is stored in the **HISTFILE** variable (default is **~/.bash_history**). The next time you start the shell, this file initializes the history list. The value of the **HISTFILESIZE** variable determines the number of lines of history saved in **HISTFILE** (see Table 9-7).

Table 9-7   History variables

Variable	Default	Function
HISTSIZE	1000 events	Maximum number of events saved during a session
HISTFILE	**~/.bash_history**	Location of the history file
HISTFILESIZE	1000 events	Maximum number of events saved between sessions

Event number   The Bourne Again Shell assigns a sequential *event number* to each command line. You can display this event number as part of the bash prompt by including \! in **PS1** (page 310). Examples in this section show numbered prompts when they help to illustrate the behavior of a command.

Enter the following command manually to establish a history list of the 100 most recent events; place it in **~/.bash_profile** to affect future sessions:

```
$ HISTSIZE=100
```

The following command causes bash to save the 100 most recent events across login sessions:

```
$ HISTFILESIZE=100
```

After you set **HISTFILESIZE**, you can log out and log in again, and the 100 most recent events from the previous login session will appear in your history list.

Enter the command **history** to display the events in the history list. This list is ordered with the oldest events at the top. The following history list includes a command to modify the bash prompt so it displays the history event number. The last event in the history list is the **history** command that displayed the list.

```
32 $ history | tail
   23  PS1="\! bash$ "
   24  ls -l
   25  cat temp
   26  rm temp
   27  vim memo
   28  lpr memo
   29  vim memo
   30  lpr memo
   31  rm memo
   32  history | tail
```

As you run commands and your history list becomes longer, it might run off the top of the screen when you use the history builtin. Pipe the output of history through less to browse through it or give the command **history 10** or **history | tail** to look at the ten most recent commands.

A handy history alias

tip   Creating the following aliases makes working with history easier. The first allows you to give the command **h** to display the ten most recent events. The second alias causes the command **hg** *string* to display all events in the history list that contain *string*. Put these aliases in your **~/.bashrc** file to make them available each time you log in. See page 334 for more information on aliases.

```
$ alias 'h=history | tail'
$ alias 'hg=history | grep'
```

RE-EXECUTING AND EDITING COMMANDS

You can re-execute any event in the history list. This feature can save you time, effort, and aggravation. Not having to re-enter long command lines allows you to re-execute events more easily, quickly, and accurately than you could if you had to retype the command line in its entirety. You can recall, modify, and re-execute previously executed events in three ways: You can use the fc builtin (next), the exclamation point commands (page 323), or the Readline Library, which uses a one-line vi- or emacs-like editor to edit and execute events (page 328).

Which method to use?

tip If you are more familiar with vi or emacs and less familiar with the C or TC Shell, use fc or the Readline Library. If you are more familiar with the C or TC Shell, use the exclamation point commands. If it is a toss-up, try the Readline Library; it will benefit you in other areas of Linux more than learning the exclamation point commands will.

fc: DISPLAYS, EDITS, AND RE-EXECUTES COMMANDS

The fc (fix command) builtin enables you to display the history list and to edit and re-execute previous commands. It provides many of the same capabilities as the command-line editors.

VIEWING THE HISTORY LIST

When you call fc with the –l option, it displays commands from the history list. Without any arguments, fc –l lists the 16 most recent commands in a numbered list, with the oldest appearing first:

```
$ fc -l
1024    cd
1025    view calendar
1026    vim letter.adams01
1027    aspell -c letter.adams01
1028    vim letter.adams01
1029    lpr letter.adams01
1030    cd ../memos
1031    ls
1032    rm *0405
1033    fc -l
1034    cd
1035    whereis aspell
1036    man aspell
1037    cd /usr/share/doc/*aspell*
1038    pwd
1039    ls
1040    ls man-html
```

The fc builtin can take zero, one, or two arguments with the –l option. The arguments specify the part of the history list to be displayed:

fc –l [first [last]]

The fc builtin lists commands beginning with the most recent event that matches *first*. The argument can be an event number, the first few characters of the command line, or a negative number, which specifies the *n*th previous command.

Without *last*, fc displays events through the most recent. If you include *last*, fc displays commands from the most recent event that matches *first* through the most recent event that matches *last*.

The next command displays the history list from event 1030 through event 1035:

```
$ fc -l 1030 1035
1030     cd ../memos
1031     ls
1032     rm *0405
1033     fc -l
1034     cd
1035     whereis aspell
```

The following command lists the most recent event that begins with **view** through the most recent command line that begins with **whereis**:

```
$ fc -l view whereis
1025     view calendar
1026     vim letter.adams01
1027     aspell -c letter.adams01
1028     vim letter.adams01
1029     lpr letter.adams01
1030     cd ../memos
1031     ls
1032     rm *0405
1033     fc -l
1034     cd
1035     whereis aspell
```

To list a single command from the history list, use the same identifier for the first and second arguments. The following command lists event 1027:

```
$ fc -l 1027 1027
1027     aspell -c letter.adams01
```

EDITING AND RE-EXECUTING PREVIOUS COMMANDS

You can use fc to edit and re-execute previous commands.

fc [–e editor] [first [last]]

When you call fc with the –e option followed by the name of an editor, fc calls the editor with event(s) in the Work buffer, assuming the editor you specify is installed. By default, fc invokes the vi(m) editor. Without *first* and *last*, it defaults to the most recent command. The next example invokes the vim editor to edit the most recent command:

```
$ fc -e vi
```

The fc builtin uses the stand-alone vim editor. If you set the **FCEDIT** variable, you do not need to use the –e option to specify an editor on the command line. Because the value of **FCEDIT** has been changed to **/usr/bin/emacs** and fc has no arguments, the following command edits the most recent command using the emacs editor (emacs package):

```
$ export FCEDIT=/usr/bin/emacs
$ fc
```

If you call it with a single argument, fc invokes the editor on the specified command. The following example starts the editor with event 1029 in the Work buffer. When you exit from the editor, the shell executes the command:

```
$ fc 1029
```

As described earlier, you can identify commands with numbers or by specifying the first few characters of the command name. The following example calls the editor to work on events from the most recent event that begins with the letters **vim** through event 1030:

```
$ fc vim 1030
```

Clean up the fc buffer

caution   When you execute an fc command, the shell executes whatever you leave in the editor buffer, possibly with unwanted results. If you decide you do not want to execute a command, delete everything from the buffer before you exit from the editor.

RE-EXECUTING COMMANDS WITHOUT CALLING THE EDITOR

You can re-execute previous commands without using an editor. If you call fc with the –s option, it skips the editing phase and re-executes the command. The following example re-executes event 1029:

```
$ fc -s 1029
lpr letter.adams01
```

The next example re-executes the previous command:

```
$ fc -s
```

When you re-execute a command, you can tell fc to substitute one string for another. The next example substitutes the string **john** for the string **adams** in event 1029 and executes the modified event:

```
$ fc -s adams=john 1029
lpr letter.john01
```

USING AN EXCLAMATION POINT (!) TO REFERENCE EVENTS

The C Shell history mechanism uses an exclamation point to reference events. This technique, which is available under bash, is frequently more cumbersome to use than fc but nevertheless has some useful features. For example, the !! command re-executes the previous event, and the shell replaces the !$ token with the last word on the previous command line.

You can reference an event by using its absolute event number, its relative event number, or the text it contains. All references to events, called event designators, begin with an exclamation point (!). One or more characters follow the exclamation point to specify an event.

You can put history events anywhere on a command line. To escape an exclamation point so that the shell interprets it literally instead of as the start of a history event, precede it with a backslash (\) or enclose it within single quotation marks.

EVENT DESIGNATORS

An event designator specifies a command in the history list. Table 9-8 lists event designators.

Table 9-8   Event designators

Designator	Meaning
!	Starts a history event unless followed immediately by SPACE, NEWLINE, =, or (.
!!	The previous command.
!*n*	Command number *n* in the history list.
!–*n*	The *n*th preceding command.
!*string*	The most recent command line that started with *string*.
!?*string*[?]	The most recent command that contained *string*. The last ? is optional.
!#	The current command (as you have it typed so far).
!{*event*}	The *event* is an event designator. The braces isolate *event* from the surrounding text. For example, !{–3}3 is the third most recently executed command followed by a **3**.

!! re-executes the previous event   You can re-execute the previous event by giving a !! command. In the following example, event 45 re-executes event 44:

```
44 $ ls -l text
-rw-rw-r--. 1 max pubs 45 04-30 14:53 text
45 $ !!
ls -l text
-rw-rw-r--. 1 max pubs 45 04-30 14:53 text
```

The !! command works whether or not your prompt displays an event number. As this example shows, when you use the history mechanism to re-execute an event, the shell displays the command it is reexecuting.

!*n* event number   A number following an exclamation point refers to an event. If that event is in the history list, the shell executes it. Otherwise, the shell displays an error message. A negative number following an exclamation point references an event relative to the current event. For example, the command !–3 refers to the third preceding event. After you issue a command, the relative event number of a given event changes (event –3 becomes event –4). Both of the following commands re-execute event 44:

```
51 $ !44
ls -l text
-rw-rw-r--. 1 max pubs 45 04-30 14:53 text
52 $ !-8
ls -l text
-rw-rw-r--. 1 max pubs 45 04-30 14:53 text
```

!*string* event text   When a string of text follows an exclamation point, the shell searches for and executes the most recent event that *began* with that string. If you enclose the string within question marks, the shell executes the most recent event that *contained* that string. The final question mark is optional if a RETURN would immediately follow it.

```
68 $ history 10
   59   ls -l text*
   60   tail text5
   61   cat text1 text5 > letter
   62   vim letter
   63   cat letter
   64   cat memo
   65   lpr memo
   66   pine zach
   67   ls -l
   68   history
69 $ !l
ls -l
...
70 $ !lpr
lpr memo
71 $ !?letter?
cat letter
...
```

optional WORD DESIGNATORS

A *word designator* specifies a word (token) or series of words from an event. (Table 9-9 on the next page lists word designators.) The words are numbered starting with 0 (the first word on the line—usually the command), continuing with 1 (the first word following the command), and ending with *n* (the last word on the line).

To specify a particular word from a previous event, follow the event designator (such as !14) with a colon and the number of the word in the previous event. For example, !14:3 specifies the third word following the command from event 14. You can specify the first word following the command (word number 1) using a caret (^) and the last word using a dollar sign ($). You can specify a range of words by separating two word designators with a hyphen.

```
72 $ echo apple grape orange pear
apple grape orange pear
73 $ echo !72:2
echo grape
grape
74 $ echo !72:^
echo apple
apple
75 $ !72:0 !72:$
echo pear
pear
76 $ echo !72:2-4
echo grape orange pear
grape orange pear
77 $ !72:0-$
echo apple grape orange pear
apple grape orange pear
```

As the next example shows, !$ refers to the last word of the previous event. You can use this shorthand to edit, for example, a file you just displayed with cat:

```
$ cat report.718
...
$ vim !$
vim report.718
...
```

If an event contains a single command, the word numbers correspond to the argument numbers. If an event contains more than one command, this correspondence does not hold for commands after the first. In the next example, event 78 contains two commands separated by a semicolon so the shell executes them sequentially; the semicolon is word number 5.

```
78 $ !72 ; echo helen zach barbara
echo apple grape orange pear ; echo helen zach barbara
apple grape orange pear
helen zach barbara
79 $ echo !78:7
echo helen
helen
80 $ echo !78:4-7
echo pear ; echo helen
pear
helen
```

Table 9-9   Word designators

Designator	Meaning
n	The *n*th word. Word 0 is normally the command name.
^	The first word (after the command name).
$	The last word.
m–n	All words from word number *m* through word number *n; m* defaults to 0 if you omit it (0–*n*).
n∗	All words from word number *n* through the last word.
∗	All words except the command name. The same as **1**∗.
%	The word matched by the most recent **?*string*?** search.

MODIFIERS

On occasion you might want to change an aspect of an event you are reexecuting. Perhaps you entered a complex command line with a typo or incorrect pathname or you want to specify a different argument. You can modify an event or a word of an event by putting one or more modifiers after the word designator or after the event designator if there is no word designator. Each modifier must be preceded by a colon (:).

Substitute modifier   The following example shows the *substitute modifier* correcting a typo in the previous event:

```
$ car /home/zach/memo.0507 /home/max/letter.0507
bash: car: command not found
$ !!:s/car/cat
cat /home/zach/memo.0507 /home/max/letter.0507
...
```

The substitute modifier has the following syntax:

[g]s/old/new/

where *old* is the original string (not a regular expression) and *new* is the string that replaces *old*. The substitute modifier substitutes the first occurrence of *old* with *new*. Placing a **g** before the **s** (as in *gs/old/new/*) causes a global substitution, replacing all occurrences of *old*. Although **/** is the delimiter in the examples, you can use any character that is not in either *old* or *new*. The final delimiter is optional if a RETURN would immediately follow it. As with the vim Substitute command, the history mechanism replaces an ampersand (&) in *new* with *old*. The shell replaces a null old string (*s//new/*) with the previous old string or string within a command that you searched for with *?string?*.

Quick substitution   An abbreviated form of the substitute modifier is *quick substitution*. Use it to re-execute the most recent event while changing some of the event text. The quick substitution character is the caret (^). For example, the command

```
$ ^old^new^
```

produces the same results as

```
$ !!:s/old/new/
```

Thus substituting **cat** for **car** in the previous event could have been entered as

```
$ ^car^cat
cat /home/zach/memo.0507 /home/max/letter.0507
...
```

You can omit the final caret if it would be followed immediately by a RETURN. As with other command-line substitutions, the shell displays the command line as it appears after the substitution.

Other modifiers   Modifiers (other than the substitute modifier) perform simple edits on the part of the event that has been selected by the event designator and the optional word designators. You can use multiple modifiers, each preceded by a colon (:).

The following series of commands uses ls to list the name of a file, repeats the command without executing it (**p** modifier), and repeats the last command, removing the last part of the pathname (**h** modifier) again without executing it:

```
$ ls /etc/sysconfig/harddisks
/etc/sysconfig/harddisks
$ !!:p
ls /etc/sysconfig/harddisks
$ !!:h:p
ls /etc/sysconfig
$
```

Table 9-10 lists event modifiers other than the substitute modifier.

Table 9-10   Event modifiers

Modifier		Function
e	(extension)	Removes all but the filename extension
h	(head)	Removes the last part of a pathname
p	(print)	Displays the command but does not execute it
q	(quote)	Quotes the substitution to prevent further substitutions on it
r	(root)	Removes the filename extension
t	(tail)	Removes all elements of a pathname except the last
x		Like **q** but quotes each word in the substitution individually

THE READLINE LIBRARY

Command-line editing under the Bourne Again Shell is implemented through the *Readline Library,* which is available to any application written in C. Any application that uses the Readline Library supports line editing that is consistent with that provided by bash. Programs that use the Readline Library, including bash, read **~/.inputrc** (page 332) for key binding information and configuration settings. The **--noediting** command-line option turns off command-line editing in bash.

vi mode You can choose one of two editing modes when using the Readline Library in bash: emacs or vi(m). Both modes provide many of the commands available in the stand-alone versions of the emacs and vim editors. You can also use the ARROW keys to move around. Up and down movements move you backward and forward through the history list. In addition, Readline provides several types of interactive word completion (page 330). The default mode is emacs; you can switch to vi mode with the following command:

```
$ set -o vi
```

emacs mode The next command switches back to emacs mode:

```
$ set -o emacs
```

vi EDITING MODE

Before you start, make sure the shell is in vi mode.

When you enter bash commands while in vi editing mode, you are in Input mode (page 174). As you enter a command, if you discover an error before you press RETURN, you can press ESCAPE to switch to vim Command mode. This setup is different from the stand-alone vim editor's initial mode. While in Command mode you can use many vim commands to edit the command line. It is as though you were using vim to edit a copy of the history file with a screen that has room for only one command. When you use the **k** command or the UP ARROW to move up a line, you access the previous command. If you then use the **j** command or the DOWN ARROW to move down a line, you return to the original command. To use the **k** and **j** keys to move between commands, you must be in Command mode; you can use the ARROW keys in both Command and Input modes.

The command-line vim editor starts in Input mode

tip The stand-alone vim editor starts in Command mode, whereas the command-line vim editor starts in Input mode. If commands display characters and do not work properly, you are in Input mode. Press ESCAPE and enter the command again.

In addition to cursor-positioning commands, you can use the search-backward (?) command followed by a search string to look *back* through the history list for the most recent command containing a string. If you have moved back in the history list, use a forward slash (/) to search *forward* toward the most recent command. Unlike the search strings in the stand-alone vim editor, these search strings cannot contain regular expressions. You can, however, start the search string with a caret (^) to force the shell to locate commands that start with the search string. As in vim, pressing **n** after a successful search looks for the next occurrence of the same string.

You can also use event numbers to access events in the history list. While you are in Command mode (press ESCAPE), enter the event number followed by a **G** to go to the command with that event number.

When you use /, ?, or **G** to move to a command line, you are in Command mode, not Input mode: You can edit the command or press RETURN to execute it.

When the command you want to edit is displayed, you can modify the command line using vim Command mode editing commands such as **x** (delete character), **r** (replace character), ~ (change case), and . (repeat last change). To change to Input mode, use an Insert (**i**, **I**), Append (**a**, **A**), Replace (**R**), or Change (**c**, **C**) command. You do not have to return to Command mode to execute a command; simply press RETURN, even if the cursor is in the middle of the command line. For more information refer to the vim tutorial on page 172.

emacs EDITING MODE

Unlike the vim editor, emacs is modeless. You need not switch between Command mode and Input mode because most emacs commands are control characters, allowing emacs to distinguish between input and commands. Like vim, the emacs command-line editor provides commands for moving the cursor on the command line and through the command history list and for modifying part or all of a command. However, in a few cases, the emacs command-line editor commands differ from those in the stand-alone emacs editor.

In emacs you perform cursor movement by using both CONTROL and ESCAPE commands. To move the cursor one character backward on the command line, press CONTROL-B.

Press CONTROL-F to move one character forward. As in vim, you can precede these movements with counts. To use a count you must first press ESCAPE; otherwise, the numbers you type will appear on the command line.

Like vim, emacs provides word and line movement commands. To move backward or forward one word on the command line, press ESCAPE b or ESCAPE f, respectively. To move several words using a count, press ESCAPE followed by the number and the appropriate escape sequence. To move to the beginning of the line, press CONTROL-A; to the end of the line, press CONTROL-E; and to the next instance of the character *c*, press CONTROL-X CONTROL-F followed by *c*.

You can add text to the command line by moving the cursor to the position you want to enter text and typing. To delete text, move the cursor just to the right of the characters you want to delete and press the erase key (page 140) once for each character you want to delete.

CONTROL-D can terminate your screen session

tip If you want to delete the character directly under the cursor, press CONTROL-D. If you enter CONTROL-D at the beginning of the line, it might terminate your shell session.

If you want to delete the entire command line, type the line kill character (page 140). You can type this character while the cursor is anywhere in the command line. Use CONTROL-K to delete from the cursor to the end of the line.

READLINE COMPLETION COMMANDS

You can use the TAB key to complete words you are entering on the command line. This facility, called *completion*, works in both vi and emacs editing modes. Several types of completion are possible, and which one you use depends on which part of a command line you are typing when you press TAB.

COMMAND COMPLETION

If you are typing the name of a command (usually the first word on the command line), pressing TAB initiates *command completion*, in which bash looks for a command whose name starts with the part of the word you have typed. If no command starts with the characters you entered, bash beeps. If there is one such command, bash completes the command name. If there is more than one choice, bash does nothing in vi mode and beeps in emacs mode. Pressing TAB a second time causes bash to display a list of commands whose names start with the prefix you typed and allows you to continue typing the command name.

In the following example, the user types **bz** and presses TAB. The shell beeps (the user is in emacs mode) to indicate that several commands start with the letters **bz**. The user enters another TAB to cause the shell to display a list of commands that start with **bz** followed by the command line as the user has entered it so far:

```
$ bz ⇨ TAB (beep) ⇨ TAB
bzcat           bzdiff        bzip2          bzless
bzcmp           bzgrep        bzip2recover   bzmore
$ bz█
```

Next the user types **c** and presses TAB twice. The shell displays the two commands that start with **bzc**. The user types **a** followed by TAB. At this point the shell completes the command because only one command starts with **bzca**.

```
$ bzc ⇨ TAB (beep) ⇨ TAB
bzcat  bzcmp
$ bzca ⇨ TAB ⇨ t ■
```

PATHNAME COMPLETION

Pathname completion, which also uses TABs, allows you to type a portion of a pathname and have bash supply the rest. If the portion of the pathname you have typed is sufficient to determine a unique pathname, bash displays that pathname. If more than one pathname would match it, bash completes the pathname up to the point where there are choices so that you can type more.

When you are entering a pathname, including a simple filename, and press TAB, the shell beeps (if the shell is in emacs mode—in vi mode there is no beep). It then extends the command line as far as it can.

```
$ cat films/dar ⇨ TAB (beep) cat films/dark_■
```

In the **films** directory every file that starts with **dar** has **k_** as the next characters, so bash cannot extend the line further without making a choice among files. The shell leaves the cursor just past the _ character. At this point you can continue typing the pathname or press TAB twice. In the latter case bash beeps, displays the choices, redisplays the command line, and again leaves the cursor just after the _ character.

```
$ cat films/dark_ ⇨ TAB (beep) ⇨ TAB
dark_passage   dark_victory
$ cat films/dark_■
```

When you add enough information to distinguish between the two possible files and press TAB, bash displays the unique pathname. If you enter **p** followed by TAB after the _ character, the shell completes the command line:

```
$ cat films/dark_p ⇨ TAB ⇨ assage
```

Because there is no further ambiguity, the shell appends a SPACE so you can either finish typing the command line or just press RETURN to execute the command. If the complete pathname is that of a directory, bash appends a slash (/) in place of a SPACE.

VARIABLE COMPLETION

When you are typing a variable name, pressing TAB results in *variable completion,* wherein bash attempts to complete the name of the variable. In case of an ambiguity, pressing TAB twice displays a list of choices:

```
$ echo $HO ⇨ TAB (beep) ⇨ TAB
$HOME        $HOSTNAME  $HOSTTYPE
$ echo $HOM ⇨ TAB ⇨ E
```

Pressing RETURN **executes the command**

caution   Pressing RETURN causes the shell to execute the command regardless of where the cursor is on the command line.

.inputrc: CONFIGURING THE READLINE LIBRARY

The Bourne Again Shell and other programs that use the Readline Library read the file specified by the **INPUTRC** environment variable to obtain initialization information. If **INPUTRC** is not set, these programs read the ~/.inputrc file. They ignore lines of **.inputrc** that are blank or that start with a hashmark (#).

VARIABLES

You can set variables in **.inputrc** to control the behavior of the Readline Library using the following syntax:

   set *variable value*

Table 9-11 lists some variables and values you can use. See "Readline Variables" in the bash man or info page for a complete list.

Table 9-11   Readline variables

Variable	Effect
editing-mode	Set to **vi** to start Readline in vi mode. Set to **emacs** to start Readline in emacs mode (the default). Similar to the **set –o vi** and **set –o emacs** shell commands (page 328).
horizontal-scroll-mode	Set to **on** to cause long lines to extend off the right edge of the display area. Moving the cursor to the right when it is at the right edge of the display area shifts the line to the left so you can see more of the line. Shift the line back by moving the cursor back past the left edge. The default value is **off**, which causes long lines to wrap onto multiple lines of the display.
mark-directories	Set to **off** to cause Readline not to place a slash (/) at the end of directory names it completes. The default value is **on**.
mark-modified-lines	Set to **on** to cause Readline to precede modified history lines with an asterisk. The default value is **off**.

KEY BINDINGS

You can map keystroke sequences to Readline commands, changing or extending the default bindings. Like the emacs editor, the Readline Library includes many commands that are not bound to a keystroke sequence. To use an unbound command, you must map it using one of the following forms:

   keyname: command_name
   "*keystroke_sequence*" : *command_name*

In the first form, you spell out the name for a single key. For example, CONTROL-U would be written as **control-u**. This form is useful for binding commands to single keys.

In the second form, you specify a string that describes a sequence of keys that will be bound to the command. You can use the emacs-style backslash escape sequences to represent the special keys CONTROL (\C), META (\M), and ESCAPE (\e). Specify a backslash by escaping it with another backslash: \\. Similarly, a double or single quotation mark can be escaped with a backslash: \" or \'.

The **kill-whole-line** command, available in emacs mode only, deletes the current line. Put the following command in **.inputrc** to bind the **kill-whole-line** command (which is unbound by default) to the keystroke sequence CONTROL-R:

```
control-r: kill-whole-line
```

bind   Give the command **bind –P** to display a list of all Readline commands. If a command is bound to a key sequence, that sequence is shown. Commands you can use in vi mode start with **vi**. For example, **vi-next-word** and **vi-prev-word** move the cursor to the beginning of the next and previous words, respectively. Commands that do not begin with **vi** are generally available in emacs mode.

Use **bind –q** to determine which key sequence is bound to a command:

```
$ bind -q kill-whole-line
kill-whole-line can be invoked via "\C-r".
```

You can also bind text by enclosing it within double quotation marks (emacs mode only):

```
"QQ": "The Linux Operating System"
```

This command causes bash to insert the string **The Linux Operating System** when you type **QQ**.

CONDITIONAL CONSTRUCTS

You can conditionally select parts of the **.inputrc** file using the **$if** directive. The syntax of the conditional construct is

> *$if test[=value]*
> > *commands*
> *[$else*
> > *commands]*
> *$endif*

where *test* is **mode**, **term**, or **bash**. If *test* equals *value* (or if *test* is *true* when *value* is not specified), this structure executes the first set of *commands*. If *test* does not equal *value* (or if *test* is *false* when *value* is not specified), this construct executes the second set of *commands* if they are present or exits from the structure if they are not present.

The power of the **$if** directive lies in the three types of tests it can perform.

1. You can test to see which mode is currently set.

```
$if mode=vi
```

The preceding test is *true* if the current Readline mode is **vi** and *false* otherwise. You can test for **vi** or **emacs**.

2. You can test the type of terminal.

```
$if term=xterm
```

The preceding test is *true* if the **TERM** variable is set to **xterm**. You can test for any value of **TERM**.

3. You can test the application name.

```
$if bash
```

The preceding test is *true* when you are running bash and not another program that uses the Readline Library. You can test for any application name.

These tests can customize the Readline Library based on the current mode, the type of terminal, and the application you are using. They give you a great deal of power and flexibility when you are using the Readline Library with bash and other programs.

The following commands in **.inputrc** cause CONTROL-Y to move the cursor to the beginning of the next word regardless of whether bash is in vi or emacs mode:

```
$ cat ~/.inputrc
set editing-mode vi
$if mode=vi
      "\C-y": vi-next-word
    $else
      "\C-y": forward-word
$endif
```

Because bash reads the preceding conditional construct when it is started, you must set the editing mode in **.inputrc**. Changing modes interactively using **set** will not change the binding of CONTROL-Y.

For more information on the Readline Library, open the bash man page and give the command /^READLINE, which searches for the word **READLINE** at the beginning of a line.

If Readline commands do not work, log out and log in again

tip   The Bourne Again Shell reads **~/.inputrc** when you log in. After you make changes to this file, you must log out and log in again before the changes will take effect.

ALIASES

An *alias* is a (usually short) name that the shell translates into another (usually longer) name or (complex) command. Aliases allow you to define new commands by substituting a string for the first token of a simple command. They are typically placed in the ~/.bashrc startup files so that they are available to interactive subshells.

The syntax of the alias builtin is

alias [name[=value]]

No SPACEs are permitted around the equal sign. If *value* contains SPACEs or TABs, you must enclose *value* within quotation marks. An alias does not accept an argument from the command line in *value*. Use a function (page 338) when you need to use an argument.

An alias does not replace itself, which avoids the possibility of infinite recursion in handling an alias such as the following:

```
$ alias ls='ls -F'
```

You can nest aliases. Aliases are disabled for noninteractive shells (that is, shell scripts). Use the unalias builtin to remove an alias. When you give an alias builtin command without any arguments, the shell displays a list of all defined aliases:

```
$ alias
alias ll='ls -l'
alias l='ls -ltr'
alias ls='ls -F'
alias zap='rm -i'
```

To view the alias for a particular name, enter the command **alias** followed by the name of the alias. Fedora/RHEL defines some aliases. Enter an **alias** command to see which aliases are in effect. You can delete the aliases you do not want from the appropriate startup file.

SINGLE VERSUS DOUBLE QUOTATION MARKS IN ALIASES

The choice of single or double quotation marks is significant in the alias syntax when the alias includes variables. If you enclose *value* within double quotation marks, any variables that appear in *value* are expanded when the alias is created. If you enclose *value* within single quotation marks, variables are not expanded until the alias is used. The following example illustrates the difference.

The **PWD** keyword variable holds the pathname of the working directory. Max creates two aliases while he is working in his home directory. Because he uses double quotation marks when he creates the **dirA** alias, the shell substitutes the value of the working directory when he creates this alias. The **alias dirA** command displays the **dirA** alias and shows that the substitution has already taken place:

```
$ echo $PWD
/home/max
$ alias dirA="echo Working directory is $PWD"
$ alias dirA
alias dirA='echo Working directory is /home/max'
```

When Max creates the **dirB** alias, he uses single quotation marks, which prevent the shell from expanding the $PWD variable. The **alias dirB** command shows that the **dirB** alias still holds the unexpanded $PWD variable:

```
$ alias dirB='echo Working directory is $PWD'
$ alias dirB
alias dirB='echo Working directory is $PWD'
```

After creating the **dirA** and **dirB** aliases, Max uses cd to make **cars** his working directory and gives each of the aliases as commands. The alias he created using double quotation marks displays the name of the directory he created the alias in as the working directory (which is wrong). In contrast, the **dirB** alias displays the proper name of the working directory:

```
$ cd cars
$ dirA
Working directory is /home/max
$ dirB
Working directory is /home/max/cars
```

How to prevent the shell from invoking an alias

tip   The shell checks only simple, unquoted commands to see if they are aliases. Commands given as relative or absolute pathnames and quoted commands are not checked. When you want to give a command that has an alias but do not want to use the alias, precede the command with a backslash, specify the command's absolute pathname, or give the command as *./command*.

EXAMPLES OF ALIASES

The following alias allows you to type **r** to repeat the previous command or **r abc** to repeat the last command line that began with **abc**:

```
$ alias r='fc -s'
```

If you use the command **ls –ltr** frequently, you can create an alias that substitutes **ls –ltr** when you give the command **l**:

```
$ alias l='ls -ltr'
$ l
-rw-r-----. 1 max pubs  3089 02-11 16:24 XTerm.ad
-rw-r--r--. 1 max pubs 30015 03-01 14:24 flute.ps
-rw-r--r--. 1 max pubs   641 04-01 08:12 fixtax.icn
-rw-r--r--. 1 max pubs   484 04-09 08:14 maptax.icn
drwxrwxr-x. 2 max pubs  1024 08-09 17:41 Tiger
drwxrwxr-x. 2 max pubs  1024 09-10 11:32 testdir
-rwxr-xr-x. 1 max pubs   485 09-21 08:03 floor
drwxrwxr-x. 2 max pubs  1024 09-27 20:19 Test_Emacs
```

Another common use of aliases is to protect yourself from mistakes. The following example substitutes the interactive version of the rm utility when you enter the command **zap**:

```
$ alias zap='rm -i'
$ zap f*
rm: remove 'fixtax.icn'? n
rm: remove 'flute.ps'? n
rm: remove 'floor'? n
```

The –i option causes rm to ask you to verify each file that would be deleted, thereby helping you avoid deleting the wrong file. You can also alias rm with the **rm –i** command: **alias rm='rm –i'**.

The aliases in the next example cause the shell to substitute **ls –l** each time you give an **ll** command and **ls –F** each time you use **ls**:

```
$ alias ls='ls -F'
$ alias ll='ls -l'
$ ll
drwxrwxr-x. 2 max pubs  1024 09-27 20:19 Test_Emacs/
drwxrwxr-x. 2 max pubs  1024 08-09 17:41 Tiger/
-rw-r-----. 1 max pubs  3089 02-11 16:24 XTerm.ad
-rw-r--r--. 1 max pubs   641 04-01 08:12 fixtax.icn
-rw-r--r--. 1 max pubs 30015 03-01 14:24 flute.ps
-rwxr-xr-x. 1 max pubs   485 09-21 08:03 floor*
-rw-r--r--. 1 max pubs   484 04-09 08:14 maptax.icn
drwxrwxr-x. 2 max pubs  1024 09-10 11:32 testdir/
```

The −F option causes ls to print a slash (/) at the end of directory names and an asterisk (*) at the end of the names of executable files. In this example, the string that replaces the alias ll (ls −l) itself contains an alias (ls). When it replaces an alias with its value, the shell looks at the first word of the replacement string to see whether it is an alias. In the preceding example, the replacement string contains the alias ls, so a second substitution occurs to produce the final command ls −F −l. (To avoid a *recursive plunge,* the ls in the replacement text, although an alias, is not expanded a second time.)

When given a list of aliases without the *=value* or *value* field, the alias builtin responds by displaying the value of each defined alias. The alias builtin reports an error if an alias has not been defined:

```
$ alias ll l ls zap wx
alias ll='ls -l'
alias l='ls -ltr'
alias ls='ls -F'
alias zap='rm -i'
bash: alias: wx: not found
```

You can avoid alias substitution by preceding the aliased command with a backslash (\):

```
$ \ls
Test_Emacs XTerm.ad  flute.ps  maptax.icn
Tiger    fixtax.icn floor    testdir
```

Because the replacement of an alias name with the alias value does not change the rest of the command line, any arguments are still received by the command that gets executed:

```
$ ll f*
-rw-r--r--. 1 max pubs   641 04-01 08:12 fixtax.icn
-rw-r--r--. 1 max pubs 30015 03-01 14:24 flute.ps
-rwxr-xr-x. 1 max pubs   485 09-21 08:03 floor*
```

You can remove an alias with the unalias builtin. When the **zap** alias is removed, it is no longer displayed with the alias builtin, and its subsequent use results in an error message:

```
$ unalias zap
$ alias
alias ll='ls -l'
alias l='ls -ltr'
alias ls='ls -F'
$ zap maptax.icn
bash: zap: command not found
```

FUNCTIONS

A shell function is similar to a shell script in that it stores a series of commands for execution at a later time. However, because the shell stores a function in the computer's main memory (RAM) instead of in a file on the disk, the shell can access it more quickly than the shell can access a script. The shell also preprocesses (parses) a function so that it starts more quickly than a script. Finally the shell executes a shell function in the same shell that called it. If you define too many functions, the overhead of starting a subshell (as when you run a script) can become unacceptable.

You can declare a shell function in the **~/.bash_profile** startup file, in the script that uses it, or directly from the command line. You can remove functions with the unset builtin. The shell does not retain functions after you log out.

Removing variables and functions that have the same name

tip If you have a shell variable and a function with the same name, using unset removes the shell variable. If you then use unset again with the same name, it removes the function.

The syntax that declares a shell function is

> *[function]* **function-name** *()*
> *{*
>   *commands*
> *}*

where the word *function* is optional, **function-name** is the name you use to call the function, and **commands** comprise the list of commands the function executes when you call it. The **commands** can be anything you would include in a shell script, including calls to other functions.

The opening brace ({) can appear on the same line as the function name. Aliases and variables are expanded when a function is read, not when it is executed. You can use the **break** statement (page 992) within a function to terminate its execution.

Shell functions are useful as a shorthand as well as to define special commands. The following function starts a process named **process** in the background, with the output normally displayed by **process** being saved in **.process.out**:

```
start_process() {
process > .process.out 2>&1 &
}
```

The next example creates a simple function that displays the date, a header, and a list of the people who are logged in on the system. This function runs the same commands as the **whoson** script described on page 289. In this example the function is being entered from the keyboard. The greater than (**>**) signs are secondary shell prompts (**PS2**); do not enter them.

```
$ function whoson ()
> {
>     date
>     echo "Users Currently Logged On"
>     who
> }

$ whoson
Tue Aug 9 15:44:58 PDT 2011
Users Currently Logged On
hls        console      2011-08-08 08:59   (:0)
max        pts/4        2011-08-08 09:33   (0.0)
zach       pts/7        2011-08-08 09:23   (guava)
```

Functions in startup files If you want the **whoson** function to be available without having to enter it each time you log in, put its definition in **~/.bash_profile**. Then run **.bash_profile**, using the **.** (dot) command to put the changes into effect immediately:

```
$ cat ~/.bash_profile
export TERM=vt100
stty kill '^u'
whoson ()
{
    date
    echo "Users Currently Logged On"
    who
}

$ . ~/.bash_profile
```

You can specify arguments when you call a function. Within the function these arguments are available as positional parameters (page 1012). The following example shows the **arg1** function entered from the keyboard:

```
$ arg1 ( ) {
> echo "$1"
> }

$ arg1 first_arg
first_arg
```

See the function **switch** () on page 284 for another example of a function. "Functions" on page 1009 discusses the use of local and global variables within a function.

optional   The following function allows you to export variables using tcsh syntax. The env builtin lists all environment variables and their values and verifies that **setenv** worked correctly:

```
$ cat .bash_profile
...
# setenv - keep tcsh users happy
function setenv()
{
    if [ $# -eq 2 ]
        then
            eval $1=$2
            export $1
        else
            echo "Usage: setenv NAME VALUE" 1>&2
    fi
}
$ . ~/.bash_profile
$ setenv TCL_LIBRARY /usr/local/lib/tcl
$ env | grep TCL_LIBRARY
TCL_LIBRARY=/usr/local/lib/tcl
```

eval   The **$#** special parameter (page 1013) takes on the value of the number of command-line arguments. This function uses the eval builtin to force bash to scan the command **$1=$2** *twice*. Because **$1=$2** begins with a dollar sign ($), the shell treats the entire string as a single token—a command. With variable substitution performed, the command name becomes **TCL_LIBRARY=/usr/local/lib/tcl**, which results in an error. With eval, a second scanning splits the string into the three desired tokens, and the correct assignment occurs.

CONTROLLING bash: FEATURES AND OPTIONS

This section explains how to control bash features and options using command-line options and the set and shopt builtins.

COMMAND-LINE OPTIONS

Short and long command-line options are available. Short options consist of a hyphen followed by a letter; long options have two hyphens followed by multiple characters. Long options must appear before short options on a command line that calls bash. Table 9-12 lists some commonly used command-line options.

Table 9-12   Command-line options

Option	Explanation	Syntax
Help	Displays a usage message.	**‑‑help**
No edit	Prevents users from using the Readline Library (page 328) to edit command lines in an interactive shell.	**‑‑noediting**

Table 9-12   Command-line options (continued)

Option	Explanation	Syntax
No profile	Prevents reading these startup files (page 282): /etc/profile, ~/.bash_profile, ~/.bash_login, and ~/.profile.	**--noprofile**
No rc	Prevents reading the ~/.bashrc startup file (page 283). This option is on by default if the shell is called as **sh**.	**--norc**
POSIX	Runs bash in POSIX mode.	**--posix**
Version	Displays bash version information and exits.	**--version**
Login	Causes bash to run as though it were a login shell.	**-l** (lowercase "l")
shopt	Runs a shell with the *opt* shopt option (page 344). A **-O** (uppercase "O") sets the option; **+O** unsets it.	**[±]O [*opt*]**
End of options	On the command line, signals the end of options. Subsequent tokens are treated as arguments even if they begin with a hyphen (–).	**--**

SHELL FEATURES

You can control the behavior of the Bourne Again Shell by turning features on and off. Different features use different methods to turn themselves on and off. The set builtin controls one group of features, and the shopt builtin controls another group. You can also control many features from the command line you use to call bash.

Features, options, variables?

tip   To avoid confusing terminology, this book refers to the various shell behaviors that you can control as *features*. The bash info page refers to them as "options" and "values of variables controlling optional shell behavior."

set ±o: TURNS SHELL FEATURES ON AND OFF

The set builtin, when used with the –o or +o option, enables, disables, and lists certain bash features. For example, the following command turns on the **noclobber** feature (page 237):

```
$ set -o noclobber
```

You can turn this feature off (the default) by giving the command

```
$ set +o noclobber
```

The command set –o without an option lists each of the features controlled by set, followed by its state (on or off). The command set +o without an option lists the same features in a form you can use as input to the shell. Table 9-13 on the next page lists bash features.

Table 9-13   bash features

Feature	Description	Syntax	Alternate syntax
allexport	Automatically exports all variables and functions you create or modify after giving this command (default is off).	**set −o allexport**	**set −a**
braceexpand	Causes bash to perform brace expansion (default is on; page 346).	**set −o braceexpand**	**set −B**
cdspell	Corrects minor spelling errors in directory names used as arguments to cd (default is off).	**shopt −s cdspell**	
cmdhist	Saves all lines of a multiline command in the same history entry, adding semicolons as needed (default is on).	**shopt −s cmdhist**	
dotglob	Causes shell special characters (wildcards; page 244) in an ambiguous file reference to match a leading period in a filename. By default special characters do not match a leading period. You must always specify the filenames . and .. explicitly because no pattern ever matches them (default is off).	**shopt −s dotglob**	
emacs	Specifies emacs editing mode for command-line editing (default is on; page 329).	**set −o emacs**	
errexit	Causes bash to exit when a simple command (not a control structure) fails (default is off).	**set −o errexit**	**set −e**
execfail	Causes a shell script to continue running when it cannot find the file that is given as an argument to exec. By default a script terminates when exec cannot find the file that is given as its argument (default is off).	**shopt −s execfail**	
expand_aliases	Causes aliases (page 334) to be expanded (default is on for interactive shells and off for noninteractive shells).	**shopt −s expand_alias**	
hashall	Causes bash to remember where commands it has found using **PATH** (page 308) are located (default is on).	**set −o hashall**	**set −h**
histappend	Causes bash to append the history list to the file named by **HISTFILE** (page 319) when the shell exits (default is off [bash overwrites this file]).	**shopt −s histappend**	
histexpand	Turns on the history mechanism (which uses exclamation points by default; page 323). Turn this feature off to turn off history expansion (default is on).	**set −o histexpand**	**set −H**

Table 9-13   bash features (continued)

Feature	Description	Syntax	Alternate syntax
history	Enables command history (default is on; page 319).	**set −o history**	
huponexit	Specifies that bash send a SIGHUP signal to all jobs when an interactive login shell exits (default is off).	**shopt −s huponexit**	
ignoreeof	Specifies that bash must receive ten EOF characters before it exits. Useful on noisy dial-up lines (default is off).	**set −o ignoreeof**	
monitor	Enables job control (default is on; page 296).	**set −o monitor**	**set −m**
nocaseglob	Causes ambiguous file references (page 244) to match filenames without regard to case (default is off).	**shopt −s nocaseglob**	
noclobber	Helps prevent overwriting files (default is off; page 237).	**set −o noclobber**	**set −C**
noglob	Disables pathname expansion (default is off; page 244).	**set −o noglob**	**set −f**
notify	With job control (page 296) enabled, reports the termination status of background jobs immediately (default is off: bash displays the status just before the next prompt).	**set −o notify**	**set −b**
nounset	Displays an error and exits from a shell script when you use an unset variable in an interactive shell (default is off: bash displays a null value for an unset variable).	**set −o nounset**	**set −u**
nullglob	Causes bash to expand ambiguous file references (page 244) that do not match a filename to a null string (default is off: bash passes these file references without expanding them).	**shopt −s nullglob**	
posix	Runs bash in POSIX mode (default is off).	**set −o posix**	
verbose	Displays command lines as bash reads them (default is off).	**set −o verbose**	**set −v**
vi	Specifies vi editing mode for command-line editing (default is off; page 328).	**set −o vi**	
xpg_echo	Causes the echo builtin to expand backslash escape sequences without the need for the −e option (default is off; page 996).	**shopt −s xpg_echo**	
xtrace	Turns on shell debugging (default is off; page 982).	**set −o xtrace**	**set −x**

shopt: TURNS SHELL FEATURES ON AND OFF

The shopt (shell option) builtin enables, disables, and lists certain bash features that control the behavior of the shell. For example, the following command causes bash to include filenames that begin with a period (.) when it expands ambiguous file references (the **–s** stands for *set*):

```
$ shopt -s dotglob
```

You can turn this feature off (the default) by giving the following command (the **–u** stands for *unset*):

```
$ shopt -u dotglob
```

The shell displays how a feature is set if you give the name of the feature as the only argument to shopt:

```
$ shopt dotglob
dotglob         off
```

Without any options or arguments, shopt lists the features it controls and their states. The command **shopt –s** without an argument lists the features controlled by shopt that are set or on. The command **shopt –u** lists the features that are unset or off. Table 9-13 on the previous page lists bash features.

Setting set ±o features using shopt

tip You can use shopt to set/unset features that are otherwise controlled by **set ±o**. Use the regular shopt syntax with **–s** or **–u** and include the **–o** option. For example, the following command turns on the **noclobber** feature:

```
$ shopt -o -s noclobber
```

PROCESSING THE COMMAND LINE

Whether you are working interactively or running a shell script, bash needs to read a command line before it can start processing it—bash always reads at least one line before processing a command. Some bash builtins, such as **if** and **case**, as well as functions and quoted strings, span multiple lines. When bash recognizes a command that covers more than one line, it reads the entire command before processing it. In interactive sessions, bash prompts with the secondary prompt (**PS2**, > by default; page 311) as you type each line of a multiline command until it recognizes the end of the command:

```
$ echo 'hi
> end'
hi
end
```

```
$ function hello () {
> echo hello there
> }
$
```

After reading a command line, bash applies history expansion and alias substitution to the line.

HISTORY EXPANSION

"Re-executing and Editing Commands" on page 320 discusses the commands you can give to modify and re-execute command lines from the history list. History expansion is the process bash uses to turn a history command into an executable command line. For example, when you enter the command !!, history expansion changes that command line so it is the same as the previous one. History expansion is turned on by default for interactive shells; **set +o histexpand** turns it off. History expansion does not apply to noninteractive shells (shell scripts).

ALIAS SUBSTITUTION

Aliases (page 334) substitute a string for the first word of a simple command. By default aliases are turned on for interactive shells and off for noninteractive shells. Enter the command **shopt –u expand_aliases** to turn aliases off.

PARSING AND SCANNING THE COMMAND LINE

After processing history commands and aliases, bash does not execute the command immediately. One of the first things the shell does is to *parse* (isolate strings of characters in) the command line into tokens or words. The shell then scans each token for special characters and patterns that instruct the shell to take certain actions. These actions can involve substituting one word or words for another. When the shell parses the following command line, it breaks it into three tokens (**cp**, **~/letter**, and **.**):

```
$ cp ~/letter .
```

After separating tokens and before executing the command, the shell scans the tokens and performs *command-line expansion*.

COMMAND-LINE EXPANSION

Both interactive and noninteractive shells transform the command line using *command-line expansion* before passing the command line to the program being called. You can use a shell without knowing much about command-line expansion, but you can use what a shell has to offer to a better advantage with an understanding of this topic. This section covers Bourne Again Shell command-line expansion.

The Bourne Again Shell scans each token for the various types of expansion and substitution in the following order. Most of these processes expand a word into a single word. Only brace expansion, word splitting, and pathname expansion can change the number of words in a command (except for the expansion of the variable "$@"—see page 1016).

1. Brace expansion (below)

2. Tilde expansion (page 348)

3. Parameter and variable expansion (page 348)

4. Arithmetic expansion (page 349)

5. Command substitution (page 351)

6. Word splitting (page 352)

7. Pathname expansion (page 352)

8. Process substitution (page 354)

Quote removal   After bash finishes with the preceding list, it removes from the command line single quotation marks, double quotation marks, and backslashes that are not a result of an expansion. This process is called *quote removal*.

ORDER OF EXPANSION

The order in which bash carries out these steps affects the interpretation of commands. For example, if you set a variable to a value that looks like the instruction for output redirection and then enter a command that uses the variable's value to perform redirection, you might expect bash to redirect the output.

```
$ SENDIT="> /tmp/saveit"
$ echo xxx $SENDIT
xxx > /tmp/saveit
$ cat /tmp/saveit
cat: /tmp/saveit: No such file or directory
```

In fact, the shell does *not* redirect the output—it recognizes input and output redirection before it evaluates variables. When it executes the command line, the shell checks for redirection and, finding none, evaluates the **SENDIT** variable. After replacing the variable with **> /tmp/saveit**, bash passes the arguments to echo, which dutifully copies its arguments to standard output. No **/tmp/saveit** file is created.

The following sections provide more detailed descriptions of the steps involved in command processing. Keep in mind that double and single quotation marks cause the shell to behave differently when performing expansions. Double quotation marks permit parameter and variable expansion but suppress other types of expansion. Single quotation marks suppress all types of expansion.

BRACE EXPANSION

Brace expansion, which originated in the C Shell, provides a convenient way to specify filenames when pathname expansion does not apply. Although brace expansion is almost always used to specify filenames, the mechanism can be used to generate arbitrary strings; the shell does not attempt to match the brace notation with the names of existing files.

Brace expansion is turned on in interactive and noninteractive shells by default; you can turn it off with **set +o braceexpand**. The shell also uses braces to isolate variable names (page 304).

The following example illustrates how brace expansion works. The ls command does not display any output because there are no files in the working directory. The echo builtin displays the strings the shell generates with brace expansion. In this case the strings do not match filenames (because there are no files in the working directory).

```
$ ls
$ echo chap_{one,two,three}.txt
chap_one.txt chap_two.txt chap_three.txt
```

The shell expands the comma-separated strings inside the braces in the echo command into a SPACE-separated list of strings. Each string from the list is prepended with the string **chap_**, called the *preamble,* and appended with the string **.txt,** called the *postscript.* Both the preamble and the postscript are optional. The left-to-right order of the strings within the braces is preserved in the expansion. For the shell to treat the left and right braces specially and for brace expansion to occur, at least one comma and no unquoted whitespace characters must be inside the braces. You can nest brace expansions.

Brace expansion is useful when there is a long preamble or postscript. The following example copies four files—**main.c, f1.c, f2.c,** and **tmp.c**—located in the **/usr/local/src/C** directory to the working directory:

```
$ cp /usr/local/src/C/{main,f1,f2,tmp}.c .
```

You can also use brace expansion to create directories with related names:

```
$ ls -F
file1  file2  file3
$ mkdir vrs{A,B,C,D,E}
$ ls -F
file1  file2  file3  vrsA/  vrsB/  vrsC/  vrsD/  vrsE/
```

The **–F** option causes ls to display a slash (**/**) after a directory and an asterisk (✳) after an executable file.

If you tried to use an ambiguous file reference instead of braces to specify the directories, the result would be different (and not what you wanted):

```
$ rmdir vrs✳
$ mkdir vrs[A-E]
$ ls -F
file1  file2  file3  vrs[A-E]/
```

An ambiguous file reference matches the names of existing files. In the preceding example, because it found no filenames matching **vrs[A–E]**, bash passed the ambiguous file reference to mkdir, which created a directory with that name. Brackets in ambiguous file references are discussed on page 247.

TILDE EXPANSION

Chapter 6 introduced a shorthand notation to specify your home directory or the home directory of another user. This section provides a more detailed explanation of *tilde expansion.*

The tilde (~) is a special character when it appears at the start of a token on a command line. When it sees a tilde in this position, bash looks at the following string of characters—up to the first slash (/) or to the end of the word if there is no slash—as a possible username. If this possible username is null (that is, if the tilde appears as a word by itself or if it is immediately followed by a slash), the shell substitutes the value of the **HOME** variable for the tilde. The following example demonstrates this expansion, where the last command copies the file named **letter** from Max's home directory to the working directory:

```
$ echo $HOME
/home/max
$ echo ~
/home/max
$ echo ~/letter
/home/max/letter
$ cp ~/letter .
```

If the string of characters following the tilde forms a valid username, the shell substitutes the path of the home directory associated with that username for the tilde and name. If the string is not null and not a valid username, the shell does not make any substitution:

```
$ echo ~zach
/home/zach
$ echo ~root
/root
$ echo ~xx
~xx
```

Tildes are also used in directory stack manipulation (page 298). In addition, ~+ is a synonym for **PWD** (the name of the working directory), and ~– is a synonym for **OLDPWD** (the name of the previous working directory).

PARAMETER AND VARIABLE EXPANSION

On a command line, a dollar sign ($) that is not followed by an open parenthesis introduces parameter or variable expansion. *Parameters* include both command-line, or positional, parameters (page 1012) and special parameters (page 1010). *Variables* include both user-created variables (page 302) and keyword variables (page 307). The bash man and info pages do not make this distinction.

The shell does not expand parameters and variables that are enclosed within single quotation marks and those in which the leading dollar sign is escaped (i.e., preceded with a backslash or enclosed within single quotation marks). The shell does expand parameters and variables enclosed within double quotation marks.

ARITHMETIC EXPANSION

The shell performs *arithmetic expansion* by evaluating an arithmetic expression and replacing it with the result. Under bash the syntax for arithmetic expansion is

   $((expression))

The shell evaluates *expression* and replaces *$((expression))* with the result of the evaluation. This syntax is similar to the syntax used for command substitution [*$(...)*] and performs a parallel function. You can use *$((expression))* as an argument to a command or in place of any numeric value on a command line.

The rules for forming *expression* are the same as those found in the C programming language; all standard C arithmetic operators are available (see Table 27-8 on page 1035). Arithmetic in bash is done using integers. Unless you use variables of type integer (page 307) or actual integers, however, the shell must convert string-valued variables to integers for the purpose of the arithmetic evaluation.

You do not need to precede variable names within *expression* with a dollar sign ($). In the following example, after read (page 1019) assigns the user's response to **age**, an arithmetic expression determines how many years are left until age 60:

```
$ cat age_check
#!/bin/bash
echo -n "How old are you? "
read age
echo "Wow, in $((60-age)) years, you'll be 60!"

$ ./age_check
How old are you? 55
Wow, in 5 years, you'll be 60!
```

You do not need to enclose the *expression* within quotation marks because bash does not perform filename expansion on it. This feature makes it easier for you to use an asterisk (*) for multiplication, as the following example shows:

```
$ echo There are $((60*60*24*365)) seconds in a non-leap year.
There are 31536000 seconds in a non-leap year.
```

The next example uses wc, cut, arithmetic expansion, and command substitution (page 351) to estimate the number of pages required to print the contents of the file **letter.txt**. The output of the wc (word count) utility used with the **–l** option is the number of lines in the file, in columns (character positions) 1 through 4, followed by a SPACE and the name of the file (the first command following). The cut utility with the **–c1–4** option extracts the first four columns.

```
$ wc -l letter.txt
351 letter.txt
$ wc -l letter.txt | cut -c1-4
351
```

The dollar sign and single parenthesis instruct the shell to perform command substitution; the dollar sign and double parentheses indicate arithmetic expansion:

```
$ echo $(( $(wc -l letter.txt | cut -c1-4)/66 + 1))
6
```

The preceding example sends standard output from wc to standard input of cut via a pipe. Because of command substitution, the output of both commands replaces the commands between the $(and the matching) on the command line. Arithmetic expansion then divides this number by 66, the number of lines on a page. A 1 is added because the integer division results in any remainder being discarded.

Fewer dollar signs ($)

tip When you use variables within **$((** and **))**, the dollar signs that precede individual variable references are optional:

```
$ x=23 y=37
$ echo $((2*$x + 3*$y))
157
$ echo $((2*x + 3*y))
157
```

Another way to get the same result without using cut is to redirect the input to wc instead of having wc get its input from a file you name on the command line. When you redirect its input, wc does not display the name of the file:

```
$ wc -l < letter.txt
    351
```

It is common practice to assign the result of arithmetic expansion to a variable:

```
$ numpages=$(( $(wc -l < letter.txt)/66 + 1))
```

let builtin   The let builtin evaluates arithmetic expressions just as the $(( )) syntax does. The following command is equivalent to the preceding one:

```
$ let "numpages=$(wc -l < letter.txt)/66 + 1"
```

The double quotation marks keep the SPACEs (both those you can see and those that result from the command substitution) from separating the expression into separate arguments to let. The value of the last expression determines the exit status of let. If the value of the last expression is 0, the exit status of let is 1; otherwise, its exit status is 0.

You can supply let with multiple arguments on a single command line:

```
$ let a=5+3 b=7+2
$ echo $a $b
8 9
```

When you refer to variables when doing arithmetic expansion with let or $(( )), the shell does not require a variable name to begin with a dollar sign ($). Nevertheless, it is a good practice to do so for consistency, because in most places you must precede a variable name with a dollar sign.

COMMAND SUBSTITUTION

Command substitution replaces a command with the output of that command. The preferred syntax for command substitution under bash follows:

> *$(command)*

Under bash you can also use the following, older syntax:

> ` *command* `

The shell executes *command* within a subshell and replaces *command*, along with the surrounding punctuation, with standard output of *command*.

In the following example, the shell executes pwd and substitutes the output of the command for the command and surrounding punctuation. Then the shell passes the output of the command, which is now an argument, to echo, which displays it.

```
$ echo $(pwd)
/home/max
```

The next script assigns the output of the pwd builtin to the variable **where** and displays a message containing the value of this variable:

```
$ cat where
where=$(pwd)
echo "You are using the $where directory."
$ ./where
You are using the /home/zach directory.
```

Although it illustrates how to assign the output of a command to a variable, this example is not realistic. You can more directly display the output of pwd without using a variable:

```
$ cat where2
echo "You are using the $(pwd) directory."
$ ./where2
You are using the /home/zach directory.
```

The following command uses find to locate files with the name **README** in the directory tree rooted at the working directory. This list of files is standard output of find and becomes the list of arguments to ls.

```
$ ls -l $(find . -name README -print)
```

The next command line shows the older ` *command* ` syntax:

```
$ ls -l `find . -name README -print`
```

One advantage of the newer syntax is that it avoids the rather arcane rules for token handling, quotation mark handling, and escaped back ticks within the old syntax. Another advantage of the new syntax is that it can be nested, unlike the old syntax. For example, you can produce a long listing of all **README** files whose size exceeds the size of **./README** with the following command:

```
$ ls -l $(find . -name README -size +$(echo $(cat ./README | wc -c)c ) -print )
```

Try giving this command after giving a **set –x** command (page 982) to see how bash expands it. If there is no **README** file, the command displays the output of **ls –l**.

For additional scripts that use command substitution, see pages 978, 997, and 1027.

$((versus $(

tip   The symbols **$((** constitute a single token. They introduce an arithmetic expression, not a command substitution. Thus, if you want to use a parenthesized subshell (page 295) within **$( )**, you must put a SPACE between the **$(** and the following **(**.

WORD SPLITTING

The results of parameter and variable expansion, command substitution, and arithmetic expansion are candidates for word splitting. Using each character of **IFS** (page 312) as a possible delimiter, bash splits these candidates into words or tokens. If **IFS** is unset, bash uses its default value (SPACE-TAB-NEWLINE). If **IFS** is null, bash does not split words.

PATHNAME EXPANSION

Pathname expansion (page 244), also called *filename generation* or *globbing,* is the process of interpreting ambiguous file references and substituting the appropriate list of filenames. Unless **noglob** (page 343) is set, the shell performs this function when it encounters an ambiguous file reference—a token containing any of the unquoted characters *, ?, [, or]. If bash cannot locate any files that match the specified pattern, the token with the ambiguous file reference remains unchanged. The shell does not delete the token or replace it with a null string but rather passes it to the program as is (except see **nullglob** on page 343).

In the first echo command in the following example, the shell expands the ambiguous file reference **tmp*** and passes three tokens (**tmp1**, **tmp2**, and **tmp3**) to echo. The echo builtin displays the three filenames it was passed by the shell. After rm removes the three **tmp*** files, the shell finds no filenames that match **tmp*** when it tries to expand it. It then passes the unexpanded string to the echo builtin, which displays the string it was passed.

```
$ ls
tmp1 tmp2 tmp3
$ echo tmp*
tmp1 tmp2 tmp3
$ rm tmp*
$ echo tmp*
tmp*
```

A period that either starts a pathname or follows a slash (/) in a pathname must be matched explicitly unless you have set **dotglob** (page 342). The option **nocaseglob** (page 343) causes ambiguous file references to match filenames without regard to case.

Quotation marks Putting double quotation marks around an argument causes the shell to suppress pathname and all other kinds of expansion except parameter and variable expansion. Putting single quotation marks around an argument suppresses all types of expansion. The second echo command in the following example shows the variable **$max** between double quotation marks, which allow variable expansion. As a result the shell expands the variable to its value: **sonar**. This expansion does not occur in the third echo command, which uses single quotation marks. Because neither single nor double quotation marks allow pathname expansion, the last two commands display the unexpanded argument **tmp∗** .

```
$ echo tmp∗ $max
tmp1 tmp2 tmp3 sonar
$ echo "tmp∗ $max"
tmp∗ sonar
$ echo 'tmp∗ $max'
tmp∗ $max
```

The shell distinguishes between the value of a variable and a reference to the variable and does not expand ambiguous file references if they occur in the value of a variable. As a consequence you can assign to a variable a value that includes special characters, such as an asterisk (∗).

Levels of expansion In the next example, the working directory has three files whose names begin with **letter**. When you assign the value **letter∗** to the variable **var**, the shell does not expand the ambiguous file reference because it occurs in the value of a variable (in the assignment statement for the variable). No quotation marks surround the string **letter∗**; context alone prevents the expansion. After the assignment the set builtin (with the help of grep) shows the value of **var** to be **letter∗** .

```
$ ls letter∗
letter1  letter2  letter3
$ var=letter∗
$ set | grep var
var='letter∗'
$ echo '$var'
$var
$ echo "$var"
letter∗
$ echo $var
letter1 letter2 letter3
```

The three **echo** commands demonstrate three levels of expansion. When **$var** is quoted with single quotation marks, the shell performs no expansion and passes the character string **$var** to echo, which displays it. With double quotation marks, the shell performs variable expansion only and substitutes the value of the **var** variable for its name, preceded by a dollar sign. No pathname expansion is performed on this command because double quotation marks suppress it. In the final command, the shell, without the limitations of quotation marks, performs variable substitution and then pathname expansion before passing the arguments to echo.

PROCESS SUBSTITUTION

A special feature of the Bourne Again Shell is the ability to replace filename arguments with processes. An argument with the syntax *<(command)* causes *command* to be executed and the output written to a named pipe (FIFO). The shell replaces that argument with the name of the pipe. If that argument is then used as the name of an input file during processing, the output of *command* is read. Similarly an argument with the syntax *>(command)* is replaced by the name of a pipe that *command* reads as standard input.

The following example uses sort (page 154) with the **–m** (merge, which works correctly only if the input files are already sorted) option to combine two word lists into a single list. Each word list is generated by a pipe that extracts words matching a pattern from a file and sorts the words in that list.

```
$ sort -m -f <(grep "[^A-Z]..$" memo1 | sort) <(grep ".*aba.*" memo2 |sort)
```

CHAPTER SUMMARY

The shell is both a command interpreter and a programming language. As a command interpreter, it executes commands you enter in response to its prompt. As a programming language, the shell executes commands from files called shell scripts. When you start a shell, it typically runs one or more startup files.

Running a shell script
Assuming the file holding a shell script is in the working directory, there are three basic ways to execute the shell script from the command line.

1. Type the simple filename of the file that holds the script.

2. Type a relative pathname, including the simple filename preceded by *./*.

3. Type **bash** followed by the name of the file.

Technique 1 requires that the working directory be in the **PATH** variable. Techniques 1 and 2 require that you have execute and read permission for the file holding the script. Technique 3 requires that you have read permission for the file holding the script.

Job control
A job is one or more commands connected by pipes. You can bring a job running in the background into the foreground using the fg builtin. You can put a foreground job into the background using the bg builtin, provided you first suspend the job by pressing the suspend key (typically CONTROL-Z). Use the jobs builtin to see which jobs are running or suspended.

Variables
The shell allows you to define variables. You can declare and initialize a variable by assigning a value to it; you can remove a variable declaration using unset. Variables are local to a process unless they are exported using the export builtin to make them available to child processes. Variables you declare are called *user-created* variables. The shell defines *keyword* variables. Within a shell script you can work with the command-line (*positional*) parameters the script was called with.

Process   Each process has a unique identification (PID) number and is the execution of a single Linux command. When you give it a command, the shell forks a new (child) process to execute the command, unless the command is built into the shell. While the child process is running, the shell is in a state called sleep. By ending a command line with an ampersand (&), you can run a child process in the background and bypass the sleep state so that the shell prompt returns immediately after you press RETURN. Each command in a shell script forks a separate process, each of which might in turn fork other processes. When a process terminates, it returns its exit status to its parent process. An exit status of zero signifies success; nonzero signifies failure.

History   The history mechanism maintains a list of recently issued command lines, also called *events,* that provides a way to re-execute previous commands quickly. There are several ways to work with the history list; one of the easiest is to use a command-line editor.

Command-line editors   When using an interactive Bourne Again Shell, you can edit a command line and commands from the history list, using either of the Bourne Again Shell's command-line editors (vim or emacs). When you use the vim command-line editor, you start in Input mode, unlike vim. You can switch between Command and Input modes. The emacs editor is modeless and distinguishes commands from editor input by recognizing control characters as commands.

Aliases   An alias is a name the shell translates into another name or (complex) command. Aliases allow you to define new commands by substituting a string for the first token of a simple command.

Functions   A shell function is a series of commands that, unlike a shell script, is parsed prior to being stored in memory. As a consequence shell functions run faster than shell scripts. Shell scripts are parsed at runtime and are stored on disk. A function can be defined on the command line or within a shell script. If you want the function definition to remain in effect across login sessions, you can define it in a startup file. Like functions in many programming languages, a shell function is called by giving its name followed by any arguments.

Shell features   There are several ways to customize the shell's behavior. You can use options on the command line when you call bash. You can use the bash set and shopt builtins to turn features on and off.

Command-line expansion   When it processes a command line, the Bourne Again Shell might replace some words with expanded text. Most types of command-line expansion are invoked by the appearance of a special character within a word (for example, a leading dollar sign denotes a variable). Table 9-6 on page 315 lists these special characters. The expansions take place in a specific order. Following the history and alias expansions, the common expansions are parameter and variable expansion, command substitution, and pathname expansion. Surrounding a word with double quotation marks suppresses all types of expansion except parameter and variable expansion. Single quotation marks suppress all types of expansion, as does quoting (escaping) a special character by preceding it with a backslash.

EXERCISES

1. Explain the following unexpected result:

```
$ whereis date
date: /bin/date ...
$ echo $PATH
.:/usr/local/bin:/usr/bin:/bin
$ cat > date
echo "This is my own version of date."
$ ./date
Sat May 21 11:45:49 PDT 2011
```

2. What are two ways you can execute a shell script when you do not have execute permission for the file containing the script? Can you execute a shell script if you do not have read permission for the file containing the script?

3. What is the purpose of the **PATH** variable?

   a. Set the **PATH** variable so it causes the shell to search the following directories in order:

   • /usr/local/bin

   • /usr/bin

   • /bin

   • /usr/kerberos/bin

   • The **bin** directory in your home directory

   • The working directory

   b. If there is a file named **doit** in **/usr/bin** and another file with the same name in your **~/bin** directory, which one will be executed? (Assume you have execute permission for both files.)

   c. If your **PATH** variable is not set to search the working directory, how can you execute a program located there?

   d. Which command can you use to add the directory **/usr/games** to the end of the list of directories in **PATH**?

4. Assume you have made the following assignment:

```
$ person=zach
```

   Give the output of each of the following commands:

   a. echo $person

   b. echo '$person'

   c. echo "$person"

5. The following shell script adds entries to a file named **journal-file** in your home directory. This script helps you keep track of phone conversations and meetings.

```
$ cat journal
# journal: add journal entries to the file
# $HOME/journal-file

file=$HOME/journal-file
date >> $file
echo -n "Enter name of person or group: "
read name
echo "$name" >> $file
echo >> $file
cat >> $file
echo "--------------------------------------------------------" >> $file
echo >> $file
```

a. What do you have to do to the script to be able to execute it?

b. Why does the script use the read builtin the first time it accepts input from the terminal and the cat utility the second time?

6. Assume the **/home/zach/grants/biblios** and **/home/zach/biblios** directories exist. Specify Zach's working directory after he executes each sequence of commands. Explain what happens in each case.

a.
```
$ pwd
/home/zach/grants
$ CDPATH=$(pwd)
$ cd
$ cd biblios
```

b.
```
$ pwd
/home/zach/grants
$ CDPATH=$(pwd)
$ cd $HOME/biblios
```

7. Name two ways you can identify the PID number of the login shell.

8. Enter the following command:

```
$ sleep 30 | cat /etc/services
```

Is there any output from sleep? Where does cat get its input from? What has to happen before the shell displays a prompt?

ADVANCED EXERCISES

9. Write a sequence of commands or a script that demonstrates variable expansion occurs before pathname expansion.

10. Write a shell script that outputs the name of the shell executing it.

11. Explain the behavior of the following shell script:

```
$ cat quote_demo
twoliner="This is line 1.
This is line 2."
echo "$twoliner"
echo $twoliner
```

   a. How many arguments does each echo command see in this script? Explain.

   b. Redefine the **IFS** shell variable so the output of the second echo is the same as the first.

12. Add the exit status of the previous command to your prompt so it behaves similarly to the following:

```
$ [0] ls xxx
ls: xxx: No such file or directory
$ [1]
```

13. The dirname utility treats its argument as a pathname and writes to standard output the path prefix—that is, everything up to but not including the last component:

```
$ dirname a/b/c/d
a/b/c
```

If you give **dirname** a simple filename (no **/** characters) as an argument, **dirname** writes a . to standard output:

```
$ dirname simple
.
```

Implement dirname as a bash function. Make sure it behaves sensibly when given such arguments as **/**.

14. Implement the basename utility, which writes the last component of its pathname argument to standard output, as a bash function. For example, given the pathname **a/b/c/d**, basename writes **d** to standard output:

```
$ basename a/b/c/d
d
```

15. The Linux basename utility has an optional second argument. If you give the command **basename** *path suffix,* basename removes the *suffix* and the prefix from *path:*

```
$ basename src/shellfiles/prog.bash .bash
prog
$ basename src/shellfiles/prog.bash .c
prog.bash
```

Add this feature to the function you wrote for exercise 14.

10

NETWORKING AND THE INTERNET

OBJECTIVES

After reading this chapter you should be able to:

▶ Discuss a variety of network types

▶ Define several network protocols

▶ List the software and hardware components of
networks

▶ Explain the features and advantages of IPv6

▶ List several network utilities

▶ Explain how ping works

▶ Use dig to determine the nameserver for a Web site

▶ Describe distributed computing

▶ Explain the role of the World Wide Web

359

INTRODUCTION TO NETWORKING

The communications facilities linking computers are continually improving, allowing faster and more economical connections. The earliest computers were unconnected stand-alone systems. To transfer information from one system to another, you had to store it in some form (usually magnetic tape, paper tape, or punch cards—called IBM or Hollerith cards), carry it to a compatible system, and read it back in. A notable advance occurred when computers began to exchange data over serial lines, although the transfer rate was slow (hundreds of bits per second). People quickly invented new ways to take advantage of this computing power, such as email, news retrieval, and bulletin board services. With the speed and ubiquity of today's networks, a piece of email can cross the country or even travel halfway around the world in a fraction of a second.

Today it would be difficult to find a computer facility that does not include a LAN to link its systems. Linux systems are typically attached to an *Ethernet* (page 1163) network. Wireless networks are also prevalent. Large computer facilities usually maintain several networks, often of different types, and almost certainly have connections to larger networks (companywide or campuswide and beyond).

Internet   The Internet is a loosely administered network of networks (an *internetwork*) that links computers on diverse LANs around the globe. An internet (small *i*) is a generic network of networks that might share some parts in common with the public Internet. It is the Internet that makes it possible to send an email message to a colleague thousands of miles away and receive a reply within minutes. A related term, *intranet*, refers to the networking infrastructure within a company or other institution. Intranets are usually private; access to them from external networks might be limited and carefully controlled, typically using firewalls (page 368).

Network services   Over the past decade many network services have emerged and become standardized. On Linux and UNIX systems, special processes called *daemons* (page 1160) support such services by exchanging specialized messages with other systems over the network. Several software systems have been created to allow computers to share filesystems with one another, making it appear as though remote files are stored on local disks. Sharing remote filesystems allows users to share information without knowing where the files physically reside, without making unnecessary copies, and without learning a new set of utilities to manipulate them. Because the files appear to be stored locally, you can use standard utilities (e.g., cat, vim, lpr, mv, or their graphical counterparts) to work with them.

Many tools take advantage of networks for more than sharing files. These tools have varied tasks, from executing programs remotely to communicating between computers, programs, and people. The ssh (secure shell, page 673) utility is the standard tool for remote command execution and remote computer access. Years ago it replaced insecure tools such as rsh, telnet, and rlogin. The ssh utility encompasses the features of these tools and includes built-in security features for safe and private access across public networks. Some devices do not implement ssh, but not many.

Previously, users communicated using command-line tools such as talk, write, and IRC (Internet Relay Chat). These tools are still around, particularly IRC, but their use has waned in preference to Facebook, Twitter, Google Talk, Skype, and older IM (Instant Messaging) tools like MSN, AIM, ICQ, and Yahoo Messenger. Many people use the Empathy IM client for Linux. Jabber is popular in private company networks.

Intranet An *intranet* is a network that connects computing resources at a school, company, or other organization but, unlike the Internet, typically restricts access to internal users. An intranet is usually composed of one or more local area networks (LANs) but could be fairly large for a regional, national, or worldwide company. An intranet can provide database, email, and Web page access to a limited group of people, regardless of their geographic location.

The ability of an intranet to connect dissimilar machines is one of its strengths. Think of all the machines you can find on the Internet: Macintosh systems, PCs running different versions of Windows, machines running UNIX and Linux, and so on. Each of these machines can communicate via the IP protocol suite (page 370). The intranet defines the communication boundaries and security trust zones that enable this communication.

Another key difference between the Internet and an intranet is that the Internet transmits only one protocol suite natively: IP. In contrast, an intranet can be set up to use a number of protocols, such as IP, AppleTalk, or other protocols developed by vendors over the years. Although these protocols cannot be transmitted directly over the Internet, you can set up gateway boxes at remote sites that tunnel or encapsulate these protocols into IP packets and then use the Internet to pass them. In practice, most of the older protocols have been rewritten to use IP as a transport. Even storage protocols and networks like SCSI and Fibre Channel have IP implementations now (iSCSI, FCoE).

You can use an *extranet* (also called a *partner net*) or a VPN (virtual private network) to improve security. These terms describe ways to connect remote sites securely to a local site, typically by using the public Internet as a carrier and employing encryption as a means of protecting data in transit. A typical use of an extranet is to link research institutions for collaboration or to link a parts supplier and a manufacturer to obtain direct inventory access.

Following are some terms you might want to become familiar with before you read the rest of this chapter:

ASP (page 1152)	*hub* (page 1169)	*packet* (page 1180)
bridge (page 1154)	*internet* (page 1170)	*router* (page 1186)
extranet (page 1164)	*Internet* (page 1170)	*sneakernet* (page 1189)
firewall (page 1165)	*intranet* (page 1170)	*switch* (page 1192)
gateway (page 1166)	*ISP* (page 1171)	*VPN* (page 1196)

TYPES OF NETWORKS AND HOW THEY WORK

Computers communicate over IP networks using unique addresses assigned by system software. An IP *packet* includes the address of the destination computer and the sender's return address. Networks can consist of many distinct *topologies,* or arrangements of computers and networking equipment. The most common topologies are broadcast, point-to-point, and switched. Ethernet is the most common topology used in LANs (local area networks, discussed shortly). Ethernet speeds range from 10 megabits per second to 100 gigabits per second (not formally accepted as of this writing). Other types of LANs include Myrinet, Infiniband, and Quadrics, but they are used mostly in high-performance computing.

Speed is critical to the proper functioning of the Internet. Newer specifications (cat 6 and cat 7) are being adopted for 10000BaseT (10 gigabits per second; also called 10GE) and faster networking. Specialized cables are required for higher speeds. SFP+ and QSFP are in common use. Many of the networks that form the backbone of the Internet run at speeds of 38 gigabits per second (OC768) to accommodate the ever-increasing demand for network services. Table 10-1 lists some of the specifications in use today.

Table 10-1   Network specifications

Specification	Speed
DS0	64 kilobits per second
ISDN	Two DS0 lines plus signaling (16 kilobits per second) or 128 kilobits per second
T-1	1.544 megabits per second (24 DS0 lines)
T-3	43.232 megabits per second (28 T-1s)
OC3	155 megabits per second (100 T-1s)
OC12	622 megabits per second (4 OC3s)
OC48	2.5 gigabits per second (4 OC12s)
OC192	9.6 gigabits per second (4 OC48s)
OC768	38.4 gigabits per second (4 OC192s)

BROADCAST NETWORKS

On a *broadcast network,* any of the many systems attached to the network cable can send a message at any time; each system examines the destination address in each message and responds only to messages addressed to it. A problem occurs on a broadcast network when multiple systems send data at the same time, resulting in a collision of the messages on the cable. When messages collide, they can become garbled. The sending system notices the garbled message and resends it after waiting a short but random amount of time. Waiting a random amount of time helps prevent those same systems from resending the data at the same moment and experiencing yet another collision. The extra traffic that results from collisions can strain the network; if the collision rate gets too high, retransmissions might result in more collisions. Ultimately the network might become unusable.

A special *broadcast* (page 1154) packet in a network requires all machines to inspect the packet. Certain protocols take advantage of this feature: The ARP protocol, which is used for IP addresses to MAC (Ethernet) addresses resolution, the PXE network boot protocol, DHCP, and some service discovery protocols all use broadcast packets.

POINT-TO-POINT NETWORKS

A point-to-point link does not seem like much of a network because only two endpoints are involved. However, most connections to WANs (wide area networks) go through point-to-point links, using wire cable, radio, or satellite links. The advantage of a point-to-point link is its simplicity: Because only two systems are involved, the traffic on the link is limited and well understood. A disadvantage is that each system can typically be equipped for only a small number of such links; it is impractical and costly to establish point-to-point links that connect each computer to all the rest. For example two hosts require one link, three hosts require three links, four hosts require six links, and five hosts require 10 links to connect a point to point network. The number of required links increases more quickly as you add more hosts. Point-to-point links often use serial links and specialized interfaces.

The most common types of point-to-point links are the ones used to connect to the Internet. When you use DSL[1] (digital subscriber line), you are using a point-to-point link to connect to the Internet. Serial lines, such as T-1, T-3, ATM links, FIOS, and ISDN, are all point-to-point. Although it might seem like a point-to-point link, a cable modem is based on broadcast technology and in that way is similar to Ethernet.

SWITCHED NETWORKS

With the introduction of switched networks, pure broadcast networks became a thing of the past. A switched network runs in full duplex mode, allowing machines and network equipment to send and receive data at the same time. Support for full duplex is built-in and required in gigabit networks and above, on 100-megabit networks it is optional, and on 10 megabit networks it is rare.

A *switch* is a device that establishes a virtual path between source and destination hosts in such a way that each path appears to be a point-to-point link, much like a old-fashioned telephone switchboard. Instead of the operator using a plug to connect

---

1. The term *DSL* incorporates the xDSL suite of technologies, which includes ADSL, IDSL, HDSL, SDSL, and XDSL.

your local line to an outgoing line, the switch inspects each packet to determine its destination and directs the packet appropriately.

The switch creates and tears down virtual paths as hosts seek to communicate with each other. Each host thinks it has a direct point-to-point path to the host it is talking to. Contrast this approach with a broadcast network, where each host also sees traffic bound for other hosts. The advantage of a switched network over a pure point-to-point network is that each host requires only one connection: the connection to the switch. Using pure point-to-point connections, each host must have a connection to every other host. Scalability is provided by further linking switches.

To achieve this reduction in traffic, Ethernet switches learn which hosts are on which ports. When traffic comes in destined for a host, the switch looks up which port that host is connected to in its CAM[2] and sends the packet out that port. When a switch has not yet heard from a host matching the destination, or if the packet is a special broadcast packet, the packet is flooded out on all ports just like a packet in a broadcast network. A switched Ethernet network is a technological enhancement over a broadcast network.

LAN: LOCAL AREA NETWORK

Local area networks (LANs) are confined to a relatively small area—a single computer facility, building, or campus. Today most LANs run over copper. Fiberoptic (glass or plastic) cable, wireless (Wi-Fi), and sometimes infrared (similar to most television remote control devices) are also common infrastructure.

If its destination address is not on the local network, a packet must be passed on to another network by a router (page 367). A router might be a general-purpose computer or a special-purpose device attached to multiple networks to act as a gateway among them.

Switching terminology

You might see references to a *layer-2 switch*, *layer-3 switch*, or *layer-4 switch*. These terms refer to the IP networking model (page 370). A layer-2 switch is what the preceding discussion of switched network describes. A layer-3 switch is equivalent to a router; it combines features of layer-2 switching and routing. A single layer-3 switch can connect multiple independent LANs. Layer-4 switches inspect higher level packets to make decisions. Most Web load balancers are layer-4 switches. They can route traffic to many devices to spread the load on the network.

ETHERNET

A Linux system connected to a LAN usually connects to a network using Ethernet. A typical Ethernet connection can support data transfer rates from 10 megabits per second to 100 gigabits per second. Transfer rates of 10 megabits per second, 100 megabits per second, and 1 gigabit per second use the same, older technology. However, 10, 40, and 100 gigabit per second transfer rates require newer technology and

---

2. A memory table used to *dereference* (page 1161) Ethernet addresses.

specialized cables. Ten gigabit per second Ethernet can be compatible with 1 gigabit per second Ethernet by using physical media adapters. Because of the need for extremely tight tolerances, 40 and 100 gigabit per second Ethernet are not backward compatible. The technology required for these higher-speed transfer rates requires very precisely defined physical interfaces. The hardware is quite expensive and common only in the network infrastructure realm and HPC (high performance computing) environments, connecting multiple switches using high speed links.

Cables As mentioned earlier, a modern Ethernet network transfers data using copper or fiber-optic cable or wireless transmitters and receivers. Originally, each computer was attached to a thick coaxial cable (called *thicknet*) at tap points spaced at six-foot intervals along the cable. The thick cable was awkward to deal with, so other solutions, including a thinner coaxial cable called *thinnet,* or 10Base2,[3] were developed.

Today most Ethernet connections are either wireless or made over UTP (unshielded twisted pair). There are a number of UTP standards, each referred to by a category and a number. Some examples are Category 5 [cat 5], Category 5e [cat 5e], and Category 6 [cat 6]. These categories specify how far the cable can carry a signal. The higher the number, the tighter the tolerances and the more expensive the cable, but the farther it can reliably carry a signal. These standards specify the physical connectors at the ends of the cables, how tightly the wires in the cable are twisted, and various other parameters. The terms 10BaseT, 100BaseT, and 100BaseT refer to Ethernet over cat-3/4/5/5e/6/7 cables. STP (shielded twisted pair) is not very common.

Segment A network *segment* is a part of a network in which all systems communicate using the same physical layer (layer 1) of the IP and OSI models (page 371). It is of arbitrary size and can be a part of a WAN, MAN, or another network.

Duplex In *half-duplex* mode, packets travel in one direction at a time over the cable. In *full-duplex* mode, packets travel in both directions.

Hub A *hub* (sometimes called a *concentrator*) is a device that connects systems so they are all part of one network segment and share the network bandwidth. Hubs work at the physical layer of the IP and OSI models (layer 1, page 371). All packets are sent to all hosts (flooded).

Switch A *switch* connects network segments. A switch inspects each data packet; it learns which devices are connected to which of its ports. The switch sends each packet only to the device it is intended for. Because a switch sends packets only to their destination devices, it can conserve network bandwidth and perform better than a hub. Some switches have buffers that hold and queue packets.

Switches work at layers 2 and higher of the IP and OSI models (page 370). A layer-2 switch works at the datalink layer, and a layer-3 switch works at the IP layer and routes packets. Layer-4 switches work at the transport and application layers and are the basis for load balancers and application proxies.

---

3. Versions of Ethernet are classified as **XBaseY**, where *X* is the data rate in megabits per second, **Base** means baseband (as opposed to radio frequency), and *Y* is the category of cabling.

All modern Ethernet switches have enough bandwidth to communicate simultaneously, in full-duplex mode, with all connected devices. A nonswitched (hub-based) broadcast network can run in only half-duplex mode. Full-duplex Ethernet further improves efficiency by eliminating collisions. Each host on a full-duplex switched network can transmit and receive simultaneously at the speed of the network (e.g., 100 megabits per second) for an effective bandwidth between hosts of twice the speed of the network (e.g., 200 megabits per second), depending on the capacity of the switch.

Bridge   A network *bridge* connects multiple network segments at the data link layer (IP layer 2) of the OSI model. A bridge is similar to a repeater or network hub, devices that connect network segments at the physical layer, however a bridge works by forwarding traffic from one network segment to another only if the destination device specified in the packet is known to be on the remote segment. A bridge does not forward traffic between LAN hosts on the same side of the bridge.

In Ethernet networks, the term *bridge* formally means a device that behaves according to the IEEE 802.1D standard. Marketing literature frequently refers to this type of device as a network switch.

Router   A *router* connects networks at layer 3 of the IP and OSI models (page 371). For example, a router can connect a LAN to a WAN (such as the Internet) or it can connect two LANs. A router determines which path packets should take to travel to a different network and forwards the packets. Routers work at the network layer of the IP and OSI models (layer 3). "Internetworking Through Gateways and Routers" on the next page covers routers in more depth.

VLAN   A VLAN (virtual local area network or virtual LAN) is a logical entity defined in software. It defines a group of hosts that share the same broadcast domain (layer 2). That is, when a host sends out a broadcast packet, such as an ARP packet, it will arrive at all other hosts in the same VLAN. All modern, managed switches, those that have a command line or Web interface, have VLAN capability. A VLAN allows an administrator to group hosts into IP ranges (LANs). VLANs commonly group hosts by department, organization, or security needs. Hosts in the same VLAN communicate with each other using layer 2, and hosts in different VLANs communicate using layer 3. The primary difference between a LAN and a VLAN is that in a LAN (a nonmanaged switch), all hosts are in the same broadcast domain, whereas in a VLAN, there can be multiple broadcast domains on a single switch.

Broadcast domains and IP protocol layer 2 segments are effectively the same thing. However, layer 2 can be confused with hosts (network addresses) being in the same IP network. Consider the classic concentrator, a device that sends out all packets on all ports all the time. These ports might include separate networks. For example, some hosts might be in network 10.0.1.0, and others might be in network 192.168.1.0. Ethernet broadcast packets do not know the difference between the networks; these packets go to all hosts regardless of IP address. This setup is sometimes referred to as a *collision domain*. VLANs enable you to place the hosts in the IP network 10.0.1.0 into one VLAN and the hosts in 192.168.1.0 into another, so the networks do not share each others' broadcasts. VLANs also enable you to connect hosts that share the same function across a corporate network.

WIRELESS

Wireless networks are becoming increasingly common. They are found in offices, homes, and public places, such as universities, coffee shops, and airports. Wireless access points provide functionality similar to an Ethernet hub. They allow multiple users to interact via a common radio frequency spectrum. A wireless, point-to-point connection allows you to wander about your home or office with a laptop, using an antenna to link to a LAN or to the Internet via an in-house base station. Linux includes drivers for many wireless devices. A wireless access point, or base station, connects a wireless network to a wired network so that no special protocol is required for a wireless connection. Refer to the *Linux Wireless LAN HOWTO* at www.hpl.hp.com/personal/Jean_Tourrilhes/Linux.

WAN: WIDE AREA NETWORK

A WAN (wide area network) covers a large geographic area. In contrast, the technologies (such as Ethernet) used for LANs were designed to work over limited distances and for a certain number of host connections. A WAN might span long distances over dedicated data lines (leased from a telephone company) or radio or satellite links. Such networks are often used to connect LANs and typically support much lower bandwidth than LANs because of the expense the connection. Major Internet service providers rely on WANs to connect to their customers within a country and around the globe.

MAN   Some networks do not fit into either the LAN or the WAN designation. A *metropolitan area network* (MAN) is a network that is contained in a smaller geographic area, such as a city. Like WANs, MANs are typically used to interconnect LANs.

INTERNETWORKING THROUGH GATEWAYS AND ROUTERS

Gateway   A LAN connects to a WAN through a *gateway,* a generic term for a computer or a special device with multiple network connections that passes data from one network to another. A gateway connects a LAN to other LANs, VLANs, or to a WAN. Data that crosses the country from one Ethernet to another over a WAN, for example, is repackaged from the Ethernet format to a different format that can be processed by the communications equipment that makes up the WAN backbone. When it reaches the end of its journey over the WAN, the data is converted by another gateway to a format appropriate for the receiving network. For the most part, these details are of concern only to the network administrators; the end user does not need to know anything about how the data transfer takes place.

Router   The modern, canonical reference to a gateway is to the default gateway, which is the *router* that connects a LAN or VLAN to other networks. Routers play an important role in internetworking. Just as you might study a map to plan your route when you need to drive to an unfamiliar place, so a computer needs to know how to deliver a message to a system attached to a distant network by passing through intermediary systems and networks along the way. Although you might envision using a giant network road map to choose the route that your data should follow, a static map of computer routes is usually a poor choice for a large network. Computers and networks along the route you choose might be overloaded or down and not provide a detour for your message.

Routers instead communicate dynamically, keeping each other informed about which routes are open for use. To extend the analogy, this situation is like heading out on a car trip without consulting a map to find a route to your destination; instead you head for a nearby gas station and ask directions. Throughout the journey you continue to stop at one gas station after another, getting directions at each to find the next one. Although it would take a while to make the stops, the owner of each gas station would advise you of bad traffic, closed roads, alternative routes, and shortcuts.

The stops made by the data are much quicker than those you would make in your car, but each message leaves each router on a path chosen based on the most current information. Think of this system as a GPS (global positioning system) setup that automatically gets updates at each intersection and tells you where to go next, based on traffic and highway conditions.

Figure 10-1 shows an example of how LANs might be set up at three sites interconnected by a WAN (the Internet). In this type of network diagram, Ethernet LANs are drawn as straight lines, with devices attached at right angles; WANs are represented as clouds, indicating the details have been left out; and wireless connections are drawn as zigzag lines with breaks, indicating the connection might be intermittent.

In Figure 10-1, a gateway or a router relays messages between each LAN and the Internet. The figure shows the three routers in the Internet that are closest to each site. Site A has a server, a workstation, a network computer, and a PC sharing a single Ethernet LAN. Site B has an Ethernet LAN that serves a printer and four Linux workstations. A firewall permits only certain traffic to pass between the Internet router and the site's local router. Site C has three LANs linked by a single router, perhaps to reduce the traffic load that would result if the LANs were combined or to keep workgroups or locations on separate networks. Site C also includes a wireless access point that enables wireless communication with nearby computers.

FIREWALL

A firewall in a car separates the engine compartment from the passenger compartment, protecting the driver and passengers from engine fires, noise, and fumes. In much the same way, computer firewalls separate computers from malicious and unwanted users.

A *firewall* prevents certain types of traffic from entering or leaving a network. For example, a firewall might prevent traffic from your IP address from leaving the network and prevent anyone except users from selected domains from using FTP

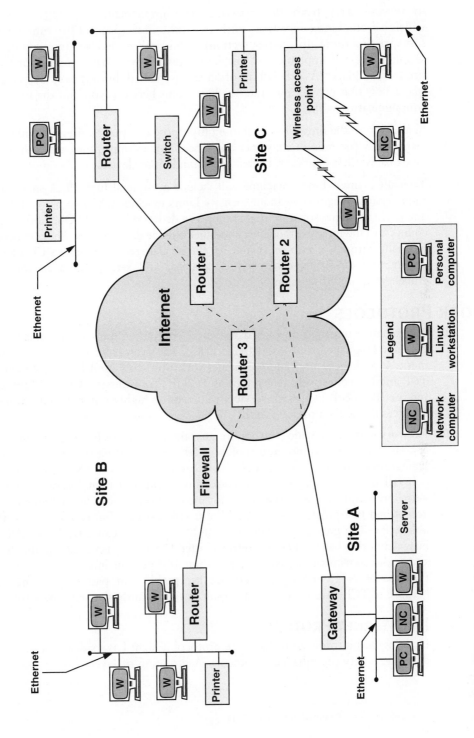

Figure 10-1   A slice of the Internet

to retrieve data from the network. The implementations of firewalls vary widely—from Linux machines with two *interfaces* (page 1170) running custom software to a router (preceding section) with simple access lists to esoteric, vendor-supplied firewall appliances. Most larger installations have at least one kind of firewall in place. A firewall is often accompanied by a proxy server/gateway (page 398) that provides an intermediate point between you and the host you are communicating with.

In addition to the firewalls found in multipurpose computers, firewalls are becoming increasingly common in consumer appliances. For example, they are built into cable modems, wireless gateways, routers, and stand-alone devices.

Typically a single Linux machine will include a minimal firewall. A small group of Linux systems might have an inexpensive Linux machine with two network interfaces and packet-filtering software functioning as a dedicated firewall. One of the interfaces connects to the Internet, modems, and other outside data sources. The other connects, normally through a hub or switch, to the local network. Refer to Chapter 25 for information on system-config-firewall, iptables, and setting up a firewall and to Appendix C for a discussion of security.

NETWORK PROTOCOLS

TCP   To exchange information over a network, computers must communicate using a common language, or *protocol* (page 1183). The protocol determines the format of message packets. The predominant network protocols used by Linux systems are TCP and IP,[4] collectively referred to as TCP/IP (Transmission Control Protocol and Internet Protocol). Network services that require highly reliable connections, such as ssh and scp, tend to use TCP/IP.

UDP   Network services that do not require guaranteed delivery but require timely delivery, such as video, audio, and time services, operate using the simpler UDP (User Datagram Protocol; UDP/IP). VoIP (voice over IP) and NTP (Network Time Protocol) fall into this category. UDP packets are sent and then forgotten. Voice and video protocols are delay sensitive, not integrity sensitive. The human ear and eye accept and interpolate loss in an audio or video stream but cannot deal with variable delay. The guaranteed delivery that TCP provides can introduce a delay on a busy network when packets are retransmitted. This delay is not acceptable for video and audio transmissions, whereas less than 100 percent integrity is acceptable. In the case of NTP, missing packets are acceptable, but packets that are delayed because of TCP retransmission can result in significantly skewed time settings.

IP: INTERNET PROTOCOL

Layering was introduced to facilitate protocol design: Layers distinguish functional differences between adjacent protocols. A grouping of layers can be standardized

---

4. All references to IP imply *IPv4* (page 1171).

into a protocol model. IP has a model that distinguishes protocol layers and that differs from the ISO seven-layer protocol model (also called the OSI model) often illustrated in networking textbooks. Specifically IP uses the following simplified five-layer model:

1. The first layer of the IP protocol, called the *physical layer,* describes the physical medium (e.g., copper, fiber, wireless) and the data encoding used to transmit signals on that medium (e.g., pulses of light, electrical waves, or radio waves).

2. The second layer, called the *data link layer,* covers media access by network devices and describes how to put data into packets, transmit the data, and check it for errors. Ethernet is found at this layer, as is *802.11* (page 1150) wireless.

3. The third layer, called the *network layer,* frequently uses IP and addresses and routes packets. It allows data to traverse the networks.

4. The fourth layer, called the *transport layer,* is where TCP and UDP exist. This layer provides a means for applications to communicate with each other. Functions commonly performed by the transport layer include guaranteed delivery, delivery of packets in the order of their transmission, flow control, error detection, and error correction. The transport layer is responsible for dividing data streams into packets. In addition, this layer performs port addressing, which allows it to distinguish among different services using the same transport protocol. Port addressing keeps the data from multiple applications using the same protocol (for example, TCP) separate.

5. Anything above the transport layer is the domain of the application and is part of the *fifth layer.* Unlike the ISO model, the Internet model does not distinguish among application, presentation, and session layers. All the upper-layer characteristics, such as character encoding, encryption, and GUIs, are part of the application. Applications choose the transport characteristics they require as well as the corresponding transport layer protocol with which to send and receive data.

TCP: TRANSMISSION CONTROL PROTOCOL

TCP is most frequently run on top of IP in a combination referred to as TCP/IP. This protocol provides error recovery and guaranteed delivery in packet transmission order; it also works with multiple ports so that it can handle more than one application. TCP is a *connection-oriented protocol* (page 1158), also known as a *stream-based* protocol. Once established, a TCP connection looks like a stream of data, not individual IP packets. The connection is assumed to remain up and be uniquely addressable. Every piece of information you write to the connection always goes to the same destination and arrives in the order it was sent. Because TCP is connection oriented and establishes a *virtual circuit* between two systems, this protocol is not suitable for one-to-many transmissions (see the discussion of UDP, following). TCP has builtin mechanisms for dealing with congestion (or flow) control over busy networks and throttles back (slows the speed of data flow) when it has to retransmit dropped packets. TCP can also deal with acknowledgments, wide area links, high-delay links, and other situations.

UDP: USER DATAGRAM PROTOCOL

UDP runs at layer 4 of the IP stack, just as TCP does, but is much simpler. Like TCP, UDP works with multiple ports and multiple applications. It has checksums for error detection but does not automatically retransmit *datagrams* (page 1160) that fail the checksum test. UDP is a datagram-oriented protocol: Each datagram must carry its own address and port information. Each router along the way examines each datagram to determine the destination, one hop at a time. You can broadcast or multicast UDP datagrams to many destinations at the same time by using special addresses.

PPP: POINT-TO-POINT PROTOCOL

PPP provides serial line point-to-point connections that support IP. It compresses data to make the most of the limited bandwidth available on these connections. PPP acts as a point-to-point layer 2/3 transport that many other types of protocols can ride on. Today it is used mostly in devices such as cable modems. Previously, it was used as a transport for TCP and UDP on dial-up modems that connected a computer to the Internet.

IPv4

Under IPv4, the network address of a machine is an IP address that is represented as one number broken into four *octets*[5] separated by periods (for example, 192.168.184.5). Domain names and IP addresses are assigned through a highly distributed system coordinated by ICANN (Internet Corporation for Assigned Names and Numbers—www.icann.org) via many registrars (see www.internic.net). ICANN is funded by the various domain name registries and registrars and by IP address registries, which supply globally unique identifiers for hosts and services on the Internet. Although you might not deal with any of these agencies directly, your Internet service provider most assuredly does.

How a company uses IP addresses is determined by the system or network administrator. For example, the two leftmost sets of numbers in an IP address might represent a large network (campuswide or companywide); the third set, a subnetwork (perhaps a department or a single floor in a building); and the rightmost number, an individual computer. The operating system uses the address in a different, lower-level form, converting it to its binary equivalent, a series of 1s and 0s. Refer to "Private address space" on page 650 for information about addresses you can use on a LAN without registering them.

---

5. Using binary notation, an eight-bit byte can represent the range of 0–255, thus the term octet.

IPv6

Getting started with IPv6

tip Even if the ISP you do business with does not provide IPv6 service, it is still easy and free to participate on the IPv6 Internet by using a tunnel broker. For more information on tunnel brokers see en.wikipedia.org/wiki/List_of_IPv6_tunnel_brokers. Setting up a small home or lab network through a tunnel broker is an excellent way to gain experience with IPv6 and experiment with its configurations and capabilities. Most tunnel brokers offer instructions on how to get various platforms working with their service.

IPv6 (Internet Protocol version 6)[6] is the next generation of the Internet Protocol. Since the introduction of IPv4 (Internet Protocol version 4) in 1980, the Internet has undergone explosive growth that has caused its needs to exceed the capabilities of IPv4. A proliferation of Internet connected devices, including cellular telephones, tablet computers, electronic book readers, and advanced televisions and set-top boxes, all of which need an IP address in order to communicate on the Internet, has fueled that growth. IPv4 uses a 32-bit address space, which is no longer sufficient to give a unique IP address to every device on the Internet. The lack of IPv4 address space has been mitigated by the use of *NAT* (page 1177) and by other techniques, but each of these techniques comes with limitations and overhead.

IPv6 uses a 128-bit address space, which ensures that all devices can have unique IP addresses without resorting to such mitigations, and provides enormous room to grow as the Internet continues to expand. While the enormous address space in IPv6 is its most compelling feature in light of the shortage of IPv4 addresses, IPv6 has many other desirable features:

- IPv6 enables stateless address autoconfiguration. With IPv4, DHCP (page 489) is usually used to automate network configuration. With IPv6, autoconfiguration makes it possible for hosts to configure their IP addresses automatically and autonomously without the need for a central service like DHCP.

- In IPv6, *multicast* (page 1177 and next) is mandatory and fundamental to its operation.

- IPv6 provides a simplified packet header that reduces router complexity by improving routing efficiency and cuts router cost by eliminating the need for much hardware acceleration.

- IPv6 reserves 20 bits in the header for advanced services, such as resource reservation protocols, better backbone routing, and improved traffic engineering.

---

6. IPv5 referred to an experimental real-time stream protocol named ST—thus the jump from IPv4 to IPv6.

IPv6 can coexist with IPv4. Even though the protocols are very similar in many ways, the network considers them to be different protocols, so one will not interfere with the other. Also, most operating systems support IPv4 and IPv6 simultaneously by using a dual-stack configuration. This configuration is likely to be common for a long time because it allows IPv6-enabled hosts to reach legacy IPv4-only hosts easily.

MULTICAST PACKETS

IPv6 does not use *broadcast* (page 1154) packets and therefore does not have a *broadcast address* (page 1155) that corresponds to the IPv4 broadcast address. IPv6 mandates the implementation and use of *multicast* (page 1177).

Multicast improves the efficiency of the network by reducing the amount of traffic that each host must process: The system network interface does not ordinarily pass to the host multicast traffic it is not registered to receive.

For example, when a host wants to discover a DHCPv6 server, it sends a packet to the "all DHCPv6 servers" well-known link-local multicast address (ff05::1:3). This packet is processed only by hosts running DHCPv6. Under IPv4 the host must send a broadcast packet to discover the DHCP server. This packet is processed by every host on the network.

Many tools, such as ssh, work with IPv6 and IPv4 without difficulty. Some tools have special versions that work with IPv6 (e.g., ping6, traceroute6, and ip6tables).

ADDRESSES

Because they are much longer, IPv6 addresses are quite different from IPv4 addresses. For brevity and clarity, IPv6 addresses are usually expressed as eight sets of four hexadecimal digits, each set separated from the next by a colon. As an example, consider the IPv6 address 2001:4860:800a:0000:0000:0000:0000:0067.

To shorten the address and allow it to remain unambiguous, you can replace any number of adjacent sets of four zeros and the colons that enclose them with two colons. After making this replacement, you can represent the example address as 2001:4860:800a::0067. With this replacement, you (or a computer) can easily expand the shortened address by adding enough sets of four zeros to fill out the eight sets in the address. You cannot make this replacement more than once in an address. If you did, when you tried to expand the address you would not know how many sets of zeros to replace each double colon with.

As an additional way of shortening an address, you can eliminate any leading zeros in any set of four digits. Using this technique, you can write the example address as 2001:4860:800a::67, which is much more manageable than the original address. You can also use CIDR notation (page 380): The example host might be in an allocation such as 2001:4860:800a::/48.

In IPv6, the network prefix is always 64 bits, and the host part is always the remaining 64 bits. In other words, all networks are the same size. If an organization were given the network allocation 2001:4860:800a::/48, it would have 16 bits of network address space to use, each network being of the form 2001:4860:800a:*xxxx*::/64, where *xxxx* is any one of the 65,536 possible numbers in 16 bits. Because of the immense size of the IPv6 address space, this allocation is considered small, although even very large organizations would fit well within it.

AUTOCONFIGURATION

A constant host address length of 64 bits allows for stateless address autoconfiguration. Using a multicast ICMPv6 packet, the router sends periodic advertisements to all hosts on the network, telling them of its ability to route for a given network prefix. At the same time, it gives hosts permission to assign themselves addresses using that prefix.

A host that hears this advertisement can construct a host address in a deterministic way by incorporating the hardware address of the network adapter (i.e., the MAC address [page 376]). Without resorting to the use of a stateful service (e.g., DHCP) to maintain a list of assigned addresses, this construction guarantees that no other host on the network will have the same address. After constructing a host address, the host finalizes the configuration by adding a default route to the router from which the advertisement came. Alternatively, when a host interface initially comes up, it can solicit router information by sending a request to all routers instead of waiting for the periodic advertisement, speeding up the process. Once it has assigned itself an address, the host expects to hear periodic advertisements from the router. If it does not hear these advertisements, the host will eventually expire its knowledge of this autoconfigured route and address.

LINK-LOCAL ADDRESSES

A *link-local* IP address can be used to communicate only with other systems on the network; a router will not forward a packet that has a link-local address. This address is autoconfigured in a manner similar to that explained in the preceding section, except the network prefix is always fe80::/64, marking it as a link-local address.

This setup contrasts with how IPv4 DHCP works: Because an IPv4 host does not have an address when it initially communicates with a DHCP server, a *hack* is needed to use a fake address for the host. Such hacks are not necessary in IPv6 because of autoconfigured link-local addresses. For example, when a host solicits router information, it uses a link-local address to do so.

Multihoming   The IPv6 specification requires *multihoming* (allowing a single network interface to have multiple addresses). Multihoming allows the link-local address to persist after a global-scope address has been assigned to a system, allowing continued access to the host via the link-local address.

Interface-local   The IPv6 loopback address is ::1 and is considered *interface-local*.

Well-known link-local addresses   Certain link-local addresses are not autoconfigured. These addresses are well-known and are registered with IANA. For a list of these addresses visit IANA at www.iana.org/assignments/ipv6-multicast-addresses/ipv6-multicast-addresses.xml.

Servers subscribe to these addresses as needed, allowing them to receive requests. For example, a DHCPv6 server will subscribe to ff05::1:3 so it receives configuration requests from hosts.

DHCPv6   DHCPv6 is a completely new implementation of DHCP (page 489) that covers IPv6. Although autoconfiguration works for most situations, network administrators who wish to have more control over their networks might choose to use DHCPv6. It enables an administrator to specify certain host addresses that can persist even if the host or network interface has to be replaced. (Autoconfigured addresses depend on the interface hardware address [NIC]).

It also allows configuration of other operational parameters, such as local DNS resolver address(es), which are not well supported with autoconfiguration. This feature is important on networks that run IPv6 only.

DHCPv6 also introduces the notion of a stateless mode, which is a way to enjoy the simplicity of autoconfiguration using router advertisements while also allowing the administrator to manage static configuration elements (e.g., DNS resolver addresses) using a very simple DHCP configuration that is easily made fault tolerant.

DNS   DNS works like in IPv4, except instead of having A records to associate names with addresses, there are AAAA records (sometimes called quad-A records; page 852). Just as a DNS name can have multiple A records, it can have multiple AAAA records and/or a combination of both. DNS does not place any restriction on which record type will be delivered based on which protocol was used by the requestor; DNS returns the record type(s) requested. This setup enables the DNS server to provide AAAA records for services that are available over IPv6, even when DNS itself has not been made available over IPv6.

Fragmentation   Under IPv6, if a router receives a packet larger than the network can support (the MTU, or maximum transmission unit), it sends a "fragmentation needed" ICMP packet back to the originator. Instead of the router bearing the burden of fragmenting the packet in-transit, the router depends on the originator to keep the packets down to a manageable size. Because the intervening routers do not have to concern themselves with fragmenting packets, they are able to work more efficiently and with less specialized hardware.

HOST ADDRESS

MAC address   Each *NIC* (page 1178) on a system connected to a network has a unique identifier[7] called a *MAC address* (page 1174), sometimes referred to as an *Ethernet address*. A system attached to more than one network has multiple interfaces—one for each network. Such a system might have one MAC address for the system, or it might have one MAC address for each interface. Both setups work as long as a given MAC address is unique on a given LAN or VLAN.

---

7. In fact, each identifier might not be unique. Vendors have been known to reuse MAC addresses for physical devices shipped to different regions. In practice, you are unlikely to run into duplicate addresses. The only requirement is that a MAC address must be unique on a given LAN or VLAN segment.

Each system on a network also has a one or more unique IP addresses. At IP layer 3 (the network layer), systems communicate using IP addresses. However, at IP layer 2 (the data link layer), they communicate using MAC addresses.

ARP For hosts to talk to each other over a network, a map between IP addresses and MAC addresses must exist. ARP (Address Resolution Protocol) is a method for finding a host's MAC (Ethernet) address from its IP address. Each host builds an ARP cache that holds a map that translates IP addresses into MAC addresses. The arp utility works with this cache; the –a option to display the cache:

```
$ arp -a
plum (172.16.192.151) at 00:0c:29:2d:eb:a9 [ether] on eth0
...
```

The preceding output shows the IP and Ethernet addresses of all hosts the local host is aware of. The example maps the IP address of **plum** (172.16.192.151) to the MAC address of the NIC on **plum** (00:0c:29:2d:eb:a9).

Each packet of information transmitted over a LAN has a destination MAC address. The NIC on each host on the network checks each packet to see if the destination address matches its MAC address. If it matches, the NIC passes the packet to the kernel for processing; if it does not match, and the packet does not have the special FF:FF:FF:FF:FF:FF destination address, the NIC silently drops the packet. All NICs examine all packets that have the special FF:FF:FF:FF:FF:FF destination address.

When the local system has a packet to send to another system, but knows only the remote system's IP address and not its MAC address, it sends an ARP broadcast packet to the special FF:FF:FF:FF:FF:FF destination address. That packet specifies the IP address the local system is trying to contact and requests the system with that IP address respond with its MAC address. When the host with the IP address the packet specifies examines the packet, it responds with its MAC address directly to the host that sent the packet. Once the systems have each other's IP addresses mapped to their MAC addresses in their ARP caches, they can communicate directly using this information. For more detail, refer to a book such as *Internetworking with TCP/IP*, Volume 1, 5th edition, by Douglas E. Comer, Prentice Hall (July 2005).

When the local system needs to send a packet to a host on another network, it sends the packet to the router (default gateway) on the local network. The local system knows the IP address of the router and uses ARP to determine its MAC address. The router and all hosts use the same process to determine the MAC address of hosts they need to send packets to. Then they can communicate directly with each of these hosts.

Each host and router keeps an ARP cache. Entries in the cache expire in about five minutes, balancing the currency of the address resolution table and the frequency of ARP requests.

STATIC VERSUS DYNAMIC IP ADDRESSES

A static IP address is one that always remains the same. A server (e.g., mail, Web) usually has a static address so clients can find the server machine on the network. See pages 493 and 652 for information on configuring a static IP address.

A dynamic IP address is one that is allocated (leased) to a client and that has a defined expiration time. Typically the client renews the lease before it expires at which time the server provides a new lease on the same IP address. A dynamic IP address can change each time a system connects to the network but frequently remains the same. End-user systems usually work well with dynamic addresses. During a given login session, these systems can function as a client (e.g., Web browser) because they maintain a constant IP address. When you log out and log in again, it does not matter that a system has a different IP address because, acting as a client, it establishes a new connection with a server. The advantage of dynamic addressing is that it allows inactive addresses to be reused, reducing the total number of IP addresses needed. Dynamic addressing is particularly popular on wireless access points.

optional SUBNETS

IP addresses are divided into two parts, the *network address*, also called the *subnet* (subnetwork address), and the *host address*, or *node address*. The network address specifies a set of computers that can communicate without sending packets through a router. The host address specifies an individual computer. IP is an internetwork protocol and was originally intended to connect networks together.

When sending a packet, a computer examines the network portion of the destination IP address. If the network address matches that of the sending computer's network, the computer can send the packet to the destination computer directly. If it does not match, the computer must send the packet to the router. The portion of the IP address used to identify the network is given by the subnet mask (next).

Terminology: subnet mask, network mask,
Although the term *subnet mask* is in common use, the preferred term is *network mask* or simply *mask*. This book uses the term subnet mask to make a clear distinction between the network prefix and the subnet prefix. Otherwise it uses the term network mask.

Subnet mask
A *subnet mask* (or *network mask*) is a bit mask that identifies which parts of an IP address correspond to the network address and the subnet portion of the address. This mask has 1s in positions corresponding to the network and subnet numbers and 0s in the host number positions. When you perform a bitwise AND on an IP address and a subnet mask, the resulting address contains everything except the host address (hostid) portion. There are several ways to represent a subnet mask: A network could have a subnet mask of 255.255.255.0 (decimal), FFFFFF00 (*hexadecimal* [page 1167]), or /24 (the number of bits used for the subnet mask).

A subnet mask of /24 has 8 bits for hosts (32-24). However, the last address in the range is reserved as a broadcast address, and the first address in the range is the network address. The second address is typically reserved for the router, although some setups use the broadcast address – 1 for this purpose. Thus there are $2^8 - 3 = 253$ IP addresses.

As another example, when you divide the address 192.25.4.0 into eight subnets, you get a subnet mask of 255.255.255.224, FFFFFFE0, or /27 (27 1s). The eight resultant networks are 192.25.4.0, 192.25.4.32, 192.25.4.64, 192.25.4.96, 192.25.4.128, 192.25.4.160, 192.25.4.192, and 192.25.4.224. You can use a Web-based subnet mask calculator to calculate subnet masks (refer to "Network Calculators" on page 1121). To use this calculator to determine the preceding subnet mask, start with an IP network address of 192.25.4.0.

Table 10-2 shows some of the computations for the IP address 131.204.027.027. Each address is shown in decimal, hexadecimal, and binary form. Binary is the easiest to work with for bitwise (binary) computations. The first three lines show the IP address. The next three lines show the *subnet mask* in three bases. Next the IP address and the subnet mask are ANDed together bitwise to yield the *subnet number* (page 1191), which is shown in three bases. The last three lines show the *broadcast address* (page 1155), which is computed by taking the subnet number and turning the hostid bits into 1s. The subnet number identifies the local network. The subnet number and the subnet mask determine what range the IP address of the machine must be in. They are also used by routers to segment traffic; see *network segment* (page 1178). A broadcast on this network goes to all hosts in the range 131.204.27.1 through 131.204.27.254 but will be acted on only by hosts that have a use for it. For more information refer to "Specifying a Subnet" on page 479.

Table 10-2   Computations for IP address 131.204.027.027

	---------------Class B-----------		netid	hostid	
	131	.204	.027	.027	decimal
IP address	83	CC	1B	1B	hexadecimal
	1000 0011	1100 1100	0001 1011	0001 1011	binary
	255	.255	.255	.000	decimal
Subnet mask	FF	FF	FF	00	hexadecimal
	1111 1111	1111 1111	1111 1111	0000 0000	binary
IP address bitwise AND	1000 0011	1100 1100	0001 1011	0001 1011	
Subnet mask	1111 1111	1111 1111	1111 1111	0000 0000	binary
= Subnet number	1000 0011	1100 1100	0001 1011	0000 0000	
	131	.204	.027	.000	decimal
Subnet number	83	CC	1B	00	hexadecimal
	1000 0011	1100 1100	0001 1011	0000 0000	binary
	131	.204	.27	.255	decimal
Broadcast address	83	CC	1B	FF	hexadecimal
(set host bits to 1)	1000 0011	1100 1100	0001 1011	1111 1111	binary

CIDR: CLASSLESS INTER-DOMAIN ROUTING

CIDR (pronounced "cider") allows groups of addresses to be assigned to an organization or ISP and then further subdivided and parceled out. In addition, it helps prevent routing tables on Internet backbone providers from becoming too large to manage by consolidating arbitrary network ranges along bit boundaries.

IPv6 (page 373) is the solution to IPv4 address exhaustion. The trend is to reclaim older, large address blocks, if possible, and recycle them into groups of smaller address blocks. Larger blocks are allocated to ISPs, which in turn subdivide these blocks and allocate them to their customers. When you request an address block, your ISP usually gives you as many addresses as you need—and no more. The ISP aggregates one or more contiguous smaller blocks to satisfy your request. This aggregation is CIDR. Without CIDR, the Internet as we know it would not function.

For example, you might be allocated the 192.168.5.0/22 IP address block, which can support 2^{10} hosts $(32 - 22 = 10)$. Your ISP would set its routers so packets going to an address in that block would be sent to your network. Internally, your own routers might further subdivide this block of 1,024 potential hosts into four networks. Four networks require an additional two bits of addressing $(2^2 = 4)$. You could therefore set up your router to support four networks with this allocation: 192.168.5.0/24, 192.168.6.0/24, 192.168.7.0/24, and 192.168.8.0/24. Each of these networks could then have 254 hosts. CIDR lets you arbitrarily divide networks and subnetworks into increasingly smaller blocks along the way. Each router has enough memory to keep track of the addresses it needs to direct and aggregates the rest.

This scheme uses memory and address space efficiently. For example, you could take 192.168.8.0/24 and further divide it into 16 networks with 14 hosts each. The 16 networks require four more bits $(2^4 = 16)$, so you would have 192.168.8.0/28, 192.168.8.16/28, 192.168.8.32/28, and so on, up through the last subnet of 192.168.8.240/16, which would have the hosts 192.168.8.241 through 192.168.8.254.

HOSTNAMES

People generally find it easier to work with names than with numbers, so Linux provides several ways to associate hostnames with IP addresses. The oldest method is to consult a list of names and addresses stored in the **/etc/hosts** file:

```
$ cat /etc/hosts
127.0.0.1      localhost
130.128.52.1   gw-example.example.com   gw-example
130.128.52.2   bravo.example.com        bravo
130.128.52.3   hurrah.example.com       hurrah
130.128.52.4   kudos.example.com        kudos
```

localhost =
127.0.0.1 The address 127.0.0.1 is reserved for the special hostname **localhost**, which serves as a hook for the system's networking software to operate on the local machine without going onto a physical network. The names of the other systems are shown in two forms: in a *fully qualified domain name* (FQDN) format that is unique on the Internet and as a nickname that is locally unique. Use of these names is a convention; the system does not check the contents of the **hosts** file.

NIS As more hosts joined networks, storing these name-to-address mappings in a text file proved to be inefficient and inconvenient. The **hosts** file grew bigger and became impossible to keep up-to-date. To solve this problem Linux supports NIS (Network Information Service; Chapter 21), which was developed for use on Sun computers. NIS stores information in a database, making it easier to find a specific address, but it is useful only for host information within a single administrative domain. Hosts outside the domain cannot access the information. Also, by default NIS is not secure and is difficult to secure.

DNS The solution to this dilemma is DNS (Domain Name Service; Chapter 24). DNS effectively addresses the efficiency and update issues by arranging the entire network *namespace* (page 1177) as a hierarchy. Each domain in the DNS manages its own namespace (addressing and name resolution), and each domain can easily query for any host or IP address by following the tree up or down the namespace until it finds the appropriate domain. By providing a hierarchical naming structure, DNS distributes name administration across the entire Internet.

COMMUNICATE OVER A NETWORK

Many commands that you can use to communicate with other users on a single computer system have been extended to work over a network. Examples of extended utilities include electronic mail programs, information-gathering utilities (e.g., finger; page 167), and communications utilities (e.g., Empathy). These utilities are examples of the UNIX philosophy: Instead of creating a new, special-purpose tool, modify an existing one.

Many utilities understand a convention for the format of network addresses: **user@host** (spoken as "user at host"). When you use an @ sign in an argument to one of these utilities, the utility interprets the text that follows as the name of a remote host. When you omit the @ sign, a utility assumes you are requesting information from or corresponding with someone on the local system.

If you frequently use more than one system over a network, you might find it difficult to keep track of which system you are interacting with at any particular moment. If you set your prompt to include the hostname of the current system, it will always be clear which system you are using. To identify the computer you are using, run hostname or give the command **uname –n**:

```
$ hostname
kudos
```

See page 310 for information on how you can change the prompt.

finger: DISPLAYS INFORMATION ABOUT REMOTE USERS

The finger utility displays information about one or more users on a system. This utility was designed for local use, but when networks became popular, it was obvious that finger should be enhanced to reach out and collect information remotely. See page 167 for examples.

The **in.fingerd** daemon

security   The finger daemon (**in.fingerd**) gives away system account information that can aid a malicious user. Some sites disable **in.fingerd** or randomize user account IDs to make a malicious user's job more difficult. Disable **in.fingerd** by setting **disable = yes** in **/etc/xinetd.d/finger** and restarting **xinetd**. For more information refer to "The xinetd Superserver" on page 481.

The finger utility (**finger** package) works by querying a standard network service, the **in.fingerd** daemon, that runs on the system being queried. Although this service is available in the **finger-server** package, many sites choose not to install and run it to minimize the load on their systems, reduce security risks, or maintain privacy. When you use finger to obtain information about someone at such a site, you will see an error message or nothing at all. The remote **in.fingerd** daemon determines how much information to share and in what format.

Mailing List Servers

A mailing list server (listserv[8]) allows you to create and manage an email list. An electronic mailing list provides a means for people interested in a particular topic to participate in an electronic discussion. One of the most powerful features of most list servers is their ability to archive email postings to the list, create an archive index, and allow users to retrieve postings from the archive based on keywords or discussion threads. Typically you can subscribe and unsubscribe from the list with or without human intervention. The owner of the list can restrict who can subscribe, unsubscribe, and post messages to the list. See page 752 for instructions on configuring the Mailman list server. Other popular list servers include LISTSERV (www.lsoft.com), phplist (www.phplist.com), Lyris (www.lyris.com), and Majordomo (www.greatcircle.com/majordomo). Fedora/RHEL maintains mailing lists and list archives for those mailing lists at www.redhat.com/mailman/listinfo. Use Google to search on **linux mailing list** to find other lists.

Network Utilities

To realize the full benefits of a networked environment, it made sense to extend certain tools, some of which have already been described. The advent of networks also created a need for new utilities to control and monitor them, spurring the development of new tools that took advantage of network speed and connectivity. This section describes concepts and utilities for systems attached to a network.

Trusted Hosts

Although they are deprecated in favor of ssh (next), some commands, such as rcp and rsh, work only if the remote system trusts the local computer (that is, if the

---

8. Although the term *listserv* is sometimes used generically to include many different list server programs, it is a specific product and a registered trademark of L-soft International, Inc.: LISTSERV (for more information visit www.lsoft.com).

remote system knows the local computer and believes that it is not pretending to be another system). The **/etc/hosts.equiv** file lists trusted systems. For reasons of security, the **root** account does not rely on this file to identify trusted privileged users from other systems.

Host-based trust is largely obsolete. Because there are many ways to circumvent trusted host security, including subverting DNS systems and *IP spoofing* (page 1171), authentication based on IP address is insecure.

In a small homogeneous network it might be tempting to use these tools, and it might suffice. However, because ssh is easy to setup, provides privacy and authentication, and does not slow down modern CPUs appreciably, it is a good idea to use it instead of the older tools.

Do not share your login account

security   It is poor practice to use a **~/.rhosts** file to allow another user to log in as you from a remote system without knowing your password. Do not compromise the security of your files or the entire system by sharing your login account. Use ssh and scp instead of rsh and rcp.

OpenSSH Tools

The OpenSSH project provides a set of tools that replace rcp, rsh, and others with secure equivalents. These tools are installed by default in Fedora/RHEL and can be used as drop-in replacements for their insecure counterparts. The OpenSSH tool suite is covered in detail in Chapter 18.

telnet: Logs In on a Remote System

You can use the TELNET protocol to interact with a remote computer. The telnet utility (**telnet** package), a user interface to this protocol, is older than ssh and is not secure. Nevertheless, it might work where ssh (page 681) is not available (there is more non-UNIX support for TELNET access than for ssh access). In addition, some legacy devices, such as terminal servers, facilities infrastructure, and network devices, still do not support ssh. The following example shows Sam using telnet to log in on a remote system that is running the **in.telnetd** daemon (controlled by **xinetd** [page 481]; **telnet-server** package):

```
[sam@guava ~]$ telnet plum
Trying 172.16.192.151...
Connected to plum.
Escape character is '^]'.
Fedora release 15 (Lovelock)
Kernel 2.6.38-1.fc15.i686 on an i686 (1)
login: sam
Password:
Last login: Tue Mar  8 13:20:14 from 172.16.192.1
...
[sam@plum ~]$ logout
Connection closed by foreign host.
[sam@guava ~]$
```

telnet versus ssh   When you connect to a remote UNIX or Linux system, telnet presents a textual **login:** prompt. Because telnet is designed to work with non-UNIX and non-Linux systems, it does not assume your remote username is the same as your local username (ssh does make this assumption). In some cases, telnet requires no login credentials.

telnet **is not secure**

security   Whenever you enter sensitive information, such as your password, while you are using telnet, it is transmitted in cleartext and can be read by someone who is eavesdropping on the session.

In addition, telnet allows you to configure special parameters, such as how RETURNs or interrupts are processed (ssh does not give you this option). When using telnet between UNIX and/or Linux systems, you rarely need to change any parameters.

When you do not specify the name of a remote host on the command line, telnet runs in an interactive mode. The following example is equivalent to the previous telnet example:

```
[sam@guava ~]$ telnet
telnet> open plum
Trying 172.16.192.151...
Connected to plum.
Escape character is '^]'.
...
```

Before connecting to a remote system, telnet tells you what the *escape character* is; in most cases, it is ^] (where ^ represents the CONTROL key). When you press CONTROL-], you escape to telnet's interactive mode. Continuing the preceding example:

```
[sam@guava ~]$ CONTROL-]
telnet> ?
Commands may be abbreviated.  Commands are:

close           close current connection
logout          forcibly logout remote user and close the connection
display         display operating parameters
mode            try to enter line or character mode ('mode ?' for more)
...
telnet> close
Connection closed.
[sam@guava ~]$
```

When you enter a question mark in response to the **telnet>** prompt, telnet lists its commands. The **close** command ends the current telnet session, returning you to the local system. To get out of telnet's interactive mode and resume communication with the remote system, press RETURN in response to a prompt.

USING telnet TO CONNECT TO OTHER PORTS

By default telnet connects to port 23, which is used for remote logins. However, you can use telnet to connect to other services by specifying a port number. In addition to standard services, many of the special remote services available on the Internet use unallocated port numbers. Unlike the port numbers for standard protocols, these port numbers can be picked arbitrarily by the administrator of the service.

Although telnet is no longer commonly employed to log in on remote systems, it is still used extensively as a debugging tool by allowing you to communicate directly with a TCP server. Some standard protocols are simple enough that an experienced user can debug problems by connecting to a remote service directly using telnet. If you are having a problem with a network server, a good first step is to try to connect to it using telnet.

If you use telnet to connect to port 25 on a host, you can interact with SMTP. In addition, port 110 connects to the POP protocol, port 80 connects with a WWW server, and port 143 connects to IMAP. All these protocols are ASCII protocols and are documented in *RFCs* (page 1185). You can read the RFCs or search the Web for examples on how to use them interactively.

In the following example, a system administrator who is debugging a problem with email delivery uses telnet to connect to the SMTP port (port 25) on the server at **example.com** to see why it is bouncing mail from the **spammer.com** domain. The first line of output indicates which IP address telnet is trying to connect to. After telnet displays the **Connected to smtpsrv.example.com** message, the user emulates an SMTP dialog, following the standard SMTP protocol. The first line, which starts with **helo**, begins the session and identifies the local system. After the SMTP server identifies itself, the user enters a line that identifies the mail sender as **user@spammer.com**. The SMTP server's response explains why the message is bouncing, so the user ends the session with **quit**.

```
$ telnet smtpsrv 25
Trying 192.168.1.1...
Connected to smtpsrv.example.com.
Escape character is '^]'.
helo example.com
220 smtpsrv.example.com ESMTP Sendmail 8.13.1/8.13.1; Wed, 4 May 2011 00:13:43 -0500 (CDT)
250 smtpsrv.example.com Hello desktop.example.com [192.168.1.97], pleased to meet you
mail from:user@spammer.com
571 5.0.0 Domain banned for spamming
quit
221 2.0.0 smtpsrv.example.com closing connection
```

The telnet utility allows you to use any protocol you want, as long as you know it well enough to type commands manually.

ftp: TRANSFERS FILES OVER A NETWORK

FTP (File Transfer Protocol) is a method of downloading files from and uploading files to a remote system using TCP/IP over a network. Most Web browsers can download files from FTP servers. Some vendors use anonymous FTP (page 707) to accept uploaded debugging sessions or to allow clients to download firmware. FTP is not a secure protocol; use it only for downloading public information from a public server. See page 702 for more information on FTP security. Use one of the

OpenSSH tools described in Chapter 18 for secure communication. Chapter 19 covers FTP clients and servers.

ping: TESTS A NETWORK CONNECTION

The ping[9] and ping6 utilities (referred to in this section as ping; read the story of ping at http://ftp.arl.mil/~mike/ping.html) send an ECHO_REQUEST packet to a remote computer. This packet causes the remote system to send back a reply. This exchange is a quick way to verify that a remote system is available and to check how well the network is operating, such as how fast it is or whether it is dropping data packets. The ping utility uses the ICMP (Internet Control Message Protocol) protocol. Without any options, ping tests the connection once per second until you abort execution using CONTROL-C.

```
$ ping www.slashdot.org
PING www.slashdot.org (216.34.181.48) 56(84) bytes of data.
64 bytes from star.slashdot.org (216.34.181.48): icmp_seq=1 ttl=238 time=70.2 ms
64 bytes from star.slashdot.org (216.34.181.48): icmp_seq=2 ttl=238 time=72.6 ms
64 bytes from star.slashdot.org (216.34.181.48): icmp_seq=3 ttl=238 time=57.5 ms
64 bytes from star.slashdot.org (216.34.181.48): icmp_seq=4 ttl=238 time=71.2 ms
CONTROL-C
--- www.slashdot.org ping statistics ---
4 packets transmitted, 4 received, 0% packet loss, time 3024ms
rtt min/avg/max/mdev = 57.553/67.899/72.605/6.039 ms
```

This example shows that a connection to **www.slashdot.org** is answered by **star.slashdot.org** (**www.slashdot.org** is an alias for **star.slashdot.org**) and that that system is up and available over the network.

By default ping sends packets containing 64 bytes (56 data bytes and 8 bytes of protocol header information). In the preceding example, four packets were sent to the system **star.slashdot.org** before the user interrupted ping by pressing CONTROL-C. The four-part number in parentheses on each line is the remote system's IP address. A packet sequence number (named **icmp_seq**) is also given. If a packet is dropped, a gap occurs in the number sequence. The round-trip time is listed last; it represents the time (in milliseconds) that elapsed from when the packet was sent from the local system to the remote system until the reply from the remote system was received by the local system. This time is affected by the distance between the two systems, network traffic, and the load on both computers. Before it terminates, ping summarizes the results, indicating how many packets were sent and received as well as the minimum, average, maximum, and mean deviation round-trip times it measured. Use ping6 to test IPv6 networks.

---

9. The name ping mimics the sound of a sonar burst used by submarines to identify and communicate with each other. The word ping also expands to packet internet groper.

When ping **cannot connect**

If it is unable to contact the remote system, ping continues trying until you interrupt it by pressing CONTROL-C. A system might not answer for any of several reasons: The remote computer might be down, the network interface or some part of the network between the systems might be broken, a software failure might have occurred, or the remote machine might be set up (for reasons of security) not to return pings (try pinging www.microsoft.com or www.ibm.com).

traceroute: TRACES A ROUTE OVER THE INTERNET

The traceroute and traceroute6 utilities (referred to in this section as traceroute; **traceroute** package) trace the route that an IP packet follows, including all intermediary points traversed (called *network hops*), to its destination (the argument to traceroute—a remote system). They display a numbered list of hostnames, if available, and IP addresses, together with the round-trip time it took for a packet to reach each router along the way and for the local system to receive a response. You can put this information to good use when you are trying to identify the location of a network bottleneck.

The traceroute utility has no concept of the path from one host to the next; instead, it simply sends UDP packets with increasing *TTL* (time to live) values. TTL is an IP header field that indicates how many more hops the packet should be allowed to make before being discarded or returned. Each router along the way inspects the TTL and decrements it by 1. When the TTL reaches 0 the router that has the packet sends back an ICMP TIME EXCEEDED to the local system, where traceroute records the IP address of the router that sent it back. The result is a list of hosts that the packet traveled through to get to its destination.

The traceroute utility can help solve routing configuration problems and locate routing path failures. When you cannot reach a host, use traceroute to discover which path the packet follows, how far it gets, and what the delay is.

The example on the next page shows the output of traceroute when it follows a route from a local computer to **www.linux.org**. The first line indicates the IP address of the target, the maximum number of hops that will be traced, and the size of the packets that will be used. Each numbered line contains the name and IP address of the intermediate destination, followed by the time it takes a packet to make a trip to that destination and back again. The traceroute utility sends three packets to each destination; thus three times appear on each line. Line 1 shows the statistics when a packet is sent to the local gateway (less than 3 milliseconds). Lines 4–6 show the packet bouncing around Mountain View (California) before it goes to San Jose. Between hops 13 and 14 the packet travels across the United States (San Francisco to somewhere in the East). By hop 18 the packet has found **www.linux.org**. The traceroute utility displays asterisks when it does not receive a response. Each asterisk indicates that traceroute has waited three seconds. Use traceroute6 to test IPv6 networks.

```
$ /usr/sbin/traceroute www.linux.org
traceroute to www.linux.org (198.182.196.56), 30 hops max, 38 byte packets
 1  gw.localco.com. (204.94.139.65)  2.904 ms  2.425 ms  2.783 ms
 2  covad-gw2.meer.net (209.157.140.1)  19.727 ms  23.287 ms  24.783 ms
 3  gw-mv1.meer.net (140.174.164.1)  18.795 ms  24.973 ms  19.207 ms
 4  d1-4-2.a02.mtvwca01.us.ra.verio.net (206.184.210.241)  59.091 ms d1-10-0-0-200.a03.
      mtvwca01.us.ra.verio.net (206.86.28.5)  54.948 ms  39.485 ms
 5  fa-11-0-0.a01.mtvwca01.us.ra.verio.net (206.184.188.1)  40.182 ms  44.405 ms 49.362 ms
 6  p1-1-0-0.a09.mtvwca01.us.ra.verio.net (205.149.170.66)  78.688 ms  66.266 ms 28.003 ms
 7  p1-12-0-0.a01.snjsca01.us.ra.verio.net (209.157.181.166) 32.424 ms 94.337 ms 54.946 ms
 8  f4-1-0.sjc0.verio.net (129.250.31.81)  38.952 ms  63.111 ms  49.083 ms
 9  sjc0.nuq0.verio.net (129.250.3.98)  45.031 ms  43.496 ms  44.925 ms
10  mae-west1.US.CRL.NET (198.32.136.10)  48.525 ms  66.296 ms  38.996 ms
11  t3-ames.3.sfo.us.crl.net (165.113.0.249)  138.808 ms  78.579 ms  68.699 ms
12  E0-CRL-SFO-02-E0X0.US.CRL.NET (165.113.55.2)  43.023 ms  51.910 ms  42.967 ms
13  sfo2-vva1.ATM.us.crl.net (165.113.0.254)  135.551 ms  154.606 ms  178.632 ms
14  mae-east-02.ix.ai.net (192.41.177.202)  158.351 ms  201.811 ms  204.560 ms
15  oc12-3-0-0.mae-east.ix.ai.net (205.134.161.2)  202.851 ms  155.667 ms  219.116 ms
16  border-ai.invlogic.com (205.134.175.254)  214.622 ms  *  190.423 ms
17  router.invlogic.com (198.182.196.1)  224.378 ms  235.427 ms  228.856 ms
18  www.linux.org (198.182.196.56)  207.964 ms  178.683 ms  179.483 ms
```

Some firewalls block UDP/traceroute. If traceroute fails, try using the **–T** (sends TCP SYN packets) or **–I** (sends ICMP ECHO packets) options. Another useful tool is mtr (**mtr** package), which provides traceroute functionality plus information about dropped packets. The mtr utility is useful for debugging packet loss along a multi-hop network path.

host AND dig: QUERY INTERNET NAMESERVERS

Given a name, the host utility looks up an IP address, or vice versa. The following example shows how to use host to look up the domain name of a machine, given an IP address:

```
$ host  64.13.141.6
6.141.13.64.in-addr.arpa domain name pointer ns.meer.net.
```

You can also use host to determine the IP address of a domain name:

```
$ host ns.meer.net
ns.meer.net has address 64.13.141.6
```

The dig (domain information groper) utility queries DNS servers and individual machines for information about a domain. A powerful utility, dig has many features you might never use. It is more complex than host. Chapter 24 on DNS has many examples of the use of host and dig.

whois: LOOKS UP INFORMATION ABOUT AN INTERNET SITE

The whois utility (**whois** package) queries a **whois** server for information about an Internet site. This utility returns site contact and InterNIC or other registry information that can help you track down the person who is responsible for a site: Perhaps that person is sending you or your company spam. Many sites on the Internet are easier to use and faster than whois. Use a browser and search engine to search on **whois** or go to www.networksolutions.com/whois or www.db.ripe.net/whois to get started.

When you do not specify a **whois** server, whois defaults to **whois.internic.net**. Use the **–h** option to whois to specify a different **whois** server. See the whois info page for more options and setup information.

To obtain information on a domain name, specify the complete domain name, as in the following example:

```
$ whois sobell.com
    Domain Name: SOBELL.COM
    Registrar: GODADDY.COM, INC.
    Whois Server: whois.godaddy.com
    Referral URL: http://registrar.godaddy.com
    Name Server: NS1.HUNGERHOST.COM
 ...
Registrant:
    Sobell Associates Inc
    660 Market Street
    Fifth Floor
    San Francisco, California 94104
    United States

    Registered through: GoDaddy.com, Inc. (http://www.godaddy.com)
    Domain Name: SOBELL.COM
        Created on: 07-Apr-95
        Expires on: 08-Apr-13
        Last Updated on: 01-Mar-10

    Administrative Contact:
        Sobell, Mark  sobell@meer.net
        Sobell Associates Inc
        660 Market Street
        Fifth Floor
        SAN FRANCISCO, California 94104
        United States
        18888446337      Fax -- 18888446337

    Technical Contact:
        W., Tim  hostmaster@meer.net
        meer.net
        po box 390804
        Mountain View, California 94039
        United States
        18888446337      Fax -- 18888446337

    Domain servers in listed order:
        NS1.HUNGERHOST.COM
        NS2.HUNGERHOST.COM
```

Several top-level registries serve various regions of the world. You are most likely to use the following ones:

North American registry	**whois.arin.net**
European registry	**www.ripe.net**
Asia-Pacific registry	**www.apnic.net**
U.S. military	**whois.nic.mil**
U.S. government	**www.nic.gov**

DISTRIBUTED COMPUTING

When many similar systems are part of a network, it is often desirable to share common files and utilities among them. For example, a system administrator might choose to keep a copy of the system documentation on one computer's disk and to make those files available to remote systems. In this case, the system administrator configures the files so users who need to access the online documentation are not aware that the files are stored on a remote system. This type of setup, which is an example of *distributed computing,* not only conserves disk space but also allows you to update one central copy of the documentation rather than tracking down and updating copies scattered throughout the network on many different systems.

Figure 10-2 illustrates a *fileserver* that stores the system manual pages and users' home directories. With this arrangement, a user's files are always available to that user no matter which system the user logs in on. Each system's disk might contain a directory to hold temporary files as well as a copy of the operating system. Chapter 22 contains instructions for setting up NFS clients and servers in networked configurations.

THE CLIENT/SERVER MODEL

Mainframe model The client/server model was not the first computational model. First came the mainframe, which follows a one-machine-does-it-all model. That is, all the intelligence resides in one system, including the data and the program that manipulates and reports on the data. Users connect to a mainframe using terminals.

File-sharing model With the introduction of PCs, file-sharing networks became available. In this scheme data is downloaded from a shared location to a user's PC, where a program then manipulates the data. The file-sharing model ran into problems as networks expanded and more users needed access to the data.

Client/server model In the client/server model, a client uses a protocol, such as HTTP or SCP, to request services, and a server provides the services the client requests. Rather than providing data files as the file-sharing model does, the server in a client/server relationship is a database that provides only those pieces of information the client needs or requests.

The client/server model dominates UNIX and Linux system networking and underlies most of the network services described in this book. FTP, NFS, DNS, email, and HTTP (the Web browsing protocol) all rely on the client/server model. Some servers, such as

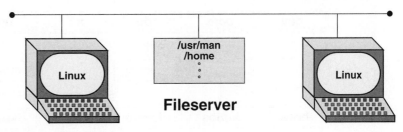

Figure 10-2   A fileserver

Web servers and browser clients, are designed to interact with specific utilities. Other servers, such as those supporting DNS, communicate with one another, in addition to answering queries from a variety of clients. Clients and servers can reside on the same or different systems running the same or different operating systems. The systems can be proximate or thousands of miles apart. A system that is a server to one system can turn around and act as a client to another. A server can reside on a single system or, as is the case with DNS, be distributed among thousands of geographically separated systems running many different operating systems.

Peer-to-peer model   The peer-to-peer (PTP) model, in which either program can initiate a transaction, stands in contrast to the client/server model. PTP protocols are common on small networks. For example, Microsoft's Network Neighborhood and Apple's Bonjour both rely on broadcast-based PTP protocols for browsing and automatic configuration. The Zeroconf multicast DNS protocol is a PTP alternative DNS for small networks. The highest-profile PTP networks are those used for file sharing, such as Kazaa and GNUtella. Many of these networks are not pure PTP topologies. Pure PTP networks do not scale well, so networks such as BitTorrent employ a hybrid approach.

DNS: DOMAIN NAME SERVICE

DNS is a distributed service: Nameservers on thousands of machines around the world cooperate to keep the DNS database up-to-date. The database itself, which maps hundreds of thousands of alphanumeric hostnames to numeric IP addresses, does not exist in one place. That is, no system has a complete copy of the database. Instead, each system that runs DNS knows which hosts are local to that site and understands how to contact other nameservers to learn about other, nonlocal hosts.

Like the Linux filesystem, DNS is organized hierarchically. Each country has an ISO (International Organization for Standardization) country code designation as its domain name. (For example, **AU** represents Australia, **IL** is Israel, and **JP** is Japan; see www.iana.org/domains/root/cctld for a complete list.) Although the United States is represented in the same way (**US**) and uses the standard two-letter Postal Service state abbreviations to identify the next level of the domain, only governments and a few organizations use these codes. Schools in the **US** domain are represented by a third- (and sometimes second-) level domain: **k12**. For example, the domain name for Myschool in New York state could be www.myschool.k12.ny.us.

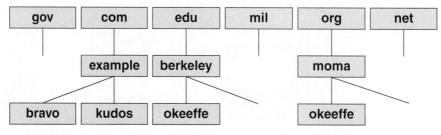

Figure 10-3   U.S. top-level domains

Following is a list of the seven original top-level domains. These domains are used extensively within the United States and, to a lesser degree, by users in other countries:

COM	Commercial enterprises
EDU	Educational institutions
GOV	Nonmilitary government agencies
INT	International organizations recognized by treaty
MIL	Military government agencies
NET	Networking organizations
ORG	Other (often nonprofit) organizations

Recently, the following additional top-level domains have been approved for use. Visit en.wikipedia.org/wiki/List_of_Internet_top-level_domains for a complete, current list.

AERO	Air-transport industry
BIZ	Business
COOP	Cooperatives
INFO	Unrestricted use
MUSEUM	Museums
NAME	Name registries

FQDN   Like Internet addresses, domain names were once assigned by the Network Information Center (NIC); now they are assigned by several companies. A system's full name, referred to as its *fully qualified domain name* (FQDN), is unambiguous in the way that a simple hostname cannot be. The system **okeeffe.berkeley.edu** at the University of California at Berkeley (Figure 10-3) is not the same as one named **okeeffe.moma.org**, which might represent a host at the Museum of Modern Art. The domain name not only tells you something about where the system is located but also adds enough diversity to the namespace to avoid confusion when different sites choose similar names for their systems.

Unlike the filesystem hierarchy, the top-level domain name appears last (reading from left to right). Also, domain names are not case sensitive, so the names **okeeffe.berkeley.edu**, **okeeffe.Berkeley.edu**, and **okeeffe.Berkeley.EDU** refer to the same computer. Once a domain has been assigned, the local site is free to extend the hierarchy to meet local needs.

With DNS, email addressed to **user@example.com** can be delivered to the computer named **example.com** that handles the corporate mail and knows how to forward messages to user mailboxes on individual machines. As the company grows, its site administrator might decide to create organizational or geographical subdomains. The name **delta.ca.example.com** might refer to a system that supports California offices, for example, while **alpha.co.example.com** is dedicated to Colorado. Functional subdomains are another choice, with **delta.sales.example.com** and **alpha.dev.example.com** representing the sales and development divisions, respectively.

BIND   On Linux systems, the most common interface to the DNS is BIND (Berkeley Internet Name Domain). BIND follows the client/server model. On any given local network, one or more systems might be running a nameserver, supporting all the local hosts as clients. When it wants to send a message to another host, a system queries the nearest nameserver to learn the remote host's IP address. The client, called a *resolver,* might be a process running on the same computer as the nameserver, or it might pass the request over the network to reach a server. To reduce network traffic and facilitate name lookups, the local nameserver maintains some knowledge of distant hosts. If the local server must contact a remote server to pick up an address, when the answer comes back, the local server adds that address to its internal table and reuses it for a while. The nameserver deletes the nonlocal information before it can become outdated. Refer to "TTL" on page 1194.

The system's translation of symbolic hostnames into IP addresses is transparent to most users; only the system administrator of a networked system needs to be concerned with the details of name resolution. Systems that use DNS for name resolution are generally capable of communicating with the greatest number of hosts—more than would be practical to maintain in a **/etc/hosts** file or private NIS database. Chapter 24 covers setting up and running a DNS server.

Three common sources are referenced for hostname resolution: NIS, DNS, and system files (such as **/etc/hosts**). Linux does not ask you to choose among these sources; rather, the **nsswitch.conf** file (page 494) allows you to choose any of these sources, in any combination, and in any order.

PORTS

Ports are logical channels on a network interface and are numbered from 1 to 65,535. Each network connection is uniquely identified by the IP address and port number of each endpoint.

In a system that has many network connections open simultaneously, the use of ports keeps *packets* (page 1180) flowing to and from the appropriate programs. A program that needs to receive data *binds* to a port and then uses that port for communication.

Privileged ports   Services are associated with specific ports, generally with numbers less than 1024. These ports are called *privileged* (or *reserved*) *ports.* For security reasons, only a process running with **root** privileges can bind to a privileged port. A service run on a privileged port provides assurance that the service is being provided by someone with authority over the system, with the exception that any user on Windows 98 and earlier Windows systems can bind to any port. Commonly used ports include 22 (SSH), 23 (TELNET), 80 (HTTP), 111 (Sun RPC), and 201–208 (AppleTalk).

Privileged ports do not provide absolute security

security | Any user who can gain **root** privileges can easily start a service on any port. Thus, it is necessary to treat privileged ports as a necessary but not sufficient component in a security policy and to be aware of which other systems are on the local network.

NIS: NETWORK INFORMATION SERVICE

NIS (Network Information Service) simplifies the maintenance of frequently used administrative files by keeping them in a central database and having clients contact the database server to retrieve information from the database. Just as DNS addresses the problem of keeping multiple copies of **hosts** files up-to-date, NIS deals with the issue of keeping system-independent configuration files (such as **/etc/passwd**) current. Although NIS has been functionally replaced by LDAP, LDAP is harder to configure, and so NIS is still in common use. Refer to Chapter 21 for coverage of NIS and LDAP.

NFS: NETWORK FILESYSTEM

The NFS (Network Filesystem) protocol allows a server to share selected local directory hierarchies with client systems on a heterogeneous network. Files on the remote fileserver appear as if they are present on the local system. Chapter 22 covers NFS.

optional
NETWORK SERVICES

Linux Internet services are provided by daemons that run continuously or by a daemon that is started automatically by the **xinetd** daemon (page 481) or by the systemd init daemon (page 426) when a service request comes in. The **/etc/services** file lists network services (for example, **telnet, ftp,** and **ssh**) and their associated numbers. Any service that uses TCP/IP or UDP/IP has an entry in this file. IANA (Internet Assigned Numbers Authority) maintains a database of all permanent, registered services. The **/etc/services** file usually lists a small, commonly used subset of services.

Most executable daemon files are stored in **/usr/sbin**. By convention the names of many daemons end with the letter **d** to distinguish them from utilities (one common daemon whose name does not end in **d** is **sendmail**). The prefix **in.** or **rpc.** is often used for daemon names. Give the command **ls /usr/sbin/*d** to see a list of many of the daemon programs on the local system. Refer to "Configuring Daemons (Services)" on page 433 (Fedora) and to "The Upstart Event-Based **init** Daemon" on page 436 (RHEL)for information about starting and stopping these daemons.

To see how a daemon works, consider what happens when you run ssh. The local system contacts the ssh daemon (**sshd**) on the remote system to establish a connection. The two systems negotiate the connection according to a fixed protocol. Each system identifies itself to the other, and they then take turns asking each other specific questions and waiting for valid replies. Each network service follows its own protocol.

COMMON DAEMONS

In addition to the daemons that support the utilities described in this chapter, many other daemons support system-level services that you will not typically interact with. Table 10-3 lists some of these daemons.

Table 10-3   Common daemons

Daemon	Used for or by	Function
acpid	Advanced configuration and power interface	Flexible daemon for delivering ACPI events. Replaces **apmd**.
anacron	anacrontab	Used for periodic execution of tasks. This daemon looks in the **/etc/anacrontab** file. When a task comes up for execution, **anacron** executes it as the user who owns the file that describes the task. See page 611.
apmd	Advanced power management	Reports and takes action on specified changes in system power, including shutdowns. Useful with machines, such as laptops, that run on batteries.
atd	at	Executes a command once at a specific time and date. See **crond** for periodic execution of a command. See page 615.
automount	Automatic mounting	Automatically mounts filesystems when they are accessed. Automatic mounting is a way of demand-mounting remote directories without having to hard-configure them into **/etc/fstab**. See page 811.
crond	cron	Used for periodic execution of tasks. This daemon looks in the **/var/spool/cron** directory for files with filenames that correspond to usernames. It also looks at the **/etc/crontab** file and at files in the **/etc/cron.d** directory. When a task comes up for execution, **crond** executes it as the user who owns the file that describes the task. See page 611.
cupsd	Printing daemon	Configures local and remote printers and handles printing jobs. See Chapter 14 for more information.

Table 10-3 Common daemons (continued)

Daemon	Used for or by	Function
dhcpd, dhcpd6	DHCP	Assigns Internet address, network mask, default gateway, DNS, and other information to hosts. This protocol answers DHCP requests and, optionally, BOOTP requests. Refer to "DHCP: Configures Network Interfaces" on page 489.
exim4	Mail programs	The **exim4** daemon came from the University of Cambridge. The **exim4** daemon listens on port 25 for incoming mail connections and then calls a local delivery agent, such as **/bin/mail**. Mail user agents (MUAs), such as KMail and Thunderbird, typically use **exim4** to deliver mail messages. See also **sendmail**.
ftpd	FTP	Handles FTP requests. Refer to "ftp: Transfers Files over a Network" on page 385. See also **vsftpd** (page 701). Can be launched by **xinetd**.
gpm	General-purpose mouse or GNU paste manager	Allows you to use a mouse to cut and paste text on console applications.
hald	Hardware Abstraction Layer (HAL) daemon	Collects and maintains system hardware information in real time. Part of the **hal** package.
httpd	HTTP	The Web server daemon (Apache; page 917).
in.fingerd	finger	Handles requests for user information from the finger utility. Launched by **xinetd**. See page 381.
inetd		Listens for service requests on network connections and starts up the appropriate daemon to respond to any particular request. Deprecated in favor of **xinetd**.
munged	Authentication daemon	Allows processes running on different machines to authenticate each other. Part of the **munge** package.
mysqld	The MySQL daemon	Supports queries on a MySQL database. It is the M in LAMP (Linux, Apache, MySQL, PHP/Perl/Python). See page 635.
named	DNS	Supports DNS. See page 845.
nfsd, statd, lockd, mountd, rquotad	NFS	These five daemons operate together to handle NFSv3 (page 791) operations. The **nfsd** daemon handles file and directory requests. The **statd** and **lockd** daemons implement network file and record locking. The **mountd** daemon converts filesystem name requests from the mount utility into NFS handles and checks access permissions. If disk quotas are enabled, **rquotad** handles those.
ntpd	NTP	Synchronizes time on network computers. For more information visit www.ntp.org.

Table 10-3   Common daemons (continued)

Daemon	Used for or by	Function
radvd	IPv6	IPv6 Router ADVertisement Daemon. Provides autoconfiguration on the network if the local system is being used as a router.
rpcbind	RPC	Maps incoming requests for RPC service numbers to TCP or UDP port numbers on the local system. Refer to "RPC Network Services" on page 398.
rsyslogd	System log	Transcribes important system events and stores them in files and/or forwards them to users or another host running the **rsyslogd** daemon. See page 623.
sendmail	Mail programs	The **sendmail** daemon came from Berkeley UNIX and has been available for a long time. The de facto mail transfer program on the Internet, the **sendmail** daemon always listens on port 25 for incoming mail connections and then calls a local delivery agent, such as **/bin/mail**. Mail user agents (MUAs), such as KMail and Thunderbird, typically use **sendmail** to deliver mail messages. See also **exim4**. See page 729.
smartd	SMART Disk Monitoring Daemon	Monitors the Self-Monitoring, Analysis and Reporting Technology (SMART) system built into many hard drives. SMART tests drive reliability, predicts failure, and performs other self tests. Part of the **smartmontools** package. See page 81.
smbd, nmbd	Samba	Allow Windows PCs to share files and printers with UNIX and Linux computers. See page 817.
sshd	ssh, scp	Enables secure logins between remote systems (page 688).
talkd	talk	Allows you to have a conversation with another user on the same or a remote machine. The **talkd** daemon handles the connections between the machines. The talk utility on each system contacts the **talkd** daemon on the other system for a bidirectional conversation. Launched by **xinetd**.
telnetd	TELNET	One of the original Internet remote access protocols. Launched by **xinetd**. See page 383.
tftpd	TFTP	Used to boot a system or get information from a network. Examples include network computers, routers, and some printers. Launched by **xinetd**.
timed	Time server	On a LAN synchronizes time with other computers that are also running **timed**.
xinetd	Internet superserver	Listens for service requests on network connections and starts up the appropriate daemon to respond to any particular request. Because of **xinetd**, a system does not need the daemons running continually to handle various network requests. See page 481.

PROXY SERVERS

A *proxy* is a network service that is authorized to act for a system while not being part of that system. A proxy server or proxy gateway provides proxy services; it is a transparent intermediary that relays communications back and forth between an application (e.g., a browser) and a server that usually resides outside of a LAN and frequently on the Internet. When more than one process uses the proxy gateway/server, the proxy must keep track of which processes are connecting to which hosts/servers so that it can route the return messages to the proper process. The most commonly encountered proxies are email and Web proxies.

A proxy server/gateway insulates the local computer from all other computers or from specified domains by using at least two IP addresses: one to communicate with the local computer and one to communicate with a server. The proxy server/gateway examines and changes the header information on all packets it handles so it can encode, route, and decode them properly. The difference between a proxy gateway and a proxy server is that the proxy server usually includes *cache* (page 1155) to store frequently used Web pages so the next request for that page is available locally and quickly; a proxy gateway typically does not use cache. The terms "proxy server" and "proxy gateway" are frequently used interchangeably.

Proxy servers/gateways are available for such common Internet services as HTTP, HTTPS, FTP, SMTP, and SNMP. When an HTTP proxy sends queries from local systems, it presents a single organizationwide IP address (the external IP address of the proxy server/gateway) to all servers. It funnels all user requests to the appropriate servers and keeps track of them. When the responses come back, the HTTP proxy fans them out to the appropriate applications using each machine's unique IP address, thereby protecting local addresses from remote/specified servers.

Proxy servers/gateways are generally just one part of an overall firewall strategy to prevent intruders from stealing information or damaging an internal network. Other functions, which can be either combined with or kept separate from the proxy server/gateway, include packet filtering, which blocks traffic based on origin and type, and user activity reporting, which helps management learn how the Internet is being used.

RPC NETWORK SERVICES

Much of the client/server interaction over a network is implemented using the RPC (Remote Procedure Call) protocol, which is implemented as a set of library calls that make network access transparent to the client and server. RPC specifies and interprets messages but does not concern itself with transport protocols; it runs on top of TCP/IP and UDP/IP. Services that use RPC include NFS and NIS. RPC was developed by Sun as ONC RPC (Open Network Computing Remote Procedure Calls) and differs from Microsoft RPC.

rpcbind   In the client/server model, a client contacts a server on a specific port (page 393) to avoid any mixup between services, clients, and servers. RPC has two possible ways of registering a port. The first works in the manner of a traditional daemon: The server binds to the port it wants to bind to but then registers with the RPC port-mapper daemon (**rpcbind**) on the server. As an example, NFS uses this mechanism to always bind to port 2049. The client's port is irrelevant most of the time, so it picks a random port.

More commonly, to avoid maintaining a long list of port numbers and to enable new clients/servers to start up without registering a port number with a central registry, when a server that uses RPC starts, it looks in **/etc/rpc** for the service number and then registers itself with **rpcbind** as just described. The **rpcbind** daemon assigns the server a TCP or UDP port number, and the server binds to that port. RPC servers typically use service numbers (**/etc/rpc**) that were defined by Sun, but the TCP or UDP port number it uses is random. When a client wants to connect to an RPC server, it first asks **rpcbind** on the server, which listens on port 111, for the name of the service it is interested in (e.g., **mountd**). If that service is registered, **rpcbind** returns the TCP or UDP port number of the server to the client. The client then contacts the RPC server daemon directly to finish the transaction.

Files   The **/etc/rpc** file (page 511) maps RPC service names to RPC numbers. The **/etc/services** file (page 511) maps system service names to TCP or UDP ports.

RPC client/server communication   The sequence of events for communication between an RPC client and server is as follows:

1. The client system needs to talk to a server application running on a remote system. The client system knows which system the server application is running on but not which port it is using. The client system looks for the service name in **/etc/rpc** to determine the service number.

2. The client system contacts **rpcbind** on port 111 of the remote system with the service number to ask which UDP or TCP port the server on the remote system is listening on.

3. The **rpcbind** daemon on the remote system checks which server applications have registered with it. If the service number the client system asked for is registered, the **rpcbind** daemon on the remote system returns the UDP or TCP port assigned to that server application.

4. The RPC libraries on the client system encode procedure calls and send them to the server application on the remote system on the specified port. (The client system issues a "read record from a file" request.)

5. The server application running on the remote system receives the call, sends it through the RPC libraries to decode it, and generates results. (The filesystem receives the "read record from file" request.)

6. The server application passes the results back through the RPC libraries, which encode the results, and then sends the encoded results to the client using the client's registered port. (The read record is returned to the calling program.)

7. The client system receives the results, passes them through the RPC libraries for decoding, and presents the decoded results to the user or application that requested them.

When RPC servers are started by the **xinetd** daemon (page 481), the **rpcbind** daemon must be started before the **xinetd** daemon is invoked. The init scripts (page 442) make sure **rpcbind** starts before **xinetd**. If the **rpcbind** daemon stops, you must restart all RPC servers on the local system.

WWW: WORLD WIDE WEB

The World Wide Web (WWW, W3, or the Web) provides a unified, interconnected interface to the vast amount of information stored on computers around the world. The idea that spawned the World Wide Web came from the mind of Tim Berners-Lee (www.w3.org/People/Berners-Lee) of the European Particle Physics Laboratory (CERN) in response to a need to improve communications throughout the high-energy physics community. The first-generation solution consisted of a notebook program named Enquire, short for *Enquire Within Upon Everything* (the name of a book from Berners-Lee's childhood), which he created in 1980 on a NeXT computer and which supported links between named nodes. Not until 1989 was the concept proposed as a global hypertext project to be known as the World Wide Web. In 1990, Berners-Lee wrote a proposal for a hypertext project, which eventually produced HTML (Hypertext Markup Language), the common language of the Web. The World Wide Web program became available on the Internet in the summer of 1991. By designing the tools to work with existing protocols, such as FTP and gopher, the researchers who created the Web produced a system that is generally useful for many types of information and across many types of hardware and operating systems.

The WWW is another example of the client/server paradigm. You use a WWW client application, or *browser,* to retrieve and display information stored on a server that might be located anywhere on the local network or the Internet. WWW clients can interact with many types of servers. For example, you can use a WWW client to contact a remote FTP server and display the list of files it offers for anonymous FTP download. Most commonly you use a WWW client to contact a WWW server, which offers support for the special features of the World Wide Web that are described in the remainder of this chapter.

The power of the Web derives from its use of *hypertext*, a way to navigate through information by following cross-references (called *links*) from one piece of information to another. To use the Web effectively, you need to run interactive network applications. The first GUI for browsing the Web was a tool named Mosaic, which was released in February 1993. Designed at the National Center for Supercomputer Applications at the University of Illinois, its introduction sparked a dramatic increase in the number of users of the World Wide Web. Marc Andreessen, who participated in the Mosaic project at the University of Illinois, later cofounded Netscape Communications with the founder of Silicon Graphics, Jim Clark. The pair created Netscape Navigator, a Web client program that was designed to perform better and support more features than the Mosaic browser. Netscape Navigator enjoyed immense success and was a popular choice for exploring the World Wide Web. Important for Linux users is the fact that from its inception Netscape has provided versions of its tools that run on Linux.

BROWSERS

Mozilla (www.mozilla.org) is the open-source counterpart to Netscape and was first released in March 1998, based on Netscape 4 code. Since then, Mozilla has been under continuous development by employees of Netscape (now a division of AOL), Red Hat, and other companies and by contributors from the community. Firefox is the Web browser component of Mozilla. KDE offers Konqueror, an all-purpose file manager and Web browser. Other browsers include Safari (www.apple.com/safari), Chrome (www.google.com/chrome), Epiphany (projects.gnome.org/epiphany) and Opera (www.opera.com). Although each Web browser is unique, all of them allow you to move about the Internet, viewing HTML documents, watching videos, and retrieving files. If you do not use the X Window System, try a text browser, such as lynx or links. The lynx browser works well with Braille terminals.

SEARCH ENGINES

Search engine is a name that applies to a group of hardware and software tools that help you search for World Wide Web sites that contain specific information. A search engine relies on a database of information collected by a *Web crawler,* a program that regularly looks through the millions of pages that make up the World Wide Web. A search engine must also have a way of collating the information the Web crawler collects so you can access it quickly, easily, and in a manner that makes it most useful to you. This part of the search engine, called an *index*, allows you to search for a word, a group of words, or a concept; it returns the URLs of Web pages that pertain to what you are searching for. Many different types of search engines are available on the Internet, each with its own set of strengths and weaknesses.

URL: UNIFORM RESOURCE LOCATOR

Consider the URL (Uniform Resource Locator) www.w3.org/Consortium/siteindex. The first component in the URL indicates the type of resource, in this case **http** (HTTP—Hypertext Transfer Protocol). Other valid resource names, such as **https** (HTTPS—secure HTTP) and **ftp** (FTP—File Transfer Protocol), represent information available on the Web using other protocols. Next come a colon and double slash (**://**). Frequently the **http://** string is omitted from a URL in print, as you seldom need to enter it to reach the URL. The next element is the full name of the host that acts as the server for the information (**www.w3.org/**). The rest of the URL consists of a relative pathname to the file that contains the information (**Consortium/siteindex**). If you enter a URL in the location bar of a Web browser, the Web server returns the page, frequently an *HTML* (page 1168) file, pointed to by this URL.

By convention many sites identify their WWW servers by prefixing a host or domain name with **www**. For example, you can reach the Web server at the New Jersey Institute of Technology at www.njit.edu. When you use a browser to explore the World Wide Web, you might never need to enter a URL. However, as more information is published in hypertext form, you cannot help but find URLs everywhere—not just online in email messages and blogs, but also in newspapers, in advertisements, and on product labels.

URI Whereas a URL indicates the location of a resource and a method of retrieving it (e.g., a network address and protocol), a URI (Uniform Resource Identifier) simply indicates something about the resource (e.g., an ISBN number). All URLs are URIs, but not all URIs are URLs. The terms are frequently used interchangeably because very few URIs that are not URLs are in common use.

CHAPTER SUMMARY

A Linux system attached to a network is probably communicating on an Ethernet network, which might in turn be linked to other local area networks (LANs) and wide area networks (WANs). Communication between LANs and WANs requires the use of gateways and routers. Gateways translate the local data into a format suitable for the WAN, and routers make decisions about the optimal routing of the data along the way. The most widely used network, by far, is the Internet.

Basic networking tools allow Linux users to log in and run commands on remote systems (ssh, telnet, rsync) and copy files quickly from one system to another (scp, ftp/sftp). Other features, such as the Network Filesystem (NFS), were created to extend the basic UNIX model and to simplify information sharing.

Concern is growing about our ability to protect the security and privacy of machines connected to networks and of data transmitted over networks. Toward this end, many tools and protocols have been created: ssh, scp, HTTPS, IPv6, firewall hardware and software, VPN, and so on. Many of these tools take advantage of newer, more impenetrable encryption techniques. In addition, some weaker concepts (such as that of trusted hosts) and some tools (such as finger and rwho) have been deprecated in the name of security.

Computer networks offer two major advantages over other ways of connecting computers: They enable systems to communicate at high speeds, and they require few physical interconnections (typically one per system). The Internet Protocol (IP), the universal language of the Internet, has made it possible for dissimilar computer systems around the world to readily communicate with one another. Technological advances continue to improve the performance of computer systems and the networks that link them.

The rapid increase of network communication speeds in recent years has encouraged the development of many new applications and services. The World Wide Web provides access to vast information stores on the Internet and makes extensive use of hypertext links to promote efficient searching through related documents. It adheres to the client/server model that is so pervasive in networking. Typically the WWW client is local to a site or is made available through an Internet service provider. WWW servers are responsible for providing the information requested by their many clients.

Mozilla/Firefox is a WWW client program that has enormous popular appeal. Firefox and other browsers use a GUI to give you access to text, picture, and audio information: Making extensive use of these hypermedia simplifies access to and enhances the presentation of information.

EXERCISES

1. Describe the similarities and differences between these utilities:

   a. scp and ftp

   b. ssh and telnet

   c. rsh and ssh

2. Describe two ways to find out who is logged in on some of the other machines attached to your network.

3. Explain the client/server model. Give three examples of services on Linux systems that take advantage of this model.

4. A software implementation of chess was developed by GNU and is available for free. How can you use the Internet to find and download this program?

5. What is the difference between the World Wide Web and the Internet?

6. If you have access to the World Wide Web, answer the following questions.

   a. Which browser do you use?

   b. What is the URL of the author of this book's home page? How many links does it have?

   c. Does your browser allow you to create bookmarks? If so, how do you create a bookmark? How can you delete one?

7. Give one advantage and two disadvantages of using a wireless network.

8. What is the fully abbreviated form of the IPv6 address 2620:0100:e000:0000:0000:0000:0000:8001?

9. IPv6 supports 128-bit addresses. What is the size of the host part of the address? How many hosts would that address space theoretically support on one LAN?

ADVANCED EXERCISES

10. Suppose the link between routers 1 and 2 is down in the Internet shown in Figure 10-1 on page 369. What happens if someone at site C sends a message to a user on a workstation attached to the Ethernet cable at site A? What happens if the router at site A is down? What does this tell you about designing network configurations?

11. If you have a class B IPv4 network and want to divide it into subnets, each with 126 hosts, which subnet mask should you use? How many networks will be available? What are the four addresses (broadcast and network number) for the network starting at 131.204.18?

12. Suppose you have 300 hosts and want to have no more than 50 hosts per subnet. What size of address block should you request from your ISP? How many /24 addresses would you need? How many subnets would you have left over from your allocation?

13. a. On the local system, find two daemons running that are not listed in this chapter and explain what purpose they serve.

b. Review which services/daemons are automatically started on your system and consider which you might turn off. Are there any services/daemons in the list in Table 10-3 on page 395 you would consider adding?

14. Determine if IPv6 is enabled on the local system by finding the link-local address of a network interface.

15. Use ssh to connect to a remote system on the local LAN using the remote system's autoconfigured link-local IPv6 address. (Hint: To specify the network interface to use for link-local addresses, append **%IFNAME** to the end of the address, where **IFNAME** is the local operating system's name for the interface.

PART IV
SYSTEM ADMINISTRATION

11

System Administration: Core Concepts

Objectives

After reading this chapter you should be able to:

▶ Explain the need for and the responsibility of the privileged user (**root**)

▶ Gain privilege using su and sudo

▶ Describe the startup sequence using systemd (Fedora) and Upstart (RHEL)

▶ Explain the history and current role of SysVinit scripts

▶ Manage which services start at boot time

▶ Start and stop services on a running system

▶ Boot into single-user mode for system maintenance

▶ Shut down a running system

▶ Secure a system by applying updates, monitoring logs, and controlling access to files using SELinux, setuid permission, and PAM

▶ Use system administration tools to monitor and maintain the system

▶ List common steps for installing, configuring, and securing a server

▶ Configure a system using a static IP address or using DHCP

The job of a system administrator is to keep one or more systems in a useful and convenient state for users. On a Linux system, the administrator and user might both be you, with you and the computer being separated by only a few feet. Alternatively, the system administrator might be halfway around the world, supporting a network of systems, with you being one of thousands of users. On the one hand, a system administrator can be one person who works part-time taking care of a system and perhaps is also a user of the system. On the other hand, several administrators can work together full-time to keep many systems running.

A well-maintained system

- Runs quickly enough so users do not get frustrated waiting for the system to respond or complete a task.

- Has enough storage to accommodate users' reasonable needs.

- Provides a working environment appropriate to each user's abilities and requirements.

- Is secure from malicious and accidental acts altering its performance or compromising the security of the data it holds and exchanges with other systems.

- Is backed up regularly, with recently backed-up files readily available to users.

- Has recent copies of the software that users need to get their jobs done.

- Is easier to administer than a poorly maintained system.

In addition, a system administrator should be available to help users with all types of system-related problems—from logging in to obtaining and installing software updates to tracking down and fixing obscure network issues.

Part IV of this book breaks system administration into seven chapters:

- Chapter 11 covers the core concepts of system administration, including working with **root** (Superuser) privileges, system operation, the Fedora/Linux configuration tools and other useful utilities, general information about setting up and securing a server (including a section on DHCP), and PAM.

- Chapter 12 covers files, directories, and filesystems from an administrator's point of view.

- Chapter 13 covers installing software on the system, including the use of yum, Red Hat Network (RHN), up2date, BitTorrent, and wget.

- Chapter 14 discusses how to set up local and remote printers that use the CUPS printing system.

- Chapter 15 explains how to rebuild the Linux kernel and work with GRUB, the Linux boot loader.

- Chapter 16 covers additional system administrator tasks and tools, including setting up users and groups, backing up files, scheduling tasks, printing system reports, and general problem solving.

- Chapter 17 goes into detail about how to set up a LAN, including setting up and configuring network hardware and configuring software.

Because Linux is readily configurable and runs on a wide variety of platforms, this chapter cannot discuss every system configuration or every action you might potentially have to take as a system administrator. Instead, this chapter seeks to familiarize you with the concepts you need to understand and the tools you will use to maintain a Fedora/RHEL system. Where it is not possible to go into depth about a subject, the chapter provides references to other sources.

This chapter assumes you are familiar with the following terms:

block device (page 1154)	*filesystem* (page 1164)	*root filesystem* (page 1186)
daemon (page 1160)	*fork* (page 1165)	*runlevel* (page 1187)
device (page 1161)	*kernel* (page 1172)	*signal* (page 1188)
device filename (page 1161)	*login shell* (page 1174)	*spawn* (page 1189)
disk partition (page 1161)	*mount* (page 1176)	*system console* (page 1192)
environment (page 1163)	*process* (page 1182)	*X server* (page 1198)

If there is a problem, check the log files

tip If something on the system is not working as expected, check the log files in **/var/log**. This directory holds many files and subdirectories. If you cannot connect to a server, also check the log files on the server.

If something does not work, see if the problem is caused by SELinux

tip If a server or other system software does not work properly, especially if it displays a permissions-related error message, the problem might lie with SELinux. To see if SELinux is the cause of the problem, put SELinux in permissive mode and run the software again. If the problem goes away, you need to modify the SELinux policy. Remember to turn SELinux back on. For more information refer to "Setting the Targeted Policy with system-config-selinux" on page 463.

RUNNING COMMANDS WITH root PRIVILEGES

The user named **root** Some commands can damage the filesystem or crash the operating system. Other commands can invade users' privacy or make the system less secure. To keep a Linux system up and running as well as secure, Fedora/RHEL is configured not to permit ordinary users to execute some commands and access certain files. Linux provides several ways for a trusted user to execute these commands and access these files. The default username of the trusted user with these systemwide powers is **root**; a user with these privileges is sometimes referred to as a *privileged user* or *Superuser*.

The Special Powers of a Privileged User

root privileges   A user running with **root** privileges has the following powers—and more:

- Some commands, such as those that add new users, partition hard drives, and change system configuration, can be executed only by a user working with **root** privileges. Such a user can configure tools, such as sudo, to give specific users permission to perform tasks that are normally reserved for a user running with **root** privileges.

- Read, write, and execute file access and directory access permissions do not affect a user with **root** privileges. A user with **root** privileges can read from, write to, and execute all files, as well as examine and work in all directories.

  Exceptions to these privileges exist. For example, SELinux mandatory access can be configured to limit **root** access to a file. Also, a user working with **root** privileges cannot read an encrypted file without possessing the key.

- Some restrictions and safeguards that are built into some commands do not apply to a user with **root** privileges. For example, a user with **root** privileges can change any user's password without knowing the old password.

prompt   When you are running with **root** privileges in a command-line environment, by convention the shell displays a special prompt to remind you of your status. By default, this prompt is (or ends with) a hashmark (#).

Console security

security   Linux is not secure from a person who has physical access to the computer. Additional security measures, such as setting boot loader and BIOS passwords, can help secure the computer. However, if someone has physical access to the hardware, as system console users typically do, it is very difficult to secure a system from that user.

Least privilege

caution   When you are working on any computer system, but especially when you are working as the system administrator (with **root** privileges), perform any task while using the least privilege possible. When you can perform a task logged in as an ordinary user, do so. When you must run a command with **root** privileges, do as much as you can as an ordinary user, log in or use su or sudo so you have **root** privileges, complete the part of the task that has to be done with **root** privileges, and revert to being an ordinary user as soon as you can. Because you are more likely to make a mistake when you are rushing, this concept becomes even more important when you have less time to apply it.

Gaining root Privileges

Classically a user gained **root** privileges by logging in as the user named **root** or by giving an su (substitute user) command and providing the **root** password. More recently the use of sudo has taken over this classic technique of gaining **root** privileges. With sudo, the user logs in as herself, gives an **sudo** command, and provides her own password (not the **root** password) to gain **root** privileges. "Security of sudo" on page 415 discusses some of the advantages of sudo.

Graphical environment   When an ordinary user executes a privileged command in a graphical environment, the system prompts for the **root** password or the user's password, depending on how the system is set up.

Some distributions lock the **root** account by not assigning a **root** password. On these systems, you cannot gain **root** privileges using a technique that requires you to supply the **root** password unless you unlock the **root** account as explained on page 425. Fedora/RHEL assigns a **root** password when the system is installed, so you can use these techniques from the start.

There is a **root** account, but no **root** password

tip   As installed, some systems (not Fedora/RHEL) lock the **root** account by not providing a **root** password. This setup prevents anyone from logging in to the **root** account (except when you bring the system up in single-user mode [page 449]). There is, however, a **root** account (a user with the username **root**—look at the first line in **/etc/passwd**). This account/user owns files (give the command **ls –l /bin**) and runs processes (give the command **ps –ef** and look at the left column of the output). The **root** account is critical to the functioning of a Linux system.

When properly set up, the sudo utility enables you to run a command as though it had been run by a user logged in as **root**. This book uses the phrase "working with **root** privileges" to emphasize that, although you are not logged in as **root**, when you use sudo you have the powers of the **root** user.

The following list describes some of the ways you can gain or grant **root** privileges. Some of these techniques depend on you supplying the password for the **root** account. Again, if the **root** account is locked, you cannot use these techniques unless you unlock the **root** account (set up a **root** password), as explained on page 425. Other of the techniques depend on the **sudoers** file being set up to allow you to gain **root** privileges. If this file is not set up in this manner, you cannot use these techniques unless you set up the **sudoers** file as explained on page 419.

- When you bring the system up in single-user/rescue mode (page 450), you are logged in as the user named **root**.

- You can give an su (substitute user) command while you are logged in as yourself. When you then provide the **root** password, you will be running with **root** privileges. See page 413.

- The sudo utility allows specified users to run selected commands with **root** privileges while they are logged in as themselves. You can set up sudo to allow certain users to perform specific tasks that require **root** privileges without granting these users systemwide **root** privileges. See page 415 for more information on sudo.

- Once the system is up and running in multiuser mode (page 451), you can log in as **root**. When you then supply the **root** password, you will be running with **root** privileges.

- Some programs ask for a password (either your password or the **root** password, depending on the command and the configuration of the system) when they start. When you provide a password, the program runs with **root** privileges. You stop running as a privileged user when you quit using the program. This setup keeps you from remaining logged in with **root** privileges when you do not need or intend to be. Refer to "consolehelper: Allows an Ordinary User to Run a Privileged Command" on page 425.

- Any user can create a *setuid* (set user ID) file. Setuid programs run on behalf of the owner of the file and have all the access privileges the owner has. While you are working with **root** privileges, you can change the permissions of a file owned by **root** to setuid. When an ordinary user executes a file that is owned by **root** and has setuid permissions, the program has *effective* **root** *privileges*. In other words, the program can do anything a program running with **root** privileges can do that the program normally does. The user's privileges do not change. Thus, when the program finishes running, all user privileges are as they were before the program started. Setuid programs owned by **root** are both extremely powerful and extremely dangerous to system security, which is why a system contains very few of them. Examples of setuid programs that are owned by **root** include passwd, at, and crontab. For more information refer to "Setuid and Setgid Permissions" on page 205.

root-owned setuid programs are extremely dangerous

security   Because **root**-owned setuid programs allow someone who does not know the **root** password and cannot use sudo to gain **root** privileges, they are tempting targets for a malicious user. Also, programming errors that make normal programs crash can become **root** exploits in setuid programs. A system should have as few of these programs as possible. You can disable setuid programs at the filesystem level by mounting a filesystem with the **nosuid** option (page 522). You can also use SELinux (page 459) to disable setuid programs. See page 459 for a find command that lists all setuid files on the local system. In future releases Fedora/RHEL will remove all setuid files; see fedoraproject.org/wiki/Features/RemoveSETUID.

Logging in   The **/etc/securetty** file controls which terminals (ttys) a user can log in on as **root**.

Using the **/etc/security/access.conf** file, PAM controls the who, when, and how of logging in. Initially this file contains only comments. See page 463, the comments in the file, and the **access.conf** man page for details.

Do not allow root access over the Internet

security   Prohibiting a user from logging in as **root** over a network is the default policy of Fedora/RHEL. The **/etc/securetty** file must contain the names of all devices you want a user to be able to log in on as **root**.

You can, however, log in as **root** over a network using ssh (page 673). As shipped by Fedora/RHEL, ssh does not follow the instructions in **securetty** or **access.conf**. Also, in **/etc/ssh/sshd_config**, Fedora/RHEL sets **PermitRootLogin** to **yes** (it is set by default) to permit **root** to log in using ssh (page 694). For a more secure system, change **PermitRootLogin** to **no**.

USING su TO GAIN root PRIVILEGES

When you install Fedora/RHEL, you assign a password to the **root** account. Thus you can use su to gain **root** privileges without any further setup.

The su (substitute user) utility can spawn a shell or execute a program with the identity and privileges of a specified user, including **root**:

- Follow **su** on the command line with the name of a user; if you are working with **root** privileges or if you know the user's password, you will then take on the identity of that user.

- When you give an su command without an argument, su defaults to spawning a shell with **root** privileges (you have to supply the **root** password).

SPAWNING A ROOT SHELL

When you give an su command to work with **root** privileges, su spawns a new shell, which displays the # prompt. You can return to your normal status (and your former shell and prompt) by terminating this shell: Press CONTROL-D or give an exit command. Giving an su command without any arguments changes your user and group IDs but makes minimal changes to the environment. For example, **PATH** has the same value as it did before you gave the su command. The id utility displays your user and group IDs and the groups you are associated with. In the following example, the information that starts with **context** pertains to SELinux:

```
$ pwd
/home/sam
$ echo $PATH
/usr/local/bin:/bin:/usr/bin:/usr/local/sbin:/usr/sbin:/sbin:/home/sam/bin
$ id
uid=500(sam) gid=500(sam) groups=500(sam) context=unconfined_u: ...
$ su
Password:
# pwd
/home/sam
# echo $PATH
/usr/local/bin:/bin:/usr/bin:/usr/local/sbin:/usr/sbin:/sbin:/home/sam/bin
# id
uid=0(root) gid=0(root) groups=0(root),1(bin),2(daemon),3(sys),4(adm) ...
# exit
exit
$
```

When you give the command **su –** (you can use **–l** or **––login** in place of the hyphen), su provides a **root** login shell: It is as though you logged in as **root**. Not only do the shell's user and group IDs match those of **root**, but the environment is the same as when you log in as **root**. The login shell executes the appropriate startup files (page 282) before displaying a prompt, and the working directory is set to what it would be if you had logged in as **root** (/**root**). **PATH** is also set as though you had logged in as **root**, typically including **/sbin** and **/usr/sbin** before **/bin** and **/usr/bin**.

```
$ su -
Password:
# pwd
/root
# echo $PATH
/usr/local/sbin:/usr/local/bin:/sbin:/bin:/usr/sbin:/usr/bin:/root/bin
```

EXECUTING A SINGLE COMMAND

You can use su with the –c option to run a command with **root** privileges, returning to the original shell when the command finishes executing. In the following example, Sam tries to set the system clock while working as himself, a nonprivileged user. The date utility displays an error message followed by the expanded version of the date Sam entered. When he uses su to run date to set the system clock, su prompts him for a password, he responds with the **root** password, and the command succeeds. The quotation marks are necessary because **su –c** takes the command it is to execute as a single argument.

```
$ date 12281448
date: cannot set date: Operation not permitted
Tue Dec 28 14:48:00 PST 2010

$ su -c "date 12281448"
Password:
Tue Dec 28 14:48:00 PST 2010
```

The next example first shows that Sam is not permitted to kill (page 470) a process. With the use of **su –c** and the **root** password, however, Sam is working with **root** privileges and is permitted to kill the process.

```
$ kill -15 4982
-bash: kill: (4982) - Operation not permitted
$ su -c "kill -15 4982"
Password:
$
```

The final example combines the – and –c options to show how to run a single command with **root** privileges in the **root** environment:

```
$ su -c pwd
Password:
/home/sam
$ su - -c pwd
Password:
/root
```

Root privileges, PATH, and security

security   The fewer directories you keep in **PATH** when you are working with **root** privileges, the less likely you will be to execute an untrusted program while working with **root** privileges. If possible, keep only the default directories, along with **/sbin** and **/usr/sbin**, in **root**'s **PATH**. *Never include the working directory in **PATH** (as . or : : anywhere in **PATH**, or : as the last element of **PATH**)*. For more information refer to "PATH: Where the Shell Looks for Programs" on page 308.

USING sudo TO GAIN root PRIVILEGES

If sudo (www.sudo.ws) is not set up so you can use it, and a **root** password exists and you know what it is, see "Quick setup" on the next page for instructions on setting up sudo so you can use it to gain **root** privileges.

ADVANTAGES OF sudo

Using sudo rather than the **root** account for system administration offers many advantages:

- When you run sudo, it requests *your* password—not the **root** password—so you have to remember only one password.

- The sudo utility logs all commands it executes. This log can be useful for retracing your steps for system auditing and if you make a mistake.

- The sudo utility logs the username of a user who issues an sudo command. On systems with more than one administrator, this log tells you which users have issued sudo commands. Without sudo, you would not know which user issued a command while working with **root** privileges.

- The sudo utility allows implementation of a finer-grained security policy than does the use of su and the **root** account. Using sudo, you can enable specific users to execute specific commands—something you cannot do with the classic **root** account setup.

- Using sudo makes it harder for a malicious user to gain access to a system. When there is an unlocked **root** account, a malicious user knows the username of the account she wants to crack before she starts. When the **root** account is locked, the user has to determine the username *and* the password to break into a system.

- Managing **root** passwords over many systems is challenging. Remembering each system's password is difficult without writing them down (and storing them in a safe), and then retrieving a password is time-consuming. Keeping track of which users know which **root** passwords is impossible. Using sudo, even for full **root**-shell access, makes the tasks of gaining **root** privileges on a large number of systems and tracking who can gain **root** privileges on each system much easier.

SECURITY OF sudo

Some users question whether sudo is less secure than su. Because both rely on passwords, they share the same strengths and weaknesses. If the password is compromised, the system is compromised. However, if the password of a user who is allowed by sudo to do one task is compromised, the entire system might not be at risk. Thus, *if used properly,* the finer granularity of sudo's permissions structure *can* make it a more secure tool than su. Also, when sudo is used to invoke a single command, it is less likely that a user will be tempted to keep working with **root** privileges than if the user opens a **root** shell with su.

Using sudo might not always be the best, most secure way to set up a system. On a system used by a single user, there is not much difference between using sudo and carefully using su and a **root** password. In contrast, on a system with several users, and especially on a network of systems with central administration, sudo can be set up to be more secure than su.

USING sudo

Quick setup The following line in the **/etc/sudoers** file allows members of the **wheel** group to use sudo to gain **root** privileges:

```
%wheel  ALL=(ALL)          ALL
```

If this line is commented out (it is in RHEL and versions of Fedora before 15), working with **root** privileges, use visudo as explained on page 419 to remove the leading hash mark (#) so members of the **wheel** group can gain **root** privileges.

Next, working with **root** privileges, run usermod with the **–a** and **–G wheel** options to add the username of the user who is to be granted **root** privileges to the **wheel** group. Substitute that username for **sam** in the following example.

```
# usermod -a -G wheel sam
# grep wheel /etc/group
wheel:x:10:root,sam
```

The grep command shows Sam as a member of the **wheel** group. See **/etc/group** on page 506 for more information.

Timestamp By default, sudo asks for *your* password (not the **root** password) the first time you run it. At that time, sudo sets your *timestamp*. After you supply a password, sudo will not prompt you again for a password for five minutes, based on your timestamp.

EXECUTING A SINGLE COMMAND

In the following example, Sam tries to set the system clock while working as himself, a nonprivileged user. The date utility displays an error message followed by the expanded version of the date Sam entered. When he uses sudo to run date to set the system clock, sudo prompts him for his password, and the command succeeds.

```
$ date 01121500
date: cannot set date: Operation not permitted
Wed Jan 12 15:00:00 PST 2011

$ sudo date 01121500
[sudo] password for sam:
Wed Jan 12 15:00:00 PST 2011
```

Next Sam uses sudo to unmount a filesystem. Because he gives this command within five minutes of the previous sudo command, he does not need to supply a password:

```
$ sudo umount /music
$
```

Now Sam uses the **–l** option to check which commands sudo will allow him to run. Because the **sudoers** file is set up as explained in "Quick setup," on the previous page, he is allowed to run any command as any user.

```
$ sudo -l
...
User sam may run the following commands on this host:
    (ALL) ALL
```

Granting root privileges to edit a file

tip   With the **–e** option, or when called as sudoedit, sudo edits with **root** privileges the file named by its argument. By default sudo uses the vi editor; see page 419 for instructions on how to specify a different editor.

Any user who can run commands with **root** privileges can use the **–e** option. To give other users permission to edit any file using **root** privileges, specify in the **sudoers** file that that user can execute the command **sudoedit**. For more information refer to "User Privilege Specifications" on page 420.

Calling an editor in this manner runs the editor in the user's environment, maintaining the concept of least privilege. The sudo utility first copies the file to be edited to a temporary file that is owned by the user. If the file does not exist, sudo creates a new file that is owned by the user. Once the user has finished editing the file, sudo copies it back in place of the original file (with the original permissions).

SPAWNING A root SHELL

When you have several commands you need to run with **root** privileges, it might be easier to spawn a **root** shell, give the commands without having to type **sudo** in front of each one, and exit from the shell. This technique defeats some of the safeguards built into sudo, so use it carefully and remember to return to a non**root** shell as soon as possible. (See the caution on least privilege on page 410.) Use the sudo **–i** option (page 419) to spawn a **root** shell:

```
$ pwd
/home/sam
$ sudo -i
# id
uid=0(root) gid=0(root) groups=0(root),1(bin),2(daemon),3(sys) ...
# pwd
/root
# exit
logout
$
```

In this example, sudo spawns a **root** shell, which displays a # prompt to remind Sam that he is running with **root** privileges. The id utility displays the identity of the user running the shell. The exit command (you can also use CONTROL-D) terminates the **root** shell, returning Sam to his normal status and his former shell and prompt.

sudo's environment   The pwd builtin in the preceding example shows one aspect of the modified environment created by the **–i** option. This option spawns a **root** login shell (a shell with the same environment as a user logging in as **root** would have) and executes **root**'s startup files (page 282). Before issuing the **sudo –i** command, the pwd builtin shows **/home/sam** as Sam's working directory; after the command, it shows **/root**, **root**'s home directory, as the working directory. Use the **–s** option (page 419) to spawn a **root** shell without modifying the environment. When you call sudo without an option, it runs the command you specify in an unmodified environment. To demonstrate this feature, the following example calls sudo without an option to run pwd. The working directory of a command run in this manner does not change.

```
$ pwd
/home/sam
$ sudo pwd
/home/sam
```

Redirecting output   The following command fails because although the shell that sudo spawns executes ls with **root** privileges, the nonprivileged shell that the user is running redirects the output. The user's shell does not have permission to write to **/root**.

```
$ sudo ls > /root/ls.sam
-bash: /root/ls.sam: Permission denied
```

There are several ways around this problem. The easiest is to pass the whole command line to a shell running under sudo:

```
$ sudo bash -c "ls > /root/ls.sam"
```

The bash **–c** option spawns a shell that executes the string following the option and then terminates. The sudo utility runs the spawned shell with **root** privileges. You must quote the string to prevent the nonprivileged shell from interpreting special characters. You can also spawn a **root** shell using **sudo –i**, execute the command, and exit from the privileged shell. (See the preceding section.)

optional   Another way to deal with the issue of redirecting output of a command run by sudo is to use tee (page 242):

```
$ ls | sudo tee /root/ls.sam
...
```

This command writes the output of ls to the file but also displays it. If you do not want to display the output, you can have the nonprivileged shell redirect the output to **/dev/null** (page 503). The next example uses this technique to do away with the displayed output and uses the **–a** option to tee to append to the file instead of overwriting it:

```
$ ls | sudo tee -a /root/ls.sam > /dev/null
```

OPTIONS

You can use command-line options to control how sudo runs a command. Following is the syntax of an sudo command line:

sudo [options] [command]

where *options* is one or more options and *command* is the command you want to execute. Without the **–u** option, sudo runs *command* with **root** privileges. Some of the more common *options* follow; see the sudo man page for a complete list.

–b (**background**) Runs *command* in the background.

–e (**edit**) With this option, *command* is a filename and not a command. This option causes sudo to edit the file named *command* with **root** privileges using the editor named by the **SUDO_EDITOR**, **VISUAL**, or **EDITOR** environment variable. Default is the **vi** editor. Alternatively, you can use the sudoedit utility without any options. Using this technique, the editor does not run with **root** privileges. See the tip on page 417.

–i (**initial login environment**) Spawns the shell that is specified for **root** (or another user specified by **–u**) in **/etc/passwd**, running **root**'s (or the other user's) startup files, with some exceptions (e.g., **TERM** is not changed). Does not take a *command*. See "Spawning a **root** Shell" on page 413 for an example.

–k (**kill**) Resets the timestamp (page 416) of the user running the command, which means the user must enter her password the next time she runs sudo.

–L (**list defaults**) Lists the parameters that you can set on a Defaults line (page 423) in the **sudoers** file. Does not take a *command*.

–l (**list commands**) Lists the commands the user who is running sudo is allowed to run on the local system. Does not take a *command*.

–s (**shell**) Spawns a new **root** (or another user specified by **–u**) shell as specified in the **/etc/passwd** file. Similar to **–i** but does not change the environment. Does not take a *command*.

–u *user* Runs *command* with the privileges of *user*. Without this option, sudo runs *command* with **root** privileges.

sudoers: CONFIGURING sudo

As installed, sudo is not as secure and robust as it can be if you configure it carefully. The sudo configuration file is **/etc/sudoers**. You can edit this file to give specific users the ability to run only certain commands with **root** privileges as opposed to any commands. You can also limit these users to running commands only with certain options or arguments. Or you can set up sudo so a specific user cannot use a specific option or argument when running a command with **root** privileges.

The best way to edit **sudoers** is to use visudo by giving the command: **su -c visudo** or **sudo visudo**. The visudo utility locks, edits, and checks the grammar of the **sudoers** file. By default, visudo calls the **vi** editor. You can set the **SUDO_EDITOR**, **VISUAL**, or **EDITOR** environment variable to cause visudo to call a different editor. The following command causes visudo to use the nano editor (**nano** package):

```
$ export EDITOR=$(which nano)
```

Replace **nano** with the textual editor of your choice. Put this command in a startup file (page 282) to set this variable each time you log in.

Always use visudo to edit the sudoers file

caution   A syntax error in the **sudoers** file can prevent you from using sudo to gain **root** privileges. If you edit this file directly (without using visudo), you will not know that you introduced a syntax error until you find you cannot use sudo. The visudo utility checks the syntax of **sudoers** before it allows you to exit. If it finds an error, it gives you the choice of fixing the error, exiting without saving the changes to the file, or saving the changes and exiting. The last choice is usually a poor one, so visudo marks the it with **(DANGER!)**.

In the **sudoers** file, comments, which start with a hashmark (#), can appear anywhere on a line. In addition to comments, this file holds three types of entries: user privilege specifications, aliases, and defaults. Each of these entries occupies a line. You can continue a line by terminating it with a backslash (\).

User Privilege Specifications

The format of a line that specifies user privileges is as follows (the whitespace around the equal sign is optional). In each case,

   user_list host_list = [(runas_list)] command_list

- The *user_list* specifies the user(s) this specification line applies to. This list can contain usernames, groups (prefixed with %), and user aliases (next section). You can use the builtin alias ALL to cause the line to apply to all users.

- The *host_list* specifies the host(s) this specification line applies to. This list can contain one or more hostnames, IP addresses, or host aliases (discussed in the next section). You can use the builtin alias ALL to cause the line to apply to all systems that refer to this **sudoers** file.

- The *runas_list* specifies the user(s) the commands in the *command_list* can be run as when sudo is called with the **−u** option (page 419). This list can contain usernames, groups (prefixed with %), and runas aliases (discussed in the next section). It must be enclosed within parentheses. Without *runas_list*, sudo assumes **root**. You can use the builtin alias ALL to cause the line to apply to all usernames and groups.

- The *command_list* specifies the utilities this specification line applies to. This comma-separated list can contain names of utilities, names of directories holding utilities, and command aliases (discussed in the next section). All names must be absolute pathnames; directory names must end with a slash (/). Precede a command with an exclamation point (!) to exclude that command. You can use the builtin alias ALL to cause the line to apply to all commands.

Including the string **sudoedit** in the *command_list* gives users in the *user_list* permission to edit files using **root** privileges. See the Tip on page 417 for more information.

If you follow a command in the *command_list* with two adjacent double quotation marks (" "), the user will not be able to specify any command-line arguments, including options to that command. Alternatively, you can specify arguments, including wildcards, to limit the arguments a user is allowed to specify with that command.

Examples The following user privilege specification allows Sam to use sudo to mount and unmount filesystems (run mount and umount with **root** privileges) on all systems (as specified by **ALL**) that refer to the **sudoers** file containing this specification:

```
sam      ALL=(root) /bin/mount, /bin/umount
```

The (root) *runas_list* is optional. If you omit it, sudo allows the user to run the commands in the *command_list* with **root** privileges. In the following example, Sam takes advantage of these permissions. He cannot run umount directly; instead, he must call sudo to run it.

```
$ whoami
sam
$ umount /music
umount: only root can unmount /dev/sdb7 from /music
$ sudo umount /music
[sudo] password for sam:
$
```

If you replace the line in **sudoers** described above with the following line, Sam is not allowed to unmount **/p03**, although he can still unmount any other filesystem and can mount any filesystem:

```
sam      ALL=(root) /bin/mount, /bin/umount, !/bin/umount /p03
```

The result of the preceding line in **sudoers** is shown next. The sudo utility does not prompt for a password because Sam has entered his password within the last five minutes.

```
$ sudo umount /p03
Sorry, user sam is not allowed to execute '/bin/umount /p03' as root on localhost.
```

The following line limits Sam to mounting and unmounting filesystems mounted on **/p01**, **/p02**, **/p03**, and **/p04**:

```
sam      ALL= /bin/mount /p0[1-4], /bin/umount /p0[1-4]
```

The following commands show the result:

```
$ sudo umount /music
Sorry, user sam is not allowed to execute '/bin/umount /music' as root on localhost.
$ sudo umount /p03
$
```

Using the privileged
wheel group
As explained under "Quick setup" on page 416, the following lines in **sudoers** allow users who are members of the **wheel** group to use sudo to gain **root** privileges:

```
## Allows people in group wheel to run all commands
%wheel  ALL=(ALL)        ALL

# Members of the admin group may gain root privileges
%admin ALL=(ALL) ALL
```

This user privilege specification applies to all systems (as indicated by the **ALL** to the left of the equal sign). As the comment indicates, this line allows members of the **wheel** group (specified by preceding the name of the group with a percent sign: **%wheel**) to run any command (the rightmost **ALL**) as any user (the **ALL** within parentheses). When you call it without the **–u** option, the sudo utility runs the command you specify with **root** privileges, which is what sudo is used for most of the time.

If you modified the preceding line in **sudoers** as follows, it would allow members of the **wheel** group to run any command as any user with one exception: They would not be allowed to run passwd to change the **root** password (although they could gain **root** privileges and edit it manually).

```
%wheel ALL=(ALL) ALL, !/usr/bin/passwd root
```

optional   In the **%wheel ALL=(ALL) ALL** line in **/etc/sudoers**, if you replaced (ALL) with (**root**) or if you omitted (**ALL**), you would still be able to run any command with **root** privileges. You would not, however, be able to use the **–u** option to run a command as another user. Typically, when you can have **root** privileges, this limitation is not an issue. Working as a user other than yourself or **root** allows you to use the least privilege possible to accomplish a task, which is a good idea.

For example, if you are in the **wheel** group, the default entry in the **sudoers** file allows you to give the following command to create and edit a file in Sam's home directory. Because you are working as Sam, he will own the file and be able to read from and write to it.

```
$ sudo -u sam vi ~sam/reminder
$ ls -l ~sam/reminder
-rw-r--r--. 1 sam pubs 15 03-09 15:29 /home/sam/reminder
```

ALIASES

An alias enables you to rename and/or group users, hosts, or commands. Following is the format of an alias definition:

alias_type alias_name = alias_list

where *alias_type* is the type of alias (**User_Alias**, **Runas_Alias**, **Host_Alias**, **Cmnd_Alias**), *alias_name* is the name of the alias (by convention in all uppercase letters), and *alias_list* is a comma-separated list of one or more elements that make up the alias. Preceding an element of an alias with an exclamation point (**!**) negates it.

User_Alias   The *alias_list* for a user alias is the same as the *user_list* for a user privilege specification (discussed in the previous section). The following lines from a **sudoers** file define three user aliases: OFFICE, ADMIN, and ADMIN2. The *alias_list* that defines the first alias includes the usernames **zach**, **sam**, and **sls**; the second includes two usernames and members of the **admin** group; and the third includes all members of the **admin** group except Max.

```
User_Alias      OFFICE = zach, sam, sls
User_Alias      ADMIN = max, zach, %admin
User_Alias      ADMIN2 = %admin, !max
```

Runas_Alias   The *alias_list* for a runas alias is the same as the *runas_list* for a user privilege specification (discussed in the previous section). The following SM runas alias includes the usernames **sam** and **sls**:

```
Runas_Alias     SM = sam, sls
```

Host_Alias   Host aliases are meaningful only when the **sudoers** file is referenced by sudo running on more than one system. The *alias_list* for a host alias is the same as the *host_list* for a user privilege specification (discussed in the previous section). The following line defines the LCL alias to include the systems named **guava** and **plum**:

```
Host_Alias      LCL = guava, plum
```

If you want to use fully qualified hostnames (**hosta.example.com** instead of just **hosta**) in this list, you must set the **fqdn** flag (next section). However, doing so might slow the performance of sudo.

Cmnd_Alias   The *alias_list* for a command alias is the same as the *command_list* for a user privilege specification (discussed in the previous section). The following command alias includes three files and by including a directory (denoted by its trailing **/**), incorporates all the files in that directory:

```
Cmnd_Alias      BASIC = /bin/cat, /usr/bin/vi, /bin/df, /usr/local/safe/
```

DEFAULTS (OPTIONS)

You can change configuration options from their default values by using the **Defaults** keyword. Most values in this list are flags that are implicitly Boolean (can either be on or off) or strings. You turn on a flag by naming it on a Defaults line, and you turn it off by preceding it with a **!**. The following line in the **sudoers** file would turn off the **lecture** and **fqdn** flags and turn on **tty_tickets**:

```
Defaults        !lecture,tty_tickets,!fqdn
```

This section lists some common flags; see the **sudoers** man page for a complete list.

env_reset   Causes sudo to reset the environment variables to contain the **LOGNAME**, **SHELL**, **USER**, **USERNAME**, **MAIL**, and **SUDO_*** variables only. Default is **on**. See the **sudoers** man page for more information.

fqdn   (**fully qualified domain name**) Performs DNS lookups on *FQDNs* (page 1165) in the **sudoers** file. When this flag is set, you can use FQDNs in the **sudoers** file, but doing so might negatively affect sudo's performance, especially if DNS is not working. When this flag is set, you must use the local host's official DNS name, not an alias. If hostname returns an FQDN, you do not need to set this flag. Default is **on**.

insults Displays mild, humorous insults when a user enters a wrong password. Default is **off**. See also **passwd_tries**.

lecture=*freq* Controls when sudo displays a reminder message before the password prompt. Possible values of *freq* are **never**, **once**, and **always**. Specifying **!lecture** is the same as specifying a *freq* of **never**. Default is **once**.

mail_always Sends email to the **mailto** user each time a user runs sudo. Default is **off**.

mail_badpass Sends email to the **mailto** user when a user enters an incorrect password while running sudo. Default is **off**.

mail_no_host Sends email to the **mailto** user when a user whose username is in the **sudoers** file but who does not have permission to run commands on the local host runs sudo. Default is **off**.

mail_no_perms Sends email to the **mailto** user when a user whose username is in the **sudoers** file but who does not have permission to run the requested command runs sudo. Default is **off**.

mail_no_user Sends email to the **mailto** user when a user whose username is not in the **sudoers** file runs sudo. Default is **on**.

mailsub=*subj* (**mail subject**) Changes the default email subject for warning and error messages from the default ✳✳✳ **SECURITY information for %h** ✳✳✳ to *subj*. The sudo utility expands **%h** within *subj* to the local system's hostname. Place *subj* between quotation marks if it contains shell special characters (page 146).

mailto=*eadd* Sends sudo warning and error messages to *eadd* (an email address; default is **root**). Place *eadd* between quotation marks if it contains shell special characters (page 146).

passwd_timeout=*mins*
The *mins* is the number of minutes before a sudo password prompt times out. A value of 0 (zero) indicates the password does not time out. Default is **5**.

passwd_tries=*num*
The *num* is the number of times the user can enter an incorrect password in response to the sudo password prompt before sudo quits. Default is **3**. See also **insults** and **lecture**.

rootpw Causes sudo to accept only the **root** password in response to its prompt. Because sudo issues the same prompt whether it is asking for your password or the **root** password, turning this flag on might confuse users. Default is **off**, causing sudo to prompt for the password of the user running sudo.

shell_noargs Causes sudo, when called without any arguments, to spawn a **root** shell without changing the environment. Default is **off**. This option is the same as the sudo **–s** option.

timestamp_timeout=*mins*
The *mins* is the number of minutes that the sudo timestamp (page 416) is valid. Set *mins* to **–1** to cause the timestamp to be valid forever; set to 0 (zero) to cause sudo to always prompt for a password. Default is **5**.

tty_tickets   Causes sudo to authenticate users on a per-tty basis, not a per-user basis. Default is **on**.

umask=*val*   The *val* is the umask (page 473) that sudo uses to run the command that the user specifies. Set *val* to 0777 to preserve the user's umask value. Default is 0022.

Locking the root Account (Removing the root Password)

If you decide you want to lock the **root** account, give the command **su -c 'passwd –l root'**. This command renders the encrypted password in **/etc/shadow** invalid by prepending two exclamation points (**!!**) to it. You can unlock the account again by removing the exclamation points or by giving the command shown in the following example.

Unlocking the **root** account   If you decide you want to unlock the **root** account after locking it, give the following command. This command assumes you can use sudo to gain **root** privileges and unlocks the **root** account by assigning a password to it:

```
$ sudo passwd root
[sudo] password for sam:
Changing password for user root.
New password:
Retype new password:
passwd: all authentication tokens updated successfully.
```

consolehelper: Allows an Ordinary User to Run a Privileged Command

The consolehelper utility makes it easier for an ordinary user to run system programs that normally can be run only by a user with **root** privileges. PAM (page 463), which authenticates users, can be set to trust all console users, to require user passwords (not the **root** password), or to require the **root** password before granting trust. The concept underlying consolehelper is that you might want to consider as trustworthy anyone who has access to the console. For example, Sam can log in on the console as himself and run reboot without knowing the **root** password.

To understand how consolehelper works, look at the two **halt** files:

```
$ file /sbin/halt /usr/bin/halt
/sbin/halt:    symbolic link to '../bin/systemctl'
/usr/bin/halt: symbolic link to 'consolehelper'
```

Under Fedora, the file in **/sbin** is a link to **/bin/systemctl**; under RHEL it is linked to **/sbin/reboot**. On both systems the file in **/usr/bin** is a link to **/usr/bin/consolehelper**. Both of these linked-to files are executable:

```
$ file /bin/systemctl /usr/bin/consolehelper
/bin/systemctl:         ELF 32-bit LSB executable, Intel 80386 ...
/usr/bin/consolehelper: ELF 32-bit LSB executable, Intel 80386 ...
```

In **root**'s **PATH** variable (page 308), **/sbin** normally precedes **/usr/bin**. Thus, when a user running with **root** privileges in a **root** login environment gives a halt command, the shell executes **/bin/systemctl reboot** under Fedora or **/sbin/reboot** under RHEL.

In an ordinary user's **PATH** variable, **/usr/bin** normally precedes **/sbin** (if **/sbin** is included in **PATH** at all). Thus, when an ordinary user gives a reboot command, the shell executes **/usr/bin/consolehelper** (the consolehelper utility).

What consolehelper does depends on how PAM is set up (see **/etc/pam.d/halt** for the modules it calls and **/usr/share/doc/pam-*/txts/*** and the **pam_console** man page for descriptions of the modules). Refer to "PAM" on page 463 for more information. By default, consolehelper does not require the **root** password; any user can give a **reboot** command to reboot the system.

THE init DAEMON

The **init** daemon is the system and service manager for Linux. As explained on page 317, it is the first true process Linux starts when it boots and as such, has a PID of 1 and is the ancestor of all processes. The **init** daemon has been around since the early days of UNIX, and many people have worked to improve it. The first Linux **init** daemon was based on the UNIX System V **init** daemon and is referred to as SysVinit (System V **init** daemon).

Because SysVinit does not deal well with modern hardware, including hotplug (page 516) devices, USB hard and flash drives, and network-mounted filesystems, Fedora/RHEL recently replaced it with the Upstart **init** daemon (upstart.ubuntu.com and upstart.ubuntu.com/wiki). The Upstart daemon as implemented by RHEL is described starting on page 436. Fedora 15 has moved past Upstart to systemd **init** daemon, which is described next. Several other replacements for SysVinit are also available. One of the most prominent is **initng** (initng.sourceforge.net/trac). In addition, Solaris uses SMF (Service Management Facility), and MacOS uses **launchd**.

THE systemd init DAEMON (FEDORA)

The name *systemd* comprises *system,* which systemd manages, followed by *d.* Under UNIX/Linux, daemon names frequently end in **d**: systemd is the system daemon. At boot time, systemd renames itself **init**, so you will not see a process named systemd. However, **init** is simply a link to systemd:

```
$ ls -l /sbin/init
lrwxrwxrwx. 1 root root 14 04-22 08:47 /sbin/init -> ../bin/systemd
```

The name is also a play on words with *System D,* a reference to the French *débrouillard* (to untangle) or *démerder.* System D is a manner of responding to challenges that requires fast thinking, adapting, and improvising.

The systemd **init** daemon is a drop-in replacement for SysVinit; most of the administration tools that worked with SysVinit and Upstart work with systemd. Although systemd is new, most of the user interfaces pertinent to administrators will remain stable (www.freedesktop.org/wiki/Software/systemd/InterfaceStabilityPromise). A GUI to systemd is under development.

MORE INFORMATION

Local   Use apropos to list man pages that pertain to systemd (**apropos systemd**). Some of the most interesting of these are **systemd**, systemctl, systemd.unit, and systemd.special.

Web   systemd home page: www.freedesktop.org/wiki/Software/systemd
Fedora systemd home page: fedoraproject.org/wiki/Systemd
Fedora systemd feature list: fedoraproject.org/wiki/Features/systemd
SysVinit to systemd conversion notes:
   fedoraproject.org/wiki/SysVinit_to_Systemd_Cheatsheet
List of services that run natively under systemd:
   fedoraproject.org/wiki/User:Johannbg/QA/Systemd/compatability
Blog about systemd by its creator, Lennart Poettering:
   0pointer.de/blog/projects/systemd.html
systemd stability promise:
   www.freedesktop.org/wiki/Software/systemd/InterfaceStabilityPromise
cgroups: www.kernel.org/doc/Documentation/cgroups/cgroups.txt

SERVICE UNITS AND TARGET UNITS

The systemd **init** daemon is based on the concept of units, each of which has a name and type. Typically information about a unit is stored in a file that has the same name as the unit (e.g., **dbus.service**). The types of units are service, socket, device, mount, automount, target, snapshot, timer, swap, and path. This section discusses service and target units, which are critical to controlling daemons and runlevel under systemd.

Service unit   A service unit refers to a daemon (service) that systemd controls, including those controlled natively by systemd and those controlled by systemd via SysVinit scripts. For example, systemd controls the **ntpd** daemon natively via the **ntpd.service** service unit.

Target unit   A target unit groups other units. Of concern in this section are targets that control the system runlevel. By default, Fedora activates **graphical.target**, which brings the system to a runlevel that equates to what was formerly called runlevel 5 (multiuser graphical mode). Activating **multi-user.target** brings the system to what was formerly called runlevel 3 (multiuser textual mode). Table 11-1 on page 448 lists all the runlevels (target units).

Terminology: server, service, daemon   A *daemon*, such as **ntpd** or **cupsd**, provides a *service* that runs on a *server*. The daemon itself is also sometimes referred to as a *server*. These three terms can be used interchangeably.

RUNLEVELS

The systemd **init** daemon does not support runlevels the way SysVinit did. It supports *target units,* which parallel runlevels but are different. To ease the transition, this book continues to use the term *runlevel* to refer to target units. One difference between SysVinit runlevels and systemd target units is that the former can be changed only when the system changes runlevels while the latter can be activated by any of a large group of triggers. Another difference is that a systemd-based system can activate more than one target unit at a time, allowing the system to be in more than one runlevel at a time. For example, **graphical.target** pulls in **multi-user.target** so they are both active at the same time.

systemd runlevels differ from SysVinit runlevels

tip   For consistency and clarity during the transition from SysVinit to systemd, this book refers to systemd *target units* as *runlevels.* Target units are not true runlevels, but they perform a function similar to the function performed by SysVinit runlevels.

WANTS AND REQUIRES

Under systemd, the terms *wants* and *requires* specify units that are to be activated when the unit that wants or requires the other unit is activated. A unit that *requires* another unit will not start if the other unit is not available and will quit if the other unit becomes unavailable while the first unit is active. Wants is similar to requires, except a unit that *wants* another unit will not fail if the wanted unit is not available.

DISPLAYING PROPERTIES

The following systemctl **show** command displays the Requires properties of the **graphical.target** unit. It shows that **graphical.target** requires **multi-user.target**:

```
$ systemctl show --property "Requires" graphical.target
Requires=multi-user.target
```

This relationship causes systemd not to start **graphical.target** if **multi-user.target** is not available. It means **graphical.target** requires units that **multi-user.target** requires and wants units that **multi-user.target** wants. Because of this relationship, **multi-user.target** (runlevel) is active at the same time **graphical.target** (runlevel) is active.

You can also use the systemctl **show** command to display the Wants properties of a target:

```
$ systemctl show --property "Wants" multi-user.target
Wants=systemd-update-utmp-runlevel.service NetworkManager.service ...
(END) q
```

The list is long. Although systemctl passes the output through a pager, it runs off the right edge of the screen. When the command displays (**END**), press **q** to return to the shell prompt. Sending the output through the fmt text formatter with a line-length specification of 10 displays the list one service per line:

```
$ systemctl show --property "Wants" multi-user.target | fmt -10
Wants=systemd-update-utmp-runlevel.service
NetworkManager.service
abrtd.service
ntpd.service
mcelog.service
rsyslog.service
...
```

To see if a target wants a specific service, send the output of the previous command through grep:

```
$ systemctl show --property "Wants" multi-user.target | fmt -10 | grep ntpd
ntpd.service
ntpdate.service
```

The output shows that **multi-user.target** wants the **ntpd.service** service. Because **graphical.target** requires **multi-user.target** and **multi-user.target** wants **ntpd.service**, systemd will start **ntpd.service** when the system enters the runlevel defined by **graphical.target**.

/etc/systemd/system HIERARCHY: CONTROLS SERVICES AND THE PERSISTENT RUNLEVEL

The services wanted by a runlevel target appear in directories named ***.wants** under the **/etc/systemd/system** directory:

```
$ ls -ld /etc/systemd/system/*.wants
...
drwxr-xr-x. 2 root root 4096 04-20 17:10 /etc/systemd/system/graphical.target.wants
drwxr-xr-x. 2 root root 4096 04-20 17:10 /etc/systemd/system/multi-user.target.wants
...
```

The following command lists the runlevel targets that want **ntpd.service**:

```
$ ls /etc/systemd/system/*.wants/ntpd.service
/etc/systemd/system/multi-user.target.wants/ntpd.service
```

As explained in the previous section, you can also display this information using the systemctl **show** command.

The directory hierarchy with its root at **/etc/systemd/system** controls the persistent runlevel of the system. That is, this directory hierarchy specifies which daemons will be started when the system boots or otherwise changes runlevel or when the daemon is activated for another reason.

All service unit files are kept in the **/lib/systemd/system** directory. All plain files in the **/etc/systemd/system** hierarchy are links to files in the **/lib/systemd/system** hierarchy. For example, **ntpd.service** shown in the preceding example is a link to the appropriate service unit file in **/lib/systemd/system**:

```
$ ls -l /etc/systemd/system/multi-user.target.wants/ntpd.service
lrwxrwxrwx. 1 root root 32 04-08 14:34 /etc/systemd/system/multi-user.target.wants/ntpd.service ->
/lib/systemd/system/ntpd.service
```

The service unit file provides systemd with information it needs to start the service and specifies the system runlevel target that wants the service:

```
$ cat /lib/systemd/system/ntpd.service
[Unit]
Description=Network Time Service
After=syslog.target ntpdate.service

[Service]
EnvironmentFile=/etc/sysconfig/ntpd
ExecStart=/usr/sbin/ntpd -n -u ntp:ntp $OPTIONS

[Install]
WantedBy=multi-user.target
```

When you instruct systemd to start a service when the system boots (make the service persistent), it places a link to the service file in the directory specified by WantedBy in the service file. Continuing with the example, systemd places a link to **ntpd.service** in the **multi-user.target.wants** directory as shown previously. When you instruct systemd to not start a service when the system boots, it removes the link. "Setting the Persistent State of a Daemon (Service)" on page 433 explains how to use systemctl to make these changes.

The persistent (default) runlevel is also controlled by a link:

```
$ ls -l /etc/systemd/system/default.target
lrwxrwxrwx. 1 root root 36 04-20 10:07 /etc/systemd/system/default.target ->
/lib/systemd/system/runlevel5.target
```

See "Setting the Persistent Runlevel" on page 432 for more information.

Custom Service Files

As explained in the previous section, files in the **/etc/systemd/system** directory hierarchy are symbolic links to files in the **/lib/systemd/system** directory hierarchy. The systemd **init** daemon treats files in the **/etc/systemd/system** directory hierarchy and files in the **/lib/systemd/system** directory hierarchy the same way, with files in **/etc/systemd/system** overriding files with the same name in **/lib/systemd/system**. An important difference between these directory hierarchies is that **/lib/systemd/system** is managed by yum/RPM while **/etc/systemd/system** is managed by the system administrator.

Put custom service files in the **/etc/systemd/system** hierarchy. If you want to modify a service file, copy it from the **/lib/systemd/system** hierarchy to the **/etc/systemd/system** hierarchy and edit the copy. The custom file in the **/etc/systemd/system** hierarchy will not be overwritten by yum/RPM and will take precedence over a file with the same name in the **/lib/systemd/system** hierarchy.

DETERMINING IF systemd RUNS A DAEMON NATIVELY

To ease migration from a SysVinit and Upstart to systemd and to provide compatibility with software intended for other distributions, systemd can control daemons via SysVinit scripts (page 442). You can use the systemctl **status** command to determine if systemd is controlling a daemon natively or via a SysVinit script. Following, systemctl displays the status of **dhcpd** and **sshd**:

```
$ systemctl status dhcpd.service
dhcpd.service - DHCPv4 Server Daemon
        Loaded: loaded (/lib/systemd/system/dhcpd.service)
        Active: inactive (dead)
        CGroup: name=systemd:/system/dhcpd.service

$ systemctl status sshd.service
sshd.service - LSB: Start up the OpenSSH server daemon
        Loaded: loaded (/etc/rc.d/init.d/sshd)
        Active: active (running) since Wed, 20 Apr 2011 19:08:32 -0700; 19h ago
      Main PID: 817 (sshd)
        CGroup: name=systemd:/system/sshd.service
                + 817 /usr/sbin/sshd
```

The systemctl utility requires a period and unit type (**.service** in the preceding example) following a unit name (**dhcpd** and **sshd** in the preceding example). The lines that start with **Loaded** name the file controlling each daemon (service). The **dhcpd** daemon is controlled by **/lib/systemd/system/dhcpd.service**. The location of the file (the **/lib/systemd** hierarchy) and its filename extension (**.service**) indicate systemd is running the daemon natively. The **sshd** daemon is controlled by **/etc/rc.d/init.d/sshd**. The location of the file (the **init.d** directory) and the lack of a filename extension indicate systemd is running the daemon via a SysVinit script. See fedoraproject.org/wiki/User:Johannbg/QA/Systemd/compatability for a list of services that have been ported to systemd (and are run natively by systemd).

You can use service to display the same information as systemctl **status**. However, service does not accept a period and unit type.

```
# service dhcpd status
dhcpd.service - DHCPv4 Server Daemon
        Loaded: loaded (/lib/systemd/system/dhcpd.service)
        Active: inactive (dead)
        CGroup: name=systemd:/system/dhcpd.service

# service sshd status
sshd.service - LSB: Start up the OpenSSH server daemon
        Loaded: loaded (/etc/rc.d/init.d/sshd)
        Active: active (running) since Wed, 20 Apr 2011 19:08:32 -0700; 19h ago
      Main PID: 817 (sshd)
        CGroup: name=systemd:/system/sshd.service
                + 817 /usr/sbin/sshd
```

SETTING AND CHANGING RUNLEVELS

The runlevel specifies which daemons are running and which interfaces are available on a system. See "Runlevels" on page 428 and Table 11-1 on page 448 for more information. This section describes how to set the persistent (default) runlevel (the runlevel the system boots to) and how to change the current runlevel.

SETTING THE PERSISTENT RUNLEVEL

Under systemd no true runlevels exist; see "Runlevels" on page 448. For example, the default runlevel under Fedora is **graphical.target** and has an alternative name of **runlevel5.target**. Under SysVinit this runlevel is referred to as runlevel 5 (multiuser graphical mode). The **/etc/systemd/system/default.target** file is a link to the file that specifies the target the system will boot to by default:

```
$ ls -l /etc/systemd/system/default.target
lrwxrwxrwx. 1 root root 36 04-20 10:07 /etc/systemd/system/default.target ->
/lib/systemd/system/runlevel5.target
```

The following command shows **runlevel5.target** is a link to **graphical.target**:

```
$ ls -l /lib/systemd/system/runlevel5.target
lrwxrwxrwx. 1 root root 16 04-08 14:33 /lib/systemd/system/runlevel5.target ->
graphical.target
```

The **multi-user.target** file (and the link to it, **runlevel3.target**) causes the system to boot to the multiuser runlevel (multiuser textual mode; SysVinit runlevel 3). The following command replaces the link shown in the previous example and will cause the system enter multiuser textual mode each time it is booted. This command does not change the current runlevel.

```
# ln -sf /lib/systemd/system/multi-user.target /etc/systemd/system/default.target
```

The **–s** (symbolic) option creates a symbolic link, and the **–f** (force) option overwrites any existing file. After giving the preceding command and rebooting the system, the systemctl **list-units** command shows the system is in multiuser mode:

```
$ systemctl list-units --type=target
...
multi-user.target          loaded active active     Multi-User
...
```

CHANGING THE CURRENT RUNLEVEL

The systemctl **isolate** command changes the current runlevel of the system. The following command changes the runlevel to multiuser graphical mode (**graphical.target**). When the system is rebooted, it will return to the default runlevel as specified by the link at **/etc/systemd/system/default.target**.

```
# systemctl isolate graphical.target
```

After a few moments, systemctl shows the system is in the runlevel specified by **graphical.target**:

```
$ systemctl list-units --type=target
...
graphical.target          loaded active active     Graphical Interface
...
```

The preceding examples were run from an ssh login. If you give these commands from a terminal emulator running in a GUI, the system will log you out each time the system changes runlevel.

CONFIGURING DAEMONS (SERVICES)

Two states are important when you consider a daemon: its current state and its persistent state (the state it will be in after the system is booted). Possible states are running and stopped. Under Fedora, daemons are stopped when they are installed and are set up to be stopped after the system is booted.

The systemctl utility controls the current and persistent states of daemons that run natively under systemd. The service and chkconfig utilities originally controlled daemons that run under SysVinit and were upgraded to control daemons that run under Upstart. Now these utilities have been retrofitted to control daemons that run under systemd, which they do by calling systemctl. You can still use service to control the current state of a daemon and chkconfig to control the persistent state of a daemon.

The next sections describe the systemctl commands that control daemons, followed by the service or chkconfig commands that perform the same functions.

SETTING THE PERSISTENT STATE OF A DAEMON (SERVICE)

The systemctl **disable** command causes a daemon not to start when the system is booted. This command has no effect on the current state of the daemon. You must specify the **.service** part of the service name.

```
# systemctl disable ntpd.service
rm '/etc/systemd/system/multi-user.target.wants/ntpd.service'
```

The preceding command removes the link that causes systemd to start **ntpd** when the system enters multi-user runlevel and, by inheritance, graphical runlevel. See "/etc/systemd/system Hierarchy: Controls Services and the Persistent Runlevel" on page 429 for a discussion of these links.

The preceding command works on the **ntpd** daemon, which is run natively by systemd. If you run the same command on a daemon controlled by a SysVinit script, such as **cups**, it calls chkconfig (covered shortly). Even though no **cups.service** service or file exists, you must specify the **.service** part of the service name.

```
# systemctl disable cups.service
cups.service is not a native service, redirecting to /sbin/chkconfig.
Executing /sbin/chkconfig cups off
```

The following commands each verify the **ntpd** daemon will not start when the system boots. The first command shows no links in the ***.wants** directories for ntpd.service. The second uses the systemctl **is-enabled**, which sets its exit status (page 1012) to 0 (zero) if the service is enabled or to nonzero otherwise. The **||** Boolean operator (OR; page 1038) executes the echo command if systemctl returns a nonzero exit status (fails).

```
# ls /etc/systemd/system/*.wants/ntpd.service
ls: cannot access /etc/systemd/system/*.wants/ntpd.service: No such file or directory

# systemctl is-enabled ntpd.service || echo ntpd is not enabled
ntpd is not enabled
```

The systemctl **enable** command causes a daemon to start when the system is booted. This command has no effect on the current state of the daemon. It creates the link that causes systemd to start **ntpd** when the system enters multiuser textual mode and, by inheritance, multiuser graphical mode. If you run the same command on a daemon that is controlled by a SysVinit script, it calls chkconfig (covered shortly).

```
# systemctl enable ntpd.service
ln -s '/lib/systemd/system/ntpd.service' '/etc/systemd/system/multi-user.target.wants/ntpd.service'
```

As in the preceding example, the next two commands check whether the daemon will start when the system is booted.

```
$ ls /etc/systemd/system/*.wants/ntpd.service
/etc/systemd/system/multi-user.target.wants/ntpd.service

$ systemctl is-enabled ntpd.service || echo ntpd is not enabled
$
```

The chkconfig **off** and **on** commands correspond to the systemctl **disable** and **enable** commands. The messages the commands display when run on daemons systemd controls natively show they call systemctl. Because the chkconfig **--list** option does not display the correct information for daemons controlled natively by systemd; you must use the preceding techniques to determine if such a daemon is enabled.

```
# chkconfig ntpd off
Note: Forwarding request to 'systemctl disable ntpd.service'.
rm '/etc/systemd/system/multi-user.target.wants/ntpd.service'

# chkconfig ntpd on
Note: Forwarding request to 'systemctl enable ntpd.service'.
ln -s '/lib/systemd/system/ntpd.service' '/etc/systemd/system/multi-user.target.wants/ntpd.service'
```

optional The preceding section discussed the systemctl **enable** command in terms of causing a daemon to start when the system boots. Most of the time this command works that way. However, the systemctl **enable** command can cause services to start based on various triggers, not just by the system booting.

For example, when **bluetooth.service** is enabled, it is controlled by the bluetooth device logic, which starts **bluetooth.service** when a bluetooth device is plugged in. If the bluetooth device is built in to the computer, this distinction is not important. However, if the bluetooth device is attached to a USB dongle, running systemctl **enable** means that in the future, the bluetooth service will be started as soon as the dongle is plugged in but not before.

In a similar vein, in future releases of Fedora the **cupsd** daemon will no longer be started when the system boots. Rather, running systemctl **enable** will only establish a communication socket for **cupsd**. The **cupsd** daemon will not start until a process tries to access it (when someone sends a job to the printer).

CHANGING THE CURRENT STATE OF A DAEMON

The systemctl **stop** command immediately stops a daemon from running. This command has no effect on whether the daemon starts when the system is booted. The following command works on the **ntpd** daemon, which is run natively by systemd. It will also work on a daemon systemd controls via a SysVinit script. You must always specify the **.service** part of the service name.

```
# systemctl stop ntpd.service
```

The preceding command stops the **ntpd** daemon. It displays no output, even if you mistype the name of the daemon. The following commands each verify the **ntpd** daemon is not running.

```
# systemctl status ntpd.service
ntpd.service - Network Time Service
        Loaded: loaded (/lib/systemd/system/ntpd.service)
        Active: inactive (dead) since Fri, 22 Apr 2011 08:50:59 -0700; 17ms ago
       Process: 1036 ExecStart=/usr/sbin/ntpd -n -u ntp:ntp $OPTIONS (code=exited, status=0/SUCCESS)
        CGroup: name=systemd:/system/ntpd.service

# systemctl is-active ntpd.service
inactive
```

The systemctl **status** command shows an **Active** status of **inactive (dead)**. The systemctl **is-active** command displays a status of **inactive**. You can also use **ps –ef | grep ntpd** to determine if the daemon is running.

The systemctl **start** command immediately starts a daemon running. This command has no effect on whether the daemon starts when the system is booted.

```
# systemctl start ntpd.service
```

The next two commands each show the daemon is running.

```
# systemctl status ntpd.service
ntpd.service - Network Time Service
        Loaded: loaded (/lib/systemd/system/ntpd.service)
        Active: active (running) since Fri, 22 Apr 2011 08:50:59 -0700; 33ms ago
      Main PID: 1562 (ntpd)
        CGroup: name=systemd:/system/ntpd.service
                + 1562 /usr/sbin/ntpd -n -u ntp:ntp -g

# systemctl is-active ntpd.service
active
```

The service **stop**, **start**, and **status** commands correspond the systemctl **stop**, **start**, and **status** commands. The messages the **stop** and **start** commands display show they simply call systemctl. You can use the service **status** command (or the systemctl **status** command) to display the status of a daemon.

```
# service ntpd stop
Stopping ntpd (via systemctl):                              [  OK  ]

# service ntpd start
Starting ntpd (via systemctl):                              [  OK  ]

# service ntpd status
ntpd.service - Network Time Service
        Loaded: loaded (/lib/systemd/system/ntpd.service)
        Active: active (running) since Fri, 22 Apr 2011 08:50:59 -0700; 102ms ago
      Main PID: 1615 (ntpd)
        CGroup: name=systemd:/system/ntpd.service
                + 1615 /usr/sbin/ntpd -n -u ntp:ntp -g
```

THE UPSTART init DAEMON (RHEL)

The runlevel-based SysVinit daemon uses runlevels (single-user, multiuser, and more) and links from the **/etc/rc.d/rc?.d** directories to the init scripts in **/etc/init.d** to start and stop system services (page 442). The event-based Upstart **init** daemon (**upstart** package) uses events to start and stop system services. This section discusses Upstart and the parts of SysVinit that remain: the **/etc/rc.d/rc?.d** and **/etc/rc.d/init.d** directories and the concept of runlevels.

The Upstart **init** daemon is event-based and runs specified programs when something on the system changes. These programs, which are frequently scripts, start and stop services. This setup is similar in concept to the links to init scripts that SysVinit calls as a system enters runlevels, except Upstart is more flexible. Instead of starting and stopping services only when the runlevel changes, Upstart can start and stop services upon receiving information that something on the system has changed. Such a change is called an *event*. For example, Upstart can take action when it learns from udev (page 516) that a filesystem, printer, or other device has been added or removed from the running system. It can also start and stop services when the system boots, when the system is shut down, or when a job changes state.

SOFTWARE PACKAGES

The Upstart system is contained in one package, which is installed by default:

- **upstart**—Provides the Upstart **init** daemon and initctl utility.

DEFINITIONS

Events   An *event* is a change in state that can be communicated to **init**. Almost any change in state—either internal or external to the system—can trigger an event. For example, the boot loader triggers the **startup** event (**startup** man page), and the telinit command (page 449) triggers the **runlevel** event (page 441). Removing and installing a hotplug (page 516) or USB device (such as a printer) can trigger an event as well. You can also trigger an event manually by giving the initctl **emit** command (page 439). For more information refer to "Events" on page 440.

Jobs A *job* is a series of instructions that **init** reads. These instructions typically include a program (binary file or shell script) and the name of an event. The Upstart **init** daemon runs the program when the event is triggered. You can run and stop a job manually by giving the initctl **start** and **stop** commands, respectively (page 440). Jobs are divided into tasks and services. A job is a service by default; you must explicitly specify a job as a task for it to run as a task.

Tasks A *task* is a job that performs its work and returns to a waiting state when it is done. A task blocks the program/process that emitted the event that triggered it until the program it specifies is finished running. The **rc** task described on page 441 is an example of a task.

Services A *service* is a job that does not normally terminate by itself. For example, the **logd** daemon and mingetty processes (page 441) are implemented as services. The **init** daemon monitors each service, restarting the service if it fails and killing the service if it is stopped either manually or by an event. A service blocks the program/process that emitted the event that triggered it until the program it specifies has started running.

Job definition files The **/etc/init** directory holds *job definition files* (files defining the jobs that the Upstart **init** daemon runs). Initially this directory is populated by the Upstart software package. The installation of some services adds files to this directory to control the service, replacing the files that were previously placed in the **/etc/rc.d/rc?.d** and **/etc/rc.d/init.d** directories when the service was installed.

init is a state machine At its core, the Upstart **init** daemon is a state machine. It keeps track of the state of jobs and, as events are triggered, tracks jobs as they change states. When **init** tracks a job from one state to another, it might execute the job's commands or terminate the job.

Runlevel emulation The System V **init** daemon used changes in runlevels (page 448) to determine when to start and stop processes. RHEL systems, which rely on the Upstart **init** daemon, have no concept of runlevels. To ease migration from a runlevel-based system to an event-based system, and to provide compatibility with software intended for other distributions, RHEL emulates runlevels using Upstart.

The **rc** task, which is defined by the **/etc/init/rc.conf** file, runs the **/etc/rc.d/rc** script. This script, in turn, runs the **init** scripts in **/etc/rc.d/init.d** from the links in the **/etc/rc.d/rc?.d** directories, emulating the functionality of these links under Sys-Vinit. The **rc** task runs these scripts as the system enters a runlevel; it normally takes no action when the system leaves a runlevel. See page 441 for a discussion of the **rc** task and page 442 for information on init scripts. Upstart implements the runlevel (page 448) and telinit (page 449) utilities to provide compatibility with SysVinit systems.

initctl The initctl (**init** control) utility communicates with the Upstart **init** daemon. An ordinary user can query the Upstart **init** daemon using the initctl **list** and **status** commands. A system administrator working with **root** privileges can both query this daemon and start and stop jobs. For example, the initctl **list** command lists jobs and their states:

```
$ initctl list
rc stop/waiting
tty (/dev/tty3) start/running, process 1271
tty (/dev/tty2) start/running, process 1269
plymouth-shutdown stop/waiting
control-alt-delete stop/waiting
system-setup-keyboard start/running, process 842
readahead-collector stop/waiting
vpnc-cleanup stop/waiting
quit-plymouth stop/waiting
rcS stop/waiting
...
```

See the initctl man page and the examples in this section for more information. You can give the command **initctl help** (no hyphens before **help**) to display a list of initctl commands. Alternatively, you can give the following command to display more information about the **list** command:

```
$ initctl list --help
Usage: initctl list [OPTION]...
List known jobs.

Options:
      --system              use D-Bus system bus to connect to init daemon
      --dest=NAME           destination well-known name on system bus
  -q, --quiet               reduce output to errors only
  -v, --verbose             increase output to include informational messages
      --help                display this help and exit
      --version             output version information and exit

The known jobs and their current status will be output.

Report bugs to <upstart-devel@lists.ubuntu.com>
```

Replace **list** with the initctl command for which you want to obtain more information. The start, stop, reload, and status utilities are links to initctl that run the initctl commands they are named for.

Jobs

Each file in the **/etc/init** directory defines a job and usually contains at least an event and a command. When the event is triggered, **init** executes the command. This section describes examples of both administrator-defined jobs and jobs installed with the **upstart** package.

Administrator-Defined Jobs

mudat example   The following administrator-defined job uses the **exec** keyword to execute a shell command. You can also use this keyword to execute a shell script stored in a file or a binary executable file.

In the first stanza (**start on runlevel 5**), **start on** is a keyword (you can use **stop on** in its place), **runlevel** is an event (page 436), and **5** is an argument to **runlevel**.

```
$ cat /etc/init/mudat.conf
start on runlevel 5
task
exec echo "Entering multiuser mode on " $(date) > /tmp/mudat.out
```

This file defines a task: It runs the echo shell command when the system enters multiuser mode (runlevel 5). This command writes a message that includes the time and date to **/tmp/mudat.out**. The shell uses command substitution (page 351) to execute the date utility. After this job runs to completion, the **mudat** task stops and enters a wait state.

In the next example, the cat utility shows the contents of the **/tmp/mudat.out** file and the initctl **list** command and the status utility report on this task:

```
$ cat /tmp/mudat.out
Entering multiuser mode on Tue Jan 18 16:04:10 PST 2011

$ initctl list | grep mudat
mudat stop/waiting
$ status mudat
mudat stop/waiting
```

If the **exec** command line contains shell special characters (page 146), **init** executes **/bin/sh** (a link to bash) and passes the command line to the shell. Otherwise, **exec** executes the command line directly. To run multiple shell commands, either use **exec** to run a shell script stored in a file or use **script...end script** (next).

The Upstart **init** daemon can monitor only jobs (services) whose programs are executed using **exec**; it cannot monitor jobs run using **script...end script**. Put another way, *services* require the use of **exec**; *tasks* can use either method to run a program. Future versions of the Upstart **init** daemon will be able to monitor these jobs.

myjob example   You can also define an event and set up a job that is triggered by that event. The **myjob.conf** job definition file defines a job that is triggered by the **hithere** event:

```
$ cat /etc/init/myjob.conf
start on hithere
script
    echo "Hi there, here I am!" > /tmp/myjob.out
    date >> /tmp/myjob.out
end script
```

The **myjob** file shows another way of executing commands: It includes two command lines between the **script** and **end script** keywords. These keywords always cause **init** to execute **/bin/sh**. The commands write a message and the date to the **/tmp/myjob.out** file. You can use the initctl **emit** command to trigger the job:

initctl **emit**
```
# initctl emit hithere

$ cat /tmp/myjob.out
Hi there, here I am!
Wed Jan 12 16:21:36 PST 2011

$ status myjob
myjob stop/waiting
```

initctl **start** and **stop**   In the preceding example, cat shows the output that **myjob** generates and initctl displays the status of the job. You can run the same job by giving the command **initctl start myjob** (or just **start myjob**). The initctl **start** command is useful when you want to run a job without triggering an event. For example, you can use the command **initctl start mudat** to run the **mudat** job from the previous example without triggering the **runlevel** event.

Events

The **upstart** package defines many events. The following command lists events and brief descriptions of each. See the corresponding man page for more information on each event.

```
$ apropos event | grep signalling
control-alt-delete (7) - event signalling console press of Control-Alt-Delete
keyboard-request (7) - event signalling console press of Alt-UpArrow
power-status-changed (7) - event signalling change of power status
runlevel (7)            - event signalling change of system runlevel
started (7)             - event signalling that a job is running
starting (7)            - event signalling that a job is starting
startup (7)             - event signalling system startup
stopped (7)             - event signalling that a job has stopped
stopping (7)            - event signalling that a job is stopping
```

apropos   The apropos utility, which is a link to whatis, is discussed on page 127.

optional

Specifying events with arguments   The telinit (page 449) and shutdown (page 453) utilities emit **runlevel** events that include arguments. For example, **shutdown** emits **runlevel 0**, and **telinit 2** emits **runlevel 2**. You can match these events within a job definition using the following syntax:

> *start|stop on **event** [arg [arg...]]*

where *event* is an event such as **runlevel** and *arg* is one or more arguments. To stop a job when the system enters runlevel 2 from runlevel 1, specify **stop on runlevel 2 1**. You can also specify **[235]** to match 2, 3, and 5 or **[!2]** to match any value except 2.

Event arguments   Although Upstart ignores additional arguments in an event, additional arguments in an event name within a job definition file must exist in the event. For example, **runlevel** (no argument) in a job definition file matches all **runlevel** events (regardless of arguments), whereas **runlevel S arg1 arg2** does not match any **runlevel** event because the **runlevel** event takes two arguments (the runlevel the system is entering and the previous runlevel).

Job Definition Files in /etc/init

As RHEL continues its transition from SysVinit to Upstart **init**, more jobs will be defined in the **/etc/init** directory. This section describes some of the jobs the **upstart** package puts in this directory.

rc task and the
runlevel event
A **runlevel** event [runlevel(7) man page] signals a change in runlevel and is emitted by telinit (page 449) and shutdown (page 453). This event sets the environment variable RUNLEVEL to the value of the new runlevel.

The **/etc/init/rc.conf** job definition file defines the **rc** task. This task monitors the **runlevel** event. The keyword **task** specifies this job as a task and not a service. Because it is a task, it blocks the call that emitted the **runlevel** event until the **rc** task has finished running.

The **exec** stanza in **rc.conf** calls the **/etc/rc.d/rc** script (not the **rc** task) with an argument of RUNLEVEL. The **rc** script calls the links in the **/etc/rc.d/rc_n_.d** directory, where _n_ is equal to RUNLEVEL (page 442). Thus the **rc** task, when called with RUNLEVEL set to 2, runs the init scripts that the links in the **/etc/rc.d/rc2.d** directory point to.

The **rc** task runs the **rc** script when the system enters a runlevel from 0 through 6 (**start on runlevel [0123456]**). Normally this task terminates when it finishes executing the **rc** script.

The stop stanza (**stop on runlevel [!$RUNLEVEL]**) takes care of the case wherein a second **runlevel** event attempts to start while an **rc** task is running the **rc** script. In this case, the value of RUNLEVEL is not equal to the value of RUNLEVEL that the **rc** task was called with and the **rc** task stops.

```
$ cat /etc/init/rc.conf# rc - System V runlevel compatibility
#
# This task runs the old sysv-rc runlevel scripts.  It
# is usually started by the telinit compatibility wrapper.

start on runlevel [0123456]

stop on runlevel [!$RUNLEVEL]

task

export RUNLEVEL
console output
exec /etc/rc.d/rc $RUNLEVEL
```

tty services
Following is the job definition file for the service that monitors the mingetty processes (page 451). The **start-ttys.conf** job starts these processes when the system enters multiuser mode.

```
$ cat /etc/init/tty.conf
# tty - getty
#
# This service maintains a getty on the specified device.

stop on runlevel [016]

respawn
instance $TTY
exec /sbin/mingetty $TTY
```

The event in the **stop on** stanza is named **runlevel**. This stanza stops the **tty** services when a **runlevel** event is emitted with an argument of 0, 1, or 6—that is, when the system enters single-user mode, is shut down, or is rebooted.

The **respawn** keyword tells **init** to restart the **tty** service if it terminates. The **exec** stanza runs a mingetty process. In the next example, the initctl utility reports that the **tty** service on device **/dev/tty2** has started and is running as process 1506; ps reports on the process:

```
$ status tty TTY=/dev/tty2
tty (/dev/tty2) start/running, process 1506

$ ps -ef | grep 1506
root      1506     1  0 15:43 tty2     00:00:00 /sbin/mingetty /dev/tty2
```

control-alt-delete task See page 454 for a discussion of the **control-alt-delete** task, which you can use to bring the system down.

Do not set the system to boot to runlevel 0 or 6

caution Never set the system to boot to runlevel 0 or 6, as it will not come up properly. To boot to multiuser graphical mode (runlevel 5), edit the **inittab** file as shown in the adjacent example, replacing the **1** with a **5**.

rcS task and inittab Under SysVinit, the **initdefault** entry in the **/etc/inittab** file tells **init** which runlevel (page 448) to bring the system to when it comes up. Fedora/RHEL includes an **inittab** file for compatibility with the old **init** daemon. Fedora ignores this file. By default under RHEL this file causes the system to boot to runlevel 5 (multiuser with a graphical login). If this file is not present, the Upstart **init** daemon (using the **rcS** task) boots the system to runlevel 3 (multiuser textual mode [no X11]). If you want the system to boot to a different runlevel, edit the **inittab** file. The following entry in the **inittab** file causes the system to boot to runlevel 1 (single user):

```
$ cat /etc/inittab
...
id:1:initdefault:
```

SysVinit (rc) Scripts: Start and Stop System Services (Fedora/RHEL)

rc scripts The SysVinit daemon is driven by init (initialization scripts). These scripts, also called rc (run command) scripts, are shell scripts located in the **/etc/rc.d/init.d** directory. A symbolic link at **/etc/init.d** points to **/etc/rc.d/init.d**. The scripts are run via symbolic links in the **/etc/rc.d/rc*n*.d** directories, where *n* is the runlevel the system is entering.

Under a system (such as RHEL) that runs SysVinit natively, the first script **init** runs is **/etc/rc.d/rc.sysinit**, which performs basic system configuration, including setting the system clock, hostname, and keyboard mapping; setting up swap partitions; checking the filesystems for errors; and turning on quota management (page 634).

Next the **/etc/rc.d/rc** init script runs the scripts for the services that need to be started when you first bring the system up and that need to be started or stopped when the system goes from single-user to multiuser mode and back down again.

Most of the files in the /etc/rc.d/rc*n*.d and /etc/rc.d/init.d directories will go away

tip Fedora: Under systemd, Fedora uses targets with the names of runlevels to aid migration and provide compatibility with software for other distributions (see Table 11-1 on page 448). This section explains how init scripts work to control system services. Over the next few distributions, most of the file in the **/etc/rc.d/rc*n*.d** and **/etc/rc.d/init.d** directories will go away as they are replaced by systemd service files.

RHEL: As explained on page 437, RHEL emulates runlevels using Upstart to aid migration and provide compatibility with software for other distributions. This section explains how init scripts work with (emulated) runlevels to control system services. Many of the scripts in the **/etc/rc.d/rc*n*.d** and **/etc/rc.d/init.d** directories described in this section suggest you use the corresponding initctl or service commands in place of the script because the links in these directories have been replaced by job definition files in **/etc/init** (page 437).

The **/etc/rc.d/rc*n*.d** directories contain scripts whose names begin with **K** (**K10cups**, **K25sshd, K83bluetooth,** and so on) and scripts whose names begin with **S** (**S90crond, S12rsyslog, S80sendmail,** and so on). When entering a new runlevel, each **K** (kill) script is executed with an argument of **stop**, and then each **S** (start) script is executed with an argument of **start**. Each of the **K** files is run in numerical order. The **S** files are run in similar fashion. This arrangement allows the person who sets up these files to control which services are stopped and which are started, and in what order, whenever the system enters a given runlevel. Using scripts with **start** and **stop** arguments promotes flexibility because it allows one script to both start and kill a process, depending on which argument it is called with.

To customize system initialization, you can add shell scripts to the **/etc/rc.d/init.d** directory and place links to these files in the **/etc/rc.d/rc*n*.d** directories (although in practice it is best to use chkconfig [page 446] or system-config-services [page 445] to create the links).

The **cups** script controls the printer daemon. The following example shows several links to the **cups** init script. These links are called to run the **cups** init script to start or stop the **cupsd** printer daemon at various runlevels:

```
$ ls -l /etc/rc.d/rc?.d/*cups*
lrwxrwxrwx. 1 root root 14 12-10 15:57 /etc/rc.d/rc0.d/K10cups -> ../init.d/cups
lrwxrwxrwx. 1 root root 14 12-10 15:57 /etc/rc.d/rc1.d/K10cups -> ../init.d/cups
lrwxrwxrwx. 1 root root 14 12-10 15:57 /etc/rc.d/rc2.d/S25cups -> ../init.d/cups
lrwxrwxrwx. 1 root root 14 12-10 15:57 /etc/rc.d/rc3.d/S25cups -> ../init.d/cups
lrwxrwxrwx. 1 root root 14 12-10 15:57 /etc/rc.d/rc4.d/S25cups -> ../init.d/cups
lrwxrwxrwx. 1 root root 14 12-10 15:57 /etc/rc.d/rc5.d/S25cups -> ../init.d/cups
lrwxrwxrwx. 1 root root 14 12-10 15:57 /etc/rc.d/rc6.d/K10cups -> ../init.d/cups
```

Each link in **/etc/rc.d/rc*n*.d** points to a file in **/etc/rc.d/init.d**. For example, the file **/etc/rc.d/rc1.d/K10cups** is a link to the file named **cups** in **/etc/rc.d/init.d**. (The numbers in the filenames of the links in the **/etc/rc.d/rc*n*.d** directories might change from one release to the next, but the scripts in **/etc/rc.d/init.d** always have the same names.) The names of files in the **init.d** directory are functional. Thus, when you want to turn NFS services on or off, you use the **nfs** script. Similarly, when you want to turn basic network services on or off, you run the **network** script. Each script takes an argument of **stop** or **start**, depending on what you want to do. Some scripts also take other arguments, such as **restart, reload,** and **status**. Most scripts, when run without an argument, display a usage message indicating which arguments they accept:

```
$ /etc/rc.d/init.d/sshd
Usage: /etc/rc.d/init.d/sshd {start|stop|restart|reload|force-reload|condrestart|try-restart|status}
```

Following are three examples of calls to init scripts. You might find it easier to use **service** (discussed next) in place of the pathnames in these commands:

```
# /etc/rc.d/init.d/nfs stop
# /etc/rc.d/init.d/network start
# /etc/rc.d/init.d/network restart
```

The first example stops all NFS server processes (processes related to serving filesystems over the network). The second example starts all processes related to basic network services. The third example stops and then restarts these same processes.

Use chkconfig to maintain the links in the /etc/rc.d/rc*n*.d directory hierarchy

tip   Refer to page 446 for information about using chkconfig to maintain the symbolic links in the **/etc/rc.d/rc*n*.d** directory hierarchy.

/etc/rc.d/rc.local   The **/etc/rc.d/rc.local** file is executed after the other init scripts when the system boots. Put commands that customize the system in **rc.local**. Although you can add any commands you like to **rc.local**, it is best to run them in the background; that way, if they hang, they will not stop the boot process.

service: CONFIGURES SERVICES I

The **service** utility can report on or change the status of any of the jobs in **/etc/init** (page 438) and any of the system services in **/etc/rc.d/init.d** (page 442). In place of the commands described at the end of the previous section, you can give the following commands from any directory:

```
# service nfs stop
# service network start
# service network restart
```

When you call **service** with the name of a job or service but no other argument, it typically displays a usage message indicating which arguments the job or service accepts:

```
$ service cups
Usage: cups {start|stop|restart|restartlog|condrestart|try-restart|reload|force-reload|status}
```

The command **service --status-all** displays the status of all system services controlled by SysVinit. It does not report accurately on services controlled natively by systemd. The next section explores yet another way to configure system services.

Figure 11-1   The Service Configuration window (RHEL)

system-config-services: CONFIGURES SERVICES II

The system-config-services utility (**system-config-services** package) displays the Service Configuration window (Figure 11-1). This utility is most useful under RHEL and has two functions: It turns system services on and off immediately, and it controls which services are stopped and started when the system enters and leaves runlevels 2–5 (but not services controlled by systemd). The system-config-services utility works with many of the services listed in **/etc/rc.d/init.d** as well as with those controlled by **xinetd** (page 481) and listed in **/etc/xinetd.d** (or specified in **/etc/xinetd.conf**). To run system-config-services, enter **system-config-services** from a command line in a graphical environment or select **Main menu: Applications⇨Other⇨Services** (Fedora; if **Applications** is not visible see "Configuring Fallback Mode" on page 92) or **Main menu: System⇨Administration⇨Services** (RHEL).

The left side of the RHEL Service Configuration window displays a scrollable list of services. At the left end of each line is a red or green circle or a small bank of three switches. A green circle indicates the service is enabled; a red circle indicates it is disabled. With the line highlighted, the same information is repeated on the right side of the window. If a bank of switches appears in place of the circle, the right side of the window displays information about which runlevels the highlighted service is enabled in.

To the right of the circle or switches is a plug that is either plugged in or unplugged to indicate the highlighted service is running or not running, respectively. Additionally, the right side of the window displays a description of the service.

Scroll to and highlight the service you want to work with. Click the buttons on the tool bar to enable, disable, customize, start, stop, or restart (stop and then start) the highlighted service.

The start, stop, and restart buttons turn the service on or off immediately; the change does not affect whether the service will run the next time you boot the system, enter another runlevel, or re-enter the current runlevel. These changes are equivalent to those you would make with the service utility (page 444).

When you click **Customize**, system-config-services displays the Customize Runlevels window. Put ticks in the check boxes labeled with the runlevels you want the service enabled in and then click **OK**. Now when the system enters one of the runlevels marked with a tick, it will turn the service on. The current state of the service is not changed.

These changes affect all runlevels and will remain in effect through changes in runlevels and reboots unless you change them again. They are equivalent to the changes you would make with the chkconfig utility (next).

SERVICES THAT DEPEND ON xinetd

Some services, such as **rsync**, depend on the **xinetd** daemon (page 481) being installed and running. (Except that the **rsync** client uses **sshd** by default and thus does not require **xinetd**.) As with other services, highlight the service to read a description of it. Click the Enable or Disable button on the toolbar to turn the service on or off. This action changes the **yes/no** parameter of the **disable** line discussed on page 483. Restart **xinetd** by scrolling to the **xinetd** service (it appears only if it is installed) and clicking **Restart**.

chkconfig: CONFIGURES SERVICES III

The chkconfig character-based utility duplicates much of what system-config-services does: It makes it easier for a system administrator to maintain the **/etc/rc***n***.d** directory hierarchy. This utility can add, remove, list startup information, and check the state of system services. It changes the configuration only—it does not change the current state of any service. Without any arguments, chkconfig displays a list of all services:

```
$ chkconfig
abrt-ccpp      0:off   1:off   2:off   3:on    4:off   5:on    6:off
auditd         0:off   1:off   2:on    3:on    4:on    5:on    6:off
cgconfig       0:off   1:off   2:off   3:off   4:off   5:off   6:off
cgred          0:off   1:off   2:off   3:off   4:off   5:off   6:off
cpuspeed       0:off   1:on    2:on    3:on    4:on    5:on    6:off
cups           0:off   1:off   2:on    3:on    4:on    5:on    6:off
...
```

All services that run their own daemons are listed, one to a line, followed by their configured state for each runlevel. You can check how a specific daemon is configured by specifying the **--list** option followed by the name of the daemon:

```
$ chkconfig --list cups
```

Note: This output shows SysV services only and does not include native
      systemd services. SysV configuration data might be overridden by
      native systemd configuration.

```
cups            0:off   1:off   2:on    3:on    4:on    5:on    6:off
```

Under Fedora, the **--list** option and not specifying an option do not accurately
report on services natively controlled by systemd.

In the next example, chkconfig configures the **/etc/rc.d** directory hierarchy so **cups**
will be off in runlevels equivalent to **2, 3, 4,** and **5** and then confirms the change. To
make changes using chkconfig, you must work with **root** privileges:

```
# chkconfig --level 2345 cups off
# chkconfig --list cups
...
cups            0:off   1:off   2:off   3:off   4:off   5:off   6:off
```

For convenience, you can omit the **--level 2345** option. When you specify an init
script and **on** or **off**, chkconfig defaults to the runlevel equivalents of **2, 3, 4,** and **5.**
The following command is equivalent to the first of the preceding commands:

```
# chkconfig cups off
```

Both ps and service confirm that even though chkconfig set it up so that **cups** would
be off in all runlevels, this daemon is still running; the chkconfig utility did not shut
down **cups**:

```
$ ps -ef | grep cups
root       836     1  0 17:44 ?        00:00:00 cupsd -C /etc/cups/cupsd.conf

$ service cups status
cups.service - LSB: The CUPS scheduler
          Loaded: loaded (/etc/rc.d/init.d/cups)
          Active: active (running) since Mon, 02 May 2011 15:39:41 -0700; 2h 43min ago
        Main PID: 836 (cupsd)
          CGroup: name=systemd:/system/cups.service
                  + 836 cupsd -C /etc/cups/cupsd.conf
```

With the preceding changes, when you reboot the system, **cups** will not start. You
can stop it without rebooting using service:

```
# service cups stop
Stopping cups (via systemctl):                          [  OK  ]

# service cups status
...
                Active: inactive (dead)
...
```

The chkconfig utility works with **xinetd**-based programs such as swat by changing
the **disable = yes** to **disable = no** in program's file in **/etc/xinetd.d.** See page 482 for
an example.

SYSTEM OPERATION

This section covers the basics of how the system functions and can help you make intelligent decisions as a system administrator. It does not examine every possible aspect of system administration in the depth necessary to enable you to set up or modify all system functions. Instead, it provides a guide to bringing a system up and keeping it running on a day-to-day basis.

RUNLEVELS

As described on page 428, Fedora has introduced systemd, which has done away with traditional runlevels although vestiges remain. As a transitional tool, RHEL has replaced runlevels with a structure that runs under Upstart and emulates runlevels (page 437). Table 11-1 lists the runlevels (target units) as they exist under Upstart and systemd.

Table 11-1   Runlevels (target units)

SysVinit runlevel	systemd runlevel (target unit)	Name/function
0	runlevel0.target, poweroff.target	Shuts down the system
1	runlevel1.target, rescue.target	Brings the system to single-user/rescue mode
2, 3, 4	runlevel2.target, runlevel3.target, runlevel4.target, multi-user.target	Brings the system to multiuser textual mode
5	runlevel5.target, graphical.target	Brings the system to multiuser graphical mode
6	runlevel6.target, reboot.target	Reboots the system
	emergency.target	Emergency shell

Default (persistent) runlevel By default, Fedora systems boot to multiuser graphical mode (**graphical.target**), and RHEL systems boot to multiuser mode (runlevel 5). See "Setting the Persistent Runlevel" on page 432 (Fedora) or "**rcS** task and **inittab**" on page 442 (RHEL) for instructions explaining how to change this default.

runlevel The runlevel utility [runlevel(8) man page; do not confuse it with the Upstart **runlevel** event described on page 441] displays the previous and current runlevels. This utility is a transitional tool; it provides compatibility with SysVinit. In the following example, the **N** indicates the system does not know which was the previous runlevel, and the **5** indicates the system is in multiuser graphical mode.

```
$ runlevel
N 5
```

who The who utility with the **–r** option also displays the current runlevel:

```
$ who -r
                    run-level 5   2011-05-02 15:28
```

telinit The telinit utility (telinit man page) allows a user working with **root** privileges to bring the system down, reboot the system, or change between runlevels. The telinit utility is a transitional tool; it provides compatibility with SysVinit. Under Fedora this utility calls systemctl; under RHEL it emits a **runlevel** event (page 441) based on its argument. The format of a telinit command is

> telinit *runlevel*

where *runlevel* is one of the runlevels described in Table 11-1.

single-user/rescue mode and the **root** password — When the system enters the single-user/rescue mode, if the **root** account is unlocked (page 425) as it is by default, **init** displays the **root** prompt without requesting a password. When the system enters multiuser mode, it displays a graphical login screen.

Booting the System

Booting a system is the process of reading the Linux *kernel* (page 1172) into system memory and starting it running. Refer to "GRUB: The Linux Boot Loader" on page 595 for more information on the initial steps of bringing a system up.

List the kernel boot messages

tip To save a list of kernel boot messages, run dmesg immediately after booting the system and logging in:

```
$ dmesg > dmesg.boot
```

This command saves the kernel messages in a file named **dmesg.boot**. This list can be educational; it can also be useful when you are having a problem with the boot process. For more information see page 597.

init daemon As the last step of the boot procedure, Linux starts the **init** daemon (page 436) as PID number 1. The **init** daemon is the first genuine process to run after booting and is the parent of all system processes. (Which is why when you kill process 1 while you are working with **root** privileges, the system dies.)

Reinstalling the MBR — If the master boot record (MBR) is overwritten, the system will not boot; you need to rewrite the MBR. See page 456 for instructions.

Single-User Mode

When the system is in single-user mode, only the system console is enabled. You can run programs from the console in single-user mode just as you would from any terminal in multiuser mode with two differences: You cannot run graphical programs (because you are working in textual mode) and few of the system daemons are running.

With the system in single-user/rescue mode, you can perform system maintenance that requires filesystems to be unmounted or that requires just a quiet system—no one except you using it, so no user programs interfere with disk maintenance and

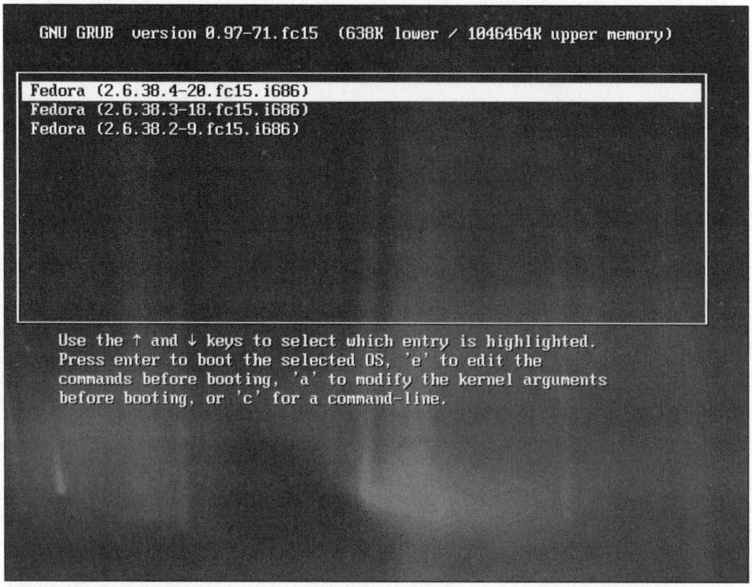

Figure 11-2 The GRUB menu

backup programs. The classical UNIX term for this state is *quiescent*. You can often boot to single-user mode when the system will not boot normally, allowing you to change or replace configuration files, check and repair partitions using fsck (page 525), rewrite boot information (page 456), and more.

BOOTING THE SYSTEM TO SINGLE-USER/RESCUE MODE

This section explains how to bring a system up to single-user/rescue mode by booting from the hard disk and giving GRUB the appropriate instructions.

Displaying the GRUB menu
The first step in bringing a system up in single-user mode from the hard disk is to display the GRUB menu (Figure 11-2). Boot the system normally (turn on the power or reboot the system). The GRUB menu will be hidden or displayed. Either way, if you hold down any key that does not move the cursor, such as the SHIFT key, as the system is booting, GRUB displays its menu and stops booting the system. As Fedora/RHEL is initially configured, you must be holding the key down as the system starts to boot.

Single-user/rescue mode versus rescuing an installed system

tip
When you bring a system up in single-user/rescue mode, Fedora/RHEL boots from the hard disk and displays a bash prompt. This section explains how to bring a system up in single-user/rescue mode.

When you bring a system up to rescue an installed system, you boot Fedora/RHEL from the first installation CD, the Net Boot CD, or the install DVD and select **Rescue installed system** from the Welcome menu as explained on page 457.

Selecting single-user/rescue mode
Unless you have modified the **/boot/grub/grub.conf** file (page 596), the GRUB menu starts with a few lines similar to the following:

```
Fedora (2.6.38.2-20.fc15.i686)
Fedora (2.6.38-3-18.fc15.i686)
```

Typically the first line is highlighted as shown in Figure 11-2.

Editing the
GRUB menu

With the GRUB menu displayed, follow these instructions to bring the system up in single-user/rescue mode:

1. Highlight the kernel you want to boot—GRUB highlights the default kernel when it displays its menu.

2. Press **a** to append to the GRUB boot command line (from **/boot/grub/grub.conf**) for the kernel you selected.

With the cursor positioned at the right end of the line, enter SPACE **single** (following **quiet** in the default setup) and press RETURN to boot the system using the modified kernel line. After a few moments, the system displays a bash root prompt (#).

GOING TO GRAPHICAL MULTIUSER MODE

Graphical multiuser mode (runlevel 5) is the default state for a Fedora/RHEL system. In this mode all appropriate filesystems are mounted, and users can log in from all connected terminals, dial-up lines, and network connections. All support services and daemons are enabled and running. With the system in multiuser mode, Fedora/RHEL displays a graphical login screen on the console.

If you booted to single-user mode to fix something, give a **reboot** command, which reboots the system starting with the BIOS. If the system entered single-user mode automatically to allow you to repair the filesystem, you can give an **exit** command which causes the system to continue booting: **init** brings the system to the default runlevel—usually multiuser graphical mode. Alternatively, you can give the following command while working with **root** privileges to bring the system to multiuser graphical mode:

```
# systemctl isolate graphical.target      (Fedora)

# telinit 5                               (RHEL)
```

The telinit (page 449) and systemctl (page 432) utilities tell **init** which runlevel to change to.

LOGGING IN

Textual login: **init**,
getty, and login

With a textual login, the system uses **init**, mingetty, and login to allow a user to log in; login uses PAM modules (page 463) to authenticate a user. When you enter your username, mingetty establishes the characteristics of the terminal. It then overlays itself with a login process and passes to the login process whatever you entered in response to the **login:** prompt. One authentication technique uses PAM: The login process consults the **/etc/passwd** file to see whether any username there matches the username you entered. Next, PAM examines the **/etc/shadow** file to see whether a password is associated with the username. If it is, login prompts you for a password; if not, it continues without requiring a password. When your username requires a password, login verifies the password you enter by checking the **/etc/shadow** file again. If either your username or your password is not correct, login displays **Login incorrect**, pauses, and prompts you to log in again.

By default, all passwords in the **/etc/shadow** file are hashed using *MD5* (page 1175). When you log in, the login process hashes the password you type at the prompt and compares it to the hashed password in **/etc/shadow**. If the two passwords match, you are authenticated. See page 630 for more information on selecting a secure password.

With NIS or LDAP, login compares the username and password with the information in the appropriate naming service instead of (or in addition to) the **passwd** and **shadow** files. If the system is configured to use both methods (**/etc/passwd** and NIS/LDAP), it checks the **/etc/nsswitch.conf** file (page 494) to see in which order it should consult them.

Graphical login   With a graphical login, the **init** daemon runs the **prefdm** (preferred display manager; **/lib/systemd/system/prefdm.service** service [Fedora] or **/etc/init/prefdm.conf** task [RHEL]), which executes the **/etc/X11/prefdm** script to determine which display manager to start. If the **/etc/sysconfig/desktop** file exists, the script obtains the name of the display manager from this file. By default it spawns gdm (the GNOME display manager) on the first free virtual terminal, providing features similar to those offered by mingetty and login. The gdm utility starts an X server and presents a login window. The gdm display manager then uses PAM to authenticate the user and runs the scripts in the **/etc/gdm/PreSession** directory. These scripts launch the user's session. The GNOME desktop environment can be set up to store the state of the last saved session and restore it when the user logs in again.

PAM   PAM (page 463)—the Pluggable Authentication Module facility—gives you greater control over user logins than the **/etc/passwd** and **/etc/shadow** files do. Using PAM, you can specify multiple levels of authentication, mutually exclusive authentication methods, or parallel methods, each of which is by itself sufficient to grant access to the system. For example, you can have different authentication methods for console logins and for ssh logins. Similarly, you can require modem users to authenticate themselves using two or more methods (such as a smartcard or badge reader and a password). PAM modules also provide security technology vendors with a convenient way to interface their hardware or software products with a system.

Initializing the session   When both the username and the password are correct, login or the scripts in **PreSession** consult the appropriate services to initialize the user and group IDs, establish the user's home directory, and determine which shell or desktop manager the user works with.

The login utility and **PreSession** scripts assign values to variables and look in the **/etc/group** file (page 506) to identify the groups the user belongs to. When login has finished its work, it overlays itself with the login shell, which inherits the variables set by login. In a graphical environment, the **PreSession** scripts start the desktop manager.

During a textual login, the login shell assigns values to additional shell variables and executes the commands in the system startup files **/etc/profile** and **/etc/bashrc**.

Some systems have other system startup files as well. Although the actions performed by these scripts are system-dependent, they typically display the contents of the /etc/motd (message of the day) and /etc/issue files, let you know if you have email, and set umask (page 473), the file-creation mask.

Along with executing the system startup commands, the shell executes the commands from the personal startup files in the user's home directory. These scripts are described on page 282. Because the shell executes some of the personal startup files *after* the system startup files, a sophisticated user can override any variables or conventions that were established by the system. A new user, by contrast, can remain uninvolved in these matters.

LOGGING OUT

With a shell prompt displayed in a textual environment, you can either execute a program or exit from the shell. If you exit from the shell, the process running the shell dies, and the parent process wakes up. When the shell is a child of another shell, the parent shell wakes up and displays a prompt. Exiting from a login shell causes the operating system to send **init** a signal that one of its children has died. Upon receiving this signal, **init** takes appropriate action. In the case of a process controlling a line for a terminal, **init** calls the appropriate tty service, which then respawns mingetty so another user can log in.

When you exit from a GUI, the GNOME display manager, gdm, initiates a new login display.

BRINGING THE SYSTEM DOWN

shutdown   The reboot and shutdown utilities perform the tasks needed to bring the system down safely. These utilities can restart the system, prepare the system to be turned off, and, on most hardware, power down the system. The halt and poweroff utilities are links to reboot. When you run halt, poweroff, or reboot while working with **root** privileges, the system executes systemctl (Fedora) or **/lib/upstart/reboot** (RHEL). Without **root** privileges, the links from these commands go through consolehelper [page 425].)

You must tell shutdown when you want to bring the system down. This time can be expressed as an absolute time of day, as in 19:15, which causes the shutdown to occur at 7:15 PM. Alternatively, you can give this time as the number of minutes from the present time, as in **+15**, which means 15 minutes from now. To bring the system down immediately (recommended for emergency shutdowns only or when you are the only user logged in), you can give the argument +0 or its synonym, **now**. When the shutdown time exceeds five minutes, all nonroot logins are disabled for the last five minutes before shutdown.

Calling shutdown with the –r option causes the system to reboot (same as reboot, except reboot implies **now**). Calling shutdown with the –h option forces the system to halt (same as halt, except halt implies **now**). A message appears once the system has been safely halted: **System halted**. Because most ATX systems power off automatically after shutdown, you are unlikely to see this message.

Do not turn the power off before bringing the system down

caution   Do not turn the power off on a Linux system without first bringing it down as described in this section. To speed up disk access, Linux keeps buffers in memory that it writes to disk periodically or when system use is momentarily low. When you turn off or reset the computer without writing the contents of these buffers to the disk, you lose information in the buffers. Running the **shutdown** utility forces these buffers to be written to disk. You can force the buffers to be written at any time by issuing a **sync** command. However, **sync** does not unmount filesystems, nor does it bring the system down. Also, turning off or resetting a system without bringing it down properly can destroy filesystems on IDE and SATA hard disks.

Because Linux is a multiuser system, **shutdown** warns all users before taking action. This warning gives users a chance to prepare for the shutdown, perhaps by writing out editor files or exiting from applications. You can replace the default shutdown message with one of your own by following the time specification on the command line with a message:

```
# shutdown -h 09:30 Going down 9:30 to install disk, up by 10am.
```

CONTROL-ALT-DEL: REBOOTS THE SYSTEM

In a textual environment, pressing the CONTROL-ALT-DEL keys simultaneously (also referred to as the *three-finger salute* or the *Vulcan death grip*) on the console causes **systemctl** to reboot the system (Fedora) or causes the kernel to trigger a **control-alt-delete** task (page 442) that causes **init** to run the commands in **/etc/init/control-alt-delete.conf** (RHEL).

In a graphical environment, the X Window System traps this key set, but the window manager does not pass it to the kernel. As a result, CONTROL-ALT-DEL does nothing in a graphical environment.

GOING TO SINGLE-USER MODE

The following steps describe a method of manually bringing the system down to single-user mode. In some cases it might be easier to simply reboot the system and bring it up in single-user mode; see page 450. Before starting, make sure you give other users enough warning before switching to single-user mode; otherwise, they might lose the data they are working on. Because going from multiuser to single-user mode can affect other users, you must work with **root** privileges to perform all these tasks.

1. Give the command **touch /etc/nologin** to prevent users from logging on as you bring the system down. See the **nologin** man page for more information.

2. Use **wall** (page 626) to warn everyone who is using the system to log out.

3. If you are sharing files via NFS, use **exportfs –ua** to disable network access to the shared filesystems. (Use **exportfs** without an argument to see which filesystems are being shared.)

4. Confirm no critical processes are running in the background (e.g., an unattended compile).

5. Give the command **systemctl isolate rescue.target** (Fedora; page 432) or **telinit 1** (RHEL; page 449) to bring the system down to single-user mode. The system displays messages about the services it is shutting down, followed by a bash **root** shell prompt (#). In single-user mode, the system kills many system services and then brings the system to runlevel S. The systemctl or runlevel utilities can confirm the current runlevel.

```
# systemctl isolate rescue.target
...
Welcome to rescue mode. Use "systemctl default" or ^D to activate default mode.
# systemctl list-units --type=target
...
rescue.target             loaded active active     Rescue Mode
...
```

6. Use **umount –a** to unmount all mounted devices that are not in use. Use **mount** without an argument to make sure no devices other than root (/) are mounted before continuing. Alternatively, you can perform maintenance tasks that do not require devices to be unmounted.

TURNING THE POWER OFF

Once the system is in single-user mode, give the command **systemctl halt** (Fedora), **telinit 0** (page 449;RHEL), **halt**, or **reboot –p** to bring the system down. If the system does not power off by itself, turn the power off when prompted to do so or when the system starts rebooting.

CRASH

A *crash* occurs when the system stops suddenly or fails unexpectedly. A crash might result from software or hardware problems or from a loss of power. As a running system loses power, it might behave in erratic or unpredictable ways. In a fraction of a second, some components are supplied with enough voltage; others are not. Buffers are not flushed, corrupt data might be written to hard disks, and so on. IDE and SATA drives do not behave as predictably as SCSI drives under these circumstances. After a crash, you must bring the operating system up carefully to minimize possible damage to the filesystems. On many occasions, little or no damage will have occurred.

REPAIRING A FILESYSTEM

Although the filesystems are checked automatically during the boot process if needed, you will have to check them manually if a problem cannot be repaired automatically.

By default, when fsck cannot repair a filesystem automatically at boot time, Linux enters single-user mode so you can run fsck manually. If necessary, you can explicitly boot the system to single-user mode (page 450). *Do not* mount any devices other than root, which Linux mounts automatically.

Back up a badly damaged filesystem *before* running fsck on it

caution   When a filesystem is badly broken, fsck sometimes makes the situation worse while trying to repair it. In these cases, it might be possible to recover *more* data by copying the readable data from the broken filesystem before attempting to repair it. When a damaged filesystem holds important data, use dd (dd man page) to make a full binary backup *before* attempting to repair it using fsck.

With the system in single-user mode, give a **mount** command to make sure none of the local filesystems you want to check are mounted. Then run fsck (page 525) on these filesystems, repairing them as needed. Make note of any ordinary files or directories that you repair (and can identify), and inform their owners that these files might not be complete or correct. Look in the **lost+found** directory (page 502) *in each filesystem* for missing files. After successfully running fsck, if the system entered single-user mode automatically, type **exit** to exit from the single-user shell and resume booting the system; otherwise, give a **reboot** command.

If files are not correct or are missing altogether, you might have to re-create them from a backup copy of the filesystem. For more information refer to "Backing Up Files" on page 605.

REINSTALLING THE MBR

To reinstall the MBR, as is necessary when it gets overwritten by a Windows installation, boot the system from the install DVD and select **Rescue installed system** (next page). Then mount the system image and run grub-install (page 597) on the appropriate device:

```
# chroot /mnt/sysimage
# grub-install /dev/sda
```

WHEN THE SYSTEM DOES NOT BOOT

When a system will not boot from the hard disk, boot the system to rescue installed system (next) or single-user/rescue mode (page 450). If the system comes up, run fsck (page 525) on the root filesystem on the hard disk and try booting from the hard disk again. If the system still does not boot, you might have to reinstall the master boot record (previous).

When all else fails, go through the install procedure and perform an "upgrade" to the current version of Linux. Fedora/RHEL systems can perform a nondestructive upgrade and can fix quite a bit of damage in the process.

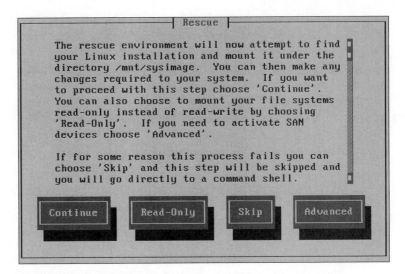

Figure 11-3   The Rescue screen

RESCUE INSTALLED SYSTEM

When you rescue an installed system you can fix a system that does not boot normally: You can change or replace configuration files, check and repair partitions using fsck (page 492), rewrite boot information, and more. To rescue an installed system, boot the system from the Net Boot CD or the install DVD and select **Rescue installed system** from the Welcome menu (Figure 3-5, page 57). When the system comes up it asks you to specify the language and keyboard you want to use and then displays the Rescue screen (Figure 11-3).

The Rescue screen first asks if you want to set up the network interface. This interface is required if you want to copy files from other systems on the LAN or download files from the Internet. When you choose to set up the network interface, you need to decide whether to have DHCP automatically configure the network connection or to manually supply the IP address and network mask of the interface, as well as the IP addresses of the gateway and DNS server(s).

If the rescue setup finds an existing Linux installation, you can choose to mount it under **/mnt/sysimage**, optionally in readonly mode. With the existing installation mounted, once the system displays a shell prompt (similar to **bash-4.2#**), you can give the command **chroot /mnt/sysimage** to access the existing installation as it would be if you had booted normally, with the existing installation's root directory available as **/** (root). See page 485 for more information on chroot. If you choose not to mount the existing installation, you are running a rescue system with standard tools mounted in standard locations (**/bin**, **/usr/bin**, and so on). You can fix or mount partitions from the local installation. When you exit from the rescue shell, the system reboots. Remove the CD or DVD if you want to boot from the hard drive.

SECURING A SYSTEM

This section describes several ways to make a client or server system more secure. It describes how to avoid a Trojan horse, the dangers of files with setuid permissions, and how to configure SELinux and PAM. See also "Securing a Server" on page 484.

AVOIDING A TROJAN HORSE

A *Trojan horse* is a program, usually embedded in or masquerading as another program. The program does something destructive and/or disruptive to a system while appearing to be benign. Because of the way it is disguised, a user typically runs it without realizing what he is doing. As an example, you could store the following script in an executable file named mkfs:

```
while true
    do
    echo 'Good Morning Mr. Jones. How are you? Ha Ha Ha.' > /dev/console
    done
```

If you are working with **root** privileges when you run this command, it will continuously write a message to the console. If the programmer were malicious, it could do something worse. The only thing missing in this plot is access permissions.

A malicious user could implement this Trojan horse by changing **root**'s **PATH** variable to include a publicly writable directory at the start of the **PATH** string. (The catch is that you need to be able to write to **/etc/profile** or **/root/.bash_profile**—where the **PATH** variable is set for **root**—and only a user with **root** privileges can do that.) Then you would need to put the bogus mkfs program file in that directory. Because the fraudulent version appears in a directory mentioned earlier than the real one in **PATH**, the shell would run it rather than the real version. Thus, the next time a user working with **root** privileges tries to run mkfs, the fraudulent version would run.

Trojan horses that lie in wait for and take advantage of the misspellings most people make are among the most insidious types. For example, you might type **sl** instead of **ls**. Because you do not regularly execute a utility named **sl** and you might not remember typing the command **sl**, it is more difficult to track down this type of Trojan horse than one that takes the name of a more familiar utility.

A good way to help prevent the execution of a Trojan horse is to make sure your **PATH** variable does not contain a single colon (:) at the beginning or end of the **PATH** string or a period (.) or double colon (::) anywhere in the **PATH** string. This precaution ensures that you will not execute a file in the working directory by accident.

To check for a possible Trojan horse, examine the filesystem periodically for files with setuid (page 205) permission. The following command lists these files:

Listing setuid files
```
# find / -perm /4000 -exec ls -lh {} \; 2> /dev/null
...
-rwsr-xr-x. 1 root root  28K 07-16 03:46 /usr/bin/passwd
---s--x--x. 2 root root 195K 11-30 03:38 /usr/bin/sudoedit
-rwsr-xr-x. 1 root root  59K 07-20 02:24 /usr/bin/chage
-rwsr-sr-x. 1 root root  45K 08-13 07:12 /usr/bin/crontab
-rwsr-xr-x. 1 root root  66K 07-20 02:24 /usr/bin/gpasswd
-rws--x--x. 1 root root  15K 11-25 04:17 /usr/bin/chsh
---s--x--x. 2 root root 195K 11-30 03:38 /usr/bin/sudo
...
```

This command uses find to locate all files that have their setuid bit set (mode 4000). The slash preceding the mode causes find to report on any file that has this bit set, regardless of how the other bits are set. The output sent to standard error is redirected to **/dev/null** so it does not clutter the screen.

Listing setgid files
You can display all files with setgid permission (page 205) by substituting 2000 for 4000 in the preceding command.

Run software only from sources you trust
Another way a Trojan horse can enter a system is via a tainted **~/.bashrc** (page 502) file. A bogus sudo command or alias in this file can capture a user's password, which might then be used to gain **root** privileges. Because a user has write permission to this file, any program the user executes can easily modify it. The best way to prevent this type of Trojan horse from entering a system is to run software only from sources you trust.

You can set up a program, such as AIDE (Advanced Intrusion Detection Environment; **aide** package), that will take a snapshot of the system and periodically check files for changes. For more information see sourceforge.net/projects/aide.

SELINUX

Traditional Linux security, called DAC (*Discretionary Access Control*), is based on users and groups. ACLs (page 208) implement DAC and can achieve fine-grain control over which users and processes can access files and how they can access them. Fine-grained access control is particularly important on servers, which often hold programs that require **root** privileges to run. The problem is that under DAC, the owner of a file has control over the permissions to the file, which is not always ideal.

SELinux (Security-Enhanced Linux), developed by the U.S. National Security Agency (NSA), implements MAC (*Mandatory Access Control*) in the Linux kernel. MAC, which is under the control of the system administrator, enforces security policies that limit what a user or program can do. It defines a security policy that controls some or all objects, such as files, devices, sockets, and ports, and some or all subjects, such as processes. Using SELinux, you can grant a process only those permissions it needs to be functional, following the principle of least privilege (page 410). Users are assigned roles that determine the primary function of the user. SELinux roles are conceptually similar to groups, except under SELinux, a user must actively switch between permitted roles. MAC is an important tool for limiting security threats that come from user errors, software flaws, and malicious users. The kernel checks MAC rules after it checks DAC rules; either can deny access.

DAC vs. MAC: who has the final say?

tip   Both DAC (Discretionary Access Control) and MAC (Mandatory Access Control) are effective at controlling access. The difference is that DAC is under the control of the user who owns a file and is therefore more easily subverted than is MAC, which is under the control of the system administrator. The kernel checks MAC rules after it checks DAC rules; either can deny access.

Modes   SELinux can be in one of three states (modes):

- **Enforcing/Active**—The default state, wherein SELinux security policy is enforced. No user or program will be able to do anything not permitted by the security policy.

- **Permissive/Warn**—The diagnostic state, wherein SELinux sends warning messages to a log but does not enforce the security policy. You can use the log to build a security policy that matches your requirements.

- **Disabled**—SELinux does not enforce a security policy nor does it issue warnings because no policy is loaded.

Running SELinux in permissive or enforcing state is estimated to degrade system performance between 0 and 7 percent, depending on tuning and usage. Although SELinux is usually of no benefit on a single-user system, you might want to consider SELinux for a server that connects to the Internet. If you are unsure whether to use SELinux, selecting permissive state allows you to change to disabled or enforcing state easily at a later date.

Policies   SELinux implements one of the following policies:

- **Targeted**—Applies SELinux MAC controls only to certain (targeted) processes (default).

- **MLS**—Multilevel Security protection.

- **Strict**—Applies SELinux MAC controls to all processes.

This section discusses the targeted policy. With this policy, daemons and system processes that do not have a specified policy are controlled by traditional Linux DACs. With the strict policy, all processes are controlled by SELinux (MACs). Setting up a system that runs under strict policy is beyond the scope of this book.

There is always a tradeoff between security and usability. The targeted policy is less secure than the strict policy, but it is much easier to maintain. When you run the strict policy, you will likely have to customize the policy so users can do their work and the system can function as you would like it to.

You can switch from one policy to the other (as explained shortly). Despite this flexibility, it is a poor idea to switch from a targeted to a strict policy on a production system. If you do so, some users might not be able to do their work. You would need to customize the policy in such a case. Changing from a strict to a targeted policy should not create any problems.

MORE INFORMATION

Web NSA: www.nsa.gov/research/selinux/docs.shtml
Fedora SELinux Wiki: fedoraproject.org/wiki/SELinux
SELinux News: selinuxnews.org
SELinux for Distributions (Sourceforge): selinux.sourceforge.net
Official FAQ: docs.fedoraproject.org/en-US/Fedora/13/html/SELinux_FAQ
Unofficial FAQ: www.crypt.gen.nz/selinux/faq.html
SELinux reference policy: oss.tresys.com/projects/refpolicy
Fedora SELinux mailing list: admin.fedoraproject.org/mailman/listinfo/selinux

Turning off SELinux

tip There are two ways to disable SELinux. You can either modify the **/etc/selinux/config** file so it includes the line **SELINUX=disabled** and reboot the system, or you can use **system-config-selinux** (as explained on the next page).

If there is a chance you will want to enable SELinux in the future, putting SELinux in permissive mode is a better choice than disabling it. This strategy allows you to turn on SELinux more quickly when you decide to do so.

config: THE SELINUX CONFIGURATION FILE

The **/etc/selinux/config** file, which has a link at **/etc/sysconfig/selinux**, controls the state of SELinux on the local system. Although you can modify this file, it might be more straightforward to work with system-config-selinux (next). In the following example, the policy is set to targeted, but that setting is of no consequence because SELinux is disabled:

```
$ cat /etc/selinux/config
# This file controls the state of SELinux on the system.
# SELINUX= can take one of these three values:
#       enforcing - SELinux security policy is enforced.
#       permissive - SELinux prints warnings instead of enforcing.
#       disabled - SELinux is fully disabled.
SELINUX=disabled
# SELINUXTYPE= type of policy in use. Possible values are:
#       targeted - Only targeted network daemons are protected.
#       strict - Full SELinux protection.
SELINUXTYPE=targeted
```

To put SELinux in enforcing mode, change the line containing the **SELINUX** assignment to **SELINUX=enforcing**. Similarly, you can change the policy by setting **SELINUXTYPE**.

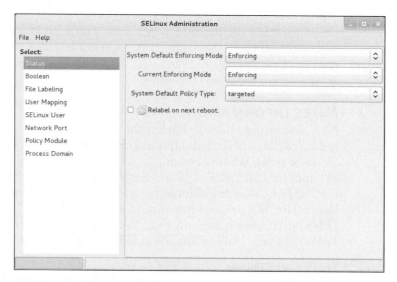

Figure 11-4   The SELinux Administration window (system-config-selinux)

If you will use SELinux in the future

tip   If you will use SELinux in the future but not now, turn it on when you install Linux and run it in permissive state with the policy set to the policy you will eventually use. Permissive state writes the required extended information to inodes, but it does not stop you from doing anything on the system.

If you turn on SELinux after it has been disabled, when you reboot the system SELinux has to add extended attributes to the files in the filesystem. This process can take a long time on a large filesystem. If you are never going to use SELinux, disable it.

getenforce, setenforce, AND sestatus: WORK WITH SELINUX

The getenforce and setenforce utilities report on and temporarily set the SELinux mode. The sestatus utility displays a summary of the state of SELinux:

```
# getenforce
Enforcing

# setenforce permissive

# sestatus
SELinux status:              enabled
SELinuxfs mount:             /selinux
Current mode:                permissive
Mode from config file:       enforcing
Policy version:              24
Policy from config file:     targeted
```

SETTING THE TARGETED POLICY WITH system-config-selinux

The system-config-selinux utility (**policycoreutils-gui** package) displays the SELinux Administration window (Figure 11-4), which controls SELinux. To run this utility, enter **system-config-selinux** from a command line in a graphical environment or select **Main menu: Applications⇨Other⇨SELinux Management** (Fedora; if **Applications** is not visible see "Configuring Fallback Mode" on page 92) or **Main menu: System⇨Administration⇨SELinux Management** (RHEL).

With **Status** highlighted on the left side of the SELinux Administration window, choose Enforcing (default), Permissive, or Disabled from the drop-down list labeled **System Default Enforcing Mode**. The mode you choose becomes effective next time you boot the system. You can use the drop-down list labeled **Current Enforcing Mode** to change between Enforcing and Permissive modes immediately. When you change the mode using this list, the system resumes the default mode when you reboot it.

To modify the SELinux policy, highlight **Boolean** on the left side of the SELinux Administration window and scroll through the list of modules. For example, the SpamAssassin (page 744) module has two policies: **Allow user spamassassin clients to use the network** and **Allow spamd to read/write user home directories**. Each of these policies does not have a tick in the check box in the column labeled **Active** (the left column), so SELinux does *not* allow user SpamAssassin clients to use the network and does *not* allow the SpamAssassin daemon (**spamd**) to read from and write to the home directories of users. Put ticks in these check boxes to turn on these policies.

To find Booleans that pertain to NFS, type **nfs** in the text box labeled **Filter** and then press RETURN. The SELinux Administration window displays all Booleans with the string **nfs** in their descriptions. The modules with tick marks in the column labeled **Active** are in use.

The last item on the left side of the SELinux Administration window, **Process Domain**, allows you put a single module into permissive mode as needed. This selection avoids putting the entire system into permissive mode when just one or two modules are not working properly with the system in enforcing mode.

PAM

PAM (Linux-PAM, or Linux Pluggable Authentication Modules) allows a system administrator to determine how applications use *authentication* (page 1152) to verify the identity of a user. PAM provides shared libraries of modules (located in **/lib/security**) that, when called by an application, authenticate a user. The configuration files kept in the **/etc/pam.d** directory determine the method of authentication and contain a list (i.e., stack) of calls to the modules. PAM might also use other files, such as **/etc/passwd**, when necessary. The term "Pluggable" in PAM's name refers to the ease with which you can add and remove modules from an authentication stack.

The configuration files stored in **/etc/pam.d** describe the authentication procedure for each application. These files usually have names that are the same as or similar to the names of the applications that they authenticate for. For example, authentication for the login utility is configured in **/etc/pam.d/login**. The name of the file is the name of the PAM service[1] that the file configures. Occasionally one file might serve two programs. PAM accepts only lowercase letters in the names of files in the **/etc/pam.d** directory.

Authentication stack The files in **/etc/pam.d** list the set of modules to be used for each application to perform each task. Each such set of the modules is called an *authentication stack* or simply a *stack*. PAM calls the modules one at a time in order, going from the top of the stack (the first module listed in the configuration file) to the bottom. Each module reports success or failure back to PAM. When all stacks of modules (with some exceptions) within a configuration file have been called, the PAM library reports success or failure back to the application.

Instead of building the authentication code into each application, PAM provides shared libraries that keep the authentication code separate from the application code. The techniques of authenticating users stay the same from application to application. In this way PAM enables a system administrator to change the authentication mechanism for a given application without modifying the application.

PAM provides authentication for a variety of system-entry services (such as login, ftp, su, and sudo). You can take advantage of its ability to stack authentication modules to integrate system-entry services with different authentication mechanisms, such as RSA, DCE, Kerberos, and smartcards.

From login to using su or sudo to shutting the system down, whenever you are asked for a password (or not asked for a password because the system trusts you are who you say you are), PAM makes it possible for the system administrator to configure the authentication process. It also makes the configuration process essentially the same for all applications that use PAM for authentication.

Do not create /etc/pam.conf

caution You might have encountered PAM on other systems where all configuration is arranged in a single file (**/etc/pam.conf**). This file does not exist on Fedora/RHEL systems. Instead, the **/etc/pam.d** directory contains individual configuration files, one per application that uses PAM. This setup makes it easy to install and uninstall applications that use PAM because you do not have to modify the **/etc/pam.conf** file each time. If you create a **/etc/pam.conf** file on a system that does not use this file, the PAM configuration might become confused. Do not use PAM documentation from a different system. Also, the **requisite** control flag is not available on some systems that support PAM.

---

1. There is no relationship between PAM services and the **/etc/services** file. The name of the PAM service is an arbitrary string that each application gives to PAM; PAM then looks up the configuration file with that name and uses it to control authentication. There is no central registry of PAM service names.

Error messages   PAM warns you about errors it encounters, logging them to **/var/log/messages** or **/var/log/secure**. Review these files if you are trying to figure out why a changed PAM file is not working properly. To prevent a malicious user from seeing information about PAM, PAM sends error messages to a file rather than to the screen.

MORE INFORMATION

Local   *Linux-PAM System Administrators' Guide:*
        /usr/share/doc/pam-1.1.1/html/Linux-PAM_SAG.html

pam man page
PAM modules: **apropos pam_** lists man pages describing PAM modules

Web   *Linux-PAM System Administrators' Guide:*
        www.kernel.org/pub/linux/libs/pam/Linux-PAM-html/Linux-PAM_SAG.html
        Description: www.netbsd.org/docs/guide/en/chap-pam.html

HOWTO   *User Authentication HOWTO*

CONFIGURATION FILES, MODULE TYPES, AND CONTROL FLAGS

Login module   Following is an example of a PAM configuration file. Comment lines begin with a hashmark (#).

```
$ cat /etc/pam.d/login
#%PAM-1.0
auth [user_unknown=ignore success=ok ignore=ignore default=bad] pam_securetty.so
auth       include      system-auth
account    required     pam_nologin.so
account    include      system-auth
password   include      system-auth
# pam_selinux.so close should be the first session rule
session    required     pam_selinux.so close
session    required     pam_loginuid.so
session    optional     pam_console.so
# pam_selinux.so open should only be followed by sessions to be executed in the user context
session    required     pam_selinux.so open
session    required     pam_namespace.so
session    optional     pam_keyinit.so force revoke
session    include      system-auth
-session   optional     pam_ck_connector.so
```

The first line is a special comment; it will become significant only if another PAM format is released. Do not use **#%** other than in the first line of the preceding example.

The rest of the lines tell PAM to do something as part of the authentication process. The first word on each line is a module type indicator: **account, auth, password,** or **session** (Table 11-2). The second is a control flag (Table 11-3) that indicates the action PAM should take if authentication fails. The rest of the line contains the name of a PAM module (located in **/lib/security**) and any arguments for that module. The PAM library itself uses the **/etc/pam.d** files to determine which modules to delegate work to.

Lines that have a control flag of **include** include the file named in the third field.

Table 11-2   Module type indicators

Module type	Description	Controls
account	Account management	Determining whether an already authenticated user is allowed to use the service she is trying to use. (That is, has the account expired? Is the user allowed to use this service at this time of day?)
auth	Authentication	Proving that the user is authorized to use the service; uses passwords or another mechanism.
password	Password modification	Updating authentication mechanisms such as user passwords.
session	Session management	Setting things up when the service is started (as when a user logs in) and breaking them down when the service is terminated (as when a user logs out).

You can use one of the control flag keywords listed in Table 11-3 to set the control flags.

Table 11-3   Control flag keywords

Keyword	Flag function
required	Success is required for authentication to succeed. Control and a failure result are returned after all modules in the stack have been executed. The technique of delaying the report to the calling program until all modules have been executed might keep attackers from knowing precisely what caused their authentication attempts to fail and tell them less about the system, making it more difficult for them to break in.
requisite	Success is required for authentication to succeed. Further module processing is aborted, and control is returned immediately after a module fails. This technique might expose information about the system to an attacker. However, if it prevents a user from giving a password over an insecure connection, it might keep information out of the hands of an attacker.
sufficient	Success indicates this module type has succeeded; no subsequent **required** modules of this type are executed. Failure is not fatal to the stack of this module type. This technique is generally used when one form of authentication or another is good enough: If one fails, PAM tries the other. For example, when you use **su** to escalate privileges, **/etc/pam.d/su** first uses **pam_rootok** to check whether you are running with a UID of zero (**root** privileges). Because **su** calls **pam_rootok** with a control flag of **sufficient**, if you are running with a UID of zero, the **pam_rootok** module reports success, and PAM immediately reports success to the **su** utility that called it. If you are not running with **root** privileges, PAM starts the authentication again and asks for a password. If this second authentication succeeds, PAM ignores the fact that the **pam_rootok** module reported failure. If both modules fail, PAM reports failure to the **su** utility that called it.
optional	Result is generally ignored. An optional module is relevant only when it is the sole module on the stack for a particular service.

PAM uses each of the module types as requested by the application. That is, the application asks PAM separately to authenticate, check account status, manage sessions, and change the password. PAM uses one or more modules from the **/lib/security** directory to accomplish each of these tasks.

EXAMPLE

Part of the login service's authentication stack follows:

```
$ cat /etc/pam.d/login
auth [user_unknown=ignore success=ok ignore=ignore default=bad] pam_securetty.so
auth       include      system-auth
account    required     pam_nologin.so
...
```

The login utility first asks for a username and then calls PAM to run this stack to authenticate the user. Refer to Table 11-2 and Table 11-3.

1. PAM first calls **pam_securetty** (secure tty; **pam_securetty** man page) as an auth (authentication) module to make sure the **root** user logs in only from an allowed terminal. This module looks at the **/etc/securetty** file for a list of terminals that the user named **root** is allowed to log in from. Thus PAM implements the long time UNIX practice of not allowing **root** to use telnet to log in on the system (telnet uses login for authentication). This technique is not used but could be added to the **sshd, vsftpd,** and other PAM configuration files.

   Within the brackets ([]) in the control flag field are *value=action* pairs. When the module returns *value*, PAM evaluates *action*. In the example, when the module returns **user_unknown,** the result of running the module is ignored, and when the module returns success, the user is allowed to continue authentication. See the **pam_securetty** man page for details.

   The **pam_securetty** module is *required* to succeed if the authentication stack is to succeed. The **pam_securetty** module reports failure only if someone is trying to log in as **root** from an unauthorized terminal. Otherwise (if the username being authenticated is not **root** or if the username is **root** and the login attempt is being made from a secure terminal), the **pam_securetty** module reports success.

   Success and failure within PAM are opaque concepts that apply only to PAM. They do not equate to "true" and "false" as used elsewhere in the operating system.

2. Next, PAM includes the **/etc/pam.d/system-auth** file (system-auth man page). This file provides a common interface with which to call PAM.

3. The **pam_nologin** module (**pam_nologin** man page) makes sure that if the **/etc/nologin** file exists, only the **root** user is allowed to log in. (That is, the **pam_nologin** module reports success only if **/etc/nologin** does not exist or if the **root** user is logging in.) Thus, when a shutdown has been scheduled to occur in the near future, the system keeps users from logging in, only to have the system shut down moments later.

The **account** module type works like the **auth** module type but is called after the user has been authenticated; it acts as an additional security check or requirement that must be met for a user to gain access to the system. For example, **account** modules might enforce a policy that a user can log in only during business hours or check whether a password has expired.

The **session** module type sets up and tears down the session (perhaps mounting and unmounting the user's home directory). One common **session** module on a Fedora/RHEL system is the **pam_console** module, which sets the system up especially for users who log in at the physical console, rather than remotely. A local user is able to access the floppy and CD drives, the sound card, and sometimes other devices as defined by the system administrator.

The **password** module type is a bit unusual: All modules in the stack are called once and told to get all information they need to store the password to persistent memory, such as a disk, but not actually to store it. If it determines that it cannot or should not store the password, a module reports failure. If all **password** modules in the stack report success, they are called a second time and told to store to persistent memory the password they obtained on the first pass. The **password** module is responsible for updating the authentication information (i.e., changing the user's password).

Any one module can act as more than one module type; many modules can act as all four module types. For example, **pam_unix** can be called as an **auth** module to check a username and password against the **passwd** and **shadow** files, as an **account** module to check password expiration, as a **password** module to update a password (i.e., if login prompts with **your password has expired, enter a new password**), or as a **session** module to record login and logout timestamps for **wtmp** (for use with the last utility).

MODIFYING THE PAM CONFIGURATION

Do not lock yourself out of the system

caution   Editing PAM configuration files correctly requires paying careful attention. It is easy to lock yourself out of the system with a single mistake. To avoid this problem, keep backup copies of the PAM configuration files you edit, test every change thoroughly, and make sure you can still log in after the change is installed. Keep a **root** shell open (use **su** or **sudo –i**) until you have finished testing. If a change fails and you cannot log in, use the **root** shell to replace the newly edited files with the backup copies.

Some UNIX systems require that a user be a member of the **wheel** group to use the su command. Although Fedora/RHEL is not configured this way by default, PAM allows you to change this behavior by editing the **/etc/pam.d/su** file:

```
$ cat /etc/pam.d/su
...
# Uncomment the following line to implicitly trust users in the "wheel" group.
#auth           sufficient      pam_wheel.so trust use_uid
# Uncomment the following line to require a user to be in the "wheel" group.
#auth           required        pam_wheel.so use_uid
...
```

The lines of the **su** module contain comments that include the lines necessary to permit only users who are in the **wheel** group to use su (required) and to permit members of the **wheel** group to run su without supplying a password (sufficient). Uncomment one of these lines when you want the system to follow one of these rules.

SYSTEM ADMINISTRATION TOOLS

This section describes a few of the textual (command-line) tools that can help you be an efficient and thorough system administrator. Some are simply mentioned here and are described in detail elsewhere in the book. It also presents a list of graphical administration tools available under Fedora/RHEL. You can learn more about these tools by reading the appropriate man or info pages.

TEXTUAL ADMINISTRATION UTILITIES

blkid: DISPLAYS BLOCK DEVICE INFORMATION

The blkid utility displays labels, UUID value, and filesystem type for block devices:

```
# blkid
/dev/sda1: UUID="7694f86e-c3ff-4e51-b677-01b3d27927a4" TYPE="ext4"
/dev/sda2: UUID="BiNaOD-AmD2-aC3r-h2tZ-Js6c-xj1L-31Z5U6" TYPE="LVM2_member"
/dev/mapper/vg_bee-lv_root: LABEL="_Fedora-14-i686-" UUID="7743cb0d-..." TYPE="ext4"
/dev/mapper/vg_bee-lv_swap: UUID="800b87ec-b333-4d51-90e5-be359421e999" TYPE="swap"
```

chsh: CHANGES THE LOGIN SHELL FOR A USER

The chsh utility changes the login shell for a user. When you call chsh without an argument, you change your login shell. When an ordinary user changes his login shell with chsh, he must specify an installed shell that is listed in the file **/etc/shells**, exactly as it is listed there; chsh rejects other entries. When working with **root** privileges, you can change any user's shell to any value by calling chsh with the username as an argument. The **chsh --list-shells** command displays the list of available shells. In the following example, a user working with **root** privileges changes Sam's shell to tcsh:

```
# chsh sam
Changing shell for sam.
New shell [/bin/bash]: /bin/tcsh
Shell changed.
```

See page 281 for more information.

clear: CLEARS THE SCREEN

The clear utility clears the screen. You can also use CONTROL-L from the bash shell to clear the screen. The value of the environment variable **TERM** (page 1122) determines how to clear the screen.

dmesg: DISPLAYS SYSTEM MESSAGES

The dmesg utility displays recent system log messages (the kernel ring buffer; page 597).

e2label: WORKS WITH VOLUME LABELS

The e2label utility displays or creates a volume label on an **ext2**, **ext3**, or **ext4** filesystem. You must run this utility with **root** privileges. An e2label command has the following format:

> e2label *device [newlabel]*

where *device* is the name of the device (e.g., **/dev/hda2, /dev/sdb1, /dev/fd0**) you want to work with. When you include the optional *newlabel* parameter, e2label changes the label on *device* to *newlabel*. Without this parameter, e2label displays the label. You can also create a volume label with the −L option of tune2fs (page 526). See also blkid on the previous page.

kill: SENDS A SIGNAL TO A PROCESS

The kill builtin sends a signal to a process. This signal might or might not terminate (kill) the process, depending on which signal it is and how the process is designed. Refer to "trap: Catches a Signal" on page 1025 for a discussion of the various signals and their interaction with a process. Running kill is definitely not the first method to try when a process needs to be aborted. See also killall (next) and pkill (page 472).

Usually a user can kill a process by working in another window or by logging in on another terminal. Sometimes, however, you might have to work with **root** privileges to kill a process for a user. To kill a process, you need to know its PID. The ps utility can provide this information once you determine the name of the program the user is running and/or the username of the user. The top utility (page 616) can also be helpful in finding and killing a runaway process (use the top **k** command).

kill: Use the kill signal (−KILL or −9) as a method of last resort

caution
When you do need to use kill, send the termination signal (**kill −TERM** or **kill −15**) first. Only if that tactic does not work should you attempt to use the kill signal (**kill −KILL** or **kill −9**).

Because of its inherent dangers, using a kill signal is a method of last resort, especially when you are working with **root** privileges. One kill command issued while working with **root** privileges can bring the system down without warning. The kill signal can also cause the target program to corrupt its configuration or state.

In the following example, Sam complains that gnome-calculator is stuck and that he cannot do anything from the gnome-calculator window—not even close it. A more experienced user could open another window and kill the process, but in this case you kill it for Sam. First you use ps to produce a long list of all processes and then use a pipe and grep to find which one is running gnome-calculator:

```
$ ps -ef | grep gnome-calculator
sam         3730  2424  0 14:07 ?        00:00:00 gnome-calculator
sam         3766  3568  0 14:14 pts/3    00:00:00 grep gnome-calculator
```

If several people are running gnome-calculator, look in the left column to find the correct username so you can kill the correct process.

You can also use the pgrep utility to list all processes owned by Sam with the string **calc** in the name of the program the process is running:

```
$ pgrep -u sam -l calc
3730 gnome-calculato
```

Now that you know Sam's process running gnome-calculator has a PID of 3730, you can use kill to terminate it. The safest way to do so is to log in as Sam (perhaps you could allow him to log in for you or su to sam [**su sam**] if you are logged in as **root**) and give any of the following commands (all of which send a termination signal to process 3730):

```
$ kill 3730
```

or

```
$ kill -15 3730
```

or

```
$ kill –TERM 3730
```

Only if this command fails should you send the kill signal:

```
$ kill –KILL 3730
```

The **–KILL** option instructs kill to send a **SIGKILL** signal, which the process cannot ignore. Although you can give the same command while you are working with **root** privileges, a typing mistake in this situation can have much more far-reaching consequences than if you make the same mistake while you are working as a nonprivileged user. A nonprivileged user can kill only her own processes, whereas a user with **root** privileges can kill any process, including system processes.

As a compromise between speed and safety, you can combine the su or sudo and kill utilities by using the su –c or the sudo –u option. The following command runs the kill command with the identity of Sam (Sam's privileges):

```
# su sam -c "kill -TERM 3730"
```

or

```
$ sudo -u sam kill -TERM 3730
```

See also killall (page 472) and pkill (page 472).

killall: KILLS A COMMAND

The killall utility is similar to kill (previous) but uses a command name instead of a PID number. Give the following command to kill all your processes that are running gnome-calculator or vi:

```
$ killall gnome-calculator vi
```

Running this command while working with **root** privileges kills all processes running gnome-calculator or vi. See also kill (previous) and pkill (page 472).

lshw: DISPLAYS HARDWARE INFORMATION

The lshw utility (**lshw** package, Fedora only) lists system hardware. The lshw utility is part of the **lshw** package. This utility provides complete information only when run with **root** privileges. Use the **–short** option to display a brief listing. See page 649 for more information.

mkfs: CREATES A FILESYSTEM

The mkfs utility creates a new filesystem on a device, destroying all data on the device as it does so. This utility is a front-end for many utilities, each of which builds a different type of filesystem. By default, mkfs builds an **ext2** filesystem and works on either a hard disk partition or a floppy diskette. Although it can take many options and arguments, you can use mkfs simply as

```
# mkfs device
```

where *device* is the name of the device (**/dev/hda2**, **/dev/sdb1**, **/dev/fd0**, and so on) you want to make a filesystem on. Use the **–t** option to specify a type of filesystem. As an example, the following command creates an **ext4** filesystem on **/dev/sda2**:

```
# mkfs -t ext4 /dev/sda2
```

pidof: DISPLAYS PID NUMBERS OF COMMANDS

The pidof utility displays the PID number of each process running the command you specify:

```
$ pidof httpd
567 566 565 564 563 562 561 560 553
```

If it is difficult to find the right process, try using top. Refer to the man pages for these utilities for more information, including lists of options.

ping: SEND A PACKET TO A REMOTE SYSTEM

The ping utility sends packets to a remote system. This utility determines whether you can reach a remote system through the network and tells you how long it takes to exchange messages with the remote system. Refer to "ping: Tests a Network Connection" on page 386.

pkill: KILLS A COMMAND

The pkill utility, which has a syntax similar to pgrep, kills a process based on the command line that initiated the process. The next command sends a termination signal to all processes owned by username **sam** that have the string **calc** in the command line that started the process.

```
$ pkill -u sam calc
```

Caution dictates that you give the same command using pgrep in place of pkill before attempting to kill a process.

reset (LINK TO tset): RESETS A TERMINAL

The reset utility, which is a link to tset, resets terminal characteristics. The value of the **TERM** environment variable (page 1122) determines how the screen will be reset. The screen is cleared, the kill and interrupt characters are set to their default values, and character echo is turned on. When given from a graphical terminal emulator, this command also changes the size of the window to its default. The reset utility is useful for restoring the screen to a sane state after it has been corrupted, such as after attempting to cat a binary file. In this sense, it is similar to an **stty sane** command.

setserial: WORK WITH A SERIAL PORT

The setserial utility gets and sets serial port information. When run with **root** privileges, this utility can configure a serial port. It does not configure the hardware. The following command sets the input address of **/dev/ttys0** to 0x100, the interrupt (IRQ) to 5, and the baud rate to 115,000 baud:

```
# setserial /dev/ttys0 port 0x100 irq 5 spd_vhi
```

You can also check the configuration of a serial port with setserial:

```
# setserial /dev/ttys0
/dev/ttyS0, UART: 16550A, Port: 0x0100, IRQ: 5, Flags: spd_vhi
```

Normally the system calls setserial as it is booting if a serial port needs custom configuration. This utility is part of the **setserial** package.

stat: DISPLAYS INFORMATION ABOUT A FILE OR FILESYSTEM

The stat utility displays information about a file or filesystem. Giving the –f (filesystem) option followed by the mount point for a filesystem displays information about the filesystem, including the maximum number of characters allowed in a filename (**Namelen** in the following example). See the stat man page for more information.

```
$ stat -f /dev/sda
  File: "/dev/sda"
    ID: 0         Namelen: 255      Type: tmpfs
Block size: 4096        Fundamental block size: 4096
Blocks: Total: 127271     Free: 127207     Available: 127207
Inodes: Total: 127271     Free: 126600
```

umask: SPECIFIES THE PERMISSION MASK

The umask shell builtin specifies the mask the system uses to set up access permissions when it creates a file. A umask command has the following format:

umask [mask]

where *mask* is a three- or four-digit octal number or a symbolic value such as you would use with chmod (page 203). A *mask* that you specify using symbolic values specifies the permissions that *are* allowed. A *mask* that you specify using octal numbers specifies the permissions that are *not* allowed; the digits correspond to the permissions for the owner of the file, members of the group the file is associated with, and everyone else. Because *mask* specifies the permissions that are *not* allowed, the system uses binary arithmetic to subtract each of the three digits from 7 when you create a file. If the file is an ordinary file (and not a directory file), the system then removes execute permissions from the file. The result is three or four octal numbers that specify the access permissions for the file (the numbers you would use with chmod).

An octal value of 1 (001 binary) represents execute permission, 2 (010 binary) write permission, and 4 (100 binary) read permission (for a file).

You must use binary or octal arithmetic when performing permissions calculations. To calculate file permissions given a umask value, subtract the umask value from octal 777.

For example, assume a umask value of 003:

```
 777      starting permissions for calculation
-003      subtract umask value
 774      resulting permissions for a directory
 111      remove execute permissions
 664      resulting permissions for an ordinary file
```

To calculate permissions for a directory, umask subtracts the umask value from 777: In the example where umask has a value of 003, octal 7 minus octal 0 equals octal 7 (for two positions). Octal 7 minus octal 3 equals octal 4. Or using binary arithmetic, 111 – 011 = 100. The result is that the system gives permissions of 774 (**rwxrwxr--**) to a directory.

To calculate permissions for an ordinary file, the system changes the execute bit (001 binary) to 0 for each position. If the execute bit is not set, the system does not change the execute bit. In the example, removing the execute bit from octal 7 yields octal 6: (removing 001 from 111 yields 110; two positions). Octal 4 remains octal 4 because the execute bit is not set (the 001 bit is not set in 100, so it remains 100). The result is that the system gives permissions of 664 (**rw--rw--r--**) to an ordinary file.

The following commands set the file-creation mask and display the mask and its effect when you create a file and a directory. The mask of 022, when subtracted from 777, gives permissions of 755 (**rwxr--xr--x**) for a directory. For an ordinary file, the system subtracts execute permissions from 755 yielding permissions of 644 (**rw--r--r--**).

```
$ umask 022
$ umask
0022
$ touch afile
$ mkdir adirectory
$ ls -ld afile adirectory
drwxr-xr-x. 2 sam pubs 4096 12-31 12:42 adirectory
-rw-r--r--. 1 sam pubs    0 12-31 12:42 afile
```

The next example sets the same mask using symbolic values. The –S option displays the mask symbolically:

```
$ umask u=rwx,g=rx,o=rx
$ umask
0022
$ umask -S
u=rwx,g=rx,o=rx
```

uname: DISPLAYS SYSTEM INFORMATION

The uname utility displays information about the system. Without arguments, it displays the name of the operating system (**Linux**). With the –a (all) option, it displays the operating system name, hostname, version number and release date of the operating system, and type of hardware you are using:

```
$ uname -a
Linux guava 2.6.38.6-27.fc15.i686.PAE #1 SMP Sun May 8 17:39:47 UTC 2011 i686 ... GNU/Linux
```

GRAPHICAL CONFIGURATION TOOLS

Most of the Fedora/RHEL configuration tools are named system-config-✳. These tools bring up a graphical display when called from a GUI; some display a textual interface when called from a non-GUI command line. Some, such as system-config-firewall-tui, use a name with a **–tui** extension for the textual interface. In general, these tools, which are listed in Table 11-4, are simple to use and require little explanation beyond what the tool presents. Some have Help selections on their toolbars. Most do not have man pages, but some have a useful **--help** option.

Table 11-4 Fedora/RHEL configuration tools

Tool	Function
system-config-authentication	Displays the Authentication Configuration window with two tabs. The Identity & Authentication tab allows you to configure user accounts to enable local accounts only or to use NIS, LDAP, FreeIPA (Fedora only), or Winbind support. This tab also allows you to specify how the system authenticates users, depending on how you configure user accounts.
	The Advanced Options tab allows you to specify local authentication options including the use of a fingerprint reader or which password hashing algorithm you want to use; it can also set up the system to create a home directory the first time a user logs in and can set up smart card authentication.
	For a pseudographical interface use authconfig-tui; for a purely textual (scriptable) interface use authconfig.
system-config-bind	Displays the BIND Configuration GUI window (**system-config-bind** package; page 861). Fedora only.

Table 11-4 Fedora/RHEL configuration tools (continued)

Tool	Function
system-config-boot	Displays the Boot Configuration window, which allows you to specify a default kernel and timeout for the **grub.conf** file (**system-config-boot** package). Fedora only.
system-config-date	Displays the Date/Time Properties window with two tabs: Date & Time and Time Zone. You can set the date and time or enable NTP (Network Time Protocol) from the first tab. The Time Zone tab allows you to specify the time zone of the system clock or set the system clock to *UTC* (page 1195).
system-config-firewall[-tui]	Displays the Firewall Configuration window (page 893).
system-config-httpd	Displays the HTTP Server Configuration window (**system-config-httpd** package). Fedora only.
system-config-keyboard	Displays the Keyboard window, which allows you to select the type of keyboard attached to the system. You use this utility to select the keyboard when you install the system.
system-config-kickstart	Displays the Kickstart Configurator window, which allows you to create a Kickstart script (**system-config-kickstart** package; page 81).
system-config-language	Displays the Language Selection window, which allows you to specify the default system language from among those that are installed. You use this utility to select the system language when you install the system.
system-config-lvm	Displays the Logical Volume Management window, which allows you to modify existing logical volumes (page 42).
system-config-netboot	Displays the Network Installation and Diskless Environment window, which allows you to configure the network installation or a diskless environment (**system-config-netboot** package). The first time you run this utility, it displays the First Time Druid window. Fedora only.
system-config-network[-tui]	Displays a pseudographical network configuration window.

Table 11-4   Fedora/RHEL configuration tools (continued)

Tool	Function
system-config-network-cmd	Displays the parameters that system-config-network uses. Has a useful **--help** option.
system-config-nfs	Displays the NFS Server Configuration window (page 802; **system-config-nfs** package). Fedora only.
system-config-printer	Displays the Printing window, which allows you to set up printers and edit printer configurations (page 562). Has a useful **--help** option.
system-config-rootpassword	Displays the Root Password window, which allows you to change the **root** password. While logged in as **root**, you can also use passwd from a command line to change the **root** password (**system-config-rootpassword** package). Fedora only.
system-config-samba	Displays the Samba Server Configuration window, which can help you configure Samba (**system-config-samba** package; page 827). Fedora only.
system-config-selinux	Displays the SELinux Administration window, which controls SELinux (**policycoreutils-gui** package; page 463).
system-config-services	Displays the Service Configuration window, which allows you to specify which daemons (services) run at each runlevel (**system-config-services** package; page 445).
system-config-users	Displays the User Manager window, which allows you to work with users and groups (page 602).
system-switch-mail	Displays the system-switch-mail pseudographical window, which allows you to choose between the **sendmail** (page 729) and Postfix (page 732) MTAs when both packages are installed (**system-switch-mail** package). Fedora only.

SETTING UP A SERVER

This section discusses issues you might need to address when setting up a server: how to write configuration files; how to specify hosts and subnets; how to use **rpcbind**, rpcinfo, and TCP wrappers (**hosts.allow** and **hosts.deny**); and how to set up a chroot jail. Chapters 14 and 18–26 cover setting up specific servers; Chapter 17 discusses setting up a LAN.

STANDARD RULES IN CONFIGURATION FILES

Most configuration files, which are typically named *.conf, rely on the following conventions:

- Blank lines are ignored.

- A # anywhere on a line starts a comment that continues to the end of the line. Comments are ignored.

- When a name contains a SPACE, you must quote the SPACE by preceding it with a backslash (\) or by enclosing the entire name within single or double quotation marks.

- To make long lines easier to read and edit, you can break them into several shorter lines. To break a line, insert a backslash (\) immediately followed by a NEWLINE (press RETURN in a text editor). When you insert the NEWLINE before or after a SPACE, you can indent the following line to make it easier to read. Do not break lines in this manner while editing on a Windows machine, as the NEWLINEs might not be properly escaped (Windows uses a RETURN-LINEFEED combination to end lines).

Configuration files that do not follow these conventions are noted in the text.

SPECIFYING CLIENTS

Table 11-5 shows some common ways to specify a host or a subnet. In most cases you can specify multiple hosts or subnets by separating their specifications with SPACEs.

Table 11-5   Specifying a client

Client name pattern	Matches
n.n.n.n	One IP address.
name	One hostname, either local or remote.
Name that starts with .	Matches a hostname that ends with the specified string. For example, **.example.com** matches the systems named **kudos.example.com** and **speedy.example.com**, among others.
IP address that ends with .	Matches a host address that starts with the specified numbers. For example, **192.168.0.** matches **192.168.0.0**–**192.168.0.255**. If you omit the trailing period, this format does not work.
n.n.n.n/m.m.m.m *or* n.n.n.n/mm	An IP address and network mask specifying a subnet.
Starts with /	An absolute pathname of a file containing one or more names or addresses as specified in this table.

Table 11-5   Specifying a client (continued)

Wildcard	Matches
* and ?	Matches one (?) or more (*) characters in a simple hostname or IP address. These wildcards do not match periods in a domain name.
ALL	Always matches.
LOCAL	Matches any hostname that does not contain a period.
Operator	
EXCEPT	Matches anything in the preceding list that is not in the following list. For example, **a b c d EXCEPT c** matches **a**, **b**, and **d**. Thus you could use **192.168. EXCEPT 192.168.0.1** to match all IP addresses that start with **192.168.** except **192.168.0.1**.

Examples   Each of the following examples specifies one or more systems:

10.10.	Matches all systems with IP addresses that start with **10.10.**
.redhat.com	Matches all named hosts on the Fedora/Linux network
localhost	Matches the local system
127.0.0.1	The loopback address; always resolves to **localhost**
192.168.*.1	Could match all routers on a network of /24 subnets (next)

SPECIFYING A SUBNET

When you set up a server, you frequently need to specify which clients are allowed to connect to it. Sometimes it is convenient to specify a range of IP addresses, called a subnet. The discussion on page 378 explains what a subnet is and how to use a network mask to specify a subnet. Usually you can specify a subnet as

> *n.n.n.n/m.m.m.m*

or

> *n.n.n.n/maskbits*

where *n.n.n.n* is the base IP address and the subnet is represented by *m.m.m.m* (the network mask) or *maskbits* (the number of bits used for the network mask). For example, **192.168.0.1/255.255.255.0** represents the same subnet as **192.168.0.1/24**. In binary, decimal **255.255.255.0** is represented by 24 ones followed by 8 zeros. The **/24** is shorthand for a network mask with 24 ones. Each line in Table 11-6 presents two notations for the same subnet, followed by the range of IP addresses the subnet includes.

Table 11-6   Different ways to represent a subnet

Bits	Mask	Range
10.0.0.0/8	10.0.0.0/255.0.0.0	10.0.0.0–10.255.255.255
172.16.0.0/12	172.16.0.0/255.240.0.0	172.16.0.0–172.16.255.255
192.168.0.0/16	192.168.0.0/255.255.0.0	192.168.0.0–192.168.255.255

rpcinfo: DISPLAYS INFORMATION ABOUT rpcbind

The rpcinfo utility (**rpcbind** package) displays information about programs registered with **rpcbind** and makes RPC calls to programs to see if they are alive. For more information on **rpcbind**, refer to "RPC Network Services" on page 398. The rpcinfo utility takes the following options and arguments:

Syntax

rpcinfo –p [host]
rpcinfo [–n port] [–u | –t] host program [version]
rpcinfo –b | –d program version

–b (**broadcast**) Makes an RPC broadcast to *version* of *program* and lists those hosts that respond.

–d (**delete**) Removes local RPC registration for *version* of *program*. Available to a user running with **root** privileges only.

–n (**port number**) With **–t** or **–u**, uses the port numbered *port* instead of the port number specified by **rpcbind**.

–p (**probe**) Lists all RPC programs registered, with **rpcbind** on *host* or on the local system when you do not specify *host*.

–t (**TCP**) Makes a TCP RPC call to *version* (if specified) of *program* on *host* and reports whether it receives a response.

–u (**UDP**) Makes a UDP RPC call to *version* (if specified) of *program* on *host* and reports whether it receives a response.

Examples

The following command displays the RPC programs registered with the rpcbind daemon on the system named **plum**:

```
$ rpcinfo -p plum
   program vers proto    port  service
   100000    4   tcp      111  portmapper
   100000    3   tcp      111  portmapper
...
   100021    1   udp    44202  nlockmgr
   100021    3   udp    44202  nlockmgr
...
   100003    2   tcp     2049  nfs
   100003    3   tcp     2049  nfs
...
```

Use the **–u** option to display a list of versions of a daemon, such as **nfs**, registered on a remote system (**plum**):

```
$ rpcinfo -u plum nfs
program 100003 version 2 ready and waiting
program 100003 version 3 ready and waiting
program 100003 version 4 ready and waiting
```

Specify **localhost** to display a list of versions of a daemon registered on the local system:

```
$ rpcinfo -u localhost ypbind
program 100007 version 1 ready and waiting
program 100007 version 2 ready and waiting
```

Locking down rpcbind Because the **rpcbind** daemon holds information about which servers are running on the local system and which port each server is running on, only trusted systems should have access to this information. One way to ensure only selected systems have access to **rpcbind** is to lock it down in the **/etc/hosts.allow** and **/etc/hosts.deny** files (page 484). Put the following line in **hosts.deny** to prevent all systems from using **rpcbind** on the local (server) system:

```
rpcbind: ALL
```

You can test this setup from a remote system by giving the following command:

```
$ rpcinfo -p hostname
rpcinfo: can't contact portmapper: RPC: Authentication error; ...
```

Replace *hostname* with the name of the remote system that you changed the **hosts.deny** file on. The change is usually immediate; in most cases you do not need to restart **rpcbind**.

Next add the following line to the **hosts.allow** file on the server system:

```
rpcbind: host-IP
```

where *host-IP* is the IP address of the trusted, remote system that you gave the preceding rpcinfo command from. Use only IP addresses with **rpcbind** in **hosts.allow**; do not use system names that **rpcbind** could get stuck trying to resolve. If you give the same command, rpcinfo should display a list of the servers that RPC knows about, including **rpcbind**. See page 766 for more examples.

Set the clocks

security The **rpcbind** daemon relies on the client's and the server's clocks being synchronized. A simple *DoS attack* (page 1162) can be initiated by setting the server's clock to the wrong time.

THE xinetd SUPERSERVER

The **xinetd** (extended Internet daemon; xinetd.org) is called a superserver or service dispatcher because it starts other daemons, such as **smbd** (Samba) and **vsftpd** (FTP), as necessary. It listens for network connections. When one is made, it identifies a server daemon based on the port the connection comes in on, sets the daemon's standard input and standard output file descriptors to the socket (page 517), and starts the daemon.

Using this superserver offers two advantages over having several servers constantly running daemons that monitor ports. First, the superserver avoids the need for daemons to run when not in use. Second, it allows developers to write servers that read from standard input and write to standard output; it handles all socket communication.

The **inetd** superserver, which originally shipped with 4.3BSD, was not particularly insecure. However, it typically opened a lot of ports and ran many servers, increasing the possibility that exploitable software would be exposed to the Internet. Its successor, **xinetd**, introduced access control and logging. This daemon allowed an administrator to limit the hours a service was available and the origin and number of incoming connections. When compiled with **libwrap**, **xinetd** can take advantage of TCP wrappers (next).

At a time when CPU power was more limited than it is today and RAM was more expensive, these superservers offered the advantage of efficient memory and CPU usage. Systems have slowly moved away from using these superservers over the past few years. Today a system can easily spare the few megabytes of memory and the minimal CPU time it takes to keep a daemon running to monitor a port: It takes fewer resources to keep a process in RAM (or swap space) than it does to restart it periodically. Also, a developer can now handle socket communications more easily using various toolkits.

The base configuration for **xinetd** is stored in the **/etc/xinetd.conf** file. If this file is not present, **xinetd** is probably not installed (**xinetd** package). The default **xinetd.conf** file is well commented. The following example **xinetd.conf** file shows some of the more common defaults:

```
$ cat /etc/xinetd.conf
# Sample configuration file for xinetd

defaults
{
        instances            = 60
        log_type             = SYSLOG authpriv
        log_on_success       = HOST PID
        log_on_failure       = HOST
        cps                  = 25 30
}
includedir /etc/xinetd.d
```

The **defaults** section specifies the default configuration of **xinetd**; the files in the included directory, **/etc/xinetd.d**, specify server-specific configurations. Defaults can be overridden by server-specific configuration files.

In the preceding file, the **instances** directive specifies that no daemon might run more than 60 copies of itself at one time. The **log_type** directive specifies that **xinetd** send messages to the system log daemon (**syslogd**; page 623) using the **authpriv** facility. The next two lines specify what to log on success and on failure. The **cps** (connections per second) directive specifies that no more than 25 connections to a specific service should be made per second and that the service should be disabled for 30 seconds if this limit is exceeded.

Following is the default rsync **xinetd** configuration file. By default, an rsync client uses ssh as the transport and does not connect to the rsync daemon. Thus it does not use **xinetd**.

```
$ cat /etc/xinetd.d/rsync
# default: off
# description: The rsync server is a good addition to an ftp server, \
#         as it allows crc checksumming etc.
```

```
service rsync
{
        disable         = yes
        flags           = IPv6
        socket_type     = stream
        wait            = no
        user            = root
        server          = /usr/bin/rsync
        server_args     = --daemon
        log_on_failure  += USERID
}
```

The **socket_type** indicates whether the socket uses TCP or UDP. TCP-based protocols establish a connection between the client and the server and are identified by the type **stream**. UDP-based protocols rely on the transmission of individual datagrams and are identified by the type **dgram**.

When **wait** is set to **no**, **xinetd** handles multiple concurrent connections to this service. Setting **wait** to **yes** causes **xinetd** to wait for the server process to complete before handling the next request for that service. In general, UDP services should be set to **yes** and TCP services to **no**. If you were to set **wait** to **yes** for a service such as telnet, only one person would be able to use the service at any given time.

The **user** specifies which user the server runs as. If this user is a member of multiple groups, you can also specify the group on a separate line with the keyword **group**. The **user** directive is ignored if **xinetd** is run without **root** permissions. The **server** provides the pathname of the server program that **xinetd** runs for this service while **server_args** specifies the arguments with which **xinetd** calls the server.

The **disable** line disables a service without removing the configuration file. As shipped by Fedora/RHEL, a number of services include an **xinetd** configuration file with **disable** set to **yes**. To run one of these services, change **disable** to **no** in the appropriate file in **xinetd.d** and restart **xinetd**:

```
# service xinetd restart
Stopping xinetd:                                    [  OK  ]
Starting xinetd:                                    [  OK  ]
```

Alternatively, when you use chkconfig (page 446) to turn a service on or off, it changes the value of the **disable** parameter in the corresponding **xinetd** configuration file and reloads **xinetd** by sending it a signal.

If you include **only_from**, it specifies which systems **xinetd** allows to use the service. It is a good idea to use IP addresses only—using hostnames can render the service unavailable if DNS fails. Zeros at the right of an IP address are treated as wildcards. For example, **192.168.0.0** allows access from any system in the **192.168** subnet.

See the **xinetd.conf** man page for more information on **xinetd** configuration parameters.

SECURING A SERVER

Two ways you can secure a server are by using TCP wrappers and by setting up a chroot jail. This section describes both techniques. Alternatively, you can use **system-config-firewall** (page 893) to secure a system. It covers protocols such as **httpd** that are not protected by **libwrap**. For more information refer to "Securing a System" on page 458.

TCP WRAPPERS: SECURE A SERVER (hosts.allow AND hosts.deny)

Follow these guidelines when you open a local system to access from remote systems:

- Open the local system only to systems you want to allow to access it.

- Allow each remote system to access only the data you want it to access.

- Allow each remote system to access data only in the appropriate manner (readonly, read/write, write only).

libwrap As part of the client/server model, TCP wrappers, which can be used for any daemon that is linked against **libwrap**, rely on the **/etc/hosts.allow** and **/etc/hosts.deny** files as the basis of a simple access control list (ACL). This access control language defines rules that selectively allow clients to access server daemons on a local system based on the client's address and the daemon the client tries to access. The output of **ldd** shows that one of the shared library dependencies of **sshd** is **libwrap**:

```
$ ldd /usr/sbin/sshd | grep libwrap
        libwrap.so.0 => /lib/libwrap.so.0 (0x00e7c000)
```

hosts.allow and **hosts.deny** Each line in the **hosts.allow** and **hosts.deny** files has the following format:

daemon_list : client_list [: command]

where *daemon_list* is a comma-separated list of one or more server daemons (e.g., **rpcbind**, **vsftpd**, **sshd**), *client_list* is a comma-separated list of one or more clients (see Table 11-5 on page 478), and the optional *command* is the command that is executed when a client from *client_list* tries to access a server daemon from *daemon_list*.

When a client requests a connection to a server, the **hosts.allow** and **hosts.deny** files on the server system are consulted in the following order until a match is found:

1. If the daemon/client pair matches a line in **hosts.allow**, access is granted.

2. If the daemon/client pair matches a line in **hosts.deny**, access is denied.

3. If there is no match in **hosts.allow** or **hosts.deny**, access is granted.

The first match determines whether the client is allowed to access the server. When either **hosts.allow** or **hosts.deny** does not exist, it is as though that file were empty. Although not recommended, you can allow access to all daemons for all clients by removing both files.

Examples   For a more secure system, put the following line in **hosts.deny** to block all access:

```
$ cat /etc/hosts.deny
...
ALL : ALL : echo '%c tried to connect to %d and was blocked' >> /var/log/tcpwrappers.log
```

This line prevents any client from connecting to any service, unless specifically permitted to do so in **hosts.allow**. When this rule is matched, it adds a line to the file named **/var/log/tcpwrappers.log**. The **%c** expands to client information, and the **%d** expands to the name of the daemon the client attempted to connect to.

With the preceding **hosts.deny** file in place, you can include lines in **hosts.allow** that explicitly allow access to certain services and systems. For example, the following **hosts.allow** file allows any client to connect to the OpenSSH daemon (ssh, scp, sftp) but allows telnet connections only from the same network as the local system and users on the 192.168. subnet:

```
$ cat /etc/hosts.allow
sshd: ALL
in.telnet: LOCAL
in.telnet: 192.168.* 127.0.0.1
...
```

The first line allows connection from any system (ALL) to **sshd**. The second line allows connection from any system in the same domain as the server (LOCAL). The third line matches any system whose IP address starts with **192.168.** as well as the local system.

SETTING UP A chroot JAIL

On early UNIX systems, the root directory was a fixed point in the filesystem. On modern UNIX variants, including Linux, you can define the root directory on a per-process basis. The chroot utility allows you to run a process with a root directory other than /.

The root directory appears at the top of the directory hierarchy and has no parent. Thus a process cannot access files above the root directory because none exists. If, for example, you run a program (process) and specify its root directory as **/home/sam/jail**, the program would have no concept of any files in **/home/sam** or above: **jail** is the program's root directory and is labeled **/** (not **jail**).

By creating an artificial root directory, frequently called a (chroot) jail, you prevent a program from accessing, executing, or modifying—possibly maliciously—files outside the directory hierarchy starting at its root. You must set up a chroot jail properly to increase security: If you do not set up the chroot jail correctly, you can make it easier for a malicious user to gain access to a system than if there were no chroot jail.

USING chroot

Creating a chroot jail is simple: Working with **root** privileges, give the command **/usr/sbin/chroot** *directory*. The *directory* becomes the root directory, and the process attempts to run the default shell. Working with **root** privileges, the following command sets up a chroot jail in the (existing) **/home/sam/jail** directory:

```
# /usr/sbin/chroot /home/sam/jail
/usr/sbin/chroot: failed to run command '/bin/bash': No such file or directory
```

This example sets up a chroot jail, but when the system attempts to run the bash shell, the operation fails. Once the jail is set up, the directory that was named **jail** takes on the name of the root directory, **/**. As a consequence, chroot cannot find the file identified by the pathname **/bin/bash**. In this situation the chroot jail works correctly but is not useful.

Getting a chroot jail to work the way you want is more complicated. To have the preceding example run bash in a chroot jail, create a **bin** directory in **jail** (**/home/sam/jail/bin**) and copy **/bin/bash** to this directory. Because the bash binary is dynamically linked to shared libraries, you need to copy these libraries into **jail** as well. The libraries go in **lib**.

The next example creates the necessary directories, copies **bash**, uses ldd to display the shared library dependencies of bash, and copies the necessary libraries to **lib**. The **linux-gate.so.1** file is a dynamically shared object (DSO) provided by the kernel to speed system calls; you do not need to copy it.

```
$ pwd
/home/sam/jail
$ mkdir bin lib
$ cp /bin/bash bin
$ ldd bin/bash
        linux-gate.so.1 =>  (0x00988000)
        libtinfo.so.5 => /lib/libtinfo.so.5 (0x0076b000)
        libdl.so.2 => /lib/libdl.so.2 (0x00afb000)
        libc.so.6 => /lib/libc.so.6 (0x00110000)
        /lib/ld-linux.so.2 (0x00923000)

$ cp /lib/{libtinfo.so.5,libdl.so.2,libc.so.6,ld-linux.so.2} lib
```

Now start the chroot jail again. Although all the setup can be done by an ordinary user, you must be working with **root** privileges to run chroot:

```
$ su
Password:
#/usr/sbin/chroot .
bash-4.1# pwd
/
bash-4.1# ls
bash: ls: command not found
bash-4.1#
```

This time chroot finds and starts **bash**, which displays its default prompt (**bash-4.1#**). The pwd command works because it is a shell builtin (page 249). However, bash cannot find the ls utility because it is not in the chroot jail. You can copy **/bin/ls** and its libraries into the jail if you want users in the jail to be able to use ls. An **exit** command allows you to escape from the jail.

If you provide chroot with a second argument, it takes that argument as the name of the program to run inside the jail. The following command is equivalent to the preceding one:

```
# /usr/sbin/chroot /home/sam/jail /bin/bash
```

To set up a useful chroot jail, first determine which utilities the users of the chroot jail need. Then copy the appropriate binaries and their libraries into the jail. Alternatively, you can build static copies of the binaries and put them in the jail without installing separate libraries. (The statically linked binaries are considerably larger than their dynamic counterparts. The size of the base system with bash and the core utilities exceeds 50 megabytes.) You can find the source code for most common utilities in the **bash** and **coreutils** SRPMS (source rpm) packages.

The chroot utility fails unless you run it with **root** privileges. The result of running chroot with **root** privileges is a **root** shell (a shell with **root** privileges) running inside a chroot jail. Because a user with **root** privileges can break out of a chroot jail, it is imperative that you run a program in the chroot jail with reduced privileges (i.e., privileges other than those of **root**).

There are several ways to reduce the privileges of a user. For example, you can put su or sudo in the jail and then start a shell or a daemon inside the jail, using one of these programs to reduce the privileges of the user working in the jail. A command such as the following starts a shell with reduced privileges inside the jail:

```
# /usr/sbin/chroot jailpath /bin/su user -c /bin/bash
```

where *jailpath* is the pathname of the jail directory, and *user* is the username under whose privileges the shell runs. The problem with this scenario is that sudo and su, as compiled for Fedora/RHEL, call PAM. To run one of these utilities you need to put all of PAM, including its libraries and configuration files, in the jail, along with sudo (or su) and the **/etc/passwd** file. Alternatively, you can recompile su or sudo. The source code calls PAM, however, so you would need to modify the source so it does not call PAM. Either one of these techniques is time-consuming and introduces complexities that can lead to an unsecure jail.

The following C program[2] runs a program with reduced privileges in a chroot jail. Because this program obtains the UID and GID of the user you specify on the command line before calling **chroot**(), you do not need to put **/etc/passwd** in the jail. The program reduces the privileges of the specified program to those of the specified user. This program is presented as a simple solution to the preceding issues so you can experiment with a chroot jail and better understand how it works.

---

2. Thanks to David Chisnall and the Étoilé Project (etoileos.com) for the **uchroot.c** program.

```
$ cat uchroot.c

/* See svn.gna.org/viewcvs/etoile/trunk/Etoile/LiveCD/uchroot.c for terms of use. */

#include <stdio.h>
#include <stdlib.h>
#include <pwd.h>

int main(int argc, char * argv[])
{
        if(argc < 4)
        {
                printf("Usage: %s {username} {directory} {program} [arguments]\n",
argv[0]);
                return 1;
        }
        /* Parse arguments */
        struct passwd * pass = getpwnam(argv[1]);
        if(pass == NULL)
        {
                printf("Unknown user %s\n", argv[1]);
                return 2;
        }
        /* Set the required UID */
        chdir(argv[2]);
        if(chroot(argv[2])
                ||
                setgid(pass->pw_gid)
                ||
                setuid(pass->pw_uid))
        {
                printf("%s must be run as root.  Current uid=%d, euid=%d\n",
                                argv[0],
                                (int)getuid(),
                                (int)geteuid()
                                );
                return 3;
        }
        return execv(argv[3], argv + 3);
}
```

The first of the following commands compiles **uchroot.c** using cc (**gcc** package),
creating an executable file named uchroot. Subsequent commands move uchroot to
/usr/local/bin and give it appropriate ownership.

```
$ cc -o uchroot uchroot.c
$ su
password:
# mv uchroot /usr/local/bin
# chown root:root /usr/local/bin/uchroot
# exit
$ ls -l /usr/local/bin/uchroot
-rwxrwxr-x. 1 root root 5704 12-31 15:00 /usr/local/bin/uchroot
```

Using the setup from earlier in this section, give the following command to run a shell with the privileges of the user **sam** inside a chroot jail:

```
# /usr/local/bin/uchroot sam /home/sam/jail /bin/bash
```

Keeping multiple chroot jails

tip If you plan to deploy multiple chroot jails, it is a good idea to keep a clean copy of the **bin** and **lib** directories somewhere other than one of the active jails.

RUNNING A SERVICE IN A chroot JAIL

Running a shell inside a jail has limited usefulness. In reality, you are more likely to want to run a specific service inside the jail. To run a service inside a jail, make sure all files needed by that service are inside the jail. Using uchroot, the format of a command to start a service in a chroot jail is

```
# /usr/local/bin/uchroot user jailpath daemonname
```

where *jailpath* is the pathname of the jail directory, *user* is the username that runs the daemon, and *daemonname* is the pathname (inside the jail) of the daemon that provides the service.

Some servers are already set up to take advantage of chroot jails. For example, you can set up DNS so that **named** runs in a jail (page 877), and the **vsftpd** FTP server can automatically start chroot jails for clients (page 717).

SECURITY CONSIDERATIONS

Some services need to be run by a user or process with **root** privileges but release their **root** privileges once started (Apache, Procmail, and **vsftpd** are examples). If you are running such a service, you do not need to use uchroot or put su or sudo inside the jail.

A process run with **root** privileges can potentially escape from a chroot jail. For this reason, you should reduce privileges before starting a program running inside the jail. Also, be careful about which setuid (page 205) binaries you allow inside a jail—a security hole in one of them could compromise the security of the jail. In addition, make sure the user cannot access executable files that he uploads to the jail.

DHCP: CONFIGURES NETWORK INTERFACES

Instead of storing network configuration information in local files on each system, DHCP (Dynamic Host Configuration Protocol) enables client systems to retrieve the necessary network configuration information from a DHCP server each time they connect to the network. A DHCP server assigns IP addresses from a pool of addresses to clients as needed. Assigned addresses are typically temporary but need not be.

This technique has several advantages over storing network configuration information in local files:

- A new user can set up an Internet connection without having to deal with IP addresses, netmasks, DNS addresses, and other technical details. An experienced user can set up a connection more quickly.

- DHCP facilitates assignment and management of IP addresses and related network information by centralizing the process on a server. A system administrator can configure new systems, including laptops that connect to the network from different locations, to use DHCP; DHCP then assigns IP addresses only when each system connects to the network. The pool of IP addresses is managed as a group on the DHCP server.

- DHCP facilitates the use of IP addresses by more than one system, reducing the total number of IP addresses needed. This conservation of addresses is important because the Internet is quickly running out of IPv4 addresses. Although a particular IP address can be used by only one system at a time, many end-user systems require addresses only occasionally, when they connect to the Internet. By reusing IP addresses, DHCP has lengthened the life of the IPv4 protocol.

DHCP is particularly useful for an administrator who is responsible for maintaining a large number of systems because new systems no longer need to be set up with unique configuration information.

MORE INFORMATION

Web   www.dhcp.org
DHCP FAQ: www.dhcp-handbook.com/dhcp_faq.html

Local   DHCP client: **/usr/share/doc/dhclient-***
DHCP server: **/usr/share/doc/dhcp-***

HOWTO   *DHCP Mini HOWTO*

HOW DHCP WORKS

Using dhclient, the client contacts the server daemon, **dhcpd,** to obtain the IP address, netmask, broadcast address, nameserver address, and other networking parameters. In turn, the server provides a *lease* on the IP address to the client. The client can request the specific terms of the lease, including its duration; the server can limit these terms. While connected to the network, a client typically requests extensions of its lease as necessary so its IP address remains the same. This lease might expire once the client is disconnected from the network, with the server giving the client a new IP address when it requests a new lease. You can also set up a DHCP server to provide static IP addresses for specific clients (refer to "Static Versus Dynamic IP Addresses" on page 378).

When you install Fedora/RHEL, the system runs a DHCP client, connects to a DHCP server if it can find one, and configures its network interface.

DHCP CLIENT

A DHCP client requests network configuration parameters from the DHCP server and uses those parameters to configure its network interface.

PREREQUISITES

Make sure the following package is installed:

- dhclient

dhclient: THE DHCP CLIENT

When a DHCP client system connects to the network, dhclient requests a lease from the DHCP server and configures the client's network interface(s). Once a DHCP client has requested and established a lease, it stores the lease information in a file named **dhclient-*-*interface*.lease**, which resides in the **/var/lib/dhclient** directory. The *interface* is the name of the interface the client uses, such as eth0. The system uses this information to reestablish a lease when either the server or the client needs to reboot. The DHCP client configuration file, **/etc/dhcp/dhclient.conf**, is required only for custom configurations.

The following **dhclient.conf** file specifies a single interface, **eth0**:

```
$ cat /etc/dhcp3/dhclient.conf
interface "eth0"
{
send dhcp-client-identifier 1:xx:xx:xx:xx:xx:xx;
send dhcp-lease-time 86400;
}
```

In the preceding file, the 1 in the **dhcp-client-identifier** specifies an Ethernet network and **xx:xx:xx:xx:xx:xx** is the *MAC address* (page 1174) of the device controlling that interface. See page 493 for instructions on how to determine the MAC address of a device. The **dhcp-lease-time** is the duration, in seconds, of the lease on the IP address. While the client is connected to the network, dhclient automatically renews the lease each time half of the lease time is up. A lease time of 86,400 seconds (one day) is a reasonable choice for a workstation.

DHCP SERVER

A DHCP server maintains a list of IP addresses and other configuration parameters. Clients request network configuration parameters from the server.

PREREQUISITES

Install the following package:

- dhcp

dhcpd init script   Run chkconfig to cause **dhcpd** to start when the system enters multiuser mode:

```
# chkconfig dhcpd on
```

After configuring the DHCP server, start or restart **dhcpd**:

```
# service dhcpd start
```

dhcpd: The DHCP Daemon

A simple DCHP server (**dhcpd**) allows you to add clients to a network without maintaining a list of assigned IP addresses. A simple network, such as a home-based LAN sharing an Internet connection, can use DHCP to assign a dynamic IP address to almost all nodes. The exceptions are servers and routers, which must be at known network locations if clients are to find them. If servers and routers are configured without DHCP, you can specify a simple DHCP server configuration in **/etc/dhcp/dhcpd.conf**:

```
$ cat /etc/dhcp/dhcpd.conf
default-lease-time 600;
max-lease-time 86400;

option subnet-mask 255.255.255.0;
option broadcast-address 192.168.1.255;
option routers 192.168.1.1;
option domain-name-servers 192.168.1.1;
option domain-name "example.com";

subnet 192.168.1.0 netmask 255.255.255.0 {
    range 192.168.1.2 192.168.1.200;
}
```

By default, **dhcpd** serves requests on all nonbroadcast network interfaces.

The preceding configuration file specifies a LAN where both the router and the DNS server are located on **192.168.1.1**. The **default-lease-time** specifies the number of seconds the dynamic IP lease will remain valid if the client does not specify a duration. The **max-lease-time** is the maximum time allowed for a lease.

The information in the **option** lines is sent to each client when it connects. The names following the word **option** specify what the following argument represents. For example, the **option broadcast-address** line specifies the broadcast address of the network. The **routers** and **domain-name-servers** options can be followed by multiple values separated by commas.

The **subnet** section includes a **range** line that specifies the range of IP addresses the DHCP server can assign. In the case of multiple subnets, you can define options, such as **subnet-mask**, inside the **subnet** section. Options defined outside all **subnet** sections are global and apply to all subnets.

The preceding configuration file assigns addresses in the range from 192.168.1.2 to 192.168.1.200. The DHCP server starts at the bottom of this range and attempts to assign a new IP address to each new client. Once the DHCP server reaches the top of the range, it starts reassigning IP addresses that have been used in the past but are not currently in use. If you have fewer systems than IP addresses, the IP address of each system should remain fairly constant. Two systems cannot use the same IP address at the same time.

Once you have configured a DHCP server, restart it using the **dhcpd** init script (page 492). When the server is running, clients configured to obtain an IP address from the server using DHCP should be able to do so. See the **/usr/share/doc/dhcp✳/✳ sample** files for sample **dhcpd.conf** files.

STATIC IP ADDRESSES

As mentioned earlier, routers and servers typically require static IP addresses. Although you can manually configure IP addresses for these systems, it might be more convenient to have the DHCP server provide them with static IP addresses. See page 652 if you want to configure a system to use a static IP address without using DHCP.

When a system that requires a specific static IP address connects to the network and contacts the DHCP server, the server needs a way to identify the system so it can assign the proper IP address to that system. The DHCP server uses the *MAC address* (page 1174) of the system's network interface card (NIC) as an identifier. When you set up the server, you must know the MAC address of each system that requires a static IP address.

Determining a MAC address The ip utility displays the MAC addresses of the Ethernet cards in a system. In the following example, the MAC address is the colon-separated series of hexadecimal number pairs following **link/ether**:

```
$ ip link show eth1
2: eth1: <BROADCAST,MULTICAST,UP,LOWER_UP> mtu 1500 qdisc pfifo_fast state UNKNOWN qlen 1000
    link/ether 00:0c:29:12:35:6e brd ff:ff:ff:ff:ff:ff
```

Run ip on each system that requires a static IP address. Once you have determined the MAC addresses of these systems, you can add a **host** section to the **/etc/dhcp/ dhcpd.conf** file for each one, instructing the DHCP server to assign a specific address to that system. The following **host** section assigns the address **192.168.1.1** to the system with the MAC address of **BA:DF:00:DF:C0:FF**:

```
$ cat /etc/dhcp/dhcpd.conf
...
host router {
    hardware ethernet BA:DF:00:DF:C0:FF;
    fixed-address 192.168.1.1;
    option host-name router;
}
```

The name following **host** is used internally by **dhcpd**. The name specified after **option host-name** is passed to the client and can be a hostname or an FQDN. After making changes to **dhcpd.conf**, restart **dhcpd** using the **dhcpd** init script (page 492).

nsswitch.conf: WHICH SERVICE TO LOOK AT FIRST

Once NIS and DNS were introduced, finding user and system information was no longer a simple matter of searching a local file. When once you looked in **/etc/passwd** to get user information and in **/etc/hosts** to find system address information, now you can use several methods to obtain this type of information. The **/etc/nsswitch.conf** (name service switch configuration) file specifies which methods to use and the order in which to use them when looking for a certain type of information. You can also specify which action the system should take based on whether a method succeeds or fails.

Syntax   Each line in **nsswitch.conf** specifies how to search for a piece of information, such as a user's password. A line in **nsswitch.conf** has the following syntax:

> *info:*   *method [[action]] [method [[action]]...]*

where *info* is the type of information the line describes, *method* is the method used to find the information, and *action* is the response to the return status of the preceding *method*. The action is enclosed within square brackets.

When called upon to supply information that **nsswitch.conf** describes, the system examines the line with the appropriate *info* field. It uses the methods specified on this line, starting with the method on the left. By default, when it finds the desired information, the system stops searching. Without an *action* specification, when a method fails to return a result, the system tries the next action. It is possible for the search to end without finding the requested information.

INFORMATION

The **nsswitch.conf** file commonly controls searches for usernames, passwords, host IP addresses, and group information. The following list describes most of the types of information (*info* in the syntax given earlier) that **nsswitch.conf** controls searches for:

automount	Automount (**/etc/auto.master** and **/etc/auto.misc**; page 811)
bootparam	Diskless and other booting options (**bootparam** man page)
ethers	MAC address (page 1174)
group	Groups of users (**/etc/group**; page 506)
hosts	System information (**/etc/hosts**; page 507)
networks	Network information (**/etc/networks**)
passwd	User information (**/etc/passwd**; page 508)
protocols	Protocol information (**/etc/protocols**; page 510)
publickey	Used for NFS running in secure mode
rpc	RPC names and numbers (**/etc/rpc**; page 511)
services	Services information (**/etc/services**; page 511)
shadow	Shadow password information (**/etc/shadow**; page 511)

Methods

Following is a list of the types of information that **nsswitch.conf** controls searches for (*method* in the syntax shown on the previous page). For each type of information, you can specify one or more of the following methods:[3]

compat	± syntax in **passwd, group,** and **shadow** files (page 496)
dns	Queries the DNS (**hosts** queries only)
files	Searches local files such as **/etc/passwd** and **/etc/hosts**
ldap	Queries an LDAP server (page 776)
nis	Searches the NIS database; **yp** is an alias for **nis**

Search Order

The information provided by two or more methods might overlap: For example, both **files** and **nis** might provide password information for the same user. With overlapping information, you need to consider which method you want to be authoritative (take precedence) and then place that method at the left of the list of methods.

The default **nsswitch.conf** file lists methods without actions, assuming no overlap (which is normal). In this case, the order is not critical: When one method fails, the system goes to the next one and all that is lost is a little time. Order becomes critical when you use actions between methods or when overlapping entries differ.

The first of the following lines from **nsswitch.conf** causes the system to search for password information in **/etc/passwd** and if that fails, to use NIS to find the information. If the user you are looking for is listed in both places, the information in the local file is used and is considered authoritative. The second line uses NIS to find an IP address given a hostname; if that fails, it searches **/etc/hosts;** if that fails, it checks with DNS to find the information.

```
passwd          files nis
hosts           nis files dns
```

Action Items

Each method can optionally be followed by an action item that specifies what to do if the method succeeds or fails. An action item has the following format:

[[!]STATUS=action]

where the opening and closing square brackets are part of the format and do not indicate that the contents are optional; *STATUS* (uppercase by convention) is the status being tested for; and *action* is the action to be taken if *STATUS* matches the status returned by the preceding method. The leading exclamation point (**!**) is optional and negates the status.

---

3. Other, less commonly used methods also exist. See the default **/etc/nsswitch.conf** file and the **nsswitch.conf** man page for more information. Although NIS+ belongs in this list, it is not implemented as a Linux server and is not discussed in this book.

STATUS *STATUS* might have any of the following values:

NOTFOUND—The method worked, but the value being searched for was not found. The default action is **continue**.

SUCCESS—The method worked, and the value being searched for was found; no error was returned. The default action is **return**.

TRYAGAIN—The method failed because it was temporarily unavailable. For example, a file might be locked or a server overloaded. The default action is **continue**.

UNAVAIL—The method failed because it is permanently unavailable. For example, the required file might not be accessible or the required server might be down. The default action is **continue**.

action There are two possible values for *action:*

return—Returns to the calling routine with or without a value.

continue—Continues with the next method. Any returned value is overwritten by a value found by a subsequent method.

Example The following line from **nsswitch.conf** causes the system first to use DNS to search for the IP address of a given host. The action item following the DNS method tests whether the status returned by the method is not (!) UNAVAIL.

```
hosts        dns [!UNAVAIL=return] files
```

The system takes the action associated with the *STATUS* (**return**) if the DNS method does not return UNAVAIL (**!UNAVAIL**)—that is, if DNS returns SUCCESS, NOTFOUND, or TRYAGAIN. As a consequence, the following method (**files**) is used only when the DNS server is unavailable. If the DNS server is *not un*available (read the two negatives as "is available"), the search returns the domain name or reports that the domain name was not found. The search uses the **files** method (checks the local **/etc/hosts** file) only if the server is not available.

compat METHOD: ± IN passwd, group, AND shadow FILES

You can put special codes in the **/etc/passwd**, **/etc/group**, and **/etc/shadow** files that cause the system, when you specify the **compat** method in **nsswitch.conf**, to combine and modify entries in the local files and the NIS maps. That is, a plus sign (**+**) at the beginning of a line in one of these files adds NIS information; a minus sign (**–**) removes information.

For example, to use these codes in the **passwd** file, specify **passwd: compat** in the **nsswitch.conf** file. The system then goes through the **passwd** file in order, adding or removing the appropriate NIS entries when it reaches each line that starts with a **+** or **–**.

Although you can put a plus sign at the end of the **passwd** file, specify **passwd: compat** in **nsswitch.conf** to search the local **passwd** file, and then go through the NIS map, it is more efficient to put **passwd: file nis** in **nsswitch.conf** and not modify the **passwd** file.

GETTING HELP

Fedora/RHEL comes with extensive documentation (page 125). Fedora maintains a page that points to many useful support documents at docs.fedoraproject.org; fedoraproject.org/en/get-help shows how to get to the fedora forums, email lists, and IRC chatrooms; Red Hat maintains a similar page at access.redhat.com. and keeps documentation at access.redhat.com/docs. Although some sections of these Red Hat sites require an account to access, anyone can get an account for free. You can also find help on the System Administrators Guild site (www.sage.org). The Internet is another rich source of information on managing a Linux system; refer to Appendix B (page 1115) and to the author's home page (www.sobell.com) for pointers to useful sites.

You need not act as a Fedora/RHEL system administrator in isolation; a large community of Fedora/RHEL experts is willing to assist you in getting the most out of a Linux system. Of course, you will get better help if you have already tried to solve a problem yourself by reading the available documentation. If you are unable to solve a problem by consulting the documentation, a well-thought-out question posed to the appropriate newsgroup, such as **comp.os.linux.misc**, or mailing list can often generate useful information. Be sure to describe the problem accurately and identify the system carefully. Include information about the version of Fedora/RHEL running on the system and any software packages and hardware you think relate to the problem. The newsgroup **comp.os.linux.answers** contains postings of solutions to common problems and periodic postings of the most up-to-date versions of FAQs and HOWTO documents. See www.catb.org/~esr/faqs/smart-questions.html for a helpful paper by Eric S. Raymond and Rick Moen titled "How to Ask Questions the Smart Way."

CHAPTER SUMMARY

A system administrator is someone who keeps the system in a useful and convenient state for its users. Much of the work you do as the system administrator will require you to work with **root** privileges. A user with these privileges (sometimes referred to as Superuser) has extensive systemwide powers that normal users do not have. A user with **root** privileges can read from and write to any file and can execute programs that ordinary users are not permitted to execute.

The system administrator controls system operation, which includes the following tasks: configuring the system; booting up; running init scripts; setting up servers; working in single-user, multiuser, and rescue modes; bringing the system down; and handling system crashes. Fedora/RHEL provides both graphical and textual configuration tools. Many of the graphical tools are named system-config-*.

When you bring up the system in single-user mode, only the system console is functional. While working in single-user mode, you can back up files and use fsck to check the integrity of filesystems before you mount them. The telinit utility can bring the system to its default multiuser state. With the system running in multiuser mode, you can still perform many administration tasks, such as adding users and printers.

When you install a Fedora/RHEL system, you specify a password for the **root** account. You use this password to gain **root** privileges, either by logging in as the user named **root** or by using su and providing the **root** password. Alternatively, you can configure sudo which grants **root** privileges based on your password. A system that does not have a **root** password and that relies on sudo to escalate permissions can be more secure than one with a **root** password.

The Upstart **init** daemon, which replaces the traditional System V **init** daemon (SysVinit), is event based: It can start and stop services upon receiving information that something on the system has changed (an *event*). Events include adding devices to and removing them from the system as well as bringing the system up and shutting it down.

The **xinetd** superserver starts server daemons as needed and can help secure a system by controlling who can use which services. You can use TCP wrappers to control who can use which system services by editing the **hosts.allow** and **hosts.deny** files in the **/etc** directory. Setting up a chroot jail limits the portion of the filesystem a user sees, so it can help control the damage a malicious user can do.

You can set up a DHCP server so you do not have to configure each system on a network manually. DHCP can provide both static and dynamic IP addresses. Whether a system uses NIS, DNS, local files, or a combination (and in what order) as a source of information is determined by **/etc/nsswitch.conf**. Linux-PAM enables you to maintain fine-grained control over who can access the system, how they can access it, and what they can do.

EXERCISES

1. How does single-user mode differ from multiuser mode?

2. How would you communicate each of the following messages?

   a. The system is coming down tomorrow at 6:00 in the evening for periodic maintenance.

   b. The system is coming down in five minutes.

   c. Zach's jobs are slowing the system down drastically, and he should postpone them.

   d. Zach's wife just had a baby girl.

3. What do the letters of the su command stand for? (*Hint:* It is not Superuser.) What can you do with su besides give yourself **root** privileges? How would you log in as Zach if you did not know his password but knew the **root** password? How would you establish the same environment that Zach has when he first logs in?

4. How would you allow a user to execute a specific, privileged command without giving the user the **root** password?

5. How do you kill process 1648? How do you kill all processes running kmail? In which instances do you need to work with **root** privileges?

6. How can you disable SELinux?

7. Develop a strategy for coming up with a password that an intruder would not be likely to guess but that you will be able to remember.

ADVANCED EXERCISES

8. Give the command

    ```
    $ /bin/fuser -uv /
    ```

    What does the output list? Why is it so long? Give the same command while working with **root** privileges (or ask the system administrator to do so and email you the results). How does this list differ from the first? Why is it different?

9. When it puts files in a **lost+found** directory, fsck has lost the directory information for the files and thus has lost the names of the files. Each file is given a new name, which is the same as the inode number for the file:

    ```
    $ ls -l lost+found
    -rw-r--r-- 1 max pubs 110 2010-06-10 10:55 51262
    ```

    How can you identify these files and restore them?

10. Take a look at **/usr/bin/lesspipe.sh**. Explain its purpose and describe six ways it works.

11. Why are setuid shell scripts inherently unsafe?

12. When a user logs in, you would like the system to first check the local **/etc/passwd** file for a username and then check NIS. How do you implement this strategy?

13. Some older kernels contain a vulnerability that allows a local user to gain **root** privileges. Explain how this kind of vulnerability negates the value of a chroot jail.

12

FILES, DIRECTORIES, AND FILESYSTEMS

OBJECTIVES

After reading this chapter you should be able to:

▶ List four important directories and describe their uses

▶ List common system startup configuration files and describe their uses

▶ List typical network configuration files and describe their uses

▶ List common login configuration files and describe their uses

▶ List a few device filenames and describe their uses

▶ Define the seven types of files found on the system

▶ Describe several filesystem types found on a Linux system

▶ View, check, tune, mount, and unmount local filesystems

Filesystems hold directories of files. These structures store user data and system data that are the basis of users' work on the system and the system's existence. This chapter discusses important files and directories, various types of files and ways to work with them, and the use and maintenance of filesystems.

IMPORTANT FILES AND DIRECTORIES

This section details the files most commonly used to administer the system. For a more general list of files, refer to "Important Standard Directories and Files" on page 199.

lost+found Holds preallocated disk blocks of directories that fsck uses to store pointers to unlinked files (files that have lost their directory [and therefore filename] information). Having these blocks available ensures that fsck does not have to allocate data blocks during recovery, a process that could further damage a corrupted filesystem. See page 525 for more information on fsck. However, fsck will allocate blocks if they do not exist.

Each **ext2**, **ext3**, and **ext4** filesystem contains a **lost+found** directory in the filesystem's root directory. If, for example, a filesystem is mounted at **/home**, there will be a **/home/lost+found** directory. There is always a **/lost+found** directory. These directories are normally created by mkfs when it writes an **ext2/ext3/ext4** filesystem to a partition. Although rarely necessary, you can create a **lost+found** directory manually using mklost+found.

~/.bash_profile Contains an individual user's *login shell* (page 1174) initialization script. The shell executes the commands in this file in the same environment as the shell each time a user logs in. (For information about executing a shell script in this manner, refer to the discussion of the . [dot] command on page 284.) The file must be located in a user's home directory. It is not run from terminal emulator windows because you do not log in in those windows.

The default Fedora/RHEL **.bash_profile** file executes the commands in **~/.bashrc**.

You can use **.bash_profile** to specify the editor you want to use, run stty to establish the terminal characteristics, set up aliases, and perform other housekeeping functions when a user logs in.

A simple **.bash_profile** file that sets **EDITOR** to vi and CONTROL-H as the erase key follows:

```
$ cat .bash_profile
export EDITOR=$(which vi)
stty erase '^h'
```

Using command substitution and **which vi** sets **EDITOR** to the absolute pathname of the vi editor. For more information refer to "Startup Files" on page 282.

~/.bashrc Contains an individual user's interactive, nonlogin shell initialization script. The shell executes the commands in this file in the same environment as the (new) shell each time a user creates a new interactive shell, including when a user opens a terminal emulator window. (For information about executing a shell script in this manner, refer to the discussion of the **. [dot]** command on page 284.) The **.bashrc** script differs from **.bash_profile** in that it is executed each time a new shell is spawned, not just when a user logs in. The default Fedora/RHEL **.bash_profile** file executes the commands in **~/.bashrc** so that these commands are executed when a user logs in. For more information refer to "Startup Files" on page 282.

/dev   Contains files representing pseudodevices and physical devices that might be attached to the system. The **/dev/sda** device was traditionally the first SCSI disk; now it is the first drive, including IDE, SATA, and USB drives. Other similar drives are named **/dev/sdb**, **/dev/sdc**, etc.

These names, such as **/dev/sda**, represent the order of the devices on the bus the devices are connected to, not the devices themselves. For example, if you swap the data cables on the disks referred to as **/dev/sda** and **/dev/sdb**, the drive's designations will change. Similarly, if you remove the device referred to as **/dev/sda**, the device that was referred to as **/dev/sdb** will now be referred to as **/dev/sda**. See **/dev/disk/by-uuid** (below) for a way to refer to specific devices and not to their order on the bus.

/dev/disk/by-path

Holds symbolic links to local devices. The names of the devices in this directory identify the devices. Each entry points to the device in **/dev** that it refers to (**sr0** is the CD/DVD drive).

```
$ ls -l /dev/disk/by-path
lrwxrwxrwx. 1 root root  9 01-25 04:17 pci-0000:00:07.1-scsi-1:0:0:0 -> ../../sr0
lrwxrwxrwx. 1 root root  9 01-25 04:17 pci-0000:00:10.0-scsi-0:0:0:0 -> ../../sda
lrwxrwxrwx. 1 root root 10 01-25 04:17 pci-0000:00:10.0-scsi-0:0:0:0-part1 -> ../../sda1
lrwxrwxrwx. 1 root root 10 01-25 04:17 pci-0000:00:10.0-scsi-0:0:0:0-part2 -> ../../sda2
```

/dev/disk/by-uuid

Holds symbolic links to local devices. The names of the devices in this directory consist of the *UUID* (page 1196) numbers of the devices. Each entry points to the device in **/dev** that it refers to. See page 524 for more information. The **dm** in the partition names stands for *device mapper*, which is used by LVM (page 42).

```
$ ls -l /dev/disk/by-uuid
lrwxrwxrwx. 1 root root 10 01-25 04:17 7694f86e-c3ff-4e51-b677-01b3d27927a4 -> ../../sda1
lrwxrwxrwx. 1 root root 10 01-25 12:17 7743cb0d-b961-4b65-b3a2-071536734d8a -> ../../dm-0
lrwxrwxrwx. 1 root root 10 01-25 12:17 800b87ec-b333-4d51-90e5-be359421e999 -> ../../dm-1
```

/dev/null   Also called a *bit bucket*. Output sent to this file disappears. The **/dev/null** file is a device file. Input you redirect to come from this file appears as null values, creating an empty file. You can create an empty file named **nothing** by giving one of the following commands:

```
$ cat /dev/null > nothing
$ cp /dev/null nothing
```

or, without explicitly using **/dev/null**,

```
$ > nothing
```

The last command redirects the output of a null command to the file with the same result as the previous commands. You can use any of these commands to truncate an existing file to zero length without changing its permissions. You can also use **/dev/null** to get rid of output you do not want:

```
$ grep portable * 2> /dev/null
```

This command displays all lines in all files in the working directory that contain the string **portable**. Any output to standard error (page 285), such as a permission or directory error, is discarded, while output to standard output appears on the screen. See also page 239.

/dev/pts A hook into the Linux kernel. This pseudofilesystem is part of the pseudoterminal support. Pseudoterminals are used by remote login programs, such as ssh and telnet, as well as xterm and other graphical terminal emulators. The following sequence of commands demonstrates that Sam is logged in on **/dev/pts/1**. After using tty to verify the pseudoterminal he is logged in on and using ls to show that this pseudoterminal exists, Sam redirects the output of an echo command to **/dev/pts/1**, whereupon the output appears on his screen:

```
$ tty
/dev/pts/1
$ ls /dev/pts
0  1  2  ptmx
$ echo Hi there > /dev/pts/1
Hi there
```

/dev/random
and
/dev/urandom Interfaces to the kernel's random number generator. You can use either file with dd to create a file filled with pseudorandom bytes. However, if there is not enough entropy, urandom can generate potentially inferior results (although for most purposes the difference is irrelevant). Following is an example:

```
$ dd if=/dev/urandom of=randfile bs=1 count=100
100+0 records in
100+0 records out
100 bytes (100 B) copied, 0.000884387 seconds, 113 kB/s
```

The preceding command reads from **/dev/urandom** and writes to the file named **randfile**. The block size is 1, and the count is 100; thus **randfile** is 100 bytes long. For bytes that are more random, you can read from **/dev/random**. See the **urandom** and **random** man pages for more information.

Using random can cause the system to hang

tip Reading from **/dev/random** can cause the system to hang for a long time if there is not enough entropy. This problem is common on virtual systems. You can create entropy and free the system by moving the mouse, typing on the keyboard, or copying files. Alternatively, you can read from **/dev/urandom**.

optional

Wiping a file   You can use a similar technique to wipe data from a file before deleting it, making it almost impossible to recover data from the deleted file. You might want to wipe a file for security reasons.

In the following example, ls shows the size of the file named **secret**. Using a block size of 1 and a count corresponding to the number of bytes in **secret**, dd wipes the file. The **conv=notrunc** argument ensures that dd writes over the data in the file and not another (erroneous) place on the disk.

```
$ ls -l secret
-rw-r--r--. 1 sam pubs 5733 01-27 13:12 secret
$ dd if=/dev/urandom of=secret bs=1 count=5733 conv=notrunc
5733+0 records in
5733+0 records out
5733 bytes (5.7 kB) copied, 0.0358146 seconds, 160 kB/s
$ rm secret
```

For added security, run sync to flush the disk buffers after running dd and repeat the two commands several times before deleting the file. See wipe.sourceforge.net for more information about wiping files.

/dev/shm   Implements shared memory, which provides an efficient way for processes to share information.

/dev/zero   Input you take from this file contains an infinite string of zeros (numerical zeros, not ASCII zeros). You can fill a file (e.g., a swap file; page 513) or overwrite a file with zeros with a command such as the following:

```
$ dd if=/dev/zero of=zeros bs=1024 count=10
10+0 records in
10+0 records out
10240 bytes (10 kB) copied, 0.000160263 seconds, 63.9 MB/s

$ od -c zeros
0000000  \0  \0  \0  \0  \0  \0  \0  \0  \0  \0  \0  \0  \0  \0  \0  \0
*
0024000
```

The od utility shows the contents of the new file.

If you try to fill a file with zeros using **/dev/null**, you fill the partition in which you are working:

```
$ cp /dev/zero bigzero
cp: writing 'bigzero': No space left on device
$ rm bigzero
```

/etc/aliases   Used by the mail delivery system to hold **aliases** for users. Edit this file to suit local needs. For more information refer to **/etc/aliases** on page 736.

/etc/alternatives   Holds symbolic links so you can call a utility by a name other than that of the file that holds the utility. For example, when you give the command **cancel**, the shell calls **cancel.cups** using the following links:

```
$ ls -l /usr/bin/cancel
lrwxrwxrwx. 1 root root 30 01-25 12:14 /usr/bin/cancel -> /etc/alternatives/print-cancel
$ ls -l /etc/alternatives/print-cancel
lrwxrwxrwx. 1 root root 20 01-25 12:14 /etc/alternatives/print-cancel -> /usr/bin/cancel.cups
```

The **alternatives** directory also allows a utility to appear in more than one directory and can ease an administrator's learning curve by providing familiar commands to do similar tasks (e.g., mailq can call sendmail or postfix commands depending on which server is being used).

In addition, this directory allows you to call one utility by several names. Although the **alternatives** directory does not allow developers to do anything they could not do without it, it provides an orderly way to keep and update these links. Use whereis (page 165) to find all links to a utility.

/etc/at.allow,   By default, users can use the at and crontab utilities. The **at.allow** and **cron.allow** files
/etc/at.deny,   list the users who are allowed to use at and crontab, respectively. The **at.deny** and
/etc/cron.allow, **cron.deny** files specify users who are not permitted to use the corresponding utilities.
and   As Fedora/RHEL is configured, an empty **at.deny** file and the absence of an **at.allow**
/etc/cron.deny   file allows anyone to use at; the absence of **cron.allow** and an empty **cron.deny** file allows anyone to use crontab. To prevent anyone except a user running with **root** privileges from using at, remove the **at.deny** file. To prevent anyone except a user running with **root** privileges from using crontab, create a **cron.allow** file with the single entry **root**. For more information on crontab, refer to "Scheduling Tasks" on page 611.

/etc/default   A directory that holds files that set default values for system services and utilities such as NFS and useradd. Look at the files in this directory for more information.

/etc/fstab   filesystem (**mount**) **table**—Contains a list of mountable devices as specified by the system administrator. See page 524 for more information.

/etc/group   Groups allow users to share files or programs without giving all system users access to those files or programs. This scheme is useful when several users are working with files that are not public. The **/etc/group** file associates one or more usernames with each group (number). Refer to "ACLs: Access Control Lists" on page 208 for a finer-grained way to control file access.

Each entry in the **/etc/group** file has four colon-separated fields that describe one group:

group-name:password:group-ID:login-name-list

The *group-name* is the name of the group. The *password* is an optional hashed (page 1167) password. This field frequently contains an **x**, indicating that group passwords are not used. The *group-ID* is a number, with 1–499 reserved for system accounts. The *login-name-list* is a comma-separated list of users who belong to the group. If an entry is too long to fit on one line, end the line with a backslash (\), which quotes the following RETURN, and continue the entry on the next line. A sample entry from a **group** file follows. The group is named **pubs**, has no password, and has a group ID of 1103:

```
pubs:x:1103:max,sam,zach,mark
```

You can use the groups utility to display the groups to which a user belongs:

```
$ groups sam
sam : sam pubs
```

Each user has a primary group, which is the group that user is assigned to in the **/etc/passwd** file. By default, Fedora/RHEL has user private groups: Each user's primary group has the same name as the user. In addition, a user can belong to other groups, depending on which *login-name-list*s the user appears on in the **/etc/group** file. In effect, you simultaneously belong both to your primary group and to any groups you are assigned to in **/etc/group**. When you attempt to access a file you do not own, Linux checks whether you are a member of the group that has access to the file. If you are, you are subject to the group access permissions for the file. If you are not a member of the group that has access to the file and you do not own the file, you are subject to the public access permissions for the file.

When you create a file, Linux assigns it to your primary group. Refer to page 604 for information on using system-config-users to work with groups.

/etc/hosts Stores the names, IP addresses, and optionally aliases of other systems. Typically, this file holds the hostname and IP address of the local system. It also holds a special entry for **localhost**. This entry supports the *loopback service*, which allows the local system to talk to itself (e.g., for RPC services). The IP address of the loopback service is always 127.0.0.1, while 127.0.1.1 names the local system. Following is a simple **/etc/hosts** file:

```
$ cat /etc/hosts
127.0.0.1       localhost
127.0.1.1       tiny
192.168.0.9     jam
192.168.0.10    plum
192.168.0.12    dog
...
```

If you are not using NIS or DNS to look up hostnames (called *hostname resolution*), you must include in **/etc/hosts** all systems that the local system should be able to contact by hostname. (A system can always contact another system by using the IP address of the system.) The **hosts** entry in the **/etc/nsswitch.conf** file (page 494) controls the order in which hostname resolution services are checked.

/etc/init Holds Upstart job definition files. See page 440 for more information.

/etc/init.d A symbolic link to **/etc/rc.d/init.d** (page 442).

/etc/inittab initialization table—Fedora ignores this file. RHEL can use the **initdefault** entry in this file to determine which runlevel it boots to. For more information see "rc-default task and **inittab**" on page 442.

/etc/motd Contains the message of the day, which can be displayed each time someone logs in using a textual login. This file typically contains site policy and legal information. Keep this file short because users tend to see the message many times.

/etc/mtab Under Fedora this file is a symbolic link to the kernel mount table at **/proc/mounts**. Under RHEL it is an ordinary text file. When you call mount without any arguments, it consults this file and displays a list of mounted devices. Each time you (or an init script) call mount or umount, these utilities make the necessary changes to **mtab**. Although this is an ASCII text file, you should not edit it. See also **/etc/fstab**.

Fixing mtab (RHEL)

tip The kernel maintains its own internal mount table. You can display this table with the command **cat /proc/mounts**. Under RHEL, the list of files in **/etc/mtab** might not be synchronized with the partitions in this table. To bring the **mtab** file in line with the operating system's mount table, you can either reboot the system or replace **/etc/mtab** with a symbolic link to **/proc/mounts** (although some information might be lost).

```
# rm /etc/mtab
# ln -s /proc/mounts /etc/mtab
```

/etc/nsswitch.conf

Specifies whether a system uses NIS, DNS, local files, or a combination as the source of certain information and in which order it consults these services (page 494).

/etc/pam.d Files in this directory specify the authentication methods used by PAM (page 463) applications.

/etc/passwd Describes users to the system. Do not edit this file directly; instead, use one of the utilities discussed in "Configuring User and Group Accounts" on page 602. Each line in **passwd** has seven colon-separated fields that describe one user:

login-name:password:user-ID:group-ID:info:directory:program

The *login-name* is the user's username—the name you enter in response to the **login:** prompt or on a GUI login screen. The value of the *password* is the character **x**. The **/etc/shadow file** (page 511) stores the real password, which is hashed (page 1167). For security reasons, every account should have a password. By convention, disabled accounts have an asterisk (✳) in this field.

The *user-ID* is a number, with 0 indicating the **root** account and 1–499 being reserved for system accounts. The *group-ID* identifies the user's primary group. It is a number, with 0–499 being reserved for system accounts; see **/etc/group** (page 506). You can change these values and set maximum values in **/etc/login.defs**.

The *info* is information that various programs, such as accounting and email programs, use to identify the user further. Normally it contains at least the first and last names of the user. It is referred to as the *GECOS* (page 1166) field.

The *directory* is the absolute pathname of the user's home directory. The *program* is the program that runs once the user logs in to a textual session. If *program* is not present, a value of **/bin/bash** is assumed. You can put **/bin/tcsh** here to log in using the TC Shell or **/bin/zsh** to log in using the Z Shell, assuming the shell you specify is installed. The chsh utility (page 469) changes this value.

The *program* is usually a shell, but it can be any program. The following line in the **passwd** file creates a "user" whose only purpose is to execute the who utility:

```
who:x:1000:1000:execute who:/usr:/usr/bin/who
```

Logging in with **who** as a username causes the system to log you in, execute the who utility, and log you out. The output of who flashes by quickly because the new login prompt clears the screen immediately after who finishes running. This entry in the **passwd** file does not provide a shell, so you cannot stay logged in after who finishes executing.

This technique is useful for providing special accounts that might do only one thing. The **ftp** account, for example, enables anonymous FTP (page 701) access to an FTP server. Because no one logs in on this account, the shell is set to **/bin/false** (which returns a false exit status) or to **/sbin/nologin** (which does not permit a nonprivileged user to log in). When you put a message in **/etc/nologin.txt**, nologin displays that message (except it has the same problem as the output of who—it is removed so quickly it is hard to see).

Do not replace a login shell with a shell script

security   Do not use shell scripts as replacements for shells in **/etc/passwd**. A user might be able to interrupt a shell script, giving him full shell access when you did not intend to do so. When installing a dummy shell, use a compiled program, not a shell script.

/etc/printcap   The printer capability database for LPD/LPR (page 560). It is not used with CUPS (Chapter 14), the Fedora/RHEL default printing system. This file describes system printers and is derived from 4.3BSD UNIX.

/etc/profile and **/etc/profile.d**   Contain systemwide interactive shell initialization scripts for environment and startup programs. When you log in, the shell immediately executes the commands in **/etc/profile**. This script executes all the commands in all the files in the **/etc/profile.d** directory (next) that have a filename extension of **.sh**. Both **profile** and the files in **profile.d** are executed in the same environment as the shell. (For information on executing a shell script in this manner, refer to the discussion of the . [dot] command on page 284.) As the comments at the beginning of **profile** say, if you want to make a systemwide change to users' environments, place a script with a filename extension of **.sh** in **profile.d**. Do not modify **profile** because it might be replaced when the system is updated; a file you create in **profile.d** will not be replaced.

The system administrator can create a file with a filename extension of **.sh** in **profile.d** to establish systemwide environment parameters that individual users can override in their **~/.bash_profile** (page 502) files. For example, this file can set shell variables, execute utilities, set up aliases, and take care of other housekeeping tasks. Following is an example of a file in **/etc/profile.d** that displays the message of the day (the

/etc/motd file), sets the file-creation mask (umask; page 473), and sets the interrupt character to CONTROL-C:

```
# cat /etc/profile.d/simple.sh
cat /etc/motd
umask 022
stty intr '^c'
```

See the **/etc/profile** file and the files in **/etc/profile.d** on the local system for more complex examples.

/etc/protocols   Provides protocol numbers, aliases, and brief definitions for DARPA Internet TCP/IP protocols. Do not modify this file.

/etc/rc.d   Holds SysVinit initialization scripts and links. See page 442 for more information.

/etc/resolv.conf   The resolver (page 848) configuration file; provides access to DNS. This file is built by NetworkManager (page 651) if it is running.

The following example shows the **resolv.conf** file for the **example.com** domain. A **resolv.conf** file usually contains at least two lines—a search line (optional) and a nameserver line:

```
$ cat /etc/resolv.conf
search example.com
nameserver 10.0.0.50
nameserver 10.0.0.51
```

The **search** keyword might be followed by a maximum of six domain names. The first domain is interpreted as the host's local domain. These names are appended one at a time to all DNS queries, shortening the time needed to query local hosts. The domains are searched in order in the process of resolving hostnames that are not fully qualified. See *FQDN* on page 1165.

When you put **search example.com** in **resolv.conf**, any reference to a host within the **example.com** domain or a subdomain (such as **marketing.example.com**) can use the abbreviated form of the host. For example, instead of issuing the command **ping speedy.marketing.example.com**, you can use **ping speedy.marketing**; however, a trailing period causes DNS to assume the name is complete so it appends no suffix. The following line in **resolv.conf** causes the **marketing** subdomain to be searched first, followed by **sales**, and finally the entire **example.com** domain:

```
search marketing.example.com sales.example.com example.com
```

It is a good idea to put the most frequently used domain names first to try to outguess possible conflicts. If both **speedy.marketing.example.com** and **speedy.example.com** exist, for example, the order of the search determines which one is selected when you invoke DNS. Do not overuse this feature: The longer the search path, the more network DNS requests generated, and the slower the response. Three or four names are typically sufficient.

Up to a maximum of three **nameserver** lines indicate which systems the local system queries to resolve hostnames to IP addresses, and vice versa. These machines are consulted in the order they appear, with a timeout between queries. The first time-out is a few seconds; each subsequent timeout is twice as long as the previous one. The preceding file causes this system to query 10.0.0.50, followed by 10.0.0.51 when the first system does not answer within a few seconds. The **resolv.conf** file might be automatically updated when a PPP (Point-to-Point Protocol) or DHCP (Dynamic Host Configuration Protocol) controlled interface is activated.

/etc/rpc   Maps RPC services to RPC numbers. The three columns in this file show the name of the server for the RPC program, the RPC program number, and any aliases.

/etc/services   Lists system services. The three columns in this file show the informal name of the service, the port number/protocol the service uses most frequently, and any aliases for the service. This file does not specify which services are running on the local system, nor does it map services to port numbers. The **services** file is used internally to map port numbers to services for display purposes; editing this file does not change which ports and protocols the local system uses.

/etc/shadow   Contains *SHA2* (page 1187) or *MD5* (page 1175) hashed user passwords, depending on system configuration. Each entry occupies one line composed of nine fields, separated by colons:

login-name:password:last-mod:min:max:warn:inactive:expire:flag

The *login-name* is the user's username—the name that the user enters in response to the **login:** prompt or on a GUI login screen. The *password* is a hashed password that passwd puts in this file. New accounts that are not set up with a password are given a value of !, !!, or * in this field to prevent the user from logging in until you assign a password to that user (page 603).

The *last-mod* field indicates when the password was last modified. The *min* is the minimum number of days that must elapse before the password can be changed; the *max* is the maximum number of days before the password must be changed. The *warn* field specifies how much advance warning (in days) will be given to the user before the password expires. The account will be closed if the number of days between login sessions exceeds the number of days specified in the *inactive* field. The account will also be closed as of the date in the *expire* field. The last field in an entry, *flag*, is reserved for future use. You can use the Password Info tab in system-config-users (page 603) or chage to modify these fields.

The **shadow** password file must be owned by **root** and must not be publicly readable or writable. Setting ownership and permissions in this way makes it more difficult for someone to break into the system by identifying accounts without passwords or by using specialized programs that try to match hashed passwords.

A number of conventions exist for creating special **shadow** entries. An entry of *LK* or **NP** in the *password* field indicates *locked* or *no password*, respectively. *No password* is different from an empty password; no password implies that this is an administrative account that no one ever logs in on directly. Occasionally programs will run with the privileges of this account for system maintenance functions. These accounts are set up under the principle of least privilege (page 410).

Entries in the **shadow** file must appear in the same order as in the **passwd** file. There must be exactly one **shadow** entry for each **passwd** entry.

/etc/hosts.deny and /etc/hosts.allow   As part of the client/server model, TCP wrappers use these files for access control. See page 484 for more information.

/etc/sysconfig   A directory containing a hierarchy of system configuration files. For more information refer to the **/usr/share/doc/initscripts✽/sysconfig.txt** file.

/etc/sysconfig/network

Describes the network setup for the local system. Set **HOSTNAME** in this file to the hostname of the system. Setting this variable changes the hostname of the system the next time it boots. Give the command **hostname** *name* to change the hostname of the system to *name* immediately. Without changing the **network** file, the hostname will revert the next time the system boots.

/proc   Provides a window into the Linux kernel. Through the **/proc** pseudofilesystem you can obtain information on any process running on the system, including its current state, memory usage, CPU usage, terminal association, parent, and group. You can extract information directly from the files in **/proc**. An example follows:

```
$ sleep 1000 &
[1] 3104
$ cd /proc/3104
$ ls -l
dr-xr-xr-x. 2 sam pubs 0 04-09 14:00 attr
-r-------- 1 sam pubs 0 04-09 14:00 auxv
-r--r--r-- 1 sam pubs 0 04-09 14:00 cgroup
--w------- 1 sam pubs 0 04-09 14:00 clear_refs
-r--r--r-- 1 sam pubs 0 04-09 14:00 cmdline
-rw-r--r-- 1 sam pubs 0 04-09 14:00 coredump_filter
-r--r--r-- 1 sam pubs 0 04-09 14:00 cpuset
lrwxrwxrwx 1 sam pubs 0 04-09 14:00 cwd -> /home/sam
-r-------- 1 sam pubs 0 04-09 14:00 environ
lrwxrwxrwx 1 sam pubs 0 04-09 14:00 exe -> /bin/sleep
dr-x------ 2 sam pubs 0 04-09 14:00 fd
...

$ cat status
Name:    sleep
State:   S (sleeping)
Tgid:    3104
Pid:     3104
PPid:    1503
TracerPid:       0
Uid:     1000    1000    1000    1000
Gid:     1000    1000    1000    1000
FDSize: 256
Groups: 4 20 24 46 105 119 122 1000
VmPeak:     3232 kB
VmSize:     3232 kB
VmLck:         0 kB
...
```

In this example, bash creates a background process (PID 3104) for sleep. Next the user changes directories to the directory in **/proc** that has the same name as the PID of the background process (**cd /proc/3104**). This directory holds information about the process it is named for—the sleep process in the example. The **ls –l** command shows that some entries in this directory are links (**cwd** is a link to the directory the process was started from, and **exe** is a link to the executable file that this process is running) and some appear to be ordinary files. All appear to be empty. However, when you use cat to display one of these pseudofiles (**status** in the example), cat displays output. Obviously it is not an ordinary file.

swap Swap space is used by the virtual memory subsystem of the kernel. When it runs low on real memory (RAM), the kernel writes memory pages from RAM to the swap space. Which pages are written and when they are written are controlled by finely tuned algorithms in the Linux kernel. When needed by running programs, the kernel brings these pages back into RAM—a technique called *paging* (page 1180). When a system is running very short on memory, an entire process might be paged out to disk.

Running an application that requires a large amount of virtual memory might result in the need for additional swap space. Swap space can be added and deleted from the system dynamically: If you run out of swap space, you can use mkswap to create a swap file and swapon to enable it. Normally the kernel uses a disk partition as swap space, but it can also use a file for this purpose. However, a disk partition provides much better performance than a file.

If you are creating a file as swap space, first use df to ensure the partition you are creating it in has adequate space for the file. The following commands first use dd and **/dev/zero** (page 505) to create an empty file (do not use cp because you might create a file with holes, which might not work) in the working directory. Next mkswap takes as an argument the name of the file created in the first step to set up the swap space. For security reasons, change the file so it cannot be read from or written to by anyone except a user with **root** privileges. Use swapon with the same argument to turn the swap file on; then use **swapon –s** to confirm the swap space is available. The final two commands turn off the swap file and remove it:

```
# dd if=/dev/zero of=swapfile bs=1024 count=65536
65536+0 records in
65536+0 records out
67108864 bytes (67 MB) copied, 0.40442 s, 166 MB/s
# mkswap swapfile
Setting up swapspace version 1, size = 65532 KiB
no label, UUID=49ec7f5b-1391-4b24-bd0a-a07e55752666
# chmod 600 swapfile
# swapon swapfile
# swapon -s
Filename                                Type        Size     Used     Priority
/dev/dm-1                               partition   2031612  0        -1
/swapfile                               file        65532    0        -2
# swapoff swapfile
# rm swapfile
rm: remove regular file 'swapfile'? y
```

/sys A pseudofilesystem that was added in the Linux 2.6 kernel to make it easy for programs running in kernelspace, such as device drivers, to exchange information with programs running in userspace. See page 516 for more information.

/usr/share/magic Most files begin with a unique identifier called a *magic number*. This file is a text database listing all known magic numbers on the system. When you use the file utility, it consults **/usr/share/magic** to determine the type of a file. Occasionally you might acquire a new tool that creates a new type of file that is unrecognized by the file utility. In this situation you need to update the **/usr/share/magic** file; refer to the **magic** man page for details. See also "magic number" on page 1174.

/var/log Holds system log files, many of which are generated by **syslogd** (page 623). You can use a text display program such as less, tail, or cat, or the graphical program gnome-system-log (**gnome-system-log** package) to view the files in this directory. To run gnome-system-log, select **Main menu: Applications⇨System Tools⇨Log File Viewer** (if **Applications** is not visible see "Configuring Fallback Mode" on page 101) or enter **gnome-system-log** from a terminal emulator or in a Run Application window (ALT-F2).

/var/log/messages
Contains messages from daemons, the Linux kernel, and security programs. For example, you will find **filesystem full** warning messages, error messages from system daemons (e.g., NFS, **ntpd**, printer daemons), SCSI and IDE disk error messages, and more in **messages**. Check **/var/log/messages** periodically to keep informed about important system events. Much of the information displayed on the system console is also sent to **messages**. If the system experiences a problem and you cannot access the console, check this file for messages about the problem. See page 623 for information on **syslogd**, which generates many of these messages.

/var/log/secure Holds messages from security-related programs such as su and the **sshd** daemon.

FILE TYPES

Linux supports many types of files. This section discusses the following types of files:

- Ordinary files, directories, links, and inodes (next)
- Symbolic links (page 515)
- Device special files (page 515)
- FIFO special files (named pipes) (page 517)
- Sockets (page 517)
- Block and character devices (page 518)
- Raw devices (page 518)

ORDINARY FILES, DIRECTORIES, LINKS, AND INODES

Ordinary and directory files
An *ordinary* file stores user data, such as textual information, programs, or images, such as a **jpeg** or **tiff** file. A *directory* is a standard-format disk file that stores information, including names, about ordinary files and other directory files.

Inodes
An *inode* is a *data structure* (page 1160), stored on disk, that defines a file's existence and is identified by an inode number. An inode contains critical information about a file, such as the UID of the owner, where it is physically located on the disk, and how many hard links point to it. In addition, SELinux (page 459) stores extended information about files in inodes. An inode that describes a directory file maps each of the filenames in the directory to the inode that describes that file. This setup allows an inode to be associated with more than one filename and to be pointed to from more than one directory.

When you move (mv) a file, including a directory file, within a filesystem, you change the filename portion of the directory entry associated with the inode that describes the file. You do not create a new inode. If you move a file to another filesystem, mv first creates a new inode on the destination filesystem and then deletes the original inode. You can also use mv to move a directory recursively from one filesystem to another. In this case mv copies the directory and all the files in it and deletes the original directory and its contents.

Hard links
When you make an additional hard link (ln; page 214) to a file, you add a directory entry that points to the inode that describes the file. You do not create a new inode. It is not possible to create a hard link to a directory.

When you remove (rm) a file, you delete the directory entry that describes the file. When you remove the last hard link to a file, the operating system puts all blocks the inode pointed to back in the *free list* (the list of blocks that are available for use on the disk) and frees the inode to be used again.

The . and .. directory entries
Every directory contains at least two entries (. and ..). The . entry is a link to the directory itself. The .. entry is a link to the parent directory. In the case of the root directory, there is no parent; the .. entry is a link to the root directory itself.

Symbolic links
Because each filesystem has a separate set of inodes, you can create hard links to a file only from within the filesystem that holds that file. To get around this limitation, Linux provides symbolic links, which are files that point to other files. Files that are linked by a symbolic link do not share an inode. As a consequence, you can create a symbolic link to a file from any filesystem. You can also create a symbolic link to a directory, device, or other special file. For more information refer to "Symbolic Links" on page 216.

DEVICE SPECIAL FILES

Device special files (also called *device files* and *special files*) represent Linux kernel routines that provide access to an operating system feature. FIFO (first in, first out) special files allow unrelated programs to exchange information. Sockets allow unrelated processes on the same or different systems to exchange information. One type of socket, the UNIX domain socket, is a special file. Symbolic links are another type of special file.

Device files   *Device files* include both block and character special files and represent device drivers that allow the system to communicate with peripheral devices, such as terminals, printers, and hard disks. By convention, device files appear in the **/dev** directory and its subdirectories. Each device file represents a device; hence, the system reads from and writes to the file to read from and write to the device it represents. The following example shows part of a listing for the **/dev** directory:

```
$ ls -l /dev
crw-rw----. 1 root video    10, 175 01-25 12:17 agpgart
crw-------. 1 root root      10, 235 01-25 12:17 autofs
drwxr-xr-x. 2 root root         640 01-25 04:17 block
drwxr-xr-x. 2 root root          80 01-25 04:17 bsg
drwxr-xr-x. 3 root root          60 01-25 04:17 bus
lrwxrwxrwx. 1 root root           3 01-25 04:17 cdrom -> sr0
drwxr-xr-x. 2 root root        2760 01-25 12:17 char
crw-------. 1 root root       5,   1 01-25 12:17 console
lrwxrwxrwx. 1 root root          11 01-25 04:17 core -> /proc/kcore
...
brw-rw----. 1 root disk       8,   0 01-25 04:17 sda
brw-rw----. 1 root disk       8,   1 01-25 12:17 sda1
brw-rw----. 1 root disk       8,   2 01-25 04:17 sda2
...
```

The first character of each line is always –, **b**, **c**, **d**, **l**, or **p**, representing the file type—ordinary (plain), block, character, directory, symbolic link, or named pipe (next), respectively. The next nine characters identify the permissions for the file, followed by the number of hard links and the names of the owner and the group. Where the number of bytes in a file would appear for an ordinary or directory file, a device file shows *major* and *minor device numbers* (page 517) separated by a comma. The rest of the line is the same as for any other **ls –l** listing (page 202).

udev   The udev utility manages device naming dynamically. It replaces **devfs** and moves the device-naming functionality from the kernel to userspace. Because devices are added to and removed from a system infrequently, the performance penalty associated with this change is minimal. The benefit of the move is that a bug in udev cannot compromise or crash the kernel.

/sys   The udev utility is part of the hotplug system (next). When a device is added to or removed from the system, the kernel creates a device name in the **/sys** pseudofilesystem and notifies hotplug of the event, which is received by udev. The udev utility then creates the device file, usually in the **/dev** directory, or removes the device file from the system. The udev utility can also rename network interfaces. See the page at www.kernel.org/pub/linux/utils/kernel/hotplug/udev.html for more information.

Hotplug   The hotplug system allows you to plug a device into a running system and use it immediately. Although hotplug was available in the Linux 2.4 kernel, the 2.6 kernel integrates hotplug with the unified device driver model framework (the *driver model core*) so any bus can report an event when a device is added to or removed from the system. User software can be notified of the event so it can take appropriate action. See linux-hotplug.sourceforge.net for more information.

FIFO SPECIAL FILE (NAMED PIPE)

A *FIFO special* file, also called a *named pipe,* represents a pipe: You read from and write to the file to read from and write to the pipe. The term *FIFO* stands for *first in, first out*—the way any pipe works. In other words, the first information you put in one end is the first information that comes out the other end. When you use a pipe on a command line to send the output of a program to the printer, the printer outputs the information in the same order that the program produced it and sent it to the pipe.

Unless you are writing sophisticated programs, you will not be working with FIFO special files. However, programs use named pipes for interprocess communication. You can create a pipe using mkfifo:

```
$ mkfifo AA
$ ls -l AA
prw-rw-r--. 1 sam pubs 0 01-27 17:55 AA
```

The **p** at the left end of the output indicates the file is a pipe.

Both UNIX and Linux systems have included pipes for many generations. Without named pipes, only processes that were children of the same ancestor could use pipes to exchange information. Using named pipes, *any* two processes on a single system can exchange information. When one program writes to a FIFO special file, another program can read from the same file. The programs do not have to run at the same time or be aware of each other's activity. The operating system handles all buffering and information storage. This type of communication is termed *asynchronous* (*async*) because the programs on the opposite ends of the pipe do not have to be synchronized.

SOCKETS

Like FIFO special files, UNIX/Linux domain *sockets* allow asynchronous processes that are not children of the same ancestor to exchange information. These sockets are the central mechanism of the interprocess communication that forms the basis of the networking facility. They differ from TCP/IP sockets, which are not represented in the filesystem. When you use networking utilities, pairs of cooperating sockets manage the communication between the processes on the local system and the remote system. Sockets form the basis of such utilities as ssh and scp.

MAJOR AND MINOR DEVICE NUMBERS

A *major device number* points to a driver in the kernel that works with a class of hardware devices: terminal, printer, tape drive, hard disk, and so on. In the listing of the **/dev** directory on page 516, all the hard disk partitions have a major device number of 8.

A *minor device number* identifies a particular piece of hardware within a class. Although all hard disk partitions are grouped together by their major device number, each has a different minor device number (**sda1** is 1, **sda2** is 2, and so on). This setup allows one piece of software (the device driver) to service all similar hardware yet still be able to distinguish among different physical units.

BLOCK AND CHARACTER DEVICES

This section describes typical device drivers. Because device drivers can be changed to suit a particular purpose, the descriptions in this section do not pertain to every system.

Block device   A *block device* is an I/O (input/output) device that has the following characteristics:

- Able to perform random access reads
- Has a specific block size
- Handles only single blocks of data at a time
- Accepts only transactions that involve whole blocks of data
- Able to have a filesystem mounted on it
- Has the Linux kernel buffer its input and output
- Appears to the operating system as a series of blocks numbered from 0 through $n - 1$, where n is the number of blocks on the device

Block devices commonly found on a Linux system include hard disks, floppy diskettes, CDs, and DVDs.

Character device   A *character device* is any device that is not a block device. Examples of character devices include printers, terminals, tape drives, and modems.

The device driver for a character device determines how a program reads from and writes to that device. For example, the device driver for a terminal allows a program to read the information you type on the terminal in two ways. First, a program can read single characters from a terminal in *raw* mode—that is, without the driver interpreting characters. (This mode has nothing to do with the raw device described next.) Alternatively, a program can read one line at a time. When a program reads one line at a time, the driver handles the erase and kill characters so the program never sees typing mistakes that have been corrected. In this case, the program reads everything from the beginning of a line to the RETURN that ends a line; the number of characters in a line can vary.

RAW DEVICES

Device driver programs for block devices usually have two entry points so they can be used in two ways: as block devices or as character devices. The character device form of a block device is called a *raw device*. A raw device is characterized by

- Direct I/O (no buffering through the Linux kernel).
- One-to-one correspondence between system calls and hardware requests.
- Device-dependent restrictions on I/O.

fsck An example of a utility that uses a raw device is fsck. It is more efficient for fsck to operate on the disk as a raw device rather than being restricted by the fixed size of blocks in the block device interface. Because it has full knowledge of the underlying filesystem structure, fsck can operate on the raw device using the largest possible units. When a filesystem is mounted, processes normally access the disk through the block device interface, which explains why it is important to allow fsck to modify only unmounted filesystems. On a mounted filesystem, there is the danger that while fsck is rearranging the underlying structure through the raw device, another process could change a disk block using the block device, resulting in a corrupted filesystem.

FILESYSTEMS

Table 12-1 lists some types of filesystems available under Linux.

Table 12-1   Filesystems

Filesystem	Features
adfs	Advanced Disc Filing System. Used on Acorn computers. The word *Advanced* differentiated this filesystem from its predecessor DFS, which did not support advanced features such as hierarchical filesystems.
affs	Amiga Fast Filesystem (FFS).
autofs	Automounting filesystem (page 811).
cifs	Common Internet Filesystem (page 1157). Formerly the Samba Filesystem (**smbfs**).
coda	CODA distributed filesystem (developed at Carnegie Mellon).
devpts	A pseudofilesystem for pseudoterminals (page 504).
ext2	A standard filesystem for Fedora/RHEL systems, usually with the **ext4** extension.
ext3	A journaling (page 1171) extension to the **ext2** filesystem. It greatly improves recovery time from crashes (it takes a lot less time to run fsck), promoting increased availability. As with any filesystem, a journaling filesystem can lose data during a system crash or hardware failure.
ext4	An extension to the **ext3** filesystem. It is backward compatible with **ext2/ext3** filesystems and provides improved performance over **ext3** the filesystem.
GFS	Global Filesystem. GFS is a journaling, clustering filesystem. It enables a cluster of Linux servers to share a common storage pool.
hfs	Hierarchical Filesystem. Used by older Macintosh systems. Newer Macintosh systems use **hfs+**.
hpfs	High-Performance Filesystem. The native filesystem for IBM's OS/2.

Table 12-1   Filesystems (continued)

Filesystem	Features
jffs2	Journaling Flash Filesystem (**jffs**). A filesystem for flash memory.
iso9660	The standard filesystem for CDs and DVDs.
minix	Very similar to Linux. The filesystem of a small operating system that was written for educational purposes by Andrew S. Tanenbaum (www.minix3.org).
msdos	Filesystem used by DOS and subsequent Microsoft operating systems. Do not use **msdos** for mounting Windows filesystems; it does not read VFAT attributes.
ncpfs	Novell NetWare NCP Protocol Filesystem. Used to mount remote filesystems under NetWare.
nfs	Network Filesystem. Developed by Sun Microsystems, this protocol allows a computer to access remote files over a network as if the files were local (page 791).
ntfs	NT Filesystem. The native filesystem of Windows NT. See www.linux-ntfs.org.
proc	An interface to several Linux kernel *data structures* (page 1160) that behaves like a filesystem (page 512).
qnx4	QNX 4 operating system filesystem.
reiserfs	A journaling (page 1171) filesystem based on balanced-tree algorithms. See **ext4** for more on journaling filesystems.
romfs	A dumb, readonly filesystem used mainly for *RAM disks* (page 1184) during installation.
smbfs	Samba Filesystem (deprecated). See **cifs**.
sysv	System V UNIX filesystem.
ufs	Default filesystem under Sun's Solaris operating system and other UNIXs.
umsdos	A full-feature UNIX-like filesystem that runs on top of a DOS FAT filesystem.
vfat	Developed by Microsoft, a standard that allows long filenames on FAT partitions.
VxFS	Veritas Extended Filesystem. The first commercial journaling (page 1171) filesystem, popular under HP-UX and Solaris.
xfs	SGI's journaling filesystem (ported from Irix).

mount: MOUNTS A FILESYSTEM

The mount utility connects directory hierarchies—typically filesystems—to the Linux directory hierarchy. These directory hierarchies can be on remote and local disks, USB flash drives, CDs, DVDs, and floppy diskettes. Linux can also mount *virtual filesystems* that have been built inside ordinary files, filesystems built for other operating systems, and the special **/proc** filesystem (page 512), which maps Linux kernel information to a pseudodirectory. This section covers mounting local filesystems; refer to page 791 for information on using NFS to mount remote directory hierarchies. See **/dev** on page 503 for information on device names.

Mount point   The *mount point* for the filesystem/directory hierarchy that you are mounting is a directory in the local filesystem. This directory must exist before you can mount a filesystem; its contents disappear as long as a filesystem is mounted on it and reappear when you unmount the filesystem. See page 36 for a discussion of mount points.

Without any arguments, mount lists the mounted filesystems, showing the physical device holding each filesystem, the mount point, the type of filesystem, and any options set when each filesystem was mounted. The mount utility gets this information from the **/etc/mtab** file (page 508).

```
$ mount
/dev/mapper/vg_bee-lv_root on / type ext4 (rw)
proc on /proc type proc (rw)
sysfs on /sys type sysfs (rw)
devpts on /dev/pts type devpts (rw,gid=5,mode=620)
tmpfs on /dev/shm type tmpfs (rw,rootcontext="system_u:object_r:tmpfs_t:s0")
/dev/sda1 on /boot type ext4 (rw)
none on /proc/sys/fs/binfmt_misc type binfmt_misc (rw)
fusectl on /sys/fs/fuse/connections type fusectl (rw)
gvfs-fuse-daemon on /home/sam/.gvfs type fuse.gvfs-fuse-daemon (rw,nosuid,nodev,user=sam)
```

The first entry in the preceding example shows an LV mounted by the LVM (page 42) device mapper on **/** (root). The next entries show the **/proc** (page 512) and **/sys** (page 516) pseudofilesystems. The line that starts with **devpts** shows the interface to pseudoterminal (pty) devices mounted at **/dev/pts/*** (page 504). The **tmpfs** device represents a shared-memory filesystem mounted at **/dev/shm** and stored in RAM. As explained on page 39, the **/boot** partition cannot reside on an LV; it is mounted on **/dev/sda1**.

binfmt_misc   The **binfmt_misc** line allows the Linux kernel to recognize and execute arbitrary executable file formats and to pass to the resulting processes user space applications, such as emulators and virtual machines. The kernel uses a file's magic number (page 514) to identify the format of the file. This feature enables you to invoke many programs (e.g., compiled Java, Python) by entering its name in response to a shell prompt. See www.kernel.org/doc/Documentation/binfmt_misc.txt for more information.

fusectl   The **fusectl** line provides FUSE (Filesystems in Userspace; fuse.sourceforge.net). FUSE is a kernel module that allows a nonprivileged user to create a custom filesystem without editing the kernel.

gvfs   The **gvfs-fuse-daemon** line uses FUSE to provide a userspace virtual filesystem that support sftp, ftp, smb, etc.

Do not mount anything on root (/)

caution Always mount network directory hierarchies and removable devices at least one level below the root level of the filesystem. The root filesystem is mounted on /; you cannot mount two filesystems in the same place. If you were to try to mount something on /, all files, directories, and filesystems that were under the root directory would no longer be available, and the system would crash.

When you add a line for a filesystem to the **/etc/fstab** file (page 506), you can mount that filesystem by giving the associated mount point or device name as the argument to mount. For example, the following command mounts a backup volume at **/backup**:

```
$ mount /backup
```

This command works because **/etc/fstab** contains the additional information needed to mount the file. A nonprivileged user is able to mount the file because of the **user** option.

```
/dev/sda7       /backup    ext4 user,noauto,rw 0 0
```

On the local system, the mount point and device name will differ from those in this example. You can specify a filesystem type of **auto** (in place of **ext4**) to cause the system to probe the filesystem to determine its type. You can also mount filesystems that do not appear in **/etc/fstab**. For example, when you insert a floppy diskette that holds a DOS filesystem into the floppy diskette drive, you can mount that filesystem using the following command:

```
# mount -t msdos /dev/fd0 /media/floppy0
```

The **-t msdos** option specifies a filesystem type of **msdos**. You can mount DOS file-systems only if the Linux kernel is configured to accept DOS filesystems (it is by default). You do not need to mount a DOS filesystem to read from and write to it, such as when you use unix2dos (page 159). However, you do need to mount a DOS filesystem to use Linux commands (other than Mtools commands) on files on the filesystem (which might be on a diskette).

MOUNT OPTIONS

The mount utility takes many options, which you can specify either on the command line or in the **/etc/fstab** file (page 524). For a complete list of mount options for local filesystems, see the mount man page; for remote directory hierarchies, see page 797 and the nfs man page.

The system mounts most filesystems specified in **fstab** when it boots. You can specify the **noauto** option to cause Linux not to mount a filesystem automatically.

Mount removable devices with the **nosuid** option

security Always mount removable devices with the **nosuid** option so a malicious user cannot, for example, put a setuid copy of bash on a disk and have a shell with **root** privileges. By default, Fedora/RHEL uses the **nosuid** option when mounting removable media. See page 796 for more information.

Unless you specify the **user, users,** or **owner** option, only a user running with **root** privileges can mount and unmount a filesystem. The **user** option allows any user to mount the filesystem, but the filesystem can be unmounted only by the user who mounted it; the **users** option allows any user to mount and unmount the filesystem. These options are frequently specified for CD, DVD, and floppy drives. The **owner** option, which is used only under special circumstances, is similar to the **user** option except that the user mounting the device must own the device.

Three options can help ensure the security of the system when you allow nonprivileged users to mount filesystems. The **noexec** option prevents a user from running an executable file on the mounted filesystem, **nosuid** forces mounted setuid and setgid executable files to run with regular permissions (no effective user or group ID change) on the mounted filesystem (page 796), and **nodev** prevents the system from recognizing a device special file on the mounted filesystem (page 797). The **user** and **users** option imply all three of these options; **owner** implies **nosuid** and **nodev**.

umount: UNMOUNTS A FILESYSTEM

The umount utility unmounts a filesystem as long as it does not contain any files or directories that are in use (open). For example, a logged-in user's working directory cannot be on the filesystem you want to unmount. The next command unmounts the CD mounted earlier:

```
$ umount /media/cdrom
```

Unmount a floppy or a remote (NFS) directory hierarchy the same way you would unmount a partition of a hard drive.

The umount utility consults **/etc/fstab** to get the necessary information and then unmounts the appropriate filesystem from its server. When a process has a file open on the filesystem you are trying to unmount, umount displays a message similar to the following:

```
umount: /home: device is busy
```

When you cannot unmount a device because it is in use

tip   When a process has a file open on a device you need to unmount, use fuser to determine which process has the file open and to kill it. For example, when you want to unmount a CD, give the command **fuser –ki /media/cdrom** (substitute the mount point for the diskette on the local system for **/media/cdrom**). After checking with you, this command kills the process(es) using the CD. You can also use lsof (page 629) to find open files.

Use the **–a** option to umount to unmount all mounted filesystems that are not in use. You can never unmount the filesystem mounted at **/**. You can combine **–a** with the **–t** option to unmount filesystems of a given type (e.g., **ext4** or **nfs**). For example, the following command unmounts all mounted **nfs** directory hierarchies that are not in use:

```
# umount -at nfs
```

fstab: KEEPS TRACK OF FILESYSTEMS

The system administrator maintains the **/etc/fstab** file, which lists local and remote directory hierarchies, most of which the system mounts automatically when it boots. The **fstab** file has six columns; a hyphen is a placeholder for a column that has no value:

1. **Name**—The name, label, or UUID number of a local block device (page 518) or a pointer to a remote directory hierarchy. When you install the system, Fedora/RHEL uses UUID numbers for fixed devices (but not for LVs). Using UUID numbers in **fstab** during installation circumvents the need for consistent device naming. Because udev (page 516) manages device naming dynamically, the installer might not be aware, for example, that the first disk is not named **/dev/hda1** but rather **/dev/sda1**, but it always knows the UUID number of a device. Using UUID numbers to identify devices also keeps partitions and mount points correctly correlated when you remove or exchange devices. When run with root privileges, blkid displays device UUID numbers. See **/dev/disk/by-uuid** (page 503) for more information on UUID numbers. You can use the volume label of a local filesystem by using the form **LABEL=*xx***, where *xx* is the volume label. For information on labeling devices, refer to e2label on page 470.

   A remote directory hierarchy appears as *hostname:pathname*, where *hostname* is the name of the remote system that houses the filesystem, and *pathname* is the absolute pathname (on the remote system) of the directory that is to be mounted.

2. **Mount point**—The name of the directory file that the filesystem/directory hierarchy is to be mounted on. If it does not already exist, create this directory using mkdir. See pages 36 and 521.

3. **Type**—The type of filesystem/directory hierarchy that is to be mounted. Local filesystems are generally of type **ext2**, **ext4**, or **iso9660**, and remote directory hierarchies are of type **nfs** or **cifs**. Table 12-1 on page 519 lists filesystem types.

4. **Mount options**—A comma-separated list of mount options, such as whether the filesystem is mounted for reading and writing (**rw**, the default) or readonly (**ro**). See pages 522 and 797 and refer to the mount and nfs man pages for lists of options.

5. **Dump**—Previously used by dump to determine when to back up the filesystem.

6. **Fsck**—Specifies the order in which fsck checks filesystems. Root (**/**) should have a **1** in this column. Filesystems that are mounted to a directory just below the root directory should have a **2**. Filesystems that are mounted on another mounted filesystem (other than root) should have a **3**. For example, if **local** is a separate filesystem from **/usr** and is mounted on **/usr** (as **/usr/local**), then **local** should have a **3**. Filesystems and directory hierarchies

that do not need to be checked (for example, remotely mounted directory hierarchies and CDs/DVDs) should have a 0.

The following example shows a typical **fstab** file:

```
# cat /etc/fstab
...
/dev/mapper/vg_bee-lv_root                   /         ext4    defaults           1 1
UUID=7694f86e-c3ff-4e51-b677-01b3d27927a4 /boot     ext4    defaults           1 2
/dev/mapper/vg_bee-lv_swap                   swap      swap    defaults           0 0
tmpfs                                        /dev/shm  tmpfs   defaults           0 0
devpts                                       /dev/pts  devpts  gid=5,mode=620     0 0
sysfs                                        /sys      sysfs   defaults           0 0
proc                                         /proc     proc    defaults           0 0
```

See page 520 for information about mount and the types of devices it mounts.

fsck: CHECKS FILESYSTEM INTEGRITY

The fsck (filesystem check) utility verifies the integrity of filesystems and, if possible, repairs problems it finds. Because many filesystem repairs can destroy data, particularly on non*journaling filesystems* (page 1171), such as **ext2**, by default fsck asks you for confirmation before making each repair.

Do not run fsck on a mounted filesystem

caution   Do not run fsck on a mounted filesystem. When you attempt to check a mounted filesystem, fsck warns you and asks whether you want to continue. Reply **no**. You can run fsck with the **–N** option on a mounted filesystem because it will not write to the filesystem; as a result, no harm can come from running it. See page 519 for more information.

When fsck repairs a damaged filesystem, it might find unlinked files: files that have lost their directory information. These files have no filenames. The fsck utility gives these files their inode numbers as names and stores them in the **lost+found** directory (page 502) in the filesystem that holds the file. You can use file (page 156) to determine the type of these files and less to view readable files. Because ls –l displays the name of the owner of these files, you can return them to their owners.

The following command checks all unmounted filesystems that are marked to be checked in **/etc/fstab** (page 524) except for the root filesystem:

```
# fsck -AR
```

The –A option causes fsck to check filesystems listed in **fstab**. When used with the –A option, the –R option causes fsck not to check the root filesystem. You can check a specific filesystem with a command similar to one of the following:

```
# fsck /home
```

or

```
# fsck /dev/sda1
```

tune2fs: CHANGES FILESYSTEM PARAMETERS

The tune2fs utility displays and modifies filesystem parameters on **ext2**, **ext3**, and **ext4** filesystems. This utility can also set up journaling on an **ext2** filesystem, turning it into an **ext3** filesystem. With the introduction of increasingly reliable hardware and software, systems tend to be rebooted less frequently, so it is important to check filesystems regularly. By default, fsck is run on each partition while the system is brought up, before the partition is mounted. (The checks scheduled by tune2fs are separate and scheduled differently from the checks that are done following a system crash or hard disk error [see the previous section].)

Depending on the flags, fsck might do nothing more than display a message saying the filesystem is clean. The larger the partition, the more time it takes to check it, assuming a nonjournaling filesystem. These checks are often unnecessary. The tune2fs utility helps you to find a happy medium between checking filesystems each time you reboot the system and never checking them. It does so by scheduling when fsck checks a filesystem (these checks occur only when the system is booted).[1] You can use two scheduling patterns: time elapsed since the last check and number of mounts since the last check. The following command causes fsck to check **/dev/sda1** after it has been mounted 8 times or after 15 days have elapsed since its last check, whichever happens first:

```
# tune2fs -c 8 -i 15 /dev/sda1
tune2fs 1.41.12 (17-May-2010)
Setting maximal mount count to 8
Setting interval between checks to 1296000 seconds
```

A maximum mount count of –1 or 0 causes fsck and the kernel to ignore the mount count information. The next tune2fs command is similar but works on a different partition (an LV) and sets the current mount count to 4. When you do not specify a current mount count, it is set to zero:

```
# tune2fs -c 8 -i 15 -C 4 /dev/mapper/vg_bee-lv_root
tune2fs 1.41.12 (17-May-2010)
Setting maximal mount count to 8
Setting current mount count to 4
Setting interval between checks to 1296000 seconds
```

The **–l** option lists a variety of information about the partition. You can combine this option with others.

```
# tune2fs -l /dev/mapper/vg_bee-lv_root
tune2fs 1.41.12 (17-May-2010)
Filesystem volume name:   _Fedora-14-i686-
Last mounted on:          /
Filesystem UUID:          7743cb0d-b961-4b65-b3a2-071536734d8a
```

---

1. For systems whose purpose in life is to run continuously, this kind of scheduling does not work. You must develop a schedule that is not based on system reboots but rather on a clock. Each filesystem must be unmounted periodically, checked with fsck (preceding section), and then remounted.

```
Filesystem magic number:   0xEF53
Filesystem revision #:      1 (dynamic)
Filesystem features:        has_journal ext_attr resize_inode dir_index
        filetype needs_recovery extent flex_bg sparse_super large_file
        huge_file uninit_bg dir_nlink extra_isize
Filesystem flags:           signed_directory_hash
Default mount options:      user_xattr acl
Filesystem state:           clean
Errors behavior:            Continue
Filesystem OS type:         Linux
Inode count:                1155072
Block count:                4603904
...
Last mount time:            Tue Jan 25 12:17:36 2011
Last write time:            Mon Jan 31 14:04:23 2011
Mount count:                4
Maximum mount count:        8
Last checked:               Tue Nov  2 14:51:57 2010
Check interval:             1296000 (2 weeks, 1 day)
...
```

Set the filesystem parameters on the local system so they are appropriate to the way you use it. When using the mount count to control when fsck checks filesystems, use the –C option to stagger the checks to ensure all checks do not occur at the same time. Always make sure new and upgraded filesystems have checks scheduled as you desire.

ext2 to ext3   To change an **ext2** filesystem to an **ext3** filesystem, you must put a *journal* (page 1171) on the filesystem, and the kernel must support **ext3** filesystems. Use the –j option to set up a journal on an unmounted filesystem:

```
# tune2fs -j /dev/sda1
tune2fs 1.41.12 (17-May-2010)
Creating journal inode: done
This filesystem will be automatically checked every 8 mounts or
15 days, whichever comes first.  Use tune2fs -c or -i to override.
```

Before you can use **fstab** (page 506) to mount the changed filesystem, you must modify its entry in the **fstab** file to reflect its new type. To do so, change the third column to **ext3**.

ext3 to ext2   The following command changes an unmounted or readonly **ext3** filesystem to an **ext2** filesystem:

```
# tune2fs -O ^has_journal /dev/sda1
tune2fs 1.41.12 (17-May-2010)
```

Speeding lookups   The **dir_index** option, which is turned off by default, adds a balanced-tree binary hash lookup method for directories. This feature improves scalability of directories with large numbers of files, although it means that the hash needs to be updated each time a directory changes. Turn on using **tune2fs –O dir_index** and reboot to create the hash.

Refer to the tune2fs man page for more details.

CHAPTER SUMMARY

Filesystems hold directories of files. These structures store user data and system data that are the basis of users' work on the system and the system's existence. Linux supports many types of files, including ordinary files, directories, links, and special files. Special files provide access to operating system features. The kernel uses major and minor device numbers to identify classes of devices and specific devices within each class. Character and block devices represent I/O devices such as hard disks and printers. Inodes, which are identified by inode numbers, are stored on disk and define a file's existence.

When the system comes up, the **/etc/fstab** file controls which filesystems are mounted and how they are mounted (readonly, read-write, and so on). After a system crash, filesystems are automatically verified and repaired if necessary by fsck. You can use tune2fs to force the system to cause fsck to verify a filesystem periodically when the system boots.

EXERCISES

1. What is the function of the **/etc/hosts** file? Which services can you use in place of or to supplement the **hosts** file?

2. What does the **/etc/resolv.conf** file do? What do the **nameserver** lines in this file do?

3. What is an inode? What happens to the inode when you move a file within a filesystem?

4. What does the **..** entry in a directory point to? What does this entry point to in the root (**/**) directory?

5. What is a device file? Where are device files located?

6. What is a FIFO? What does FIFO stand for? What is another name for a FIFO? How does a FIFO work?

ADVANCED EXERCISES

7. Write a line for the **/etc/fstab** file that mounts the **/dev/sdb1 ext4** filesystem on **/extra** with the following characteristics: The filesystem will not be mounted automatically when the system boots, and anyone can mount and unmount the filesystem.

8. Without using rm, how can you delete a file? (*Hint:* How do you rename a file?)

9. After burning an ISO image file named **image.iso** to a CD on **/dev/hdc**, how can you can verify the copy from the command line?

10. Why should **/var** reside on a separate partition from **/usr**?

11. Create a FIFO. Using the shell, demonstrate that two users can use this FIFO to communicate asynchronously.

12. How would you mount an ISO image so you could copy files from it without burning it to a CD?

13

FINDING, DOWNLOADING, AND INSTALLING SOFTWARE

OBJECTIVES

After reading this chapter you should be able to:

▶ Explain the purpose of a software package, a package management system, and a software repository

▶ List the uses and benefits of yum

▶ Use yum to list installed and available packages

▶ Use yum to search for packages containing specific applications or utilities

▶ Use yum to install and remove a software package

▶ Use yum to update all software packages on the local system.

▶ Download large files with BitTorrent

▶ Use rpm to display information about a package and install software

▶ List common steps for installing non-RPM software from source

▶ Describe the role of Red Hat Network in software management

531

INTRODUCTION

Linux is based on millions of lines of code and includes thousands of programs. Each of these programs is updated periodically, and most depend on other programs or files to run. The source code for each program must be compiled for each processor architecture and each release of each Linux distribution. With the first releases of Linux, these tasks were done by hand. Over time, this process has been automated. This chapter explains how you can make your life easier by taking advantage of the facilities Fedora/RHEL provides for finding, installing, updating, and removing software.

Software package   A *software package*, or simply *package*, is the collection of scripts, programs, files, and directories required to install and run an application, utility, server, or system software. A package also includes a list of other packages the package depends on (*dependencies*). Using software packages makes it easier to install, update, and uninstall software. A package contains either executable files or source code files. Executable files are precompiled for a specific processor architecture and operating system, whereas source files need to be compiled but will run on a wide range of machines and operating systems.

PMS   A *PMS*, or *package management system*, is a set of utilities that allow you to install, upgrade, remove, and search software packages easily and in a consistent manner. It is based on a local database that holds information about each installed package, including its dependencies and version information.

One of the biggest advantages of a PMS is how easy it makes it to uninstall a package. If you compile from source, a **make install** command typically installs the files, but there is frequently no **make uninstall** command. A PMS keeps track of all the files that belong to a package. These files might be distributed among many directories throughout a system. This tracking allows you to remove all files belonging to a package with a single command. A PMS also enables you to query packages, a great troubleshooting tool that does not come with manual installation. When you manually install a package, you must obtain the source code (again, and in some cases the same version as you installed) to learn which files are a part of the package, what was done during installation, and how to remove the software.

Software package formats   Software packages come in different formats. Fedora/RHEL and SUSE use RPM (RPM Package Manager; page 547). Ubuntu and Debian use **dpkg** (Debian package), which was the first Linux packaging system to incorporate dependency information. Other formats include the GNU Configure and Build System (page 552), and compressed tar. Formats such as compressed tar, which were popular before the introduction of RPM, are used less often today because they require more work on the part of the installer (you) and do not provide the dependency and compatibility checking RPM offers.

yum Early releases of Red Hat Linux did not include a tool for managing updates. Although RPM could install or upgrade individual software packages, it was up to the user to locate a package and any packages it was dependent on. When Terra Soft produced its Red Hat–based Linux distribution for the PowerPC, the company created the Yellow Dog Updater to fill this gap. This program has since been ported to other architectures and distributions. The result, named Yellow Dog Updater, Modified (yum; yum.baseurl.org), is included with Fedora/RHEL. This chapter covers many yum commands and features.

PackageKit PackageKit (www.packagekit.org) is a front end for several PMSs, providing a uniform interface. Fedora, Kubuntu, and SUSE use PackageKit. The **gnome-packagekit** package holds graphical tools designed for the GNOME desktop; each of these tools is named **gpk***.

Graphical interfaces This chapter describes yum, which provides a textual interface. The yumex utility (yum extender; **yumex** package), which this book does not cover, provides a graphical interface to **yum**. The gpk-application utility, part of PackageKit (previous), also provides a way to work with software packages graphically.

Kernel source code Chapter 15 discusses downloading, configuring, compiling, and installing kernel source code. See page 586 for an example of downloading kernel source code using yumdownloader.

Repositories The yum utility downloads package headers and packages from servers, called *repositories,* that can reside on the Internet, a CD, a DVD, or the local network. See page 543 for more information. RHEL uses Red Hat Network (page 554) as a repository. If you need to distribute locally built packages to a group of systems, you might want to consider setting up a local repository.

Keeping software up-to-date Of the many reasons to keep software up-to-date, one of the most important is security. Although you often hear about software-based security breaches after the fact, you rarely hear about the fixes that were available but never installed before the breach occurred. Timely installation of software updates is critical to system security. Linux open-source software is the ideal environment to find and fix bugs and make repaired software available quickly. When you keep a system and application software up-to-date, you keep abreast of bug fixes, new features, support for new hardware, speed enhancements, and more.

As shipped, Fedora/RHEL checks for updates daily, automatically installs security updates, and advises you when other updates are available. Use the Software Update Preferences window, Update Settings tab to change these options; see "Updates" on page 123.

Bug tracking Fedora/RHEL uses Bugzilla (bugzilla.redhat.com), which belongs to a class of programs formally known as *defect tracking systems,* to track bugs. You can use Bugzilla to read about existing bugs and to report new ones. See page 554 for information on how Fedora/RHEL handles errata.

JumpStart: Installing and Removing Packages Using yum

This section explains how to use yum to install packages on and remove packages from the local system. The yum utility provides a textual interface; see "Graphical interfaces" on page 533 if you want to use a GUI.

Work with **root** privileges when you install and remove packages

tip   Because installing and removing packages involves writing to directories that only a user working with **root** privileges can write to, you must work with **root** privileges when you install and remove packages.

If you do not know the name of the package you want to install, see page 537. If you want yum to download a package that is not supported by Fedora/RHEL, you must add to the **/etc/yum.repos.d** directory (page 543) a file that specifies the repository that holds the package.

Before using yum to install a package, work with **root** privileges to give the command **yum update** (page 539) to update the local RPM installation database. By default, the system updates this database daily. Even so, it is a good idea to give this command periodically until you are sure the script is updating the database properly.

yum **install**   The following example calls yum to install the tcsh shell, which is part of the **tcsh** package. After yum determines what it needs to do, it asks for confirmation. Reply **y** if you want to continue or **n** to quit.

```
# yum install tcsh
Loaded plugins: langpacks, presto, refresh-packagekit
Setting up Install Process
Resolving Dependencies
--> Running transaction check
---> Package tcsh.i686 0:6.17-15.fc15 will be installed
--> Finished Dependency Resolution

Dependencies Resolved

================================================================================
 Package        Arch         Version            Repository              Size
================================================================================
Installing:
 tcsh           i686         6.17-15.fc15       updates-testing         403 k

Transaction Summary
================================================================================
Install       1 Package(s)

Total download size: 403 k
Installed size: 1.1 M
```

```
Is this ok [y/N]: y
Downloading Packages:
Setting up and reading Presto delta metadata
Processing delta metadata
Package(s) data still to download: 403 k
tcsh-6.17-15.fc15.i686.rpm                            | 403 kB     00:01
Running rpm_check_debug
Running Transaction Test
Transaction Test Succeeded
Running Transaction
  Installing : tcsh-6.17-15.fc15.i686                                    1/1

Installed:
  tcsh.i686 0:6.17-15.fc15

Complete!
```

Automatically
installs
dependencies

The next command installs the **ypbind** (NIS) package. Because this package depends on other packages that are not installed (**rpcbind** and **yp-tools**), yum lists the package under **Installing for dependencies** and installs them automatically. The yum utility asks for confirmation before installing the packages.

```
# yum install ypbind
Loaded plugins: langpacks, presto, refresh-packagekit
Setting up Install Process
Resolving Dependencies
--> Running transaction check
---> Package ypbind.i686 3:1.32-5.fc15 will be installed
--> Processing Dependency: yp-tools for package: 3:ypbind-1.32-5.fc15.i686
--> Processing Dependency: rpcbind for package: 3:ypbind-1.32-5.fc15.i686
--> Running transaction check
---> Package rpcbind.i686 0:0.2.0-10.fc15 will be installed
---> Package yp-tools.i686 0:2.12-4.fc15 will be installed
--> Finished Dependency Resolution

Dependencies Resolved

================================================================================
 Package          Arch         Version              Repository        Size
================================================================================
Installing:
 ypbind           i686         3:1.32-5.fc15        fedora            55 k
Installing for dependencies:
 rpcbind          i686         0.2.0-10.fc15        fedora            47 k
 yp-tools         i686         2.12-4.fc15          fedora            69 k

Transaction Summary
================================================================================
Install       3 Package(s)

Total download size: 171 k
Installed size: 345 k
Is this ok [y/N]: y
...
```

yum remove   You can also use yum to remove packages, using a similar syntax. The following example removes the **tcsh** package:

```
# yum remove tcsh
Loaded plugins: langpacks, presto, refresh-packagekit
Setting up Remove Process
Resolving Dependencies
--> Running transaction check
---> Package tcsh.i686 0:6.17-15.fc15 will be erased
--> Finished Dependency Resolution

Dependencies Resolved


================================================================================
 Package        Arch        Version            Repository              Size
================================================================================
Removing:
 tcsh           i686        6.17-15.fc15       @updates-testing        1.1 M

Transaction Summary
================================================================================
Remove         1 Package(s)

Installed size: 1.1 M
Is this ok [y/N]: y
Downloading Packages:
Running rpm_check_debug
Running Transaction Test
Transaction Test Succeeded
Running Transaction
  Erasing    : tcsh-6.17-15.fc15.i686                                    1/1
Removed:
  tcsh.i686 0:6.17-15.fc15

Complete!
```

Automatically removes dependencies   When yum removes a package, it also removes packages that are dependent on the package it is removing. The following example removes **ypbind** and its dependency, **yp-tools**. It does not remove **rpcbind** because another installed package might depend on **rpcbind**.

```
# yum remove ypbind
Loaded plugins: langpacks, presto, refresh-packagekit
Setting up Remove Process
Resolving Dependencies
--> Running transaction check
---> Package ypbind.i686 3:1.32-5.fc15 will be erased
--> Processing Dependency: ypbind for package: yp-tools-2.12-4.fc15.i686
--> Running transaction check
---> Package yp-tools.i686 0:2.12-4.fc15 will be erased
--> Finished Dependency Resolution

Dependencies Resolved


================================================================================
 Package        Arch        Version            Repository              Size
```

```
================================================================================
Removing:
 ypbind              i686          3:1.32-5.fc15           @fedora          91 k
Removing for dependencies:
 yp-tools            i686          2.12-4.fc15            @fedora          167 k

Transaction Summary
================================================================================
Remove        2 Package(s)

Installed size: 258 k

Is this ok [y/N]: y
...
```

FINDING THE PACKAGE THAT HOLDS AN APPLICATION OR FILE YOU NEED

You might know the name of an application, utility, or file you need but not know the name of the package that holds the file. This section describes several ways you can locate the package.

Finding a package with a name that sounds like...

tip   The yum **search** command (next page) searches package names, descriptions, and summaries. The yum **list** command (next page) searches package names only.

Fedora package database   Visit admin.fedoraproject.org/pkgdb. After entering the string you are searching for in the text box labeled **Search**, click **APPLICATIONS** or **PACKAGES** to display software packages with the string you entered in their names or descriptions.

gpk-application   You can use gpk-application to search for packages by filename, program or application name, or package name. When you find the package you want, this program will install it.

yum **whatprovides**   You can also use yum to search repositories for a package that contains a specified file. For example, suppose you are compiling a program and get the following error message:

```
xv.h:174:22: error: X11/Xlib.h: No such file or directory
```

Following, the yum **whatprovides** (or just **provides**) command displays a list of packages that contain the file named **Xlib.h** in the **X11** directory:

```
$ yum whatprovides "*X11/Xlib.h"
Loaded plugins: langpacks, presto, refresh-packagekit
...
libX11-devel-1.4.2-1.fc15.i686 : Development files for libX11
Repo        : fedora
Matched from:
Filename    : /usr/include/X11/Xlib.h
...
```

The most likely candidate is the entry shown in the preceding example, which is the most generic. You can install this package using the following command:

```
# yum install libX11-devel
```

yum **search** The yum **search** command searches for a string in the package description, summary, and name fields. The following example searches for packages that have the string **vim** in these fields:

```
$ yum search vim
Loaded plugins: langpacks, presto, refresh-packagekit
updates-testing/pkgtags                              |  44 kB     00:00
============================= N/S Matched: vim ================================
glusterfs-vim.i686 : Vim syntax file
perl-Text-VimColor.noarch : Syntax color text in HTML or XML using Vim
uzbl-vim.i686 : Vim highlighting for uzbl's config
vim-X11.i686 : The VIM version of the vi editor for the X Window System
vim-clustershell.noarch : VIM files for ClusterShell
vim-common.i686 : The common files needed by any version of the VIM editor
...
```

yum **list** The yum **list** command searches for a package name field that matches a string. Specify **list available** without an argument to list all packages that can be installed from the yum repositories. The following example searches for packages whose name fields match the string **＊emacs＊**:

```
$ yum list '＊emacs＊'
Loaded plugins: langpacks, presto, refresh-packagekit
Available Packages
clips-emacs.noarch              6.30.0-0.3.20090722svn.fc15     fedora
coq-emacs.i686                  8.2p11-1.fc12                   fedora
crm114-emacs.i686               0-2.14.20100106.fc15           fedora
cvc3-emacs.noarch               2.2-3.fc15                      fedora
cvc3-emacs-el.noarch            2.2-3.fc15                      fedora
cvc3-xemacs.noarch              2.2-3.fc15                      fedora
cvc3-xemacs-el.noarch           2.2-3.fc15                      fedora
emacs.i686                      1:23.2-17.fc15                  fedora
...
```

yum: KEEPS THE SYSTEM UP-TO-DATE

This section continues to describe yum. It covers updating installed packages, yum commands and groups, downloading RPM package files, configuring yum, and adding a repository specification. Refer to yum.baseurl.org for more information.

Do not upgrade to a new release using yum

caution   Using yum to upgrade a system from one release to another can be problematic and is not recommended. Visit fedoraproject.org/wiki/YumUpgradeFaq for more information.

UPDATING PACKAGES

In the following example, yum determines that two packages need to be updated and checks dependencies. By default, Fedora/RHEL notifies you when packages need to be updated. The yum **update** command, without additional parameters, updates all installed packages. It downloads package headers for installed packages, determines which packages need to be updated, prompts you to continue, and downloads and installs the updated packages.

```
# yum update
Loaded plugins: langpacks, presto, refresh-packagekit
Setting up Update Process
Resolving Dependencies
--> Running transaction check
---> Package gnome-games.i686 1:2.91.93-1.fc15 will be updated
---> Package gnome-games.i686 1:2.91.94-0.20110331.1.fc15 will be an update
---> Package xorg-x11-server-Xorg.i686 0:1.10.0-3.fc15 will be updated
---> Package xorg-x11-server-Xorg.i686 0:1.10.0-7.fc15 will be an update
--> Finished Dependency Resolution

Dependencies Resolved

================================================================================
 Package              Arch Version                  Repository      Size
================================================================================
Updating:
 gnome-games          i686 1:2.91.94-0.20110331.1.fc15   updates-testing 2.4 M
 xorg-x11-server-Xorg i686 1.10.0-7.fc15                  updates-testing 1.4 M

Transaction Summary
================================================================================
Upgrade     2 Package(s)

Total download size: 3.8 M
Is this ok [y/N]: y
Downloading Packages:
Setting up and reading Presto delta metadata
Processing delta metadata
Download delta size: 1.2 M
(1/2): gnome-games-2.91.93-1.fc15_2.91.94-0.20110331.1.f | 341 kB    00:02
(2/2): xorg-x11-server-Xorg-1.10.0-3.fc15_1.10.0-7.fc15. | 870 kB    00:06
Finishing rebuild of rpms, from deltarpms
<delta rebuild>                                          | 3.8 MB    00:02
Presto reduced the update size by 69% (from 3.8 M to 1.2 M).
Running rpm_check_debug
Running Transaction Test
Transaction Test Succeeded
Running Transaction
  Updating    : 1:gnome-games-2.91.94-0.20110331.1.fc15.i686        1/4
  Updating    : xorg-x11-server-Xorg-1.10.0-7.fc15.i686             2/4
  Cleanup     : 1:gnome-games-2.91.93-1.fc15.i686                   3/4
  Cleanup     : xorg-x11-server-Xorg-1.10.0-3.fc15.i686             4/4

Updated:
  gnome-games.i686 1:2.91.94-0.20110331.1.fc15
  xorg-x11-server-Xorg.i686 0:1.10.0-7.fc15

Complete!
```

You can update specific packages by specifying the names of the packages on the command line following the word **update**. The yum **check-update** command (next) lists packages that can be updated.

yum COMMANDS

This section describes a few commonly used yum commands. The yum man page contains a complete list.

check Reports on problems in the local RPM database.

check-update Lists packages that are installed on the local system and have updates available in the yum repositories.

clean all Removes header files that yum uses for resolving dependencies. Also removes cached packages. However, because yum removes packages after they have been installed, typically no cached packages exist (see **keepcache** on page 542).

clean metadata Removes the files yum uses to determine remote package availability. Using this command forces yum to download all metadata the next time you run it.

grouplist Lists yum groups (next).

groupinfo *group* Lists information about the yum group named *group* (next).

groupinstall *group*
Installs the packages in the yum group named *group* (next).

info *word* Displays information about packages in the yum repositories named *word*. Specify *word* as " *＊word＊* " to search for *word* anywhere in the package name.

list *word* Lists packages in the yum repositories whose name is *word*. Specify *word* as " *＊word＊* " to search for *word* anywhere in the package name. See page 538 for an example.

list available Lists all packages that can be installed from the yum repositories. Use a pipe and grep to search for packages (e.g., **yum list available | grep samba**).

provides Same as **whatprovides**.

search *word* Lists packages in the yum repositories that have *word* in their descriptions, summaries, or names. See page 538 for an example.

whatprovides *word*
Searches repositories and displays a list of packages that provides a feature or file that matches *word*. Specify *word* as " *＊word＊* " to search for *word* anywhere in a feature or filename. See page 537 for an example.

yum GROUPS

In addition to working with single packages, yum can work with groups of packages. The next example shows how to display a list of installed and available groups:

```
$ yum grouplist
Loaded plugins: langpacks, presto, refresh-packagekit
Setting up Group Process
Installed Groups:
   Administration Tools
   Dial-up Networking Support
   Fonts
```

```
        GNOME Desktop Environment
        ...
        Window Managers
        X Window System
Installed Language Groups:
    Arabic Support [ar]
    Armenian Support [hy]
Available Groups:
        ...
        MySQL Database
        ...
    Done
```

The command **yum groupinfo** followed by the name of a group displays information about the group, including a description of the group and a list of mandatory, default, and optional packages. The next example displays information about the MySQL Database group of packages. You must quote group names that include SPACEs.

```
# yum groupinfo "MySQL Database"
Loaded plugins: langpacks, presto, refresh-packagekit
Setting up Group Process

Group: MySQL Database
 Description: This package group contains packages useful for use with MySQL.
 Mandatory Packages:
   mysql
 Default Packages:
   MySQL-python
   libdbi-dbd-mysql
   mysql-connector-odbc
   mysql-server
   perl-DBD-MySQL
   unixODBC
 Optional Packages:
   mod_auth_mysql
   mysql-bench
   mysql-devel
   mysqlreport
   mysqltuner
   php-mysql
   qt-mysql
   qt3-MySQL
```

To install a group of packages, give the command **yum groupinstall** followed by the name of the group.

DOWNLOADING RPM PACKAGE FILES WITH yumdownloader

The yumdownloader utility (**yum-utils** package) locates and downloads—but does not install—RPM files. Because it does not install software, you do not need to work with **root** privileges to run it; you need only permission to write to the working directory.

The following example downloads the **samba** RPM file to the working directory:

```
$ yumdownloader samba
Loaded plugins: langpacks, presto, refresh-packagekit
samba-3.6.0-64pre1.fc15.1.i686.rpm                              | 4.5 MB        00:04
```

Downloading
source files

You can use yumdownloader with the **−−source** option to download RPM source package files. The yumdownloader utility automatically enables the necessary source repositories. See page 586 for an example that downloads in the working directory the RPM file for the latest version of the kernel source code for the release installed on the local system. Without the **−−source** option, yumdownloader would have downloaded an executable RPM file. See page 551 for information on installing this type of file.

yum.conf: CONFIGURES yum

You do not need to configure yum: As installed, it is ready to use. This section describes the yum configuration files for users who want to modify them. The primary configuration file, **/etc/yum.conf**, holds global settings. As distributed with Fedora/RHEL, files in the **/etc/yum.repos.d** directory define repositories. Following is the default **yum.conf** file:

```
$ cat /etc/yum.conf
[main]
cachedir=/var/cache/yum/$basearch/$releasever
keepcache=0
debuglevel=2
logfile=/var/log/yum.log
exactarch=1
obsoletes=1
gpgcheck=1
plugins=1
installonly_limit=3
color=never
...
# PUT YOUR REPOS HERE OR IN separate files named file.repo
# in /etc/yum.repos.d
```

The section labeled [**main**] defines global configuration options. The **cachedir** specifies the directory where yum stores downloaded packages, although with **keepcache** set to 0, yum does not store these packages after installing them. The amount of information logged is specified by **debuglevel**, with a value of 10 producing the most information. The **logfile** specifies where yum keeps its log.

Setting **exactarch** to **1** causes yum to update packages only with packages of the same architecture, thereby preventing an i686 package from replacing an i386 package, for example. You can use **retries** to specify the number of times yum will try to retrieve a file before returning an error (the default is 6). Set this parameter to 0 to cause yum to continue trying forever.

Setting **obsoletes** to **1** causes yum to replace obsolete packages when updating packages; it has no effect when you install packages. When **gpgcheck** is set to **1**, yum checks the GPG (page 1130) signatures on packages it installs. This check verifies the authenticity of the packages. Setting **plugins** to **1** enables yum plugins, which extend yum functionality. The **metadata_expire** parameter specifies the number of seconds (or minutes if the value is followed by **m**) that yum uses the metadata (about packages it downloads from the repository) before it downloads the information again. This parameter defaults to 90 minutes.

Although the balance of the yum configuration information, which specifies the yum repositories, can appear in the **yum.conf** file, Fedora/RHEL puts this information in **/etc/yum.repos.d**.

optional   Some packages should only be installed; they should not be updated. The parameter **installonlypkgs** in **/etc/yum.conf** identifies these packages. Packages related to the kernel default to **installonlypkgs**: Typically you do not want to update a kernel; you want to install a new one and keep the old one around in case you need it. The **installonly_limit** parameter specifies the number of versions of **installonlypkgs** packages that yum keeps. See the **yum.conf** man page for more information.

yum REPOSITORIES

As noted in **/etc/yum.conf**, Fedora/RHEL stores information about each repository in a separate file in the **/etc/yum.repos.d** directory:

```
$ ls /etc/yum.repos.d
fedora.repo  fedora-updates.repo  fedora-updates-testing.repo
```

A parameter set in one of these files overrides the same parameter set in the [**main**] section (in **yum.conf**). Each of these files contains a header, such as [**fedora**], which provides a unique name for the repository. The name of the file is generally similar to the repository name, with the addition of a **fedora-** prefix and a **.repo** filename extension. Commonly used repositories include **fedora** (held in the **fedora.repo** file), which contains the packages present on the installation DVD (stable packages); **updates** (held in the **fedora-updates.repo** file), which contains updated versions of the stable packages; and **updates-testing** (held in the **fedora-updates-testing.repo** file), which contains updates that are not ready for release. This last repository is not enabled; do not enable it unless you are testing unstable packages. Never enable the **updates-testing** repository on a production system.

optional   Each **∗.repo** file includes specifications for several related repositories, which are usually disabled. For example, the **fedora.repo** file holds [**fedora-debuginfo**] and [**fedora-source**] in addition to [**fedora**]. You cannot download source files using yum. Instead, use **yumdownloader** (page 541) for this task.

The next example shows part of the **fedora.repo** file that specifies the parameters for the **fedora** repository:

```
$ cat /etc/yum.repos.d/fedora.repo
[fedora]
name=Fedora $releasever - $basearch
failovermethod=priority
#baseurl=http://download.fedoraproject.org/pub/fedora/linux/releases/$releasever/Everything/$basearch/os/
mirrorlist=https://mirrors.fedoraproject.org/metalink?repo=fedora-$releasever&arch=$basearch
enabled=1
#metadata_expire=7d
gpgcheck=1
gpgkey=file:///etc/pki/rpm-gpg/RPM-GPG-KEY-fedora-$basearch
...
```

Repository specification files

Each repository specification file contains the name of the repository enclosed in brackets ([]), a **name**, a **failovermethod**, a **baseurl**, and a **mirrorlist**. The **name** provides an informal name for the repository that yum displays. The **failover-method** determines the order in which yum contacts an initial mirror site and additional mirror sites if the first one fails; **priority** selects the sites in the order in which they appear, while **roundrobin** selects sites randomly. The **baseurl** indicates the location of the main repository; it is commented out by default. The **mirrorlist** specifies the URL of a file that holds a list of **baseurl**s, or mirrors of the main repository. Only **baseurl** or **mirrorlist** can be enabled at one time. These definitions use two variables: yum sets **$basearch** to the architecture of the system (e.g., **i686**) and **$releasever** to the version of the release (e.g., **15** for Fedora 15).

The repository described by the file is enabled (yum will use it) if **enabled** is set to **1** and is disabled if **enabled** is set to **0**. The **metadata_expire** specifies how long yum considers metadata valid: After this amount of time, yum downloads fresh metadata. Default is six hours. As described earlier, **gpgcheck** determines whether yum checks GPG signatures on files it downloads. The **gpgkey** specifies the location of the GPG key. Refer to the **yum.conf** man page for more options.

Adding a repository

There are many repositories of software packages. For more information and a list of repositories, visit fedoraproject.org/wiki/Third_party_repositories. You can also search the Internet for **fedora repositories**. One of the most interesting of these sites is repos.fedorapeople.org. These sites provide repository specification files for their repositories. Add a repository to the local system by placing a repository specification file in the **/etc/yum.repos.d** directory but see the following security tip.

Use repositories you trust

security

Be selective in which repositories you add to a system: When you add a repository, you are trusting the person who runs the repository not to put malicious software in packages you download. In addition, packages that are not supported by Fedora/RHEL can conflict with other packages and/or cause upgrades to fail.

BitTorrent

The easiest way to download a BitTorrent file is to click the torrent file object in a Web browser or in the Nautilus File Browser; this action opens a GUI. This section describes how BitTorrent works and explains how to download a BitTorrent file from the command line.

The BitTorrent protocol implements a hybrid client/server and *P2P* (page 1180) file transfer mechanism. BitTorrent efficiently distributes large amounts of static data, such as the Fedora/RHEL installation ISO images. It can replace protocols such as anonymous FTP, where client authentication is not required. Each BitTorrent client that downloads a file provides additional bandwidth for uploading the file, thereby reducing the load on the initial source. In general, BitTorrent downloads proceed faster than FTP downloads. Unlike protocols such as FTP, BitTorrent groups multiple files into a single package: a BitTorrent file.

Tracker, peer, seed, and swarm BitTorrent, like other P2P systems, does not use a dedicated server. Instead, the functions of a server are performed by the tracker, peers, and seeds. The *tracker* is a server that allows clients to communicate with each other. Each client—called a *peer* when it has downloaded part of the BitTorrent file and a *seed* after it has downloaded the entire BitTorrent file—acts as an additional source for the BitTorrent file. Peers and seeds are collectively called a *swarm*. As with a P2P network, a member of a swarm uploads to other clients the sections of the BitTorrent file it has already downloaded. There is nothing special about a seed: It can be removed at any time after the torrent is available for download from other seeds.

The torrent The first step in downloading a BitTorrent file is to locate or acquire the *torrent*, a file with the filename extension of **.torrent**. A torrent contains pertinent information (metadata) about the BitTorrent file to be downloaded, such as its size and the location of the tracker. You can obtain a torrent by accessing its URI, or you can acquire it via the Web, an email attachment, or other means. The BitTorrent client can then connect to the tracker to learn the locations of other members of the swarm it can download the BitTorrent file from.

Manners After you have downloaded a BitTorrent file (the local system has become a seed), it is good manners to allow the local BitTorrent client to continue to run so peers (clients that have not downloaded the entire BitTorrent file) can upload *at least* as much information as you have downloaded.

Prerequisites

If necessary, use yum (page 534) to install the **bittorrent** package. Normally you do not have to edit **/etc/sysconfig/bittorrent**, which configures the BitTorrent executables described in this section. Because the BitTorrent utilities are written in Python (**python** package) and run on any platform with a Python interpreter, they are not dependent on system architecture. See **/usr/share/doc/bittorrent*** for more information.

USING BITTORRENT

The bittorrent-curses utility is a textual BitTorrent client that provides a pseudo-graphical interface. When you have a torrent, enter a command such as the following, substituting the name of the torrent you want to download for the Fedora torrent in the example:

```
$ bittorrent-curses Fedora-15-i386-DVD.torrent
```

A torrent can download one or more files; the torrent specifies the filename(s) for the downloaded file(s) and, in the case of a multifile torrent, a directory to hold the files. The torrent in the preceding command saves the BitTorrent files in the **Fedora-15-i386-DVD** directory in the working directory.

The following example shows bittorrent-curses running. Depending on the speed of the Internet connection and the number of seeds, downloading a large BitTorrent file can take from hours to days.

```
------------------------------------------------------------------------
| file:     Fedora-15-i386-DVD                                          |
| size:     3,634,693,220 (3 GiB)                                       |
| dest:     /home/sam/Fedora-15-i386-DVD                                |
| progress: #####_____             |
| status:   finishing in 0:57:25 (7.7%)                                 |
| dl speed: 874.2 KB/s                                                  |
| ul speed: 0.0 KB/s                                                    |
| sharing:  0.000  (0.0 MB up / 25.1 MB down)                           |
| seeds:    17 seen now, plus 0 distributed copies(1:99.5%, 2:6.5%, 3:0.0%) |
| peers:    2 seen now                                                  |
|                                                                       |
|                                                                       |
|                                                                       |
------------------------------------------------------------------------
```

You can abort the download by pressing **q** or CONTROL-C. The download will automatically resume from where it left off when you download the same torrent to the same location again.

Make sure you have enough room to download the torrent

caution   Some torrents are huge. Make sure the partition you are working in has enough room to hold the BitTorrent file you are downloading.

Enter the command **bittorrent-curses | less** for a list of options (no man page exists). One of the most useful options is **--max_upload_rate**, which limits how much bandwidth in kilobytes per second the swarm can use while downloading the torrent *from the local system* (upstream bandwidth). Default is **20**. A value of zero (0) means there is no limit to the bandwidth the swarm can use. The following command prevents BitTorrent from using more than 100 kilobytes per second of upstream bandwidth:

```
$ bittorrent-curses --max_upload_rate 100 Fedora-15-i386-DVD.torrent
```

BitTorrent usually allows higher download rates for members of the swarm that upload more data, so it is to your advantage to increase this value if you have spare bandwidth. You need to leave enough free upstream bandwidth for the acknowledgment packets from your download to get through or the download will be very slow.

The argument to **--max_uploads** specifies the number of concurrent uploads that bittorrent-curses will permit. Default is **2**. If you are downloading over a very slow connection, try setting **--max_upload_rate** to 3 and leaving **--max_uploads** at its default value.

The name of the file or directory BitTorrent saves a file or files in is specified by the torrent. You can specify a different file or directory name by using the **--save_as** option. The torrentinfo-console utility displays the name the BitTorrent file will be saved as, the size of the file, the name of the torrent (**metainfo file**), and other information:

```
$ torrentinfo-console Fedora-15-i386-DVD.torrent
torrentinfo-console 4.4.0 - decode BitTorrent metainfo files

metainfo file.......: Fedora-15-i386-DVD.torrent
info hash...........: 12574b1ebcbf5a38d39969811860b672c9433c1f
directory name......: Fedora-15-i386-DVD
files...............:
    Fedora-15-i386-CHECKSUM (1124)
    Fedora-15-i386-DVD.iso (3634692096)
archive size........: 3634693220 (13865 * 262144 + 66660)
tracker announce url: http://torrent.fedoraproject.org:6969/announce
comment.............:
```

RPM: THE RPM PACKAGE MANAGER

RPM (RPM Package Manager; www.rpm.org) works only with software packages built for processing by RPM; it can download, install, uninstall, upgrade, query, and verify RPM packages. The files that hold these packages have a filename extension of **.rpm**. RPM uses the local RPM installation database to track the locations where software packages are installed, the versions of the installed packages, and the dependencies between the packages. RPM uses the Berkeley Database (Berkeley DB or BDB) and stores the database files in **/var/lib/rpm**. RPM forms the basis for yum: yum finds packages, downloads them from repositories, and then calls RPM to install/upgrade/remove the packages.

Source RPM packages are frequently found in a directory named **SRPMS** (source RPMs), whereas binary RPM packages usually reside in **Packages**. When you download binary packages, make sure they are relevant to the local operating system (both distribution and release—for example, Fedora 15).[1] They should also be compiled for the appropriate processor architecture:

Processor architectures

- **i386** covers all Intel- and most AMD-based systems; the N and Z Series Atom processors are also based on this architecture.

- **i586** covers Pentium-class or higher processors.

- **i686** refers to Pentium II or better and includes MMX extensions.

- **S390x** is for IBM System/390.

- **ia64** is for the Intel 64-bit Intel Itanium (not compatible with x86_64)

- **alpha** is for the DEC/Compaq Alpha chip.

- **ppc** and **ppc64** denotes the Power PC 32- and 64-bit processors.

- **x86_64** is for Intel and AMD 64-bit processors (not Itanium); the 230 and 330 Series Atom processors are also based on this architecture.

- **sparc** covers the Sun Sparc processor.

noarch   The name of the rpm file contains almost all the necessary information. Packages marked **noarch** ("no architecture") contain resources, such as images or scripts, that are run by an interpreter. You can install and run **noarch** packages on any architecture.

yumdownloader   See page 541 for instructions on using yumdownloader to download RPM package files.

QUERYING PACKAGES AND FILES

The following rpm command displays a list of one-line summaries of all packages installed on the system:

```
$ rpm -qa
mtools-4.0.15-2.fc15.i686
iwl6000-firmware-9.221.4.1-2.fc15.noarch
gnome-desktop3-2.91.93-1.fc15.i686
libmusicbrainz3-3.0.3-3.fc15.i686
dejavu-fonts-common-2.32-2.fc15.noarch
pptp-1.7.2-12.fc15.i686
...
```

The **–q** option queries the package database; the **–a** option specifies all packages. Without **–a**, **–q** takes the name of a package as an argument and displays information about that package only. For instance, **rpm –q ypserv** tells you whether the **ypserv** package is installed and, if so, which version is installed. Use the **–ql** options to list the files in a package.

---

1. Many RPM packages run on releases and even distributions other than the ones they were compiled for. However, installing packages intended for other distributions can create problems.

```
$ rpm -q ypserv
package ypserv is not installed

$ rpm -ql logrotate
/etc/cron.daily/logrotate
/etc/logrotate.conf
/etc/logrotate.d
/usr/sbin/logrotate
/usr/share/doc/logrotate-3.7.9
/usr/share/doc/logrotate-3.7.9/CHANGES
/usr/share/doc/logrotate-3.7.9/COPYING
/usr/share/man/man5/logrotate.conf.5.gz
/usr/share/man/man8/logrotate.8.gz
/var/lib/logrotate.status
```

With the **–qi** options, rpm displays information about a package:

```
$ rpm -qi logrotate
Name        : logrotate
Version     : 3.7.9
Release     : 8.fc15
Architecture: i686
Install Date: Wed 23 Mar 2011 05:37:59 PM PDT
Group       : System Environment/Base
Size        : 84226
License     : GPL+
Signature   : RSA/SHA256, Mon 21 Mar 2011 03:05:16 PM PDT, Key ID b4ebf579069c8460
Source RPM  : logrotate-3.7.9-8.fc15.src.rpm
Build Date  : Mon 21 Mar 2011 06:28:12 AM PDT
Build Host  : x86-06.phx2.fedoraproject.org
Relocations : (not relocatable)
Packager    : Fedora Project
Vendor      : Fedora Project
Summary     : Rotates, compresses, removes and mails system log files
Description :
The logrotate utility is designed to simplify the administration of
log files on a system which generates a lot of log files.  Logrotate
allows for the automatic rotation compression, removal and mailing of
log files.  Logrotate can be set to handle a log file daily, weekly,
monthly or when the log file gets to a certain size.  Normally,
logrotate runs as a daily cron job.

Install the logrotate package if you need a utility to deal with the
log files on your system.
```

You can use the **–qf** options to determine which package a file belongs to; it works with installed packages only. Use the yum **whatprovides** command (page 537) to search repositories for the same information. The following command shows that more is part of the **util-linux** package:

```
$ rpm -qf /bin/more
util-linux-2.19-3.fc15.i686
```

Include the **–p** option with other options to query an uninstalled RPM package file:

```
$ ls ypser*
ypserv-2.24-2.fc15.i686.rpm

$ rpm -qip ypserv-2.24-2.fc15.i686.rpm
Name        : ypserv
Version     : 2.24
Release     : 2.fc15
...
```

INSTALLING, UPGRADING, AND REMOVING PACKAGES

Although it is frequently easier to use yum or gpk-application, you can use rpm to download, install, upgrade, or remove a package. Run rpm with **root** privileges; although you can run rpm as a nonprivileged user, you will not have permission to write to the necessary directories during an install or uninstall, and the procedure will fail. During a query, you do not need to work with **root** privileges, so you can and should work as a nonprivileged user. Give the **–U** (upgrade) option, followed by the name of the file that contains the RPM version of the package you want to install. The **–U** option upgrades existing packages and installs new packages (as though you had used the **–i** option). For kernels, use **–i** (not **–U**) to leave the old kernel intact when you install a new kernel. Add the **–v** (verbose) option to display more information about what is happening and the **–h** (or **––hash**) option to display hash marks as the package is unpacked and installed.

Installing a package   For example, the following command installs the **samba** package on the local system:

```
# ls samba*
samba-3.6.0-64pre1.fc15.1.i686.rpm
# rpm -Uvh samba-3.6.0-64pre1.fc15.1.i686.rpm
Preparing...                ########################################### [100%]
   1:samba                  ########################################### [100%]
```

When you install a package, the rpm file must be in the working directory, or you must use a pathname that points to the rpm file. If you specify an FTP or HTTP URL, rpm will download the package before installing it (but it will not download or install dependencies):

```
# rpm -Uvh http://download.fedora.redhat.com/pub/fedora/linux/updates/15/i386/bind-9.8.0-5.P2.fc15.i686.rpm
```

Removing a package   The following command removes the **samba** package. You can give the command from any directory:

```
# rpm -e samba
error: Failed dependencies:
        samba is needed by (installed) system-config-samba-1.2.91-2.fc15.noarch
```

When you run this command, rpm reports that another package, **system-config-samba**, is dependent on the **samba** package. To remove the **samba** package, you have two choices: You can ignore the dependency by including the rpm **––nodeps** option or you can remove the dependent package and then remove the **samba** package.

```
# rpm -e system-config-samba
# rpm -e samba
```

If you remove the samba package without removing the package that is dependent on it, the utilities within the dependent package will not work. In the preceding example, the system-config-samba utility will not work.

When you use rpm to remove a package, rpm queries package database to find the information it needs to uninstall the package and removes links, unloads device drivers, and stops daemons as necessary. Refer to the rpm man page for more rpm options.

INSTALLING A LINUX KERNEL BINARY

The following steps install a Linux kernel binary from an RPM package. If you simply want to install the latest kernel for the local system, give the command **yum install kernel** instead. Refer to Chapter 15 when you want to configure and rebuild a kernel from source files, rather than installing a new, prebuilt kernel binary.

1. Run rpm with the **–i** option to install the new kernel. Do not use the **–U** option: You are installing a new kernel that has a different name than the old kernel; you are not upgrading the existing kernel.

2. Make sure the new kernel works before you remove the old kernel. To verify the new kernel works, reboot the system using the new kernel. You might want to wait a while before removing the old kernel to make sure that no problems arise with the new one.

3. When you are satisfied with the new kernel, remove the old kernel using rpm with the **–e** option; you must specify the kernel version number. If necessary, you can manually remove an old kernel by removing files whose names contain the release number from **/boot** or **/** (root). Remove information about the old kernel from **grub.conf** (page 595). Removing the kernel manually is not recommended because it is too easy to miss a file and because it does not remove the kernel from the RPM database.

INSTALLING NON-rpm SOFTWARE

Most software that is not in RPM format comes with detailed instructions on how to configure, build (if necessary), and install it. Some binary distributions (those containing prebuilt executables that run on Fedora/RHEL) require you to unpack the software from the root directory (i.e., you must cd to **/** before unpacking it).

THE /opt AND /usr/local DIRECTORIES

Some newer application packages include scripts that install themselves automatically into a directory hierarchy under **/opt**, with files in a **/opt** subdirectory that is named after the package and executables in **/opt/bin** or **/opt/**package**/bin**.

Other software packages allow you to choose where you unpack them. Because many different people develop software for Linux, there is no consistent method for installing it. As you acquire software, install it on the local system in as consistent and predictable a manner as possible. The standard Linux file structure has a directory hierarchy under **/usr/local** for binaries (**/usr/local/bin**), manual pages (**/usr/local/man**), and so forth. Because many GNU buildtools search the **/usr/local** hierarchy by default and could find the wrong version of a utility if you install developer tools there, putting these tools in **/opt** is a good idea.

To prevent confusion later and to avoid overwriting or losing the software when you install standard software upgrades, avoid installing nonstandard software in standard system directories (such as **/usr/bin**). On a multiuser system, make sure users know where to find the local software and advise them whenever you install, change, or remove local tools.

GNU Configure and Build System

The GNU Configure and Build System makes it easy to build a program that is distributed as source code (see www.gnu.org/software/autoconf). This process requires a shell, make (**make** package), and gcc (the GNU C compiler; **gcc** package). You do not need to work with **root** privileges except to install the program.

The following example assumes you have downloaded the GNU which program (ftp.gnu.org/pub/gnu/which; page 164) to the working directory. First unpack and decompress the file and cd to the new directory:

```
$ tar -xvzf which-2.20.tar.gz
which-2.20/
which-2.20/EXAMPLES
which-2.20/posixstat.h
...
which-2.20/configure.ac
which-2.20/COPYING

$ cd which-2.20
```

After reading the **README** and **INSTALL** files, run the **configure** script, which gathers information about the local system and generates the **Makefile** file:

```
$ ./configure
checking for a BSD-compatible install... /usr/bin/install -c
checking whether build environment is sane... yes
checking for a thread-safe mkdir -p... /bin/mkdir -p
checking for gawk... gawk
checking whether make sets $(MAKE)... yes
checking whether to enable maintainer-specific portions of Makefiles... no
...
config.status: creating Makefile
config.status: creating maintMakefile
config.status: creating tilde/Makefile
config.status: creating config.h
config.status: executing depfiles commands
```

Refer to the **configure** info page, specifically the **--prefix** option, which causes the install phase to place the software in a directory other than **/usr/local**. For package-specific options enter the command **configure --help**. Next, run make:

```
$ make
make  all-recursive
make[1]: Entering directory `/home/sam/which-2.20'
Making all in tilde
make[2]: Entering directory `/home/sam/which-2.20/tilde'
source='tilde.c' object='tilde.o' libtool=no \
        DEPDIR=.deps depmode=pch /bin/bash ../depcomp \
        gcc -DHAVE_CONFIG_H -I. -I..     -g -O2 -c tilde.c
source='shell.c' object='shell.o' libtool=no \
        DEPDIR=.deps depmode=pch /bin/bash ../depcomp \
        gcc -DHAVE_CONFIG_H -I. -I..     -g -O2 -c shell.c
rm -f libtilde.a
ar cru libtilde.a tilde.o shell.o
...
source='which.c' object='which.o' libtool=no \
        DEPDIR=.deps depmode=pch /bin/bash ./depcomp \
        gcc -DHAVE_CONFIG_H -I.      -g -O2 -c which.c
gcc  -g -O2    -o which getopt.o getopt1.o bash.o which.o ./tilde/libtilde.a
make[2]: Leaving directory `/home/sam/which-2.20'
make[1]: Leaving directory `/home/sam/which-2.20'

$ ls which
which
```

After make finishes, the which executable is in the working directory. Some packages place the executable in a subdirectory. If you want to install it, give the following command while running with **root** privileges. By default this command installs which in **/usr/local/bin** so it is known to be the local version of which.

```
$ su -c "make install"
Password:
make  install-recursive
make[1]: Entering directory `/home/sam/which-2.20'
Making install in tilde
make[2]: Entering directory `/home/sam/which-2.20/tilde'
make[3]: Entering directory `/home/sam/which-2.20/tilde'
...
```

You can complete the entire task with the following command line:

```
$ su -c "./configure && make && make install"
```

The Boolean AND operator (&&) allows the execution of a subsequent command only if the previous step returned a successful exit status.

KEEPING SOFTWARE UP-TO-DATE

See page 533 for a discussion of why it is important to keep software up-to-date.

BUGS

A *bug* is an unwanted and unintended program property, especially one that causes the program to malfunction (definition courtesy of foldoc.org). Bugs have been around forever, in many types of systems, machinery, thinking, and so on. All sophisticated software contains bugs. Bugs in system software or application packages can cause the system to crash or programs not to run correctly. Security holes (a type of bug) can compromise the security of the system, allowing malicious users to read and write files, send mail to your contacts in your name, or destroy all data on the system, rendering the system useless.

Even if the engineers fixed all the bugs, there would still be feature requests as long as anyone used the software. Bugs, feature requests, and security holes are here to stay. Thus they must be properly tracked if developers are to fix the most dangerous/important bugs first, users are to research and report bugs in a logical manner, and administrators are to apply the developers' fixes quickly and easily.

Bug tracking   Early on, Netscape used an internal bug-tracking system named BugSplat. Later, after Netscape created Mozilla (mozilla.org) as an open-source browser project, the Mozilla team decided that it needed its own bug-tracking system. Netscape's IS department wrote a very short-lived version of Bugzilla. Terry Weissman, who had been maintaining BugSplat, then wrote a new open-source version of Bugzilla in Tcl, rewriting it in Perl a couple of months later.

Bugzilla belongs to a class of programs formally known as *defect-tracking systems*, of which Bugzilla is preeminent. Almost all Linux developers use this tool to track problems and enhancement requests for their software. Fedora/RHEL uses Bugzilla to track bugs and bug fixes for its Linux distributions; Red Hat Network takes advantage of Bugzilla to notify users of and distribute these fixes. To use Bugzilla, visit bugzilla.redhat.com.

ERRATA

As the Linux community, including Red Hat and the Fedora Project, finds and fixes operating system and software package bugs, including security holes, Red Hat and the Fedora Project generate RPM files (page 547) that contain the code that fixes the problems. When you upgrade a system software package, rpm renames modified configuration files with a **.rpmsave** extension. You must manually merge the changes you made to the original files into the new files. The easiest way to learn about, obtain, and install updates is to use yum.

The Fedora Announce List (admin.fedoraproject.org/mailman/listinfo/announce) holds information about Fedora updates. Under Fedora/RHEL, **packagkitd** via gpk-update-icon notifies you when updates are available.

RED HAT NETWORK (RHEL)

Red Hat Network (rhn.redhat.com), a service provided by Red Hat (for a fee), is an Internet-based system that can keep the software on one or more RHEL systems up-to-date with minimal work on your part. You must subscribe to the RHN service to use it. Red Hat uses the term *entitle* to indicate that a system subscribes to RHN: A system must be entitled before it can take advantage of RHN. You can choose to make RHN more or less automated, giving you varying degrees of control over the update process.

The entitled systems are the clients; Red Hat maintains the RHN server. The RHN server is much more than a single server: It involves many systems and databases that are replicated and located in different areas. For the purpose of understanding how to use the client tools on the local system, picture the RHN server as a single server. For additional information, refer to the Red Hat Network manuals at www.redhat.com/docs/manuals/RHNetwork.

Security is a priority with RHN. Whenever you allow a remote system to put a program on a system and run it, the setup must be very close to the theoretical ideal of absolutely secure. Toward this end, RHN never initiates communication with a system. After a program running on a system sends a message to the RHN server, the server can respond, and the system can trust the response.

rhnsd: THE RHN DAEMON

The RHN daemon (**rhnsd**) is a background service that periodically queries the RHN server to determine whether any new packages are available to be downloaded. This daemon is one of the keys to RHN security: It initiates contact with the RHN server so the server never has to initiate contact with the local system. Refer to "service: Configures Services I" on page 444 for information on how to start, stop, or display the status of **rhnsd** immediately; refer to "system-config-services: Configures Services II" on page 445 or "chkconfig: Configures Services III" on page 446 for information on how to start or stop **rhnsd** at specified runlevels.

wget: DOWNLOADS FILES NONINTERACTIVELY

The wget utility (**wget** package) is a noninteractive, command-line utility that retrieves files from the Web using HTTP, HTTPS, or FTP. In the following example, wget downloads the Fedora Project home page, named **index.html**, to a file in the working directory with the same name.

```
$ wget http://fedoraproject.org/index.html
--2011-03-31 10:28:12--  http://fedoraproject.org/index.html
Resolving fedoraproject.org... 140.211.169.196, 152.19.134.142, 209.132.181.15, ...
Connecting to fedoraproject.org|140.211.169.196|:80... connected.
HTTP request sent, awaiting response... 200 OK
Length: 22188 (22K) [text/html]
Saving to: "index.html"

100%[=====================================================>] 22,188      --.-K/s   in 0.09s

2011-03-31 10:28:12 (234 KB/s) - "index.html" saved [22188/22188]
```

With the **--recursive** (**-r**) option, wget downloads the directory hierarchy under the URI you specify. Be careful with this option because it can download a lot of data (which could completely fill the partition you are working in). The **--background** (**–b**) option runs wget in the background and redirects its standard error to a file named **wget-log**:

```
$ wget --recursive --background http://fedoraproject.org/index.html
Continuing in background, pid 15982.
Output will be written to 'wget-log'.
$
```

The wget utility does not overwrite log files. When **wget-log** exists, wget writes subsequent logs to **wget-log.1, wget-log.2,** and so on.

Running wget in the background is useful when you need to download a large file to a remote system. You can start it running from an ssh (page 681) session and then disconnect, allowing the download to complete without any interaction.

The wget **--continue** (**–c**) option continues an interrupted download. For example, if you decide to stop a download so you can run it in the background, you can continue it from where it left off with this option.

CHAPTER SUMMARY

As a system administrator, you need to keep applications and system software current. Of the many reasons to keep the software on a system up-to-date, one of the most important is system security.

A PMS (package management system) is a set of utilities that allow you to install, upgrade, remove, and search software packages easily and in a consistent manner. It is based on a local database that holds information about each installed package, including its dependencies and version information. The development of the RPM PMS has made the process of adding and removing the software packages quite easy. You can use yum, a front end to RPM, to install and upgrade software packages. The yum utility is installed by default and is easy to configure and use.

In addition, you can use the rpm utility to install, uninstall, upgrade, query, and verify RPM packages. For packages distributed as source code, the GNU Configure and Build System makes it easy to build executable files.

BitTorrent is a handy tool for downloading large static data files such as the Fedora installation ISO images. BitTorrent can replace protocols such as anonymous FTP, where client authentication is not required.

Red Hat Network (RHN), a service provided by Red Hat, is an Internet-based system that can keep the software on one or more Red Hat Enterprise Linux systems up-to-date.

EXERCISES

1. Why would you use HTTP or FTP instead of BitTorrent for downloading large files?

2. Which command would you give to update all installed packages using yum?

3. Why would you build a package from its source code when a (binary) rpm file is available?

4. Suggest two advantages that rpm files have over source distributions.

ADVANCED EXERCISES

5. When you compile a package yourself, rather than from an rpm file, which directory hierarchy should you put it in?

6. What are some steps you should take before performing an upgrade on a mission-critical server? When should you use **rpm –i** instead of **rpm –U**?

14

PRINTING WITH CUPS

OBJECTIVES

After reading this chapter you should be able to:

▶ Explain Fedora/RHEL in the purpose of a printing subsystem

▶ Describe the capabilities of CUPS

▶ Define IPP and explain its role with CUPS

▶ Use system-config-printer to install and manage local and remote printers

▶ Use the CUPS Web interface to install and manage local or remote printers

▶ Share local printers

▶ Print from a Windows system to a Fedora/RHEL printer

▶ Print from a Fedora/RHEL system to a Windows printer

▶ Use command line tools to submit, list, and cancel print jobs

▶ Limit printing with quotas

A *printing system* handles the tasks involved in getting a print job from an application (or the command line) through the appropriate *filters* (page 1164) and into a queue for a suitable printer and then getting it printed. When a printer fails, the printing system can redirect jobs to other, similar printers.

INTRODUCTION

LPD and LPR   Traditionally, UNIX had two printing systems: the BSD Line Printer Daemon (LPD) and the System V Line Printer system (LPR). Linux adopted these systems at first, and both UNIX and Linux have seen modifications to and replacements for these systems. Today CUPS is the default printing system under Fedora/RHEL.

CUPS   CUPS (Common UNIX Printing System) is a cross-platform print server built around IPP (next). CUPS provides many printer drivers and can print different types of files, including PostScript. Because it is built on IPP and written to be portable, CUPS runs under many operating systems, including Linux and Windows. Other UNIX variants, including Mac OS X, use CUPS; recent versions of Windows include the ability to print to IPP printers. Thus CUPS is an ideal solution for printing in a heterogeneous environment. CUPS provides System V and BSD command-line interfaces and, in addition to IPP, supports LPD/LPR, HTTP, SMB, and JetDirect (socket) protocols, among others.

If the printer you are configuring is on an older Linux system or another UNIX-like operating system that does not run CUPS, the system probably runs LPD/LPR. Most devices that connect printers directly to a network support LPR/LPD; some support IPP.

IPP   The IPP project (Internet Printing Protocol; www.pwg.org/ipp) began in 1996, when Novell and several other companies designed a protocol for printing over the Internet. IPP enables users to

- Determine the capabilities of a printer.
- Submit jobs to a printer.
- Determine the status of a printer.
- Determine the status of a print job.
- Cancel a print job.

IPP is an HTTP-based client/server protocol in which the server side can be a print server or a network-capable stand-alone printer.

Network printers   Printers connected directly to a network are functionally equivalent to printers connected to a system running a print server: They listen on the same ports as systems running print servers, and they queue jobs.

Printers and queues   On a modern computing system, when you "send a job to the printer," you actually add the job to the list of jobs waiting their turn to be printed on a printer. This list is called a *print queue* or simply a *queue*. The phrase *configuring* (or *setting up*) *a printer* is often used to mean *configuring a (print) queue*. This chapter uses these phrases interchangeably.

Configuration tools This chapter explores two tools you can use to configure a print queue: system-config-printer (page 562) and the CUPS Web interface (page 568), with an emphasis on the former. Using the CUPS Web interface is very similar to using system-config-printer; thus much of the discussion of system-config-printer applies to the CUPS Web interface. However, system-config-printer is a native application written in Python, not a Web interface.

PREREQUISITES

Make sure the following packages are installed (most are installed with the base Fedora/RHEL system):

- **cups**

- **system-config-printer** (optional)

- **cups-pdf** (optional; Fedora only; sets up a virtual PDF printer)

The CUPS Web interface requires an X server and a Web browser. Although it is a poor solution, a text Web browser such as elinks (**elinks** package) will work too.

cups init script Run chkconfig to cause CUPS (the **cupsd** daemon) to start when the system goes into multiuser mode:

```
# chkconfig cups on
```

Start CUPS:

```
# service cups start
```

MORE INFORMATION

Local CUPS Documentation: With the CUPS Web interface up (page 571), point a local browser at localhost:631/help.

Web Information on printers and printing under Linux, including forums and articles: www.linuxfoundation.org/collaborate/workgroups/openprinting:
A support database with details about many printers, including notes and driver information: www.openprinting.org/printers
CUPS home page: www.cups.org
IPP information: www.pwg.org/ipp

HOWTO The *SMB HOWTO* has a section titled "Sharing a Windows Printer with Linux Machines."

NOTES

SELinux When SELinux is set to use a targeted policy, CUPS is protected by SELinux. You can disable this protection if necessary. For more information refer to "Setting the Targeted Policy with system-config-selinux" on page 463.

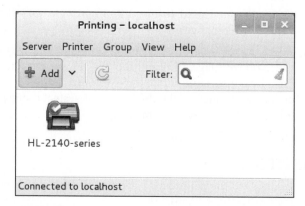

Figure 14-1 The Printing window

Firewall A CUPS server normally uses TCP port 631 for an IPP connection and port 80 for an LPR/LPD connection. If the CUPS server system accepts print jobs from remote systems and is running a firewall, you need to open one or both of these ports. Using the Fedora/RHEL system-config-firewall utility, select **Network Printing Server (IPP)** from the Trusted Services tab (page 894) to open these ports. For more general information, see Chapter 25 (page 891), which covers iptables.

PDF printer You can set up a virtual PDF printer by installing the **cups-pdf** package, or you can set up this printer manually.

FEDORA/RHEL CONFIGURES A LOCAL PRINTER AUTOMATICALLY

In most cases, when you connect a printer to the local system and turn it on, Fedora/RHEL asks twice if you want to install drivers. When the drivers are installed, the printer is ready for use. Use system-config-printer (next) to verify the printer is installed, send a test page to the printer, and change the configuration of the printer.

JUMPSTART I: CONFIGURING A PRINTER USING system-config-printer

The Printing window (Figure 14-1) enables you to add, remove, and configure local and remote printers. This JumpStart explains how to modify the configuration of an existing printer. See page 565 for information on how to set up a new printer. To display this window, select **Main menu: Applications⇨Other⇨Printing** (Fedora; if **Applications** is not visible see "Configuring Fallback Mode" on page 92) or **Main menu: System⇨Administration⇨Printing** (RHEL) or give the command **system-config-printer** from a terminal emulator or Run Application window (ALT-F2).

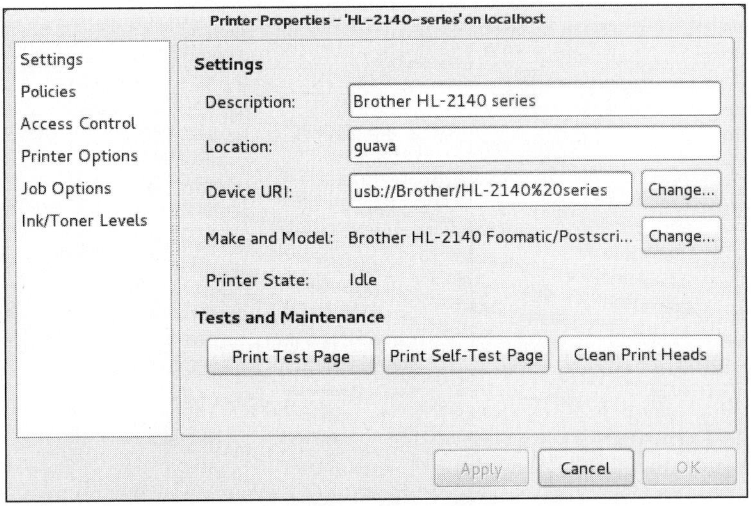

Figure 14-2   The Printer Properties window

Default printer   Highlight a printer in the Printing window and select **menubar: Printer⇨Set as Default** from the window menu to specify the highlighted printer as the default printer. If just one printer appears in the Printing window, it is the default printer; you do not have to set it up as such. The tick on the printer in Figure 14-1 indicates the default printer.

Server Settings   Select **menubar: Server⇨Settings** from the Printing window to display the Server Settings window. The top two check boxes in this window specify whether system-config-printer displays printers that are shared by other systems and whether the local system publishes printers it shares. You control whether a specific printer is shared from the Policies selection of the Printer Properties window (next).

Configuration Selections

Double-click a printer in the Printing window or highlight a printer and select **menubar: Printer⇨Properties** to display the Printer Properties window (Figure 14-2) for that printer.

This section describes the six selections found in the frame at the left side of the Printer Properties window. These selections allow you to configure the printer you chose in the Printing window.

Settings   Figure 14-2 shows the Settings selection for a Brother printer. The text boxes labeled **Description** and **Location** hold information that can help users identify the printer. The system does not use this information; change it as you like. For example, it might be helpful to put the physical location of the printer, such as **Sam's Office,** in the text box labeled **Location.** The text boxes labeled **Device URI** and **Make and Model** specify the location of the printer on the computer or network and type of the printer.

Figure 14-3   The New Printer window, Select Device screen I

Policies   The Policies selection enables you to control printer state, sharing, and banners. Under the word **State** are check boxes labeled **Enabled, Accepting jobs,** and **Shared.** Table 14-1 describes the effects of putting ticks in the first two check boxes. Putting a tick in the check box labeled **Shared** shares the printer with other systems if the local system publishes shared printers (see "Server Settings"). The Policies tab also controls whether the printer prints banners before and after jobs and what CUPS does when the printer reports an error.

Access Control   The Access Control selection enables you to set the policy for printer access. By default, anyone can use the printer. To restrict access, you can create a blacklist of users who *are not* allowed to use it. Alternatively, you can prohibit anyone from using the printer and then create a whitelist of users who *are* allowed to use it.

Printer Options   The Printer Options selection controls image quality, paper size and source (tray), and other generic printer options.

Job Options   The Job Options selection controls the number of copies, orientation (portrait or landscape), scaling, margins, and more. Options specified by an application sending a job to the printer override options you set in this tab. Scroll down to see all options.

Table 14-1   Printer status

	Enabled	**Disabled**
Accepting jobs	Accepts new jobs into the queue.	Accepts new jobs into the queue.
	Prints jobs from the queue.	Does not print jobs from the queue until the printer is enabled.
Rejecting jobs	Rejects new jobs.	Rejects new jobs.
	Prints jobs from the queue.	Does not print jobs from the queue until the printer is enabled.

Figure 14-4   The New Printer window, Select Device screen II

Ink/Toner Levels   The Ink/Toner Levels selection reports on ink/toner (marker) levels and displays status messages.

JumpStart II: Setting Up a Local or Remote Printer

This section describes how to set up three types of printers for local use: a printer attached to the local system, a printer hosted by another system, and a printer that resides on the local network (a network printer). For instructions on how to use the CUPS Web interface to perform the same tasks, see page 568.

To add a printer to the local system, click **Add** (Fedora) or **New** (RHEL) on the toolbar in the Printing window (Figure 14-1, page 562). The system-config-printer utility looks for printers attached to the system or the local network. It then asks if you want to adjust the firewall so the local system can detect printers on the network (Fedora only) and displays the New Printer window (Figure 14-3).

To configure a printer, highlight the printer in the frame labeled **Select Device**. Click the triangle to the left of **Network Printers** to display network printers. The system-config-printer utility displays a description of the printer you highlight.

Specifying a URI   The easiest way to locate a remote printer that is not listed is to select **Find Network Printer** under **Network Printer** in the frame labeled **Select Device**. Then enter in the text box labeled **Host** the name of the host the printer is attached to (the server) or, for a network printer, the name of the printer. You can specify an IP address instead of a hostname. Click **Find**. If it finds a printer, system-config-printer displays the name of the printer under **Network Printer** and fills in information about the printer on the right side of the window (Figure 14-4). For IPP printers, system-config-printer displays

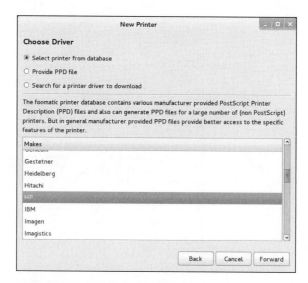

Figure 14-5   Selecting a printer manufacturer

a *URI* (page 1195), which is the printer's location on the network; see page 572 for more information.

If the printer is not listed, select **Other** (for a local printer) or one of the selections under Network Printer (for a remote printer) from the frame labeled **Select Device**; system-config-printer displays appropriate text boxes on the right side of the window. All selections under Network Printer require you to specify a Host and a Queue or Port number. These values locate the printer on the network.

To specify the queue for an LPD/LPR printer, use the form *printer-name*; for an IPP printer, use the form **/printers/***printer-name*; for an HP JetDirect-compatible network printer, specify the *printer-name* and Port number. Replace *printer-name* with the name of the printer on the server.

If you are unsure of the name of a printer, give the command **lpstat –p** on the server to display the names of all printers on that system. After selecting or specifying a printer, click the button labeled **Verify** (if present) to make sure the printer is accessible and then click **Forward**. The system-config-printer utility searches for the printer driver.

Next the utility might ask you which printer options you want to install. Specify the options and click **Forward**.

If system-config-printer displays the Choose Driver screen of the New Printer window (Figure 14-5), you can specify a printer manufacturer (such as HP). Typically system-config-printer selects the manufacturer automatically. Alternatively, you can specify a PPD file (page 572) or search for a driver to download. Click **Forward**.

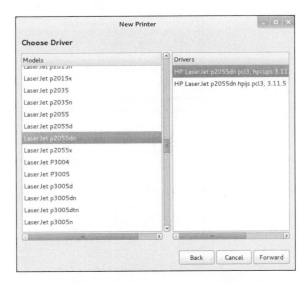

Figure 14-6 Selecting a printer model and driver

The next screen (Choose Driver; Figure 14-6), which system-config-printer might not display, allows you to specify the model of the printer and select which driver you want to use (if more than one is available). A selection is usually highlighted automatically.

The system-config-printer utility might display a screen showing installable (printer-specific) options. Generally you do not need to make changes to this screen. Click **Forward**.

If a printer is not listed...

tip   If the printer you are configuring is not listed, you can select **Generic** (at the top of the list) as the printer manufacturer and choose a type of generic printer from the list box labeled **Models**. Choose **PostScript Printer** from the list if the printer is PostScript-capable. Alternatively, you can select a PostScript printer such as the Apple LaserWriter 12/640ps. Then select a PostScript driver from the list box labeled **Drivers**.

If the printer is not PostScript capable, check whether the printer supports PCL; if it does, select another, similar PCL printer. If it does not support PCL, choose **text-only printer** from the list box labeled **Models**; you will not be able to print graphics, but you should be able to print text.

Or you can check whether the printer can emulate another printer (i.e., if it has an *emulation mode*). If it can, check whether the manufacturer and model of the printer it can emulate are listed and set it up that way.

If all else fails, determine which listed printer is most similar to the one you are configuring and specify that printer. You can also try configuring the printer using the CUPS Web interface (page 568), which offers a different choice of models.

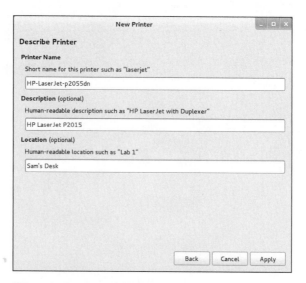

Figure 14-7 Specifying the name of the printer

On the next screen (Describe Printer; Figure 14-7), you must specify a name for the printer; specifying the description and location is optional. The name of the printer must start with a letter and cannot contain SPACEs. If you use only one printer, the name you choose is not important. If you use two or more printers, the name should help users distinguish between them. The printer name is the name of the print queue on the local system. Click **Apply**.

At this point, the system-config-printer utility closes the New Printer window, asks if you want to print a test page, and displays the new printer in the Printing window. If you have more than one print queue and want to set up the new print queue to be the default, highlight the printer and select **menubar: Printer➾Set As Default**.

WORKING WITH THE CUPS WEB INTERFACE

The CUPS Web interface allows you to do the same things as system-config-printer (pages 562 and 565). Because the two interfaces are functionally similar, this section does not go into as much detail as the section on system-config-printer. This section describes how to configure/reconfigure for local use a printer attached to the local system, a printer hosted by another system, or a printer that resides on the local network (a network printer).

Username and password At some point the CUPS Web interface asks for a username and password. Supply **root** and the **root** password.

Remote administration

security When you provide a username and password to the CUPS Web interface, they are transmitted in cleartext over HTTP. The lack of encryption is a security issue when you are administrating printers over an unsecure network.

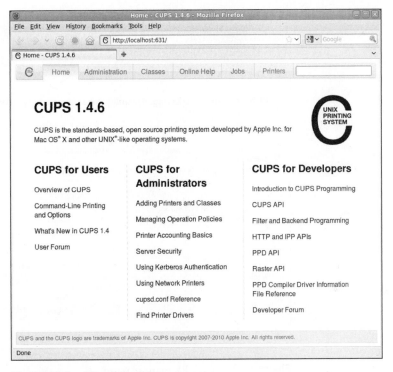

Figure 14-8 The Cups Home page

Display the CUPS Web interface by pointing a Web browser at **localhost:631** on the system on which you are configuring the printer (Figure 14-8).

Clicking the **Administration** tab at the top of the page displays the Administration page. On this page click **Add Printer** (under the word **Printers**) to display the first Add Printer page. This page is functionally equivalent to the Select Device screen of the New Printer window displayed by system-config-printer (Figure 14-3, page 564).

Clicking the **Printers** tab at the top of the page displays a page that lists the configured printers. Clicking the name of the printer in the column labeled **Queue Name** displays a page that allows you to work with that printer and queue (Figure 14-9 on the next page).

On the Printer page, select **Print Test Page** from the **Maintenance** drop-down list to test the printer. If you want to make this printer the default printer, select **Set As Server Default** from the **Administration** drop-down list. The **Maintenance** drop-down list allows you to pause the printer and to cancel, reject, and move jobs in the queue. The **Administration** drop-down list allows you to change the printer options and to modify and delete the printer. The buttons at the bottom of this page enable you to cancel or move jobs in the print queue. In addition to these tasks, you might be able to reprint jobs.

Figure 14-9 A CUPS printer page

CONFIGURING PRINTERS

You can use the CUPS Web interface, the CUPS command-line interface, or system-config-printer to manage printers and queues.

MODIFYING A PRINTER

"JumpStart II: Setting Up a Local or Remote Printer" (page 565) explains how to configure a printer using system-config-printer. "Working with the CUPS Web Interface" (page 568) discusses how to configure a printer using the CUPS Web interface. This section explains how to use either of these tools to modify a printer that is already configured. In both cases, modifying a printer takes you through the same steps as setting up a printer, except the fields are filled in so you can modify the ones that need to be changed.

Using system-config-printer

Open the Printing window, select the printer whose configuration you want to modify, and proceed as explained on page 562. Reconfiguring an existing printer follows the same steps as installing a new printer.

Using the CUPS Web interface

Open the CUPS Web interface as explained on page 568. To modify a printer, click the **Printers** tab at the top of the page and then click the name of the printer you want to modify. The CUPS Web interface displays two drop-down lists near the top of the page: **Administration** and **Maintenance** (Figure 14-9, page 570). These lists allow you to work with the selected printer. The Administration drop-down list allows you to modify the printer; this selection takes you through the same steps as when you set up a new printer. From this list you can also delete and set default options for the printer as well as set the printer as the default printer and specify which users are allowed to use the printer. From the **Maintenance** drop-down list, you can print a test page and pause the printer. You can also reject, move, and cancel all jobs.

THE CUPS WEB INTERFACE

To connect to the CUPS Web interface (page 568), point a Web browser running on the local system at **localhost:631**. You must supply the username **root** and the **root** password to change a printer configuration using the CUPS Web interface.

This section describes two tasks: modifying jobs and setting up printer classes. You can also perform these tasks from the command line using lpadmin (page 573) or from system-config-printer (page 562) by selecting **menu bar: Printer⇨View Print Queue** or **menu bar: Group**, respectively.

JOBS

Click the **Jobs** tab near the top of the page to display the Jobs page, which lists jobs in the print queues. From this page you can cancel print jobs and move them to other queues. Click **Show Completed Jobs** to display a list of recently completed jobs. In some cases, you can reprint completed jobs from this page. You can perform the same tasks from the Printer page.

CLASSES

CUPS allows you to organize similar printers into a group called a *class*. To clients, a class of printers appears as a single printer. For each class, you must specify a name; optionally, you can specify a location and description. A printer can belong to more than one class. CUPS prints jobs sent to a class on the first available printer in the class. For example, you might be able to divide your print jobs into black-and-white jobs and color jobs. If more than one printer can fulfill each of these roles, you can allow users to select a printer manually, or you can define two printer classes (black-and-white and color) and have users send their jobs to a certain class of printers. Place printers that are members of the same class physically close to each other so users can easily find their output.

Plan for the future

tip If you expect to add printers to the network, you might want to configure classes containing the existing printers when you set up the network. You can then add printers later without having to change printer configurations on client systems.

To define a class, first click the **Administration** tab at the top of the page and then click **Add Class**. At a minimum, you must enter a name for the class. You might also enter a description and location. The Members list displays the names of all CUPS printers and classes. Highlight the printers you want to be members of the class you are defining; hold SHIFT and click another printer to highlight more than one printer. To define a class that includes printers that are not adjacent in the list, define the class to have a single printer and then modify the class after you create it to add other printers. To modify existing classes, click **Manage Classes** in the Administration tab.

CUPS ON THE COMMAND LINE

In addition to using system-config-printer and the CUPS Web interface, you can control CUPS and manage print queues from the command line. This section describes the utilities that enable you to manage printers and print queues and establish printing quotas.

lpinfo: DISPLAYS AVAILABLE DRIVERS

PPD files   The lpinfo utility provides information about the printer drivers and interfaces available to CUPS. The **–m** option displays the list of available PostScript Printer Definition (PPD) files/drivers.

```
$ lpinfo -m | head
gutenprint.5.2://pcl-apollo-p2100/expert Apollo P-2100 - CUPS+Gutenprint v5.2.6
gutenprint.5.2://pcl-apollo-p2100/simple Apollo P-2100 - CUPS+Gutenprint v5.2.6 Simplified
gutenprint.5.2://pcl-apollo-p2150/expert Apollo P-2150 - CUPS+Gutenprint v5.2.6
gutenprint.5.2://pcl-apollo-p2150/simple Apollo P-2150 - CUPS+Gutenprint v5.2.6 Simplified
gutenprint.5.2://pcl-apollo-p2200/expert Apollo P-2200 - CUPS+Gutenprint v5.2.6
gutenprint.5.2://pcl-apollo-p2200/simple Apollo P-2200 - CUPS+Gutenprint v5.2.6 Simplified
gutenprint.5.2://pcl-apollo-p2250/expert Apollo P-2250 - CUPS+Gutenprint v5.2.6
gutenprint.5.2://pcl-apollo-p2250/simple Apollo P-2250 - CUPS+Gutenprint v5.2.6 Simplified
gutenprint.5.2://pcl-apollo-p2500/expert Apollo P-2500 - CUPS+Gutenprint v5.2.6
gutenprint.5.2://pcl-apollo-p2500/simple Apollo P-2500 - CUPS+Gutenprint v5.2.6 Simplified
```

URIs   CUPS uses URIs (page 565) to identify printer ports by type and location, just as a Web browser identifies documents by protocol and location. A parallel port has a URI with the format **parallel:/dev/lp0**; a remote LPD printer uses the format **lpd://192.168.0.101**, and a USB printer uses the format **usb://Brother/HL-2140%20series**. When run with **root** privileges, lpinfo with the **–v** option displays a list of available connections:

```
# lpinfo -v
direct scsi
network https
network ipp
network lpd
network http
network socket
serial serial:/dev/ttyS0?baud=115200
serial serial:/dev/ttyS1?baud=115200
direct usb://Brother/HL-2140%20series
```

The **–v** option to lpinfo does not display every possible network address for the socket, HTTP, IPP, LPD, and SMB protocols because there are more than 4 billion of these addresses in the IPv4 address space.

lpadmin: CONFIGURES PRINTERS

You can use the lpadmin utility to add and remove printers from the system, modify printer configurations, and manage printer classes. This utility has three major options: **–d** (set the default printer), **–x** (remove a printer), and **–p** (add or modify a printer). The first two options are simple; examples follow the next subsection. Each of these three options takes the name of a printer as an argument. The name of the printer must start with a letter and cannot contain SPACEs.

ADDING OR MODIFYING A PRINTER

Add a printer or modify an existing printer by giving a command in the following format:

> # *lpadmin –p printer-name options*

where ***printer-name*** is the name of the printer and ***options*** is a combination of options from the following list:

–c *class*   Adds the printer to the class *class,* creating the class if necessary.

–D *info*   The *info* is a string that describes the printer for the benefit of users; it has no meaning to the system. Enclose *info* within quotation marks if it contains SPACEs.

–E   Enables the printer, instructing CUPS to accept jobs into its print queue.

–L *loc*   The *loc* is a string that indicates the physical location of the printer (e.g., office, building, floor). It has no meaning to the system. Enclose *loc* within quotation marks if it contains SPACEs.

–m *model*   The *model* is the name of the PPD file (page 572) that describes the printer. Use **lpinfo –m** to display a list of installed PPD files. If you have a manufacturer-provided PPD file, copy it to **/usr/share/cups/model**. Use the **–P** option to specify the pathname of the file. Specifying **–m postscript.ppd.gz**, for example, is the same as specifying **–P /usr/share/cups/model/postscript.ppd.gz**.

–P *file*   The *file* is the absolute pathname of the PPD file (page 572) that describes the printer. Use **lpinfo –m** to display a list of installed PPD files. If you have a manufacturer-provided PPD file, copy it to **/usr/share/cups/model**. See **–m** for an alternative way to specify a PPD file.

–r *class*   Removes the printer from the class *class*. This option removes the class if, after removing the printer, the class would be empty.

–v *URI*   The *URI* is the device to which the printer is attached. Use **lpinfo –v** to list possible devices.

EXAMPLE lpadmin COMMANDS

At a minimum, you need to provide a device and a model when you add a printer to the system. The following command adds a Brother HL-2140 printer to the system and enables it for use. This printer is connected locally to a USB port and is named HL2140.

```
# lpadmin -p HL2140 -E -v usb://Brother/HL-2140%20series -m Brother-HL-2140-hpijs-pcl5e.ppd
```

The printer information generated by the preceding command is stored in the /etc/cups/printers.conf file:

```
# cat /etc/cups/printers.conf
# Printer configuration file for CUPS v1.4.6
# Written by cupsd on 2011-04-12 15:40
# DO NOT EDIT THIS FILE WHEN CUPSD IS RUNNING
<DefaultPrinter HL-2140-series>
Info Brother HL-2140 series
Location guava
MakeModel Brother HL-2140 Foomatic/hpijs-pcl5e (recommended)
DeviceURI usb://Brother/HL-2140%20series
State Idle
StateTime 1302648023
Type 8433684
Product (HL-2140 series)
Filter application/vnd.cups-raw 0 -
Filter application/vnd.cups-postscript 100 foomatic-rip
Filter application/vnd.cups-pdf 0 foomatic-rip
Filter application/vnd.cups-command 0 commandtops
Accepting Yes
Shared Yes
JobSheets none none
QuotaPeriod 0
PageLimit 0
KLimit 0
OpPolicy default
ErrorPolicy stop-printer
</Printer>
```

The lpadmin command decompresses and copies the printer driver information from the /usr/share/cups/model/stcolor.ppd.gz file to /etc/cups/ppd. The resulting file is given the printer's name: /etc/cups/ppd/HL-2140-series.ppd.

You can modify a printer configuration with lpadmin using the same options that you used to add it. When you specify the name of an existing printer, lpadmin modifies the printer rather than creating a new one.

The next command configures an HP LaserJet–compatible printer with a JetDirect interface that is connected directly to the LAN at 192.168.1.103 and names this printer HPLJ. Specifying **socket** in the protocol part of the URI instructs CUPS to use the JetDirect protocol, a proprietary protocol developed by HP for printers connected directly to a network.

```
# lpadmin -p HPLJ -E -v socket://192.168.1.103 -m laserjet.ppd.gz
```

The lpstat utility with the **–d** option displays the name of the default printer:

```
#lpstat -d
system default destination: MainPrinter
```

CUPS automatically makes the first printer you define the default printer. The following command makes HPLJ the default printer:

```
#-d HPLJ
```

The following command removes the configuration for the HL2140 printer:

```
#-x HL2140
```

PRINTING QUOTAS

CUPS provides rudimentary printing quotas. You can define two forms of quotas: page count and file size. File size quotas are almost meaningless because a small PostScript file can take a long time to interpret and can require a lot more ink to print than a large one. Page quotas are more useful, although their implementation is flawed. To determine the number of pages in a document, CUPS examines the PostScript input. If a job is submitted in the printer's native language, such as PCL, CUPS bypasses this accounting mechanism. Also, if mpage is used to create a Post-Script file with multiple pages printed on each sheet, CUPS counts each page in the original document, rather than each sheet of paper it prints on.

Use **job-quota-period** and either **job-page-limit** or **job-k-limit** to establish a quota for each user on a given printer. The **job-quota-period** option specifies the number of seconds that the quota remains valid. The following command establishes a quota of 20 pages per day per user for the printer named HPLJ:

```
#lpadmin -p HPLJ -o job-quota-period=86400 -o job-page-limit=20
```

The **job-k-limit** option works similarly but defines a file size limit in kilobytes. The limit is the total number of kilobytes that each user can print during the quota period. After a user has exceeded her quota, she will not be allowed to print until the next quota period.

MANAGING PRINT QUEUES

When a printer is operating normally, it accepts jobs into its print queue and prints those jobs in the order they are received. You can give the command **cupsreject** followed by the name of a printer to cause a printer to not accept jobs into its print queue; enter the command **cupsaccept** to re-enable it. You can also use system-config-printer to control the print queue; refer to "Settings" on page 563. Two factors determine how a printer handles a job: if the printer is accepting jobs and if it is enabled. Table 14-1 on page 564 describes what happens with the various combinations of the two factors.

The utilities that change these factors are cupsdisable, cupsenable, cupsreject, and cupsaccept. Each utility takes the name of a printer as an argument. The following commands first disable and then enable the printer named HPLJ:

```
#cupsdisable HPLJ
#cupsenable HPLJ
```

The next commands cause HPLJ to reject and then accept jobs:

```
#cupsreject HPLJ
#cupsaccept HPLJ
```

SHARING CUPS PRINTERS

The section describes how to use textual tools to share local printers. Alternatively, you can use system-config-printer (page 562) to share printers: Display the Server Settings window by selecting **menubar: Server⇨Settings** and put a tick in the check box labeled **Publish shared printers connected to this system**. Using this technique allows you to chose whether to share each printer.

IPP facilitates remote printing. The Listen directive in the CUPS configuration file, **/etc/cups/cupsd.conf**, specifies which IP address and port or which domain socket path CUPS binds to and accepts requests on. The Listen directive has the following format:

Listen *IP:port* | *path*

where *IP* is the IP address that CUPS accepts connections on, *port* is the port number that CUPS listens on for connections on *IP*, and *path* is the pathname of the domain socket CUPS uses to communicate with printers. CUPS typically uses port 631 and by default binds to **localhost**. Thus it accepts connections from the loopback service of the local system only. CUPS uses **/var/run/cups/cups.sock**, a local domain socket, to communicate with local printers. It can also use a Port directive to specify the port number it listens to for HTTP requests.

```
$ grep -i listen /etc/cups/cupsd.conf
# Only listen for connections from the local machine.
Listen localhost:631
Listen /var/run/cups/cups.sock
```

To allow other systems to connect to the CUPS server on the local system, you must instruct CUPS to bind to an IP address that the other systems can reach. First remove or comment out the **Listen localhost:631** directive; leave the other Listen directive in place:

```
# Listen localhost:631
Listen /var/run/cups/cups.sock
```

In place of the commented-out Listen directive, use an access control list to permit only selected machines to connect to local printers. An access control list is defined inside a <Location> container (see page 934 for the Apache equivalent). The following example allows only the system at IP address 192.168.1.101 and the local system to print to the specified printer.

```
<Location />
Order Allow,Deny
# Allow access from the local system and 192.168.1.101
Allow from localhost
Allow from 192.168.1.101
# Uncomment the following line to permit access from all systems
# Allow @LOCAL
</Location>
```

The **@LOCAL** macro is internal to CUPS and specifies the local system. This macro accepts communication from any address that resolves to the local system. Specify **Allow @LOCAL** to share the printer with all systems.

When you change **cupsd.conf**, you must restart the **cupsd** daemon (page 561).

The Order Allow,Deny directive denies print requests by default and allows requests from specified addresses. An Order Deny,Allow directive would allow access by default and denies access only to clients specified in Deny from directives. You can use domain names, including wildcards, and IP ranges with either wildcards or netmasks in Allow from and Deny from directives. These directives work the same way they do in Apache. For more information refer to "Order" on page 946.

With the Order Deny,Allow directive, **Deny from** specifies the only IP addresses CUPS does not accept connections from. When you use the Order Allow,Deny directive, **Allow from** specifies the only IP addresses CUPS accepts connections from.

After you restart **cupsd**, remote systems can print on the local system's printers using the IP address and port number specified by the Listen directive. If the server is running a firewall, you need to allow remote systems to connect through it on port 631; see page 562. You might also need to modify the SELinux policy (page 463) depending on the system setup.

TRADITIONAL UNIX PRINTING

Before the advent of GUIs and *WYSIWYG* (page 1198) word processors, UNIX users would create documents using an editor such as vi and a typesetting markup language such as TeX or nroff/troff, convert the resulting files to PostScript using an interpreter, and send the PostScript files to the printer using lpr (BSD) or lp (System V). Fedora/RHEL implements both BSD and System V command-line printing utilities for compatibility. However, these utilities are now wrappers around the equivalent functionality in CUPS rather than core components of the printing system. The corresponding utilities are functionally equivalent; use whichever you prefer (Table 14-2).

Table 14-2   BSD and System V command-line print utilities

BSD/SysV	Purpose
lpr/lp	Sends job(s) to the printer
lpq/lpstat	Displays the status of the print queue
lprm/cancel	Removes job(s) from the print queue

From the command line, you can print a text, PostScript, or PDF file using lp:

```
$ lp memo.txt
request id is MainPrinter-25 (1 file(s))
```

The preceding command adds **memo.txt** to the print queue of the default printer and assigns it job number 25. When this printer is available, it prints the file. You can specify a printer using the **–d** option:

```
$ lp -d HL2140 graph.ps
request id is HL2140-26 (1 file(s))
```

The lpr **–P** option is equivalent to the lp **–d** option.

Without arguments, lp and lpr send their standard input to the printer:

```
$ cat memo2.txt | lp
request id is MainPrinter-27 (1 file(s))
```

The lpq and lpstat commands display information about the print queue:

```
$ lpstat
MainPrinter-25          zach            13312   Sun Feb 21 18:28:38 2010
HL2140-26               zach            75776   Sun Feb 21 18:28:48 2010
MainPrinter-27          zach             8192   Sun Feb 21 18:28:57 2010
```

Use cancel or lprm to remove jobs from the print queue. By default, only the owner of a print job or a user working with **root** privileges can remove a job.

```
$ cancel 27
$ lpstat
MainPrinter-25          zach            13312   Sun Feb 21 18:28:38 2010
HL2140-26               zach            75776   Sun Feb 221 18:28:48 2010
```

While working with **root** privileges, give the command **cancel –a** or **lprm –** to remove all jobs from the print queues.

PRINT FROM WINDOWS

This section explains how to use printers on Linux CUPS servers from Windows machines. CUPS is easier to manage and can be made more secure than using Samba to print from Windows.

PRINT USING CUPS

Modern versions of Windows (2000 and later) support IPP and as a result can communicate directly with CUPS. To use this feature, you must have CUPS configured on the Linux print server to allow remote IPP printing; you also need to create a new printer on the Windows system that points to the IP address of the Linux print server.

First set up the **/etc/cups/cupsd.conf** file to allow network printing from a client, as explained in "Sharing CUPS Printers" on page 576. Setting up CUPS to allow printing from a Windows machine is exactly the same as setting it up to allow printing from a Linux client system. If necessary, open the firewall as explained on page 562.

Windows XP   From Windows XP, go to **Control Panel⇨Printers and Faxes** and click **Add Printer**. Click **Next** in the introductory window and select **A network printer or a printer attached to another computer**. Click **Next**. Select **Connect to a printer on the Internet or on a home or office network**. Continue following the next paragraph at "Enter URL."

Windows 7   From Windows 7, go to **Control Panel⇨Devices and Printers** and click **Add a printer**. Click **Add a network, wireless, or Bluetooth printer**. Assuming Windows does not find the printer, click **The printer that I want isn't listed**. Click the radio button labeled **Select a shared printer by name**.

Enter URL   Enter the following information in the text box (under Windows XP it is labeled **URL**):

http://hostname:631/printers/printer-name

where *hostname* is the name or IP address of the Linux CUPS server system and *printer-name* is the name of the printer on that system. For example, for the printer named **dog88** on the system named **dog** at IP address 192.168.0.12, you could enter **http://dog:631/printers/dog88** or **http://192.168.0.12:631/printers/dog88**. If you use a hostname, it must be defined in the **hosts** file on the Windows machine. Click **Next**. Windows requests that you specify the manufacturer and model of printer or provide a driver for the printer. If you supply a printer driver, use the Windows version of the driver.

After Windows copies some files, the printer appears in the Printers and Faxes/Devices and Printers window. Under Windows 7 you need to click through two more screens. Right-click the printer and select **Set as Default Printer** to make it the default printer. You can specify comments, a location, and other attributes of the printer by right-clicking the printer and selecting **Properties** or **Printer Properties**.

PRINT USING SAMBA

This section assumes that Samba (page 817) is installed and working on the Linux system that controls the printer you want to use from Windows. Samba must be set up so that the Windows user who will be printing is mapped to a Linux user (including mapping the Windows **guest** user to the Linux user **nobody**). Make sure these users have Samba passwords. Refer to "Samba Users, User Maps, and Passwords" on page 820.

Windows supports printer sharing via SMB, which allows a printer to be shared transparently between Windows systems using the same mechanism as file sharing. Samba allows Windows users to use printers connected to Linux systems just as they would use any other shared printers. Because all Linux printers traditionally appear to be PostScript printers, the Linux print server appears to share a PostScript printer. Windows does not include a generic PostScript printer driver. Instead, Windows users must select a printer driver for a PostScript printer. The Apple LaserWriter 12/640ps driver is a good choice.

When you use rpm to install Samba, it creates a directory named **/var/spool/samba** that is owned by the **root** account and that anyone can read from and write to. The sticky bit (page 1190) is set for this directory, allowing a Windows user who starts a print job as a Linux user to be able to delete that job, but denying users the ability to delete the print jobs of other users. Make sure this directory is in place and has the proper ownership and permissions:

```
$ ls -ld /var/spool/samba
drwxrwxrwt. 2 root root 4096 02-03 15:23 /var/spool/samba
```

Under Fedora, put the following two lines in the **[global]** section of the **/etc/samba/smb.conf** file. Under RHEL, these lines are set up by default, you need only change the **printcap name** as shown.

```
[global]
...
printing = cups
printcap name = cups
```

The printer's share is listed in the **[printers]** section in **smb.conf**. In the following example, the **path** is the path Samba uses as a spool directory and is not a normal share path. The settings allow anyone, including **guest**, to use the printer. The **[printers]** section in the default **smb.conf** file has the following entries, which are appropriate for most setups:

```
[printers]
        comment = All Printers
        path = /var/spool/samba
        browseable = no
        guest ok = no
        writable = no
        printable = yes
```

Ideally each user who plans to print should have an account. Otherwise, when multiple users share the same account (for example, the **nobody** account), they can delete one another's print jobs.

PRINTING TO WINDOWS

CUPS views a printer on a Windows machine exactly the same way it views any other printer. The only difference is the URI you need to specify when connecting it. To configure a printer connected to a Windows machine, click the **Administration** tab in the CUPS Web interface and select **Add Printer**, just as you would for a local printer.

When you are asked to select the device, choose **Windows Printer via SAMBA**. Enter the URI of the printer in the following format:

> *smb://windows_system/printer_name*

where *windows_system* can be an IP address or a hostname. After you have added the printer, you can use it as you would any other printer.

Alternatively, you can use system-config-printer (page 562) to set up a Windows printer. When you chose to install a Windows Printer, you can specify a URL as described previously, or you can click **Browse**. By default, this setup prompts the user if authentication is required; you can chose **Set authentication details now** if you prefer.

CHAPTER SUMMARY

A printing system such as CUPS sets up printers. It also moves print jobs from an application or the command line through the appropriate filters and into a queue for a suitable printer and then prints those jobs.

CUPS is a cross-platform print server built around IPP (Internet Printing Protocol). It handles setting up and sending jobs through print queues. The easiest way to configure printers is via the Printing window (system-config-printer). You can also configure CUPS using the Web interface, which you can access by pointing a Web browser at **localhost:631** on the system the printer is connected to. From the Web interface, you can configure print queues and modify print jobs in the queues.

You can use the traditional UNIX commands from a command line to send jobs to a printer (lpr/lp), display a print queue (lpq/lpstat), and remove jobs from a print queue (lprm/cancel). In addition, CUPS provides the lpinfo and lpadmin utilities, which allow you to configure printers from the command line.

CUPS and Samba enable you to print on a Linux printer from a Windows machine, and vice versa.

EXERCISES

1. Which commands can you use from the command line to send a file to the default printer?

2. Which command would you give to cancel all print jobs on the system?

3. Which commands list your outstanding print jobs?

4. What is the purpose of sharing a Linux printer using Samba?

5. Name three printing protocols that CUPS supports. Which is the CUPS native protocol?

ADVANCED EXERCISES

6. Which command lists the installed printer drivers available to CUPS?

7. How would you send a text file to a printer connected to the first parallel port without using a print queue? Why is doing so a bad idea?

8. Assume you have a USB printer with a manufacturer-supplied PostScript printer definition file named **newprinter.ppd.** Which command would you use to add this printer to the system on the first USB port with the name USBPrinter?

9. How would you define a quota that allows each user to print up to 50 pages per week to the printer named LaserJet?

10. Define a set of access control rules for a <Location> container inside **/etc/cups/cupsd.conf** that would allow anyone to print to all printers as long as they were either on the local system or in the **mydomain.com** domain.

15

BUILDING A LINUX KERNEL

OBJECTIVES

After reading this chapter you should be able to:

▸ Download, install, and prep the kernel source code

▸ Choose kernel compile options

▸ Configure the system to use the newly compiled kernel

▸ Explain the purpose of the GRUB bootloader

▸ Modify the bootloader configuration

▸ Troubleshoot kernel messages using dmesg

After you have installed Fedora/RHEL, you might want to reconfigure and build a new Linux kernel. Fedora/RHEL comes with a prebuilt kernel that simplifies the installation process. However, this kernel might not be properly configured for all system features. By configuring and building a new kernel, you can create one that is customized for a system and its unique needs. A customized kernel is typically smaller than a generic one. However, compiling and maintaining a custom kernel takes a lot of time and work.

Sometimes you do not need to build a new kernel. Instead, you can dynamically change many aspects of the installed kernel. Two ways to make these changes are by using boot command-line parameters (page 67) or by modifying **/etc/sysctl.conf**, which sysctl (next) reads when the system boots.

You can add the same parameters you use on the boot command line to **/boot/grub/grub.conf** or to its symbolic link, **/etc/grub.conf**. For example, **acpi=off** prevents **acpid** (the advanced configuration and power interface daemon) from starting. See page 67 for more information.

sysctl   The sysctl utility can modify kernel parameters while the system is running. This utility takes advantage of the facilities of **/proc/sys**, which defines the parameters that sysctl can modify.

The command **sysctl –a** displays a complete list of sysctl parameters. An example of displaying and changing the **domainname** kernel parameter follows. The double quotation marks are not required in this example, but you must quote any characters that would otherwise be interpreted by the shell. You must work with **root** privileges when you change a parameter.

```
$ sysctl kernel.domainname
kernel.domainname = tcorp.com
$ su -c 'sysctl -w kernel.domainname="example.com"'
kernel.domainname = example.com
$ sysctl kernel.domainname
kernel.domainname = example.com
```

Have the first installation CD or the installation DVD handy when you build a new kernel

caution   When you build a new Linux kernel to install a new version or to change the configuration of the existing version, make sure you have the first installation CD or the installation DVD handy. These disks allow you to reboot the system, even when you have destroyed the system software completely. Having this CD/DVD available can mean the difference between momentary panic and a full-scale nervous breakdown. Refer to "Rescue Installed System" on page 457 for instructions on bringing the system up in rescue mode.

Before you can start building a new kernel, you must download, install, and prep the source code. You also need to build a configuration file that describes the new kernel you want to build. This chapter describes the steps involved in completing these tasks.

DOWNLOADING, INSTALLING, AND PREPPING THE KERNEL SOURCE CODE

This section describes how to download kernel source code on the local system. If you want to download code that has not been customized (patched) by Fedora/RHEL, visit kernel.org/pub. It also covers prepping and installing the kernel source code. See "Configuring and Compiling the Linux Kernel" on page 588 for information on how to proceed after you have downloaded, installed, and prepped the kernel source code.

PREREQUISITES

Install the following packages:

- **rpmdevtools**
- **yum-utils** (installed with the default system)
- **ncurses-devel** (used to configure the kernel using **make menuconfig**)
- **libglade2-devel** (used to configure the kernel using **make gconfig**)

Compiling a kernel takes a lot of disk space

tip Make sure you have enough disk space before you compile a kernel. When you compile a default kernel, it occupies approximately 3.5 gigabytes. This disk space must be available on the filesystem in which you compile the kernel.

MORE INFORMATION

Local The kernel package includes the latest documentation, some of which might not be available in other documents. You might wish to review the **README** files included within the source code directories and the relevant files in the **Documentation** subdirectory.

Howto Detailed, somewhat dated, generic guide to installing and configuring the Linux kernel: *Linux Kernel-HOWTO*

Web Kernel source code: kernel.org
Fedora source code: download.fedora.redhat.com
All builds of all packages for multiple architectures plus source code: koji.fedoraproject.org

DOWNLOADING THE SOURCE CODE

rpmdev-setuptree After you download the required packages (previous section), run rpmdev-setuptree. This utility sets up an SRPM build environment comprising an **rpmbuild** directory hierarchy in your home directory:

```
$ rpmdev-setuptree
$ ls rpmbuild
BUILD  RPMS  SOURCES  SPECS  SRPMS
```

After you compile the kernel, the five directories rpmdev-setuptree creates will hold files as follows: **BUILD** holds the results of compiling the kernel, **RPMS** holds compiled RPM files, **SOURCES** holds source and patch files, **SPECS** holds the kernel specification file, and **SRPMS** holds source RPM files, if any.

Do not work with **root** privileges

caution   You do not need to—nor should you—work as a user with **root** privileges for any portion of configuring or building the kernel except for installing software packages and installing the kernel (the last step). The kernel **README** file says, "Don't take the name of **root** in vain."

The sections on building, customizing, and installing the kernel use **su –c** when it is necessary to work with root privileges. This practice helps keep you from working with **root** privileges when you do not mean to. It also provides a better record for you to review in the shell history (page 319) should something go wrong. For more information on **su –c**, refer to "Executing a Single Command" on page 414.

Fedora   **Fedora only:** The easiest way to download the updated kernel source code for the
yumdownloader   most recently released version of the Fedora kernel is to use yumdownloader. Work in and download kernel source code RPM file to your home directory:

```
$ cd
$ yumdownloader --source kernel
Loaded plugins: langpacks, presto, refresh-packagekit
Enabling updates-testing-source repository
Enabling fedora-source repository
kernel-2.6.38.2-9.fc15.src.rpm                          |  72 MB      02:48
```

The download.fedora.redhat.com site holds the kernel source code for other Fedora releases.

RHEL   **RHEL only:** To download the source code for a RHEL kernel, point a browser or FTP client at ftp://ftp.redhat.com/pub/redhat/linux/enterprise and select the version of RHEL you want, following the links until you get to the **SRPMS** directory. For the RHEL 6 server kernel, go to

```
ftp://ftp.redhat.com/pub/redhat/linux/enterprise/6Server/en/os/SRPMS
```

From the SRPMS page, search for or scroll down until you find the files named **kernel∗src.rpm**. Click and download the RPM file for the kernel source code. Typically you will want to download the most recent version. It will have a name similar to **kernel-2.6.32-71.18.1.el6.src.rpm**. The **src** indicates the package contains source files. Alternatively, if you have an account with Red Hat Network (page 554) you can download the kernel source code RPM file from rhn.redhat.com.

About the examples in this section

The examples in this section show Sam, whose home directory is **/home/sam** (**~sam**), working with the kernel named **kernel-2.6.35.11-83.fc14**. When you build a kernel, you will probably work in your home directory, and the name of the kernel you work with will differ from the name of Sam's kernel. Make the necessary substitutions as you follow the examples.

INSTALLING THE SOURCE CODE

yum-builddep   With the kernel source code RPM package file in your home directory, run yum-builddep to download and install the packages needed to build the source code package (dependencies). Because you are installing packages, you must work with **root** privileges. Replace **sam** and **2.6.35.11-83.fc14** in the following example with your username and the name of the kernel you are using to specify the location of the RPM file on the system.

```
$ su -c 'yum-builddep ~sam/kernel-2.6.38.2-9.fc15.src.rpm'
password:
Loaded plugins: langpacks, presto, refresh-packagekit
Adding en_US to language list
Getting requirements for kernel-2.6.38.2-9.fc15.src
...
Install      29 Package(s)

Total download size: 26 M
Installed size: 77 M
Is this ok [y/N]: y
...
Complete!
```

Finally, working from your home directory as a nonprivileged user, use rpm to install the kernel source code in the **rpmbuild** directory hierarchy in your home directory:

```
$ rpm -Uvh kernel-2.6.38.2-9.fc15.src.rpm
   1:kernel                 warning: user mockbuild does not exist - using root
warning: group mockbuild does not exist - using root
warning: user mockbuild does not exist - using root
...
   1:kernel                 ######################################## [100%]
```

You can ignore errors, such as those shown above, about groups and users that do not exist.

PREPPING THE SOURCE CODE

The final step before you can work with the source code is to prep it. Prepping unpacks compressed files and applies patches. The following rpmbuild command uses the **–bp** option to prep the source code:

```
$ cd /home/sam/rpmbuild/SPECS
$ rpmbuild -bp --target $(arch) kernel.spec
Building target platforms: i686
Building for target i686
Executing(%prep): /bin/sh -e /var/tmp/rpm-tmp.SJXxg1
+ umask 022
+ cd /home/sam/rpmbuild/BUILD
...
```

If rpmbuild cannot find a package it needs to prep the code, it displays a message such as the following:

```
error: Failed build dependencies:
        elfutils-libelf-devel is needed by kernel-2.6.32-71.18.1.el6.i686
        zlib-devel is needed by kernel-2.6.32-71.18.1.el6.i686
        binutils-devel is needed by kernel-2.6.32-71.18.1.el6.i686
```

In this case, install the needed packages (you might have to install different packages than those in the example):

```
$ su -c 'yum install elfutils-libelf-devel zlib-devel binutils-devel'
```

After you install the packages, give the preceding rpmbuild command again. With the kernel source code installed and prepped on the local system, you can configure, compile, and install it.

CONFIGURING AND COMPILING THE LINUX KERNEL

This section describes how to configure and compile the kernel.

Where are the kernel source code and the kernel specification file?

tip   After installing and prepping the source code as described in the previous section, Sam's source code is in **/home/sam/rpmbuild/BUILD/kernel-2.6.38.fc15/linux-2.6.38.i686**, and his kernel specification file is in **/home/sam/rpmbuild/SPECS**. Your source code will be in a similarly named directory (**~/rpmbuild/BUILD/kernel∗/linux∗**) and your kernel specification file will be in the directory named **~/rpmbuild/SPECS**.

Most of the work in this section is done in the directory in which the source code is located (**linux∗**). Labeling and installing the kernel is done in the **SPECS** directory.

LABELING THE KERNEL

To prevent overwriting existing kernel files and to identify various compilations of the kernel, you can change the **buildid** variable in the **kernel.spec** file. This variable is initially set to **.local**. Whatever value you assign to this variable is placed at the end of the kernel name and release number to identify the kernel. You can make note of patches applied to the kernel in this string to help people track down problems later on. Use cd to change directories to **~/rpmbuild/SPECS**, edit **kernel.spec**, and change **local** in the line

```
#% define buildid .local
```

to a value that identifies the kernel you are building. You must also remove the leading hash mark (#), the SPACE following the hash mark, and the SPACE between **%** and **define**:

```
%define buildid .sam1104181000
```

.config: CONFIGURES THE KERNEL

Before you can compile the code and create a Linux kernel, you must decide on and specify which features you want the kernel to support. You can configure the kernel to support most features in one of two ways: by building the feature into the kernel or by specifying the feature as a loadable kernel module (page 593), which is loaded into the kernel only as needed. In deciding which method to use, you must weigh the size of the kernel against the time it takes to load a module. Make the kernel as small as possible while minimizing how often modules have to be loaded.

The **.config** file in the **~/rpmbuild/BUILD/kernel**✻**/linux**✻ directory controls which features the new kernel will support and how it will support them. The next section provides instructions for replacing an existing custom kernel. "Customizing a Kernel" on page 590 explains how to create a default version of the **.config** file if it does not exist and how to edit the file if it does exist.

REPLACING A CUSTOM KERNEL

If you have already configured a custom kernel, you might want to replace it with a similarly configured, newer kernel. Each kernel potentially has new configuration options, however—which explains why it is poor practice to use an old **.config** file for compiling a new kernel. This section explains how to upgrade an existing **.config** file so it includes options that are new to the new kernel and maintains the existing configuration for the old options.

Work in the **~/rpmbuild/BUILD/kernel**✻**/linux**✻ directory. The system keeps a copy of the configuration file for the kernel the local system is running in **/boot**. The following command copies this file to **.config** in the working directory:

```
$ pwd
/home/sam/rpmbuild/BUILD/kernel-2.6.38.fc15/linux-2.6.38.i686
$ cp /boot/config-$(uname -r) .config
```

In this command, the shell executes **uname –r** and uses command substitution (page 351) to replace **$(uname –r)** with the output of the command, which is the name of the release of the kernel running on the local system.

Next give the command **make oldconfig** to patch the **.config** file with options from the new kernel that are not present in the old kernel. This command displays each kernel option that is the same in the new and old kernels and automatically sets the state of the option in the new kernel the same way it was set in the old kernel. It stops when it finds an option that appears in the new kernel but not in the old kernel. It then displays a prompt, which is similar to [**N/y/?**] (**NEW**), showing possible responses and indicating this option is new. The prompt shows the default response as an uppercase letter; you can type this letter (uppercase or lowercase) and press RETURN, or just press RETURN to select this response. In the example, the Tickless System option is new, and the default response is **Y** for *yes, include the option in the new kernel.* To select a nondefault response (**n** means *no, do not include the option,* and **m** means *include the option as a module*), you must type the letter and press RETURN. Enter **?** followed by RETURN to display more information about the option.

```
$ make oldconfig
scripts/kconfig/conf --oldconfig Kconfig
*
* Linux Kernel Configuration
*
*
* Code maturity level options
*
Prompt for development and/or incomplete code/drivers (EXPERIMENTAL) [Y/n/?] y
*
* General setup
*
Local version - append to kernel release (LOCALVERSION) []
Automatically append version information to version string (LOCALVERSION_AUTO) [N/y/?] n
...
*
* Processor type and features
*
Tickless System (Dynamic Ticks) (NO_HZ) [Y/n/?] (NEW) ? ?
This option enables a tickless system: timer interrupts will
only trigger on an as-needed basis both when the system is
busy and when the system is idle.

Tickless System (Dynamic Ticks) (NO_HZ) [Y/n/?] (NEW) ? RETURN
High Resolution Timer Support (HIGH_RES_TIMERS) [Y/n/?] y
Symmetric multi-processing support (SMP) [Y/n/?] y
Subarchitecture Type
> 1. PC-compatible (X86_PC)
  2. AMD Elan (X86_ELAN)
...
#
# configuration written to .config
#
```

CUSTOMIZING A KERNEL

The **~/rpmbuild/BUILD/kernel*****/linux*** directory and the **configs** subdirectory provide sample configuration files for various processors, multiple processors, and configurations. You might want to look at these files before you get started or use one of them as your starting point. To use one of these files, copy it to **.config**.

You can use one of three standard commands to build the **.config** file that configures a Linux kernel:

Figure 15-1   The Linux Kernel Configuration window, split view

```
$ make config
$ make menuconfig
$ make gconfig
```

See "Prerequisites" on page 585 for a list of packages required to run all but the first of these commands.

If a **.config** file does not exist in the working directory, each of these commands except the first sets up a **.config** file that matches the kernel the local system is running and then allows you to modify that configuration. The commands can set up this **.config** file only if the configuration file for the locally running kernel is at **/boot/config-$(uname –r)**. See the preceding section if you want to build a new kernel with a configuration similar to that of an existing kernel.

The **make config** command is the simplest of the three commands, uses a textual interface, and does not require additional software. It is, however, the most unforgiving and hardest to use of the configuration interfaces. The **make menuconfig** command uses a pseudographical interface and also displays a textual interface. The **make gconfig** command uses GTK+ (www.gtk.org) and displays a graphical interface.

Each command asks the same questions and produces the same result, given the same responses. The first and second commands work in character-based environments; the third command works in graphical environments. For many administrators working with a GUI, the third method is the easiest to use.

The **make gconfig** command displays the Linux Kernel Configuration window, which you can view in three configurations: single, split, or full view. Choose a view by clicking one of the three icons to the right of the save icon on the toolbar. Figure 15-1 shows the split view. In this view, the left frame shows the options and the top-right view lists the features for each option. The bottom-right view describes the highlighted option or feature. Figure 15-2 on the next page shows the full view.

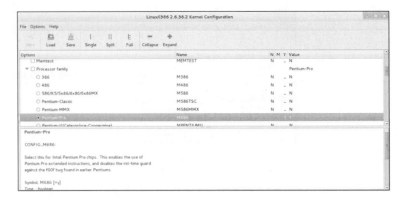

Figure 15-2   The Linux Kernel Configuration window, full view

At the far right of all views are four columns labeled **N**, **M**, **Y**, and **Value**. An **N** appears in the **N** column if the feature on that line is not being used. An **M** in the **M** column means the feature is included as a module. A **Y** in the **Y** column means the feature is compiled in the kernel. An underscore in any of these columns means that the value that would appear in that column is valid for the feature (e.g., an underscore in the column labeled **M** means that that feature can be included as a module, although it is not included as a module). The Value column holds the value of the feature (**N**, **M**, or **Y**).

In any view, you can double-click the check boxes and radio buttons next to the features to select or deselect that feature. An empty check box/radio button indicates the feature is disabled, a tick indicates it is to be compiled in the kernel, and a minus sign means it is to be compiled as a module. With a choice highlighted, you can also press **M** for module, **N** for not included, and **Y** for compiled into the kernel. Select **Menubar: Options⇨Show All Options** to display all options and features.

Go through the options and mark the features as you would like them to be configured in the new kernel. At any time during the configuration process, you can store the currently defined configuration to a file, load a configuration from a file, or exit with or without saving your changes. The selections to do so are available in **Menubar: File**. When you are done, select **Menubar: File⇨Save** and close the window.

CLEANING THE SOURCE TREE

After generating a **.config** file, but before compiling or recompiling the kernel, purge the source tree of all potentially stale ***.o** files using the following command:

```
$ make clean
    CLEAN    arch/x86/boot/compressed
    CLEAN    arch/x86/boot
    CLEAN    /home/sam/rpmbuild/BUILD/kernel-2.6.38.fc15/linux-2.6.38.i686
    CLEAN    arch/x86/kernel/acpi/realmode
    CLEAN    arch/x86/kernel/cpu
```

```
...
    CLEAN    Documentation/watchdog/src
    CLEAN    .tmp_versions
    CLEAN    vmlinux System.map .tmp_kallsyms3.o .tmp_kallsyms3.S ...
```

This command ensures that make correctly applies any numbering scheme you use when you compile the kernel.

COPYING THE CONFIGURATION FILE

Before compiling the kernel, you must copy the .config file you want to use to the directory you will compile the kernel in. This file must have a name that corresponds to the kernel in use on the local system (e.g., **config-i686-generic**):

```
$ cp .config ~/rpmbuild/SOURCES/config-$(arch)-generic
```

COMPILING A KERNEL IMAGE FILE AND LOADABLE MODULES

The next command compiles the kernel and modules. Compiling the kernel will take upwards of several hours, depending on the power of the system you are using.

```
$ pwd
/home/sam/rpmbuild/SPECS
$ rpmbuild -bb --target $(arch) kernel.spec
Building target platforms: i686
Building for target i686
Executing(%prep): /bin/sh -e /var/tmp/rpm-tmp.JoAIFx
+ umask 022
+ cd /home/sam/rpmbuild/BUILD
...
Wrote: /home/sam/rpmbuild/RPMS/i686/kernel-debug-devel-2.6.38.2-9.sam1 .... fc15.i686.rpm
Wrote: /home/sam/rpmbuild/RPMS/i686/kernel-debug-debuginfo-2.6.38.2-9.s ... fc15.i686.rpm
Executing(%clean): /bin/sh -e /var/tmp/rpm-tmp.gZcEvK
+ umask 022
+ cd /home/sam/rpmbuild/BUILD
+ cd kernel-2.6.38.fc15
+ rm -rf /home/sam/rpmbuild/BUILDROOT/kernel-2.6.38.2-9.sam1104181000.fc15.i386
+ exit 0
```

USING LOADABLE KERNEL MODULES

A *loadable kernel module* (page 1173) (sometimes called a *module* or *loadable module*) is an object file—part of the kernel—that is linked into the kernel at runtime. Modules can be inserted into and removed from a running kernel at almost any time (except when a module is being used). This ability gives the kernel the flexibility to be as small as possible at any given time. Modules are a good way to code some kernel features, including drivers that are not used continually (such as a tape driver). Module filenames end in **.ko** and are stored in subdirectories in **/lib/modules**. Under Fedora/RHEL, kernel modules are compiled along with the kernel as explained in the preceding section.

Table 15-1 lists some of the tools available to help you work with modules. Refer to the corresponding man pages for options and more information.

Table 15-1   Tools for working with modules

Tool/utility	Function
depmod	Works with dependencies for modules.
insmod	Loads modules in a running kernel.
lsmod	Lists information about all loaded modules.
modinfo	Lists information about a module.
modprobe	Loads, unloads, and reports on modules. When it loads a module, it also loads dependencies.
rmmod	Unloads modules from a running kernel.

INSTALLING THE KERNEL, MODULES, AND ASSOCIATED FILES

The next step, which you must execute with **root** privileges, is to copy the compiled kernel, modules, and associated files to the appropriate directories—usually **/boot** and a subdirectory of **/lib/modules**. When you have a partition mounted at **/boot**, the files are kept in the root of this partition (**/boot**). Because you have created an RPM package, installing these files is quite easy. The following command installs the new kernel files from the **rpmbuild** directory hierarchy in Sam's home directory into the proper directories:

```
$ su -c 'rpm -ivh --force ~sam/rpmbuild/RPMS/i686/kernel-2.6.38.2-9.sam1104181000.fc15.i686.rpm'
Password:
Preparing...               ########################################## [100%]
   1:kernel                 ########################################## [100%]
```

Installing the kernel in this manner updates the **grub.conf** (page 596) GRUB configuration file to include the new kernel.

Reboot   Reboot the system by clicking your name at the upper-right corner of the screen and selecting **Shut Down** and then selecting **Restart**. If you are working at the console, press CONTROL-ALT-DEL. You can also give a **reboot** command from the console, a character-based terminal, or a terminal emulator. When the system is rebooted, you can use uname to verify the new kernel is loaded:

```
$ uname -r
2.6.38.2-9.sam1104181000.fc15.i686
```

GRUB: The Linux Boot Loader

MBR   A boot loader is a very small program that the *bootstrap* (page 1154) process uses as it brings a computer from off or reset to a fully functional state. The boot loader frequently resides on the starting sectors of a hard disk called the MBR (master boot record).

BIOS   The *BIOS* (page 1153), which is stored in an *EEPROM* (page 1163) on the system's motherboard, gains control of a system when you turn on or reset the computer. After testing the hardware, the BIOS transfers control to the MBR, which usually passes control to the partition boot record. This transfer of control starts the boot loader, which is responsible for locating the operating system kernel (kept in the **/** or **/boot** directory), loading that kernel into memory, and starting it running. If you use a **/boot** directory, which might be mounted on a separate partition, this directory or partition must be present for the system to boot Linux. Refer to "Booting the System" on page 449 for more information on what happens from this point forward.

LBA addressing mode and the **/boot** partition   All newer hard disks support LBA (logical block addressing) mode. LBA permits the **/boot** directory to appear anywhere on the hard disk. For LBA to work, it must be supported by the hard disk, the BIOS, and the operating system (GRUB in the case of Linux). Although GRUB supports LBA addressing mode, some BIOSes do not. For this reason, it is a good idea to place the **/boot** directory in its own partition located near the beginning of the hard disk. With this setup, the root (**/**) filesystem can be anywhere on any hard drive that Linux can access regardless of LBA support. In some instances, without a separate **/boot** partition, the system might boot at first but then fail as you update the kernel and the kernel files move further from the beginning of the disk.

LVM   Systems with LVM require a separate boot partition that is not an LV. For more information on LVM see page 42.

GRUB   GRUB stands for Grand Unified Boot loader. Although GRUB 2 has been released, Fedora/RHEL use GRUB, which is sometimes referred to as GRUB legacy. GRUB 2 is a complete rewrite of GRUB legacy; few of the configuration files are the same.

A product of the GNU project, the GRUB loader conforms to the *multiboot specification* (page 1176), which allows it to load many free operating systems directly as well as to *chain load* (page 1156) proprietary operating systems. The GRUB loader can recognize various types of filesystems and kernel executable formats, allowing it to load an arbitrary operating system. When you boot the system, GRUB can display a menu of choices that is generated by the **/boot/grub/grub.conf** file (next page). At this point you can modify a menu selection, choose which operating system or kernel to boot, or do nothing and allow GRUB to boot the default system.

When you install GRUB at the time you install Linux, the installation program configures GRUB automatically. See the grub info page and www.gnu.org/software/grub for more information on GRUB.

CONFIGURING GRUB

The **/boot/grub/grub.conf** file, with its link at **/etc/grub.conf**, is the default GRUB configuration file. The **grub.conf** file in the following example is from a system that had its kernel replaced (there are two versions of **vmlinuz** and **initrd**). The system has a separate **boot** partition so that all kernel and **initrd** (for systems using loadable modules; page 593) image paths are relative to **/boot** (see the NOTICE in the file). Without a separate **boot** partition, the boot files reside in the root partition (**/**) so that kernel and **initrd** paths are relative to **/**.

The file starts with comments that Anaconda, the graphical installer, puts there, followed by three assignments and **hiddenmenu**. The **default** is the section number of the default boot specification. This numbering starts with 0. The example includes two boot specifications: The first, numbered 0, is for the **2.6.38.2-9.sam1104181000.fc15.i686** kernel; the second, numbered 1, is for the **2.6.38.2-9.fc15.i686** kernel. The **timeout** is the number of seconds that grub waits after it has prompted for a boot specification before it boots the system with the default boot specification. The **splashimage** is the grub menu interface background GRUB displays when the system boots. When you specify **hiddenmenu,** grub boots the default entry and does not display the menu interface unless you press ESCAPE while the system is booting.

```
# cat /boot/grub/grub.conf
# grub.conf generated by anaconda
#
# Note that you do not have to rerun grub after making changes to this file
# NOTICE:  You have a /boot partition.  This means that
#          all kernel and initrd paths are relative to /boot/, eg.
#          root (hd0,0)
#          kernel /vmlinuz-version ro root=/dev/mapper/vg_guava-lv_root
#          initrd /initrd-[generic-]version.img
#boot=/dev/sda
default=0
timeout=0
splashimage=(hd0,0)/grub/splash.xpm.gz
hiddenmenu
title Fedora (2.6.38.2-9.sam1104181000.fc15.i686)
        root (hd0,0)
        kernel /vmlinuz-2.6.38.2-9.sam1104181000.fc15.i686 ro
root=/dev/mapper/vg_guava-lv_root rd_LVM_LV=vg_guava/lv_root rd_LVM_LV=vg_guava/lv_swap
rd_NO_LUKS rd_NO_MD rd_NO_DM LANG=en_US.UTF-8 SYSFONT=latarcyrheb-sun16 KEYTABLE=us
rhgb quiet
        initrd /initramfs-2.6.38.2-9.sam1104181000.fc15.i686.img
title Fedora (2.6.38.2-9.fc15.i686)
        root (hd0,0)
        kernel /vmlinuz-2.6.38.2-9.fc15.i686 ro root=/dev/mapper/vg_guava-lv_root
  rd_LVM_LV=vg_guava/lv_root rd_LVM_LV=vg_guava/lv_swap rd_NO_LUKS rd_NO_MD rd_NO_DM
  LANG=en_US.UTF-8 SYSFONT=latarcyrheb-sun16 KEYTABLE=us rhgb quiet
        initrd /initramfs-2.6.38.2-9.fc15.i686.img
```

Following the **hiddenmenu** assignment in the preceding example are two boot specifications, differentiated by the **title** lines. The three logical lines following the title line in each specification specify the location of the **root** (drive hd0, partition 0), **kernel**, and **initrd** images. In this case because there is a **/boot** partition, the pathnames are relative to **/boot**. For the default boot specification (the first one, numbered 0), the absolute pathname of the kernel is **/boot/vmlinuz-2.6.35.11-83.F1103021130.fc14.i686**, which is specified with options that tell grub it is to be mounted readonly and that root (**/**) is mounted on the specified logical volume. The **rhgb** (Red Hat graphical boot) software generates a graphical display that tells you what is happening as the system boots. The **quiet** option produces less debugging output so it is easier to tell what is happening. You specify the **initrd** (initialize *RAM disk;* page 1184) image in a manner similar to the kernel. Substitute the local kernel and **initrd** names and version numbers for the ones in the example. Make sure when you install a new kernel manually, its **title** line is different from the others in **grub.conf**.

grub-install: INSTALLS THE MBR AND GRUB FILES

The grub-install utility installs the MBR (page 595) and the files that GRUB needs to boot the system. This utility takes a single argument—the name of the device that is to hold the MBR. You can specify the device name as a GRUB device name (e.g., **hd0**) or a device filename (e.g., **/dev/sda**). The following example shows grub-install installing files in the default location (**/boot/grub**) and the MBR on device **/dev/sda**:

```
# grub-install /dev/sda
Installation finished. No error reported.
This is the contents of the device map /boot/grub/device.map.
Check if this is correct or not. If any of the lines is incorrect,
fix it and re-run the script 'grub-install'.

# this device map was generated by anaconda
(hd0)     /dev/sda
```

See page 456 for instructions on how to reinstall the MBR.

dmesg: DISPLAYS KERNEL MESSAGES

The dmesg utility displays the kernel-ring buffer, where the kernel stores messages. When the system boots, the kernel fills this buffer with messages related to hardware and module initialization. Messages in the kernel-ring buffer are often useful for diagnosing system problems.

When you run dmesg, it displays a lot of information. It is frequently easier to pipe the output of dmesg through less or grep to find what you are looking for. For example, if you find that your hard disks are performing poorly, you can use dmesg to check whether they are running in DMA mode:

```
$ dmesg | grep DMA
...
[    1.398073] ata1: PATA max UDMA/33 cmd 0x1f0 ctl 0x3f6 bmdma 0x10c0 irq 14
[    1.398078] ata2: PATA max UDMA/33 cmd 0x170 ctl 0x376 bmdma 0x10c8 irq 15
...
```

The preceding lines tell you which mode each ATA device is operating in. If you are having problems with the Ethernet connection, search the dmesg buffer for **eth**:

```
$ dmesg | grep eth
[    5.060499] pcnet32: eth0: registered as PCnet/PCI II 79C970A
[   84.527758] pcnet32 0000:02:01.0: eth0: link up
[   95.458834] eth0: no IPv6 routers present
```

If everything is working properly, dmesg displays the hardware configuration information for each network interface.

dmesg log   Boot messages are also logged to **/var/log/dmesg**. This file is overwritten each time the system is booted, but the previous version of the file is saved as **dmesg.old**. This log is a good place to start when diagnosing faults. If you have configured a system service incorrectly, this log quickly fills with errors.

Chapter Summary

You can build a Linux kernel from the source code. Sometimes you do not need to build a kernel; instead, you can change many aspects of the kernel by using boot options in **/etc/grub.conf**. You can dynamically change options by modifying **/etc/sysctl.conf**.

Before you can build a Linux kernel, you must download the kernel source files to the local system. After you have downloaded the source files, you need to install and prep the source code, configure and compile the kernel and the loadable modules, and install the kernel and loadable modules.

The GRUB boot loader is a small program that controls the process of bringing the system up. You must configure the boot loader so that it recognizes the new kernel.

The dmesg utility displays the kernel-ring buffer, where the kernel stores messages. You can use this utility to help diagnose boot-time problems.

Exercises

1. What is the purpose of the kernel?

2. How would you display a list of all loaded modules in the current kernel?

3. Which command would you give to upgrade the kernel from an rpm file, and how is this different from upgrading other packages?

4. How would you display information from the kernel about the hard disk on the first SATA channel?

5. The **acpi=off** kernel argument prevents **acpid** from starting. How would you use this argument?

6. What is a boot loader?

ADVANCED EXERCISES

7. How would you label the kernel before compiling it? Why would you want to label the kernel?

8. You have just installed an Adaptec SCSI card. How can you find out whether it has been recognized and which entry in **/dev** represents it?

9. When you install an experimental kernel for testing purposes, how do you instruct GRUB not to load it by default?

10. How would you obtain a list of all network-related kernel parameters?

16

ADMINISTRATION TASKS

OBJECTIVES

After reading this chapter you should be able to:

▶ Add and manage user accounts using
  system-config-users

▶ Add and manage user accounts from the
  command line

▶ Backup files using tar and cpio

▶ Schedule tasks in the future using **crond**, anacron,
  and at

▶ Monitor the system with various tools including
  vmstat and top

▶ Monitor and manage log files

▶ Manage disk partitions with parted

▶ Communicate with users

▶ Deploy a MySQL server and perform basic changes
  and queries

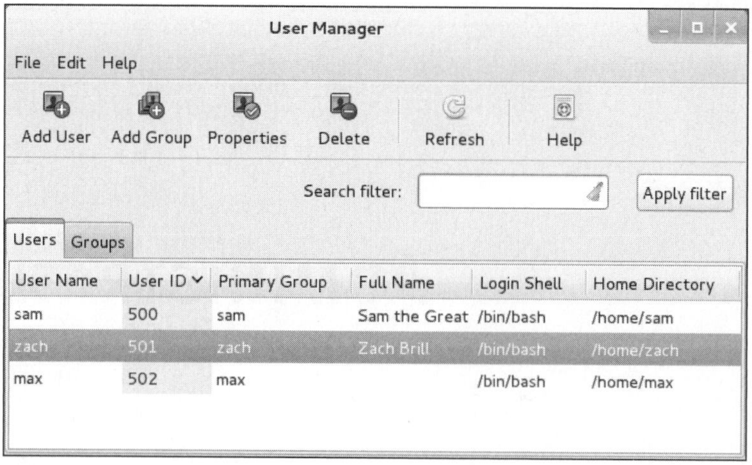

Figure 16-1   The User Manager window, Users tab

The system administrator has many responsibilities. This chapter discusses tasks not covered in Chapter 11, including configuring user and group accounts, backing up files, scheduling tasks, general problem solving, and using the system log daemon, **rsyslogd**. The chapter concludes with a section on installing and using MySQL.

CONFIGURING USER AND GROUP ACCOUNTS

More than a username is required for a user to be able to log in on and use a system: A user must have the necessary files, directories, permissions, and usually a password to log in. At a minimum a user must have an entry in the **/etc/passwd** and **/etc/shadow** files and a home directory. This section describes several ways you can work with user accounts. Refer to Chapter 21 if you want to run NIS to manage the **passwd** database.

system-config-users: MANAGES USER ACCOUNTS

The system-config-users utility displays the User Manager window and enables you to add, delete, and modify system users and groups. To display the User Manager window, enter **system-config-users** on a command line or select **Main menu: Applications⇨Other⇨Users and Groups** (Fedora; if **Applications** is not visible see "Configuring Fallback Mode" on page 92) or **Main menu: System⇨Administration⇨Users and Groups** (RHEL). This window has two tabs: Users and Groups, where each tab displays information appropriate to its name. Figure 16-1 shows the Users tab.

By default, system-config-users **does not display system users and groups**

tip   By default, system-config-users does not display users with UIDs less than 500 and groups with GIDs less than 500. To display these users and groups, click **Menubar: Edit⇨Preferences** and remove the tick from the check box labeled **Hide system users and groups**.

Figure 16-2   The User Properties window, User Data tab

Authentication   Because you can use **system-config-users** to make changes to the system that affect other users, this utility asks you for the **root** password.

Search filter   The Search filter, located just below the toolbar, selects users or groups whose names match the string you enter in the text box labeled **Search filter**. The string can include wildcards. The string matches the beginning of a name. For example, *nob matches **nobody** and **nfsnobody**, whereas **nob** matches only **nobody**. After you enter the string, click **Apply filter** or press RETURN. If you have only a few users, you will not need to use the Search filter.

ADDING A USER

To add a user to the system, click the button on the toolbar labeled **Add User**. The User Manager window displays the Add New User window, which gathers much of the same information as the User Data tab of the User Properties window (Figure 16-2). Enter the information for the new user and click **OK**. After you create a user, you can modify information related to that user.

MODIFYING A USER

To modify a user, highlight the user in the User Manager window and click **Properties** on the toolbar; the utility displays the User Properties window (Figure 16-2), which has four tabs. The User Data tab holds basic user information such as name and password. The Account Info tab allows you to specify an expiration date for the account and to lock the account so the user cannot log in locally. The Password Info tab allows you to turn on password expiration and specify various related parameters. In the Groups tab, you can specify which groups the user is a member of. Click **OK** when you are done making changes in this window.

WORKING WITH GROUPS

Click the **Groups** tab in the User Manager window to work with groups. To create a group, click **Add Group** on the toolbar and specify the name of the group. To change the name of a group or to add or remove users from a group, highlight the group and click **Properties** on the toolbar. Click the appropriate tab, make the changes you want, and click **OK**. See page 506 for more information on groups.

Help   To obtain assistance, click **Help** on the toolbar.

When you are done working with users and groups, close the window.

MANAGING USER ACCOUNTS FROM THE COMMAND LINE

In addition to using the graphical system-config-users to manage user accounts, you can use the command-line tools described in this section.

useradd: ADDS A USER ACCOUNT

The useradd utility adds a user account to the system. By default, useradd assigns the next highest unused user ID to a new account and specifies bash as the user's login shell. The following example adds entries to the **/etc/passwd** and **/etc/shadow** files, creates the user's home directory (in **/home**), specifies the user's group ID as 1105, and puts the user's full name in the comment field in **passwd**. The group ID you specify must exist in **/etc/group** or the command will fail. Use groupadd (next page) to add a group.

```
# useradd -g 1105 -c "Max R." max
```

The useradd utility puts a **!!** in the password field of the **shadow** file (page 511) to prevent the user from logging in until you use passwd to assign a password to that user. Based on the **/etc/login.defs** and **/etc/default/useradd** files, useradd creates a home directory for the new user. When doing so, it copies the contents of **/etc/skel** to that directory. For more information on adding user information, see the useradd man page.

userdel: REMOVES A USER ACCOUNT

The userdel utility deletes a user account. If appropriate, back up the files belonging to the user before deleting them. The following command removes Max's account. The **--remove** (**-r**) option causes the command to remove his home directory hierarchy:

```
# userdel --remove max
```

See the userdel man page for more information.

usermod: MODIFIES A USER ACCOUNT

To turn off a user's account temporarily, you can use usermod to change the expiration date for the account. Because it specifies that his account expired in the past (December 31, 2010), the following command prevents Max from logging in:

```
# usermod -e "12/31/10" max
```

chage You can also use chage to view and modify account expiry information. The **--list** (**-l**) option displays information about password expiration, and **--expiredate** (**-E**) changes the date an account expires. The following command has the same effect as the preceding one:

```
# chage -E "12/31/10" max
```

See the usermod and chage man pages for more information.

groupadd: ADDS A GROUP

Just as useradd adds a new user to the system, so groupadd adds a new group by adding an entry to **/etc/group** (page 506). The following example creates a group named **pubs** with a group ID of 1024:

```
# groupadd -g 1024 pubs
```

Unless you use the **-g** option to assign a group ID, the system picks the next available sequential number greater than 500. The **-o** option allows the group ID to be non-unique, which allows you to assign multiple names to a group ID.

groupdel AND groupmod: REMOVE AND MODIFY A GROUP

The analogue of userdel for groups is groupdel, which takes a group name as an argument. You can also use groupmod to change the name or group ID of a group, as in the following examples:

```
# groupmod -g 1025 pubs
# groupmod -n manuals pubs
```

The first example changes the group ID number of the previously created **pubs** group. The second example renames the **pubs** group to **manuals**.

Changing group ID numbers

caution The groupmod utility does not change group numbers in **/etc/passwd** when you renumber a group. Instead, you must edit **/etc/passwd** and change the entries manually. If you change the number of a group, files that are associated with the group will no longer be associated with the group. Rather, they might be associated with no group or with another group with the old group ID number.

BACKING UP FILES

One of the most neglected tasks of system administration is making backup copies of files on a regular basis. The backup copies are vital in three instances: when the system malfunctions and files are lost, when a catastrophic disaster (fire, earthquake, and so on) occurs, and when a user or the system administrator deletes or corrupts a file by accident. Even when you set up RAID (page 41), you still need to back up files. Although RAID can provide fault tolerance (helpful in the event of disk failure), it does not help when a catastrophic disaster occurs or when a file is corrupted or removed accidentally. It is a good idea to have a written backup policy and to keep copies of backups offsite (in another building, at home, or at a different facility or campus) in a fireproof vault or safe.

The time to start thinking about backups is when you partition the disk. Refer to "Partitioning a Disk" on page 37. Make sure the capacity of the backup device and your partition sizes are comparable. Although you can back up a partition onto multiple volumes, it is easier not to—and it is much easier to restore data from a single volume.

You must back up filesystems regularly. Backup files are usually kept on magnetic tape, external hard disk, or another removable medium. Alternatively, you can keep backup files on a remote system. How often and which files you back up depend on the system and your needs. Use this criterion when determining a backup schedule: If the system crashes, how much work are you willing to lose? Ideally you would back up all files on the system every few minutes so you would never lose more than a few minutes of work.

Of course, there is a tradeoff: How often are you willing to back up the files? The backup procedure typically slows the system for users, takes a certain amount of your time, and requires that you have and store the media holding the backup. Avoid backing up an active filesystem; the results might be inconsistent, and restoring from the backup might be impossible. This requirement is a function of the backup program and the filesystem you are backing up.

Another question is when to run the backup. Unless you plan to kick users off and bring the system down to single-user mode (not a user-friendly practice), you will want to perform this task when the machine is at its quietest. Depending on the use of the system, sometime in the middle of the night can work well. Then the backup is least likely to affect users, and the files are not likely to change as they are being read for backup.

A *full* backup makes copies of all files, regardless of when they were created or accessed. An *incremental* backup makes copies of those files that have been created or modified since the last (usually full) backup.

The more people using the system, the more often you should back up the filesystems. One popular schedule is to perform an incremental backup one or two times a day and a full backup one or two times a week.

Choosing a Backup Medium

If the local system is connected to a network, you can write backups to a drive on another system. This technique is often used with networked computers to avoid the cost of having a backup drive on each computer in the network and to simplify management of backing up many computers in a network. Although tapes are still used for backups, hard disks are being used more frequently. Backing up to a hard disk on a remote system is cost-effective, reliable, and practical. Because hard disks hold many gigabytes of data, using them simplifies the task of backing up the system, making it more likely that you will take care of this important task regularly. Other options for holding backups are writable CDs and DVDs. These devices, although not as cost-effective or able to store as much information as hard disk or tape systems, offer the benefit of convenience.

BACKUP UTILITIES

A number of utilities are available to help you back up a system, and most work with any media. Most Linux backup utilities are based on one of the archive programs—tar or cpio—and augment these basic programs with bookkeeping support for managing backups conveniently.

You can use any of the tar, cpio, or dump/restore utilities to construct full or partial backups of a system. Each utility constructs a large file that contains, or archives, other files. In addition to file contents, an archive includes header information for each file it holds. This header information can be used when extracting files from the archive to restore file permissions and modification dates. An archive file can be saved to disk, written to tape, or shipped across the network while it is being created.

In addition to helping you back up the system, these programs offer a convenient way to bundle files for distribution to other sites. The tar program is often used for this purpose, and some software packages available on the Internet are bundled as tar archive files.

amanda The amanda (Advanced Maryland Automatic Network Disk Archiver) utility (www.amanda.org), which is one of the more popular backup systems, uses dump or tar and takes advantage of Samba to back up Windows systems. The amanda utility backs up a LAN of heterogeneous hosts to a hard disk or tape. Relevant software packages are **amanda-common**, **amanda-client**, and **amanda-server**.

tar: ARCHIVES FILES

The tar (tape archive) utility writes files to and retrieves files from an archive; it can compress this archive to conserve space. If you do not specify an archive device, tar writes to standard output and reads from standard input. With the –f (––file) option, tar uses the argument to –f as the name of the archive device. You can use this option to refer to a device on another system on the network. Although tar has many options, you need only a few in most situations. The following command displays a complete list of options:

```
$ tar --help | less
```

Most options for tar can be given either in a short form (a single letter) or as a descriptive word. Descriptive-word options are preceded by two hyphens, as in ––help. Single-letter options can be combined into a single command-line argument and need not be preceded by a hyphen (for consistency with other utilities, it is good practice to use the hyphen anyway).

Although the following two commands look quite different, they specify the same tar options in the same order. The first version combines single-letter options into a single command-line argument; the second version uses descriptive words for the same options:

```
# tar -ztvf /dev/st0
# tar --gzip --list --verbose --file /dev/st0
```

Both commands tell tar to generate a (**v, verbose**) table of contents (**t, list**) from the tape on **/dev/st0** (**f, file**), using gzip (**z, gzip**) to decompress the files.

Unlike the original UNIX tar utility, when you specify an absolute pathname when you archive a file, the GNU version strips the leading **/** from the file pathname. Also, when it extracts files from a compressed archive, it decompresses them automatically. The first of the following commands shows tar compressing (**j** causes tar to compress using bzip2; page 160) and archiving some files from the **/etc** directory; it displays a message telling you it is stripping the leading **/**s. The second command extracts the files to the working directory. Because tar strips the leading **/** from each pathname, the files are not restored to their original locations in the root directory (**/**). The third command shows the extracted files in the working directory.

```
$ tar cvjf etc.gnome /etc/gnome*
tar: Removing leading `/' from member names
/etc/gnome-settings-daemon/
/etc/gnome-settings-daemon/xrandr/
/etc/gnome-vfs-2.0/
/etc/gnome-vfs-2.0/modules/
/etc/gnome-vfs-2.0/modules/ssl-modules.conf
/etc/gnome-vfs-2.0/modules/default-modules.conf

$ tar xvf etc.gnome
etc/gnome-settings-daemon/
etc/gnome-settings-daemon/xrandr/
etc/gnome-vfs-2.0/
etc/gnome-vfs-2.0/modules/
etc/gnome-vfs-2.0/modules/ssl-modules.conf
etc/gnome-vfs-2.0/modules/default-modules.conf

$ ls etc
gnome-settings-daemon  gnome-vfs-2.0
```

You can use the **–C** option to cause tar to extract files to a directory other than the working directory. The argument to this option specifies the directory tar extracts the files to.

The options in Table 16-1 tell the tar program what to do. You must include exactly one of these options in a tar command. The **–c**, **–t**, and **–x** options are used most frequently. See page 162 for more examples of tar.

Table 16-1   tar options

Option	Effect
––append (–r)	Appends files to an archive
––catenate (–A)	Adds one or more archives to the end of an existing archive

Table 16-1   tar options (continued)

Option	Effect
--create (-c)	Creates a new archive
--delete	Deletes files in an archive (not on tapes)
--diff (-d)	Compares files in an archive with disk files
--extract (-x)	Extracts files from an archive
--help	Displays a help list of tar options
--list (-t)	Lists the files in an archive
--update (-u)	Like the **-r** option, but the file is not appended if a newer version is already in the archive

cpio: ARCHIVES FILES

The cpio (copy in/out) program is similar to tar but can read and write archive files in various formats, including the one used by tar. Normally cpio reads the names of the files to add to the archive from standard input and produces the archive file as standard output. When extracting files from an archive, it reads the archive as standard input.

While tar takes the name of a directory as an argument and traverses the directory hierarchy recursively to archive the directory, cpio must be presented with each filename it is to archive. For example, the following commands each back up the **/bin** directory:

```
$ tar cf bin.tar.bak /bin
```

```
$ find /bin -print | cpio -o > bin.cpio.bak
```

In the second command, find sends a list of files in the **/bin** directory hierarchy to standard output; cpio reads this list from standard input and creates an archive of these files.

Another difference between these two utilities is that cpio does not strip the leading **/** from each pathname when it creates an archive. Restoring the cpio archive created in the preceding example will attempt to overwrite the files in **/bin**; it fails because the files in **/bin** are the same age as the files in the archive. Even if the files in the archive were newer, it would fail because the user does not have permission to overwrite the files in **/bin**.

As with tar, some options can be given in both a short, single-letter form and a more descriptive word form. However, unlike with tar, the syntax of the two forms in cpio differs when the option must be followed by additional information. In the short form, you must include a SPACE between the option and the additional information; with the word form, you must separate the two with an equal sign and no SPACEs.

Running cpio with the **--help** option displays a complete list of options. See the next section for more examples of cpio.

PERFORMING A SIMPLE BACKUP

When you prepare to make a major change to a system, such as replacing a disk drive, upgrading to a new release, or updating the Linux kernel, it is a good idea to archive some or all of the files so you can restore any that become damaged if something goes wrong. For this type of backup, tar or cpio works well. For example, if you have a SCSI tape drive as device **/dev/st0** (or it could be a hard disk at **/dev/sda**) that is capable of holding all the files on a single tape, you can use the following commands to construct a backup tape of the entire system:

```
# cd /
# tar -cf /dev/st0 .
```

All the commands in this section start by using cd to change to the root directory so you are sure to back up the entire system. The tar command then creates an archive (c) on the device **/dev/st0** (f). To compress the archive, replace the preceding tar command with the following command, which uses **j** to call bzip2:

```
# tar -cjf /dev/st0 .
```

You can back up a system with a combination of find and cpio. The following commands create an output file and set the I/O block size to 5120 bytes (the default is 512 bytes):

```
# cd /
# find . -depth | cpio -oB > /dev/st0
```

The next command restores the files in the **/home** directory from the preceding backup. The options extract files from an archive (**–i**) in verbose mode (**–v**), keeping the modification times (**–m**), and creating directories (**–d**) as needed. The asterisk is escaped (preceded by a backslash) so the shell does not expand it but rather passes it to cpio.

```
# cd /
# cpio -ivmd /home/\* < /dev/st0
```

Although all the archive programs work well for simple backups, utilities such as amanda (page 607) provide more sophisticated backup and restore systems. For example, to determine whether a file is in an archive, you must read the entire archive. If the archive is split across several tapes, this process is particularly tiresome. More sophisticated utilities, including amanda, assist you in several ways, including keeping a table of contents of the files in a backup.

Exclude some directories from a backup

tip In practice, you will likely want to exclude some directories from the backup process. For example, not backing up **/tmp** or **/var/tmp** (or its link, **/usr/tmp**) can save room in the archive. Also, do not back up the files in **proc**. Because the **/proc** pseudofilesystem is not a true disk filesystem but rather a way for the Linux kernel to provide information about the operating system and system memory, you need not back up **/proc**; you cannot restore it later. Similarly, you do not need to back up filesystems that are mounted from disks on other systems on the network. Do not back up FIFOs; the results are unpredictable.

dump, restore The dump utility (**dump** package) first appeared in UNIX version 6. It backs up either an entire **ext2**, **ext3**, or **ext4** filesystem or only those files that have changed since a recent dump. The restore utility can then restore an entire filesystem, a directory hierarchy, or an individual file. Although it is available, not many people use this utility. Refer to dump.sourceforge.net and the dump and restore man pages for more information.

SCHEDULING TASKS

It is a good practice to schedule certain routine tasks to run automatically. For example, you might want to remove old core files once a week, summarize accounting data daily, and rotate system log files monthly.

crond **stops for no one; try** anacron

tip The **crond** daemon assumes the system is always running. A similar utility, anacron, does not make that assumption and is well suited to portable and home computers that are frequently turned off. The anacron utility takes its instructions from the **/etc/anacrontab** file unless you specify otherwise. It is enabled by default and is set up to catch any missed **cron.daily**, **cron.weekly**, and **cron.monthly** run-parts commands as described in the following sections. Refer to the anacron and anacrontab man pages for more information.

crond AND anacron: SCHEDULE ROUTINE TASKS

The **crond** daemon executes scheduled commands periodically. This daemon can execute commands at specific times on systems that are always running. The anacron utility executes scheduled commands when it is called. It works well on laptops and other systems that are not on all the time. The 0anacron script (page 613), which calls anacron, will not run commands when a system is running on batteries (i.e., not on AC).

SELinux When SELinux is set to use a targeted policy, it protects the **crond** daemon. You can disable this protection if necessary. For more information refer to "Setting the Targeted Policy with system-config-selinux" on page 463.

CRONTAB FILES

The **crond** daemon reads the commands it is to execute from crontab files. System crontab files are kept in the **/etc/cron.d** directory and in **/etc/crontab**. Users can use the crontab utility to set up personal crontab files in **/var/spool/cron**. (The term *crontab* has three meanings: It refers to a text file in a specific format [a crontab file; crontab(5) man page], it is the name of a utility [crontab; crontab(1) man page], and it is the name of a file [**/etc/crontab**].)

By default, Fedora/RHEL is set up with no restrictions on which users can have **crond** run commands in their personal crontab files. See **cron.allow** and **cron.deny** on page 506 for ways of restricting this access.

System crontab files   Crontab files specify how often **crond** is to run a command. Within these files, comments begin with a hashmark (#). Crontab files frequently include assignments to several environment variables: The **SHELL** and **PATH** environment variables are described on page 308; **MAILTO** determines which user receives output (via email) from jobs run by the file.

A line describing a job in a system crontab file, such as **/etc/crontab**, has the following format:

minute hour day-of-month month day-of-week user command

The first five fields indicate when **crond** will execute the *command*. The *minute* is the number of minutes after the start of the hour, the *hour* is the hour of the day based on a 24-hour clock, the *day-of-month* is a number from 1 to 31, and the *day-of-week* is a number from 0 to 7, with 0 and 7 indicating Sunday. An asterisk (*) substitutes for any value in a field. The *user* is the username or user ID of the user that the *command* will run as. Specify *command* as an absolute pathname to ensure **crond** executes the correct *command*.

Following are some examples:

```
20 1 * * *     root    /usr/local/bin/checkit
25 9 17 * *    root    /usr/local/bin/monthly.check
40 23 * * 7    root    /usr/local/bin/sunday.check
10/* * * * *   root    /usr/local/bin/tenmin.check
```

All four lines run their commands with **root** privileges. The first line runs **checkit** every day at 1:20 AM. The second line runs **monthly.check** at 9:25 AM on day 17 of every month. The third line runs **sunday.check** at 11:40 PM every Sunday. The fourth line uses the step syntax to run **tenmin.check** every ten minutes; the **10/*** is equivalent to **0,10,20,30,40,50**. Enter the command **man 5 crontab** to obtain more information on crontab files.

User crontab files   A user crontab file has the same format as a system crontab file except it does not include the *user* field because it always runs as the user who is running it. Users can work with their own crontab files by giving the command **crontab** followed by **–l** to list the file, **–r** to remove the file, or **–e** to edit the file. The **–e** option uses the vi editor by default; if you prefer, export (page 1008) and set the **VISUAL** or **EDITOR** environment variable to the textual editor of your choice. See the crontab man page for more information.

/etc/crontab   The **crond** daemon looks for crontab files at **/etc/crontab** and in the **/etc/cron.d** directory. Following is the default **/etc/crontab** file, which does not run any jobs:

```
$ cat /etc/crontab
SHELL=/bin/bash
PATH=/sbin:/bin:/usr/sbin:/usr/bin
MAILTO=root

# For details see man 4 crontabs

# Example of job definition:
# .---------------- minute (0 - 59)
# |  .------------- hour (0 - 23)
# |  |  .---------- day of month (1 - 31)
# |  |  |  .------- month (1 - 12) OR jan,feb,mar,apr ...
# |  |  |  |  .---- day of week (0 - 6) (Sunday=0 or 7) OR sun,mon,tue,wed,thu,fri,sat
# |  |  |  |  |
# *  *  *  *  * user-name  command to be executed
```

/etc/cron.d/0hourly As installed, the **/etc/cron.d** directory holds two crontab files: **smolt**, which tracks hardware, and **0hourly**. Following is the default **/etc/cron.d/0hourly** crontab file:

```
$ cat /etc/cron.d/0hourly
SHELL=/bin/bash
PATH=/sbin:/bin:/usr/sbin:/usr/bin
MAILTO=root
01 * * * * root run-parts /etc/cron.hourly
```

run-parts After setting some variables, this script executes run-parts with **root** privileges. The 01 * * * * at the beginning of the line causes **crond** to run the job one minute past the start of every hour. The run-parts utility runs the executable files in the directory named by its argument (**/etc/cron.hourly**). Output from the execution of these files is sent to the user named by **MAILTO** (**root**).

/etc/cron.hourly/ 0anacron As installed, there is one file in **/etc/cron.hourly**: 0anacron. Following is the default **/etc/cron.hourly/0anacron** shell script:

```
$ cat /etc/cron.hourly/0anacron
#!/bin/bash
#in case file doesn't exist
if test -r /var/spool/anacron/cron.daily; then
    day=`cat /var/spool/anacron/cron.daily`
fi
if [ `date +%Y%m%d` = "$day" ]; then
    exit 0;
fi

# in case anacron is already running,
# there will be log (daemon won't be running twice).
if test -x /usr/bin/on_ac_power; then
    /usr/bin/on_ac_power &> /dev/null
    if test $? -eq 1; then
    exit 0
    fi
fi
/usr/sbin/anacron -s
```

The anacron utility keeps track of the last time it ran each of its jobs so when it is called, it can tell which jobs need to be run. The **/var/spool/anacron/cron.daily** file holds the date anacron last ran the job with the jobID of **cron.daily**. The 0anacron script first tests to see if today's date is the same as the one held by the **cron.daily** file. If it is, anacron has already run today, so the script exits. Next the script tests to see if the system is running on AC power. If it is not, the script exits. Thus, if the **cron.daily** job has not been run today and if the system is running on AC power, the script executes anacron. The –s option causes anacron to run its jobs serially (not all at once).

/etc/anacrontab When anacron is run, it reads the commands it is to execute from the **/etc/anacrontab** file. This file is where the files in the **/etc/cron.daily**, **/etc/cron.weekly**, and **/etc/cron.monthly** directories get executed on a system running anacron. The **anacrontab** file specifies how often **anacron** is to run one or more jobs, but has a different syntax from a crontab file. Within the **anacrontab** file, comments begin with a hash-mark (#). Several variables that establish the environment a job runs in can appear within the **anacrontab** file: The **SHELL** and **PATH** environment variables are described on page 308; **MAILTO** determines which user receives output (via email) from jobs; **RANDOM_DELAY** delays the start of jobs by a random number of minutes up to the value of this variable; and **START_HOURS_RANGE** specifies the hours during which **anacron** can start a job.

A job entry in the **anacrontab** file has the following format:

> *period delay jobID* **command**

where the *period* is the frequency in days (how often) that anacron executes the *command*, the *delay* is the number of minutes after anacron starts that it executes the *command*, and the *jobID* is the name of the file in **/var/spool/anacron** that anacron uses to keep track of when it last executed the *command*.

Following is the default **anacrontab** file. Based on the value of the variable named **START_HOURS_RANGE**, **anacron** can start jobs in this file between 3 AM and 10 PM (3–22).

```
$ cat /etc/anacrontab
# /etc/anacrontab: configuration file for anacron

# See anacron(8) and anacrontab(5) for details.

SHELL=/bin/sh
PATH=/sbin:/bin:/usr/sbin:/usr/bin
MAILTO=root
# the maximal random delay added to the base delay of the jobs
RANDOM_DELAY=45
# the jobs will be started during the following hours only
START_HOURS_RANGE=3-22

#period in days   delay in minutes   job-identifier   command
1        5           cron.daily            nice run-parts /etc/cron.daily
7        25          cron.weekly           nice run-parts /etc/cron.weekly
@monthly 45          cron.monthly          nice run-parts /etc/cron.monthly
```

The line that begins with **1** specifies the job with the jobID of **cron.daily**. This job is run once a day with a delay of 5 minutes. It runs nice, which executes run-parts (page 613) with a low priority; the job passes run-parts an argument of **/etc/cron.daily**. Similarly, the next line runs **cron.weekly** every seven days with a delay of 25 minutes. Because a month does not have a fixed number of days, the last line uses the **@monthly** macro to run **cron.monthly** once a month with a delay of 45 minutes.

As explained earlier, the **crond** daemon runs the shell scripts in the **/etc/cron.hourly** directory.

at: RUNS OCCASIONAL TASKS

Like the **crond** daemon, at runs a job sometime in the future. Unlike **crond**, at runs a job only once. For instance, you can schedule an at job that will reboot the system at 3:00 AM (when all users are probably logged off):

```
# at 3am
at> reboot
at> <EOT>
job 1 at Wed Jan 26 03:00:00 2011
```

It is also possible to run an at job from within an at job. For instance, an at job might check for new patches every 18 days—something that would be more difficult with **crond**. See the at man page for more information.

By default, Fedora/RHEL is not set up with restrictions that prevent users from running at. See **at.allow** and **at.deny** on page 506 for more information.

SYSTEM REPORTS

Many utilities report on one thing or another. The who, finger, ls, ps, and other utilities, for example, generate simple end-user reports. In some cases, these reports can help with system administration. This section describes utilities that generate more in-depth reports that can provide greater assistance with system administration tasks. Linux has many other report utilities, including sar (system activity report), iostat (input/output and CPU statistics), and mpstat (processor statistics), all part of the **sysstat** package; netstat (network report; **net-tools** package); and nfsstat (NFS statistics; **nfs-utils** package).

vmstat: REPORTS VIRTUAL MEMORY STATISTICS

The vmstat utility (virtual memory statistics; **procps** package) generates virtual memory information along with (limited) disk and CPU activity data. The following example shows virtual memory statistics at three-second intervals for seven iterations (from the arguments 3 7). The first line covers the time since the system was booted; each subsequent line covers the period since the previous line.

```
$ vmstat 3 7
procs -----------memory---------- ---swap-- -----io---- --system-- ----cpu----
 r  b   swpd   free   buff  cache   si   so    bi    bo   in    cs us sy id wa
 0  2      0 684328  33924 219916    0    0   430   105 1052   134  2  4 86  8
 0  2      0 654632  34160 248840    0    0  4897  7683 1142   237  0  5  0 95
 0  3      0 623528  34224 279080    0    0  5056  8237 1094   178  0  4  0 95
 0  2      0 603176  34576 298936    0    0  3416   141 1161   255  0  4  0 96
 0  2      0 575912  34792 325616    0    0  4516  7267 1147   231  0  4  0 96
 1  2      0 549032  35164 351464    0    0  4429    77 1120   210  0  4  0 96
 0  2      0 523432  35448 376376    0    0  4173  6577 1135   234  0  4  0 95
```

The following list explains the column heads displayed by vmstat:

- **procs**   Process information
  - **r**   Number of waiting, runnable processes
  - **b**   Number of blocked processes (in uninterruptable sleep)
- **memory**   Memory information (in kilobytes)
  - **swpd**   Used virtual memory
  - **free**   Idle memory
  - **buff**   Memory used as buffers
  - **cache**   Memory used as cache
- **swap**   System paging activity (in kilobytes per second)
  - **si**   Memory swapped in from disk
  - **so**   Memory swapped out to disk
- **io**   System I/O activity (in blocks per second)
  - **bi**   Blocks received from a block device
  - **bo**   Blocks sent to a block device
- **system**   (Values are per second)
  - **in**   Interrupts (including the clock)
  - **cs**   Context switches
- **cpu**   Percentage of total CPU time spent in each of these states
  - **us**   User (nonkernel)
  - **sy**   System (kernel)
  - **id**   Idle
  - **wa**   Waiting for I/O
  - **st**   Stolen from a virtual machine (only on virtual machines)

top: LISTS PROCESSES USING THE MOST RESOURCES

The top utility is a useful supplement to ps. At its simplest, top displays system information followed by the most CPU-intensive processes. The top utility updates itself periodically; type **q** to quit. Although you can use command-line options, the interactive commands are often more helpful. Refer to Table 16-2 and to the top man page for more information.

Table 16-2   top: interactive commands

Command	Function
h or **?**	Displays a Help screen.
k	(**kill**) Prompts for a PID number and type of signal and sends the process that signal. Defaults to signal 15 (SIGTERM); specify 9 (SIGKILL) only when 15 does not work.

Table 16-2   top: interactive commands (continued)

Command	Function
F	Displays a page that allows you to specify a sort field.
f	Displays a page that allows you to specify which fields top displays.
o	Displays a page that allows you to specify the order of the displayed fields.
q	Quits top.
s	Prompts for time between updates in seconds. Use 0 (zero) for continuous updates; such updates can slow the system by consuming a lot of resources.
SPACE	Updates the display immediately.
u	Prompts for username and displays only processes owned by that user.
W	Writes a startup file named ~/.toprc so that the next time you start top, it uses the same parameters it is currently using.

```
$ top
top - 17:58:53 up 3 days,  4:20,  1 user,  load average: 2.16, 1.61, 0.83
Tasks: 167 total,   5 running, 162 sleeping,   0 stopped,   0 zombie
Cpu(s):  1.5%us,  0.5%sy, 1.3%ni, 96.0%id,  0.2%wa,  0.6%hi, 0.0%si, 0.0%st
Mem:   2076092k total,  1990652k used,    85440k free,    18416k buffers
Swap:  7815580k total,    34908k used,  7780672k free,  1330008k cached

  PID USER      PR  NI  VIRT  RES  SHR S %CPU %MEM    TIME+  COMMAND
31323 zach      25   0  9020 6960  396 R   63  0.3   0:17.58 bzip2
31327 zach      18   0  2092  596  492 R   57  0.0   0:00.92 cp
31311 root      15   0     0    0    0 S   16  0.0   0:00.38 pdflush
 6870 zach      27  12  331m 190m  37m R    2  9.4 198:42.98 firefox-bin
31303 root      15   0     0    0    0 S    2  0.0   0:00.42 pdflush
    1 root      15   0  2912 1808  488 S    0  0.1   0:01.55 init
...
```

MAINTAINING THE SYSTEM

This section discusses several tools and concepts that are important to a system administrator. It covers using parted to work with partitions on a hard disk, how to avoid creating problems, and how to solve system problems.

parted: REPORTS ON AND PARTITIONS A HARD DISK

The parted (partition editor) utility reports on and manipulates hard disk partitions from the command line. The palimpsest utility (page 77) allows you to perform the same tasks using a GUI. Following, the parted **print** command displays information about the partitions on the **/dev/sda** drive:

```
# parted /dev/sda print
Model: ATA Hitachi HDS12345 (scsi)
Disk /dev/sda: 165GB
Sector size (logical/physical): 512B/512B
Partition Table: msdos

Number  Start   End     Size    Type      File system  Flags
1       32kB    1045MB  1045MB  primary   ext4         boot
2       1045MB  12GB    10GB    primary   ext4
3       12GB    22GB    10GB    primary   ext4
4       22GB    165GB   143GB   extended
5       22GB    23GB    1045MB  logical   linux-swap(v1)
6       23GB    41GB    18GB    logical   ext4
7       41GB    82GB    41GB    logical   ext4
```

Figure 16-3 graphically depicts the partitions shown in this example. The first few lines that parted displays present the model name, device name, device capacity, and the type of partition table on the device. Following that information, the **print** command displays the these columns:

- **Number**—The minor device number (page 517) of the device holding the partition. This number is the same as the last number in the device name. In the example, 5 corresponds to **/dev/sda5**.

- **Start**—The location on the disk where the partition starts. The parted utility specifies a location on the disk as the distance (in bytes) from the start of the disk. Thus partition 3 starts 12 gigabytes from the start of the disk.

- **End**—The location on the disk where the partition stops. Although partition 2 ends 12 gigabytes from the start of the disk and partition 3 starts at the same location, parted takes care that the partitions do not overlap at this single byte.

- **Size**—The size of the partition in kilobytes (kB), megabytes (MB), or gigabytes (GB).

- **Type**—The partition type: primary, extended, or logical. See Figure 16-3 and page 35 for information on partitions.

- **File system**—The filesystem type: **ext2**, **ext3**, **ext4**, **fat32**, **linux-swap**, and so on. See Table 12-1 on page 519 for a list of filesystem types.

- **Flags**—The flags that are turned on for the partition, including **boot**, **raid**, and **lvm**. In the example, partition 1 is bootable.

In the preceding example, partition 4 defines an extended partition that includes 143 gigabytes of the 165-gigabyte disk (Figure 16-3). You cannot make changes to an extended partition without affecting all logical partitions within it.

In addition to reporting on the layout and size of a hard disk, you can use parted interactively to modify the disk layout. Be *extremely* careful when using parted in this manner and always back up the system before starting to work with this utility. Changing the partition information (the *partition table*) on a disk can destroy the information on the disk. Read the parted info page before you attempt to modify a partition table.

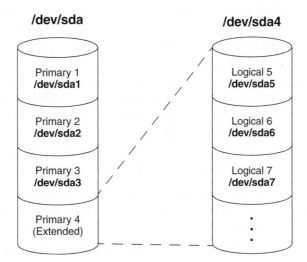

/dev/sda

Primary 1
/dev/sda1

Primary 2
/dev/sda2

Primary 3
/dev/sda3

Primary 4
(Extended)

/dev/sda4

Logical 5
/dev/sda5

Logical 6
/dev/sda6

Logical 7
/dev/sda7

Figure 16-3   The primary and extended partitions from the example

parted **can destroy everything**

caution   Be as careful with **parted** as you would be with a utility that formats a hard disk. Changes you make with **parted** can easily result in the loss of large amounts of data. If you are using **parted** and have any question about what you are doing, quit with a **q** command before making any changes. When you enter a command, **parted** immediately makes the change you requested.

To partition a disk, give the command **parted** followed by the name of the device you want to work with. In the following example, after starting parted, the user enters a **help** (or just **h**) command, which displays a list of parted commands:

```
# parted /dev/sda
GNU Parted 2.3
Using /dev/sda
Welcome to GNU Parted! Type 'help' to view a list of commands.
(parted) help
  align-check TYPE N                        check partition N for TYPE(min|opt) alignment
  check NUMBER                              do a simple check on the file system
  cp [FROM-DEVICE] FROM-NUMBER TO-NUMBER    copy file system to another partition
  help [COMMAND]                            print general help, or help on COMMAND
  mklabel,mktable LABEL-TYPE                create a new disklabel (partition table)
  mkfs NUMBER FS-TYPE                       make a FS-TYPE file system on partition NUMBER
  mkpart PART-TYPE [FS-TYPE] START END      make a partition
  mkpartfs PART-TYPE FS-TYPE START END      make a partition with a file system
  move NUMBER START END                     move partition NUMBER
  name NUMBER NAME                          name partition NUMBER as NAME
  print [devices|free|list,all|NUMBER]      display the partition table, available devices, free ...
  quit                                      exit program
  rescue START END                          rescue a lost partition near START and END
  resize NUMBER START END                   resize partition NUMBER and its file system
  rm NUMBER                                 delete partition NUMBER
  select DEVICE                             choose the device to edit
  set NUMBER FLAG STATE                     change the FLAG on partition NUMBER
  toggle [NUMBER [FLAG]]                    toggle the state of FLAG on partition NUMBER
  unit UNIT                                 set the default unit to UNIT
  version                                   display the version number and copyright information of ...
(parted)
```

Follow the command **help** with the name of a parted command to display more information about that command. When you enter a **print** (or just **p**) command, parted displays current partition information, just as a **print** command on the command line does.

The parted utility will not allow you to set up overlapping partitions (except for logical partitions overlapping their containing extended partition). Similarly, it will not allow you to create a partition that starts at the very beginning of the disk (cylinder 0). Both of these situations can cause loss of data.

Following are guidelines to remember when defining a partition table for a disk. For more information refer to "Partitioning a Disk" on page 37.

- Do not delete or modify the partition that defines the extended partition unless you are willing to lose all data on all the logical partitions within the extended partition.

- If you put **/boot** on a separate partition, it is a good idea to put it at the beginning of the drive (partition 1) so there is no issue of Linux having to boot from a partition located too far into the drive. When you can afford the disk space, it is desirable to put each major filesystem on a separate partition. Many people choose to combine / (root), **/var**, and **/usr** into a single partition, which generally results in less wasted space but can on rare occasions cause problems. For more information refer to "Manual Partitioning: Planning Partitions" on page 38.

- Although parted can create some types of filesystems, it is typically easiest to use parted to create partitions and then use mkfs and mkswap to create filesystems on the partitions.

The following sequence of commands defines a 300-megabyte, bootable, Linux partition as partition 1 on a clean disk:

```
#/sbin/parted /dev/sdb
...
Using /dev/sdb
(parted) mkpart                                 (create new partition)
Partition type?  primary/extended? primary      (select primary partition)
File system type?  [ext2]?                       (default to an ext2 filesystem)
Start? 1                                          (start at the beginning of the disk)
End? 300m                                         (specify a 300-megabyte partition)
(parted) help set                                (use help to check the syntax of the set command)
  set NUMBER FLAG STATE         change a flag on partition NUMBER

        NUMBER is the partition number used by Linux.  On msdos disk labels, the primary
        partitions number from 1 to 4, logical partitions from 5 onwards.
        FLAG is one of: boot, root, swap, hidden, raid, lvm, lba, hp-service, palo,
        prep, msftres
        STATE is one of: on, off
```

```
(parted) set 1 boot on                    (turn on the boot flag on partition 1)
(parted) print                            (verify that the partition is correct)
Disk geometry for /dev/sdb: 0kB - 250GB
Disk label type: msdos
Number  Start   End    Size   Type     File system  Flags
1       1kB     300MB  300MB  primary  ext2         boot
(parted) quit
Information: Don't forget to update /etc/fstab, if necessary.
```

When you specify a size within parted, you can use a suffix of **k** (kilobytes), **m** (megabytes), or **g** (gigabytes). After creating a partition, enter a **print** command to see where the partition ends. Perform this task before defining the next contiguous partition so you do not waste space. After setting up all the partitions, exit from parted with a **quit** command.

Next make a filesystem (mkfs, page 472) on each partition that is to hold a filesystem (not swap). Make all partitions, except swap, of type **ext4**, unless you have a reason to do otherwise. Use mkswap (page 513) to set up a swap area on a partition. You can use e2label (page 470) to label a partition.

logrotate: MANAGES LOG FILES

Rather than deleting or truncating log files, you might want to keep these files for a while in case you need to refer to them. The logrotate utility manages system log (and other) files automatically by *rotating* (page 1186), compressing, mailing, and removing each file as you specify. The logrotate utility is controlled by the **/etc/logrotate.conf** file, which sets default values and can optionally specify files to be rotated. Typically **logrotate.conf** has an **include** statement that points to utility-specific specification files in **/etc/logrotate.d**. Following is the default **logrotate.conf** file:

```
$ cat /etc/logrotate.conf
# see "man logrotate" for details
# rotate log files weekly
weekly

# keep 4 weeks worth of backlogs
rotate 4

# create new (empty) log files after rotating old ones
create

# use date as a suffix of the rotated file
dateext

# uncomment this if you want your log files compressed
#compress

# RPM packages drop log rotation information into this directory
include /etc/logrotate.d
```

```
# no packages own wtmp and btmp -- we'll rotate them here
/var/log/wtmp {
    monthly
    create 0664 root utmp
        minsize 1M
    rotate 1
}

/var/log/btmp {
    missingok
    monthly
    create 0600 root utmp
    rotate 1
}

# system-specific logs may be also be configured here.
```

The **logrotate.conf** file sets default values for common parameters. Whenever logrotate reads another value for one of these parameters, it resets the default value. You have a choice of rotating files **daily, weekly,** or **monthly.** The number following the **rotate** keyword specifies the number of rotated log files you want to keep. The **create** keyword causes logrotate to create a new log file with the same name and attributes as the newly rotated log file. The **dateext** keyword causes logrotate to use the date as a filename extension. The **compress** keyword (commented out in the default file) causes log files to be compressed using gzip. The **include** keyword specifies the standard **/etc/logrotate.d** directory for program-specific logrotate specification files. When you install a program using rpm (page 550) or an rpm-based utility such as yum (Chapter 13), rpm puts the logrotate specification file in this directory.

The last sets of instructions in **logrotate.conf** take care of the **/var/log/wtmp** and **/var/log/btmp** log files (**wtmp** holds login records and **btmp** holds records of failed [bad] login attempts); you can view these files using **who**). The keyword **missingok** overrides the implicit default value of **nomissingok** *for this file only.* This keyword causes logrotate to continue without issuing an error message if the log file is missing. The keyword **monthly** overrides the default value of **weekly** *for this file only.* The **create** keyword is followed by the arguments establishing the permissions, owner, and group for the new file. Finally **rotate** establishes that one rotated log file should be kept.

The **/etc/logrotate.d/httpd** file is an example of a utility-specific logrotate specification file:

```
$ cat /etc/logrotate.d/httpd
/var/log/httpd/*log {
    missingok
    notifempty
    sharedscripts
    delaycompress
    postrotate
        /sbin/service httpd reload > /dev/null 2>/dev/null || true
    endscript
}
```

This file, which is installed by the **httpd** package install script and incorporated in **/etc/logrotate.d** because of the **include** statement in **logrotate.conf**, works with each of the files in **/var/log/httpd** that has a filename ending in **log** (*****log**). The **notifempty** keyword causes logrotate not to rotate the log file if it is empty, overriding the default action of rotating empty log files. The **sharedscripts** keyword causes logrotate to execute the command(s) in the **prerotate** and **postrotate** sections one time only—not one time for each log that is rotated. The **delaycompress** keyword causes logrotate to delay compression for one cycle. Although it does not appear in this example, the **copytruncate** keyword causes logrotate to truncate the original log file immediately after it copies it. This keyword is useful for programs that cannot be instructed to close and reopen their log files because they might continue writing to the original file even after it has been moved. The logrotate utility executes the commands between **prerotate** and **endscript** before the rotation begins. Similarly, commands between **postrotate** and **endscript** are executed after the rotation is complete.

The logrotate utility works with a variety of keywords, many of which take arguments and have side effects. Refer to the logrotate man page for details.

rsyslogd: LOGS SYSTEM MESSAGES

Traditionally, UNIX programs sent log messages to standard error. If a more permanent log was required, the output was redirected to a file. Because of the limitations of this approach, 4.3BSD introduced the system log daemon (**rsyslogd**; www.rsyslog.com) now used by Linux. This daemon listens for log messages and stores them in the **/var/log** hierarchy. In addition to providing logging facilities, **rsyslogd** allows a single machine to serve as a log repository for a network and allows arbitrary programs to process specific log messages.

rsyslog.conf   The **/etc/rsyslog.conf** file stores configuration information for **rsyslogd**. Each line in this file contains one or more *selectors* and an *action* separated by whitespace. The selectors define the origin and type of the messages; the action specifies how **rsyslogd** processes the message. Sample lines from **rsyslog.conf** follow (a **#** begins a comment):

```
# Log all kernel messages to the console.
kern.*                                    /dev/console
# Log all the mail messages in one place.
mail.*                                    /var/log/maillog
# Log cron stuff
cron.*                                    /var/log/cron
# Everybody gets emergency messages
*.emerg                                   *
# Save boot messages also to boot.log
local7.*                                  /var/log/boot.log
```

Selectors   A selector is split into two parts, a *facility* and a *priority*, which are separated by a period. The facility indicates the origin of the message. For example, **kern** messages come from the kernel, and **mail** messages come from the mail subsystem.

Following is a list of facility names used by **rsyslogd** and the systems that generate these messages:

Facilities

auth	Authorization and security systems including login
authpriv	Same as **auth,** but should be logged to a secure location
cron	**crond**
daemon	System and network daemons without their own categories
kern	Kernel
lpr	Printing subsystem
mail	Mail subsystem
news	Network news subsystem
user	Default facility; all user programs use this facility
uucp	The UNIX-to-UNIX copy protocol subsystem
local0 to **local7**	Reserved for local use

The priority indicates the severity of the message. The following list of the priority names and the conditions they represent appears in ascending priority order:

Priorities

debug	Debugging information
info	Information that does not require intervention
notice	Conditions that might require intervention
warning	Warnings
err	Errors
crit	Critical conditions such as hardware failure
alert	Conditions that require immediate attention
emerg	Emergency conditions

A selector consisting of a single facility and priority, such as **kern.info**, causes the corresponding action to be applied to every message from that facility with that priority *or higher* (more urgent). Use **.=** to specify a single priority; for example, **kern.=info** applies the action to kernel messages of **info** priority. An exclamation point specifies that a priority is not matched. Thus **kern.!info** matches kernel messages with a priority lower than **info**, and **kern.!=info** matches kernel messages with a priority other than **info**.

A line with multiple selectors, separated by semicolons, applies the action if any of the selectors is matched. Each of the selectors on a line with multiple selectors constrains the match, with subsequent selectors frequently tightening the constraints. For example, the selectors **mail.info;mail.!err** match mail subsystem messages with **debug, info, notice**, or **warning** priorities.

You can replace either part of the selector with an asterisk to match anything. The keyword **none** in either part of the selector indicates no match is possible. The selector **∗.crit;kern.none** matches all critical or higher-priority messages, except those from the kernel.

Actions   The action specifies how **rsyslogd** processes a message that matches the selector. The simplest actions are ordinary files, which are specified by their absolute pathnames; **rsyslogd** appends messages to these files. Specify **/dev/console** to send messages to the system console. If you want a hardcopy record of messages, specify a device file that represents a dedicated printer. Precede a filename with a hyphen (–) to keep **rsyslogd** from writing each message to the file as it is generated (syncing). Doing so might improve performance, but you might lose data if the system crashes after the message is generated but before it gets written to a file.

You can write important messages to users' terminals by specifying one or more usernames separated by commas. Very important messages can be written to every logged-in terminal by using an asterisk.

To forward messages to **rsyslogd** on a remote system, specify the name or IP address of the system preceded by @ (sends messages to UDP port 514) or @@ (sends messages to TCP port 514). It is a good idea to forward critical messages from the kernel to another system because these messages often precede a system crash and might not be saved to the local disk. The following line from **rsyslog.conf** sends critical kernel messages to **plum**:

```
kern.crit       @plum
```

On the remote system edit **/etc/rsyslog.conf** and one or both sets of the following lines depending on whether you want to use UDP or TCP. Do not remove the hash marks from the comments. After editing this file restart the **rsyslogd** daemon using **rsyslog.service**.

```
# Provides UDP syslog reception
#$ModLoad imudp
#$UDPServerRun 514

# Provides TCP syslog reception
#$ModLoad imtcp
#$InputTCPServerRun 514
```

KEEPING USERS INFORMED

One of your primary responsibilities as a system administrator is communicating with system users. You need to make announcements, such as when the system will be down for maintenance, when a class on some new software will be held, and how users can access the new system printer. You can even start to fill the role of a small local newspaper, letting users know about new employees, RIFs, births, the company picnic, and so on.

Different communications have different priorities. For example, information about the company picnic in two months is not as time sensitive as the fact that you are bringing the system down in five minutes. To meet these differing needs, Linux provides different ways of communicating. The most common methods are described and contrasted in the following list. These methods are generally available to all users, except for the message of the day, which is typically reserved for a user with **root** privileges.

write   Use the write utility (page 170) to communicate with a user who is logged in on the local system. You might use it, for example, to ask a user to stop running a program that is slowing the system; the user might reply that he will be done in three minutes. Users can also use write to ask the system administrator to mount a tape or restore a file. Messages sent from write might not appear in a graphical environment.

IM   The Empathy IM (Internet Messaging; live.gnome.org/Empathy) utility supports text, voice, and video chat and file transfers using Google Talk, MSN, IRC, AIM, Facebook, Yahoo!, ICQ, and other protocols. It is available from **Main menu: Applications⇨Internet⇨Empathy Internet Messaging**. IM is common in many workplaces, and you can use it to contact Red Hat support.

wall   The wall (write all) utility effectively communicates immediately with all users who are logged in. This utility takes its input from standard input and works much like write, except that users cannot use wall to write back to only you. Use wall when you are about to bring the system down or are in another crisis situation. Users who are not logged in will not get the message.

Run wall as a user with **root** privileges *only* in a crisis situation; it interrupts anything anyone is doing. Messages sent by wall might not appear in a graphical environment.

Email   Email is useful for communicating less urgent information to one or more systems and/or remote users. When you send mail, you have to be willing to wait for each user to read it. Email is useful for reminding users that they are forgetting to log out, their bills are past due, or they are using too much disk space.

Users can easily make permanent records of messages they receive via email, as opposed to messages received via write, so they can keep track of important details. For instance, it would be appropriate to use email to inform users about a new, complex procedure so each user could keep a copy of the information for reference.

Message of the day   Users see the message of the day each time they log in in a textual environment but not when they open a terminal emulator window. You can edit the **/etc/motd** file to change this message as necessary. The message of the day can alert users to upcoming periodic maintenance, new system features, or a change in procedures.

CREATING PROBLEMS

Even experienced system administrators make mistakes; new system administrators just make more mistakes. Although you can improve your odds of avoiding problems by carefully reading and following the documentation provided with software, many things can still go wrong. A comprehensive list, no matter how long, is not possible because new and exciting ways to create problems are discovered every day. This section describes a few of the more common techniques.

Failing to perform regular backups   Few feelings are more painful to a system administrator than realizing that important information is lost forever. If the local system supports multiple users, having a recent backup might be your only protection from a public lynching. If it is a single-user system, having a recent backup certainly keeps you happier when you lose a hard disk or erase a file by mistake.

Not reading and following instructions

Software developers provide documentation for a reason. Even when you have installed a software package before, carefully read the instructions again. They might have changed, or you might simply remember them incorrectly. Software changes more quickly than books are revised, so no book should be taken as offering foolproof advice. Instead, look for the latest documentation online. The **/usr/share/doc** directory has information on many utilities, libraries, and software packages.

Failing to ask for help when instructions are not clear

If something does not seem to make sense, try to find out what does make sense—do not attempt to guess. See Appendix B for a list of places you might be able to find assistance.

Deleting or mistyping information in a critical file

One sure way to give yourself nightmares is to execute the command

> `# rm -rf /etc`   ← *do not do this*

Perhaps no other command renders a Linux system useless so quickly. The only recourse is to boot from installation media to rescue an installed system (page 457) and restore the missing files from a recent backup. Although this example depicts an extreme case, many files are critical to proper operation of a system. Deleting one of these files or mistyping information in one of them is almost certain to cause problems. If you directly edit **/etc/passwd**, for example, entering the wrong information in a field can make it impossible for one or more users to log in. Do not use **rm -rf** with an argument that includes wildcard characters; do pause after typing the command and read it before you press RETURN. Check everything you do carefully, and make a copy of a critical file before you edit it.

Be careful when using a wildcard character with rm

caution When you must use a wildcard character, such as ∗, in an argument to an rm command, specify the **–i** option to cause rm to prompt you before removing each file. Alternatively, you can use echo with the same argument to see exactly which files you will be deleting. This check is especially important when you are working with **root** privileges.

SOLVING PROBLEMS

As the system administrator, it is your responsibility to keep the system secure and running smoothly. When a user is having a problem, it usually falls to the administrator to help the user get back on track. This section suggests ways to keep users happy and the system functioning at peak performance.

HELPING WHEN A USER CANNOT LOG IN

When a user has trouble logging in on the system, the source might be a user error or a problem with the system software or hardware. The following steps can help determine where the problem is:

- Check the log files in **/var/log**. The **/var/log/messages** file accumulates system errors, messages from daemon processes, and other important information. It might indicate the cause or more symptoms of a problem.

Also check the system console. Occasionally messages about system problems that are not written to **/var/log/messages** (for instance, a full disk) are displayed on the system console.

- Determine whether only that one user or only that one user's terminal/ workstation has a problem or if the problem is more widespread.

- Check that the user's CAPS LOCK key is not on.

- Make sure the user's home directory exists and corresponds to that user's entry in the **/etc/passwd** file. Verify that the user owns her home directory and startup files and that they are readable (and, in the case of the user's home directory, executable). Confirm that the entry for the user's login shell in the **/etc/passwd** file is accurate and the shell exists as specified.

- Change the user's password if there is a chance that he has forgotten it.

- Check the user's startup files (**.profile, .login, .bashrc,** and so on). The user might have edited one of these files and introduced a syntax error that prevents login.

- Check the terminal or monitor data cable from where it plugs into the terminal to where it plugs into the computer (or as far as you can follow it). Try turning the terminal or monitor off and then turning it back on.

- When the problem appears to be widespread, check whether you can log in from the system console. Make sure the system is not in single-user mode. If you cannot log in, the system might have crashed; reboot it and perform any necessary recovery steps (the system usually does quite a bit automatically).

- Use df to check for full filesystems. If the **/tmp** filesystem or the user's home directory is full, login sometimes fails in unexpected ways. In some cases you might be able to log in to a textual environment but not a graphical one. When applications that start when the user logs in cannot create temporary files or cannot update files in the user's home directory, the login process itself might terminate.

- If the user is logging in over a network connection

  ◆ Restart the service the user is trying to use (e.g., ssh). See "Changing the Current State of a Daemon" on page 435 (Fedora) or run the appropriate init script (RHEL; page 442).

  ◆ Make sure the system clocks on the two systems are synchronized. Clocks set to different times can cause login failures when using encrypted login methods such as HTTPS, ssh, LDAP, and especially kerberos.

  ◆ Make sure DNS is working properly. Some network services are particular about name resolution including reverse lookups (i.e., slow connections via ssh can be caused by a name resolution problem).

SPEEDING UP THE SYSTEM

When the system is running slowly for no apparent reason, perhaps a process did not exit when a user logged out. Symptoms of this problem include poor response time and a system load, as shown by w or uptime, greater than 1.0. Running top (page 616) is an excellent way to find rogue processes quickly. Use **ps –ef** to list all processes. One thing to look for in **ps –ef** output is a large number in the **TIME** column. For example, if a Firefox process has a **TIME** field greater than 100.0, this process has likely run amok. However, if the user is doing a lot of Java work and has not logged out for a long time, this value might be normal. Look at the **STIME** field to see when the process was started. If the process has been running for longer than the user has been logged in, it is a good candidate to be killed.

When a user gets stuck and leaves her terminal unattended without notifying anyone, it is convenient to kill (page 470) all processes owned by that user. If the user is running a GUI on the console, kill the process that started the desktop environment or the window manager itself. Processes to look for include **gnome-session**, **startkde**, or another process name that ends in **wm**. Usually the window manager is either the first or last thing to be run, and exiting from the window manager logs the user out. If killing the window manager does not work, try killing the X server process. This process is typically listed as **/usr/bin/Xorg**. If that fails, you can kill all processes owned by a user by giving the command **kill –15 –1** or, equivalently, **kill –TERM –1** *while you are logged in as that user*. Using **–1** (one) in place of the process ID tells kill to send the signal to all processes that are owned by that user. For example, as **root** you could enter the following command:

```
# su zach -c 'kill -TERM -1'
```

If this does not kill all processes (sometimes TERM does not kill a process), you can use the KILL signal (**–9**). The following line will definitely kill all processes owned by Zach and will not be friendly about it:

```
# su zach -c 'kill -KILL -1'
```

If you do not include **su zach –c**, this command brings the system down.

lsof: FINDS OPEN FILES

The lsof (list open files) utility displays the names of open files. Its options display only certain processes, only certain file descriptors of a process, or only certain network connections (network connections use file descriptors just as normal files do and lsof can show these as well). After you have identified a suspect process using **ps –ef**, enter the following command:

```
# lsof -s -p pid
```

Replace *pid* with the process ID of the suspect process; lsof displays a list of file descriptors that process *pid* has open. The **–s** option displays the sizes of all open files, and the **–p** option allows you to specify the PID number of the process of interest (lsof does not work if you combine these options). This size information is helpful in determining whether the process has a very large file open. If it does, contact the owner of the process or, if necessary, kill the process. The **–rn** option redisplays the output of lsof every *n* seconds.

KEEPING A MACHINE LOG

A machine log that includes the information shown in Table 16-3 can help you find and fix system problems. It it useful to note the time and date of each entry in the log. Avoid the temptation to keep the log *only* on the computer—it will be most useful to you when the system is down. Also keep email that details user problems. One strategy is to save this mail to a separate file or folder as you read it. Another approach is to set up a mail alias that users can send mail to when they have problems. This alias can then forward mail to you and also store a copy in an archive file. Following is an example of an entry in the **/etc/aliases** file (page 736) that sets up this type of alias:

```
trouble: admin,/var/spool/mail/admin.archive
```

Email sent to the **trouble** alias will be forwarded to the **admin** user as well as stored in the file **/var/spool/mail/admin.archive**.

Table 16-3   Machine log

Entry	Function
Hardware modifications	Keep track of the system hardware configuration: which devices hold which partitions, the model of the new NIC you added, and so on.
System software modifications	Keep track of the options used when building Linux. Print such files as **/usr/src/linux/.config** (Linux kernel configuration). The file hierarchy under **/etc/sysconfig** contains valuable information about the network configuration, among other things.
Hardware malfunctions	Keep as accurate a list as possible of any problems with the system. Make note of any error messages or numbers the system displays on the system console and identify what users were doing when the problem occurred.
User complaints	Make a list of all reasonable complaints made by knowledgeable users (for example, "Machine is abnormally slow").

KEEPING THE SYSTEM SECURE

No system with dial-in lines or public access to terminals is absolutely secure. Nevertheless, you can make a system as secure as possible by changing the passwords of the **root** password frequently and by choosing passwords that are difficult to guess. Do not tell anyone who does not *absolutely* need to know the **root** password. You can also encourage system users to choose difficult passwords and to change them periodically.

Passwords   By default, passwords on Fedora/RHEL use *MD5* (page 1175) hashing, which makes them more difficult to crack than passwords encrypted with DES (page 1129). Of course, it makes little difference how well encrypted your password is if you make it easy for someone to find out or guess what the password is. The system-config-authentication utility allows you to specify a local password hashing algorithm: Select the Advanced Options tab and make a selection from the drop-down box labeled **Password Hashing Algorithm**.

A password that is difficult to guess is one that someone else would not be likely to think you would have chosen. Do not use words from the dictionary (spelled forward or backward); names of relatives, pets, or friends; or words from a foreign language. A good strategy is to choose a couple of short words, include some punctuation (for example, put a ^ between them), mix the case, and replace some of the letters in the words with numbers. If it were not printed in this book, an example of a good password would be **C&yGram5** (candygrams). Ideally you would use a random combination of ASCII characters, but that would be difficult to remember.

You can use one of several password-cracking programs to find users who have chosen poor passwords. These programs work by repeatedly hashing words from dictionaries, phrases, names, and other sources. If the hashed password matches the output of the program, then the program has found the password of the user. Two programs that crack passwords are crack (**crack** package) and john (John the Ripper; www.openwall.com/john; **john** package). These and many other programs and security tips are available from CERT (www.cert.org), which was originally called the Computer Emergency Response Team. Specifically, look at www.cert.org/tech_tips.

It takes a lot of computational power to crack a good password. Password-cracking programs generally start by looking at the character set comprising uppercase and lowercase letters and numbers. When you add symbols, they have to do more work to crack a password. Also, the longer the password, the more computational power it takes to crack. Make your password long enough so it will be harder to crack and short enough so you can remember it; 8–20 characters is usually a good length. Include a few symbols such as **#**, **@**, and **%**. If it takes too long to crack your password, the person or machine doing the dirty work might move on to easier accounts.

Setuid files Make sure no one except a user with **root** privileges can write to files containing programs that are owned by **root** and run in setuid mode (for example, passwd and su). Also make sure users do not transfer programs that run in setuid mode and are owned by **root** onto the system by means of mounting tapes or disks. These programs can be used to circumvent system security. One technique that prevents users from having setuid files is to use the **nosuid** flag to mount, which you can set in the flags section in the **fstab** file. Refer to "Mount Options" on page 522.

BIOS The BIOS in many machines gives you some degree of protection from an unauthorized person who tries to modify the BIOS or reboot the system. When you set up the BIOS, look for a section named **Security**. You can probably add a BIOS password. If you depend on the BIOS password, lock the computer case—it is usually a simple matter to reset the BIOS password by using a jumper on the motherboard.

LOG FILES AND MAIL FOR root

Users frequently email **root** and **postmaster** to communicate with the system administrator. If you do not forward **root**'s mail to yourself (**/etc/aliases** on page 736), remember to check **root**'s mail periodically. You will not receive reminders about mail that arrives for **root** when you use su to perform system administration tasks. However, you can use the command su –c 'mail –u root' to look at **root**'s mail.

Review the system log files regularly for evidence of problems. Some important files are **/var/log/messages**, where the operating system and some applications record errors; **/var/log/secure**, which holds messages pertaining to system security; **/var/log/maillog**, which contains errors from the mail system; and **/var/log/cron**, which contains messages from **crond**.

The logwatch utility (**logwatch** package) is a report writer that is written in Perl and sends email reports about log files. By default, **/etc/cron.daily/0logwatch** runs this script daily and emails its output to **root**. Refer to the logwatch man page and to the script itself for more information.

MONITORING DISK USAGE

Sooner or later you will probably start to run out of disk space. Do not fill up a partition; Linux can write to files significantly faster if at least 5 to 30 percent of the space in a partition remains free. Using more than the maximum optimal disk space in a partition can degrade system performance.

Fragmentation   As a filesystem becomes full, it can become fragmented. This is similar to the DOS concept of fragmentation but is not nearly as pronounced and is typically rare on modern Linux filesystems; by design Linux filesystems are resistant to fragmentation. If you keep filesystems from running near full capacity, you might never need to worry about fragmentation. If there is no space on a filesystem, you cannot write to it at all.

To check for filesystem fragmentation, unmount the filesystem and run fsck (page 525) on it; use the **–f** option on **ext2**, **ext3**, and **ext4** filesystems. The output of fsck includes a percent fragmentation figure for the filesystem. You can defragment a filesystem by backing it up; using mkfs (page 472) to make a clean, empty image; and then restoring the filesystem. Which utility you use to perform the backup and restore—dump/restore, tar, cpio, or a third-party backup program—is not important.

Reports   Linux provides several programs that report on who is using how much disk space on which filesystems. Refer to the du, quota, and df man pages and the **–size** option in the find utility man page. In addition to these utilities, you can use the disk quota system (page 634) to manage disk space.

Four strategies to increase the amount of free space on a filesystem are to compress files, delete files, grow LVM-based filesystems, and condense directories. This section contains some ideas on ways to maintain a filesystem so it does not become overloaded.

Files that grow quickly   Some files, such as log files and temporary files, inevitably grow over time. Core dump files, for example, take up substantial space and are rarely needed. Also, users occasionally run programs that accidentally generate huge files. As the system administrator, you must review these files periodically so they do not get out of hand.

If a filesystem is running out of space quickly (that is, over a period of an hour rather than weeks or months), first figure out why it is running out of space. Use a **ps –ef** command to determine if a user has created a runaway process that is creating a huge file. When evaluating the output of **ps**, look for a process that has consumed a large amount of CPU time. If such a process is running and creating a large file, the file will continue to grow as you free up space. If you remove the huge file, the space it occupied will not be freed until the process terminates, so you need to kill the process. Try to contact the user running the process and ask him to kill it. If you cannot contact the user, use **root** privileges to kill the process yourself. Refer to kill on page 470 for more information.

You can also truncate a large log file rather than remove it, although you can better deal with this recurring situation using logrotate (page 621). For example, if the **/var/log/messages** file has become very large because a system daemon is misconfigured, you can use **/dev/null** to truncate it:

```
# cp /dev/null /var/log/messages
```

or

```
# cat /dev/null > /var/log/messages
```

or, without spawning a new process,

```
# : > /var/log/messages
```

If you remove **/var/log/messages**, you have to restart the **rsyslogd** daemon. If you do not restart **rsyslogd**, the space on the filesystem will not be released.

When no single process is consuming the disk space but capacity has instead been used up gradually, locate unneeded files and delete them. You can archive these files by using cpio, dump, or tar before you delete them. You can safely remove most files named **core** that have not been accessed for several days. The following command line performs this function without removing necessary files named **core** (such as **/dev/core**):

```
# find / -type f -name core | xargs file | grep 'B core file' | sed 's/:ELF.*//g' | xargs rm -f
```

The find command lists all ordinary files named **core** and sends its output to xargs, which runs file on each of the files in the list. The file utility displays a string that includes **B core file** for files created as the result of a core dump. These files need to be removed. The grep command filters out from file any lines that do not contain this string. Finally sed removes everything following the colon so that all that is left on the line is the pathname of the **core** file; xargs then removes the file.

To free up more disk space, look through the **/tmp** and **/var/tmp** directories for old temporary files and remove them. Keep track of disk usage in **/var/mail**, **/var/spool**, and **/var/log**.

Removing Unused Space from Directories

A directory that contains too many filenames is inefficient. The point at which a directory on an **ext2**, **ext3**, or **ext4** filesystem becomes inefficient varies, depending partly on the length of the filenames it contains. Best practice is to keep directories relatively small. Having fewer than several hundred files (or directories) in a directory is generally a good idea, and having more than several thousand is generally a bad idea. Additionally, Linux uses a caching mechanism for frequently accessed files that speeds the process of locating an inode from a filename. This caching mechanism works only on filenames of up to 30 characters in length, so avoid giving frequently accessed files extremely long filenames.

When a directory becomes too large, you can usually break it into several smaller directories by moving its contents to those new directories. Make sure you remove the original directory after you have moved its contents.

Because Linux directories do not shrink automatically, removing a file from a directory does not shrink the directory, even though it frees up space on the disk. To remove unused space and make a directory smaller, you must copy or move all the files to a new directory *and* remove the original directory.

The following procedure removes unused directory space. First remove all unneeded files from the large directory. Then create a new, empty directory. Next move or copy all remaining files from the old large directory to the new empty directory. Remember to copy hidden files. Finally delete the old directory and rename the new directory.

```
# mkdir /home/max/new
# mv /home/max/large/* /home/max/large/.[A-z]* /home/max/new
# rmdir /home/max/large
# mv /home/max/new /home/max/large
```

optional Disk Quota System

The disk quota system (**quota** package) limits the disk space and number of files owned by individual users. You can choose to limit each user's disk space, the number of files each user can own, or both. Each resource that is limited has a lower limit and an upper limit. The user can exceed the lower limit, or *quota*, although a warning is given each time the user logs in when he is above the quota. After a certain number of warnings (one warning per day; the number of days is set by the system administrator), the system behaves as if the user had reached the upper limit. When the upper limit is reached or the user has received the specified number of warnings, the user will not be allowed to create any more files or use any more disk space. The user's only recourse at that point is to remove files.

Users can review their usage and limits with the quota utility. A user running with **root** privileges can use repquota to display quota information on multiple users.

You can turn on quotas only if the filesystem is mounted with the **usrquota** and/or **grpquota** options (**ext3** and **ext4** filesystems).

First you must decide which filesystems to limit and how to allocate space among users. Typically only filesystems that contain users' home directories, such as **/home**, are limited. Use the edquota utility to set the quotas and then use quotaon to start the quota system. You will probably want to put a quotaon command in the appropriate init script so that the quota system will be enabled when you bring up the system (page 442). Unmounting a filesystem automatically disables the quota system for that filesystem.

MySQL

MySQL (My Structured Query Language) is the world's most popular open-source database. It is the M in LAMP (Linux, Apache, MySQL, PHP/Perl/Python), an open-source enterprise software stack. Many programming languages provide an interface to MySQL (e.g., C, PHP, Perl).

Michael Widenius and David Axmark started development of MySQL in 1994. Today the MySQL database is owned and supported by Oracle Corporation (which acquired the former owner, Sun Microsystems, in 2010).

This section explains how to set up and work with MySQL; it does not explain SQL

tip SQL (Structured Query Language) is the language used to work with SQL databases, including MySQL. This chapter explains how to install and set up MySQL in a Fedora/RHEL environment. Although it includes some SQL statements in this explanation, it makes no attempt to explain SQL. See dev.mysql.com/doc for SQL documentation.

More Information

Home page: www.mysql.com
MySQL documentation: dev.mysql.com/doc
Introduction: dev.mysql.com/tech-resources/articles/mysql_intro.html
Backing up databases: www.webcheatsheet.com/SQL/mysql_backup_restore.php

Terminology

This section briefly describes some basic terms used when working with a relational database. See also Figure 16-4 on page 640.

database A structured set of persistent data comprising one or more tables.

table A collection of rows in a relational database.

row An ordered set of columns in a table. Also *record*.

column A set of one type of values, one per row in a table. Also *field*.

Syntax and Conventions

A MySQL program comprises one or more statements, each terminated by a semicolon (;). Although keywords in statements are not case sensitive, this book shows keywords in uppercase letters for clarity. Database and table names are case sensitive.

The following example shows a multiline MySQL statement that includes both the primary interpreter prompt (**mysql>**) and the secondary interpreter prompt (**–>**). This statement displays the values of three columns from the table named **people** in rows that meet specified criteria.

```
mysql> SELECT person,password,executeperm
    -> FROM people
    -> WHERE password IS NULL AND executeperm=true;
```

Prerequisites

Install the following packages:

- mysql
- mysql-server

Run chkconfig to cause the MySQL daemon (**mysqld**) to start when the system enters multiuser mode:

```
# chkconfig mysqld on
```

mysqld init script   Start **msqld**:

```
# service mysqld start
Starting mysqld (via systemctl):                              [  OK  ]
```

Notes

Unlike Oracle, when you create a user, MySQL does not automatically create a database. Under MySQL, users and databases are not as rigidly bound as they are under Oracle.

MySQL has a separate set of users from Linux users. As installed, the name of the MySQL administrator is **root**. Because the MySQL **root** user is not the same as the Linux **root** user, it can have a different password.

JumpStart: Setting Up MySQL

You must assign a password to the MySQL user named root

tip   The examples in this section will not work unless you assign a password to the MySQL user named **root**. See the following instructions.

MySQL is installed with test databases, an anonymous user, and no password for the MySQL user named **root**. For a more secure setup, remove the anonymous user and assign a password to MySQL **root**. The mysql_secure_installation utility asks questions that allows you to assign a password to the MySQL user named **root**, remove the anonymous user, and perform other housekeeping tasks. If you have just installed MySQL, enter RETURN in response to the prompt for the current password for **root**.

```
# mysql_secure_installation
...
Enter current password for root (enter for none):
OK, successfully used password, moving on...
...
Set root password? [Y/n] y
New password:
Re-enter new password:
Password updated successfully!
Reloading privilege tables..
 ... Success!
...
Remove anonymous users? [Y/n] y
...
Disallow root login remotely? [Y/n] y
...
Remove test database and access to it? [Y/n] y
...
Reload privilege tables now? [Y/n] y
...
```

Alternatively, you can use the following command to assign *mysql-password* as the password for the MySQL user named **root**:

```
# mysqladmin -u root password 'mysql-password'
```

OPTIONS

This section describes some of the options you can use on the mysql command line. The options preceded by a single hyphen and those preceded by a double hyphen are equivalent.

––disable-reconnect

>Does not attempt to connect to the server again if the connection is dropped. See **––reconnect**.

––host=*hostname* –h *hostname*

>Specifies the address of the MySQL server as ***hostname***. Without this option MySQL connects to the server on the local system (127.0.0.1).

––password[=*passwd*]
>**–p[*passwd*]**

>Specifies the MySQL password as ***passwd***. For improved security, do not specify the password on the command line; MySQL will prompt for it. By default, MySQL does not use a password. In the short form of this option, do not put a SPACE between the **–p** and ***passwd***.

    ––reconnect   Attempts to connect to the server again if the connection is dropped (default). Disable this behavior using **––disable-reconnect**.

  ––user=_usr_ **–u** _usr_

            Specifies the MySQL user as _usr_. When you first install MySQL, there is one user, **root**, and that user does not have a password.

    ––verbose   **–v** Increases the amount of information MySQL displays. Use this option multiple times to increase verbosity.

The .my.cnf Configuration File

You can use the **~/.my.cnf** file to set MySQL options. The following example shows Max's **.my.cnf** file. The **[mysql]** specifies the MySQL group. The next line sets Max's password to **mpassword**. With this setup, Max does not have to use **–p** on the command line; MySQL logs him in automatically.

```
$ cat /home/max/.my.cnf
[mysql]
password="mpassword"
```

Working with MySQL

Adding a user Before starting to work with the database, create a user so you do not have to work as the MySQL **root** user. If the MySQL username you add is the same as your Linux username, you will not have to specify a username on the MySQL command line. In the following example, Max works as the MySQL **root** user (**–u root**) to create a database named **maxdb** and add the MySQL user named **max** with a password of **mpassword**. In response to the **Enter password** prompt, Max supplies the password for the MySQL user named **root**. The GRANT statement gives Max the permissions he needs to work with the **maxdb** database. You must work as the MySQL **root** user to set up a MySQL user. The **–p** option causes MySQL to prompt for the password. When using the MySQL interpreter, **Query OK** indicates that the preceding statement was syntactically correct. You must enclose all character and date data within quotation marks.

```
$ mysql -u root -p
Enter password:
Welcome to the MySQL monitor.  Commands end with ; or \g.
Your MySQL connection id is 12
Server version: 5.5.10 MySQL Community Server (GPL)
...
Type 'help;' or '\h' for help. Type '\c' to clear the current input
statement.

mysql> CREATE DATABASE maxdb;
Query OK, 1 row affected (0.00 sec)

mysql> GRANT ALL PRIVILEGES
    -> ON maxdb.* to 'max'
    -> IDENTIFIED BY 'mpasswd'
    -> WITH GRANT OPTION;
Query OK, 0 rows affected (0.00 sec)
```

```
mysql> SELECT user, password
    -> FROM mysql.user;
+------+-------------------------------------------+
| user | password                                  |
+------+-------------------------------------------+
| root | *81F5E21E35407D884A6CD4A731AEBFB6AF209E1B |
| root | *81F5E21E35407D884A6CD4A731AEBFB6AF209E1B |
| max  | *34432555DD6C778E7CB4A0EE4551425CE3AC0E16 |
+------+-------------------------------------------+
3 rows in set (0.00 sec)

mysql> quit
Bye
$
```

In the preceding example, after creating the database and setting up the new user, Max queries the **user** table of the **mysql** database to display the **user** and **password** columns. Two users now exist: **root** and **max**. Max gives the command **quit** to exit from the MySQL interpreter.

Working as the MySQL user **max**, Max can now set up a simple database to keep track of users. He does not need to use the **–u** option on the command line because his Linux username and his MySQL username are the same.

Specifying the default database   For subsequent commands, if you do not tell MySQL which database you are working with, you must prefix the names of tables with the name of the database. For example, you would need to specify the **people** table in the **maxdb** database as **maxdb.people**. When you specify the **maxdb** database with a USE statement, you can refer to the same table as **people**. In the following example, Max specifies **maxdb** as the database he is working with:

```
mysql> USE maxdb;
Database changed
```

Creating a table   Next Max creates a table named **people** in the **maxdb** database. This table has six columns of various types. After creating the table, Max uses a DESCRIBE statement to display a description of the table.

```
mysql> CREATE TABLE people ( person VARCHAR(20), password CHAR(41),
    -> created DATE, readperm BOOL, writeperm BOOL, executeperm BOOL);
Query OK, 0 rows affected (0.01 sec)

mysql> DESCRIBE people;
+-------------+-------------+------+-----+---------+-------+
| Field       | Type        | Null | Key | Default | Extra |
+-------------+-------------+------+-----+---------+-------+
| person      | varchar(20) | YES  |     | NULL    |       |
| password    | char(41)    | YES  |     | NULL    |       |
| created     | date        | YES  |     | NULL    |       |
| readperm    | tinyint(1)  | YES  |     | NULL    |       |
| writeperm   | tinyint(1)  | YES  |     | NULL    |       |
| executeperm | tinyint(1)  | YES  |     | NULL    |       |
+-------------+-------------+------+-----+---------+-------+
6 rows in set (0.00 sec)
```

	person	password	created
	topsy	31fdca65565 ...	2011-01-25
Rows	bailey	NULL	2011-01-25
	percy	NULL	2011-01-25

Figure 16-4   Part of the **people** table in the **maxdb** database

MySQL changed the columns Max specified as BOOL (Boolean) to type tinyint(1), an 8-bit integer, because MySQL does not have native (bit) Boolean support. With tinyint(1), 0 evaluates as FALSE, and 1–255 evaluate as TRUE. Figure 16-4 shows part of the **people** table after data has been entered in it.

Modifying a table Max decides that the **readperm**, **writeperm**, and **executeperm** columns should default to 0. He uses an ALTER TABLE statement to modify the table so he does not have to delete it and start over. He then checks his work using a DESCRIBE statement.

```
mysql> ALTER TABLE people
    -> MODIFY readperm BOOL DEFAULT 0,
    -> MODIFY writeperm BOOL DEFAULT 0,
    -> MODIFY executeperm BOOL DEFAULT 0;
Query OK, 0 rows affected (0.01 sec)
Records: 0  Duplicates: 0  Warnings: 0

mysql> DESCRIBE people;
+-------------+-------------+------+-----+---------+-------+
| Field       | Type        | Null | Key | Default | Extra |
+-------------+-------------+------+-----+---------+-------+
| person      | varchar(20) | YES  |     | NULL    |       |
| password    | char(41)    | YES  |     | NULL    |       |
| created     | date        | YES  |     | NULL    |       |
| readperm    | tinyint(1)  | YES  |     | 0       |       |
| writeperm   | tinyint(1)  | YES  |     | 0       |       |
| executeperm | tinyint(1)  | YES  |     | 0       |       |
+-------------+-------------+------+-----+---------+-------+
6 rows in set (0.00 sec)
```

Entering data You can enter information into a database in several ways. The following command adds three rows to **maxdb** from a Linux text file. In the file, each row is on a separate line, a TAB separates each column from the next, and \N specifies a null character. The file is not terminated with a NEWLINE.

```
$ cat /home/max/people_to_add
max     \N      2008-02-17      1       1       1
zach    \N      2009-03-24      1       1       0
sam     \N      2009-01-28      1       0       0

mysql> LOAD DATA LOCAL INFILE '/home/max/people_to_add'
    -> INTO TABLE people;
Query OK, 3 rows affected (0.00 sec)
Records: 3  Deleted: 0  Skipped: 0  Warnings: 0
```

The next command adds a row using an INSERT statement:

```
mysql> INSERT INTO people
    -> VALUES ('topsy',NULL,CURDATE(),1,1,1);
Query OK, 1 row affected (0.01 sec)
```

Within an INSERT statement you can specify which columns you want to enter data into:

```
mysql> INSERT INTO people (person,created,readperm)
    -> VALUES ('bailey',CURDATE(),1), ('percy',CURDATE(),0);
Query OK, 2 rows affected (0.01 sec)
Records: 2  Duplicates: 0  Warnings: 0

mysql> SELECT * FROM people;
+--------+----------+------------+----------+-----------+-------------+
| person | password | created    | readperm | writeperm | executeperm |
+--------+----------+------------+----------+-----------+-------------+
| max    | NULL     | 2008-02-17 |        1 |         1 |           1 |
| zach   | NULL     | 2009-03-24 |        1 |         1 |           0 |
| sam    | NULL     | 2009-01-28 |        1 |         0 |           0 |
| topsy  | NULL     | 2011-01-25 |        1 |         1 |           1 |
| bailey | NULL     | 2011-01-25 |        1 |         0 |           0 |
| percy  | NULL     | 2011-01-25 |        0 |         0 |           0 |
+--------+----------+------------+----------+-----------+-------------+
6 rows in set (0.00 sec)
```

The CURDATE() function returns today's date. Because the default values for **readperm**, **writeperm**, and **executeperm** are 0, you do not have to specify values for those fields.

Deleting rows using a WHERE clause — Next a DELETE FROM statement deletes rows that meet the specified criteria. Here the criteria are specified using equalities in a WHERE clause:

```
mysql> DELETE FROM people
    -> WHERE person='bailey' OR person='percy';
Query OK, 2 rows affected (0.02 sec)
```

Selecting rows using LIKE — You can also use a LIKE clause to specify criteria. The following SELECT statement displays all rows that contain the letter **m** in the **person** column. The % operators are wildcards; they match any characters.

```
mysql> SELECT * FROM people
    -> WHERE person LIKE '%m%';
+--------+----------+------------+----------+-----------+-------------+
| person | password | created    | readperm | writeperm | executeperm |
+--------+----------+------------+----------+-----------+-------------+
| max    | NULL     | 2008-02-17 |        1 |         1 |           1 |
| sam    | NULL     | 2009-01-28 |        1 |         0 |           0 |
+--------+----------+------------+----------+-----------+-------------+
2 rows in set (0.00 sec)
```

Modifying data — In the next example, the PASSWORD() function returns a *hash* (page 1167) of the text given as its argument. The UPDATE statement assigns this hash to the **password** column in rows in which the **person** column holds a value of **sam**. This example does not change the MySQL password information because that information is kept in the database named **mysql**; this statement works with the **maxdb** database.

```
mysql> UPDATE people
    -> SET password=PASSWORD("sampass")
    -> WHERE person='sam';
Query OK, 1 row affected (0.00 sec)
Rows matched: 1  Changed: 1  Warnings: 0
```

More queries   The next query searches for rows where the **password** is null (IS NULL) and (AND) **executeperm** is true (=true).

```
mysql> SELECT person,password,executeperm
    -> FROM people
    -> WHERE password IS NULL AND executeperm=true;
+--------+----------+-------------+
| person | password | executeperm |
+--------+----------+-------------+
| max    | NULL     |           1 |
| topsy  | NULL     |           1 |
+--------+----------+-------------+
2 rows in set (0.00 sec)
```

Because PASSWORD() is a *one-way hash function* (page 1179), you cannot retrieve the plaintext password from the password hash. However, you can check whether any users have their usernames as their passwords:

```
mysql> SELECT * FROM people
    -> WHERE password=PASSWORD(person);
+--------+-----------+------------+----------+-----------+-------------+
| person | password  | created    | readperm | writeperm | executeperm |
+--------+-----------+------------+----------+-----------+-------------+
| topsy  | 31fdca6...| 2009-12-08 |        1 |         1 |           1 |
+--------+-----------+------------+----------+-----------+-------------+
+1 row in set (0.00 sec)
```

Use an UPDATE statement to give Topsy a NULL password:

```
mysql> UPDATE people
    -> SET password=NULL
    -> WHERE person="topsy";
Query OK, 1 row affected (0.00 sec)
Rows matched: 1  Changed: 1  Warnings: 0

mysql> SELECT person,password
    -> FROM people
    -> WHERE password IS NULL;
+--------+----------+
| person | password |
+--------+----------+
| max    | NULL     |
| zach   | NULL     |
| topsy  | NULL     |
+--------+----------+
3 rows in set (0.00 sec)
```

CHAPTER SUMMARY

The system-config-users utility adds new users and groups to the system and modifies existing users' accounts. You can also use the equivalent command-line tools (useradd, usermod, userdel, chage, groupadd, and groupmod) to work with user accounts.

Backing up files on the system is a critical but often-overlooked part of system administration. Linux includes the tar, cpio, dump, and restore utilities to back up and restore files. You can also use more sophisticated packages such as amanda and various commercial products.

The system scheduling daemon, **crond**, periodically executes scheduled tasks. You can schedule tasks using crontab, anacrontab, and at.

System reports present information on the health of the system. Two useful tools that generate these reports are vmstat, which details virtual memory, I/O, and CPU usage, and top, which reports on how the system is performing from moment to moment and can help you figure out what might be slowing it down.

Another aspect of system administration is solving problems. Linux includes several tools that can help track down system problems. One of the most important of these tools is **rsyslogd**, the system log daemon. Using **/etc/rsyslog.conf**, you can control which error messages appear on the console or a user's terminal, which are sent to a remote system and which go to one of several log files.

System administrators are frequently called upon to set up and administrate MySQL databases. MySQL is the M in LAMP (Linux, Apache, MySQL, PHP/Perl/Python), an open-source enterprise software stack. Many programming languages provide an interface to MySQL, including C, PHP, and Perl.

EXERCISES

1. How would you list all the processes running vi?

2. How would you use kill to log Max off the system?

3. From the command line, how would you create a user named John Doe who has the username **jd** and who belongs to group 65535?

4. How would you notify users that you are going to reboot the system in ten minutes?

5. Give a command that creates a gzip compressed tar backup of the **/usr** filesystem on **/dev/sdg**. Which command would you use to make the same backup using bzip2? Using cpio?

ADVANCED EXERCISES

6. If the system is less responsive than normal, what is a good first step in figuring out where the problem is?

7. A process stores its PID number in a file named **process.pid**. Write a command line that terminates this process.

8. Working with **root** privileges, you are planning to delete some files but want to make sure that the wildcard expression you use is correct. Suggest two ways you could make sure you delete the correct files.

17

CONFIGURING AND MONITORING A LAN

OBJECTIVES

After reading this chapter you should be able to:

▶ List and describe the uses of each hardware component of wired and wireless LANs

▶ Determine which network interface card is installed in the local Linux system

▶ List the software settings required to communicate on a LAN

▶ Use Network Manager to configure the system to use static network settings

▶ List several types of network services and their uses

▶ Monitor the network using Cacti

Networks allow computers to communicate and share resources. A local area network (LAN) connects computers at one site, such as an office, home, or library, and can allow the connected computers to share an Internet connection, files, and a printer. Of course, one of the most important reasons to set up a LAN is to allow systems to communicate while users enjoy multiplayer games.

This chapter covers the two aspects of configuring a LAN: setting up the hardware and configuring the software. It is not necessarily organized in the order you will perform the tasks involved in setting up a particular LAN. Instead, read the chapter through, figure out how you will set up your LAN, and then read the parts of the chapter in the order appropriate to your setup. The final section discusses how to monitor devices on a network using Cacti.

SETTING UP THE HARDWARE

Each system, or *node,* on a LAN must have a network interface card (NIC), and each system must connect to a central hub or switch. If the LAN is connected to another network, such as the Internet, it must also have a router.

CONNECTING THE COMPUTERS

Computers are connected to a network using cables (wired; page 365) or radio waves (wireless or Wi-Fi, page 367). The cables can connect to a variety of devices, some of which are described in this section. See "LAN: Local Area Network" on page 364 for an explanation of cables and definitions of *hub, switch,* and *router.*

In the simple network shown in Figure 17-1, four computers are connected to a single hub or switch. Assume computers 1 and 2 are communicating at the same time as computers 3 and 4. With a hub (page 365), each conversation is limited to a maximum of half the network bandwidth. With a switch (page 365), each conversation can theoretically use the full network bandwidth.

Hubs are usually less expensive than switches, although switches are getting cheaper all the time and hubs are becoming less available. If you plan to use the network for sharing an Internet connection and light file sharing, a hub is likely to be fast enough. If systems on the network will exchange files regularly, a switch might be a better choice.

Wireless access point (WAP) A wireless access point (WAP) connects a wireless network to a wired one. Typically a WAP acts as a transparent bridge, forwarding packets between the two networks as if they were one. If you connect multiple WAPs in different locations to the same wired network, wireless clients can roam transparently between the WAPs.

Wireless networks do not require a hub or switch, although a WAP can optionally fill the role of a hub. In a wireless network, the bandwidth is shared among all nodes within range of one another; the maximum speed is limited by the slowest node.

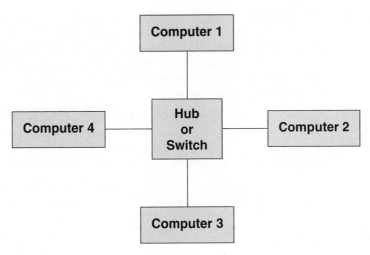

Figure 17-1   A simple network

ROUTERS

A router (page 367) connects a LAN to another network, such as the Internet. A router can perform several functions, the most common of which is allowing several systems to share a single Internet connection and IP address (NAT; page 896). When a router uses NAT, the packets from each system on the LAN appear to come from a single IP address; the router passes return packets to the correct system. A router can also act as a firewall.

You have several choices for routers:

- A simple hardware router is relatively cheap and does most of the things required by a small network.

- You can set up a Fedora/RHEL system as a router. The Linux kernel can use iptables (page 895) to implement a firewall to help protect a system.

- You can use a special-purpose distribution/operating system tailored for use as a router. For example, SmoothWall (www.smoothwall.org), pfSense (www.pfsense.com), and m0n0wall (m0n0.ch/wall) provide browser-based configurations in the style of a hardware router.

NIC: NETWORK INTERFACE CARD

Each system's NIC might be a separate Ethernet card (wired or wireless), or the NIC might be built into the motherboard.

Supported NICs   Linux supports most wired and many wireless Ethernet NICs.

Unsupported wireless NICs   If a wireless network card is not supported under Linux directly, you might be able to get it to work with NdisWrapper (sourceforge.net/projects/ndiswrapper), which uses Win32 drivers. NdisWrapper is a kernel module that provides a subset of the Windows network driver API. No Fedora/RHEL package contains this program.

Wireless bridge   An alternative to a wireless NIC is a wireless bridge. A wireless bridge forwards packets between wired and wireless interfaces, eliminating the need for wireless drivers. This simple device has an Ethernet port that plugs into a NIC and an 802.11 (wireless) controller. Although carrying a bridge around is usually not feasible for mobile users, a wireless bridge is an easy way to migrate a desktop computer to a wireless configuration.

Ad hoc and infrastructure modes   Wireless networks operate in either ad hoc or infrastructure mode. In ad hoc mode, individual nodes in the network communicate directly with one another. In infrastructure mode, nodes communicate via a WAP (page 646). Infrastructure mode is generally more reliable if the wireless LAN must communicate with a wired LAN.

If you do not want to use a WAP, it might be possible to set up a wireless bridge so it acts as a WAP. Consult the NIC/driver documentation for more information.

TOOLS

This section describes three tools you can use to examine system hardware.

lspci: LISTS PCI INFORMATION

The lspci utility (**pciutils** package) lists PCI device information:

```
$ lspci
00:00.0 Host bridge: Intel Corporation 440BX/ZX/DX - 82443BX/ZX/DX Host bridge (rev 01)
00:01.0 PCI bridge: Intel Corporation 440BX/ZX/DX - 82443BX/ZX/DX AGP bridge (rev 01)
00:07.0 ISA bridge: Intel Corporation 82371AB/EB/MB PIIX4 ISA (rev 08)
00:07.1 IDE interface: Intel Corporation 82371AB/EB/MB PIIX4 IDE (rev 01)
00:07.3 Bridge: Intel Corporation 82371AB/EB/MB PIIX4 ACPI (rev 08)
00:07.7 System peripheral: VMware Virtual Machine Communication Interface (rev 10)
00:0f.0 VGA compatible controller: VMware SVGA II Adapter
00:10.0 SCSI storage controller: LSI Logic / Symbios Logic 53c1030 PCI-X Fusion-MPT Dual
Ultra320 SCSI (rev 01)
...
02:00.0 USB Controller: Intel Corporation 82371AB/EB/MB PIIX4 USB
02:01.0 Ethernet controller: Advanced Micro Devices [AMD] 79c970 [PCnet32 LANCE] (rev 10)
02:02.0 Multimedia audio controller: Ensoniq ES1371 [AudioPCI-97] (rev 02)
02:03.0 USB Controller: VMware USB2 EHCI Controller
```

With the **–v** option, lspci is more verbose. You can use the **–vv** or **–vvv** option to display even more information.

```
$ lspci -v | head -14
00:00.0 Host bridge: Intel Corporation 440BX/ZX/DX - 82443BX/ZX/DX Host bridge (rev 01)
        Subsystem: VMware Virtual Machine Chipset
        Flags: bus master, medium devsel, latency 0
        Kernel driver in use: agpgart-intel

00:01.0 PCI bridge: Intel Corporation 440BX/ZX/DX - 82443BX/ZX/DX AGP bridge (rev 01)
(prog-if 00 [Normal decode])
        Flags: bus master, 66MHz, medium devsel, latency 0
        Bus: primary=00, secondary=01, subordinate=01, sec-latency=64
```

```
00:07.0 ISA bridge: Intel Corporation 82371AB/EB/MB PIIX4 ISA (rev 08)
        Subsystem: VMware Virtual Machine Chipset
        Flags: bus master, medium devsel, latency 0

00:07.1 IDE interface: Intel Corporation 82371AB/EB/MB PIIX4 IDE (rev 01) (prog-if 8a
[Master SecP PriP])
```

lshw: LISTS HARDWARE INFORMATION (FEDORA ONLY)

The lshw utility (**lshw** package; Fedora only) lists information about the hardware configuration of the local system. Run this utility with **root** privileges to display a more detailed report. The **–short** option displays a brief report.

```
# lshw -short
H/W path            Device         Class      Description
=========================================================
                                   system     Computer
/0                                 bus        440BX Desktop Reference Platform
/0/0                               memory     87KiB BIOS
/0/4                               processor  Intel(R) Core(TM)2 Quad CPU    Q9650  @ 3.00GHz
/0/4/1c                            memory     16KiB L1 cache
...
/0/100                             bridge     440BX/ZX/DX - 82443BX/ZX/DX Host bridge
/0/100/1                           bridge     440BX/ZX/DX - 82443BX/ZX/DX AGP bridge
/0/100/7                           bridge     82371AB/EB/MB PIIX4 ISA
/0/100/7.1          scsi1          storage    82371AB/EB/MB PIIX4 IDE
/0/100/7.1/0.0.0    /dev/cdrom     disk       SCSI CD-ROM
/0/100/7.3                         bridge     82371AB/EB/MB PIIX4 ACPI
...
/0/100/f                           display    SVGA II Adapter
/0/100/10           scsi2          storage    53c1030 PCI-X Fusion-MPT Dual Ultra320 SCSI
/0/100/10/0.0.0     /dev/sda       disk       42GB SCSI Disk
/0/100/10/0.0.0/1   /dev/sda1      volume     500MiB EXT4 volume
/0/100/10/0.0.0/2   /dev/sda2      volume     39GiB Linux LVM Physical Volume partition
/0/100/11                          bridge     PCI bridge
/0/100/11/0                        bus        82371AB/EB/MB PIIX4 USB
```

You can also use lshal (**hal** package) to display hardware information, where the report is based on the HAL (hardware abstraction layer) device database. See www.freedesktop.org/wiki/Software/hal.

lsusb: LISTS USB DEVICES

The lsusb utility (**usbutils** package) displays information about USB buses and USB devices. Use the **–v** (**--verbose**) option to display additional information.

```
$ lsusb
Bus 002 Device 005: ID 04f9:0033 Brother Industries, Ltd
Bus 002 Device 004: ID 051d:0002 American Power Conversion Uninterruptible Power Supply
Bus 002 Device 003: ID 045e:00dd Microsoft Corp.
Bus 002 Device 002: ID 046d:c018 Logitech, Inc.
```

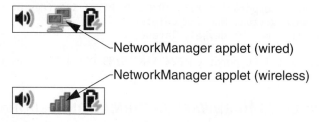

Figure 17-2   The NetworkManager applet on the Top panel

CONFIGURING THE SYSTEMS

After the hardware is in place, you need to configure each system so it knows about the NIC that connects it to the network. Normally the system detects and configures new hardware automatically when you install Fedora/RHEL or the first time you boot it after you install a NIC. You can use nm-connection-editor (next page) to augment the information Fedora/RHEL collects or to set up things differently: For a server, you might want to assign a static IP address to the NIC and not use DHCP (page 652).

System information   In addition to information about the NIC, each system needs the following data:

- The system's IP address
- The netmask (network mask or subnet mask) for the system's address (page 479)
- The IP address of the gateway (page 647)
- The IP addresses of the nameservers (DNS addresses—specify two or three for more reliable network connections)
- The system's hostname (set when you install Fedora/RHEL)

If a DHCP server (page 489) distributes network configuration information to systems on the LAN, you do not need to specify the preceding information on each system. Instead, you just specify that the system is using DHCP to obtain this information (which Fedora/RHEL does by default). You must specify this information when you set up the DHCP server.

Private address   When you set up a LAN, the IP addresses of the systems on the LAN are generally not
space   made public on the Internet. Special IP addresses, which are part of the *private address space* defined by *IANA* (page 1169), are reserved for private use and are appropriate to use on a LAN (Table 17-1). Unless you have been assigned IP addresses for the systems on the LAN, choose addresses from the private address space.

Table 17-1   Private IP ranges (defined in RFC 1918)

Range of IP addresses	From IP address	To IP address
10.0.0.0/8	10.0.0.1	10.255.255.254
172.16.0.0/12	172.16.0.1	172.31.255.254
192.168.0.0/16	192.168.0.1	192.168.255.254

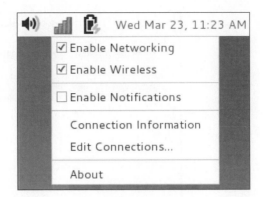

Figure 17-3   The Network Manager applet right-click menu

NETWORKMANAGER: CONFIGURES NETWORK CONNECTIONS

By default, the **NetworkManager** daemon (projects.gnome.org/NetworkManager) manages the network. When it detects a new wired or wireless connection, it starts the appropriate interface. For a wireless connection, it prompts for and stores keys and passphrases. It also detects new hardware—for example, when you plug a USB wireless adapter into the system.

NetworkManager applet
The NetworkManager applet appears toward the right end of the Top panel. It appears as a double monitor when the system is using a wired connection and as a series of vertical bars when the system is using a wireless connection (Figure 17-2). Exactly what appears when you click the NetworkManager applet depends on the system hardware and the items that you have previously set up. Right- and left-clicking the NetworkManager applet display different menus.

THE NETWORKMANAGER APPLET RIGHT-CLICK MENU

Right-click the NetworkManager applet to display a menu that allows you to turn on/off networking and, if available, wireless (networking). See Figure 17-3. Click either **Enable Networking** or **Enable Wireless** to place or remove a tick next to the entry; a tick indicates the service is enabled. You can also select **Connection Information** to display a window showing information about the active connection. Select **Edit Connections** to display the Network Connections window (next).

THE NETWORK CONNECTIONS WINDOW (nm-connection-editor)

Selecting **Edit Connections** from the NetworkManager applet right-click menu runs the nm-connection-editor utility, which displays the Network Connections window

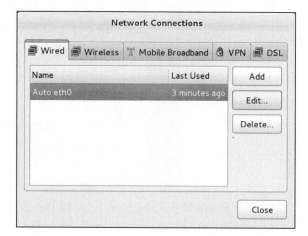

Figure 17-4   The Network Connections window

(Figure 17-4). Alternatively, you can give the command **nm-connection-editor** from a terminal emulator or Run Application window (ALT-F2). From the Network Connections window you can modify the configuration of wired and wireless NICs.

The Network Connections window has five tabs that allow you to configure wired, wireless, and other types of network connections. After the system identifies and configures new network hardware, you can use this window to modify the configuration.

To modify the configuration of a NIC, select the appropriate tab, highlight the description of the connection you want to modify, and click **Edit**; nm-connection-editor displays the Editing window (Figures 17-5 and 17-6 [page 654]). To add a NIC, select a tab and click **Add**; nm-connection-editor displays the same window. When you are finished working in the Editing window, click **Save**.

CONFIGURING A STATIC IP ADDRESS FOR A NIC

By default, Fedora/RHEL runs DHCP (page 489), which typically assigns a *dynamic IP address* to a NIC, so the IP address might not stay the same over time. To make the server easy for clients to find on the Internet, it must have the same IP address all the time (a *static IP address*). See page 378 for information on static IP addresses and page 493 if you want to set up a static IP address using DHCP.

This section describes how to configure a static IPv4 address that does not use DHCP. You can perform the same task by editing the appropriate configuration file in **/etc/sysconfig/network-scripts** (e.g., **ifcfg-eth0** or **ifcfg-Auto_eth0**); see the sample file on page 654.

First, select the Wired tab of the Network Connections window, highlight the NIC you want to configure, and click **Edit**. Or click **Add** if the NIC has not yet been configured. The nm-connection-editor utility displays the **Editing** *xxx* window, where *xxx* is the name of the NIC you are configuring (Figure 17-5).

Figure 17-5   The Editing window, IPv4 Setting tab

If you are setting up an IPv4 address, select the IPv4 Settings tab; for an IPv6 address, select the IPv6 Settings tab. Select **Manual** from the drop-down list labeled **Method**, click **Add** to the right of the box labeled **Addresses**, and enter the IP address of the NIC, the netmask, and the IP address of the gateway for the connection you are setting up. Enter the IP address(es), separated by commas, of the DNS server(s) in the text box labeled **DNS servers**. These actions set the values of IPADDR, PREFIX, GATEWAY, and DNS1 in **/etc/sysconfig/network-scripts/ifcfg***.

A tick in the check box labeled **Require IPv4 addressing for this connection to complete** causes the connection to fail if it cannot obtain an IPv4 address and sets IPV4_FAILURE_FATAL=yes in **/etc/sysconfig/network-scripts/ifcfg***. Put a tick in this check box if the system does not have IPv6 set up. Without a tick, if IPv4 fails, the system tries IPv6 addressing.

A tick in the check box labeled **Available to all users** causes the connection to be available to all users and to be up even when the user who set up the connection is not logged in. Without a tick, the connection is up only when the user who set up the connection is logged in. Typically you will want a tick in this check box.

A tick in the check box labeled **Connect automatically** causes the system to bring up the connection when it boots and sets ONBOOT=yes in **/etc/sysconfig/network-scripts/ifcfg***. Without a tick the connection must be brought up manually. When you are finished, click **Save**.

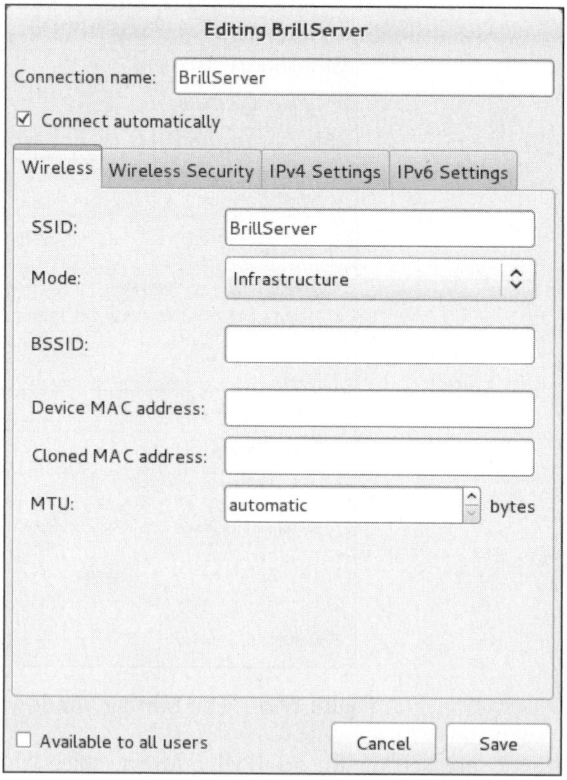

Figure 17-6   The Editing window, wireless tab

Following is the **ifcfg*** file that results from running nm-connection-editor and following the preceding instructions. For more information about this type of file, see **/usr/share/doc/initscripts-*/sysconfig.txt**.

```
$ cat /etc/sysconfig/network-scripts/ifcfg-Auto_eth0
TYPE=Ethernet
BOOTPROTO=none
IPADDR=172.16.192.151
PREFIX=24
GATEWAY=172.16.192.2
DNS1=172.16.192.2
DEFROUTE=yes
IPV4_FAILURE_FATAL=yes
IPV6INIT=no
NAME="Auto eth0"
UUID=bdb28e80-e8e6-4af6-a7c4-90b27f5c6023
ONBOOT=yes
HWADDR=00:0C:29:2D:EB:A9
LAST_CONNECT=1300744981
```

WIRELESS SETTINGS

It is usually easier to configure a wireless connection using the NetworkManager applet (next section) than it is to use the Editing window (Figure 17-6). To use the

Figure 17-7   The NetworkManager applet left-click menu

Editing window to configure wireless settings, click the **Wireless** tab, click **Add** (or highlight the connection and click **Edit**), and enter the appropriate information. When you are finished entering information in the Editing window, click **Apply**.

THE NETWORKMANAGER APPLET LEFT-CLICK MENU

Left-clicking the NetworkManager applet displays a menu that lists the available wireless networks. It also displays selections labeled **More networks, Connect to Hidden Wireless Network**, and **Create New Wireless Network** (if the system has a wireless connection), **Wired Network, Disconnect**, and **VPN Connections**. In Figure 17-7, **disconnected** appears below **Wired Network**, and **mgs3** appears below **Wireless Networks**, meaning that the system is using the wireless connection named **mgs3** and is not using a wired connection.

Click the name of a wireless network (under the word **Available**) to connect to a network. The NetworkManager applet shows activity while it connects to the new network. It then displays the wireless icon (Figure 17-2; page 650). To disable a network, click the word **Disconnect** below the name of the connection you want to disable.

system-config-network   The system-config-network utility presents a simple, pseudographical window you can use to configure a device or DNS.

SETTING UP SERVERS

Setting up local clients and servers can make a LAN both easier to use and more useful. The following list briefly describes some clients and servers and references the pages that describe them in detail.

Firewall   Although not a server, a firewall—which is typically installed on the router—is an important part of a LAN. See system-config-firewall (page 893) and iptables (page 895) for more information.

NIS   NIS can provide a uniform login regardless of which system you log in on. The NIS authentication server is covered on page 769 and the client on page 763. NIS is often combined with home directories that are mounted using NFS. Although still popular, NIS is coming to the end of its life: If you are setting up a new system, choose LDAP over NIS.

NFS   NFS allows you to share directory hierarchies. Sharing directories using NFS requires that the server export the directory hierarchy (page 804) and that clients mount the directory hierarchy (page 796).

Using NFS, you can store all home directories on one system and mount them from other systems as needed. This configuration works well with NIS login authentication. With this setup, it can be convenient to create a world-writable directory—for example, /home/shared—that users can use to exchange files. If you set the sticky bit (page 1190) on this directory (**chmod 1777 /home/shared**), users can delete only files they created. If you do not set the sticky bit, any user can delete any file.

OpenSSH   OpenSSH tools include ssh (logs in on a remote system; page 681) and scp (copies files to and from a remote system; page 683). You can also set up automatic logins with OpenSSH: If you set up a shared home directory with NFS, each user's ~/.ssh directory (page 676) is the same on each system; a user who sets up a personal authentication key (page 689) will be able to use OpenSSH tools between systems without entering a password. See page 688 for information on how to set up an OpenSSH server. You can just use the ssh and scp clients—you do not have to set them up.

DNS cache   Setting up a local cache can reduce the traffic between the LAN and the Internet and can improve response times. For more information refer to "JumpStart I: Setting Up a DNS Cache" on page 860.

DHCP   DHCP enables a client system to retrieve network configuration information from a server each time it connects to a network. See page 489 for more information.

LDAP   LDAP is a database server that can hold names and addresses, authentication information, and other types of data. See page 776 for more information.

Samba   Samba allows Linux systems to participate in a Windows network, sharing directories and printers, and accessing those directories and printers shared by Windows systems. Samba includes a special share for accessing users' home directories. For more information on the [**homes**] share see page 835.

You can also use Samba to set up a shared directory similar to the one described under "NFS." To share a Linux directory with Windows computers, the value of **Workgroup** in **/etc/samba/smb.conf** must be the same as that of the Windows workgroup (frequently MSHOME or WORKGROUP by default). Place the following code in **smb.conf** (page 836):

```
[public]
    comment = Public file space
    path = /home/shared
    read only = no
    public = yes
    browseable = yes
```

Any Windows or Mac user can access this share, which can be used to exchange files between users and among Linux, Mac, and Windows systems.

INTRODUCTION TO CACTI

Cacti (cacti.net) is a network monitoring tool that graphs system and network information over time (*time-series data*) and provides a comprehensive Web interface for browsing and examining the ongoing performance of the devices on a network.

For example, you can configure Cacti to monitor the network traffic passing through the network ports on local servers and the switch and router ports on the local network. Cacti graphs provide information on traffic levels on the various parts of the network. When the network is slow, for example, you can refer to the historical graphs and see if anything out of the ordinary has occurred. In addition to network traffic levels, Cacti can collect data on CPU utilization, disk space usage, page views on a Web server, and almost any other data points available on the local network.

Cacti collects baseline (typical) data over time. You can use that information to gain insight into the ongoing behavior of a system and network and help you resolve problems. The information can even predict what might happen in the future (e.g., when a disk is likely to become full).

When Cacti is installed and configured, it periodically polls devices on a network for the data it needs and stores the data in RRD files for use with RRDtool (round-robin database tool; oss.oetiker.ch/rrdtool). The Cacti Web interface allows you to browse a list of devices and graphs and see visual representations of the devices over time.

Cacti is part of the next generation of monitoring tools. It builds on the lessons learned from tools such as MRTG (oss.oetiker.ch/mrtg; page 964) and Cricket (sourceforge.net/projects/cricket). Each of these tools has the following capabilities:

- Periodically polls tracked devices for data. The tool most commonly used to collect this data is SNMP (Simple Network Management Protocol; www.net-snmp.org).

- Stores the data in an RRD file.

- Has a Web interface that allows you to examine graphs generated from the stored data. These graphs typically display daily, weekly, monthly, and yearly information.

Cacti's configuration is performed through its Web interface, whereas MRTG and Cricket are configured by editing text files.

RRD files and RRDtool are the key to much of Cacti's functionality. The Cacti Web site describes Cacti as "the complete RRDtool-based graphing solution." RRD files store time-series data efficiently and, through the use of aggregation functions, make it easy to keep a lot of detail for recent time periods but progressively less detail as the data in the files ages. RRDtool easily generates both simple and complex graphs from RRD files.

Extending Cacti   Many extensions and plugins are available for Cacti. When you are familiar with the basic use and operation of Cacti, visit cacti.net/additional_scripts.php for a partial list of these additions. Also visit the documentation and the user forums at the same site to obtain more information about Cacti and to learn how you can add functionality and support for different devices and data sources.

CONFIGURING SNMP

If you want to monitor data sources on the local system, install and run the SNMP daemon on the local system as explained under "Setting Up a Remote Data Source" on page 664.

SETTING UP LAMP

Cacti is a LAMP (Linux, Apache, MySQL, PHP) application; you must install and configure these applications before you can configure Cacti. This section explains how to set up the software on the system running Cacti. See "Setting Up a Remote Data Source" on page 664 for an explanation of how to set up a system that Cacti will query and report on. By default, Cacti sets up the local system to run Cacti *and* be a data source.

NOTES

When you set up LAMP, you use the MySQL databases named **mysql** and **cacti**. Fedora/RHEL sets up the **mysql** database when you install MySQL. You set up and populate the **cacti** database as explained under "Configuring MySQL" on page 659.

You need to set up the following database users. Each of these accounts should have a password:

- A user named **root** for the database named **mysql**. This user must be named **root**. The MySQL installation script sets up this user.

- A user named **cactiuser** for the database named **mysql**. You can change this username, but as installed, Cacti is set up to use **cactiuser**.

- A Cacti administrative user for the database named **cacti**. As set up when you install Cacti, this user has the name **admin** and the password **admin**. You can set up additional Cacti user accounts.

As of this writing, Fedora/RHEL has Cacti 0.8.7g-2 in its repositories. Do not be misled by the pre-1.0 version number: Cacti is stable and in use on many systems.

PREREQUISITES

Install the following packages:

- **cacti** (Fedora only; download cacti for RHEL from fedoraproject.org/wiki/EPEL)

- **mysql** (page 635)

- **mysql-server** (page 635)

- **php** (installed with **cacti**)

- **httpd** (Apache; page 917; installed with **cacti**)

- **rrdtool** (installed with **cacti**)

- **net-snmp** (optional; needed only to monitor the local system)

- **net-snmp-utils** (optional)

Firewall   The **snmpd** daemon, which runs on systems monitored by Cacti, uses UDP port 161. If the monitored system is running a firewall or is behind a firewall, you must open this port. Using system-config-firewall (page 893), select the Other Ports tab, put a tick in the check box labeled **User Defined**, and add UDP port 161. For more information refer to "Other Ports" on page 894. If you want to work with Cacti from a browser on a system other than the one running Cacti, you need to open TCP port 80 on the system running Cacti (refer to "Firewall" on page 920).

SELinux   When SELinux is set to use a targeted policy, both **httpd** (on the system running Cacti) and **snmpd** (on the systems being monitored) are protected by SELinux. You can disable this protection if necessary. For more information refer to "Setting the Targeted Policy with system-config-selinux" on page 463.

CONFIGURING MYSQL

Install MySQL, run chkconfig, and start the **mysqld** daemon using service as explained starting at "Prerequisites" on page 636. Be sure to assign a password to the MySQL user named **root** by using either mysql_secure_installation or mysqladmin.

Create the **cacti** database   Next, issue the following commands to create a database named **cacti**, create a mysql database user named **cactiuser**, grant that user the necessary privileges, and assign a password to that user. Replace *cactipassword* in the following example with your choice of a password. Although the FLUSH PRIVILEGES statement is not required, it is good practice to include it.

```
# mysql -p
Enter password:
Welcome to the MySQL monitor.  Commands end with ; or \g.
Your MySQL connection id is 5
Server version: 5.5.10 MySQL Community Server (GPL)
...
mysql> CREATE DATABASE cacti;
Query OK, 1 row affected (0.00 sec)

mysql> GRANT ALL ON cacti.*
    -> TO cactiuser@localhost
    -> IDENTIFIED BY 'cactipassword';
Query OK, 0 rows affected (0.00 sec)

mysql> FLUSH PRIVILEGES;
Query OK, 0 rows affected (0.00 sec)

mysql> exit
Bye
```

Set up and populate the cacti database Give the following command to set up and populate the database named **cacti**. When MySQL prompts for a password, provide the password for the MySQL user named **root** (not the MySQL user named **cactiuser**).

```
# mysql -p cacti < /usr/share/doc/cacti*/cacti.sql
Enter password:
```

As this book went to press, the preceding command would fail with an SQL syntax error. To work around this error, edit **cacti.sql** and remove all occurrences of the string **TYPE=MyISAM** (i.e., substitute a null string for each **TYPE=MyISAM** string: s/TYPE=MyISAM//).

Edit db.php Most of the information in the **/etc/cacti/db.php** file is correct as installed. Edit this file to change the value assigned to **$database_password** from **cactiuser** to the same value you used for *cactipassword* when you created the **cacti** database (the password for the MySQL user named **cactiuser**). Do not change the value assigned to **$database_username**.

```
$database_type = "mysql";
$database_default = "cacti";
$database_hostname = "localhost";
$database_username = "cactiuser";
$database_password = "cactiuser";
$database_port = "3306";
```

CONFIGURING APACHE

Install Apache as explained under "Running an Apache Web Server" on page 920. Modify the **httpd.conf** file as explained on page 922; if you do not make this modification, Apache will display errors when it starts but will work anyway. Run chkconfig and use service to start the **httpd** daemon. Cacti supplies the content.

The **/etc/httpd/conf.d/cacti.conf** file controls the location and accessibility of Cacti on the Apache server. By default, Cacti is available as **127.0.0.1/cacti** (based on the Alias statement), and only a user on **127.0.0.1** (and not **localhost**; based on the Allow from statement) can access Cacti. The default **cacti.conf** file follows:

```
$ cat /etc/httpd/conf.d/cacti.conf
#
# Cacti: An rrd based graphing tool
#
Alias /cacti    /usr/share/cacti

<Directory /usr/share/cacti/>
        Order Deny,Allow
        Deny from all
        Allow from 127.0.0.1
</Directory>
```

To follow the example in this section, add an **Allow from localhost** line immediately below the **Allow from 127.0.0.1** line. You can add additional lines to allow access from other systems. The following <Directory> container allows access from **127.0.0.1, localhost,** and the remote system at **172.16.192.150**:

```
<Directory /usr/share/cacti/>
        Order Deny,Allow
        Deny from all
        Allow from 127.0.0.1
        Allow from localhost
        Allow from 172.16.192.150
</Directory>
```

See "Alias" (page 939), "<Directory>" (page 931), and "Allow" (page 945) for more information.

ENABLING THE CACTI POLLER

Enable the Cacti poller by removing the hash mark from the left end of the line in the **/etc/cron.d/cacti** crontab file. The ***/5** entry in this file causes **crond** to execute the script every five minutes. For more information refer to "Crontab Files" on page 611.

```
$ cat /etc/cron.d/cacti
*/5 * * * * cacti /usr/bin/php /usr/share/cacti/poller.php > /dev/null 2>&1
```

CONFIGURING CACTI

After starting or restarting Apache, point a Web browser on the machine running Cacti at **localhost/cacti**; Apache redirects the browser to the Cacti installation page at **localhost/cacti/install** and displays the Cacti Installation Page screen. Click **Next**.

Confirm the information on the Cacti Installation Guide screen (Figure 17-8, next page) and click **Next**.

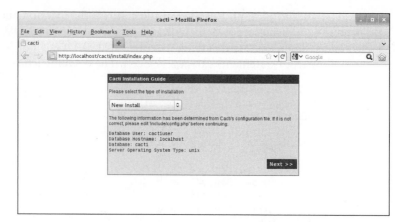

Figure 17-8 The Cacti Installation Guide screen

The next screen displays several pathnames and information about which versions of Net-SNMP and RRDTool are installed. Review this information and click **Finish**.

Next Cacti displays the User Login screen. Log in with the username **admin** and the password **admin**. Cacti then forces you to change the password for the **cacti** database user named **admin**. After you change the password, Cacti displays the main Console screen (Figure 17-9). The name of the screen appears just below the Console tab at the upper-left corner of the screen.

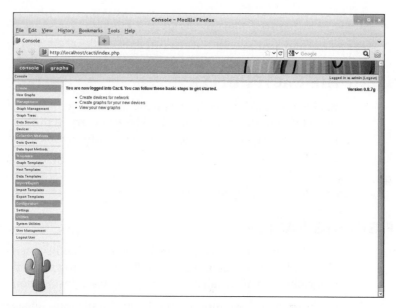

Figure 17-9 The Cacti main Console screen

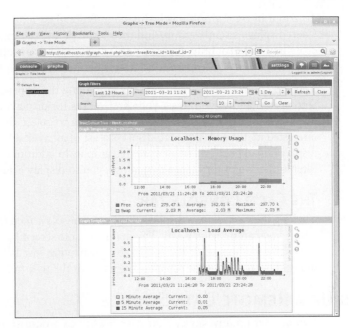

Figure 17-10 Default graphs for **localhost**

BASIC CACTI ADMINISTRATION

By default, Cacti collects data from **localhost** (the system it is installed on). After a few poller cycles have passed (approximately 15 minutes after you added the **crond** job for Cacti), Cacti will display this information. You must install **snmpd** on the local system if you want to monitor the local system (next page).

You must install **snmpd** on the local system to monitor the local system

tip You must install and configure **snmpd** on the local system, just as you would on a remote system, if you want to monitor the local system. For more information refer to "Setting Up a Remote Data Source" on the next page.

From the main Console screen, click **View your new graphs** or click the Graphs tab at the top of the screen. Cacti displays the default graphs in tree mode for **localhost** (Figure 17-10).

Cacti creates graphs for the following data sources: memory usage, load average, logged-in users, and number of processes. If you click one of the graphs, Cacti displays a page with four graphs for the data source you clicked: daily, weekly, monthly, and yearly. These graphs will mostly be blank until Cacti collects sufficient data to fill them.

To store the data it collects and to display graphs, Cacti uses RRDTool. Cacti graphs show more detail over short time spans and less detail (averaged, or otherwise aggregated) over longer time spans.

To zoom in on a graph, click the magnifying glass icon on the right side of a graph; Cacti displays a single graph, and the mouse pointer changes to a cross hairs. Drag the cross hairs horizontally over the part of the graph that represents the time period you are interested in. In response, Cacti regenerates the graph for that time period.

You can control the graphs using the tabs along the upper-right edge of the screen. The Settings tab allows you to set your preferences for displaying graphs; the Tree View tab displays a hierarchy of graphs, allowing you to select the devices or graphs you are interested in; the List View tab displays a list of all available graphs; and the Preview tab displays small previews of all available graphs. In addition, each of these tabs provides a filter at the top of the screen that allows you to display a subset of graphs.

THE CACTI CONSOLE TAB

Clicking the Console tab displays the main Console screen (Figure 17-9; page 662) from which you can manage Cacti. The main Console screen has a menu on the left side and shows the pathname of the screen it is displaying just below the Console tab. At the upper-right corner of the screen is the name of the user (**admin**) and a Logout button.

SETTING UP A REMOTE DATA SOURCE

You can set up any device that runs SNMP as a data source that Cacti can monitor and report on. This section explains how to set up a remote system on the local network as a data source and how to set up Cacti to monitor that source. Setting up a local data source is similar to setting up a remote data source.

PREREQUISITES

Install the following packages on the remote system that Cacti will monitor. You must install and configure these packages on the local system if you want to monitor the local system; they are not installed with the **cacti** package.

- **net-snmp**

- **net-snmp-utils** (optional)

snmpd.conf The **/etc/snmp/snmpd.conf** file controls the **snmpd** daemon. Save the installed **snmpd.conf** file so you can refer to it later. Set up the following **snmpd.conf** file, which sets the SNMP community to **public** and allows queries from **localhost** and **172.16.192.151** (the system running Cacti; replace this address with that of the local Cacti server):

```
$ cat /etc/snmp/snmpd.conf
rocommunity public localhost
rocommunity public 172.16.192.151
```

Run chkconfig to cause **snmpd** to start when the system enters multiuser mode:

```
# chkconfig snmpd on
```

/etc/default/snmpd Under Ubuntu and other Debian-based systems, the **/etc/default/snmpd** file controls various aspects of the **snmpd** daemon. For example, it specifies which address(es) **snmpd** listens for queries on. Fedora/RHEL systems do not use this file. You must

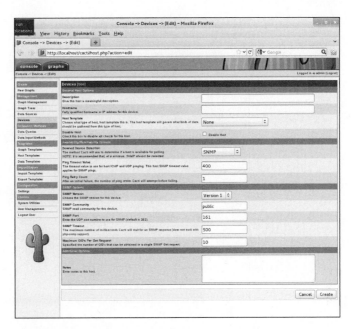

Figure 17-11   Adding a new device

edit the following line, which specifies the options **snmpd** is run with, if you want **snmpd** to listen for queries from a remote system:

```
$ cat /etc/default/snmpd
...
SNMPDOPTS='-Lsd -Lf /dev/null -u snmp -g snmp -I -smux -p /var/run/snmpd.pid 127.0.0.1'
...
```

Change the **127.0.0.1** to the IP address of the local system, as this is the address the system running Cacti will query the local system on. If you do not make this change, the local system will not respond to **snmpd** queries from a remote system.

Firewall If the local system is running a firewall, see page 659.

snmpd init script Use **service** to start the **snmpd** daemon.

ADDING A DEVICE

In the Web browser connected to Cacti, click the **Console** tab and select **Configuration⇨Settings** and then click the **General** tab and select **Version 1** from the drop-down list labeled **SNMP Version** (not **SNMP Utility Version**). By default, SNMP runs with community set to **public**; do not change this setting unless you have reason to do so. Click **Save**.

Next select **Management⇨Devices** and click the word **Add** (it is small) at the upper-right corner of the screen. Alternatively, you can select **Create⇨New Graphs** and then click **Create New Host**. Cacti displays a screen that allows you to specify a new device (Figure 17-11).

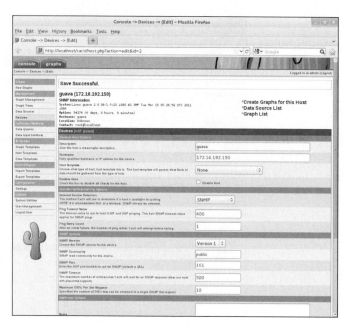

Figure 17-12   Information about the new system

If you have set the SNMP Version as just explained (i.e., Version 1), the SNMP settings will appear as shown in Figure 17-11 (previous page). Fill in the text box labeled **Description** with an appropriate description of the system to be monitored. Enter the IP address or fully qualified domain name in the text box labeled **Hostname**. Select an appropriate item from the drop-down list labeled **Host Template**. The example uses **Generic SNMP-enabled Host**. Alternatively, you can use **Local Linux Machine**. Make sure **Downed Device Detection** is set to **SNMP** and **SNMP Version** is set to **Version 1**. Click **Create**.

Cacti uses SNMP to collect information from the device. If all goes well, it will report **Save Successful** and display the information about the new system near the top of the screen (Figure 17-12).

Creating a graph
Click **Create Graphs for this Host**. Cacti displays the Create New Graph page, which holds a drop-down list labeled **Create**. Select a type of graph to create from the drop-down list (e.g., Unix—Load Average) and click **Create**. Cacti displays a message at the top of the screen that tells you which graphs it created (Figure 17-13). Repeat for each graph you want to create.

Adding a node to the graph tree
Select **Management⇨Graph Trees** and click **Add** to add a node to the graph tree. Enter a name for the new node (e.g., **Servers**) and click **Create**.

Now click **Add** (on the right) to add a Tree Item, select Host from the drop-down list labeled **Tree Item Type**, select the host you just added (Cacti might add **Host** for you), and click **Create**.

Wait
Take a break for 10 or 15 minutes to allow Cacti to poll the new device a few times.

Displaying the graph
Click the **Graphs** tab. The name for the new node appears in the device tree on the left side of the screen. When you click the plus sign (**+**) that appears to the left of the

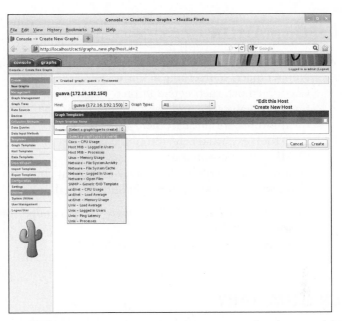

Figure 17-13   A list of queries and data sources for the new device

node name, Cacti expands the tree and displays the node you just added. Click the node name to display the graphs for that device (Figure 17-14).

You can now browse through the graphs that are being generated, choose time periods you are interested in, and learn more about the behavior of the devices and networks.

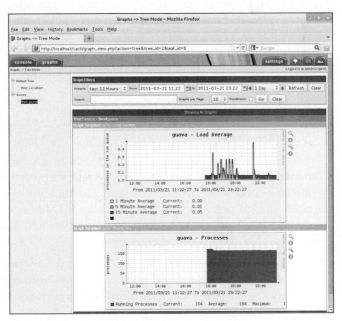

Figure 17-14   Cacti graphs for new devices

MORE INFORMATION

Web   Router operating systems: www.smoothwall.org, www.pfsense.com, m0n0.ch/wall
NdisWrapper: sourceforge.net/projects/ndiswrapper
Cacti: cacti.net, cacti.net/additional_scripts.php
Cacti manual: cacti.net/downloads/docs/html
Cacti forums: forums.cacti.net
RRDTool: oss.oetiker.ch/rrdtool
SNMP: www.net-snmp.org
Hardware compatibility list: hardware.redhat.com
HAL: www.freedesktop.org/wiki/Software/hal

HOWTOs   *Linux Wireless Lan HOWTO:* www.hpl.hp.com/personal/Jean_Tourrilhes/Linux
Wireless HOWTO
Linux Hardware Compatibility HOWTO

CHAPTER SUMMARY

A local area network (LAN) connects computers at one site and can allow the connected computers to share an Internet connection, files, and a printer. Each system, or node, on a LAN must have a network interface card (NIC). NICs can be connected to the network via cables (wired) or radio waves (wireless).

An Ethernet-based LAN has a connection between each computer and a central hub or switch. Hubs are generally slower than switches, but either is usually satisfactory for a small LAN. A wireless access point (WAP) connects a wireless network to a wired one. If the LAN you are setting up is connected to another network, such as the Internet, the LAN requires a router. A router can perform several functions, the most common of which is allowing several systems to share a single Internet connection and IP address; this function is called NAT.

Several tools are useful when you are setting up a LAN. In particular, the Network Connections window (nm-connection-editor) and the nm-applet enable you to configure NICs (wired or wireless).

You can configure the systems on the LAN to use NIS as a login server so you do not have to set up accounts on each system. You can use NFS, which allows you to mount remote directory hierarchies, to set up a universal home directory. Samba is an important part of many LANs: It allows Linux systems to participate in a Windows network, sharing directories and printers and accessing those directories and printers shared by Windows systems.

Cacti is a network monitoring tool that graphs system and network information over time and provides a comprehensive Web interface for browsing and examining the ongoing performance of the devices on a network.

EXERCISES

1. What advantage does a switch have over a hub?

2. Which server would you set up to allow users to log in with the same username and password on all computers on a LAN?

3. Name two servers that allow you to share directories between systems.

4. What is a WAP, and what does it do?

5. What is a common function of a router? What is this function called?

6. What does a wireless bridge do?

7. Which tool can you use to configure a wireless NIC (rather than having it be configured automatically)?

8. What is the private address space? When would you use a private address?

ADVANCED EXERCISES

9. If you set a system's network mask to 255.255.255.0, how many computers can you put on the network without using a router?

10. Which file stores information about which DNS servers the system uses?

PART V

Using Clients and Setting Up Servers

18

OpenSSH: Secure Network Communication

OBJECTIVES

After reading this chapter you should be able to:

▶ Explain the need for encrypted services

▶ Log in on a remote OpenSSH server system using ssh

▶ Copy files and directories to and from a remote system securely

▶ Set up an OpenSSH server

▶ Configure OpenSSH server options

▶ Set up a client/server so you do not need to use a password to log in using ssh or scp

▶ Enable trusted X11 tunneling between the client and the OpenSSH server

▶ Remove a known host record from the **~/.ssh/known_hosts** file

▶ Use ssh and scp without password authentication

▶ Enable trusted X11 forwarding

▶ List the uses of ssh tunneling (port forwarding)

OpenSSH is a suite of secure network connectivity tools that replaces telnet/**telnetd**, rcp, rsh/**rshd**, rlogin/**rlogind**, and ftp/**ftpd**. Unlike the tools they replace, OpenSSH tools encrypt all traffic, including passwords. In this way they can thwart malicious users who attempt to eavesdrop, hijack connections, and steal passwords.

This chapter covers the following OpenSSH tools:

- scp—Copies files to and from a remote system
- sftp—Copies files to and from a remote system (a secure replacement for ftp)
- ssh—Runs a command on or logs in on a remote system
- **sshd**—The OpenSSH daemon (runs on the server)
- ssh-keygen—Creates, manages, and converts RSA or DSA host/user authentication keys

INTRODUCTION TO OPENSSH

Using public key encryption (page 1127), OpenSSH provides two levels of authentication: server and client/user. First the client verifies it is connected to the correct server. Then OpenSSH encrypts communication between the systems. When a secure, encrypted connection has been established, OpenSSH makes sure the user is authorized to log in on or copy files to and from the server. After verifying the system and user, OpenSSH allows different services to be passed through the connection. These services include interactive shell sessions (ssh), remote command execution (ssh), file copying (scp), FTP services (sftp), X11 client/server connections, and TCP/IP port tunneling.

SSH1 versus SSH2   SSH protocol version 2 (SSH2) is a complete rewrite of SSH protocol version 1 (SSH1) that offers improved security, performance, and portability. The two protocols are not compatible. Because SSH1 is being rapidly supplanted by SSH2 and because SSH1 is vulnerable to a man-in-the-middle attack (page 1130), this chapter does not discuss SSH1. Because version 2 is floating-point intensive, version 1 does have a place on systems without FPUs (floating-point units or accelerators), such as old 486SX systems. As installed, the OpenSSH tools supplied with Fedora/RHEL support both protocols; you need run only one server to communicate with systems using either protocol.

ssh   The ssh utility allows you to log in on a remote system over a network. You might choose to use a remote system to access a special-purpose application or to take advantage of a device that is available only on that system, or you might use a remote system because you know it is faster or less busy than the local system. While traveling, many businesspeople use ssh on a laptop to log in on a system at company headquarters. From a GUI you can use several systems simultaneously by logging in on each one from a different terminal emulator window.

X11 forwarding   When you turn on trusted X11 forwarding on an ssh client, it is a simple matter to run a graphical program over an ssh connection to a server that has X11 forwarding enabled: Run ssh from a terminal emulator running on an X11 server and give an X11 command such as **gnome-calculator**; the graphical output appears on the local display. For more information refer to "Forwarding X11" on page 696.

HOW OPENSSH WORKS

When OpenSSH starts, it first establishes an encrypted connection and then authenticates the user. When these two tasks are complete, OpenSSH allows the two systems to send information back and forth.

keys   OpenSSH uses a *host key* pair and a *session key* to negotiate an encrypted session. The host key pair is a set of public/private keys that is established the first time the server system runs **sshd** (page 688). The session key is a symmetric key that the server and client share. For more information on keys see "Encryption" on page 1126.

The first time an OpenSSH client connects with an OpenSSH server, OpenSSH asks you to verify the client is connected to the correct server (see "First-time authentication" on page 679). This verification helps prevent a man-in-the-middle attack (page 1130). After verification, the client makes a copy of the server's public host key. On subsequent connections, the client compares the key provided by the server with the original key it stored. Although this test is not foolproof, the next one is quite secure.

The client then generates a random key, which it encrypts with both the server's public host key and the session key. The client sends this encrypted key to the server. The server, in turn, uses its private keys to decrypt the encrypted key. This process creates the session key, a key that is known only to the client and the server and is used to encrypt the rest of the session.

FILES

OpenSSH clients and servers rely on many files. Global files are kept in **/etc/ssh** and user files in **~/.ssh**. In this section, the first word in the description of each file indicates whether the client or the server uses the file.

rhost authentication is a security risk

security   Although OpenSSH can get authentication information from **/etc/hosts.equiv**, **/etc/shosts.equiv**, **~/.rhosts**, and **~/.shosts**, this chapter does not cover the use of these files because they present security risks. The default settings in the **/etc/ssh/sshd_config** configuration file prevent their use.

/etc/ssh: GLOBAL FILES

Global files listed in this section appear in the **/etc/ssh** directory. They affect all users, but a user can override them with files in her **~/.ssh** directory.

moduli **client and server**   Contains key exchange information that OpenSSH uses to establish a secure connection. Do not modify this file.

ssh_config **client**   The global OpenSSH configuration file (page 686). Entries here can be overridden by entries in a user's **~/.ssh/config** file.

sshd_config **server**   The configuration file for **sshd** (page 692).

ssh_host_dsa_key,
ssh_host_dsa_key.pub

server   SSH protocol version 2 DSA host keys. Both files should be owned by **root**. The **ssh_host_dsa_key.pub** public file should be readable by anyone but writable only by its owner (644 permissions). The **ssh_host_dsa_key** private file should not be readable or writable by anyone except its owner (600 permissions).

ssh_host_key,
ssh_host_key.pub

server   SSH protocol version 1 host keys. Both files should be owned by **root**. The **ssh_host_key.pub** public file should be readable by anyone but writable only by its owner (644 permissions). The **ssh_host_key** private file should not be readable or writable by anyone except its owner (600 permissions).

ssh_host_rsa_key,
ssh_host_rsa_key.pub

server   SSH protocol version 2 RSA host keys. Both files should be owned by **root**. The **ssh_host_rsa_key.pub** public file should be readable by anyone but writable only by its owner (644 permissions). The **ssh_host_rsa_key** private file should not be readable or writable by anyone except its owner (600 permissions).

ssh_known_hosts

client   Contains public RSA (by default) keys of hosts that users on the local system can connect to. This file contains information similar to that found in **~/.ssh/known_hosts** but is set up by the administrator and is available to all users. This file should be owned by **root** and should be readable by anyone but writable only by its owner (644 permissions).

~/.ssh: USER FILES

OpenSSH creates the **~/.ssh** directory and the **known_hosts** file therein automatically when a user connects to a remote system.

authorized_keys **server**   Enables a user to log in on or copy files to and from another system without supplying a user login password (page 689). However, the user might need to supply a passphrase, depending on how the key was set up. No one except the owner should be able to write to this file.

config **client**   A user's private OpenSSH configuration file (page 686). Entries here override those in **/etc/ssh/ssh_config**.

environment **server**   Contains assignment statements that define environment variables on a server when a user logs in using **ssh**.

id_dsa, **client** User authentication DSA keys generated by ssh-keygen (page 689). Both
id_dsa.pub files should be owned by the user in whose home directory they appear. The
id_dsa.pub public file should be readable by anyone but writable only by its owner
(644 permissions). The **id_dsa** private file should not be readable or writable by
anyone except its owner (600 permissions).

id_rsa, **client** User authentication RSA keys generated by ssh-keygen (page 689). Both
id_rsa.pub files should be owned by the user in whose home directory they appear. The
id_rsa.pub public file should be readable by anyone but writable only by its owner
(644 permissions). The **id_rsa** private file should not be readable or writable by
anyone except its owner (600 permissions).

known_hosts **client** Contains public RSA keys (by default) of hosts the user has connected to.
OpenSSH automatically adds entries each time the user connects to a new server
(page 678). Refer to "HostKeyAlgorithms" (page 687) for information on using
DSA keys. If **HashKnownHosts** (page 687) is set to **yes**, the hostnames and
addresses in this file are hashed to improve security.

MORE INFORMATION

Local man pages: ssh, scp, sftp, ssh-keygen, ssh_config, sshd, sshd_config

Web OpenSSH home page: www.openssh.com
Search on **ssh** to find various HOWTOs and other documents: tldp.org

Books *Implementing SSH: Strategies for Optimizing the Secure Shell* by Dwivedi; John
Wiley & Sons (October 2003)
SSH, The Secure Shell: The Definitive Guide by Barrett, Silverman, & Byrnes;
O'Reilly Media (May 2005)

RUNNING THE ssh, scp, AND sftp OpenSSH CLIENTS

This section covers setting up and using the ssh, scp, and sftp clients.

PREREQUISITES

Install the following package (both are installed by default):

- **openssh**
- **openssh-clients**

There is no **init** script for OpenSSH clients.

JUMPSTART: USING ssh AND scp TO CONNECT TO AN OpenSSH SERVER

The ssh and scp clients do not require setup beyond installing the requisite packages,
although you can create and edit files that facilitate their use. To run a secure shell on or

securely copy a file to or from a remote system, the following criteria must be met: The remote system must be running the OpenSSH daemon (**sshd**), you must have an account on the remote system, and the server must positively identify itself to the client.

ssh   The following example shows Zach using ssh to log in on the remote host named **plum**, running who, and finally giving an **exit** command to return to the shell on the local system. The who utility displays the IP address of the system Zach logged in from.

```
$ ssh zach@plum
zach@plum's password:
[zach@plum ~]$ who am i
zach      pts/2        2010-12-03 11:43 (172.16.192.150)
[zach@plum ~]$ exit
logout
Connection to plum closed.
```

You can omit *user@* (**zach@** in the preceding example) from the command line if you want to log in as yourself and you have the same username on both systems. The first time you connect to a remote OpenSSH server, ssh or scp asks you to confirm that you are connected to the right system. Refer to "First-time authentication" on page 679.

scp   The following example uses scp to copy **ty1** from the working directory on the local system to Zach's home directory on **plum**:

```
$ scp ty1 zach@plum:
zach@plum's password:
ty1                                        100%  162     0.2KB/s    00:00
```

Remember to follow the system name with a colon (**:**). If you omit the colon, scp copies the file locally; in the example you would end up with a copy of **ty1** named **zach@plum**.

CONFIGURING OPENSSH CLIENTS

This section describes how to set up OpenSSH on the client side.

RECOMMENDED SETTINGS

X11 forwarding   The configuration files provided by Fedora/RHEL establish a mostly secure system that might or might not meet your needs. One OpenSSH parameter you might want to change is ForwardX11Trusted, which is set to **yes** in the **/etc/ssh/ssh_config** configuration file (page 686). To increase security, and in some cases reduce usability, set ForwardX11Trusted to **no**. See page 696 for more information on X11 forwarding.

SERVER AUTHENTICATION/KNOWN HOSTS

Two files list the hosts the local system has connected to and positively identified: **~/.ssh/known_hosts** (user) and **/etc/ssh/ssh_known_hosts** (global). No one except the owner (**root** in the case of the second file) should be able to write to either of these files. No one except the owner should have any access to a **~/.ssh** directory.

First-time authentication When you connect to an OpenSSH server for the first time, the OpenSSH client prompts you to confirm that you are connected to the right system. This behavior is controlled by **StrictHostKeyChecking** (page 687). This check can help prevent a man-in-the-middle attack (page 1130):

```
The authenticity of host 'plum (172.16.192.151)' can't be established.
RSA key fingerprint is d1:9d:1b:5b:97:5c:80:e9:4b:41:9a:b7:bc:1a:ea:a1.
Are you sure you want to continue connecting (yes/no)? yes
Warning: Permanently added 'plum,172.16.192.151' (RSA) to the list of
known hosts.
```

Before you respond to the preceding query, make sure you are logging in on the correct system and not on an imposter. If you are not sure, a telephone call to someone who logs in on that system locally can help verify that you are on the intended system. When you answer **yes** (you must spell it out), the client appends the server's public host key (the single line in the **/etc/ssh/ssh_host_rsa_key.pub** or **/etc/ssh/ssh_host_dsa_key.pub** file on the server) to the user's **~/.ssh/known_hosts** file on the local system, creating the **~/.ssh** directory if necessary. So that it can keep track of which line in **known_hosts** applies to which server, OpenSSH prepends the name of the server and the server's IP address to the line.

When you subsequently use OpenSSH to connect to that server, the client verifies it is connected to the correct server by comparing this key to the one supplied by the server.

known_hosts file The **~/.ssh/known_hosts** file uses one or two very long lines to identify each host it keeps track of. Each line starts with the hostname and IP address of the system the line corresponds to, followed by the type of encryption being used and the server's public host key. When **HashKnownHosts** (page 687) is set to **yes** (the default is **no**), OpenSSH hashes the system name and address to improve security. Because **HashKnownHosts** hashes the hostname and IP address separately, OpenSSH puts two lines in **known_hosts** for each host. The following line (it is one logical line that wraps on to several physical lines) from **known_hosts** is used to connect to **plum** at 172.16.192.151 using *RSA* (page 1186) encryption:

```
$ cat ~/.ssh/known_hosts
plum,172.16.192.151 ssh-rsa AAAAB3NzaC1yc2EAAAADAQABAAABAQDbhLRVTfI
v9gy7oP+5T3HjZmrKt2q6ydyKmLlHNUjZFXM4hCdkJlpTfJ4wy260UAZBWvrBLP6N9k
...
```

You can use ssh-keygen with the **–R** option followed by the hostname to remove an entry, even a hashed one. Alternatively, you can use a text editor to remove an entry. The **–F** option to ssh-keygen displays a line in a **known_hosts** file that corresponds to a specified system, even if the entry is hashed:

```
$ ssh-keygen -F plum
# Host plum found: line 1 type RSA
plum ssh-rsa AAAAB3NzaC1yc2EAAAADAQABAAABAQDbhLRVTfIv9gy7oP+5T3HjZmr
Kt2q6ydyKmLlHNUjZFXM4hCdkJlpTfJ4wy260UAZBWvrBLP6N9kYA+KRG1FyuwROUwXQ
...
```

ssh_known_hosts OpenSSH automatically stores keys from servers it has connected to in user-private files (*~/.ssh/known_hosts*). These files work only for the user whose directory they appear in. Working with **root** privileges and using a text editor, you can copy nonhashed lines from a user's private list of known hosts to the public list in **/etc/ssh/ssh_known_hosts** to make a server known globally on the local system.

The following example shows how Sam puts the hashed entry from his **known_hosts** file into the global **ssh_known_hosts** file. First, working as himself, Sam sends the output of ssh-keygen through tail to strip off the **Host plum found** line and redirects the output to a file named **tmp_known_hosts** in his home directory. Next, working with **root** privileges, Sam appends the contents of the file he just created to **/etc/ssh/ssh_known_hosts**. This command creates this file if it does not exist. Finally, Sam returns to working as himself and removes the temporary file he created.

```
$ ssh-keygen -F plum | tail -1 > ~sam/tmp_known_hosts
$ su
Password:
# cat ~sam/tmp_known_hosts >> /etc/ssh/ssh_known_hosts
# exit
exit
$ rm ~/tmp_known_hosts
```

If, after a remote system's public key is stored in one of the known-hosts files, the remote system supplies a different fingerprint when the systems connect, OpenSSH displays the following message and does not complete the connection:

```
@@@@@@@@@@@@@@@@@@@@@@@@@@@@@@@@@@@@@@@@@@@@@@@@@@@@@@@@@@@
@    WARNING: REMOTE HOST IDENTIFICATION HAS CHANGED!     @
@@@@@@@@@@@@@@@@@@@@@@@@@@@@@@@@@@@@@@@@@@@@@@@@@@@@@@@@@@@
IT IS POSSIBLE THAT SOMEONE IS DOING SOMETHING NASTY!
Someone could be eavesdropping on you right now (man-in-the-middle attack)!
It is also possible that the RSA host key has just been changed.
The fingerprint for the RSA key sent by the remote host is
f1:6f:ea:87:bb:1b:df:cd:e3:45:24:60:d3:25:b1:0a.
Please contact your system administrator.
Add correct host key in /home/sam/.ssh/known_hosts to get rid of this message.
Offending key in /home/sam/.ssh/known_hosts:1
RSA host key for plum has changed and you have requested strict checking.
Host key verification failed.
```

If you see this message, you might be the subject of a man-in-the-middle attack. More likely, however, something on the remote system has changed, causing it to supply a new fingerprint. Check with the remote system's administrator. If all is well, remove the offending key from the specified file (the third line from the bottom in the preceding message points to the line you need to remove) and try connecting again. You can use ssh-keygen with the **–R** option followed by the name of a host to remove a hashed entry. You will be subject to first-time authentication (page 679) again as OpenSSH verifies you are connecting to the correct system. Follow the same steps as when you initially connected to the remote host.

ssh: LOGS IN OR EXECUTES COMMANDS ON A REMOTE SYSTEM

The format of an ssh command line is

ssh [options] [user@]host [command]

where *host,* the name of the OpenSSH server (the remote system) you want to connect to, is the only required argument. The *host* can be a local system name, the *FQDN* (page 1165) of a system on the Internet, or an IP address.

With the command **ssh *host,*** you log in on the remote system *host* with the same username you are using on the local system. The remote system displays a shell prompt, and you can run commands on *host.* Enter the command **exit** to close the connection to *host* and return to the local system's prompt. Include *user@* when you want to log in with a username other than the one you are using on the local system. Depending on how the server is set up, you might need to supply the password you use on the remote system.

When you include *command,* ssh logs in on *host,* executes *command,* closes the connection to *host,* and returns control to the local system. The remote system never displays a shell prompt.

Opening a remote shell

In the following example, Sam, who is logged in on **guava,** uses ssh to log in on **plum,** gives a **uname** command that shows the name and type of the system, and uses **exit** to close the connection to **plum** and return to the local system's prompt:

```
[sam@guava ~]$ ssh plum
sam@plum's password:
[sam@plum ~]$ uname -nm
plum i686
[sam@plum ~]$ exit
logout
Connection to plum closed.
[sam@guava ~]$
```

Running commands remotely

The following example uses ls to display a listing of the files in the **memos** directory on the remote system **plum.** The example assumes the user running the command (Sam) has a login on **plum** and that the **memos** directory is in Sam's home directory on **plum:**

```
$ ssh plum ls memos
sam@plum's password:
memo.0921
memo.draft
$
```

When you run ssh, standard output of the command run on the remote system is passed to the local shell as though the command had been run on the local system. As with all shell commands, you must quote special characters you do not want the local shell to interpret.

In the next example, standard output of the ls command, which is run on the remote system, is sent to **ls.out** on the local system.

```
$ ssh plum ls memos > ls.out
sam@plum's password:
$ cat ls.out
memo.0921
memo.draft
```

In the preceding ssh command the redirect symbol (>) is not quoted, so it is interpreted by the local shell and creates the **ls.out** file on the local system.

The next command is similar, but the redirect symbol is quoted, so the local shell does not interpret it but passes it to the remote shell. The first command creates the **ls.out2** file on the remote system, and the second command displays the file.

```
$ ssh plum 'ls memos > ls.out2'
sam@plum's password:
$ ssh plum cat ls.out2
sam@plum's password:
memo.0921
memo.draft
```

For the next example, assume the working directory on the local system holds a file named **memo.new**. You cannot remember whether this file contains certain changes or whether you made these changes to the file named **memo.draft** in the **memos** directory on **plum**. You could copy **memo.draft** to the local system and run diff (page 154) on the two files, but then you would have three similar copies of the file spread across two systems. If you are not careful about removing the old copies when you are done, you might just become confused again in a few days. Instead of copying the file, you can use ssh. This example shows that only the date line differs between the two files:

```
$ ssh plum cat memos/memo.draft | diff memo.new -
sam@plum's password:
1c1
< Fri Dec  4 12:06:22 PST 2010
---
> Fri Dec  3 14:27:06 PST 2010
```

In the preceding example, the output of the cat command on **plum** is sent through a pipe on the local system to diff (running on the local system), which compares the local file **memos.new** to standard input (–). The following command line has the same effect but causes diff to run on the remote system:

```
$ cat memo.new | ssh plum diff - memos/memo.draft
sam@plum's password:
1c1
< Fri Dec  4 12:06:22 PST 2010
---
> Fri Dec  3 14:27:06 PST 2010
```

Standard output from diff on the remote system is sent to the local shell, which displays it on the screen (because it is not redirected).

OPTIONS

This section describes some of the options you can use with ssh.

–C (**compression**) Enables compression (page 698). In the commercial version of ssh, –C disables compression and +C enables compression.

–f (**not foreground**) Sends ssh to the background after asking for a password and before executing the *command*. Useful when you want to run the *command* in the background but must supply a password. Implies **–n**.

–L Forwards a port on the local system to a remote system. For more information refer to "Tunneling/Port Forwarding" on page 696.

–l *user* (**login**) Attempts to log in as *user*.

–n (**null**) Redirects standard input to ssh to come from **/dev/null**. Required when running ssh in the background (**–f** option).

–o *option* (**option**) Specifies *option* in the format used in configuration files (page 686).

–p (**port**) Specifies the port on the remote host that the connection is made to. Using the **host** declaration (page 687) in the configuration file, you can specify a different port for each system you connect to.

–R Forwards a port on the remote system to the local client. For more information refer to "Tunneling/Port Forwarding" on page 696.

–t (**tty**) Allocates a pseudo-tty (terminal) to the ssh process on the remote system. Without this option, when you run a command on a remote system, ssh does not allocate a tty (terminal) to the process. Instead, it attaches standard input and standard output of the remote process to the ssh session—which is normally, but not always, what you want. This option forces ssh to allocate a tty on the remote system so programs that require a tty will work.

–v (**verbose**) Displays debugging messages about the connection and transfer. Useful if things are not going as expected. Repeat this option up to a total of three times to increase verbosity.

–X (**X11**) Turns on nontrusted X11 forwarding. This option is not necessary if you turn on X11 nontrusted forwarding in the configuration file. For more information refer to "Forwarding X11" on page 696.

–x (**X11**) Turns off X11 forwarding.

–Y (**X11trusted**) Turns on trusted X11 forwarding. This option is not necessary if you turn on trusted X11 forwarding in the configuration file. For more information refer to "Forwarding X11" on page 696.

scp: COPIES FILES TO AND FROM A REMOTE SYSTEM

The scp (secure copy) utility copies an ordinary or directory file from one system to another over a network; both systems can be remote. This utility uses ssh to transfer files and employs the same authentication mechanism as ssh; thus it provides the same security as ssh. The scp utility asks for a password when one is required. The format of an scp command is

scp [[user@]from-host:]source-file [[user@]to-host:][destination-file] where *from-host* is the name of the system you are copying files from and *to-host* is the system you are copying to. The *from-host* and *to-host* arguments can be local system names, *FQDNs* (page 1165) of systems on the Internet, or IP addresses. When you do not specify a host, scp assumes the local system. The *user* on either system defaults to the user on the local system who is giving the command; you can specify a different user with *user@*.

The *source-file* is the file you are copying, and the *destination-file* is the resulting copy. Make sure you have read permission for the file you are copying and write permission for the directory you are copying it into. You can specify plain or directory files as relative or absolute pathnames. (A relative pathname is relative to the specified directory or to the implicit user's home directory.) When the *source-file* is a directory, you must use the **–r** option to copy its contents. When the *destination-file* is a directory, each of the source files maintains its simple filename. When the *destination-file* is missing, scp assumes the user's home directory.

Suppose Sam has an alternate username, **sls**, on **plum**. In the following example, Sam uses scp to copy **memo.txt** from the home directory of his **sls** account on **plum** to the **allmemos** directory in the working directory on the local system. If **allmemos** were not the name of a directory, **memo.txt** would be copied to a file named **allmemos** in the working directory.

```
[sam@guava ~]$ scp sls@plum:memo.txt allmemos
sls@plum's password:
memo.txt                                       100%    12KB   12.3KB/s    00:00
```

As the transfer progresses, the percentage and number of bytes transferred increase, and the time remaining decreases.

rsync **is much more versatile than** scp

tip The rsync utility is more configurable than scp and uses OpenSSH security by default. It has many options; the most commonly used are **–a** and **–v**. The **–a** option causes rsync to copy ordinary files and directories, preserving the ownership, group, permissions, and modification times associated with the files. It usually does no harm to specify the **–a** option and frequently helps. The **–v** option causes rsync to list files as it copies them. For example, Sam could have given the preceding command as

```
$ rsync -av sls@plum:memo.txt allmemos
sls@plum's password:
receiving incremental file list
memo.txt

sent 30 bytes  received 87495 bytes  19450.00 bytes/sec
total size is 87395  speedup is 1.00
```

The rsync utility is also smarter than scp. If the source and destination files exist, rsync copies only the parts of the source file that are different from the destination file. This feature can save a lot of time when copying large files with few changes, such as when making backups. The number following **speedup** in the output indicates how much rsync's algorithm has speeded up the process of copying a file.

In the next example, Sam, while working from **guava**, copies the same file as in the previous example to the directory named **old** in his home directory on **speedy**. For this example to work, Sam must be able to use ssh to log in on **speedy** from **plum** without using a password. For more information refer to "Authorized Keys: Automatic Login" on page 689.

```
[sam@guava ~]$ scp sls@plum:memo.txt speedy:old
sls@plum's password:
```

OPTIONS

This section describes some of the options you can use with scp.

–C   (**compression**) Enables compression (page 698).

–o *option*   (**option**) Specifies *option* in the format used in configuration files (discussed shortly).

–P *port*   (**port**) Connects to port *port* on the remote host. This option is uppercase for scp and in lowercase for ssh.

–p   (**preserve**) Preserves the modification and access times as well as the modes of the original file.

–q   (**quiet**) Does not display the progress information as scp copies a file.

–r   (**recursive**) Recursively copies a directory hierarchy (follows symbolic links).

–v   (**verbose**) Displays debugging messages about the connection and transfer. Useful if things are not going as expected.

sftp: A SECURE FTP CLIENT

As part of OpenSSH, Fedora/RHEL provides sftp, a secure alternative to ftp (page 701). Functionally the same as ftp, sftp maps ftp commands to OpenSSH commands. You can replace ftp with sftp when you are logging in on a server that is running the OpenSSH daemon, sshd. When you are connected to a system with sftp, enter the command **?** to display a list of commands. For secure communication, use sftp or scp to perform all file transfers requiring authentication. Refer to the sftp man page for more information.

lftp   Fedora/RHEL also offers lftp, which is more sophisticated than sftp and supports sftp. The lftp utility provides a shell-like command syntax that has many features, including support for tab completion and the ability to run jobs in the background. Place the following **.lftprc** file in your home directory to ensure lftp uses OpenSSH to connect to a server.

```
$ cat ~/.lftprc
set default-protocol sftp
```

You can also use **/etc/lftp.conf** to configure lftp; see the lftp man page for more information.

~/.ssh/config AND /etc/ssh/ssh_config CONFIGURATION FILES

It is rarely necessary to modify OpenSSH client configuration files. For a given user there might be two configuration files: **~/.ssh/config** (user) and **/etc/ssh/ssh_config** (global). These files are read in this order and, for a given parameter, the first one found is the one OpenSSH uses. A user can override a global parameter setting by setting the same parameter in her user configuration file. Parameters given on the ssh or scp command line take precedence over parameters set in either of these files.

For security, a user's **~/.ssh/config** file should be owned by the user in whose home directory they appear and should not be writable by anyone except the owner. This file is typically set to mode 600 as there is no reason for anyone except its owner to be able to read it.

Lines in the configuration files contain declarations. Each of these declarations starts with a keyword that is not case sensitive. Some keywords must be followed by whitespace and one or more case-sensitive arguments. You can use the **Host** keyword to cause declarations to apply to a specific system. A Host declaration applies to all the lines between it and the next Host declaration.

Following are some of the keywords and arguments you can specify:

CheckHostIP yes | no

Identifies a remote system using the IP address in addition to a hostname from the **known_hosts** file when set to **yes**. Set it to **no** to use a hostname only. Setting CheckHostIP to **yes** can improve system security. Default is **yes**.

ForwardX11 yes | no

When set to **yes**, automatically forwards X11 connections over a secure channel in non-trusted mode and sets the **DISPLAY** shell variable. Fedora/RHEL allows this keyword to default to **no** so X11 forwarding is *not* initially enabled. If ForwardX11Trusted is also set to **yes**, the connections are made in trusted mode. Alternatively, you can use **–X** on the command line to redirect X11 connections in nontrusted mode. For X11 forwarding to work, you must also set X11Forwarding to **yes** in the **/etc/sshd_config** file on the server (page 694). For more information refer to "Forwarding X11" on page 696.

ForwardX11Trusted yes | no

Works in conjunction with ForwardX11, which must be set to **yes** for this keyword to have any effect. When this keyword is set to **yes** (as it is under Fedora/RHEL) and ForwardX11 is set to **yes**, this keyword gives remote X11 clients full access to the original (server) X11 display. Alternatively, you can use **–Y** on the command line to redirect X11 connections in trusted mode. For X11 forwarding to work, X11Forwarding must also be set to **yes** in the **/etc/sshd_config** file on the server (page 694). Default value is **no**, but Fedora/RHEL sets this keyword to **yes**. For more information refer to "Forwarding X11" on page 696.

HashKnownHosts

Causes OpenSSH to hash hostnames and addresses in the **~/.ssh/known_hosts** file when set to **yes**. When set to **no**, the hostnames and addresses are written in cleartext. Default is **no**. See page 679 for more information on the **known_hosts** file.

Host *hostnames*   Specifies that the following declarations, until the next Host declaration, apply only to hosts that *hostnames* matches. The *hostnames* is a whitespace-separated list that can include **?** and **✻** wildcards. A single **✻** specifies all hosts. Without this keyword, all declarations apply to all hosts.

HostbasedAuthentication yes | no

Tries **rhosts** authentication when set to **yes**. For a more secure system, set to **no**. Default is **no**.

HostKeyAlgorithms *algorithms*

The *algorithms* is a comma-separated list of algorithms the client uses in order of preference. Choose *algorithms* from **ssh-rsa** or **ssh-dss**. Default is **ssh-rsa,ssh-dss**.

Port *num*   Causes OpenSSH to connect to the remote system on port *num*. Default is 22.

StrictHostKeyChecking yes | no | ask

Determines whether and how OpenSSH adds host keys to a user's **known_hosts** file. Set this option to **ask** to ask whether to add a host key when connecting to a new system, set it to **no** to add a host key automatically, and set it to **yes** to require host keys to be added manually. The **yes** and **ask** arguments cause OpenSSH to refuse to connect to a system whose host key has changed. For a more secure system, set to **yes** or **ask**. Default is **ask**.

TCPKeepAlive yes | no

Periodically checks whether a connection is alive when set to **yes**. Checking causes the ssh or scp connection to be dropped when the server crashes or the connection dies for another reason, even if it is only temporary. This option tests the connection at the transport (TCP) layer (page 371). Setting this parameter to **no** causes the client not to check whether the connection is alive. Default is **yes**.

This declaration uses the TCP **keepalive** option, which is not encrypted and is susceptible to *IP spoofing* (page 1171). Refer to **ClientAliveInterval** on page 693 for a server-based nonspoofable alternative.

User *name*   Specifies a username to use when logging in on a system. You can specify a system with the Host declaration. This option means you do not have to enter a username on the command line when you are using a username that differs from your username on the local system.

VisualHostKey yes | no

Displays an ASCII art representation of the key of the remote system in addition to displaying the hexadecimal representation of the key when set to **yes**. When set to **no**, this declaration displays the hexadecimal key only. For more information refer to "Randomart" on page 691. Default is **no**.

Setting Up an OpenSSH Server (sshd)

This section describes how to set up an OpenSSH server.

Prerequisites

Install the following packages (both are installed by default):

- openssh
- openssh-server

Under Fedora (and not RHEL) you must run chkconfig to cause **sshd** to start when the system enters multiuser mode:

```
# chkconfig sshd on
```

sshd init script   Under Fedora (and not RHEL), after you configure the **sshd** server (you might not need to do anything), call the **sshd init** script to start the **sshd** daemon:

```
# service sshd start
```

After changing **sshd** configuration files, use **reload** in place of **start** to reload the **sshd** configuration files.

Under Fedora, when you start the **sshd** daemon for the first time it automatically creates host key files (page 675) in **/etc/ssh** (under RHEL **sshd** creates these files when the system is booted just after RHEL is installed). OpenSSH uses the files it creates to identify the server.

Notes

Firewall   An OpenSSH server normally uses TCP port 22. Under RHEL, this port is open when the system is installed. If the OpenSSH server system is running a firewall, you need to open this port. Using the Fedora graphical firewall tool (page 893), select **SSH** from the Trusted Services frame to open this port. The first time you run the graphical firewall tool, SSH is selected but not operative. Click **Disable, Enable,** and **Apply** to cause the system to accept inbound SSH packets.

SELinux   When SELinux is set to use a targeted policy, **sshd** is protected by SELinux. You can disable this protection if necessary. For more information refer to "Setting the Targeted Policy with system-config-selinux" on page 463.

JumpStart: Starting an OpenSSH Server

Install the requisite packages and start the OpenSSH server (**sshd**) daemon as described under "Install the following packages (both are installed by default):" (page 688). You can look in **/var/log/secure** and **/var/log/messages** to make sure everything is working properly.

RECOMMENDED SETTINGS

The configuration files provided by Fedora/RHEL establish a mostly secure system that might or might not meet your needs. The Fedora/RHEL **/etc/ssh/sshd_config** file turns on X11 forwarding (page 696). It is important to set PermitRootLogin (page 694) to **no**, which prevents a known-name, privileged account from being exposed to the outside world with only password protection.

AUTHORIZED KEYS: AUTOMATIC LOGIN

You can configure OpenSSH so you do not have to enter a password each time you connect to a server (remote system). To set up this feature, you need to generate a personal authentication key on the client (local system), place the public part of the key on the server, and keep the private part of the key on the client. When you connect to the server, it issues a challenge based on the public part of the key. OpenSSH then uses the private part of the key to respond to this challenge. If the client provides the appropriate response, the server logs you in.

The first step in setting up an automatic login is to generate your personal authentication keys. First check whether these authentication keys already exist on the local system (client) by looking in **~/.ssh** for either **id_dsa** and **id_dsa.pub** or **id_rsa** and **id_rsa.pub**. If one of these pairs of files is present, skip the next step (do not create a new key).

ssh-keygen   On the client, the ssh-keygen utility creates the public and private parts of an RSA key. The key's randomart image is a visual representation of the public key; see page 691.

```
$ ssh-keygen -t rsa
Generating public/private rsa key pair.
Enter file in which to save the key (/home/sam/.ssh/id_rsa):
Enter passphrase (empty for no passphrase):
Enter same passphrase again:
Your identification has been saved in /home/sam/.ssh/id_rsa.
Your public key has been saved in /home/sam/.ssh/id_rsa.pub.
The key fingerprint is:
23:8f:99:2e:43:36:93:ed:c6:38:fe:4d:04:61:27:28 sam@guava
The key's randomart image is:
+--[ RSA 2048]----+
|       .+ .       |
|   E .. +         |
|    .  .          |
|       .          |
|     o. S         |
|     * .B .       |
|    o *+ o        |
|     =.+o         |
|     ..*o .       |
+-----------------+
```

Replace **rsa** with **dsa** to generate DSA keys. In this example, the user pressed RETURN in response to each query. You have the option of specifying a passphrase (10–30 characters is a good length) to encrypt the private part of the key. There is no way to recover a lost passphrase. See the security tip on page 691 for more information about the passphrase.

The ssh-keygen utility generates two keys: a private key or identification in **~/.ssh/id_rsa** and a public key in **~/.ssh/id_rsa.pub**. No one except the owner should be able to write to either of these files, and only the owner should be able to read from the private key file.

You can display the local server's RSA key fingerprint using ssh-keygen:

```
$ ssh-keygen -lf /etc/ssh/ssh_host_rsa_key.pub
2048 d1:9d:1b:5b:97:5c:80:e9:4b:41:9a:b7:bc:1a:ea:a1 /etc/ssh/ssh_host_rsa_key.pub (RSA)
```

Or you can display the fingerprint of the public key you just created:

```
$ ssh-keygen -lf ~/.ssh/id_rsa.pub
2048 23:8f:99:2e:43:36:93:ed:c6:38:fe:4d:04:61:27:28 /home/sam/.ssh/id_rsa.pub (RSA)
```

ssh-copy-id   To log in on or copy files to and from another system without supplying a password, you must copy the **~/.ssh/id_rsa.pub** from the client (local system) to a file named **~/.ssh/authorized_keys** on the server (remote system). The ssh-copy-id utility creates the **~/.ssh** directory on the server if necessary, copies **id_rsa.pub**, and makes sure permissions are correct. The following example shows Sam setting up automatic login on the system named **plum**:

```
$ ssh-copy-id sam@plum
sam@plum's password:
Now try logging into the machine, with "ssh 'sam@plum'", and check in:

    .ssh/authorized_keys

to make sure we haven't added extra keys that you weren't expecting.

$ ssh sam@plum
$
```

Sam must supply his password to copy the file to **plum**. After running ssh-copy-id, Sam can log in on **plum** without providing a password. To make the server even more secure, disable password authentication (see the adjacent tip). Automatic login will fail if anyone other than the owner has permission to read from or write to the **~/.ssh** directory on the server.

Use a personal authentication key instead of a password

security   Using a personal authentication key is more secure than using a password. When you turn off password authentication, brute force authentication attacks become very unlikely.

Disable password authentication by setting **PasswordAuthentication** to **no** in **/etc/ssh/sshd_config** (remove the # from the beginning of the **PasswordAuthentication** line and change the **yes** to **no**; page 693).

Randomart   The *randomart* image of a system is an experimental OpenSSH ASCII visualization of the system's host key. This image is displayed by OpenSSH utilities, including ssh, scp, and ssh-keygen. Its display is controlled by the **VisualHostKey** keyword in the **ssh_config** file (page 687). With this keyword set to **yes**, OpenSSH displays a system's randomart image when you connect:

```
$ ssh plum
Host key fingerprint is 0b:90:12:02:97:fb:93:6e:d4:14:f8:e0:ac:f3:26:36
+--[ RSA 2048]----+
|+ o. .           |
| o..o..          |
|  .+oo .         |
|  ..o.o          |
|   o +. S        |
|  o = .. .       |
|   = . .         |
|  E =            |
|  . =            |
+-----------------+

sam@plum's password:
...
```

The randomart image renders a system's host key in a visual format that can be easier to recall than a host key fingerprint (see the preceding example). Making it easier for a user to detect a change in the fingerprint can mean that a user will be aware when he is connecting to a system other than the one he intended to connect to.

ssh-agent: HOLDS YOUR PRIVATE KEYS

Personal key encryption, passphrase, and ssh-agent

security   The private part of your personal authentication key is kept in a file that only you can read. When you set up automatic login on a remote system, any user who has access to your account on the local system also has access to your account on the remote system because that user can read the private part of your personal key. Thus, if a malicious user compromises your account or the **root** account on the local system, that user then has access to your account on the remote system.

Encrypting the private part of your personal key protects the key and, therefore, restricts access to the remote system should someone compromise your local account. However, if you encrypt your personal key, you must supply the passphrase you used to encrypt the key each time you use the key, negating the benefit of not having to type a password when logging in on the remote system.

You can use ssh-agent to remember the private part of your personal key for the duration of a session; you supply your passphrase once, at the beginning of the session.

Storing private keys on a removable medium

security   You can store the private keys on a removable medium, such as a USB flash drive, and use your **~/.ssh** directory as the mount point for the filesystem stored on this drive. You might want to encrypt these keys with a passphrase in case you lose the flash drive.

When you use ssh-keygen to generate a public/private key pair, you have the option of specifying a passphrase. If you specify a passphrase, you must supply that passphrase each time you use the key. The result is, when you set up a key pair to avoid specifying your password when you log in on a remote system using ssh, you end up supplying the passphrase instead.

The ssh-agent utility allows you to use a passphrase with your personal key while entering the key one time, at the beginning of each session. When you log out, ssh-agent forgets the key. Because Fedora/RHEL is set up with ssh-agent enabled for X sessions, it is very easy to use in a graphical environment. It is also easy to set up in a textual environment.

If you are running a textual session (not within a terminal emulator window), you must give the following command to enable ssh-agent. If you are running a graphical session, skip this step (ssh-agent is set up in the files in **/etc/X11/xinitrc**).

```
$ eval $(ssh-agent -s)
Agent pid 9882
```

ssh-add   Once ssh-agent is enabled, use ssh-add to specify the passphrase for a key pair:

```
$ ssh-add ~/.ssh/id_rsa
Enter passphrase for /home/sam/.ssh/id_rsa:
Identity added: /home/sam/.ssh/id_rsa (/home/sam/.ssh/id_rsa)
```

If you omit the argument to ssh-add, it adds a passphrase for each of the **~/.ssh/id_rsa**, **~/.ssh/id_dsa**, and **~/.ssh/identity** files that exist.

With this setup, you can use ssh to work on a remote system without supplying a login password and by supplying your passphrase one time per session.

COMMAND-LINE OPTIONS

Command-line options override declarations in the configuration files. Following are descriptions of some of the more useful **sshd** options.

–d   (**debug**) Sets debug mode so that **sshd** sends debugging messages to the system log and the server stays in the foreground (implies –D). You can specify this option a maximum of three times to increase the verbosity of the output. See also –e. (The ssh client uses –v for debugging; page 683.)

–e   (**error**) Sends output to standard error, not to the system log. Useful with –d.

–f *file*   Specifies *file* as the configuration file instead of **/etc/ssh/sshd_config**.

–t   (**test**) Checks the configuration file syntax and the sanity of the key files.

–D   (**noDetach**) Keeps **sshd** in the foreground. Useful for debugging; implied by –d.

/etc/ssh/sshd_config CONFIGURATION FILE

Lines in the **/etc/ssh/sshd_config** configuration file contain declarations. Each of these declarations starts with a keyword that is not case sensitive. Some keywords must be followed by whitespace and one or more case-sensitive arguments. You must reload the **sshd** server before these changes will take effect.

AllowUsers *userlist*

The *userlist* is a SPACE-separated list of usernames that specifies which users are allowed to log in using **sshd**. This list can include * and ? wildcards. You can specify a user as *user* or *user@host*. If you use the second format, make sure you specify the host as returned by hostname. Without this declaration, any user who can log in locally can log in using an OpenSSH client. Does not work with numeric user IDs.

ClientAliveCountMax *n*

The *n* specifies the number of client-alive messages that can be sent without receiving a response before **sshd** disconnects from the client. See **ClientAliveInterval**. Default is 3.

ClientAliveInterval *n*

Sends a message through the encrypted channel after *n* seconds of not receiving a message from the client. See **ClientAliveCountMax**. The default is 0, meaning that no messages are sent.

This declaration passes messages over the encrypted channel (application layer; page 371) and is not susceptible to *IP spoofing* (page 1171). It differs from **TCPKeepAlive**, which uses the TCP **keepalive** option (transport layer; page 371) and is susceptible to IP spoofing.

DenyUsers *userlist*

The *userlist* is a SPACE-separated list of usernames that specifies users who are not allowed to log in using **sshd**. This list can include * and ? wildcards. You can specify a user as *user* or *user@host*. If you use the second format, make sure you specify the host as returned by hostname. Does not work with numeric user IDs.

ForceCommand *command*

Executes *command*, ignoring commands specified by the client and commands in the optional ~/.ssh/ssh/rc file.

HostbasedAuthentication yes | no

Tries **rhosts** and **/etc/hosts.equiv** authentication when set to **yes**. For a more secure system, set this declaration to **no**. Default is **no**.

IgnoreRhosts yes | no

Ignores **.rhosts** and **.shosts** files for authentication. Does not affect the use of **/etc/hosts.equiv** and **/etc/ssh/shosts.equiv** files for authentication. For a more secure system, set this declaration to **yes**. Default is **yes**.

LoginGraceTime *n*

Waits *n* seconds for a user to log in on the server before disconnecting. A value of 0 means there is no time limit. Default is 120 seconds.

LogLevel *val*   Specifies how detailed the log messages are. Choose *val* from QUIET, FATAL, ERROR, INFO, and VERBOSE. Default is INFO.

PasswordAuthentication yes | no

Permits a user to use a password for authentication. For a more secure system, set up automatic login (page 689) and set this declaration to **no**. Default is **yes**.

PermitEmptyPasswords yes | no

Permits a user to log in on an account that has an empty password. Default is **no**.

PermitRootLogin yes | without-password | forced-commands-only | no
> Permits **root** to log in using an OpenSSH client. Default is **yes**.
>
> Setting this declaration to **yes** allows a user to log in as a privileged user by suppling the **root** password. This setup allows the **root** password to be sent over the network, although it is encrypted, so it is not a big security risk. It also requires all users connecting as a privileged user to know the **root** password.
>
> Setting this declaration to **no** does not allow **root** to authenticate directly; privilege must come from sudo or su after a user has logged in. Given the number of brute-force attacks on a typical system connected to the Internet, this is a good choice.
>
> Setting this declaration to **without-password** means the only way for a user to authenticate as **root** is by using an authorized key (page 689). This choice eliminates the need for a group of people to know the **root** password. However, one user must be able to run with **root** privileges so new keys can be added as needed.
>
> Setting this declaration to **forced-commands** works with an authorized key but forces a specific command after authentication instead of starting an interactive shell. The command is specified by **ForceCommand** (page 693).

PermitUserEnvironment yes | no
> Permits a user to modify the environment he logs in to on the remote system. Default is **no**. See **environment** on page 676.

Port *num* Specifies that the **sshd** server listen on port *num*. It might improve security to change *num* to a nonstandard port. Default is 22.

StrictModes yes | no
> Checks modes and ownership of the user's home directory and files. Login fails for users other than the owner if the directories and/or files can be written to by anyone other than the owner. For a more secure system, set this declaration to **yes**. Default is **yes**.

SyslogFacility *val*
> Specifies the facility name (page 624) **sshd** uses when logging messages. Set *val* to **daemon, user, auth, authpriv, local0, local1, local2, local3, local4, local5, local6,** or **local7**. Default is **auth**.

TCPKeepAlive yes | no
> Periodically checks whether a connection is alive when set to **yes**. Checking causes the ssh or scp connection to be dropped when the client crashes or the connection dies for another reason, even if it is only temporary. Setting this parameter to **no** causes the server not to check whether the connection is alive. Default is **yes**.
>
> This declaration tests the connection at the transport (TCP) layer (page 371). It uses the TCP **keepalive** option, which is not encrypted and is susceptible to *IP spoofing* (page 1171). Refer to **ClientAliveInterval** (page 693) for a nonspoofable alternative.

X11Forwarding yes | no
> Allows X11 forwarding when set to **yes**. For trusted X11 forwarding to work, the ForwardX11 or the ForwardX11Trusted declaration must also be set to **yes** in either the **~/.ssh/config** or **/etc/ssh/ssh_config** client configuration file (page 686). The

default is **no**, but Fedora/RHEL sets X11Forwarding to **yes**. For more information refer to "Forwarding X11" on page 696.

TROUBLESHOOTING

Log files   There are several places to look for clues when you have a problem connecting with ssh or scp. First look for **sshd** entries in **/var/log/secure** and **/var/log/messages** on the server. Following are messages you might see when you are using an **AllowUsers** declaration but have not included the user who is trying to log in (page 693). The messages that are marked **pam_unix** originate with PAM (page 463).

```
# grep sshd /var/log/secure | tail -6
guava sshd[10244]: Server listening on :: port 22.
guava sshd[10248]: User sam from 172.16.192.150 not allowed because not listed in AllowUsers
guava sshd[10249]: input_userauth_request: invalid user sam
guava sshd[10248]: pam_unix(sshd:auth): authentication failure; logname= uid=0 euid=0 tty=ssh ruser=
rhost=172.16.192.150  user=sam
guava sshd[10248]: Failed password for invalid user sam from 172.16.192.150 port 59088 ssh2
guava sshd[10249]: Connection closed by 172.16.192.150
```

Check the   You can use the **sshd –t** option to check the syntax of the server configuration file.
configuration file

Debug the client   If entries in these files do not help solve the problem, try connecting with the **–v** option (either ssh or scp—the results should be the same). OpenSSH displays a lot of debugging messages, one of which might help you figure out what the problem is. You can use a maximum of three **–v** options to increase the number of messages that OpenSSH displays.

```
$ ssh -v plum
OpenSSH_5.6p1, OpenSSL 1.0.0d-fips 8 Feb 2011
debug1: Reading configuration data /etc/ssh/ssh_config
debug1: Applying options for *
debug1: Connecting to plum [172.16.192.151] port 22.
debug1: Connection established.
debug1: identity file /home/sam/.ssh/id_rsa type 1
debug1: identity file /home/sam/.ssh/id_rsa-cert type -1
...
debug1: Host 'plum' is known and matches the RSA host key.
debug1: Found key in /home/sam/.ssh/known_hosts:1
debug1: ssh_rsa_verify: signature correct
...
debug1: Authentications that can continue: publickey,gssapi-keyex,gssapi-with-mic,password
...
debug1: Next authentication method: publickey
debug1: Offering public key: /home/sam/.ssh/id_rsa
debug1: Authentications that can continue: publickey,gssapi-keyex,gssapi-with-mic,password
debug1: Trying private key: /home/sam/.ssh/id_dsa
debug1: Next authentication method: password
sam@plum's password:
```

Debug the server   You can debug from the server side by running **sshd** with the **–de** options. The server will run in the foreground, and its display might help you solve the problem.

TUNNELING/PORT FORWARDING

The ssh utility can forward a port (*port forwarding*; page 1182) through the encrypted connection it establishes. Because the data sent across the forwarded port uses the encrypted ssh connection as its data link layer (page 371), the term *tunneling* (page 1194) is applied to this type of connection: "The connection is tunneled through ssh." You can secure protocols—including POP, X, IMAP, VNC, and WWW—by tunneling them through ssh.

FORWARDING X11

The ssh utility makes it easy to tunnel the X11 protocol. For X11 tunneling to work, you must enable it on both the server and the client, and the client must be running the X Window System.

SERVER

On the ssh server, enable X11 forwarding by setting the X11Forwarding declaration (page 694) to **yes** (the default) in the **/etc/ssh/sshd_config** file.

TRUSTED CLIENT

On a client, enable trusted X11 forwarding by setting the ForwardX11 (default is **no**; page 686) *and* ForwardX11Trusted (default is **no**, but set to **yes** as installed; page 686) declarations to **yes** in the **/etc/ssh/ssh_config** or ~/.ssh/sshconfig file. Alternatively, you can specify the **–Y** option (page 683) on the command line to start the client in trusted mode.

When you enable X11 forwarding on a client, the client connects as a trusted client, which means the client trusts the server and is given full access to the X11 display. With full access to the X11 display, in some situations a client might be able to modify other clients of the X11 display. Make a trusted connection only when you trust the remote system. (You do not want someone tampering with your client.) If this concept is confusing, see the tip "The roles of X client and server might be counterintuitive" on page 259.

NONTRUSTED CLIENT

On a client, enable nontrusted X11 forwarding by setting the ForwardX11 (default is **no**; page 686) declaration to **yes** *and* the ForwardX11Trusted (default is **no**, but set to **yes** as installed; page 686) declaration to **no** in the **/etc/ssh/ssh_config** or ~/.ssh/sshconfig file. Alternatively, you can specify the **–X** option (page 683) on the command line to start the client in trusted mode.

A nontrusted client is given limited access to the X11 display and cannot modify other clients of the X11 display. Few clients work properly when they are run in nontrusted mode. If you are running an X11 client in nontrusted mode and encounter problems, try running in trusted mode (assuming you trust the remote system). Fedora/RHEL sets up ssh clients to run in trusted mode.

RUNNING ssh

With X11 forwarding turned on, ssh tunnels the X11 protocol, setting the **DISPLAY** environment variable on the system it connects to and forwarding the required port. Typically you will be running from a GUI, which usually means that you are using ssh in a terminal emulator window to connect to a remote system. When you give an X11 command from an ssh prompt, OpenSSH creates a new secure channel that carries the X11 data, and the graphical output from the X11 program appears on the screen. Typically you will need to start the client in trusted mode.

```
[sam@guava ~]$ ssh plum
[sam@plum ~]$ echo $DISPLAY
localhost:10.0
```

By default, ssh uses X Window System display numbers 10 and higher (port numbers 6010 and higher) for forwarded X sessions. After you connect to a remote system using **ssh**, you can give a command to run an X application. The application will then run on the remote system with its display appearing on the local system, such that it appears to run locally.

PORT FORWARDING

You can forward arbitrary ports using the –L and –R options. The –L option forwards a local port to a remote system, so a program that tries to connect to the forwarded port on the local system transparently connects to the remote system. The –R option does the reverse: It forwards remote ports to the local system. The –N option, which prevents ssh from executing remote commands, is generally used with –L and –R. When you specify –N, ssh works only as a private network to forward ports. An ssh command line using the –L or –R option has the following format:

$ *ssh –N –L | –R local-port:remote-host:remote-port target*

where *local-port* is the number of the local port that is being forwarded to or from *remote-host*, *remote-host* is the name or IP address of the system that *local-port* gets forwarded to or from, *remote-port* is the number of the port on *remote-host* that is being forwarded from or to the local system, and *target* is the name or IP address of the system ssh connects to.

As an example, assume there is a POP mail client on the local system and that the POP server is on a remote network, on a system named **pophost**. POP is not a secure protocol; passwords are sent in cleartext each time the client connects to the server. You can make it more secure by tunneling POP through ssh (POP-3 connects on port 110; port 1550 is an arbitrary port on the local system):

```
$ ssh -N -L 1550:pophost:110 pophost
```

After giving the preceding command, you can point the POP client at **localhost:1550**. The connection between the client and the server will then be encrypted. (When you set up an account on the POP client, specify the location of the server as **localhost, port 1550**; details vary with different mail clients.)

FIREWALLS

In the preceding example, *remote-host* and *target* were the same system. However, the system specified for port forwarding (*remote-host*) does not have to be the same as the destination of the ssh connection (*target*). As an example, assume the POP server is behind a firewall and you cannot connect to it via ssh. If you can connect to the firewall via the Internet using ssh, you can encrypt the part of the connection over the Internet:

```
$ ssh -N -L 1550:pophost:110 firewall
```

Here *remote-host* (the system receiving the port forwarding) is **pophost**, and *target* (the system that ssh connects to) is **firewall**.

You can also use ssh when you are behind a firewall (that is running **sshd**) and want to forward a port into your system without modifying the firewall settings:

```
$ ssh -R 1678:localhost:80 firewall
```

The preceding command forwards connections from the outside to port 1678 on the firewall to the local Web server. Forwarding connections in this manner allows you to use a Web browser to connect to port 1678 on the firewall when you connect to the Web server on the local system. This setup would be useful if you ran a Web-mail program (page 749) on the local system because it would allow you to check your mail from anywhere using an Internet connection.

COMPRESSION

Compression, which is enabled with the –C option, can speed up communication over a low-bandwidth connection. This option is commonly used with port forwarding. Compression can increase latency to an extent that might not be desirable for an X session forwarded over a high-bandwidth connection.

CHAPTER SUMMARY

OpenSSH is a suite of secure network connectivity tools that encrypts all traffic, including passwords, thereby helping to thwart malicious users who might otherwise eavesdrop, hijack connections, and steal passwords. The **sshd** server daemon accepts connections from clients including ssh (runs a command on or logs in on another system), scp (copies files to and from another system), and sftp (securely replaces ftp). Helper programs including ssh-keygen (creates, manages, and converts authentication keys), ssh-agent (manages keys during a session) and ssh-add (works with ssh-agent) create and manage authentication keys.

To ensure secure communications, when an OpenSSH client opens a connection, it verifies that it is connected to the correct server. Then OpenSSH encrypts communication between the systems. Finally, OpenSSH makes sure the user is authorized to log in on or copy files to and from the server. You can secure many protocols—including POP, X, IMAP, VNC, and WWW—by tunneling them through ssh.

When it is properly set up, OpenSSH also enables secure X11 forwarding. With this feature, you can run securely a graphical program on a remote system and have the display appear on the local system.

EXERCISES

1. What is the difference between the scp and sftp utilities?

2. How can you use ssh to find out who is logged in on a remote system?

3. How would you use scp to copy your ~/.bashrc file from the system named **plum** to the local system?

4. How would you use ssh to run xterm on **plum** and show the display on the local system?

5. What problem can enabling compression present when you are using ssh to run remote X applications on a local display?

6. When you try to connect to a remote system using an OpenSSH client and you see a message warning you that the remote host identification has changed, what has happened? What should you do?

ADVANCED EXERCISES

7. Which scp command would you use to copy your home directory from **plum** to the local system?

8. Which single command could you give to log in as **root** on the remote system named **plum**, if **plum** has remote **root** logins disabled?

9. How could you use ssh to compare the contents of the ~/**memos** directories on **plum** and the local system?

10. How would you use rsync with OpenSSH authentication to copy the **memos12** file from the working directory on the local system to your home directory on **plum**? How would you copy the **memos** directory from the working directory on the local system to your home directory on **plum** and cause rsync to display each file as it copied the file?

19

FTP: Transferring Files Across a Network

Objectives

After reading this chapter you should be able to:

▶ Download files from and upload files to an FTP server

▶ Download files from an anonymous FTP server

▶ Automate FTP logins using a **.netrc** file

▶ Explain the difference between binary and ASCII transfers

▶ Install and configure the **vsftpd** server

FTP   FTP (File Transfer Protocol) is a method of downloading files from and uploading files to another system using TCP/IP over a network. FTP is the name of a client/server protocol (FTP) and a client utility (ftp) that invokes the protocol. In addition to the original ftp utility, there are many textual and graphical FTP client programs, including most browsers, that run under many different operating systems. There are also many FTP server programs.

Introduction to FTP

This chapter starts with an introduction to FTP that discusses security, describes types of FTP connections, and presents a list of FTP clients. The first JumpStart section covers basic ftp commands and includes a tutorial on using the ftp client. Next is a section that presents more details of ftp. The final section describes how to set up a **vsftpd** FTP server.

History   First implemented under 4.2BSD, FTP has played an essential role in the propagation of Linux; this protocol/program is frequently used to distribute free software.

FTP site   The term *FTP site* refers to an FTP server that is connected to a network, usually the Internet. FTP sites can be public, allowing anonymous users to log in and download software and documentation. In contrast, private FTP sites require you to log in with a username and password. Some sites allow you to upload programs.

ftp and **vsftpd**   Although most FTP clients are similar, the servers differ quite a bit. This chapter describes the ftp client with references to sftp, a secure FTP client. It also covers the **vsftpd** (very secure FTP daemon) server which Fedora/RHEL uses internally and offers as part of its distribution.

ftp utility   The ftp utility is a user interface to FTP, a standard protocol used to transfer files between systems that communicate over a network.

Security

FTP is not a secure protocol: All usernames and passwords exchanged in setting up an FTP connection are sent in cleartext, data exchanged over an FTP connection is not encrypted, and the connection is subject to hijacking. Given these facts, FTP is best used for downloading public files. In most cases, the OpenSSH clients, ssh (page 681), scp (page 683), and sftp (page 685), offer secure alternatives to FTP.

Use FTP only to download public information

security   FTP is not secure. The sftp utility provides better security for all FTP functions other than allowing anonymous users to download information. Because sftp uses an encrypted connection, user passwords and data cannot be sniffed when you use this utility. You can replace all instances of ftp in this chapter with sftp because sftp uses the same commands as ftp. See page 685 for more information on sftp.

The **vsftpd** server does *not* make usernames, passwords, data, and connections more secure. However, it is secure in that a malicious user finds it more difficult to compromise directly the system running it, even if **vsftpd** is poorly implemented.

One feature that makes **vsftpd** more secure than **ftpd** is the fact that it does not run with **root** privileges. See also "Security" on page 713.

FTP CONNECTIONS

FTP uses two connections: one for control (you establish this connection when you log in on an FTP server) and one for data transfer (FTP sets up this connection when you ask it to transfer a file). An FTP server listens for incoming connections on port 21 by default and handles user authentication and file exchange.

Passive versus active connections
A client can ask an FTP server to establish either a PASV (passive—the default) or a PORT (active) connection for data transfer. Some servers are limited to one type of connection. The difference between a passive and an active FTP connection lies in whether the client or the server initiates the data connection. In passive mode, the client initiates the connection to the server (on port 20 by default); in active mode, the server initiates the connection (there is no default port; see "Connection Parameters" on page 723 for the parameters that determine which ports a server uses). Neither approach is inherently more secure than the other. Passive connections are more common because a client behind a NAT (page 896) can connect to a passive server and it is simpler to program a scalable passive server.

FTP CLIENTS

ftp
Fedora/RHEL supplies several FTP clients, including ftp (an older version of the BSD ftp utility). This section discusses ftp because it is commonly used and most other FTP clients, including sftp and lftp, provide a superset of ftp commands.

sftp
Part of the OpenSSH suite, sftp (**openssh-clients** package) is a secure and functionally equivalent alternative to ftp. The sftp utility is not a true FTP client—it does not understand the FTP protocol. It maps ftp commands to OpenSSH commands. See page 685 for more information.

lftp
The lftp utility (**lftp** package) provides the same security as sftp but offers more features. See the lftp man page for more information.

gFTP
The gftp utility (**gftp** package) is a graphical client that works with FTP, SSH, and HTTP servers. This client has many useful features, including the ability to resume an interrupted file transfer. See www.gftp.org and freshmeat.net/projects/gftp for more information.

NcFTP
The ncftp utility (**ncftp** package) is a textual client that offers many more features than ftp, including filename completion and command-line editing. For details see www.ncftp.com and freshmeat.net/projects/ncftp.

MORE INFORMATION

Local
Type **help** or **?** at an **ftp>** prompt to display a list of commands. Follow the **?** with a SPACE and an **ftp** command to display information about that command.
Files: **/usr/share/doc/vsftpd-***
man pages: ftp, sftp, lftp, **netrc, vsftpd.conf**

Web
vsftpd home page: vsftpd.beasts.org

HOWTO
FTP mini-HOWTO

NOTES

A Linux system running ftp can exchange files with any of the many operating systems that support FTP. Many sites offer archives of free information on an FTP server, although for many it is just an alternative to an easier-to-access Web site (see, for example, ftp://ftp.ibiblio.org/pub/Linux and http://www.ibiblio.org/software/linux). Most browsers can connect to and download files from FTP servers.

The ftp utility makes no assumptions about filesystem nomenclature or structure because you can use ftp to exchange files with non-UNIX/Linux systems (which might use different filenaming conventions).

RUNNING THE ftp AND sftp FTP CLIENTS

This section describes how to use the ftp and sftp FTP clients. The commands covered here work with both utilities.

PREREQUISITES

Install the following packages:

- **openssh-clients** (installed by default; contains sftp)
- **ftp**

There is no **init** script for ftp or sftp clients.

JUMPSTART I: DOWNLOADING FILES USING ftp

This JumpStart section is broken into two parts: a description of the basic commands and a tutorial session that shows a user working with ftp.

BASIC COMMANDS

Give the command

```
$ ftp hostname
```

where *hostname* is the name of the FTP server you want to connect to. If you have an account on the server, log in with your username and password. If it is a public system, log in as the user **anonymous** (or **ftp**) and give your email address as your password. Use the **ls** and **cd** ftp commands on the server as you would use the corresponding utilities from a shell. The command **get** *file* copies *file* from the server to the local system, **put** *file* copies *file* from the local system to the server, **status** displays information about the FTP connection, and **help** displays a list of commands.

The preceding commands, except for **status**, are also available in sftp, lftp, and ncftp.

TUTORIAL SESSION

Following are two ftp sessions wherein Sam transfers files from and to a **vsftpd** server named **plum**. When Sam gives the command **ftp plum**, the local ftp client connects to the server, which asks for a username and password. Because he is logged in on his local system as **sam**, ftp suggests that Sam log in on **plum** as **sam**. To log in as **sam**, he could just press RETURN. Because his username on **plum** is **sls**, however, he types **sls** in response to the **Name (plum:sam):** prompt. After Sam responds to the **Password:** prompt with his normal system password, the **vsftpd** server greets him and informs him that it is **Using binary mode to transfer files**. With ftp in binary mode, Sam can transfer ASCII and binary files (page 708).

Connect and log in

```
$ ftp plum
Connected to plum (172.16.192.151).
220 (vsFTPd 2.3.4)
Name (plum:sam): sls
331 Please specify the password.
Password:
230 Login successful.
Remote system type is UNIX.
Using binary mode to transfer files.
ftp>
```

After logging in, Sam uses the ftp **ls** command to see what is in his remote working directory, which is his home directory on **plum**. Then he cds to the **memos** directory and displays the files there.

ls and cd

```
ftp> ls
227 Entering Passive Mode (172,16,192,131,245,127).
150 Here comes the directory listing.
drwxrwxr-x    2 501      501          4096 Mar 03 02:52 expenses
drwxrwxr-x    2 501      501          4096 Mar 03 02:54 memos
drwxrwxr-x    2 501      501          4096 Mar 03 02:52 tech
226 Directory send OK.

ftp> cd memos
250 Directory successfully changed.

ftp> ls
227 Entering Passive Mode (172,16,192,131,49,131).
150 Here comes the directory listing.
-rw-rw-r--    1 501      501         87499 Mar 03 02:53 memo.0514
-rw-rw-r--    1 501      501         58235 Mar 03 02:54 memo.0628
-rw-rw-r--    1 501      501         58531 Mar 03 02:54 memo.0905
-rw-rw-r--    1 501      501        128546 Mar 03 02:54 memo.0921
-rw-rw-r--    1 501      501         76271 Mar 03 02:54 memo.1102
226 Directory send OK.
```

Next Sam uses the ftp **get** command to copy **memo.1102** from the server to the local system. His use of binary mode ensures that he will get a good copy of the file regardless of whether it is binary or ASCII. The server confirms that the file was copied successfully and reports on its size and the time required to copy it. Sam then copies the local file **memo.1114** to the remote system. This file is copied into his remote working directory, **memos**.

get and **put**

```
ftp> get memo.1102
local: memo.1102 remote: memo.1102
227 Entering Passive Mode (172,16,192,131,151,7).
150 Opening BINARY mode data connection for memo.1102 (76271 bytes).
226 Transfer complete.
76271 bytes received in 0.0136 secs (5588.44 Kbytes/sec)

ftp> put memo.1114
local: memo.1114 remote: memo.1114
227 Entering Passive Mode (172,16,192,131,213,13).
150 Ok to send data.
226 Transfer complete.
137023 bytes sent in 0.0266 secs (5156.09 Kbytes/sec)
```

Now Sam decides he wants to copy all the files in the **memo** directory on **plum** to a new directory on his local system. He gives an **ls** command to make sure he will copy the right files, but ftp has timed out. Instead of exiting from ftp and giving another ftp command from the shell, he gives ftp an **open plum** command to reconnect to the server. After logging in, he uses the ftp **cd** command to change directories to **memos** on the server.

Timeout and open

```
ftp> ls
No control connection for command: Success
Passive mode refused.
ftp> open plum
Connected to plum (172.16.192.151).
220 (vsFTPd 2.3.4)
Name (plum:sam): sls
...
ftp> cd memos
250 Directory successfully changed.
```

Local cd (lcd) At this point, Sam realizes he has not created the new directory to hold the files he wants to download. Giving an ftp **mkdir** command would create a new directory on the server, but Sam wants a new directory on the local system. He uses an exclamation point (!) followed by a **mkdir memos.hold** command to invoke a shell and run mkdir on the local system, thereby creating a directory named **memos.hold** in his working directory on the local system. (You can display the name of the working directory on the local system using !**pwd**.) Next, because Sam wants to copy files from the server to the **memos.hold** directory on his local system, he has to change his working directory on the local system. Giving the command !**cd memos.hold** will not accomplish what Sam wants to do because the exclamation point will spawn a new shell on the local system and the **cd** command would be effective only in the new shell, which is not the shell that ftp is running under. For this situation, ftp provides the **lcd** (local cd) command, which changes the working directory for ftp and reports on the new local working directory:

```
ftp> !mkdir memos.hold

ftp> lcd memos.hold
Local directory now /home/sam/memos.hold
```

Sam uses the ftp **mget** (multiple get) command followed by the asterisk (*) wildcard to copy all files from the remote **memos** directory to the **memos.hold** directory on the local system. When ftp prompts him for the first file, Sam realizes that he forgot to turn off the prompts, so he responds with **n** and presses CONTROL-C to stop copying files in response to the second prompt. The server checks whether he wants to continue with his **mget** command.

Next Sam gives the ftp **prompt** command, which toggles the prompt action (turns it off if it is on and turns it on if it is off). Now when he gives a **mget** * command, ftp copies the files without prompting him. After getting the desired files, Sam gives a **quit** command to close the connection with the server, exit from ftp, and return to the local shell prompt.

mget and prompt

```
ftp> mget *
mget memo.0514? n
mget memo.0628? CONTROL-C
Continue with mget? n

ftp> prompt
Interactive mode off.

ftp> mget *
local: memo.0514 remote: memo.0514
227 Entering Passive Mode (172,16,192,131,207,88).
150 Opening BINARY mode data connection for memo.0514 (87499 bytes).
226 Transfer complete.
87499 bytes received in 0.0127 secs (6912.55 Kbytes/sec)
local: memo.0628 remote: memo.0628
227 Entering Passive Mode (172,16,192,131,182,100).
150 Opening BINARY mode data connection for memo.0628 (58235 bytes).
226 Transfer complete.
58235 bytes received in 0.0204 secs (2860.97 Kbytes/sec)
...
150 Opening BINARY mode data connection for memo.1114 (137023 bytes).
226 Transfer complete.
137023 bytes received in 0.0212 secs (6460.30 Kbytes/sec)
ftp> quit
221 Goodbye.
```

ANONYMOUS FTP

Many systems—most notably those from which you can download free software—allow you to log in as **anonymous**. Most systems that support anonymous logins accept the name **ftp** as an easier-to-spell and quicker-to-enter synonym for **anonymous**. An anonymous user is usually restricted to a portion of a filesystem set aside to hold files that are to be shared with remote users. When you log in as an anonymous user, the server prompts you to enter a password. Although the system accepts any password, by convention you are expected to supply your email address. Do not use an important address if you are logging into a public site because that address could receive spam based on this login.

Many systems that permit anonymous access store interesting files in the **pub** directory. Most browsers, such as Firefox, log in on an anonymous FTP site and transfer a file when you click on the filename.

AUTOMATIC LOGIN

.netrc   You can store server-specific FTP username and password information so you do not have to enter it each time you visit an FTP site. Each line of ~/.netrc identifies a server. When you connect to an FTP server, ftp reads the ~/.netrc file to determine whether you have an automatic login set up for that server. The format of a line in ~/.netrc is

> machine **server** login **username** password **passwd**

where **server** is the name of the server, **username** is your username, and **passwd** is your password on **server**. Replace **machine** with **default** on the last line of the file to specify a username and password for systems not listed in ~/.netrc. The **default** line is useful for logging in on anonymous servers. A sample ~/.netrc file follows:

```
$ cat ~/.netrc
machine plum login sls password mypassword
default login anonymous password sam@example.com
```

To protect the account information in .netrc, make it readable only by the user whose home directory it appears in. Refer to the **netrc** man page for more information.

BINARY VERSUS ASCII TRANSFER MODE

The **vsftpd** FTP server can—but does not always—provide two modes to transfer files. Binary mode transfers always copy an exact, byte-for-byte image of a file and never change line endings. Transfer all binary files using binary mode. Unless you need to convert line endings, use binary mode to transfer ASCII files as well.

These descriptions do not apply to files created by word processors such as Word or LibreOffice because those programs generate binary files. The **vsftpd** server can map Linux line endings to Windows line endings as you upload files and Windows line endings to Linux line endings as you download files.

To use ASCII mode on an FTP server that allows it, give an **ascii** command (page 710) after you log in and set **cr** to ON (the default; page 711). If the server does not allow you to change line endings as you transfer a file, you can use the unix2dos (page 159) utility before or after you transfer a file in binary mode.

Security   To enhance security, by default **vsftpd** transfers every file in binary mode, even when it appears to be using ASCII mode. On the server side, you can enable *real* ASCII mode transfers by setting the **ascii_upload_enable** and **ascii_download_enable** parameters (page 720) to YES. With the server set to allow ASCII transfers, the client controls whether line endings are mapped by using the **ascii**, **binary**, and **cr** commands (page 710).

ftp SPECIFICS

This section covers the details of using ftp.

FORMAT

An ftp command line has the following format:

ftp [options] [ftp-server]

where *options* is one or more options from the list in the next section and *ftp-server* is the name or IP address of the FTP server you want to exchange files with. If you do not specify an *ftp-server,* you will need to use the ftp **open** command to connect to a server once ftp is running.

COMMAND-LINE OPTIONS

–g (**globbing**) Turns off globbing. See **glob** (page 711).

–i (**interactive**) Turns off prompts during file transfers with **mget** (page 710) and **mput** (page 710). See also **prompt** (page 711).

–n (**no automatic login**) Disables automatic logins (page 708).

–v (**verbose**) Tells you more about how ftp is working. Displays responses from the server and reports information on how quickly files are transferred. See also **verbose** (page 712).

ftp COMMANDS

The ftp utility is interactive: After you start ftp, it prompts you to enter commands to set parameters or transfer files. You can abbreviate commands as long as the abbreviations are unique. Program help is available with the **help** command (page 712).

SHELL COMMAND

![command] Without *command*, escapes to (spawns) a shell on the local system. Use CONTROL-D or **exit** to return to ftp when you are finished using the local shell. Follow the exclamation point with *command* to execute that command only; ftp will display an **ftp>** prompt when execution of the command finishes. Because the shell that ftp spawns with this command is a child of the shell that is running ftp, no changes you make in this shell are preserved when you return to ftp. Specifically, when you want to copy files to a local directory other than the directory that you started ftp from, you need to use the ftp **lcd** command to change the local working directory: Issuing a **cd** command in the spawned shell will not make the change you desire. See "Local cd (**lcd**)" on page 706 for an example.

Transfer Files

In the following descriptions, *remote-file* and *local-file* can be pathnames.

append *local-file* [*remote-file*]

Appends *local-file* to the file with the same name on the remote system or to *remote-file* if specified.

get *remote-file* [*local-file*]

Copies *remote-file* to the local system under the name *local-file*. Without *local-file*, ftp uses *remote-file* as the filename on the local system.

mget *remote-file-list*

(**multiple get**) Copies several files to the local system, with each file maintaining its original filename. You can name the remote files literally or use wildcards (see **glob**). Use **prompt** (page 711) to turn off the prompts during transfers.

mput *local-file-list*

(**multiple put**) Copies several files to the server, with each file maintaining its original filename. You can name the local files literally or use wildcards (see **glob**). Use **prompt** (page 711) to turn off the prompts during transfers.

newer *remote-file* [*local-file*]

If the modification time of *remote-file* is more recent than that of *local-file* or if *local-file* does not exist, copies *remote-file* to the local system under the name *local-file*. Without *local-file*, ftp uses *remote-file* as the filename on the local system. This command is similar to **get** but will not overwrite a newer file with an older one.

put *local-file* [*remote-file*]

Copies *local-file* to the remote system under the name *remote-file*. Without *remote-file*, ftp uses *local-file* as the filename on the remote system.

reget *remote-file* [*local-file*]

If *local-file* exists and is smaller than *remote-file*, assumes that a previous **get** of *local-file* was interrupted and continues from where the previous **get** left off. Without *local-file*, ftp uses *remote-file* as the filename on the local system. This command can save time when a **get** of a large file fails partway through the transfer.

Status

ascii   Sets the file transfer type to ASCII. The **cr** command must be ON for **ascii** to work (page 708).

binary   Sets the file transfer type to binary (page 708).

bye   Closes the connection to the server and terminates ftp. Same as **quit**.

case   Toggles and displays the case mapping status. The default is OFF. When it is ON, for **get** and **mget** commands, this command maps filenames that are all uppercase on the server to all lowercase on the local system.

close   Closes the connection to the server without exiting from ftp.

cr (**carriage** RETURN) Toggles and displays the (carriage) RETURN stripping status. Effective only when the file transfer type is **ascii**. Set **cr** to ON (default) to remove RETURN characters from RETURN/LINEFEED line termination sequences used by Windows, yielding the standard Linux line termination of LINEFEED. Set **cr** to OFF to leave line endings unmapped (page 708).

debug [*n*] Toggles/sets and displays the debugging status/level, where *n* is the debugging level. OFF or 0 (zero) is the default. When *n* > 0, ftp displays each command it sends to the server.

glob Toggles and displays the filename expansion (page 244) status for **mdelete** (page 712), **mget** (page 710), and **mput** (page 710) commands.

hash Toggles and displays the hashmark (#) display status. When it is ON, ftp displays one hashmark for each 1024-byte data block it transfers.

open [*hostname*]

Specifies *hostname* as the name of the server to connect to. Without *hostname*, prompts for the name of the server. This command is useful when a connection times out or otherwise fails. See page 706 for an example.

passive Toggles between passive (PASV—the default) and active (PORT) transfer modes and displays the transfer mode. For more information refer to "Passive versus active connections" on page 703.

prompt Toggles and displays the prompt status. When it is ON (default), **mdelete** (page 712), **mget** (page 710), and **mput** (page 710) ask for verification before transferring each file. Set **prompt** to OFF to turn off these prompts.

quit Closes the connection to the server and terminates ftp. Same as **bye**.

umask [*nnn*] Changes the umask (page 473) applied to files created on the server to *nnn*. Without *nnn*, displays the umask.

user [*username*] [*password*]

Prompts for or accepts the *username* and *password* that enable you to log in on the server. When you call it with the **–n** option, ftp prompts you for a username and password automatically. For more information refer to "Automatic Login" on page 708.

DIRECTORIES

cd *remote-directory*

Changes the working directory on the server to *remote-directory*.

cdup Changes the working directory on the server to the parent of the working directory.

lcd [*local_directory*]

(**local change directory**) Changes the working directory on the local system to *local_directory*. Without an argument, this command changes the working directory on the local system to your home directory (just as the **cd** shell builtin does without an argument). See "Local cd (**lcd**)" on page 706 for an example.

FILES

chmod *mode remote-file*

> Changes the access permissions of *remote-file* on the server to *mode*. See chmod on page 203 for more information on how to specify the *mode*.

delete *remote-file*

> Removes *remote-file* from the server.

mdelete *remote-file-list*

> (**multiple delete**) Deletes the files specified by *remote-file-list* from the server.

DISPLAY INFORMATION

?   (**question mark**) Same as **help**.

dir [*remote-directory*] [*file*]

> Displays a listing of *remote-directory* from the server. When you do not specify *remote-directory*, displays the working directory. When you specify *file*, the listing is saved on the local system in a file named *file*.

help [*command*]   Displays information about *command*. Without *command*, displays a list of local ftp commands. Also **?**.

ls [*remote-directory*] [*file*]

> Similar to **dir** but produces a more concise listing from some servers. When you specify *file*, the listing is saved on the local system in a file named *file*.

pwd   Displays the pathname of the working directory on the server. Use **!pwd** to display the pathname of the local working directory.

rstatus   Displays ftp connection and status information for the local system (client).

status   Displays ftp connection and status information for the remote system (server).

verbose   Toggles and displays verbose mode, which displays responses from the server and reports how quickly files are transferred. The effect of this command is the same as specifying the **–v** option on the command line.

SETTING UP AN FTP SERVER (vsftpd)

This section explains how to set up an FTP server implemented by the **vsftpd** daemon as supplied by Fedora/RHEL.

PREREQUISITES

Install the following package:

- **vsftpd**

vsftpd init script   Run chkconfig to cause **vsftpd** to start when the system enters multiuser mode.

```
# chkconfig vsftpd on
```

Start **vsftpd**:

```
# service vsftpd start
```

If you change the **vsftpd.conf** configuration file, you need to restart **vsftpd**.

NOTES

The **vsftpd** server can run in normal mode (the **xinetd** daemon [page 481], which is not installed by default, calls **vsftpd** each time a client tries to make a connection) or it can run in stand-alone mode (**vsftpd** runs as a daemon and handles connections directly).

Stand-alone mode   Although by default **vsftpd** runs in normal mode, Fedora/RHEL sets it up to run in stand-alone mode by setting the **listen** parameter (page 715) to YES in the **vsftpd.conf** file. Under Fedora/RHEL, with **vsftpd** running in stand-alone mode, you start and stop the server using service and the **vsftpd** init script.

Normal mode   The **xinetd** superserver (page 481) must be installed and running and you must install an **xinetd** control file to run **vsftpd** in normal mode. A sample control file is located at **/usr/share/doc/vsftpd✱/vsftpd.xinetd**. Copy the sample file to the **/etc/xinetd.d** directory, rename it **vsftpd**, and edit the file to change the **disable** parameter to **no**. With the **listen** parameter in **vsftpd.conf** set to NO, **xinetd** starts **vsftpd** as needed.

Security   The safest policy is not to allow users to authenticate against FTP: Instead, use FTP for anonymous access only. If you do allow local users to authenticate and upload files to the server, be sure to put local users in a chroot jail (page 717). Because FTP sends usernames and passwords in cleartext, a malicious user can easily *sniff* (page 1189) them. Armed with a username and password, the same user can impersonate a local user, upload a *Trojan horse* (page 1194), and compromise the system.

Firewall   An FTP server normally uses TCP port 21. If the FTP server system is running a firewall, you need to open this port. Using system-config-firewall (page 893), select **FTP** from the Trusted Services frame to open this port.

SELinux   When SELinux is set to use a targeted policy, FTP is protected by SELinux. You can disable this protection if necessary. For more information refer to "Setting the Targeted Policy with system-config-selinux" on page 463.

JUMPSTART II: STARTING A vsftpd FTP SERVER

By default, under Fedora/RHEL **vsftpd** allows local and anonymous users only to log in on the server; it does not set up a guest account. When someone logs in as an anonymous user, that person works in the **/var/ftp** directory. You do not have to configure anything.

TROUBLE SHOOTING

Make sure **vsftpd** is working by logging in from the server system. You can refer to the server as **localhost** or by using its hostname on the command line. Log in as a user and provide that user's password:

```
$ ftp localhost
Connected to localhost (127.0.0.1).
220 (vsFTPd 2.3.4)
Name (localhost:sam): sls
331 Please specify the password.
Password:
230 Login successful.
Remote system type is UNIX.
Using binary mode to transfer files.
ftp> quit
221 Goodbye.
```

If you are not able to connect to the server, first make sure the server is running:

```
$ service vsftpd status
vsftpd (pid 2348) is running...

$ ps -ef | grep vsftpd
root      2348     1  0 18:45 ?        00:00:00 /usr/sbin/vsftpd /etc/vsftpd/vsftpd.conf
```

If you want to allow users to log in as **anonymous** or **ftp, anonymous_enable** must be set to YES in **/etc/vsftpd/vsftpd.conf** (it is by default; page 717). Restart the **vsftpd** daemon (page 712) if you change **vsftpd.conf**. Any password is acceptable with these login names.

```
$ ftp localhost
Connected to localhost (127.0.0.1).
220 (vsFTPd 2.3.4)
Name (localhost:sam): anonymous
331 Please specify the password.
Password:
230 Login successful.
Remote system type is UNIX.
Using binary mode to transfer files.
```

Next check that permissions on **/var/ftp**, or the home directory of ftp as specified in **/etc/passwd**, are set to 755 and that the directory is not owned by **ftp**. If the **ftp** user can write to **/var/ftp**, connections will fail.

```
$ ls -ld /var/ftp
drwxr-xr-x. 3 root root 4096 03-05 19:03 /var/ftp
```

Once you are able to log in from the local system, log in from another system—either one on the LAN or another system with access to the server. On the command line, use the hostname from within the LAN or the *FQDN* (page 1165) from outside the LAN. The dialog should appear the same as in the previous example. If you cannot log in from a system that is not on the LAN, use ping (page 386) to test the connection and then make sure the firewall is set up to allow FTP access. See "FTP Connections" on page 703 for a discussion of active and passive modes and the ports that each mode uses.

CONFIGURING A vsftpd SERVER

The configuration file for **vsftpd**, **/etc/vsftpd/vsftpd.conf**, lists Boolean, numeric, and string name-value pairs of configuration parameters, called directives. Each name-value pair is joined by an equal sign with no SPACEs on either side. Fedora/RHEL provides a well-commented **vsftpd.conf** file that changes many of the compiled-in defaults. This section covers many of the parameters, noting their default values and their values as specified in the **vsftpd.conf** file supplied with Fedora/RHEL.

Set Boolean parameters to YES or NO and numeric parameters to a nonnegative integer. Octal numbers, which are useful for setting umask parameters, must have a leading 0 (zero). Numbers without a leading zero are treated as base 10 numbers. Following are examples of setting each type of parameter:

```
anonymous_enable=YES
local_umask=022
xferlog_file=/var/log/vsftpd.log
```

Descriptions of the directives are broken into the following groups:

- Stand-alone mode (page 715)
- Logging in (page 716)
- Working directory and the chroot jail (page 717)
- Downloading and uploading files (page 719)
- Messages (page 721)
- Display (page 721)
- Logs (page 722)
- Connection parameters (page 723)
- Miscellaneous (page 724)
- Other configuration files (page 725)

STAND-ALONE MODE

Refer to "Notes" on page 713 for a discussion of normal and stand-alone modes. This section describes the parameters that affect stand-alone mode.

listen   YES runs **vsftpd** in stand-alone mode; NO runs it in normal mode.

Default: NO
Fedora/RHEL: YES

listen_address   In stand-alone mode, specifies the IP address of the local interface that **vsftpd** listens on for incoming connections. When this parameter is not set, **vsftpd** uses the default network interface.

Default: none

listen_port   In stand-alone mode, specifies the port that **vsftpd** listens on for incoming connections.

Default: 21

max_clients   In stand-alone mode, specifies the maximum number of clients. Zero (0) indicates unlimited clients.

Default: 0

max_per_ip   In stand-alone mode, specifies the maximum number of clients from the same IP address. Zero (0) indicates unlimited clients from the same IP address.

Default: 0

LOGGING IN

Three classes of users can log in on a **vsftpd** server: anonymous, local, and guest. The guest user is rarely used and is not covered in this chapter. A local user logs in using his system username and password. An anonymous user logs in using **anonymous** or **ftp** and his email address as a password. You can control whether each of these classes of users can log in on the server and what they can do once they log in. You can also specify what a local user can do on a per-user basis; for more information refer to **user_config_dir** on page 725.

LOCAL USERS

userlist_enable   The **/etc/vsftpd/user_list** file (page 725), or another file specified by **userlist_file**, contains a list of zero or more users. YES consults this list and takes action based on **userlist_deny**, either granting or denying users in the list permission to log in on the server. To prevent the transmission of cleartext passwords, access is denied immediately after the user enters her username. NO does not consult the list. Set to NO for a more secure system.

Default: NO
Fedora/RHEL: YES

userlist_deny   YES prevents users listed in **/etc/vsftpd/user_list** (page 725) from logging in on the server. NO allows *only* users listed in **/etc/vsftpd/user_list** to log in on the server. Use **userlist_file** to change the name of the file that this parameter consults. This parameter is checked only when **userlist_enable** is set to YES.

Default: YES

userlist_file   The name of the file consulted when **userlist_enable** is set to YES.

Default: /etc/vsftpd/user_list

local_enable   YES permits local users (users listed in **/etc/passwd**) to log in on the server.

Default: NO
Fedora/RHEL: YES

ANONYMOUS USERS

anonymous_enable

YES allows anonymous logins. NO disables anonymous logins.

Default: YES

no_anon_password

YES skips asking anonymous users for passwords.

Default: NO

deny_email_enable

YES checks whether the password (email address) that an anonymous user enters is listed in **/etc/vsftpd.banned_emails** or another file specified by **banned_email_file**. If it is, the user is not allowed to log in on the system. NO does not perform this check. Using system-config-firewall (page 893) or iptables (page 891) to block specific hosts is generally more productive than using this parameter.

Default: NO

banned_email_file

The name of the file consulted when **deny_email_enable** is set to YES.

Default: **/etc/vsftpd/vsftpd.banned_emails**

THE WORKING DIRECTORY AND THE chroot JAIL

When a user logs in on a **vsftpd** server, standard filesystem access permissions control which directories and files the user can access and how the user can access them. Three basic parameters control a user who is logged in on a **vsftpd** server:

- The user ID (UID)
- The initial working directory
- The root directory

By default, the **vsftpd** server sets the UID of a local user to that user's UID and sets the UID of an anonymous user to that of the user named **ftp**. A local user starts in her home directory and an anonymous user starts in **/var/ftp**.

By default, anonymous users are placed in a chroot jail for security; local users are not. For example, when an anonymous user logs in on a **vsftpd** server, his home directory is **/var/ftp**. All that user sees, however, is that his home directory is **/**. The user sees the directory at **/var/ftp/upload** as **/upload**. The user cannot see or work with, for example, the **/home**, **/usr/local**, or **/tmp** directory because the user is in a chroot jail. For more information refer to "Setting Up a chroot Jail" on page 485.

You can use the **chroot_local_user** parameter to put each local user in a chroot jail whose root is the user's home directory. You can use **chroot_list_enable** to put selected local users in chroot jails.

chroot_list_enable

Upon login, YES checks whether a local user is listed in **/etc/vsftpd/chroot_list** (page 725) or another file specified by **chroot_list_file**.

When a user is in the list and **chroot_local_user** is set to NO, the user is put in a chroot jail in his home directory. Only users listed in **/etc/vsftpd/chroot_list** are put in chroot jails.

When a user is in the list and **chroot_local_user** is set to YES, that user is not put in a chroot jail. Users not listed in **/etc/vsftpd/chroot_list** are put in chroot jails.

Default: NO

chroot_local_user

See **chroot_list_enable**. Set to NO for a more open system but remember to add new users to the **chroot_list_file** as needed when you add users to the system. Set to YES for a more secure system. New users are automatically restricted unless you add them to **chroot_list_file**.

Default: NO

chroot_list_file   The name of the file consulted when **chroot_list_enable** is set to YES.

Default: **/etc/vsftpd/chroot_list**

passwd_chroot_enable

YES enables you to change the location of the chroot jail that the **chroot_list_enable** and **chroot_local_user** settings impose on a local user.

The location of the chroot jail can be moved up the directory structure by including a **/./** within the home directory string for that user in **/etc/passwd**. This change has no effect on the standard system login, just as a **cd .** command has no effect on the working directory.

For example, changing the home directory field in **/etc/passwd** (page 508) for Sam from **/home/sam** to **/home/./sam** allows Sam to cd to **/home** after logging in using **vsftpd**. Given the proper permissions, Sam can now view files and collaborate with another user.

Default: NO

secure_chroot_dir   The name of an empty directory that is not writable by the user **ftp**. The **vsftpd** server uses this directory as a secure chroot jail when the user does not need access to the filesystem.

Default: **/usr/share/empty**

local_root   After a local user logs in on the server, this directory becomes the user's working directory. No error results if the specified directory does not exist.

Default: none

DOWNLOADING AND UPLOADING FILES

By default, any user—whether local or anonymous—can download files from the **vsftpd** server, assuming proper filesystem access and permissions. The **write_enable** parameter must be set to YES (Fedora/RHEL sets it this way) to permit local users to upload files. The **local_umask** parameter defaults to 077, although Fedora/RHEL sets it to 022, giving uploaded files 644 permissions (page 202). These permissions allow users to download other users' files. Change **local_umask** to 077 to allow only the user who created a file to download and overwrite it.

Security   Refer to "Security" on page 713 for information on the security hole that is created when you allow local users to upload files.

The following actions set up **vsftpd** to allow anonymous users to upload files:

1. Set **write_enable** (below) to YES. (Fedora/RHEL sets this parameter to YES.)

2. Create a directory under **/var/ftp** that an anonymous user can write to but not read from (mode 333). You do not want a malicious user to be able to see, download, modify, and upload a file that another user originally uploaded. The following commands create a **/var/ftp/uploads** directory that anyone can write to but no one can read from:

```
# mkdir /var/ftp/uploads
# chmod 333 /var/ftp/uploads
```

Because of the security risk, **vsftpd** prevents anonymous connections when an anonymous user (**ftp**) can write to **/var/ftp**.

3. Set **anon_upload_enable** (page 720) to YES.

4. See the other parameters in this section.

DOWNLOAD/UPLOAD FOR LOCAL USERS

local_umask   The umask (page 473) setting for local users.

Default: 077
Fedora/RHEL: 022

file_open_mode   Uploaded file permissions for local users. The umask (page 473) is applied to this value. Change to 0777 to make uploaded files executable.

Default: 0666

write_enable   YES permits users to create and delete files and directories (assuming appropriate filesystem permissions). NO prevents users from making changes to the filesystem.

Default: NO
Fedora/RHEL: YES

Anonymous Users

anon_mkdir_write_enable

YES permits an anonymous user to create new directories when **write_enable** is set to YES and the anonymous user has permission to write to the working directory.

Default: NO

anon_other_write_enable

YES grants an anonymous user write permission in addition to the permissions granted by **anon_mkdir_write_enable** and **anon_upload_enable**. For example, YES allows an anonymous user to delete and rename files, assuming she has permission to write to the working directory. For a more secure site, do not set this parameter to YES.

Default: NO

anon_root   After an anonymous user logs in on the server, this directory becomes the user's working directory. No error results if the specified directory does not exist.

Default: none

anon_umask   The umask (page 473) setting for anonymous users. The default setting gives only anonymous users access to files uploaded by anonymous users; set this parameter to 022 to give everyone read access to these files.

Default: 077

anon_upload_enable

YES allows anonymous users to upload files when **write_enable=YES** and the anonymous user has permission to write to the directory.

Default: NO

anon_world_readable_only

YES limits the files that a user can download to those that are readable by the owner of the file, members of the group the file is associated with, and others. It might not be desirable to allow one anonymous user to download a file that another anonymous user uploaded. Setting this parameter to YES can avoid this scenario.

Default: YES

ascii_download_enable

YES allows a user to download files using ASCII mode (page 708). Setting this parameter to YES can create a security risk (page 708).

Default: NO

ascii_upload_enable

YES allows a user to upload files using ASCII mode (page 708).

Default: NO

chown_uploads   YES causes files uploaded by anonymous users to be owned by **root** (or another user specified by **chown_username**). To improve security, change **chown_username** to a name other than **root** if you set this parameter to YES.

Default: NO

chown_username See **chown_uploads**.

> Default: **root**

ftp_username The username of anonymous users.

> Default: **ftp**

nopriv_user The name of the user with minimal privileges, as used by **vsftpd**. Because other programs use **nobody**, to enhance security you can replace **nobody** with the name of a dedicated user such as **ftp**.

> Default: **nobody**

MESSAGES

You can replace the standard greeting banner that **vsftpd** displays when a user logs in on the system (**banner_file** and **ftpd_banner**). You can also display a message each time a user enters a directory (**dirmessage_enable** and **message_file**). When you set **dirmessage_enable=YES**, each time a user enters a directory using cd, **vsftpd** displays the contents of the file in that directory named **.message** (or another file specified by **message_file**).

dirmessage_enable

> YES displays **.message** or another file specified by **message_file** as an ftp user enters a new directory by giving a **cd** command.

> Default: NO
> Fedora/RHEL: YES

message_file See **dirmessage_enable**.

> Default: **.message**

banner_file The absolute pathname of the file that is displayed when a user connects to the server. Overrides **ftpd_banner**.

> Default: none

ftpd_banner Overrides the standard **vsftpd** greeting banner displayed when a user connects to the server.

> Default: none; uses standard **vsftpd** banner

DISPLAY

This section describes parameters that can improve security and performance by controlling how **vsftpd** displays information.

hide_ids YES lists all users and groups in directory listings as **ftp**. NO lists the real owners.

> Default: NO

setproctitle_enable

> NO causes ps to display the process running **vsftpd** as **vsftpd**. YES causes ps to display what **vsftpd** is currently doing (uploading and so on). Set to NO for a more secure system.

> Default: NO

text_userdb_names
NO improves performance by displaying numeric UIDs and GIDs in directory listings. YES displays names.

Default: NO

use_localtime   NO causes the **ls, mls,** and **modtime** FTP commands to display *UTC* (page 1195). YES causes these commands to display the local time.

Default: NO

ls_recurse_enable   YES permits users to give **ls –R** commands. Setting this parameter to YES might pose a security risk because giving an **ls –R** command at the top of a large directory hierarchy can consume a lot of system resources.

Default: NO

Logs

By default, logging is turned off. However, the **vsftpd.conf** file distributed with Fedora/RHEL turns it on. This section describes parameters that control the details and locations of logs.

A **vsftpd** server can generate logs in two formats: **vsftpd** and **xferlog**. The default **vsftpd** log format is more readable than **xferlog** format but cannot be processed by programs that generate statistical summaries of **xferlog** files. Search for **xferlog** on the Internet to obtain more information on this command.

log_ftp_protocol   YES logs FTP requests and responses in the default **vsftpd** log format, provided that **xferlog_std_format** is set to NO.

Default: NO

xferlog_enable   YES maintains a transfer log in **/var/log/vsftpd.log** (or another file specified by **xferlog_file**). NO does not create a log.

Default: NO
Fedora/RHEL: YES

xferlog_std_format
YES causes a transfer log (not covering connections) to be written in standard **xferlog** format, as used by wu-ftpd, as long as **xferlog_file** is explicitly set. If **xferlog_std_format** is set to YES and **xferlog_file** is not explicitly set, logging is turned off. Setting this parameter to NO causes **vsftpd** to generate logs in **vsftpd** log format, provided **log_ftp_protocol** is set to YES.

Default: NO
Fedora/RHEL: YES

xferlog_file   See **xferlog_enable** and **xferlog_std_format**.

Default: **/var/log/xferlog**

CONNECTION PARAMETERS

You can allow clients to establish passive and/or active connections (page 703). Setting timeouts and maximum transfer rates can improve server security and performance. This section describes parameters that control the types of connections that a client can establish, the length of time **vsftpd** will wait while establishing a connection, and the speeds of connections for different types of users.

PASSIVE (PASV) CONNECTIONS

pasv_enable   NO prevents the use of PASV connections.

Default: YES

pasv_promiscuous

NO causes PASV to perform a security check that ensures that the data and control connections originate from a single IP address. YES disables this check. Set to NO for a more secure system.

Default: NO

pasv_max_port   The highest port number **vsftpd** will allocate for a PASV data connection; useful in setting up a firewall.

Default: 0 (use any port)

pasv_min_port   The lowest port number **vsftpd** will allocate for a PASV data connection; useful in setting up a firewall.

Default: 0 (use any port)

pasv_address   Specifies an IP address other than the one used by the client to contact the server.

Default: none; the address is the one used by the client

ACTIVE (PORT) CONNECTIONS

port_enable   NO prevents the use of PORT connections.

Default: YES

port_promiscuous

NO causes PORT to perform a security check that ensures that outgoing data connections connect only to the client. YES disables this check. Set to NO for a more secure system.

Default: NO

connect_from_port_20

YES specifies port 20 (**ftp-data**, a privileged port) on the server for PORT connections, as required by some clients. NO allows **vsftpd** to run with fewer privileges (on a non-privileged port).

Default: NO
Fedora/RHEL: YES

ftp_data_port   With **connect_from_port_20** set to NO, specifies the port that **vsftpd** uses for PORT connections.

Default: 20

TIMEOUTS

accept_timeout   The number of seconds the server waits for a client to establish a PASV data connection.

Default: 60

connect_timeout   The number of seconds the server waits for a client to respond to a PORT data connection.

Default: 60

data_connection_timeout

The number of seconds the server waits for a stalled data transfer to resume before disconnecting.

Default: 300

idle_session_timeout

The number of seconds the server waits between FTP commands before disconnecting.

Default: 300

local_max_rate   For local users, the maximum data transfer rate in bytes per second. Zero (0) indicates no limit.

Default: 0

anon_max_rate   For anonymous users, the maximum data transfer rate in bytes per second. Zero (0) indicates no limit.

Default: 0

one_process_model

YES establishes one process per connection, which improves performance but degrades security. NO allows multiple processes per connection. Set to NO for a more secure system.

Default: NO

MISCELLANEOUS

This section describes parameters not discussed elsewhere.

pam_service_name

The name of the PAM service used by **vsftpd**.

Default: **ftp**
Fedora/RHEL: **vsftpd**

rsa_cert_file   Specifies where the RSA certificate for SSL-encrypted connections is kept.

Default: **/usr/share/ssl/certs/vsftpd.pem**

rsa_private_key_file

Specifies where the RSA key for SSL-encrypted connections is kept.

Default: none

tcp_wrappers YES causes incoming connections to use **tcp_wrappers** (page 484) if **vsftpd** was compiled with **tcp_wrappers** support. When **tcp_wrappers** sets the environment variable **VSFTPD_LOAD_CONF**, **vsftpd** loads the configuration file specified by this variable, allowing per-IP configuration.

Default: NO
Fedora/RHEL: YES

user_config_dir Specifies a directory that contains files named for local users. Each of these files, which mimic **vsftpd.conf**, contains parameters that override, on a per-user basis, default parameters and parameters specified in **vsftpd.conf**. For example, assume **user_config_dir** is set to **/etc/vsftpd/user_conf**. Further suppose the default configuration file, **/etc/vsftpd/vsftpd.conf**, sets **idlesession_timeout=300** and Sam's individual configuration file, **/etc/vsftpd/user_conf/sam**, sets **idlesession_timeout=1200**. Then all users' sessions except for Sam's will time out after 300 seconds of inactivity. Sam's sessions will time out after 1,200 seconds.

Default: none

Other Configuration Files

In addition to **/etc/vsftpd/vsftpd.conf**, the following files control the functioning of **vsftpd**. The directory hierarchy that **user_config_dir** points to is not included in this list because it has no default name.

/etc/vsftpd/ftpusers

Lists users, one per line, who are never allowed to log in on the FTP server, regardless of how **userlist_enable** (page 716) is set and regardless of the users listed in the **user_list** file. The default file lists **root, bin, daemon,** and others.

/etc/vsftpd/user_list

Lists either the only users who can log in on the server or the only users who are not allowed to log in on the server. The **userlist_enable** (page 716) parameter must be set to YES for **vsftpd** to examine the list of users in this file. Setting **userlist_enable** to YES and **userlist_deny** (page 716) to YES (or not setting it) prevents listed users from logging in on the server. Setting **userlist_enable** to YES and **userlist_deny** to NO permits only the listed users to log in on the server.

/etc/vsftpd/chroot_list

Depending on the **chroot_list_enable** (page 718) and **chroot_local_user** (page 718) settings, lists either users who are forced into a chroot jail in their home directories or users who are not placed in a chroot jail.

/var/log/xferlog

Log file. For more information refer to "Logs" on page 722.

CHAPTER SUMMARY

File Transfer Protocol is a protocol for downloading files from and uploading files to another system over a network. FTP is the name of both a client/server protocol (FTP) and a client utility (ftp) that invokes this protocol. Because FTP is not a secure protocol, it should be used only to download public information. You can run the **vsftpd** FTP server in the restricted environment of a chroot jail to make it significantly less likely that a malicious user can compromise the system.

Many servers and clients implement the FTP protocol. The ftp utility is the original client implementation; sftp and lftp are secure implementations that use OpenSSH facilities to encrypt the connection. Although they do not understand the FTP protocol, they map ftp commands to OpenSSH commands. The **vsftpd** daemon is a secure FTP server; it better protects the server from malicious users than do other FTP servers.

Public FTP servers allow you to log in as **anonymous** or **ftp**. By convention, you supply your email address as a password when you log in as an anonymous user. Public servers frequently have interesting files in the **pub** directory.

FTP provides two modes of transferring files: binary and ASCII. It is safe to use binary mode to transfer all types of files, including ASCII files. If you transfer a binary file using ASCII mode, the transfer will fail.

EXERCISES

1. What changes does FTP make to an ASCII file when you download it in ASCII mode to a Windows machine from a Linux server? What changes are made when you download the file to a Mac?

2. What happens if you transfer an executable program file in ASCII mode?

3. When would ftp be a better choice than sftp?

4. How would you prevent a local user from logging in on a **vsftpd** server using her system username and password?

5. What advantage does sftp have over ftp?

6. What is the difference between cd and lcd in ftp?

ADVANCED EXERCISES

7. Why might you have problems connecting to an FTP server in PORT mode?

8. Why is it advantageous to run **vsftpd** in a chroot jail?

9. After downloading a file, you find that it does not match the MD5 checksum provided. Downloading the file again gives the same incorrect checksum. What have you done wrong and how would you fix it?

10. How would you configure **vsftpd** to run through **xinetd**, and what would be the main advantage of this approach?

20

sendmail: SETTING UP MAIL SERVERS, CLIENTS, AND MORE

OBJECTIVES

After reading this chapter you should be able to:

▶ Explain what **sendmail** is

▶ Explain the purpose and give examples of an MUA, an MTA, and an MDA

▶ Describe the role of SMTP, IMAP, and POP

▶ Configure the local SMTP service to use a smarthost for outgoing mail

▶ Configure the local SMTP server to accept incoming mail, relay outgoing mail for specific hosts, and deliver mail directly to the remote systems

▶ Configure mail aliases and mail forwarding

▶ Install and configure SpamAssassin on a mail client and a mail server

▶ Install and configure a Webmail service (SquirrelMail)

▶ Setup a mailing list (Mailman)

▶ Install and configure an IMAP server (Dovecot)

▶ Describe the process and purpose of authenticated relaying

729

Sending and receiving email require three pieces of software. At each end, there is a client, called an MUA (mail user agent), which is a bridge between a user and the mail system. Common MUAs are Evolution, KMail, Thunderbird, mutt, and Outlook. When you send an email, the MUA hands it to an MTA (mail transfer agent, such as **exim4** or **sendmail**), which transfers it to the destination server. At the destination, an MDA (mail delivery agent, such as **procmail**) puts the mail in the recipient's mailbox file. On Linux systems, the MUA on the receiving system either reads the mailbox file or retrieves mail from a remote MUA or MTA, such as an ISP's SMTP (Simple Mail Transfer Protocol) server, using POP (Post Office Protocol) or IMAP (Internet Message Access Protocol).

SMTP Most Linux MUAs expect a local MTA such as **sendmail** to deliver outgoing email. On some systems, including those with a dial-up connection to the Internet, the MTA sends email to an ISP's mail server. Because most MTAs use SMTP (Simple Mail Transfer Protocol) to deliver email, they are often referred to as SMTP servers.

You do not need to set up **sendmail** to send and receive email

tip Most MUAs can use POP or IMAP to receive email from an ISP's server. These protocols do not require an MTA such as **sendmail**. As a consequence, you do not need to install or configure **sendmail** (or another MTA) to receive email. Although you still need SMTP to send email, the SMTP server can be at a remote location, such as your ISP. Thus you might not need to concern yourself with it either.

In the default Fedora setup, the **sendmail** MTA uses **procmail** as the local MDA. In turn, **procmail** writes email to the end of the recipient's mailbox file. You can also use **procmail** to sort email according to a set of rules, either on a per-user basis or globally. The global filtering function is useful for systemwide filtering to detect spam and for other tasks, but the per-user feature is largely superfluous on a modern system. Traditional UNIX MUAs were simple programs that could not filter mail and thus delegated this function to MDAs such as **procmail**. Modern MUAs, by contrast, incorporate this functionality. Although by default RHEL uses **postfix** as the MTA, this chapter explains how to set up **sendmail** as the MTA.

INTRODUCTION TO sendmail

When the network that was to evolve into the Internet was first set up, it connected a few computers, each serving a large number of users and running several services. Each computer was capable of sending and receiving email and had a unique hostname, which was used as a destination for email.

Today the Internet has a large number of transient clients. Because these clients do not have fixed IP addresses or hostnames, they cannot receive email directly. Users on these systems usually maintain an account on an email server run by their employer or an ISP, and they collect email from this account using POP or IMAP. Unless you own a domain where you want to receive email, you will not need to set up **sendmail** to receive mail from nonlocal systems.

OUTBOUND EMAIL

When used as a server, **sendmail** accepts outbound email and directs it to the system it is addressed to (the destination system). This section describes the different ways you can set up **sendmail** to perform this task.

ACCEPTING EMAIL FOR DELIVERY

You can set up a **sendmail** server so it accepts outbound email from the local system only, from specified systems (such as a LAN), or from all systems. Accepting email from unknown systems makes it likely the server will propagate spam.

DELIVERING EMAIL

Direct connection   You can set up a **sendmail** server so it connects directly to the SMTP server on nonlocal destination systems. This SMTP server then delivers the email. Typically, **sendmail** delivers local email directly.

Smarthost   Alternatively, you can set up a **sendmail** server so it sends email bound for nonlocal systems to an SMTP server that relays the mail to its destination. This type of server is called a *smarthost* or *SMTP relay*.

Port 25   By default, SMTP uses port 25. Some Windows viruses use a simple, self-contained SMTP server to propagate themselves. As a partial defense against these types of viruses, some ISPs and larger organizations block all outgoing connections that originate or terminate on port 25, with the exception of connections to their own SMTP server (smarthost). Blocking this port prevents local systems from making a direct connection to send email. These organizations require you to use a smarthost for email bound for nonlocal systems.

INBOUND EMAIL

Although not typical, you can set up **sendmail** to accept email for a registered domain name as specified in the domain's DNS MX record (page 853). However, most mail clients (MUAs) do not interact directly with **sendmail** to receive email. Instead, they use POP or IMAP—protocols that include features for managing mail folders, leaving messages on the server, and reading only the subject of an email without downloading the entire message. If you want to collect email from a system other than the one running the incoming mail server, you might need to set up a POP or IMAP server, as discussed on page 754.

ALTERNATIVES TO sendmail

Over the years, **sendmail** has grown to be enormously complex. Its complexity makes it challenging to configure if you want to set up something more than a simple mail server. Its size and complexity also add to its vulnerability. For optimal security, make sure you run the latest version of **sendmail** and always keep **sendmail** up-to-date. Or you might want to consider using one of the following alternatives.

exim4   The default MTA under Ubuntu, **exim4** (www.exim.org; **exim** package), was introduced in 1995 by the University of Cambridge. It can be configured in several different ways and includes many features other MTAs lack.

Postfix   Postfix (www.postfix.org; **postfix** package) is an alternative MTA. Postfix is fast and easy to administer but is compatible enough with **sendmail** to not upset **sendmail** users. Postfix has a good reputation for ease of use and security and is a drop-in replacement for **sendmail**.

Qmail   Qmail (www.qmail.org) is a direct competitor of Postfix and has the same objectives. By default, Qmail stores email using the **maildir** format as opposed to the **mbox** format that other MTAs use (page 735).

MORE INFORMATION

Web   **sendmail:** www.sendmail.org
exim4: www.exim.org, www.exim-new-users.co.uk, wiki.debian.org/PkgExim4
procmail: www.procmail.org
IMAP and POP3: www.dovecot.org, cyrusimap.org
SpamAssassin: spamassassin.apache.org, wiki.apache.org/spamassassin
Spam database: razor.sourceforge.net
Mailman: www.list.org
SquirrelMail: www.squirrelmail.org
Dovecot: www.dovecot.org
Postfix: www.postfix.org
Qmail: www.qmail.org

Local   **exim4: /usr/share/doc/exim4**/*
Dovecot: **/usr/share/doc/dovecot**
man pages: **sendmail, aliases, makemap, exim4 exim4_files** update-exim4.conf
update-exim4defaults spamassassin spamc **spamd**
SpamAssassin: **/usr/share/doc/spamassassin**, install the **perl** (page 1059) and **spamassassin** packages and give the following command:

```
$ perldoc Mail::SpamAssassin::Conf
```

SETTING UP A sendmail MAIL SERVER

This section explains how to set up a **sendmail** mail server. Under RHEL, before you start **sendmail,** you must stop the Postfix **master** daemon and run chkconfig so the **master** daemon does not start when the system enters multiuser mode:

```
# service postfix stop
Shutting down postfix:                                    [  OK  ]
# chkconfig postfix off
```

Prerequisites

Install the following packages:

- **sendmail**

- **sendmail-cf** (required to configure **sendmail**)

sendmail init script   As installed, **sendmail** is set up to run when the system enters multiuser mode. Give the following command to cause **sendmail** to reread its configuration files:

```
# service sendmail restart
Restarting sendmail (via systemctl):                          [  OK  ]
```

Notes

Firewall   An SMTP server normally uses TCP port 25. If an SMTP server system that receives nonlocal mail is running a firewall, you need to open this port. Using the Fedora/RHEL graphical firewall tool (page 893), select **Mail (SMTP)** from the Trusted Services frame to open this port. For more general information see Chapter 25, which details iptables.

cyrus   This chapter covers the IMAP and POP3 servers included in the **dovecot** package. Fedora/RHEL also provides IMAP and POP3 servers in the **cyrus-imapd** package.

JumpStart I: Configuring sendmail on a Client

You might not need to configure sendmail to send email

tip   With **sendmail** running, give the command described under "Test" on page 734. As long as **sendmail** can connect to port 25 outbound, you should not need to set up **sendmail** to use an SMTP relay as described in this section. If you receive the mail sent by the test, you can skip this section.

This JumpStart configures an outbound **sendmail** server. This server

- Uses a remote SMTP server—typically an ISP—to relay outbound email to its destination (a smarthost or SMTP relay).

- Sends to the SMTP server email originating from the local system only. It does not forward email originating from other systems.

- Does not handle inbound email. As is frequently the case, you need to use POP or IMAP to receive email.

Change   To set up this server, you must edit **/etc/mail/sendmail.mc** and restart **sendmail**.
sendmail.mc
The **dnl** (page 739) at the start of the following line in **sendmail.mc** indicates that this line is a comment:

```
dnl define(`SMART_HOST', `smtp.your.provider')dnl
```

You can ignore the **dnl** at the end of the line. To specify a remote SMTP server, you must open **sendmail.mc** in an editor and change the preceding line, deleting **dnl** from the beginning of the line and replacing **smtp.your.provider** with the FQDN of your ISP's SMTP server (obtain this name from your ISP). Be careful not to alter the back ticks (`) and the single quotation marks (') in this line. If your ISP's SMTP server is at **smtp.myisp.com**, you would change the line to

```
define(`SMART_HOST', `smtp.myisp.com')dnl
```

Do not alter the back ticks (`) or the single quotation marks (')

tip   Be careful not to alter the back ticks (`) or the single quotation marks (') in any line in **sendmail.mc**. These symbols control the way the m4 preprocessor converts **sendmail.mc** to **sendmail.cf**; **sendmail** will not work properly if you do not preserve these symbols.

Restart sendmail   When you restart it, **sendmail** regenerates the **sendmail.cf** file from the **sendmail.mc** file you edited:

```
# service sendmail restart
```

Test   Test **sendmail** with the following command:

```
$ echo "my sendmail test" | /usr/sbin/sendmail user@remote.host
```

Replace *user@remote.host* with an email address on *another system* where you receive email. You need to send email to a remote system to make sure that **sendmail** is relaying your email.

JumpStart II: Configuring sendmail on a Server

If you want to receive inbound email sent to a registered domain that you own, you need to set up **sendmail** as an incoming mail server. This JumpStart describes how to set up such a server. This server

- Accepts outbound email from the local system only.
- Delivers outbound email directly to the recipient's system, without using an SMTP relay (smarthost).
- Accepts inbound email from any system.

This server does not relay outbound email originating on other systems. Refer to "access: Sets Up a Relay Host" on page 742 if you want the local system to act as a relay. For this configuration to work, you must be able to make outbound connections from and receive inbound connections to port 25.

The line in **sendmail.mc** that limits **sendmail** to accepting inbound email from the local system only is

```
DAEMON_OPTIONS(`Port=smtp,Addr=127.0.0.1, Name=MTA')dnl
```

To allow **sendmail** to accept inbound email from other systems, remove the parameter **Addr=127.0.0.1,** from the preceding line:

```
DAEMON_OPTIONS(`Port=smtp, Name=MTA')dnl
```

By default, **sendmail** does not use a remote SMTP server to relay email, so there is nothing to change to cause **sendmail** to send email directly to recipients' systems. (JumpStart I set up a SMART_HOST to relay email.)

Once you have restarted **sendmail**, it will accept mail addressed to the local system, as long as a DNS MX record (page 853) points at the local system. If you are not running a DNS server, you must ask your ISP to set up an MX record.

WORKING WITH sendmail MESSAGES

Outbound email | When you send email, the MUA passes the email to **sendmail**, which creates in the **/var/spool/mqueue** (mail queue) directory two files that hold the message while **sendmail** processes it. To create a unique filename for a particular piece of email, **sendmail** generates a random string and uses that string in filenames pertaining to the email. The **sendmail** daemon stores the body of the message in a file named **df** (data file) followed by the generated string. It stores the headers and envelope information in a file named **qf** (queue file) followed by the generated string.

If a delivery error occurs, **sendmail** creates a temporary copy of the message that it stores in a file whose name starts with **tf** (temporary file) and logs errors in a file whose name starts **xf**. Once an email has been sent successfully, **sendmail** removes all files pertaining to that email from the **mqueue** directory.

Mail addressed to the local system | By default, **sendmail** delivers email addressed to the local system to users' files in the mail spool directory, **/var/spool/mail**, in **mbox** format. Within this directory, each user has a mail file named with the user's username. Mail remains in these files until it is collected, typically by an MUA. Once an MUA collects the mail from the mail spool, the MUA stores the mail as directed by the user, usually in the user's home directory.

Mail addressed to nonlocal systems | The scheme that **sendmail** uses to process email addressed to a nonlocal system depends on how it is configured: It can send the email to a smarthost, it can send the email to the system pointed to by the DNS MX record of the domain the email is addressed to, or it can refuse to send the email.

mbox versus **maildir** | The **mbox** format holds all messages for a user in a single file. To prevent corruption, a process must lock this file while it is adding messages to or deleting messages from the file; thus the MUA cannot delete a message at the same time the MTA is adding messages. A competing format, **maildir**, holds each message in a separate file. This format does not use locks, allowing an MUA to delete messages from a user at the same time as mail is delivered to the same user. In addition, the **maildir** format is better able to handle larger mailboxes. The downside is that the **maildir** format adds overhead when you are using a protocol such as IMAP to check messages. The **dovecot** package supports both **mbox** and **maildir** formats. Qmail (page 732), an alternative to **sendmail**, supports the **maildir** format only.

MAIL LOGS

The **sendmail** daemon stores log messages in **/var/log/maillog**. Other mail servers, such as Dovecot, might also log information to this file. Following is a sample log entry:

/var/log/maillog

```
# cat /var/log/maillog
...
Dec 14 15:37:27 plum sendmail[4466]: oBENbP2Q004464:
to=<mgs@sobell.com>, ctladdr=<sams@example.com> (500/500),
delay=00:00:02, xdelay=00:00:02, mailer=relay, pri=120289,
relay=smtp.gmail.com [72.14.213.109], dsn=2.0.0, stat=Sent (OK
id=1PSeQx-0001uM-3e)
```

Each log entry starts with a timestamp, the name of the system sending the email, the name of the mail server (**sendmail**), and a unique identification number. The address of the recipient follows the **to=** label and the address of the sender follows **ctladdr=**. Additional fields provide the name of the mailer and the time it took to send the message. If a message is sent correctly, the **stat=** label is followed by **Sent**.

A message is marked **Sent** when **sendmail** sends it; **Sent** does not indicate the message has been delivered. If a message is not delivered because an error occurred farther down the line, the sender usually receives an email saying that it was not delivered and giving a reason why.

See the **sendmail** documentation for more information on log files. If you send and receive a lot of email, the **maillog** file can grow quite large. The logrotate (page 621) **syslog** entry archives and rotates these files regularly.

ALIASES AND FORWARDING

You can use the **aliases**, **~/.forward** (page 737), and **virtusertable** (page 743) files to forward email. Table 20-1 on page 743 compares the three files.

/etc/aliases   Most of the time when you send email, it goes to a specific person; the recipient, **user@system**, maps to a real user on the specified system. Sometimes, however, you might want email to go to a class of users and not to a specific recipient. Examples of classes of users include **postmaster**, **webmaster**, **root**, and **tech_support**. Different users might receive this email at different times or the email might go to a group of users. You can use the **/etc/aliases** file to map local addresses and classes to local users, files, commands, and local as well as to nonlocal addresses.

Each line in **/etc/aliases** contains the name of a local (pseudo)user, followed by a colon, whitespace, and a comma-separated list of destinations. The default installation includes a number of aliases that redirect messages for certain pseudousers to **root**. These have the form

```
adm:        root
```

Sending messages to the **root** account is a good way to make them easy to review. However, because **root**'s email is rarely checked, you might want to send copies to a real user. You can set up an alias to forward email to more than one user. The following line forwards mail sent to **abuse** on the local system to **sam** and **max** in addition to **root**:

```
abuse:    root, sam, max
```

It is common to forward mail sent to many special accounts to **root**. If Zach is to read mail sent and forwarded to **root**, you could fix each alias individually. Alternatively, you can simply add the following line *to the end* of the **aliases** file (order does matter in this case). This line forwards to Zach all mail sent and forwarded to **root**:

```
...
root:     zach
```

You can create simple mailing lists with this type of alias. For example, the following alias sends copies of all email sent to **admin** on the local system to several users, including Zach, who is on a different system:

```
admin:    sam, helen, max, zach@example.com
```

You can direct email to a file by specifying an absolute pathname in place of a destination address. The following alias, which is quite popular among less conscientious system administrators, redirects email sent to **complaints** to **/dev/null** (page 503), where it disappears:

```
complaints:    /dev/null
```

You can also send email to standard input of a command by preceding the command with the pipe character (|). This technique is commonly used by mailing list software such as Mailman (page 752). For each list it maintains, Mailman has entries, such as the following one for **painting_class**, in the **aliases** file:

```
painting_class:    "|/var/lib/mailman/mail/mailman post painting_class"
```

newaliases After you edit **/etc/aliases**, you must either run newaliases while you are working with **root** privileges or restart **sendmail** to recreate the **/etc/aliases.db** file that **sendmail** reads.

praliases You can use praliases to list aliases currently loaded by **sendmail**:

```
# praliases | head -5
@:@
abuse:root
adm:root
amanda:root
daemon:root
```

~/.forward Systemwide aliases are useful in many cases, but non**root** users cannot make or change them. Sometimes you might want to forward your own mail: Maybe you want mail from several systems to go to one address, or perhaps you want to forward your mail while you are working at another office. The **~/.forward** file allows ordinary users to forward their email.

Lines in a **.forward** file are the same as the right column of the **aliases** file explained earlier in this section: Destinations are listed one per line and can be a local user, a remote email address, a filename, or a command preceded by the pipe character (|).

Mail that you forward does not go to your local mailbox. If you want to forward mail and keep a copy in your local mailbox, you must specify your local username preceded by a backslash to prevent an infinite loop. The following example sends Sam's email to himself on the local system and on the system at **example.com**:

```
$cat ~sam/.forward
sams@example.com
\sam
```

RELATED PROGRAMS

sendmail   The **sendmail** packages include several programs. The primary program, **sendmail**, reads from standard input and sends an email to the recipient specified by its argument. You can use **sendmail** from the command line to check that the mail delivery system is working and to email the output of scripts. See page 734 for an example. The command **apropos sendmail** displays a list of **sendmail**-related files and utilities.

mailq   The mailq utility displays the status of the outgoing mail queue. When there are no messages in the queue, it reports the queue is empty. Unless they are transient, messages in the queue usually indicate a problem with the local or remote MTA configuration or a network problem.

```
# mailq
/var/spool/mqueue is empty
            Total requests: 0
```

mailstats   The mailstats utility reports on the number and sizes of messages **sendmail** has sent and received since the date it displays on the first line:

```
# mailstats
Statistics from Fri Dec 24 16:02:34 2010
M   msgsfr  bytes_from    msgsto    bytes_to  msgsrej msgsdis  Mailer
0        0          0K     17181     103904K        0       0  prog
4   368386    4216614K    136456    1568314K    20616       0  esmtp
9   226151   26101362K    479025   12776528K     4590       0  local
=============================================================
T   594537   30317976K    632662   14448746K    25206       0
C   694638               499700                146185
```

In the preceding output, each mailer is identified by the first column, which displays the mailer number, and by the last column, which displays the name of the mailer. The second through fifth columns display the number and total sizes of messages sent and received by the mailer. The sixth and seventh columns display the number of messages rejected and discarded respectively. The row that starts with **T** lists the column totals, and the row that starts with **C** lists the number of TCP connections.

CONFIGURING sendmail

The **sendmail** configuration files reside in **/etc/mail**, where the primary configuration file is **sendmail.cf**. This directory contains other text configuration files, such as **access**, **mailertable**, and **virtusertable**. The **sendmail** daemon does not read these files but instead reads the corresponding ✳**.db** files in the same directory.

makemap   You can use makemap or give the command **make** from the **/etc/mail** directory to generate the ✳**.db** files, although this step is not usually necessary: When you run the **sendmail** init script (page 733), it automatically generates these files.

THE sendmail.mc AND sendmail.cf FILES

The **sendmail.cf** file is not intended to be edited and contains a large warning to this effect:

```
$ cat /etc/mail/sendmail.cf
...
######################################################################
#####
#####     DO NOT EDIT THIS FILE!  Only edit the source .mc file.
#####
######################################################################
...
```

EDITING sendmail.mc AND GENERATING sendmail.cf

The **sendmail.cf** file is generated from **sendmail.mc** using the m4 macro processor. It can be helpful to use a text editor that supports syntax highlighting, such as vim, to edit **sendmail.mc**.

dnl   Many of the lines in **sendmail.mc** start with **dnl**, which stands for **delete to new line**; this token causes m4 to delete from the **dnl** to the end of the line (the next NEWLINE character). Because m4 ignores anything on a line after a **dnl** instruction, you can use **dnl** to introduce comments; it works the same way as # does in a shell script.

Many of the lines in **sendmail.mc** *end* with **dnl**. Because NEWLINEs immediately follow these **dnls**, these **dnls** are superfluous; you can remove them if you like.

After you edit **sendmail.mc**, you need to regenerate **sendmail.cf** to make your changes take effect. When you restart **sendmail**, the **sendmail** init script regenerates **sendmail.cf**.

ABOUT sendmail.mc

Lines near the beginning of **sendmail.mc** provide basic configuration information:

```
divert(-1)dnl
include(`/usr/share/sendmail-cf/m4/cf.m4')dnl
VERSIONID(`setup for linux')dnl
OSTYPE(`linux')dnl
```

The line that starts with **divert** tells m4 to discard extraneous output it might generate when processing this file.

The **include** statement tells m4 where to find the macro definition file it will use to process the rest of this file; it points to the file named **cf.m4**. The **cf.m4** file contains other **include** statements that include parts of the **sendmail** configuration rule sets.

The **VERSIONID** statement defines a string that indicates the version of this configuration. You can change this string to include a brief comment about changes you have made to this file or other information. The value of this string is not significant to **sendmail**.

Do not change the **OSTYPE** statement unless you are migrating a **sendmail.mc** file from another operating system.

Other statements you might want to change are explained in the following sections and in the **sendmail** documentation.

Quoting m4 strings

tip   The m4 macro processor, which converts **sendmail.mc** to **sendmail.cf**, requires strings to be preceded by a back tick (`) and closed with a single quotation mark ('). Make sure not to change these characters when you edit the file or **sendmail** will not work properly.

MASQUERADING

Typically you want your email to appear to come from the user and the domain where you receive email; sometimes the outbound server is in a different domain than the inbound server. You can cause **sendmail** to alter outbound messages so that they appear to come from a user and/or domain other than the one they are sent from: In other words, you *masquerade* (page 1175) the message.

Several lines in **sendmail.mc** pertain to this type of masquerading. Each is commented out in the file distributed by Fedora/RHEL:

```
dnl MASQUERADE_AS(`mydomain.com')dnl
dnl MASQUERADE_DOMAIN(localhost)dnl
dnl FEATURE(masquerade_entire_domain)dnl
```

The MASQUERADE_AS statement causes email you send from the local system to appear to come from the specified domain (**mydomain.com** in the commented-out line). Remove the leading **dnl** and change **mydomain.com** to the domain name you want mail to appear to come from.

The MASQUERADE_DOMAIN statement causes email from the specified system or domain to be masqueraded, just as local email is. That is, email from the system specified in this statement is treated as though it came from the local system: It is changed so that it appears to come from the domain specified in the MASQUERADE_AS statement. Remove the leading **dnl** and change **localhost** to the name of the system or domain that sends the email you want to masquerade. If the name you specify has a leading period, it specifies a domain. If there is no leading period, the name specifies a system or host. The **sendmail.mc** file can include as many MASQUERADE_DOMAIN statements as necessary.

The **masquerade_entire_domain** feature statement causes **sendmail** also to masquerade subdomains of the domain specified in the MASQUERADE_DOMAIN statement. Remove the leading **dnl** to masquerade entire domains.

ACCEPTING EMAIL FROM UNKNOWN HOSTS

As configured by Fedora/RHEL, **sendmail** accepts email from domains it cannot resolve (and that might not exist). To turn this feature off and cut down the amount of spam you receive, add **dnl** to the beginning of the following line:

```
FEATURE(`accept_unresolvable_domains')dnl
```

When this feature is off, **sendmail** uses DNS to look up the domains of all email it receives. If it cannot resolve the domain, it rejects the email.

SETTING UP A BACKUP SERVER

You can set up a backup mail server to hold email when the primary mail server experiences problems. For maximum coverage, the backup server should be on a different connection to the Internet from the primary server.

Setting up a backup server is easy. Just remove the leading **dnl** from the following line in the *backup* mail server's **sendmail.mc** file:

```
dnl FEATURE(`relay_based_on_MX')dnl
```

DNS MX records (page 853) specify where email for a domain should be sent. You can have multiple MX records for a domain, each pointing to a different mail server. When a domain has multiple MX records, each record usually has a different priority; the priority is specified by a two-digit number, where lower numbers specify higher priorities.

When attempting to deliver email, an MTA first tries to deliver email to the highest-priority server. If that delivery attempt fails, it tries to deliver to a lower-priority server. If you activate the **relay_based_on_MX** feature and point a low-priority MX record at a secondary mail server, the mail server will accept email for the domain. The mail server will then forward email to the server identified by the highest-priority MX record for the domain when that server becomes available.

OTHER FILES IN /etc/mail

The **/etc/mail** directory holds most of the files that control **sendmail**. This section discusses three of those files: **mailertable**, **access**, and **virtusertable**.

mailertable: FORWARDS EMAIL FROM ONE DOMAIN TO ANOTHER

When you run a mail server, you might want to send mail destined for one domain to a different location. The **sendmail** daemon uses the **/etc/mail/mailertable** file for this purpose. Each line in **mailertable** holds the name of a domain and a destination mailer separated by whitespace; when **sendmail** receives email for the specified domain, it forwards it to the mailer specified on the same line. Fedora/RHEL enables this feature by default: Put an entry in the **mailertable** file and restart **sendmail** to use it.

The following line in **mailertable** forwards email sent to **tcorp.com** to the mailer at **plum.com**:

```
$ cat /etc/mail/mailertable
tcorp.com          smtp:[plum.com]
```

The square brackets in the example instruct **sendmail** not to use MX records but rather to send email directly to the SMTP server. Without the brackets, email could enter an infinite loop.

A period in front of a domain name acts as a wildcard and causes the name to match any domain that ends in the specified name. For example, **.tcorp.com** matches **sales.tcorp.com**, **mktg.tcrop.com**, and so on.

The **sendmail** init script regenerates **mailertable.db** from **mailertable** each time you run it, as when you restart **sendmail**.

access: SETS UP A RELAY HOST

On a LAN, you might want to set up a single server to process outbound mail, keeping local mail inside the network. A system that processes outbound mail for other systems is called a *relay host*. The **/etc/mail/access** file specifies which systems the local server relays email for. As configured by Fedora/RHEL, this file lists only the local system:

```
$ cat /etc/mail/access
...
# by default we allow relaying from localhost...
Connect:localhost.localdomain        RELAY
Connect:localhost                    RELAY
Connect:127.0.0.1                    RELAY
```

You can add systems to the list in **access** by adding an IP address followed by whitespace and the word **RELAY**. The following line adds the 192.168. subnet to the list of hosts the local system relays mail for:

```
Connect:192.168.                     RELAY
```

The **sendmail** init script regenerates **access.db** from **access** each time you run it, as when you restart **sendmail**.

virtusertable: SERVES EMAIL TO MULTIPLE DOMAINS

You can set up DNS MX records (page 853) so a single system serves email to multiple domains. On a system that serves mail to many domains, you need a way to sort the incoming mail so it goes to the correct places. The **/etc/mail/virtusertable** file can forward inbound email addressed to different domains (**aliases** cannot do this).

As **sendmail** is configured by Fedora/RHEL, **virtusertable** is enabled. You need to put forwarding instructions in the **virtusertable** file and restart **sendmail** to serve the specified domains. The **virtusertable** file is similar to the **aliases** file (page 736), except the left column contains full email addresses, not just local ones. Each line in **virtusertable** starts with the address the email was sent to, followed by whitespace and the address **sendmail** will forward the email to. As with **aliases**, the destination can be a local user, an email address, a file, or a pipe symbol (l), followed by a command.

The following line from **virtusertable** forwards mail addressed to zach@tcorp.com to **zcs**, a local user:

```
zach@tcorp.com      zcs
```

You can also forward email for a user to a remote email address:

```
sams@plum.com      sams@tcorp.com
```

You can forward all email destined for a domain to another domain without specifying each user individually. To forward email for every user at **plum.com** to **tcorp.com**, specify **@plum.com** as the first address on the line. When **sendmail** forwards email, it replaces the **%1** in the destination address with the name of the recipient. The next line forwards all email addressed to **plum.com** to **tcorp.com**, keeping the original recipients' names:

```
@plum.com      %1@tcorp.com
```

Finally you can specify that email intended for a specific user should be rejected by using the **error** namespace in the destination. The next example bounces email addressed to **spam@tcorp.com** with the message **5.7.0:550 Invalid address**:

```
spam@tcorp.com      error:5.7.0:550 Invalid address
```

.forward, aliases, and virtusertable   The **.forward** (page 737), **aliases** (page 736), and **virtusertable** files all do the same thing: They forward email addressed to one user to another user. They can also redirect email to a file or to serve as input to a program. The difference between them is scope and ownership; see Table 20-1.

Table 20-1   Comparison of forwarding techniques

	.forward	aliases	virtusertable
Controlled by	non**root** user	**root**	**root**
Forwards email addressed to	non**root** user	Any real or virtual user on the local system	Any real or virtual user on any domain recognized by **sendmail**
Order of precedence	Third	Second	First

SpamAssassin

Spam—or more correctly UCE (unsolicited commercial email)—accounts for more than three-fourths of all email. SpamAssassin evaluates each piece of incoming email and assigns it a number that indicates the likelihood that the email is spam. The higher the number, the more likely the email is spam. You can filter email based on its rating. SpamAssassin is effective as installed, but you can modify its configuration files to make it better fit your needs. See page 732 for sources of more information on SpamAssassin.

How SpamAssassin Works

spamc and **spamd**   SpamAssassin comprises the **spamd** daemon and the spamc client. Although it includes the spamassassin utility, the SpamAssassin documentation suggests using spamc and not spamassassin to filter mail because spamc is much quicker to load than spamassassin. While spamassassin works alone, spamc calls **spamd**. The **spamd** daemon spawns children; when **spamd** is running, ps displays several **spamd child** processes in addition to the parent **spamd** process:

```
# ps -ef | grep spam
root      4254       1  0 14:17 ?         00:00:02 /usr/bin/spamd -d -c -m5 -H -r ...
root      4256    4254  0 14:17 ?         00:00:00 spamd child
root      4257    4254  0 14:17 ?         00:00:00 spamd child
root      4689    4662  0 16:48 pts/1     00:00:00 grep --color=auto spam
```

The spamc utility is a filter: It reads each piece of email from standard input, sends the email to **spamd** for processing, and writes the modified email to standard output. The **spamd** daemon uses several techniques to identify spam:

- **Header analysis**—Checks for tricks people who send spam use to make you think email is legitimate.

- **Text analysis**—Checks the body of an email for characteristics of spam.

- **Blacklists**—Checks lists to see whether the sender is known for sending spam email.

- **Database**—Checks the signature of the message against Vipul's Razor (razor.sourceforge.net), a spam-tracking database.

You can set up SpamAssassin on a mail server so it processes all email being delivered to local systems before it is sent to users (page 747). Alternatively, individual users can run it from their mail clients (page 748). Either way, the local system must run **spamd** and each email message must be filtered through this daemon using spamc.

PREREQUISITES

Install the following packages (both are installed by default):

- **spamassassin**

- **procmail** (needed to run SpamAssassin on a mail server; page 747)

spamassassin init   Run chkconfig to cause **spamassassin** to start when the system enters multiuser mode.
script

```
# chkconfig spamassassin on
```

Start **spamassassin**:

```
# service spamassassin start
```

TESTING SPAMASSASSIN

With **spamd** running, you can see how **spamc** works by sending it a string:

```
$ echo "hi there" | spamc
X-Spam-Checker-Version: SpamAssassin 3.3.2-r929478 (2010-03-31) on sobell.com
X-Spam-Flag: YES
X-Spam-Level: ******
X-Spam-Status: Yes, score=6.9 required=5.0 tests=EMPTY_MESSAGE,MISSING_DATE,
        MISSING_HEADERS,MISSING_MID,MISSING_SUBJECT,NO_HEADERS_MESSAGE,NO_RECEIVED,
        NO_RELAYS autolearn=no version=3.3.2-r929478
X-Spam-Report:
        *  -0.0 NO_RELAYS Informational: message was not relayed via SMTP
        *   1.2 MISSING_HEADERS Missing To: header
        *   0.1 MISSING_MID Missing Message-Id: header
        *   1.8 MISSING_SUBJECT Missing Subject: header
        *   2.3 EMPTY_MESSAGE Message appears to have no textual parts and no
        *       Subject: text
        *  -0.0 NO_RECEIVED Informational: message has no Received headers
        *   1.4 MISSING_DATE Missing Date: header
        *   0.0 NO_HEADERS_MESSAGE Message appears to be missing most RFC-822
        *       headers
hi there
Subject: [SPAM]
X-Spam-Prev-Subject: (nonexistent)
```

Of course, SpamAssassin complains because the string you gave it did not contain standard email headers. The logical line that starts with **X-Spam-Status** contains the heart of the report on the string **hi there**. First it says **Yes** (it considers the message to be spam). SpamAssassin uses a rating system that assigns a number of hits to a piece of email. If the email receives more than the required number of hits (5.0 by default), SpamAssassin marks it as spam. The string failed for many reasons that are enumerated on this status line. The reasons are detailed in the section labeled X-Spam-Report.

The following listing is from a real piece of spam processed by SpamAssassin. It received 24.5 hits, indicating that it is almost certainly spam.

```
X-Spam-Status: Yes, hits=24.5 required=5.0
    tests=DATE_IN_FUTURE_06_12,INVALID_DATE_TZ_ABSURD,
          MSGID_OE_SPAM_4ZERO,MSGID_OUTLOOK_TIME,
          MSGID_SPAMSIGN_ZEROES,RCVD_IN_DSBL,RCVD_IN_NJABL,
          RCVD_IN_UNCONFIRMED_DSBL,REMOVE_PAGE,VACATION_SCAM,
          X_NJABL_OPEN_PROXY
    version=2.55

X-Spam-Level: *************************
X-Spam-Checker-Version: SpamAssassin 2.55 (1.174.2.19-2003-05-19-exp)
X-Spam-Report:   This mail is probably spam.  The original message has been attached
   along with this report, so you can recognize or block similar unwanted
   mail in future.  See http://spamassassin.org/tag/ for more details.
   Content preview:  Paradise SEX Island Awaits! Tropical 1 week vacations
   where anything goes! We have lots of WOMEN, SEX, ALCOHOL, ETC! Every
   man's dream awaits on this island of pleasure. [...]
   Content analysis details:   (24.50 points, 5 required)
   MSGID_SPAMSIGN_ZEROES (4.3 points)  Message-Id generated by spam tool (zeroes variant)
   INVALID_DATE_TZ_ABSURD (4.3 points)  Invalid Date: header (timezone does not exist)
   MSGID_OE_SPAM_4ZERO (3.5 points)  Message-Id generated by spam tool (4-zeroes variant)
   VACATION_SCAM         (1.9 points)  BODY: Vacation Offers
   REMOVE_PAGE           (0.3 points)  URI: URL of page called "remove"
   MSGID_OUTLOOK_TIME (4.4 points)  Message-Id is fake (in Outlook Express format)
   DATE_IN_FUTURE_06_12 (1.3 points)  Date: is 6 to 12 hours after Received: date
   RCVD_IN_NJABL         (0.9 points)  RBL: Received via a relay in dnsbl.njabl.org
   [RBL check: found 94.99.190.200.dnsbl.njabl.org.]
   RCVD_IN_UNCONFIRMED_DSBL (0.5 points)  RBL: Received via a relay in unconfirmed.dsbl.org
   [RBL check: found 94.99.190.200.unconfirmed.dsbl.org.]
   X_NJABL_OPEN_PROXY (0.5 points)  RBL: NJABL: sender is proxy/relay/formmail/spam-source
   RCVD_IN_DSBL          (2.6 points)  RBL: Received via a relay in list.dsbl.org
   [RBL check: found 211.157.63.200.list.dsbl.org.]
X-Spam-Flag: YES
Subject: [SPAM] re: statement
```

CONFIGURING SPAMASSASSIN

SpamAssassin looks in many locations for configuration files; for details, refer to the spamassassin man page. The easiest configuration file to work with is **/etc/mail/spamassassin/local.cf**. You can edit this file to configure SpamAssassin globally. Users can override these global options and add their own options in the **~/.spamassassin/user_prefs** file. You can put the options discussed in this section in either of these files.

For example, you can configure SpamAssassin to rewrite the Subject line of email it rates as spam. The **rewrite_header** keyword in the configuration files controls this behavior. The word **Subject** following this keyword tells SpamAssassin to rewrite Subject lines. Remove the **#** from the following line to turn on this behavior:

```
# rewrite_header Subject *****SPAM*****
```

The **required_score** keyword specifies the minimum score a piece of email must receive before SpamAssassin considers it to be spam. The default is 5.00. Set the value of this keyword to a higher number to cause SpamAssassin to mark fewer pieces of email as spam.

```
required_score 5.00
```

Sometimes mail from addresses that should be marked as spam is not, or mail from addresses that should not be marked as spam is. Use the **whitelist_from** keyword to specify addresses that should never be marked as spam and **blacklist_from** to specify addresses that should always be marked as spam:

```
whitelist_from sams@example.com
blacklist_from *@spammer.net
```

You can specify multiple addresses, separated by SPACEs, on the **whitelist_from** and **blacklist_from** lines. Each address can include wildcards. To whitelist everyone sending email from the example.com domain, use **whitelist_from *@example.com**. You can use multiple **whitelist_from** and **blacklist_from** lines.

RUNNING SPAMASSASSIN ON A MAIL SERVER

This section explains how to set up SpamAssassin on a mail server so it processes all email being delivered to local systems before it is sent to users. It shows how to use **procmail** as the MDA and have **procmail** send email through spamc.

First, make sure the MTA (**sendmail**) uses **procmail** as the MDA. The first two of the following lines in **sendmail.mc** specify the **procmail** path, command, and flags. The MAILER line defines **procmail** as the mailer. You should not have to make changes to these lines.

```
define(`PROCMAIL_MAILER_PATH', `/usr/bin/procmail')dnl
FEATURE(local_procmail, `', `procmail -t -Y -a $h -d $u')dnl
MAILER(procmail)dnl
```

Also make sure the **procmail** package is installed on the server system. Next, if the **/etc/procmailrc** configuration file does not exist, create it so it is owned by **root** and has 644 permissions and the following contents. If it does exist, append the last two lines from the following file to it:

```
$ cat /etc/procmailrc
DROPPRIVS=yes
:0 fw
| /usr/bin/spamc
```

The first line of this file ensures that **procmail** runs with the least possible privileges. The next two lines implement a rule that pipes each user's incoming email through spamc. The **:0** tells **procmail** that a rule follows. The **f** flag indicates a filter; the **w** flag causes **procmail** to wait for the filter to complete and check the exit code. The last line specifies the **/usr/bin/spamc** utility as the filter.

With this file in place, all email the server receives for local delivery passes through SpamAssassin, which rates it according to the options in the global configuration file. Users with accounts on the server system can override the global SpamAssassin configuration settings in their **~/.spamassassin/user_prefs** files.

When you run SpamAssassin on a server, you typically want to rate the email conservatively so fewer pieces of good email are marked as spam. Setting **required_hits** in

Figure 20-1   Evolution Preferences window

the range of 6–10 is generally appropriate. Also, you do not want to remove any email automatically because you could prevent a user from getting a piece of non-spam email. When the server marks email as possibly being spam, users can manually or automatically filter the spam and decide what to do with it.

USING SPAMASSASSIN WITH A MAIL CLIENT

Alternatively, individual users can run it from their mail clients.

With the SpamAssassin (**spamd**) daemon running and the configuration files set up, you are ready to have SpamAssassin filter your email. To do so, you need to set up two rules in your mail client: The first passes each piece of email through SpamAssassin using **spamc** (page 744), and the second filters email based on whether the X-Spam-Flag line has a YES or NO on it.

This section explains how to set up Evolution to work with SpamAssassin. You can set up other mail clients similarly. Evolution is set up to work with SpamAssassin only when you use an IMAP server. With this setup, you must specify you want to use SpamAssassin in two places: Mail Preferences and Mail Accounts. If you have multiple accounts, you must specify each account you want to check for spam.

Open the Evolution Preferences window by selecting **Evolution menubar: Edit⇨Preferences**. Click the Mail Preferences icon and then the Junk tab. See Figure 20-1. Put a tick in the check box labeled **Check custom headers for junk**. Two custom header tests that work with SpamAssassin are installed by default. The first checks if **X-Spam-Flag** is set to **YES**; the second checks if **X-Spam-Level** is set to **✳✳✳✳✳**. One of these tests will return a true value if SpamAssassin has rated a piece of email as spam.

Next, display the Account Editor window by clicking the Mail Accounts icon in the Evolution Preferences window, highlighting the account you want to work with,

Figure 20-2   Account Editor window, Receiving Options tab

and clicking **Edit**. In the Receiving Email tab the Server Type must be IMAP for these instructions to work. Click the Receiving Options tab (Figure 20-2). Under Options, put a tick in the check box labeled **Apply filters to new messages in Inbox on this server**. Click **OK** to close the Account Editor window. Click **Close** to close the Evolution Preferences window.

SELinux   When SELinux is set to use a targeted policy, the SpamAssassin daemon, **spamd**, is protected by SELinux. You can disable this protection if necessary. For more information refer to "Setting the Targeted Policy with system-config-selinux" on page 463.

ADDITIONAL EMAIL TOOLS

This section covers Webmail and mailing lists. In addition, it discusses how to set up IMAP and POP3 servers.

WEBMAIL

Traditionally you read email using a dedicated email client such as mail or Evolution. Recently it has become more common to use a Web application to read email. If you have an email account with a commercial provider such as Gmail, HotMail, or Yahoo! Mail, you use a Web browser to read email. Email read in this manner is called *Webmail*. Unlike email you read on a dedicated client, you can read Webmail from anywhere you can open a browser on the Internet: You can check your email from an Internet cafe or a friend's computer, for example.

SquirrelMail SquirrelMail provides Webmail services. It is written in PHP and supports the IMAP and SMTP protocols. For maximum compatibility across browsers, SquirrelMail renders pages in HTML 4.0 without the use of JavaScript.

SquirrelMail is modular, meaning you can easily add functionality using plugins. Plugins can allow you to share a calendar, for example, or give you the ability to change passwords using the Webmail interface. See the plugins section of the SquirrelMail Web site (www.squirrelmail.org) for more information.

To use SquirrelMail, you must run IMAP (page 754) because SquirrelMail uses IMAP to receive and authenticate email. You must also run Apache (Chapter 26) so a user can use a browser to connect to SquirrelMail.

Prerequisites Install the following packages:

- **squirrelmail**
- **httpd** (page 921)
- **sendmail** (page 730)
- **dovecot** (page 754) or another IMAP server

Startup You do not need to start SquirrelMail, nor do you have to open any ports for it. However, you need to configure, start, and open ports (if the server is running on a system with a firewall) for **sendmail** (page 733), IMAP (page 754), and Apache (page 921).

Configuration The SquirrelMail files reside in **/usr/share/squirrelmail**. Create the following link to make SquirrelMail accessible from the Web:

```
# ln -s /usr/share/squirrelmail /var/www/html/mail
```

Give the following commands to configure SquirrelMail:

```
# cd /usr/share/squirrelmail/config
# ./conf.pl
SquirrelMail Configuration : Read: config_default.php (1.4.0)
---------------------------------------------------------
Main Menu --
1.  Organization Preferences
2.  Server Settings
3.  Folder Defaults
4.  General Options
5.  Themes
6.  Address Books
7.  Message of the Day (MOTD)
8.  Plugins
9.  Database
10. Languages

D.  Set pre-defined settings for specific IMAP servers

C   Turn color on
S   Save data
Q   Quit

Command >>
```

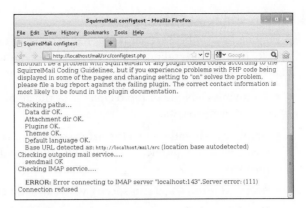

Figure 20-3   SquirrelMail running a configuration test

This menu has multiple levels. When you select a setting (and not a submenu), conf.pl displays information that can help you decide how to answer the question it poses. Set the server's domain name (number **1** on the Server Settings page) and the name of the IMAP server you are using (**D** on the main menu). SquirrelMail provides several themes; if you do not like the way SquirrelMail looks, choose another theme from Themes (number 5). When you are finished making changes, exit from conf.pl. Run conf.pl whenever you want to change the configuration of SquirrelMail.

SquirrelMail provides a Web page that tests its configuration. Point a browser on the server at **localhost/mail/src/configtest.php**. Replace **localhost** with the IP address or FQDN of the server to view the page from another system. SquirrelMail checks its configuration and displays the results on this page. Figure 20-3 shows that SquirrelMail cannot connect to the IMAP server on the local system, probably because IMAP has not been installed.

Logging in   Point a Web browser at **localhost/mail** or **localhost/mail/src/login.php** to display the SquirrelMail login page (Figure 20-4). Replace **localhost** with the IP address or FQDN of the server to view the page from another system. Enter the username and password of a user who has an account on the server system.

Figure 20-4   SquirrelMail login page

MAILING LISTS

A mailing list can be an asset if you regularly send email to the same large group of people. It offers several advantages over listing numerous recipients in the To or Cc field of an email or sending the same email individually to many people:

- **Anonymity**—None of the recipients of the email can see the addresses of the other recipients.

- **Archiving**—Email sent to the list is stored in a central location where list members or the public, as specified by the list administrator, can browse through it.

- **Access control**—You can specify who can send email to the list.

- **Consistency**—When you send mail to a group of people using To or Cc, it is easy to forget people who want to be on the list and to erroneously include people who want to be off the list.

- **Efficiency**—A mailing list application spreads email transmissions over time so it does not overload the mail server.

Mailman   Mailman, the GNU list manager, is written mostly in Python and manages email discussions and email newsletter lists. Because it is integrated with the Web, Mailman makes it easy for users to manage their accounts and for administrators to manage lists. For more information, see the Mailman home page (www.list.org) and, once you have installed Mailman, the files in the **/usr/share/doc/mailman✳** directory.

Prerequisites   Install the **mailman** package and an MTA such as **sendmail** (page 733). To use the Web interface you must install Apache (page 921).

Mailman site list   Give the following newlist command to create a site list, substituting the name of your mailing site for **painting_class**. You must also create a site list named **mailman** (substitute **mailman** for **painting_class**); otherwise Mailman will not start.

```
# /usr/lib/mailman/bin/newlist
Enter the name of the list: painting_class
Enter the email of the person running the list: helen@example.com
Initial painting_class password:
To finish creating your mailing list, you must edit your /etc/aliases (or equivalent) file
by adding the following lines, and possibly running the 'newaliases' program:

## painting_class mailing list
painting_class:              "|/usr/lib/mailman/mail/mailman post painting_class"
painting_class-admin:        "|/usr/lib/mailman/mail/mailman admin painting_class"
painting_class-bounces:      "|/usr/lib/mailman/mail/mailman bounces painting_class"
painting_class-confirm:      "|/usr/lib/mailman/mail/mailman confirm painting_class"
painting_class-join:         "|/usr/lib/mailman/mail/mailman join painting_class"
painting_class-leave:        "|/usr/lib/mailman/mail/mailman leave painting_class"
painting_class-owner:        "|/usr/lib/mailman/mail/mailman owner painting_class"
painting_class-request:      "|/usr/lib/mailman/mail/mailman request painting_class"
painting_class-subscribe:    "|/usr/lib/mailman/mail/mailman subscribe painting_class"
painting_class-unsubscribe:  "|/usr/lib/mailman/mail/mailman unsubscribe painting_class"

Hit enter to notify painting_class owner...
```

Before users on the list can receive email, you need to copy the lines generated by newlist (the ones that start with the name of the new mailing site) to the end of **/etc/aliases** (page 736) and run newaliases (page 737).

You must create a site list named **mailman**

tip With recent versions of mailman, you must use the newlist utility to create a site list named **mailman** in addition to the site lists you want to set up. If you do not create this site list, Mailman will display the error **Starting mailman: Site list is missing: mailman** when you try to start the **qrunner** daemon.

mm_cfg.py The main Mailman configuration file is **/etc/mailman/mm_cfg.py**. When you install Mailman, it assigns the value of **fqdn** to **DEFAULT_EMAIL_HOST** (the default domain for mailing lists) and **DEFAULT_URL_HOST** (the default Web server for Mailman) in this file. Change the values assigned to these variables as needed, making sure to enclose the values within single quotation marks, and start or restart Mailman. The following example uses www.example.com as the default Web server and mail.example.com as the default mail server:

```
# grep '^DEFAULT' /etc/mailman/mm_cfg.py
DEFAULT_URL_HOST   = 'www.example.com'
DEFAULT_EMAIL_HOST = 'mail.example.com'
```

mailman configuration file You can configure many aspects of Mailman mailing lists by modifying the file named **/etc/mailman/sitelist.cfg**. See the comments in this file for more information.

mailman init script After setting up the **mailman** site list and a site list of your choice, start the Mailman **qrunner** daemon with the following command:

```
# service mailman start
Starting mailman:                                          [  OK  ]
```

After modifying any Mailman configuration files or adding a new site list, give the same command but replace **start** with **restart** to cause Mailman to reread its configuration files. Remember also to start **sendmail** and Apache as needed.

Web interface You must modify the last line of the **/etc/httpd/conf.d/mailman.conf** file before the Mailman Web interface will work. Remove the leading hashmark (#) and change the domain name to that of the host for the Web interface as previously established in **mm_cfg.py**:

```
# tail -1 /etc/httpd/conf.d/mailman.conf
RedirectMatch ^/mailman[/]*$ http://www.example.com/mailman/listinfo
```

Restart Apache. Assuming the host for the Web interface is **example.com**, anyone can point a browser at **example.com/mailman** to display a list of available mailing lists. Click the name of a mailing list to display a page that allows you to view the list's archives, send a message, or subscribe to the list. At the bottom of the page is a link to the administrative interface for the list.

If Mailman says **there are no publicly-advertised Mailman mailing lists**, add the following line to **mm_cfg.py** and restart Mailman.

```
VIRTUAL_HOST_OVERVIEW = Off
```

SETTING UP AN IMAP OR POP3 MAIL SERVER

Dovecot   IMAP (Internet Message Access Protocol) and POP (Post Office Protocol) allow users to retrieve and manipulate email remotely. This section explains how to set up servers for these protocols. Dovecot (www.dovecot.org and wiki.dovecot.org) implements these protocols. After you install Dovecot, see **/usr/share/doc/dovecot*** for more information.

Prerequisites   Install the **dovecot** package. The rpm installation script creates the self-signed certificates **dovecot** requires in the files named **/etc/pki/dovecot/certs/dovecot.pem** and **/etc/pki/dovecot/private/dovecot.pem**. Typically, you do not need to modify the **dovecot** configuration file (**/etc/dovecot/dovecot.conf**).

Use chkconfig to cause the **dovecot** daemons to start when the system enters multiuser mode:

```
# chkconfig dovecot on
```

dovecot init script   After configuring **dovecot**, start the **dovecot** daemon with the following command:

```
# service dovecot start
```

Despite **dovecot** reporting that it started the IMAP server only, it also starts the POP3 server. After modifying a **dovecot** configuration file, give the same command, replacing **start** with **restart,** to cause **dovecot** to reread its configuration files.

AUTHENTICATED RELAYING

If you travel with a portable computer such as a laptop, you might connect to the Internet through a different connection at each location where you work. Perhaps you travel for work, or maybe you just bring your laptop home at night.

This section does not apply if you always dial in to the network through your ISP. In that case, you are always connected to your ISP's network and it is as though you never moved your computer.

On a laptop you do not use a local instance of **sendmail** to send email. Instead, you use SMTP to connect to an ISP or to a company's SMTP server (a smarthost), which then relays your outgoing mail. To avoid relaying email for anyone, including malicious users who would send spam, SMTP servers restrict who they relay email for, based on IP address. By implementing authenticated relaying, you can cause the SMTP server to authenticate, based on user identification. In addition, SMTP can encrypt communication when you send mail from your email client and use an SMTP server.

An authenticated relay provides several advantages over a plain connection:

* You can send email from any Internet connection.
* The secure connection makes it more difficult to intercept email as it traverses the Internet.
* The outgoing mail server requires authentication, preventing it from being used for spam.

You set up authenticated relaying by creating an SSL certificate or using an existing one, enabling SSL in **sendmail**, and telling your email client to connect to the SMTP server using SSL. If you have an SSL certificate from a company such as VeriSign, you can skip the next section in which you create a self-signed certificate.

CREATING A SELF-SIGNED CERTIFICATE FOR sendmail

The default location for SSL certificates is **/etc/pki/tls/certs** (PKI stands for public key infrastructure). Working with **root** privileges, give the command **make sendmail.pem** in this directory to generate the required certificates. Apache uses a similar procedure for creating a certificate (page 959).

```
# cd /etc/pki/tls/certs
# make sendmail.pem
...
Generating a 2048 bit RSA private key
...............................+++
..........................................................+++
writing new private key to '/tmp/openssl.snxDr0'
-----
You are about to be asked to enter information that will be incorporated
into your certificate request.
What you are about to enter is what is called a Distinguished Name or a DN.
There are quite a few fields but you can leave some blank
For some fields there will be a default value,
If you enter '.', the field will be left blank.
-----
Country Name (2 letter code) [XX]:US
State or Province Name (full name) []:California
Locality Name (eg, city) [Default City]:San Francisco
Organization Name (eg, company) [Default Company Ltd]:Sobell Associates Inc.
Organizational Unit Name (eg, section) []:
Common Name (eg, your name or your server's hostname) []:sobell.com
Email Address []:mgs@sobell.com

..............++++++
```

You can enter any information you wish in the certificate.

ENABLING SSL IN sendmail

Once you have a certificate, instruct **sendmail** to use it by uncommenting (removing the leading **dnl** from) the following lines in **sendmail.mc**:

```
TRUST_AUTH_MECH(`EXTERNAL DIGEST-MD5 CRAM-MD5 LOGIN PLAIN')dnl
define(`confAUTH_MECHANISMS', `EXTERNAL GSSAPI DIGEST-MD5 CRAM-MD5 LOGIN PLAIN')dnl
```

These lines specify the authentication mechanisms.

Next, uncomment the following lines in **sendmail.mc** to tell **sendmail** where the certificate is:

```
        define(`confCACERT_PATH', `/etc/pki/tls/certs')dnl
        define(`confCACERT', `/etc/pki/tls/certs/ca-bundle.crt')dnl
        define(`confSERVER_CERT', `/etc/pki/tls/certs/sendmail.pem')dnl
        define(`confSERVER_KEY', `/etc/pki/tls/certs/sendmail.pem')dnl
```

Encrypted connections are made in one of two ways: SSL (simpler) or TLS. SSL requires a dedicated port and has the client and the server negotiate a secure connection and continue the transaction as if the connection were not encrypted. TLS has the client connect to the server using an insecure connection and then issue a STARTTLS command to negotiate a secure connection. TLS runs over the same port as an unencrypted connection. Because many clients support only SSL, it is a good idea to instruct **sendmail** to listen on the SMTPS port. The final line you must uncomment in **sendmail.mc** instructs **sendmail** to listen on the SMTPS (SMTP secure) port:

```
DAEMON_OPTIONS(`Port=smtps, Name=TLSMTA, M=s')dnl
```

ENABLING SSL IN THE MAIL CLIENT

Enabling SSL in a mail client is usually quite simple. For example, Evolution provides the **Edit⇨Preferences⇨Mail Accounts⇨Edit⇨Receiving Email⇨Security⇨ Use Secure Connection** combo box that allows you to choose the type of encryption you want to use: **No encryption, TLS encryption,** or **SSL encryption.** There is a similar combo box under the **Sending Email** tab. Alternatively, you can specify the type of encryption you want to use when you set up Evolution.

CHAPTER SUMMARY

The **sendmail** daemon is an MTA (mail transfer agent). When you send a message, **sendmail** works with other software to get the email to the proper recipients. You can set up **sendmail** to send email to an SMTP server that then relays the email to its destination or you can have **sendmail** send email directly to the SMTP servers for the domains receiving the email. By default, **sendmail** stores incoming messages in the mail spool directory, **/var/spool/mail.**

The file that controls many aspects of how **sendmail** works is **sendmail.cf.** If you edit this file, when you restart **sendmail,** the **sendmail** init script generates **sendmail.cf.** The system administrator can use the **/etc/aliases** file and ordinary users can use **~/.forward** files to reroute email to one or more local or remote addresses, to files, or as input to programs.

You can use a program such as SpamAssassin to grade and mark email as to the likelihood of it being spam. You can then decide what to do with the marked email: You can look at each piece of potential spam and decide where to put it, or you can have your MUA automatically put potential spam in a special mailbox for spam.

Other programs that can help with email include SquirrelMail, which provides Webmail services, and Mailman, which provides mailing list support. IMAP (Internet Message Access Protocol) and POP (Post Office Protocol) allow users to retrieve and manipulate email remotely. The Dovecot system provides IMAP and POP servers.

EXERCISES

1. By default, email addressed to **system** goes to **root**. How would you also save a copy in **/var/logs/systemmail**?

2. How would Max store a copy of his email in **~/mbox** and send a copy to **max@example.com**?

3. If your firewall allowed only the machine with the IP address 192.168.1.1 to send email outside the network, how would you instruct the local copy of **sendmail** to use this server as a relay?

4. What does **dnl** stand for in the m4 macro language? What are **dnl** commands used for?

5. SpamAssassin is installed on your mail server, with the threshold set to an unusually low value of 3, resulting in a lot of false positives. What rule could you give to your mail client to allow it to identify spam with a score of 5 or higher?

6. Describe the software and protocols used when Max sends an email to Sam on a remote Linux system.

ADVANCED EXERCISES

7. Your company's current mail server runs on a commercial UNIX server, and you are planning to migrate it to Linux. After copying the configuration files across to the Linux system, you find that it does not work. What might you have forgotten to change?

8. Assume a script stores certain information in a variable named **RESULT**. What line could you put in the script that would send the contents of **RESULT** to the email address specified by the first argument on the command line?

9. Give a simple way of reading your email that does not involve the use of an MUA.

10. If you accidentally delete the **/etc/aliases** file, how could you easily re-create it (assuming that you had not restarted **sendmail**)?

NIS and LDAP

Objectives

After reading this chapter you should be able to:

▶ Describe the architecture and use of NIS

▶ List advantages and disadvantages of NIS

▶ Install an NIS server using static port assignments

▶ Port existing local users to an NIS server

▶ Configure a client to use the NIS server for authentication

▶ Describe the architecture and use of LDAP

▶ List advantages and disadvantages of LDAP

▶ Install and configure an openldap server to hold contact information

▶ Determine required and optional attributes from a published schema

▶ Create an LDIF file to add, modify, or delete an entry

▶ Query an LDAP server with multiple clients

NIS (Network Information Service) simplifies the maintenance of common administrative files by keeping them in a central database and having clients contact the database server to retrieve information from the database. Developed by Sun Microsystems, NIS is an example of the client/server paradigm.

Just as DNS addresses the problem of keeping multiple copies of **/etc/hosts** files up-to-date, so NIS deals with the issue of keeping system-independent configuration files (such as **/etc/passwd**) current. Most networks today are *heterogeneous* (page 1167); even though they run different varieties of UNIX or Linux, they have certain common attributes, such as a **passwd** file.

An LDAP (Lightweight Directory Access Protocol) directory can hold many types of information, including names and addresses, lists of network services, and authentication data. Another example of the client/server paradigm, LDAP is appropriate for any type of relatively static, structured information where fast lookups are required. Many types of clients are set up to communicate with LDAP servers, including email clients, browsers, and authentication servers.

INTRODUCTION TO NIS

A primary goal of a LAN administrator is to make the network transparent to users. One aspect of this transparency is presenting users with similar environments, including usernames and passwords, when they log in on different machines. From the administrator's perspective, the information that supports a user's environment should not be replicated but rather should be kept in a central location and distributed as required. NIS simplifies this task.

As with DNS, users need not be aware that NIS is managing system configuration files. Setting up and maintaining NIS databases are tasks for the system administrator; individual users and users on single-user Linux systems rarely need to work directly with NIS.

Yellow Pages   NIS used to be called the *Yellow Pages,* and some people still refer to it by this name. Sun renamed the service because another corporation holds the trademark to the Yellow Pages name. The names of NIS utilities and files, however, are reminiscent of the old name: ypcat displays and ypmatch searches an NIS file, and the server daemon is named **ypserv**.

HOW NIS WORKS

No encryption   NIS does not encrypt data it transfers over the network—it transfers data as plain text.

NIS domain   NIS makes a common set of information available to systems on a network. The network, referred to as an *NIS domain,* is characterized by each system having the same *NIS domain name* (different than a DNS *domain name* [page 1162]). Technically an NIS domain is a set of NIS maps (database files).

Master and slave servers Each NIS domain must have exactly one master server; larger networks might have slave servers. Each slave server holds a copy of the NIS database from the master server. The need for slave servers is based on the size of the NIS domain and the reliability of the systems and network. A system can belong to only one NIS domain at a time.

When a client determines that a server is down or is not responding fast enough, it selects another server, as specified in the configuration file. If it cannot reach a server, the **ypbind** NIS client daemon terminates with an error.

nsswitch.conf Whether a system uses NIS, DNS, local files, or a combination of these as the source of certain information, and in which order, is determined by the **/etc/nsswitch.conf** file (page 494). When it needs information from the NIS database, a client requests the information from the NIS server. For example, when a user attempts to log in, the client system might authenticate the user with username and password information from the NIS server.

You can configure **nsswitch.conf** to cause **/etc/passwd** to override NIS password information for the local system. When you do not export the **root** account to NIS (and you should not), this setup allows you to have a unique **root** password for each system.

Source files Under Fedora/RHEL, NIS derives the information it offers—such as usernames, passwords, and local system names and IP addresses—from local ASCII configuration files such as **/etc/passwd** and **/etc/hosts**. These files are called *source files* or *master files*. (Some administrators avoid confusion by using different files to hold local configuration information and NIS source information.) An NIS server can include information from one or more of the following source files:

/etc/group	Defines groups and their members
/etc/gshadow	Provides shadow passwords for groups
/etc/hosts	Maps local systems and IP addresses
/etc/passwd	Lists user information
/etc/printcap	Lists printer information
/etc/rpc	Maps RPC program names and numbers
/etc/services	Maps system service names and port numbers
/etc/shadow	Provides shadow passwords for users

The information that NIS offers is based on files that change from time to time. NIS is responsible for making the updated information available in a timely manner to all systems in the NIS domain.

NIS maps Before NIS can store the information contained in a source file, it must be converted to a *dbm* (page 1160) format file called a *map*. Each map is indexed on one field (column). Records (rows) from a map can be retrieved by specifying a value from the indexed field. Some files generate two maps, each indexed on a different field. For example, the **/etc/passwd** file generates two maps: one indexed by username, the other indexed by UID. These maps are named **passwd.byname** and **passwd.byuid**, respectively.

optional   NIS maps correspond to C library functions. The **getpwnam()** and **getpwuid()** functions obtain username and UID information from **/etc/passwd** on non-NIS systems. On NIS systems, these functions place RPC calls to the NIS server in a process that is transparent to the application calling the function.

Map names   The names of the maps NIS uses correspond to the files in the **/var/yp/***nisdomainname* directory on the master server, where *nisdomainname* is the name of the NIS domain. The examples in this chapter use the NIS domain named **mgs**:

```
$ ls /var/yp/mgs
group.bygid    mail.aliases    protocols.byname    services.byname
group.byname   netid.byname    protocols.bynumber  services.byservicename
hosts.byaddr   passwd.byname   rpc.byname          ypservers
hosts.byname   passwd.byuid    rpc.bynumber
```

Map nicknames   To make it easier to refer to NIS maps, you can assign nicknames to them. The **/var/yp/nicknames** file on clients holds a list of commonly used nicknames:

```
$ cat /var/yp/nicknames
passwd        passwd.byname
group         group.byname
networks      networks.byaddr
hosts         hosts.byname
protocols     protocols.bynumber
services      services.byname
aliases       mail.aliases
ethers        ethers.byname
```

You can also use the command **ypcat –x** to display the list of nicknames. Each line in **nicknames** contains a nickname followed by whitespace and the name of the map corresponding to the nickname. You can add, remove, or modify nicknames by changing the **nicknames** file.

Displaying maps   The ypcat and ypmatch utilities display information from the NIS maps on the server. Using the nickname **passwd**, the following command, which you can run on any NIS client in the local domain, displays the information contained in the **passwd.byname** map:

```
$ ypcat passwd
sam:$6$Verpa3R1Ju/ag ... rOysHi.:500:500:Sam the Great:/home/sam:/bin/bash
sls:$6$CMP4baC4WqZ6w ... 7CAiZU0:501:501:Sam the Great:/home/sls:/bin/bash
...
```

By default, NIS stores passwords only for users with UIDs greater than or equal to 500 (see MINUID on page 772). Thus ypcat does not display lines for **root, bin,** and other system entries. You can display password information for a single user with ypmatch:

```
$ ypmatch sam passwd
sam:$6$Verpa3R1Ju/ag ... rOysHi.:500:500:Sam the Great:/home/sam:/bin/bash
```

You can retrieve the same information by filtering the output of ypcat through grep, but ypmatch is more efficient because it searches the map directly, using a single process. The ypmatch utility works on the key for the map only. To match members of the group or other fields not in a map, such as the *GECOS* (page 1166) field in **passwd**, you need to use ypcat and grep:

```
$ ypcat passwd | grep Great
sam:$6$Verpa3R1Ju/ag ... rOysHi.:500:500:Sam the Great:/home/sam:/bin/bash
```

Terminology This chapter uses the following definitions:

NIS source files   The ASCII files that NIS obtains information from
NIS maps   The dbm-format files created from NIS source files
NIS database   The collection of NIS maps

MORE INFORMATION

Local   man pages: domainname, makedbm, **netgroup**, revnetgroup, **ypbind**, ypcat, ypinit, ypmatch, yppasswd, yppoll, yppush, ypset, **ypserv**, **ypserv.conf**, ypwhich, ypxfr, **ypxfrd** (Some of these are installed only when you install **ypserv**, which is needed when you run an NIS server [page 769].)

Web   www.linux-nis.org
NIS-HOWTO

RUNNING AN NIS CLIENT

This section explains how to set up an NIS client on the local system.

PREREQUISITES

Install the following packages:

- **ypbind**
- **yp-tools** (installed automatically with **ypbind**)
- **rpcbind** (installed automatically with **ypbind**)

No server   If there is no NIS server for the NIS client to bind to when you start an NIS client or boot the system, the client spends several minutes trying to find a server and then fails.

rpcbind init script   Run chkconfig to cause the **rpcbind** daemon to start when the system enters multiuser mode:

```
# chkconfig rpcbind on
```

Start the **rpcbind** daemon using service:

```
# service rpcbind start
```

ypbind init script   Run chkconfig to cause the **ypbind** daemon to start when the system enters multiuser mode:

```
# chkconfig ypbind on
```

After you have configured **ypbind**, start it using service. This daemon will fail to start if it cannot connect to an NIS server.

```
# service ypbind start
```

NOTES

If there is no NIS server for the local system's NIS domain, you need to set one up (page 769). If there is an NIS server, you need to know the name of the NIS domain the system belongs to and the name or IP address of one or more NIS servers for the NIS domain.

An NIS client can run on the same system as an NIS server.

SELinux   When SELinux is set to use a targeted policy, NIS is protected by SELinux. You can disable this protection if necessary. For more information refer to "Setting the Targeted Policy with system-config-selinux" on page 463.

CONFIGURING AN NIS CLIENT

This section explains how to set up and start an NIS client.

/etc/sysconfig/network: SPECIFIES THE NIS DOMAIN NAME

A DNS domain name is different from an NIS domain name

tip   The DNS domain name is used throughout the Internet to refer to a group of systems. DNS maps these names to IP addresses to enable systems to communicate with one another.

The NIS domain name is used strictly to identify systems that share an NIS server and is normally not seen or used by users and other programs. Although some administrators use one name as both a DNS domain name and an NIS domain name, this practice can degrade security.

Add the following line to the **/etc/sysconfig/network** file to specify the NIS domain name of the local system:

NISDOMAIN=nisdomainname

The *nisdomainname* is the name of the NIS domain the local system belongs to. The **ypbind** and **ypserv** init scripts execute the **network** file and set the name of the system's NIS domain. You can use the nisdomainname utility to set or view the NIS domain name, but setting it in this manner does not maintain the name when the system is rebooted:

```
# nisdomainname
nisdomainname: Local domain name not set
# nisdomainname mgs
# nisdomainname
mgs
```

To avoid confusion, use nisdomainname, not domainname

tip The domainname and nisdomainname utilities do the same thing: They display or set the system's NIS domain name. Use nisdomainname to avoid confusion when you are also working with DNS domain names.

You must set the local system's NIS domain name

tip If you do not set the local system's NIS domain name, when you start **ypbind**, it logs an error and quits.

/etc/yp.conf: SPECIFIES AN NIS SERVER

Edit **/etc/yp.conf** to specify one or more NIS servers (masters and/or slaves). As explained by comments in the file, you can use one of three formats to specify each server:

> domain **nisdomain** *server* **server_name**

> domain **nisdomain** *broadcast* (**do not use**)

> *ypserver* **server_name**

where **nisdomain** is the name of the NIS domain that the local (client) system belongs to and **server_name** is the hostname of the NIS server that the local system queries. It is best to specify **server_name** as an IP address or a hostname from **/etc/hosts**. If you specify a hostname that requires a DNS lookup and DNS is down, NIS will not find the server. The second format puts **ypbind** in broadcast mode and is less secure than the first and third formats because it exposes the system to rogue servers by broadcasting a request for a server to identify itself.

Following is a simple **yp.conf** file for a client in the **mgs** domain with a server at 172.16.192.151:

```
$ cat /etc/yp.conf
domain mgs server 172.16.192.151
```

You can use multiple lines to specify multiple servers for one or more domains. Specifying multiple servers for a single domain allows the system to change to another server when its current server is slow or down.

When you specify more than one NIS domain, you must set the system's NIS domain name before starting **ypbind** so the client queries the proper server. Specifying the NIS domain name in **/etc/sysconfig/network** before running the **ypbind** init script takes care of this issue (page 764).

START ypbind

The **ypbind** daemon is **ypbind-mt** renamed—that is, a newer, multithreaded version of the older **ypbind** daemon. Use chkconfig to cause **ypbind** to start each time the system enters multiuser mode and service to start **ypbind** immediately. For more information refer to "Prerequisites" on page 763.

TROUBLESHOOTING THE CLIENT

After starting **ypbind**, use nisdomainname to make sure the correct NIS domain name is set. Refer to page 764 if you need to set the NIS domain name. Next use ypwhich to check whether the system is set up to connect to the proper server; the name of this server is set in **/etc/yp.conf** (page 765):

```
$ ypwhich
plum
```

Use rpcinfo to make sure the NIS server is up and running (replace **plum** with the name of the server that ypwhich returned):

```
$ rpcinfo -u plum ypserv
program 100004 version 1 ready and waiting
program 100004 version 2 ready and waiting
```

After starting **ypbind**, check that it is registered with **rpcbind**:

```
$ rpcinfo -u localhost ypbind
program 100007 version 1 ready and waiting
program 100007 version 2 ready and waiting
```

If rpcinfo does not report that **ypbind** is **ready and waiting,** check that **ypbind** is running (message is from a Fedora system, REHL provides a different message):

```
$ service ypbind status
ypbind.service - SYSV: This is a daemon which runs on NIS/YP clients and
binds them to a NIS domain. It must be running for systems based on
glibc to work as NIS clients, but it should not be enabled on systems
which are not using NIS.
        Loaded: loaded (/etc/rc.d/init.d/ypbind)
        Active: active (running) since Tue, 15 Mar 2011 17:51:30
            -0700; 1min 55s ago
       Process: 15967 ExecStart=/etc/rc.d/init.d/ypbind start
            (code=exited, status=0/SUCCESS)
      Main PID: 15981 (ypbind)
        CGroup: name=systemd:/system/ypbind.service
            + 15981 /usr/sbin/ypbind
```

If NIS still does not work properly, use service to stop the **ypbind** daemon and then start it manually with debugging turned on:

```
# service ypbind stop
Stopping ypbind (via systemctl):                          [  OK  ]

# ypbind -debug
15232: parsing config file
15232: Trying entry: domain mgs server 172.16.192.151
15232: parsed domain 'mgs' server '172.16.192.151'
15232: add_server() domain: mgs, host: 172.16.192.151, slot: 0
15232: [Welcome to ypbind-mt, version 1.32]
```

```
       15232: ping interval is 20 seconds

       15234: NetworkManager is running.

       15234: Network is available.
       15234: Switch to online mode
       15234: Going online, reloading config file.
       15234: parsing config file
       15234: Trying entry: domain mgs server 172.16.192.151
       15234: parsed domain 'mgs' server '172.16.192.151'
       15234: add_server() domain: mgs, host: 172.16.192.151, slot: 0
       15234: ping host '172.16.192.151', domain 'mgs'
       15234: Answer for domain 'mgs' from server '172.16.192.151'
       15234: interface: org.freedesktop.DBus, object path:
               /org/freedesktop/DBus, method: NameAcquired
       15235: ping host '172.16.192.151', domain 'mgs'
       15235: Entry for mgs unchanged, skipping writeout
       15235: Answer for domain 'mgs' from server '172.16.192.151'
       15235: Pinging all active servers.
       15235: Pinging all active servers.
       ...
```

The **–debug** option keeps **ypbind** in the foreground and causes it to send error messages and debugging output to standard error. Use CONTROL-C to stop **ypbind** when it is running in the foreground.

yppasswd: CHANGES NIS PASSWORDS

The yppasswd utility—not to be confused with the **yppasswdd** daemon (two **d**'s; page 775) that runs on the NIS server—replaces the functionality of passwd on clients when you use NIS for passwords. Where passwd changes password information in the **/etc/shadow** file on the local system, yppasswd changes password information in the **/etc/shadow** file on the NIS master server *and* in the NIS **shadow.byname** map. Optionally, yppasswd can also change user information in the **/etc/passwd** file and the **passwd.byname** map.

The yppasswd utility changes the way you log in on all systems in the NIS domain that use NIS to authenticate passwords. It cannot change **root** and system passwords; by default, NIS does not store passwords of users with UIDs less than 500. You have to use passwd to change these users' passwords locally.

To use yppasswd, the **yppasswdd** daemon must be running on the NIS master server.

passwd VERSUS yppasswd

When a user who is authenticated using NIS passwords runs passwd to change her password, all appears to work properly, yet the user's password is not changed: The user needs to use yppasswd. The **root** and system accounts, in contrast, must use passwd to change their passwords. A common solution to this problem is first to rename passwd—for example, to rootpasswd—and then to change its permissions so only a user working with **root** privileges can execute it.[1] Second, create a link to yppasswd named passwd. You must work with **root** privileges when you make these changes.

```
# ls -l /usr/bin/passwd
-rwsr-xr-x. 1 root root 28216 02-08 07:41 /usr/bin/passwd
# mv /usr/bin/passwd /usr/bin/rootpasswd
# chmod 700 /usr/bin/rootpasswd
# ln -s /usr/bin/yppasswd /usr/bin/passwd
# ls -l /usr/bin/{yppasswd,passwd,rootpasswd}
lrwxrwxrwx. 1 root root    17 03-15 18:03 /usr/bin/passwd -> /usr/bin/yppasswd
-rwx------. 1 root root 28216 03-08 07:41 /usr/bin/rootpasswd
-rwxr-xr-x. 3 root root 18664 03-08 02:00 /usr/bin/yppasswd
```

With this setup, a non**root** user changing his password using passwd will run yppasswd, which is appropriate. If **root** or a system account user runs passwd (really yppasswd), yppasswd displays an error that reminds the administrator to run rootpasswd.

MODIFYING USER INFORMATION

As long as the **yppasswdd** daemon is running on the NIS master server, a user can use the yppasswd utility from an NIS client to change her NIS password while a user running with **root** privileges can change any user's password (except that of **root** or a system account). A user can also use yppasswd to change his login shell and *GECOS* (page 1166) information if the **yppasswdd** daemon is set up to permit these changes. Refer to "**yppasswdd**: The NIS Password Update Daemon" on page 775 for information on how to configure **yppasswdd** to permit users to change these values. Use the **–p** option with yppasswd to change the password, **–f** to change GECOS information, and **–l** to change the login shell:

```
$ yppasswd -l
Changing NIS account information for sam on plum.
Please enter password:

Changing login shell for sam on plum.
To accept the default, simply press return. To use the
system's default shell, type the word "none".
Login shell [/bin/bash]: /bin/tcsh

The login shell has been changed on plum.
```

```
$ ypmatch sam passwd
sam:$6$Verpa3R1Ju/ag ... rOysHi.:500:500:Sam the Great:/home/sam:/bin/tcsh
```

If yppasswd does not work and the server system is running a firewall, refer to "Firewall" on page 770.

ADDING AND REMOVING USERS

There are several ways to add and remove users from the NIS **passwd** map. The simplest approach is to keep the **/etc/passwd** file on the NIS master server synchronized

---

1. The passwd utility has setuid permission with read and execute permissions for all users and read, write, and execute permissions for **root**. If, after changing its name and permissions, you want to restore its original name and permissions, first change its name and then give the command **chmod 4755 /usr/bin/passwd**. You must work with **root** privileges to make these changes.

with the **passwd** map. You can keep these files synchronized by first making changes to the **passwd** file using standard tools such as useradd and userdel, or their graphical counterparts, and then running ypinit (page 774) to update the map.

SETTING UP AN NIS SERVER

This section explains how to install and configure an NIS server.

PREREQUISITES

Decide on an NIS domain name (page 764) and install the following packages:

- **ypserv**
- **rpcbind** (installed with **ypserv**)

rpcbind init script   Run chkconfig to cause the **rpcbind** daemon to start when the system enters multiuser mode:

```
# chkconfig rpcbind on
```

Start the **rpcbind** daemon:

```
# service rpcbind start
```

ypserv init script   Run chkconfig to cause the **ypserv** daemon to start when the system enters multiuser mode:

```
# chkconfig ypserv on
```

After configuring **ypserv**, start it using the **ypserv** init script:

```
# service ypserv start
```

ypxfrd init script   The **ypxfrd** map server daemon speeds up the process of copying large NIS databases from the master server to slaves. It allows slaves to copy the maps, thereby avoiding the need for each slave to copy the raw data and then compile the maps. When an NIS slave receives a message from the server saying there is a new map, it starts ypxfr, which reads the map from the server.

On the master server only, run chkconfig to cause the **ypxfrd** daemon to start when the system enters multiuser mode:

```
# chkconfig ypxfrd on
```

Next start the **ypxfrd** daemon on the system running the master server:

```
# service ypxfrd start
```

yppasswdd init script   In addition, on the master server only, run chkconfig to cause the NIS password update daemon, **yppasswdd** (page 775), to start when the system enters multiuser mode:

```
# chkconfig yppasswdd on
```

Now start the **yppasswdd** daemon (page 775) on the master server:

```
# service yppasswdd start
```

Notes

An NIS client can run on the same system as an NIS server.

There must be only one master server for each domain.

You can run multiple NIS domain servers (for different domains) on a single system.

An NIS server serves the NIS domains listed in **/var/yp**. For a more secure system, remove the **maps** directories from **/var/yp** when disabling an NIS server.

SELinux When SELinux is set to use a targeted policy, NIS is protected by SELinux. You can disable this protection if necessary. For more information refer to "Setting the Targeted Policy with system-config-selinux" on page 463.

Firewall The NIS server (**ypserv**), the map server daemon (**ypxfrd**), and the NIS password daemon (**yppasswdd**) use **rpcbind** (page 480) to choose which ports they accept queries on. The **rpcbind** server uses port 111 and hands out a random unused port below 1024 when a service, such as **ypserv**, requests a port. Having **ypserv**, **ypxfrd**, and **yppasswdd** use random port numbers makes it difficult to set up a firewall on an NIS server. You can specify ports by editing the **/etc/sysconfig/network** file and adding the lines shown following (choose any unused ports less than 1024; see page 776 for instructions on specifying a port for **yppasswdd**):

```
# cat /etc/sysconfig/network
...
YPSERV_ARGS='--port 114'
YPXFRD_ARGS='--port 116'
```

Using system-config-firewall (page 893), select the Other Ports tab, put a tick in the check box labeled **User Defined**, and add the ports you specified (both TCP and UDP) in the **network** file. For more information refer to "Other Ports" on page 894. You must also add TCP and UDP ports 111 for **rpcbind**.

Configuring the Server

This section explains how to configure an NIS server.

Specify the System's NIS Domain Name

Specify the system's NIS domain name as explained on page 764.

/etc/ypserv.conf: Configures the NIS Server

The **/etc/ypserv.conf** file, which holds NIS server configuration information, specifies options and access rules. Option rules specify server options and have the following format:

option: value

Options

Following is a list of *option*s and their default *value*s:

files Specifies the maximum number of map files that **ypserv** caches. Set to 0 to turn off caching. The default is 30.

trusted_master On a slave server, the name/IP address of the master server from which the slave accepts new maps. The default is no master server, meaning no new maps are accepted.

xfer_check_port YES (default) requires the master server to run on a *privileged port* (page 1182). NO allows the master server to run on any port.

ACCESS RULES

Access rules, which specify which hosts and domains can access which maps, have the following format:

host:domain:map:security

where *host* and *domain* specify the IP address and NIS domain this rule applies to; *map* is the name of the map this rule applies to; and *security* is either **none** (always allow access), **port** (allow access from a privileged port), or **deny** (never allow access).

The following lines appear in the **ypserv.conf** file supplied with Fedora/RHEL:

```
$ cat /etc/ypserv.conf
...
# Not everybody should see the shadow passwords, not secure, since
# under MSDOG everbody is root and can access ports < 1024 !!!
*                        : *       : shadow.byname    : port
*                        : *       : passwd.adjunct.byname : port
...
# *                      : *       : *                : none
```

These lines restrict the **shadow.byname** and **passwd.adjunct.byname** (the **passwd** map with shadow [asterisk] entries) maps to access from ports numbered less than 1024. However, anyone using a DOS or early Windows system on the network can read the maps because they can access ports numbered less than 1024. If you uncomment it, the last line allows access to the other maps from any port on any host.

The following example describes a LAN with some addresses you want to grant NIS access from and some that you do not; perhaps you have a wireless segment or some public network connections you do not want to expose to NIS. You can list the systems or an IP subnet that you want to grant access to in **ypserv.conf**. Anyone logging in on another IP address will then be denied NIS services. The following line from **ypserv.conf** grants access to anyone logging in from an IP address in the range of 192.168.0.1 to 192.168.0.255 (specified as 192.168.0.1 with a network mask [page 479] of /24):

```
$ cat /etc/ypserv.conf
...
  192.168.0.1/24 : * : * : none
```

/var/yp/securenets: Enhances Security

To enhance system security, you can create the **/var/yp/securenets** file, which prevents unauthorized systems from sending RPC requests to the NIS server and retrieving NIS maps. Notably **securenets** prevents unauthorized users from retrieving the **shadow** map, which contains encrypted passwords. When **securenets** does not exist or is empty, an NIS server accepts requests from any system.

Each line of **securenets** lists a netmask and IP address. NIS accepts requests from systems whose IP addresses are specified in **securenets**; it ignores and logs requests from other addresses. You must include the (local) server system as **localhost** (127.0.0.1) in **securenets**. A simple **securenets** file follows:

```
$ cat /var/yp/securenets
# you must accept requests from localhost
255.255.255.255        127.0.0.1
#
# accept requests from IP addresses 192.168.0.1 - 192.168.0.62
255.255.255.192        192.168.0.0
#
# accept requests from IP addresses starting with 192.168.14
255.255.255.0          192.168.14.0
```

/var/yp/Makefile: Creates Maps

The make utility, which is controlled by **/var/yp/Makefile**, uses makedbm to create the NIS maps that hold the information distributed by NIS. When you run ypinit (page 774) on the master server, ypinit calls make: You do not need to run make manually.

Edit **/var/yp/Makefile** to set options and specify which maps to create. The following sections discuss **/var/yp/Makefile** in more detail.

Variables

Following is a list of variables you can set in **/var/yp/Makefile**. The values following Fedora/RHEL are the values set in the file distributed by Fedora/RHEL.

B   Do not change.

Fedora/RHEL: not set

NOPUSH   Specifies that **ypserv** is not to copy (push) maps to slave servers. Set to TRUE if you do not have any slave NIS servers; set to FALSE to cause NIS to copy maps to slave servers.

Fedora/RHEL: TRUE

MINUID,
MINGID   Specify the lowest UID and GID numbers, respectively, to include in NIS maps. In the **/etc/passwd** and **/etc/group** files, lower ID numbers belong to **root** and system accounts and groups. To enhance security, NIS does not distribute password and group information about these users and groups. Set **MINUID** to the lowest UID

number you want to include in the NIS maps and set **MINGID** to the lowest GID number you want to include.

Fedora/RHEL: 500/500

NFSNOBODYUID,
NFSNOBODYGID

Specify the UID and GID, respectively, of the user named **nfsnobody**. NIS does not export values for this user. Set to 0 to export maps for **nfsnobody**.

Fedora/RHEL: 65534/65534

MERGE_PASSWD,
MERGE_GROUP

When set to TRUE, merge the **/etc/shadow** and **/etc/passwd** files and the **/etc/gshadow** and **/etc/group** files in the **passwd** and **group** maps, respectively, enabling shadow user passwords and group passwords.

Fedora/RHEL: TRUE/TRUE

FILE LOCATIONS

The next sections of **/var/yp/Makefile** specify standard file locations; you do not normally need to change these entries. This part of the makefile is broken into the following groups:

Commands—Locates gawk and make and sets a value for umask (page 473)
Source directories—Locates directories that contain NIS source files
NIS source files—Locates NIS source files used to build the NIS database
Servers—Locates the file that lists NIS servers

Two **ALIASES** lines appear in the NIS source files section. To avoid getting an error message in the next step, uncomment the line with the leading hash sign and comment the other so they look like this:

```
ALIASES    = $(YPSRCDIR)/aliases  # aliases could be in /etc or /etc/mail
#ALIASES    = /etc/mail/aliases
```

THE all: TARGET

The **all:** target in **/var/yp/Makefile** specifies the maps that make is to build for NIS:

```
all:  passwd group hosts rpc services netid protocols mail \
        # netgrp shadow publickey networks ethers bootparams printcap \
        # amd.home auto.master auto.home auto.local passwd.adjunct \
        # timezone locale netmasks
```

The first line of the **all:** target lists the maps that make builds by default. This line starts with the word **all**, followed by a colon (:) and a TAB. Because each of the first three lines of the **all:** target ends with a backslash, each of the four physical lines in the **all:** target is part of one long logical line. The last three physical lines are commented out. Uncomment lines and delete or move map names until the list matches your needs.

As your needs change, you can edit the **all:** target in **Makefile** and run make in the **/var/yp** directory to modify the list of maps distributed by NIS.

START THE SERVERS

Start the master server and then the slave servers after completing the preceding steps. See page 769 for details.

ypinit: BUILDS OR IMPORTS THE MAPS

The ypinit utility builds or imports and then installs the NIS database. On the master server, ypinit gathers information from the **passwd, group, hosts, networks, services, protocols, netgroup,** and **rpc** files in **/etc** and builds the database. On a slave server, ypinit copies the database from the master server.

You must run ypinit by giving its absolute pathname (**/usr/lib/yp/ypinit**). Use the **–m** option to create the domain subdirectory under **/var/yp** and build the maps that go in it on the master server; use the **–s** *master* option on slave servers to import maps from the master server named *master*. In the following example, ypinit asks for the name of each of the slave servers; it already has the name of the master server because this command is run on the system running the master server (**plum** in the example). Terminate the list with CONTROL-D on a line by itself. After you respond to the query about the list of servers being correct, ypinit builds the **ypservers** map and calls make with **/var/yp/Makefile**, which builds the maps specified in **Makefile**. On 64-bit systems use **/usr/lib64/yp/ypinit –m** in place of the command in the example.

```
# /usr/lib/yp/ypinit -m

At this point, we have to construct a list of the hosts which will run NIS
servers.  plum is in the list of NIS server hosts.  Please continue to add
the names for the other hosts, one per line.  When you are done with the
list, type a <control D>.
        next host to add:  plum
        next host to add:  CONTROL-D
      The current list of NIS servers looks like this:
plum

Is this correct?  [y/n: y]  y
We need a few minutes to build the databases...
Building /var/yp/mgs/ypservers...
Running /var/yp/Makefile...
gmake[1]: Entering directory `/var/yp/mgs'
Updating passwd.byname...
Updating passwd.byuid...
Updating group.byname...
Updating group.bygid...
Updating hosts.byname...
Updating hosts.byaddr...
Updating rpc.byname...
Updating rpc.bynumber...
Updating services.byname...
Updating services.byservicename...
```

```
Updating netid.byname...
Updating protocols.bynumber...
Updating protocols.byname...
Updating mail.aliases...
gmake[1]: Leaving directory `/var/yp/mgs'

plum has been set up as a NIS master server.

Now you can run ypinit -s guava on all slave server.
```

After running **ypinit,** you must restart the server (page 769).

TROUBLESHOOTING THE SERVER

This section suggests some ways to troubleshoot an NIS server. See "Troubleshooting the Client" on page 766 for techniques you can use to troubleshoot an NIS client.

From the server, check that **ypserv** is connected to **rpcbind:**

```
$ rpcinfo -p | grep ypserv
    100004    2    udp    819    ypserv
    100004    1    udp    819    ypserv
    100004    2    tcp    822    ypserv
    100004    1    tcp    822    ypserv
```

Again from the server system, make sure the NIS server is up and running:

```
$ rpcinfo -u localhost ypserv
program 100004 version 1 ready and waiting
program 100004 version 2 ready and waiting
```

If the server is not working properly, use **service** to stop the NIS server. Then start **ypserv** manually in the foreground with debugging turned on:

```
# service ypserv stop
# ypserv --debug
[ypserv (ypserv) 2.24]

ypserv.conf: files: 30
ypserv.conf: xfr_check_port: 1
ypserv.conf: 0.0.0.0/0.0.0.0:*:shadow.byname:2
ypserv.conf: 0.0.0.0/0.0.0.0:*:passwd.adjunct.byname:2
...
```

The **--debug** option keeps **ypserv** in the foreground and causes it to send error messages and debugging output to standard error. Press CONTROL-C to stop **ypserv** when it is running in the foreground.

yppasswdd: THE NIS PASSWORD UPDATE DAEMON

The NIS password update daemon, **yppasswdd,** runs on the master server only; it is not necessary to run it on slave servers. If the master server is down and you try to change your password from a client, **yppasswd** displays an error message. When a user runs **yppasswd** (page 767) on a client, this utility exchanges information with the **yppasswdd** daemon to update the user's password (and optionally other) information in the NIS **shadow** (and optionally **passwd**) map and in the **/etc/shadow** (and optionally **/etc/passwd**) file on the NIS master server. Password change requests are sent to **syslogd** (page 623).

If the server system is running a firewall, open a port for **yppasswdd**. Refer to "Firewall" on page 770.

START yppasswdd

Start **yppasswdd** as explained on page 769.

ALLOW GECOS AND LOGIN SHELL MODIFICATION

As shipped, **yppasswdd** does not allow users to change their login shell or *GECOS* (page 1166) information. You can change these settings with options on the command line when you start **yppasswdd** or, more conveniently, by modifying the **/etc/sysconfig/yppasswdd** configuration file. The **–e chfn** option to **yppasswdd** allows users to change their GECOS information; **–e chsh** allows users to change their login shell. When you set the options in **/etc/sysconfig/yppasswdd**, these values are set automatically each time **yppasswdd** is run. The following example causes **yppasswdd** to accept calls on port 112 and allows users to change both their GECOS information and their login shell:

```
# cat /etc/sysconfig/yppasswdd
...
YPPASSWDD_ARGS='--port 112 -e chfn -e chsh'
```

LDAP

LDAP (Lightweight Directory Access Protocol) is an alternative to the older X.500 DAP (Directory Access Protocol). It runs over TCP/IP and is network aware, standards-based, and available on many platforms. A client queries an LDAP server, specifying the data it wants. For example, a query could ask for the first names and email addresses of all people with a last name of Smith who live in San Francisco.

Directory   Because LDAP is designed to work with data that does not change frequently, the server holds a search and read optimized database, called a *directory*. LDAP clients query and update this directory.

In addition to name and address information, an LDAP directory can hold lists of network services. Or, other services can use it for authentication. LDAP is appropriate for any kind of relatively static structured information where fast lookups are required. Many types of clients are set up to communicate with LDAP servers, including LDAP-specific clients (page 784), email clients, and authentication servers.

OpenLDAP   Fedora/RHEL provides the OpenLDAP (www.openldap.org) implementation of LDAP. OpenLDAP uses the Sleepycat Berkeley Database (Berkeley DB, or BDB, now owned by Oracle), which meets the needs of an LDAP database. It supports distributed architecture, replication, and encryption. BDB differs from a relational database (RDBMS) in that instead of holding information in rows and columns,

BDB implements an LDAP directory as a hierarchical data structure that groups information with similar attributes. This section describes OpenLDAP.

In addition to BDB, Fedora/RHEL supplies HDB (Hash Database), which is based on BDB but which organizes data in a true hierarchical fashion. HDB provides faster writes than does BDB. It also supports subtree renaming, which allows subtrees to be moved efficiently within a database.

Fedora/RHEL Directory Servers In addition to OpenLDAP, Fedora provides the 389 Directory Server (**389-ds** package) and RHEL provides the Red Hat Directory Server, both of which are LDAP servers. For more information see the references on page 778.

Entries and attributes An *entry* (a node in the LDAP directory hierarchy, or a container) is the basic unit of information in an LDAP directory. Each entry holds one or more *attributes*. Each attribute has a name (an attribute type or description) and one or more values. Attribute names come from a standard schema that is held in files found in the **/etc/openldap/schema** directory. This schema is standard across many implementations of LDAP, enabling LDAP clients to obtain data from many LDAP servers. Although it is not usually necessary or advisable, you can augment or modify the standard schema.

DN A Distinguished Name (DN) uniquely identifies each entry in an LDAP directory. A DN comprises a Relative Distinguished Name (RDN), which is constructed from one or more attributes in the entry, followed by the DN of the parent entry. Because a DN can change (e.g., a woman might change her last name), and because a consistent, unique identifier is sometimes required, the server assigns a UUID (an unambiguous identifier) to each entry.

DSE and DC The DSE (DSA-Specific Entry) is the root, or top-level, entry in an LDAP directory. (DSA stands for Directory System Agent.) The DSE is defined in the file named **/etc/openldap/slapd.d/cn=config/olcDatabase={1}bdb.ldif** and specifies the domain name of the server. LDAP defines a domain name in terms of its component parts. The following line defines the DSE comprising the Domain Component (DC) **brillserve** and the DC **com**:

```
# grep brillserve /etc/openldap/slapd.d/cn=config/olcDatabase={1}bdb.ldif
olcSuffix: dc=brillserve,dc=com
```

LDIF and CN The LDAP directory specified by the example DSE could contain the following entry, which is specified in LDAP Data Interchange Format (LDIF; see the **ldif** man page for more information):

```
dn: cn=Sam the Great,dc=brillserve,dc=com
cn: Sam the Great
cn: the great
objectClass: inetOrgPerson
mail: sam@brillserve.com
givenName: Sam
sn: the Great
displayName: Sam the Great
telephoneNumber: 888 888 8888
homePhone: 111 111 1111
initials: SLS
```

Each line except the first specifies an attribute. The word on each line preceding the colon is the attribute name. Following the colon and a SPACE is the attribute value. The first line in this example specifies the DN of the entry. The attribute value used in the RDN is a CN (Common Name) from the entry: **Sam the Great**. This second-level entry is a child of the top-level entry; thus the DN of the parent entry is the DN of the top-level entry (**dc=brillserve,dc=com**). You can uniquely identify this entry by its DN: **cn=Sam the Great,dc=brillserve,dc=com**.

Because this entry defines two CNs, a search for **Sam the Great** or **the Great** will return this entry. This entry also defines a given name, a surname (**sn**), an email address (**mail**), and other attributes.

objectClass attribute   Entries inherit object class attributes from their parents. In addition, each entry must have at least one **objectClass** attribute. Each **objectClass** value must be a class defined in the schema. The schema specifies both mandatory and optional (allowed) attributes for an object class. For example, the following entry in the schema defines the object class named **person**. The MUST and MAY lines specify which attributes the **person** object class requires (**sn** [surname] and **cn**; attribute names are separated by a dollar sign) and which attributes are optional (**userPassword, telephoneNumber, seeAlso,** and **description**).

```
$ cat /etc/openldap/schema/core.schema
...
objectclass ( 2.5.6.6 NAME 'person'
        DESC 'RFC2256: a person'
        SUP top STRUCTURAL
        MUST ( sn $ cn )
        MAY ( userPassword $ telephoneNumber $ seeAlso $ description ) )
...
```

Abbreviations   The following list summarizes the abbreviations mentioned in this section.

CN	Common Name
DC	Domain Component
DN	Distinguished Name
DSE	DSA-Specific Entry
LDIF	LDAP Data Interchange Format
RDN	Relative Distinguished Name

MORE INFORMATION

Local   man pages: **ldap.conf,** ldapmodify, ldapsearch, **ldif, slapd, slapd.conf,** slappasswd

Web   LDAP home page: www.openldap.org
Administrator's Guide: www.openldap.org/doc/admin24
389 Directory Server home page: directory.fedoraproject.org
Red Hat Directory Server manuals: docs.redhat.com/docs/en-US/
    Red_Hat_Directory_Server/7.1/html/Administrators_Guide/adminTOC.htm
    (these manuals apply to both the Fedora and Red Hat Directory Servers)
OpenLDAP Faq-O-Matic: www.openldap.org/faq

book: www.zytrax.com/books/ldap
gq: sourceforge.net/projects/gqclient

HOWTO   *LDAP Linux HOWTO*

SETTING UP AN LDAP SERVER

This section explains how to set up an LDAP server.

PREREQUISITES

Install the following packages:

- **openldap-clients**
- **openldap-servers**

slapd init script   Run chkconfig to cause the LDAP daemon, **slapd** (stand-alone LDAP daemon—the abbreviation does not quite work), to start when the system enters multiuser mode. Do not confuse **ldap** and **slapd** in the names of utilities, daemons, and init scripts.

```
# chkconfig slapd on
```

After configuring **slapd**, start it with the following command.

```
# service slapd start
```

Replace **start** with **restart** when you need to restart the daemon, such as after changing an LDAP configuration file.

NOTE

Firewall   The **slapd** LDAP server normally listens on TCP port 389, which is not encrypted. If you are using LDAP for authentication, use LDAP over SSL on port 636. If the LDAP server system is running a firewall, you need to open one of these ports. Using system-config-firewall (page 893), select the Other Ports tab, put a tick in the check box labeled **User Defined**, and open TCP port 389 or 636. For more information refer to "Other Ports" on page 894.

STEP-BY-STEP SETUP

This section lists the steps involved in setting up an LDAP server at the brillserve.com domain. When you set up an LDAP server, substitute the domain name of the server you are setting up for **brillserve.com** in the examples. The example in this section is quite simple, so you will probably need different entries in the directory you set up.

To experiment with and learn about LDAP, set up and run locally the example server described in this section. Although the example uses brillserve.com, when working from the server system you can refer to the LDAP server as **localhost**.

CONFIGURE THE SERVER

1. Rename **ldap.conf** so it does not interfere with the server you are setting up:

   ```
   # mv /etc/openldap/ldap.conf /etc/openldap/ldap.conf.0
   ```

2. The other files you need to change are in the **cn=config** directory; cd to that directory:

   ```
   # cd /etc/openldap/slapd.d/cn=config
   ```

3. Make the following changes to the **olcDatabase={1}bdb.ldif** file:

   a. The **olcSuffix** line defines the DSE (page 777). Change the existing **olcSuffix** line as follows:

   ```
   olcSuffix: dc=brillserve,dc=com
   ```

   b. The **olcRootDN** line establishes the user (the LDAP administrator) who can read any information from and write any information to the LDAP directory. The value on this line is the DN for this user. The RDN is the name of the LDAP administrator; the DN includes the DN of the parent node (the DSE as specified in step 3a).

   In this example, the name of this user is **ldapadmin** and the password is **porcupine**. This user does not need to exist as a user on the system (i.e., the user does not need to be listed in **/etc/passwd**).

   ```
   olcRootDN: cn=ldapadmin,dc=brillserve,dc=com
   ```

   c. The **olcRootPW** line sets up a password for the LDAP administrator specified in step 3b. Add an **olcRootPW** line as shown next. This example sets up **porcupine** as a cleartext password.

   ```
   olcRootPW: porcupine
   ```

   If you will be administrating LDAP over a network, use an encrypted password. First use slappasswd to encrypt a password:

   ```
   # slappasswd
   New password:
   Re-enter new password:
   {SSHA}7h060/qgeUrXl/Tsqy80lTbGYBOXdc/+
   ```

   Then copy the output of slappasswd to a new **olcRootPW** line:

   ```
   olcRootPW: {SSHA}7h060/qgeUrXl/Tsqy80lTbGYBOXdc/+
   ```

4. Make the following change to the **olcDatabase={2}monitor.ldif** file:

```
olcAccess: {0}to * by dn.base="cn=ldapadmin,dc=brillserve,dc=com" read  by * none
```

START AND TEST THE SERVER

Start the **slapd** daemon as explained under "Prerequisites" on page 769. Then test the server with the following query:

```
$ ldapsearch -x -s base namingContexts
# extended LDIF
#
# LDAPv3
# base <> (default) with scope baseObject
# filter: (objectclass=*)
# requesting: namingContexts
#

#
dn:
namingContexts: dc=brillserve,dc=com

# search result
search: 2
result: 0 Success

# numResponses: 2
# numEntries: 1
```

The **–x** on the command line specifies simple authentication, **–s base** specifies the scope of the search as the base object, and **namingContexts** is the attribute you are searching for. The output of this command should look similar to that shown in the preceding example. The **namingContexts** returned by the search should be the same as the DSE you specified when you configured the server.

ADD ENTRIES TO THE DIRECTORY

You can use many tools, both graphical and textual, to add information to and query an LDAP directory. This section explains how to use the ldapmodify command-line utility to set up an employee LDAP directory. See page 784 for descriptions of other tools.

When you specify the following file on an ldapmodify command line, ldapmodify adds a second-level entry (one below the DSE entry) to the directory:

```
$ cat one.ldif
dn: dc=brillserve,dc=com
changetype: add
dc: brillserve
objectClass: dcObject
objectClass: organization
organizationName: ZBrill Associates Inc.
```

The first line of **one.ldif** specifies the root DN for the entry you are adding. The **changetype** instruction tells ldapmodify to add the entry to the directory. You can omit this instruction if you use the **–a** option on the ldapmodify command line or if you use the ldapadd utility in place of ldapmodify. The line that starts with **dc** specifies the DC (domain component). The **objectClass** lines specify the object classes this entry belongs to. The **organizationName** specifies the name of the organization this entry is part of.

The following command modifies the LDAP directory based on the **one.ldif** file. The **ldif** filename extension is commonly used but is not required for files holding LDIF entries.

```
$ ldapmodify -xD "cn=ldapadmin,dc=brillserve,dc=com" -w porcupine -f one.ldif
adding new entry "dc=brillserve,dc=com"
```

The **–x** option causes the server to use simple authentication. The argument following **–D** specifies the DN of the LDAP administrator of the directory the command is to work with (specified in step b on page 780). By specifying this user, this argument also specifies the DSE of the LDAP directory. (The DN of the parent of the LDAP administrator's entry specifies the DSE.) The argument following **–w** is the password for the LDAP administrator. For better security, you can use **–W** to cause ldapmodify to prompt for this password. The name of the input file follows the **–f** option. The ldapmodify utility reports the DN of the new entry.

The **slapcat** utility, which must be run as the **root** user of the system (not the administrator of the LDAP directory), displays all entries in the LDAP directory in LDIF format. After the executing the preceding command, there is one entry:

```
$ su -c slapcat
dn: dc=brillserve,dc=com
dc: brillserve
objectClass: dcObject
objectClass: organization
o: ZBrill Associates Inc.
structuralObjectClass: organization
entryUUID: 341413f4-e44b-102f-9480-97daa3d0714e
creatorsName: cn=ldapadmin,dc=brillserve,dc=com
createTimestamp: 20110316185902Z
entryCSN: 20110316185902.781196Z#000000#000#000000
modifiersName: cn=ldapadmin,dc=brillserve,dc=com
modifyTimestamp: 20110316185902Z
```

The **o** attribute name is an abbreviation for **organizationName**. The server adds additional information to the entry, including a UUID number that remains constant throughout the life of the entry, timestamps, and the names of the users who created and modified the entry. In this case they are the same person.

You can put as many entries in a file as you like, but each must be separated from the next by a blank line. For clarity, the examples in this section show one entry per file.

The next file adds to the LDAP directory the object class **organizationalUnit** named **employees** (**ou=employees**). The DN is **ou=employees** followed by the DSE:

```
$ cat two.ldif
dn: ou=employees,dc=brillserve,dc=com
changetype: add
objectClass: organizationalUnit
ou: employees
```

```
$ ldapmodify -xD "cn=ldapadmin,dc=brillserve,dc=com" -w porcupine -f two.ldif
adding new entry "ou=employees,dc=brillserve,dc=com"
```

With this object class in place, you can add employees to the LDAP directory. You can use the following file to add an employee:

```
$ cat three.ldif
dn: cn=Zach Brill,ou=employees,dc=brillserve,dc=com
changetype: add
cn: Zach Brill
cn: brillserve
objectClass: inetOrgPerson
mail: zbrill@brillserve.com
givenName: Zach
surname: Brill
displayName: Zach Brill
telephoneNumber: 999 999 9999
homePhone: 000 000 0000
initials: ZCB
```

```
$ ldapmodify -xD "cn=ldapadmin,dc=brillserve,dc=com" -w porcupine -f three.ldif
adding new entry "cn=Zach Brill,ou=employees,dc=brillserve,dc=com"
```

Now slapcat shows the employee you just added:

```
$ su -c slapcat
dn: dc=brillserve,dc=com
dc: brillserve
...
dn: cn=Zach Brill,ou=employees,dc=brillserve,dc=com
cn: Zach Brill
cn: brillserveobjectClass: inetOrgPerson
mail: zbrill@brillserve.com
givenName: Zach
sn: Brill
displayName: Zach Brill
telephoneNumber: 999 999 9999
homePhone: 000 000 0000
initials: ZCB
structuralObjectClass: inetOrgPerson
entryUUID: c03f3f4c-e44c-102f-9482-97daa3d0714e
creatorsName: cn=ldapadmin,dc=brillserve,dc=com
createTimestamp: 20110316191007Z
entryCSN: 20110316191007.441864Z#000000#000#000000
modifiersName: cn=ldapadmin,dc=brillserve,dc=com
modifyTimestamp: 20110316191007Z
```

The DN shows that the new employee is at the third level of the directory structure: The first level is **dc=brillserve,dc=com**; **ou=employees,dc=brillserve,dc=com** is at the second level; and **cn=Zach Brill,ou=employees,dc=brillserve,dc=com**, the employee, is at the third level.

The following example adds another employee at the third level:

```
$ cat four.ldif
dn: cn=Sam the Great,ou=employees,dc=brillserve,dc=com
changetype: add
cn: Sam the Great
cn: the great
objectClass: inetOrgPerson
mail: sam@brillserve.com
givenName: Sam
surname: the Great
displayName: Sam the Great
telephoneNumber: 888 888 8888
homePhone: 111 111 1111
initials: SLS

$ ldapmodify -xD "cn=ldapadmin,dc=brillserve,dc=com" -w porcupine -f four.ldif
adding new entry "cn=Sam the Great,ou=employees,dc=brillserve,dc=com"
```

The next example uses the ldapmodify **modify** instruction to replace the **mail** attribute value and add a **title** attribute for the employee named Sam the Great. The hyphen on a line by itself separates multiple modifications in a single file. Because the file specifies Sam's DN, the server knows which entry to modify.

```
$ cat five.ldif
dn: cn=Sam the Great,ou=employees,dc=brillserve,dc=com
changetype: modify
replace: mail
mail: sls@brillserve.com
-
add: title
title: CTO

$ ldapmodify -xD "cn=ldapadmin,dc=brillserve,dc=com" -w porcupine -f five.ldif
modifying entry "cn=Sam the Great,ou=employees,dc=brillserve,dc=com"
```

You can use slapcat to verify the change. The final example deletes Sam from the LDAP directory:

```
$ cat six.ldif
dn: cn=Sam the Great,ou=employees,dc=brillserve,dc=com
changetype: delete

$ ldapmodify -xD "cn=ldapadmin,dc=brillserve,dc=com" -w porcupine -f six.ldif
deleting entry "cn=Sam the Great,ou=employees,dc=brillserve,dc=com"
```

TOOLS FOR WORKING WITH LDAP

You can use a variety of tools to work with LDAP. For example, most email clients are able to retrieve data from an LDAP database.

Figure 21-1   The New Address Book window, General tab

EVOLUTION MAIL

This section explains how to use Evolution (Mail) to retrieve data from the example LDAP database created earlier. Evolution must be configured on the local system before you can follow the example in this section. If you just want to experiment with Evolution, you can set it up with an email address such as **user@localhost**. If you are running KDE, you can use KAddressBook, which is integrated into many KDE tools, including Kontact.

Open the Mail-Evolution window by selecting **Main menu: Applications⇨Office⇨ Evolution Mail and Calendar** (if **Applications** is not visible see "Configuring Fallback Mode" on page 92) or by giving the command **evolution** from a terminal emulator or Run Application window (ALT-F2). To query an LDAP database, select **Menubar: File⇨New⇨Address Book**. Evolution displays the General tab of the New Address Book window (Figure 21-1).

General tab   Select **On LDAP Servers** from the drop-down list labeled **Type**. Enter the name Evolution Mail will use to refer to this LDAP directory in the text box labeled **Name**; the example uses **employees**. Enter the FQDN of the LDAP server in the text box labeled **Server**. If you are experimenting on the local system, enter **localhost** in this box. If appropriate, change the value in the text box labeled **Port**. To follow the

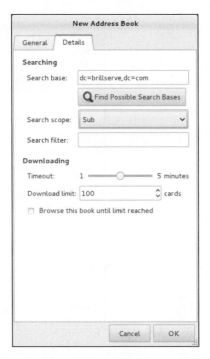

Figure 21-2   The New Address Book window, Details tab

example in this chapter, select **No encryption** from the drop-down list labeled **Use secure connection**.

In the section labeled **Authentication**, select **Using distinguished name (DN)** from the drop-down list labeled **Login method**. Enter the DN of the LDAP administrator in the text box labeled **Login** (the example uses **cn=ldapadmin,dc=brillserve,dc=com**).

Details tab   Next click the tab labeled **Details** (Figure 21-2). Click **Find Possible Search Bases**. If all is working properly, Evolution will display the Supported Search Bases window. Highlight the DN of the directory you want to use and click **OK**. Evolution displays the selected DN in the text box labeled **Search base**. Select **Sub** from the drop-down list labeled **Search scope** to enable searches at all levels of the directory. Click **OK**.

Next click the **Contacts** button at the lower-left corner of the Mail-Evolution window. **On LDAP Servers** appear at the left side of the window. If the name of the address book you specified (**employees** in the example) does not appear below **On LDAP servers**, click the plus sign (**+**; Fedora) or triangle (RHEL) to the left of this label. Then click the name of the address book you want to work with. Evolution prompts for the LDAP administrator password. Enter the password and click **OK**. Evolution highlights the name of the address book; you can now search the LDAP database.

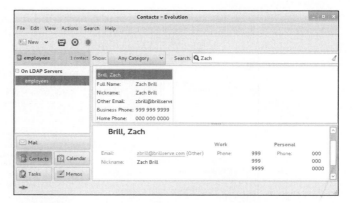

Figure 21-3   Contacts, Evolution window

Enter the name of an entry in the text box labeled **Search** at the upper-right corner of the window and press RETURN. Evolution displays the entry. Figure 21-3 shows the result of following the example in this chapter and entering **Zach** in the **Search** text box.

gq: AN LDAP CLIENT (FEDORA)

The gq utility (sourceforge.net/projects/gqclient; **gq** package) is a graphical (GTK+-based) LDAP client you can use to display and modify entries. Before you can work with gq, you must specify the DN for the administrator. Select **menubar: File⇨Preferences**, click the Servers tab, highlight the server (**localhost** in the example), click **Edit**, click the **Connections** tab, and set Bind DN to the DN for the administrator (**cn=ldapadmin,dc=brillserve,dc=com** in the example). Figure 21-4 shows gq displaying an entry from the example LDAP directory.

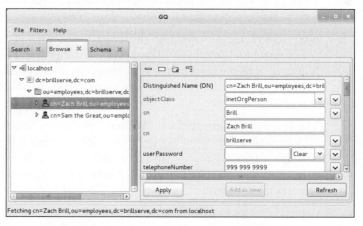

Figure 21-4   Using gq to browse an LDAP directory

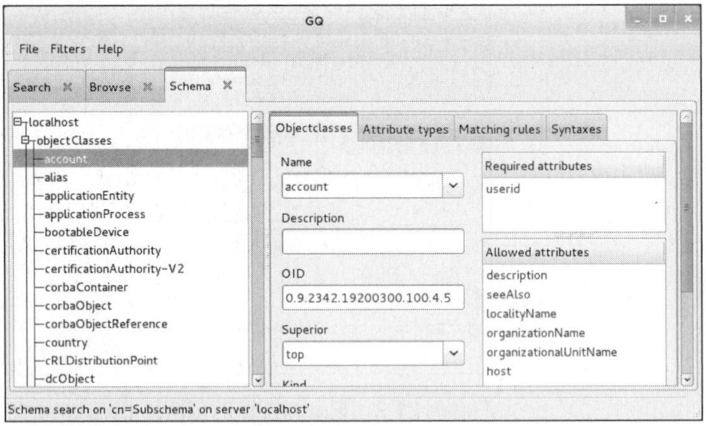

Figure 21-5   The gq Schema tab

You can also use **gq** for browsing the schema: Click the Schema tab and select the server from the left side of the window (**localhost** in Figure 21-5). Select **objectClasses** and then an object class to view information about that object class, including a list of required and optional attributes.

Chapter Summary

NIS (Network Information Service) simplifies the management of common administrative files by maintaining them in a central database and having clients contact the database server to retrieve information from the database. The network that NIS serves is called an NIS domain. Each NIS domain has one master server; larger networks might have slave servers.

NIS derives the information it offers from local configuration files, such as **/etc/passwd** and **/etc/hosts**. These files are called source files or master files. Before NIS can store the information contained in a source file, it must be converted to dbm-format files, called maps. The **ypcat** and **ypmatch** utilities display information from NIS maps.

The **yppasswd** utility replaces the functionality of **passwd** on clients when you use NIS to authenticate passwords. The **/etc/ypserv.conf** file, which holds NIS server configuration information, specifies options and access rules for the NIS server. To enhance system security, you can create a **/var/yp/securenets** file, which prevents unauthorized systems from retrieving NIS maps.

An LDAP (Lightweight Directory Access Protocol) server holds a search- and read-optimized database, called a directory. LDAP clients, such as email clients, query and update this directory. In addition, authentication servers can use an LDAP directory to authenticate users.

Fedora/RHEL provide the OpenLDAP implementation of LDAP. OpenLDAP uses the Sleepycat Berkeley Database, which supports distributed architecture, replication, and encryption.

EXERCISES

1. What is the difference between the passwd and yppasswd utilities?

2. How would you prevent NIS from exporting the **root** user and other system users to clients?

3. How would you make NIS user information override local user information on client systems?

4. Why does the **/etc/passwd** file need two NIS maps?

5. How does an LDAP directory differ from a relational database system?

6. What is the basic unit of information in an LDAP directory? What is the structure of an attribute?

ADVANCED EXERCISES

7. How can you use NIS to mirror the functionality of a private DNS server for a small network? Why should NIS not be used this way on a large network?

8. How can you determine whether the working directory is the home directory of an NIS user?

9. a. What advantage does NIS provide when you use it with NFS?

   b. Suggest a way to implement NIS maps so they can be indexed on more than one field.

10. Where is the LDAP **device** object class defined? Which of its attributes are mandatory and which are optional?

11. How would you determine the longer name for the l (lowercase "l") LDAP object class?

22

NFS: Sharing Directory Hierarchies

Objectives

After reading this chapter you should be able to:

▶ Describe the use, history, and architecture of NFS

▶ Mount remote NFS shares

▶ Configure an NFS server to share directories with specific clients

▶ Troubleshoot mount failures

▶ Set up automount to mount directories on demand

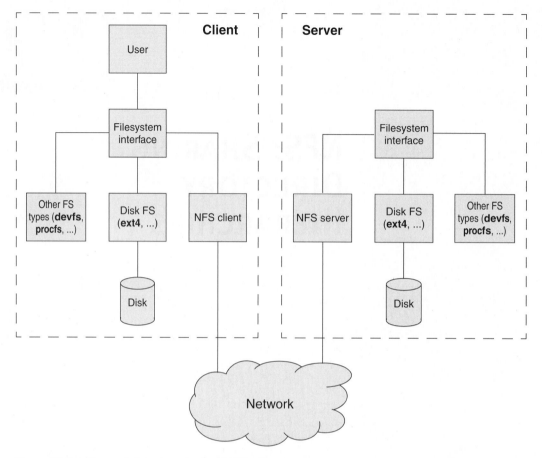

Figure 22-1   Flow of data in a typical NFS client/server setup

The NFS (Network Filesystem) protocol, a UNIX de facto standard developed by Sun Microsystems, allows a server to share selected local directory hierarchies with client systems on a heterogeneous network. NFS runs on UNIX, DOS, Windows, VMS, Linux, and more. Files on the remote computer (the server) appear as if they are present on the local system (the client). Most of the time, the physical location of a file is irrelevant to an NFS user; all standard Linux utilities work with NFS remote files the same way as they operate with local files.

NFS reduces storage needs and system administration workload. As an example, each system in a company traditionally holds its own copy of an application program. To upgrade the program, the administrator needs to upgrade it on each system. NFS allows you to store a copy of a program on a single system and give other users access to it over the network. This scenario minimizes storage requirements by reducing the number of locations that need to maintain the same data. In addition to boosting efficiency, NFS gives users on the network access to the same data (not just application programs), thereby improving data consistency and reliability. By consolidating data, it reduces administrative overhead and provides a convenience to users.

NFS has been pejoratively referred to as the *Nightmare Filesystem,* but NFSv4 has fixed many of the shortcomings of NFSv3. NFSv4

- Performs well over high-latency, low-bandwidth Internet connections.
- Because it uses a single port, NFSv4 is much easier to set up with firewalls and NAT than NFSv3 was.
- Has strong, built-in security.
- Has lock and mount protocols integrated into the NFS protocol.
- Handles client and server crashes better than NFSv3 because it provides stateful operations.
- Improves performance by making extensive use of caching on the client.
- Supports ACLs (Access Control Lists).

AUTH_SYS authentication   NFSv4 supports AUTH_SYS authentication, the standard method of authentication under NFSv3. Because AUTH_SYS uses UIDs and GIDs to authenticate users, it is easy to crack. NFSv4 uses AUTH_SYS security by default. See the **sec** option (page 806) for more information.

RPCSEC_GSS authentication   NFSv4 also supports the newer RPCSEC_GSS (see the **rpc.gssd** man page and www.citi.umich.edu/projects/nfsv4/gssd), which provides secure authentication as well as verification and encryption. RPCSEC_GSS is based on GSS-API (Generic Security Services Application Programming Interface; www.faqs.org/faqs/kerberos-faq/general/section-84.html) and can use Kerberos 5 (best for enterprise or LAN use) and LIBKEY (based on SPKM-3; best for Internet use) among other authentication protocols.

This chapter describes setting up an NFSv4 client and server using AUTH_SYS authentication, the Fedora/RHEL default mode.

INTRODUCTION TO NFS

Figure 22-1 shows the flow of data in a typical NFS client/server setup. An NFS directory hierarchy appears to users and application programs as just another directory hierarchy. By looking at it, you cannot tell a given directory holds a remotely mounted NFS directory hierarchy and not a local filesystem. The NFS server translates commands from the client into operations on the server's filesystem.

Diskless systems   In many computer facilities, user files are stored on a central fileserver equipped with many large-capacity disk drives and devices that quickly and easily make backup copies of the data. A *diskless* system boots from a fileserver (netboots—discussed next) or a CD/DVD and loads system software from a fileserver. The Linux Terminal Server Project (LTSP.org) Web site says it all: "Linux makes a great platform for deploying diskless workstations that boot from a network server. The LTSP is all about running thin client computers in a Linux environment." Because a diskless workstation does not require a lot of computing power, you can give older, retired computers a second life by using them as diskless systems.

Netboot/PXE   You can *netboot* (page 1177) systems that are appropriately set up. Fedora/RHEL includes TFTP (Trivial File Transfer Protocol; **tftp-server** package) that you can use to set up a PXE (Preboot Execution Environment) boot server for Intel systems. Non-Intel architectures have historically included netboot capabilities, which Fedora/RHEL also supports. In addition, you can build the Linux kernel so it mounts **root** (**/**) using NFS. Given the many ways to set up a system, the one you choose depends on what you want to do. See the *Remote-Boot mini-HOWTO* for more information.

Dataless systems   Another type of Linux system is a *dataless* system, in which the client has a disk but stores no user data (only Linux and the applications are kept on the disk). Setting up this type of system is a matter of choosing which directory hierarchies are mounted remotely.

df: shows where directory hierarchies are mounted   The df utility displays a list of the directory hierarchies available on the system, along with the amount of disk space, free and used, on each. The **–h** (human) option makes the output more intelligible. Device names in the left column that are prepended with *hostname:* specify directory hierarchies that are available through NFS.

```
[zach@guava ~]$ cd; pwd
/home/zach
[zach@guava ~]$ df -h
Filesystem             Size  Used Avail Use% Mounted on
...
/dev/mapper/vg_guava-lv_root
                        20G  2.4G   18G  13% /
plum:/home/zach         37G  2.3G   35G   7% /home/zach
/dev/sda1              485M   50M  410M  11% /boot
```

When Zach logs in on **guava**, his home directory, **/home/zach**, is on the remote system **plum**. Using NFS, the **/home/zach** directory hierarchy on **plum** is mounted on **guava** as **/home/zach**. Any files in the **zach** directory on **guava** are hidden while the **zach** directory from **plum** is mounted; they reappear when the directory is unmounted. The **/** filesystem is local to **guava**.

The df **–T** option adds a Type column to the display. The following output shows the directory mounted at **/home/zach** is an **nfs4** directory hierarchy; **/** and **/boot** are local **ext4** filesystems.

```
$ df -hT
Filesystem      Type   Size  Used Avail Use% Mounted on
...
/dev/mapper/vg_guava-lv_root
                ext4    20G  2.4G   18G  13% /
plum:/home/zach
                nfs4    37G  2.3G   35G   7% /home/zach
/dev/sda1       ext4   485M   50M  410M  11% /boot
```

The df **–t** option displays a single filesystem type. With an argument of **nfs4** it displays NFS directory hierarchies:

```
$ df -ht nfs4
Filesystem          Size  Used  Avail  Use%  Mounted on
plum:/home/zach     37G   2.3G  35G    7%    /home/zach
```

Security   By default, an NFS server uses AUTH_SYS (page 793) authentication which is based on the trusted-host paradigm (page 382) and has all the security shortcomings that plague other services based on this paradigm. In addition, in this mode NFS file transfers are not encrypted. Because of these issues, you should implement NFS on a single LAN segment only, where you can be (reasonably) sure systems on the LAN segment are what they claim to be. Make sure a firewall blocks NFS traffic from outside the LAN and never use NFS over the Internet. To improve security, make sure UIDs and GIDs are the same on the server and clients (page 807).

Alternatively, you can use RPCSEC_GSS (page 793) authentication, one of the new security features available under NFSv4. RPCSEC_GSS provides authentication, verification, and encryption. This chapter does not cover setting up an NFS server that uses RPCSEC_GSS authentication.

MORE INFORMATION

Web   NFSv4 home page: www.nfsv4.org
NFSv4 secure installation tutorial:
   nfsv4.bullopensource.org/doc/kerberosnfs/krbnfs_howto_v3.pdf
Mostly NFSv3 with some NFSv4 information: nfs.sourceforge.net
NFSv4 information: www.citi.umich.edu/projects/nfsv4
Up-to-date NFSv4 information including documentation: http://wiki.linux-nfs.org
GSS-API: www.faqs.org/faqs/kerberos-faq/general/section-84.html
PXE boot server tutorial (TFTP):
   wiki.alteeve.com/index.php/Setting_Up_a_PXE_Server_in_Fedora
autofs tutorial: www.linuxhq.com/lg/issue24/nielsen.html

Local   man pages: **autofs** (sections 5 and 8), **automount, auto.master,** exportfs, **exports,** mountstats, **nfs** (especially see SECURITY CONSIDERATIONS), **rpc.idmapd, rpc.gssd, rpc.mountd, rpc.nfsd,** and showmount

HOWTO   NFS-HOWTO: nfs.sourceforge.net/nfs-howto

Book   *NFS Illustrated* by Callaghan, Addison-Wesley (January 2000)

RUNNING AN NFS CLIENT

This section describes how to set up an NFS client, mount remote directory hierarchies, and improve NFS performance. See page 810 for a list of error messages and troubleshooting tips.

PREREQUISITES

Install the following package:

- **nfs-utils**

- **rpcbind** (installed with **nfs-utils**)

rpcbind init script   Run chkconfig to cause the **rpcbind** daemon to start when the system enters multiuser mode:

```
# chkconfig rpcbind on
```

Start the **rpcbind** daemon:

```
# service rpcbind start
```

JUMPSTART I: MOUNTING A REMOTE DIRECTORY HIERARCHY

To set up an NFS client, mount the remote directory hierarchy the same way you mount a local directory hierarchy (page 520).

The following examples show two ways to mount a remote directory hierarchy, assuming **dog** is on the same network as the local system and is sharing **/home** and **/export** with the local system. The **/export** directory on **dog** holds two directory hierarchies you want to mount: **/export/progs** and **/export/oracle**. The example mounts **dog**'s **/home** directory on **/dog.home** on the local system, **/export/progs** on **/apps**, and **/export/oracle** on **/oracle**.

First run mkdir on the local (client) system to create the directories that are the mount points for the remote directory hierarchies:

```
# mkdir /dog.home /apps /oracle
```

You can mount any directory hierarchy from an exported directory hierarchy. In this example, **dog** exports **/export** and the local system mounts **/export/progs** and **/export/oracle**. The following commands manually mount the directory hierarchies one time:

```
# mount dog:/home /dog.home
# mount -o ro,nosuid dog:/export/progs /apps
# mount -o ro dog:/export/oracle /oracle
```

By default, directory hierarchies are mounted read-write, assuming the NFS server is exporting them with read-write permissions. The first of the preceding commands mounts the **/home** directory hierarchy from **dog** on the local directory **/dog.home**. The second and third commands use the **–o ro** option to force a readonly mount. The second command adds the **nosuid** option, which forces setuid (page 205) executables in the mounted directory hierarchy to run with regular permissions on the local system.

nosuid option   If a user has the ability to run a setuid program, that user has the power of a user with **root** privileges. This ability should be limited. Unless you know a user will need to run a program with setuid permissions from a mounted directory hierarchy, always mount a directory hierarchy with the **nosuid** option. For example, you would need to mount a directory hierarchy with setuid privileges when the root partition of a diskless workstation is mounted using NFS.

nodev option   Mounting a device file creates another potential security hole. Although the best policy is not to mount untrustworthy directory hierarchies, it is not always possible to implement this policy. Unless a user needs to use a device on a mounted directory hierarchy, mount directory hierarchies with the **nodev** option, which prevents character and block special files (page 518) on the mounted directory hierarchy from being used as devices.

fstab file   If you mount directory hierarchies frequently, you can add entries for the directory hierarchies to the **/etc/fstab** file (page 801). (Alternatively, you can use **automount**; see page 811.) The following **/etc/fstab** entries mount the same directory hierarchies as in the previous example at the same time that the system mounts the local filesystems:

```
$ cat /etc/fstab
...
dog:/home          /dog.home    nfs4    rw            0  0
dog:/export/progs  /apps        nfs4    ro,nosuid     0  0
dog:/export/oracle /oracle      nfs4    ro            0  0
```

A file mounted using NFS is always of type **nfs4** on the local system, regardless of what type it is on the remote system. Typically you do not run fsck on or back up an NFS directory hierarchy. The entries in the third, fifth, and sixth columns of **fstab** are usually **nfs** (filesystem type), **0** (do not back up this directory hierarchy with dump [page 610]), and **0** (do not run fsck [page 525] on this directory hierarchy). The options for mounting an NFS directory hierarchy differ from those for mounting an **ext4** or other type of filesystem. See the section on mount (next) for details.

Unmounting directory hierarchies   Use umount to unmount a remote directory hierarchy the same way you unmount a local filesystem (page 523).

mount: MOUNTS A DIRECTORY HIERARCHY

The mount utility (page 520) associates a directory hierarchy with a mount point (a directory). You can use mount to mount an NFS (remote) directory hierarchy. This section describes some mount options. It lists default options first, followed by nondefault options (enclosed in parentheses). You can use these options on the command line or set them in **/etc/fstab** (page 801). For a complete list of options, refer to the mount and nfs man pages.

Following are two examples of mounting a remote directory hierarchy. Both mount the **/home/public** directory from the system **plum** on the **/plum.public** mount point on the local system. When called without arguments, mount displays a list of mounted filesystems, including the options the filesystem is mounted with.

The first mount command mounts the remote directory without specifying options. The output from the second mount command, which lists the mounted filesystems, is sent through a pipe to grep, which displays the single (very long) logical line that provides information about the remotely mounted directory. All the options, starting with **rw** (read-write) are defaults or are specified by mount.

```
# mount plum:/home/public /plum.public
# mount | grep plum
plum:/home/public on /plum.public type nfs4 (rw,relatime,vers=4,rsize=131072,wsize=131072
,namlen=255,hard,proto=tcp,port=0,timeo=600,retrans=2,sec=sys,clientaddr=172.16.192.150,m
inorversion=0,local_lock=none,addr=172.16.192.151)
# umount /plum.public
```

The next mount command mounts the remote directory specifying the **noac** option (**–o noac**; next). The output from the second mount command shows the addition of the **noac** option. When you specify **noac**, mount adds the **acregmin**, **acregmax**, **acdirmin**, and **acdirmax** options (all next) and sets them to 0.

```
# mount -o noac plum:/home/public /plum.public
# mount | grep plum
plum:/home/public on /plum.public type nfs4 (rw,relatime,sync,vers=4,rsize=131072,wsize=1
31072,namlen=255,acregmin=0,acregmax=0,acdirmin=0,acdirmax=0,hard,noac,proto=tcp,port=0,t
imeo=600,retrans=2,sec=sys,clientaddr=172.16.192.150,minorversion=0,local_lock=none,addr=
172.16.192.151)
```

Attribute Caching

A file's inode (page 515) stores file attributes that provide information about a file, such as file modification time, size, links, and owner. File attributes do not include the data stored in a file. Typically file attributes do not change very often for an ordinary file; they change even less often for a directory file. Even the size attribute does not change with every write instruction: When a client is writing to an NFS-mounted file, several write instructions might be given before the data is transferred to the server. In addition, many file accesses, such as that performed by **ls**, are readonly operations and, therefore, do not change the file's attributes or its contents. Thus a client can cache attributes and avoid costly network reads.

The kernel uses the modification time of the file to determine when its cache is out-of-date. If the time the attribute cache was saved is later than the modification time of the file itself, the data in the cache is current. The server must periodically refresh the attribute cache of an NFS-mounted file to determine whether another process has modified the file. This period is specified as a minimum and maximum number of seconds for ordinary and directory files. Following is a list of options that affect attribute caching:

ac (noac)   (**attribute cache**) Permits attribute caching. The **noac** option disables attribute caching. Although **noac** slows the server, it avoids stale attributes when two NFS clients actively write to a common directory hierarchy. See the example in the preceding section that shows that when you specify **noac**, mount sets each of the following four options to 0, which in effect specifies that attributes will not be cached. Default is **ac**.

acdirmax=n (**attribute cache directory file maximum**) The n is the number of seconds, at a maximum, that NFS waits before refreshing directory file attributes. Default is 60 seconds.

acdirmin=*n* (**attribute cache directory file minimum**) The *n* is the number of seconds, at a minimum, that NFS waits before refreshing directory file attributes. Default is **30** seconds.

acregmax=*n* (**attribute cache regular file maximum**) The *n* is the number of seconds, at a maximum, that NFS waits before refreshing regular file attributes. Default is **60** seconds.

acregmin=*n* (**attribute cache regular file minimum**) The *n* is the number of seconds, at a minimum, that NFS waits before refreshing regular file attributes. Default is **3** seconds.

actimeo=*n* (**attribute cache timeout**) Sets **acregmin**, **acregmax**, **acdirmin**, and **acdirmax** to *n* seconds. Without this option, each individual option takes on its assigned or default value.

ERROR HANDLING

The following options control what NFS does when the server does not respond or when an I/O error occurs. To allow for a mount point located on a mounted device, a missing mount point is treated as a timeout.

fg (bg) (**foreground**) Exits with an error status if a foreground NFS mount fails. The **bg** (background) option retries failed NFS mount attempts in the background. Default is **fg**.

hard (soft) With the **hard** option, NFS retries indefinitely when an NFS request times out. With the **soft** option, NFS retries the connection **retrans** times and then reports an I/O error to the calling program. In general, it is not advisable to use **soft**. As the mount man page says of **soft**, "Usually it just causes lots of trouble." For more information refer to "Improving Performance" on page 800. Default is **hard**.

retrans=*n* (**retransmission value**) NFS generates a **server not responding** message after *n* timeouts. NFS continues trying after *n* timeouts if **hard** is set and fails if **soft** is set. Default is **3**.

retry=*n* (**retry value**) The number of minutes that NFS retries a mount operation before giving up. Set to **0** to cause mount to exit immediately if it fails. Default is **2** minutes for foreground mounts (**fg**) and **10,000** minutes for background mounts (**bg**).

timeo=*n* (**timeout value**) The *n* is the number of tenths of a second NFS waits for a response before retransmitting. For NFS over TCP, the default is **60** seconds. See the **nfs** man page for information about the defaults used by NFS over UDP. On a busy network, in case of a slow server, or when the request passes through multiple routers, increasing this value might improve performance. See "Timeouts" on the next page for more information.

MISCELLANEOUS OPTIONS

Following are additional useful options:

lock (nolock) Permits NFS locking. The **nolock** option disables NFS locking and is useful with older servers that do not support NFS locking. Default is **lock**.

nfsvers=*n* The *n* specifies the NFS version number used to contact the NFS server (**2**, **3**, or **4**). The mount fails if the server does not support the specified version. By default, the client negotiates the version number, starting with **4**, followed by **3** and then **2**.

port=*n*   The *n* specifies the number of the port used to connect to the NFS server. Under NFSv4, the default is 0, causing NFS to query rpcbind on the server to determine the port number, which is typically 2049. NFSv4 does not use rpcbind.

rsize=*n*   (**read block size**) The *n* specifies the number of bytes read at one time from an NFS server. Refer to "Improving Performance." Default is negotiated by the client and server and is the largest both can support.

wsize=*n*   (**write block size**) The *n* specifies the number of bytes written at one time to an NFS server. Refer to "Improving Performance." Default is negotiated by the client and server and is the largest both can support.

udp   Uses UDP for an NFS mount. Default is **tcp**.

tcp   Uses TCP for an NFS mount. Default is **tcp**.

IMPROVING PERFORMANCE

hard/soft   Several parameters can affect the performance of NFS, especially over slow connections such as a line with a lot of traffic or a line controlled by a modem. If you have a slow connection, make sure **hard** (default; page 799) is set so timeouts do not abort program execution.

Block size   One of the easiest ways to improve NFS performance is to increase the block size—that is, the number of bytes NFS transfers at a time. Try not specifying **rsize** and **wsize** (previous) so the client and server set these options to their maximum values. Experiment until you find the optimal block size. Unmount and mount the directory hierarchy each time you change an option. See the *Linux NFS-HOWTO* at nfs.sourceforge.net/nfs-howto for more information on testing different block sizes.

Timeouts   NFS waits the amount of time specified by the **timeo** (timeout; page 799) option for a response to a transmission. If it does not receive a response in this amount of time, NFS sends another transmission. The second transmission uses bandwidth that, over a slow connection, might slow things down even more. You might be able to increase performance by increasing **timeo**.

You can test the speed of a connection with the size of packets you are sending (**rsize** and **wsize**; both above) by using ping with the –s (size) option:

```
$ ping -s 4096 plum
PING plum (172.16.192.151) 4096(4124) bytes of data.
4104 bytes from plum (172.16.192.151): icmp_req=1 ttl=64 time=0.469 ms
4104 bytes from plum (172.16.192.151): icmp_req=2 ttl=64 time=0.540 ms
4104 bytes from plum (172.16.192.151): icmp_req=3 ttl=64 time=0.459 ms
4104 bytes from plum (172.16.192.151): icmp_req=4 ttl=64 time=0.520 ms
...
4104 bytes from plum (172.16.192.151): icmp_req=25 ttl=64 time=0.545 ms
4104 bytes from plum (172.16.192.151): icmp_req=26 ttl=64 time=0.501 ms
^C
--- plum ping statistics ---
26 packets transmitted, 26 received, 0% packet loss, time 25014ms
rtt min/avg/max/mdev = 0.443/0.506/0.550/0.032 ms
```

The preceding example uses a packet size of 4096 bytes and shows a fast average packet round-trip time of about one-half of a millisecond. Over a modem line, you can expect times of several seconds. If the connection is dealing with other traffic, the time will be even longer. Run the test during a period of heavy traffic. Try increasing **timeo** to three or four times the average round-trip time (to allow for unusually bad network conditions, such as when the connection is made) and see whether performance improves. Remember that the **timeo** value is given in tenths of a second (100 milliseconds = one-tenth of a second).

/etc/fstab: MOUNTS DIRECTORY HIERARCHIES AUTOMATICALLY

The **/etc/fstab** file (page 524) lists directory hierarchies that the system might mount automatically as it comes up. You can use the options discussed in the preceding sections on the command line or in the **fstab** file.

The following line from the **fstab** file on **guava** mounts the **/home/public** directory from **plum** on the **/plum.public** mount point on **guava**:

```
plum:/home/public  /plum.public  nfs    rsize=8192,wsize=8192  0 0
```

A mount point should be an empty, local directory. (Files in a mount point are hidden when a directory hierarchy is mounted on it.) The type of a filesystem mounted using NFS is always **nfs4**, regardless of its type on its local system. You can increase the **rsize** and **wsize** options to improve performance. Refer to "Improving Performance" on page 800.

The next example from **fstab** mounts a filesystem from **dog**:

```
dog:/export      /dog.export   nfs4   timeo=50,hard          0 0
```

Because the local system connects to **dog** over a slow connection, **timeo** is increased to 5 seconds (50-tenths of a second). Refer to "Timeouts" on page 800. In addition, **hard** is set to make sure NFS keeps trying to communicate with the server after a major timeout. Refer to **hard/soft** on page 800.

The final example from **fstab** shows a remote-mounted home directory. Because **dog** is a local server and is connected via a reliable, high-speed connection, **timeo** is decreased and **rsize** and **wsize** are increased substantially:

```
dog:/home       /dog.home     nfs4 timeo=4,rsize=16384,wsize=16384 0 0
```

SETTING UP AN NFS SERVER

PREREQUISITES

Install the following package:

- **nfs-utils**
- **rpcbind** (installed with **nfs-utils**)
- **system-config-nfs** (Fedora; optional)

rpcbind   The **rpcbind** daemon must be running before you can start the **nfsd** daemon.

rpcbind init script   Run chkconfig to cause the **rpcbind** daemon to start when the system enters multiuser mode:

```
# chkconfig rpcbind on
```

Start the **rpcbind** daemon:

```
# service rpcbind start
```

nfs init script   Run chkconfig to cause the **nfsd** daemon to start when the system enters multiuser mode:

```
# chkconfig nfs on
```

Start the **nfsd** daemon:

```
# service nfs start
```

The **nfs** init script starts **mountd**, **nfsd**, and optionally **rquotad**. Use **restart** in place of **start** to restart these daemons once they are running.

After changing the NFS configuration on an active server, use **reload** in place of **restart** to reexport directory hierarchies without disturbing clients connected to the server.

NOTES

Troubleshooting   See page 810 for a list of error messages and troubleshooting tips.

SELinux   When SELinux is set to use a targeted policy, NFS is protected by SELinux. You can disable this protection if necessary. For more information refer to "Setting the Targeted Policy with **system-config-selinux**" on page 463.

Firewall   When NFSv4 is using AUTH_SYS authentication, as it does by default, it uses TCP port 2049. If the NFS server system is running a firewall or is behind a firewall, you must open this port. Using **system-config-firewall**, select **NFS4** from the Trusted Services tab (page 894) to open this port.

Security   NFSv3 (and not NFSv4) uses TCP wrappers to control client access to the server. As explained on page 484, you can set up **/etc/hosts.allow** and **/etc/hosts.deny** files to specify which clients can contact **rpc.mountd** on the server and thereby use NFS. The name of the daemon to use in these files is **mountd**. However, as of this writing, there is a bug that causes TCP wrappers not to protect the server in some cases For more information see bugzilla.redhat.com/show_bug.cgi?id=480420#c17.

JUMPSTART II: CONFIGURING AN NFS SERVER USING system-config-nfs (FEDORA)

To display the NFS Server Configuration window (Figure 22-2), enter the command **system-config-nfs** or select **Main menu: System⇨Applications⇨Other⇨NFS** (Fedora; if **Applications** is not visible see "Configuring Fallback Mode" on page 92) or **Main menu: System⇨Administration⇨Server Settings⇨NFS** (RHEL). From this

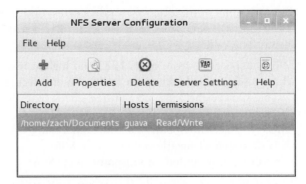

Figure 22-2   NFS Server Configuration window

window you can generate an **/etc/exports** file, which is almost all there is to setting up an NFS server. If the system is running a firewall, see "Firewall" in the preceding section. The system-config-nfs utility allows you to specify which directory hierarchies you want to share and how they are shared using NFS. Each exported hierarchy is called a *share*.

To add a share, click **Add** on the toolbar. To modify a share, highlight the share and click **Properties** on the toolbar. Clicking **Add** displays the Add NFS Share window; clicking **Properties** displays the Edit NFS Share window. These windows are identical except for their titles.

The Add/Edit NFS Share window has three tabs: Basic, General Options, and User Access. On the Basic tab (Figure 22-3) you can specify the pathname of the root of the shared directory hierarchy, the names or IP addresses of the systems (clients) the hierarchy will be shared with, and whether users from the specified systems will be able to write to the shared files.

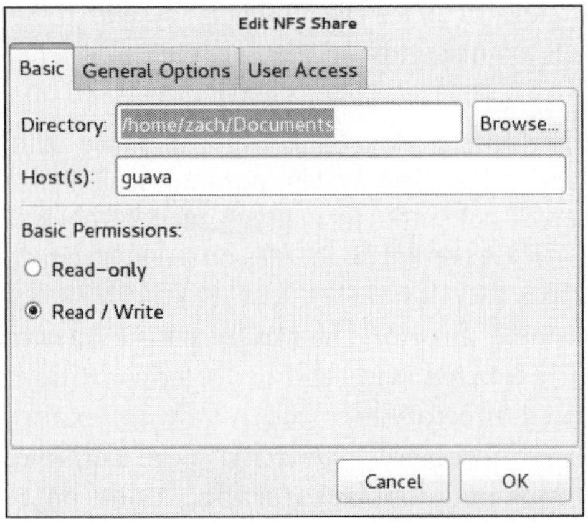

Figure 22-3   Edit NFS Share window

The selections in the other two tabs correspond to options you can specify in the /etc/exports file. Following is a list of the check box descriptions in these tabs and the option each corresponds to:

General Options tab   Allow connections from ports 1023 and higher: **insecure** (page 806)
Allow insecure file locking: **no_auth_nlm** or **insecure_locks** (page 805)
Disable subtree checking: **no_subtree_check** (page 806)
Sync write operations on request: **sync** (page 806)
Force sync of write operations immediately: **no_wdelay** (page 806)
Hide filesystems beneath: **nohide** (page 806)
Export only if mounted: **mountpoint** (page 806)

User Access tab   Treat remote root user as local root: **no_root_squash** (page 807)
Treat all client users as anonymous users: **all_squash** (page 807)
Local user ID for anonymous users: **anonuid** (page 808)
Local group ID for anonymous users: **anongid** (page 808)

After making the changes you want, click **OK** to close the Add/Edit NFS Share window and click **OK** again to close the NFS Server Configuration window. There is no need to restart any daemons.

MANUALLY EXPORTING A DIRECTORY HIERARCHY

Exporting a directory hierarchy makes the directory hierarchy *available* for mounting by designated systems via a network. "Exported" does not mean "mounted": When a directory hierarchy is exported, it is placed in the list of directory hierarchies that can be mounted by other systems. An exported directory hierarchy might be mounted (or not) at any given time.

Exporting symbolic links and device files

tip   When you export a directory hierarchy that contains a symbolic link, make sure the object of the link is available on the client (remote) system. If the object of the link does not exist on a client system, you must export and mount it along with the exported link. Otherwise, the link will not point to the same file it points to on the server.

A device file refers to a Linux kernel interface. When you export a device file, you export that interface. If the client system does not have the same type of device available, the exported device will not work. To improve security on a client, you can use mount's **nodev** option (page 797) to prevent device files on mounted directory hierarchies from being used as devices.

Exported partition holding a mount point   A mounted directory hierarchy whose mount point is within an exported partition is not exported with the exported partition. You need to explicitly export each mounted directory hierarchy you want exported, even if it resides within an already exported directory hierarchy. For example, assume two directory hierarchies, **/opt/apps** and **/opt/apps/oracle**, reside on two partitions. You must export each directory hierarchy explicitly, even though **oracle** is a subdirectory of **apps**. Most other subdirectories and files are exported automatically. See also **mountpoint** and **nohide**, both on page 806.

/etc/exports: HOLDS A LIST OF EXPORTED DIRECTORY HIERARCHIES

The **/etc/exports** file is the ACL (access control list) for exported directory hierarchies that NFS clients can mount; it is the only file you need to edit to set up an NFS server. The exportfs utility (page 809) reads this file when it updates the files in **/var/lib/nfs** (page 808), which the kernel uses to keep its mount table current. The **exports** file controls the following NFS characteristics:

- Which clients can access the server (see also "Security" on page 795)
- Which directory hierarchies on the server each client can access
- How each client can access each directory hierarchy
- How client usernames are mapped to server usernames
- Various NFS parameters

Each line in the **exports** file has the following format:

export-point client1(option-list) [client2(option-list) ...]

where *export-point* is the absolute pathname of the root directory of the directory hierarchy to be exported. The *client1-n* are the names or IP addresses of one or more clients, separated by SPACEs, that are allowed to mount the *export-point*. The *option-list* is a comma-separated list of options (next) that applies to the preceding *client*; it must not contain any SPACEs. There must not be any SPACE between each client name and the open parenthesis that starts the *option-list*.

You can either use system-config-nfs (page 802) to make changes to **exports** or edit this file manually. The following **exports** file gives the system at 172.16.192.150 read-write access to **/home/public** and **/home/zach**:

```
$ cat /etc/exports
/home/public 172.16.192.150(rw,sync)
/home/zach 172.16.192.150(rw,sync)
```

The specified directories are on the local server. In each case, access is implicitly granted for the directory hierarchy rooted at the exported directory. You can specify IP addresses or hostnames and you can specify more than one client system on a line. By default, directory hierarchies are exported in readonly mode.

GENERAL OPTIONS

The left column of this section lists default options, followed by nondefault options enclosed in parentheses. Refer to the **exports** man page for more information.

auth_nlm (no_auth_nlm) or secure_locks (insecure_locks)

Setting the **auth_nlm** or **secure_locks** option (these two options are the same) causes the server to require authentication of lock requests. Use **no_auth_nlm** for older clients when you find that only files that anyone can read can be locked. Default is **auth_nlm**.

mountpoint[=*path*]
Allows a directory to be exported only if it has been mounted. This option prevents a mount point that does not have a directory hierarchy mounted on it from being exported and prevents the underlying mount point from being exported. Also **mp**.

nohide (hide)
When a server exports two directory hierarchies, one of which is mounted on the other, the **hide** option requires a client to mount both directory hierarchies explicitly to access both. When the second (child) directory hierarchy is not explicitly mounted, its mount point appears as an empty directory and the directory hierarchy is hidden. The **nohide** option causes the underlying second directory hierarchy to appear when it is not explicitly mounted, but this option does not work in all cases. See "Exported partition holding a mount point" on page 804. Default is **nohide**.

ro (rw)
(**readonly**) The **ro** option permits only read requests on an NFS directory hierarchy. Use **rw** to permit read and write requests. Default is **ro**.

secure (insecure)
The **secure** option requires NFS requests to originate on a *privileged port* (page 1182) so a program running without **root** privileges cannot mount a directory hierarchy. This option does not guarantee a secure connection. Default is **secure**.

no_subtree_check (subtree_check)
The **subtree_check** option checks subtrees for valid files. Assume you have an exported directory hierarchy that has its root below the root of the filesystem that holds it (that is, an exported subdirectory of a filesystem). When the NFS server receives a request for a file in that directory hierarchy, it performs a subtree check to confirm the file is in the exported directory hierarchy.

Subtree checking can cause problems with files that are renamed while opened and, when **no_root_squash** is used, files that only a process running with **root** privileges can access. The **no_subtree_check** option disables subtree checking and can improve reliability in some cases.

For example, you might need to disable subtree checking for home directories. Home directories are frequently subtrees (of **/home**), are written to often, and can have files within them frequently renamed. You would probably not need to disable subtree checking for directory hierarchies that contain files that are mostly read, such as **/usr**. Default is **no_subtree_check**.

sec=*mode*
The *mode* is the type of RPCGSS security to use to access files on this mount point and can be **sys** (AUTH_SYS), **krb5**, **krb5i**, **krb5p**, **lkey**, **lkeyi**, **lkeyp**, **spkm**, **spkmi**, or **spkmp**. Refer to SECURITY CONSIDERATIONS in the **nfs** man page for more information. Default is **sys**.

sync (async)
(**synchronize**) The **sync** option specifies that the server should reply to requests only after disk changes made by the request are written to disk. The **async** option specifies that the server does not have to wait for information to be written to disk and can improve performance, albeit at the cost of possible data corruption if the server crashes or the connection is interrupted. Default is **sync**.

wdelay (no_wdelay)
(**write delay**) The **wdelay** option causes the server to delay committing write requests when it anticipates that another, related request will follow, thereby

improving performance by committing multiple write requests within a single operation. The **no_wdelay** option does not delay committing write requests and can improve performance when the server receives multiple, small, unrelated requests. Default is **wdelay**.

USER ID MAPPING OPTIONS

Each user has a UID number and a primary GID number on the server. The **/etc/passwd** and **/etc/group** files on the server might map these numbers to names. When a user on a client makes a request of an NFS server, the server uses these numbers to identify the user on the client, raising several issues:

- The user might not have the same ID numbers on both systems. As a consequence, the user might have owner access to files of another user and not have owner access to his own files (see "NIS and NFS" [below] for a solution).

- You might not want a user with **root** privileges on the client system to have owner access to **root**-owned files on the server.

- You might not want a remote user to have owner access to some important system files that are not owned by **root** (such as those owned by **bin**).

Owner access to a file means the remote user can execute or—worse—modify the file. NFS gives you two ways to deal with these cases:

- You can use the **root_squash** option to map the ID number of the **root** account on a client to the **nfsnobody** user (UID 65534) on the server.

- You can use the **all_squash** option to map all NFS users on the client to **nfsnobody** (UID 65534) on the server.

The **/etc/passwd** file shows that **nfsnobody** has a UID and GID of 65534. Use the **anonuid** and **anongid** options to override these values.

NIS and NFS   When you use NIS (page 759) for user authorization, users automatically have the same UIDs on both systems. If you are using NFS on a large network, it is a good idea to use a directory service such as NIS or LDAP (page 776) for authorization. Without such a service, you must synchronize the **passwd** files on all systems manually.

root_squash (no_root_squash)
  The **root_squash** option maps requests from **root** on a client so they appear to come from the UID for **nfsnobody** (UID 65534), a nonprivileged user on the server, or as specified by **anonuid**. This option does not affect other sensitive UIDs such as **bin**. The **no_root_squash** option turns off this mapping so requests from **root** appear to come from **root**. Default is **root_squash**.

no_all_squash   The **no_all_squash** option does not change the mapping of users on clients making
  (all_squash)   requests of the NFS server. The **all_squash** option maps requests from all users—not just **root**—on client systems to appear to come from the UID for **nfsnobody** (UID 65534), a nonprivileged user on the server, or as specified by **anonuid**. This option is useful for controlling access to exported public FTP, news, and other directories.

Critical files in NFS-mounted directories should be owned by root

security   Despite the mapping done by the **root_squash** option, a user with **root** privileges on a client system can use sudo or su to assume the identity of any user on the system and then access that user's files on the server. Thus, without resorting to **all_squash**, you can protect only files owned by **root** on an NFS server. Make sure that **root**—and not **bin** or another user—owns and is the only user who can modify or delete critical files within any NFS-mounted directory hierarchy.

Taking this precaution does not completely protect the system against an attacker with **root** privileges, but it can help thwart an attack from a less experienced malicious user.

anonuid=*un* and   Set the UID or the GID of the anonymous account to *un* or *gn*, respectively. NFS uses
anongid=*gn*   these accounts when it does not recognize an incoming UID or GID and when it is instructed to do so by **root_squash** or **all_squash**. Both options default to **nfsnobody** (UID 65534).

WHERE THE SYSTEM KEEPS NFS MOUNT INFORMATION

A server holds several lists of directory hierarchies it can export. The list that you as a system administrator work with is **/etc/exports**. This section describes the important files and pseudofiles that NFS works with. The following discussion assumes that the server, **plum**, is exporting the **/home/public** and **/home/zach** directory hierarchies.

/var/lib/nfs/etab   (**export table**) On the server, **/var/lib/nfs/etab** holds a lists of the directory hierarchies that are exported (can be mounted but are not necessarily mounted at the moment) and the options they are exported with:

```
$ cat /var/lib/nfs/etab
/home/zach 172.16.192.150(rw,sync,wdelay,hide,nocrossmnt,secure,root_sq
uash,no_all_squash,no_subtree_check,secure_locks,acl,anonuid=65534,anon
gid=65534)

/home/public 172.16.192.150(rw,sync,wdelay,hide,nocrossmnt,secure,root_
squash,no_all_squash,no_subtree_check,secure_locks,acl,anonuid=65534,an
ongid=65534)
```

The preceding output shows that 172.16.192.150 can mount **/home/zach** and **/home/public**. The **etab** file is initialized from **/etc/exports** when the system is brought up, read by **mountd** when a client asks to mount a directory hierarchy, and modified by exportfs (page 809) as the list of exported directory hierarchies changes. The **/proc/fs/nfsd/exports** pseudofile holds similar information.

/proc/mounts   On the client, this pseudofile displays the kernel mount table, which lists filesystems mounted by the local system. In the following example, grep displays lines that contain the string **nfs4**:

```
$ grep nfs4 /proc/mounts
plum:/home/public /plum.public nfs4 rw,relatime,vers=4,rsize=131072,wsi
ze=131072,namlen=255,hard,proto=tcp,port=0,timeo=600,retrans=2,sec=sys,
clientaddr=172.16.192.150,minorversion=0,local_lock=none,addr=172.16.19
2.151 0 0
```

exportfs: MAINTAINS THE LIST OF EXPORTED DIRECTORY HIERARCHIES

The exportfs utility maintains the **/var/lib/nfs/etab** file (page 808). When **mountd** is called, it checks this file to see if it is allowed to mount the requested directory hierarchy. Typically exportfs is called with simple options and modifies the **etab** file based on changes in **/etc/exports**. When called with client and directory arguments, it can add to or remove the directory hierarchies specified by those arguments from the list kept in **etab**, without reference to the **exports** file. An exportfs command has the following format:

exportfs [options] [client:dir ...]

where *options* is one or more options (next), *client* is the name of the system that *dir* is exported to, and *dir* is the absolute pathname of the directory at the root of the directory hierarchy being exported. Without any arguments, exportfs reports which directory hierarchies are exported to which systems:

```
# exportfs
/home/public    172.16.192.150
/home/zach      172.16.192.150
```

The system executes the following command when it starts the **nfsd** daemon (it is in the **nfs** init script). This command reexports the entries in **/etc/exports** and removes invalid entries from **/var/lib/nfs/etab** so **etab** is synchronized with **/etc/exports**:

```
# exportfs -r
```

OPTIONS

–a (**all**) Exports directory hierarchies specified in **/etc/exports**. This option does not *unexport* entries you have removed from **exports** (that is, it does not remove invalid entries from **/var/lib/nfs/etab**); use **–r** to perform this task.

–f (**flush**) Removes everything from the kernel's export table.

–i (**ignore**) Ignores **/etc/exports**; uses what is specified on the command line only.

–o (**options**) Specifies options. You can specify options following **–o** the same way you do in the **exports** file. For example, **exportfs –i –o ro dog:/home/sam** exports **/home/sam** on the local system to **dog** for readonly access.

–r (**reexport**) Synchronizes **/var/lib/nfs/etab** with **/etc/exports**, removing invalid entries from **/var/lib/nfs/etab**.

–u (**unexport**) Makes an exported directory hierarchy no longer exported. If a directory hierarchy is mounted when you unexport it, users see the message **Stale NFS file handle** when they try to access the directory hierarchy from a remote system.

–v (**verbose**) Provides more information. Displays export options when you use exportfs to display export information.

TROUBLESHOOTING

This section describes NFS error messages and what you can do to fix the problems they report on. It also suggests some ways to test an NFS server.

ERROR MESSAGES

Sometimes a client might lose access to files on an NFS server. For example, a network problem or a remote system crash might make these files temporarily unavailable. If you try to access a remote file in these circumstances, you will get an error message, such as **NFS server *xxx* not responding**. When the local system can contact the server again, NFS will display another message, such as **NFS server *xxx* OK**. A stable network and server (or not using NFS) is the best defense against this problem.

The **mount: RPC: Program not registered** message might mean NFS is not running on the server. Start the **nfsd** and **rpcbind** daemons on the server.

The **Stale NFS filehandle** message appears when a file that is opened on a client is removed, renamed, or replaced. Try remounting the directory hierarchy.

TESTING THE SERVER

From the server, run the **nfs** init script with an argument of **status**. If all is well, the system displays something similar to the following:

```
$ service nfs status
...
nfs.service - LSB: Start up the NFS server sevice
        Loaded: loaded (/etc/rc.d/init.d/nfs)
        Active: active (running) since Wed, 09 Mar 2011 04:29:23 -0800; 42min ago
       Process: 14431 ExecStop=/etc/rc.d/init.d/nfs stop (code=exited, status=0/SUCCESS)
       Process: 14532 ExecStart=/etc/rc.d/init.d/nfs start (code=exited, status=0/SUCCESS)
        CGroup: name=systemd:/system/nfs.service
                + 2191 rpc.idmapd
                + 14583 rpc.mountd
...
```

Also check that **mountd** is running:

```
$ ps -ef | grep mountd
root      14583     1  0 04:29 ?        00:00:00 rpc.mountd
```

Next, from the server, use rpcinfo to make sure NFS is registered with rpcbind:

```
$ rpcinfo -p localhost | grep nfs
    100003    2   tcp   2049  nfs
    100003    3   tcp   2049  nfs
    100003    4   tcp   2049  nfs
    100227    2   tcp   2049  nfs_acl
    100227    3   tcp   2049  nfs_acl
    100003    2   udp   2049  nfs
    100003    3   udp   2049  nfs
    100003    4   udp   2049  nfs
    100227    2   udp   2049  nfs_acl
    100227    3   udp   2049  nfs_acl
```

Repeat the preceding command from the client, replacing **localhost** with the name of the server. The results should be the same.

If you get a permission denied message, check that

- You have not specified **rw** access in **/etc/exports** when the client has only read permission to the directory hierarchy.

- You have specified the directory hierarchy and client correctly in **/etc/exports**.

- You have not edited **/etc/exports** since you last ran **exportfs –r**.

- You are not trying to export a directory hierarchy and a subdirectory of that hierarchy. From the client you can mount a directory hierarchy and a subdirectory of that hierarchy separately, but you cannot export both from the server. Export the higher-level directory only.

Finally, try mounting directory hierarchies from remote systems and verify access.

automount: Mounts Directory Hierarchies on Demand

In a distributed computing environment, when you log in on any system on the network, all your files—including startup scripts—are available. All systems are also commonly able to mount all directory hierarchies on all servers: Whichever system you log in on, your home directory is waiting for you.

As an example, assume **/home/zach** is a remote directory hierarchy that is mounted on demand. When Zach logs in or when you issue the command ls **/home/zach**, autofs goes to work: It looks in the **/etc/auto.misc** map, finds **/home/zach** is a key that says to mount **plum:/home/zach**, and mounts the remote directory hierarchy. Once the directory hierarchy is mounted, ls displays the list of files in that directory.

NIS and LDAP   The automount maps can be stored on NIS and LDAP servers in addition to the local filesystem. Unless you change the **automount** entry in the **/etc/nsswitch.conf** file (page 494), the **automount** daemon will look for maps as files on the local system.

Prerequisites

Install the following package:

- **autofs**

Run chkconfig to cause the **automount** daemon to start when the system enters multiuser mode:

```
# chkconfig autofs on
```

autofs init script   Start the **automount** daemon:

```
# service autofs start
```

After changing the **automount** configuration on an active server, use **reload** in place of **restart** to reload **automount** configuration files without disturbing automatically mounted directory hierarchies.

autofs: AUTOMATICALLY MOUNTED DIRECTORY HIERARCHIES

An **autofs** directory hierarchy is like any other directory hierarchy but remains unmounted until it is needed, at which time the system mounts it automatically (*demand mounting*). The system unmounts an **autofs** directory hierarchy when it is no longer needed—by default, after five minutes of inactivity. Automatically mounted directory hierarchies are an important part of managing a large collection of systems in a consistent way. The **automount** daemon is particularly useful when an installation includes a large number of servers or a large number of directory hierarchies. It also helps to remove server-server dependencies (next).

Server-server dependency
When you boot a system that uses traditional **fstab**-based mounts and an NFS server is down, the system can take a long time to come up as it waits for the server to time out. Similarly, when you have two servers, each mounting directory hierarchies from the other, and both systems are down, both might hang as they are brought up while each tries to mount a directory hierarchy from the other. This situation is called a *server–server dependency*. The **automount** facility gets around these issues by mounting a directory hierarchy from another system only when a process tries to access it.

When a process attempts to access one of the files within an unmounted **autofs** directory hierarchy, the kernel notifies the **automount** daemon, which mounts the directory hierarchy. You must give a command, such as **cd /home/zach**, that accesses the **autofs** mount point (in this case **/home/zach**) to create the demand that causes **automount** to mount the **autofs** directory hierarchy; only then can the system display or use the **autofs** directory hierarchy. Before you issue this **cd** command, **zach** does not appear in **/home**.

The main file that controls the behavior of **automount** is **/etc/auto.master**. Each line in this file describes a mount point and refers to an **autofs** map that specifies the directory that is to be mounted on the mount point. A simple example follows:

```
$ cat /etc/auto.master
/-       /etc/auto.misc --timeout=60
/plum    /etc/auto.plum
```

Mount point
The **auto.master** file has three columns. The first column names the parent of the **autofs** *mount point*—the location where the **autofs** directory hierarchy is to be mounted. A **/–** in the first column means the mount point is the root directory.

Map files
The second column names the file, called a *map file*, that stores supplemental configuration information. The optional third column holds **autofs** options for the map entry. In the preceding example, the first line sets the timeout (the length of time a directory stays mounted when it is not in use) to 60 seconds; the default timeout is 300 seconds. You can change **autofs** default values in **/etc/sysconfig/autofs**.

Although the map files can have any names, one is traditionally named **auto.misc**. Following are the two map files specified in the preceding **auto.master** file:

```
$ cat /etc/auto.misc
/music          -fstype=ext4      :/dev/mapper/vg_guava-music
/home/zach      -fstype=nfs       plum:/home/zach

$ cat /etc/auto.plum
public          -fstype=nfs4 plum:/home/public
```

Relative mount point   The first column of a map file holds the absolute or relative **autofs** mount point. A pathname other than **/–** appearing in the first column of **auto.master** specifies a relative **autofs** mount point. A relative mount point is appended to the corresponding **autofs** mount point from column 1 of the **auto.master**. In this example, **public** (from **auto.plum**) is appended to **/plum** (from **auto.master**) to form **/plum/public**.

Absolute mount point   A **/–** appearing in the first column of **auto.master** specifies an absolute **autofs** mount point. In this example, **auto.master** specifies **/–** as the mount point for the **auto.misc** map file, so the mount points specified in this map file are absolute and are specified entirely in **auto.misc** map file. The **auto.misc** file specifies the **autofs** mount points **/music** and **/home/zach**.

The second column holds autofs options, and the third column shows the server and directory hierarchy to be mounted.

The **auto.misc** file specifies a local filesystem (**/dev/mapper/vg_guava-music**; an LV (page 42) and a remote NFS directory (**plum:/home/zach**). You can identify a local directory hierarchy by the absence of a system name before the colon and usually the **ext4** filesystem type. A system name appears before the colon of a remote directory hierarchy filesystem and the filesystem type is always **nfs4**.

Before the new setup can work, you must reload the **automount** daemon using the **autofs** init script (page 811). This script creates the directories that hold the mount points if necessary.

The following example starts with the automount daemon not running. The first **ls** command shows that the **/music** and **/plum** directories are empty. The next command, run with **root** privileges, starts the **automount** daemon using the **autofs** init script. Now when you list **/music**, autofs mounts it and **ls** displays its contents. The **/plum** listing shows nothing: It is not an **autofs** mount point.

```
$ ls /music /plum
/music:

/plum:

$ su -c 'service autofs start'
Starting autofs (via systemctl):                        [  OK  ]

$ ls /music /plum
/music:
```

```
lost+found   mp3   ogg

/plum:
```

When you give an ls command and specify the mount point (**/plum/public**), **automount** mounts it and ls displays its contents. Once **public** is mounted on **/plum**, ls **/plum** shows the **public** directory is in place.

```
$ ls /plum/public
memos   personal
$ ls /plum
public
```

A df command shows the remotely mounted directory hierarchy and the locally mounted filesystem:

```
$ df -h
Filesystem              Size  Used Avail Use% Mounted on
...
plum:/home/public        37G  2.3G   35G   7% /plum/public
/dev/mapper/vg_guava-music
                         18G  172M   17G   2% /music
```

CHAPTER SUMMARY

NFS allows a server to share selected local directory hierarchies with client systems on a heterogeneous network, thereby reducing storage needs and administrative overhead. NFS defines a client/server relationship in which a server provides directory hierarchies that clients can mount.

On the server, the **/etc/exports** file lists the directory hierarchies that the system exports. Each line in **exports** specifies a directory hierarchy and the client systems that are allowed to mount it, including options for each client (readonly, read-write, and so on). An **exportfs –r** command causes NFS to reread this file.

From a client, a **mount** command mounts an exported NFS directory hierarchy. Alternatively, you can put an entry in **/etc/fstab** to have the system automatically mount the directory hierarchy when it mounts the local filesystems.

Automatically mounted directory hierarchies help manage large groups of systems containing many servers and directory hierarchies in a consistent way and can help remove server–server dependencies. The **automount** daemon automatically mounts **autofs** directory hierarchies when they are needed and unmounts them when they are no longer needed.

EXERCISES

1. What are three reasons to use NFS?

2. Which command would you give to mount on the local system the **/home** directory hierarchy that resides on the file server named **plum**? Assume the mounted directory hierarchy will appear as **/plum.home** on the local system. How would you mount the same directory hierarchy if it resided on the fileserver at 192.168.1.1? How would you unmount **/home**?

3. How would you list the mount points on the remote server named **plum** that the local client named **guava** can mount?

4. Which command line lists the currently mounted NFS directory hierarchies?

5. What does the **/etc/fstab** file do?

6. From a server, how would you allow readonly access to **/opt** for any system in **example.com**?

ADVANCED EXERCISES

7. When is it a good idea to disable attribute caching?

8. Describe the difference between the **root_squash** and **all_squash** options in **/etc/exports**.

9. Why does the **secure** option in **/etc/exports** not really provide any security?

10. Some diskless workstations use NFS as swap space. Why is this approach useful? What is the downside?

11. NFS maps users on the client to users on the server. Explain why this mapping is a security risk.

12. What does the mount **nosuid** option do? Why would you want to use this option?

23

Samba: Linux and Windows File and Printer Sharing

Objectives

After reading this chapter you should be able to:

▶ Describe the use, history, and components of Samba

▶ List capabilities of the Samba Server

▶ Use a variety of Samba client tools

▶ Describe Samba authentication methods

▶ Configure a Samba share for local accounts

▶ Troubleshoot Samba connections

Samba is a suite of programs that enables UNIX-like operating systems, including Linux, Solaris, FreeBSD, and Mac OS X, to share files and printers with other operating systems, such as OS/2 and Windows, as both a server and a client.

As a server, Samba shares Linux files and printers with Windows systems. As a client, Samba gives Linux users access to files and printers on Windows systems. Its ability to share files across operating systems makes Samba an ideal tool in a heterogeneous computing environment.

Refer to pages 579 and 581 for information about printing to and from a Windows machine using CUPS and Samba.

INTRODUCTION TO SAMBA

This chapter starts by providing a list of Samba tools followed by some basic information about Samba. The section on Samba clients explains how to use Samba to work with files and printers on a remote system. The next section describes three ways to configure a Samba server. First, a JumpStart section explains how to use the system-config-samba GUI (Fedora only) to set up a Samba server. The next sections cover using the swat Web-based configuration tool to set up a Samba Server and using a text editor to edit Samba configuration files. The final section, "Troubleshooting" (page 840), offers tips on what to do when Samba does not work properly.

Table 23-1 lists some of the utilities and daemons that make up the Samba suite of programs. See the **samba** man page for a complete list.

Table 23-1   Samba utilities and daemons

Utility or daemon	Function
net	This utility has the same syntax as the DOS **net** command and, over time, will eventually replace other Samba utilities such as **smbpasswd**.
nmbd	The *NetBIOS* (page 1177) nameserver program, run as a daemon by default. Provides NetBIOS over IP naming services for Samba clients. Also provides browsing support for Samba shares on remote systems.
nmblookup	Queries the *NetBIOS* (page 1177) name; see page 842.
pdbedit	Maintains the Samba user database (page 821).
smbclient	Displays shares on a Samba server such as a Windows machine; uses ftp-like commands (page 823).
smbd	The Samba program, run as a daemon by default. Provides file and print services for Samba and Windows clients.
smbpasswd	Changes Windows NT password hashes on Samba and Windows NT servers (page 821).

Table 23-1   Samba utilities and daemons (continued)

Utility or daemon	Function
smbstatus	Displays information about current **smbd** connections.
smbtar	Backs up and restores data from Samba servers; similar to tar.
smbtree	Displays a hierarchical diagram of available shares (page 823).
swat	Samba Web Administration Tool. A browser-based editor for the **smb.conf** file (page 830).
testparm	Checks the syntax of the **smb.conf** file (page 841).

More Information

Local Documentation: Samba/swat home page has links to local documentation (page 830). Documentation: With the **samba-doc** package installed, point a browser at **/usr/share/doc/samba-doc-x.y.z** (substitute the correct version number for *x.y.z*).

Web Samba: www.samba.org (mailing lists, documentation, downloads, and more) CIFS: www.samba.org/cifs

HOWTO *Samba HOWTO*: With the **samba-doc** package installed, point a browser at /usr/share/doc/samba-doc-3.5.6/htmldocs/Samba3-HOWTO/index.html. *Unofficial Samba HOWTO*: www.oregontechsupport.com/samba.

Notes

Server firewall The Samba *server* normally uses UDP ports 137 and 138 and TCP ports 139 and 445. If the Samba server system is running a firewall, you need to open at least port 445 and in some cases all of these ports. Using system-config-firewall (page 893), select **Samba** from the Trusted Services frame to open these ports.

Client firewall The Samba *clients* normally use UDP ports 137 and 138. If the Samba server system is running a firewall, you might need to open these ports. Using system-config-firewall (page 893), open these ports by selecting **Samba Client** from the Trusted Services frame.

swat firewall If you want to access swat (page 830) from a remote system and the server system is running a firewall, you must open port 901 on the server. See page 830 for more information.

SELinux When SELinux is set to use a targeted policy, Samba is protected by SELinux. You can use system-config-selinux (page 463) to disable this protection if necessary. If you want to allow users to share their home directories, see "SELinux" on page 835.

Share Under Samba and Windows, an exported directory hierarchy is called a *share*.

Mapping a share The Samba/Windows term *mapping a share* is equivalent to the Linux term *mounting a directory hierarchy*.

Samba The name *Samba* is derived from *SMB* (page 1188), the protocol that is the native method of file and printer sharing for Windows. Also CIFS (next).

CIFS   *CIFS* (page 1157) is an Internet filesystem protocol based on SMB (previous). The terms SMB and CIFS are used interchangeably.

Printing   Using CUPS to print on a printer connected to a Linux system is easier and can be made more secure than using Samba to print from Windows. For more information refer to "Print from Windows" on page 579.

Troubleshooting   If the server does not work properly, see "Troubleshooting" on page 840.

SAMBA USERS, USER MAPS, AND PASSWORDS

Authentication   For a Windows user to access Samba services on a Linux system, the user must provide a Windows username and a Samba password. In some cases, Windows supplies the username and password for you. Alternatively, you can log in as the user named **guest** (the Anonymous user; below). It is also possible to authenticate using other methods. For example, Samba can use *LDAP* (page 1172) or PAM (page 463) instead of the default password file. Refer to the Samba documentation for more information on authentication methods.

Windows users   The username supplied by Windows must be the same as a Linux username or must map to a Linux username (see "User maps," below).

Samba users   A Samba user must have the same name as a Linux user (the username must appear in **/etc/passwd**). You can use pdbedit (page 821) to display Samba users.

Samba passwords   By default, under Fedora/RHEL Samba uses Samba passwords to authenticate users. As installed, no Samba passwords exist. You can use smbpasswd (page 821) to work with Samba passwords. Each Samba user, except for **nobody**, must have a Samba password. See the next page for more information.

Linux passwords   By default, Linux passwords are different from Samba passwords.

No password   By default, a Windows user logging in without a password logs in as the Samba/Linux user **nobody** (the Anonymous user); you do not have to add this user as a Samba user. You need to add users and passwords for all other users who want to access shares on the Samba server

The user named **guest**   When the **guest ok** (page 840) parameter in the **smb.conf** configuration file (page 834) is set to YES and **guest account** (page 836) is set to **nobody** (default), Samba gives a Windows user logging in as **guest** the privileges of the Linux user named **nobody**. This user does not need to supply a password. The Samba user named **nobody** does not need to exist, but the user named **nobody** must appear in the **/etc/passwd** file. This user is referred to as the Anonymous user.

User maps   You can create a file, called a *user map*, that maps Windows usernames to Linux usernames. The **username map** (page 838) parameter in the **smb.conf** configuration file (page 834) specifies the location of this file. The default Samba configuration does not specify a user map. However, a sample map appears at **/etc/samba/smbusers**.

A user map can map Windows usernames to Linux usernames and/or map multiple Windows usernames to a single Linux username to facilitate file sharing. Each line in a user map file starts with a server (Linux) username, followed by a SPACE, an equal sign, another SPACE, and one or more SPACE-separated client (Windows) usernames. An asterisk (*) on the client side matches any client username. Following is the sample file (that by default Samba does not use) included with the **samba** package:

```
$ cat /etc/samba/smbusers
# Unix_name = SMB_name1 SMB_name2 ...
root = administrator admin
nobody = guest pcguest smbguest
```

The first entry maps the two Windows usernames (**administrator** and **admin**) to the Linux username **root**. The second entry maps three Windows usernames to the Linux username **nobody**.

Add the following line to the file the **username map** parameter points to, creating the file if necessary, to map the Windows username **sam** to the Linux username **sls**:

```
sls = sam
```

After you add a user to this file, you must give the user a password using smbpasswd (next). When Sam logs in as **sam**, Samba now maps **sam** to **sls** and looks up **sls** in the Samba password database. Assuming Sam provides the correct password, he logs in on the Samba server as **sls**.

smbpasswd AND pdbedit: WORK WITH SAMBA USERS AND PASSWORDS

Samba passwords Samba can use Linux passwords or Samba passwords to authenticate users. The **passdb backend** (page 837) parameter in the **smb.conf** (page 834) configuration file controls which type of passwords Samba uses. Setting **passdb backend** to **tdbsam** (default) causes Samba to use Samba passwords. Samba stores the passwords in a Trivial Database (tdb.sourceforge.net). Setting **passdb backend** to **smbpasswd** cause Samba to use Linux passwords that are stored in the text file named **/etc/samba/smbpasswd**. This section discusses how to use smbpasswd to work with Samba passwords and how to use pdbedit to display Samba users.

pdbedit With the **–L** option, pdbedit displays a list of Samba users; when you install Samba, no Samba users are defined:

```
# pdbedit -L
#
```

The Samba user named **nobody** does not have to exist for a the Windows user named **guest** to log in as the Anonymous user. See the "The user named **guest**" in the preceding section for more information.

Adding a Samba user and password As installed, no users have Samba passwords (there are no Samba users). You can add Samba users and optionally passwords only for users listed in **/etc/passwd**.

Working with **root** privileges, use smbpasswd with the **–a** option to add a Samba user and password for a Linux user (a user listed in **/etc/passwd**):

```
# smbpasswd –a sam
New SMB password:
Retype new SMB password:
```

The pdbedit utility shows the Samba user you just added, although it does not display password information:

```
# pdbedit -L
sam:500:Sam the Great
```

Changing your own Samba password

Once a user has a Samba password, he can use smbpasswd without any arguments to change his password. The smbpasswd utility will display a nondescriptive error message if the new password is too simple or if the two passwords you enter do not match.

```
$ smbpasswd
Old SMB password:
New SMB password:
Retype new SMB password:
```

If a user has different usernames on the Linux and Windows systems, you must map the Windows username to a Linux username (see **username map** on page 838). Except for the Windows user specified by the **guest** account (page 836), make sure all Linux users who will log in using Samba have Samba passwords.

RUNNING SAMBA CLIENTS

To run a Samba client under Linux you need to install a package and open a couple of ports on the client firewall. No Samba daemon runs on a client. Samba clients run on Linux and Windows. Under Linux you can use smbtree (page 823) to display shares, smbclient (page 823) to connect to shares in a manner similar to ftp, browse shares using Nautilus (page 824), and mount shares (page 824). Under Windows you can browse (page 825) and map (mount; page 826) shares.

PREREQUISITES

Install the following packages:

- **samba-client** (needed to run Samba clients)
- **samba-common** (installed with **samba-client**)
- **samba-doc** (optional documentation)

The **samba-client** package has no daemon, and therefore you do not have to run chkconfig or service when you install it.

Firewall   Open the client firewall as explained on see page 819.

Usernames and passwords   You might have to set up a user and password on the server. For more information refer to "Samba Users, User Maps, and Passwords" on page 820.

WORKING WITH SHARES FROM LINUX

Samba enables you to view and work with files on a server system from a Linux system (client). This section discusses several ways of accessing Windows files from Linux.

smbtree: DISPLAYS SHARES

The smbtree utility displays a hierarchical diagram of available shares. Unless you use the **–N** option, smbtree prompts you for a password; use the **–N** option or do not enter a password (just press RETURN) if you want to browse shares that are visible to the Anonymous user (browseable). The password allows you to view restricted shares, such as a user's home directory in the [**homes**] share. Following is sample output from smbtree:

```
$ smbtree -N
MGS
        \\PLUM                          Samba Server Version 3.5.6-71.fc14
           \\PLUM\HL-2140-series        Brother HL-2140 series
           \\PLUM\IPC$                  IPC Service (Samba Server Version 3.5.6-71.fc14)
           \\PLUM\tmp                   Temporary Directory
```

In the preceding output, **MGS** is the name of the workgroup and **PLUM** is the name of the Samba server. Workgroup and machine names are always shown in uppercase letters. If smbtree does not display output, set the **workgroup** (page 836) and **wins server** (page 840) parameters in **smb.conf**. Refer to the smbtree man page for more information.

smbclient: CONNECTS TO SHARES

The smbclient utility functions similarly to ftp (page 701) and connects to a share. However, smbclient uses Linux-style forward slashes (/) as path separators rather than Windows-style backslashes (\). As with smbtree, entering a password allows you to view restricted shares. The **–N** option prevents smbclient from requesting a password. The next example connects to a restricted share on **PLUM**:

```
$ smbclient //plum/sam
Enter sam's password: password RETURN
Domain=[MGS] OS=[Unix] Server=[Samba 3.5.6-71.fc14]
smb: \> ls
  .                               D        0  Wed Feb 16 18:56:49 2011
  ..                              D        0  Fri Dec 10 17:16:00 2010
  .pulse                          DH       0  Tue Nov  2 14:54:58 2010
  .setroubleshoot                 H       95  Tue Nov  2 14:56:32 2010
  .mozilla                        DH       0  Fri Oct 22 11:15:42 2010
  .imsettings.log                 H      631  Thu Feb  3 15:23:16 2011
  .fontconfig                     DH       0  Tue Dec 21 10:43:32 2010
  .nautilus                       DH       0  Tue Nov  2 14:54:55 2010
  .cache                          DH       0  Tue Nov  2 14:54:54 2010
  Public                          D        0  Tue Nov  2 14:54:52 2010
  ...

        35401 blocks of size 524288. 29912 blocks available
smb: \>
```

You can use most ftp commands from smbclient. Refer to "Tutorial Session" on page 705 for examples of ftp commands. Alternatively, give the command **help** to display a list of commands or **help** followed by a command for information on a specific command:

```
smb: \> help history
HELP history:
        displays the command history
```

BROWSING SHARES

Browsing shares using smbtree and smbclient is quite awkward compared with the ease of browsing a network from Windows; GNOME provides a more user-friendly alternative. Select **Menubar: Places⇨Connect to Server** to display the Connect to Server window. Select **Windows share** from the drop-down list labeled **Service type** and enter the name or IP address of the server in the text box labeled **Server**. If you want to view a particular share, enter the name of the share. If the share is restricted, enter the name of the user who has permission to view the share. Click **Connect**. If necessary, Nautilus prompts for a domain (workgroup) and password. Nautilus displays the share in a file browser window.

Nautilus uses virtual filesystem add-ons, which are part of the desktop environment and not part of the native Linux system. As a consequence, only native GNOME applications can open files on remote shares; normal Linux programs cannot. For example, gedit can open files on remote shares; LibreOffice, mplayer, and xedit cannot.

MOUNTING SHARES

The mount utility (page 520) with a **–t cifs** option mounts a share as if it were a Linux directory hierarchy. See page 1157 for more information on the CIFS protocol. When you mount a share, you can write to the files on the share; you cannot write to files on a share using smbclient.

A mount command that mounts a share has the following syntax (you must run this command with **root** privileges):

   mount -t cifs //host/share dir

where *host* is the name of the system the share is on, *share* is the name of the share you want to mount, and *dir* is the absolute pathname of the Linux directory you are mounting the share on (the mount point).

The following command, when run with **root** privileges, mounts on the **/plum.sam** directory the **sam** share on **plum**:

```
# mount -t cifs //plum/sam /plum.sam -o username=sam
Password: password RETURN
# ls /plum.sam
Desktop  Documents  Downloads  Music  Pictures  Public ...
```

Omit the **username** argument and provide a blank password to mount shares that are visible to an anonymous user.

Use the **uid**, **file_mode**, and **dir_mode** mount options with type **cifs** filesystems to establish ownership and permissions of mounted files:

```
# mount -t cifs //plum/sam /plum.sam -o username=sam,uid=sam,file_mode=0644,dir_mode=0755
```

Permissions must be expressed as octal numbers preceded by a zero. For more information refer to the mount.cifs man page.

Credentials file You can also store the username, password, and optionally the workgroup (domain) in a credentials file. To prevent another user from mounting this share, a credentials file should be owned by **root** and readable and writable only by a user working with **root** privileges (600 permissions). When you specify the credentials file in **fstab** (page 524), the share can be mounted automatically when the system is booted. Following is the credentials file for the share in the preceding example:

```
# cat /etc/plum.sam.credentials
username=sam
password=password
domain=MGS

# ls -l /etc/plum.sam.credentials
-rw------- 1 root root 26 01-11 12:52 /etc/plum.sam.credentials
```

The following command mounts this share using the credential file:

```
# mount -t cifs //plum/sam /plum.sam -o credentials=/etc/plum.sam.credentials
```

The following line in **/etc/fstab** would cause the share to be mounted when the system boots:

```
//plum/sam      /plum.sam      cifs      defaults,credentials=/etc/plum.sam.credentials
```

Each share must have its own credentials file unless it uses the same login information as another share, in which case the files can use the same credentials file.

Working with Shares from Windows

This section describes how to access Linux (or Windows) directories from a Windows machine. You do not need to set up a Linux client to browse or map Linux shares from a Windows machine.

Browsing Shares

To access a share on a Samba server from Windows, open My Computer or Explorer on the Windows system, and in the text box labeled **Address**, enter \\ followed by the Net-BIOS name (or just the hostname if you have not assigned a different NetBIOS name) of the Samba server. Windows then displays the share names of the directories the remote system is sharing. To view the shares on the Linux system named **plum**, for example, enter **\\plum**. From this window, you can view and, if permitted, browse the shares available on the remote system. If you set a share on the server so it is not browseable, you need to enter the path of the share using the format *servername**sharename* to display the share.

MAPPING A SHARE

Another way to access a share on a Samba server from a Windows machine is by mapping (mounting) a share. Open My Computer or Explorer on the Windows system and click **Map Network Drive** from one of the drop-down lists on the menubar (found on the **Tools** menu on many Windows machines). Windows displays the Map Network Drive window. Select an unused Windows drive letter from the list box labeled **Drive** and enter the Windows path to the share you want to map in the text box labeled **Folder**. (When you use system-config-samba [Fedora only] to create a share, the share has the same name as the name of the directory you are sharing.) The format of the windows path is *hostname**sharename*. For example, to map **/tmp** on **plum** to Windows drive J, assuming the share is named **tmp**, select **J** in the list box labeled **Drive**, enter **\\plum\tmp** in the text box labeled **Folder**, and click **Finish**. After supplying a username and password, you should be able to access the **/tmp** directory from **plum** as **J** (**tmp**) on the Windows machine. If you cannot map the drive, refer to "Troubleshooting" on page 840.

SETTING UP A SAMBA SERVER

This section describes how to install and configure a Samba server using the system-config-samba GUI (Fedora only), the swat browser-based configuration tool, and an editor to edit the configuration files.

PREREQUISITES

Install the following packages:

- **samba**
- **system-config-samba** (optional; Fedora only)
- **samba-common** (installed with **samba**)
- **samba-swat** (optional)
- **xinetd** (needed to run swat; installed with **samba-swat**)
- **samba-doc** (optional documentation; installed with **samba-swat**)

smb init script   Run chkconfig to cause **smbd** to start when the system enters multiuser mode:

```
# chkconfig smb on
```

Start **smb**:

```
# service smb start
```

nmb init script   Run chkconfig to cause **nmbd** to start when the system enters multiuser mode:

```
# chkconfig nmb on
```

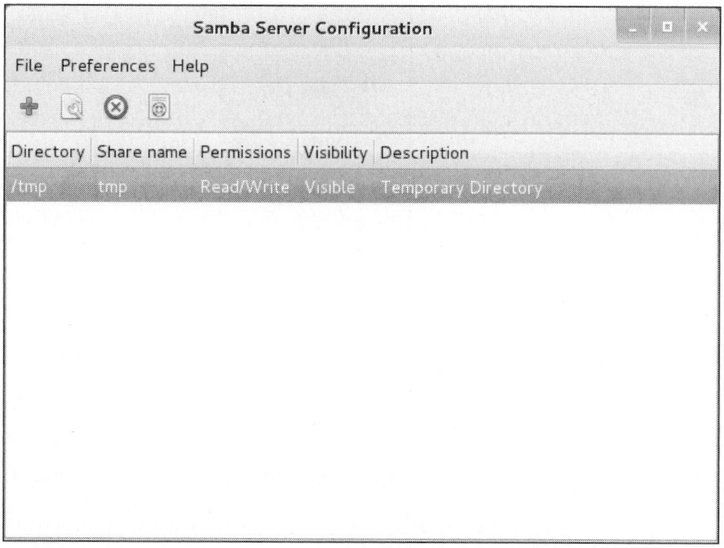

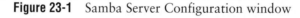

Figure 23-1   Samba Server Configuration window

Start **nmb**:

```
# service nmb start
```

Although it is not usually necessary to reload the Samba daemons, you can use **reload** with service to reload Samba configuration files without disturbing clients connected to the server.

Firewall   Open the server firewall as explained on page 819.

Printers   The default **smb.conf** configuration file shares printers on the Samba server; no configuration is necessary.

Home directories   The default **smb.conf** configuration file shares home directories of users on the Samba server; no configuration is necessary.

Configuration   The **/etc/sysconfig/samba** file causes **smbd** and **nmbd** each to start with the **–D** option, causing the **smbd** and **nmbd** processes to run as daemons.

JUMPSTART: CONFIGURING A SAMBA SERVER USING system-config-samba (FEDORA)

The system-config-samba utility, which is not available under RHEL, can set up only basic features of a Samba server. It is, however, the best tool to use if you are not familiar with Samba and you want to set up a simple Samba server quickly. The system-config-samba utility performs three basic functions: configuring the server, configuring users, and setting up shares (directory hierarchies) that are exported to Windows machines.

Figure 23-2   Server Settings window, Basic tab

To display the Samba Server Configuration window (Figure 23-1), select **Main menu: Applications⇨Other⇨Samba** or enter **system-config-samba** from a terminal emulator or Run Application window (ALT-F2).

Configure the server   Select **Menubar: Preferences⇨Server Settings** to display the Server Settings window Basic tab (Figure 23-2). Change the workgroup to the one in use on the Windows machines. Change the description of the server if you like. Click the **Security** tab and make sure Authentication Mode is set to **User**; you do not need to specify an Authentication Server or a Kerberos Realm. If you are using Windows 98 or later, set Encrypt Passwords to **Yes**. When you specify a username in the Guest Account, anyone logging in on the Samba server as **guest** maps to that user's ID. Click **OK**.

Add or modify Samba users   Select **Menubar: Preferences⇨Samba Users** to display the Samba Users window (Figure 23-3). If the user you want to log in as is not listed in this window, click **Add User**. When you have the proper permissions, the Create New Samba User window displays a combo box labeled **Unix Username** that allows you to select a Linux user; otherwise, your username is displayed as the Unix Username. The Windows Username is the Windows username that you want to map to the specified Linux (UNIX) username. The Samba Password is the password this user or Windows enters to gain access to the Samba server.

If Sam's username is **sam** on both the Linux and Windows systems, you would select **sam** from the Unix Username combo box and enter **sam** in the Windows Username text box. If his username were **sls** under Linux and **sam** under Windows, you would select **sls** from the Unix Username combo box and enter **sam** in the Windows Username text box. Finally you would enter Sam's Windows password in the two Samba Password text boxes. Click **OK** to close the Create New Samba User window, then click **OK** to close the Samba Users window.

User map   If you are mapping a Windows username to a *different* Linux username, you must add the following **username map** (page 838) parameter to the **[global]** section of **/etc/samba/smb.conf** (page 834):

```
username map = /etc/samba/smbusers
```

Figure 23-3   Samba Users window

Without this line in **smb.conf**, Samba will not consult the user map file.

Linux shares Next you need to add a *share,* which is the directory hierarchy you export from the server (Linux) system to the client (Windows) system. Click the plus sign (**+**) on the toolbar to display the Basic tab of the Create Samba Share window (Figure 23-4). In the text box labeled **Folder,** enter the absolute pathname of the directory you want to share (**/tmp** is an easy directory to practice with). Enter a description if you like. It can be useful to enter the Linux hostname and the pathname of the directory you are sharing here. Put a tick in the check box labeled **Writable** if you want to be able to write to the directory from the client machine; putting a tick in the check box labeled **Visible** allows the share to be seen (browsed) from the client machine. Click the Access tab and specify whether you want to limit access to specified users or whether you want to allow anyone to access this share. Click **OK**. Close the Samba Server Configuration window.

Figure 23-4   Create Samba Share window, Basic tab

You should now be able to access the share from a Windows machine (page 825). There is no need to start or restart the Samba server.

Troubleshooting If the server does not work properly, see "Troubleshooting" on page 840.

swat: CONFIGURES A SAMBA SERVER

Make a copy of **smb.conf**

tip As installed, the **/etc/samba/smb.conf** file contains extensive comments (page 834). The swat utility overwrites this file, removing the comments. Make a copy of **smb.conf** for safekeeping before you run this utility for the first time.

The swat (Samba Web Administration Tool; **samba-swat** package) utility is a browser-based graphical editor for the **/etc/samba/smb.conf** file. For each of the configurable parameters, it provides Help links, default values, and a text box to change the value. The swat utility is a well-designed tool in that lines in the swat GUI correspond to the lines in the **smb.conf** file you edit: You can use and learn from swat, so that if you want to use a text editor to modify **smb.conf**, the transition will be straightforward.

CONFIGURING swat

The swat utility is run from **xinetd** (**xinetd** package, installed with **samba-swat**; page 481). If you want to run swat from the local system only, give the following command:

```
# chkconfig swat on
```

This command changes **disable = yes** to **disable = no** in the **/etc/xinetd.d/swat** file. Start or restart the **xinetd** daemon as explained below.

If you want to run swat from a system other than the local system, you must open the firewall and edit the **swat** file so swat responds to the remote system. Open **/etc/xinetd.d/swat** with a text editor. If necessary, change the **yes** that follows **disable =** to **no**. Next, modify the line that starts with **only_from**. As swat is installed, this line permits access from the local system only (127.0.0.1). Add the names or IP addresses of the other system(s) you want to access swat from to this line. Separate the system names or IP addresses with SPACEs.

```
only_from  = 127.0.0.1 172.16.192.150
```

Restart **xinetd** Restart **xinetd** so it rereads the **swat** file:

```
# service xinetd restart
Restarting xinetd (via systemctl):                      [  OK  ]
```

Firewall If you are running swat from a system other than the server and the server is running a firewall, you must allow the remote system access to port 901 on the server so it can communicate with swat: Run system-config-firewall, select the Other Ports tab, and select **901 TCP swat** as explained on page 894.

Now you should be able to run swat: From the local system, open a browser and enter either **http://127.0.0.1:901** or **http://localhost:901** in the location bar. When prompted, enter the username **root** and the **root** password. (If you provide a username

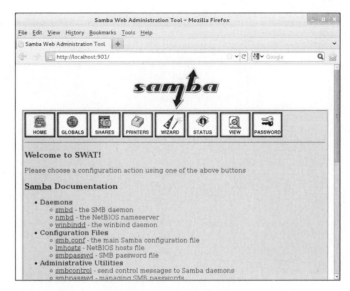

Figure 23-5   The local swat home page

other than **root,** you will be able to view some configuration information but will not be able to make changes. From a remote system, replace **127.0.0.1** with the name or IP address of the server (but see the adjacent security tip).

Do not allow unencrypted remote access to swat

security Do not allow access to swat from a remote system on an insecure network. When you do so and log in, the **root** password is sent in cleartext over whatever connection you are using and can easily be sniffed. If you want to access swat over an insecure network, use ssh to forward port 901 (page 696).

The browser displays the local Samba/swat home page (Figure 23-5). This page includes links to local Samba documentation and the buttons listed below.

HOME   Links to local Samba documentation. When you click the word **Samba** (not the logo, but the one just before the word **Documentation** in the Samba/swat home page), swat displays the Samba man page, which defines each Samba program.

GLOBALS   Edits global parameters (variables) in **smb.conf.**

SHARES   Edits share information in **smb.conf.**

PRINTERS   Edits printer information in **smb.conf.**

WIZARD   Rewrites the **smb.conf** file, removing all comment lines and lines that specify default values.

STATUS   Shows the active connections, active shares, and open files. Allows you to stop and restart the **smbd** and **nmbd** daemons.

VIEW   Displays a subset of the configuration parameters as determined by the default values and settings in **smb.conf.** Click **Full View** for a complete list.

PASSWORD   Manages Samba passwords.

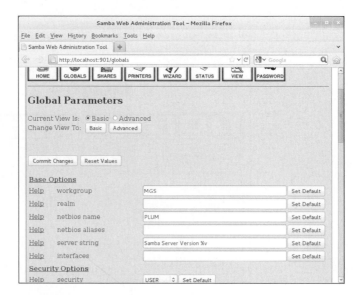

Figure 23-6   Global Parameters page

SAMPLE SETUP

It is quite easy to establish a basic Samba setup so you can work with a Linux directory hierarchy from a Windows system. More work is required to set up a secure connection or one with special features. The following example creates a basic setup based on default values and the sample **smb.conf** file included with Fedora/RHEL.

swat Help and   Each of the parameters swat displays has a button labeled **Help** next to it. Click
defaults   **Help** to open a new browser window containing an explanation of that parameter. Each parameter also has a **Set Default** button that sets the parameter to its default value (not necessarily the initial value as supplied by Fedora/RHEL).

For this example, do not click any of the **Set Default** buttons. Be sure to click **Commit Changes** at the top of each page after you finish making changes on a page but before you click a menu button at the top of the page. Otherwise, swat will discard your changes.

GLOBALS page   To follow this example, first click **GLOBALS** at the top of the Samba/swat home page to display the Global Parameters page (Figure 23-6). Leave everything at its current setting with three exceptions: **workgroup, hosts allow,** and **hosts deny.** Setting these parameters makes the server more secure by limiting the clients Samba responds to.

workgroup   Set **workgroup** to the workgroup used on the Windows systems. (If you followed the preceding JumpStart, the workgroup is already set.)

hosts allow and   Scroll near the bottom of the Security Options and set **hosts deny** to **ALL.** Set **hosts**
hosts deny   **allow** to the names or IP addresses of systems you want to allow to access the local system's shares and printers (including **localhost** [127.0.0.1]). If there are any addresses in **hosts allow** or if you set **hosts deny** to ALL, you must also add 127.0.0.1 to **hosts allow** to be able to connect to swat from the local system. Separate the entries

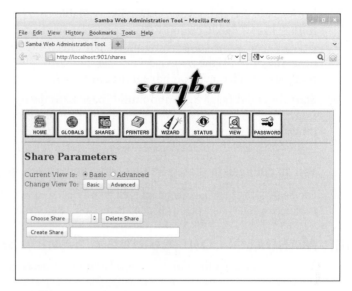

Figure 23-7   Share Parameters page

with SPACEs or commas. See page 836 for more information on the various ways you can set **hosts allow.** Click **Commit Changes** (near the top of the page) when you are done with the Global Parameters page.

If you can no longer use swat

tip   If you can no longer use swat, you probably changed the **hosts allow** setting incorrectly. In this case you need to edit **/etc/samba/smb.conf** manually and fix the line with the words **hosts allow** in it:

```
$ grep hosts smb.conf
        hosts allow = 127.0.0.1, 172.16.192.150
        hosts deny = ALL
```

The preceding entries allow access from the local system and from 172.16.192.150 only. They also allow swat to work. You do not need to restart Samba after changing **smb.conf**.

SHARES page   Next click **SHARES** at the top of the page. A few buttons and boxes appear near the bottom of the page (Figure 23-7). In the text box adjacent to the button labeled **Create Share,** enter the name you want to assign to the share you are setting up. You will use this share name from Windows when you map (mount) the share. Click **Create Share.** To modify an existing share, display the name of the share in the drop-down list labeled **Choose Share** and click **Choose Share.** Either of these actions expands the Share Parameters page so it displays information about the selected share.

Set **path** to the absolute pathname on the Linux server of the share and, if you like, set **comment** to a string that will help you remember where the share is located. The values for **hosts allow** and **hosts deny,** if any, are taken from the global parameters that you set previously. Make sure **read only, guest ok,** and

browseable are set as you desire. Set **available** to YES or you will not have access to the share. Click **Commit Changes** when you are done with the Share Parameters page. If you want to see how many parameters there really are, click **Advanced** near the top of the page. Switching between the Basic and Advanced views removes any changes you have not committed.

Troubleshooting   Start the **smbd** (page 826) and **nmbd** (page 826) daemons, open the firewalls as necessary (page 819), and add users and passwords as necessary (page 821). From a Windows machine, you should now be able to access the share you just created (page 825). If the server does not work properly, see "Troubleshooting" on page 840.

You do not need to restart Samba when you change smb.conf

tip   Samba rereads its configuration files each time a client connects. Unless you change the **security** parameter (page 837), you do not need to restart Samba when you change **smb.conf**.

smb.conf: MANUALLY CONFIGURING A SAMBA SERVER

The **/etc/samba/smb.conf** file controls most aspects of how Samba works and is divided into sections. Each section begins with a line that holds some text between brackets ([...]). The text within the brackets identifies the section. Typical sections are

[global]	Defines global parameters
[printers]	Defines printers
[homes]	Defines shares in user home directories
[*share name*]	Defines a share (you can have more than one of these sections)

smb.conf   As installed under Fedora/RHEL, the **smb.conf** sample configuration file contains
comments   extensive comments and commented-out examples. Comment lines start with either a hashmark (#) or a semicolon (;). The sample file uses hashmarks to begin lines that are intended to remain as comments. Semicolons begin lines you might want to mimic or use as is by removing the semicolons.

Basic **smb.conf** file   Following is a basic **smb.conf** file. It depends on default values for many parameters. To make the code clearer, important default values are written as comments beginning with a semicolon as they are in the default **smb.conf** file. To make the system more secure, change the default **server string** to eliminate the Samba version number; this value might aid hackers in penetrating the system. The **hosts allow** and **hosts deny** parameters are not required. When included, they prevent systems other than those listed from contacting the Samba server. If you uncomment these lines, replace 172.16.192.150 with the IP address of the system you want to allow to connect to the Samba server. You must open the firewall (page 819) and start the **smbd** and **nmbd** daemons (page 826) before a client can contact the server.

```
$ cat /etc/samba/smb.conf
[global]
        workgroup = MGS
        server string = Samba Server Version %v
        log file = /var/log/samba/log.%m
        max log size = 50
;       hosts allow = 127.0.0.1, 172.16.192.150
```

```
;               hosts deny = ALL
;               security = user
;               encrypt passwords = YES
;               guest ok = NO
;               guest account = nobody

[homes]
                comment = Home Directories
                read only = NO
                browseable = NO

[tmp]
                comment = Temporary Directory
                path = /tmp
                read only = NO
                guest ok = YES
;               available = YES
;               browseable = YES
```

The **[homes]** share   The sample **smb.conf** file includes the **[homes]** share, which allows users to share their Linux home directories with a Windows machine. The default **smb.conf** file includes the same share. This share causes each user's home directory to be shared with the specified parameters. The pathname of the share is */username*; Sam's share on **plum** would be **/plum/sam**. The default settings, which are used in the file shown above, prevent users other than the owners from browsing or accessing home directories while allowing logged-in owners full access.

SELinux   If the system is running SELinux with a targeted policy and you want to allow users to share their home directories as explained in this section, you must modify the SELinux policy to allow this access. You can use system-config-selinux (page 463) to allow this access: In the Boolean tab, **samba** module, put a tick mark adjacent to **Allow samba to share users home directories.**

Defining a share   The **tmp** share in the preceding **smb.conf** file enables a user on a Windows system to be able to read from and write to the **/tmp** directory on the server. The name of the share under Windows is **tmp**; the path under Linux is **/tmp**. Any Windows user who can log in on Samba, including **guest**, can read from and write to this directory, assuming the user's Linux permissions allow it. To allow a user to log in on Samba, you must run smbpasswd (page 821). The **browseable** parameter, which defaults to **YES**, causes the share to appear as a share on the server. The Linux permissions that apply to a Windows user using Samba are the same permissions that apply to the Linux user that the Windows user logs in as or maps to.

Troubleshooting   Start the **smbd** (page 826) and **nmbd** (page 826) daemons, open the firewalls as necessary (page 819), and add users and passwords as necessary (page 821). From a Windows machine, you should now be able to access the share you just created (page 825). If the server does not work properly, see "Troubleshooting" on page 840.

PARAMETERS IN THE smbd.conf FILE

The **smb.conf** man page and the Help feature of swat list all the parameters you can set in **smb.conf**. The following sections identify some of the parameters you might need to change.

GLOBAL PARAMETERS

interfaces   A SPACE-separated list of networks Samba listens on. Specify as interface names (such as **lo** and **eth0**) or as IP address/net mask pairs (page 479).

Default: all active interfaces except 127.0.0.1

server string   The string the client (Windows) machine displays in various places. Within the string, Samba replaces **%v** with the Samba version number and **%h** with the hostname of the server. To make the system more secure, eliminate the Samba version number; this value might aid hackers in penetrating the system.

Default: Samba %v
Fedora/RHEL: Samba Server Version %v

workgroup   The workgroup the server belongs to. Set to the same workgroup as the Windows clients that use the server. This parameter controls the domain name that Samba uses when **security** (page 837) is set to DOMAIN.

Default: WORKGROUP
Fedora/RHEL: MYGROUP

SECURITY PARAMETERS

encrypt passwords   YES accepts only encrypted passwords from clients. Windows 98 and Windows NT 4.0 Service Pack 3 and later use encrypted passwords by default. This parameter uses smbpasswd to authenticate passwords unless you set **security** to SERVER or DOMAIN, in which case Samba authenticates using another server.

Default: YES

guest account   The username that is assigned to users logging in as **guest** or mapped to **guest**; applicable only when **guest ok** (page 840) is set to YES. This username should be present in **/etc/passwd** but should not be able to log in on the system. Typically **guest account** is assigned a value of **nobody** because the user **nobody** can access only files that any user can access. If you are using the **nobody** account for other purposes on the server system, set this parameter to a name other than **nobody**. See page 820 for more information.

Default: **nobody**

hosts allow   Analogous to the **/etc/hosts.allow** file (page 484); specifies hosts that are allowed to connect to the server. Overrides hosts specified in **hosts deny**. A good strategy is to specify ALL in **hosts deny** and to specify the hosts you want to grant access to in this file. Specify hosts in the same manner as in the **hosts.allow** file.

Default: none (all hosts permitted access)

hosts deny Analogous to the **/etc/hosts.deny** file (page 484); specifies hosts that are not allowed to connect to the server. Overridden by hosts specified in **hosts allow**. If you specify ALL in this parameter, remember to include the local system (127.0.0.1) in **hosts allow**. Specify hosts in the same manner as in the **hosts.deny** file.

Default: none (no hosts excluded)

invalid users Lists users who are not allowed to log in using Samba.

Default: none (all users are permitted to log in)

map to guest Defines when a failed login is mapped to the **guest account**. Useful only when security (below) is not set to SHARE or SERVER.

Never: Allows **guest** to log in only when the user explicitly provides **guest** as the username and a blank password.

Bad User: Treats any attempt to log in as a user who does not exist as a **guest** login. This parameter is a security risk because it allows a malicious user to retrieve a list of users on the system quickly.

Bad Password: Silently logs in as **guest** any user who incorrectly enters her password. This parameter might confuse a user when she mistypes her password and is unknowingly logged in as **guest** because she will suddenly see fewer shares than she is used to seeing.

Default: never

passdb backend Specifies how Samba stores passwords. Set to **ldapsam** for LDAP, **smbpasswd** for Samba, or **tdbsam** for TDB (Trivial Database) password storage. See page 821 for instructions on using smbpasswd to change or add Samba passwords.

Default: **tdbsam**

passwd chat The chat script Samba uses to converse with the program defined by **passwd program** (next). If this script is not followed, Samba does not change the password. Used only when **unix password sync** (page 838) is set to YES.

Default: *new*password* %n\n*new*password* %n\n *changed*

passwd program The program Samba uses to set *Linux* passwords. Samba replaces **%u** with the user's username.

Default: none

security Specifies if and how clients transfer user and password information to the server. Choose one of the following:

USER: Causes Samba to require a username and password from Windows users when logging in on the Samba server. With this setting you can use

- **username map** (page 838) to map Samba usernames to Linux usernames
- **encrypt passwords** (page 836) to encrypt passwords (recommended)
- **guest account** (page 836) to map users to the **guest** account

SHARE: Causes Samba not to authenticate clients on a per-user basis. Instead, Samba uses the Windows 9*x* setup, in which each share can have an individual password for either read or full access. This option is not compatible with recent versions of Windows.

SERVER: Causes Samba to use another SMB server to validate usernames and passwords. If the remote validation fails, the local Samba server tries to validate usernames and passwords as though **security** were set to USER.

DOMAIN: Samba passes an encrypted password to a Windows NT domain controller for validation. The **workgroup** parameter (page 836) must be properly set in **smb.conf** for DOMAIN to work.

ADS: Instructs Samba to use an Active Directory server for authentication, allowing a Samba server to participate as a native Active Directory member. (Active Directory is the centralized information system that Windows 2000 and later use. It replaces Windows Domains, which was used by Windows NT and earlier.)

Default: USER

unix password sync YES causes Samba to change a user's Linux password when the associated user changes the encrypted Samba password.

Default: NO

update encrypted YES allows users to migrate from cleartext passwords to encrypted passwords without logging in on the server and using smbpasswd. To migrate users, set to YES and set **encrypt passwords** to NO. As each user logs in on the server with a cleartext Linux password, smbpasswd encrypts and stores the password. Set to NO and set **encrypt passwords** to YES after all users have been converted.

Default: NO

username map Points to a user map file that maps Windows usernames to Linux usernames. See "User maps" on page 820 for more information.

Default: no map

LOGGING PARAMETERS

log file The name of the Samba log file. Samba replaces **%m** with the name of the client system, allowing you to generate a separate log file for each client.

Default: none
Fedora/RHEL: **/var/log/samba/log.%m**

log level Sets the log level, with 0 (zero) being off and higher numbers being more verbose.

Default: 0 (off)

max log size An integer specifying the maximum size of the log file in kilobytes. A 0 (zero) specifies no limit. When a file reaches this size, Samba appends **.old** to the filename and starts a new log, deleting any old log file.

Default: 5000
Fedora/RHEL: 50

BROWSER PARAMETERS

The *domain master browser* is the system responsible for maintaining the list of machines on a network used when browsing. *SMB* (page 1188) uses weighted elections every 11–15 minutes to determine which machine is the domain master browser.

Whether a Samba server wins this election depends on two parameters:

- Setting **domain master** to YES instructs the Samba server to enter the election.

- The **os level** determines how much weight the Samba server's vote receives. The maximum setting for **os level** is 255, although setting it to 65 should ensure that the Samba server wins. NT Server series domain controllers—including Windows 2000, XP, and 2003—use an **os level** of 32.

domain master   YES causes **nmbd** to attempt to be the domain master browser. If a domain master browser exists, then local master browsers will forward copies of their browse lists to it. If there is no domain master browser, then browse queries might not be able to cross subnet boundaries. A Windows PDC (primary domain controller) will always try to become the domain master and might behave in unexpected ways if it fails. Refer to the preceding discussion for more information.

Default: AUTO

local master   YES causes **nmbd** to enter elections for the local master browser on a subnet. A local master browser stores a cache of the *NetBIOS* (page 1177) names of entities on the local subnet, allowing browsing. Windows machines automatically enter elections; for browsing to work, the network must have at least one Windows machine or one Samba server with **local master** set to YES. It is poor practice to set **local master** to NO. If you do not want a computer to act as a local master, set its **os level** to a lower number, allowing it to be used as the local master if all else fails.

Default: YES

os level   An integer that controls how much Samba advertises itself for browser elections and how likely **nmbd** is to become the local master browser for its workgroup. A higher number increases the chances of the local server becoming the local master browser. Refer to the discussion at the beginning of this section for more information.

Default: 20

preferred master   YES forces **nmbd** to hold an election for local master and enters the local system with a slight advantage. With **domain master** set to YES, this parameter helps ensure the local Samba server becomes the domain master. Setting this parameter to YES on more than one server causes the servers to compete to become master, generating a lot of network traffic and sometimes leading to unpredictable results. A Windows PDC automatically acts as if this parameter is set to YES.

Default: AUTO

COMMUNICATION PARAMETERS

dns proxy   When acting as a *WINS server* (page 1197), YES causes **nmbd** to use DNS if *NetBIOS* (page 1177) resolution fails.

Default: YES

socket options   Tunes the network parameters used when exchanging data with a client.

Default: TCP_NODELAY

wins server   The IP address of the WINS server **nmbd** should register with.

Default: not enabled

wins support   YES specifies **nmbd** is to act as a WINS server.

Default: NO

SHARE PARAMETERS

Each of the following parameters can appear many times in **smb.conf**, once in each share definition.

available   YES specifies the share as active. Set this parameter to NO to disable the share but continue logging requests for it.

Default: YES

browseable   Determines whether the share can be browsed, for example, in Windows My Network Places.

Default: YES

comment   A description of the share, shown when browsing the network from Windows.

Default: none
Fedora/RHEL: varies

guest ok   Allows a user who logs in as **guest** to access this share.

Default: NO

path   The path of the directory being shared.

Default: none
Fedora/RHEL: various

read only   Does not allow write access. Use **writable** to allow read-write access.

Default: YES

TROUBLESHOOTING

Samba and Windows provide tools that can help troubleshoot a connection. This section discusses these tools and suggests other techniques that can help narrow down the problem when you cannot get Samba to work.

1. Restart the Samba daemons. Normally you do not need to restart these daemons after changing the **smb.conf** file. Make sure **smbd** and **nmbd** are running.

```
# service smb restart
Restarting smb (via systemctl):                              [  OK  ]
# service nmb restart
Restarting nmb (via systemctl):                              [  OK  ]
# ps -ef | grep mbd
root     13009     1  0 13:49 ?        00:00:00 smbd -D
root     13011 13009  0 13:49 ?        00:00:00 smbd -D
root     13031     1  0 13:49 ?        00:00:00 nmbd -D
```

testparm 2. Run testparm to confirm that the **smb.conf** file is syntactically correct:

```
$ testparm
Load smb config files from /etc/samba/smb.conf
Processing section "[homes]"
Processing section "[tmp]"
Loaded services file OK.
Server role: ROLE_STANDALONE
Press enter to see a dump of your service definitions
...
```

You can ignore an error message about **rlimit_max**. If you misspell a keyword in **smb.conf**, you get an error such as the following:

```
$ testparm
Load smb config files from /etc/samba/smb.conf
Unknown parameter encountered: "workgruop"
Ignoring unknown parameter "workgruop"
...
```

Log files 3. Check the log files in **/var/samba/log** (page 838).

ping 4. Use ping (page 386) from both sides of the connection to make sure the network is up.

Firewall 5. Confirm the firewall on the server is not blocking the Samba connection on either the server or the client (page 819).

User 6. Make sure the user who is trying to log in exists as a Samba user. See pdbedit on page 821.

Password 7. Make sure you have set up a password for the Samba user who is trying to log in. See smbpasswd on page 821.

SELinux 8. You might need to modify the SELinux policy. See pages 819 and 835.

hosts allow 9. If you specify a value for **hosts deny**, be sure to specify values for **hosts allow**, including 127.0.0.1 so you can access Samba from the local system. See page 832 for more information.

net view 10. From a Windows command prompt, use net view to display a list of shares available from the server (**plum** in this example):

```
C:>net view \\plum
Shared resources at \\plum

Samba Server Version 3.5.6-71.fc14

Share name   Type   Used as  Comment

--------------------------------------------------------------------
sam          Disk            Home Directories
tmp          Disk            Temporary Directory
The command completed successfully.
```

net use 11. Try to map (mount) the drive from a Windows command prompt. The
following command attempts to mount the share named **sam** on **plum** as
drive X:

```
C:>net use x: \\plum\sam
Enter the user name for 'plum': sam
Enter the password for plum:
The command completed successfully.
```

nmblookup 12. From the Samba server, use nmblookup (**samba-client** package) to query the
nmbd server, using the special name __SAMBA__ for the server's NetBIOS
name. The **–d 2** option turns the debugger on at level 2, which generates a
moderate amount of output. The **–B** option specifies the server you are
querying.

```
$ nmblookup -d 2 -B localhost __SAMBA__
...
querying __SAMBA__ on 127.0.0.1
Got a positive name query response from 127.0.0.1 ( 172.16.192.151 )
172.16.192.151 __SAMBA__<00>
```

The next example uses nmblookup, without setting the debug level, to
query the local system for all NetBIOS names.

```
$ nmblookup -B localhost \*
querying * on 127.0.0.1
172.16.192.151 *<00>
```

To query for the master browser from the local server, run nmblookup with
the **–A** option followed **localhost** or the name of the server:

```
$ nmblookup -A localhost
Looking up status of 127.0.0.1
        PLUM            <00> -          H <ACTIVE>
        PLUM            <03> -          H <ACTIVE>
        PLUM            <20> -          H <ACTIVE>
        ..__MSBROWSE__. <01> - <GROUP> H <ACTIVE>
        MGS             <1d> -          H <ACTIVE>
        MGS             <1e> - <GROUP> H <ACTIVE>
        MGS             <00> - <GROUP> H <ACTIVE>

        MAC Address = 00-00-00-00-00-00
```

smbclient 13. From the Samba server, use smbclient (**samba-client** package) with the **–L** option followed by the name of the server to generate a list of shares offered by the server. When you do not enter a password, smbclient displays shares available to the Anonymous user. When you enter a password, it also displays restricted shares including the [**homes**] share for the user.

```
$ smbclient -L localhost
Enter sam's password: RETURN  (do not enter a password)
Anonymous login successful
Domain=[MGS] OS=[Unix] Server=[Samba 3.5.6-71.fc14]

        Sharename       Type        Comment
        ---------       ----        -------
        tmp             Disk        Temporary Directory
        IPC$            IPC         IPC Service (Samba Server Version 3. ...)
Anonymous login successful
Domain=[MGS] OS=[Unix] Server=[Samba 3.5.6-71.fc14]

        Server                  Comment
        ---------               -------
        PEACH
        PLUM                    Samba Server Version 3.5.6-71.fc14

        Workgroup               Master
        ---------               -------
        MGS                     PLUM
```

CHAPTER SUMMARY

Samba is a suite of programs that enables a server to share directory hierarchies and printers with a client. Typically the server is a Linux system and the client is a Windows machine. A directory hierarchy or printer that Samba shares between server and client systems is called a *share*. To access a share on a Linux system, a Windows user must supply a username and password. Usernames must correspond to Linux usernames either directly or as mapped by the file that is pointed to by the **username map** parameter in **smb.conf**, often **/etc/samba/smbusers**. Samba passwords are generated by smbpasswd and kept in a Trivial Database named **tdbsam**.

The main Samba configuration file is **/etc/samba/smb.conf**, which you can edit using system-config-samba (Fedora only), the swat Web-based administration utility, or a text editor. The swat utility is a powerful configuration tool that provides integrated online documentation and clickable default values to help you set up Samba.

From a Windows machine, you can access a share on a Samba server by opening a directory or Explorer window and, in the location text box near the top of the window, entering \\ followed by the name of the server. In response, Windows displays the shares on the server. You can work with these shares as though they were Windows files.

From a Linux system, you can use any of several Samba tools to access shares. These tools include smbtree (displays shares), smbclient (similar to ftp), and mount with the **–t cifs** option (mounts shares). In addition, you can use **Menubar: Places**⇨**Connect to Server** to browse shares.

EXERCISES

1. Which two daemons are part of the Samba suite? What does each do?

2. What steps are required for mapping a Windows user to a Linux user?

3. How can a system administrator add a Samba password for a new user?

4. What is the purpose of the [**homes**] share? Should this share be browseable? Why?

ADVANCED EXERCISES

5. Describe how Samba's handling of users differs from that of NFS.

6. Which configuration changes would you need to apply to routers if you wanted to allow SMB/CIFS browsing across multiple subnets without configuring master browsers?

7. How could you use swat securely from a remote location?

8. WINS resolution allows hosts to define their own names. Suggest a way to use Samba to assign names from a centralized list.

24

DNS/BIND: TRACKING DOMAIN NAMES AND ADDRESSES

OBJECTIVES

After reading this chapter you should be able to:

▶ Explain what DNS does, how it is structured, and why it is necessary

▶ Describe the purpose of a resolver, forward and reverse name resolution, and an FQDN

▶ Describe the differences between an iterative query and a recursive query

▶ Use dig to determine the IP address and mail server address for a domain

▶ Describe each the three types of DNS servers

▶ List the components of the **named.conf** configuration files and explain their purpose

▶ Describe the use and required components of a zone file

▶ Explain the use of several types of resource records

▶ Configure a DNS Cache server

▶ Discuss security options within DNS including allow_transfer directives, views, chroot jails, and dnssec keys

845

DNS (Domain Name System) maps domain names to IP addresses, and vice versa. It reduces the need for humans to work with IP addresses, which, with the introduction of IPv6, are complex. The DNS specification defines a secure, general-purpose database that holds Internet host information. It also specifies a protocol that is used to exchange this information. Further, DNS defines library routines that implement the protocol. Finally, DNS provides a means for routing email. Under DNS, *nameservers* work with clients, called *resolvers,* to distribute host information in the form of *resource records* in a timely manner as needed.

This chapter describes BIND (Berkeley Internet Name Domain) version 9, a popular open-source implementation of DNS. Part of Fedora/RHEL, BIND includes the DNS server daemon (**named**), a DNS resolver library, and tools for working with DNS. Although DNS can be used for private networks, this chapter covers DNS as used by the Internet.

INTRODUCTION TO DNS

You typically use DNS when you display a Web page. For example, to display Red Hat's home page, you enter its name, www.redhat.com, in a browser; the browser then displays the page you want. You never enter or see the IP address for the displayed page. However, without the IP address, the browser could not display the page. DNS works behind the scenes to find the IP address when you enter the name in the browser. The DNS database is

- **Hierarchical,** so it provides quick responses to queries. DNS has a root, branches, and nodes.

- **Distributed,** so it offers fast access to servers. The DNS database is spread across thousands of systems worldwide; each system is referred to as a *DNS server* (or a *domain server* or *nameserver*).

- **Replicated,** to enhance reliability. Because many systems hold the same information, when some systems fail, DNS does not stop functioning.

As implemented, DNS is

- **Secure,** so your browser or email is directed to the correct location.

- **Flexible,** so it can adapt to new names, deleted names, and names whose information changes.

- **Fast,** so Internet connections are not delayed by slow DNS lookups.

History The mapping that DNS does was originally handled statically in a **/etc/hosts** file (page 507) on each system on a network. Small LANs still make use of this file. As networks—specifically the Internet—grew, a dynamic mapping system was required. DNS was specified in 1983 and BIND became part of BSD in 1985. Today BIND is by far the most popular implementation of DNS.

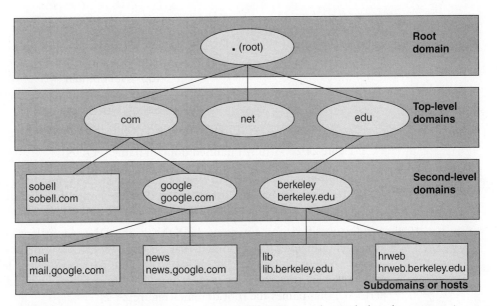

Figure 24-1   The DNS domain structure (FQDNs are shown below hostnames.)

Security   Historically BIND has not been very secure. Recently, however, developers have focused on improving the security of BIND. You might want to run BIND inside a chroot jail (page 877) or under SELinux (page 459) and use transaction signatures (TSIG, page 875) to improve security.

host and dig   The host and dig utilities (page 388) query DNS servers. When called without any options, the host utility is simpler, is easier to use, and returns less information than dig. The –v option causes host to display full RFC-format output. This chapter uses both tools to explore DNS.

NODES, DOMAINS, AND SUBDOMAINS

Node   Each node in the hierarchical DNS database is called a *domain* and is labeled with a (domain) name. As with the Linux file structure, the node at the top of the DNS hierarchy is called the *root node* or *root domain*. While the Linux file structure separates the nodes (directory and ordinary files) with slashes (/) and labels the root node (directory) with a slash, the DNS structure uses periods in place of the file structure's slashes (Figure 24-1).

You read an absolute pathname in a Linux filesystem from left to right: It starts with the root directory (represented by /) at the left and, as you read to the right, describes the path to the file being identified (for example, **/var/spool/cups**). Unlike a Linux pathname, you read a DNS domain name from right to left: It starts with the root domain at the right (represented by a period [.]) and, as you read to the left, works its way down through the top-level and second-level domains to a subdomain or host. Frequently the name of the root domain (the period at the right) is omitted from a domain name.

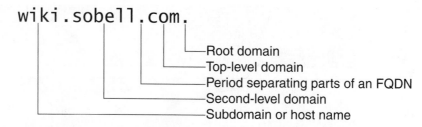

Figure 24-2   A fully qualified domain name (FQDN)

Domain   The term *domain* refers both to a single node in the DNS domain structure and to a catenated, period-separated list (path) of domain names that describes the location of a domain.

FQDN   A fully qualified domain name (FQDN) is the DNS equivalent of a filesystem's absolute pathname: It is a pointer that positively locates a domain on the Internet. Just as you (and Linux) can identify an absolute pathname by its leading slash (**/**) that represents the root directory, so an FQDN can be identified by its trailing period (.) that names the root domain (Figure 24-2).

Resolver   The resolver comprises the routines that turn an unqualified domain name into an FQDN that is passed to DNS to be mapped to an IP address. The resolver can append several domains, one at a time, to an unqualified domain name, producing several FQDNs that it then passes, one at a time, to DNS. For each FQDN, DNS reports success (it found the FQDN and is returning the corresponding IP address) or failure (the FQDN does not exist).

The resolver always appends the root domain (.) to an unqualified domain name first, thereby allowing you to type **www.sobell.com** instead of **www.sobell.com.** (including the trailing period) in a browser. You can specify other domains for the resolver to try if the root domain fails. Put the domain names, in the order you want them tried, after the **search** keyword in **/etc/resolv.conf** (page 510). For example, if your search domains include **sobell.com.**, then the domains **wiki** and **wiki.sobell.com.** will resolve to the same address.

Subdomains   Each node in the domain hierarchy is a domain. Each domain that has a parent (that is, every domain except the root domain) is also a subdomain, regardless of whether it has children. All subdomains *can* resolve to hosts—even those with children. For example, the **sobell.com.** domain resolves to the host that serves the Sobell Web site, without preventing its children—domains such as **wiki.sobell.com**—from resolving. The leftmost part of an FQDN is often called the *hostname*.

Hostnames   In the past, hostnames could contain only characters from the set a–z, A–Z, 0–9, and –. As of March 2004, however, hostnames can include various accents, umlauts, and so on (www.switch.ch/id/idn). DNS considers uppercase and lowercase letters to be the same (it is not case sensitive), so www.sobell.com is the same as WWW.sObEll.coM.

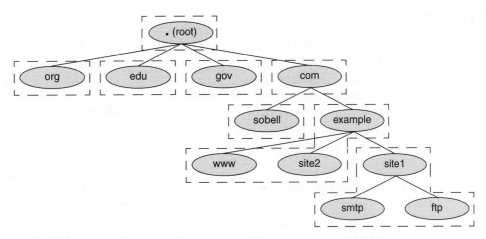

Figure 24-3 DNS structure showing zones

ZONES

For administrative purposes, domains are grouped into zones that extend downward from a domain (Figure 24-3). A single DNS server is responsible for (holds the information required to resolve) all domains within a zone. The DNS server for a zone also holds pointers to DNS servers that are responsible for the zones immediately below the zone it is responsible for. Information about zones originates in zone files, one zone per file.

Root domain   The highest zone—the one containing the root domain—does not contain any hosts. Instead, this domain delegates to the DNS servers for the top-level domains (Figure 24-1, page 847).

Authority   Each zone has at least one authoritative DNS server. This server holds all information about the zone. A DNS query returns information about a domain and specifies which DNS server is authoritative for that domain.

DNS employs a hierarchical structure to keep track of names and authority. At the top or root of the structure is the root domain, which employs 13 authoritative nameservers. These are the only servers that are authoritative for the root and top-level domains.

Delegation of   When referring to DNS, the term *delegation* means *delegation of authority*. ICANN
authority   (Internet Corporation for Assigned Names and Numbers, www.icann.org) delegates authority to the root and top-level domains. In other words, ICANN says which servers are authoritative for these domains. Authority is delegated to each domain below the top-level domains by the authoritative server at the next-higher-level domain. ICANN is not authoritative for most second-level domains. For example, Sobell Associates is authoritative for the sobell.com domain. This scheme of delegating authority allows for local control over segments of the DNS database while making all segments available to the public.

QUERIES

There are two types of DNS queries: *iterative* and *recursive*.[1]

Iterative queries   An iterative query sends a domain name to a DNS server and asks the server to return either the IP address of the domain or the name of the DNS server that is authoritative for the domain or one of its parents: The server does not query other servers when seeking an answer. Nameservers typically send each other iterative queries.

Recursive queries   A recursive query sends a domain name to a DNS server and asks the server to return the IP address of the domain. The server might need to query other servers to get the answer.

Both iterative and recursive queries can fail. In case of failure, the server returns a message saying it is unable to locate the domain.

When a client, such as a browser, needs the IP address that corresponds to a domain name, the client queries a resolver. Most resolvers are quite simple and require a DNS server to do most of the work—that is, they send recursive queries. The resolver communicates with a single DNS server, which can perform multiple iterative queries in response to the resolver's recursive query.

All DNS servers must answer iterative queries. DNS servers can also be set up to answer recursive queries. A DNS server that is not set up to answer recursive queries treats a recursive query as though it is an iterative query.

In Figure 24-4, the resolver on a client system is trying to discover the IP address of the server ftp.site1.example.com. on the network with the DNS layout shown in Figure 24-3 on page 849. The resolver on the client sends a recursive query to its primary DNS server. This server interrogates the root server and one additional server for each zone until it receives an answer, which it returns to the resolver on the client. In practice, the query would not start with the root server because most servers have the location of the authoritative nameserver for the **com.** domain stored in cache (memory).

SERVERS

There are three main types of DNS servers: primary (master), secondary (slave), and caching-only.

- A *primary master server,* also called a *primary server* or *master server,* is the authoritative server that holds the master copy of zone data. It copies information from the *zone* or *master file,* a local file that the server administrator maintains. For security and efficiency, a primary master server should provide iterative answers only. A primary master server

---

1. A third type of query is not covered in this book: *inverse.* An inverse query provides a domain name given a resource record. Reverse name resolution (page 856), not an inverse query, is used to query for a domain name given an IP address.

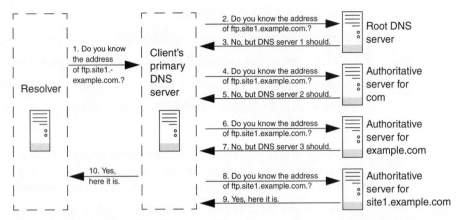

Figure 24-4 A recursive query that starts several iterative queries to find the answer

that provides recursive answers is more easily subverted by a *DoS attack* (page 1162) than one that provides iterative answers only.

- *Slave servers,* also called *secondary servers,* are authoritative and copy zone information from the primary master server or another slave server. On some systems, when information on the primary master server changes, the primary master server notifies the slave servers. When a slave receives such a message, it uses a process called *zone transfer* to copy the new zone information from the master server to itself.

- *DNS caches,* also called *caching-only servers,* are not authoritative. These servers store answers to previous queries in cache (memory). When a DNS cache receives a query, it answers it from cache if it can. If the DNS cache does not have the answer in cache, it forwards the query to an authoritative server.

Do not make a primary server also function as a DNS cache

security It is possible—but for security reasons not recommended—for the same server to be the primary master server (authoritative) for some zones and a DNS cache for others. When the same server acts as both a DNS cache and a master server, if a malicious local user or malfunctioning resolver on the local network floods the DNS cache with more traffic than it can handle (a DoS attack), users might be prevented from accessing the public servers handled by the primary master server. Conversely, if the authoritative server is compromised, the attacker can subvert all traffic leaving the network.

RESOURCE RECORDS

Resource records store information about nodes (domains) in the DNS database and are kept in zone files (page 868). The zone that a resource record pertains to is defined by the zone file that contains the resource record. The zone is named in the **named.conf** file (page 866) that references the zone file.

A resource record has the following fields:

- **Name**—The domain name or IP address
- **TTL**—Time to live (not in all resource records; see page 1194)
- **Class**—Always IN for Internet (the only class supported by DNS)
- **Type**—Record type (discussed in the next section)
- **Data**—Varies with record type

If the Name field is missing, the resource record inherits the name from the previous resource record in the same file. If the Name field ends in a period (.), it specifies an FQDN; otherwise it is relative to the zone named in **named.conf**.

Cached resource records become out-of-date when the information in the record changes on the authoritative server. The TTL field indicates the maximum amount of time a server might keep a record in cache before checking whether a newer one is available. Typically the TTL is on the order of days. A TTL of 0 (zero) means that the resource record should not be cached.

More than 30 types of resource records exist, ranging from common types, such as address records that store the address of a host, to those that contain geographical information. The following paragraphs describe the types of resource records you are most likely to encounter.

A   **IPv4 Address** Maps a domain name to the IPv4 address of a host. There must be at least one address record for each domain; multiple address records can point to the same IP address. The Name field holds the domain name, which is assumed to be in the same zone as the domain. The Data field holds the IP address associated with the name. The following address resource record maps the **ns** domain in the zone to 192.168.0.1:

```
ns      IN      A       192.168.0.1
```

AAAA   **IPv6 Address** Maps a domain name to the IPv6 address of a host. The following address resource record maps the **ns** domain in the zone to an IPv6 address:

```
ns      IN      AAAA    2001:630:d0:131:a00:20ff:feb5:ef1e
```

CNAME   **Canonical Name** Maps an alias or nickname to a domain name. The Name field holds the alias or nickname; the Data field holds the official or canonical name. CNAME is useful for specifying an easy-to-remember name or multiple names for the same domain. It is also useful when a system changes names or IP addresses. In this case the alias can point to the real name that must resolve to an IP address.

When a query returns a CNAME, a client or DNS tool performs a DNS lookup on the domain name returned with the CNAME. It is acceptable to provide multiple CNAME records all pointing to the name that has the A record. The following resource record maps **ftp** in the zone to www.sam.net.:

```
ftp     IN      CNAME   www.sam.net.
```

MX   **Mail Exchange** Specifies a destination for mail addressed to the domain. MX records must always point to A (or AAAA) records. The Name field holds the domain name, which is assumed to be in the zone; the Data field holds the name of a mail server preceded by its priority. Unlike A records, MX records contain a priority number that allows mail delivery agents to fall back to a backup server if the primary server is down. Several mail servers can be ranked in priority order, where the lowest number has the highest priority. DNS selects randomly from among mail servers with the same priority. The following resource records forward mail sent to **speedy** in the zone first to **mail** in the zone and then, if that attempt fails, to **mail.sam.net.**. The value of **speedy** in the Name field on the second line is implicit.

```
speedy IN     MX      10 mail
       IN     MX      20 mail.sam.net.
```

NS   **Nameserver** Specifies the name of the system that provides domain service (DNS records) for the domain. The Name field holds the domain name; the Data field holds the name of the DNS server. Each domain must have at least one NS record. DNS servers do not need to reside in the domain, and in fact, it is better if at least one does not. The system name **ns** is frequently used to specify a nameserver, but this name is not required and does not have any significance beyond assisting humans in identifying a nameserver. The following resource record specifies **ns.max.net.** as a nameserver for **peach** in the zone:

```
peach  IN     NS      ns.max.net.
```

PTR   **Pointer** Maps an IP address to a domain name and is used for reverse name resolution. The Name field holds the IP address; the Data field holds the domain name. Do not use PTR resource records with aliases. The following resource record maps 3 in a reverse zone (for example, 3 in the 0.168.192.in-addr.arpa zone is 192.168.0.3) to **peach** in the zone:

```
3      IN     PTR     peach
```

For more information refer to "Reverse Name Resolution" on page 856.

SOA   **Start of Authority** Designates the start of a zone. Each zone must have exactly one SOA record. An authoritative server maintains the SOA record for the zone it is authoritative for.

All zone files must have one SOA resource record, which must be the first resource record in the file. The Name field holds the name of the domain at the start of the zone. The Data field holds the name of the host the data was created on, the email address of the person responsible for the zone, and the following information, which must be enclosed within parentheses if the record does not fit on one line. If this information is enclosed within parentheses (and it usually is), the opening parenthesis must appear on the first physical line of the SOA record:

serial A value in the range 1 to 2,147,483,647. A change in this number indicates the zone data has changed. By convention, this field is set to the string **yyyymmddnn** (year, month, day, change number). Along with the date, the final two digits—that is, the change number—should be incremented each time you change the SOA record.

refresh The elapsed time after which the primary master server notifies slave (secondary) servers to refresh the record; the amount of time between updates.

retry The time to wait after a refresh fails before trying to refresh again.

expiry The elapsed time after which the zone is no longer authoritative and the root servers must be queried. The expiry applies to slave servers only.

minimum The *negative caching* (page 1177) TTL, which is the amount of time that a non-existent domain error (NXDOMAIN) can be held in a slave server's cache. A negative caching TTL is the same as a normal TTL except that it applies to domains that do not exist rather than to domains that do exist.

The $TTL directive (page 869) specifies the default zone TTL (the maximum amount of time data stays in a slave server's cache). Jointly, the default zone TTL and the negative caching TTL encompass all types of replies the server can generate. If you will be adding subdomains or modifying existing domains frequently, set the negative caching TTL to a low number. A short TTL increases traffic to DNS for clients requesting domains that do not exist, but allows new domains to propagate quickly, albeit at the expense of increased traffic.

The following two SOA resource records are equivalent (the parentheses in the first record are optional because the record fits on one physical line):

```
@ IN SOA ns.zach.net. mgs@sobell.com. ( 2010111247 8H 2H 4W 1D )
```

```
@       IN      SOA     ns.zach.net. mgs@sobell.com. (
                        2010111247      ; serial
                        8H              ; refresh
                        2H              ; retry
                        4W              ; expire
                        1D )            ; minimum
```

The second format is more readable because of its layout and the comments. The at symbol (**@**) at the start of the SOA resource record stands for the zone name (also called the *origin*) as specified in the **named.conf** file. Because the **named.conf** file specifies the zone name to be **zach.net**, you could rewrite the first line as follows:

```
zach.net.   IN SOA      ns.zach.net. mgs@sobell.com. (
```

The **host** utility returns something closer to the first format with each of the times specified in seconds:

```
$ host -t soa zach.net
zach.net. SOA ns.zach.net. mgs\@sobell.com. 03111 28800 7200 2419200 86400
```

TXT **Text** Associates a character string with a domain. The Name field holds the domain name. The data field can contain up to 256 characters and must be enclosed within quotation marks. TXT records can contain any arbitrary text value. As well as general information, they can be used for things such as public key distribution. Following is a TXT resource record that specifies a company name:

```
zach.net.   IN TXT      "Sobell Associates Inc."
```

DNS Queries and Responses

Queries A DNS query has three parts:

1. Name—Domain name, FQDN, or, for reverse name resolution, IP address

2. Type—Type of record requested (page 851)

3. Class—Always IN for Internet class

Cache Most DNS servers store in cache memory the query responses from other DNS servers. When a DNS server receives a query, it first tries to resolve the query from its cache. If that attempt fails, the server might query other servers to get an answer. Because DNS uses cache, when you make a change to a DNS record, the change takes time—sometimes a matter of days—to propagate throughout the DNS hierarchy.

Responses A DNS message sent in response to a query can hold the following records:

- Header record—Information about this message

- Query record—Repeats the query

- Answer records—Resource records that answer the query

- Authority records—Resource records for servers that have authority for the answers

- Additional records—Additional resource records, such as NS records

The dig and host utilities do not consult **/etc/nsswitch.conf** (page 494) to determine which server to query. The following example uses dig to query a DNS server. The **+all** option causes dig to query for all records.

```
$ dig +all google.com
...
;; QUESTION SECTION:
;google.com.                    IN      A

;; ANSWER SECTION:
google.com.             5       IN      A       74.125.19.147
google.com.             5       IN      A       74.125.19.99
google.com.             5       IN      A       74.125.19.103
google.com.             5       IN      A       74.125.19.104

;; AUTHORITY SECTION:
google.com.             5       IN      NS      ns3.google.com.
google.com.             5       IN      NS      ns4.google.com.
google.com.             5       IN      NS      ns1.google.com.
google.com.             5       IN      NS      ns2.google.com.

;; ADDITIONAL SECTION:
ns1.google.com.         5       IN      A       216.239.32.10
ns2.google.com.         5       IN      A       216.239.34.10
...
```

REVERSE NAME RESOLUTION

In addition to normal or forward name resolution, DNS provides *reverse name resolution* (also referred to as *inverse mapping* or *reverse mapping*) so you can look up domain names given an IP address. Because resource records in the forward DNS database are indexed hierarchically by domain name, DNS cannot perform an efficient search by IP address on this database.

DNS implements reverse name resolution by means of special domains named **in-addr.arpa** (IPv4) and **ip6.int** (IPv6). Resource records in these domains have Name fields that hold IP addresses; the records are indexed hierarchically by IP address. The Data fields hold the FQDNs that correspond to these IP addresses.

Reverse name resolution can verify that someone is who he says he is or at least is from the domain he says he is from. In general, it allows a server to retrieve and record the domain names of the clients it provides services to. For example, legitimate mail contains the domain of the sender and the IP address of the sending machine. A mail server can verify the stated domain of a sender by checking the domain associated with the IP address. Reverse name resolution can also be used by anonymous FTP servers to verify that a domain specified in an email address used as a password is legitimate.

For example, to determine the domain name that corresponds to the IP address 209.132.183.42 in Figure 24-5, a resolver would query DNS for information about the domain named 42.183.132.209.in-addr.arpa.

The following example uses dig to query DNS for the IP address that corresponds to www.sobell.com, which is 209.157.128.22. The second command line uses the dig utility to query the same IP address, reversed and appended with **.in-addr.arpa** (22.128.157.209.in-addr.arpa) to display a PTR resource record (page 853). The data portion of the resultant resource record is the domain name from the original query: www.sobell.com.

```
$ dig www.sobell.com
...
;; QUESTION SECTION:
;www.sobell.com.                    IN      A

;; ANSWER SECTION:
www.sobell.com.         2274   IN      A       209.157.128.22
...

$ dig 22.128.157.209.in-addr.arpa PTR
...
;; QUESTION SECTION:
;22.128.157.209.in-addr.arpa.   IN      PTR

;; ANSWER SECTION:
22.128.157.209.in-addr.arpa. 2244 IN    PTR     www.sobell.com.
...
```

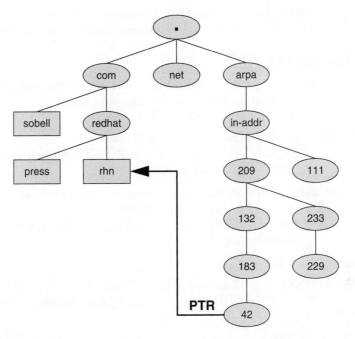

Figure 24-5   Reverse name resolution and the **in-addr.arpa** domain

Instead of reformatting the IP address as in the preceding example, you can use the **–x** option to dig to perform a reverse query:

```
$ dig -x 209.157.128.22
...
;; QUESTION SECTION:
;22.128.157.209.in-addr.arpa.    IN      PTR

;; ANSWER SECTION:
22.128.157.209.in-addr.arpa. 2204 IN    PTR     www.sobell.com.
...
```

Alternatively, you can just use host:

```
$ host 209.157.128.22
22.128.157.209.in-addr.arpa domain name pointer www.sobell.com.
```

How DNS Works

Application programs do not issue DNS queries directly but rather use the **gethostbyname**() system call. How the system comes up with the corresponding IP address is transparent to the calling program. The **gethostbyname**() call examines the **hosts** line in **/etc/nsswitch.conf** (page 494) to determine which files it should examine and/or which services it should query and in what order to obtain the IP address corresponding to a domain name. When it needs to query DNS, the local system (i.e., the

DNS client) queries the DNS database by calling the resolver library on the local system. This call returns the required information to the application program.

MORE INFORMATION

DNS for Rocket Scientists is an excellent site that makes good use of links to present information on DNS in a very digestible form. The same information is available in the *Pro DNS and BIND* book.

Local *Bind Administrator Reference Manual:*
/usr/share/doc/bind9-doc/arm/Bv9ARM.html or see the tip "Using this JumpStart" on page 862.

Web DNS for Rocket Scientists: www.zytrax.com/books/dns
BIND: www.isc.org/products/BIND
DNS security: www.sans.org/reading_room/whitepapers/dns/1069.php
(downloadable PDF file)

HOWTO *DNS HOWTO*

Book *DNS & BIND*, fifth edition, by Albitz & Liu, O'Reilly & Associates (May 2006)
Pro DNS and BIND, first edition, by Ron Aitchison, Apress (August 2005)

SETTING UP A DNS SERVER

This section explains how to set up the simplest type of DNS server, a DNS cache. See page 879 for information on setting up other types of DNS servers.

PREREQUISITES

Install the following packages:

- **bind**

- **bind-utils** (installed by default)

- **system-config-bind** (Fedora), optional, page 861)

- **bind-chroot** (optional, used to set up BIND to run in a chroot jail, page 877)

Before you set up a BIND server

tip Before you configure a BIND server, set up a static IP address for the server system. See "Configuring a Static IP Address for a NIC" on page 652 for instructions.

named init script   Run chkconfig to cause **named** to start when the system enters multiuser mode:

```
# chkconfig named on
```

After you have configured **named**, start it with service:

```
# service named start
Starting named (via systemctl):                          [  OK  ]
```

After changing the BIND configuration on an active server, you can use **reload** in place of **start** to reload **named** configuration files without disturbing clients connected to the server. Although it will interrupt clients, **restart** generates better error messages than **reload**: After giving the command **service named restart**, look in **/var/log/messages** for information about loading zone files, updated serial numbers, and so on.

NOTES

Terms:
DNS and **named**

The name of the DNS server is **named**. This chapter uses "DNS" and "**named**" interchangeably.

Firewall

The **named** server normally accepts queries on TCP and UDP port 53. If the server system is running a firewall, you need to open these ports. Using the Fedora/RHEL system-config-firewall utility, select **DNS** from the Trusted Services tab (page 894) to open these ports. For more general information, see Chapter 25, which details iptables.

SELinux

According to the Fedora/RHEL **named** man page, the default Fedora/RHEL SELinux policy for **named** is very secure and prevents known BIND security vulnerabilities from being exploited. This setup has some limitations, however. Refer to the **named** man page for more information.

If the system is running SELinux with a targeted policy and you want to modify the SELinux **named** settings, you must turn on one or more of the SELinux settings under the **Name Service** clause as displayed by system-config-selinux (page 463).

chroot jail

The **bind-chroot** package sets up **named** to run in a chroot jail. With this package installed, all files that control BIND are located within this jail.

named options

See the comments in the **/etc/sysconfig/named** file for information about **named** options that you can set there. One of the most important of these options sets the value of the **ROOTDIR** variable that controls the location of the chroot jail (page 877) that BIND runs in.

named.conf

The Fedora/RHEL **named** daemon obtains configuration information from the file named **/etc/named.conf** (page 869).

Error messages

In some situations **named** generates error messages regarding files it cannot find. These messages generally appear in **/var/log/messages**. To eliminate these messages, you can try creating an empty file with the name specified in the log. For example, if **named** generates the message

```
managed-keys.bind failed: file not found
```

give these commands to create the file and make **named** the owner of the file:

```
# touch /var/named/managed-keys.bind
# chown named:named /var/named/managed-keys.bind
```

Restart **named** and see if it still generates the error.

You can safely ignore the **working directory is not writable** error message.

JUMPSTART I: SETTING UP A DNS CACHE

As explained earlier, a DNS cache is a bridge between a resolver and authoritative DNS servers: It is not authoritative but simply stores the results of its queries in memory. Most ISPs provide a DNS cache for the use of their customers. Setting up a local cache can reduce the traffic between the LAN and the outside world, thereby improving response times. While it is possible to set up a DNS cache on each system on a LAN, setting up a single DNS cache on a LAN prevents multiple systems on the LAN from having to query a remote server for the same information.

After installing BIND (the **bind** package), you have most of a caching-only nameserver ready to run. Refer to "Setting Up a DNS Cache" on page 869 for an explanation of which files this nameserver uses and how it works.

ifcfg-eth0 and resolv.conf Before you start the DNS cache, set up a static IP address for the server system; see page 652 for instructions.

Next, add **localhost** (127.0.0.1) as the primary nameserver in the **/etc/resolv.conf** file (page 510). Modify the **/etc/sysconfig/network-scripts/ifcfg-eth0** file, or whichever **ifcfg-✳** file the server uses, to effect this change.

Finally, change the current primary nameserver to be the secondary nameserver. This change makes room for the local DNS Cache to be the primary nameserver. To make this change, change the **1** to a **2** in the existing line that starts with **DNS1** in the **ifcfg-✳** file. If the file specifies additional nameservers, demote each (change **DNS2** to **DNS3**, etc.) For example, if the **ifcfg-eth0** file has the line **DNS1=192.0.32.10**, change it to **DNS2=192.0.32.10**. Then add the following line to the same file:

```
DNS1=127.0.0.1
```

This line tells the resolver to use the local system (**localhost** or 127.0.0.1) as the primary nameserver. To experiment with using the local system as the only nameserver, comment out other DNS lines in the **ifcfg-✳** file by preceding each with a hashmark (#).

In some cases you might need to comment out the three lines that start with **dnssec** (put a hash mark [#] at the left end of the line) and add a **forwarders** line (page 867) that points to a remote DNS server in the options clause.

The last step is to start or restart the **named** daemon using **service** (page 858).

Once you have started or restarted **named**, you can see the effect of the local cache by using dig to look up the IP address of a remote system:

```
$ dig www.sobell.com
...
;; QUESTION SECTION:
;www.sobell.com.                        IN      A

;; ANSWER SECTION:
www.sobell.com.         14400   IN      CNAME   sobell.com.
sobell.com.             14400   IN      A       216.38.53.176
...
;; Query time: 84 msec
;; SERVER: 216.38.53.176#53(216.38.53.176)
;; WHEN: Mon Oct 18 13:36:21 2010
;; MSG SIZE  rcvd: 141
```

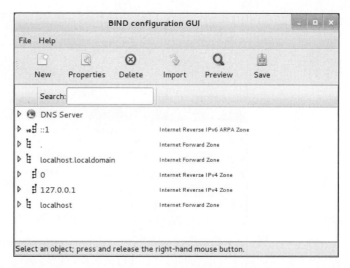

Figure 24-6 The BIND Configuration GUI window

The fourth line from the bottom of the preceding example shows this query took 84 milliseconds (a little less than one-tenth of a second). The third line from the bottom of the same example shows the IP address of the DNS server that dig queried. When you run the same query again, it runs more quickly because the DNS cache has saved the information locally in memory. This time dig shows the time of the query as 1 millisecond and the DNS server as 127.0.0.1:

```
$ dig www.sobell.com
...
;; Query time: 1 msec
;; SERVER: 127.0.0.1#53(127.0.0.1)
;; WHEN: Mon Oct 18 13:36:23 2010
...
```

If the DNS cache does not improve the query time

tip If the DNS cache does not improve the query time, you might already be using a DNS cache provided by your ISP. Try specifying a different secondary nameserver in **ifcfg-***. Alternatively, you can try using a public DNS server; see the lists of servers at code.google.com/speed/public-dns, www.tech-faq.com/public-dns-servers.html, and www.opennicproject.org/publictier2servers.

JUMPSTART II: SETTING UP A DOMAIN USING system-config-bind (FEDORA)

The BIND Configuration GUI window (Figure 24-6) enables you to set up a DNS server. To display this window, select **Main menu: Applications⇨System Tools⇨ Domain Name System** (under Fedora, if **Applications** is not visible see "Configuring Fallback Mode" on page 92) or give the command **system-config-bind** from a terminal emulator or Run Application window (ALT-F2).

If **/etc/named.conf** does not exist, system-config-bind displays a dialog box that informs you it is installing a default configuration. Click **OK**.

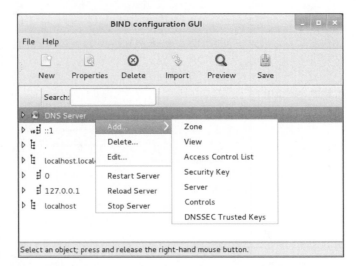

Figure 24-7   The BIND Configuration GUI window with a right-click menu

Using this JumpStart

tip   The system-config-bind utility is a complex tool you might find helpful for setting up BIND. Run this utility and click **Help⇨Manual** on the menubar to display the Fedora/RHEL manual for this utility. Click **Help⇨ISC ARM** to display the BIND 9 Administrator Reference Manual. You might want to experiment with this utility after you have set up one of the servers described at the end of this chapter, as its configuration information might make more sense after you go through the process of manually configuring BIND.

This section explains how to use system-config-bind but does not go into detail about what each of the files and settings does; that information is covered elsewhere in this chapter.

NOTES

Each zone file that system-config-bind creates has a filename extension of **.db**.

Because the windows displayed by system-config-bind contain a lot of information, you might find it helpful to expand or maximize these windows so that you can view the information more easily.

USING THE BIND CONFIGURATION GUI WINDOW

Right-click an object (line) in the BIND Configuration GUI window to display a pop-up context menu. This menu always has an Edit selection, which displays a window in which you can edit information pertaining to the object you clicked. You can display the same window by double-clicking the object or by highlighting the object and clicking **Properties** on the Icon menu. This pop-up menu also always has an Add selection that displays a submenu with choices appropriate to the object you are working with. Figure 24-7 shows the pop-up menu for the DNS Server object along with the Add submenu.

Figure 24-8   The first New Zone window

In the BIND Configuration GUI window, a triangle at the left end of a line indicates that the object holds other objects. Click a triangle so that it points down to expand an entry. Click it so that it points to the right to collapse an entry.

SETTING UP A DOMAIN SERVER

Highlight DNS Server in the BIND Configuration GUI window and click **New⇨Zone** on the toolbar (or right-click and select **Add⇨Zone**) to add a new zone (page 849) and its associated nameserver. In response, system-config-bind displays the first New Zone window (Figure 24-8), which allows you to specify information about the zone you are setting up. With the Class combo box displaying **IN Internet**, click OK under this box.

Next select the origin type from the combo box under Origin Type. The most common choices are Forward or IPV4 Reverse. Click **OK** under this box. Assuming you selected a forward zone, the Forward Zone Origin text box replaces the origin type information. Enter the domain name of the zone, including a trailing period, in the text box.

Finally select the type of zone you want to set up by clicking the combo box in the Zone Type frame. You can select from master, slave, forward, hint, and other types of zones. Refer to "Servers" on page 850 and **type** on page 868 for information on types of zones.

After you make your selections and click OK, system-config-bind displays the second New Zone window (Figure 24-9 on the next page). This window enables you to set up SOA information for the zone. Refer to "SOA" on page 853 for information about the fields in the SOA record, including the serial number and the various times (refresh intervals). In this window, the authoritative (primary) nameserver (page 850) defaults to the local system and the email address of the person responsible for the zone defaults to **root** on the local system. If you enter names that do not end with a period in these text boxes, system-config-bind appends the domain name of the zone to the name you have entered. Change the values in this window as necessary. All zone files that system-config-bind creates have a filename extension of **.db** by default. The default filename for the zone file is the name of the domain you are setting up with an extension of **.db**. Click **OK** to close the window when you are done making changes.

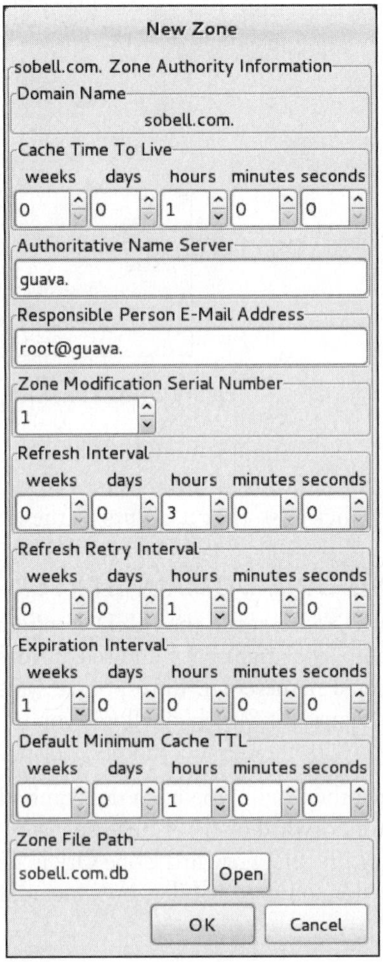

New Zone

sobell.com. Zone Authority Information

Domain Name

sobell.com.

Cache Time To Live

weeks	days	hours	minutes	seconds
0	0	1	0	0

Authoritative Name Server

guava.

Responsible Person E-Mail Address

root@guava.

Zone Modification Serial Number

1

Refresh Interval

weeks	days	hours	minutes	seconds
0	0	3	0	0

Refresh Retry Interval

weeks	days	hours	minutes	seconds
0	0	1	0	0

Expiration Interval

weeks	days	hours	minutes	seconds
1	0	0	0	0

Default Minimum Cache TTL

weeks	days	hours	minutes	seconds
0	0	1	0	0

Zone File Path

sobell.com.db   Open

OK   Cancel

Figure 24-9   The second New Zone window

After you add a new zone, the information about this zone appears in the BIND Configuration GUI window (Figure 24-6, page 861). Click **Save** on the toolbar to save the changes you made before you close the window.

To view information about the new zone, you can expand the object that holds the name of the new zone. You can further expand the Zone Authority Information and Name Server objects that appear when you expand the new zone object. Right-click any object to add to or modify the information in the object or to delete the object.

ADDING RESOURCE RECORDS

You can add any of an extensive list of resource records to a domain. Right-click the object representing the domain you just added to display a pop-up menu. Slide the

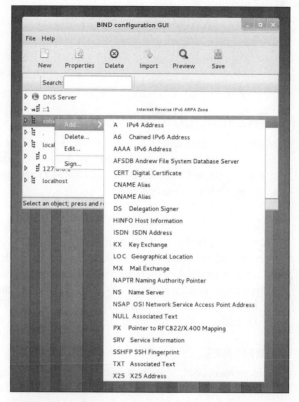

Figure 24-10 The domain Add drop-down menu

mouse pointer over **Add** to display the domain Add menu (Figure 24-10). The uppercase letters at the left end of each selection specify the type of resource record (page 851) the selection adds to the domain. Following are some of the choices available on this menu:

- **A**   IPv4 Address record (page 852)
- **CNAME**   Alias record (page 852)
- **MX**   Mail Exchange record (page 853)
- **NS**   Nameserver record (page 853)
- **TXT**   Text record (page 854)

To add a reverse zone (a PTR record [page 853]), add a new zone as before, but this time select **IPv4** (or **IPv6**) **Reverse** as the origin type. For more information refer to "Reverse Name Resolution" on page 856.

Click **Save** when you are done, close the BIND Configuration GUI window, and start or restart the **named** daemon as explained on page 858.

CONFIGURING A DNS SERVER

This section discusses the **/etc/bind/named.conf** file, zone files, implementation of a DNS cache, DNS glue records, transaction signatures (TSIGs), and running BIND in a chroot jail.

named.conf: THE named CONFIGURATION FILE

Configuration information for **named** is kept in **/etc/named.conf**. By default, the zone files reside in **/var/named**. If you are running **named** in a chroot jail (page 877), these files are also available as **/var/named/chroot/etc/named.conf** and **/var/named/chroot/var/named**.

IP-list

In the descriptions in this section, *IP-list* is a semicolon-separated list of IP addresses, where each IP address is optionally followed by a slash and a network mask length (page 479). Prefix an *IP-list* with an exclamation point (!) to negate it. Builtin names you can use in *IP-list* include **any**, **none**, and **localhost**; these names must be enclosed within double quotation marks. The **localhost** builtin name refers to all IP addresses on the local system, not just 127.0.0.1.

COMMENTS

Within **named.conf**, specify a comment by preceding it with a hashmark (#) as in a Perl or shell program, preceding it with a double slash (//) as in a C++ program, or enclosing it between /* and */ as in a C program. Within a zone file, a comment starts with a semicolon (;).

INCLUDED FILES

An **include** statement within the **named.conf** file includes the file named as its argument as though its contents appeared inline in the **named.conf** file. The default **named.conf** file includes the **/etc/named.rfc1912.zones** and **/etc/named.root.key** files.

OPTIONS CLAUSE

Option statements can appear in two sections of **named.conf**: Options and Zone. Option statements within the Options clause apply globally. When an option statement appears in a Zone clause, the option applies to the zone and, within that zone, overrides a corresponding global option.

An Options clause starts with the keyword **options** and continues with a pair of braces surrounding one or more statements. Following is a list of some option statements. Statements that can appear only in an Options clause and statements that cannot appear in a View clause (page 884) are so noted.

allow-query {*IP-list*}

Allows queries from *IP-list* only. Without this option, the server responds to all queries.

allow-recursion {*IP-list*}

Specifies systems for which this server will perform recursive queries (page 850). For systems not in *IP-list*, the server performs iterative queries only. Without this option, the server performs recursive queries for any system. This statement might be overridden by the **recursion** statement.

allow-transfer {*IP-list*}

Specifies systems that are allowed to perform zone transfers from this server. Specify an *IP-list* of **"none"** (include the quotation marks) to prevent zone transfers. For a more secure network, include only trusted systems in *IP-list* because systems on the list can obtain a list of all systems on the network.

directory *path*   Specifies the absolute pathname of the directory containing the zone files. Under Fedora/RHEL, this directory is initially **/var/named**. Relative pathnames specified in **named.conf** are relative to this directory. Options clause only; not in View clause.

forward ONLY|FIRST

ONLY forwards all queries and fails if it does not receive an answer. **FIRST** forwards all queries and, if a query does not receive an answer, attempts to find an answer using additional queries. Valid with the **forwarders** statement only.

forwarders {*IP* [*port*] [; ...]}

Specifies IP addresses and optionally port numbers that queries are forwarded to. See the **forward** statement.

notify YES|NO   **YES** sends a message to slave servers for the zone when zone information changes. Master servers only. See page 884.

recursion YES|NO

YES (default) provides recursive queries (page 850) if the client requests. **NO** provides iterative queries only (page 850). An answer is always returned if it appears in the server's cache. This statement overrides **allow-recursion** statements. Options clause only.

ZONE CLAUSE

A Zone clause defines a zone and can include any of the statements listed for the Options clause except as noted. A Zone clause is introduced by the keyword **zone**, the name of the zone enclosed within double quotation marks, and the class (always IN). The body of the Zone clause consists of a pair of braces surrounding one or more Zone statements. See the listing of **named.rfc1912.zones** on page 871 for examples of Zone clauses. Following is a list of some Zone statements:

allow-update {*IP-list*}

>Specifies systems that are allowed to update this zone dynamically. This statement might be useful when hosting a master DNS server for a domain owned by someone other than the local administrator because it allows a remote user to update the DNS entry without granting the user access to the server.

file *filename*

>Specifies the *zone file*—the file that specifies the characteristics of the zone. The *filename* is relative to the directory specified by the **directory** statement in the Options clause. The **file** statement is mandatory for master and hint zones. Including it for slave zones is a good idea (see **type**).

masters (*IP-list*)

>Specifies systems that a slave zone can use to update zone files. Slave zones only.

type *ztype*

>Specifies the type of zone defined by this clause. Choose *ztype* from the following list:

> - **forward**—Specifies a forward zone, which forwards queries directed to this zone. See the **forward** and/or **forwarders** statements in the Options clause.

> - **hint**—Specifies a hint zone. A hint zone lists root servers that the local server queries when it starts and when it cannot find an answer in its cache.

> - **master**—Specifies the local system as a primary master server (page 850) for this zone.

> - **slave**—Specifies the local system as a slave server (page 850) for this zone.

ZONE FILES

Zone files define zone characteristics. The name of the zone is typically specified in **named.conf**. In contrast to **named.conf**, zone files use periods at the ends of domain names. See page 872 for example zone files. To improve security, master and hint zone files should be kept in **/var/named**, which is owned by **root** and is not writable by processes running with a UID of **named**. Slave zone files should be kept in **/var/named/slaves**, which is owned by **named** and is writable by processes running with a UID of **named**. This configuration enables SELinux to offer better security. When you set up a chroot jail, the slaves directory is not put in the jail. Both of these setups ensure that master and hint zone files cannot be updated by dynamic DNS updates or by zone transfers. See the **named** man page for more information.

TIME FORMATS

All times in BIND files are given in seconds, unless they are followed by one of these letters (uppercase or lowercase): S (seconds), M (minutes), H (hours), D (days), or W (weeks). You can combine formats. For example, the time 2h25m30s means 2 hours, 25 minutes, and 30 seconds and is the same as 8,730 seconds.

DOMAIN QUALIFICATION

An unqualified domain in a zone file is assumed to be in the current zone (the zone defined by the zone file and named by the **named.conf** file that refers to the zone file). The name **zach** in the zone file for **myzone.com**, for example, would be expanded to the FQDN **zach.myzone.com..** Use an FQDN (include the trailing period) to specify a domain that is not in the current zone. Any name that does not end with a period is regarded as a subdomain of the current zone.

ZONE NAME

Within a zone file, an at sign (@) is replaced with the zone name specified by the $ORIGIN directive (next). If there is no $ORIGIN directive in the zone file, an at sign is replaced with the zone name specified by the Zone clause in the **named.conf** file that refers to the zone file. For documentation and clarity, it is common practice to put an $ORIGIN directive near the top of all zone files, even if the $ORIGIN matches the zone name in **named.conf**. The zone name is also referred to as the *origin*.

ZONE FILE DIRECTIVES

The following directives can appear within a zone file. Each directive is identified by a leading dollar sign. The $TTL directive is mandatory and must be the first entry in a zone file.

$TTL   Defines the default time to live for all resource records in the zone. This directive must appear in a zone file before any resource records it applies to. Any resource record can include a TTL value that overrides this value, except for the resource record in the root zone (.).

$ORIGIN   Changes the zone name from that specified in the **named.conf** file. This name, or the zone name if this directive does not appear in the zone file, replaces an @ sign in the Name field of a resource record.

$INCLUDE   Includes a file as though it were part of the zone file. The scope of an $ORIGIN directive within an included file is the included file. That is, an $ORIGIN directive within an included file does not affect the file that holds the $INCLUDE directive.

SETTING UP A DNS CACHE

You install a DNS cache (also called a resolving, caching nameserver) when you install the **bind** package. The section "JumpStart I: Setting Up a DNS Cache" (page 860) explains how to run this server. This section describes how the files provided by Fedora/RHEL implement this server.

named.conf: THE named CONFIGURATION FILE

The default **/etc/named.conf** file follows.

```
# cat /etc/named.conf//
// named.conf
//
// Provided by Red Hat bind package to configure the ISC BIND named(8) DNS
// server as a caching only nameserver (as a localhost DNS resolver only).
//
// See /usr/share/doc/bind*/sample/ for example named configuration files.
//

options {
        listen-on port 53 { 127.0.0.1; };
        listen-on-v6 port 53 { ::1; };
        directory       "/var/named";
        dump-file       "/var/named/data/cache_dump.db";
        statistics-file "/var/named/data/named_stats.txt";
        memstatistics-file "/var/named/data/named_mem_stats.txt";
        allow-query     { localhost; };
        recursion yes;

        dnssec-enable yes;
        dnssec-validation yes;
        dnssec-lookaside auto;

        /* Path to ISC DLV key */
        bindkeys-file "/etc/named.iscdlv.key";

        managed-keys-directory "/var/named/dynamic";
};

logging {
        channel default_debug {
                file "data/named.run";
                severity dynamic;
        };
};

zone "." IN {
        type hint;
        file "named.ca";
};

include "/etc/named.rfc1912.zones";
include "/etc/named.root.key";
```

Options clause   The first two lines of the Options clause instruct **named** to listen on port 53 (the default **named** port) on the local system for incoming queries. The **directory** statement specifies the directory that all relative pathnames in this file are relative to. Specifically, the files named in the Zone clauses (of the included **named.rfc1912.zones** file) are in the **/var/named** directory. If you are running **named** in a chroot jail, this directory is located under **/var/named/chroot** (page 877). The file also specifies the locations of the **dump-file** (cache dump), **statistics-file** (statistics file), and **memstatistics-file** (memory statistics file). The **allow-query** statement specifies the IP addresses that are allowed to query the server. This file specifies that only **localhost** can query the server. The **recursion** statement specifies that this server perform recursive queries. The **dnssec** statements implement DNSSEC (DNS Security Extensions), which adds security to DNS.

Logging section   The Logging section causes debugging messages to be sent to **data/named.run**. For more information refer to "Logging" on page 881.

Zone clause   The Zone clause specifies the hint zone, whose name is a period. This zone specifies that when the server starts or when it does not know which server to query, it should look in the **/var/named/named.ca** (**ca** stands for *cache*) file to find the addresses of authoritative servers for the root domain.

Include statement   The **include** statements incorporate **/etc/named.rfc1912.zones** (specifies additional zones; next section) and **/etc/named.root.key** (provides the DNS key for the root zone) as though they were present in this file.

named.rfc1912.zones: THE ZONE CONFIGURATION FILE

The **/etc/named.rfc1912.zones** file, which the **named.conf** file incorporates with an **include** statement, holds five Zone clauses. The comments in this file are out-of-date.

```
# cat /etc/named.rfc1912.zones
// named.rfc1912.zones:
//
// Provided by Red Hat caching-nameserver package
//
// ISC BIND named zone configuration for zones recommended by
// RFC 1912 section 4.1 : localhost TLDs and address zones
// and http://www.ietf.org/internet-drafts/draft-ietf-dnsop-default-local-zones-02.txt
// (c)2007 R W Franks
//
// See /usr/share/doc/bind*/sample/ for example named configuration files.
//

zone "localhost.localdomain" IN {
        type master;
        file "named.localhost";
        allow-update { none; };
};

zone "localhost" IN {
        type master;
        file "named.localhost";
        allow-update { none; };
};

zone "1.0.0.0.0.0.0.0.0.0.0.0.0.0.0.0.0.0.0.0.0.0.0.0.0.0.0.0.0.0.0.0.ip6.arpa" IN {
        type master;
        file "named.loopback";
        allow-update { none; };
};

zone "1.0.0.127.in-addr.arpa" IN {
        type master;
        file "named.loopback";
        allow-update { none; };
};

zone "0.in-addr.arpa" IN {
        type master;
        file "named.empty";
        allow-update { none; };
};
```

Zone clauses   Each of the five Zone clauses has an **allow-update** statement that specifies dynamic updates of the zone are not allowed. All filenames in the **named.rfc1912.zones** file are relative to **/var/named**, the directory specified by the **directory** statement in the Options section of **named.conf**.

- **localhost.localdomain**—Specifies that **localhost.localdomain** points to 127.0.0.1, preventing the local server from looking upstream for this information.

- **localhost**—Sets up the normal server on the local system.

- **1.0 ... 0.0.ip6.arpa**—Sets up IPv6 reverse name resolution.

- **1.0.0.127.in-addr.arpa**—Sets up IPv4 reverse name resolution.

- **0.in-addr.arpa**—Specifies that IP addresses that start with 0 have their reverse lookup handled by the local server, preventing the local server from looking upstream for this information.

ZONE FILES

There are four zone files in **/var/named**:

The root zone: The hint zone file, **named.ca** (**named** cache), is an edited copy of the output of a query
named.ca   of the root domain (**dig +bufsize=1200 +norec NS . @a.root-servers.net**). This information does not change frequently. See ftp://ftp.internic.net/domain/named.cache for more information. The **named.ca** file specifies authoritative servers for the root domain. The DNS server initializes its cache from this file and can determine an authoritative server for any domain from this information.

The root zone is required only for servers that answer recursive queries: If a server responds to recursive queries, it needs to perform a series of iterative queries starting at the root domain. Without the root domain hint file, it would not know where to find the root domain servers.

```
# cat /var/named/named.ca; <<>> DiG 9.5.0b2 <<>> +bufsize=1200 +norec
NS . @a.root-servers.net
;; global options:  printcmd
;; Got answer:
;; ->>HEADER<<- opcode: QUERY, status: NOERROR, id: 34420
;; flags: qr aa; QUERY: 1, ANSWER: 13, AUTHORITY: 0, ADDITIONAL: 20

;; OPT PSEUDOSECTION:
; EDNS: version: 0, flags:; udp: 4096
;; QUESTION SECTION:
;.                                IN     NS

;; ANSWER SECTION:
.                     518400     IN     NS     M.ROOT-SERVERS.NET.
.                     518400     IN     NS     A.ROOT-SERVERS.NET.
.                     518400     IN     NS     B.ROOT-SERVERS.NET.
...
```

```
;; ADDITIONAL SECTION:
A.ROOT-SERVERS.NET.        3600000 IN      A         198.41.0.4
A.ROOT-SERVERS.NET.        3600000 IN      AAAA      2001:503:ba3e::2:30
B.ROOT-SERVERS.NET.        3600000 IN      A         192.228.79.201
C.ROOT-SERVERS.NET.        3600000 IN      A         192.33.4.12
D.ROOT-SERVERS.NET.        3600000 IN      A         128.8.10.90
E.ROOT-SERVERS.NET.        3600000 IN      A         192.203.230.10
...
;; Query time: 147 msec
;; SERVER: 198.41.0.4#53(198.41.0.4)
;; WHEN: Mon Feb 18 13:29:18 2008
;; MSG SIZE  rcvd: 615
```

named.empty

```
# cat /var/named/named.empty
$TTL 3H
@   IN      SOA     @ rname.invalid. (
                                  0         ; serial
                                  1D        ; refresh
                                  1H        ; retry
                                  1W        ; expire
                                  3H )      ; minimum
            NS      @
            A       127.0.0.1
            AAAA    ::1
```

named.localhost The **named.localhost** zone file defines the **localhost** zone, the normal server on the local system. It starts with a $TTL directive and holds four resource records: SOA, NS, A, and AAAA. The $TTL directive in the following file specifies that the default time to live for the resource records specified in this file is one day (1D):

```
# cat /var/named/named.localhost
$TTL 1D
@   IN      SOA     @ rname.invalid. (
                                  0         ; serial
                                  1D        ; refresh
                                  1H        ; retry
                                  1W        ; expire
                                  3H )      ; minimum
            NS      @
            A       127.0.0.1
            AAAA    ::1
```

As explained earlier, the @ stands for the origin (the name of the zone), which is **localhost**, as specified in **named.rfc1912.zones**. The last three lines are the NS resource record that specifies the nameserver for the zone as **localhost** (@), the A resource record that specifies the IPv4 address of the host as 127.0.0.1, and the AAAA resource record that specifies the IPv6 address of the host as ::1. Because these three records have blank Name fields, each inherits this value from the preceding resource record—in this case, @.

named.loopback The **named.loopback** zone file provides information about the 1.0.0.127.in-addr.arpa reverse lookup zone and the equivalent IPv6 zone. It follows the same pattern as the

localhost zone file, with one exception: In addition to the A resource record, this file has a PTR record that provides the name the zone associates with the IP address (localhost):

```
# cat /var/named/named.loopback
$TTL    1D
@       IN      SOA     @ rname.invalid. (
                                0                   ; serial
                                1D                  ; refresh
                                1H                  ; retry
                                1W                  ; expire
                                3H )                ; minimum
        NS      @
        A       127.0.0.1
        AAAA    ::1
        PTR     localhost.
```

Once **named** is started (page 858), you can use the tests described under "Trouble-shooting" on page 878 to make sure the server is working.

DNS GLUE RECORDS

It is common practice to put the nameserver for a zone inside the zone it serves. For example, you might put the nameserver for the zone starting at site1.example.com (Figure 24-3, page 849) in ns.site1.example.com. When a DNS cache tries to resolve www.site1.example.com, the authoritative server for example.com gives it the NS record pointing to ns.site1.example.com. In an attempt to resolve ns.site1.example.com, the DNS cache again queries the authoritative server for example.com, which points back to ns.site1.example.com. This loop does not allow ns.site1.example.com to be resolved.

The simplest solution to this problem is to prohibit any nameserver from residing inside the zone it points to. Because every zone is a child of the root zone, this solution means every domain would be served by the root server and would not scale at all.

A better solution is to use *glue* records. A glue record is an A record for a nameserver that is returned in addition to the NS record when an NS query is performed. Because the A record provides an IP address for the nameserver, it does not need to be resolved and does not create the problematic loop.

The nameserver setup for google.com illustrates the use of glue records. When you query for NS records for google.com, DNS returns four NS records. In addition, it returns four A records that provide the IP addresses for hosts that the NS records point to:

```
$ dig -t NS google.com...
;; QUESTION SECTION:
;google.com.                        IN      NS

;; ANSWER SECTION:
```

```
google.com.              5      IN      NS      ns4.google.com.
google.com.              5      IN      NS      ns1.google.com.
google.com.              5      IN      NS      ns2.google.com.
google.com.              5      IN      NS      ns3.google.com.

;; ADDITIONAL SECTION:
ns4.google.com.          5      IN      A       216.239.38.10
ns1.google.com.          5      IN      A       216.239.32.10
ns2.google.com.          5      IN      A       216.239.34.10
ns3.google.com.          5      IN      A       216.239.36.10
...
```

You can create a glue record by providing an A record for the nameserver inside the delegating domain's zone file:

```
site1.example.com                 IN      NS      ns.site1.example.com
ns.site1.example.com              IN      A       1.2.3.4
```

TSIGs: TRANSACTION SIGNATURES

Interaction between DNS components is based on the query–response model: One part queries another and receives a reply. Traditionally a server determines whether and how to reply to a query based on the client's IP address. *IP spoofing* (page 1171) is relatively easy to carry out, making this situation less than ideal. Recent versions of BIND support transaction signatures (TSIGs), which allow two systems to establish a trust relationship by using a shared secret key.

TSIGs provide an additional layer of authentication between master and slave servers for a zone. When a slave server is located at a different site than the master server (as it should be), a malicious person operating a router between the sites can spoof the IP address of the master server and change the DNS data on the slave (a man-in-the-middle scenario). With TSIGs, this person would need to know the secret key to change the DNS data on the slave.

CREATING A SECRET KEY

If dnssec-keygen hangs

tip   Running dnssec-keygen can cause the system to hang for a long time if there is not enough entropy. This problem is common on virtual systems. You can create entropy and free the system by moving the mouse, typing on the keyboard, or copying files. Alternatively, you can read from **/dev/urandom** (page 504):

```
$ dnssec-keygen -r /dev/urandom -a hmac-md5 -b 512 -n HOST keyname
```

A secret key is an encoded string of up to 512 bits. The dnssec-keygen utility, which is included with BIND, generates this key. The following command, which might take a while to run, generates a 512-bit random key using MD5, a *one-way hash function* (page 1179):

```
$ dnssec-keygen -a hmac-md5 -b 512 -n HOST keyname
Kkeyname.+157+47586
```

In the preceding command, replace *keyname* with a string that is unique yet meaningful. This command creates a key in a file whose name is similar to the string **K*keyname*.+157+47586.private**, where *keyname* is replaced by the name of the key, **+157** indicates the algorithm used, and **+47586** is a hash of the key. If you run the same command again, the hash part will be different.

The key file is not used directly. Use cat with an argument of the private filename to display the algorithm and key information you will need in the next step:

```
$ cat Kkeyname.+157+47586.private
Private-key-format: v1.3
Algorithm: 157 (HMAC_MD5)
Key: uNPDouqVwR7fvo/zFyjkqKbQhcTd6Prm...
...
```

USING THE SHARED SECRET

The next step is to tell the nameservers about the shared secret by inserting the following code in the **/etc/named.conf** file on both servers. This code is a top-level clause in **named.conf**; insert it following the Options clause:

```
key keyname {
    algorithm "hmac-md5";
    secret "uNPDouqVwR7fvo/zFyjkqKbQhcTd6Prm...";
};
```

The *keyname* is the name of the key you created. The **algorithm** is the string that appears within parentheses in the output of cat, above. The **secret** is the string that follows **Key:** in the output of cat. You must enclose each string within double quotation marks. Be careful when you copy the key; although it is long, you must not break it into multiple lines.

Because key names are unique, you can insert any number of Key clauses into **named.conf**. To keep the key a secret, make sure users other than **root** cannot read it: Either give **named.conf** permissions such that no one except **root** has access to it or put the key in a file that only **root** can read and incorporate it in **named.conf** using an **include** statement.

Once both servers know about the key, use a **server** statement in **named.conf** to tell them when to use it:

```
server 1.2.3.4 {
# 1.2.3.4 is the IP address of the other server using this key
    keys {
        "keyname";
    };
};
```

Each server must have a Server clause, each containing the IP address of the other server. The servers will now communicate with each other only if they first authenticate each other using the secret key.

RUNNING BIND IN A chroot JAIL

To increase security, you can run BIND in a chroot jail. See page 485 for information about the security advantages of, and ways to set up, a chroot jail. See also the note about SELinux on page 859 and the **named** man page for information about BIND, SELinux, and chroot jails. The **bind-chroot** package, which sets up BIND to run in a chroot jail, creates a directory named **/var/named/chroot** that takes the place of the root directory (**/**) for all BIND files.

With the **bind-chroot** package installed, the **ROOTDIR** shell variable is set to **/var/named/chroot** in the **/etc/sysconfig/named** file, which is executed by the **named** init script. While **named** is running, all files that control BIND are mounted (available) in two places. For example, the **/var/named** directory is also mounted at **/var/named/chroot/var/named**:

```
# ls -li /var/named /var/named/chroot/var/named
/var/named:
660026 drwxr-x---. 6 root   named 4096 10-22 12:30 chroot
660006 drwxrwx---. 2 named  named 4096 10-22 12:30 data
660007 drwxrwx---. 2 named  named 4096 10-22 13:30 dynamic
660008 -rw-r-----. 1 root   named 1892 02-18  2008 named.ca
660009 -rw-r-----. 1 root   named  152 12-15  2009 named.empty
660010 -rw-r-----. 1 root   named  152 06-21  2007 named.localhost
660011 -rw-r-----. 1 root   named  168 12-15  2009 named.loopback
660012 drwxrwx---. 2 named  named 4096 09-29 00:53 slaves

/var/named/chroot/var/named:
660026 drwxr-x---. 6 root   named 4096 10-22 12:30 chroot
660006 drwxrwx---. 2 named  named 4096 10-22 12:30 data
660007 drwxrwx---. 2 named  named 4096 10-22 13:30 dynamic
660008 -rw-r-----. 1 root   named 1892 02-18  2008 named.ca
660009 -rw-r-----. 1 root   named  152 12-15  2009 named.empty
660010 -rw-r-----. 1 root   named  152 06-21  2007 named.localhost
660011 -rw-r-----. 1 root   named  168 12-15  2009 named.loopback
660012 drwxrwx---. 2 named  named 4096 09-29 00:53 slaves
```

Similarly, **/etc/named.conf** is also mounted at **/var/named/chroot/etc/named.conf**:

```
# ls -li /etc/named.conf /var/named/chroot/etc/named.conf
52364 -rw-r-----. 1 root named 1008 07-19 06:34 /etc/named.conf
52364 -rw-r-----. 1 root named 1008 07-19 06:34 /var/named/chroot/etc/named.conf
```

When you stop **named**, the **named init** script unmounts the second copy of the files:

```
# service named stop
Stopping named (via systemctl):                         [  OK  ]

# ls -li /etc/named.conf /var/named/chroot/etc/named.conf
ls: cannot access /var/named/chroot/etc/named.conf: No such file or directory
52364 -rw-r-----. 1 root named 1008 07-19 06:34 /etc/named.conf
```

optional   The **named** init script uses the mount **--bind** option to remount part of a directory hierarchy (which can be a single file) in another location. This option allows you to do what you cannot do with hard links: access a directory hierarchy from another location in a filesystem. It also bypasses some of the limitations of symbolic links, including permissions issues. However, it does not create another link to a file—see the preceding listing for **named.conf:** The links count (page 202) to each file is 1. See the mount man page for more information.

TROUBLESHOOTING

When you start a DNS cache, the **/var/log/messages** file contains lines similar to the following:

```
# cat /var/log/messages
...
13:46:07 shark named[4221]: starting BIND 9.8.0-RedHat-9.8.0-2.fc15 -u named -t
/var/named/chroot
13:46:07 shark named[4221]: found 1 CPU, using 1 worker thread
13:46:07 shark named[4221]: using up to 4096 sockets
13:46:07 shark named[4221]: loading configuration from '/etc/named.conf'
13:46:07 shark named[4221]: reading built-in trusted keys from file
'/etc/named.iscdlv.key'
13:46:07 shark named[4221]: using default UDP/IPv4 port range: [1024, 65535]
13:46:07 shark named[4221]: using default UDP/IPv6 port range: [1024, 65535]
13:46:07 shark named[4221]: listening on IPv4 interface lo, 127.0.0.1#53
13:46:07 shark named[4221]: listening on IPv6 interface lo, ::1#53
13:46:07 shark named[4221]: generating session key for dynamic DNS
13:46:07 shark named[4221]: using built-in trusted-keys for view _default
13:46:07 shark named[4221]: set up managed keys zone for view _default, file
'/var/named/dynamic/managed-keys.bind'
13:46:07 shark named[4221]: automatic empty zone: 127.IN-ADDR.ARPA
13:46:07 shark named[4221]: automatic empty zone: 254.169.IN-ADDR.ARPA
13:46:07 shark named[4221]: automatic empty zone: 2.0.192.IN-ADDR.ARPA
...
13:46:07 shark named[4221]: zone localhost/IN: loaded serial 0
13:46:07 shark named[4221]: managed-keys-zone ./IN: loaded serial 24
13:46:07 shark named[4221]: running
```

With an argument of **status,** the **named** init script displays useful information:

```
# service named status
version: 9.8.0-RedHat-9.8.0-2.fc15
CPUs found: 1
worker threads: 1
number of zones: 19
debug level: 0
xfers running: 0
xfers deferred: 0
soa queries in progress: 0
query logging is OFF
```

```
recursive clients: 0/0/1000
tcp clients: 0/100
server is up and running
named (pid  4221) is running...
```

When you create or update DNS information, you can use dig or host to test whether the server works as planned. The most useful part of the output from dig is usually the answer section, which gives the nameserver's reply to your query:

```
$ dig example.com
...
;; ANSWER SECTION:
example.com.             172800  IN      A        192.0.32.10
...
```

The preceding output shows that the **example.com** domain has a single A record that points to 192.0.32.10. The TTL of this record, which tells you how long the record can be held in cache, is 172,800 seconds (two days). You can also use dig to query other record types by using the **–t** option followed by the type of record you want to query for (**–t** works with host, too):

```
$ # dig -t MX tldp.com
...
;; ANSWER SECTION:
tldp.com.  5       IN      MX      0 mx1.sub5.homie.mail.dreamhost.com.
tldp.com.  5       IN      MX      0 mx2.sub5.homie.mail.dreamhost.com.
...
```

If you query for a domain that does not exist, dig returns the SOA record for the authority section of the highest-level domain in your query that does exist:

```
$ dig domaindoesnotexist.info
...
;; AUTHORITY SECTION:
info.    900  IN  SOA  a0.info.afilias-nst.info. noc.afilias-nst.info. ...
...
```

Because it tells you the last zone that was queried correctly, this information can be useful in tracing faults.

TSIGs   If two servers using TSIGs (page 875) fail to communicate, confirm the system clock is set to the same time on both servers. The TSIG authentication mechanism is dependent on the current time. If the clocks on the two servers are not synchronized, TSIG will fail. Consider setting up *NTP* (page 1179) on the servers to prevent this problem.

SETTING UP DIFFERENT TYPES OF DNS SERVERS

This section describes how to set up a full-functioned nameserver, a slave server, and a split-horizon server.

A FULL-FUNCTIONED NAMESERVER

Because the IP addresses used in this example are part of the *private address space* (page 1182), you can copy the example and run the server without affecting global DNS. Also, to prevent contamination of the global DNS, each zone has the **notify** option set to NO. When you build a nameserver that is integrated with the Internet, you will want to use IP addresses that are unique to your installation. You might want to change the settings of the **notify** statements.

named.conf   The **named.conf** file in this example limits the IP addresses that **named** answers queries from and sets up logging.

```
$ cat /etc/named.conf
options {
    directory "/var/named";
    allow-query {127.0.0.1; 192.168.0.0/24;};};

zone "." IN {
    type    hint;
    file    "named.ca";};

zone "0.168.192.in-addr.arpa" IN {
    type    master;
    file    "named.local";
    notify  NO;
};

zone "sam.net" IN {
    type    master;
    file    "sam.net";
    notify  NO;
};

logging{
    channel "misc" {
        file "/var/log/bind/misc.log" versions 4 size 4m;
        print-time YES;
        print-severity YES;
        print-category YES;
    };
    channel "query" {
        file "/var/log/bind/query.log" versions 4 size 4m;
        print-time YES;
        print-severity NO;
        print-category NO;
    };
    category default {
        "misc";
    };
    category queries {
        "query";
    };
};
```

The **allow-query** statement in the Options clause specifies the IP addresses of systems the server answers queries from. You must include the local system as 127.0.0.1 if it will be querying the server. The server is authoritative for the zone **sam.net**; the zone file for **sam.net** is **/var/named/sam.net**.

Logging Logging is turned on by the Logging clause. Logging is separate from **named** messages, which go to **syslogd**. The Logging clause in the preceding example opens two logging channels: one that logs information to **/var/log/bind/misc.log** and one that logs information to **/var/log/bind/query.log**. When either of these logs grows to 4 megabytes (**size 4m** in the file statement), it is renamed by appending **.1** to its filename and a new log is started. The numbers at the ends of other, similarly named logs are incremented. Any log that would have a larger number than that specified by the **versions** keyword (**4** in the example) is removed. See logrotate (page 621) for another way to maintain log files.

The print statements determine whether the time, severity, and category of the information are sent to the log; specify each as YES or NO. The category determines what information is logged to the channel. In the previous example, default information is sent to the **misc** channel and queries are sent to the **query** channel. Refer to the **named.conf** man page for more choices.

named.local The origin for the reverse zone file (**named.local**) is 0.168.192.in-addr.arpa (as specified in the Zone clause that refers to this file in **named.**). Following the SOA and NS resource records, the first three PTR resource records equate address 1 in the subnet 0.168.192.in-addr.arpa (192.168.0.1) with the names **gw.sam.net.**, **www.sam.net.**, and **ftp.sam.net.**, respectively. The next three PTR records equate 192.168.0.3 with **mark.sam.net.**, 192.168.0.4 with **mail.sam.net.**, and 192.168.0.6 with **ns.sam.net.**.

```
$ cat named.local
; zone "0.168.192.in-addr.arpa"
;
$TTL    3D
@       IN      SOA     ns.sam.net. mgs@sobell.com. (
                                2005110501      ; serial
                                8H              ; refresh
                                2H              ; retry
                                4W              ; expire
                                1D)             ; minimum
        IN      NS      ns.sam.net.
1       IN      PTR     gw.sam.net.
3       IN      PTR     mark.sam.net.
4       IN      PTR     mail.sam.net.
6       IN      PTR     ns.sam.net.
```

sam.net The zone file for **sam.net** takes advantage of many BIND features and includes TXT (page 854), CNAME (page 852), and MX (page 853) resource records. When you query for resource records, **named** returns the TXT resource record along with the records you requested. The first of the two NS records specifies an unqualified name (**ns**) to which BIND appends the zone name (**sam.net**), yielding an FQDN of

ns.sam.net. The second nameserver is specified with an FQDN name that BIND does not alter. The MX records specify mail servers in a similar manner and include a priority number at the start of the data field, where lower numbers indicate preferred servers.

```
$ cat sam.net
; zone "sam.net"
;
$TTL    3D
@       IN      SOA     ns.sam.net. mgs@sobell.com. (
                                2010110501      ; serial
                                8H              ; refresh
                                2H              ; retry
                                4W              ; expire
                                1D )            ; minimum

                TXT     "Sobell Associates Inc."
                NS      ns          ; Nameserver address (unqualified)
                NS      ns.max.net.; Nameserver address (qualified)
                MX      10 mail     ; Mail exchange (primary/unqualified)
                MX      20 mail.max.net.; Mail exchange (2nd/qualified)

localhost IN    A       127.0.0.1

www     IN      CNAME   ns
ftp     IN      CNAME   ns

gw      IN      A       192.168.0.1
                TXT     "Router"

ns      IN      A       192.168.0.6
                MX      10 mail
                MX      20 mail.max.net.

mark    IN      A       192.168.0.3
                MX      10 mail
                MX      20 mail.max.net.
                TXT     "MGS"

mail    IN      A       192.168.0.4
                MX      10 mail
                MX      20 mail.max.net.
```

Some resource records have a value in the Name field; those without a name inherit the name from the previous resource record. In a similar manner, the previous resource record might have an inherited name value, and so on. The five resource records following the SOA resource record inherit the @, or zone name, from the SOA resource record. These resource records pertain to the zone as a whole. In the preceding example, the first TXT resource record inherits its name from the SOA resource record; it is the TXT resource record for the **sam.net** zone (give the command **host –t TXT sam.net** to display the TXT resource record).

Following these five resource records are resource records that pertain to a domain within the zone. For example, the MX resource records that follow the A resource record with the Name field set to **mark** are resource records for the **mark.sam.net.** domain.

The A resource record for **localhost** is followed by two CNAME resource records that specify www(.sam.net.) and ftp(.sam.net.) as aliases for the nameserver **ns.sam.net.**. For example, a user connecting to ftp.sam.net will connect to 192.168.0.6. The resource records named **gw**, **ns**, **mark**, and **mail** are resource records for domains within the **sam.net** zone.

Log files   Before restarting **named**, create the directory for the log files and give it permissions and ownership as shown below. If you are running **named** in a chroot jail, create the **bind** directory in **/var/named/chroot/var/log**.

```
# mkdir /var/log/bind
# chmod 744 /var/log/bind
# chown named /var/log/bind
# ls -ld /var/log/bind
drwxr--r--. 2 named root 4096 10-19 14:43 /var/log/bind
```

With the log directory in place, **named.conf** in **/etc** (or in **/var/named/chroot/etc** if you are running **named** in a chroot jail), **named.ca**, **named.local**, and **sam.net** zone files in **/var/named** (or in **/var/named/chroot/var/named** if you are running **named** in a chroot jail), restart **named** and check the log files. The file **/var/log/messages** should show something like the following:

```
# cat /var/log/messages
...
15:11:40 shark named[9824]: starting BIND 9.8.0-RedHat-9.8.0-2.fc15 -u named
...
15:11:40 shark named[9824]: loading configuration from '/etc/named.conf'
15:11:40 shark named[9824]: using default UDP/IPv4 port range: [1024, 65535]
15:11:40 shark named[9824]: using default UDP/IPv6 port range: [1024, 65535]
15:11:40 shark named[9824]: listening on IPv4 interface lo, 127.0.0.1#53
...
shark named[9824]: command channel listening on 127.0.0.1#953
15:11:40 shark named[9824]: command channel listening on ::1#953
15:11:40 shark named[9824]: the working directory is not writable
```

You can safely ignore the **working directory is not writable** error message. The **misc.log** file might show errors that do not appear in the **messages** file:

```
# cat /var/log/bind/misc.log
15:11:40.594 general: info: zone 0.168.192.in-addr.arpa/IN: loaded serial 2005110501
15:11:40.596 general: info: zone sam.net/IN: loaded serial 2010110501
15:11:40.596 general: info: managed-keys-zone ./IN: loaded serial 0
15:11:40.600 general: notice: running
```

See "Error messages" on page 859 if **named** generates an error message.

A SLAVE SERVER

To set up a slave server, copy the **/etc/named.conf** file from the master server to the slave server, replacing the **type master** statement with **type slave** and adding a **masters { *1.2.3.4*; };** directive. Remove any zones the slave server will not be acting as a slave for, including the root (.) zone, if the slave server will not respond to recursive queries. If necessary, create the **/var/log/bind** directory for log files as explained at the end of the previous section.

notify statement   Slave servers copy zone information from the primary master server or another slave server. The **notify** statement specifies whether you want a master server to notify slave servers when information on the master server changes. Set the (global) value of **notify** in the Options clause or set it within a Zone clause, which overrides a global setting for a given zone. The format is

> *notify YES | NO | EXPLICIT*

YES causes the master server to notify all slaves listed in NS resource records for the zone as well as servers at IP addresses listed in an **also-notify** statement. When you set **notify** to *EXPLICIT,* the server notifies servers listed in the **also-notify** statement only. *NO* turns off notification.

When you start **named**, it copies the zone files to **/var/named**. If you specify **notify YES** on the master server, the zone files on the slave server will be updated each time you change the serial field of the SOA resource record in a zone. You must manually distribute changes to **/etc/named.conf** and included files.

A SPLIT HORIZON SERVER

Assume you want to set up a LAN that provides all of its systems and services to local users on internal systems, which might be behind a firewall, but only certain public services—such as Web, FTP, and mail—to Internet (public) users. A *split horizon* (also called *DMZ*) DNS server takes care of this situation by treating queries from internal systems differently from queries from public systems (systems on the Internet).

View clauses   BIND 9 introduced View clauses in **named.conf**. View clauses facilitate the implementation of a split DNS server. Each view provides a different perspective of the DNS namespace to a group of clients. When there is no View clause, all zones specified in **named.conf** are part of the implicit default view.

Assume an office has several systems on a LAN and public Web, FTP, DNS, and mail servers. The single connection to the Internet is NATed (page 1177), so it is shared by the local systems and the servers. The system connected directly to the Internet is a router, firewall, and server. This scenario takes advantage of the View clauses in **named.conf** and supports separate secondary nameservers for local and public users. Although public users need access to the DNS server as the authority on the domain that supports the servers, they do not require the DNS server to support recursive queries. Not supporting recursion for public users limits the load on

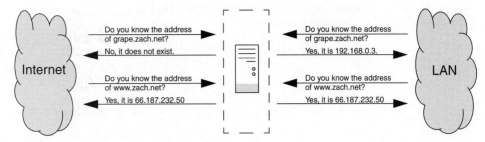

Figure 24-11   A split horizon DNS server

the DNS server and the Internet connection. For security reasons, public users must not have access to information about local systems other than the servers. Local users should have access to information about local systems and should be able to use the DNS server recursively.

Figure 24-11 shows that the server responds differently to queries from the LAN and from the Internet.

The **system-config-firewall** (page 893) or **iptables** utility (page 895) controls which ports on which systems users on internal and external systems can access. DNS controls which systems are advertised to which users.

The **named.conf** file has four clauses: an Options clause, two View clauses, and a Logging clause. The Options clause specifies that the zone files be located in the **/var/named** directory. The View clauses specify the characteristics and zones that a resolver is given access to, which depend on the resolver's address. One zone is for use by the LAN/local users; the other is used by Internet/public users. The Logging clause sets up the **misc2.log** file for default messages; you must create a **/var/log/bind** directory as explained under "Log files" (page 883).

There are several ways to specify which clients see a view. The following **named.conf** file uses **match-clients** statements:

```
$ cat /etc/named.conf
options {
    directory "/var/named";
}; //end options


view "local" IN {                        // start local view
match-clients { 127.0.0.1; 192.168.0.0/24;};
recursion YES;


zone"zach.net" IN {
    type    master;
    file    "local.net";
    notify YES;
};
```

```
zone "0.168.192.in-addr.arpa" IN {
    type    master;
    file    "named.local";
    notify YES;
};

zone "." IN {
    type    hint;
    file    "named.ca";
};

};                                    // end local view

view "public" IN {                    // start public view
match-clients { "any";};
recursion NO;

zone"zach.net" IN {
    type    master;
    file    "public.net";
    notify YES;
};

zone "0.168.192.in-addr.arpa" IN {
    type    master;
    file    "named.public";
    notify YES;
};

zone "." IN {
    type    hint;
    file    "named.ca";
};

};                                        // end public view

logging{
    channel "misc" {
        file "/var/log/bind/misc2.log" versions 2 size 1m;
        print-time YES;
        print-severity YES;
        print-category YES;
    };
    category default {
        "misc";
    };
};                                    //end logging
```

The ordering of View clauses within **named.conf** is critical because the view that is presented to a client is the first view that the client matches. The preceding **named.conf** file holds two View clauses: one for local users and one for public users, in that order. Local users are defined to be those on the 192.168.0.0/24 subnet or **localhost** (127.0.0.1); public users are defined to be any users. If you reversed the order of the View clauses, all users—including local users—would get the view intended for the public and no users would see the local view.

Many statements from the Options clause can be used within View clauses, where they override statements in the (global) Options clause. The **recursion** statement, which can appear within an Options clause, appears in each View clause. This **named.conf** file sets up a server that provides recursive answers to queries that originate locally and iterative answers to queries from the public. This setup provides quick, complete answers to local users, limiting the network and processor bandwidth that is devoted to other users while continuing to provide authoritative name service for the local servers.

To make **named.conf** easier to understand and maintain, zones in different View clauses can have the same name but different zone files. Both the local and public View clauses in the example have zones named **zach.net**: The public **zach.net** zone file is named **public.net** and the local one is named **local.net**.

The Logging clause is described on page 881.

The zone files defining **zach.net** are similar to the ones in the previous examples; the public file is a subset of the local one. Following the SOA resource record in both files is a TXT, two NS, and two MX resource records. Next are three CNAME resource records that direct queries addressed to www.zach.net, ftp.zach.net, and mail.zach.net to the system named **ns.zach.net**. The next four resource records specify two nameserver addresses and two mail servers for the ns.zach.net domain.

The final four resource records appear in the local **zach.net** zone file and not in the public zone file; they are address (A) resource records for local systems. Instead of keeping this information in **/etc/hosts** files on each system, you can keep it on the DNS server, where it can be updated easily. When you use DNS instead of **/etc/hosts**, you must change the **hosts** line in **/etc/nsswitch.conf** (page 494) accordingly.

```
$ cat local.net
; zach.net local zone file
;
$TTL    3D
@       IN      SOA     ns.zach.net. mgs@sobell.com. (
                            201011118       ; serial
                            8H              ; refresh
                            2H              ; retry
                            4W              ; expire
                            1D )            ; minimum

        IN      TXT     "Sobell Associates Inc."
        IN      NS      ns          ; Nameserver address (unqualified)
        IN      NS      ns.speedy.net.; Nameserver address (qualified)
        IN      MX      10 mail     ; Mail exchange (primary/unqualified)
        IN      MX      20 mail.max.net.; Mail exchange (2nd/qualified)
```

```
ns      IN      A       192.168.0.1
mail    IN      A       192.168.0.2

www     IN      CNAME   mail
ftp     IN      CNAME   mail
gw      IN      CNAME   ns

speedy  IN      A       192.168.0.5
grape   IN      A       192.168.0.3
potato  IN      A       192.168.0.4
peach   IN      A       192.168.0.6
```

The public version of the **zach.net** zone file follows:

```
$ cat public.net
; zach.net public zone file
;
$TTL    3D
@       IN      SOA     ns.zach.net. mgs@sobell.com. (
                                201011118       ; serial
                                8H              ; refresh
                                2H              ; retry
                                4W              ; expire
                                1D )            ; minimum

        IN      TXT     "Sobell Associates Inc."
        IN      NS      ns              ; Nameserver address (unqualified)
        IN      NS      ns.speedy.net.; Nameserver address (qualified)

        IN      MX      10 mail ; Mail exchange (primary/unqualified)
        IN      MX      20 mail.max.net.; Mail exchange (2nd/qualified)
www     IN      CNAME   mail
ftp     IN      CNAME   mail
gw      IN      CNAME   ns

ns      IN      A       192.168.0.1
mail    IN      A       192.168.0.2
```

Here there are two reverse zone files, each of which starts with SOA and NS resource records, followed by PTR resource records for each of the names of the servers. The local version of this file also lists the names of the local systems:

```
$ cat named.local
;"0.168.192.in-addr.arpa" reverse zone file
;
$TTL    3D
@       IN      SOA     ns.zach.net. mgs@sobell.com. (
                                2010110501      ; serial
                                8H              ; refresh
                                2H              ; retry
                                4W              ; expire
                                1D)             ; minimum
```

```
                 IN      NS       ns.zach.net.
                 IN      NS       ns.speedy.net.
         1       IN      PTR      ns.zach.net.
         2       IN      PTR      mail.zach.net.
         3       IN      PTR      grape.zach.net.
         4       IN      PTR      potato.zach.net.
         5       IN      PTR      speedy.zach.net.
         6       IN      PTR      peach.zach.net.

$ cat named.public
;"0.168.192.in-addr.arpa" reverse zone file
;
$TTL     3D
@        IN      SOA      ns.zach.net. mgs@sobell.com. (
                                  2010110501      ; serial
                                  8H              ; refresh
                                  2H              ; retry
                                  4W              ; expire
                                  1D)             ; minimum
                 IN      NS       ns.zach.net.
                 IN      NS       ns.speedy.net.
         1       IN      PTR      ns.zach.net.
         2       IN      PTR      mail.zach.net.
```

CHAPTER SUMMARY

DNS maps domain names to IP addresses, and vice versa. It is implemented as a hierarchical, distributed, and replicated database on the Internet. You can improve the security of BIND, which implements DNS, by running it inside a chroot jail and using transaction signatures (TSIGs) and SELinux.

When a program on the local system needs to look up an IP address that corresponds to a domain name, it calls the resolver. The resolver queries the local DNS cache, if available, and then queries DNS servers on the LAN or Internet. There are two types of queries: iterative and recursive. When a server responds to an iterative query, it returns whatever information it has at hand; it does not query other servers. Recursive queries cause a server to query other servers if necessary to respond with an answer.

There are three types of servers. Master servers, which hold the master copy of zone data, are authoritative for a zone. Slave servers are also authoritative and copy their data from a master server or other slave servers. DNS caches are not authoritative and either answer queries from cache or forward queries to another server.

The DNS database holds resource records for domains. Many types of resource records exist, including A (address), MX (mail exchange), NS (nameserver), PTR (pointer for performing reverse name resolution), and SOA (start of authority, which describes the zone).

EXERCISES

1. What kind of server responds to recursive queries? How does this server work?

2. What kind of DNS record is likely to be returned when a Web browser tries to resolve the domain part of a URI?

3. What are MX resource records for?

4. How would you find the IP address of example.com from the command line?

5. How would you instruct a Linux system to use the local network's DNS cache, located at 192.168.1.254, or the ISP's DNS cache, located at 1.2.3.4, if the LAN nameserver is unavailable?

6. How would you instruct a DNS server to respond only to queries from the **137.44.*** IP range?

7. How might a resolver attempt to find the IP address of the **example** domain?

ADVANCED EXERCISES

8. How would you set up a private domain name hierarchy that does not include any of the official InterNIC-assigned domain names?

9. Which part of DNS is most vulnerable to an attack from a malicious user and why?

10. It is often irritating to have to wait for DNS records to update around the world when you change DNS entries. You could prevent this delay by setting the TTL to a small number. Why is setting the TTL to a small number a bad idea?

11. Outline a method by which DNS could be used to support encryption.

25

system-config-firewall AND iptables: SETTING UP A FIREWALL

OBJECTIVES

After reading this chapter you should be able to:

- ▶ Explain the purpose of a packet filtering firewall
- ▶ Define and explain the uses of NAT
- ▶ Configure a basic firewall using system-config-firewall
- ▶ Copy firewall rules to and from the kernel
- ▶ Configure NAT so several clients on a LAN can use a single Internet connection

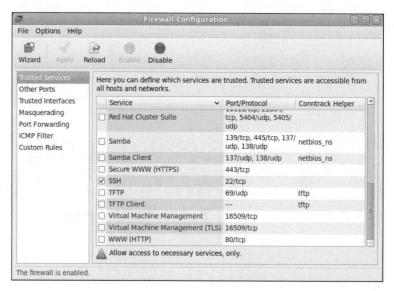

Figure 25-1   Firewall Configuration window

The system-config-firewall is a user-friendly, graphical front-end for iptables and ip6tables (both referred to in this chapter as iptables); iptables builds and manipulates network *packet filtering* (page 1180) rules in the Linux kernel. You can use system-config-firewall or iptables directly to create a firewall that protects a system from malicious users and to set up *NAT* (Network Address Translation, page 1177), which can allow several systems to share a single Internet connection.

The iptables utility is flexible and extensible, allowing you to set up both simple and complex network packet filtering solutions. It provides connection tracking (stateful packet filtering), allowing you to handle *packets* (page 1180) based on the state of their connection. For example, you can set up rules that reject inbound packets trying to open a new connection and accept inbound packets that are responses to a locally initiated connection. Many features not included in the base **iptables** package are available as patches via the patch-o-matic program.

Some of the concepts required to fully understand iptables are beyond the scope of this book. You can use iptables at different levels; this chapter presents the fundamentals. Some sections of this chapter, however, delve into areas that might require additional understanding or explanation. If a concept is not clear, refer to one of the resources in "More Information" on page 898.

Routers have firewalls too

tip   Many systems are already protected by a firewall located in a router. If you use a router that has a firewall, you might need to open ports on the router firewall in addition to opening ports on any firewall you set up on the local system.

If several systems are connected to the router, you might want to set up different, more restrictive rules on the systems than you set up on the router.

JumpStart: Building a Firewall Using system-config-firewall

The firewall is enabled by default

tip   When you install Fedora/RHEL, **iptables** is installed on the system; the firewall is running and blocks most inbound traffic. For information about the initial firewall setup, see "Copying Rules to and from the Kernel" on page 908.

On a RHEL system, **iptables** accepts inbound traffic on TCP port 22, allowing remote systems to connect to the **sshd** daemon on the local system. See page 688 for information on setting up an OpenSSH server.

To display the Firewall Configuration window (Figure 25-1), enter **system-config-firewall** on a command line or select **Main menu: Applications⇨Other⇨Firewall** (Fedora; if **Applications** is not visible see "Configuring Fallback Mode" on page 92) or **Main menu: System⇨Administration⇨Firewall** (RHEL). The system-config-firewall utility allows you to build a simple firewall; use iptables (page 895) for more complex firewalls.

system-config-firewall overwrites custom firewall configurations

caution   As the Firewall Configuration Startup window warns, system-config-firewall overwrites any firewall setup you have configured using other tools, including **iptables**. It also removes the mDNS rule (page 910) that is established when you install Fedora (not RHEL). If you run this utility and do not want to overwrite an existing firewall setup, exit the utility without clicking **Apply** (the green check mark) and without selecting **menubar: File⇨Apply**.

Before allowing you to work with the Firewall Configuration window, system-config-firewall displays the Firewall Configuration Startup window, which holds a warning. See the adjacent caution box. Once you close this window, system-config-firewall displays the Authenticate window; enter the **root** password and click **Authenticate**. The Firewall Configuration window displays the Trusted Services tab as shown in Figure 25-1. The tabs are listed on the left side of the window with the content of each tab on the right.

Firewall is enabled by default   The firewall is enabled by default: It allows packets that originate locally through to the outside (generally the Internet) and allows responses to those packets back in. Under RHEL it also allows traffic in on TCP port 22, which is typically used for OpenSSH traffic.

Applying changes   The system-config-firewall utility allows you to make as many changes to the firewall configuration as you like, including enabling/disabling the firewall, without implementing the changes. The changes are implemented when you click the green **Apply** tick icon or select **menubar: File⇨Apply**. When you do so, system-config-firewall warns you again that you will be overwriting any custom firewall configuration. Click **Yes** to proceed.

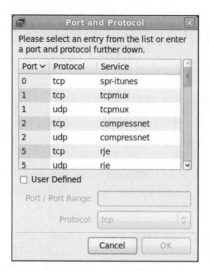

Figure 25-2   The Port and Protocol window

Disabling the firewall

Click the red **Disable** button or select **menubar: Options⇨Disable Firewall** and then click **Apply** to disable the firewall.

The Firewall Configuration window presents the following seven tabs:

Trusted Services

With the Trusted Services frame displayed, click the check boxes next to the services that the local system provides and that you want to allow inbound through the firewall. Ticks in these check boxes set up a firewall that allows the local system to function as one or more types of servers, including FTP, Mail (SMTP), Samba, Secure WWW (HTTPS), SSH, and WWW (HTTP). Click **Apply** when you are done making changes.

ssh is enabled when you run system-config-firewall

caution

In the Trusted Services tab, the check box labeled SSH has a tick in it by default. Unless you clear this tick, when you restart the firewall using **system-config-firewall**, TCP port 22 will be open.

Other Ports

Performs the same function as Trusted Services, except it gives you more options. Enter other ports you want to open by clicking **Other Ports** on the left side of the window and then clicking **Add** to open the Port and Protocol window (Figure 25-2). This window allows you to select from a list or, if you put a tick in the check box labeled **User Defined**, specify a port to open and the protocol that port uses (TCP or UDP).

For example, to open TCP port 616 for a service on the local system, click **Other Ports** and then click **Add** on the right side of the window; system-config-firewall opens the Port and Protocol window shown in Figure 25-2. Put a tick in the check box labeled **User Defined**, enter **616** in the text box labeled **Port/Port Range**, select **tcp** from the drop-down list labeled **Protocol**, and click **OK**. The new, open port appears in the Firewall Configuration window.

Trusted Interfaces Allows you to specify network interfaces. The firewall gives packets coming in on each selected interface full access to the local system.

Masquerading Allows you set up the local system to connect the local network to the Internet. For more information refer to "Connecting Several Clients to a Single Internet Connection" on page 911.

Port Forwarding Allows you to set up the local system to forward ports on the local system or from the local system to a remote system.

ICMP Filter By default the firewall allows inbound *ICMP* (page 1169) packets, such as those sent by ping (page 386), through. You can use the selections in this tab to block these packets. Put tick marks in the check boxes adjacent to the types of packets you want the firewall to block. To block ping packets, put a tick in the check box labeled **Echo Request**. Click **Apply** when you are done making changes.

Custom Rules Allows you to read in files containing iptables rules. The files must be in the iptables-save format. For more information refer to "Copying Rules to and from the Kernel" on page 908.

INTRODUCTION TO iptables

netfilter and iptables The functionality referred to as iptables and ip6tables is composed of two components: **netfilter** and iptables. Running in *kernelspace* (page 1172), the **netfilter** component is a set of tables that hold rules the kernel uses to control network packet filtering. Running in *userspace* (page 1195), the iptables utility sets up, maintains, and displays the rules stored by **netfilter**.

Rules, matches, targets, and chains A *rule* comprises one or more criteria (*matches* or *classifiers*) and a single action (a *target*). If, when a rule is applied to a network packet, the packet matches all the criteria, the action is applied to the packet. Rules are stored in *chains*. Each rule in a chain is applied, in order, to a packet until a match is found. If there is no match, the chain's *policy*, or default action, is applied to the packet (page 903).

History In the kernel, iptables replaces the earlier ipchains as a method of filtering network packets. It provides multiple chains for increased filtration flexibility. The iptables utility also provides stateful packet inspection (page 897).

Example rules As an example of how rules work, assume a chain has two rules (Figure 25-3 on the next page). The first rule tests whether a packet's destination is port 23 (TELNET) and drops the packet if it is. The second rule tests whether a packet was received from the IP address 192.168.1.1 and alters the packet's destination if it was. When a packet is processed by the example chain, the kernel applies the first rule in the chain to see whether the packet arrived on port 23. If the answer is yes, the packet is dropped and that is the end of processing for that packet. If the answer is no, the kernel applies the second rule in the chain to see whether the packet came from the specified IP address. If the answer is yes, the destination in the packet's header is changed and the modified packet is sent on its way. If the answer is no, the packet is sent on without being changed.

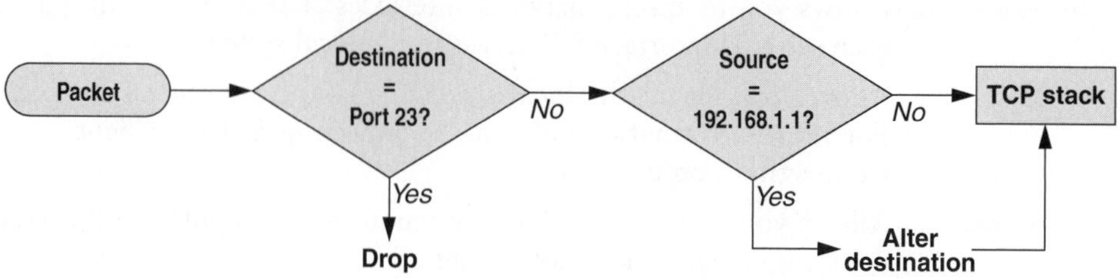

Figure 25-3 Example of how rules in a chain work

Chains are collected in three tables: Filter, NAT, and Mangle. Each of these tables has builtin chains (described next). You can create additional, user-defined chains in Filter, the default table.

Filter table   The default table. This table is mostly used to DROP or ACCEPT packets based on their content; it does not alter packets. Builtin chains are INPUT, FORWARD, and OUTPUT. All user-defined chains go in this table.

NAT table   The Network Address Translation table. Packets that create new connections are routed through this table, which is used exclusively to translate the source or destination fields of packets. Builtin chains are PREROUTING, OUTPUT, and POSTROUTING. Use this table with DNAT, SNAT, and MASQUERADE targets only.

- **DNAT** (destination NAT) alters the destination IP address of the first inbound packet in a connection so it is rerouted to another host. Subsequent packets in the connection are automatically DNATed. DNAT is useful for redirecting packets from the Internet that are bound for a firewall or a NATed server (page 913).

- **SNAT** (source NAT) alters the source IP address of the first outbound packet in a connection so it appears to come from a fixed IP address—for example, a firewall or router. Subsequent packets in the connection are automatically SNATed. Replies to SNATed packets are automatically de-SNATed so they go back to the original sender. SNAT is useful for hiding LAN addresses from systems outside the LAN and using a single IP address to serve multiple local hosts.

- **MASQUERADE** differs from SNAT only in that it checks for an IP address to apply to each outbound packet, making it suitable for use with dynamic IP addresses such as those provided by DHCP (page 489). MASQUERADE is slightly slower than SNAT.

Mangle table   Used exclusively to alter the TOS (type of service), TTL (time to live), and MARK fields in a packet. Builtin chains are PREROUTING and OUTPUT.

Network packets   When a packet from the network enters the kernel's network protocol stack, it is given some basic sanity tests, including checksum verification. After passing these tests, the packet goes through the PREROUTING chain, where its destination address can be changed (Figure 25-4).

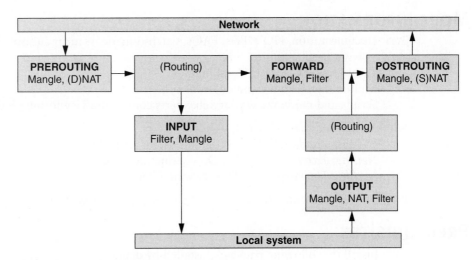

Figure 25-4 Filtering a packet in the kernel

Next the packet is routed based on its destination address. If it is bound for the local system, it first goes through the INPUT chain, where it can be filtered (accepted, dropped, or sent to another chain) or altered. If the packet is not addressed to the local system (the local system is forwarding the packet), it goes through the FORWARD and POSTROUTING chains, where it can again be filtered or altered.

Packets created locally pass through the OUTPUT and POSTROUTING chains, where they can be filtered or altered before being sent to the network.

State The connection tracking machine (also called the state machine) provides information on the state of a packet, allowing you to define rules that match criteria based on the state of the connection the packet is part of. For example, when a connection is opened, the first packet is part of a NEW connection, whereas subsequent packets are part of an ESTABLISHED connection. Connection tracking is handled by the **conntrack** module.

The OUTPUT chain handles connection tracking for locally generated packets. The PREROUTING chain handles connection tracking for all other packets. For more information refer to "State" on page 906.

Before the advent of connection tracking, it was sometimes necessary to open many or all nonprivileged ports to make sure that the system accepted all RETURN and RELATED traffic. Because connection tracking allows you to identify these kinds of traffic, you can keep many more ports closed to general traffic, thereby increasing system security.

Jumps and targets A *jump* or *target* (page 906) specifies the action the kernel takes if a network packet matches all the match criteria (page 901) for the rule being processed.

MORE INFORMATION

Web Documentation, HOWTOs, FAQs, patch-o-matic, security information:
www.netfilter.org
Tutorial: www.faqs.org/docs/iptables
Multicast DNS: www.multicastdns.org
Scripts and more: www.yourwebexperts.com/forum/viewforum.php?f=35

HOWTO *KernelAnalysis-HOWTO*
IP-Masquerade-HOWTO (contains useful scripts)
Netfilter Extensions HOWTO: www.netfilter.org
Netfilter Hacking-HOWTO: www.netfilter.org

Book *TCP/IP Illustrated* by W. Richard Stevens, Addison-Wesley, January 2002

PREREQUISITES

Install the following package (installed by default):

• iptables

iptables init script   As Fedora/RHEL is installed, iptables is set up to run while the system is in runlevels 2–5. You can use chkconfig to prevent iptables from starting when the system comes up (but you probably do not want to):

```
# chkconfig iptables off
```

To ensure maximum protection, the **iptables** init script starts packet filtering by running iptables very soon after the system enters runlevels 2–5; this script does not stop packet filtering almost until the system leaves runlevels 0, 1, and 6. See page 442 for more information on init scripts. You can save and reload iptables rules as explained in "Saving rules" on the next page.

You can use the **iptables init** script with an argument of **status** to display the rules iptables is running.

```
# service iptables status
Table: filter
Chain INPUT (policy ACCEPT)
num  target     prot opt source               destination
1    ACCEPT     all  --  0.0.0.0/0            0.0.0.0/0            state RELATED,ESTABLISHED
2    ACCEPT     icmp --  0.0.0.0/0            0.0.0.0/0
3    ACCEPT     all  --  0.0.0.0/0            0.0.0.0/0
4    ACCEPT     tcp  --  0.0.0.0/0            0.0.0.0/0            state NEW tcp dpt:22
5    REJECT     all  --  0.0.0.0/0            0.0.0.0/0            reject-with icmp-host-prohibited

Chain FORWARD (policy ACCEPT)
num  target     prot opt source               destination
1    REJECT     all  --  0.0.0.0/0            0.0.0.0/0            reject-with icmp-host-prohibited

Chain OUTPUT (policy ACCEPT)
num  target     prot opt source               destination
```

You can also use the **iptables init** script to turn iptables off:

```
# service iptables stop
iptables: Flushing firewall rules:                         [  OK  ]
iptables: Setting chains to policy ACCEPT: filter          [  OK  ]
iptables: Unloading modules:                               [  OK  ]
```

With iptables off, no rules are in effect:

```
# service iptables status
Table: filter
Chain INPUT (policy ACCEPT)
num  target     prot opt source                destination

Chain FORWARD (policy ACCEPT)
num  target     prot opt source                destination

Chain OUTPUT (policy ACCEPT)
num  target     prot opt source                destination
```

Give the command **service iptables save** to save the rules iptables is running. See the next section for more information.

Emergency disconnect An argument of **panic** severs all connections with the network. This command unloads all iptables modules from the kernel and sets a policy of DROP for all tables. It locks down the local system so no traffic can get in or out of it. You would use this command if the system was under attack and you wanted to stop all network traffic in and out of the system immediately. Make sure you have backed up firewall rules you want to save before giving this command.

```
# service iptables panic
iptables: Flushing firewall rules:                          [  OK  ]
iptables: Setting chains to policy DROP: filter             [  OK  ]
```

NOTES

Startup The iptables utility is a tool that manipulates rules in the kernel. It differs from daemons (servers) in its setup and use. Whereas Linux daemons such as Apache, **vsftpd,** and **sshd** read the data that controls their operation from a configuration file, you must provide iptables with a series of commands that build a set of packet filtering rules that are kept in the kernel.

Displaying rules Give the command **iptables –L** or **service iptables status** to display the rules iptables is running.

Saving rules There are two ways to set up the same set of rules each time you bring the system up. First, you can put iptables commands in a script and run that script each time the system boots. You can call this script from **/etc/rc.d/rc.local.**

Second, you can put the arguments to the iptables commands you want to execute in **/etc/sysconfig/iptables.** The system-config-firewall utility (page 909) and the Anaconda installer (page 58) both use this technique, building sets of rules and storing the corresponding iptables command arguments in **/etc/sysconfig/iptables.** These rules are read into the kernel when the system boots. If you use the **/etc/sysconfig/iptables** file in this manner, be aware that system-config-firewall overwrites this file.

See page 908 for information on copying packet filtering rules to and from the kernel.

iptables-config The **iptables init** script executes the **/etc/sysconfig/iptables-config** file. Refer to the comments in this file for options you can set.

Resetting iptables   If you encounter problems related to the firewall rules, you can return the packet processing rules in the kernel to their default state without rebooting by giving the following commands:

```
# iptables --flush
# iptables --delete-chain
```

These commands delete all rules from all chains and delete any user-defined chains; they do not change policy. Therefore, if the policy is ACCEPT (**–P ACCEPT**), flushing opens the firewall so it accepts all packets; if the policy is DROP (**–P DROP**), flushing causes the firewall to drop all packets.

See "Emergency disconnect" on page 899 if you need to lock down the system quickly.

ANATOMY OF AN iptables COMMAND

Command line   This section describes the components of an iptables command line that follow the name of the utility, iptables. Except as noted, the iptables utility is not sensitive to the positions of arguments on the command line. The examples in this chapter reflect a generally accepted syntax that allows commands to be easily read, understood, and maintained. Not all commands have all components.

Many tokens on an iptables command line have two forms: a short form, consisting of a single letter preceded by a single hyphen, and a long form, consisting of a word preceded by two hyphens. Most scripts use the short forms for brevity; lines using the long forms can get unwieldy. The following iptables command lines are equivalent and are used as examples in this section:

```
# iptables --append FORWARD --in-interface eth1 --out-interface eth0 --jump ACCEPT
# iptables -A FORWARD -i eth1 -o eth0 -j ACCEPT
```

Table   The table specifies the name of the table the command operates on: Filter, NAT, or Mangle. You can specify a table name in any iptables command. When you do not specify a table name, the command operates on the Filter table. Most examples in this chapter do not specify table names and, therefore, work on the Filter table. Specify a table as **–t** *tablename* or **––table** *tablename*.

Command   The command tells iptables what to do with the rest of the command line—for example, add or delete a rule, display rules, or add a chain. The example commands, **–A** and **––append**, append the rule specified by the command line to the specified table (defaults to Filter table) and chain. See page 902 for information on commands.

Chain   The chain specifies the name of the chain that this rule belongs to or that this command works on. The chain is INPUT, OUTPUT, FORWARD, PREROUTING, POSTROUTING, or the name of a user-defined chain. Specify a chain by putting the name of the chain on the command line without any preceding hyphens. The examples at the beginning of this section work with the FORWARD chain.

Match criteria   There are two kinds of match criteria: *packet match* criteria, which match a network packet, and *rule match* criteria, which match an existing rule.

Packet match criteria/rule specifications   Packet match criteria identify network packets and implement rules that take action on packets that match the criteria. The combination of packet match criteria and an action is called a *rule specification*. Rule specifications form the basis for packet filtering. The first example at the beginning of this section uses the **--in-interface eth1 --out-interface eth0** rule match criteria. The second example uses the short form of the same criteria: **-i eth1 -o eth0**. Both of these rules forward packets that come in on device **eth1** and go out on device **eth0**.

Rule match criteria   Rule match criteria identify existing rules. An iptables command can modify, remove, or position a new rule adjacent to a rule specified by a rule match criterion. There are two ways to identify an existing rule: You can use the same rule specification that was used to create the rule or you can use the rule's ordinal number, called a *rule number*. Rule numbers begin with 1, signifying the first rule in a chain, and can be displayed using **iptables –L --line-numbers**. The first command below deletes the rule listed at the beginning of this section; the second command replaces (**–R**) INPUT chain rule number 3 with a rule that rejects all packets from IP address 192.168.0.10:

```
# iptables --delete -A FORWARD -i eth1 -o eth0 -j ACCEPT
# iptables -R INPUT 3 --source 192.168.0.10 --jump REJECT
```

A jump or target specifies what action the kernel takes on packets that match all match criteria for a rule. Specify a jump or target as **–j** *target* or **--jump** *target*. The examples at the beginning of this section specify the ACCEPT target using the following commands: **--jump ACCEPT** and **–j ACCEPT**.

Jumps   A jump transfers control to a different chain within the same table. The following command adds (**--append**) a rule to the INPUT chain that transfers packets that use the TCP protocol (**--protocol tcp**) to a user-defined chain named **tcp_rules** (**--jump tcp_rules**):

```
# iptables --append INPUT --protocol tcp --jump tcp_rules
```

When the packet finishes traversing the **tcp_rules** chain, assuming it has not been dropped or rejected, it continues traversing the INPUT chain from the rule following the one it jumped from.

Targets   A target specifies an action the kernel takes on the packet; the simplest actions are ACCEPT, DROP, and REJECT. The following command adds a rule to the FORWARD chain that rejects TCP packets coming from the FTP port (**/etc/services**, the file iptables consults to determine which port to use, shows that FTP uses port 21):

```
# iptables --append FORWARD -p tcp --sport ftp --jump REJECT
```

Some targets, such as LOG, are *nonterminating*: Control passes to the next rule after the target is executed. See page 906 for information on how to use targets.

BUILDING A SET OF RULES USING iptables

This section describes the specifics that comprise an iptables rule. It starts with iptables commands; continues with packet match criteria, display criteria, and match extensions; and concludes with targets.

To specify a table, it is common practice to put the table declaration on the command line immediately following **iptables**. For example, the following command flushes (deletes all the rules from) the NAT table:

```
# iptables -t NAT -F
```

COMMANDS

Following is a list of iptables commands:

--append   **–A**   Adds rule(s) specified by *rule-specifications* to the end of *chain*. When a packet matches all of the *rule-specifications, target* processes it.

> *iptables –A chain rule-specifications --jump target*

--delete   **–D**   Removes one or more rules from *chain,* as specified by the *rule-numbers* or *rule-specifications*.

> *iptables –D chain rule-numbers | rule-specifications*

--insert   **–I**   Adds rule(s) specified by *rule-specifications* and *target* to the location in *chain* specified by *rule-number*. If you do not specify *rule-number,* it defaults to 1, the head of the chain.

> *iptables –I chain rule-number | rule-specifications --jump target*

--replace   **–R**   Replaces rule number *rule-number* in *chain* with *rule-specification* and *target*. The command fails if *rule-number* or *rule-specification* resolves to more than one address.

> *iptables –R chain rule-number | rule-specification --jump target*

--list   **–L**   Displays the rules in *chain*. Omit *chain* to display the rules for all chains. Use **--line-numbers** to display rule numbers or select other display criteria from the list on page 904.

> *iptables –L [chain] display-criteria*

--flush   **–F**   Deletes all rules from *chain*. Omit *chain* to delete all rules from all chains. This command does not change policy; see "Resetting iptables" on page 900 for more information.

> *iptables –F [chain]*

--zero   **–Z**   Changes to zero the value of all packet and byte counters in *chain* or in all chains when you do not specify *chain*. Use with **–L** to display the counters before clearing them.

> *iptables –Z [–L] [chain]*

--delete-chain **–X** Removes the user-defined chain named *chain*. If you do not specify *chain*, removes all user-defined chains. You cannot delete a chain that a target points to.

> *iptables –X chain*

--policy **–P** Sets the default target or policy *builtin-target* for the builtin chain *builtin-chain*. This policy is applied to packets that do not match any rule in the chain. If a chain does not have a policy, unmatched packets are ACCEPTed.

> *iptables –P builtin-chain builtin-target*

--rename-chain **–E** Changes the name of the chain *old* to *new*.

> *iptables –E old new*

--help **–h** Displays a summary of the iptables command syntax.

> *iptables –h*

Follow a match extension protocol with **–h** to display options you can use with that protocol. For more information refer to "Help with extensions" on the next page.

PACKET MATCH CRITERIA

The following criteria match network packets. When you precede a criterion with an exclamation point (**!**), the rule matches packets that do not match the criterion.

--protocol [!] *proto*

> **–p** Matches if the packet uses the *proto* protocol. This criterion is a match extension (next page).

--source [!] *address[/mask]*

> **–s** or **--src** Matches if the packet came from *address*. The *address* should be an IP address and not a name because, when the system boots, iptables starts before the network and will not be able to resolve a name. See page 479 for formats of the optional *mask* (only with an IP address).

--destination [!] *address[/mask]*

> **–d** or **--dst** Matches if the packet is going to *address*. The *address* should be an IP address and not a name because, when the system boots, iptables starts before the network and will not be able to resolve a name. See page 479 for formats of the optional *mask* (only with an IP address).

--in-interface [!] *iface[+]*

> **–i** For the INPUT, FORWARD, and PREROUTING chains, matches if *iface* is the name of the interface the packet was received from. Append a plus sign (**+**) to *iface* to match any interface whose name begins with *iface*. When you do not specify **in-interface**, the rule matches packets coming from any interface.

--out-interface [!] *iface[+]*

> **–o** For the OUTPUT, FORWARD, and POSTROUTING chains, matches if *iface* is the interface the packet will be sent to. Append a plus sign (**+**) to *iface* to match any interface whose name begins with *iface*. When you do not specify **out-interface**, the rule matches packets going to any interface.

[!] –fragment   –f   Matches the second and subsequent fragments of fragmented packets. Because these packets do not contain source or destination information, they do not match any other rules.

DISPLAY CRITERIA

The following criteria display information. All packets match these criteria.

--verbose   –v   Displays additional output.

--numeric   –n   Displays IP addresses and port numbers as numbers, not names.

--exact   –x   Use with –L to display exact packet and byte counts instead of rounded values.

--line-numbers   Displays line numbers when listing rules. These line numbers are also the rule numbers that you can use in rule match criteria (page 901).

MATCH EXTENSIONS

Rule specification (packet match criteria) extensions, called *match extensions*, add matches based on protocols and state to the matches described previously. Each of the protocol extensions is kept in a module that must be loaded before that match extension can be used. The command that loads the module must appear in the same rule specification as, and to the left of, the command that uses the module. There are two types of match extensions: implicit and explicit.

IMPLICIT MATCH EXTENSIONS

Help with extensions   Implicit extensions are loaded (somewhat) automatically when you use a --protocol command (described below). Each protocol has its own extensions. Follow the protocol with –h to display extensions you can use with that protocol. For example, the following command displays TCP extensions *at the end* of the Help output:

```
$ iptables -p tcp -h
...
tcp match options:
 --tcp-flags [!] mask comp      match when TCP flags & mask == comp
                                (Flags: SYN ACK FIN RST URG PSH ALL NONE)
 [!] --syn                      match when only SYN flag set
                                (equivalent to --tcp-flags SYN,RST,ACK SYN)
 --source-port [!] port[:port]
 --sport ...
                                match source port(s)
 --destination-port [!] port[:port]
 --dport ...
                                match destination port(s)
 --tcp-option [!] number        match if TCP option set
```

This section does not describe all extensions. Use –h, as in the preceding example, to display a complete list.

--protocol [!] *proto*

–p   Loads the *proto* module and matches if the packet uses the *proto* protocol. The *proto* can be a name or number from **/etc/protocols**, including **tcp**, **udp**, and **icmp** (page 1169). Specifying **all** or **0** (zero) matches all protocols and is the same as not including this match in a rule.

The following criteria load the TCP module and match TCP protocol packets coming from port 22 (ssh packets):

```
--protocol tcp --source-port 22
```

The following command expands the preceding match to cause the kernel to drop all incoming ssh packets. This command uses **ssh**, which iptables looks up in **/etc/services**, in place of **22**:

```
# iptables --protocol tcp --source-port ssh --jump DROP
```

TCP

The extensions in this section are loaded when you specify **--protocol tcp**.

--destination-port [!] [*port*[:*port*]] | port: | :port

--dport Matches a destination port number or service name (see **/etc/services**). You can also specify a range of port numbers. Specifically, *:port* specifies ports 0 through *port,* and *port:* specifies ports *port* through 65535.

--source-port [!] [*port*[:*port*]] | port: | :port

--sport Matches a source port number or service name (see **/etc/services**). You can also specify a range of port numbers. Specifically, *:port* specifies ports 0 through *port,* and *port:* specifies ports *port* through 65535.

[!] **--syn** Matches packets with the SYN bit set and the ACK and FIN bits cleared. This match extension is shorthand for **--tcp-flags SYN,RST,ACK SYN.**

--tcp-flags [!] *mask comp*

Defines which TCP flag settings constitute a match. Valid flags are SYN, ACK, FIN, RST, URG, PSH, ALL, and NONE. The *mask* is a comma-separated list of flags to be examined; *comp* is a comma-separated subset of *mask* that specifies the flags that must be set for a match to occur. Flags not specified in *mask* must be unset.

--tcp-option [!] *n* Matches a TCP option with a decimal value of *n*.

UDP

When you specify **--protocol udp**, you can specify a source and/or destination port in the same manner as described under "TCP" on the preceding page.

ICMP

The extension in this section is loaded when you specify **--protocol icmp**. *ICMP* (page 1169) packets carry messages only.

--icmp-type [!] *name*

Matches when the packet is an ICMP packet of type *name*. The *name* can be a numeric ICMP type or one of the names returned by

```
$ iptables -p icmp -h
```

EXPLICIT MATCH EXTENSIONS

Explicit match extensions differ from implicit match extensions in that you must use a **–m** or **––match** option to specify a module before you can use the extension. Many explicit match extension modules are available; this section covers **state**, one of the most important.

STATE

The **state** extension matches criteria based on the state of the connection the packet is part of (page 897).

––state *state*   Matches a packet whose state is defined by *state*, a comma-separated list of states from the following list:

- ESTABLISHED—Any packet, within a specific connection, following the exchange of packets in both directions for that connection.

- INVALID—A stateless or unidentifiable packet.

- NEW—The first packet within a specific connection, typically a SYN packet.

- RELATED—Any packets exchanged in a connection spawned from an ESTABLISHED connection. For example, an FTP data connection might be related to the FTP control connection. (The **ip_conntrack_ftp** module is required for FTP connection tracking.)

The following command loads the **state** extension and establishes a rule that matches and drops both invalid packets and packets from new connections:

```
# iptables --match state --state INVALID,NEW --jump DROP
```

TARGETS

All targets are built in; there are no user-defined targets. This section lists some of the targets available with iptables. Applicable target options are listed following each target.

ACCEPT   Causes the packet to leave the chain. The packet can then be processed by another chain or be up the TCP stack.

DNAT   **Destination Network Address Translation**   Rewrites the destination address of the packet (page 896).

––to-destination *ip[-ip][:port-port]*

Same as SNAT (next page) with **to-source**, except it changes the destination addresses of packets to the specified addresses and ports and is valid only in the PREROUTING or OUTPUT chains of the NAT table and any user-defined chains called from those chains. The following command adds to the PREROUTING chain of the NAT table a rule that changes the destination in the headers of TCP packets with a destination of 66.187.232.50 to 192.168.0.10:

```
# iptables -t NAT -A PREROUTING -p tcp -d 66.187.232.50 -j DNAT --to-destination 192.168.0.10
```

DROP   Ends the packet's life without notice.

LOG   Turns on logging for the packet being processed. The kernel uses **syslogd** (page 623) to process output generated by this target. LOG is a nonterminating target, so processing continues with the next rule. Use two rules to LOG packets that you REJECT or DROP, one each with the targets LOG and REJECT or DROP, with the same matching criteria.

--log-level *n*   Specifies logging level *n* as per **syslog.conf** (page 623).

--log-prefix *string*

Prefixes log entries with *string*, which can be a maximum of 14 characters long.

--log-tcp-options   Logs options from the TCP packet header.

--log-ip-options   Logs options from the IP packet header.

MASQUERADE   Similar to SNAT (below) with **--to-source**, except that it grabs the IP information from the interface on the specified port. For use on systems with dynamically assigned IP addresses, such as those using DHCP, including most dial-up lines. Valid only in rules in the POSTROUTING chain of the NAT table.

--to-ports *port[-port]*

Specifies the port for the interface you want to masquerade. Forgets connections when the interface goes down, as is appropriate for dial-up lines. You must specify the TCP or UDP protocol (**--protocol tcp** or **udp**) with this target.

REJECT   Similar to DROP, except it notifies the sending system that the packet was blocked.

--reject-with *type*   Returns the error *type* to the originating system. The *type* can be any of the following, all of which return the appropriate *ICMP* (page 1169) error: **icmp-net-unreachable**, **icmp-host-unreachable**, **icmp-port-unreachable**, **icmp-proto-unreachable**, **icmp-net-prohibited**, or **icmp-host-prohibited**. You can specify *type* as **echo-reply** from rules that require an ICMP ping (page 386) packet to return a ping reply. You can specify **tcp-reset** from rules in or called from the INPUT chain to return a TCP RST packet. This parameter is valid in the INPUT, FORWARD, and OUTPUT chains and user-defined chains called from these chains.

RETURN   Stops traversing this chain and returns the packet to the calling chain.

SNAT   **Source Network Address Translation**   Rewrites the source address of the packet. Appropriate for hosts on a LAN that share an Internet connection.

--to-source *ip[-ip][:port-port]*

Alters the source IP address of an outbound packet, and the source IP addresses of all future packets in this connection, to *ip*. Skips additional rules, if any exist. Returning packets are automatically de-SNATed so they return to the originating host. Valid only in the POSTROUTING chain of the NAT table.

When you specify a range of IP addresses (*ip-ip*) or use multiple **to-source** targets, iptables assigns the addresses in a round-robin fashion, cycling through the addresses, one for each new connection.

When the rule specifies the TCP or UDP protocol (**–p tcp** or **–p udp**), you can specify a range of ports. When you do not specify a range of ports, the rule matches all ports. Every connection on a NATed subnet must have a unique IP address and port combination. If two systems on a NATed subnet try to use the same port, the kernel maps one of the ports to another (unused) port. Ports less than 512 are mapped to other ports less than 512, ports from 512 to 1024 are mapped to other ports from 512 to 1024, and ports above 1024 are mapped to other ports above 1024.

COPYING RULES TO AND FROM THE KERNEL

The iptables-save utility copies packet filtering rules from the kernel to standard output; you can redirect the output to a file. The iptables-restore utility copies rules from standard input, as written by iptables-save, to the kernel. Following is the output from iptables-save as the system is installed (system-config-firewall has not been run):

```
# iptables-save# Generated by iptables-save v1.4.9 on Tue Nov  2 14:57:10 2010
*filter
:INPUT ACCEPT [0:0]
:FORWARD ACCEPT [0:0]
:OUTPUT ACCEPT [78:7254]
-A INPUT -m state --state RELATED,ESTABLISHED -j ACCEPT
-A INPUT -p icmp -j ACCEPT
-A INPUT -i lo -j ACCEPT
-A INPUT -d 224.0.0.251/32 -p udp -m state --state NEW -m udp --dport 5353 -j ACCEPT
-A INPUT -j REJECT --reject-with icmp-host-prohibited
-A FORWARD -j REJECT --reject-with icmp-host-prohibited
COMMIT
# Completed on Tue Nov  2 14:57:10 2010
```

Most lines that iptables-save writes are iptables command lines without the **iptables** at the beginning. Lines that begin with a hashmark (**#**) are comments. Lines that begin with an asterisk (*****) are names of tables that the following commands work on; the commands in the preceding example work on the Filter table. The COMMIT line must appear at the end of all commands for a table; it executes the preceding commands. Lines that begin with colons specify chains in the following format:

:chain policy [packets:bytes]

where ***chain*** is the name of the chain, ***policy*** is the policy (default target) for the chain, and ***packets*** and ***bytes*** are the packet and byte counters, respectively. The square brackets must appear in the line; they do not indicate optional parameters.

Refer to the next section and visit www.faqs.org/docs/iptables/iptables-save.html for more information.

system-config-firewall: GENERATES A SET OF RULES

This section describes the set of rules generated by system-config-firewall (page 893) when you ask it to create a firewall with only ssh (TCP port 22) running as a trusted service and no other ports specified. The system-config-firewall utility writes the rules in the format used by iptables-save (see the preceding section) to the **/etc/sysconfig/iptables** file, which is read by the **iptables** init script so that the firewall is implemented each time the system boots.

In the following listing, ***filter** indicates that the commands appearing after it work on the Filter table. The first line that begins with a colon specifies that the policy for the INPUT chain in the Filter table is ACCEPT. FORWARD and OUTPUT chains are specified similarly. Because the counters for all the chains are zero, the counters will be reset to zero each time the system boots and initializes iptables from this file. The system-config-firewall utility works mostly with the INPUT chain.

```
# cat /etc/sysconfig/iptables# Firewall configuration written by
system-config-firewall
# Manual customization of this file is not recommended.
*filter
:INPUT ACCEPT [0:0]
:FORWARD ACCEPT [0:0]
:OUTPUT ACCEPT [0:0]
-A INPUT -m state --state ESTABLISHED,RELATED -j ACCEPT
-A INPUT -p icmp -j ACCEPT
-A INPUT -i lo -j ACCEPT
-A INPUT -m state --state NEW -m tcp -p tcp --dport 22 -j ACCEPT
-A INPUT -j REJECT --reject-with icmp-host-prohibited
-A FORWARD -j REJECT --reject-with icmp-host-prohibited
COMMIT
```

Most of the lines append rules to the INPUT chain. Following is a description of what these lines do.

The first line that works with the INPUT chain uses **–m** to specify the **state** module and accepts ESTABLISHED and RELATED packets:

```
-A INPUT -m state --state ESTABLISHED,RELATED -j ACCEPT
```

The next line accepts all ICMP packets:

```
-A INPUT -p icmp -j ACCEPT
```

This line accepts packets from the local interface:

```
-A INPUT -i lo -j ACCEPT
```

This line allows new TCP connections on port 22 (ssh):

```
-A INPUT -m state --state NEW -m tcp -p tcp --dport 22 -j ACCEPT
```

These lines reject all packets that have not been accepted and return ICMP error **icmp-host-prohibited** to the system that sent the packet:

```
-A INPUT -j REJECT --reject-with icmp-host-prohibited
-A FORWARD -j REJECT --reject-with icmp-host-prohibited
```

mDNS Running system-config-firewall (see the previous section), added the rule that accepts TCP packets on port 22 and removed the default rule that accepts multicast DNS (mDNS; www.multicastdns.org) packets:

```
-A INPUT -d 224.0.0.251/32 -p udp -m state --state NEW -m udp --dport 5353 -j ACCEPT
```

COMMIT executes the preceding commands. With the preceding rules loaded, you can use iptables to list the rules and see the defaults that iptables puts in place:

```
# iptables -L
Chain INPUT (policy ACCEPT)
target     prot opt source              destination
ACCEPT     all  --  anywhere            anywhere             state RELATED,ESTABLISHED
ACCEPT     icmp --  anywhere            anywhere
ACCEPT     all  --  anywhere            anywhere
ACCEPT     tcp  --  anywhere            anywhere             state NEW tcp dpt:ssh
REJECT     all  --  anywhere            anywhere             reject-with icmp-host-prohibited

Chain FORWARD (policy ACCEPT)
target     prot opt source              destination
REJECT     all  --  anywhere            anywhere             reject-with icmp-host-prohibited

Chain OUTPUT (policy ACCEPT)
target     prot opt source              destination
```

Sharing an Internet Connection Using NAT

Many scripts that set up Internet connection sharing using iptables are available on the Internet. Each of these scripts boils down to the same few basic iptables commands, albeit with minor differences. This section discusses those few statements to explain how a connection can be shared. You can use the statements presented in this section or refer to the *Linux IP Masquerade HOWTO* for complete scripts. The tldp.org/HOWTO/IP-Masquerade-HOWTO/firewall-examples.html Web page holds the simplest of these scripts.

There are two ways you can share a single connection to the Internet (one IP address), both of which involve setting up NAT to alter addresses in packets and then forward them. The first allows clients (browsers, mail readers, and so on) on several systems on a LAN to share a single IP address to connect to servers on the Internet. The second allows servers (mail, Web, FTP, and so on) on different systems on a LAN to provide their services over a single connection to the Internet. You can use iptables to set up one or both of these configurations. In both cases, you need to set up a system that is a router: It must have two network connections—one connected to the Internet and the other to the LAN.

For optimal security, use a dedicated system as a router. Because data transmission over a connection to the Internet—even over a broadband connection—is relatively slow, using a slower, older system as a router does not generally slow down a LAN. This setup also offers some defense against intrusion from the Internet. A workstation on the LAN can function as a router as well, but this setup means that you maintain data on a system that is directly connected to the Internet. The following sections discuss the security of each setup.

The examples in this section assume the device named **eth0** connects to the Internet on 10.255.255.255 and that **eth1** connects to the LAN on 192.168.0.1. Substitute the devices and IP addresses that the local systems use. If you use a modem to connect to the Internet, you need to substitute **ppp0** (or another device) for **eth0** in the examples.

For the examples in this section to work, you must turn on IP forwarding. First give the following command and make sure everything is working:

```
# sysctl -w net.ipv4.ip_forward=1
net.ipv4.ip_forward = 1
```

If you want to forward IPv6 packets, give this command instead:

```
# sysctl -w net.ipv6.conf.all.forwarding=1net.ipv6.conf.all.forwarding = 1
```

Once you know that iptables is working correctly, change the 0 to a 1 in the following line in **/etc/sysctl.conf** to make the kernel always perform IP forwarding:

```
net.ipv4.ip_forward = 0
```

After making this change, give the command **/sbin/sysctl –e –p** to apply the change and to make sure that there are no typographical errors in the configuration file.

CONNECTING SEVERAL CLIENTS TO A SINGLE INTERNET CONNECTION

Configuring the kernel of the router system to allow clients on multiple local systems on the LAN to connect to the Internet requires you to set up *IP masquerading,* or *SNAT* (source NAT). IP masquerading translates the source and destination addresses in the headers of network packets that originate on local systems and the packets that remote servers send in response to those packets. These packets are part of connections that originate on a local system. The example in this section does nothing to packets that are part of connections that originate on the remote systems (on the Internet): These packets cannot get past the router system, which provides some degree of security.

The point of rewriting the packet headers is to allow systems with different local IP addresses to share a single IP address on the Internet. The router system translates the source or origin address of packets from the local systems to that of the Internet connection, so all packets passing from the router to the Internet appear to come from a single system—10.255.255.255 in the example. All packets sent in response by remote systems on the Internet to the router system have the address of the Internet connection—10.255.255.255 in the example—as their destination address. The router system remembers each connection and alters the destination address of each response packet to that of the local, originating system.

The router system is established by four iptables commands, one of which sets up a log of masqueraded connections. The first command puts the first rule in the FORWARD chain of the Filter (default) table (**–A FORWARD**):

```
# iptables -A FORWARD -i eth0 -o eth1 -m state --state ESTABLISHED,RELATED -j ACCEPT
```

To match this rule, a packet must be

1. Received on **eth0** (coming in from the Internet): **–i eth0**

2. Going to be sent out on **eth1** (going out to the LAN): **–o eth1**

3. Part of an established connection or a connection that is related to an established connection: **––state ESTABLISHED,RELATED**

The kernel accepts (**–j ACCEPT**) packets that meet these three criteria. Accepted packets pass to the next appropriate chain or table. Packets from the Internet that attempt to create a new connection are not matched and, therefore, are not accepted by this rule. Packets that are not accepted pass to the next rule in the FORWARD chain.

The second command puts the second rule in the FORWARD chain of the Filter table:

```
# iptables -A FORWARD -i eth1 -o eth0 -j ACCEPT
```

To match this rule, a packet must be

1. Received on **eth1** (coming in from the LAN): **–i eth1**

2. Going to be sent out on **eth0** (going out to the Internet): **–o eth0**

The kernel accepts packets that meet these two criteria, which means all packets that originate locally and are going to the Internet are accepted. Accepted packets pass to the next appropriate chain/table; packets that are not accepted pass to the next rule in the FORWARD chain.

The third command puts the third rule in the FORWARD chain of the Filter table:

```
# iptables -A FORWARD -j LOG
```

Because this rule has no match criteria, it acts on all packets it processes. This rule's action is to log packets—that is, it logs packets from the Internet that attempt to create a new connection.

Packets that reach the end of the FORWARD chain of the Filter table are done with the rules set up by iptables and are handled by the local TCP stack. Packets from the Internet that attempt to create a new connection on the router system are accepted or returned, depending on whether the service they are trying to connect to is available on the router system.

The fourth command puts the first rule in the POSTROUTING chain of the NAT table. Only packets that are establishing a new connection are passed to the NAT table. Once a connection has been set up for SNAT or MASQUERADE, the headers on all subsequent ESTABLISHED and RELATED packets are altered the same way as the header of the first packet. Packets sent in response to these packets automatically have their headers adjusted so they return to the originating local system.

```
# iptables -t NAT -A POSTROUTING -o eth0 -j MASQUERADE
```

To match this rule, a packet must be

1. Establishing a new connection (otherwise it would not have come to the NAT table)

2. Going to be sent out on **eth0** (going out to the Internet): **–o eth0**

The kernel MASQUERADEs all packets that meet these criteria. In other words, all locally originating packets that are establishing new connections have their source address changed to the address that is associated with **eth0** (10.255.255.255 in the example). If the local system has a static IP address, substitute SNAT for MASQUERADE.

The following example shows all four commands together:

```
# iptables -A FORWARD -i eth0 -o eth1 -m state --state ESTABLISHED,RELATED -j ACCEPT
# iptables -A FORWARD -i eth1 -o eth0 -j ACCEPT
# iptables -A FORWARD -j LOG
# iptables -t NAT -A POSTROUTING -o eth0 -j MASQUERADE
```

See page 899 for instructions on how to save these rules so the firewall comes up each time the system boots. To limit the local systems that can connect to the Internet, you can add a **–s** (source) match criterion to the last command:

```
# iptables -t NAT -A POSTROUTING -o eth0 -s 192.168.0.0-192.168.0.32 -j MASQUERADE
```

In the preceding command, **–s 192.168.0.0-192.168.0.32** causes only packets from an IP address in the specified range to be MASQUERADEd.

CONNECTING SEVERAL SERVERS TO A SINGLE INTERNET CONNECTION

DNAT (destination NAT) can set up rules that allow clients from the Internet to send packets to servers on the LAN. This example sets up an SMTP mail server on 192.168.1.33 and an HTTP (Web) server on 192.168.1.34. Both protocols use TCP. SMTP uses port 25 and HTTP uses port 80, so the rules match TCP packets with destination ports of 25 and 80. The example assumes the mail server does not make outgoing connections and uses another server on the LAN for DNS and mail relaying. Both commands put rules in the PREROUTING chain of the NAT table (**–A PREROUTING –t NAT**):

```
# iptables -A PREROUTING -t NAT -p tcp --dport 25 -j DNAT --to-destination 192.168.0.33:25
# iptables -A PREROUTING -t NAT -p tcp --dport 80 -j DNAT --to-destination 192.168.0.34:80
```

To match these rules, the packet must use the TCP protocol (**–p tcp**) and have a destination port of either 25 (first rule, **––dport 25**) or 80 (second rule, **––dport 80**).

The **--to-destination** is a target specific to the PREROUTING and OUTPUT chains of the NAT table; it alters the destination address and port of matched packets as specified. As with MASQUERADE and SNAT, subsequent packets in the same and related connections are altered the same way.

The fact that the servers cannot originate connections means that neither server can be exploited to participate in a *DDoS attack* (page 1160) on systems on the Internet, nor can they send private data from the local system back to a malicious user's system.

CHAPTER SUMMARY

A firewall, as implemented by iptables, is designed to prevent unauthorized access to a system or network. The system-config-firewall utility is a graphical tool for building and maintaining an iptables firewall. Such a firewall can protect just the single system it runs on or can protect the system it runs on plus other systems on a LAN that connect to the Internet through the system running the firewall.

The iptables utility creates firewalls intended to prevent unauthorized access to a system or network. An iptables command sets up or maintains in the kernel rules that control the flow of network packets; rules are stored in chains. Each rule includes a criteria part and an action part, called a target. When the criteria part matches a network packet, the kernel applies the action from the rule to the packet.

Chains are collected in three tables: Filter, NAT, and Mangle. Filter (the default table) DROPs or ACCEPTs packets based on their content. NAT (the Network Address Translation table) translates the source or destination field in packet headers. Mangle is used exclusively to alter the TOS (type of service), TTL (time to live), and MARK fields in a packet. The connection tracking machine, which is handled by the **conntrack** module, defines rules that match criteria based on the state of the connection a packet is part of.

In an emergency you can give the following command to unload all iptables modules from the kernel and set a policy of DROP for all tables:

```
# service iptables panic
```

EXERCISES

1. How would you remove all iptables rules and chains, but not change policy?

2. How would you list all current iptables rules?

3. How is configuring iptables different from configuring most Linux services?

4. Define an iptables rule that will reject incoming connections on the TELNET port.

5. What does NAT stand for? What does the NAT table do?

ADVANCED EXERCISES

6. What does the **conntrack** module do?

7. What do rule match criteria do? What are they used for?

8. What do packet match criteria do? What are they used for?

9. Which utilities copy packet filtering rules to and from the kernel? How do they work?

10. Write a rule that will silently block incoming SMTP connections from **10.10.0.10**.

APACHE (httpd): SETTING UP A WEB SERVER

OBJECTIVES

After reading this chapter you should be able to:

▶ Explain the purpose of Apache and describe the use of several available modules

▶ Configure an Apache server to listen on the network and provide simple content

▶ Customize names, addresses, ports, and the location of content, logs, and scripts of an Apache server

▶ Allow users to publish content from their home directories

▶ Configure virtual hosts to display different content

▶ Configure password protected directory hierarchies, host based access control, directory options, and SELinux Booleans to secure access to Web content

The World Wide Web (WWW or Web for short), is a collection of servers that hold material, called *content,* that (Web) browsers can display. Each of the servers on the Web is connected to the Internet, a network of networks (an *internetwork*). Much of the content on the Web is coded in HTML (Hypertext Markup Language, page 1168). *Hypertext,* the links you click on a Web page, allows browsers to display and react to links that point to other Web pages on the Internet.

Apache is the most popular Web server on the Internet. It is both robust and extensible. The ease with which you can install, configure, and run it in the Linux environment makes it an obvious choice for publishing content on the World Wide Web. The Apache server and related projects are developed and maintained by the Apache Software Foundation (ASF), a not-for-profit corporation formed in June 1999. The ASF grew out of the Apache Group, which was established in 1995 to develop the Apache server.

This chapter starts by providing introductory information about Apache. Following this information is the first JumpStart section, which describes the minimal steps needed to get Apache up and running. Next is "Filesystem Layout," which tells you where the various Apache files are located.

Configuration directives (referred to simply as directives) are a key part of Apache and are discussed starting on page 925. This section includes coverage of contexts and containers, two features/concepts that are critical to understanding Apache. The next section, which starts on page 947, explains the main Apache configuration file, **httpd.conf,** as distributed by Fedora/RHEL. The final pages of the chapter cover advanced Apache configuration: redirects, content negotiation, directory indexing, virtual hosts, troubleshooting, and modules you can use with Apache, including CGI and SSL.

INTRODUCTION

Apache is a server that responds to requests from Web browsers, or *clients,* such as Firefox, Netscape, lynx, elinks, and Internet Explorer. When you enter the address of a Web page (a *URI,* page 1195) in a Web browser's location bar, the browser sends a request over the Internet to the (Apache) server at that address. In response, the server sends (serves) the requested content back to the browser. The browser then displays or plays the content, which might be a textual document, song, picture, video clip, or other information.

Content   Aside from add-on modules that can interact with the content, Apache looks only at the type of data it is sending so that it can specify the correct *MIME* (page 1176) type; otherwise it remains oblivious to the content itself. Server administration and content creation are two different aspects of bringing up a Web site. This chapter concentrates on setting up and running an Apache server; it spends little time discussing content creation.

Modules   Apache, like the Linux kernel, uses external modules to increase load-time flexibility and allow parts of its code to be recompiled without recompiling the whole program. Rather than being part of the Apache binary, modules are stored as separate files that can be loaded when Apache is started.

Apache uses external modules, called dynamic shared objects (DSOs), for basic and advanced functions; there is not much to Apache without these modules. Apache also uses modules to extend its functionality. For example, modules can process scripts written in Perl, PHP, Python, and other languages; use several different methods to authenticate users; facilitate publishing content; and process nontextual content, such as audio. The list of modules written by the ASF and third-party developers is constantly growing. For more information refer to "Modules" on page 957.

MORE INFORMATION

Local   Apache documentation: With Apache running and the **httpd-manual** package installed, point a browser at *server*/**manual**. On the server system, substitute **localhost** for *server*; from a remote system, substitute the name or IP address of the Apache server for *server*. If Apache is not running, point a browser on the server system only at **/var/www/manual/index.html**.
Apache directives: *server*/**manual/mod/directives.html**
SSI directives: *server*/**manual/howto/ssi.html**

Web   Apache documentation: httpd.apache.org/docs/2.2
Apache directives: httpd.apache.org/docs/2.2/mod/directives.html
Apache Software Foundation (newsletters, mailing lists, projects, module registry, and more): www.apache.org
webalizer: www.mrunix.net/webalizer
awstats: awstats.sourceforge.net
mod_perl: perl.apache.org
mod_php: www.php.net
mod_python: www.modpython.org
mod_ssl: www.modssl.org
mod_wsgi: code.google.com/p/modwsgi
MRTG: oss.oetiker.ch/mrtg
SNMP: net-snmp.sourceforge.net
SSI directives: httpd.apache.org/docs/2.2/howto/ssi.html

NOTES

Terms: Apache and **httpd**   Apache is the name of a server that serves HTTP and other content. The Apache daemon is named **httpd** because it is an HTTP server daemon. This chapter uses the terms *Apache* and *httpd* interchangeably.

Terms: server and process   An Apache *server* is the same thing as an Apache *process*. An Apache child process exists to handle incoming client requests; hence it is referred to as a server.

Firewall   An Apache server normally uses TCP port 80; a secure server uses TCP port 443. If the Apache server system is running a firewall or is behind a firewall, you must open one or both of these ports. To get started, open port 80 (HTTP). Using system-config-firewall, select **WWW (HTTPD)** and/or **Secure WWW (HTTPS)** from the Trusted Services tab (page 894) to open these ports.

SELinux   When SELinux is set to use a targeted policy, **httpd** is protected by SELinux. You can disable this protection if necessary. For more information refer to "Setting the Targeted Policy with system-config-selinux" on page 463.

Running with **root** privileges   Because Apache serves content on privileged ports, you must start it running with **root** privileges. For security reasons, Fedora/RHEL sets up Apache to spawn processes that run as the user and group **apache**.

Locale   The **httpd** daemon starts using the C locale by default. You can modify this behavior—for example, to use the configured system locale—by setting the **HTTPD_LANG** variable in the **/etc/sysconfig/httpd** file.

Document root   The root of the directory hierarchy that Apache serves content from is called the *document root* and is controlled by the DocumentRoot directive (page 928). This directive defines a directory on the server that maps to **/**. This directory appears to users who are browsing a Web site as the root directory. As distributed by Fedora/RHEL, the document root is **/var/www/html**.

Modifying content   With the default Fedora/RHEL configuration of Apache, only a user working with **root** privileges can add or modify content in **/var/www/html**. To avoid having people work with **root** privileges when they are manipulating content, create a group (**webwork**, for example), put people who need to work with Web content in this group, and make the directory hierarchy starting at **/var/www/html** (or another document root) writable by that group. In addition, if you give the directory hierarchy setgid permission, all new files created within this hierarchy will belong to the group, which facilitates sharing files. The first three commands below add the new group, change the mode of the document root to setgid, and change the group that the document root belongs to. The last command adds *username* to the **webwork** group; you must repeat this command for each user you want to add to the group.

```
# groupadd webwork
# chmod g+rws /var/www/html
# chown :webwork /var/www/html

# usermod -aG webwork username
```

See page 604 for more information about working with groups.

Version   Fedora/RHEL runs Apache version 2.2.

RUNNING AN APACHE WEB SERVER

This section explains how to install, test, and configure a basic Web server.

PREREQUISITES

Minimal installation Install the following packages:

- **httpd**
- **apr** (Apache portable runtime; installed with **httpd**)
- **apr-util** (installed with **httpd**)

Before you set up an Apache server

tip Before you configure an Apache server, set up a static IP address for the server system. See "Configuring a Static IP Address for a NIC" on page 652 for instructions.

httpd init script Run chkconfig to cause **httpd** to start when the system enters multiuser mode:

```
# chkconfig httpd on
```

After you configure Apache, use service to start **httpd**:

```
# service httpd start
```

After changing the Apache configuration, restart **httpd** with the following command, which will not disturb clients connected to the server:

```
# service httpd graceful
```

Optional packages You might want to install the following optional packages:

- **httpd-manual**—The Apache manual; see "Local" on page 919 for more information
- **webalizer**—Web server log analyzer (page 963)
- **awstats**—Web server log analyzer
- **mod_perl**—Embedded Perl scripting language
- **mod_python**—Metapackage that installs the embedded Python scripting language (Fedora only)
- **mod_wsgi**—Alternative Python scripting language
- **mod_ssl**—Secure Sockets Layer extension (page 958)
- **mod-php**—Embedded PHP scripting language, including IMAP and LDAP support
- **mrtg**—MRTG traffic monitor (page 964)
- **net-snmp** and **net-snmp-utils**—SNMP, required for MRTG (page 964)

JumpStart I: Getting Apache Up and Running

To get Apache up and running, modify the **/etc/httpd/conf/httpd.conf** configuration file as described in this section. "Directives I: Directives You Might Want to Modify as You Get Started" on page 925 explains more about this file and explores other changes you might want to make to it.

MODIFYING THE httpd.conf CONFIGURATION FILE

Apache runs as installed, but it is a good idea to add/modify the three lines of the **/etc/httpd/conf/httpd.conf** configuration file described in this section before starting Apache. If you do not add/modify these lines, Apache will assign values that might not work on the server.

ServerName   The ServerName line establishes a name for the server. Add one of the following lines to **httpd.conf** to set the name of the server to the domain name of the server or, if you do not have a domain name, to the IP address of the server. Add the line just below the commented out ServerName line in the **httpd.conf** file. The commented-out line specifies port 80 (**:80** at the end of the line); port 80 is the default so you do not need to specify it.

> ServerName *example.com*

or

> ServerName *IP_address*

where *example.com* is the domain name of the server and *IP_address* is the IP address of the server. If you are not connected to a network, you can use the **localhost** address, 127.0.0.1, so you can start the server and experiment with it. See page 928 for more information on the ServerName directive.

ServerAdmin and ServerSignature   When a client has trouble getting information from a server, the server typically displays an error page that identifies the problem. For example, when Apache cannot find a requested page, it displays an error page that says **Error 404: Not Found**. The ServerSignature directive (page 942) enables you to add a signature line to server-generated pages, including error pages. You can turn the signature line on or off using this directive. You can also specify that the signature line include a **mailto:** link that the user can click to send mail to the server's administrator. This link appears as the domain name the user called in the Browser. The ServerAdmin (page 927) directive specifies the email address that the server sends mail to when a user clicks the link on an error page. Change these two lines in **httpd.conf**.

> ServerAdmin *email_address*

> ServerSignature *EMail*

where *email_address* is the email address of the person who needs to know when people are having trouble using the server. Make sure that someone checks this email account frequently. But also see the tip "ServerAdmin attracts spam" on page 927.

It can make system administration much easier if you use a role alias (for example, **webmaster@example.com**) instead of a specific username (e.g., **max@example.com**) as an *email_address*. See the discussion of email aliases on page 736.

After making changes to **httpd.conf**, start or restart **httpd** as explained on page 921.

TESTING APACHE

Once you start the **httpd** daemon, you can confirm that Apache is working correctly by pointing a browser on the local (server) system to **http://localhost/**. From a remote system, point a browser to **http://** followed by the ServerName you specified in the previous section. If you are displaying a page from a system other than the local one, the local system must know how to resolve a domain name you enter (e.g., by using DNS or the **/etc/hosts** file). For example, you might use either of these URI formats: **http://192.168.0.16** or **http://example.org**.

The browser should display the Fedora/RHEL test page, which is actually an error page that says there is no content. For more information refer to "Fedora/RHEL test page" on page 949. If the server is behind a firewall, open TCP port 80 (page 920). If you are having problems getting Apache to work, see "Troubleshooting" on page 956.

PUTTING CONTENT IN PLACE

Place the content you want Apache to serve in **/var/www/html**. Apache automatically displays the file named **index.html** in this directory. Working with **root** privileges (or as a member of the group you set up for this purpose [e.g., **webwork**]), create such a page:

```
# cat /var/www/html/index.html
<html><body><p>This is <i>my</i> test page.</p></body></html>
```

After you create this file, either refresh the page on the browser (if it is still running) or restart the browser and point it at the server. The browser should display the page you created.

FILESYSTEM LAYOUT

This section lists the locations and uses of files you can work with to configure Apache and serve Web pages.

Binaries, scripts, and modules   The Apache server and related binary files are kept in several directories:

/usr/sbin/httpd—The Apache server (daemon).

/usr/sbin/apachectl—Starts and stops Apache. The **httpd** init script calls apachectl.

/usr/bin/htpasswd—Creates and maintains the password files used by the Apache authentication module (page 961).

/usr/sbin/rotatelogs—Rotates Apache log files so that these files do not get too large. See logrotate (page 621) for more information.

/etc/httpd/modules—Holds module binaries. Two of the most frequently used module binary files are **mod_perl.so** (**mod_perl** package) and **mod_python.so** or **mod_wsgi.so** (**mod_python** or **mod_wsgi** packages). This directory is a symbolic link to **/usr/lib/httpd/modules** (page 957).

Configuration files   Apache configuration files are kept in the **/etc/httpd/conf** and **/etc/httpd/conf.d** directories:

> **/etc/httpd/conf/httpd.conf**—Holds local configuration directives. This file is the main Apache configuration file. The discussion of configuration directives starts on page 925. Refer to "The Fedora/RHEL **httpd.conf** File" on page 947 for a description of the **httpd.conf** file.

> **/etc/httpd/conf/magic**—Provides *MIME* (page 1176) file type identification (the MIME hints file). It is not normally changed. See *magic number* (page 1174) for more information.

> **/etc/pki/tls/certs**—Holds files and directories used by **mod_ssl** (page 958).

> **/etc/httpd/conf.d**—Holds configuration files including **php** and **mod_perl**.

Logs   Log files are kept in **/var/log/httpd** (there is a symbolic link at **/etc/httpd/logs**):

> **/var/log/httpd/access_log**—Logs requests made to the server.

> **/var/log/httpd/error_log**—Logs request and runtime server errors.

> **/var/log/httpd/ssl_*_log**—Holds **mod_ssl** logs.

Web documents   Web documents (including the Web pages displayed by client browsers), custom error messages, and CGI scripts are kept in **/var/www** by default:

> **/var/www/cgi-bin**—Holds CGI scripts (page 958).

> **/var/www/error**—Holds default error documents. You can modify these documents to conform to the style of your Web site. This directory is aliased to **/error/**. See ErrorDocument (page 939).

> **/var/www/icons**—Holds icons used to display directory entries. This directory is aliased to **/icons/**.

> **/var/www/manual**—Holds the Apache Server Manual. Present only if the **httpd-manual** package is installed.

Document root   By default, the document root (page 920) is **/var/www/html**. You can change this location with the DocumentRoot directive (page 928). In addition to content for the Web pages that Apache serves, this directory can house the **usage** directory, which holds webalizer (page 963) output.

.htaccess files   A **.htaccess** file contains configuration directives and can appear in any directory in the document root hierarchy. The location of a **.htaccess** file is critical: The directives in a **.htaccess** file apply to all files in the hierarchy rooted at the directory that holds the **.htaccess** file. You must use an AllowOverride directive to cause Apache to examine **.htaccess** files and process directives in those files. This protection is duplicated and enhanced in the **httpd.conf** file distributed by Fedora/RHEL, where a directive instructs Apache not to serve files whose names start with **.ht**. Because of this directive, Apache does not serve **.htaccess** files (nor does it serve **.htpasswd** files).

CONFIGURATION DIRECTIVES

Configuration directives, or simply *directives,* are lines in a configuration file that control some aspect of how Apache functions. A configuration directive is composed of a keyword followed by one or more arguments separated by SPACEs. For example, the following configuration directive sets **Timeout** to 300 (seconds):

```
Timeout 300
```

You must enclose arguments that contain SPACEs within double quotation marks. Keywords are not case sensitive, but arguments (pathnames, filenames, and so on) often are.

httpd.conf   The main file that holds Apache configuration directives is, by default, **/etc/httpd/conf/httpd.conf**. This file holds global directives that affect all content served by Apache. An Include directive (page 943) within **httpd.conf** can incorporate the contents of another file as though it were part of **httpd.conf**.

.htaccess   Local directives can appear in **.htaccess** files. A **.htaccess** file can appear in any directory within the document root hierarchy; it affects files in the directory hierarchy rooted at the directory it appears in.

Pathnames   When you specify an absolute pathname in a configuration directive, the directive uses that pathname without modifying it. When you specify a relative pathname, such as a simple filename or the name of a directory, Apache prepends to that name the value specified by the ServerRoot (page 941) directive (**/etc/httpd** by default).

DIRECTIVES I: DIRECTIVES YOU MIGHT WANT TO MODIFY AS YOU GET STARTED

When it starts, Apache reads the **/etc/httpd/conf/httpd.conf** configuration file (by default) for instructions governing every aspect of how Apache runs and serves content. The **httpd.conf** file shipped with Fedora/RHEL is more than 1,000 lines long.

This section details some directives you might want to change as you are getting started with Apache. You can use each of the following directives in **httpd.conf**. The **Context** line in each explanation tells you which locations the directives can appear in; contexts are explained on page 930. The section titled "Directives II: Advanced Directives" on page 935 describes more directives.

Listen   *Specifies the IP address and port that Apache listens for requests on.*

Listen [IP-address:]portnumber

where **IP-address** is the IP address that Apache listens on and **portnumber** is the number of the port that Apache listens on for the given **IP-address**. When **IP-address** is absent or is set to 0.0.0.0, Apache listens on all network interfaces. At least one Listen directive must appear in the configuration files or Apache will not work.

The following minimal directive from the **httpd.conf** file listens for requests on all interfaces on port 80:

```
Listen 80
```

The next directive changes the port from the default value of 80 to 8080:

```
Listen 8080
```

When you specify a port other than 80, each request to the server must include a port number (as in **www.example.org:8080**) or the kernel will return a **Connection Refused** message. Use multiple Listen directives to have Apache listen on multiple IP addresses and ports. For example,

```
Listen 80
Listen 192.168.1.1:8080
Listen 192.168.1.2:443
```

accepts connections on all network interfaces on port 80, on 192.168.1.1 on port 8080, and on 192.168.1.2 on port 443.

Context: **server config**
Default: none (Apache will not start without this directive)
Fedora/RHEL: Listen 80

Redirect   *Tells the client to fetch a requested resource from a different, specified location.*

*Redirect [**status**] **requested-path** [**new-URI**]*

where *status* is the status that Apache returns along with the redirect. If you omit *status*, Apache assumes **temp**. The *status* can be an Apache error code in the range 300–399 or one of the following:

permanent	Returns status 301 (the resource has moved permanently)
temp	Returns status 302 (the resource has moved temporarily)
seeother	Returns status 303 (the resource has been replaced)
gone	Returns status 410 (the resource has been removed—does not take a *new-URI* argument)

The *requested-path* is the absolute pathname of the ordinary file or directory that Apache is to redirect requests for. Apache redirects all requests that start with the absolute pathname specified by *requested-path* (see the example below). Use RedirectMatch (discussed next) if you want to use a regular expression in this argument.

The *new-URI* is the URI that Apache redirects requests to. If the *new-URI* starts with a slash (**/**) and not **http://**, **ftp://**, or a similar prefix, Apache uses the same prefix it was called with. Most Redirect directives require a *new-URI* argument.

A request must match all segments of the *requested-path* argument. Assume the following directive:

```
Redirect /www.example.com/pictures http://pictures.example.com/
```

Apache will redirect a request for **http://www.example.com/pictures/mom.jpg** to **http://pictures.example.com/mom.jpg** but, because the final segment does not match, it will not redirect a request for **http://www.example.com/pictures_mom.jpg**.

Contexts: **server config, virtual host, directory, .htaccess**
Default: none
Fedora/RHEL: none

RedirectMatch   *Tells the client to fetch a requested resource from a different location specified by a regular expression.*

*RedirectMatch [**status**] **requested-path-re** [**new-URI**]*

This directive is the same as Redirect (discussed on the previous page), except you can use a regular expression (Appendix A) in *requested-path-re*.

Contexts: **server config, virtual host, directory, .htaccess**
Default: none
Fedora/RHEL: none

ServerAdmin   *Sets the email address used in **mailto:** links on error pages.*

*ServerAdmin **email-address***

where ***email-address*** is the email address of the person who is responsible for managing the Web content. Apache includes this address as a link on Apache-generated error pages. However, Fedora/RHEL sets ServerSignature (page 942) to **On**, which causes Apache to display information about the server—rather than a link to an email address—on error pages. If you want Apache to display the link on error pages, set ServerSignature to **EMail**. Make sure *email-address* points to an email account that someone checks frequently. Users can use this address to get help with the Web site or to inform the administrator of problems. There is no default value for ServerAdmin; if you do not use this directive and ServerSignature is set to **EMail**, the **mailto:** link on error pages points to [**no address given**].

ServerAdmin attracts spam

security   The email address you put in ServerAdmin often attracts spam. Use a spam-guarded address such as **"mgs at sobell dot com"** (you must use the quotation marks) or use a custom error page to point to a Web page with a form for sending mail to the right person.

You can use a role alias such as **webmaster** at your domain and use a mail alias to forward mail that is sent to **webmaster** to the person who is responsible for maintaining the Web site. See the discussion of mail aliases on page 736.

Contexts: **server config, virtual host**
Default: none
Fedora/RHEL: **root@localhost**

ServerName   *Specifies the server's name and the port it listens on.*

ServerName FQDN [:port]

where *FQDN* is the fully qualified domain name or IP address of the server and *port* is the optional port number Apache listens on. The domain name of the server must be able to be resolved (by DNS or **/etc/hosts**) and might differ from the hostname of the system running the server. If you do not specify a ServerName, Apache performs a DNS reverse name resolution (page 856) on the system's IP address and assigns that value to ServerName. If the reverse lookup fails, Apache assigns the system's IP address to ServerName.

Fedora/RHEL provides the following ServerName template in the **httpd.conf** file:

```
#ServerName www.example.com:80
```

Copy this line, remove the **#**, and substitute the FQDN or IP address of the server for **www.example.com**. You can omit the **:80** because it specifies the default port. Change the 80 to the port number Apache listens on if it does not listen on port 80.

```
ServerName www.example.com:80
```

The ports specified by ServerName and Listen (page 925) must be the same if you want the FQDN specified by ServerName to be tied to the IP address specified by the Listen directive.

Apache uses ServerName to construct a URI when it redirects a client (page 950). See also UseCanonicalName (page 937).

Contexts: **server config, virtual host**
Default: none
Fedora/RHEL: none

DocumentRoot   *Points to the root of the directory hierarchy that holds the server's content.*

DocumentRoot dirname

where *dirname* is the absolute pathname of the directory at the root of the directory hierarchy that holds the content Apache serves. Do not use a trailing slash. The FHS (page 199) specifies **/srv** as the top-level directory for this purpose. You can put the document root wherever you like, as long as the user **apache** has read access to the ordinary files and execute access to the directory files in the directory hierarchy. Access control includes both discretionary access controls (chmod, including ACLs for the user **apache**) and mandatory access controls (selinux for **httpd**). The following directive puts the document root at **/srv/www**:

```
DocumentRoot /srv/www
```

Contexts: **server config, virtual host**
Default: **/usr/local/apache/htdocs**
Fedora/RHEL: **/var/www/html**

You might want to change the location of the document root

tip By design, the **/var** directory hierarchy (page 39) is designed to hold data that changes frequently, which is not usually the case with static Web site data. Data in such a partition is more likely to become corrupted than data in a partition that holds static data. Thus you might want to place Web site data in a different partition. Good candidates for the document root include **/usr/local** (holds site-specific data), **/home/www** (the home directory is frequently backed up while other directories might not be, and **/srv/www** (specified by FHS).

UserDir   *Allows users to publish content from their home directories.*

*UserDir **dirname** | disabled | enabled **user-list***

where ***dirname*** is the name of a directory that, if it appears in a local user's home directory, Apache publishes to the Web. When you do not specify a ***dirname***, Apache publishes content in **~/public_html**. The ***disabled*** keyword prevents content from being published from users' home directories; ***enabled*** causes content to be published from the home directories of users specified in the SPACE-separated ***user-list***.

Apache can combine the effects of multiple UserDir directives. For example, assume you use the following directives:

```
UserDir disabled
UserDir enabled user1 user2 user3
UserDir web
```

The first directive turns off user publishing for all users. The second directive enables user publishing for three users. The third directive makes **web** the name of the directory that, if it appears in one of the specified users' home directories, Apache publishes to the Web.

To cause a browser to display the content published by a user, specify in the location bar the name of the Web site followed by a **/~** and the user's username. For example, if Sam published content in the **public_html** directory in his home directory and the URI of the Web site was **www.example.com**, you would enter **http://www.example.com/~sam** to display Sam's Web page. To display a user's Web page, Apache must have execute permission (as user **apache**) for the user's home directory and the directory holding the content, and read permission for the content files.

Fedora/RHEL provides the following ServerName directive and template in the **httpd.conf** file. Because the statements are in an IfModule container (page 948), they are executed only if the **mod_userdir** module is loaded, which it is by default.

```
<IfModule mod_userdir.c>
    UserDir disabled
    #UserDir public_html
</IfModule>
```

Put a hashmark (#) in front of the first line and remove the hashmark from the second line to allow users to publish content from directories named **public_html** in their home directories.

Contexts: **server config, virtual host**
Default: none
Fedora/RHEL: disabled

DirectoryIndex   *Specifies which file Apache serves when a user requests a directory.*

*DirectoryIndex **filename** [**filename** ...]*

where **filename** is the name of the file that Apache serves.

This directive specifies a list of filenames. When a client requests a directory, Apache attempts to find a file in the specified directory whose name matches a file in the list. When Apache finds a match, it returns that file. When this directive is absent or when none of the files specified by this directive exists in the specified directory, Apache displays a directory listing as specified by the IndexOptions directive (page 940).

Fedora/RHEL provides the following DirectoryIndex directive in the **httpd.conf** file:

```
DirectoryIndex index.html index.html.var
```

This directive causes Apache to search the specified directory and return the file named **index.html**, which is the name of the standard, default HTML document. If you supply CGI documents, you might want to add the **index.cgi** value to this directive. The name **index** is standard but arbitrary.

A **.var** filename extension denotes a content-negotiated document that allows Apache to serve documents in one of several languages as specified by the client. If you are not providing content in different languages, you can omit this filename extension from the DirectoryIndex directive. For more information refer to "Type Maps" on page 951.

Contexts: **server config, virtual host**
Default: **index.html**
Fedora/RHEL: **index.html index.html.var**

CONTEXTS AND CONTAINERS

To make it flexible and easy to customize, Apache uses configuration directives, contexts, and containers. Configuration directives were covered in the previous section. This section discusses contexts and containers, which are critical to managing an Apache server.

CONTEXTS

Four locations, called *contexts*, define where configuration directives can appear. This chapter marks each configuration directive to indicate which context(s) it can appear in. Table 26-1 describes each of these contexts.

Table 26-1 Contexts

Context	Location(s) directives can appear
server config	In the **httpd.conf** file or included files only, but not inside <VirtualHost> or <Directory> containers (next section) unless so marked
virtual host	Inside <VirtualHost> containers in the **httpd.conf** file or included files only
directory	Inside <Directory>, <Location>, and <Files> containers in the **httpd.conf** file or included files only
.htaccess	In **.htaccess** files (page 924) only

Directives in files incorporated by means of an Include directive (page 943) are part of the context they are included in and must be allowed in that context.

Putting a directive in the wrong context generates a configuration error and can cause Apache not to serve content correctly or not to start.

CONTAINERS

Containers, or *special directives*, are directives that group other directives. Containers are delimited by XML-style tags. Three examples are shown here:

```
<Directory> ... </Directory>

<Location> ... </Location>

<VirtualHost> ... </VirtualHost>
```

Look in **httpd.conf** for examples of containers. Like other directives, containers are limited to use within specified contexts. This section describes some of the more frequently used containers.

<Directory> *Applies directives to all directories within the specified directory hierarchy.*

*<Directory **directory**> ... </Directory>*

where ***directory*** is an absolute pathname specifying the root of the directory hierarchy that holds the directories the directives in the container apply to. The ***directory*** can include wildcards; a * does not match a /.

A <Directory> container provides the same functionality as a **.htaccess** file. While an administrator can use a <Directory> container in Apache configuration files, regular users cannot. Regular users can use **.htaccess** files to control access to their own directories.

The directives in the <Directory> container shown in the following example apply to the **/var/www/html/corp** directory hierarchy. The Deny directive denies access to all clients, the Allow directive grants clients from the 192.168.10. subnet access, and the AllowOverride directive (page 945) enables Apache to process directives in **.htaccess** files in the hierarchy:

```
<Directory /var/www/html/corp>
    Deny from all
    Allow from 192.168.10.
    AllowOverride All
</Directory>
```

Contexts: **server config, virtual host**

<Files> *Applies directives to specified ordinary files.*

*<Files **directory**> ... </Files>*

where **directory** is an absolute pathname specifying the root of the directory hierarchy that holds the ordinary files the directives in the container apply to. The **directory** can include wildcards; a * does not match a /. This container is similar to <Directory> but applies to ordinary files rather than to directories.

The following directive, from the Fedora/RHEL **httpd.conf** file, denies access to all files whose filenames start with **.ht**, meaning that Apache will not serve these files. The tilde (~) changes how Apache interprets the following string. Without a tilde, the string is a simple shell match that interprets shell special characters (page 244). With a tilde, Apache interprets the string as a regular expression (page 1105):

```
Files ~ "^\.ht">
    Order allow,deny
    Deny from all
    Satisfy All
</Files>
```

Contexts: **server config, virtual host, directory, .htaccess**

<IfModule> *Applies directives if a specified module is loaded.*

*<IfModule [!]**module-name**> ... </IfModule>*

where **module-name** is the name of the module (page 957) tested for. Apache executes the directives in this container if **module-name** is loaded or with **!** if **module-name** is not loaded.

Apache will not start if you specify a configuration directive that is specific to a module that is not loaded.

The following <IfModule> container, which is located in the Fedora/RHEL **httpd.conf** file, depends on the **mod_mime_magic.c** module being loaded. If this module is loaded, Apache runs the MIMEMagicFile directive, which tells the **mod_mime_magic.c** module where its hints file is located.

```
<IfModule mod_mime_magic.c>
#   MIMEMagicFile /usr/share/magic.mime
    MIMEMagicFile conf/magic
</IfModule>
```

See page 948 for another example of an <IfModule> container.

Contexts: **server config, virtual host, directory, .htaccess**

<Limit>   *Limits access-control directives to specified HTTP methods.*

*<Limit **method** [**method**] ... > ... </Limit>*

where **method** is an HTTP method. An HTTP method specifies which action is to be performed on a URI. The most frequently used methods are GET, PUT, POST, and OPTIONS; method names are case sensitive. GET (the default method) sends any data indicated by the URI. PUT stores data from the body section of the communication at the specified URI. POST creates a new document containing the body of the request at the specified URI. OPTIONS requests information about the capabilities of the server.

The <Limit> container binds a group of access-control directives to specified HTTP methods: Only methods named by this container are affected by this group of directives.

The following example disables HTTP uploads (PUTs) from systems that are not in a subdomain of **example.com**:

```
<Limit PUT>
    order deny,allow
    deny from all
    allow from .example.com
</Limit>
```

Contexts: **server config, virtual host, directory, .htaccess**

Use <LimitExcept> instead of <Limit>

caution   It is safer to use the <LimitExcept> container than to use the <Limit> container, as the former protects against arbitrary methods. When you use <Limit>, you must be careful to name explicitly all possible methods that the group of directives could affect.

<LimitExcept>   *Limits access-control directives to all except specified HTTP methods.*

*<LimitExcept **method** [**method**] ... > ... </LimitExcept>*

where **method** is an HTTP method. See <Limit> for a discussion of methods.

This container causes a group of access-control directives *not* to be bound to specified HTTP methods. Thus methods *not* named in <LimitExcept> are affected by this group of directives.

The access-control directives within the following <LimitExcept> container affect HTTP methods other than GET, POST, and OPTIONS. You could put this container in a <Directory> container to limit its scope:

```
<LimitExcept GET POST OPTIONS>
    Order deny,allow
    Deny from all
</LimitExcept>
```

Contexts: **server config, virtual host, directory, .htaccess**

<Location>   *Applies directives to specified URIs.*

<Location URI> ... </Location>

where *URI* points to content; it specifies a file or the root of the directory hierarchy that the directives in the container apply to. While the <Directory> container points within the local filesystem, <Location> points outside the local filesystem. The *URI* can include wildcards; a * does not match a /.

The following <Location> container limits access to **http://*server*/pop** to clients from the **example.net** domain, where *server* is the FQDN of the server:

```
<Location /pop>
    Order deny,allow
    Deny from all
    Allow from .example.net
</Location>
```

Contexts: **server config, virtual host**

Use <Location> with care

caution   Use this powerful container with care. Do not use it to replace the <Directory> container: When several URIs point to the same location in a filesystem, a client might be able to circumvent the desired access control by using a URI not specified by this container.

<LocationMatch>   *Applies directives to URIs specified by a regular expression.*

<LocationMatch regexp> ... </LocationMatch>

where *regexp* is a regular expression that matches one or more URIs. This container works the same way as <Location>, except that it applies to any URIs that *regexp* matches.

Contexts: **server config, virtual host**

<VirtualHost>   *Applies directives to a specified virtual host.*

<VirtualHost addr[:port] [addr[:port]] ... > ... </VirtualHost>

where *addr* is the IP address (or FQDN, although it is not recommended) of the virtual host (or * to represent all addresses) and *port* is the port that Apache listens on for the virtual host. This directive does not control which addresses and ports Apache listens on; use a Listen directive (page 925) for that purpose. This container holds commands that Apache applies to a virtual host. For more information see "NameVirtualHost" on page 936 and "Virtual Hosts" on page 953.

Context: **server config**

DIRECTIVES II: ADVANCED DIRECTIVES

This section discusses configuration directives that you might want to use after you have gained some experience with Apache.

DIRECTIVES THAT CONTROL PROCESSES

MaxClients *Specifies the maximum number of child processes.*

*MaxClients **num***

where **num** is the maximum number of child processes (servers) Apache runs at one time, including idle processes and processes serving requests. When Apache is running **num** processes and there are no idle processes, Apache issues **Server too busy** errors to new connections; it does not start new child processes.

Context: **server config**
Default: 256
Fedora/RHEL: 256

MaxRequestsPerChild

Specifies the maximum number of requests a child process can serve.

*MaxRequestsPerChild **num***

where **num** is the maximum number of requests a child process (server) can serve during its lifetime. After a child process serves **num** requests, it does not process any more requests but dies after it finishes processing its current requests. Apache can start another child process to replace the one that dies. Additional requests are processed by other processes from the server pool.

Set **num** to 0 to not set a limit on the number of requests a child can process, except for the effects of MinSpareServers. By limiting the lives of processes, this directive can prevent memory leaks from consuming too much system memory. However, setting MaxRequestsPerChild to a too-small value can hurt performance by causing Apache to create new child servers constantly.

Context: **server config**
Default: 10000
Fedora/RHEL: 4000

MaxSpareServers *Specifies the maximum number of idle processes.*

*MaxSpareServers **num***

where **num** is the maximum number of idle processes (servers) Apache keeps running to serve requests as they come in. Do not set this number too high, as each process consumes system resources.

Context: **server config**
Default: 10
Fedora/RHEL: 20

MinSpareServers *Specifies the minimum number of idle processes.*

MinSpareServers **num**

where **num** is the minimum number of idle processes (servers) Apache keeps running to serve requests as they come in. More idle processes occupy more computer resources; increase this value for busy sites only.

Context: **server config**
Default: 5
Fedora/RHEL: 5

NameVirtualHost

Specifies the address and port for a name-based (host-by-name) virtual host.

NameVirtualHost **addr[:port]**

where **addr** is the IP address (or FQDN, although it is not recommended) that Apache will use for serving a name-based virtual host and **port** is the port that Apache listens on for that virtual host. Specify **addr** as * to cause the server to process requests on all interfaces as name-based virtual hosts.

This directive does not control which addresses and ports Apache listens on; use a Listen directive (page 925) for that purpose. For more information see "<VirtualHost>" on page 934 and "Virtual Hosts" on page 953.

Context: **server config**
Default: none
Fedora/RHEL: none

StartServers *Specifies the number of child processes that Apache starts with.*

StartServers **num**

where **num** is the number of child processes (servers) that Apache starts when it is brought up. This value is significant only when Apache starts; MinSpareServers and MaxSpareServers control the number of idle processes once Apache is up and running. Starting Apache with multiple servers ensures that a pool of servers is waiting to serve requests immediately.

Context: **server config**
Default: 5
Fedora/RHEL: 8

NETWORKING DIRECTIVES

HostnameLookups

Specifies whether Apache puts a client's hostname or its IP address in the logs.

HostnameLookups On | Off | Double

On: Performs DNS reverse name resolution (page 856) to determine the hostname of each client for logging purposes.

Off: Logs each client's IP address.

Double: To provide greater security, performs DNS reverse name resolution (page 856) to determine the hostname of each client, performs a forward DNS lookup to verify the original IP address, and logs the hostname. Denies access if it cannot verify the original IP address.

Contexts: **server config, virtual host, directory**
Default: Off
Fedora/RHEL: Off

Lookups can consume a lot of system resources

tip Use the **On** and **Double** options with caution: They can consume a lot of resources on a busy system. You can use a program such as logresolve to perform reverse name resolution offline for statistical purposes.

If you perform hostname resolution offline, you run the risk that the name might have changed; you usually want the name that was current at the time of the request. To minimize this problem, perform the hostname resolution as soon as possible after writing the log.

Timeout *Specifies the amount of time Apache waits for network operations to complete.*

Timeout num

where **num** is the number of seconds that Apache waits for network operations to finish. You can usually set this directive to a lower value; five minutes is a long time to wait on a busy server. The Apache documentation says the default is not lower "because there may still be odd places in the code where the timer is not reset when a packet is sent."

Context: **server config**
Default: 300
Fedora/RHEL: 60

UseCanonicalName

Specifies the method the server uses to identify itself.

UseCanonicalName On | Off | DNS

On: Apache uses the value of the ServerName directive (page 928) as its identity.

Off: Apache uses the name and port from the incoming request as its identity.

DNS: Apache performs a DNS reverse name resolution (page 856) on the IP address from the incoming request and uses the result as its identity. Rarely used.

This directive is important when a server has more than one name and needs to perform a redirect. Fedora/RHEL sets this directive to Off because the ServerName directive (page 928) is commented out. Once you set ServerName, change UseCanonicalName to **On**. See page 951 for a discussion of redirects and this directive.

Contexts: **server config, virtual host, directory**
Default: Off
Fedora/RHEL: Off

LOGGING DIRECTIVES

ErrorLog *Specifies where Apache sends error messages.*

*ErrorLog **filename** | syslog[:**facility**]*

where **filename** specifies the name of the file, relative to ServerRoot (page 941), that Apache sends error messages to. The *syslog* keyword specifies that Apache send errors to **syslogd** (page 623); **facility** specifies which **syslogd** facility to use. The default facility is **local7**.

Contexts: **server config, virtual host**
Default: **logs/error_log**
Fedora/RHEL: **logs/error_log**

LogLevel *Specifies the level of error messages that Apache logs.*

*LogLevel **level***

where **level** specifies that Apache log errors of that level and higher (more urgent). Choose **level** from the following list, which is presented here in order of decreasing urgency and increasing verbosity:

emerg   System unusable messages
alert   Need for immediate action messages
crit   Critical condition messages
error   Error condition messages
warn   Nonfatal warning messages
notice   Normal but significant messages
info   Operational messages and recommendations
debug   Messages for finding and solving problems

Contexts: **server config, virtual host**
Default: warn
Fedora/RHEL: warn

DIRECTIVES THAT CONTROL CONTENT

AddHandler *Creates a mapping between filename extensions and a builtin Apache handler.*

*AddHandler **handler extension** [**extension**] ...*

where **handler** is the name of a builtin handler and **extension** is a filename extension that maps to the **handler**. Handlers are actions that are built into Apache and are directly related to loaded modules. Apache uses a handler when a client requests a file with a specified filename extension.

For example, the following AddHandler directive causes Apache to process files that have a filename extension of **.cgi** with the **cgi-script** handler:

```
AddHandler cgi-script .cgi
```

See "Type Maps" on page 951 for another example of an AddHandler directive.

Contexts: **server config, virtual host, directory, .htaccess**
Default: none
Fedora/RHEL: type-map var

Alias   *Maps a URI to a directory or file.*

*Alias **alias pathname***

where ***alias*** must match part of the URI that the client requested to invoke the alias. The ***pathname*** is the absolute pathname of the target of the alias, usually a directory.

For example, the following alias causes Apache to serve **/usr/local/pix/milk.jpg** when a client requests **http://www.example.com/pix/milk.jpg**:

```
Alias /pix /usr/local/pix
```

In some cases, you need to use a <Directory> container (page 931) to grant access to aliased content.

Contexts: **server config, virtual host**
Default: none
Fedora/RHEL: **/icons/ /var/www/icons/** and **/error/ /var/www/error/**

ErrorDocument   *Specifies the action Apache takes when the specified error occurs.*

*ErrorDocument **code action***

where ***code*** is the error code (page 964) this directive defines a response for and ***action*** is one of the following:

string—Defines the message that Apache returns to the client.

absolute pathname—Points to a local script or other content that Apache redirects the client to.

URI—Points to an external script or other content that Apache redirects the client to.

When you do not specify this directive for a given error code, Apache returns a hardcoded error message when that error occurs. See page 949 for an explanation of how an ErrorDocument directive returns the Fedora/RHEL test page when Apache is first installed.

Some examples of ErrorDocument directives follow:

```
ErrorDocument 403 "Sorry, access is forbidden."
ErrorDocument 403 /cgi-bin/uh-uh.pl
ErrorDocument 403 http://errors.example.com/not_allowed.html
```

Contexts: **server config, virtual host, directory, .htaccess**
Default: none; Apache returns hardcoded error messages
Fedora/RHEL: 403 /error/noindex.html; refer to "Fedora/RHEL test page" on page 949

IndexOptions *Specifies how Apache displays directory listings.*

IndexOptions [±]option [[±]option] ...

where **option** can be any combination of the following:

DescriptionWidth=*n*—Sets the width of the description column to *n* characters. Use ✳ in place of *n* to accommodate the widest description.

FancyIndexing—In directory listings, displays column headers that are links. When you click one of these links, Apache sorts the display based on the content of the column. Clicking the link a second time reverses the order.

FoldersFirst—Sorts the listing so that directories come before plain files. Use only with FancyIndexing.

HTMLTable—Displays a directory listing in a table.

IconsAreLinks—Makes the icons clickable. Use only with FancyIndexing.

IconHeight=*n*—Sets the height of icons to *n* pixels. Use only with IconWidth.

IconWidth=*n*—Sets the width of icons to *n* pixels. Use only with IconHeight.

IgnoreCase—Ignores case when sorting names.

IgnoreClient—Ignores options the client supplied in the URI.

NameWidth=*n*—Sets the width of the filename column to *n* characters. Use ✳ in place of *n* to accommodate the widest filename.

ScanHTMLTitles—Extracts and displays titles from HTML documents. Use only with FancyIndexing. Not normally used because it is CPU- and disk-intensive.

SuppressColumnSorting—Suppresses clickable column headings that can be used for sorting columns. Use only with FancyIndexing.

SuppressDescription—Suppresses file descriptions. Use only with FancyIndexing.

SuppressHTMLPreamble—Suppresses the contents of the file specified by the HeaderName directive, even if that file exists.

SuppressIcon—Suppresses icons. Use only with FancyIndexing.

SuppressLastModified—Suppresses the modification date. Use only with Fancy-Indexing.

SuppressRules—Suppresses horizontal lines. Use only with FancyIndexing.

SuppressSize—Suppresses file sizes. Use only with FancyIndexing.

VersionSort—Sorts version numbers (in filenames) in a natural way; character strings, except for substrings of digits, are not affected.

As an example of the use of IndexOptions, suppose a client requests a URI that points to a directory (such as **http://www.example.com/support/**) and none of the files specified by the DirectoryIndex directive (page 930) is present in that directory. If the directory hierarchy is controlled by a **.htaccess** file and AllowOverride (page 945) has been set to allow indexes, Apache displays a directory listing according to the options specified by this directive.

When an IndexOptions directive appears more than once within a directory, Apache merges the options from the directives. Use **+** and **−** to merge IndexOptions options with options from higher-level directories. (Unless you use **+** or **−** with all options, Apache discards any options set in higher-level directories.) For example, the following directives and containers set the options for **/custsup/download** to VersionSort; Apache discards FancyIndexing and IgnoreCase in the **download** directory because there is no **+** or **−** before VersionSort in the second <Directory> container:

```
<Directory /custsup>
    IndexOptions FancyIndexing
    IndexOptions IgnoreCase
</Directory>

<Directory /custsup/download>
    IndexOptions VersionSort
</Directory>
```

Because **+** appears before VersionSort, the following directives and containers set the options for **/custsup/download** to FancyIndexing, IgnoreCase, and VersionSort:

```
<Directory /custsup>
    IndexOptions FancyIndexing
    IndexOptions IgnoreCase
</Directory>

<Directory /custsup/download>
    IndexOptions +VersionSort
</Directory>
```

Contexts: **server config, virtual host, directory, .htaccess**
Default: none; lists only filenames
Fedora/RHEL: FancyIndexing VersionSort NameWidth=* HTMLTable
       Charset=UTF-8

ServerRoot *Specifies the root directory for server files (not content).*

ServerRoot **directory**

where **directory** specifies the pathname of the root directory for the files that make up the server. Apache prepends **directory** to relative pathnames in **httpd.conf**. This directive does not specify the location of the content that Apache serves; the DocumentRoot directive (page 928) performs that function. Do not change this value unless you move the server files.

Context: **server config**
Default: **/usr/local/apache**
Fedora/RHEL: **/etc/httpd**

ServerTokens   *Specifies the server information that Apache returns to a client.*

ServerTokens Prod | Major | Minor | Min | OS | Full

Prod: Returns the product name: **Apache**; also *ProductOnly*.

Major: Returns the major release number of the server: **Apache/2**.

Minor: Returns the major and minor release numbers of the server: **Apache/2.2**.

Min: Returns the complete version: **Apache/2.2.16**; also *Minimal*.

OS: Returns the name of the operating system and the complete version: **Apache/2.2.16 (Fedora)**. Provides less information that might help a malicious user than *Full* does.

Full: Same as *OS*, except that *Full* also sends the names and versions of non-ASF modules: **Apache/2.2.16 (Fedora) PHP/5.2.14**.

Unless you want clients to know the details of the software you are running, set ServerTokens to reveal as little as possible.

Context: **server config**
Default: Full
Fedora/RHEL: OS

ServerSignature   *Adds a line to server-generated pages.*

ServerSignature On | Off | EMail

On: Turns the signature line on. The signature line contains the server version as specified by the ServerTokens directive (above) and the name specified by the <VirtualHost> container (page 934).

Off: Turns the signature line off.

EMail: To the signature line, adds a **mailto:** link to the server email address. This option produces output that can attract spam. See ServerAdmin (page 927) for information on specifying an email address.

Contexts: **server config, virtual host, directory, .htaccess**
Default: Off
Fedora/RHEL: On

CONFIGURATION DIRECTIVES

Group   *Sets the GID of the processes that run the servers.*

Group #groupid | groupname

where *groupid* is a GID value, preceded by **#**, and *groupname* is the name of a group. The processes (servers) that Apache spawns are run as the group specified by this directive. See the User directive (page 944) for more information.

Context: **server config**
Default: #–1
Fedora/RHEL: apache

Include *Loads directives from files.*

Include *filename* | **directory**

where *filename* is the relative pathname of a file that contains directives. Apache prepends ServerRoot (page 941) to *filename*. The directives in *filename* are included in the file holding this directive at the location of the directive. Because *filename* can include wildcards, it can specify more than one file.

The *directory* is the relative pathname that specifies the root of a directory hierarchy that holds files containing directives. Apache prepends ServerRoot to *directory*. The directives in ordinary files in this hierarchy are included in the file holding this directive at the location of the directive. The *directory* can include wildcards.

When you install Apache and its modules, rpm puts configuration files, which have a filename extension of **conf**, in the **conf.d** directory within the ServerRoot directory. The Include directive in the Fedora/RHEL **httpd.conf** file incorporates module configuration files for whichever modules are installed.

Contexts: **server config, virtual host, directory**
Default: none
Fedora/RHEL: **conf.d/*.conf**

LoadModule *Loads a module.*

LoadModule **module** *filename*

where **module** is the name of an external DSO module and *filename* is the relative pathname of the named module. Apache prepends ServerRoot (page 941) to *filename* and loads the external module specified by this directive. For more information refer to "Modules" on page 957.

Context: **server config**
Default: none; nothing is loaded by default if this directive is omitted
Fedora/RHEL: loads more than 40 modules; refer to **httpd.conf** for a list

Options *Controls server features by directory.*

Options *[±]***option** *[[±]***option** *...]*

This directive controls which server features are enabled for a directory hierarchy. The directory hierarchy is specified by the container this directive appears in. A **+** or the absence of a **–** turns an option on, and a **–** turns it off.

The *option* might be one of the following:

None—None of the features this directive can control are enabled.

All—All of the features this directive can control are enabled, except for MultiViews, which you must explicitly enable.

ExecCGI—Apache can execute CGI scripts (page 958).

FollowSymLinks—Apache follows symbolic links.

Includes—Permits SSIs (server-side includes). SSIs are containers embedded in HTML pages that are evaluated on the server before the content is passed to the client.

IncludesNOEXEC—The same as Includes but disables the **#exec** and **#exec cgi** commands that are part of SSIs. Does *not* prevent the **#include** command from referencing CGI scripts.

Indexes—Generates a directory listing if DirectoryIndex (page 930) is not set.

MultiViews—Allows MultiViews (page 952).

SymLinksIfOwnerMatch—The same as FollowSymLinks but follows the link only if the file or directory being pointed to has the same owner as the link.

The following Options directive from the Fedora/RHEL **httpd.conf** file sets the Indexes and FollowSymLinks options and, because the <Directory> container specifies the **/var/www/html** directory hierarchy (the document root), affects all content:

```
<Directory "/var/www/html">
    Options Indexes FollowSymLinks
...
<Directory>
```

Context: **directory**
Default: All
Fedora/RHEL: Indexes, FollowSymLinks

ScriptAlias   *Maps a URI to a directory or file and declares the target to be a server (CGI) script.*

*ScriptAlias **alias pathname***

where **alias** must match part of the URI the client requested to invoke the Script-Alias. The **pathname** is the absolute pathname of the target of the alias, usually a directory. Similar to the Alias directive, this directive specifies the target is a CGI script (page 958).

The following ScriptAlias directive from the Fedora/RHEL **httpd.conf** file maps client requests that include **/cgi-bin/** to the **/var/www/cgi-bin** directory (and indicates that these requests will be treated as CGI requests):

```
ScriptAlias /cgi-bin/ "/var/www/cgi-bin/"
```

Contexts: **server config, virtual host**
Default: none
Fedora/RHEL: /cgi-bin/ "/var/www/cgi-bin"

User   *Sets the UID of the processes that run the servers.*

*User #**userid** | **username***

where **userid** is a UID value, preceded by **#**, and **username** is the name of a local user. The processes that Apache spawns are run as the user specified by this directive.

Apache must start with **root** privileges to listen on a privileged port. For reasons of security, Apache's child processes (servers) run as nonprivileged users. The default UID of –1 does not map to a user under **Fedora/RHEL**. Instead, the **Fedora/RHEL httpd** package creates a user named **apache** during installation and sets User to that user.

Context: **server config**
Default: #–1
Fedora/RHEL: **apache**

Do not set User to root or 0

security   For a more secure system, do not set User to **root** or **0** (zero) and do not allow the **apache** user to have write access to the DocumentRoot directory hierarchy (except as needed for storing data), especially not to configuration files.

SECURITY DIRECTIVES

Allow   *Specifies which clients can access specified content.*

Allow from All | host [host ...] | env=var [env=var ...]

This directive, which must be written as **Allow from**, grants access to a directory hierarchy to the specified clients. The directory hierarchy is specified by the container or **.htaccess** file this directive appears in. See the Order directive (page 946) for an example.

All—Serves content to any client.

host: Serves content to the client(s) specified by *host,* which can take several forms: an FQDN, a partial domain name (such as **example.com**), an IP address, a partial IP address, or a network/netmask pair.

var: Serves content when the environment variable named *var* is set. You can set a variable with the SetEnvIf directive. See the Order directive (page 946) for an example.

Contexts: **directory, .htaccess**
Default: none; default behavior depends on the Order directive
Fedora/RHEL: All

AllowOverride   *Specifies whether Apache examines .htaccess files and which classes of directives in those files it processes.*

AllowOverride All | None | directive-class [directive-class ...]

This directive specifies whether Apache examines **.htaccess** files in the directory hierarchy specified by its container. If Apache does examine **.htaccess** files, this directive specifies which classes of directives within **.htaccess** files Apache processes. See the tip on page 962 for performance considerations.

All—Processes all classes of directives in **.htaccess** files.

None—Ignores directives in **.htaccess** files. However, Apache will still serve the content of **.htaccess** files, possibly exposing sensitive information. This choice does not affect **.htpasswd** files. The example in the description of the <Files> container (page 932) shows how to prevent Apache from serving the content of files whose names begin with **.ht**.

The *directive-class* is one of the following directive class identifiers:

AuthConfig—Class of directives that control authorization (AuthName, AuthType, Require, and so on). This class is used mostly in **.htaccess** files to require a username and password to access the content. For more information refer to "Authentication Modules and **.htaccess**" on page 961.

FileInfo—Class of directives that controls document types (DefaultType, Error-Document, SetHandler, and so on).

Indexes—Class of directives relating to directory indexing (DirectoryIndex, Fancy-Indexing, IndexOptions, and so on).

Limit—Class of client-access directives (Allow, Deny, and Order).

Options—Class of directives controlling directory features.

Context: **directory**
Default: All
Fedora/RHEL: None

Deny *Specifies which clients are not allowed to access specified content.*

Deny from All | host [host ...] | env=var [env=var ...]

This directive, which must be written as **Deny from**, denies access to a directory hierarchy to the specified clients. The directory hierarchy is specified by the container or **.htaccess** file this directive appears in. See the Order directive (next) for an example.

All—Denies content to all clients.

host: Denies content to the client(s) specified by *host,* which can take several forms: an FQDN, a partial domain name (such as **example.com**), an IP address, a partial IP address, or a network/netmask pair.

var: Denies content when the environment variable named *var* is set. You can set a variable with the SetEnvIf directive.

Contexts: **directory, .htaccess**
Default: none
Fedora/RHEL: none

Order *Specifies the default access and the order in which Allow and Deny directives are evaluated.*

Order Deny,Allow | Allow,Deny

Deny,Allow—Allows access by default; denies access only to clients specified in Deny directives (first evaluates Deny directives and then evaluates Allow directives).

Allow,Deny—Denies access by default; allows access only to clients specified in Allow directives (first evaluates Allow directives and then evaluates Deny directives).

There must not be SPACEs on either side of the comma. Access defaults to the second entry in the pair (Deny,Allow defaults to Allow) if there is no Allow from or Deny from directive that matches the client. If a single Allow from or Deny from directive matches the client, that directive overrides the default. If multiple Allow from and Deny from directives match the client, Apache evaluates the directives in the order specified by the Order directive; the last match takes precedence.

Access granted or denied by this directive applies to the directory hierarchy specified by the container or **.htaccess** file this directive appears in. Although Fedora/RHEL has a default of Allow,Deny, which denies access to all clients not specified by Allow directives, the next directive in **httpd.conf**, **Allow from all**, grants access to all clients:

```
Order allow,deny
Allow from all
```

You can restrict access by specifying Deny,Allow to deny all access and then specifying only those clients you want to grant access to in an Allow directive. The following directives grant access to clients from the **example.net** domain only and would typically appear within a <Directory> container (page 931):

```
Order deny,allow
Deny from all
Allow from .example.net
```

Contexts: **directory, .htaccess**
Default: Deny,Allow
Fedora/RHEL: Allow,Deny (for **/var/www/html**)

THE FEDORA/RHEL httpd.conf FILE

This section highlights some of the important features of the Fedora/RHEL **httpd.conf** file, which is based on the **httpd.conf** file distributed by Apache. This heavily commented file is broken into the following parts (as is this section):

1. **Global Environment**—Controls the overall functioning of the Apache server.

2. **Main Server Configuration**—Configures the default server (as opposed to virtual hosts) and provides default configuration information for virtual hosts.

3. **Virtual Hosts**—Configures virtual hosts (page 953).

SECTION 1: GLOBAL ENVIRONMENT

ServerTokens   The ServerTokens directive (page 942) is set to **OS**, which causes Apache, when queried, to return the name of the operating system and the complete version number of Apache:

```
ServerTokens OS
```

ServerRoot   The ServerRoot directive (page 941) is set to **/etc/httpd**, which is the pathname that Apache prepends to relative pathnames in **httpd.conf**:

```
ServerRoot "/etc/httpd"
```

<IfModule>   The <IfModule> containers (page 932) allow you to use the same **httpd.conf** file with different multiprocessing modules (MPMs, page 962). Apache executes the directives in an <IfModule> container only if the specified module is loaded. The **httpd.conf** file holds two <IfModule> containers that configure Apache differently, depending on which module—**prefork** or **worker**—is loaded. Fedora/RHEL ships with the **prefork** module loaded; this section does not discuss the <IfModule> container for the **worker** module. (The **worker** module does not work with PHP. See the comments in the **/etc/sysconfig/httpd** file if you want to load the **worker** module.)

```
# prefork MPM
...
<IfModule prefork.c>
StartServers         8
MinSpareServers      5
MaxSpareServers     20
ServerLimit        256
MaxClients         256
MaxRequestsPerChild 4000
</IfModule>

# worker MPM
...
<IfModule worker.c>
StartServers         4
MaxClients         300
MinSpareThreads     25
MaxSpareThreads     75
ThreadsPerChild     25
MaxRequestsPerChild 0
</IfModule>
```

For more information refer to "Multiprocessing Modules (MPMs)" on page 962.

User   The User directive causes Apache to run as the user named **apache**:

```
User apache
```

TypesConfig   The TypesConfig directive specifies the file that defines the *MIME* (page 1176) types that Apache uses for content negotiation (page 951). It is used to match filename extensions with MIME types (e.g., **.png** with **image/png**).

```
TypesConfig /etc/mime.types
```

DefaultType The DefaultType directive specifies the content-type Apache sends if it cannot determine a type.

```
DefaultType text/plain
```

Listen The Listen directive (page 925) does not specify an IP address, causing Apache to listen on all network interfaces:

```
Listen 80
```

Include an IP address in this directive to prevent Apache from listening on all network interfaces:

```
Listen 192.0.32.10:80
```

LoadModule There are many LoadModule directives (page 943) in **httpd.conf**; these directives load the Apache DSO modules (page 957).

Include The Include directive (page 943) includes the files that match ***.conf** in the **/etc/httpd/conf.d** directory, as though they were part of **httpd.conf**:

```
Include conf.d/*.conf
```

Fedora/RHEL test page When you install Apache, there is no **index.html** file in **/var/www/html**; when you point a browser at the local Web server, Apache generates error 403 (Forbidden), which returns the Fedora/RHEL test page. The mechanism by which this page is returned is convoluted: The Fedora/RHEL **httpd.conf** file holds an Include directive that includes all files with a filename extension of **.conf** that reside in the **conf.d** directory that is in the ServerRoot directory (**/etc/httpd**; page 941). The **/etc/httpd/conf.d/welcome.conf** file contains an ErrorDocument 403 directive (page 939) that redirects users who receive this error to **error/noindex.html** in the DocumentRoot directory (**/var/www**; page 928). (The **httpd.conf** file holds an Alias directive (page 939) that causes **/var/www/error** to appear as **/error**.) The **noindex.html** file is the Fedora/RHEL test page that confirms the server is working but there is no content to display.

SECTION 2: MAIN SERVER CONFIGURATION

ServerAdmin and ServerName As Fedora/RHEL Apache is installed, ServerAdmin is set to **root@localhost** and the ServerName directive is commented out. Uncomment ServerName and change both to useful values as suggested in the ServerAdmin (page 927) and ServerName (page 928) sections.

DocumentRoot The DocumentRoot directive (page 928) appears as follows:

```
DocumentRoot "/var/www/html"
```

Modify this directive only if you want to put content somewhere other than in the **/var/www/html** directory.

<Directory> The following <Directory> container (page 931) sets up a restrictive environment for the entire local filesystem (specified by **/**):

```
<Directory />
    Options FollowSymLinks
    AllowOverride None
</Directory>
```

The Options directive (page 943) allows Apache to follow symbolic links but disallows many options. The AllowOverride directive (page 945) causes Apache not to process directives in .htaccess files. You must explicitly enable less restrictive options if you want them, but be aware that doing so can expose the root filesystem and compromise system security.

Next, another <Directory> container sets up less restrictive options for the Document-Root (/var/www/html). The code in **httpd.conf** is interspersed with many comments. Without the comments it looks like this:

```
<Directory "/var/www/html">
    Options Indexes FollowSymLinks
    AllowOverride None
    Order allow,deny
    Allow from all
</Directory>
```

The Indexes option in the Options directive allows Apache to display directory listings. The Order (page 946) and Allow (page 945) directives combine to allow requests from all clients. This container is slightly less restrictive than the preceding one, although it still does not allow Apache to follow directives in .htaccess files.

DirectoryIndex   As explained on page 930, the DirectoryIndex directive causes Apache to return the file named **index.html** from a requested directory. Because Options Indexes is specified in the preceding <Directory> container, if this file does not exist in a queried directory, Apache returns a directory listing:

```
DirectoryIndex  index.html index.html.var
```

A **.var** filename extension denotes a content-negotiated document that allows Apache to serve the Apache manual and other documents in one of several languages as specified by the client. For more information refer to "Type Maps" on page 951.

There are many more directives in this part of the **httpd.conf** file. The comments in the file provide a guide as to what they do. There is nothing here you need to change as you get started using Apache.

SECTION 3: VIRTUAL HOSTS

All lines in this section are comments or commented-out directives. See page 953 for instructions on setting up virtual hosts.

ADVANCED CONFIGURATION

This section describes how to configure some advanced features of Apache.

REDIRECTS

Apache can respond to a request for a URI by asking the client to request a different URI. This response is called a *redirect*. A redirect works because redirection is part of the HTTP implementation: Apache sends the appropriate response code and the new URI, and a compliant browser requests the new location.

The Redirect directive can establish an explicit redirect that sends a client to a different page when a Web site is moved. Or, when a user enters the URI of a directory in a browser but leaves off the trailing slash, Apache can automatically redirect the client to the same URI terminated with a slash.

UseCanonicalName The ServerName directive (page 928), which establishes the name of the server, and the UseCanonicalName directive (page 937) are both important when a server has more than one name and needs to perform an automatic redirect. For example, assume the server with the name **zach.example.com** and the alias **www.example.com** has ServerName set to **www.example.com**. When a client specifies a URI of a directory but leaves off the trailing slash (**zach.example.com/dir**), Apache has to perform a redirect to determine the URI of the requested directory. When UseCanonicalName is set to On, Apache uses the value of ServerName and returns **www.example.com/dir/**. With UseCanonicalName set to Off, Apache uses the name from the incoming request and returns **zach.example.com/dir/**.

CONTENT NEGOTIATION

Apache can serve multiple versions of the same page, using a client's preference to determine which version to send. The process Apache uses to determine which version of a page (file) to send is called *content negotiation*. Apache supports two methods of content negotiation: type maps and MultiViews search, which can work together.

TYPE MAPS

The following AddHandler directive from **httpd.conf** tells Apache to use any filename ending in **.var** as a type map:

```
AddHandler type-map var
```

To see how type maps work, create the following files in **/var/www/html**:

```
$ cat /var/www/html/index.html.en
<html><body><h1>Hello</h1></body></html>

$ cat /var/www/html/index.html.fr
<html><body><h1>Bonjour</h1><body></html>

$ cat /var/www/html/index.html.var
URI: index.html.en
Content-Language: en
Content-type: text/html; charset=ISO-8859-1

URI: index.html.fr
Content-Language: fr
Content-type: text/html; charset=ISO-8859-1
```

If your browser's preferred language is set to English (**en**), it will display the **Hello** page when you browse to **http://localhost/index.html.var**. If your browser's preferred language is set to French (**fr**), it will display the **Bonjour** page. (With the MultiViews option turned on, as it is by default, the browser displays the correct page when you browse to **http://localhost**. See the next section.) You can change the default language in Firefox by selecting **Edit⇨Preferences** from the menubar, clicking the Content icon, and finally clicking **Choose** from the Languages frame. Select a language from the **Select a language to add** combo box, if necessary, and then move the preferred language to the top of the list. In the example, the **charset** assignments are not necessary. However, they would be helpful if you were sending pages using different encodings such as English, Russian, and Korean.

Type maps are used for more than selecting among different languages. Instead of matching **Content-Language** as in the preceding example, the map could match **Content-type** and send **jpeg** or **png** images depending on how the browser's preferences are set.

MULTIVIEWS

When you set the MultiViews option on a directory, Apache attempts to deliver the correct page when a requested resource does not exist. In **httpd.conf**, add **MultiViews** to the Options line in the Directory container as shown following:

```
<Directory "/var/www/html">
...
    Options Indexes FollowSymLinks MultiViews
...
```

To see how MultiViews work, remove the **/var/www/html/index.html.var** type map file you created in the preceding section. Now browse to **http://localhost**. The proper language page is displayed, but why?

When a browser sends Apache a request for a directory, Apache looks for a file named **index.html** in that directory. In the example, Apache does not find the file. If MultiViews is enabled, Apache looks for files named **index.html.❋**. In the example it finds **index.html.en** and **index.html.fr**. Apache effectively creates a type map on the fly, mapping the **index.html.❋** files to various languages, and sends its best guess as to the page you want.

Which to use: MultiViews or type maps?

caution   MultiViews provides an easy way to serve multiple versions of the same file without having to create a type map. However, MultiViews is slower than type maps. Also, if you require finer-grained control over which version of a resource should be sent, type maps is a better solution.

SERVER-GENERATED DIRECTORY LISTINGS (INDEXING)

When a client requests a directory, the Apache configuration determines what is returned to the client. Apache can return a file as specified by the DirectoryIndex directive (page 930), a directory listing if no file matches DirectoryIndex and the Options Indexes directive (page 943) is set, or an error message if no file matches DirectoryIndex and Options Indexes is not set. Figure 26-1 shows the server-generated directory listing.

Figure 26-1   A server-generated directory listing

VIRTUAL HOSTS

Apache supports *virtual hosts,* which means that one instance of Apache can respond to requests directed to multiple IP addresses or hostnames as though it were multiple servers. Each IP address or hostname can then provide different content and be configured differently.

There are two types of virtual hosts: *host-by-name* (also called *host-based*) and *host-by-IP*. Host-by-name relies on the FQDN the client uses in its request to Apache—for example, **www.example.com** versus **www2.example.com**. Host-by-IP examines the IP address the host resolves as and responds according to that match.

Host-by-name is handy if there is only one IP address, but Apache must support multiple FQDNs. Although you can use host-by-IP if a given Web server has aliases, Apache should serve the same content regardless of which name is used.

The NameVirtualHost directive specifies which IP address supports host-by-name virtual hosting; the ServerName (or ServerAlias) directive must match the client request to match that virtual host. Without a NameVirtualHost directive, the virtual host is a host-by-IP virtual host; the ServerName directive specifies the name the server uses to identify itself.

Virtual hosts inherit their configurations from **httpd.conf** Section 1 (page 948) and Section 2 (page 949). In Section 3, commented-out <VirtualHost> containers create the virtual hosts and specify directives that override inherited and default values. You can specify many virtual hosts for a single instance of Apache.

EXAMPLES

The following examples of host-by-name virtual hosting use wildcards (✱) to remain as flexible as possible. You might want to replace the wildcards with the IP address of the server for more precise control when Apache is serving multiple virtual hosts.

The first <VirtualHost> container sets up host-by-name for the site named **example.com**. This virtual host handles requests that are directed to **example.com**. The ServerAlias directive allows it to also process requests directed to **www.example.com**.

```
<VirtualHost *>
    ServerName      example.com
    ServerAlias     www.example.com
    ServerAdmin     webmaster@example.com
    DocumentRoot    /var/www/html/example.com
    CustomLog       /var/log/httpd/example.com.log combined
    ErrorLog        /var/log/httpd/example.com.err
</VirtualHost>
```

The next example is similar to the previous one. It adds a Directory directive that prevents remote users (users not coming from the 192.168. subnet) from accessing the Web site.

```
<VirtualHost *>
    ServerName      intranet.example.com
    ServerAdmin     webmaster@example.com
    DocumentRoot    /var/www/html
    ErrorLog        /var/log/httpd/intra.error_log
    CustomLog       /var/log/httpd/example.com.log combined
    <Directory      /var/www/html>
        Order deny,allow
        Deny from all
        Allow from 192.168.  # allow from private subnet only
    </Directory>
</VirtualHost>
```

The next example sets up two virtual hosts. The VirtualHost containers accept all traffic directed to the server by specifying ✱. The ServerName directives accept traffic for **sam.example.com** (or the alias **www.example.com/sam**) and **mail.example.com**. The first virtual host serves documents from Sam's **public_html** directory; the second is a Webmail server with its content at **/var/www/html/squirrelmail**. This example works because all three addresses resolve to the IP address of the server.

```
NameVirtualHost *:
<VirtualHost *>
    ServerName      sam.example.com
    ServerAlias     www.example.com/sam
    ServerAdmin     webmaster@example.com
    DocumentRoot    /home/sam/public_html
</VirtualHost>
```

```
<VirtualHost *:>
    ServerName      mail.example.com
    ServerAdmin     webmaster2@example.com
    DocumentRoot    /var/www/html/squirrelmail
</VirtualHost>
```

If the user specifies an IP address and not a URI, that address might match more than one of the virtual hosts, as in the example. In this case, Apache serves the virtual host that best matches. If none of the virtual host addresses matches the IP address better than another, Apache serves the first virtual host. In the preceding example, both virtual hosts match an IP address the same way; neither is a better match, so Apache serves the first virtual host (**sam.example.com**). If **mail.example.com** was defined as <VirtualHost 192.168.1.102> and a user specified that IP address, Apache would serve **mail.example.com** because it is a better match for the IP address than the wildcard that the other virtual host specifies.

The next example shows VirtualHost containers for a host-by-IP server. The example assumes that 111.111.0.0 and 111.111.0.1 point to the local server. Here each virtual host has its own IP/port combination. The third virtual host is distinguished from the first by the port that a request comes in on.

```
<VirtualHost 111.111.0.0:80>
    DocumentRoot /var/www/html/www0
</VirtualHost>

<VirtualHost 111.111.0.1:80>
    DocumentRoot /var/www/html/www1
</VirtualHost>

<VirtualHost 111.111.0.0:8080>
    DocumentRoot /var/www/html/www2
    Listen 8080
</VirtualHost>
```

The final example sets up a virtual server for Webmail that can be accessed only over SSL. To use this example you must create an SSL certificate (page 959).

```
<VirtualHost mail.example.com:80>
    Redirect permanent / https://mail.example.com/
</VirtualHost>
<VirtualHost mail.example.com:443>
    ServerName      mail.example.com
    ServerAdmin     postmaster@example.com
    DocumentRoot    /var/www/html/mail.example.com
    ErrorLog        /var/log/httpd/mail.example.com.err
    CustomLog       /var/log/httpd/mail.example.com.log combined
    SSLEngine On
    SSLCertificateFile /etc/pki/tls/certs/apache.pem
</VirtualHost>
```

TROUBLESHOOTING

If the browser does not display the information you expect, make sure it is not displaying a cached version of the page. Try clearing the browser's cache and reloading the page. Also make sure that Apache has permission to read the files it is serving and the scripts it is running.

The **httpd** init script checks the syntax of the Apache configuration files and logs an error if there is a problem. You can also call apache2ctl directly to check the syntax:

```
$ apache2ctl configtest
Syntax OK
```

Or you can use service and the **httpd** init script to check the syntax of the Apache configuration files:

```
$ service httpd configtest
Syntax OK
```

Once you start the **httpd** daemon, you can confirm Apache is working correctly by pointing a browser on the local system at **http://localhost/**. From a remote system, use **http://*server/***, substituting the hostname or IP address of the server for *server*. In response, Apache displays the Fedora/RHEL test page (page 949) unless you have added an index file or changed the default virtual host.

If the browser does not display the test page, it will display one of two errors: **Connection refused** or an error page. If it displays **Connection refused**, make sure port 80 is not blocked by a firewall (page 920) and check that the server is running:

```
# service httpd status
httpd (pid 21406) is running...
```

If the server is running, confirm that you did not specify a port other than 80 in a Listen directive. If you did, the URI you specify in the browser must reflect this port number (**http://localhost:*port*** specifies port *port*). Otherwise, check the error log (**/var/log/httpd/error_log**) for information about what is not working.

To verify the browser is not at fault, use telnet to try to connect to port 80 of the server:

```
$ telnet www.example.com 80
Trying 192.0.34.166...
Connected to www.example.com.
Escape character is '^]'.
CONTROL-]
telnet> quit
Connection closed.
```

If telnet displays **Connection refused**, it means the local system cannot connect to the server.

MODULES

Apache is a skeletal program that relies on external modules, called dynamic shared objects (DSOs), to provide most of its functionality. In addition to the modules included with Fedora/RHEL, many other modules are available. For more information see httpd.apache.org/modules and httpd.apache.org/docs/2.2/mod.

Following is a list of some of the modules that are available under Apache.

actions (mod_actions.so) Allows execution of CGI scripts based on the request method.
alias (mod_alias.so) Allows outside directories to be mapped to DocumentRoot.
asis (mod_asis.so) Allows sending files that contain their own headers.
auth (mod_auth.so) Provides user authentication via **.htaccess**.
authn_anon (mod_authn_anon.so) Provides anonymous user access to restricted areas.
authn_dbd (mod_authn_dbd.so) Uses SQL files for authentication.
auth_digest (mod_auth_digest.so) Uses MD5 digest for authentication.
autoindex (mod_autoindex.so) Allows directory indexes to be generated.
cern_meta (mod_cern_meta.so) Allows the use of CERN **httpd** metafile semantics.
cgi (mod_cgi.so) Allows the execution of CGI scripts.
dav (mod_dav.so) Allows Distributed Authoring and Versioning.
dav_fs (mod_dav_fs.so) Provides a filesystem for mod_dav.
dir (mod_dir.so) Allows directory redirects and listings as index files.
env (mod_env.so) Allows CGI scripts to access environment variables.
expires (mod_expires.so) Allows generation of Expires HTTP headers.
headers (mod_headers.so) Allows customization of request and response headers.
include (mod_include.so) Provides server-side includes (SSIs).
info (mod_info.so) Allows the server configuration to be viewed.
log_config (mod_log_config.so) Allows logging of requests made to the server.
mime (mod_mime.so) Allows association of file extensions with content.
mime_magic (mod_mime_magic.so) Determines MIME types of files.
negotiation (mod_negotiation.so) Allows content negotiation.
proxy (mod_proxy.so) Allows Apache to act as a proxy server.
proxy_connect (mod_proxy_connect.so) Allows connect request handling.
proxy_ftp (mod_proxy_ftp.so) Provides an FTP extension proxy.
proxy_http (mod_proxy_http.so) Provides an HTTP extension proxy.
rewrite (mod_rewrite.so) Allows on-the-fly URI rewriting based on rules.
setenvif (mod_setenvif.so) Sets environment variables based on a request.
speling (mod_speling.so) Auto-corrects spelling if the requested URI has incorrect capitalization and one spelling mistake.
status (mod_status.so) Allows the server status to be queried and viewed.
unique_id (mod_unique_id.so) Generates a unique ID for each request.
userdir (mod_userdir.so) Allows users to have content directories (public_html).
usertrack (mod_usertrack.so) Allows tracking of user activity on a site.
vhost_alias (mod_vhost_alias.so) Allows the configuration of virtual hosting.

mod_cgi AND CGI SCRIPTS

The CGI (Common Gateway Interface) allows external application programs to interface with Web servers. Any program can be a CGI program if it runs in real time (at the time of the request) and relays its output to the requesting client. Various kinds of scripts, including shell, Perl, Python, and PHP, are the most commonly encountered CGI programs because a script can call a program and reformat its output in HTML for a client.

Apache can handle requests for CGI programs in several different ways. The most common method is to put a CGI program in the **cgi-bin** directory and then enable its execution from that directory only. The location of the **cgi-bin** directory, as specified by the ScriptAlias directive (page 944), is **/var/www/cgi-bin**. Alternatively, an AddHandler directive (page 938) can identify the filename extensions of scripts, such as **.cgi** or **.pl**, within the regular content (for example, **AddHandler cgi-script .cgi**). If you use AddHandler, you must also specify the ExecCGI option in an Options directive within the appropriate <Directory> container. The **mod_cgi** module must be loaded to access and execute CGI scripts.

The following Perl CGI script displays the Apache environment. This script should be used for debugging only because it presents a security risk if remote clients can access it:

```
#!/usr/bin/perl
##
##   printenv -- demo CGI program that prints its environment
##

print "Content-type: text/plain\n\n";
foreach $var (sort(keys(%ENV))) {
    $val = $ENV{$var};
    $val =~ s|\n|\\n|g;
    $val =~ s|"|\\"|g;
    print "${var}=\"${val}\"\n";
}
```

mod_ssl

SSL (Secure Sockets Layer), which is implemented by the **mod_ssl** module, has two functions: It allows a client to verify the identity of a server and it enables secure two-way communication between a client and a server. SSL is used on Web pages in conjunction with forms that require passwords, credit card numbers, or other sensitive data.

Apache uses the HTTPS protocol—not HTTP—for SSL communication. When Apache uses SSL, it listens on a second port (443 by default) for a connection and performs a handshaking sequence before sending the requested content to the client.

Server verification is critical for financial transactions: You do not want to give your credit card number to a fraudulent Web site posing as a known company. SSL uses a certificate to positively identify a server. Over a public network such as the Internet, the identification is reliable only if the certificate contains a digital signature from an authoritative source such as VeriSign or Thawte. SSL Web pages are denoted by a URI beginning with **https://**.

Data encryption prevents malicious users from eavesdropping on Internet connections and copying personal information. To encrypt communication, SSL sits between the network and an application and encrypts communication between the server and the client.

SETTING UP mod_ssl

You must install the **mod_ssl** package to run SSL. The **/etc/httpd/conf.d/ssl.conf** file configures and loads **mod_ssl**. The first few directives in this file load the **mod_ssl** module, instruct Apache to listen on port 443, and set various parameters for SSL operation. About a third of the way through the file is a section labeled **SSL Virtual Host Context** that sets up virtual hosts (page 953).

As with any virtual host, a virtual host for SSL holds directives such as ServerName and ServerAdmin that need to be configured. In addition, it holds some SSL-related directives. See the example on page 955.

USING A SELF-SIGNED CERTIFICATE FOR ENCRYPTION

If you require SSL for encryption and not verification—that is, if the client already trusts the server—you can generate and use a self-signed certificate, bypassing the time and expense involved in obtaining a digitally signed certificate. Self-signed certificates generate a warning when you connect to the server: Most browsers display a dialog box that allows you to examine and accept the certificate. The **sendmail** daemon also uses certificates (page 755).

The self-signed certificate depends on two files: a private key and the certificate. The location of each file is specified in **/etc/httpd/conf.d/ssl.conf**:

```
# grep '^SSLCertificate' /etc/httpd/conf.d/ssl.conf
SSLCertificateFile /etc/pki/tls/certs/localhost.crt
SSLCertificateKeyFile /etc/pki/tls/private/localhost.key
```

The following example creates a self-signed certificate. To generate the private key that the encryption relies on, cd to **/etc/pki/tls/certs** and enter a make command:

```
# cd /etc/pki/tls/certs
# make localhost.key
umask 77 ; \
/usr/bin/openssl genrsa -aes128 2048 > localhost.key
Generating RSA private key, 2048 bit long modulus
.+++
...................+++
e is 65537 (0x10001)
Enter pass phrase:
Verifying - Enter pass phrase:
```

The preceding command generates a file named **localhost.key** that is protected by the pass phrase you entered: *You will need this passphrase to start the server*. Keep the **localhost.key** file secret.

The next command generates the certificate. This process uses the private key you just created. You need to supply the same pass phrase you entered when you created the private key.

```
# make localhost.crt
umask 77 ; \
/usr/bin/openssl req -utf8 -new -key localhost.key -x509 -days 365 -out
localhost.crt -set_serial 0
Enter pass phrase for localhost.key:
You are about to be asked to enter information that will be incorporated
into your certificate request.
What you are about to enter is what is called a Distinguished Name or a DN.
There are quite a few fields but you can leave some blank
For some fields there will be a default value,
If you enter '.', the field will be left blank.
-----
Country Name (2 letter code) [GB]:US
State or Province Name (full name) [Berkshire]:California
Locality Name (eg, city) [Newbury]:San Francisco
Organization Name (eg, company) [My Company Ltd]:Sobell Associates Inc.
Organizational Unit Name (eg, section) []:
Common Name (eg, your name or your server's hostname) []:www.sobell.com
Email Address []:mgs@sobell.com
```

The answers to the first five questions are arbitrary: They can help clients identify a site when they examine the certificate. The answer to the sixth question (**Common Name**) is critical. Because certificates are tied to the name of the server, you must enter the server's FQDN accurately. If you mistype this information, the server name and that of the certificate will not match. The browser will then generate a warning message each time a connection is made.

As specified by **ssl.conf**, Apache looks for the files in the directory that you created them in. Do not move these files. After you restart Apache, the new certificate will be in use.

NOTES ON CERTIFICATES

- As long as the server is identified by the name for which the certificate was issued, you can use the certificate on another server or IP address.

- A root certificate is the certificate that identifies the root certificate authority (root CA). Every browser contains a database of the public keys for the root certificates of the major signing authorities, including VeriSign and Thawte.

- It is possible to generate a root certificate and sign all your server certificates with this root CA. Regular clients can import the public key of the root CA so that they recognize every certificate signed by that root CA.

This setup is convenient for a server with multiple SSL-enabled virtual hosts and no commercial certificates. For more information see www.modssl.org/docs/2.8/ssl_faq.html#ToC29.

- A self-signed certificate does not enable clients to verify the identity of the server.

AUTHENTICATION MODULES AND .htaccess FILES

To restrict access to a Web page, Apache and third parties provide authentication modules and methods that can verify a user's credentials, such as a username and password. Some modules support authentication against various databases including NIS (page 760) and LDAP (page 776).

User authentication directives are commonly placed in a **.htaccess** file. A basic **.htaccess** file that uses the Apache default authentication module (**mod_auth**) follows. When placed in **/var/www**, this file causes Apache to request a password before a browser can access content in the **/var/www** directory hierarchy. Substitute appropriate values for the local server.

```
# cat .htaccess
AuthUserFile /var/www/.htpasswd
AuthGroupFile /dev/null
AuthName "Browser dialog box query"
AuthType Basic
require valid-user
```

The **/var/www/.htpasswd** is a typical absolute pathname of a **.htpasswd** file and **Browser dialog box query** is the string that the user will see as part of the dialog box that requests a username and password.

The second line of the preceding **.htaccess** file turns off the group function. The fourth line specifies the user authentication type **Basic**, which is implemented by the default **mod_auth** module. The last line tells Apache which users can access the protected directory. The entry **valid-user** grants access to the directory to any user whose username appears in the Apache password file and who enters the correct password.

You can put the Apache password file anywhere on the system, as long as Apache can read it. It is safe to put this file in the same directory as the **.htaccess** file because, by default, Apache will not answer any requests for files whose names start with **.ht**. However, be sure you have not changed the **httpd.conf** configuration file to allow Apache to answer requests for files whose names begin with **.ht**. See page 924 for more information on **.htaccess** files.

The following command creates (–c) a **.htpasswd** file with an entry for Sam in the working directory. Omit the –c option to add a user or to change a password in an existing **.htpasswd** file.

```
$ htpasswd -c .htpasswd sam
New password:
Re-type new password:
Adding password for user sam
```

The **default httpd.conf** file includes an **AllowOverride None** directive (page 945) for **/var/www**. You must change this directive to at least **AllowOverride AuthConfig** or remove it to enable Apache to process user authentication directives (such as reading an **.htaccess** file).

.htaccess files can degrade performance

tip   With Apache configured to process **.htaccess** files, when it receives a request for a file, it has to traverse the directory hierarchy from the requested file upward, toward the root, looking for a **.htacess** file to determine if it can serve the requested file. This search can affect performance. Typically performance degradation is not severe, but this issue can become important if performance is critical.

SCRIPTING MODULES

Apache can process content before serving it to a client. In earlier versions of Apache, only CGI scripts could process content. In the current version, *scripting modules* can work with scripts embedded in HTML documents. The downside is that major bugs in scripting modules can affect the stability of Apache processes.

Scripting modules manipulate content before Apache serves it to a client. Because they are built into Apache, scripting modules are fast. Scripting modules are especially efficient at working with external data sources such as relational databases. Clients can pass data to a scripting module that modifies the information that Apache serves.

Scripting modules stand in contrast to CGI scripts that are run externally to Apache. In particular, CGI scripts do not allow client interaction and are slow because they must make external calls.

You can embed Perl (**mod_perl**), Python, and PHP code in HTML content. Perl and Python are general-purpose scripting languages and are implemented in the **mod_perl** and **mod_python** or **mod_wsgi** (code.google.com/p/modwsgi) modules.

PHP, which was developed for manipulating Web content, outputs HTML by default. It is encapsulated for use directly in Apache, easy to set up, has a syntax similar to that of Perl and C, and comes with a large number of Web-related functions.

MULTIPROCESSING MODULES (MPMs)

If Apache were to execute in only one process, every time a client requested a page, Apache would have to ignore other requests while it read that page from disk (or waited for a CGI script to generate it). After it read the page, it could send the page to the client and respond to the next request. With this setup, Apache could serve only one client at a time.

prefork MPM   Apache 1.3 and earlier forked servers to respond to multiple clients. Apache 2 moved the forking behavior to the **prefork** multiprocessing module (MPM). MPMs introduced the ability to switch between various multiprocessing techniques.

The **prefork** MPM uses the **fork**() system call to create an exact copy of the running Apache process to serve each request. The MaxServers, MaxSpareServers, and similar directives control how many copies of Apache run at the same time. Because the operating system has to spend time context switching between Apache processes, and because each process has its own memory, the **prefork** MPM generates considerable overhead on a busy server. Fedora/RHEL runs the **prefork** MPM by default.

worker MPM The **worker** MPM reduces this overhead by using **threads**. A thread is similar to a process in that it can execute independently of other threads or processes. Waiting for a read to complete in one thread does not stop (block) other threads from executing. The difference between threads and processes is that all the threads running under one process share the same memory, and the program—rather than the operating system—is responsible for managing the threads. The **worker** MPM maintains a pool of threads it can use to serve each request. Instead of the parent Apache process forking a child to serve each request for content as in **prefork**, the **worker** MPM uses threads to serve requests for content.

Threads Because all these threads run under the same process, they share the same memory. Code that is not *thread safe* (see *reentrant* on page 1184) can return inconsistent results. For example, some PHP library functions use the **strtok**() C function to convert a string to tokens. This function maintains internal variables. If it is called by multiple threads sharing the same memory, **strtok**()'s internal variables are put in an inconsistent state.

PHP If you want to use PHP, either you must use the **prefork** MPM or, if you want to use the **worker** MPM and PHP, you must remove **mod_php** and run PHP as a CGI script (page 958).

To run the **worker** MPM, uncomment the following line in **/etc/sysconfig/httpd**:

```
HTTPD=/usr/sbin/httpd.worker
```

Use **service** to stop the **httpd** daemon before changing this file; restart it after making the change.

webalizer: ANALYZES WEB TRAFFIC

The **webalizer** package creates a directory at **/var/www/usage**, a cron file (page 611) at **/etc/cron.daily/00webalizer**, a webalizer configuration file at **/etc/webalizer.conf**, and an Apache configuration file at **/etc/httpd/conf.d/webalizer.conf**. After installing the package, use **service** to restart the **httpd** daemon. Once a day, the cron file generates usage data and puts it in the **usage** directory; you can view this data by pointing a browser at **http://*server*/usage/**, where *server* is the name or IP address of the server.

The **/etc/webalizer.conf** file controls the behavior of the webalizer utility. If you want information on virtual hosts (which by definition change the location of the DocumentRoot and often change the location of log files), you must modify the **/etc/webalizer.conf** file. The **/etc/httpd/conf.d/webalizer.conf** file includes Deny from ALL and Allow from 127.0.0.1 directives. If you want to view statistics from a remote browser, you must add an Allow directive to this file. For more information on webalizer, refer to the webalizer man page and the sites listed under "More Information" on page 919.

MRTG: MONITORS TRAFFIC LOADS

Multi Router Traffic Grapher (MRTG; **mrtg** package) is an open-source application that graphs statistics available through SNMP (Simple Network Management Protocol). SNMP information is available on all high-end routers and switches as well as on some other networked equipment, such as printers and wireless access points. You can use the **net-snmp** and **net-snmp-utils** packages supplied by Fedora/RHEL to install SNMP on a system. You also need to install the **mrtg** package. The **/etc/httpd/conf.d/mrtg.conf** file includes Deny from ALL and Allow from 127.0.0.1 directives. If you want to view statistics from a remote browser, you must add an Allow directive to this file.

Once MRTG and SNMP are installed and running, you can view the reports at **http://*server*/mrtg**, where *server* is the hostname of the server. For more information see the mrtg man page and the sites listed under "More Information" on page 919. See also "Introduction to Cacti" on page 657 on capturing and displaying SNMP information.

ERROR CODES

Following is a list of Apache error codes:

100 Continue	404 Not Found
101 Switching Protocols	405 Method Not Allowed
200 OK	406 Not Acceptable
201 Created	407 Proxy Authentication Required
202 Accepted	408 Request Timed out
203 Non-Authoritative Info...	409 Conflict
204 No Content	410 Gone
205 Reset Content	411 Length Required
206 Partial Content	412 Precondition Failed
300 Multiple Choices	413 Request Entity Too Large
301 Moved Permanently	414 Request-URI Too Large
302 Moved Temporarily	415 Unsupported Media Type
303 See Other	500 Internal Server Error
304 Not Modified	501 Not Implemented
305 Use Proxy	502 Bad Gateway
400 Bad Request	503 Service Unavailable
401 Unauthorized	504 Gateway Time-out
402 Payment Required	505 HTTP Version Not Supported
403 Forbidden	

CHAPTER SUMMARY

Apache is the most popular Web server on the Internet. It is both robust and extensible. The **/etc/httpd/conf/httpd.conf** configuration file controls many aspects of how Apache runs. The Fedora/RHEL **httpd.conf** file, which is based on the **httpd.conf** file distributed by Apache, is heavily commented and broken into three parts: Global Environment, Main Server Configuration, and Virtual Hosts.

Content to be served is typically placed in **/var/www/html**, called the document root. Apache automatically displays the file named **index.html** in this directory.

Configuration directives, or simply directives, are lines in a configuration file that control some aspect of how Apache functions. Four locations, called contexts, define where a configuration directive can appear: **server config**, **virtual host**, **directory**, and **.htaccess**. Containers, or special directives, are directives that group other directives.

To restrict access to a Web page, Apache and third parties provide authentication modules and methods that can verify a user's credentials, such as a username and password. Some modules enable authentication against various databases, including LDAP and NIS.

Apache can respond to a request for a URI by asking the client to request a different URI. This response is called a redirect. Apache can also process content before serving it to a client using scripting modules that work with scripts embedded in HTML documents.

Apache supports virtual hosts, which means that one instance of Apache can respond to requests directed to multiple IP addresses or hostnames as though it were multiple servers. Each IP address or hostname can provide different content and be configured differently.

The CGI (Common Gateway Interface) allows external application programs to interface with Web servers. Any program can be a CGI program if it runs in real time and relays its output to the requesting client.

SSL (Secure Sockets Layer) has two functions: It allows a client to verify the identity of a server and it enables secure two-way communication between a client and server.

EXERCISES

1. How would you tell Apache that your content is in **/usr/local/www**?

2. How would you instruct an Apache server to listen on port 81 instead of port 80?

3. How would you enable Sam to publish Web pages from his **~/website** directory but not allow anyone else to publish to the Web?

4. Apache must be started with **root** privileges. Why? Why does this action not present a security risk?

Advanced Exercises

5. If you are running Apache on a firewall system, perhaps to display a Web front-end for firewall configuration, how would you make sure that it is accessible only from inside the local network?

6. Why is it more efficient to run scripts using **mod_perl** than to run them through CGI?

7. What two things does SSL provide and how does this situation differ if the certificate is self-signed?

8. Some Web sites generate content by retrieving data from a database and inserting it into a template using PHP or CGI each time the site is accessed. Why is this practice often a poor idea?

9. Assume you want to provide Webmail access for employees on the same server that hosts the corporate Web site. The Web site address is example.com, you want to use mail.example.com for Webmail, and the Webmail application is located in **/var/www/webmail**. Describe two ways you can set up this configuration.

10. Part of a Web site is a private intranet. Describe how you would prevent people outside the company's internal 192.168.0.0/16 network from accessing this site. The site is defined as follows:

```
<VirtualHost *>
  ServerName example.com
  DocumentRoot /var/www
  <Directory /var/www/intranet>
      AllowOverride AuthConfig
  </Directory>
</VirtualHost>
```

PART VI

PROGRAMMING TOOLS

27

PROGRAMMING THE BOURNE AGAIN SHELL

OBJECTIVES

After reading this chapter you should be able to:

▶ Use control structures to add decision making and repetition in scripts

▶ Handle input and output of scripts

▶ Use local and environment variables

▶ Evaluate the value of variables

▶ Use bash builtin commands to call other scripts inline, trap signals, and kill processes

▶ Use arithmetic and logical expressions

▶ List standard programming practices that result in well written scripts

Chapter 7 introduced the shells and Chapter 9 went into detail about the Bourne Again Shell. This chapter introduces additional Bourne Again Shell commands, builtins, and concepts that carry shell programming to a point where it can be useful. Although you might make use of shell programming as a system administrator, you do not have to read this chapter to perform system administration tasks. Feel free to skip this chapter and come back to it if and when you like.

The first part of this chapter covers programming control structures, also called control flow constructs. These structures allow you to write scripts that can loop over command-line arguments, make decisions based on the value of a variable, set up menus, and more. The Bourne Again Shell uses the same constructs found in such high-level programming languages as C.

The next part of this chapter discusses parameters and variables, going into detail about array variables, local versus global variables, special parameters, and positional parameters. The exploration of builtin commands covers type, which displays information about a command, and read, which allows a shell script to accept user input. The section on the exec builtin demonstrates how to use exec to execute a command efficiently by replacing a process and explains how to use exec to redirect input and output from within a script.

The next section covers the trap builtin, which provides a way to detect and respond to operating system signals (such as the signal generated when you press CONTROL-C). The discussion of builtins concludes with a discussion of kill, which can abort a process, and getopts, which makes it easy to parse options for a shell script. Table 27-6 on page 1031 lists some of the more commonly used builtins.

Next the chapter examines arithmetic and logical expressions as well as the operators that work with them. The final section walks through the design and implementation of two major shell scripts.

This chapter contains many examples of shell programs. Although they illustrate certain concepts, most use information from earlier examples as well. This overlap not only reinforces your overall knowledge of shell programming but also demonstrates how you can combine commands to solve complex tasks. Running, modifying, and experimenting with the examples in this book is a good way to become comfortable with the underlying concepts.

Do not name a shell script **test**

tip   You can unwittingly create a problem if you give a shell script the name **test** because a Linux utility has the same name. Depending on how the **PATH** variable is set up and how you call the program, you might run either your script or the utility, leading to confusing results.

This chapter illustrates concepts with simple examples, which are followed by more complex ones in sections marked "Optional." The more complex scripts illustrate traditional shell programming practices and introduce some Linux utilities often used in scripts. You can skip these sections without loss of continuity. Return to them when you feel comfortable with the basic concepts.

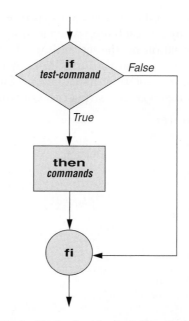

Figure 27-1   An **if...then** flowchart

CONTROL STRUCTURES

The *control flow* commands alter the order of execution of commands within a shell script. Control structures include the **if...then, for...in, while, until,** and **case** statements. In addition, the **break** and **continue** statements work in conjunction with the control structures to alter the order of execution of commands within a script.

if...then

The **if...then** control structure has the following syntax:

> *if* **test-command**
>   *then*
>   **commands**
> *fi*

The **bold** words in the syntax description are the items you supply to cause the structure to have the desired effect. The *nonbold* words are the keywords the shell uses to identify the control structure.

test builtin Figure 27-1 shows that the **if** statement tests the status returned by the *test-command* and transfers control based on this status. The end of the **if** structure is marked by a **fi** statement (*if* spelled backward). The following script prompts for two words, reads them, and then uses an **if** structure to execute commands based on the result returned by the test builtin when it compares the two words. (See the test info page for information on the test utility, which is similar to the test builtin.) The test builtin returns a status of *true* if the two words are the same and *false* if they are not. Double quotation marks around **$word1** and **$word2** make sure test works properly if you enter a string that contains a SPACE or other special character:

```
$ cat if1
echo -n "word 1: "
read word1
echo -n "word 2: "
read word2

if test "$word1" = "$word2"
    then
        echo "Match"
fi
echo "End of program."
$ ./if1
word 1: peach
word 2: peach
Match
End of program.
```

In the preceding example the ***test-command*** is test **"$word1" = "$word2"**. The test builtin returns a *true* status if its first and third arguments have the relationship specified by its second argument. If this command returns a *true* status (= 0), the shell executes the commands between the **then** and **fi** statements. If the command returns a *false* status (not = 0), the shell passes control to the statement following **fi** without executing the statements between **then** and **fi**. The effect of this **if** statement is to display **Match** if the two words are the same. The script always displays **End of program.**

Builtins   In the Bourne Again Shell, test is a builtin—part of the shell. It is also a stand-alone utility kept in **/usr/bin/test**. This chapter discusses and demonstrates many Bourne Again Shell builtins. You typically use the builtin version if it is available and the utility if it is not. Each version of a command might vary slightly from one shell to the next and from the utility to any of the shell builtins. See page 1018 for more information on shell builtins.

Checking arguments   The next program uses an **if** structure at the beginning of a script to confirm that you have supplied at least one argument on the command line. The test **–eq** operator compares two integers; the **$#** special parameter (page 1013) takes on the value of the number of command-line arguments. This structure displays a message and exits from the script with an exit status of 1 if you do not supply at least one argument:

```
$ cat chkargs
if test $# -eq 0
    then
        echo "You must supply at least one argument."
        exit 1
fi
```

```
echo "Program running."
$ ./chkargs
You must supply at least one argument.
$ ./chkargs abc
Program running.
```

A test like the one shown in **chkargs** is a key component of any script that requires arguments. To prevent the user from receiving meaningless or confusing information from the script, the script needs to check whether the user has supplied the appropriate arguments. Some scripts simply test whether arguments exist (as in **chkargs**). Other scripts test for a specific number or specific kinds of arguments.

You can use test to verify the status of a file argument or the relationship between two file arguments. After verifying that at least one argument has been given on the command line, the following script tests whether the argument is the name of an ordinary file (not a directory or other type of file) in the working directory. The test builtin with the **–f** option and the first command-line argument (**$1**) checks the file:

```
$ cat is_ordfile
if test $# -eq 0
    then
        echo "You must supply at least one argument."
        exit 1
fi
if test -f "$1"
    then
        echo "$1 is an ordinary file in the working directory"
    else
        echo "$1 is NOT an ordinary file in the working directory"
fi
```

You can test many other characteristics of a file using test options; see Table 27-1.

Table 27-1   Options to the test builtin

Option	Tests file to see if it
–d	Exists and is a directory file
–e	Exists
–f	Exists and is an ordinary file (not a directory)
–r	Exists and is readable
–s	Exists and has a size greater than 0 bytes
–w	Exists and is writable
–x	Exists and is executable

Other test options provide ways to test relationships between two files, such as whether one file is newer than another. Refer to later examples in this chapter for more information.

Always test the arguments

tip To keep the examples in this book short and focused on specific concepts, the code to verify arguments is often omitted or abbreviated. It is good practice to test arguments in shell programs that other people will use. Doing so results in scripts that are easier to run and debug.

[] is a synonym for test The following example—another version of **chkargs**—checks for arguments in a way that is more traditional for Linux shell scripts. This example uses the bracket ([]) synonym for test. Rather than using the word test in scripts, you can surround the arguments to test with brackets. The brackets must be surrounded by whitespace (SPACEs or TABs).

```
$ cat chkargs2
if [ $# -eq 0 ]
    then
        echo "Usage: chkargs2 argument..." 1>&2
        exit 1
fi
echo "Program running."
exit 0
$ ./chkargs2
Usage: chkargs2 argument...
$ ./chkargs2 abc
Program running.
```

Usage messages The error message that **chkargs2** displays is called a *usage message* and uses the **1>&2** notation to redirect its output to standard error (page 285). After issuing the usage message, **chkargs2** exits with an exit status of 1, indicating an error has occurred. The **exit 0** command at the end of the script causes **chkargs2** to exit with a 0 status after the program runs without an error. The Bourne Again Shell returns a 0 status if you omit the status code.

The usage message is commonly employed to specify the type and number of arguments the script takes. Many Linux utilities provide usage messages similar to the one in **chkargs2**. If you call a utility or other program with the wrong number or wrong kind of arguments, it will often display a usage message. Following is the usage message that **cp** displays when you call it without any arguments:

```
$ cp
cp: missing file operand
Try 'cp --help' for more information.
```

if...then...else

The introduction of an **else** statement turns the **if** structure into the two-way branch shown in Figure 27-2. The **if...then...else** control structure has the following syntax:

> *if test-command*
> > *then*
> > > *commands*
> > *else*
> > > *commands*
> *fi*

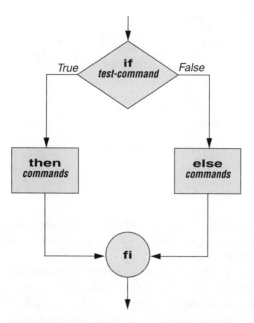

Figure 27-2 An **if...then...else** flowchart

Because a semicolon (;) ends a command just as a NEWLINE does, you can place **then** on the same line as **if** by preceding it with a semicolon. (Because **if** and **then** are separate builtins, they require a command separator between them; a semicolon and NEWLINE work equally well [page 292].) Some people prefer this notation for aesthetic reasons; others like it because it saves space.

    *if **test-command**; then*
           commands
      else
           commands
  fi

If the **test-command** returns a *true* status, the **if** structure executes the commands between the **then** and **else** statements and then diverts control to the statement following **fi**. If the **test-command** returns a *false* status, the **if** structure executes the commands following the **else** statement.

When you run the **out** script with arguments that are filenames, it displays the files on the terminal. If the first argument is **–v** (called an option in this case), **out** uses less (page 149) to display the files one screen at a time. After determining that it was called with at least one argument, **out** tests its first argument to see whether it is **–v**. If the result of the test is *true* (the first argument is **–v**), **out** uses the shift builtin (page 1014) to shift the arguments to get rid of the **–v** and displays the files using less. If the result of the test is *false* (the first argument is *not* **–v**), the script uses cat to display the files:

```
$ cat out
if [ $# -eq 0 ]
    then
        echo "Usage: out [-v] filenames..." 1>&2
        exit 1
fi

if [ "$1" = "-v" ]
    then
        shift
        less -- "$@"
    else
        cat -- "$@"
fi
```

optional   In **out** the **––** argument to cat and less tells these utilities that no more options follow on the command line and not to consider leading hyphens (–) in the following list as indicating options. Thus **––** allows you to view a file with a name that starts with a hyphen. Although not common, filenames beginning with a hyphen do occasionally occur. (You can create such a file by using the command **cat > –fname**.) The **––** argument works with all Linux utilities that use the getopts builtin (page 1028) to parse their options; it does not work with more and a few other utilities. This argument is particularly useful when used in conjunction with rm to remove a file whose name starts with a hyphen (**rm –– –fname**), including any you create while experimenting with the **––** argument.

if...then...elif

The **if...then...elif** control structure (Figure 27-3) has the following syntax:

> *if test-command*
> > *then*
> > > *commands*
> > *elif test-command*
> > > *then*
> > > > *commands*
> > . . .
> > *else*
> > > *commands*
> *fi*

The **elif** statement combines the **else** statement and the **if** statement and enables you to construct a nested set of **if...then...else** structures (Figure 27-3). The difference between the **else** statement and the **elif** statement is that each **else** statement must be paired with a **fi** statement, whereas multiple nested **elif** statements require only a single closing **fi** statement.

The following example shows an **if...then...elif** control structure. This shell script compares three words that the user enters. The first **if** statement uses the Boolean

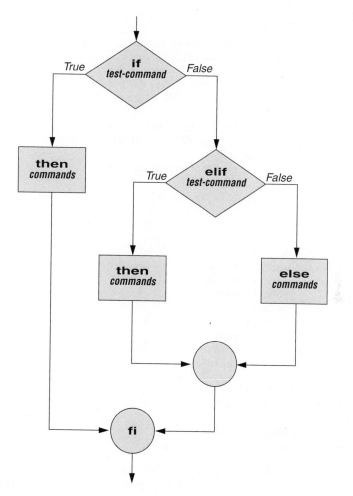

Figure 27-3   An **if...then...**elif flowchart

AND operator (**–a**) as an argument to test. The test builtin returns a *true* status only if the first and second logical comparisons are *true* (that is, **word1** matches **word2** and **word2** matches **word3**). If test returns a *true* status, the script executes the command following the next **then** statement, passes control to the statement following **fi**, and terminates.

```
$ cat if3
echo -n "word 1: "
read word1
echo -n "word 2: "
read word2
echo -n "word 3: "
read word3
```

```
if [ "$word1" = "$word2" -a "$word2" = "$word3" ]
    then
        echo "Match: words 1, 2, & 3"
    elif [ "$word1" = "$word2" ]
    then
        echo "Match: words 1 & 2"
    elif [ "$word1" = "$word3" ]
    then
        echo "Match: words 1 & 3"
    elif [ "$word2" = "$word3" ]
    then
        echo "Match: words 2 & 3"
    else
        echo "No match"
fi
```

```
$ ./if3
word 1: apple
word 2: orange
word 3: pear
No match
$ ./if3
word 1: apple
word 2: orange
word 3: apple
Match: words 1 & 3
$ ./if3
word 1: apple
word 2: apple
word 3: apple
Match: words 1, 2, & 3
```

If the three words are not the same, the structure passes control to the first **elif**, which begins a series of tests to see if any pair of words is the same. As the nesting continues, if any one of the **if** statements is satisfied, the structure passes control to the next **then** statement and subsequently to the statement following **fi**. Each time an **elif** statement is not satisfied, the structure passes control to the next **elif** statement. The double quotation marks around the arguments to echo that contain ampersands (**&**) prevent the shell from interpreting the ampersands as special characters.

optional   THE lnks SCRIPT

The following script, named **lnks**, demonstrates the **if...then** and **if...then...elif** control structures. This script finds hard links to its first argument, a filename. If you provide the name of a directory as the second argument, **lnks** searches for links in the directory hierarchy rooted at that directory. If you do not specify a directory, **lnks** searches the working directory and its subdirectories. This script does not locate symbolic links.

```
$ cat lnks
#!/bin/bash
# Identify links to a file
# Usage: lnks file [directory]

if [ $# -eq 0 -o $# -gt 2 ]; then
    echo "Usage: lnks file [directory]" 1>&2
    exit 1
fi
if [ -d "$1" ]; then
    echo "First argument cannot be a directory." 1>&2
    echo "Usage: lnks file [directory]" 1>&2
    exit 1
else
    file="$1"
fi
if [ $# -eq 1 ]; then
        directory="."
    elif [ -d "$2" ]; then
        directory="$2"
    else
        echo "Optional second argument must be a directory." 1>&2
        echo "Usage: lnks file [directory]" 1>&2
        exit 1
fi

# Check that file exists and is an ordinary file
if [ ! -f "$file" ]; then
    echo "lnks: $file not found or special file" 1>&2
    exit 1
fi
# Check link count on file
set -- $(ls -l "$file")

linkcnt=$2
if [ "$linkcnt" -eq 1 ]; then
    echo "lnks: no other hard links to $file" 1>&2
    exit 0
fi

# Get the inode of the given file
set $(ls -i "$file")

inode=$1

# Find and print the files with that inode number
echo "lnks: using find to search for links..." 1>&2
find "$directory" -xdev -inum $inode -print
```

Max has a file named **letter** in his home directory. He wants to find links to this file in his and other users' home directory file trees. In the following example, Max calls **lnks** from his home directory to perform the search. The second argument to **lnks**, **/home**, is the pathname of the directory where he wants to start the search. The **lnks** script reports that **/home/max/letter** and **/home/zach/draft** are links to the same file:

```
$ ./lnks letter /home
lnks: using find to search for links...
/home/max/letter
/home/zach/draft
```

In addition to the **if...then...elif** control structure, **lnks** introduces other features that are commonly used in shell programs. The following discussion describes **lnks** section by section.

Specify the shell   The first line of the **lnks** script uses **#!** (page 290) to specify the shell that will execute the script:

```
#!/bin/bash
```

In this chapter, the **#!** notation appears only in more complex examples. It ensures that the proper shell executes the script, even when the user is running a different shell or the script is called from a script running a different shell.

Comments   The second and third lines of **lnks** are comments; the shell ignores text that follows a hashmark (#) up to the next NEWLINE character. These comments in **lnks** briefly identify what the file does and explain how to use it:

```
# Identify links to a file
# Usage: lnks file [directory]
```

Usage messages   The first **if** statement tests whether **lnks** was called with zero arguments or more than two arguments:

```
if [ $# -eq 0 -o $# -gt 2 ]; then
    echo "Usage: lnks file [directory]" 1>&2
    exit 1
fi
```

If either of these conditions is *true,* **lnks** sends a usage message to standard error and exits with a status of 1. The double quotation marks around the usage message prevent the shell from interpreting the brackets as special characters. The brackets in the usage message indicate that the **directory** argument is optional.

The second **if** statement tests whether the first command-line argument (**$1**) is a directory (the **−d** argument to test returns *true* if the file exists and is a directory):

```
if [ -d "$1" ]; then
    echo "First argument cannot be a directory." 1>&2
    echo "Usage: lnks file [directory]" 1>&2
    exit 1
else
    file="$1"
fi
```

If the first argument is a directory, **lnks** displays a usage message and exits. If it is not a directory, **lnks** saves the value of **$1** in the **file** variable because later in the script set resets the command-line arguments. If the value of **$1** is not saved before the set command is issued, its value is lost.

Test the arguments   The next section of **lnks** is an **if...then...elif** statement:

```
    if [ $# -eq 1 ]; then
        directory="."
    elif [ -d "$2" ]; then
        directory="$2"
    else
        echo "Optional second argument must be a directory." 1>&2
        echo "Usage: lnks file [directory]" 1>&2
        exit 1
fi
```

The first *test-command* determines whether the user specified a single argument on the command line. If the *test-command* returns 0 (*true*), the **directory** variable is assigned the value of the working directory (.). If the *test-command* returns *false*, the **elif** statement tests whether the second argument is a directory. If it is a directory, the **directory** variable is set equal to the second command-line argument, **$2**. If **$2** is not a directory, **lnks** sends a usage message to standard error and exits with a status of 1.

The next **if** statement in **lnks** tests whether **$file** does not exist. This test keeps **lnks** from wasting time looking for links to a non-existent file. The **test** builtin, when called with the three arguments **!**, **–f**, and **$file**, evaluates to *true* if the file **$file** does *not* exist:

```
[ ! -f "$file" ]
```

The **!** operator preceding the **–f** argument to **test** negates its result, yielding *false* if the file **$file** *does* exist and is an ordinary file.

Next **lnks** uses **set** and **ls –l** to check the number of links **$file** has:

```
# Check link count on file
set -- $(ls -l "$file")

linkcnt=$2
if [ "$linkcnt" -eq 1 ]; then
    echo "lnks: no other hard links to $file" 1>&2
    exit 0
fi
```

The **set** builtin uses command substitution (page 351) to set the positional parameters to the output of **ls –l**. The second field in this output is the link count, so the user-created variable **linkcnt** is set equal to **$2**. The **––** used with **set** prevents **set** from interpreting as an option the first argument produced by **ls –l** (the first argument is the access permissions for the file and typically begins with **–**). The **if** statement checks whether **$linkcnt** is equal to 1; if it is, **lnks** displays a message and exits. Although this message is not truly an error message, it is redirected to standard error. The way **lnks** has been written, all informational messages are sent to standard error. Only the final product of **lnks**—the pathnames of links to the specified file—is sent to standard output, so you can redirect the output as you please.

If the link count is greater than 1, **lnks** goes on to identify the *inode* (page 1169) for **$file**. As explained on page 216, comparing the inodes associated with filenames is a good way to determine whether the filenames are links to the same file. The **lnks** script uses **set** to set the positional parameters to the output of **ls –i**. The first argument to **set** is the inode number for the file, so the user-created variable named **inode** is assigned the value of **$1**:

```
# Get the inode of the given file
set $(ls -i "$file")

inode=$1
```

Finally **lnks** uses the find utility to search for files having inode numbers that match **$inode**:

```
# Find and print the files with that inode number
echo "lnks: using find to search for links..." 1>&2
find "$directory" -xdev -inum $inode -print
```

The find utility searches the directory hierarchy rooted at the directory specified by its first argument (**$directory**) for files that meet the criteria specified by the remaining arguments. In this example, the remaining arguments send the names of files having inodes matching **$inode** to standard output. Because files in different filesystems can have the same inode number yet not be linked, find must search only directories in the same filesystem as **$directory**. The **–xdev** (cross-device) argument prevents find from searching directories on other filesystems. Refer to page 213 for more information about filesystems and links.

The echo command preceding the find command in **lnks**, which tells the user that find is running, is included because find can take a long time to run. Because **lnks** does not include a final exit statement, the exit status of **lnks** is that of the last command it runs, find.

DEBUGGING SHELL SCRIPTS

When you are writing a script such as **lnks**, it is easy to make mistakes. You can use the shell's **–x** option to help debug a script. This option causes the shell to display each command before it runs the command. Tracing a script's execution in this way can give you information about where a problem lies.

You can run **lnks** as in the previous example and cause the shell to display each command before it is executed. Either set the **–x** option for the current shell (**set –x**) so all scripts display commands as they are run or use the **–x** option to affect only the shell running the script called by the command line.

```
$ bash -x lnks letter /home
+ '[' 2 -eq 0 -o 2 -gt 2 ']'
+ '[' -d letter ']'
+ file=letter
+ '[' 2 -eq 1 ']'
+ '[' -d /home ']'
+ directory=/home
+ '[' '!' -f letter ']'
...
```

PS4 Each command the script executes is preceded by the value of the **PS4** variable—a plus sign (**+**) by default, so you can distinguish debugging output from script-produced output. You must export **PS4** if you set it in the shell that calls the script. The next command sets **PS4** to **>>>>** followed by a SPACE and exports it:

```
$ export PS4='>>>> '
```

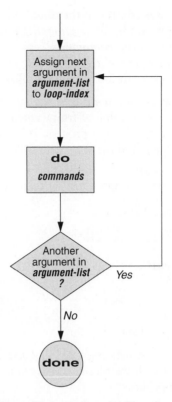

Figure 27-4 A **for...in** flowchart

You can also set the **–x** option of the shell running the script by putting the following set command near the beginning of the script:

```
set -x
```

Put **set –x** anywhere in the script you want to turn debugging on. Turn the debugging option off with a plus sign:

```
set +x
```

The **set –o xtrace** and **set +o xtrace** commands do the same things as **set –x** and **set +x**, respectively.

for...in

The **for...in** control structure has the following syntax:

for loop-index in argument-list
do
        commands
done

The **for...in** structure (Figure 27-4) assigns the value of the first argument in the *argument-list* to the *loop-index* and executes the *commands* between the **do** and **done** statements. The **do** and **done** statements mark the beginning and end of the **for** loop.

After it passes control to the **done** statement, the structure assigns the value of the second argument in the *argument-list* to the *loop-index* and repeats the *commands*. It then repeats the *commands* between the **do** and **done** statements one time for each argument in the *argument-list*. When the structure exhausts the *argument-list*, it passes control to the statement following **done**.

The following **for...in** structure assigns **apples** to the user-created variable **fruit** and then displays the value of **fruit**, which is **apples**. Next the structure assigns **oranges** to **fruit** and repeats the process. When it exhausts the argument list, the structure transfers control to the statement following **done**, which displays a message.

```
$ cat fruit
for fruit in apples oranges pears bananas
do
    echo "$fruit"
done
echo "Task complete."

$ ./fruit
apples
oranges
pears
bananas
Task complete.
```

The next script lists the names of the directory files in the working directory by looping through the files in the working directory and using test to determine which are directory files:

```
$ cat dirfiles
for i in *
do
    if [ -d "$i" ]
        then
            echo "$i"
    fi
done
```

The ambiguous file reference character * matches the names of all files (except hidden files) in the working directory. Prior to executing the **for** loop, the shell expands the * and uses the resulting list to assign successive values to the index variable **i**.

for

The **for** control structure has the following syntax:

for loop-index
do
    commands
done

In the **for** structure, the *loop-index* takes on the value of each of the command-line arguments, one at a time. The **for** structure is the same as the **for...in** structure

(Figure 27-4, page 983) except in terms of where it gets values for the *loop-index*. The **for** structure performs a sequence of commands, usually involving each argument in turn.

The following shell script shows a **for** structure displaying each command-line argument. The first line of the script, **for arg**, implies **for arg in "$@"**, where the shell expands **"$@"** into a list of quoted command-line arguments **"$1" "$2" "$3"** and so on. The balance of the script corresponds to the **for...in** structure.

```
$ cat for_test
for arg
do
    echo "$arg"
done
$ for_test candy gum chocolate
candy
gum
chocolate
```

optional THE whos SCRIPT

The following script, named **whos**, demonstrates the usefulness of the implied **"$@"** in the **for** structure. You give **whos** one or more users' full names or usernames as arguments, and **whos** displays information about the users. The **whos** script gets the information it displays from the first and fifth fields in the **/etc/passwd** file. The first field contains a username, and the fifth field typically contains the user's full name. You can provide a username as an argument to **whos** to identify the user's name or provide a name as an argument to identify the username. The **whos** script is similar to the finger utility, although **whos** delivers less information.

```
$ cat whos
#!/bin/bash

if [ $# -eq 0 ]
    then
        echo "Usage: whos id..." 1>&2
        exit 1
fi
for id
do
    gawk -F: '{print $1, $5}' /etc/passwd |
    grep -i "$id"
done
```

In the next example, **whos** identifies the user whose username is **chas** and the user whose name is **Marilou Smith**:

```
$ ./whos chas "Marilou Smith"
chas Charles Casey
msmith Marilou Smith
```

Use of "$@"   The **whos** script uses a **for** statement to loop through the command-line arguments. In this script the implied use of **"$@"** in the **for** loop is particularly beneficial because it causes the **for** loop to treat an argument that contains a SPACE as a single argument. This example encloses **Marilou Smith** in quotation marks, which causes the shell to pass it to the script as a single argument. Then the implied **"$@"** in the **for** statement causes the shell to regenerate the quoted argument **Marilou Smith** so that it is again treated as a single argument.

gawk   For each command-line argument, **whos** searches the **/etc/passwd** file. Inside the **for** loop, the gawk utility extracts the first (**$1**) and fifth (**$5**) fields from each line in **/etc/passwd**. The **–F:** option causes gawk to use a colon (**:**) as a field separator when it reads **/etc/passwd**, allowing it to break each line into fields. The gawk command sets and uses the **$1** and **$5** arguments; they are included within single quotation marks and are not interpreted by the shell. Do not confuse these arguments with positional parameters, which correspond to command-line arguments. The first and fifth fields are sent to grep (page 152) via a pipe. The grep utility searches for **$id** (to which the shell has assigned the value of a command-line argument) in its input. The **–i** option causes grep to ignore case as it searches; grep displays each line in its input that contains **$id**.

| at the end of a line   An interesting syntactical exception that bash makes for the pipe symbol (**|**) appears on the line with the gawk command: You do not have to quote a NEWLINE that immediately follows a pipe symbol (that is, a pipe symbol that is the last character on a line) to keep the NEWLINE from executing a command. Try giving the command **who |** and pressing RETURN. The shell displays a secondary prompt. If you then enter **sort** followed by another RETURN, you see a sorted who list. The pipe works even though a NEWLINE follows the pipe symbol.

while

The **while** control structure has the following syntax:

> *while* **test-command**
> *do*
>   *commands*
> *done*

As long as the **test-command** (Figure 27-5) returns a *true* exit status, the **while** structure continues to execute the series of **commands** delimited by the **do** and **done** statements. Before each loop through the **commands**, the structure executes the **test-command**. When the exit status of the **test-command** is *false*, the structure passes control to the statement after the **done** statement.

test builtin   The following shell script first initializes the **number** variable to zero. The test builtin then determines whether **number** is less than 10. The script uses test with the **–lt** argument to perform a numerical test. For numerical comparisons, you must use **–ne** (not equal), **–eq** (equal), **–gt** (greater than), **–ge** (greater than or equal to), **–lt** (less than), or **–le** (less than or equal to). For string comparisons, use **=** (equal) or **!=** (not equal) when you are working with test. In this example, test has an exit status of 0 (*true*) as long as **number** is less than 10. As long as test returns

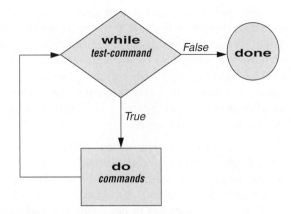

Figure 27-5 A **while** flowchart

true, the structure executes the commands between the **do** and **done** statements. See page 971 for information on the test builtin.

```
$ cat count
#!/bin/bash
number=0
while [ "$number" -lt 10 ]
    do
        echo -n "$number"
        ((number +=1))
    done
echo
$ ./count
0123456789
$
```

The echo command following **do** displays **number**. The **–n** prevents echo from issuing a NEWLINE following its output. The next command uses arithmetic evaluation [((...)); page 1032] to increment the value of **number** by 1. The **done** statement terminates the loop and returns control to the **while** statement to start the loop over again. The final echo causes **count** to send a NEWLINE character to standard output, so the next prompt occurs in the leftmost column on the display (rather than immediately following 9).

optional THE spell_check SCRIPT

The aspell utility (**aspell** package) checks the words in a file against a dictionary of correctly spelled words. With the **list** command, aspell runs in list mode: Input comes from standard input and aspell sends each potentially misspelled word to standard output. The following command produces a list of possible misspellings in the file **letter.txt**:

```
$ aspell list < letter.txt
quikly
portible
frendly
```

The next shell script, named **spell_check**, shows another use of a **while** structure. To find the incorrect spellings in a file, **spell_check** calls aspell to check a file against a system dictionary. But it goes a step further: It enables you to specify a list of correctly spelled words and removes these words from the output of aspell. This script is useful for removing words you use frequently, such as names and technical terms, that do not appear in a standard dictionary. Although you can duplicate the functionality of **spell_check** by using additional aspell dictionaries, the script is included here for its instructive value.

The **spell_check** script requires two filename arguments: the file containing the list of correctly spelled words and the file you want to check. The first **if** statement verifies the user specified two arguments. The next two **if** statements verify both arguments are readable files. (The exclamation point negates the sense of the following operator; the **–r** operator causes test to determine whether a file is readable. The result is a test that determines whether a file is *not readable*.)

```
$ cat spell_check
#!/bin/bash
# remove correct spellings from aspell output

if [ $# -ne 2 ]
    then
        echo "Usage: spell_check file1 file2" 1>&2
        echo "file1: list of correct spellings" 1>&2
        echo "file2: file to be checked" 1>&2
        exit 1
fi

if [ ! -r "$1" ]
    then
        echo "spell_check: $1 is not readable" 1>&2
        exit 1
fi
if [ ! -r "$2" ]
    then
        echo "spell_check: $2 is not readable" 1>&2
        exit 1
fi

aspell list < "$2" |
while read line
do
    if ! grep "^$line$" "$1" > /dev/null
        then
            echo $line
    fi
done
```

The **spell_check** script sends the output from aspell (with the **list** argument, so it produces a list of misspelled words on standard output) through a pipe to standard input of a **while** structure, which reads one line at a time (each line has one word on it) from standard input. The *test-command* (that is, **read line**) returns a *true* exit status as long as it receives a line from standard input.

Inside the **while** loop, an **if** statement[1] monitors the return value of grep, which determines whether the line that was read is in the user's list of correctly spelled words. The pattern grep searches for (the value of **$line**) is preceded and followed by special characters that specify the beginning and end of a line (^ and **$**, respectively). These special characters ensure that grep finds a match only if the **$line** variable matches an entire line in the file of correctly spelled words. (Otherwise, grep would match a string, such as **paul**, in the output of aspell if the file of correctly spelled words contained the word **paulson**.) These special characters, together with the value of the **$line** variable, form a regular expression (Appendix A).

The output of grep is redirected to **/dev/null** (page 239) because the output is not needed; only the exit code is important. The **if** statement checks the negated exit status of grep (the leading exclamation point negates or changes the sense of the exit status—*true* becomes *false,* and vice versa), which is 0 or *true* (*false* when negated) when a matching line is found. If the exit status is *not* 0 or *false* (*true* when negated), the word was *not* in the file of correctly spelled words. The echo builtin sends a list of words that are not in the file of correctly spelled words to standard output.

Once it detects the EOF (end of file), the read builtin returns a *false* exit status, control passes out of the **while** structure, and the script terminates.

Before you use **spell_check**, create a file of correct spellings containing words you use frequently but that are not in a standard dictionary. For example, if you work for a company named **Blinkenship and Klimowski, Attorneys,** you would put **Blinkenship** and **Klimowski** in the file. The following example shows how **spell_check** checks the spelling in a file named **memo** and removes **Blinkenship** and **Klimowski** from the output list of incorrectly spelled words:

```
$ aspell list < memo
Blinkenship
Klimowski
targat
hte
$ cat word_list
Blinkenship
Klimowski
$ ./spell_check word_list memo
targat
hte
```

Refer to the aspell manual (in the **/usr/share/doc/aspell** directory or at aspell.net) for more information.

---

1. This **if** statement can also be written as

```
if ! grep -qw "$line" "$1"
```

The –q option suppresses the output from grep so it returns only an exit code. The –w option causes grep to match only a whole word.

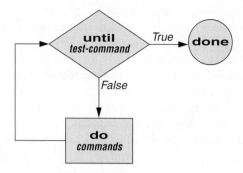

Figure 27-6   An **until** flowchart

until

The **until** and **while** structures are very similar, differing only in the sense of the test performed at the top of the loop. Figure 27-6 shows that **until** continues to loop *until* the *test-command* returns a *true* exit status. The **while** structure loops *while* the *test-command* continues to return a *true* or nonerror condition. The **until** control structure has the following syntax:

> *until test-command*
> *do*
>   *commands*
> *done*

The following script demonstrates an **until** structure that includes read. When the user enters the correct string of characters, the *test-command* is satisfied and the structure passes control out of the loop.

```
$ cat until1
secretname=zach
name=noname
echo "Try to guess the secret name!"
echo
until [ "$name" = "$secretname" ]
do
    echo -n "Your guess: "
    read name
done
echo "Very good."

$ ./until1
Try to guess the secret name!

Your guess: helen
Your guess: barbara
Your guess: rachael
Your guess: zach
Very good
```

The following **locktty** script is similar to the lock command on Berkeley UNIX and the **Lock Screen** menu selection in GNOME. The script prompts for a key (password) and uses an **until** control structure to lock the terminal. The **until** statement causes the system to ignore any characters typed at the keyboard until the user types the key followed by a RETURN on a line by itself, which unlocks the terminal. The **locktty** script can keep people from using your terminal while you are away from it for short periods of time. It saves you from having to log out if you are concerned about other users using your login.

```
$ cat locktty
#! /bin/bash

trap '' 1 2 3 18
stty -echo
echo -n "Key: "
read key_1
echo
echo -n "Again: "
read key_2
echo
key_3=
if [ "$key_1" = "$key_2" ]
    then
        tput clear
        until [ "$key_3" = "$key_2" ]
        do
            read key_3
        done
    else
        echo "locktty: keys do not match" 1>&2
fi
stty echo
```

Forget your password for **locktty**?

tip If you forget your key (password), you will need to log in from another (virtual) terminal and kill the process running **locktty**.

trap builtin The trap builtin (page 1025) at the beginning of the **locktty** script stops a user from being able to terminate the script by sending it a signal (for example, by pressing the interrupt key). Trapping signal 18 means that no one can use CONTROL-Z (job control, a stop from a tty) to defeat the lock. Table 27-5 on page 1025 provides a list of signals. The **stty −echo** command causes the terminal not to display characters typed at the keyboard, preventing the key the user enters from appearing on the screen. After turning off keyboard echo, the script prompts the user for a key, reads it into the user-created variable **key_1**, prompts the user to enter the same key again, and saves it in **key_2**. The statement **key_3=** creates a variable with a NULL value. If **key_1** and **key_2** match, **locktty** clears the screen (with the tput command) and starts an **until** loop. The **until** loop keeps attempting to read from the terminal and assigning the input to the **key_3** variable. Once the user types a string that matches one of the original keys (**key_2**), the **until** loop terminates and keyboard echo is turned on again.

break AND continue

You can interrupt a for, while, or until loop by using a break or continue statement. The break statement transfers control to the statement after the done statement, thereby terminating execution of the loop. The continue command transfers control to the done statement, continuing execution of the loop.

The following script demonstrates the use of these two statements. The for...in structure loops through the values 1–10. The first if statement executes its commands when the value of the index is less than or equal to 3 ($index –le 3). The second if statement executes its commands when the value of the index is greater than or equal to 8 ($index –ge 8). In between the two ifs, echo displays the value of the index. For all values up to and including 3, the first if statement displays continue, executes a continue statement that skips echo $index and the second if statement, and continues with the next for statement. For the value of 8, the second if statement displays break and executes a break statement that exits from the for loop.

```
$ cat brk
for index in 1 2 3 4 5 6 7 8 9 10
    do
        if [ $index -le 3 ] ; then
            echo "continue"
            continue
        fi
#
    echo $index
#
    if [ $index -ge 8 ] ; then
        echo "break"
        break
    fi
done

$ ./brk
continue
continue
continue
4
5
6
7
8
break
$
```

case

The case structure (Figure 27-7) is a multiple-branch decision mechanism. The path taken through the structure depends on a match or lack of a match between the *test-string* and one of the *patterns*. The case control structure has the following syntax:

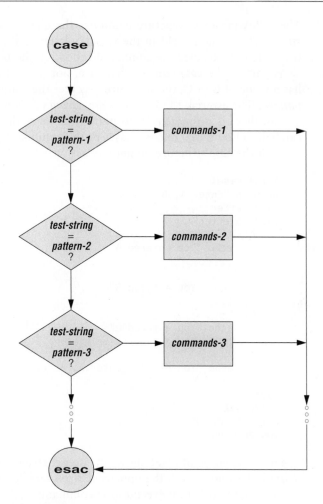

Figure 27-7   A case flowchart

```
case test-string in
    pattern-1)
        commands-1
        ;;
    pattern-2)
        commands-2
        ;;
    pattern-3)
        commands-3
        ;;
. . .
esac
```

The following **case** structure examines the character the user enters as the *test-string*. This value is held in the variable **letter**. If the *test-string* has a value of **A**, the structure executes the command following the *pattern* **A**. The right parenthesis is part of the **case** control structure, not part of the *pattern*. If the *test-string* has a value of **B** or **C**, the structure executes the command following the matching *pattern*. The asterisk (*****) indicates *any string of characters* and serves as a catchall in case there is no match. If no *pattern* matches the *test-string* and if there is no catchall (*****) *pattern*, control passes to the command following the **esac** statement, without the **case** structure taking any action.

```
$ cat case1
echo -n "Enter A, B, or C: "
read letter
case "$letter" in
    A)
        echo "You entered A"
        ;;
    B)
        echo "You entered B"
        ;;
    C)
        echo "You entered C"
        ;;
    *)
        echo "You did not enter A, B, or C"
        ;;
esac
$ ./case1
Enter A, B, or C: B
You entered B
```

The next execution of **case1** shows the user entering a lowercase **b**. Because the *test-string* **b** does not match the uppercase **B** *pattern* (or any other *pattern* in the **case** statement), the program executes the commands following the catchall *pattern* and displays a message:

```
$ ./case1
Enter A, B, or C: b
You did not enter A, B, or C
```

The *pattern* in the **case** structure is analogous to an ambiguous file reference. It can include any special characters and strings shown in Table 27-2.

The next script accepts both uppercase and lowercase letters:

```
$ cat case2
echo -n "Enter A, B, or C: "
read letter
```

```
case "$letter" in
    a|A)
        echo "You entered A"
        ;;
    b|B)
        echo "You entered B"
        ;;
    c|C)
        echo "You entered C"
        ;;
    *)
        echo "You did not enter A, B, or C"
        ;;
esac

$ ./case2
Enter A, B, or C: b
You entered B
```

Table 27-2 Patterns

Pattern	Function
*	Matches any string of characters. Use for the default case.
?	Matches any single character.
[...]	Defines a character class. Any characters enclosed within brackets are tried, one at a time, in an attempt to match a single character. A hyphen between two characters specifies a range of characters.
|	Separates alternative choices that satisfy a particular branch of the **case** structure.

optional The following example shows how you can use the **case** structure to create a simple menu. The **command_menu** script uses echo to present menu items and prompt the user for a selection. (The **select** control structure [page 999] is a much easier way of coding a menu.) The **case** structure then executes the appropriate utility depending on the user's selection.

```
$ cat command_menu
#!/bin/bash
# menu interface to simple commands

echo -e "\n        COMMAND MENU\n"
echo "  a.  Current date and time"
echo "  b.  Users currently logged in"
echo "  c.  Name of the working directory"
echo -e "  d.  Contents of the working directory\n"
echo -n "Enter a, b, c, or d: "
read answer
echo
```

```
        #
        case "$answer" in
            a)
                date
                ;;
            b)
                who
                ;;
            c)
                pwd
                ;;
            d)
                ls
                ;;
            *)
                echo "There is no selection: $answer"
                ;;
        esac

$ ./command_menu

            COMMAND MENU

        a.  Current date and time
        b.  Users currently logged in
        c.  Name of the working directory
        d.  Contents of the working directory

    Enter a, b, c, or d: a

    Wed Jan  6 12:31:12 PST 2010
```

echo –e   The –e option causes echo to interpret \n as a NEWLINE character. If you do not include this option, echo does not output the extra blank lines that make the menu easy to read but instead outputs the (literal) two-character sequence \n. The –e option causes echo to interpret several other backslash-quoted characters (Table 27-3). Remember to quote (i.e., place double quotation marks around the string) the backslash-quoted character so the shell does not interpret it but passes the backslash and the character to echo. See **xpg_echo** (page 343) for a way to avoid using the –e option.

Table 27-3   Special characters in echo (must use **–e**)

Quoted character	echo **displays**
\a	Alert (bell)
\b	BACKSPACE
\c	Suppress trailing NEWLINE
\f	FORMFEED
\n	NEWLINE
\r	RETURN

Table 27-3   Special characters in echo (must use **-e**) (continued)

Quoted character	echo **displays**
\t	Horizontal TAB
\v	Vertical TAB
\\	Backslash
\nnn	The character with the ASCII octal code *nnn;* if *nnn* is not valid, echo displays the string literally

You can also use the **case** control structure to take various actions in a script, depending on how many arguments the script is called with. The following script, named **safedit**, uses a **case** structure that branches based on the number of command-line arguments ($#). It saves a backup copy of a file you are editing with vim.

```
$ cat safedit
#!/bin/bash

PATH=/bin:/usr/bin
script=$(basename $0)
case $# in

    0)
        vim
        exit 0
        ;;

    1)
        if [ ! -f "$1" ]
            then
                vim "$1"
                exit 0
            fi
        if [ ! -r "$1" -o ! -w "$1" ]
            then
                echo "$script: check permissions on $1" 1>&2
                exit 1
            else
                editfile=$1
            fi
        if [ ! -w "." ]
            then
                echo "$script: backup cannot be " \
                    "created in the working directory" 1>&2
                exit 1
            fi
        ;;
    *)
        echo "Usage: $script [file-to-edit]" 1>&2
        exit 1
        ;;
esac
```

```
                    tempfile=/tmp/$$.$script
                    cp $editfile $tempfile
                    if vim $editfile
                        then
                            mv $tempfile bak.$(basename $editfile)
                            echo "$script: backup file created"
                        else
                            mv $tempfile editerr
                            echo "$script: edit error--copy of " \
                                "original file is in editerr" 1>&2
          fi
```

If you call **safedit** without any arguments, the **case** structure executes its first branch and calls vim without a filename argument. Because an existing file is not being edited, **safedit** does not create a backup file. If you call **safedit** with one argument, it runs the commands in the second branch of the **case** structure and verifies that the file specified by **$1** does not yet exist or is the name of a file for which the user has read and write permission. The **safedit** script also verifies that the user has write permission for the working directory. If the user calls **safedit** with more than one argument, the third branch of the **case** structure presents a usage message and exits with a status of 1.

Set **PATH**   In addition to using a **case** structure for branching based on the number of command-line arguments, the **safedit** script introduces several other features. At the beginning of the script, the **PATH** variable is set to search **/bin** and **/usr/bin**. Setting **PATH** in this way ensures that the commands executed by the script are standard utilities, which are kept in those directories. By setting this variable inside a script, you can avoid the problems that might occur if users have set **PATH** to search their own directories first and have scripts or programs with the same names as the utilities the script calls. You can also include absolute pathnames within a script to achieve this end, although this practice can make a script less portable.

Name of the   The next line creates a variable named **script** and uses command substitution to
program   assign the simple filename of the script to it:

```
          script=$(basename $0)
```

The basename utility sends the simple filename component of its argument to standard output, which is assigned to the **script** variable, using command substitution. The **$0** holds the command the script was called with (page 1013). No matter which of the following commands the user calls the script with, the output of basename is the simple filename **safedit**:

```
$ /home/max/bin/safedit memo
$ ./safedit memo
$ safedit memo
```

After the **script** variable is set, it replaces the filename of the script in usage and error messages. By using a variable that is derived from the command that invoked the script rather than a filename that is hardcoded into the script, you can create links to the script or rename it, and the usage and error messages will still provide accurate information.

Naming temporary files

Another feature of **safedit** relates to the use of the **$$** parameter in the name of a temporary file. The statement following the **esac** statement creates and assigns a value to the **tempfile** variable. This variable contains the name of a temporary file that is stored in the **/tmp** directory, as are many temporary files. The temporary filename begins with the PID number of the shell and ends with the name of the script. Using the PID number ensures that the filename is unique. Thus **safedit** will not attempt to overwrite an existing file, as might happen if two people were using **safedit** at the same time. The name of the script is appended so that, should the file be left in **/tmp** for some reason, you can figure out where it came from.

The PID number is used in front of—rather than after—**$script** in the filename because of the 14-character limit placed on filenames by some older versions of UNIX. Linux systems do not have this limitation. Because the PID number ensures the uniqueness of the filename, it is placed first so that it cannot be truncated. (If the **$script** component is truncated, the filename is still unique.) For the same reason, when a backup file is created inside the **if** control structure a few lines down in the script, the filename consists of the string **bak.** followed by the name of the file being edited. On an older system, if **bak** were used as a suffix rather than a prefix and the original filename were 14 characters long, **.bak** might be lost and the original file would be overwritten. The basename utility extracts the simple filename of **$editfile** before it is prefixed with **bak.**.

The **safedit** script uses an unusual *test-command* in the **if** structure: **vim $editfile**. The *test-command* calls vim to edit **$editfile**. When you finish editing the file and exit from vim, vim returns an exit code. The **if** control structure uses that exit code to determine which branch to take. If the editing session completed successfully, vim returns 0 and the statements following the **then** statement are executed. If vim does not terminate normally (as would occur if the user killed [page 470] the vim process), vim returns a nonzero exit status and the script executes the statements following **else**.

select

The **select** control structure is based on the one found in the Korn Shell. It displays a menu, assigns a value to a variable based on the user's choice of items, and executes a series of commands. The **select** control structure has the following syntax:

```
select varname [in arg . . . ]
do
     commands
done
```

The **select** structure displays a menu of the *arg* items. If you omit the keyword **in** and the list of arguments, **select** uses the positional parameters in place of the *arg* items. The menu is formatted with numbers before each item. For example, a **select** structure that begins with

```
select fruit in apple banana blueberry kiwi orange watermelon STOP
```

displays the following menu:

```
1) apple      3) blueberry   5) orange      7) STOP
2) banana     4) kiwi        6) watermelon
```

The **select** structure uses the values of the **LINES** and **COLUMNS** variables to specify the size of the display. (**LINES** has a default value of 24; **COLUMNS** has a default value of 80.) With **COLUMNS** set to 20, the menu looks like this:

```
1) apple
2) banana
3) blueberry
4) kiwi
5) orange
6) watermelon
7) STOP
```

PS3   After displaying the menu, **select** displays the value of **PS3**, the **select** prompt. The default value of **PS3** is ?#, but it is typically set to a more meaningful value. When you enter a valid number (one in the menu range) in response to the **PS3** prompt, **select** sets *varname* to the argument corresponding to the number you entered. An invalid entry causes the shell to set *varname* to null. Either way, **select** stores your response in the keyword variable **REPLY** and then executes the *commands* between **do** and **done**. If you press RETURN without entering a choice, the shell redisplays the menu and the **PS3** prompt.

The **select** structure continues to issue the **PS3** prompt and execute the *commands* until something causes it to exit—typically a **break** or **exit** statement. A **break** statement exits from the loop and an **exit** statement exits from the script.

The following script illustrates the use of **select**:

```
$ cat fruit2
#!/bin/bash
PS3="Choose your favorite fruit from these possibilities: "
select FRUIT in apple banana blueberry kiwi orange watermelon STOP
do
    if [ "$FRUIT" == "" ]; then
        echo -e "Invalid entry.\n"
        continue
    elif [ $FRUIT = STOP ]; then
        echo "Thanks for playing!"
        break
    fi
echo "You chose $FRUIT as your favorite."
echo -e "That is choice number $REPLY.\n"
done
```

```
$ ./fruit2
1) apple        3) blueberry   5) orange       7) STOP
2) banana       4) kiwi        6) watermelon
Choose your favorite fruit from these possibilities: 3
You chose blueberry as your favorite.
That is choice number 3.

Choose your favorite fruit from these possibilities: 99
Invalid entry.

Choose your favorite fruit from these possibilities: 7
Thanks for playing!
```

After setting the **PS3** prompt and establishing the menu with the **select** statement, **fruit2** executes the *commands* between **do** and **done**. If the user submits an invalid entry, the shell sets *varname* (**$FRUIT**) to a null value. If $FRUIT is null, echo displays an error; **continue** then causes the shell to redisplay the **PS3** prompt. If the entry is valid, the script tests whether the user wants to stop. If so, echo displays a message and **break** exits from the **select** structure (and from the script). If the user enters a valid response and does not want to stop, the script displays the name and number of the user's response. (See page 996 for information about the echo –e option.)

HERE DOCUMENT

A Here document allows you to redirect input to a shell script from within the shell script itself. A Here document is so named because it is *here*—immediately accessible in the shell script—instead of *there*, perhaps in another file.

The following script, named **birthday**, contains a Here document. The two less than symbols (<<) in the first line indicate a Here document follows. One or more characters that delimit the Here document follow the less than symbols—this example uses a plus sign. Whereas the opening delimiter must appear adjacent to the less than symbols, the closing delimiter must be on a line by itself. The shell sends everything between the two delimiters to the process as standard input. In the example it is as though you have redirected standard input to grep from a file, except that the file is embedded in the shell script:

```
$ cat birthday
grep -i "$1" <<+
Max     June 22
Barbara February 3
Darlene May 8
Helen   March 13
Zach    January 23
Nancy   June 26
+
$ ./birthday Zach
Zach    January 23
$ ./birthday june
Max     June 22
Nancy   June 26
```

When you run **birthday**, it lists all the Here document lines that contain the argument you called it with. In this case the first time **birthday** is run, it displays Zach's birthday because it is called with an argument of **Zach**. The second run displays all the birthdays in June. The –i argument causes grep's search not to be case sensitive.

optional The next script, named **bundle**,[2] includes a clever use of a Here document. The **bundle** script is an elegant example of a script that creates a shell archive (**shar**) file. The script creates a file that is itself a shell script containing several other files as well as the code to re-create the original files:

```
$ cat bundle
#!/bin/bash
# bundle:  group files into distribution package

echo "# To unbundle, bash this file"
for i
do
    echo "echo $i 1>&2"
    echo "cat >$i <<'End of $i'"
    cat $i
    echo "End of $i"
done
```

Just as the shell does not treat special characters that occur in standard input of a shell script as special, so the shell does not treat the special characters that occur between the delimiters in a Here document as special.

As the following example shows, the output of **bundle** is a shell script, which is redirected to a file named **bothfiles**. It contains the contents of each file given as an argument to **bundle** (**file1** and **file2** in this case) inside a Here document. To extract the original files from **bothfiles**, you simply give it as an argument to a bash command. Before each Here document is a cat command that causes the Here document to be written to a new file when **bothfiles** is run:

```
$ cat file1
This is a file.
It contains two lines.
$ cat file2
This is another file.
It contains
three lines.

$ ./bundle file1 file2 > bothfiles
$ cat bothfiles
# To unbundle, bash this file
echo file1 1>&2
cat >file1 <<'End of file1'
```

---

2. Thanks to Brian W. Kernighan and Rob Pike, *The Unix Programming Environment* (Englewood Cliffs, N.J.: Prentice-Hall, 1984), 98. Reprinted with permission.

```
              This is a file.
              It contains two lines.
              End of file1
              echo file2 1>&2
              cat >file2 <<'End of file2'
              This is another file.
              It contains
              three lines.
              End of file2
```

In the next example, **file1** and **file2** are removed before **bothfiles** is run. The **bothfiles** script echoes the names of the files it creates as it creates them. The ls command then shows that **bothfiles** has re-created **file1** and **file2**:

```
$ rm file1 file2
$ bash bothfiles
file1
file2
$ ls
bothfiles
file1
file2
```

FILE DESCRIPTORS

As discussed on page 286, before a process can read from or write to a file, it must open that file. When a process opens a file, Linux associates a number (called a *file descriptor*) with the file. A file descriptor is an index into the process's table of open files. Each process has its own set of open files and its own file descriptors. After opening a file, a process reads from and writes to that file by referring to its file descriptor. When it no longer needs the file, the process closes the file, freeing the file descriptor.

A typical Linux process starts with three open files: standard input (file descriptor 0), standard output (file descriptor 1), and standard error (file descriptor 2). Often these are the only files the process needs. Recall that you redirect standard output with the symbol > or the symbol **1>** and that you redirect standard error with the symbol **2>**. Although you can redirect other file descriptors, because file descriptors other than 0, 1, and 2 do not have any special conventional meaning, it is rarely useful to do so. The exception is in programs that you write yourself, in which case you control the meaning of the file descriptors and can take advantage of redirection.

Opening a file descriptor   The Bourne Again Shell opens files using the exec builtin as follows:

exec n> outfile
exec m< infile

The first line opens *outfile* for output and holds it open, associating it with file descriptor *n*. The second line opens *infile* for input and holds it open, associating it with file descriptor *m*.

Duplicating a file descriptor The `<&` token duplicates an input file descriptor; `>&` duplicates an output file descriptor. You can duplicate a file descriptor by making it refer to the same file as another open file descriptor, such as standard input or output. Use the following format to open or redirect file descriptor *n* as a duplicate of file descriptor *m*:

> *exec n<&m*

Once you have opened a file, you can use it for input and output in two ways. First, you can use I/O redirection on any command line, redirecting standard output to a file descriptor with `>&n` or redirecting standard input from a file descriptor with `<&n`. Second, you can use the read (page 1019) and echo builtins. If you invoke other commands, including functions (page 338), they inherit these open files and file descriptors. When you have finished using a file, you can close it using

> *exec n<&–*

When you invoke the shell function in the next example, named **mycp**, with two arguments, it copies the file named by the first argument to the file named by the second argument. If you supply only one argument, the script copies the file named by the argument to standard output. If you invoke **mycp** with no arguments, it copies standard input to standard output.

A function is not a shell script

tip The **mycp** example is a shell function; it will not work as you expect if you execute it as a shell script. (It will work: The function will be created in a very short-lived subshell, which is probably of little use.) You can enter this function from the keyboard. If you put the function in a file, you can run it as an argument to the . (dot) builtin (page 284). You can also put the function in a startup file if you want it to be always available (page 339).

```
function mycp ()
{
case $# in
    0)
        # Zero arguments
        # File descriptor 3 duplicates standard input
        # File descriptor 4 duplicates standard output
        exec 3<&0 4<&1
        ;;
    1)
        # One argument
        # Open the file named by the argument for input
        # and associate it with file descriptor 3
        # File descriptor 4 duplicates standard output
        exec 3< $1 4<&1
        ;;
    2)
        # Two arguments
        # Open the file named by the first argument for input
        # and associate it with file descriptor 3
        # Open the file named by the second argument for output
        # and associate it with file descriptor 4
        exec 3< $1 4> $2
        ;;
```

```
          *)
                echo "Usage: mycp [source [dest]]"
                return 1
                ;;
      esac

      # Call cat with input coming from file descriptor 3
      # and output going to file descriptor 4
      cat <&3 >&4

      # Close file descriptors 3 and 4
      exec 3<&- 4<&-
      }
```

The real work of this function is done in the line that begins with cat. The rest of the script arranges for file descriptors 3 and 4, which are the input and output of the cat command, to be associated with the appropriate files.

optional The next program takes two filenames on the command line, sorts both, and sends the output to temporary files. The program then merges the sorted files to standard output, preceding each line by a number that indicates which file it came from.

```
$ cat sortmerg
#!/bin/bash
usage ()
{
if [ $# -ne 2 ]; then
    echo "Usage: $0 file1 file2" 2>&1
    exit 1
    fi
}

# Default temporary directory
: ${TEMPDIR:=/tmp}

# Check argument count
usage "$@"

# Set up temporary files for sorting
file1=$TEMPDIR/$$.file1
file2=$TEMPDIR/$$.file2

# Sort
sort $1 > $file1
sort $2 > $file2

# Open $file1 and $file2 for reading. Use file descriptors 3 and 4.
exec 3<$file1
exec 4<$file2

# Read the first line from each file to figure out how to start.
read Line1 <&3
status1=$?
read Line2 <&4
status2=$?
```

```
# Strategy: while there is still input left in both files:
#    Output the line that should come first.
#    Read a new line from the file that line came from.
while [ $status1 -eq 0 -a $status2 -eq 0 ]
    do
        if [[ "$Line2" > "$Line1" ]]; then
            echo -e "1.\t$Line1"
            read -u3 Line1
            status1=$?
        else
            echo -e "2.\t$Line2"
            read -u4 Line2
            status2=$?
        fi
    done

# Now one of the files is at end-of-file.
# Read from each file until the end.
# First file1:
while [ $status1 -eq 0 ]
    do
        echo -e "1.\t$Line1"
        read Line1 <&3
        status1=$?
    done
# Next file2:
while [[ $status2 -eq 0 ]]
    do
        echo -e "2.\t$Line2"
        read Line2 <&4
        status2=$?
    done

# Close and remove both input files
exec 3<&- 4<&-
rm -f $file1 $file2
exit 0
```

PARAMETERS AND VARIABLES

Shell parameters and variables were introduced on page 301. This section adds to the previous coverage with a discussion of array variables, global versus local variables, special and positional parameters, and expansion of null and unset variables.

ARRAY VARIABLES

The Bourne Again Shell supports one-dimensional array variables. The subscripts are integers with zero-based indexing (i.e., the first element of the array has the subscript 0). The following format declares and assigns values to an array:

name=(element1 element2 ...)

The following example assigns four values to the array **NAMES**:

```
$ NAMES=(max helen sam zach)
```

You reference a single element of an array as follows:

```
$ echo ${NAMES[2]}
sam
```

The subscripts [*] and [@] both extract the entire array but work differently when used within double quotation marks. An @ produces an array that is a duplicate of the original array; an * produces a single element of an array (or a plain variable) that holds all the elements of the array separated by the first character in **IFS** (normally a SPACE). In the following example, the array A is filled with the elements of the **NAMES** variable using an *, and B is filled using an @. The declare builtin with the –a option displays the values of the arrays (and reminds you that bash uses zero-based indexing for arrays):

```
$ A=("${NAMES[*]}")
$ B=("${NAMES[@]}")

$ declare -a
declare -a A='([0]="max helen sam zach")'
declare -a B='([0]="max" [1]="helen" [2]="sam" [3]="zach")'
...
declare -a NAMES='([0]="max" [1]="helen" [2]="sam" [3]="zach")'
```

From the output of declare, you can see that **NAMES** and B have multiple elements. In contrast, A, which was assigned its value with an * within double quotation marks, has only one element: A has all its elements enclosed between double quotation marks.

In the next example, echo attempts to display element 1 of array A. Nothing is displayed because A has only one element and that element has an index of 0. Element 0 of array A holds all four names. Element 1 of B holds the second item in the array and element 0 holds the first item.

```
$ echo ${A[1]}

$ echo ${A[0]}
max helen sam zach
$ echo ${B[1]}
helen
$ echo ${B[0]}
max
```

You can apply the ${#*name*[*]} operator to array variables, returning the number of elements in the array:

```
$ echo ${#NAMES[*]}
4
```

The same operator, when given the index of an element of an array in place of *, returns the length of the element:

```
$ echo ${#NAMES[1]}
5
```

You can use subscripts on the left side of an assignment statement to replace selected elements of the array:

```
$ NAMES[1]=max
$ echo ${NAMES[*]}
max max sam zach
```

LOCALITY OF VARIABLES

By default variables are local to the process in which they are declared. Thus a shell script does not have access to variables declared in your login shell unless you explicitly make the variables available (global). Under bash, export makes a variable available to child processes.

export   Once you use the export builtin with a variable name as an argument, the shell places the value of the variable in the calling environment of child processes. This *call by value* gives each child process a copy of the variable for its own use.

The following **extest1** shell script assigns a value of **american** to the variable named **cheese** and then displays its filename (**extest1**) and the value of **cheese**. The **extest1** script then calls **subtest**, which attempts to display the same information. Next **subtest** declares a **cheese** variable and displays its value. When **subtest** finishes, it returns control to the parent process, which is executing **extest1**. At this point **extest1** again displays the value of the original **cheese** variable.

```
$ cat extest1
cheese=american
echo "extest1 1: $cheese"
subtest
echo "extest1 2: $cheese"
$ cat subtest
echo "subtest 1: $cheese"
cheese=swiss
echo "subtest 2: $cheese"
$ ./extest1
extest1 1: american
subtest 1:
subtest 2: swiss
extest1 2: american
```

The **subtest** script never receives the value of **cheese** from **extest1**, and **extest1** never loses the value. In bash—unlike in the real world—a child can never affect its parent's attributes. When a process attempts to display the value of a variable that has not been declared, as is the case with **subtest**, the process displays nothing; the value of an undeclared variable is that of a null string.

The following **extest2** script is the same as **extest1** except it uses **export** to make **cheese** available to the **subtest** script:

```
$ cat extest2
export cheese=american
echo "extest2 1: $cheese"
subtest
echo "extest2 2: $cheese"
$ ./extest2
extest2 1: american
subtest 1: american
subtest 2: swiss
extest2 2: american
```

Here the child process inherits the value of **cheese** as **american** and, after displaying this value, changes *its copy* to **swiss**. When control is returned to the parent, the parent's copy of **cheese** retains its original value: **american**.

An **export** builtin can optionally include an assignment:

```
export cheese=american
```

The preceding statement is equivalent to the following two statements:

```
cheese=american
export cheese
```

Although it is rarely done, you can export a variable before you assign a value to it. You do not need to export an already-exported variable a second time after you change its value.

FUNCTIONS

Because functions run in the same environment as the shell that calls them, variables are implicitly shared by a shell and a function it calls.

```
$ function nam () {
> echo $myname
> myname=zach
> }

$ myname=sam
$ nam
sam
$ echo $myname
zach
```

In the preceding example, the **myname** variable is set to **sam** in the interactive shell. The **nam** function then displays the value of **myname** (**sam**) and sets **myname** to **zach**. The final **echo** shows that, in the interactive shell, the value of **myname** has been changed to **zach**.

Function local variables

Local variables are helpful in a function written for general use. Because the function is called by many scripts that might be written by different programmers, you need to make sure the names of the variables used within the function do not conflict with (i.e., duplicate) the names of the variables in the programs that call the function. Local variables eliminate this problem. When used within a function, the typeset builtin declares a variable to be local to the function it is defined in.

The next example shows the use of a local variable in a function. It features two variables named **count**. The first is declared and assigned a value of 10 in the interactive shell. Its value never changes, as echo verifies after **count_down** is run. The other **count** is declared, using typeset, to be local to the function. Its value, which is unknown outside the function, ranges from 4 to 1, as the echo command within the function confirms.

The following example shows the function being entered from the keyboard; it is not a shell script. See the tip "A function is not a shell script" on page 1004.

```
$ function count_down () {
> typeset count
> count=$1
> while [ $count -gt 0 ]
> do
> echo "$count..."
> ((count=count-1))
> sleep 1
> done
> echo "Blast Off."
> }
$ count=10
$ count_down 4
4...
3...
2...
1...
Blast Off.
$ echo $count
10
```

The ((count=count-1)) assignment is enclosed between double parentheses, which cause the shell to perform an arithmetic evaluation (page 1032). Within the double parentheses you can reference shell variables without the leading dollar sign ($).

SPECIAL PARAMETERS

Special parameters enable you to access useful values pertaining to command-line arguments and the execution of shell commands. You reference a shell special parameter by preceding a special character with a dollar sign ($). As with positional parameters, it is not possible to modify the value of a special parameter by assignment.

$$: PID NUMBER

The shell stores in the **$$** parameter the PID number of the process that is executing it. In the following interaction, echo displays the value of this variable and the ps utility confirms its value. Both commands show that the shell has a PID number of 5209:

```
$ echo $$
5209
$ ps
  PID TTY          TIME CMD
 5209 pts/1    00:00:00 bash
 6015 pts/1    00:00:00 ps
```

Because echo is built into the shell, the shell does not create another process when you give an echo command. However, the results are the same whether echo is a builtin or not, because the shell substitutes the value of **$$** *before* it forks a new process to run a command. Try using the echo utility (**/bin/echo**), which is run by another process, and see what happens. In the following example, the shell substitutes the value of **$$** and passes that value to cp as a prefix for a filename:

```
$ echo $$
8232
$ cp memo $$.memo
$ ls
8232.memo memo
```

Incorporating a PID number in a filename is useful for creating unique filenames when the meanings of the names do not matter; this technique is often used in shell scripts for creating names of temporary files. When two people are running the same shell script, having unique filenames keeps the users from inadvertently sharing the same temporary file.

The following example demonstrates that the shell creates a new shell process when it runs a shell script. The **id2** script displays the PID number of the process running it (not the process that called it—the substitution for **$$** is performed by the shell that is forked to run **id2**):

```
$ cat id2
echo "$0 PID= $$"
$ echo $$
8232
$ id2
./id2 PID= 8362
$ echo $$
8232
```

The first echo displays the PID number of the interactive shell. Then **id2** displays its name (**$0**) and the PID number of the subshell that it is running in. The last echo shows that the PID number of the interactive shell has not changed.

$!** The shell stores the value of the PID number of the last process that ran in the background in **$!. The following example executes sleep as a background task and uses echo to display the value of **$!**:

```
$ sleep 60 &
[1] 8376
$ echo $!
8376
```

$?: EXIT STATUS

When a process stops executing for any reason, it returns an *exit status* to its parent process. The exit status is also referred to as a *condition code* or a *return code*. The $? variable stores the exit status of the last command.

By convention a nonzero exit status represents a *false* value and means the command failed. A zero is *true* and indicates the command executed successfully. In the following example, the first ls command succeeds and the second fails, as demonstrated by the exit status:

```
$ ls es
es
$ echo $?
0
$ ls xxx
ls: xxx: No such file or directory
$ echo $?
1
```

You can specify the exit status that a shell script returns by using the exit builtin, followed by a number, to terminate the script. If you do not use exit with a number to terminate a script, the exit status of the script is that of the last command the script ran.

```
$ cat es
echo This program returns an exit status of 7.
exit 7
$ es
This program returns an exit status of 7.
$ echo $?
7
$ echo $?
0
```

The es shell script displays a message and terminates execution with an exit command that returns an exit status of 7, the user-defined exit status in this script. The first echo then displays the value of the exit status of es. The second echo displays the value of the exit status of the first echo. This value is 0, indicating the first echo was successful.

POSITIONAL PARAMETERS

Positional parameters comprise the command name and command-line arguments. These parameters are called *positional* because within a shell script, you refer to them by their position on the command line. Only the set builtin (page 1014) allows you to change the values of positional parameters. However, you cannot change the value of the command name from within a script.

$#: NUMBER OF COMMAND-LINE ARGUMENTS

The $# parameter holds the number of arguments on the command line (positional parameters), not counting the command itself:

```
$ cat num_args
echo "This script was called with $# arguments."
$ ./num_args sam max zach
This script was called with 3 arguments.
```

$0: NAME OF THE CALLING PROGRAM

The shell stores the name of the command you used to call a program in parameter $0. This parameter is numbered zero because it appears before the first argument on the command line:

```
$ cat abc
echo "The command used to run this script is $0"
$ ./abc
The command used to run this script is ./abc
$ /home/sam/abc
The command used to run this script is /home/sam/abc
```

The preceding shell script uses echo to verify the name of the script you are executing. You can use the basename utility and command substitution to extract and display the simple filename of the command:

```
$ cat abc2
echo "The command used to run this script is $(basename $0)"
$ /home/sam/abc2
The command used to run this script is abc2
```

$1–$n: COMMAND-LINE ARGUMENTS

The first argument on the command line is represented by parameter $1, the second argument by $2, and so on up to $n. For values of n greater than 9, the number must be enclosed within braces. For example, the twelfth command-line argument is represented by ${12}. The following script displays positional parameters that hold command-line arguments:

```
$ cat display_5args
echo First 5 arguments are $1 $2 $3 $4 $5

$ ./display_5args zach max helen
First 5 arguments are zach max helen
```

The **display_5args** script displays the first five command-line arguments. The shell assigns a null value to each parameter that represents an argument that is not present on the command line. Thus the **$4** and **$5** parameters have null values in this example.

shift: PROMOTES COMMAND-LINE ARGUMENTS

The shift builtin promotes each command-line argument. The first argument (which was **$1**) is discarded. The second argument (which was **$2**) becomes the first argument (now **$1**), the third becomes the second, and so on. Because no "unshift" command exists, you cannot bring back arguments that have been discarded. An optional argument to shift specifies the number of positions to shift (and the number of arguments to discard); the default is 1.

The following **demo_shift** script is called with three arguments. Double quotation marks around the arguments to echo preserve the spacing of the output. The program displays the arguments and shifts them repeatedly until no more arguments are left to shift:

```
$ cat demo_shift
echo "arg1= $1     arg2= $2     arg3= $3"
shift
echo "arg1= $1     arg2= $2     arg3= $3"
shift
echo "arg1= $1     arg2= $2     arg3= $3"
shift
echo "arg1= $1     arg2= $2     arg3= $3"
shift
$ ./demo_shift alice helen zach
arg1= alice    arg2= helen    arg3= zach
arg1= helen    arg2= zach     arg3=
arg1= zach     arg2=     arg3=
arg1=     arg2=     arg3=
```

Repeatedly using shift is a convenient way to loop over all command-line arguments in shell scripts that expect an arbitrary number of arguments. See page 976 for a shell script that uses shift.

set: INITIALIZES COMMAND-LINE ARGUMENTS

When you call the set builtin with one or more arguments, it assigns the values of the arguments to the positional parameters, starting with **$1**. The following script uses set to assign values to the positional parameters **$1**, **$2**, and **$3**:

```
$ cat set_it
set this is it
echo $3 $2 $1
$ ./set_it
it is this
```

Combining command substitution (page 351) with the set builtin is a convenient way to get standard output of a command in a form that can be easily manipulated in a shell script. The following script shows how to use date and set to provide the date in a useful format. The first command shows the output of date. Then cat displays the contents of the **dateset** script. The first command in this script uses command substitution to set the positional parameters to the output of the date utility. The next command, **echo $***, displays all positional parameters resulting from the previous set. Subsequent commands display the values of parameters **$1, $2, $3,** and **$6**. The final command displays the date in a format you can use in a letter or report:

```
$ date
Wed Aug 14 17:35:29 PDT 2010
$ cat dateset
set $(date)
echo $*
echo
echo "Argument 1: $1"
echo "Argument 2: $2"
echo "Argument 3: $3"
echo "Argument 6: $6"
echo
echo "$2 $3, $6"
$ ./dateset
Wed Aug 14 17:35:34 PDT 2010

Argument 1: Wed
Argument 2: Aug
Argument 3: 14
Argument 6: 2010

Aug 14, 2010
```

You can also use the +*format* argument to date to modify the format of its output.

When used without any arguments, set displays a list of the shell variables that are set, including user-created variables and keyword variables. Under bash, this list is the same as that displayed by declare and typeset when they are called without any arguments.

The set builtin also accepts options that let you customize the behavior of the shell. For more information refer to "set ±o: Turns Shell Features On and Off" on page 341.

$* AND $@: REPRESENT ALL COMMAND-LINE ARGUMENTS

The **$*** parameter represents all command-line arguments, as the **display_all** program demonstrates:

```
$ cat display_all
echo All arguments are $*

$ ./display_all a b c d e f g h i j k l m n o p
All arguments are a b c d e f g h i j k l m n o p
```

It is a good idea to enclose references to positional parameters between double quotation marks. The quotation marks are particularly important when you are using positional parameters as arguments to commands. Without double quotation marks, a positional parameter that is not set or that has a null value disappears:

```
$ cat showargs
echo "$0 was called with $# arguments, the first is :$1:."

$ ./showargs a b c
./showargs was called with 3 arguments, the first is :a:.
$ echo $xx

$ ./showargs $xx a b c
./showargs was called with 3 arguments, the first is :a:.
$ ./showargs "$xx" a b c
./showargs was called with 4 arguments, the first is ::.
```

The **showargs** script displays the number of arguments (**$#**) followed by the value of the first argument enclosed between colons. In the preceding example, **showargs** is initially called with three simple arguments. Next the echo command demonstrates that the **$xx** variable, which is not set, has a null value. In the final two calls to **showargs**, the first argument is **$xx**. In the first case the command line becomes **showargs a b c**; the shell passes **showargs** three arguments. In the second case the command line becomes **showargs "" a b c**, which results in calling **showargs** with four arguments. The difference in the two calls to **showargs** illustrates a subtle potential problem that you should keep in mind when using positional parameters that might not be set or that might have a null value.

"$∗" versus "$@"   The **$∗** and **$@** parameters work the same way except when they are enclosed within double quotation marks. Using **"$∗"** yields a single argument (with SPACEs or the value of the first character of IFS [page 312] between the positional parameters), whereas using **"$@"** produces a list wherein each positional parameter is a separate argument. This difference typically makes **"$@"** more useful than **"$∗"** in shell scripts.

The following scripts help explain the difference between these two special parameters. In the second line of both scripts, the single quotation marks keep the shell from interpreting the enclosed special characters so they are passed to echo and displayed as themselves. The **bb1** script shows that **set "$∗"** assigns multiple arguments to the first command-line parameter:

```
$ cat bb1
set "$∗"
echo $# parameters with '"$∗"'
echo 1: $1
echo 2: $2
echo 3: $3
$ ./bb1 a b c
1 parameters with "$∗"
1: a b c
2:
3:
```

The **bb2** script shows that **set "$@"** assigns each argument to a different command-line parameter:

```
$ cat bb2
set "$@"
echo $# parameters with '"$@"'
echo 1: $1
echo 2: $2
echo 3: $3

$ ./bb2 a b c
3 parameters with "$@"
1: a
2: b
3: c
```

EXPANDING NULL AND UNSET VARIABLES

The expression ${name} (or just $name if it is not ambiguous) expands to the value of the **name** variable. If name is null or not set, bash expands ${name} to a null string. The Bourne Again Shell provides the following alternatives to accepting the expanded null string as the value of the variable:

- Use a default value for the variable.
- Use a default value and assign that value to the variable.
- Display an error.

You can choose one of these alternatives by using a modifier with the variable name. In addition, you can use **set –o nounset** (page 343) to cause bash to display an error and exit from a script whenever an unset variable is referenced.

:– USES A DEFAULT VALUE

The :– modifier uses a default value in place of a null or unset variable while allowing a nonnull variable to represent itself:

${name:–default}

The shell interprets :– as "If *name* is null or unset, expand *default* and use the expanded value in place of *name*; else use *name*." The following command lists the contents of the directory named by the **LIT** variable. If **LIT** is null or unset, it lists the contents of **/home/max/literature**:

```
$ ls ${LIT:-/home/max/literature}
```

The default can itself have variable references that are expanded:

```
$ ls ${LIT:-$HOME/literature}
```

:= ASSIGNS A DEFAULT VALUE

The :– modifier does not change the value of a variable. However, you can change the value of a null or unset variable to its default in a script by using the := modifier:

${name:=default}

The shell expands the expression *${name:=default}* in the same manner as it expands *${name:-default}* but also sets the value of *name* to the expanded value of *default*. If a script contains a line such as the following and **LIT** is unset or null at the time this line is executed, **LIT** is assigned the value **/home/max/literature**:

```
$ ls ${LIT:=/home/max/literature}
```

: (null) builtin Shell scripts frequently start with the : (null) builtin followed on the same line by the := expansion modifier to set any variables that might be null or unset. The : builtin evaluates each token in the remainder of the command line but does not execute any commands. Without the leading colon (:), the shell evaluates and attempts to execute the "command" that results from the evaluation.

Use the following syntax to set a default for a null or unset variable in a shell script (a SPACE follows the first colon):

: *${name:=default}*

When a script needs a directory for temporary files and uses the value of **TEMPDIR** for the name of this directory, the following line assigns to **TEMPDIR** the value **/tmp** if **TEMPDIR** is null:

```
: ${TEMPDIR:=/tmp}
```

:? DISPLAYS AN ERROR MESSAGE

Sometimes a script needs the value of a variable, but you cannot supply a reasonable default at the time you write the script. If the variable is null or unset, the :? modifier causes the script to display an error message and terminate with an exit status of 1:

${name:?message}

If you omit *message,* the shell displays the default error message (**parameter null or not set**). Interactive shells do not exit when you use :?. In the following command, **TESTDIR** is not set, so the shell displays on standard error the expanded value of the string following :?. In this case the string includes command substitution for date with the %T format, followed by the string **error, variable not set**.

```
cd ${TESTDIR:?$(date +%T) error, variable not set.}
bash: TESTDIR: 16:16:14 error, variable not set.
```

BUILTIN COMMANDS

Builtin commands, which were introduced in Chapter 7, do not fork a new process when you execute them. This section discusses the type, read, exec, trap, kill, and getopts builtins. Table 27-6 on page 1031 lists many bash builtin commands.

type: DISPLAYS INFORMATION ABOUT A COMMAND

The type builtin provides information about a command:

```
$ type cat echo who if lt
cat is hashed (/bin/cat)
echo is a shell builtin
who is /usr/bin/who
if is a shell keyword
lt is aliased to 'ls -ltrh | tail'
```

The preceding output shows the files that would be executed if you gave **cat** or **who** as a command. Because cat has already been called from the current shell, it is in the *hash table* (page 1167) and type reports that **cat is hashed**. The output also shows that a call to **echo** runs the echo builtin, **if** is a keyword, and **lt** is an alias.

read: ACCEPTS USER INPUT

One of the most common uses for user-created variables is storing information that a user enters in response to a prompt. Using read, scripts can accept input from the user and store that input in variables. The read builtin reads one line from standard input and assigns the words on the line to one or more variables:

```
$ cat read1
echo -n "Go ahead: "
read firstline
echo "You entered: $firstline"
$ ./read1
Go ahead: This is a line.
You entered: This is a line.
```

The first line of the **read1** script uses echo to prompt for a line of text. The **–n** option suppresses the following NEWLINE, allowing you to enter a line of text on the same line as the prompt. The second line reads the text into the variable **firstline**. The third line verifies the action of read by displaying the value of **firstline**. The variable is quoted (along with the text string) in this example because you, as the script writer, cannot anticipate which characters the user might enter in response to the prompt. Consider what would happen if the variable were not quoted and the user entered ✳ in response to the prompt:

```
$ cat read1_no_quote
echo -n "Go ahead: "
read firstline
echo You entered: $firstline
$ ./read1_no_quote
Go ahead: ✳
You entered: read1 read1_no_quote script.1
$ ls
read1    read1_no_quote     script.1
```

The ls command lists the same words as the script, demonstrating that the shell expands the asterisk into a list of files in the working directory. When the variable **$firstline** is surrounded by double quotation marks, the shell does not expand the asterisk. Thus the **read1** script behaves correctly:

```
$ ./read1
Go ahead: *
You entered: *
```

REPLY The read builtin includes several features that can make it easier to use. For example, when you do not specify a variable to receive read's input, bash puts the input into the variable named **REPLY**. You can use the **–p** option to prompt the user instead of using a separate echo command. The following **read1a** script performs exactly the same task as **read1**:

```
$ cat read1a
read -p "Go ahead: "
echo "You entered: $REPLY"
```

The **read2** script prompts for a command line, reads the user's response, and assigns it to the variable **cmd**. The script then attempts to execute the command line that results from the expansion of the **cmd** variable:

```
$ cat read2
read -p "Enter a command: " cmd
$cmd
echo "Thanks"
```

In the following example, **read2** reads a command line that calls the echo builtin. The shell executes the command and then displays **Thanks**. Next **read2** reads a command line that executes the who utility:

```
$ ./read2
Enter a command: echo Please display this message.
Please display this message.
Thanks
$ ./read2
Enter a command: who
max        pts/4        2010-06-17 07:50   (:0.0)
sam        pts/12       2010-06-17 11:54   (bravo.example.com)
Thanks
```

If **cmd** does not expand into a valid command line, the shell issues an error message:

```
$ ./read2
Enter a command: xxx
./read2: line 2: xxx: command not found
Thanks
```

The **read3** script reads values into three variables. The read builtin assigns one word (a sequence of nonblank characters) to each variable:

```
$ cat read3
read -p "Enter something: " word1 word2 word3
echo "Word 1 is: $word1"
echo "Word 2 is: $word2"
echo "Word 3 is: $word3"
```

```
$ ./read3
Enter something: this is something
Word 1 is: this
Word 2 is: is
Word 3 is: something
```

When you enter more words than read has variables, read assigns one word to each variable, assigning all leftover words to the last variable. Both **read1** and **read2** assigned the first word and all leftover words to the one variable the scripts each had to work with. In the following example, read assigns five words to three variables: It assigns the first word to the first variable, the second word to the second variable, and the third through fifth words to the third variable.

```
$ ./read3
Enter something: this is something else, really.
Word 1 is:  this
Word 2 is:  is
Word 3 is:  something else, really.
```

Table 27-4 lists some of the options supported by the read builtin.

Table 27-4   read options

Option	Function
–a *aname*	(array) Assigns each word of input to an element of array ***aname***.
–d *delim*	(delimiter) Uses ***delim*** to terminate the input instead of NEWLINE.
–e	(Readline) If input is coming from a keyboard, uses the Readline Library (page 328) to get input.
–n *num*	(number of characters) Reads ***num*** characters and returns. As soon as the user types ***num*** characters, read returns; there is no need to press RETURN.
–p *prompt*	(prompt) Displays ***prompt*** on standard error without a terminating NEWLINE before reading input. Displays ***prompt*** only when input comes from the keyboard.
–s	(silent) Does not echo characters.

–u*n*	(file descriptor) Uses the integer ***n*** as the file descriptor that read takes its input from. Thus
	
	    `read –u4 arg1 arg2`
	
	is equivalent to
	
	    `read arg1 arg2 <&4`
	
	See "File Descriptors" (page 1003) for a discussion of redirection and file descriptors.

The read builtin returns an exit status of 0 if it successfully reads any data. It has a nonzero exit status when it reaches the EOF (end of file).

The following example runs a **while** loop from the command line. It takes its input from the **names** file and terminates after reading the last line from **names**.

```
$ cat names
Alice Jones
Robert Smith
Alice Paulson
John Q. Public

$ while read first rest
> do
> echo $rest, $first
> done < names
Jones, Alice
Smith, Robert
Paulson, Alice
Q. Public, John
$
```

The placement of the redirection symbol (<) for the **while** structure is critical. It is important that you place the redirection symbol at the **done** statement and not at the call to read.

optional   Each time you redirect input, the shell opens the input file and repositions the read pointer at the start of the file:

```
$ read line1 < names; echo $line1; read line2 < names; echo $line2
Alice Jones
Alice Jones
```

Here each read opens **names** and starts at the beginning of the **names** file. In the following example, **names** is opened once, as standard input of the subshell created by the parentheses. Each read then reads successive lines of standard input:

```
$ (read line1; echo $line1; read line2; echo $line2) < names
Alice Jones
Robert Smith
```

Another way to get the same effect is to open the input file with **exec** and hold it open (refer to "File Descriptors" on page 1003):

```
$ exec 3< names
$ read -u3 line1; echo $line1; read -u3 line2; echo $line2
Alice Jones
Robert Smith
$ exec 3<&-
```

exec: EXECUTES A COMMAND OR REDIRECTS FILE DESCRIPTORS

The **exec** builtin has two primary purposes: to run a command without creating a new process and to redirect a file descriptor—including standard input, output, or error—of a shell script from within the script (page 1003). When the shell executes a command that is not built into the shell, it typically creates a new process. The new process inherits environment (global or exported) variables from its parent but does not inherit variables that are not exported by the parent. (For more information refer to "Locality of Variables" on page 1008.) In contrast, exec executes a command in place of (overlays) the current process.

exec: EXECUTES A COMMAND

The exec builtin used for running a command has the following syntax:

exec command arguments

exec versus . (dot) Insofar as exec runs a command in the environment of the original process, it is similar to the . (dot) command (page 284). However, unlike the . command, which can run only shell scripts, exec can run both scripts and compiled programs. Also, whereas the . command returns control to the original script when it finishes running, exec does not. Finally, the . command gives the new program access to local variables, whereas exec does not.

exec does not return control Because the shell does not create a new process when you use exec, the command runs more quickly. However, because exec does not return control to the original program, it can be used only as the last command in a script. The following script shows that control is not returned to the script:

```
$ cat exec_demo
who
exec date
echo "This line is never displayed."

$ ./exec_demo
zach      pts/7    May 20  7:05 (bravo.example.com)
hls       pts/1    May 20  6:59 (:0.0)
Mon May 24 11:42:56 PDT 2010
```

The next example, a modified version of the **out** script (page 976), uses exec to execute the final command the script runs. Because **out** runs either cat or less and then terminates, the new version, named **out2**, uses exec with both cat and less:

```
$ cat out2
if [ $# -eq 0 ]
    then
        echo "Usage: out2 [-v] filenames" 1>&2
        exit 1
fi
if [ "$1" = "-v" ]
    then
        shift
        exec less "$@"
    else
        exec cat -- "$@"
fi
```

exec: REDIRECTS INPUT AND OUTPUT

The second major use of exec is to redirect a file descriptor—including standard input, output, or error—from within a script. The next command causes all subsequent input to a script that would have come from standard input to come from the file named **infile**:

```
exec < infile
```

Similarly the following command redirects standard output and standard error to **outfile** and **errfile**, respectively:

```
exec > outfile 2> errfile
```

When you use **exec** in this manner, the current process is not replaced with a new process, and **exec** can be followed by other commands in the script.

/dev/tty   When you redirect the output from a script to a file, you must make sure the user sees any prompts the script displays. The **/dev/tty** device is a pseudonym for the screen the user is working on; you can use this device to refer to the user's screen without knowing which device it is. (The tty utility displays the name of the device you are using.) By redirecting the output from a script to **/dev/tty**, you ensure that prompts and messages go to the user's terminal, regardless of which terminal the user is logged in on. Messages sent to **/dev/tty** are also not diverted if standard output and standard error from the script are redirected.

The **to_screen1** script sends output to three places: standard output, standard error, and the user's screen. When run with standard output and standard error redirected, **to_screen1** still displays the message sent to **/dev/tty** on the user's screen. The **out** and **err** files hold the output sent to standard output and standard error.

```
$ cat to_screen1
echo "message to standard output"
echo "message to standard error" 1>&2
echo "message to the user" > /dev/tty

$ ./to_screen1 > out 2> err
message to the user
$ cat out
message to standard output
$ cat err
message to standard error
```

The following command redirects the output from a script to the user's screen:

```
exec > /dev/tty
```

Putting this command at the beginning of the previous script changes where the output goes. In **to_screen2**, **exec** redirects standard output to the user's screen so the **> /dev/tty** is superfluous. Following the **exec** command, all output sent to standard output goes to **/dev/tty** (the screen). Output to standard error is not affected.

```
$ cat to_screen2
exec > /dev/tty
echo "message to standard output"
echo "message to standard error" 1>&2
echo "message to the user" > /dev/tty

$ ./to_screen2 > out 2> err
message to standard output
message to the user
```

One disadvantage of using **exec** to redirect the output to **/dev/tty** is that all subsequent output is redirected unless you use **exec** again in the script.

You can also redirect the input to read (standard input) so that it comes from **/dev/tty** (the keyboard):

```
read name < /dev/tty
```

or

```
exec < /dev/tty
```

trap: CATCHES A SIGNAL

A *signal* is a report to a process about a condition. Linux uses signals to report interrupts generated by the user (for example, pressing the interrupt key) as well as bad system calls, broken pipes, illegal instructions, and other conditions. The trap builtin catches (traps) one or more signals, allowing you to direct the actions a script takes when it receives a specified signal.

This discussion covers six signals that are significant when you work with shell scripts. Table 27-5 lists these signals, the signal numbers that systems often ascribe to them, and the conditions that usually generate each signal. Give the command **kill –l** (lowercase "ell"), **trap –l** (lowercase "ell"), or **man 7 signal** to display a list of all signal names.

Table 27-5   Signals

Type	Name	Number	Generating condition
Not a real signal	EXIT	0	Exit because of **exit** command or reaching the end of the program (not an actual signal but useful in **trap**)
Hang up	SIGHUP or HUP	1	Disconnect the line
Terminal interrupt	SIGINT or INT	2	Press the interrupt key (usually CONTROL-C)
Quit	SIGQUIT or QUIT	3	Press the quit key (usually CONTROL-SHIFT-| or CONTROL-SHIFT-\)
Kill	SIGKILL or KILL	9	The **kill** builtin with the **–9** option (cannot be trapped; use only as a last resort)
Software termination	SIGTERM or TERM	15	Default of the **kill** command
Stop	SIGTSTP or TSTP	20	Press the suspend key (usually CONTROL-Z)
Debug	DEBUG		Executes ***commands*** specified in the **trap** statement after each command (not an actual signal but useful in **trap**)
Error	ERR		Executes ***commands*** specified in the **trap** statement after each command that returns a nonzero exit status (not an actual signal but useful in **trap**)

When it traps a signal, a script takes whatever action you specify: It can remove files or finish other processing as needed, display a message, terminate execution immediately, or ignore the signal. If you do not use trap in a script, any of the six actual signals listed in Table 27-5 (not EXIT, DEBUG, or ERR) will terminate the script. Because a process cannot trap a KILL signal, you can use kill –KILL (or kill –9) as a last resort to terminate a script or other process. (See page 1028 for more information on kill.)

The trap command has the following syntax:

trap ['commands'] [signal]

The optional *commands* specifies the commands that the shell executes when it catches one of the signals specified by *signal*. The *signal* can be a signal name or number—for example, INT or 2. If *commands* is not present, trap resets the trap to its initial condition, which is usually to exit from the script.

Quotation marks The trap builtin does not require single quotation marks around *commands* as shown in the preceding syntax, but it is a good practice to use them. The single quotation marks cause shell variables within the *commands* to be expanded when the signal occurs, rather than when the shell evaluates the arguments to trap. Even if you do not use any shell variables in the *commands*, you need to enclose any command that takes arguments within either single or double quotation marks. Quoting *commands* causes the shell to pass to trap the entire command as a single argument.

After executing the *commands*, the shell resumes executing the script where it left off. If you want trap to prevent a script from exiting when it receives a signal but not to run any commands explicitly, you can specify a null (empty) *commands* string, as shown in the **locktty** script (page 991). The following command traps signal number 15, after which the script continues:

```
trap '' 15
```

The following script demonstrates how the trap builtin can catch the terminal interrupt signal (2). You can use SIGINT, INT, or 2 to specify this signal. The script returns an exit status of 1:

```
$ cat inter
#!/bin/bash
trap 'echo PROGRAM INTERRUPTED; exit 1' INT
while true
do
    echo "Program running."
    sleep 1
done
$ ./inter
Program running.
Program running.
Program running.
CONTROL-C
PROGRAM INTERRUPTED
$
```

: (null) builtin   The second line of **inter** sets up a trap for the terminal interrupt signal using INT. When trap catches the signal, the shell executes the two commands between the single quotation marks in the trap command. The echo builtin displays the message **PROGRAM INTERRUPTED**, exit terminates the shell running the script, and the parent shell displays a prompt. If exit were not there, the shell would return control to the **while** loop after displaying the message. The **while** loop repeats continuously until the script receives a signal because the true utility always returns a *true* exit status. In place of true you can use the : (null) builtin, which is written as a colon and always returns a 0 (*true*) status.

The trap builtin frequently removes temporary files when a script is terminated prematurely, thereby ensuring the files are not left to clutter the filesystem. The following shell script, named **addbanner**, uses two traps to remove a temporary file when the script terminates normally or owing to a hangup, software interrupt, quit, or software termination signal:

```
$ cat addbanner
#!/bin/bash
script=$(basename $0)

if [ ! -r "$HOME/banner" ]
    then
        echo "$script: need readable $HOME/banner file" 1>&2
        exit 1
fi

trap 'exit 1' 1 2 3 15
trap 'rm /tmp/$$.$script 2> /dev/null' 0

for file
do
    if [ -r "$file" -a -w "$file" ]
        then
            cat $HOME/banner $file > /tmp/$$.$script
            cp /tmp/$$.$script $file
            echo "$script: banner added to $file" 1>&2
        else
            echo "$script: need read and write permission for $file" 1>&2
    fi
done
```

When called with one or more filename arguments, **addbanner** loops through the files, adding a header to the top of each. This script is useful when you use a standard format at the top of your documents, such as a standard layout for memos, or when you want to add a standard header to shell scripts. The header is kept in a file named **~/banner**. Because **addbanner** uses the **HOME** variable, which contains the pathname of the user's home directory, the script can be used by several users without modification. If Max had written the script with **/home/max** in place of **$HOME** and then given the script to Zach, either Zach would have had to change it or **addbanner** would have used Max's **banner** file when Zach ran it (assuming Zach had read permission for the file).

The first trap in **addbanner** causes it to exit with a status of 1 when it receives a hangup, software interrupt (terminal interrupt or quit signal), or software termination signal. The second trap uses a 0 in place of **signal-number**, which causes trap to execute its command argument *whenever* the script exits because it receives an exit command or reaches its end. Together these traps remove a temporary file whether the script terminates normally or prematurely. Standard error of the second trap is sent to **/dev/null** whenever trap attempts to remove a non-existent temporary file. In those cases rm sends an error message to standard error; because standard error is redirected, the user does not see the message.

See page 991 for another example that uses trap.

kill: ABORTS A PROCESS

The kill builtin sends a signal to a process or job. The kill command has the following syntax:

kill [–signal] PID

where *signal* is the signal name or number (for example, INT or 2) and *PID* is the process identification number of the process that is to receive the signal. You can specify a job number (page 242) as **%n** in place of *PID*. If you omit *signal*, kill sends a TERM (software termination, number 15) signal. For more information on signal names and numbers, see Table 27-5 on page 1025.

The following command sends the TERM signal to job number 1, regardless of whether it is in the foreground (running) or in the background (running or stopped):

```
$ kill -TERM %1
```

Because TERM is the default signal for kill, you can also give this command as **kill %1**. Give the command **kill –l** (lowercase "l") to display a list of signal names.

A program that is interrupted can leave matters in an unpredictable state: Temporary files might be left behind (when they are normally removed), and permissions might be changed. A well-written application traps, or detects, signals and cleans up before exiting. Most carefully written applications trap the INT, QUIT, and TERM signals.

To terminate a program, first try INT (press CONTROL-C, if the job running is in the foreground). Because an application can be written to ignore these signals, you might need to use the KILL signal, which cannot be trapped or ignored; it is a "sure kill." For more information refer to "kill: Sends a Signal to a Process" on page 470.

getopts: PARSES OPTIONS

The getopts builtin parses command-line arguments, making it easier to write programs that follow the Linux argument conventions. The syntax for getopts is

getopts optstring varname [arg ...]

where *optstring* is a list of the valid option letters, *varname* is the variable that receives the options one at a time, and *arg* is the optional list of parameters to be processed. If *arg* is not present, getopts processes the command-line arguments. If *optstring* starts with a colon (:), the script must take care of generating error messages; otherwise, getopts generates error messages.

The getopts builtin uses the **OPTIND** (option index) and **OPTARG** (option argument) variables to track and store option-related values. When a shell script starts, the value of **OPTIND** is 1. Each time getopts is called and locates an argument, it increments **OPTIND** to the index of the next option to be processed. If the option takes an argument, bash assigns the value of the argument to **OPTARG**.

To indicate that an option takes an argument, follow the corresponding letter in *optstring* with a colon (:). The option string **dxo:lt:r** indicates that getopts should search for –d, –x, –o, –l, –t, and –r options and that the –o and –t options take arguments.

Using getopts as the *test-command* in a **while** control structure allows you to loop over the options one at a time. The getopts builtin checks the option list for options that are in *optstring*. Each time through the loop, getopts stores the option letter it finds in *varname*.

Suppose that you want to write a program that can take three options:

1. A –**b** option indicates that the program should ignore whitespace at the start of input lines.

2. A –**t** option followed by the name of a directory indicates that the program should store temporary files in that directory. Otherwise, it should use **/tmp**.

3. A –**u** option indicates that the program should translate all output to uppercase.

In addition, the program should ignore all other options and end option processing when it encounters two hyphens (––).

The problem is to write the portion of the program that determines which options the user has supplied. The following solution does not use getopts:

```
SKIPBLANKS=
TMPDIR=/tmp
CASE=lower
while [[ "$1" = -* ]] # [[ = ]] does pattern match
do
    case $1 in
        -b)    SKIPBLANKS=TRUE ;;
        -t)    if [ -d "$2" ]
                   then
                   TMPDIR=$2
                   shift
               else
                   echo "$0: -t takes a directory argument." >&2
                   exit 1
               fi ;;
        -u)    CASE=upper ;;
        --)    break   ;;      # Stop processing options
        *)     echo "$0: Invalid option $1 ignored." >&2 ;;
    esac
    shift
done
```

This program fragment uses a loop to check and shift arguments while the argument is not --. As long as the argument is not two hyphens, the program continues to loop through a **case** statement that checks for possible options. The -- **case** label breaks out of the **while** loop. The * **case** label recognizes any option; it appears as the last **case** label to catch any unknown options, displays an error message, and allows processing to continue. On each pass through the loop, the program uses shift to access the next argument. If an option takes an argument, the program uses an extra shift to get past that argument.

The following program fragment processes the same options, but uses getopts:

```
SKIPBLANKS=
TMPDIR=/tmp
CASE=lower

while getopts :bt:u arg
do
    case $arg in
        b)      SKIPBLANKS=TRUE ;;
        t)      if [ -d "$OPTARG" ]
                    then
                        TMPDIR=$OPTARG
                else
                    echo "$0: $OPTARG is not a directory." >&2
                    exit 1
                fi ;;
        u)      CASE=upper ;;
        :)      echo "$0: Must supply an argument to -$OPTARG." >&2
                exit 1 ;;
        \?)     echo "Invalid option -$OPTARG ignored." >&2 ;;
    esac
done
```

In this version of the code, the **while** structure evaluates the getopts builtin each time control transfers to the top of the loop. The getopts builtin uses the **OPTIND** variable to keep track of the index of the argument it is to process the next time it is called. There is no need to call shift in this example.

In the getopts version of the script, the **case** patterns do not start with a hyphen because the value of **arg** is just the option letter (getopts strips off the hyphen). Also, getopts recognizes -- as the end of the options, so you do not have to specify it explicitly, as in the **case** statement in the first example.

Because you tell getopts which options are valid and which require arguments, it can detect errors in the command line and handle them in two ways. This example uses a leading colon in *optstring* to specify that you check for and handle errors in your code; when getopts finds an invalid option, it sets *varname* to ? and **OPTARG** to the option letter. When it finds an option that is missing an argument, getopts sets *varname* to : and **OPTARG** to the option lacking an argument.

The \? **case** pattern specifies the action to take when getopts detects an invalid option. The : **case** pattern specifies the action to take when getopts detects a missing option argument. In both cases getopts does not write any error message but rather leaves that task to you.

If you omit the leading colon from *optstring*, both an invalid option and a missing option argument cause *varname* to be assigned the string **?**. **OPTARG** is not set and getopts writes its own diagnostic message to standard error. Generally this method is less desirable because you have less control over what the user sees when an error occurs.

Using getopts will not necessarily make your programs shorter. Its principal advantages are that it provides a uniform programming interface and that it enforces standard option handling.

A Partial List of Builtins

Table 27-6 lists some of the bash builtins. You can use type (page 1019) to see if a command runs a builtin. See "Listing bash builtins" on page 249 for instructions on how to display complete lists of builtins.

Table 27-6   bash builtins

Builtin	Function
:	Returns 0 or *true* (the null builtin; page 1027)
. (dot)	Executes a shell script as part of the current process (page 284)
bg	Puts a suspended job in the background (page 297)
break	Exits from a looping control structure (page 992)
cd	Changes to another working directory (page 196)
continue	Starts with the next iteration of a looping control structure (page 992)
echo	Displays its arguments (page 157)
eval	Scans and evaluates the command line (page 340)
exec	Executes a shell script or program in place of the current process (page 1022)
exit	Exits from the current shell (usually the same as CONTROL-D from an interactive shell; page 1012)
export	Places the value of a variable in the calling environment (makes it global; page 1008)
fg	Brings a job from the background into the foreground (page 296)
getopts	Parses arguments to a shell script (page 1028)
jobs	Displays a list of background jobs (page 296)
kill	Sends a signal to a process or job (page 470)
pwd	Displays the name of the working directory (page 190)

Table 27-6   bash builtins (continued)

Builtin	Function
read	Reads a line from standard input (page 1019)
readonly	Declares a variable to be readonly (page 305)
set	Sets shell flags or command-line argument variables; with no argument, lists all variables (pages 341 and 1014)
shift	Promotes each command-line argument (page 1014)
test	Compares arguments (page 971)
times	Displays total times for the current shell and its children
trap	Traps a signal (page 1025)
type	Displays how each argument would be interpreted as a command (page 1019)
umask	Returns the value of the file-creation mask (page 473)
unset	Removes a variable or function (page 305)
wait	Waits for a background process to terminate

EXPRESSIONS

An expression comprises constants, variables, and operators that the shell can process to return a value. This section covers arithmetic, logical, and conditional expressions as well as operators. Table 27-8 on page 1035 lists the bash operators.

ARITHMETIC EVALUATION

The Bourne Again Shell can perform arithmetic assignments and evaluate many different types of arithmetic expressions, all using integers. The shell performs arithmetic assignments in a number of ways. One is with arguments to the let builtin:

```
$ let "VALUE=VALUE * 10 + NEW"
```

In the preceding example, the variables **VALUE** and **NEW** contain integer values. Within a let statement you do not need to use dollar signs ($) in front of variable names. Double quotation marks must enclose a single argument, or expression, that contains SPACEs. Because most expressions contain SPACEs and need to be quoted, bash accepts *((expression))* as a synonym for *let "expression"*, obviating the need for both quotation marks and dollar signs:

```
$ ((VALUE=VALUE * 10 + NEW))
```

You can use either form wherever a command is allowed and can remove the SPACEs if you like. In the following example, the asterisk (*) does not need to be quoted because the shell does not perform pathname expansion on the right side of an assignment (page 304):

```
$ let VALUE=VALUE*10+NEW
```

Because each argument to let is evaluated as a separate expression, you can assign values to more than one variable on a single line:

```
$ let "COUNT = COUNT + 1" VALUE=VALUE*10+NEW
```

You need to use commas to separate multiple assignments within a set of double parentheses:

```
$ ((COUNT = COUNT + 1, VALUE=VALUE*10+NEW))
```

Arithmetic evaluation versus arithmetic expansion

tip   Arithmetic evaluation differs from arithmetic expansion. As explained on page 349, arithmetic expansion uses the syntax *$((expression))*, evaluates *expression*, and replaces *$((expression))* with the result. You can use arithmetic expansion to display the value of an expression or to assign that value to a variable.

Arithmetic evaluation uses the *let expression* or *((expression))* syntax, evaluates *expression*, and returns a status code. You can use arithmetic evaluation to perform a logical comparison or an assignment.

Logical expressions   You can use the *((expression))* syntax for logical expressions, although that task is frequently left to *[[expression]]*. The next example expands the **age_check** script (page 349) to include logical arithmetic evaluation in addition to arithmetic expansion:

```
$ cat age2
#!/bin/bash
echo -n "How old are you? "
read age
if ((30 < age && age < 60)); then
        echo "Wow, in $((60-age)) years, you'll be 60!"
    else
        echo "You are too young or too old to play."
fi

$ ./age2
How old are you? 25
You are too young or too old to play.
```

The *test-statement* for the **if** structure evaluates two logical comparisons joined by a Boolean AND and returns 0 (*true*) if they are both *true* or 1 (*false*) otherwise.

LOGICAL EVALUATION (CONDITIONAL EXPRESSIONS)

The syntax of a conditional expression is

[[expression]]

where *expression* is a Boolean (logical) expression. You must precede a variable name with a dollar sign ($) within *expression*. The result of executing this builtin, as with the test builtin, is a return status. The *conditions* allowed within the brackets are almost a superset of those accepted by test (page 971). Where the test builtin uses −a as a Boolean AND operator, *[[expression]]* uses &&. Similarly, where test uses −o as a Boolean OR operator, *[[expression]]* uses ||.

To see how conditional expressions work, replace the line that tests **age** in the **age2** script with the following conditional expression. You must surround the [[and]] tokens with whitespace or a command terminator, and place dollar signs before the variables:

```
if [[ 30 < $age && $age < 60 ]]; then
```

You can also use **test**'s relational operators **–gt, –ge, –lt, –le, –eq,** and **–ne**:

```
if [[ 30 -lt $age && $age -lt 60 ]]; then
```

String comparisons The **test** builtin tests whether strings are equal. The *[[expression]]* syntax adds comparison tests for string operators. The **>** and **<** operators compare strings for order (for example, **"aa" < "bbb"**). The **=** operator tests for pattern match, not just equality: *[[string = pattern]]* is *true* if **string** matches **pattern**. This operator is not symmetrical; the **pattern** must appear on the right side of the equal sign. For example, [[**artist = a***∗]] is *true* (= 0), whereas [[**a**∗ = **artist**]] is *false* (= 1):

```
$ [[ artist = a* ]]
$ echo $?
0
$ [[ a* = artist ]]
$ echo $?
1
```

The next example uses a command list that starts with a compound condition. The condition tests that the directory **bin** and the file **src/myscript.bash** exist. If this is *true,* **cp** copies **src/myscript.bash** to **bin/myscript**. If the copy succeeds, **chmod** makes **myscript** executable. If any of these steps fails, **echo** displays a message.

```
$ [[ -d bin && -f src/myscript.bash ]] && cp src/myscript.bash \
bin/myscript && chmod +x bin/myscript || echo "Cannot make \
executable version of myscript"
```

STRING PATTERN MATCHING

The Bourne Again Shell provides string pattern-matching operators that can manipulate pathnames and other strings. These operators can delete from strings prefixes or suffixes that match patterns. Table 27-7 lists the four operators.

Table 27-7   String operators

Operator	Function
#	Removes minimal matching prefixes
##	Removes maximal matching prefixes
%	Removes minimal matching suffixes
%%	Removes maximal matching suffixes

The syntax for these operators is

${varname op pattern}

where *op* is one of the operators listed in Table 27-7 and *pattern* is a match pattern similar to that used for filename generation. These operators are commonly used to manipulate pathnames to extract or remove components or to change suffixes:

```
$ SOURCEFILE=/usr/local/src/prog.c
$ echo ${SOURCEFILE#/*/}
local/src/prog.c
$ echo ${SOURCEFILE##/*/}
prog.c
$ echo ${SOURCEFILE%/*}
/usr/local/src
$ echo ${SOURCEFILE%%/*}

$ echo ${SOURCEFILE%.c}
/usr/local/src/prog
$ CHOPFIRST=${SOURCEFILE#/*/}
$ echo $CHOPFIRST
local/src/prog.c
$ NEXT=${CHOPFIRST%%/*}
$ echo $NEXT
local
```

Here the string-length operator, **${#*name*}**, is replaced by the number of characters in the value of **name**:

```
$ echo $SOURCEFILE
/usr/local/src/prog.c
$ echo ${#SOURCEFILE}
21
```

OPERATORS

Arithmetic expansion and arithmetic evaluation in bash use the same syntax, precedence, and associativity of expressions as in the C language. Table 27-8 lists operators in order of decreasing precedence (priority of evaluation); each group of operators has equal precedence. Within an expression you can use parentheses to change the order of evaluation.

Table 27-8   Operators

Type of operator/operator	Function
Post	
var++ Postincrement	
var–– Postdecrement	
Pre	
++*var* Preincrement	
––*var* Predecrement	

Table 27-8   Operators (continued)

Type of operator/operator	Function
Unary	
−	Unary minus
+	Unary plus
Negation	
!	Boolean NOT (logical negation)
~	Complement (bitwise negation)
Exponentiation	
**	Exponent
Multiplication, division, remainder	
*	Multiplication
/	Division
%	Remainder
Addition, subtraction	
−	Subtraction
+	Addition
Bitwise shifts	
<<	Left bitwise shift
>>	Right bitwise shift
Comparison	
<=	Less than or equal
>=	Greater than or equal
<	Less than
>	Greater than
Equality, inequality	
==	Equality
!=	Inequality
Bitwise	
&	Bitwise AND
^	Bitwise XOR (exclusive OR)
|	Bitwise OR

Table 27-8 Operators (continued)

Type of operator/operator	Function
Boolean (logical)	
&& Boolean AND	
|| Boolean OR	
Conditional evaluation	
? : Ternary operator	
Assignment	
=, *=, /=, %=, +=, −=, Assignment **<<=, >>=, &=, ^=, |=**	
Comma	
, Comma	

Pipe The pipe token has higher precedence than operators. You can use pipes anywhere in a command that you can use simple commands. For example, the command line

```
$ cmd1 | cmd2 || cmd3 | cmd4 && cmd5 | cmd6
```

is interpreted as if you had typed

```
$ ((cmd1 | cmd2) || (cmd3 | cmd4)) && (cmd5 | cmd6)
```

Do not rely on rules of precedence: use parentheses

tip Do not rely on the precedence rules when you use compound commands. Instead, use parentheses to explicitly state the order in which you want the shell to interpret the commands.

Increment and decrement The postincrement, postdecrement, preincrement, and predecrement operators work with variables. The pre- operators, which appear in front of the variable name (as in **++COUNT** and **−−VALUE**), first change the value of the variable (**++** adds 1; **−−** subtracts 1) and then provide the result for use in the expression. The post- operators appear after the variable name (as in **COUNT++** and **VALUE−−**); they first provide the unchanged value of the variable for use in the expression and then change the value of the variable.

```
$ N=10
$ echo $N
10
$ echo $((--N+3))
12
$ echo $N
9
$ echo $((N++ - 3))
6
$ echo $N
10
```

Remainder   The remainder operator (%) yields the remainder when its first operand is divided by its second. For example, the expression $((15\%7))$ has the value 1.

Boolean   The result of a Boolean operation is either 0 (*false*) or 1 (*true*).

The && (AND) and || (OR) Boolean operators are called *short-circuiting* operators. If the result of using one of these operators can be decided by looking only at the left operand, the right operand is not evaluated. The && operator causes the shell to test the exit status of the command preceding it. If the command succeeded, bash executes the next command; otherwise, it skips the remaining commands on the command line. You can use this construct to execute commands conditionally.

```
$ mkdir bkup && cp -r src bkup
```

This compound command creates the directory **bkup**. If mkdir succeeds, the contents of directory **src** is copied recursively to **bkup**.

The || separator also causes bash to test the exit status of the first command but has the opposite effect: The remaining command(s) are executed only if the first one failed (that is, exited with nonzero status).

```
$ mkdir bkup || echo "mkdir of bkup failed" >> /tmp/log
```

The exit status of a command list is the exit status of the last command in the list. You can group lists with parentheses. For example, you could combine the previous two examples as

```
$ (mkdir bkup && cp -r src bkup) || echo "mkdir failed" >> /tmp/log
```

In the absence of parentheses, && and || have equal precedence and are grouped from left to right. The following examples use the true and false utilities. These utilities do nothing and return *true* (0) and *false* (1) exit statuses, respectively:

```
$ false; echo $?
1
```

The $? variable holds the exit status of the preceding command (page 1012). The next two commands yield an exit status of 1 (*false*):

```
$ true || false && false
$ echo $?
1
$ (true || false) && false
$ echo $?
1
```

Similarly the next two commands yield an exit status of 0 (*true*):

```
$ false && false || true
$ echo $?
0
$ (false && false) || true
$ echo $?
0
```

Because || and && have equal precedence, the parentheses in the two preceding pairs of examples do not change the order of operations.

Because the expression on the right side of a short-circuiting operator might never be executed, you must be careful when placing assignment statements in that location. The following example demonstrates what can happen:

```
$ ((N=10,Z=0))
$ echo $(( (N || ((Z+=1)) ))
1
$ echo $Z
0
```

Because the value of **N** is nonzero, the result of the || (OR) operation is 1 (*true*), no matter what the value of the right side is. As a consequence, ((Z+=1)) is never evaluated and **Z** is not incremented.

Ternary   The ternary operator, **? :**, decides which of two expressions should be evaluated, based on the value returned by a third expression:

   expression1 ? expression2 : expression3

If *expression1* produces a *false* (0) value, *expression3* is evaluated; otherwise, *expression2* is evaluated. The value of the entire expression is the value of *expression2* or *expression3*, depending on which is evaluated. If *expression1* is *true*, *expression3* is not evaluated. If *expression1* is *false*, *expression2* is not evaluated.

```
$ ((N=10,Z=0,COUNT=1))
$ ((T=N>COUNT?++Z:--Z))
$ echo $T
1
$ echo $Z
1
```

Assignment   The assignment operators, such as **+=**, are shorthand notations. For example, **N+=3** is the same as **((N=N+3))**.

Other bases   The following commands use the syntax *base#n* to assign base 2 (binary) values. First **v1** is assigned a value of 0101 (5 decimal) and then **v2** is assigned a value of 0110 (6 decimal). The echo utility verifies the decimal values.

```
$ ((v1=2#0101))
$ ((v2=2#0110))
$ echo "$v1 and $v2"
5 and 6
```

Next the bitwise AND operator (**&**) selects the bits that are on in both 5 (0101 binary) and 6 (0110 binary). The result is binary 0100, which is 4 decimal.

```
$ echo $(( v1 & v2 ))
4
```

The Boolean AND operator (&&) produces a result of 1 if both of its operands are nonzero and a result of 0 otherwise. The bitwise inclusive OR operator (I) selects the bits that are on in either 0101 or 0110, resulting in 0111, which is 7 decimal. The Boolean OR operator (II) produces a result of 1 if either of its operands is nonzero and a result of 0 otherwise.

```
$ echo $(( v1 && v2 ))
1
$ echo $(( v1 | v2 ))
7
$ echo $(( v1 || v2 ))
1
```

Next the bitwise exclusive OR operator (^) selects the bits that are on in either, but not both, of the operands 0101 and 0110, yielding 0011, which is 3 decimal. The Boolean NOT operator (!) produces a result of 1 if its operand is 0 and a result of 0 otherwise. Because the exclamation point in $((! v1)) is enclosed within double parentheses, it does not need to be escaped to prevent the shell from interpreting the exclamation point as a history event. The comparison operators produce a result of 1 if the comparison is *true* and a result of 0 otherwise.

```
$ echo $(( v1 ^ v2 ))
3
$ echo $(( ! v1 ))
0
$ echo $(( v1 < v2 ))
1
$ echo $(( v1 > v2 ))
0
```

Shell Programs

The Bourne Again Shell has many features that make it a good programming language. The structures that bash provides are not a random assortment, but rather have been chosen to provide most of the structural features that are found in other procedural languages, such as C or Perl. A procedural language provides the following abilities:

- Declare, assign, and manipulate variables and constant data. The Bourne Again Shell provides string variables, together with powerful string operators, and integer variables, along with a complete set of arithmetic operators.

- Break large problems into small ones by creating subprograms. The Bourne Again Shell allows you to create functions and call scripts from other scripts. Shell functions can be called recursively; that is, a Bourne Again Shell function can call itself. You might not need to use recursion often, but it might allow you to solve some apparently difficult problems with ease.

- Execute statements conditionally using statements such as **if**.

- Execute statements iteratively using statements such as **while** and **for**.

- Transfer data to and from the program, communicating with both data files and users.

Programming languages implement these capabilities in different ways but with the same ideas in mind. When you want to solve a problem by writing a program, you must first figure out a procedure that leads you to a solution—that is, an *algorithm*. Typically you can implement the same algorithm in roughly the same way in different programming languages, using the same kinds of constructs in each language.

Chapter 9 and this chapter have introduced numerous bash features, many of which are useful for both interactive use and shell programming. This section develops two complete shell programs, demonstrating how to combine some of these features effectively. The programs are presented as problems for you to solve, with sample solutions provided.

A RECURSIVE SHELL SCRIPT

A recursive construct is one that is defined in terms of itself. Alternatively, you might say that a recursive program is one that can call itself. This concept might seem circular, but it need not be. To avoid circularity, a recursive definition must have a special case that is not self-referential. Recursive ideas occur in everyday life. For example, you can define an ancestor as your mother, your father, or one of their ancestors. This definition is not circular; it specifies unambiguously who your ancestors are: your mother or your father, or your mother's mother or father or your father's mother or father, and so on.

A number of Linux system utilities can operate recursively. See the **–R** option to the chmod, chown, and cp utilities for examples.

Solve the following problem by using a recursive shell function:

Write a shell function named **makepath** that, given a pathname, creates all components in that pathname as directories. For example, the command **makepath a/b/c/d** should create directories **a**, **a/b**, **a/b/c**, and **a/b/c/d**. (The mkdir **–p** option creates directories in this manner. Solve the problem without using **mkdir –p**.)

One algorithm for a recursive solution follows:

1. Examine the path argument. If it is a null string or if it names an existing directory, do nothing and return.

2. If the path argument is a simple path component, create it (using mkdir) and return.

3. Otherwise, call **makepath** using the path prefix of the original argument. This step eventually creates all the directories up to the last component, which you can then create using mkdir.

In general, a recursive function must invoke itself with a simpler version of the problem than it was given until it is finally called with a simple case that does not need to call itself. Following is one possible solution based on this algorithm:

makepath
```
# This is a function
# Enter it at the keyboard, do not run it as a shell script
#
function makepath()
{
    if [[ ${#1} -eq 0 || -d "$1" ]]
        then
            return 0        # Do nothing
    fi
    if [[ "${1%/*}" = "$1" ]]
        then
            mkdir $1
            return $?
    fi
    makepath ${1%/*} || return 1
    mkdir $1
    return $?
}
```

In the test for a simple component (the **if** statement in the middle of the function), the left expression is the argument after the shortest suffix that starts with a **/** character has been stripped away (page 1034). If there is no such character (for example, if **$1** is **max**), nothing is stripped off and the two sides are equal. If the argument is a simple filename preceded by a slash, such as **/usr**, the expression **${1%/*}** evaluates to a null string. To make the function work in this case, you must take two precautions: Put the left expression within quotation marks and ensure that the recursive function behaves sensibly when it is passed a null string as an argument. In general, good programs are robust: They should be prepared for borderline, invalid, or meaningless input and behave appropriately in such cases.

By giving the following command from the shell you are working in, you turn on debugging tracing so that you can watch the recursion work:

```
$ set -o xtrace
```

(Give the same command, but replace the hyphen with a plus sign [**+**] to turn debugging off.) With debugging turned on, the shell displays each line in its expanded form as it executes the line. A **+** precedes each line of debugging output.

In the following example, the first line that starts with **+** shows the shell calling **makepath**. The **makepath** function is initially called from the command line with arguments of **a/b/c**. It then calls itself with arguments of **a/b** and finally **a**. All the work is done (using **mkdir**) as each call to **makepath** returns.

```
$ ./makepath a/b/c
+ makepath a/b/c
+ [[ 5 -eq 0 ]]
+ [[ -d a/b/c ]]
+ [[ a/b = \a\/\b\/\c ]]
+ makepath a/b
+ [[ 3 -eq 0 ]]
+ [[ -d a/b ]]
+ [[ a = \a\/\b ]]
```

```
+ makepath a
+ [[ 1 -eq 0 ]]
+ [[ -d a ]]
+ [[ a = \a ]]
+ mkdir a
+ return 0
+ mkdir a/b
+ return 0
+ mkdir a/b/c
+ return 0
```

The function works its way down the recursive path and back up again.

It is instructive to invoke **makepath** with an invalid path and see what happens. The following example, which is run with debugging turned on, tries to create the path **/a/b**. Creating this path requires that you create directory **a** in the root directory. Unless you have permission to write to the root directory, you are not permitted to create this directory.

```
$ ./makepath /a/b
+ makepath /a/b
+ [[ 4 -eq 0 ]]
+ [[ -d /a/b ]]
+ [[ /a = \/\a\/\b ]]
+ makepath /a
+ [[ 2 -eq 0 ]]
+ [[ -d /a ]]
+ [[ '' = \/\a ]]
+ makepath
+ [[ 0 -eq 0 ]]
+ return 0
+ mkdir /a
mkdir: cannot create directory '/a': Permission denied
+ return 1
+ return 1
```

The recursion stops when **makepath** is denied permission to create the **/a** directory. The error returned is passed all the way back, so the original **makepath** exits with nonzero status.

Use local variables with recursive functions

tip The preceding example glossed over a potential problem that you might encounter when you use a recursive function. During the execution of a recursive function, many separate instances of that function might be active simultaneously. All but one of them are waiting for their child invocation to complete.

Because functions run in the same environment as the shell that calls them, variables are implicitly shared by a shell and a function it calls. As a consequence, all instances of the function share a single copy of each variable. Sharing variables can give rise to side effects that are rarely what you want. As a rule, you should use typeset to make all variables of a recursive function be local variables. See page 1010 for more information.

THE quiz SHELL SCRIPT

Solve the following problem using a bash script:

Write a generic multiple-choice quiz program. The program should get its questions from data files, present them to the user, and keep track of the number of correct and incorrect answers. The user must be able to exit from the program at any time and receive a summary of results to that point.

The detailed design of this program and even the detailed description of the problem depend on a number of choices: How will the program know which subjects are available for quizzes? How will the user choose a subject? How will the program know when the quiz is over? Should the program present the same questions (for a given subject) in the same order each time, or should it scramble them?

Of course, you can make many perfectly good choices that implement the specification of the problem. The following details narrow the problem specification:

- Each subject will correspond to a subdirectory of a master quiz directory. This directory will be named in the environment variable **QUIZDIR**, whose default will be **~/quiz**. For example, you could have the following directories correspond to the subjects engineering, art, and politics: **~/quiz/engineering**, **~/quiz/art**, and **~/quiz/politics**. Put the **quiz** directory in **/usr/games** if you want all users to have access to it (requires **root** privileges).

- Each subject can have several questions. Each question is represented by a file in its subject's directory.

- The first line of each file that represents a question holds the text of the question. If it takes more than one line, you must escape the NEWLINE with a backslash. (This setup makes it easy to read a single question with the read builtin.) The second line of the file is an integer that specifies the number of choices. The next lines are the choices themselves. The last line is the correct answer. Following is a sample question file:

      Who discovered the principle of the lever?
      4
      Euclid
      Archimedes
      Thomas Edison
      The Lever Brothers
      Archimedes

- The program presents all the questions in a subject directory. At any point the user can interrupt the quiz using CONTROL-C, whereupon the program will summarize the results up to that point and exit. If the user does not interrupt the program, the program summarizes the results and exits when it has asked all questions for the chosen subject.

- The program scrambles the questions in a subject before presenting them.

Following is a top-level design for this program:

1. Initialize. This involves a number of steps, such as setting the counts of the number of questions asked so far and the number of correct and wrong answers to zero. It also sets up the program to trap CONTROL-C.

2. Present the user with a choice of subjects and get the user's response.

3. Change to the corresponding subject directory.

4. Determine the questions to be asked (that is, the filenames in that directory). Arrange them in random order.

5. Repeatedly present questions and ask for answers until the quiz is over or is interrupted by the user.

6. Present the results and exit.

Clearly some of these steps (such as step 3) are simple, whereas others (such as step 4) are complex and worthy of analysis on their own. Use shell functions for any complex step, and use the trap builtin to handle a user interrupt.

Here is a skeleton version of the program with empty shell functions:

```
function initialize
{
# Initializes variables.
}

function choose_subj
{
# Writes choice to standard output.
}

function scramble
{
# Stores names of question files, scrambled,
# in an array variable named questions.
}

function ask
{
# Reads a question file, asks the question, and checks the
# answer. Returns 1 if the answer was correct, 0 otherwise. If it
# encounters an invalid question file, exit with status 2.
}

function summarize
{
# Presents the user's score.
}

# Main program
initialize                          # Step 1 in top-level design

subject=$(choose_subj)              # Step 2
[[ $? -eq 0 ]] || exit 2            # If no valid choice, exit
```

```
cd $subject || exit 2              # Step 3
echo                               # Skip a line
scramble                           # Step 4

for ques in ${questions[*]}; do    # Step 5
    ask $ques
    result=$?
    (( num_ques=num_ques+1 ))
    if [[ $result == 1 ]]; then
        (( num_correct += 1 ))
    fi
    echo                           # Skip a line between questions
    sleep ${QUIZDELAY:=1}
done

summarize                          # Step 6
exit 0
```

To make reading the results a bit easier for the user, a sleep call appears inside the question loop. It delays **$QUIZDELAY** seconds (default = 1) between questions.

Now the task is to fill in the missing pieces of the program. In a sense this program is being written backward. The details (the shell functions) come first in the file but come last in the development process. This common programming practice is called top-down design. In top-down design you fill in the broad outline of the program first and supply the details later. In this way you break the problem up into smaller problems, each of which you can work on independently. Shell functions are a great help in using the top-down approach.

One way to write the **initialize** function follows. The cd command causes **QUIZDIR** to be the working directory for the rest of the script and defaults to **~/quiz** if **QUIZDIR** is not set.

```
function initialize ()
{
trap 'summarize ; exit 0' INT    # Handle user interrupts
num_ques=0                        # Number of questions asked so far
num_correct=0                     # Number answered correctly so far
first_time=true                   # true until first question is asked
cd ${QUIZDIR:=~/quiz} || exit 2
}
```

Be prepared for the cd command to fail. The directory might be unsearchable or conceivably another user might have removed it. The preceding function exits with a status code of 2 if cd fails.

The next function, **choose_subj**, is a bit more complicated. It displays a menu using a **select** statement:

```
function choose_subj ()
{
subjects=($(ls))
PS3="Choose a subject for the quiz from the preceding list: "
select Subject in ${subjects[*]}; do
    if [[ -z "$Subject" ]]; then
        echo "No subject chosen.  Bye." >&2
        exit 1
    fi
    echo $Subject
    return 0
done
}
```

The function first uses an ls command and command substitution to put a list of subject directories in the **subjects** array. Next the **select** structure (page 999) presents the user with a list of subjects (the directories found by ls) and assigns the chosen directory name to the **Subject** variable. Finally the function writes the name of the subject directory to standard output. The main program uses command substitution to assign this value to the **subject** variable [**subject=$(choose_subj)**].

The **scramble** function presents a number of difficulties. In this solution it uses an array variable (**questions**) to hold the names of the questions. It scrambles the entries in an array using the **RANDOM** variable (each time you reference **RANDOM**, it has the value of a [random] integer between 0 and 32767):

```
function scramble ()
{
typeset -i index quescount
questions=($(ls))
quescount=${#questions[*]}              # Number of elements
((index=quescount-1))
while [[ $index > 0 ]]; do
    ((target=RANDOM % index))
    exchange $target $index
    ((index -= 1))
done
}
```

This function initializes the array variable **questions** to the list of filenames (questions) in the working directory. The variable **quescount** is set to the number of such files. Then the following algorithm is used: Let the variable index count down from **quescount – 1** (the index of the last entry in the array variable). For each value of **index**, the function chooses a random value target between 0 and **index**, inclusive. The command

```
((target=RANDOM % index))
```

produces a random value between 0 and **index – 1** by taking the remainder (the % operator) when **$RANDOM** is divided by **index**. The function then exchanges the elements of **questions** at positions **target** and **index**. It is convenient to take care of this step in another function named **exchange**:

```
function exchange ()
{
temp_value=${questions[$1]}
questions[$1]=${questions[$2]}
questions[$2]=$temp_value
}
```

The **ask** function also uses the **select** structure. It reads the question file named in its argument and uses the contents of that file to present the question, accept the answer, and determine whether the answer is correct. (See the code that follows.)

The **ask** function uses file descriptor 3 to read successive lines from the question file, whose name was passed as an argument and is represented by **$1** in the function. It reads the question into the **ques** variable and the number of questions into **num_opts**. The function constructs the variable **choices** by initializing it to a null string and successively appending the next choice. Then it sets **PS3** to the value of **ques** and uses a **select** structure to prompt the user with **ques**. The **select** structure places the user's answer in **answer**, and the function then checks that response against the correct answer from the file.

The construction of the **choices** variable is done with an eye toward avoiding a potential problem. Suppose that one answer has some whitespace in it—then it might appear as two or more arguments in **choices**. To avoid this problem, make sure that **choices** is an array variable. The **select** statement does the rest of the work:

quiz
```
$ cat quiz
#!/bin/bash

# remove the # on the following line to turn on debugging
# set -o xtrace

#==================
function initialize ()
{
trap 'summarize ; exit 0' INT        # Handle user interrupts
num_ques=0                           # Number of questions asked so far
num_correct=0                        # Number answered correctly so far
first_time=true                      # true until first question is asked
cd ${QUIZDIR:=~/quiz} || exit 2
}

#==================
function choose_subj ()
{
subjects=($(ls))
PS3="Choose a subject for the quiz from the preceding list: "
select Subject in ${subjects[*]}; do
    if [[ -z "$Subject" ]]; then
        echo "No subject chosen.  Bye." >&2
        exit 1
    fi
    echo $Subject
    return 0
done
}
```

```
#==================
function exchange ()
{
temp_value=${questions[$1]}
questions[$1]=${questions[$2]}
questions[$2]=$temp_value
}

#==================
function scramble ()
{
typeset -i index quescount
questions=($(ls))
quescount=${#questions[*]}              # Number of elements
((index=quescount-1))
while [[ $index > 0 ]]; do
    ((target=RANDOM % index))
    exchange $target $index
    ((index -= 1))
done
}

#==================
function ask ()
{
exec 3<$1
read -u3 ques || exit 2
read -u3 num_opts || exit 2

index=0
choices=()
while (( index < num_opts )) ; do
    read -u3 next_choice || exit 2
    choices=("${choices[@]}" "$next_choice")
    ((index += 1))
done
read -u3 correct_answer || exit 2
exec 3<&-

if [[ $first_time = true ]]; then
    first_time=false
    echo -e "You may press the interrupt key at any time to quit.\n"
fi

PS3=$ques" "                            # Make $ques the prompt for select
                                        # and add some spaces for legibility.
select answer in "${choices[@]}"; do
    if [[ -z "$answer" ]]; then
            echo  Not a valid choice. Please choose again.
        elif [[ "$answer" = "$correct_answer" ]]; then
            echo "Correct!"
            return 1
        else
            echo "No, the answer is $correct_answer."
            return 0
    fi
done
}
```

```
#==================
function summarize ()
{
echo                            # Skip a line
if (( num_ques == 0 )); then
    echo "You did not answer any questions"
    exit 0
fi

(( percent=num_correct*100/num_ques ))
echo "You answered $num_correct questions correctly, out of \
$num_ques total questions."
echo "Your score is $percent percent."
}

#==================
# Main program
initialize                      # Step 1 in top-level design

subject=$(choose_subj)          # Step 2
[[ $? -eq 0 ]] || exit 2        # If no valid choice, exit

cd $subject || exit 2           # Step 3
echo                            # Skip a line
scramble                        # Step 4

for ques in ${questions[*]}; do # Step 5
    ask $ques
    result=$?
    (( num_ques=num_ques+1 ))
    if [[ $result == 1 ]]; then
        (( num_correct += 1 ))
    fi
    echo                        # Skip a line between questions
    sleep ${QUIZDELAY:=1}
done

summarize                       # Step 6
exit 0
```

Chapter Summary

The shell is a programming language. Programs written in this language are called shell scripts, or simply scripts. Shell scripts provide the decision and looping control structures present in high-level programming languages while allowing easy access to system utilities and user programs. Shell scripts can use functions to modularize and simplify complex tasks.

Control structures The control structures that use decisions to select alternatives are if...then, if...then...else, and if...then...elif. The case control structure provides a multiway branch and can be used when you want to express alternatives using a simple pattern-matching syntax.

The looping control structures are for...in, for, until, and while. These structures perform one or more tasks repetitively.

The **break** and **continue** control structures alter control within loops: **break** transfers control out of a loop, and **continue** transfers control immediately to the top of a loop.

The Here document allows input to a command in a shell script to come from within the script itself.

File descriptors   The Bourne Again Shell provides the ability to manipulate file descriptors. Coupled with the read and echo builtins, file descriptors allow shell scripts to have as much control over input and output as do programs written in lower-level languages.

Variables   The typeset builtin assigns attributes, such as readonly, to bash variables. The Bourne Again Shell provides operators to perform pattern matching on variables, provide default values for variables, and evaluate the length of variables. This shell also supports array variables and local variables for functions and provides built-in integer arithmetic, using the let builtin and an expression syntax similar to that found in the C programming language.

Builtins   Bourne Again Shell builtins include type, read, exec, trap, kill, and getopts. The type builtin displays information about a command, including its location; read allows a script to accept user input.

The exec builtin executes a command without creating a new process. The new command overlays the current process, assuming the same environment and PID number of that process. This builtin executes user programs and other Linux commands when it is *not* necessary to return control to the calling process.

The trap builtin catches a signal sent by Linux to the process running the script and allows you to specify actions to be taken upon receipt of one or more signals. You can use this builtin to cause a script to ignore the signal that is sent when the user presses the interrupt key.

The kill builtin terminates a running program. The getopts builtin parses command-line arguments, making it easier to write programs that follow standard Linux conventions for command-line arguments and options.

Utilities in scripts   In addition to using control structures, builtins, and functions, shell scripts generally call Linux utilities. The find utility, for instance, is commonplace in shell scripts that search for files in the system hierarchy and can perform a vast range of tasks, from simple to complex.

Expressions   There are two basic types of expressions: arithmetic and logical. Arithmetic expressions allow you to do arithmetic on constants and variables, yielding a numeric result. Logical (Boolean) expressions compare expressions or strings, or test conditions to yield a *true* or *false* result. As with all decisions within Linux shell scripts, a *true* status is represented by the value zero; *false*, by any nonzero value.

Good programming practices   A well-written shell script adheres to standard programming practices, such as specifying the shell to execute the script on the first line of the script, verifying the number and type of arguments that the script is called with, displaying a standard usage message to report command-line errors, and redirecting all informational messages to standard error.

EXERCISES

1. Rewrite the **journal** script of Chapter 9 (exercise 5, page 357) by adding commands to verify that the user has write permission for a file named **journal-file** in the user's home directory, if such a file exists. The script should take appropriate actions if **journal-file** exists and the user does not have write permission to the file. Verify that the modified script works.

2. The special parameter "**$@**" is referenced twice in the **out** script (page 976). Explain what would be different if the parameter "**$∗**" were used in its place.

3. Write a filter that takes a list of files as input and outputs the basename (page 998) of each file in the list.

4. Write a function that takes a single filename as an argument and adds execute permission to the file for the user.

   a. When might such a function be useful?

   b. Revise the script so it takes one or more filenames as arguments and adds execute permission for the user for each file argument.

   c. What can you do to make the function available every time you log in?

   d. Suppose that, in addition to having the function available on subsequent login sessions, you want to make the function available in your current shell. How would you do so?

5. When might it be necessary or advisable to write a shell script instead of a shell function? Give as many reasons as you can think of.

6. Write a shell script that displays the names of all directory files, but no other types of files, in the working directory.

7. Write a script to display the time every 15 seconds. Read the date man page and display the time, using the **%r** field descriptor. Clear the window (using the clear command) each time before you display the time.

8. Enter the following script named **savefiles**, and give yourself execute permission to the file:

```
$ cat savefiles
#! /bin/bash
echo "Saving files in current directory in file savethem."
exec > savethem
for i in *
        do
        echo "=================================================="
        echo "File: $i"
        echo "=================================================="
        cat "$i"
        done
```

a. Which error message do you get when you execute this script? Rewrite the script so that the error does not occur, making sure the output still goes to **savethem**.

b. What might be a problem with running this script twice in the same directory? Discuss a solution to this problem.

9. Read the bash man or info page, try some experiments, and answer the following questions:

a. How do you export a function?

b. What does the hash builtin do?

c. What happens if the argument to exec is not executable?

10. Using the find utility, perform the following tasks:

a. List all files in the working directory and all subdirectories that have been modified within the last day.

b. List all files you have read access to on the system that are larger than 1 megabyte.

c. Remove all files named **core** from the directory structure rooted at your home directory.

d. List the inode numbers of all files in the working directory whose filenames end in .c.

e. List all files you have read access to on the root filesystem that have been modified in the last 30 days.

11. Write a short script that tells you whether the permissions for two files, whose names are given as arguments to the script, are identical. If the permissions for the two files are identical, output the common permission field. Otherwise, output each filename followed by its permission field. (*Hint:* Try using the cut utility.)

12. Write a script that takes the name of a directory as an argument and searches the file hierarchy rooted at that directory for zero-length files. Write the names of all zero-length files to standard output. If there is no option on the command line, have the script delete the file after displaying its name, asking the user for confirmation, and receiving positive confirmation. A –f (force) option on the command line indicates that the script should display the filename but not ask for confirmation before deleting the file.

ADVANCED EXERCISES

13. Write a script that takes a colon-separated list of items and outputs the items, one per line, to standard output (without the colons).

14. Generalize the script written in exercise 13 so that the character separating the list items is given as an argument to the function. If this argument is absent, the separator should default to a colon.

15. Write a function named **funload** that takes as its single argument the name of a file containing other functions. The purpose of **funload** is to make all functions in the named file available in the current shell; that is, **funload** loads the functions from the named file. To locate the file, **funload** searches the colon-separated list of directories given by the environment variable **FUNPATH**. Assume that the format of **FUNPATH** is the same as **PATH** and that searching **FUNPATH** is similar to the shell's search of the **PATH** variable.

16. Rewrite **bundle** (page 1002) so the script it creates takes an optional list of filenames as arguments. If one or more filenames are given on the command line, only those files should be re-created; otherwise, all files in the shell archive should be re-created. For example, suppose all files with the filename extension **.c** are bundled into an archive named **srcshell**, and you want to unbundle just the files **test1.c** and **test2.c**. The following command will unbundle just these two files:

    ```
    $ bash srcshell test1.c test2.c
    ```

17. What kind of links will the **lnks** script (page 979) not find? Why?

18. In principle, recursion is never necessary. It can always be replaced by an iterative construct, such as **while** or **until**. Rewrite **makepath** (page 1042) as a nonrecursive function. Which version do you prefer? Why?

19. Lists are commonly stored in environment variables by putting a colon (:) between each of the list elements. (The value of the **PATH** variable is an example.) You can add an element to such a list by catenating the new element to the front of the list, as in

    ```
    PATH=/opt/bin:$PATH
    ```

    If the element you add is already in the list, you now have two copies of it in the list. Write a shell function named **addenv** that takes two arguments: (1) the name of a shell variable and (2) a string to prepend to the list that is the value of the shell variable only if that string is not already an element of the list. For example, the call

    ```
    addenv PATH /opt/bin
    ```

    would add **/opt/bin** to **PATH** only if that pathname is not already in **PATH**. Be sure your solution works even if the shell variable starts out empty. Also make sure you check the list elements carefully. If **/usr/opt/bin** is in **PATH** but **/opt/bin** is not, the example just given should still add **/opt/bin** to **PATH**. (*Hint:* You might find this exercise easier to complete if you first write a function **locate_field** that tells you whether a string is an element in the value of a variable.)

20. Write a function that takes a directory name as an argument and writes to standard output the maximum of the lengths of all filenames in that directory. If the function's argument is not a directory name, write an error message to standard output and exit with nonzero status.

21. Modify the function you wrote for exercise 20 to descend all subdirectories of the named directory recursively and to find the maximum length of any filename in that hierarchy.

22. Write a function that lists the number of ordinary files, directories, block special files, character special files, FIFOs, and symbolic links in the working directory. Do this in two different ways:

    a. Use the first letter of the output of **ls –l** to determine a file's type.

    b. Use the file type condition tests of the *[[expression]]* syntax to determine a file's type.

23. Modify the **quiz** program (page 1048) so that the choices for a question are randomly arranged.

28

THE PERL SCRIPTING LANGUAGE

OBJECTIVES

After reading this chapter you should be able to:

▶ Use perldoc to display Perl documentation

▶ Run a Perl program on the command line and from a file

▶ Explain the use of the **say** function

▶ Name and describe the three types of Perl variables

▶ Write a Perl program that uses each type of variable

▶ Describe the Perl control structures

▶ Write programs that read from and write to files

▶ Use regular expressions in a Perl program

▶ Write a Perl program that incorporates a CPAN module

▶ Demonstrate several Perl functions

In 1987 Larry Wall created the Perl (Practical Extraction and Report Language) programming language for working with text. Perl uses syntax and concepts from awk, sed, C, the Bourne Shell, Smalltalk, Lisp, and English. It was designed to scan and extract information from text files and generate reports based on that information. Since its introduction in 1987, Perl has expanded enormously—its documentation growing up with it. Today, in addition to text processing, Perl is used for system administration, software development, and general-purpose programming.

Perl code is portable because Perl has been implemented on many operating systems (see www.cpan.org/ports). Perl is an informal, practical, robust, easy-to-use, efficient, complete, and down-and-dirty language that supports procedural and object-oriented programming. It is not necessarily elegant.

One of the things that distinguishes Perl from many other languages is its linguistic origins. In English you say, "I will buy a car if I win the lottery." Perl allows you to mimic that syntax. Another distinction is that Perl has singular and plural variables, the former holding single values and the latter holding lists of values.

INTRODUCTION TO PERL

A couple of quotes from the manual shed light on Perl's philosophy:

> Many of Perl's syntactic elements are optional. Rather than requiring you to put parentheses around every function call and declare every variable, you can often leave such explicit elements off and Perl will frequently figure out what you meant. This is known as Do What I Mean, abbreviated DWIM. It allows programmers to be lazy and to code in a style with which they are comfortable.
>
> The Perl motto is "There's more than one way to do it." Divining how many more is left as an exercise to the reader.

One of Perl's biggest assets is its support by thousands of third-party modules. The Comprehensive Perl Archive Network (CPAN; www.cpan.org) is a repository for many of the modules and other information related to Perl. See page 1095 for information on downloading, installing, and using these modules in Perl programs.

The best way to learn Perl is to work with it. Copy and modify the programs in this chapter until they make sense to you. Many system tools are written in Perl. The first line of most of these tools begins with **#!/usr/bin/perl**, which tells the shell to pass the program to Perl for execution. Most files that contain the string

/usr/bin/perl are Perl programs. The following command uses grep to search the /usr/bin and /usr/sbin directories recursively (–r) for files containing the string /usr/bin/perl; it lists many local system tools written in Perl:

```
$ grep -r /usr/bin/perl /usr/bin /usr/sbin | head -4
/usr/bin/defoma-user:#! /usr/bin/perl -w
/usr/bin/pod2latex:#!/usr/bin/perl
/usr/bin/pod2latex:    eval 'exec /usr/bin/perl -S $0 ${1+"$@"}'
/usr/bin/splain:#!/usr/bin/perl
```

Review these programs—they demonstrate how Perl is used in the real world. Copy a system program to a directory you own before modifying it. Do not run a system program while running with **root** privileges unless you know what you are doing.

MORE INFORMATION

Local man pages: See the perl and perltoc man pages for lists of Perl man pages

Web Perl home page: www.perl.com
CPAN: www.cpan.org
blog: perlbuzz.com

Book *Programming Perl,* third edition, by Wall, Christiansen, & Orwant, O'Reilly & Associates (July 2000)

HELP

Perl is a forgiving language. As such, it is easy to write Perl code that runs but does not perform as you intended. Perl includes many tools that can help you find coding mistakes. The **–w** option and the **use warnings** statement can produce helpful diagnostic messages. The **use strict** statement (see the **perldebtut** man page) can impose order on a program by requiring, among other things, that you declare variables before you use them. When all else fails, you can use Perl's builtin debugger to step through a program. See the **perldebtut** and **perldebug** man pages for more information.

perldoc

The perldoc utility (**perl** package; installed by default) locates and displays local Perl documentation. It is similar to man (page 126) but specific to Perl. It works with files that include lines of **pod** (plain old documentation), a clean and simple documentation language. When embedded in a Perl program, **pod** enables you to include documentation for the entire program, not just code-level comments.

Following is a simple Perl program that includes **pod**. The two lines following **=cut** are the program; the rest is **pod**-format documentation.

```
$ cat pod.ex1.pl
#!/usr/bin/perl

=head1 A Perl Program to Say I<Hi there.>

This simple Perl program includes documentation in B<pod> format.
The following B<=cut> command tells B<perldoc> that what follows
is not documentation.

=cut
# A Perl program
print "Hi there.\n";

=head1 pod Documentation Resumes with Any pod Command

See the B<perldoc.perl.org/perlpod.html> page for more information
on B<pod> and B<perldoc.perl.org> for complete Perl documentation.
```

You can use Perl to run the program:

```
$ perl pod.ex1.pl
Hi there.
```

Or you can use perldoc to display the documentation:

```
$ perldoc pod.ex1.pl
POD.EX1(1)           User Contributed Perl Documentation           POD.EX1(1)



A Perl Program to Say Hi there.
    This simple Perl program includes documentation in pod format.  The
    following =cut command tells perldoc that what follows is not
    documentation.

pod Documentation Resumes with Any pod Command
    See the perldoc.perl.org/perlpod.html page for more information on pod
    and perldoc.perl.org for complete Perl documentation.



perl v5.10.0                     2008-10-14                     POD.EX1(1)
```

Most publicly distributed modules and scripts, as well as Perl itself, include
embedded **pod**-format documentation. For example, the following command
displays information about the Perl **print** function:

```
$ perldoc -f print
    print FILEHANDLE LIST
    print LIST
    print       Prints a string or a list of strings.  Returns true if
                successful.  FILEHANDLE may be a scalar variable containing the
                name of or a reference to the filehandle, thus introducing one
                level of indirection.  (NOTE: If FILEHANDLE is a variable and the
                next token is a term, it may be misinterpreted as an operator
                unless you interpose a "+" or put parentheses around the
    ...
```

Once you have installed a module (page 1095), you can use perldoc to display documentation for that module. The following example shows perldoc displaying information on the locally installed **Timestamp::Simple** module:

```
$ perldoc Timestamp::Simple
Timestamp::Simple(3)  User Contributed Perl Documentation Timestamp::Simple(3)

NAME
       Timestamp::Simple - Simple methods for timestamping

SYNOPSIS
           use Timestamp::Simple qw(stamp);
           print stamp, "\n";
...
```

Give the command **man perldoc** or **perldoc perldoc** to display the perldoc man page and read more about this tool.

Make Perl programs readable

tip   Although Perl has many shortcuts that are good choices for one-shot programming, this chapter presents code that is easy to understand and easy to maintain.

TERMINOLOGY

This section defines some of the terms used in this chapter.

Module   A Perl *module* is a self-contained chunk of Perl code, frequently containing several functions that work together. A module can be called from another module or from a Perl program. A module must have a unique name. To help ensure unique names, Perl provides a hierarchical *namespace* (page 1177) for modules, separating components of a name with double colons (::). Example module names are **Timestamp::Simple** and **WWW::Mechanize**.

Distribution   A Perl *distribution* is a set of one or more modules that perform a task. You can search for distributions and modules at search.cpan.org. Examples of distributions include **Timestamp-Simple** (the **Timestamp-Simple-1.01.tar.gz** archive file contains the **Timestamp::Simple** module only) and **WWW-Mechanize** (**WWW-Mechanize-1.34.tar.gz** contains the **WWW::Mechanize** module, plus supporting modules including **WWW::Mechanize::Link** and **WWW::Mechanize::Image**).

Package   A *package* defines a Perl namespace. For example, in the variable with the name **$WWW::Mechanize::ex**, $ex is a scalar variable in the **WWW::Mechanize** package, where "package" is used in the sense of a namespace. Using the same name, such as **WWW::Mechanize**, for a distribution, a package, and a module can be confusing.

Block   A *block* is zero or more statements, delimited by curly braces ({}), that defines a scope. The shell control structure syntax explanations refer to these elements as *commands*. See the **if...then** control structure on page 971 for an example.

Package variable   A *package variable* is defined within the package it appears in. Other packages can refer to package variables by using the variable's fully qualified name (for example, **$Text::Wrap::columns**). By default, variables are package variables unless you define them as lexical variables.

Lexical variable   A *lexical variable,* which is defined by preceding the name of a variable with the keyword **my** (see the tip on page 1067), is defined only within the block or file it appears in. Other languages refer to a lexical variable as a local variable. Because Perl 4 used the keyword **local** with a different meaning, Perl 5 uses the keyword **lexical** in its place. When programming using bash, variables that are not exported (page 1008) are local to the program they are used in.

List   A *list* is a series of zero or more scalars. The following list has three elements—two numbers and a string:

```
(2, 4, 'Zach')
```

Array   An *array* is a variable that holds a list of elements in a defined order. In the following line of code, **@a** is an array. See page 1069 for more information about array variables.

```
@a = (2, 4, 'Zach')
```

Compound statement   A *compound statement* is a statement made up of other statements. For example, the **if** compound statement (page 1074) incorporates an **if** statement that normally includes other statements within the block it controls.

RUNNING A PERL PROGRAM

There are several ways you can run a program written in Perl. The −e option enables you to enter a program on the command line:

```
$ perl -e 'print "Hi there.\n"'
Hi there.
```

The −e option is a good choice for testing Perl syntax and running brief, one-shot programs. This option requires that the Perl program appear as a single argument on the command line. The program must immediately follow this option—it is an argument to this option. An easy way to write this type of program is to enclose the program within single quotation marks.

Because Perl is a member of the class of utilities that take input from a file or standard input (page 236), you can give the command **perl** and enter the program terminated by CONTROL-D (end of file). Perl reads the program from standard input:

```
$ perl
print "Hi there.\n";
CONTROL-D
Hi there.
```

The preceding techniques are useful for quick, one-off command-line programs but are not helpful for running more complex programs. Most of the time, a Perl program is stored in a text file. Although not required, the file typically has a filename extension of **.pl**. Following is the same simple program used in the previous examples stored in a file:

```
$ cat simple.pl
print "Hi there.\n";
```

You can run this program by specifying its name as an argument to Perl:

```
$ perl simple.pl
Hi there.
```

Most commonly and similarly to most shell scripts, the file containing the Perl program is executable. In the following example, chmod (page 288) makes the **simple2.pl** file executable. As explained on page 290, the **#!** at the start of the first line of the file instructs the shell to pass the rest of the file to **/usr/bin/perl** for execution.

```
$ chmod 755 simple2.pl
$ cat simple2.pl
#!/usr/bin/perl -w
print "Hi there.\n";

$ ./simple2.pl
Hi there.
```

In this example, the **simple2.pl** program is executed as **./simple2.pl** because the working directory is not in the user's **PATH** (page 308). The **–w** option tells Perl to issue warning messages when it identifies potential errors in the code.

PERL VERSION 5.10

All examples in this chapter were run under Perl 5.10. Give the following command to see which version of Perl the local system is running:

```
$ perl -v

This is perl 5, version 12, subversion 3 (v5.12.3) built for i386-linux-thread-multi
...
```

use feature 'say' The **say** function is a Perl 6 feature available in Perl 5.10. It works the same way **print** does, except it adds a NEWLINE (**\n**) at the end of each line it outputs. Some versions of Perl require you to tell Perl explicitly that you want to use **say**. The **use** function in the following example tells Perl to enable **say**. Try running this program without the **use** line to see if the local version of Perl requires it.

```
$ cat 5.10.pl
use feature 'say';
say 'Output by say.';
print 'Output by print.';
say 'End.'

$ perl 5.10.pl
Output by say.
Output by print.End.
$
```

Earlier versions of Perl   If you are running an earlier version of Perl, you will need to replace **say** in the examples in this chapter with **print** and terminate the **print** statement with a quoted **\n**:

```
$ cat 5.8.pl
print 'Output by print in place of say.', "\n";
print 'Output by print.';
print 'End.', "\n";

$ perl 5.8.pl
Output by print in place of say.
Output by print.End.
```

SYNTAX

This section describes the major components of a Perl program.

Statements   A Perl program comprises one or more *statements*, each terminated by a semicolon (;). These statements are free-form with respect to *whitespace* (page 1196), except for whitespace within quoted strings. Multiple statements can appear on a single line, each terminated by a semicolon. The following programs are equivalent. The first occupies two lines, the second only one; look at the differences in the spacing around the equal and plus signs. See **use feature 'say'** (on the previous page) if these programs complain about **say** not being available.

```
$ cat statement1.pl
$n=4;
say "Answer is ", $n + 2;
$ perl statement1.pl
Answer is 6

$ cat statement2.pl
$n = 4; say "Answer is ", $n+2;
$ perl statement2.pl
Answer is 6
```

Expressions   The syntax of Perl expressions frequently corresponds to the syntax of C expressions but is not always the same. Perl expressions are covered in examples throughout this chapter.

Quotation marks   All character strings must be enclosed within single or double quotation marks. Perl differentiates between the two types of quotation marks in a manner similar to the way the shell does (page 303): Double quotation marks allow Perl to interpolate enclosed variables and interpret special characters such as **\n** (NEWLINE), whereas single quotation marks do not. Table 28-1 lists some of Perl's special characters.

The following example demonstrates how different types of quotation marks, and the absence of quotation marks, affect Perl in converting scalars between numbers and strings. The single quotation marks in the first **print** statement prevent Perl from interpolating the **$string** variable and from interpreting the **\n** special character. The leading **\n** in the second **print** statement forces the output of that statement to appear on a new line.

```
$ cat string1.pl
$string="5";        # $string declared as a string, but it will not matter

print '$string+5\n';    # Perl displays $string+5 literally because of
                        # the single quotation marks
print "\n$string+5\n";  # Perl interpolates the value of $string as a string
                        # because of the double quotation marks
print $string+5, "\n";  # Lack of quotation marks causes Perl to interpret
                        # $string as a numeric variable and to add 5;
                        # the \n must appear between double quotation marks

$ perl string1.pl
$string+5\n
5+5
10
```

Slash   By default, regular expressions are delimited by slashes (/). The following example tests whether the string **hours** contains the pattern **our**; see page 1090 for more information on regular expression delimiters in Perl.

```
$ perl -e 'if ("hours" =~ /our/) {say "yes";}'
```

The local version of Perl might require **use feature 'say'** (page 1063) to work properly:

```
$ perl -e 'use feature "say"; if ("hours" =~ /our/) {say "yes";}'
```

Backslash   Within a string enclosed between double quotation marks, a backslash escapes (quotes) another backslash. Thus Perl displays "\\n" as \n. Within a regular expression, Perl does not expand a metacharacter preceded by a backslash. See the **string1.pl** program above.

Comments   As in the shell, a comment in Perl begins with a hashmark (#) and ends at the end of the line (just before the NEWLINE character).

Special characters   Table 28-1 lists some of the characters that are special within strings in Perl. Perl interpolates these characters when they appear between double quotation marks but not when they appear between single quotation marks. Table 28-3 on page 1092 lists metacharacters, which are special within regular expressions.

Table 28-1   Some Perl special characters

Character	When within double quotation marks, interpolated as
\0xx (zero)	The ASCII character whose octal value is **xx**
\a	An alarm (bell or beep) character (ASCII 7)
\e	An ESCAPE character (ASCII 27)
\n	A NEWLINE character (ASCII 10)
\r	A RETURN character (ASCII 13)
\t	A TAB character (ASCII 9)

VARIABLES

Like human languages, Perl distinguishes between singular and plural data. Strings and numbers are singular; lists of strings or numbers are plural. Perl provides three types of variables: *scalar* (singular), *array* (plural), and *hash* (plural; also called *associative arrays*). Perl identifies each type of variable by a special character preceding its name. The name of a scalar variable begins with a dollar sign ($), an array variable begins with an at sign (@), and a hash variable begins with a percent sign (%). As opposed to the way the shell identifies variables, Perl requires the leading character to appear each time you reference a variable, including when you assign a value to the variable:

```
$ name="Zach" ; echo "$name"              (bash)
Zach

$ perl -e '$name="Zach" ; print "$name\n";'  (perl)
Zach
```

Variable names, which are case sensitive, can include letters, digits, and the underscore character (_). A Perl variable is a package variable (page 1061) unless it is preceded by the keyword **my**, in which case it is a lexical variable (page 1062) that is defined only within the block or file it appears in. See "Subroutines" on page 1087 for a discussion of the locality of Perl variables.

Lexical variables overshadow package variables

caution   If a lexical variable and a package variable have the same name, within the block or file in which the lexical variable is defined, the name refers to the lexical variable and not to the package variable.

A Perl variable comes into existence when you assign a value to it—you do not need to define or initialize a variable, although it might make a program more understandable to do so. Normally, Perl does not complain when you reference an uninitialized variable:

```
$ cat variable1.pl
#!/usr/bin/perl
my $name = 'Sam';
print "Hello, $nam, how are you?\n"; # Typo, e left off of name

$ ./variable1.pl
Hello, , how are you?
```

use strict   Include **use strict** to cause Perl to require variables to be declared before being assigned values. See the **perldebtut man** page for more information. When you include **use strict** in the preceding program, Perl displays an error message:

```
$ cat variable1b.pl
#!/usr/bin/perl
use strict;
my $name = 'Sam';
print "Hello, $nam, how are you?\n"; # Typo, e left off of name
```

```
$ ./variable1b.pl
Global symbol "$nam" requires explicit package name at ./variable1b.pl line 4.
Execution of ./variable1b.pl aborted due to compilation errors.
```

Using my: lexical versus package variables

tip   In **variable1.pl**, **$name** is declared to be lexical by preceding its name with the keyword **my**; its name and value are known within the file **variable1.pl** only. Declaring a variable to be lexical limits its scope to the block or file it is defined in. Although not necessary in this case, declaring variables to be lexical is good practice. This habit becomes especially useful when you write longer programs, subroutines, and packages, where it is harder to keep variable names unique. Declaring all variables to be lexical is mandatory when you write routines that will be used within code written by others. This practice allows those who work with your routines to use whichever variable names they like, without regard to which variable names you used in the code you wrote.

The shell and Perl scope variables differently. In the shell, if you do not **export** a variable, it is local to the routine it is used in (page 1008). In Perl, if you do not use **my** to declare a variable to be lexical, it is defined for the package it appears in.

–w and   The **–w** option and the **use warnings** statement perform the same function: They
use warnings   cause Perl to generate an error message when it detects a syntax error. In the following example, Perl displays two warnings. The first tells you that you have used the variable named **$nam** once, on line 3, which probably indicates an error. This message is helpful when you mistype the name of a variable. Under Perl 5.10, the second warning specifies the name of the uninitialized variable. This warning refers to the same problem as the first warning. Although it is not hard to figure out which of the two variables is undefined in this simple program, doing so in a complex program can take a lot of time.

```
$ cat variable1a.pl
#!/usr/bin/perl -w
my $name = 'Sam';
print "Hello, $nam, how are you?\n"; # Prints warning because of typo and -w

$ ./variable1a.pl
Name "main::nam" used only once: possible typo at ./variable1a.pl line 3.
Use of uninitialized value $nam in concatenation (.) or string at ./variable1a.pl line 3.
Hello, , how are you?
```

You can also use **–w** on the command line. If you use **–e** as well, make sure the argument that follows this option is the program you want to execute (e.g., **–e –w** does not work). See the tip on page 1090.

```
$ perl -w -e 'my $name = "Sam"; print "Hello, $nam, how are you?\n"'
Name "main::nam" used only once: possible typo at -e line 1.
Use of uninitialized value $nam in concatenation (.) or string at -e line 1.
Hello, , how are you?
```

undef and defined   An undefined variable has the special value **undef**, which evaluates to zero (0) in a numeric expression and expands to an empty string (" ") when you print it. Use the **defined** function to determine whether a variable has been defined. The following example, which uses constructs explained later in this chapter, calls **defined** with an argument of **$name** and negates the result with an exclamation point (**!**). The result is that the **print** statement is executed if **$name** is *not* defined.

```
$ cat variable2.pl
#!/usr/bin/perl
if (!defined($name)) {
print "The variable '\$name' is not defined.\n"
};

$ ./variable2.pl
The variable '$name' is not defined.
```

Because the **−w** option causes Perl to warn you when you reference an undefined variable, using this option would generate a warning.

SCALAR VARIABLES

A scalar variable has a name that begins with a dollar sign (**$**) and holds a single string or number: It is a singular variable. Because Perl converts between the two when necessary, you can use strings and numbers interchangeably. Perl interprets scalar variables as strings when it makes sense to interpret them as strings, and as numbers when it makes sense to interpret them as numbers. Perl's judgment in these matters is generally good.

The following example shows some uses of scalar variables. The first two lines of code (lines 3 and 4) assign the string **Sam** to the scalar variable **$name** and the numbers **5** and **2** to the scalar variables **$n1** and **$n2**, respectively. In this example, multiple statements, each terminated with a semicolon (**;**), appear on a single line. See **use feature 'say'** on page 1063 if this program complains about **say** not being available.

```
$ cat scalars1.pl
#!/usr/bin/perl -w

$name = "Sam";
$n1 = 5; $n2 = 2;

say "$name $n1 $n2";
say "$n1 + $n2";
say '$name $n1 $n2';
say $n1 + $n2, " ", $n1 * $n2;
say $name + $n1;

$ ./scalars1.pl
Sam 5 2
5 + 2
$name $n1 $n2
7 10
Argument "Sam" isn't numeric in addition (+) at ./scalers1.pl line 11.
5
```

Double quotation marks   The first **say** statement sends the string enclosed within double quotation marks to standard output (the screen unless you redirect it). Within double quotation marks,

Perl expands variable names to the value of the named variable. Thus the first **say** statement displays the values of three variables, separated from each other by SPACEs. The second **say** statement includes a plus sign (**+**). Perl does not recognize operators such as **+** within either type of quotation marks. Thus Perl displays the plus sign between the values of the two variables.

Single quotation marks The third **say** statement sends the string enclosed within single quotation marks to standard output. Within single quotation marks, Perl interprets all characters literally, so it displays the string exactly as it appears between the single quotation marks.

In the fourth **say** statement, the operators are not quoted, and Perl performs the addition and multiplication as specified. Without the quoted SPACE, Perl would catenate the two numbers (**710**). The last **say** statement attempts to add a string and a number; the **–w** option causes Perl to display an error message before displaying 5. The 5 results from adding **Sam**, which Perl evaluates as 0 in a numerical context, to the number 5 (0 + 5 = 5).

ARRAY VARIABLES

An array variable is an ordered container of scalars whose name begins with an at sign (**@**) and whose first element is numbered zero (zero-based indexing). Because an array can hold zero or more scalars, it is a plural variable. Arrays are ordered; hashes (page 1072) are unordered. In Perl, arrays grow as needed. If you reference an uninitialized element of an array, such as an element beyond the end of the array, Perl returns **undef**.

The first statement in the following program assigns the values of two numbers and a string to the array variable named **@arrayvar**. Because Perl uses zero-based indexing, the first **say** statement displays the value of the second element of the array (the element with the index 1). This statement specifies the variable **$arrayvar[1]** as a scalar (singular) because it refers to a single value. The second **say** statement specifies the variable **@arrayvar[1,2]** as a list (plural) because it refers to multiple values (the elements with the indexes 1 and 2).

```
$ cat arrayvar1.pl
#!/usr/bin/perl -w
@arrayvar = (8, 18, "Sam");
say $arrayvar[1];
say "@arrayvar[1,2]";

$ perl arrayvar1.pl
18
18 Sam
```

The next example shows a couple of ways to determine the length of an array and presents more information on using quotation marks within **print** statements. The first assignment statement in **arrayvar2.pl** assigns values to the first six elements of the **@arrayvar2** array. When used in a scalar context, Perl evaluates the name of an array as the length of the array. The second assignment statement assigns the number of elements in **@arrayvar2** to the scalar variable **$num**.

```
$ cat arrayvar2.pl
#!/usr/bin/perl -w
@arrayvar2 = ("apple", "bird", 44, "Tike", "metal", "pike");

$num = @arrayvar2;                    # number of elements in array
print "Elements: ", $num, "\n";       # two equivalent print statements
print "Elements: $num\n";

print "Last: $#arrayvar2\n";          # index of last element in array

$ ./arrayvar2.pl
Elements: 6
Elements: 6
Last: 5
```

The first two **print** statements in **arrayvar2.pl** display the string **Elements:**, a SPACE, the value of **$num**, and a NEWLINE, each using a different syntax. The first of these statements displays three values, using commas to separate them within the **print** statement. The second **print** statement has one argument and demonstrates that Perl expands a variable (replaces the variable with its value) when the variable is enclosed within double quotation marks.

$#array The final **print** statement in **arrayvar2.pl** shows that Perl evaluates the variable **$#array** as the index of the last element in the array named **array**. Because Perl uses zero-based indexing by default, this variable evaluates to one less than the number of elements in the array.

The next example works with elements of an array and uses a dot (.; the string catenation operator). The first two lines assign values to four scalar variables. The third line shows that you can assign values to array elements using scalar variables, arithmetic, and catenated strings. The dot operator catenates strings, so Perl evaluates **$va . $vb** as **Sam** catenated with **uel**—that is, as **Samuel** (see the output of the last **print** statement).

```
$ cat arrayvar3.pl
#!/usr/bin/perl -w
$v1 = 5; $v2 = 8;
$va = "Sam"; $vb = "uel";
@arrayvar3 = ($v1, $v1 * 2, $v1 * $v2, "Max", "Zach", $va . $vb);

print $arrayvar3[2], "\n";        # one element of an array is a scalar
print @arrayvar3[2,4], "\n";      # two elements of an array are a list
print @arrayvar3[2..4], "\n\n";   # a slice
```

```
print "@arrayvar3[2,4]", "\n";     # a list, elements separated by SPACEs
print "@arrayvar3[2..4]", "\n\n";  # a slice, elements separated by SPACEs

print "@arrayvar3\n";              # an array, elements separated by SPACEs
```

```
$ ./arrayvar3.pl
40
40Zach
40MaxZach

40 Zach
40 Max Zach

5 10 40 Max Zach Samuel
```

The first **print** statement in **arrayvar3.pl** displays the third element (the element with an index of 2) of the **@arrayvar3** array. This statement uses **$** in place of **@** because it refers to a single element of the array. The subsequent **print** statements use **@** because they refer to more than one element. Within the brackets that specify an array subscript, two subscripts separated by a comma specify two elements of an array. The second **print** statement, for example, displays the third and fifth elements of the array.

Array slice
When you separate two elements of an array with two dots (**..**; the range operator), Perl substitutes all elements between and including the two specified elements. A portion of an array comprising elements is called a *slice*. The third **print** statement in the preceding example displays the elements with indexes 2, 3, and 4 (the third, fourth, and fifth elements) as specified by **2..4**. Perl puts no SPACEs between the elements it displays.

Within a **print** statement, when you enclose an array variable, including its subscripts, within double quotation marks, Perl puts a SPACE between each of the elements. The fourth and fifth **print** statements in the preceding example illustrate this syntax. The last **print** statement displays the entire array, with elements separated by SPACEs.

shift, push, pop, and splice
The next example demonstrates several functions you can use to manipulate arrays. The example uses the **@colors** array, which is initialized to a list of seven colors. The **shift** function returns and removes the first element of an array, **push** adds an element to the end of an array, and **pop** returns and removes the last element of an array. The **splice** function replaces elements of an array with another array; in the example, **splice** inserts the **@ins** array starting at index 1 (the second element), replacing two elements of the array. See **use feature 'say'** on page 1063 if this program complains about **say** not being available. See the **perlfunc** man page for more information on the functions described in this paragraph.

```
$ cat ./shift1.pl
#!/usr/bin/perl -w

@colors = ("red", "orange", "yellow", "green", "blue", "indigo", "violet");

say "                              Display array: @colors";
say " Display and remove first element of array: ", shift (@colors);
say "       Display remaining elements of array: @colors";

push (@colors, "WHITE");
say "   Add element to end of array and display: @colors";

say "  Display and remove last element of array: ", pop (@colors);
say "       Display remaining elements of array: @colors";

@ins = ("GRAY", "FERN");
splice (@colors, 1, 2, @ins);
say "Replace second and third elements of array: @colors";

$ ./shift1.pl
                              Display array: red orange yellow green blue indigo violet
 Display and remove first element of array: red
        Display remaining elements of array: orange yellow green blue indigo violet
    Add element to end of array and display: orange yellow green blue indigo violet WHITE
  Display and remove last element of array: WHITE
        Display remaining elements of array: orange yellow green blue indigo violet
Replace second and third elements of array: orange GRAY FERN blue indigo violet
```

HASH VARIABLES

A hash variable, sometimes called an associative array variable, is a plural data structure that holds an array of key-value pairs. It uses strings as keys (indexes) and is optimized to return a value quickly when given a key. Each key must be a unique scalar. Hashes are unordered; arrays (page 1069) are ordered. When you assign a hash to a list, the key-value pairs are preserved, but their order is neither alphabetical nor the order in which they were inserted into the hash; instead, the order is effectively random.

Perl provides two syntaxes to assign values to a hash. The first uses a single assignment statement for each key-value pair:

```
$ cat hash1.pl
#!/usr/bin/perl -w
$hashvar1{boat} = "tuna";
$hashvar1{"number five"} = 5;
$hashvar1{4} = "fish";

@arrayhash1 = %hashvar1;
say "@arrayhash1";

$ ./hash1.pl
boat tuna 4 fish number five 5
```

Within an assignment statement, the key is located within braces to the left of the equal sign; the value is on the right side of the equal sign. As illustrated in the preceding example, keys and values can take on either numeric or string values. You do not need to quote string keys unless they contain SPACEs. This example also shows that you can display the keys and values held by a hash, each separated from the next by a SPACE, by assigning the hash to an array variable and then printing that variable enclosed within double quotation marks.

The next example shows the other way of assigning values to a hash and illustrates how to use the **keys** and **values** functions to extract keys and values from a hash. After assigning values to the **%hash2** hash, **hash2.pl** calls the **keys** function with an argument of **%hash2** and assigns the resulting list of keys to the **@array_keys** array. The program then uses the **values** function to assign values to the **@array_values** array.

```
$ cat hash2.pl
#!/usr/bin/perl -w

%hash2 = (
    boat => "tuna",
    "number five" => 5,
    4 => "fish",
    );

@array_keys = keys(%hash2);
say "  Keys: @array_keys";

@array_values = values(%hash2);
say "Values: @array_values";
$ ./hash2.pl
  Keys: boat 4 number five
Values: tuna fish 5
```

Because Perl automatically quotes a single word that appears to the left of the **=>** operator, you do not need quotation marks around **boat** in the third line of this program. However, removing the quotation marks from around **number five** would generate an error because the string contains a SPACE.

CONTROL STRUCTURES

Control flow statements alter the order of execution of statements within a Perl program. Starting on page 971, Chapter 27 discusses bash control structures in detail and includes flow diagrams. Perl control structures perform the same functions as their bash counterparts, although the two languages use different syntaxes. The description of each control structure in this section references the discussion of the same control structure under bash.

In this section, the *bold italic* words in the syntax description are the items you supply to cause the structure to have the desired effect, the *nonbold italic* words are the keywords Perl uses to identify the control structure, and *{...}* represents a block (page 1061) of statements. Many of these structures use an expression, denoted as *expr*, to control their execution. See **if/unless** (next) for an example and explanation of a syntax description.

if/unless

The **if** and **unless** control structures are compound statements that have the following syntax:

if (expr) {...}

unless (expr) {...}

These structures differ only in the sense of the test they perform. The **if** structure executes the block of statements *if expr* evaluates to *true*; **unless** executes the block of statements *unless expr* evaluates to *true* (i.e., if *expr* is *false*).

The *if* appears in nonbold type because it is a keyword; it must appear exactly as shown. The *expr* is an expression; Perl evaluates it and executes the block (page 1061) of statements represented by *{...}* if the expression evaluates as required by the control structure.

File test operators   The *expr* in the following example, **–r memo1**, uses the **–r** file test operator to determine if a file named **memo1** exists in the working directory and if the file is readable. Although this operator tests only whether you have read permission for the file, the file must exist for you to have read permission; thus it implicitly tests that the file is present. (Perl uses the same file test operators as bash; see Table 27-1 on page 973.) If this expression evaluates to *true*, Perl executes the block of statements (in this case one statement) between the braces. If the expression evaluates to *false*, Perl skips the block of statements. In either case, Perl then exits and returns control to the shell.

```
$ cat if1.pl
#!/usr/bin/perl -w
if (-r "memo1") {
    say "The file 'memo1' exists and is readable.";
    }

$ ./if1.pl
The file 'memo1' exists and is readable.
```

Following is the same program written using the postfix **if** syntax. Which syntax you use depends on which part of the statement is more important to someone reading the code.

```
$ cat if1a.pl
#!/usr/bin/perl -w
say "The file 'memo1' exists and is readable." if (-r "memo1");
```

The next example uses a **print** statement to display a prompt on standard output and uses the statement **$entry = <>;** to read a line from standard input and assign the line to the variable **$entry**. Reading from standard input, working with other files, and use of the magic file handle (<>) for reading files specified on the command line are covered on page 1082.

Comparison operators

Perl uses different operators to compare numbers from those it uses to compare strings. Table 28-2 lists numeric and string comparison operators. In the following example, the expression in the **if** statement uses the **==** numeric comparison operator to compare the value the user entered and the number **28**. This operator performs a numeric comparison, so the user can enter **28**, **28.0**, or **00028** and in all cases the result of the comparison will be *true*. Also, because the comparison is numeric, Perl ignores both the whitespace around and the NEWLINE following the user's entry. The **–w** option causes Perl to issue a warning if the user enters a nonnumeric value and the program uses that value in an arithmetic expression; without this option Perl silently evaluates the expression as *false*.

```
$ cat if2.pl
#!/usr/bin/perl -w
print "Enter 28: ";
$entry = <>;
if ($entry == 28) {                    # use == for a numeric comparison
    print "Thank you for entering 28.\n";
    }
print "End.\n";

$ ./if2.pl
Enter 28: 28.0
Thank you for entering 28.
End.
```

Table 28-2 Comparison operators

Numeric operators	String operators	Value returned based on the relationship between the values preceding and following the operator
==	eq	True if equal
!=	ne	True if not equal
<	lt	True if less than
>	gt	True if greater than
<=	le	True if less than or equal
>=	ge	True if greater than or equal
<=>	cmp	0 if equal, 1 if greater than, –1 if less than

The next program is similar to the preceding one, except it tests for equality between two strings. The **chomp** function (page 1084) removes the trailing NEWLINE from the user's entry—without this function the strings in the comparison would never match. The **eq** comparison operator compares strings. In this example the result of the string comparison is *true* when the user enters the string **five**. Leading or trailing whitespace will yield a result of *false*, as would the string 5, although none of these entries would generate a warning because they are legitimate strings.

```
$ cat if2a.pl
#!/usr/bin/perl -w
print "Enter the word 'five': ";
$entry = <>;
chomp ($entry);
if ($entry eq "five") {              # use eq for a string comparison
    print "Thank you for entering 'five'.\n";
    }
print "End.\n";

$ ./if2a.pl
Enter the word 'five': five
Thank you for entering 'five'.
End.
```

if...else

The **if...else** control structure is a compound statement that is similar to the bash **if...then...else** control structure (page 974). It implements a two-way branch using the following syntax:

if (expr) {...} else {...}

die The next program prompts the user for two different numbers and stores those numbers in **$num1** and **$num2**. If the user enters the same number twice, an **if** structure executes a **die** function, which sends its argument to standard error and aborts program execution.

If the user enters different numbers, the **if...else** structure reports which number is larger. Because *expr* performs a numeric comparison, the program accepts numbers that include decimal points.

```
$ cat ifelse.pl
#!/usr/bin/perl -w
print "Enter a number: ";
$num1 = <>;
print "Enter another, different number: ";
$num2 = <>;

if ($num1 == $num2) {
    die ("Please enter two different numbers.\n");
    }
if ($num1 > $num2) {
    print "The first number is greater than the second number.\n";
    }
else {
```

```
        print "The first number is less than the second number.\n";
        }
```

```
$ ./ifelse.pl
Enter a number: 8
Enter another, different number: 8
Please enter two different numbers.
```

```
$ ./ifelse.pl
Enter a number: 5.5
Enter another, different number: 5
The first number is greater than the second number.
```

if...elsif...else

Similar to the bash **if...then...elif** control structure (page 976), the Perl **if...elsif...else** control structure is a compound statement that implements a nested set of **if...else** structures using the following syntax:

*if (**expr**) {...} elsif {...} ... else {...}*

The next program implements the functionality of the preceding **ifelse.pl** program using an **if...elsif...else** structure. A **print** statement replaces the **die** statement because the last statement in the program displays the error message; the program terminates after executing this statement anyway. You can use the STDERR handle (page 1082) to cause Perl to send this message to standard error instead of standard output.

```
$ cat ifelsif.pl
#!/usr/bin/perl -w
print "Enter a number: ";
$num1 = <>;
print "Enter another, different number: ";
$num2 = <>;
if ($num1 > $num2) {
        print "The first number is greater than the second number.\n";
        }
    elsif ($num1 < $num2) {
        print "The first number is less than the second number.\n";
        }
    else {
        print "Please enter two different numbers.\n";
        }
```

foreach/for

The Perl **foreach** and **for** keywords are synonyms; you can replace one with the other in any context. These structures are compound statements that have two syntaxes. Some programmers use one syntax with **foreach** and the other syntax with the **for**, although there is no need to do so. This book uses **foreach** with both syntaxes.

foreach: SYNTAX 1

The first syntax for the **foreach** structure is similar to the shell's **for...in** structure (page 983):

foreach\for [var] (list) {...}

where *list* is a list of expressions or variables. Perl executes the block of statements once for each item in *list*, sequentially assigning to *var* the value of one item in *list* on each iteration, starting with the first item. If you do not specify *var*, Perl assigns values to the $_ variable (page 1082).

The following program demonstrates a simple **foreach** structure. On the first pass through the loop, Perl assigns the string **Mo** to the variable **$item** and the **say** statement displays the value of this variable followed by a NEWLINE. On the second and third passes through the loop, **$item** is assigned the value of **Larry** and **Curly**. When there are no items left in the list, Perl continues with the statement following the **foreach** structure. In this case, the program terminates. See **use feature 'say'** on page 1063 if this program complains about **say** not being available.

```
$ cat foreach.pl
foreach $item ("Mo", "Larry", "Curly") {
    say "$item says hello.";
    }

$ perl foreach.pl
Mo says hello.
Larry says hello.
Curly says hello.
```

Using $_ (page 1082), you can write this program as follows:

```
$ cat foreacha.pl
foreach ("Mo", "Larry", "Curly") {
    say "$_ says hello.";
    }
```

Following is the program using an array:

```
$ cat foreachb.pl
@stooges = ("Mo", "Larry", "Curly");
foreach (@stooges) {
    say "$_ says hello.";
    }
```

Following is the program using the **foreach** postfix syntax:

```
$ cat foreachc.pl
@stooges = ("Mo", "Larry", "Curly");
say "$_ says hello." foreach @stooges;
```

The loop variable (**$item** and $_ in the preceding examples) references the elements in the *list* within the parentheses. When you modify the loop variable, you modify the element in the list. The **uc** function returns an upshifted version of its argument.

The next example shows that modifying the loop variable **$stooge** modifies the **@stooges** array:

```
$ cat foreachd.pl
@stooges = ("Mo", "Larry", "Curly");
foreach $stooge (@stooges) {
    $stooge = uc $stooge;
    say "$stooge says hello.";
    }
say "$stooges[1] is uppercase"

$ perl foreachd.pl
MO says hello.
LARRY says hello.
CURLY says hello.
LARRY is uppercase
```

See page 1085 for an example that loops through command-line arguments.

last **AND** next

Perl's **last** and **next** statements allow you to interrupt a loop; they are analogous to the Bourne Again Shell's **break** and **continue** statements (page 992). The **last** statement transfers control to the statement following the block of statements controlled by the loop structure, terminating execution of the loop. The **next** statement transfers control to the end of the block of statements, which continues execution of the loop with the next iteration.

In the following program, the **if** structure tests whether **$item** is equal to the string **two**; if it is, the structure executes the **next** command, which skips the **say** statement and continues with the next iteration of the loop. If you replaced **next** with **last**, Perl would exit from the loop and not display **three**. See **use feature 'say'** on page 1063 if this program complains about **say** not being available.

```
$ cat foreach1.pl
foreach $item ("one", "two", "three") {
    if ($item eq "two") {
        next;
        }
    say "$item";
    }

$ perl foreach1.pl
one
three
```

foreach: SYNTAX 2

The second syntax for the **foreach** structure is similar to the C **for** structure:

foreach|for (expr1; expr2; expr3) {...}

The *expr1* initializes the **foreach** loop; Perl evaluates *expr1* one time, before it executes the block of statements. The *expr2* is the termination condition; Perl evaluates it before each pass through the block of statements and executes the block of statements if *expr2* evaluates as *true*. Perl evaluates *expr3* after each pass through the block of statements—it typically increments a variable that is part of *expr2*.

In the next example, the **foreach2.pl** program prompts for three numbers; displays the first number; repeatedly increments this number by the second number, displaying each result until the result would be greater than the third number; and quits. See page 1083 for a discussion of the magic file handle (**<>**).

```
$ cat ./foreach2.pl
#!/usr/bin/perl -w

print "Enter starting number: ";
$start = <>;

print "Enter ending number: ";
$end = <>;

print "Enter increment: ";
$incr = <>;

if ($start >= $end || $incr < 1) {
    die ("The starting number must be less than the ending number\n",
    "and the increment must be greater than zero.\n");
    }

foreach ($count = $start+0; $count <= $end; $count += $incr) {
    say "$count";
    }
$ ./foreach2.pl
Enter starting number: 2
Enter ending number: 10
Enter increment: 3
2
5
8
```

After prompting for three numbers, the preceding program tests whether the starting number is greater than or equal to the ending number or if the increment is less than 1. The ll is a Boolean OR operator; the expression within the parentheses following **if** evaluates to *true* if either the expression before or the expression after this operator evaluates to *true*.

The **foreach** statement begins by assigning the value of **$start+0** to **$count**. Adding 0 (zero) to the string **$start** forces Perl to work in a numeric context, removing the trailing NEWLINE when it performs the assignment. Without this fix, the program would display an extra NEWLINE following the first number it displayed.

while/until

The **while** (page 986) and **until** (page 990) control structures are compound statements that implement conditional loops using the following syntax:

*while (**expr**) {...}*

*until (**expr**) {...}*

These structures differ only in the sense of their termination conditions. The **while** structure repeatedly executes the block of statements *while **expr** evaluates to *true*; **until** continues *until **expr** evaluates to *true* (i.e., while **expr** remains *false*).

The following example demonstrates one technique for reading and processing input until there is no more input. Although this example shows input coming from the user (standard input), the technique works the same way for input coming from a file (see the example on page 1084). The user enters CONTROL-D on a line by itself to signal the end of file.

In this example, *expr* is **$line = <>**. This statement uses the magic file handle (**<>**; page 1083) to read one line from standard input and assigns the string it reads to the **$line** variable. This statement evaluates to *true* as long as it reads data. When it reaches the end of file, the statement evaluates to *false*. The **while** loop continues to execute the block of statements (in this example, only one statement) as long as there is data to read.

```
$ cat while1.pl
#!/usr/bin/perl -w
$count = 0;
while ($line = <>) {
    print ++$count, ". $line";
    }
print "\n$count lines entered.\n";
$ ./while1.pl
Good Morning.
1. Good Morning.
Today is Monday.
2. Today is Monday.
CONTROL-D

2 lines entered.
```

In the preceding example, **$count** keeps track of the number of lines the user enters. Putting the **++** increment operator before a variable (**++$count**; called a preincrement operator) increments the variable before Perl evaluates it. Alternatively, you could initialize **$count** to 1 and increment it with **$count++** (postincrement), but then in the final **print** statement **$count** would equal one more than the number of lines entered.

$. The **$.** variable keeps track of the number of lines of input a program has read. Using **$.** you can rewrite the previous example as follows:

```
$ cat while1a.pl
#!/usr/bin/perl -w
while ($line = <>) {
        print $., ". $line";
        }
print "\n$. lines entered.\n";
```

$_** Frequently you can simplify Perl code by using the **$_ variable. You can use **$_** many places in a Perl program—think of **$_** as meaning *it*, the object of what you are doing. It is the default operand for many operations. For example, the following section of code processes a line using the **$line** variable. It reads a line into **$line**, removes any trailing NEWLINE from **$line** using **chomp** (page 1084), and checks whether a regular expression matches **$line**.

```
while (my $line = <>) {
    chomp $line;
    if ($line =~ /regex/) ...
}
```

You can rewrite this code by using **$_** to replace **$line**:

```
while (my $_ = <>) {
    chomp $_;
    if ($_ =~ /regex/) ...
}
```

Because **$_** is the default operand in each of these instances, you can also omit **$_** altogether:

```
while (<>) {          # read into $_
    chomp;            # chomp $_
    if (/regex/) ...  # if $_ matches regex
}
```

WORKING WITH FILES

Opening a file and assigning a handle

A *handle* is a name you can use in a Perl program to refer to a file or process that is open for reading and/or writing. When you are working with the shell, handles are referred to as *file descriptors* (page 1003). As when you are working with the shell, the kernel automatically opens handles for standard input (page 232), standard output (page 232), and standard error (page 285) before it runs a program. The kernel closes these descriptors after a program finishes running. The names for these handles are **STDIN**, **STDOUT**, and **STDERR**, respectively. You must manually open handles to read from or write to other files or processes. The syntax of an **open** statement is

> *open (file-handle, ['mode',] "file-ref");*

where *file-handle* is the name of the handle or a variable you will use in the program to refer to the file or process named by *file-ref*. If you omit *mode* or specify a *mode* of <, Perl opens the file for input (reading). Specify *mode* as > to truncate and write to a file or as >> to append to a file.

See page 1098 for a discussion of reading from and writing to processes.

Writing to a file   The **print** function writes output to a file or process. The syntax of a **print** statement is

> *print [file-handle] "text";*

where *file-handle* is the name of the handle you specified in an **open** statement and *text* is the information you want to output. The *file-handle* can also be **STDOUT** or **STDERR**, as explained earlier. Except when you send information to standard output, you must specify a handle in a **print** statement. Do not place a comma after *file-handle*. Also, do not enclose arguments to **print** within parentheses because doing so can create problems.

Reading from a file   The following expression reads one line, including the NEWLINE (**\n**), from the file or process associated with *file-handle*:

> *<file-handle>*

This expression is typically used in a statement such as

```
$line = <IN>;
```

which reads into the variable **$line** one line from the file or process identified by the handle **IN**.

Magic file handle (<>)   To facilitate reading from files named on the command line or from standard input, Perl provides the *magic file handle*. This book uses this file handle in most examples. In place of the preceding line, you can use

```
$line = <>;
```

This file handle causes a Perl program to work like many Linux utilities: It reads from standard input unless the program is called with one or more arguments, in which case it reads from the files named by the arguments. See page 236 for an explanation of how this feature works with cat.

The **print** statement in the first line in the next example includes the optional handle **STDOUT**; the next **print** statement omits this handle; the final **print** statement uses the **STDERR** file handle, which causes **print**'s output to go to standard error. The first **print** statement prompts the user to enter something. The string that this statement outputs is terminated with a SPACE, not a NEWLINE, so the user can enter information on the same line as the prompt. The second line then uses a magic file handle to read one line from standard input, which it assigns to **$userline**. Because of the magic file handle, if you call **file1.pl** with an argument that is a filename, it reads one line from that file instead of from standard input. The command line that runs **file1.pl** uses **2>** (see "File descriptors" on page 286) to redirect standard error (the output of the third **print** statement) to the **file1.err** file.

```
$ cat file1.pl
print STDOUT "Enter something: ";
$userline = <>;
print "1>>>$userline<<<\n";
chomp ($userline);
print "2>>>$userline<<<\n";
print STDERR "3. Error message.\n";
```

```
$ perl file1.pl 2> file1.err
Enter something: hi there
1>>>hi there
<<<
2>>>hi there<<<

$ cat file1.err
3. Error message.
```

chomp/chop   The two **print** statements following the user input in **file1.pl** display the value of **$userline** immediately preceded by greater than signs (>) and followed by less than signs (<). The first of these statements demonstrates that **$userline** includes a NEWLINE: The less than signs following the string the user entered appear on the line following the string. The **chomp** function removes a trailing NEWLINE, if it exists, from a string. After **chomp** processes **$userline**, the **print** statement shows that this variable no longer contains a NEWLINE. (The **chop** function is similar to **chomp**, except it removes *any* trailing character from a string.)

The next example shows how to read from a file. It uses an **open** statement to assign the lexical file handle **$infile** to the file **/usr/share/dict/words**. Each iteration of the **while** structure evaluates an expression that reads a line from the file represented by **$infile** and assigns the line to **$line**. When **while** reaches the end of file, the expression evaluates to *false*; control then passes out of the **while** structure. The block of one statement displays the line as it was read from the file, including the NEWLINE. This program copies **/usr/share/dict/words** to standard output. A pipe (|; page 156) is then used to send the output through head (page 152), which displays the first four lines of the file (the first line is blank).

```
$ cat file2.pl
open (my $infile, "/usr/share/dict/words") or die "Cannot open dictionary: $!\n";
while ($line = <$infile>) {
    print $line;
    }
```

```
$ perl file2.pl | head -4

A
A's
AOL
```

$!**   The **$! variable holds the last system error. In a numeric context, it holds the system error number; in a string context, it holds the system error string. If the **words** file is not present on the system, **file2.pl** displays the following message:

```
Cannot open dictionary: No such file or directory
```

If you do not have read permission for the file, the program displays this message:

```
Cannot open dictionary: Permission denied
```

Displaying the value of **$!** gives the user more information about what went wrong than simply saying that the program could not open the file.

Always check for an error when opening a file

When a Perl program attempts to open a file and fails, the program does not display an error message unless it checks whether **open** returned an error. In **file2.pl**, the **or** operator in the **open** statement causes Perl to execute **die** (page 1076) if **open** fails. The **die** statement sends the message **Cannot open the dictionary** followed by the system error string to standard error and terminates the program.

@ARGV The **@ARGV** array holds the arguments from the command line Perl was called with. When you call the following program with a list of filenames, it displays the first line of each file. If the program cannot read a file, **die** (page 1076) sends an error message to standard error and quits. The **foreach** structure loops through the command-line arguments, as represented by **@ARGV**, assigning each argument in turn to **$filename**. The **foreach** block starts with an **open** statement. Perl executes the **open** statement that precedes the OR Boolean operator (**or**) or, if that fails, Perl executes the statement following the **or** operator (**die**). The result is that Perl either opens the file named by **$filename** and assigns **IN** as its handle or, if it cannot open that file, executes the **die** statement and quits. The **print** statement displays the name of the file followed by a colon and the first line of the file. When it accepts **$line = <IN>** as an argument to **print**, Perl displays the value of **$line** following the assignment. After reading a line from a file, the program closes the file.

```
$ cat file3.pl
foreach $filename (@ARGV) {
    open (IN, $filename) or die "Cannot open file '$filename': $!\n";
    print "$filename: ", $line = <IN>;
    close (IN);
    }
$ perl file3.pl f1 f2 f3 f4
f1: First line of file f1.
f2: First line of file f2.
Cannot open file 'f3': No such file or directory
```

The next example is similar to the preceding one, except it takes advantage of several Perl features that make the code simpler. It does not quit when it cannot read a file. Instead, Perl displays an error message and continues. The first line of the program uses **my** to declare **$filename** to be a lexical variable. Next, **while** uses the magic file handle to open and read each line of each file named by the command-line arguments; **$ARGV** holds the name of the file. When there are no more files to read, the **while** condition [(**<>**)] is *false,* **while** transfers control outside the **while** block, and the program terminates. Perl takes care of all file opening and closing operations; you do not have to write code to take care of these tasks. Perl also performs error checking.

The program displays the first line of each file named by a command-line argument. Each time through the **while** block, **while** reads another line. When it finishes with one file, it starts reading from the next file. Within the **while** block, **if** tests whether it is processing a new file. If it is, the **if** block displays the name of the file and the (first) line from the file and then assigns the new filename (**$ARGV**) to **$filename**.

```
$ cat file3a.pl
my $filename;
while (<>) {
    if ($ARGV ne $filename) {
        print "$ARGV: $_";
        $filename = $ARGV;
    }
}

$ perl file3a.pl f1 f2 f3 f4
f1: First line of file f1.
f2: First line of file f2.
Can't open f3: No such file or directory at file3a.pl line 3, <> line 3.
f4: First line of file f4.
```

Sort

reverse The **sort** function returns elements of an array ordered numerically or alphabetically, based on the *locale* (page 1173) environment. The **reverse** function is not related to **sort**; it simply returns the elements of an array in reverse order.

The first two lines of the following program assign values to the **@colors** array and display these values. Each of the next two pairs of lines uses **sort** to put the values in the **@colors** array in order, assign the result to **@scolors**, and display **@scolors**. These sorts put uppercase letters before lowercase letters. Observe the positions of **Orange** and **Violet**, both of which begin with an uppercase letter, in the sorted output. The first assignment statement in these two pairs of lines uses the full sort syntax, including the block {$a cmp $b} that tells Perl to use the **cmp** subroutine, which compares strings, and to put the result in ascending order. When you omit the block in a **sort** statement, as is the case in the second assignment statement, Perl also performs an ascending textual sort.

```
$ cat sort3.pl
@colors = ("red", "Orange", "yellow", "green", "blue", "indigo", "Violet");

say "@colors";

@scolors = sort {$a cmp $b} @colors;        # ascending sort with
say "@scolors";                             # an explicit block

@scolors = sort @colors;                    # ascending sort with
say "@scolors";                             # an implicit block

@scolors = sort {$b cmp $a} @colors;        # descending sort
say "@scolors";

@scolors = sort {lc($a) cmp lc($b)} @colors; # ascending folded sort
say "@scolors";
```

```
$ perl sort3.pl
red Orange yellow green blue indigo Violet
Orange Violet blue green indigo red yellow
Orange Violet blue green indigo red yellow
yellow red indigo green blue Violet Orange
blue green indigo Orange red Violet yellow
```

The third sort in the preceding example reverses the positions of **$a** and **$b** in the block to specify a descending sort. The last sort converts the strings to lowercase before comparing them, providing a sort wherein the uppercase letters are folded into the lowercase letters. As a result, **Orange** and **Violet** appear in alphabetical order.

To perform a numerical sort, specify the **<=>** subroutine in place of **cmp**. The following example demonstrates ascending and descending numerical sorts:

```
$ cat sort4.pl
@numbers = (22, 188, 44, 2, 12);

print "@numbers\n";

@snumbers = sort {$a <=> $b} @numbers;
print "@snumbers\n";

@snumbers = sort {$b <=> $a} @numbers;
print "@snumbers\n";
$ perl sort4.pl
22 188 44 2 12
2 12 22 44 188
188 44 22 12 2
```

SUBROUTINES

All variables are package variables (page 1061) unless you use the **my** function to define them to be lexical variables (page 1062). Lexical variables defined in a subroutine are local to that subroutine.

The following program includes a main part and a subroutine named **add**(). This program uses the variables named **$one**, **$two**, and **$ans**, all of which are package variables: They are available to both the main program and the subroutine. The call to the subroutine does not pass values to the subroutine and the subroutine returns no values. This setup is not typical: It demonstrates that all variables are package variables unless you use **my** to declare them to be lexical variables.

The **subroutine1.pl** program assigns values to two variables and calls a subroutine. The subroutine adds the values of the two variables and assigns the result to another variable. The main part of the program displays the result.

```
$ cat subroutine1.pl
$one = 1;
$two = 2;
add();
print "Answer is $ans\n";

sub add {
    $ans =$one + $two
    }
```

```
$ perl subroutine1.pl
Answer is 3
```

The next example is similar to the previous one, except the subroutine takes advantage of a **return** statement to return a value to the main program. The program assigns the value returned by the subroutine to the variable **$ans** and displays that value. Again, all variables are package variables.

```
$ cat subroutine2.pl
$one = 1;
$two = 2;
$ans = add();
print "Answer is $ans\n";

sub add {
    return ($one + $two)
    }
```

```
$ perl subroutine2.pl
Answer is 3
```

Keeping variables local to a subroutine is important in many cases. The subroutine in the next example changes the values of variables and insulates the calling program from these changes by declaring and using lexical variables. This setup is more typical.

@_   When you pass values in a call to a subroutine, Perl makes those values available in the array named **@_** in the subroutine. Although **@_** is local to the subroutine, its elements are aliases for the parameters the subroutine was called with. Changing a value in the **@_** array changes the value of the underlying variable, which might not be what you want. The next program avoids this pitfall by assigning the values passed to the subroutine to lexical variables.

The **subroutine3.pl** program calls the **addplusone()** subroutine with two variables as arguments and assigns the value returned by the subroutine to a variable. The first statement in the subroutine declares two lexical variables and assigns to them the values from the **@_** array. The **my** function declares these variables to be lexical. (See the tip on lexical and package variables on page 1066.) Although you can use **my** without assigning values to the declared variables, the syntax in the example is more commonly used. The next two statements increment the lexical variables **$lcl_one** and **$lcl_two**. The **print** statement displays the value of **$lcl_one** within the subroutine. The **return** statement returns the sum of the two incremented, lexical variables.

```
$ cat subroutine3.pl
$one = 1;
$two = 2;
$ans = addplusone($one, $two);
print "Answer is $ans\n";
print "Value of 'lcl_one' in main: $lcl_one\n";
print "Value of 'one' in main: $one\n";

sub addplusone {
    my ($lcl_one, $lcl_two) = @_;
    $lcl_one++;
    $lcl_two++;
    print "Value of 'lcl_one' in sub: $lcl_one\n";
    return ($lcl_one + $lcl_two)
    }

$ perl subroutine3.pl
Value of 'lcl_one' in sub: 2
Answer is 5
Value of 'lcl_one' in main:
Value of 'one' in main: 1
```

After displaying the result returned by the subroutine, the **print** statements in the main program demonstrate that **$lcl_one** is not defined in the main program (it is local to the subroutine) and that the value of **$one** has not changed.

The next example illustrates another way to work with parameters passed to a subroutine. This subroutine does not use variables other than the @_ array it was passed and does not change the values of any elements of that array.

```
$ cat subroutine4.pl
$one = 1;
$two = 2;
$ans = addplusone($one, $two);
print "Answer is $ans\n";
sub addplusone {
    return ($_[0] + $_[1] + 2);
    }

$ perl subroutine4.pl
Answer is 5
```

The final example in this section presents a more typical Perl subroutine. The subroutine **max**() can be called with any number of numeric arguments and returns the value of the largest argument. It uses the **shift** function to assign to **$biggest** the value of the first argument the subroutine was called with and to shift the rest of the arguments. After using **shift**, argument number 2 becomes argument number 1 (**8**), argument 3 becomes argument 2 (**64**), and argument 4 becomes argument 3 (**2**). Next, **foreach** loops over the remaining arguments (@_). Each time through the

foreach block, Perl assigns to $_ the value of each of the arguments, in order. The **$biggest** variable is assigned the value of $_ if $_ is bigger than **$biggest**. When **max()** finishes going through its arguments, **$biggest** holds the maximum value, which **max()** returns.

```
$ cat subroutine5.pl
$ans = max (16, 8, 64, 2);
print "Maximum value is $ans\n";

sub max {
    my $biggest = shift;  # Assign first and shift the rest of the arguments to max()
    foreach (@_) {        # Loop through remaining arguments
    $biggest = $_ if $_ > $biggest;
    }
return ($biggest);
}

$ perl subroutine5.pl
Maximum value is 64
```

REGULAR EXPRESSIONS

Appendix A defines and discusses regular expressions you can use in many Linux utilities. All of the material in Appendix A applies to Perl, except as noted. In addition to the facilities described in Appendix A, Perl offers regular expression features that allow you to perform more complex string processing. This section reviews some of the regular expressions covered in Appendix A and describes some of the additional features of regular expressions available in Perl. It also introduces the syntax Perl uses for working with regular expressions.

SYNTAX AND THE =~ OPERATOR

The –l option   The Perl –l option applies **chomp** to each line of input and places \n at the end of each line of output. The examples in this section use the Perl –l and –e (page 1062) options. Because the program must be specified as a single argument, the examples enclose the Perl programs within single quotation marks. The shell interprets the quotation marks and does not pass them to Perl.

Using other options with –e

tip   When you use another option with **–e**, the program must immediately follow the **–e** on the command line. Like many other utilities, Perl allows you to combine options following a single hyphen; if **–e** is one of the combined options, it must appear last in the list of options. Thus you can use **perl –l –e** or **perl –le** but not **perl –e –l** or **perl –el**.

/ is the default delimiter   By default, Perl delimits a regular expression with slashes (/). The first program uses the =~ operator to search for the pattern **ge** in the string **aged**. You can think of the =~ operator as meaning "contains." Using different terminology, the =~ operator determines whether the regular expression **ge** has a match in the string **aged**. The regular expression in this example contains no special characters; the string **ge** is part of the string **aged**. Thus the expression within the parentheses evaluates to *true* and Perl executes the **print** statement.

```
$ perl -le 'if ("aged" =~ /ge/) {print "true";}'
true
```

You can achieve the same functionality by using a postfix **if** statement:

```
$ perl -le 'print "true" if "aged" =~ /ge/'
true
```

!~ The **!~** operator works in the opposite sense from the **=~** operator. The expression in the next example evaluates to *true* because the regular expression **xy** does *not* match any part of **aged**:

```
$ perl -le 'print "true" if ("aged" !~ /xy/)'
true
```

As explained on page 1107, a period within a regular expression matches any single character, so the regular expression **a..d** matches the string **aged**:

```
$ perl -le 'print "true" if ("aged" =~ /a..d/)'
true
```

You can use a variable to hold a regular expression. The following syntax quotes *string* as a regular expression:

qr/string/

The next example uses this syntax to assign the regular expression **/a..d/** (including the delimiters) to the variable **$re** and then uses that variable as the regular expression:

```
$ perl -le '$re = qr/a..d/; print "true" if ("aged" =~ $re)'
true
```

If you want to include the delimiter within a regular expression, you must quote it. In the next example, the default delimiter, a slash (**/**), appears in the regular expression. To keep Perl from interpreting the **/** in **/usr** as the end of the regular expression, the **/** that is part of the regular expression is quoted by preceding it with a backslash (****). See page 1109 for more information on quoting characters in regular expressions.

```
$ perl -le 'print "true" if ("/usr/doc" =~ /\/usr/)'
true
```

Quoting several characters by preceding each one with a backslash can make a complex regular expression harder to read. Instead, you can precede a delimited regular expression with **m** and use a paired set of characters, such as {}, as the delimiters. In the following example, the caret (**^**) anchors the regular expression to the beginning of the line (page 1108):

```
$ perl -le 'print "true" if ("/usr/doc" =~ m{^/usr})'
true
```

You can use the same syntax when assigning a regular expression to a variable:

```
$ perl -le '$pn = qr{^/usr}; print "true" if ("/usr/doc" =~ $pn)'
true
```

Replacement string and assignment

Perl uses the syntax shown in the next example to substitute a string (the *replacement string*) for a matched regular expression. The syntax is the same as that found in vim and sed. In the second line of the example, an **s** before the regular expression instructs Perl to substitute the string between the second and third slashes (**worst**; the replacement string) for a match of the regular expression between the first two slashes (**best**). Implicit in this syntax is the notion that the substitution is made in the string held in the variable on the left of the **=~** operator.

```
$ cat re10a.pl
$stg = "This is the best!";
$stg =~ s/best/worst/;
print "$stg\n";

$ perl re10a.pl
This is the worst!
```

Table 28-3 lists some of the characters, called metacharacters, that are considered special within Perl regular expressions. Give the command **perldoc perlre** for more information.

Table 28-3   Some Perl regular expression metacharacters

Character	Matches
^ (caret)	Anchors a regular expression to the beginning of a line (page 1108)
$ (dollar sign)	Anchors a regular expression to the end of a line (page 1108)
(...)	Brackets a regular expression (page 1094)
. (period)	Any single character except NEWLINE (**\n**; page 1107)
****	A backslash (\\)
\b	A word boundary (zero-width match)
\B	A nonword boundary (**[^\b]**)
\d	A single decimal digit (**[0–9]**)
\D	A single nondecimal digit (**[^0–9]** or **[^\d]**)
\s (lowercase)	A single whitespace character SPACE, NEWLINE, RETURN, TAB, FORMFEED
\S (uppercase)	A single nonwhitespace character (**[^\s]**)
\w (lowercase)	A single word character (a letter or digit; **[a–zA–Z0–9]**)
\W (uppercase)	A single nonword character (**[^\w]**)

GREEDY MATCHES

By default Perl performs *greedy matching,* which means a regular expression matches the longest string possible (page 1109). In the following example, the regular expression /{.*} / matches an opening brace followed by any string of characters, a closing brace, and a SPACE ({**remove me**} **might have two** {**keep me**}). Perl substitutes a null string (//) for this match.

```
$ cat 5ha.pl
$string = "A line {remove me} might have two {keep me} pairs of
braces.";
$string =~ s/{.*} //;
print "$string\n";
```

```
$ perl 5ha.pl
A line pairs of braces.
```

Nongreedy matches   The next example shows the classic way of matching the shorter brace-enclosed string from the previous example. This type of match is called *nongreedy* or *parsimonious matching.* Here the regular expression matches

1. An opening brace followed by

2. A character belonging to the character class (page 1107) that includes all characters except a closing brace ([^}]) followed by

3. Zero or more occurrences of the preceding character (*) followed by

4. A closing brace followed by

5. A SPACE

(A caret as the first character of a character class specifies the class of all characters that do not match the following characters, so [^}] matches any character that is not a closing brace.)

```
$ cat re5b.pl
$string = "A line {remove me} might have two {keep me} pairs of braces.";
$string =~ s/{[^}]*} //;
print "$string\n";
```

```
$ perl re5b.pl
A line might have two {keep me} pairs of braces.
```

Perl provides a shortcut that allows you to specify a nongreedy match. In the following example, the question mark in {.*?} causes the regular expression to match the shortest string that starts with an opening brace followed by any string of characters followed by a closing brace.

```
$ cat re5c.pl
$string = "A line {remove me} might have two {keep me} pairs of braces.";
$string =~ s/{.*?} //;
print "$string\n";
```

```
$ perl re5c.pl
A line might have two {keep me} pairs of braces.
```

BRACKETING EXPRESSIONS

As explained on page 1110, you can bracket parts of a regular expression and recall those parts in the replacement string. Most Linux utilities use quoted parentheses [i.e., \(and \)] to bracket a regular expression. In Perl regular expressions, parentheses are special characters. Perl omits the backslashes and uses unquoted parentheses to bracket regular expressions. To specify a parenthesis as a regular character within a regular expression in Perl, you must quote it (page 1109).

The next example uses unquoted parentheses in a regular expression to bracket part of the expression. It then assigns the part of the string that the bracketed expression matched to the variable that held the string in which Perl originally searched for the regular expression.

First the program assigns the string **My name is Sam** to **$stg**. The next statement looks for a match for the regular expression **/My name is (.*)/** in the string held by **$stg**. The part of the regular expression bracketed by parentheses matches **Sam**; the **$1** in the replacement string matches the first (and only in this case) matched bracketed portion of the regular expression. The result is that the string held in **$stg** is replaced by the string **Sam**.

```
$ cat re11.pl
$stg = "My name is Sam";
$stg =~ s/My name is (.*)/$1/;
print "Matched: $stg\n";

$ perl re11.pl
Matched: Sam
```

The next example uses regular expressions to parse a string for numbers. Two variables are initialized to hold a string that contains two numbers. The third line of the program uses a regular expression to isolate the first number in the string. The **\D*** matches a string of zero or more characters that does not include a digit: The **\D** special character matches any single nondigit character. The trailing asterisk makes this part of the regular expression perform a greedy match that does not include a digit (it matches **What is**). The bracketed regular expression **\d+** matches a string of one or more digits. The parentheses do not affect what the regular expression matches; they allow the **$1** in the replacement string to match what the bracketed regular expression matched. The final **.*** matches the rest of the string. This line assigns the value of the first number in the string to **$string**.

The next line is similar but assigns the second number in the string to **$string2**. The **print** statements display the numbers and the result of subtracting the second number from the first.

```
$ cat re8.pl
$string = "What is 488 minus 78?";
$string2 = $string;
$string =~ s/\D*(\d+).*/$1/;
$string2 =~ s/\D*\d+\D*(\d+).*/$1/;
```

```
print "$string\n";
print "$string2\n";
print $string - $string2, "\n";

$ perl re8.pl
488
78
410
```

The next few programs show some of the pitfalls of using unquoted parentheses in regular expressions when you do not intend to bracket part of the regular expression. The first of these programs attempts to match parentheses in a string with unquoted parentheses in a regular expression, but fails. The regular expression **ag(e** matches the same string as the regular expression **age** because the parenthesis is a special character; the regular expression does not match the string **ag(ed)**.

```
$ perl -le 'if ("ag(ed)" =~ /ag(ed)/) {print "true";} else {print "false";}'
false
```

The regular expression in the next example quotes the parentheses by preceding each with a backslash, causing Perl to interpret them as regular characters. The match is successful.

```
$ perl -le 'if ("ag(ed)" =~ /ag\(ed\)/) {print "true";} else {print "false";}'
true
```

Next, Perl finds an unmatched parenthesis in a regular expression:

```
$ perl -le 'if ("ag(ed)" =~ /ag(e/) {print "true";} else {print "false";}'
Unmatched ( in regex; marked by <-- HERE in m/ag( <-- HERE e/ at -e line 1.
```

When you quote the parenthesis, all is well and Perl finds a match:

```
$ perl -le 'if ("ag(ed)" =~ /ag\(e/) {print "true";} else {print "false";}'
true
```

CPAN MODULES

CPAN (Comprehensive Perl Archive Network) provides Perl documentation, FAQs, modules (page 1061), and scripts on its Web site (www.cpan.org). It holds more than 16,000 distributions (page 1061) and provides links, mailing lists, and versions of Perl compiled to run under various operating systems (ports of Perl). One way to locate a module is to visit search.cpan.org and use the search box or click one of the classes of modules listed on that page.

This section explains how to download a module from CPAN and how to install and run the module. Perl provides a hierarchical namespace for modules, separating components of a name with double colons (::). The example in this section uses the module named **Timestamp::Simple**, which you can read about and download from search.cpan.org/dist/Timestamp-Simple. The timestamp is the date and time in the format YYYYMMDDHHMMSS.

To use a Perl module, you first download the file that holds the module. For this example, the search.cpan.org/~shoop/Timestamp-Simple-1.01/Simple.pm Web page has a link on the right side labeled **Download**. Click this link and save the file to the directory you want to work in. You do not need to work as a privileged user until the last step of this procedure, when you install the module.

Most Perl modules come as compressed tar files (page 162). With the downloaded file in the working directory, decompress the file:

```
$ tar xzvf Timestamp-Simple-1.01.tar.gz
Timestamp-Simple-1.01/
Timestamp-Simple-1.01/Simple.pm
Timestamp-Simple-1.01/Makefile.PL
Timestamp-Simple-1.01/README
Timestamp-Simple-1.01/test.pl
Timestamp-Simple-1.01/Changes
Timestamp-Simple-1.01/MANIFEST
Timestamp-Simple-1.01/ARTISTIC
Timestamp-Simple-1.01/GPL
Timestamp-Simple-1.01/META.yml
```

The **README** file in the newly created directory usually provides instructions for building and installing the module. Most modules follow the same steps.

```
$ cd Timestamp-Simple-1.01
$ perl Makefile.PL
Checking if your kit is complete...
Looks good
Writing Makefile for Timestamp::Simple
```

If the module you are building depends on other modules that are not installed on the local system, running **perl Makefile.PL** will display one or more warnings about prerequisites that are not found. This step writes out the makefile even if modules are missing. In this case the next step will fail, and you must build and install missing modules before continuing.

The next step is to run make on the makefile you just created. After you run **make**, run **make test** to be sure the module is working.

```
$ make
cp Simple.pm blib/lib/Timestamp/Simple.pm
Manifying blib/man3/Timestamp::Simple.3pm

$ make test
PERL_DL_NONLAZY=1 /usr/bin/perl "-Iblib/lib" "-Iblib/arch" test.pl
1..1
# Running under perl version 5.100000 for linux
# Current time local: Fri Sep  3 18:20:41 2010
# Current time GMT:   Sat Sep  4 01:20:41 2010
# Using Test.pm version 1.25
ok 1
ok 2
ok 3
```

Finally, running with **root** privileges, install the module:

```
# make install
Installing /usr/local/share/perl/5.10.0/Timestamp/Simple.pm
Installing /usr/local/man/man3/Timestamp::Simple.3pm
Writing /usr/local/lib/perl/5.10.0/auto/Timestamp/Simple/.packlist
Appending installation info to /usr/local/lib/perl/5.10.0/perllocal.pod
```

Once you have installed a module, you can use perldoc to display the documentation that tells you how to use the module. See page 1059 for an example.

Some modules contain SYNOPSIS sections. If the module you installed includes such a section, you can test the module by putting the code from the SYNOPSIS section in a file and running it as a Perl program:

```
$ cat times.pl
use Timestamp::Simple qw(stamp);
print stamp, "\n";

$ perl times.pl
20100904182627
```

You can then incorporate the module in a Perl program. The following example uses the timestamp module to generate a unique filename:

```
$ cat fn.pl
use Timestamp::Simple qw(stamp);

# Save timestamp in a variable
$ts = stamp, "\n";

# Strip off the year
$ts =~ s/....(.*)/\1/;

# Create a unique filename
$fn = "myfile." . $ts;

# Open, write to, and close the file
open (OUTFILE, '>', "$fn");
print OUTFILE "Hi there.\n";
close (OUTFILE);

$ perl fn.pl
$ ls myf*
myfile.0905183010
```

substr   You can use the **substr** function in place of the regular expression to strip off the year. To do so, replace the line that starts with **$ts =~** with the following line. Here, **substr** takes on the value of the string **$ts** starting at position 4 and continuing to the end of the string:

```
$ts = substr ($ts, 4);
```

EXAMPLES

This section provides some sample Perl programs. First try running these programs as is, and then modify them to learn more about programming with Perl.

The first example runs under Linux and displays the list of groups that the user given as an argument is a member of. Without an argument, it displays the list of groups that the user running the program is a member of. In a Perl program, the **%ENV** hash holds the environment variables from the shell that called Perl. The keys in this hash are the names of environment variables; the values in this hash are the values of the corresponding variables. The first line of the program assigns a username to **$user**. The **shift** function (page 1071) takes on the value of the first command-line argument and shifts the rest of the arguments, if any remain. If the user runs the program with an argument, that argument is assigned to **$user**. If no argument appears on the command line, **shift** fails and Perl executes the statement following the Boolean OR (||). This statement extracts the value associated with the **USER** key in **%ENV**, which is the name of the user running the program.

Accepting output from a process
The third statement initializes the array **@list**. Although this statement is not required, it is good practice to include it to make the code easier to read. The next statement opens the **$fh** lexical handle. The trailing pipe symbol (|) in the *file-ref* (page 1082) portion of this **open** statement tells Perl to pass the command line preceding the pipe symbol to the shell for execution and to accept standard output from the command when the program reads from the file handle. In this case the command uses grep to filter the **/etc/group** file (page 506) for lines containing the username held in **$user**. The **die** statement displays an error message if Perl cannot open the handle.

```
$ cat groupfind.pl
$user = shift || $ENV{"USER"};
say "User $user belongs to these groups:";
@list = ();
open (my $fh, "grep $user /etc/group |") or die "Error: $!\n";
while ($group = <$fh>) {
    chomp $group;
    $group =~ s/(.*?):.*/$1/;
    push @list, $group;
}
close $fh;
@slist = sort @list;
say "@slist";

$ perl groupfind.pl
User sam belongs to these groups:
adm admin audio cdrom dialout dip floppy kvm lpadmin ...
```

The **while** structure in **groupfind.pl** reads lines from standard output of grep and terminates when grep finishes executing. The name of the group appears first on each line in **/etc/group**, followed by a colon and other information, including the names of the users who belong to the group. Following is a line from this file:

```
sam:x:1000:max,zach,helen
```

The line

```
$group =~ s/(.*?):.*/$1/;
```

uses a regular expression and substitution to remove everything except the name of the group from each line. The regular expression .*: would perform a greedy match of zero or more characters followed by a colon; putting a question mark after the asterisk causes the expression to perform a nongreedy match (page 1093). Putting parentheses around the part of the expression that matches the string the program needs to display enables Perl to use the string that the regular expression matches in the replacement string. The final .* matches the rest of the line. Perl replaces the **$1** in the replacement string with the string the bracketed portion of the regular expression (the part between the parentheses) matched and assigns this value (the name of the group) to **$group**.

The **chomp** statement removes the trailing NEWLINE (the regular expression did not match this character). The **push** statement adds the value of **$group** to the end of the **@list** array. Without **chomp**, each group would appear on a line by itself in the output. After the **while** structure finishes processing input from grep, **sort** orders **@list** and assigns the result to **@slist**. The final statement displays the sorted list of groups the user belongs to.

opendir and readdir The next example introduces the **opendir** and **readdir** functions. The **opendir** function opens a directory in a manner similar to the way **open** opens an ordinary file. It takes two arguments: the name of the directory handle and the name of the directory to open. The **readdir** function reads the name of a file from an open directory.

In the example, **opendir** opens the working directory (specified by .) using the **$dir** lexical directory handle. If **opendir** fails, Perl executes the statement following the **or** operator: **die** sends an error message to standard error and terminates the program. With the directory opened, **while** loops through the files in the directory, assigning the filename that **readdir** returns to the lexical variable **$entry**. An **if** statement executes **print** only for those files that are directories (**–d**). The **print** function displays the name of the directory unless the directory is named **.** or **..** When **readdir** has read all files in the working directory, it returns *false* and control passes to the statement following the **while** block. The **closedir** function closes the open directory and **print** displays a NEWLINE following the list of directories the program displayed.

```
$ cat dirs2a.pl
#!/usr/bin/perl
print "The working directory contains these directories:\n";

opendir my $dir, '.' or die "Could not open directory: $!\n";
while (my $entry = readdir $dir) {
    if (-d $entry) {
        print $entry, ' ' unless ($entry eq '.' || $entry eq '..');
    }
}
closedir $dir;
print "\n";

$ ./dirs2a.pl
The working directory contains these directories:
two one
```

split　The **split** function divides a string into substrings as specified by a delimiter. The syntax of a call to **split** is

　　*split (/re/, **string**);*

where *re* is the delimiter, which is a regular expression (frequently a single regular character), and *string* is the string that is to be divided. As the next example shows, you can assign the list that **split** returns to an array variable.

The next program runs under Linux and lists the usernames of users with UIDs greater than or equal to 100 listed in the **/etc/passwd** (page 508) file. It uses a **while** structure to read lines from **passwd** into **$user**, and it uses **split** to break the line into substrings separated by colons. The line that begins with **@row** assigns each of these substrings to an element of the **@row** array. The expression the **if** statement evaluates is *true* if the third substring (the UID) is greater than or equal to 100. This expression uses the **>=** numeric comparison operator because it compares two numbers; an alphabetic comparison would use the **ge** string comparison operator.

The **print** statement sends the UID number and the associated username to the **$sortout** file handle. The **open** statement for this handle establishes a pipe that sends its output to **sort –n**. Because the **sort** utility (page 154) does not display any output until it finishes receiving all of the input, **split3.pl** does not display anything until it closes the **$sortout** handle, which it does when it finishes reading the **passwd** file.

```
$ cat split3.pl
#!/usr/bin/perl -w

open ($pass, "/etc/passwd");
open ($sortout, "| sort -n");
while ($user = <$pass>) {
    @row = split (/:/, $user);
    if ($row[2] >= 100) {
        print $sortout "$row[2] $row[0]\n";
        }
    }
close ($pass);
close ($sortout);
```

```
$ ./split3.pl
100 libuuid
101 syslog
102 klog
103 avahi-autoipd
104 pulse
...
```

The next example counts and displays the arguments it was called with, using **@ARGV** (page 1085). A **foreach** structure loops through the elements of the **@ARGV** array, which holds the command-line arguments. The **++** preincrement operator increments **$count** before it is displayed.

```
$ cat 10.pl
#!/usr/bin/perl -w

$count = 0;
$num = @ARGV;
print "You entered $num arguments on the command line:\n";
foreach $arg (@ARGV) {
    print ++$count, ". $arg\n";
    }
```

```
$ ./10.pl apple pear banana watermelon
You entered 4 arguments on the command line:
1. apple
2. pear
3. banana
4. watermelon
```

CHAPTER SUMMARY

Perl was written by Larry Wall in 1987. Since that time Perl has grown in size and functionality and is now a very popular language used for text processing, system administration, software development, and general-purpose programming. One of Perl's biggest assets is its support by thousands of third-party modules, many of which are stored in the CPAN repository.

The perldoc utility locates and displays local Perl documentation. It also allows you to document a Perl program by displaying lines of **pod** (plain old documentation) that you include in the program.

Perl provides three types of variables: scalar (singular variables that begin with a $), array (plural variables that begin with an @), and hash (also called associative arrays; plural variables that begin with a %). Array and hash variables both hold lists, but arrays are ordered while hashes are unordered. Standard control flow statements allow you to alter the order of execution of statements within a Perl program. In addition, Perl programs can take advantage of subroutines that can include variables local to the subroutines (lexical variables).

Regular expressions are one of Perl's strong points. In addition to the same facilities that are available in many Linux utilities, Perl offers regular expression features that allow you to perform more complex string processing.

EXERCISES

1. What are two different ways to turn on warnings in Perl?

2. What is the difference between an array and a hash?

3. In each example, when would you use a hash and when would you use an array?

   a. Counting the number of occurrences of an IP address in a log file.

   b. Generating a list of users who are over disk quota for use in a report.

4. Write a regular expression to match a quoted string, such as

   ```
   He said, "Go get me the wrench," but I didn't hear him.
   ```

5. Write a regular expression to match an IP address in a log file.

6. Many configuration files contain many comments, including commented-out default configuration directives. Write a program to remove these comments from a configuration file.

ADVANCED EXERCISES

7. Write a program that removes *~ and *.ico files from a directory hierarchy. (*Hint:* Use the **File::Find** module.)

8. Describe a programming mistake that Perl's warnings do not report on.

9. Write a Perl program that counts the number of files in the working directory and the number of bytes in those files, by filename extension.

10. Describe the difference between quoting strings using single quotation marks and using double quotation marks.

11. Write a program that copies all files with a **.ico** filename extension in a directory hierarchy to a directory named **icons** in your home directory. (*Hint:* Use the **File::Find** and **File::Copy** modules.)

12. Write a program that analyzes Apache logs. Display the number of bytes served by each path. Ignore unsuccessful page requests. If there are more than ten paths, display the first ten only.

    Following is a sample line from an Apache access log. The two numbers following the HTTP/1.1 are the response code and the byte count. A response code of 200 means the request was successful. A byte count of – means no data was transferred.

```
__DATA__
92.50.103.52 - - [19/Aug/2008:08:26:43 -0400] "GET /perl/automated-testing/next_active.gif
HTTP/1.1" 200 980 "http://example.com/perl/automated-testing/navigation_bar.htm"
"Mozilla/5.0 (X11; U; Linux x86_64; en-US; rv:1.8.1.6) Gecko/20061201 Firefox/3.0.0.6
(Fedora); Blazer/4.0"
```

PART VII

APPENDIXES

REGULAR EXPRESSIONS

A *regular expression* defines a set of one or more strings of characters. A simple string of characters is a regular expression that defines one string of characters: itself. A more complex regular expression uses letters, numbers, and special characters to define many different strings of characters. A regular expression is said to *match* any string it defines.

This appendix describes the regular expressions used by ed, vim, emacs, grep, mawk/gawk, sed, Perl, and many other utilities. Refer to page 1090 for more information on Perl regular expressions. The regular expressions used in shell ambiguous file references are different and are described in "Filename Generation/Pathname Expansion" on page 244.

CHARACTERS

As used in this appendix, a *character* is any character *except* a NEWLINE. Most characters represent themselves within a regular expression. A *special character*, also called a *metacharacter,* is one that does not represent itself. If you need to use a special character to represent itself, you must quote it as explained on page 1109.

DELIMITERS

A character called a *delimiter* usually marks the beginning and end of a regular expression. The delimiter is always a special character for the regular expression it delimits (that is, it does not represent itself but marks the beginning and end of the expression). Although vim permits the use of other characters as a delimiter and grep does not use delimiters at all, the regular expressions in this appendix use a forward slash (/) as a delimiter. In some unambiguous cases, the second delimiter is not required. For example, you can sometimes omit the second delimiter when it would be followed immediately by RETURN.

SIMPLE STRINGS

The most basic regular expression is a simple string that contains no special characters except the delimiters. A simple string matches only itself (Table A-1). In the examples in this appendix, the strings that are matched are underlined and look like this.

Table A-1   Simple strings

Regular expression	Matches	Examples
/ring/	ring	ring, spring, ringing, stringing
/Thursday/	Thursday	Thursday, Thursday's
/or not/	or not	or not, poor nothing

SPECIAL CHARACTERS

You can use special characters within a regular expression to cause the regular expression to match more than one string. A regular expression that includes a special character always matches the longest possible string, starting as far toward the beginning (left) of the line as possible.

PERIODS

A period (.) matches any character (Table A-2).

Table A-2 Periods

Regular expression	Matches	Examples
/ .alk/	All strings consisting of a SPACE followed by any character followed by alk	will talk, might balk
/.ing/	All strings consisting of any character preceding ing	sing song, ping, before inglenook

BRACKETS

Brackets ([]) define a *character class*[1] that matches any single character within the brackets (Table A-3). If the first character following the left bracket is a caret (^), the brackets define a character class that matches any single character not within the brackets. You can use a hyphen to indicate a range of characters. Within a character-class definition, backslashes and asterisks (described in the following sections) lose their special meanings. A right bracket (appearing as a member of the character class) can appear only as the first character following the left bracket. A caret is special only if it is the first character following the left bracket. A dollar sign is special only if it is followed immediately by the right bracket.

Table A-3 Brackets

Regular expression	Matches	Examples
/[bB]ill/	Member of the character class b and B followed by ill	bill, Bill, billed
/t[aeiou].k/	t followed by a lowercase vowel, any character, and a k	talkative, stink, teak, tanker
/# [6–9]/	# followed by a SPACE and a member of the character class 6 through 9	# 60, # 8:, get # 9
/[^a–zA–Z]/	Any character that is not a letter (ASCII character set only)	1, 7, @, ., }, Stop!

---

1. GNU documentation and POSIX call these List Operators and defines Character Class operators as expressions that match a predefined group of characters, such as all numbers (page 1156).

ASTERISKS

An asterisk can follow a regular expression that represents a single character (Table A-4). The asterisk represents *zero* or more occurrences of a match of the regular expression. An asterisk following a period matches any string of characters. (A period matches any character, and an asterisk matches zero or more occurrences of the preceding regular expression.) A character-class definition followed by an asterisk matches any string of characters that are members of the character class.

Table A-4   Asterisks

Regular expression	Matches	Examples
/ab*c/	a followed by zero or more b's followed by a c	ac, abc, abbc, debbcaabbbc
/ab.*c/	ab followed by zero or more characters followed by c	abc, abxc, ab45c, xab 756.345 x cat
/t.*ing/	t followed by zero or more characters followed by ing	thing, ting, I thought of going
/[a–zA–Z]*/	A string composed only of letters and SPACES	1. any string without numbers or punctuation!
/(.*)/	As long a string as possible between (and)	Get (this) and (that);
/([^)]*)/	The shortest string possible that starts with (and ends with)	(this), Get (this and that)

CARETS AND DOLLAR SIGNS

A regular expression that begins with a caret (^) can match a string only at the beginning of a line. In a similar manner, a dollar sign ($) at the end of a regular expression matches the end of a line. The caret and dollar sign are called anchors because they force (anchor) a match to the beginning or end of a line (Table A-5).

Table A-5   Carets and dollar signs

Regular expression	Matches	Examples
/^T/	A T at the beginning of a line	This line..., That Time..., In Time
/^+[0–9]/	A plus sign followed by a digit at the beginning of a line	+5 +45.72, +759 Keep this...
/:$/	A colon that ends a line	...below:

QUOTING SPECIAL CHARACTERS

You can quote any special character (but not parentheses [except in Perl; page 1094] or a digit) by preceding it with a backslash (Table A-6). Quoting a special character makes it represent itself.

Table A-6   Quoted special characters

Regular expression	Matches	Examples
/end\./	All strings that contain <u>end</u> followed by a period	The <u>end.</u>, s<u>end.</u>, pret<u>end.</u>mail
/ \\/	A single backslash	<u>\</u>
/ */	An asterisk	<u>*</u>.c, an asterisk (<u>*</u>)
/ \[5\]/	<u>[5]</u>	it was five <u>[5]</u>
/and\/or/	<u>and/or</u>	<u>and/or</u>

RULES

The following rules govern the application of regular expressions.

LONGEST MATCH POSSIBLE

A regular expression always matches the longest possible string, starting as far toward the beginning (left end) of the line as possible. Perl calls this type of match a *greedy match* (page 1093). For example, given the string

```
This (rug) is not what it once was (a long time ago), is it?
```

the expression **/Th.*is/** matches

```
This (rug) is not what it once was (a long time ago), is
```

and **/(.*)/** matches

```
(rug) is not what it once was (a long time ago)
```

However, **/([^)]*)/** matches

```
(rug)
```

Given the string

```
singing songs, singing more and more
```

the expression **/s.*ing/** matches

```
singing songs, singing
```

and **/s.*ing song/** matches

```
singing song
```

EMPTY REGULAR EXPRESSIONS

Within some utilities, such as vim and less (but not grep), an empty regular expression represents the last regular expression you used. For example, suppose you give vim the following Substitute command:

```
:s/mike/robert/
```

If you then want to make the same substitution again, you can use the following command:

```
:s//robert/
```

Alternatively, you can use the following commands to search for the string **mike** and then make the substitution

```
/mike/
:s//robert/
```

The empty regular expression (**//**) represents the last regular expression you used (**/mike/**).

BRACKETING EXPRESSIONS

You can use quoted parentheses, \(and \), to *bracket* a regular expression. (However, Perl uses unquoted parentheses to bracket regular expressions; page 1094.) The string the bracketed regular expression matches can be recalled, as explained in "Quoted Digit." on the next page. A regular expression does not attempt to match quoted parentheses. Thus a regular expression enclosed within quoted parentheses matches what the same regular expression without the parentheses would match. The expression **/\(rexp\)/** matches what **/rexp/** would match; **/a\(b✳\)c/** matches what **/ab✳c/** would match.

You can nest quoted parentheses. The bracketed expressions are identified only by the opening \(, so no ambiguity arises in identifying them. The expression **/\([a–z]\([A–Z]✳\)x\)/** consists of two bracketed expressions, one nested within the other. In the string **3 t dMNORx7 l u**, the preceding regular expression matches **dMNORx**, with the first bracketed expression matching **dMNORx** and the second matching **MNOR**.

THE REPLACEMENT STRING

The vim and sed editors use regular expressions as search strings within Substitute commands. You can use the ampersand (**&**) and quoted digits (***n***) special characters to represent the matched strings within the corresponding replacement string.

AMPERSAND

Within a replacement string, an ampersand (&) takes on the value of the string that the search string (regular expression) matched. For example, the following vim Substitute command surrounds a string of one or more digits with **NN**. The ampersand in the replacement string matches whatever string of digits the regular expression (search string) matched:

>   :s/[0-9][0-9]*/NN&NN/

Two character-class definitions are required because the regular expression [0–9]* matches *zero* or more occurrences of a digit, and *any* character string constitutes zero or more occurrences of a digit.

QUOTED DIGIT

Within the search string, a bracketed regular expression, \(**xxx**\) [(**xxx**) in Perl], matches what the regular expression would have matched without the quoted parentheses, **xxx**. Within the replacement string, a quoted digit, *n*, represents the string that the bracketed regular expression (portion of the search string) beginning with the *n*th \(matched. Perl accepts a quoted digit for this purpose, but the preferred style is to precede the digit with a dollar sign (**$***n*; page 1094). For example, you can take a list of people in the form

>   last-name, first-name initial

and put it in the form

>   first-name initial last-name

with the following vim command:

>   :1,$s/\([^,]*\), \(.*\)/\2 \1/

This command addresses all the lines in the file (**1,$**). The Substitute command (**s**) uses a search string and a replacement string delimited by forward slashes. The first bracketed regular expression within the search string, \([^,]*\), matches what the same unbracketed regular expression, [^,]*, would match: zero or more characters not containing a comma (the **last-name**). Following the first bracketed regular expression are a comma and a SPACE that match themselves. The second bracketed expression, \(.*\), matches any string of characters (the **first-name** and **initial**).

The replacement string consists of what the second bracketed regular expression matched (\2), followed by a SPACE and what the first bracketed regular expression matched (\1).

EXTENDED REGULAR EXPRESSIONS

This section covers patterns that use an extended set of special characters. These patterns are called *full regular expressions* or *extended regular expressions*. In addition to ordinary regular expressions, Perl and vim provide extended regular expressions. The three utilities egrep, grep when run with the –E option (similar to egrep), and mawk/gawk provide all the special characters included in ordinary regular expressions, except for \(and \), as well those included in extended regular expressions.

Two of the additional special characters are the plus sign (+) and the question mark (?). They are similar to *, which matches *zero* or more occurrences of the previous character. The plus sign matches *one* or more occurrences of the previous character, whereas the question mark matches *zero* or *one* occurrence. You can use any one of the special characters *, +, and ? following parentheses, causing the special character to apply to the string surrounded by the parentheses. Unlike the parentheses in bracketed regular expressions, these parentheses are not quoted (Table A-7).

Table A-7 Extended regular expressions

Regular expression	Matches	Examples
/ab+c/	<u>a</u> followed by one or more <u>b</u>'s followed by a <u>c</u>	<u>y</u><u>abc</u>w, <u>abbc</u>57
/ab?c/	<u>a</u> followed by zero or one <u>b</u> followed by <u>c</u>	b<u>ac</u>k, <u>abc</u>def
/(ab)+c/	One or more occurrences of the string <u>ab</u> followed by <u>c</u>	z<u>abc</u>d, <u>ababc</u>!
/(ab)?c/	Zero or one occurrence of the string <u>ab</u> followed by <u>c</u>	x<u>c</u>, <u>abcc</u>

In full regular expressions, the vertical bar (|) special character is a Boolean OR operator. Within vim, you must quote the vertical bar by preceding it with a backslash to make it special (\|). A vertical bar between two regular expressions causes a match with strings that match the first expression, the second expression, or both. You can use the vertical bar with parentheses to separate from the rest of the regular expression the two expressions that are being ORed (Table A-8).

Table A-8 Full regular expressions

Regular expression	Meaning	Examples
/ab|ac/	Either <u>ab</u> or <u>ac</u>	<u>ab</u>, <u>ac</u>, <u>abac</u> (***abac*** *is two matches of the regular expression*)
/^Exit|^Quit/	Lines that begin with <u>Exit</u> or <u>Quit</u>	<u>Exit</u>, <u>Quit</u>, No Exit
/(D|N)\. Jones/	<u>D. Jones</u> or <u>N. Jones</u>	P.<u>D. Jones</u>, <u>N. Jones</u>

APPENDIX SUMMARY

A regular expression defines a set of one or more strings of characters. A regular expression is said to match any string it defines.

In a regular expression, a special character is one that does not represent itself. Table A-9 lists special characters.

Table A-9   Special characters

Character	Meaning
.	Matches any single character
*	Matches zero or more occurrences of a match of the preceding character
^	Forces a match to the beginning of a line
$	A match to the end of a line
\	Quotes special characters
\<	Forces a match to the beginning of a word
\>	Forces a match to the end of a word

Table A-10 lists ways of representing character classes and bracketed regular expressions.

Table A-10   Character classes and bracketed regular expressions

Class	Defines
[*xyz*]	Defines a character class that matches *x*, *y*, or *z*
[^*xyz*]	Defines a character class that matches any character except *x*, *y*, or *z*
[*x–z*]	Defines a character class that matches any character *x* through *z* inclusive
\(*xyz*\)	Matches what *xyz* matches (a bracketed regular expression; not Perl)
(*xyz*)	Matches what *xyz* matches (a bracketed regular expression; Perl only)

In addition to the preceding special characters and strings (excluding quoted parentheses, except in vim), the characters in Table A-11 are special within full, or extended, regular expressions.

Table A-11   Extended regular expressions

Expression	Matches
+	Matches one or more occurrences of the preceding character
?	Matches zero or one occurrence of the preceding character

Table A-11   Extended regular expressions (continued)

Expression	Matches
(*xyz*)+	Matches one or more occurrences of what *xyz* matches
(*xyz*)?	Matches zero or one occurrence of what *xyz* matches
(*xyz*)✻	Matches zero or more occurrences of what *xyz* matches
xyz|*abc*	Matches either what *xyz* or what *abc* matches (use \\| in vim)
(*xy*|*ab*)*c*	Matches either what *xyc* or what *abc* matches (use \\| in vim)

Table A-12 lists characters that are special within a replacement string in sed and vim.

Table A-12   Replacement strings

String	Represents
&	Represents what the regular expression (search string) matched
n	A quoted number, *n*, represents what the *n*th bracketed regular expression in the search string matched
$*n*	A number preceded by a dollar sign, *n*, represents what the *n*th bracketed regular expression in the search string matched (Perl only)

B

HELP

You need not be a user or system administrator in isolation. A large community of Linux experts is willing to assist you in learning about, helping you solve problems with, and getting the most out of a Linux system. Before you ask for help, however, make sure you have done everything you can to solve the problem yourself. No doubt, someone has experienced the same problem before you and the answer to your question exists somewhere on the Internet. Your job is to find it. This appendix lists resources and describes methods that can help you in that task.

SOLVING A PROBLEM

Following is a list of steps that can help you solve a problem without asking someone for help. Depending on your understanding of and experience with the hardware and software involved, these steps might lead to a solution.

1. Fedora/RHEL comes with extensive documentation. Read the documentation on the specific hardware or software you are having a problem with. If it is a GNU product, use info; otherwise, use man to find local information. Also look in **/usr/share/doc** for documentation on specific tools. For more information refer to "Where to Find Documentation" on page 125.

2. When the problem involves some type of error or other message, use a search engine, such as Google (www.google.com/linux) or Google Groups (groups.google.com), to look up the message on the Internet. If the message is long, pick a unique part of the message to search for; 10 to 20 characters should be enough. Enclose the search string within double quotation marks. See "Using the Internet to Get Help" on page 132 for an example of this kind of search.

3. Check whether the Linux Documentation Project (www.tldp.org) has a HOWTO or mini-HOWTO on the subject in question. Search its site for keywords that relate directly to the product and problem. Read the FAQs.

4. See Table B-1 for other sources of documentation.

5. Use Google or Google Groups to search on keywords that relate directly to the product and problem.

6. When all else fails (or perhaps before you try anything else), examine the system logs in **/var/log**. First look at the end of the **messages** file using the following command:

```
#tail -20 /var/log/messages
```

If **messages** contains nothing useful, run the following command. It displays the names of the log files in chronological order, with the most recently modified files appearing at the bottom of the list:

```
$ ls -ltr /var/log
```

Look at the files at the bottom of the list first. If the problem involves a network connection, review the **secure** file on the local and remote systems. Also look at **messages** on the remote system.

7. The **/var/spool** directory contains subdirectories with useful information: **cups** holds the print queues, **mail** or **exim4** holds the user's mail files, and so on.

If you are unable to solve a problem yourself, a thoughtful question to an appropriate newsgroup (page 1119) or mailing list (page 1119) can elicit useful information. When you send or post a question, make sure you describe the problem and identify the local system carefully. Include the version numbers of Fedora/RHEL and any software packages that relate to the problem. Describe the hardware, if appropriate. There is an etiquette to posting questions—see www.catb.org/~esr/faqs/smart-questions.html for a good paper by Eric S. Raymond and Rick Moen titled "How To Ask Questions the Smart Way." For a fee, Red Hat provides many types of support.

The author's home page (www.sobell.com) contains corrections to this book, answers to selected chapter exercises, and pointers to other Linux sites.

FINDING LINUX-RELATED INFORMATION

Fedora/RHEL comes with reference pages stored online. You can read these documents by using the man or info (page 128) utility. You can read man and info pages to get more information about specific topics while reading this book or to determine which features are available with Linux. To search for topics, use apropos (see page 127 or give the command **man apropos**).

DOCUMENTATION

Good books are available on various aspects of using and managing UNIX systems in general and Linux systems in particular. In addition, you might find the sites listed in Table B-1 useful.[1]

Table B-1   Documentation

Site	About the site	URL
freedesktop.org	Creates standards for interoperability between open-source desktop environments.	freedesktop.org
GNOME	GNOME home page.	www.gnome.org
GNU Manuals	GNU manuals.	www.gnu.org/manual
info	Instructions for using the info utility.	www.gnu.org/software/texinfo/manual/info
Internet FAQ Archives	Searchable FAQ archives.	www.faqs.org

---

1. The right-hand columns of most of the tables in this appendix show Internet addresses (URLs). All sites have an implicit http:// prefix unless ftp:// or https:// is shown. Refer to "URLs (Web addresses)" on page 20.

Table B-1   Documentation (continued)

Site	About the site	URL
KDE Documentation	KDE documentation.	kde.org/documentation
KDE News	KDE news.	dot.kde.org
Linux Documentation Project	All things related to Linux documentation (in many languages): HOW-TOs, guides, FAQs, **man** pages, and magazines. This is the best overall source for Linux documentation. Make sure to visit the Links page.	www.tldp.org
Red Hat Documentation and Support	This site has a link to the Red Hat Knowledgebase that can help answer questions. It also has links to online documentation for Red Hat products and to a support guide.	www.redhat.com/apps/support
RFCs	Requests for comments; see *RFC* (page 1185).	www.rfc-editor.org
System Administrators Guild (SAGE)	SAGE is a group for system administrators.	www.sage.org

USEFUL LINUX SITES

Sometimes the sites listed in Table B-2 are so busy you cannot connect to them. In this case, you are usually given a list of alternative, or *mirror*, sites to try.

Table B-2   Useful Linux sites

Site	About the site	URL
DistroWatch	A survey of many Linux distributions, including news, reviews, and articles.	distrowatch.com
GNU	GNU Project Web server.	www.gnu.org
ibiblio	A large library and digital archive. Formerly Metalab; formerly Sunsite.	www.ibiblio.org www.ibiblio.org/pub/linux www.ibiblio.org/pub/historic-linux
Linux Standard Base (LSB)	A group dedicated to standardizing Linux.	www.linuxfoundation.org/en/LSB

Table B-2   Useful Linux sites (continued)

Site	About the site	URL
Rpmfind.Net	A good source for rpm files, especially when you need a specific version.	rpmfind.net
Sobell	The author's home page contains useful links, errata for this book, code for many of the examples in this book, and answers to selected exercises.	www.sobell.com
USENIX	A large, well-established UNIX group. This site has many links, including a list of conferences.	www.usenix.org
X.Org	The X Window System home.	www.x.org

LINUX NEWSGROUPS

One of the best ways of getting specific information is through a newsgroup. You can often find the answer to a question by reading postings to the newsgroup. Try using Google Groups (groups.google.com) to search through newsgroups to see whether the question has already been asked and answered. Or open a newsreader program and subscribe to appropriate newsgroups. If necessary, you can post a question for someone to answer. Before you do so, make sure you are posting to the correct group and that your question has not already been answered.

The newsgroup **comp.os.linux.answers** provides postings of solutions to common problems and periodic postings of the most up-to-date versions of FAQ and HOWTO documents. The **comp.os.linux.misc** newsgroup has answers to miscellaneous Linux-related questions.

MAILING LISTS

Subscribing to a mailing list (page 752) allows you to participate in an electronic discussion. With most lists, you can send and receive email dedicated to a specific topic to and from a group of users. Moderated lists do not tend to stray as much as unmoderated lists, assuming the list has a good moderator. The disadvantage of a moderated list is that some discussions might be cut off when they get interesting if the moderator deems that the discussion has gone on for too long. Mailing lists described as bulletins are strictly unidirectional: You cannot post information to these lists but can only receive periodic bulletins. If you have the subscription address for a mailing list but are not sure how to subscribe, put the word **help** in the body and/or header of email you send to the address. You will usually receive instructions via return email. Red Hat hosts several mailing lists; go to www.redhat.com/mailman/listinfo for more information. You can also use a search engine to search for **mailing list linux**.

WORDS

Many dictionaries, thesauruses, and glossaries are available online. Table B-3 lists a few of them.

Table B-3   Looking up words

Site	About the site	URL
DICT.org	Multiple-database search for words	www.dict.org
Dictionary.com	Everything related to words	dictionary.reference.com
DNS Glossary	DNS glossary	www.menandmice.com/knowledgehub/dnsglossary/default.aspx
FOLDOC	The Free On-Line Dictionary of Computing	foldoc.org
The Jargon File	An online version of *The New Hacker's Dictionary*	www.catb.org/~esr/jargon
Merriam-Webster	English language	www.merriam-webster.com
OneLook	Multiple-site word search with a single query	www.onelook.com
Roget's Thesaurus	Thesaurus	machaut.uchicago.edu/rogets
Webopedia	Commercial technical dictionary	www.webopedia.com
Wikipedia	An open-source (user-contributed) encyclopedia project	wikipedia.org
Wordsmyth	Dictionary and thesaurus	www.wordsmyth.net
Yahoo Reference	Search multiple sources at the same time	education.yahoo.com/reference

SOFTWARE

There are many ways to learn about interesting software packages and their availability on the Internet. Table B-4 lists sites you can download software from. For security-related programs, refer to Table C-1 on page 1140. Another way to learn about software packages is through a newsgroup (page 1119).

Table B-4   Software

Site	About the site	URL
BitTorrent	BitTorrent efficiently distributes large amounts of static data	azureus.sourceforge.net
CVS	CVS (Concurrent Versions System) is a version control system	www.nongnu.org/cvs

Table B-4   Software (continued)

Site	About the site	URL
ddd	The ddd utility is a graphical front-end for command-line debuggers such as gdb	www.gnu.org/software/ddd
Firefox	Web browser	www.mozilla.com/firefox
Free Software Directory	Categorized, searchable lists of free software	directory.fsf.org
Freshmeat	A large index of UNIX and cross-platform software and themes	freshmeat.net
gdb	The gdb utility is a command-line debugger	www.gnu.org/software/gdb
GNOME Project	Links to all GNOME projects	www.gnome.org/projects
IceWALKERS	Categorized, searchable lists of free software	www.icewalkers.com
kdbg	The kdbg utility is a graphical user interface to gdb	freshmeat.net/projects/kdbg
Linux Software Map	A database of packages written for, ported to, or compiled for Linux	www.boutell.com/lsm
Mtools	A collection of utilities to access DOS floppy diskettes from Linux without mounting the diskettes	www.gnu.org/software/mtools/intro.html
Network Calculators	Subnet/network mask calculator	www.subnetmask.info
rpmfind.net	Searchable list of rpm files for various Linux distributions and versions	rpmfind.net/linux/RPM
Savannah	Central point for development, distribution, and maintenance of free software	savannah.gnu.org
SourceForge	A development Web site with a large repository of open-source code and applications	sourceforge.net
strace	The strace utility is a system call trace debugging tool	sourceforge.net/projects/strace/
Thunderbird	Mail application	www.mozilla.com/thunderbird
ups	The ups utility is a graphical source-level debugger	ups.sourceforge.net
yum	The yum utility installs, removes, and updates system software packages	linux.duke.edu/projects/yum apt.freshrpms.net

OFFICE SUITES AND WORD PROCESSORS

Several office suites and many word processors are available for Linux. Table B-5 lists a few of them. If you are exchanging documents with people using Windows, make sure the import from/export to MS Word functionality covers your needs.

Table B-5   Office suites and word processors

Product name	What it does	URL
AbiWord	Word processor	www.abisource.com
KOffice	Integrated suite of office applications, including the KWord word processing program	www.koffice.org
LibreOffice	A multiplatform and multilingual office suite	www.libreoffice.org/
OpenOffice.org	A multiplatform and multilingual office suite	www.openoffice.org www.gnome.org/projects/ooo

SPECIFYING A TERMINAL

Because vim, emacs, and other textual and pseudographical programs take advantage of features specific to various kinds of terminals and terminal emulators, you must tell these programs the name of the terminal you are using or the terminal your terminal emulator is emulating. Most of the time the terminal name is set for you. If the terminal name is not specified or is not specified correctly, the characters on the screen will be garbled or, when you start a program, the program will ask which type of terminal you are using.

Terminal names describe the functional characteristics of a terminal or terminal emulator to programs that require this information. Although terminal names are referred to as either Terminfo or Termcap names, the difference relates to the method each system uses to store the terminal characteristics internally—not to the manner in which you specify the name of a terminal. Terminal names that are often used with Linux terminal emulators and with graphical monitors while they are run in textual mode include **ansi**, **linux**, **vt100**, **vt102**, **vt220**, and **xterm**.

When you are running a terminal emulator, you can specify the type of terminal you want to emulate. Set the emulator to either **vt100** or **vt220**, and set **TERM** to the same value.

When you log in, you might be prompted to identify the type of terminal you are using:

```
TERM = (vt100)
```

You can respond to this prompt in one of two ways. First you can press RETURN to set your terminal type to the name in parentheses. If that name does not describe the terminal you are using, you can enter the correct name and then press RETURN.

```
TERM = (vt100) ansi
```

You might also receive the following prompt:

```
TERM = (unknown)
```

This prompt indicates that the system does not know which type of terminal you are using. If you plan to run programs that require this information, enter the name of the terminal or terminal emulator you are using before you press RETURN.

TERM If you do not receive a prompt, you can give the following command to display the value of the **TERM** variable and check whether the terminal type has been set:

```
$ echo $TERM
```

If the system responds with the wrong name, a blank line, or an error message, set or change the terminal name. From the Bourne Again Shell (bash), enter a command similar to the following to set the **TERM** variable so the system knows which type of terminal you are using:

export TERM=name

Replace *name* with the terminal name for the terminal you are using, making sure you do not put a SPACE before or after the equal sign. If you always use the same type of terminal, you can place this command in your **~/.bashrc** file (page 282), causing the shell to set the terminal type each time you log in. For example, give the following command to set your terminal name to **vt100**:

```
$ export TERM=vt100
```

LANG For some programs to display information correctly, you might need to set the **LANG** variable (page 314). Frequently you can set this variable to C. Under bash use the command

```
$ export LANG=C
```

C

SECURITY

Security is a major part of the foundation of any system that is not totally cut off from other machines and users. Some aspects of security have a place even on isolated machines. Examples of these measures include periodic system backups, BIOS or power-on passwords, and self-locking screensavers.

A system that is connected to the outside world requires other mechanisms to secure it: tools to check files (tripwire), audit tools (tiger/cops), secure access methods (kerberos/ssh), services that monitor logs and machine states (swatch/watcher), packet-filtering and routing tools (ipfwadm/iptables), and more.

System security has many dimensions. The security of a system as a whole depends on the security of individual components, such as email, files, network, login, and remote access policies, as well as the physical security of the host itself. These dimensions frequently overlap, and their borders are not always static or clear. For instance, email security is affected by the security of both files and the network. If the medium (the network) over which you send and receive your email is not secure, then you must take extra steps to ensure the security of your messages. If you save your secure email in a file on the local system, then you rely on the filesystem and host access policies for file security. A failure in any one of these areas can start a domino effect, diminishing reliability and integrity in other areas and potentially compromising system security as a whole.

This short appendix cannot cover all facets of system security in depth, but provides an overview of the complexity of setting up and maintaining a secure system. This appendix offers some specifics, concepts, guidelines to consider, and many pointers to security resources (Table C-1 on page 1140).

Other sources of system security information

security   Depending on how important system security is to you, you might want to purchase one or more books dedicated to system security, visit some of the Internet sites that are dedicated to security, or hire someone who is an expert in the field.

Do not rely on this appendix as your sole source of information on system security.

ENCRYPTION

One of the building blocks of security is *encryption,* which provides a means of scrambling data for secure transmission to other parties. In cryptographic terms, the data or message to be encrypted is referred to as *plaintext,* and the resulting encrypted block of text as *ciphertext.* Processes exist for converting plaintext into ciphertext through the use of *keys,* which are essentially random numbers of a specified length used to *lock* and *unlock* data. This conversion is achieved by applying the keys to the plaintext according to a set of mathematical instructions, referred to as the *encryption algorithm.*

Developing and analyzing strong encryption software is extremely difficult. Many nuances exist, many standards govern encryption algorithms, and a background in mathematics is requisite. Also, unless an algorithm has undergone public scrutiny for a significant period of time, it is generally not considered secure; it is often impossible to know an algorithm is completely secure but possible to know that it is not secure. Ultimately time is the best test of any algorithm. Also, a solid algorithm does not guarantee an effective encryption mechanism because the fallibility of an encryption scheme frequently arises from problems with its implementation and distribution.

An encryption algorithm uses a key that is a certain number of bits long. Each bit added to the length of a key effectively doubles the *key space* (the number of combinations allowed by the number of bits in the key—2 to the power of the length of the key in bits[1]) and means it will take twice as long for an attacker to decrypt a message (assuming the scheme lacks any inherent weaknesses or vulnerabilities to

---

1. A 2-bit key would have a key space of 4 (2^2), a 3-bit key would have a key space of 8 (2^3), and so on.

exploit). However, it is a mistake to compare algorithms based only on the number of bits used. In some cases an algorithm that uses a 64-bit key can be more secure than an algorithm that uses a 128-bit key.

The two primary classifications of encryption schemes are *public key (asymmetric) encryption* and *symmetric (secret) key encryption.* Public key encryption, also called *asymmetric encryption,* uses two keys: a public key and a private key. These keys are uniquely associated with a specific user. Public key encryption schemes are used mostly to exchange keys and signatures. Symmetric key encryption, also called *symmetric encryption* or *secret key encryption,* uses one key that you and the person you are communicating with (hereafter referred to as your *friend*) share as a secret. Symmetric key encryption is typically used to encrypt large amounts of data because it is fast. Public key algorithm keys typically have a length of 512 bits to 2,048 bits, whereas symmetric key algorithms use keys in the range of 64 bits to 512 bits.

Asymmetric and symmetric algorithms complement each other. Asymmetric algorithms are good at providing digital signatures and authentication, but are slower. Symmetric algorithms are good at encrypting large blocks of data using a shared key and are faster. The algorithms are often combined to provide the best of both worlds: Text can first be processed using symmetric encryption and a random key. Then the random key can be encrypted using your friend's public key (so your friend can read it) and signed with your private key (to prove it came from you). The next sections cover these concepts in detail.

When you are choosing an encryption scheme, realize that security comes at a price. There is usually a tradeoff between resilience of the cryptosystem and ease of administration.

The practicality of a security solution is a far greater factor in encryption, and in security in general, than most people realize. With enough time and effort, nearly every algorithm can be broken. In fact, you can often unearth the mathematical instructions for a widely used algorithm by flipping through a cryptography book, reviewing a vendor's product specifications, or performing a quick search on the Internet. The challenge is to ensure the effort required to follow the twists and turns taken by an encryption algorithm and its resulting encryption solution outweighs the worth of the information it is protecting.

How much time and money should you spend on encryption?

tip   When the cost of obtaining the information exceeds the value realized by its possession, the solution is an effective one.

PUBLIC KEY (ASYMMETRIC) ENCRYPTION

To use public key encryption, you must generate two keys: a public key and a private key. You keep the private key for yourself and give the public key to the world. In a similar manner, each of your friends will generate a pair of keys and give you their public keys. Public key encryption is marked by two distinct features:

1. When you encrypt data with someone's public key, only that person's private key can decrypt it.

2. When you encrypt data with your private key, anyone can decrypt it with your public key.

You might wonder why the second point is useful: Why would you want everyone else to be able to decrypt something you just encrypted? The answer lies in the purpose of the encryption. Although encryption changes the original message into unreadable ciphertext, its purpose is to provide a *digital signature*. If the message can be properly decrypted with your public key, *only you* could have encrypted it with your private key, proving the message is authentic. Combining these two modes of operation yields privacy and authenticity. You can sign a message with your private key so it can be verified as authentic, and then you can encrypt it with your friend's public key so that only your friend can decrypt it.

Public key encryption has three major shortcomings:

1. Public key encryption algorithms are generally much slower than symmetric key algorithms and usually require a much larger key size and a way to generate large prime numbers[2] to use as components of the key, making them more resource intensive.

2. The private key must be stored securely and its integrity safeguarded. If a person's private key is obtained by another party, that party can encrypt, decrypt, and sign messages while impersonating the original owner of the key. If the private key is lost or becomes corrupted, any messages previously encrypted with it are also lost, and a new keypair must be generated.

3. It is difficult to authenticate the origin of a key—that is, to prove whom it originally came from. This so-called key-distribution problem is the raison d'être for such companies as VeriSign (www.verisign.com).

Algorithms such as RSA, Diffie-Hellman, and El-Gamal implement public key encryption methodology. Today a 512-bit key is considered barely adequate for RSA encryption and offers marginal protection; 1,024-bit keys are expected to hold off determined attackers for several more years. Keys that are 2,048 bits long are now becoming commonplace and are rated as *espionage strength*. A mathematical paper published in late 2001 and reexamined in spring 2002 describes how a machine can be built—for a very large sum of money—that could break 1,024-bit RSA encryption in seconds to minutes (this point is debated in an article at www.schneier.com/crypto-gram-0203.html#6). Although the cost of such a machine exceeds the resources available to most individuals and smaller corporations, it is well within the reach of large corporations and governments. Since the publication of that paper, subsequent algorithmic and

---

2. In particular, RSA public key encryption is based on the property that if you take two large prime numbers and multiply them together you get a much larger number. Identifying the factors of this number is a very difficult computational problem. When you keep one prime number and give away the other, the numbers act like a private key and public key.

hardware improvements have led to designs of machines that can be built for around $10,000.

SYMMETRIC KEY ENCRYPTION

Symmetric key encryption is generally fast and simple to deploy. First you and your friend agree on which algorithm to use and a key you will share. Then either of you can decrypt or encrypt a file with the chosen key. Behind the scenes, symmetric key encryption algorithms are most often implemented as a network of black boxes, which can involve hardware components, software, or a combination of the two. Each box imposes a reversible transformation on the plaintext and passes it to the next box, where another reversible transformation further alters the data. The security of a symmetric key algorithm relies on the difficulty of determining which boxes were used and the number of times the data was fed through the set of boxes. A good algorithm will cycle the plaintext through a given set of boxes many times before yielding the result, and there will be no obvious mapping from plaintext to ciphertext.

The disadvantage of symmetric key encryption is that it depends heavily on the availability of a secure channel through which to send the key to your friend. For example, you would not use email to send your key; if your email is intercepted, a third party is in possession of your secret key, and your encryption is useless. You could relay the key over the phone, but your call could be intercepted if your phone were tapped or someone overheard your conversation.

Common implementations of symmetric key algorithms include DES (Data Encryption Standard), 3-DES (triple DES), IDEA, RC5, Blowfish, and AES (Advanced Encryption Standard). AES is the new Federal Information Processing Standard (FIPS-197) algorithm endorsed for governmental use and has been selected to replace DES as the de facto encryption algorithm. AES uses the Rijndael algorithm, chosen after a thorough evaluation of 15 candidate algorithms by the cryptographic research community.

None of the aforementioned algorithms has undergone more scrutiny than DES, which has been in use since the late 1970s. However, the use of DES has drawbacks and is no longer considered secure because the weakness of its 56-bit key makes it unreasonably easy to break. Given the advances in computing power and speed since DES was developed, the small size of this algorithm's key renders it inadequate for operations requiring more than basic security for a relatively short period of time. For a few thousand dollars, you can link off-the-shelf computer systems so they can crack DES keys in a few hours.

The 3-DES application of DES is intended to combat its degenerating resilience by running the encryption three times; it is projected to be secure for years to come. DES is probably sufficient for such tasks as sending email to a friend when you need it to be confidential or secure for only a few days (for example, to send a notice of a meeting that will take place in a few hours). It is unlikely anyone is sufficiently interested in your email to invest the time and money to decrypt it. Because of 3-DES's wide availability and ease of use, it is advisable to use it instead of DES.

Encryption Implementation

Most of today's commercial software packages use both public and symmetric key encryption algorithms, taking advantage of the strengths of each and avoiding their weaknesses. The public key algorithm is used first, as a means of negotiating a randomly generated secret key and providing for message authenticity. Then a secret key algorithm, such as 3-DES, IDEA, AES, or Blowfish, encrypts and decrypts the data on both ends for speed. Finally a hash algorithm, such as DSA (Digital Signature Algorithm), generates a message digest that provides a signature that can alert you to tampering. The digest is digitally signed with the sender's private key.

GnuPG/PGP

The most popular personal encryption packages available today are GnuPG (GNU Privacy Guard, also called GPG; www.gnupg.org) and PGP (Pretty Good Privacy; www.symantec.com/business/theme.jsp?themeid=pgp). GNU Privacy Guard was designed as a free replacement for PGP, a security tool that made its debut during the early 1990s. Phil Zimmerman developed PGP as a Public Key Infrastructure (PKI), featuring a convenient interface, ease of use and management, and the security of digital certificates. One critical characteristic set PGP apart from the majority of cryptosystems then available: PGP functions entirely without certification authorities (CAs). Until the introduction of PGP, PKI implementations were built around the concept of CAs and centralized key management controls.

Both PGP and GnuPG rely on the notion of a web of trust:[3] If you trust someone and that person trusts someone else, the person you trust can provide an introduction to the third party. When you trust someone, you perform an operation called *key signing*. By signing someone else's key, you verify that the person's public key is authentic and safe for you to use to send email. When you sign a key, you are asked whether you trust this person to introduce other keys to you. It is common practice to assign this trust based on several criteria, including your knowledge of a person's character or a lasting professional relationship with the person. The best practice is to sign someone's key only after you have met face to face to avert any chance of a man-in-the-middle scenario (see the adjacent tip). The disadvantage of this scheme is the lack of a central registry for associating with people you do not already know.

Man-in-the-middle (MITM) attack

security   If Max and Zach try to carry on a secure email exchange over a network, Max first sends Zach his public key. However, suppose Mr. X sits between Max and Zach on the network and intercepts Max's public key. Mr. X then sends *his* public key to Zach. Zach then sends his public key to Max, but once again Mr. X intercepts it and substitutes *his* public key and sends that to Max. Without some kind of active protection (a piece of shared information), Mr. X, the *man-in-the-middle*, can decrypt all traffic between Max and Zach, reencrypt it, and send it on to the other party.

---

3. For more information see www.gnupg.org/gph/en/manual/x334.html.

Symantec owns PGP. Although it is available without cost for personal use, its deployment in a commercial environment requires the purchase of a license. GnuPG is a free and compatible implementation of PGP.

GnuPG supports most features and implementations made available by PGP and complies with the OpenPGP Message Format standard. Because GnuPG does not use the patented IDEA algorithm but rather relies on BUGS (Big and Useful Great Security; www.gnu.org/directory/bugs.html), you can use it almost without restriction: It is released under the GNU GPL (refer to "The Code Is Free" on page 5). PGP and GnuPG are considered to be interchangeable and interoperable. The command sequences for and internal workings of these two tools are very similar.

The GnuPG system includes the gpg program

tip GnuPG is frequently referred to as gpg, but gpg is actually the main program for the GnuPG system.

GNU offers a good introduction to privacy, *The GNU Privacy Handbook,* which is available in several languages and listed at www.gnupg.org (click **Documentation⇨ Guides**). Click **Documentation⇨HOWTOs** on the same Web page to view the *GNU Privacy Guard (GnuPG) Mini Howto,* which steps through the setup and use of gpg. And, of course, there is a gpg info page.

In addition to providing encryption, gpg is useful for authentication. For example, you can use it to verify the person who signed a piece of email is the person who sent it.

FILE SECURITY

From an end user's perspective, file security is one of the most critical areas of security. Some file security is built into Linux: chmod (page 203) gives you basic security control. ACLs (Access Control Lists) allow more fine-grained control of file access permissions. ACLs are part of Solaris, Windows NT/2000/XP, VAX/VMS, and mainframe operating systems. Fedora/RHEL supports ACLs (page 208). Even these tools are insufficient, however, when your account is compromised (for example, by someone watching your fingers on the keyboard as you type your password). To provide maximum file security, you must encrypt your files. Then even someone who knows your login password cannot read your files. Of course, if someone knows your key, that person can decrypt your files if she can get to them.

EMAIL SECURITY

Email security overlaps file security and, as discussed later, network security. GnuPG is the tool most frequently used for email security, although you can also use PGP.

MTAs (Mail Transfer Agents)

An increasingly common protocol option is STARTTLS (Start Transport Layer Security; www.sendmail.org/~ca/email/starttls.html). TLS itself usually refers to SSL (Secure Sockets Layer) and has become the de facto method for encrypting TCP/IP traffic on the Internet. The **sendmail** (Chapter 20) and **exim4** daemons fully support STARTTLS, and much documentation exists on how to configure them. STARTTLS enhancements are also available for Qmail (page 732) and Postfix (page 732) and other popular MTAs. This capability provides encryption between two mail servers but not necessarily between the local system and the mail server. Also, the advantages of using TLS are negated if the email must pass through a relay that does not support TLS.

MUAs (Mail User Agents)

Many popular mail user agents, such as mutt, elm, Thunderbird, and emacs, include the ability to use PGP or GnuPG for encryption. Evolution, the default Fedora/RHEL MUA, has built-in GnuPG support. This approach has become the default way to exchange email securely.

Network Security

Network security is a vital component for ensuring the security of a computing site. However, without the right infrastructure, providing network security is difficult, if not impossible. For example, if you run a shared network topology,[4] such as wireless, without the latest security implementation to prevent snooping, how can you prevent someone from plugging in a machine and capturing all the *packets* (page 1180) that traverse the network?[5] You cannot—so you have a potential security hole. Another common security hole relates to the use of telnet for logins. Because telnet sends and receives cleartext, anyone "listening in" on the line can easily capture usernames and passwords, compromising security. Fortunately, this problem is serious only for legacy devices that support only telnet.

Do not allow any unauthenticated PC (any PC that does not require users to supply a local name and password) on a network. On UNIX/Linux, only a user working with **root** privileges can put the network interface in promiscuous mode and collect packets. On UNIX/Linux, ports numbered less than 1024[6] are privileged—that is, normal user protocols cannot bind to these ports. This is an important but regrettable means

---

4. Shared network topology: A network in which each packet might be seen by machines other than its destination. "Shared" means that the network bandwidth is shared by all users.

5. Do not make the mistake of assuming the local network is secure just because you have a switch. Switches are designed to allocate bandwidth, not to guarantee security.

6. The term *port* has many meanings; here it is a number assigned to a program. This number links incoming data with a specific service. For example, port 21 is used by FTP traffic, and port 23 is used by TELNET.

of security for some protocols, such as NIS, NFS, RSH, and LPD. Normally a data switch on a LAN automatically protects machines from people snooping on the network for data. In high-load situations, switches have been known to behave unpredictably, directing packets to the wrong ports. Certain programs can overload the switch tables that hold information about which machine is on which port. When these tables are overloaded, the switch becomes a repeater and broadcasts all packets to all ports. An attacker on the same switch as you can potentially see the traffic the local system sends and receives.

NETWORK SECURITY SOLUTIONS

One solution to shared-network problems is to encrypt messages that travel between machines. IPSec (Internet Protocol Security Protocol) provides an appropriate technology. IPSec is commonly used to establish a secure point-to-point virtual network (*VPN*, page 1196) that allows two hosts to communicate securely over an unsecure channel, such as the Internet. This protocol provides integrity, confidentiality, authenticity, and flexibility of implementation that supports multiple vendors.

IPSec is an amalgamation of protocols (IPSec = AH + ESP + IPComp + IKE):

- **Authentication Header (AH)**—A cryptographically secure, irreversible *checksum* (page 1156) for an entire packet. AH guarantees that the packet is authentic.

- **Encapsulating Security Payload (ESP)**—Encrypts a packet to make the data unreadable.

- **IP Payload Compression (IPComp)**—Compresses a packet. Encryption can increase the size of a packet, and IPComp counteracts this increase in size.

- **Internet Key Exchange (IKE)**—Provides a way for the endpoints to negotiate a common key securely. For AH to work, both ends of the exchange must use the same key to prevent a "man-in-the-middle" (see the tip on page 1130) from spoofing the connection.

While IPSec is an optional part of IPv4, IPv6 (page 373) mandates its use.

NETWORK SECURITY GUIDELINES

The following list of general guidelines for establishing and maintaining a secure system is not a complete list, but rather is meant as a guide.

- Fiberoptic cable is more secure than copper cable. Copper is subject to both active and passive eavesdropping. With access to copper cable, all a data thief needs to monitor your network traffic is a passive device for measuring magnetic fields. In contrast, it is much more difficult to tap a fiberoptic cable without interrupting the signal. Sites requiring top security keep fiberoptic cable in pressurized conduits, where a change in pressure signals that the physical security of the cable has been breached.

- Avoid leaving unused ports available in public areas. If a malicious user can plug a laptop into the network without being detected, you are at risk of a serious security problem. Network drops that will remain unused for extended periods should be disabled at the switch, preventing them from accepting or passing network traffic.

- Use the latest in wireless encryption. At the time of this writing, WEP is totally broken and WPA with TKIP is seriously flawed. WPA2 with AES is generally believed to be relatively secure.

- Many network switches have provisions for binding a hardware address to a port for enhanced security. If someone unplugs one machine and plugs in another machine to capture traffic, chances are that the second machine will have a different hardware address. When it detects a device with a different hardware address, the switch can disable the port. Even this solution is no guarantee, however, as some programs enable you to change or mask the hardware address of a network interface. This setup can be inconvenient when you need to swap out a machine for repair.

Install a small kernel and run only the programs you need

security   Linux systems contain a huge number of programs that, although useful, significantly reduce the security of the host. Install the smallest operating system kernel that meets your needs. For servers, install only the needed components and do not install a graphical interface. Fewer packages mean fewer urgent security patches. Users might require additional packages.

- Do not allow NFSv3 or NIS access outside the local network. Otherwise, it is a simple matter for a malicious user to steal the password map. Default NFSv3 security is marginal to non-existent (a common joke is that NFS stands for No File Security or Nightmare File System) so such access should not be allowed outside your network to machines you do not trust. Versions of NFS for Linux that support much better authentication algorithms are available. Use IPSec, NFSv4 (which includes improved authentication), or firewalls to provide access outside of the local domain. Kerberos, when combined with NFSv4 or NFSv3 provides very good security, but configuring Kerberos requires a book unto itself.

- Support for VPN configuration is often built into new firewalls or provided as a separate product, enabling your system to join securely with the systems of your customers or partners. If you must allow business partners, contractors, or other outside parties to access local files, consider using a secure filesystem, such as NFS with *Kerberos* (page 1172), secure NFS (encrypts authentication, not traffic), NFS over a VPN such as IPSec, or **cfs** (cryptographic filesystem).

- Specify **/usr** as readonly (**ro**) in **/etc/fstab**. Following is an example of such a configuration:

```
/dev/sda6      /usr      ext2      ro     0    0
```

This approach is not suitable for all operating systems, or even all Linux distributions. Some applications put changeable files in **/usr**. Also, this setup entrenches security flaws and makes the system difficult to update.

- Mount filesystems other than **/** and **/usr nosuid** to prevent setuid programs from executing on this filesystem. For example:

```
/dev/sda4       /var        ext4    nosuid  0   0
/dev/sda5       /usr/local  ext4    nosuid  0   0
```

- Use a barrier or firewall product between the local network and the Internet. Several valuable mailing lists cover firewalls, including the free firewalls Web site (www.freefire.org). Fedora/RHEL includes system-config-firewall (page 893) and iptables (page 895), which allow you to set up a firewall.

- Use a program that checks file integrity. Some examples are tripwire, samhain, and AIDE. These tools include a database of checksums of files you want to monitor and alert you when any of the monitored files change.

HOST SECURITY

Your host must be secure. Simple security steps include preventing remote logins and leaving the **/etc/hosts.equiv** and individual users' **~/.rhosts** files empty (or not having them at all). Complex security steps include installing IPSec for VPNs between hosts. Many other security measures, some of which are discussed in this section, fall somewhere between these extremes. See Table C-1 on page 1140 for relevant URLs.

- Although potentially tricky to implement and manage, intrusion detection systems (IDSs) are an excellent way to keep an eye on the integrity of a device. An IDS can warn of possible attempts to subvert security on the host on which it runs. The great-granddaddy of intrusion detection systems is tripwire. This host-based system checks modification times and integrity of files by using strong algorithms (cryptographic checksums or signatures) that can detect even the most minor modifications. A commercial version of tripwire is also available. Another commercial IDS is DragonSquire. Other free, popular, and flexible IDSs include samhain and AIDE. The last two IDSs offer even more features and means of remaining invisible to users than tripwire does. Commercial IDSs that are popular in enterprise environments include Cisco Secure IDS (formerly NetRanger), Enterasys Dragon, and ISS RealSecure.

- Keep Fedora systems up-to-date by downloading and installing the latest updates. Use yum to update the system regularly (page 534) or allow the system to update itself every night automatically.

- Red Hat Network (RHN, page 554) can automatically or semiautomatically keep one or more systems up-to-date, preventing the system from becoming prey to fixed security bugs.

- Complementing host-based IDSs are network-based IDSs. The latter programs monitor the network and nodes on the network and report suspicious occurrences (attack signatures) via user-defined alerts. These signatures can be matched based on known worms, overflow attacks against programs, or unauthorized scans of network ports. Such programs as snort, klaxon, and NFR are used in this capacity. Commercial programs, such as DragonSentry, also fill this role.

- Provided with Fedora/RHEL is PAM, which allows you to set up different methods and levels of authentication in many ways (page 463).

- Process accounting—a good supplement to system security—can provide a continuous record of user actions on your system. See the accton man page (part of the acct package) for more information.

- Emerging standards for things such as Role-Based Access Control (RBAC) allow tighter delegation of privileges along defined organizational boundaries. You can delegate roles to each user as appropriate to the access required.

- General mailing lists and archives are useful repositories of security information, statistics, and papers. The most useful are the bugtraq mailing list and CERT.[7] The bugtraq site and email service offer immediate notifications about specific vulnerabilities, whereas CERT provides notice of widespread vulnerabilities and useful techniques to fix them, plus links to vendor patches.

- The syslog facility can direct messages from system daemons to specific files such as those in /var/log. On larger groups of systems, you can send all important syslog information to a secure host, where that host's only function is to store syslog data so it cannot be tampered with. See page 397 and the syslogd man page for more information.

LOGIN SECURITY

Without a secure host, good login security cannot add much protection. Table C-1 on page 1140 lists some of the best login security tools, including replacement daemons for **telnetd**, **rlogind**, and **rshd**. Many sites use ssh, which comes as both freeware and a commercially supported package that works on UNIX/Linux, Windows, and Macintosh platforms.

---

7. CERT is slow but useful as a medium for coordination between sites. It acts as a tracking agency to document the spread of security problems.

The PAM facility (page 463) allows you to set up multiple authentication methods for users in series or in parallel. In-series PAM requires multiple methods of authentication for a user. In-parallel PAM uses any one of a number of methods for authentication.

Although not the most popular choice, you can configure a system to take advantage of one-time passwords. S/Key is the original implementation of one-time passwords by Bellcore. OPIE (one-time passwords in everything), which was developed by the U.S. Naval Research Labs, is an improvement over the original Bellcore system. In one permutation of one-time passwords, the user gets a piece of paper listing a set of one-time passwords. Each time a user logs in, she enters a password from the piece of paper. Once used, a password becomes obsolete, and the next password in the list is the only one that will work. Even if a malicious user compromises the network and sees your password, this information will be of no use because the password can be used only once. This setup makes it very difficult for someone to log in as you but does nothing to protect the data you type at the keyboard. One-time passwords is a good solution if you are at a site where no encrypted login is available. A truly secure (or paranoid) site will combine one-time passwords and encrypted logins.

Another type of secure login that is becoming more common is facilitated by a token or a *smartcard*. Smartcards are credit-card-like devices that use a challenge–response method of authentication. Smartcard and token authentication rely on something you have (the card) and something you know (a pass phrase, user ID, or PIN). For example, you might enter your username in response to the login prompt and get a password prompt. You would then enter your PIN and the number displayed on the access token. The token has a unique serial number that is stored in a database on the authentication server. The token and the authentication server use this serial number as a means of computing a challenge every 30 to 60 seconds. If the PIN and token number you enter match what they should be as computed by the access server, you are granted access to the system.

REMOTE ACCESS SECURITY

Issues and solutions surrounding remote access security overlap with those pertaining to login and host security. Local logins might be secure with simply a username and password, whereas remote logins (and all remote access) should be made more secure. Many break-ins can be traced back to reusable passwords. It is a good idea to use an encrypted authentication client, such as ssh or kerberos. You can also use smartcards for remote access authentication.

Modem pools can also be an entry point into a system. Most people are aware of how easy it is to monitor a network line, but they might take for granted the security of the public switched telephone network (PSTN, also known as POTS—plain old telephone service). You might want to set up an encrypted channel after dialing in to a modem pool. One way to do so is by running ssh over PPP.

There are ways to implement stringent modem authentication policies so unauthorized users cannot use local modems. The most common techniques are PAP (Password Authentication Protocol), CHAP (Challenge Handshake Authentication Protocol), and Radius. PAP and CHAP are relatively weak as compared to Radius, so the latter has rapidly gained in popularity. Cisco also provides a method of authentication called TACACS/TACACS+ (Terminal Access Controller Access Control System).

One or more of these authentication techniques are available in a RAS (remote access server—in a network, a computer that provides network access to remote users via modem).

Two other techniques for remote access security can be built into a modem (or RAS if it has integrated modems). One is callback: After you dial in, you get a password prompt. Once you type your password, the modem hangs up and calls you back at a phone number it has stored internally. Unfortunately this technique is not foolproof. Some modems have a built-in callback table that holds about ten entries, so this strategy works for small sites with only a few modems. If you use more modems, the RAS software must provide the callback.

The second technique is to use CLID (caller line ID) or ANI (automatic number identification) to decide whether to answer the call. Depending on your wiring and the local phone company, you might not be able to use ANI. ANI information is provided before the call, whereas CLID information is provided in tandem with the call.

VIRUSES AND WORMS

Viruses spread through systems by infecting executable files. Examples of UNIX/Linux viruses include the Bliss virus/worm released in 1997 and the RST.b virus discovered in December 2001. Both are discussed in detail in articles on the Web. In the cases of Bliss and RST.b, the Linux native executable format, ELF, was used as a propagation vector.

Just after 5 PM on November 2, 1988, Robert T. Morris, Jr., a graduate student at Cornell University, released the first big virus onto the Internet. Called an Internet worm, this virus was designed to propagate copies of itself over many machines on the Internet. The worm was a piece of code that exploited four vulnerabilities, including one in finger, to force a buffer to overflow on a system. Once the buffer overflowed, the code was able to get a shell and then recompile itself on the remote machine. The worm spread around the Internet very quickly and was not disabled, despite many people's efforts, for 36 hours.

The chief characteristic of any worm is propagation over a public network, such as the Internet. A virus propagates by infecting executables on the machine, whereas a worm tends to prefer exploiting known security holes in network servers to gain **root** access and then tries to infect other machines in the same way.

UNIX/Linux file permissions help to inoculate systems against many viruses. Windows NT is resistant for similar reasons. You can easily protect the local system against many viruses and worms by keeping its system patches up-to-date, not executing untrusted binaries from the Internet, limiting **PATH** (page 308) to include only necessary system directories, and doing as little as possible while working with **root** privileges. You can prevent a disaster in case a virus strikes by frequently backing up the local system.

PHYSICAL SECURITY

Often overlooked as a defense against intrusion, physical security covers access to the computer itself and to the console or terminal attached to the machine. If the machine is unprotected in an unlocked room, there is very little hope for physical security. (A simple example of physical vulnerability is someone walking into the room where the computer is, removing the hard drive from the computer, taking it home, and analyzing it.) You can take certain steps to improve the physical security of a computer.

- Keep servers in a locked room with limited access. A key, a combination, or a swipe card should be required to gain access. Protect windows as well as doors. Maintain a single point of entry. (Safety codes might require multiple exits, but only one must be an entry.)

- For public machines, use a security system, such as a fiberoptic security system, that can secure a lab full of machines. With such a system, you run a fiberoptic cable through each machine such that the machine cannot be removed (or opened) without cutting the cable. When the cable is cut, an alarm goes off. Some machines—for example, PCs with plastic cases—are much more difficult to secure than others. Although it is not a perfect solution, a fiberoptic security system might improve local security enough to persuade a would-be thief to go somewhere else.

- Most modern PCs have a BIOS password. You can set the order in which a PC searches for a boot device, preventing the PC from being booted from a floppy disk or CD/DVD. Some BIOSs can prevent the machine from booting altogether without a proper password. The password protects the BIOS from unauthorized modification. Beware, however: Many BIOSs have well-known *back doors* (page 1152). In addition, you can blank the BIOS password by setting the clear-CMOS jumper on a PC motherboard; if you are relying on a BIOS password, lock the case.

- Run only fiberoptic cable between buildings. This strategy is not only more secure but also safer in the event of lightning strikes and is required by many commercial building codes.

- Maintain logs of who goes in and out of secure areas. Sign-in/out sheets are useful only if everyone uses them. Sometimes a guard is warranted. Often a simple proximity badge or smartcard can tell when anyone has entered or left an area and keep logs of these events.

- Anyone who has access to the physical hardware has the keys to the palace. Someone with direct access to a computer system can do such things as swap components and insert boot media, all of which are security threats.

- Avoid having activated, unused network jacks in public places. Such jacks provide unnecessary risk.

- Many modern switches can lock a particular switch port so it accepts only traffic from an NIC (network interface card) with a particular hardware address and shuts down the port if another address is seen. However, commonly available programs can enable someone to reset this address.

- Make periodic security sweeps. Check doors for proper locking. If you must have windows, make sure they are locked or are permanently sealed.

- Waste receptacles are often a source of information for intruders. Have policies for containment and disposal of sensitive documents.

- Use a UPS (uninterruptable power supply). Without a clean source of power, your system is vulnerable to corruption.

SECURITY RESOURCES

Many free and commercial programs can enhance system security. Some of these are listed in Table C-1. Many of these sites have links to other, interesting sites that are worth looking at.

Table C-1   Security resources

Tool	What it does	Where to get it
AIDE	Advanced Intrusion Detection Environment. Similar to tripwire with extensible verification algorithms.	sourceforge.net/projects/aide
bugtraq	A moderated mailing list for the announcement and detailed discussion of all aspects of computer security vulnerabilities.	www.securityfocus.com/archive/1
CERT	Computer Emergency Response Team. A repository of papers and data about major security events and a list of security tools.	www.cert.org
chkrootkit	Checks for signs of a rootkit indicating that the machine has been compromised.	www.chkrootkit.org
dsniff	Sniffing and network audit tool suite. Free.	monkey.org/~dugsong/dsniff

Table C-1 Security resources (continued)

Tool	What it does	Where to get it
freefire	Supplies free security solutions and supports developers of free security solutions.	www.freefire.org
fwtk	Firewall toolkit. A set of proxies that can be used to construct a firewall.	www.fwtk.org
GIAC	A security certification and training Web site.	www.giac.org
hping	Multipurpose network auditing and packet analysis tool.	www.hping.org
ISC^2	Educates and certifies industry professionals and practitioners under an international standard.	www.isc2.org
John	John the Ripper: a fast, flexible, weak password detector.	www.openwall.com/john
Kerberos	Complete, secure network authentication system.	web.mit.edu/kerberos/www
LIDS	Intrusion detection and active defense system.	www.lids.org
LinuxSecurity.com	A solid news site dedicated to Linux security issues.	www.linuxsecurity.com
LWN.net	Security alert database for all major Linux distributions.	lwn.net/Alerts
Microsoft Security	Microsoft security information.	www.microsoft.com/security
nessus	A plugin-based remote security scanner that can perform more than 370 security checks. Free.	www.nessus.org
netcat	Explores, tests, and diagnoses networks.	freshmeat.net/projects/netcat
nmap	Scans hosts to see which ports are available. It can perform stealth scans, determine operating system type, find open ports, and more.	nmap.org
RBAC	Role-Based Access Control. Assigns roles and privileges associated with the roles.	csrc.nist.gov/groups/SNS/rbac

Table C-1   Security resources (continued)

Tool	What it does	Where to get it
Red Hat Security	Red Hat security information.	www.redhat.com/security
Rootkit Hunter (RKH)	Checks system for rootkits and other unwanted tools.	rkhunter.sourceforge.net
SAINT	Security Administrator's Integrated Network Tool. Assesses and analyzes network vulnerabilities. This tool follows satan.	www.saintcorporation.com
samhain	A file integrity checker. Has a GUI configurator, client/server capability, and real-time reporting capability.	www.la-samhna.de
SANS	Security training and certification.	www.sans.org
SARA	The Security Auditor's Research Assistant security analysis tool.	www-arc.com/sara
Schneier, Bruce	Security visionary.	www.schneier.com
Secunia	Monitors a broad spectrum of vulnerabilities.	secunia.com
SecurityFocus	Home for security tools, mail lists, libraries, and cogent analysis.	www.securityfocus.com
snort	A flexible IDS.	www.snort.org
ssh	A secure rsh, ftp, and rlogin replacement with encrypted sessions and other options. Supplied with Fedora/RHEL.	openssh.org
swatch	A Perl-based log parser and analyzer.	sourceforge.net/projects/swatch
Treachery	A collection of tools for security and auditing.	www.treachery.net/tools
tripwire	Checks for possible signs of intruder activity. Supplied with Fedora/RHEL.	www.tripwire.com
wireshark	Network protocol analyzer. Free.	www.wireshark.org

APPENDIX SUMMARY

Security is inversely proportional to usability. There must be a balance between users' requirements to get their work done and the amount of security that is implemented. It is often unnecessary to provide top security for a small business with only a few employees. By contrast, if you work for a government military contractor, you are bound to have extreme security constraints and an official audit policy to determine whether security policies are being implemented correctly.

Review your own security requirements periodically. Several of the tools mentioned in this appendix can help you monitor a system's security measures. Tools such as nessus, samhain, and SAINT, for example, provide auditing mechanisms.

Some companies specialize in security and auditing. Hiring one of them to examine your site can be costly but might yield specific recommendations for areas you might have overlooked in your initial setup. When you hire someone to audit your security, recognize you might be providing both physical and **root** access to local systems. Make sure the company that you hire has a good history, has been in business for several years, and has impeccable references. Check up on the company periodically: Things change over time. Avoid the temptation to hire former system crackers as consultants. Security consultants should have an irreproachable ethical background or you will always have doubts about their intentions.

Your total security package is based on your risk assessment of local vulnerabilities. Strengthen those areas that are most important for your business. For example, many sites rely on a firewall to protect them from the Internet, whereas internal hosts might receive little or no security attention. Crackers refer to this setup as "the crunchy outside surrounding the soft chewy middle." Yet this setup is entirely sufficient to protect some sites. Perform your own risk assessment and address your needs accordingly. If need be, hire a full-time security administrator whose job it is to design and audit local security policies.

D

THE FREE SOFTWARE DEFINITION[1]

We maintain this free software definition to show clearly what must be true about a particular software program for it to be considered free software.

"Free software" is a matter of liberty, not price. To understand the concept, you should think of "free" as in "free speech," not as in "free beer."

Free software is a matter of the users' freedom to run, copy, distribute, study, change and improve the software. More precisely, it refers to four kinds of freedom, for the users of the software:

- The freedom to run the program, for any purpose (freedom 0).

---

1. This material is at www.gnu.org/philosophy/free-sw.html on the GNU Web site. Because GNU requests a verbatim copy, links remain in place (underlined). View the document on the Web to ensure you are reading the latest copy and to follow the links.

- The freedom to study how the program works, and adapt it to your needs (freedom 1). Access to the source code is a precondition for this.

- The freedom to redistribute copies so you can help your neighbor (freedom 2).

- The freedom to improve the program, and release your improvements to the public, so that the whole community benefits (freedom 3). Access to the source code is a precondition for this.

A program is free software if users have all of these freedoms. Thus, you should be free to redistribute copies, either with or without modifications, either gratis or charging a fee for distribution, to <u>anyone anywhere</u>. Being free to do these things means (among other things) that you do not have to ask or pay for permission.

You should also have the freedom to make modifications and use them privately in your own work or play, without even mentioning that they exist. If you do publish your changes, you should not be required to notify anyone in particular, or in any particular way.

The freedom to use a program means the freedom for any kind of person or organization to use it on any kind of computer system, for any kind of overall job, and without being required to communicate subsequently with the developer or any other specific entity.

The freedom to redistribute copies must include binary or executable forms of the program, as well as source code, for both modified and unmodified versions. (Distributing programs in runnable form is necessary for conveniently installable free operating systems.) It is ok if there is no way to produce a binary or executable form for a certain program (since some languages don't support that feature), but you must have the freedom to redistribute such forms should you find or develop a way to make them.

In order for the freedoms to make changes, and to publish improved versions, to be meaningful, you must have access to the source code of the program. Therefore, accessibility of source code is a necessary condition for free software.

One important way to modify a program is by merging in available free subroutines and modules. If the program's license says that you cannot merge in an existing module, such as if it requires you to be the copyright holder of any code you add, then the license is too restrictive to qualify as free.

In order for these freedoms to be real, they must be irrevocable as long as you do nothing wrong; if the developer of the software has the power to revoke the license, without your doing anything to give cause, the software is not free.

However, certain kinds of rules about the manner of distributing free software are acceptable, when they don't conflict with the central freedoms. For example, copyleft (very simply stated) is the rule that when redistributing the program, you cannot add restrictions to deny other people the central freedoms. This rule does not conflict with the central freedoms; rather it protects them.

You may have paid money to get copies of free software, or you may have obtained copies at no charge. But regardless of how you got your copies, you always have the freedom to copy and change the software, even to <u>sell copies</u>.

"Free software" does not mean "non-commercial". A free program must be available for commercial use, commercial development, and commercial distribution. Commercial development of free software is no longer unusual; such free commercial software is very important.

Rules about how to package a modified version are acceptable, if they don't substantively block your freedom to release modified versions, or your freedom to make and use modified versions privately. Rules that "if you make your version available in this way, you must make it available in that way also" can be acceptable too, on the same condition. (Note that such a rule still leaves you the choice of whether to publish your version at all.) Rules that require release of source code to the users for versions that you put into public use are also acceptable. It is also acceptable for the license to require that, if you have distributed a modified version and a previous developer asks for a copy of it, you must send one, or that you identify yourself on your modifications.

In the GNU project, we use "<u>copyleft</u>" to protect these freedoms legally for everyone. But <u>non-copylefted free software</u> also exists. We believe there are important reasons why <u>it is better to use copyleft</u>, but if your program is non-copylefted free software, we can still use it.

See <u>Categories of Free Software</u> for a description of how "free software," "copylefted software" and other categories of software relate to each other.

Sometimes government <u>export control regulations</u> and trade sanctions can constrain your freedom to distribute copies of programs internationally. Software developers do not have the power to eliminate or override these restrictions, but what they can and must do is refuse to impose them as conditions of use of the program. In this way, the restrictions will not affect activities and people outside the jurisdictions of these governments.

Most free software licenses are based on copyright, and there are limits on what kinds of requirements can be imposed through copyright. If a copyright-based license respects freedom in the ways described above, it is unlikely to have some other sort of problem that we never anticipated (though this does happen occasionally). However, some free software licenses are based on contracts, and contracts can impose a much larger range of possible restrictions. That means there are many possible ways such a license could be unacceptably restrictive and non-free.

We can't possibly list all the ways that might happen. If a contract-based license restricts the user in an unusual way that copyright-based licenses cannot, and which isn't mentioned here as legitimate, we will have to think about it, and we will probably conclude it is non-free.

When talking about free software, it is best to avoid using terms like "give away" or "for free", because those terms imply that the issue is about price, not freedom. Some common terms such as "piracy" embody opinions we hope you won't endorse. See <u>Confusing Words and Phrases that are Worth Avoiding</u> for a discussion of these terms. We also have a list of <u>translations of "free software"</u> into various languages.

Finally, note that criteria such as those stated in this free software definition require careful thought for their interpretation. To decide whether a specific software license qualifies as a free software license, we judge it based on these criteria to determine whether it fits their spirit as well as the precise words. If a license includes unconscionable restrictions, we reject it, even if we did not anticipate the issue in these criteria. Sometimes a license requirement raises an issue that calls for extensive thought, including discussions with a lawyer, before we can decide if the requirement is acceptable. When we reach a conclusion about a new issue, we often update these criteria to make it easier to see why certain licenses do or don't qualify.

If you are interested in whether a specific license qualifies as a free software license, see our list of licenses. If the license you are concerned with is not listed there, you can ask us about it by sending us email at licensing@gnu.org.

If you are contemplating writing a new license, please contact the FSF by writing to that address. The proliferation of different free software licenses means increased work for users in understanding the licenses; we may be able to help you find an existing Free Software license that meets your needs.

If that isn't possible, if you really need a new license, with our help you can ensure that the license really is a Free Software license and avoid various practical problems.

Another group has started using the term "open source" to mean something close (but not identical) to "free software". We prefer the term "free software" because, once you have heard it refers to freedom rather than price, it calls to mind freedom. The word "open" never does that.

Other Texts to Read

Translations of this page:

[Català | Chinese (Simplified) | Chinese (Traditional) | Czech | Dansk | Deutsch | English | Español | Persian/Farsi | Français | Galego | Hebrew | Hrvatski | Bahasa Indonesia | Italiano | Japanese | Korean | Magyar | Nederlands | Norsk | Polski | Português | Romāna | Russian | Slovinsko | Serbian | Tagalog | Türkçe]

Return to the GNU Project home page.

Please send FSF & GNU inquiries to gnu@gnu.org. There are also other ways to contact the FSF.

Please send broken links and other corrections (or suggestions) to webmasters@gnu.org

Please see the Translations README for information on coordinating and submitting translations of this article.

- Updated: $Date: 2005/11/26 13:16:40 $ $Author: rms $

GLOSSARY

All entries marked with ᶠᵒˡᵈᵒᶜ are based on definitions in the Free On-Line Dictionary of Computing (foldoc.org), Denis Howe, editor. Used with permission.

10.0.0.0	See *private address space* on page 1182.
172.16.0.0	See *private address space* on page 1182.
192.168.0.0	See *private address space* on page 1182.
802.11	A family of specifications developed by IEEE for wireless LAN technology, including 802.11 (1–2 megabits per second), 802.11a (54 megabits per second), 802.11b (11 megabits per second), and 802.11g (54 megabits per second).
absolute pathname	A pathname that starts with the root directory (represented by /). An absolute pathname locates a file without regard to the working directory.
access	In computer jargon, a verb meaning to use, read from, or write to. To access a file means to read from or write to the file.
Access Control List	See *ACL*.
access permissions	Permission to read from, write to, or execute a file. If you have write access permission to a file (usually just called *write permission*), you can write to the file. Also *access privilege*.
ACL	Access Control List. A system that performs a function similar to file permissions but with much finer-grain control.
active window	On a desktop, the window that receives the characters you type on the keyboard. Same as *focus, desktop* (page 1165).
address mask	See *network mask* on page 1178.
alias	A mechanism of a shell that enables you to define new commands.
alphanumeric character	One of the characters, either uppercase or lowercase, from A to Z and 0 to 9, inclusive.
ambiguous file reference	A reference to a file that does not necessarily specify any one file but can be used to specify a group of files. The shell expands an ambiguous file reference into a list of filenames. Special characters represent single characters (?), strings of zero or more characters (*), and character classes ([]) within ambiguous file references. An ambiguous file reference is a type of *regular expression* (page 1185).
angle bracket	A left angle bracket (<) and a right angle bracket (>). The shell uses < to redirect a command's standard input to come from a file and > to redirect the standard output. The shell uses the characters << to signify the start of a Here document and >> to append output to a file.
animate	When referring to a window action, means that the action is slowed down so the user can view it. For example, when you minimize a window, it can disappear all at once (not animated) or it can slowly telescope into the panel so you can get a visual feel for what is happening (animated).

anti-aliasing   Adding gray pixels at the edge of a diagonal line to get rid of the jagged appearance and thereby make the line look smoother. Anti-aliasing sometimes makes type on a screen look better and sometimes worse; it works best on small and large fonts and is less effective on fonts from 8 to 15 points. See also *subpixel hinting* (page 1191).

API   Application program interface. The interface (calling conventions) by which an application program accesses an operating system and other services. An API is defined at the source code level and provides a level of abstraction between the application and the kernel (or other privileged utilities) to ensure the portability of the code.FOLDOC

append   To add something to the end of something else. To append text to a file means to add the text to the end of the file. The shell uses >> to append a command's output to a file.

applet   A small program that runs within a larger program. Examples are Java applets that run in a browser and panel applets that run from a desktop panel.

archive   A file that contains a group of smaller, typically related, files. Also, to create such a file. The tar and cpio utilities can create and read archives.

argument   A number, letter, filename, or another string that gives some information to a command and is passed to the command when it is called. A command-line argument is anything on a command line following the command name that is passed to the command. An option is a kind of argument.

arithmetic expression   A group of numbers, operators, and parentheses that can be evaluated. When you evaluate an arithmetic expression, you end up with a number. The Bourne Again Shell uses the expr command to evaluate arithmetic expressions; the TC Shell uses @, and the Z Shell uses let.

ARP   Address Resolution Protocol. A method for finding a host's *MAC address* (page 1174; also Ethernet address) from its IP address. ARP allows the IP address to be independent of the MAC address. See page 377 for more information.FOLDOC

array   An arrangement of elements (numbers or strings of characters) in one or more dimensions. The Bourne Again, TC, and Z Shells and awk/mawk/gawk can store and process arrays.

ASCII   American Standard Code for Information Interchange. A code that uses seven bits to represent both graphic (letters, numbers, and punctuation) and CONTROL characters. You can represent textual information, including program source code and English text, in ASCII code. Because ASCII is a standard, it is frequently used when exchanging information between computers. See the file **/usr/pub/ascii** or give the command **man ascii** to see a list of ASCII codes.

Extensions of the ASCII character set use eight bits. The seven-bit set is common; the eight-bit extensions are still coming into popular use. The eighth bit is sometimes referred to as the *metabit*.

ASCII terminal   A textual terminal. Contrast with *graphical display* (page 1166).

ASP   Application service provider. A company that provides applications over the Internet.

asynchronous event   An event that does not occur regularly or synchronously with another event. Linux system signals are asynchronous; they can occur at any time because they can be initiated by any number of nonregular events.

attachment   A file that is attached to, but is not part of, a piece of email. Attachments are frequently opened by programs (including your Internet browser) that are called by your mail program so you might not be aware that they are not an integral part of an email message.

authentication   The verification of the identity of a person or process. In a communication system, authentication verifies that a message really comes from its stated source, like the signature on a (paper) letter. The most common form of authentication is typing a user name (which might be widely known or easily guessable) and a corresponding password that is presumed to be known only to the individual being authenticated. Other methods of authentication on a Linux system include the **/etc/passwd** and **/etc/shadow** files, LDAP, biometrics, Kerberos 5, and SMB.ᶠᴼᴸᴰᴼᶜ

automatic mounting   A way of demand mounting directories from remote hosts without having them hard configured into **/etc/fstab**. Also called *automounting*.

avoided   An object, such as a panel, that should not normally be covered by another object, such as a window.

back door   A security hole deliberately left in place by the designers or maintainers of a system. The motivation for creating such holes is not always sinister; some operating systems, for example, come out of the box with privileged accounts intended for use by field service technicians or the vendor's maintenance programmers.

Ken Thompson's 1983 Turing Award lecture to the ACM revealed the existence, in early UNIX versions, of a back door that might be the most fiendishly clever security hack of all time. The C compiler contained code that would recognize when the **login** command was being recompiled and would insert some code recognizing a password chosen by Thompson, giving him entry to the system whether or not an account had been created for him.

Normally such a back door could be removed by removing it from the source code for the compiler and recompiling the compiler. But to recompile the compiler, you have to *use* the compiler, so Thompson arranged that the compiler would *recognize when it was compiling a version of itself*. It would insert into the recompiled compiler the code to insert into the recompiled **login** the code to allow Thompson entry, and, of course, the code to recognize itself and do the whole thing again the next time around. Having done this once, he was then able to recompile the compiler from the original sources; the hack perpetuated itself invisibly, leaving the back door in place and active but with no trace in the sources.

Sometimes called a wormhole. Also *trap door*.ᶠᴼᴸᴰᴼᶜ

background process	A process that is not run in the foreground. Also called a *detached process,* a background process is initiated by a command line that ends with an ampersand (&). You do not have to wait for a background process to run to completion before giving the shell additional commands. If you have job control, you can move background processes to the foreground, and vice versa.
basename	The name of a file that, in contrast with a pathname, does not mention any of the directories containing the file (and therefore does not contain any slashes [/]). For example, **hosts** is the basename of **/etc/hosts.**FOLDOC
baud	The maximum information-carrying capacity of a communication channel in symbols (state transitions or level transitions) per second. It coincides with bits per second only for two-level modulation with no framing or stop bits. A symbol is a unique state of the communication channel, distinguishable by the receiver from all other possible states. For example, it might be one of two voltage levels on a wire for a direct digital connection, or it might be the phase or frequency of a carrier.FOLDOC Baud is often mistakenly used as a synonym for bits per second.
baud rate	Transmission speed. Usually used to measure terminal or modem speed. Common baud rates range from 110 to 38,400 baud. See *baud.*
Berkeley UNIX	One of the two major versions of the UNIX operating system. Berkeley UNIX was developed at the University of California at Berkeley by the Computer Systems Research Group and is often referred to as *BSD* (Berkeley Software Distribution).
BIND	Berkeley Internet Name Domain. An implementation of a *DNS* (page 1162) server developed and distributed by the University of California at Berkeley.
BIOS	Basic Input/Output System. On PCs, *EEPROM*-based (page 1163) system software that provides the lowest-level interface to peripheral devices and controls the first stage of the *bootstrap* (page 1154) process, which loads the operating system. The BIOS can be stored in different types of memory. The memory must be nonvolatile so that it remembers the system settings even when the system is turned off. Also BIOS ROM.
bit	The smallest piece of information a computer can handle. A *bit* is a binary digit: either 1 or 0 (*on* or *off*).
bit depth	Same as *color depth* (page 1157).
bit-mapped display	A graphical display device in which each pixel on the screen is controlled by an underlying representation of zeros and ones.
blank character	Either a SPACE or a TAB character, also called *whitespace* (page 1196). In some contexts, NEWLINEs are considered blank characters.
block	A section of a disk or tape (usually 1,024 bytes long but shorter or longer on some systems) that is written at one time.

block device   A disk or tape drive. A block device stores information in blocks of characters and is represented by a block device (block special) file. Contrast with *character device* (page 1156).

block number   Disk and tape *blocks* are numbered so that Linux can keep track of the data on the device.

blocking factor   The number of logical blocks that make up a physical block on a tape or disk. When you write 1K logical blocks to a tape with a physical block size of 30K, the blocking factor is 30.

Boolean   The type of an expression with two possible values: *true* and *false*. Also, a variable of Boolean type or a function with Boolean arguments or result. The most common Boolean functions are AND, OR, and NOT._{FOLDOC}

boot   See *bootstrap*.

boot loader   A very small program that takes its place in the *bootstrap* process that brings a computer from off or reset to a fully functional state. See "GRUB: The Linux Boot Loader" on page 595.

bootstrap   Derived from "Pull oneself up by one's own bootstraps," the incremental process of loading an operating system kernel into memory and starting it running without any outside assistance. Frequently shortened to *boot*.

Bourne Again Shell   bash. GNU's command interpreter for UNIX, bash is a POSIX-compliant shell with full Bourne Shell syntax and some C Shell commands built in. The Bourne Again Shell supports emacs-style command-line editing, job control, functions, and online help._{FOLDOC}

Bourne Shell   sh. This UNIX command processor was developed by Steve Bourne at AT&T Bell Laboratories.

brace   A left brace ({) and a right brace (}). Braces have special meanings to the shell.

bracket   A *square bracket* (page 1190) or an *angle bracket* (page 1150).

branch   In a tree structure, a branch connects nodes, leaves, and the root. The Linux filesystem hierarchy is often conceptualized as an upside-down tree. The branches connect files and directories. In a source code control system, such as SCCS or RCS, a branch occurs when a revision is made to a file and is not included in subsequent revisions to the file.

bridge   Typically a two-port device originally used for extending networks at layer 2 (data link) of the Internet Protocol model.

broadcast   A transmission to multiple, unspecified recipients. On Ethernet, a broadcast packet is a special type of *multicast* (page 1177) packet; it has a special address indicating that all devices that receive it should process it. Broadcast traffic exists at several layers of the network stack, including Ethernet and IP. Broadcast traffic has one source but indeterminate destinations (all hosts on the local network).

broadcast address	The last address on a subnet (usually 255), reserved as shorthand to mean all hosts.
broadcast network	A type of network, such as Ethernet, in which any system can transmit information at any time, and all systems receive every message.
BSD	See *Berkeley UNIX* on page 1153.
buffer	An area of memory that stores data until it can be used. When you write information to a file on a disk, Linux stores the information in a disk buffer until there is enough to write to the disk or until the disk is ready to receive the information.
bug	An unwanted and unintended program property, especially one that causes the program to malfunction.FOLDOC
builtin (command)	A command that is built into a shell. Each of the three major shells—the Bourne Again, TC, and Z Shells—has its own set of builtins.
byte	A component in the machine data hierarchy, usually larger than a bit and smaller than a word; now most often eight bits and the smallest addressable unit of storage. A byte typically holds one character.FOLDOC
C programming language	A modern systems language that has high-level features for efficient, modular programming as well as lower-level features that make it suitable for use as a systems programming language. It is machine independent so that carefully written C programs can be easily transported to run on different machines. Most of the Linux operating system is written in C, and Linux provides an ideal environment for programming in C.
C Shell	csh. The C Shell command processor was developed by Bill Joy for BSD UNIX. It was named for the C programming language because its programming constructs are similar to those of C. See *shell* on page 1188.
cable modem	A type of modem that allows you to access the Internet by using your cable television connection.
cache	Holding recently accessed data, a small, fast memory designed to speed up subsequent access to the same data. Most often applied to processor-memory access but also used for a local copy of data accessible over a network, from a hard disk, and so on.FOLDOC
calling environment	A list of variables and their values that is made available to a called program. Refer to "Executing a Command" on page 318.
cascading stylesheet	See *CSS* on page 1159.
cascading windows	An arrangement of windows such that they overlap, generally with at least part of the title bar visible. Opposite of *tiled windows* (page 1193).
case sensitive	Able to distinguish between uppercase and lowercase characters. Unless you set the **ignorecase** parameter, vim performs case-sensitive searches. The grep utility performs case-sensitive searches unless you use the –i option.

catenate
: To join sequentially, or end to end. The Linux cat utility catenates files: It displays them one after the other. Also *concatenate*.

chain loading
: The technique used by a boot loader to load unsupported operating systems. Used for loading such operating systems as DOS or Windows, it works by loading another boot loader.

character-based
: A program, utility, or interface that works only with *ASCII* (page 1151) characters. This set of characters includes some simple graphics, such as lines and corners, and can display colored characters. It cannot display true graphics. Contrast with *GUI* (page 1166).

character-based terminal
: A terminal that displays only characters and very limited graphics. See *character-based*.

character class
: In a regular expression, a group of characters that defines which characters can occupy a single character position. A character-class definition is usually surrounded by square brackets. The character class defined by [**abcr**] represents a character position that can be occupied by **a, b, c,** or **r**. Also *list operator*.

In GNU documentation and POSIX, used to refer to sets of characters with a common characteristic, denoted by the notation [:*class*:]; for example, [:upper:] denotes the set of uppercase letters.

This book uses the term character class as explained under "Brackets" on page 1107.

character device
: A terminal, printer, or modem. A character device stores or displays characters one at a time. A character device is represented by a character device (character special) file. Contrast with *block device* (page 1154).

check box
: A GUI widget, usually the outline of a square box with an adjacent caption, that a user can click to display or remove a *tick* (page 1193). When the box holds a tick, the option described by the caption is on or true. Also *tick box*.

checksum
: A computed value that depends on the contents of a block of data and is transmitted or stored along with the data to detect corruption of the data. The receiving system recomputes the checksum based on the received data and compares this value with the one sent with the data. If the two values are the same, the receiver has some confidence that the data was received correctly.

The checksum might be 8, 16, or 32 bits, or some other size. It is computed by summing the bytes or words of the data block, ignoring overflow. The checksum might be negated so that the total of the data words plus the checksum is zero.

Internet packets use a 32-bit checksum.FOLDOC

child process
: A process that is created by another process, the parent process. Every process is a child process except for the first process, which is started when Linux begins execution. When you run a command from the shell, the shell spawns a child process to run the command. See *process* on page 1182.

CIDR	Classless Inter-Domain Routing. A scheme that allocates blocks of Internet addresses in a way that allows summarization into a smaller number of routing table entries. A CIDR block is a block of Internet addresses assigned to an ISP by the Internic. Refer to "CIDR: Classless Inter-Domain Routing" on page 380._{FOLDOC}
CIFS	Common Internet File System. An Internet filesystem protocol based on *SMB* (page 1188). CIFS runs on top of TCP/IP, uses DNS, and is optimized to support slower dial-up Internet connections. SMB and CIFS are used interchangeably._{FOLDOC}
CIPE	Crypto IP *Encapsulation* (page 1163). This *protocol* (page 1183) *tunnels* (page 1194) IP packets within encrypted *UDP* (page 1194) packets, is lightweight and simple, and works over dynamic addresses, *NAT* (page 1177), and *SOCKS* (page 1189) *proxies* (page 1183).
cipher (cypher)	A cryptographic system that uses a key to transpose/substitute characters within a message, the key itself, or the message.
ciphertext	Text that is encrypted. Contrast with *plaintext* (page 1181). See also "Encryption" on page 1126.
Classless Inter-Domain Routing	See *CIDR* on page 1157.
cleartext	Text that is not encrypted. Also *plaintext*. Contrast with *ciphertext*.
CLI	Command-line interface. See also *character-based* (page 1156). Also *textual interface*.
client	A computer or program that requests one or more services from a server.
CODEC	Coder/decoder or compressor/decompressor. A hardware and/or software technology that codes and decodes data. MPEG is a popular CODEC for computer video.
color depth	The number of bits used to generate a pixel—usually 8, 16, 24, or 32. The color depth is directly related to the number of colors that can be generated. The number of colors that can be generated is 2 raised to the color-depth power. Thus a 24-bit video adapter can generate about 16.7 million colors.
color quality	See *color depth*.
combo box	A combination of a *drop-down list* (page 1163) and *text box* (page 1192). You can enter text in a combo box. Or, you can click a combo box, cause it to expand and display a static list of selections for you to choose from.
command	What you give the shell in response to a prompt. When you give the shell a command, it executes a utility, another program, a builtin command, or a shell script. Utilities are often referred to as commands. When you are using an interactive utility, such as vim or mail, you use commands that are appropriate to that utility.
command line	A line containing instructions and arguments that executes a command. This term usually refers to a line you enter in response to a shell prompt on a character-based terminal or terminal emulator.

command substitution Replacing a command with its output. The shells perform command substitution when you enclose a command between $(and) or between a pair of back ticks (` `), also called grave accent marks.

component architecture A notion in object-oriented programming where "components" of a program are completely generic. Instead of having a specialized set of methods and fields, they have generic methods through which the component can advertise the functionality it supports to the system into which it is loaded. This strategy enables completely dynamic loading of objects. JavaBeans is an example of a component architecture.FOLDOC

concatenate See *catenate* on page 1156.

condition code See *exit status* on page 1164.

connection- oriented protocol A type of transport layer data communication service that allows a host to send data in a continuous stream to another host. The transport service guarantees that all data will be delivered to the other end in the same order as sent and without duplication. Communication proceeds through three well-defined phases: connection establishment, data transfer, and connection release. The most common example is *TCP* (page 1192).

Also called connection-based protocol and stream-oriented protocol. Contrast with *connectionless protocol* and *datagram* (page 1160).FOLDOC

connectionless protocol The data communication method in which communication occurs between hosts with no previous setup. Packets sent between two hosts might take different routes. There is no guarantee that packets will arrive as transmitted or even that they will arrive at the destination at all. *UDP* (page 1194) is a connectionless protocol. Also called packet switching. Contrast with circuit switching and *connection-oriented protocol.*FOLDOC

console The main system terminal, usually directly connected to the computer and the one that receives system error messages. Also *system console* and *console terminal*.

console terminal See *console*.

control character A character that is not a graphic character, such as a letter, number, or punctuation mark. Such characters are called control characters because they frequently act to control a peripheral device. RETURN and FORMFEED are control characters that control a terminal or printer.

The word CONTROL is shown in this book in THIS FONT because it is a key that appears on most terminal keyboards. Control characters are represented by ASCII codes less than 32 (decimal). See also *nonprinting character* on page 1179.

control structure	A statement used to change the order of execution of commands in a shell script or other program. Each shell provides control structures (for example, **if** and **while**) as well as other commands that alter the order of execution (for example, **exec**). Also *control flow commands*.
cookie	Data stored on a client system by a server. The client system browser sends the cookie back to the server each time it accesses that server. For example, a catalog shopping service might store a cookie on your system when you place your first order. When you return to the site, it knows who you are and can supply your name and address for subsequent orders. You might consider cookies to be an invasion of privacy.
CPU	Central processing unit. The part of a computer that controls all the other parts. The CPU includes the control unit and the arithmetic and logic unit (ALU). The control unit fetches instructions from memory and decodes them to produce signals that control the other parts of the computer. These signals can cause data to be transferred between memory and ALU or peripherals to perform input or output. A CPU that is housed on a single chip is called a microprocessor. Also *processor* and *central processor*.
cracker	An individual who attempts to gain unauthorized access to a computer system. These individuals are often malicious and have many means at their disposal for breaking into a system. Contrast with *hacker* (page 1167).ᶠᵒˡᴰᴼᶜ
crash	The system suddenly and unexpectedly stops or fails. Derived from the action of the hard disk heads on the surface of the disk when the air gap between the two collapses.
cryptography	The practice and study of encryption and decryption—encoding data so that only a specific individual or machine can decode it. A system for encrypting and decrypting data is a cryptosystem. Such systems usually rely on an algorithm for combining the original data (plaintext) with one or more keys—numbers or strings of characters known only to the sender and/or recipient. The resulting output is called *ciphertext* (page 1157).

The security of a cryptosystem usually depends on the secrecy of keys rather than on the supposed secrecy of an algorithm. Because a strong cryptosystem has a large range of keys, it is not possible to try all of them. Ciphertext appears random to standard statistical tests and resists known methods for breaking codes.ᶠᵒˡᴰᴼᶜ |
| .cshrc file | In your home directory, a file that the TC Shell executes each time you invoke a new TC Shell. You can use this file to establish variables and aliases. |
| CSS | Cascading stylesheet. Describes how documents are presented on screen and in print. Attaching a stylesheet to a structured document can affect the way it looks without adding new HTML (or other) tags and without giving up device independence. Also *stylesheet*. |

current (process, line, character, directory, event, etc.)	The item that is immediately available, working, or being used. The current process is the program you are running, the current line or character is the one the cursor is on, and the current directory is the working directory.
cursor	A small lighted rectangle, underscore, or vertical bar that appears on a terminal screen and indicates where the next character will appear. Differs from the *mouse pointer* (page 1176).
daemon	A program that is not invoked explicitly but lies dormant, waiting for some condition(s) to occur. The perpetrator of the condition need not be aware that a daemon is lurking (although often a program will commit an action only because it knows that it will implicitly invoke a daemon). From the mythological meaning, later rationalized as the acronym Disk And Execution MONitor.FOLDOC
data structure	A particular format for storing, organizing, working with, and retrieving data. Frequently, data structures are designed to work with specific algorithms that facilitate these tasks. Common data structures include trees, files, records, tables, arrays, etc.
datagram	A self-contained, independent entity of data carrying sufficient information to be routed from the source to the destination computer without reliance on earlier exchanges between this source and destination computer and the transporting network. *UDP* (page 1194) uses datagrams; *IP* (page 1170) uses *packets* (page 1180). Packets are indivisible at the network layer; datagrams are not.FOLDOC See also *frame* (page 1165).
dataless	A computer, usually a workstation, that uses a local disk to boot a copy of the operating system and access system files but does not use a local disk to store user files.
dbm	A standard, simple database manager. Implemented as **gdbm** (GNU database manager), it uses hashes to speed searching. The most common versions of the **dbm** database are **dbm**, **ndbm**, and **gdbm**.
DDoS attack	Distributed denial of service attack. A *DoS attack* (page 1162) from many systems that do not belong to the perpetrator of the attack.
debug	To correct a program by removing its bugs (that is, errors).
default	Something that is selected without being explicitly specified. For example, when used without an argument, ls displays a list of the files in the working directory by default.
delta	A set of changes made to a file that has been encoded by the Source Code Control System (SCCS).
denial of service	*See DoS attack* on page 1162.

dereference	To access the thing to which a pointer points, that is, to follow the pointer. At first sight the word *dereference* might be thought to mean "to cause to stop referring," but its meaning is well established in jargon. FOLDOC
	When speaking of symbolic links, dereference means to follow the link rather than working with the reference to the link. For example, the –L or ––**dereference** option causes ls to list the entry that a symbolic link points to rather than the symbolic link (the reference) itself.
desktop	A collection of windows, toolbars, icons, and buttons, some or all of which appear on your display. A desktop comprises one or more *workspaces* (page 1197).
desktop manager	An icon- and menu-based user interface to system services that allows you to run applications and use the filesystem without using the system's command-line interface.
detached process	See *background process* on page 1153.
device	A disk drive, printer, terminal, plotter, or other input/output unit that can be attached to the computer. Short for *peripheral device*.
device driver	Part of the Linux kernel that controls a device, such as a terminal, disk drive, or printer.
device file	A file that represents a device. Also *special file*.
device filename	The pathname of a device file. All Linux systems have two kinds of device files: block and character device files. Linux also has FIFOs (named pipes) and sockets. Device files are traditionally located in the **/dev** directory.
device number	See *major device number* (page 1174) and *minor device number* (page 1176).
DHCP	Dynamic Host Configuration Protocol. A protocol that dynamically allocates IP addresses to computers on a LAN. FOLDOC
dialog box	In a GUI, a special window, usually without a titlebar, that displays information. Some dialog boxes accept a response from the user.
directory	Short for *directory file*. A file that contains a list of other files.
directory hierarchy	A directory, called the root of the directory hierarchy, and all the directory and ordinary files below it (its children).
directory service	A structured repository of information on people and resources within an organization, facilitating management and communication. FOLDOC
disk partition	See *partition* on page 1180.
diskless	A computer, usually a workstation, that has no disk and must contact another computer (a server) to boot a copy of the operating system and access the necessary system files.

distributed
computing
A style of computing in which tasks or services are performed by a network of cooperating systems, some of which might be specialized.

DMZ
Demilitarized zone. A host or small network that is a neutral zone between a LAN and the Internet. It can serve Web pages and other data to the Internet and allow local systems access to the Internet while preventing LAN access to unauthorized Internet users. Even if a DMZ is compromised, it holds no data that is private and none that cannot be easily reproduced.

DNS
Domain Name Service. A distributed service that manages the correspondence of full hostnames (those that include a domain name) to IP addresses and other system characteristics.

DNS domain
name
See *domain name*.

document
object model
See *DOM*.

DOM
Document Object Model. A platform-/language-independent interface that enables a program to update the content, structure, and style of a document dynamically. The changes can then be made part of the displayed document. Go to www.w3.org/DOM for more information.

domain name
A name associated with an organization, or part of an organization, to help identify systems uniquely. Technically, the part of the *FQDN* (page 1165) to the right of the leftmost period. Domain names are assigned hierarchically. The domain berkeley.edu refers to the University of California at Berkeley, for example; it is part of the top-level edu (education) domain. Also *DNS domain name*. Different than *NIS domain name* (page 1178).

Domain Name
Service
See *DNS*.

door
An evolving filesystem-based *RPC* (page 1186) mechanism.

DoS attack
Denial of service attack. An attack that attempts to make the target host or network unusable by flooding it with spurious traffic.

DPMS
Display Power Management Signaling. A standard that can extend the life of CRT monitors and conserve energy. DPMS supports four modes for a monitor: Normal, Standby (power supply on, monitor ready to come to display images almost instantly), Suspend (power supply off, monitor takes up to ten seconds to display an image), and Off.

drag
The motion part of *drag-and-drop*.

drag-and-drop
To move an object from one position or application to another within a GUI. To drag an object, the user clicks a mouse button (typically the left one) while the mouse pointer *hovers* (page 1168) over the object. Then, without releasing the

mouse button, the user drags the object, which stays attached to the mouse pointer, to a different location. The user can then drop the object at the new location by releasing the mouse button.

drop-down list A *widget* (page 1197) that displays a static list for a user to choose from. When the list is not active, it appears as text in a box, displaying the single selected entry. When a user clicks the box, a list appears; the user can move the mouse cursor to select an entry from the list. Different from a *list box* (page 1173).

druid In role-playing games, a character that represents a magical user. Fedora/RHEL uses the term *druid* at the ends of names of programs that guide you through a task-driven chain of steps. Other operating systems call these types of programs *wizards*.

DSA Digital Signature Algorithm. A public key cipher used to generate digital signatures.

DSL Digital Subscriber Line/Loop. Provides high-speed digital communication over a specialized, conditioned telephone line. See also *xDSL* (page 1198).

Dynamic Host Configuration Protocol See *DHCP* on page 1161.

editor A utility, such as vim or emacs, that creates and modifies text files.

EEPROM Electrically erasable, programmable, readonly memory. A *PROM* (page 1182) that can be written to.

effective user ID The user ID that a process appears to have; usually the same as the user ID. For example, while you are running a setuid program, the effective user ID of the process running the program is that of the owner of the program.

element One thing; usually a basic part of a group of things. An element of a numeric array is one of the numbers stored in the array.

emoticon See *smiley* on page 1188.

encapsulation See *tunneling* on page 1194.

environment See *calling environment* on page 1155.

EOF End of file.

EPROM Erasable programmable readonly memory. A *PROM* (page 1182) that can be written to by applying a higher than normal voltage.

escape See *quote* on page 1183.

Ethernet A type of *LAN* (page 1172) capable of transfer rates as high as 1,000 megabits per second. Refer to "Ethernet" on page 364.

Ethernet address See *MAC address* on page 1174.

event
An occurrence, or happening, of significance to a task or program—for example, the completion of an asynchronous input/output operation, such as a keypress or mouse click.[FOLDOC]

exabyte
2^{60} bytes or about 10^{18} bytes. See also *large number* (page 1172).

exit status
The status returned by a process; either successful (usually 0) or unsuccessful (usually 1).

exploit
A security hole or an instance of taking advantage of a security hole.[FOLDOC]

expression
See *logical expression* (page 1174) and *arithmetic expression* (page 1151).

extranet
A network extension for a subset of users (such as students at a particular school or engineers working for the same company). An extranet limits access to private information even though it travels on the public Internet.

failsafe session
A session that allows you to log in on a minimal desktop in case your standard login does not work well enough to allow you to log in to fix a login problem.

FDDI
Fiber Distributed Data Interface. A type of *LAN* (page 1172) designed to transport data at the rate of 100 million bits per second over fiberoptic cable.

file
A collection of related information referred to with a *filename* and frequently stored on a disk. Text files typically contain memos, reports, messages, program source code, lists, or manuscripts. Binary or executable files contain utilities or programs that you can run. Refer to "Directory Files and Ordinary Files" on page 187.

filename
The name of a file. A filename refers to a file.

filename completion
Automatic completion of a filename after you specify a unique prefix.

filename extension
The part of a filename following a period.

filename generation
What occurs when the shell expands ambiguous file references. See *ambiguous file reference* on page 1150.

filesystem
A *data structure* (page 1160) that usually resides on part of a disk. All Linux systems have a root filesystem, and many have other filesystems. Each filesystem is composed of some number of blocks, depending on the size of the disk partition that has been assigned to the filesystem. Each filesystem has a control block, named the superblock, that contains information about the filesystem. The other blocks in a filesystem are inodes, which contain control information about individual files, and data blocks, which contain the information in the files.

filling
A variant of maximizing in which window edges are pushed out as far as they can go without overlapping another window.

filter
A command that can take its input from standard input and send its output to standard output. A filter transforms the input stream of data and sends it to standard output. A

pipe usually connects a filter's input to standard output of one command, and a second pipe connects the filter's output to standard input of another command. The grep and sort utilities are commonly used as filters.

firewall A device for policy-based traffic management used to keep a network secure. A firewall can be implemented in a single router that filters out unwanted packets, or it can rely on a combination of routers, proxy servers, and other devices. Firewalls are widely used to give users access to the Internet in a secure fashion and to separate a company's public WWW server from its internal network. They are also employed to keep internal network segments more secure.

Recently the term has come to be defined more loosely to include a simple packet filter running on an endpoint machine.

See also *proxy server* on page 1183.

firmware Software built into a computer, often in *ROM* (page 1186). May be used as part of the *bootstrap* (page 1154) procedure.

focus, desktop On a desktop, the window that is active. The window with the desktop focus receives the characters you type on the keyboard. Same as *active window* (page 1150).

footer The part of a format that goes at the bottom (or foot) of a page. Contrast with *header* (page 1167).

foreground process When you run a command in the foreground, the shell waits for the command to finish before giving you another prompt. You must wait for a foreground process to run to completion before you can give the shell another command. If you have job control, you can move background processes to the foreground, and vice versa. See *job control* on page 1171. Contrast with *background process* (page 1153).

fork To create a process. When one process creates another process, it forks a process. Also *spawn*.

FQDN Fully qualified domain name. The full name of a system, consisting of its hostname and its domain name, including the top-level domain. Technically the name that **gethostbyname**(2) returns for the host named by **gethostname**(2). For example, **speedy** is a hostname and **speedy.example.com** is an FQDN. An FQDN is sufficient to determine a unique Internet address for a machine on the Internet.FOLDOC

frame A data link layer packet that contains, in addition to data, the header and trailer information required by the physical medium. Network layer packets are encapsulated to become frames.FOLDOC See also *datagram* (page 1160) and *packet* (page 1180).

free list In a filesystem, the list of blocks that are available for use. Information about the free list is kept in the superblock of the filesystem.

free space The portion of a hard disk that is not within a partition. A new hard disk has no partitions and contains all free space.

full duplex   The ability to receive and transmit data simultaneously. A *network switch* (page 1178) is typically a full-duplex device. Contrast with *half-duplex* (page 1167).

fully qualified domain name   See *FQDN*.

function   See *shell function* on page 1188.

gateway   A generic term for a computer or a special device connected to more than one dissimilar type of network to pass data between them. Unlike a router, a gateway often must convert the information into a different format before passing it on. The historical usage of gateway to designate a router is deprecated.

GCOS   See *GECOS*.

GECOS   General Electric Comprehensive Operating System. For historical reasons, the user information field in the **/etc/passwd** file is called the GECOS field. Also *GCOS*.

gibibyte   Giga binary byte. A unit of storage equal to 2^{30} bytes = 1,073,741,824 bytes = 1024 *mebibytes* (page 1175). Abbreviated as GiB. Contrast with *gigabyte*.

gigabyte   A unit of storage equal to 10^9 bytes. Sometimes used in place of *gibibyte*. Abbreviated as GB. See also *large number* on page 1172.

glyph   A symbol that communicates a specific piece of information nonverbally. A *smiley* (page 1188) is a glyph.

GMT   Greenwich Mean Time. See *UTC* on page 1195.

graphical display   A bitmapped monitor that can display graphical images. Contrast with *ASCII terminal* (page 1152).

graphical user interface   See *GUI*.

group (of users)   A collection of users. Groups are used as a basis for determining file access permissions. If you are not the owner of a file and you belong to the group the file is assigned to, you are subject to the group access permissions for the file. A user can simultaneously belong to several groups.

group (of windows)   A way to identify similar windows so they can be displayed and acted on similarly. Typically windows started by a given application belong to the same group.

group ID   A unique number that identifies a set of users. It is stored in the password and group databases (**/etc/passwd** and **/etc/group** files or their NIS equivalents). The group database associates group IDs with group names. Also *GID*.

GUI   Graphical user interface. A GUI provides a way to interact with a computer system by choosing items from menus or manipulating pictures drawn on a display screen instead of by typing command lines. Under Linux, the X Window System provides a graphical display and mouse/keyboard input. GNOME and KDE are two popular desktop managers that run under X. Contrast with *character-based* (page 1156).

hacker

A person who enjoys exploring the details of programmable systems and learning how to stretch their capabilities, as opposed to users, who prefer to learn only the minimum necessary. One who programs enthusiastically (even obsessively) or who enjoys programming rather than just theorizing about programming.ᶠᵒᴸᴰᴼᶜ Contrast with *cracker* (page 1159).

half-duplex

A half-duplex device can only receive or transmit at a given moment; it cannot do both. A *hub* (page 1169) is typically a half-duplex device. Contrast with *full duplex* (page 1166).

hard link

A directory entry that contains the filename and inode number for a file. The inode number identifies the location of control information for the file on the disk, which in turn identifies the location of the file's contents on the disk. Every file has at least one hard link, which locates the file in a directory. When you remove the last hard link to a file, you can no longer access the file. See *link* (page 1173) and *symbolic link* (page 1192).

hash

A string that is generated from another string. See *one-way hash function* on page 1179. When used for security, a hash can prove, almost to a certainty, that a message has not been tampered with during transmission: The sender generates a hash of a message, encrypts the message and hash, and sends the encrypted message and hash to the recipient. The recipient decrypts the message and hash, generates a second hash from the message, and compares the hash that the sender generated to the new hash. When they are the same, the message has probably not been tampered with. Hashed versions of passwords can be used to authenticate users. A hash can also be used to create an index called a *hash table*. Also *hash value*.

hash table

An index created from hashes of the items to be indexed. The hash function makes it highly unlikely that two items will create the same hash. To look up an item in the index, create a hash of the item and search for the hash. Because the hash is typically shorter than the item, the search is more efficient.

header

When you are formatting a document, the header goes at the top, or head, of a page. In electronic mail the header identifies who sent the message, when it was sent, what the subject of the message is, and so forth.

Here document

A shell script that takes its input from the file that contains the script.

hesiod

The nameserver of project Athena. Hesiod is a name service library that is derived from *BIND* (page 1153) and leverages a DNS infrastructure.

heterogeneous

Consisting of different parts. A heterogeneous network includes systems produced by different manufacturers and/or running different operating systems.

hexadecimal number

A base 16 number. Hexadecimal (or *hex*) numbers are composed of the hexadecimal digits 0–9 and A–F. Computers use *bits* (page 1153) to represent data. A group of 4 bits represents 16 possible values, 0 through F. A hexadecimal digit provides a convenient way to represent a group of 4 bits. See Table G-1 on the next page.

hidden
filename

A filename that starts with a period. These filenames are called hidden because the ls utility does not normally list them. Use the **–a** option of ls to list all files, including those with hidden filenames. The shell does not expand a leading asterisk (*) in an ambiguous file reference to match files with hidden filenames. Also *hidden file*, *invisible file*.

hierarchy

An organization with a few things, or thing—one at the top—and with several things below each other thing. An inverted tree structure. Examples in computing include a file tree where each directory might contain files or other directories, a hierarchical network, and a class hierarchy in object-oriented programming.^{FOLDOC} Refer to "The Hierarchical Filesystem" on page 186.

Table G-1 Decimal, octal, and hexadecimal numbers

Decimal	Octal	Hex	Decimal	Octal	Hex
1	1	1	17	21	11
2	2	2	18	22	12
3	3	3	19	23	13
4	4	4	20	24	14
5	5	5	21	25	15
6	6	6	31	37	1F
7	7	7	32	40	20
8	10	8	33	41	21
9	11	9	64	100	40
10	12	A	96	140	60
11	13	B	100	144	64
12	14	C	128	200	80
13	15	D	254	376	FE
14	16	E	255	377	FF
15	17	F	256	400	100
16	20	10	257	401	101

history

A shell mechanism that enables you to modify and re-execute recent commands.

home
directory

The directory that is the working directory when you first log in. The pathname of this directory is stored in the **HOME** shell variable.

hover

To leave the mouse pointer stationary for a moment over an object. In many cases hovering displays a *tooltip* (page 1193).

HTML

Hypertext Markup Language. A *hypertext* document format used on the World Wide Web. Tags, which are embedded in the text, consist of a less than sign (<), a directive, zero or more parameters, and a greater than sign (>). Matched pairs of directives, such as <TITLE> and </TITLE>, delimit text that is to appear in a special place or style.^{FOLDOC} For more information on HTML, go to www.htmlhelp.com/faq/html/all.html.

HTTP	Hypertext Transfer Protocol. The client/server TCP/IP protocol used on the World Wide Web for the exchange of *HTML* documents.
hub	A multiport repeater. A hub rebroadcasts all packets it receives on all ports. This term is frequently used to refer to small hubs and switches, regardless of the device's intelligence. It is a generic term for a layer 2 shared-media networking device. Today the term *hub* is sometimes used to refer to small intelligent devices, although that was not its original meaning. Contrast with *network switch* (page 1178).
hypertext	A collection of documents/nodes containing (usually highlighted or underlined) cross-references or links, which, with the aid of an interactive browser program, allow the reader to move easily from one document to another.ᶠᴼᴸᴰᴼᶜ
Hypertext Markup Language	See *HTML*.
Hypertext Transfer Protocol	See *HTTP*.
i/o device	Input/output device. See *device* on page 1161.
IANA	Internet Assigned Numbers Authority. A group that maintains a database of all permanent, registered system services (www.iana.org).
ICMP	Internet Control Message Protocol. A type of network packet that carries only messages, no data. The most common ICMP packet is the echo request which is sent by the ping utility.
icon	In a GUI, a small picture representing a file, directory, action, program, and so on. When you click an icon, an action, such as opening a window and starting a program or displaying a directory or Web site, takes place. From miniature religious statues.ᶠᴼᴸᴰᴼᶜ
iconify	To change a window into an *icon*. Contrast with *restore* (page 1185).
ignored window	A state in which a window has no decoration and therefore no buttons or titlebar to control it with.
indentation	See *indention*.
indention	The blank space between the margin and the beginning of a line that is set in from the margin.
inode	A *data structure* (page 1160) that contains information about a file. An inode for a file contains the file's length, the times the file was last accessed and modified, the time the inode was last modified, owner and group IDs, access privileges, number of links, and pointers to the data blocks that contain the file itself. Each directory entry associates a filename with an inode. Although a single file might have several filenames (one for each link), it has only one inode.
input	Information that is fed to a program from a terminal or other file. See *standard input* on page 1190.

installation   A computer at a specific location. Some aspects of the Linux system are installation dependent. Also *site*.

interactive   A program that allows ongoing dialog with the user. When you give commands in response to shell prompts, you are using the shell interactively. Also, when you give commands to utilities, such as vim and mail, you are using the utilities interactively.

interface   The meeting point of two subsystems. When two programs work together, their interface includes every aspect of either program that the other deals with. The *user interface* (page 1195) of a program includes every program aspect the user comes into contact with: the syntax and semantics involved in invoking the program, the input and output of the program, and its error and informational messages. The shell and each of the utilities and built-in commands have a user interface.

International Organization for Standardization   See *ISO*.

internet   A large network that encompasses other, smaller networks.

Internet   The largest internet in the world. The Internet (uppercase "I") is a multilevel hierarchy composed of backbone networks (ARPANET, NSFNET, MILNET, and others), midlevel networks, and stub networks. These include commercial (**.com** or **.co**), university (**.ac** or **.edu**), research (**.org** or **.net**), and military (**.mil**) networks and span many different physical networks around the world with various protocols, including the Internet Protocol (IP). Outside the United States, country code domains are popular (**.us**, **.es**, **.mx**, **.de**, and so forth), although you will see them used within the United States as well.

Internet Protocol   See *IP*.

Internet service provider   See *ISP*.

intranet   An inhouse network designed to serve a group of people such as a corporation or school. The general public on the Internet does not have access to an intranet. See page 361.

invisible file   See *hidden filename* on page 1168.

IP   Internet Protocol. The network layer for TCP/IP. IP is a best-effort, packet-switching, *connectionless protocol* (page 1158) that provides packet routing, fragmentation, and reassembly through the data link layer. *IPv4* is slowly giving way to *IPv6*.FOLDOC

IP address   Internet Protocol address. A four-part address associated with a particular network connection for a system using the Internet Protocol (IP). A system that is attached to multiple networks that use the IP will have a different IP address for each network interface.

IP multicast	See *multicast* on page 1177.
IP spoofing	A technique used to gain unauthorized access to a computer. The would-be intruder sends messages to the target machine. These messages contain an IP address indicating that the messages are coming from a trusted host. The target machine responds to the messages, giving the intruder (privileged) access to the target.
IPC	Interprocess communication. A method to communicate specific information between programs.
IPv4	*IP* version 4. See *IP* and *IPv6*.
IPv6	*IP* version 6. The next generation of Internet Protocol, which provides a much larger address space (2^{128} bits versus 2^{32} bits for IPv4) that is designed to accommodate the rapidly growing number of Internet addressable devices. IPv6 also has built-in autoconfiguration, enhanced security, better multicast support, and many other features.
iSCSI	Internet Small Computer System Interface. A network storage protocol that encapsulates SCSI data into TCP packets. You can use this protocol to connect a system to a storage array using an Ethernet connection.
ISDN	Integrated Services Digital Network. A set of communications standards that allows a single pair of digital or standard telephone wires to carry voice, data, and video at a rate of 64 kilobits per second.
ISO	International Organization for Standardization. A voluntary, nontreaty organization founded in 1946. It is responsible for creating international standards in many areas, including computers and communications. Its members are the national standards organizations of 89 countries, including the American National Standards Institute.FOLDOC
ISO9660	The *ISO* standard defining a filesystem for CD-ROMs.
ISP	Internet service provider. Provides Internet access to its customers.
job control	A facility that enables you to move commands from the foreground to the background, and vice versa. Job control enables you to stop commands temporarily.
journaling filesystem	A filesystem that maintains a noncached log file, or journal, which records all transactions involving the filesystem. When a transaction is complete, it is marked as complete in the log file.
	The log file results in greatly reduced time spent recovering a filesystem after a crash, making it particularly valuable in systems where high availability is an issue.
JPEG	Joint Photographic Experts Group. This committee designed the standard image-compression algorithm. JPEG is intended for compressing either full-color or gray-scale digital images of natural, real-world scenes and does not work as well on nonrealistic images, such as cartoons or line drawings. Filename extensions: **.jpg**, **.jpeg**.FOLDOC

justify   To expand a line of type in the process of formatting text. A justified line has even margins. A line is justified by increasing the space between words and sometimes between letters on the line.

Kerberos   An MIT-developed security system that authenticates users and machines. It does not provide authorization to services or databases; it establishes identity at logon, which is used throughout the session. Once you are authenticated, you can open as many terminals, windows, services, or other network accesses as you like until your session expires.

kernel   The part of the operating system that allocates machine resources, including memory, disk space, and *CPU* (page 1159) cycles, to all other programs that run on a computer. The kernel includes the low-level hardware interfaces (drivers) and manages *processes* (page 1182), the means by which Linux executes programs. The kernel is the part of the Linux system that Linus Torvalds originally wrote (see the beginning of Chapter 1).

kernelspace The part of memory (RAM) where the kernel resides. Code running in kernelspace has full access to hardware and all other processes in memory. See the *KernelAnalysis-HOWTO*.

key binding A *keyboard* key is said to be bound to the action that results from pressing it. Typically keys are bound to the letters that appear on the keycaps: When you press **A**, an **A** appears on the screen. Key binding usually refers to what happens when you press a combination of keys, one of which is CONTROL, ALT, META, or SHIFT, or when you press a series of keys, the first of which is typically ESCAPE.

keyboard   A hardware input device consisting of a number of mechanical buttons (keys) that the user presses to input characters to a computer. By default a keyboard is connected to standard input of a shell.FOLDOC

kilo-   In the binary system, the prefix *kilo-* multiplies by 2^{10} (i.e., 1,024). Kilobit and kilobyte are common uses of this prefix. Abbreviated as *k*.

Korn Shell ksh. A command processor, developed by David Korn at AT&T Bell Laboratories, that is compatible with the Bourne Shell but includes many extensions. See also *shell* on page 1188.

LAN   Local area network. A network that connects computers within a localized area (such as a single site, building, or department).

large number Visit mathworld.wolfram.com/LargeNumber.html for a comprehensive list.

LDAP   Lightweight Directory Access Protocol. A simple protocol for accessing online directory services. LDAP is a lightweight alternative to the X.500 Directory Access Protocol (DAP). It can be used to access information about people, system users, network devices, email directories, and systems. In some cases, it can be used as an alternative for services such as NIS. Given a name, many mail clients can use LDAP to discover the corresponding email address. See *directory service* on page 1161.

leaf In a tree structure, the end of a branch that cannot support other branches. When the Linux filesystem hierarchy is conceptualized as a tree, files that are not directories are leaves. See *node* on page 1179.

least privilege, concept of Mistakes made by a user working with **root** privileges can be much more devastating than those made by an ordinary user. When you are working on the computer, especially when you are working as the system administrator, always perform any task using the least privilege possible. If you can perform a task logged in as an ordinary user, do so. If you must work with **root** privileges, do as much as you can as an ordinary user, log in as **root** or give an su or sudo command so you are working with **root** privileges, do as much of the task that has to be done with **root** privileges, and revert to being an ordinary user as soon as you can.

Because you are more likely to make a mistake when you are rushing, this concept becomes more important when you have less time to apply it.

Lightweight Directory Access Protocol See *LDAP*.

link A pointer to a file. Two kinds of links exist: *hard links* (page 1167) and *symbolic links* (page 1192) also called *soft links*. A hard link associates a filename with a place on the disk where the contents of the file is located. A symbolic link associates a filename with the pathname of a hard link to a file.

Linux-PAM See *PAM* on page 1180.

Linux-Pluggable Authentication Modules See *PAM* on page 1180.

list box A *widget* (page 1197) that displays a static list for a user to choose from. The list appears as multiple lines with a *scrollbar* (page 1187) if needed. The user can scroll the list and select an entry. Different from a *drop-down list* (page 1163).

loadable kernel module See *loadable module*.

loadable module A portion of the operating system that controls a special device and that can be loaded automatically into a running kernel as needed to access that device.

local area network See *LAN*.

locale The language; date, time, and currency formats; character sets; and so forth that pertain to a geopolitical place or area. For example, en_US specifies English as spoken in the United States and dollars; en_UK specifies English as spoken in the United Kingdom and pounds. See the **locale** man page in section 5 of the system manual for more information. Also the locale utility.

log in	To gain access to a computer system by responding correctly to the **login:** and **Password:** prompts. Also *log on, login*.
log out	To end your session by exiting from your login shell. Also *log off*.
logical expression	A collection of strings separated by logical operators (>, >=, =, !=, <=, and <) that can be evaluated as *true* or *false*. Also *Boolean* (page 1154) *expression*.
.login file	A file in a user's home directory that the TC Shell executes when you log in. You can use this file to set environment variables and to run commands that you want executed at the beginning of each session.
login name	See *username* on page 1195.
login shell	The shell you are using when you log in. The login shell can fork other processes that can run other shells, utilities, and programs. See page 282.
.logout file	A file in a user's home directory that the TC Shell executes when you log out, assuming that the TC Shell is your login shell. You can put in the **.logout** file commands that you want run each time you log out.
MAC address	Media Access Control address. The unique hardware address of a device connected to a shared network medium. Each network adapter has a globally unique MAC address that it stores in ROM. MAC addresses are 6 bytes long, enabling 256^6 (about 300 trillion) possible addresses or 65,536 addresses for each possible IPv4 address.

A MAC address performs the same role for Ethernet that an IP address performs for TCP/IP: It provides a unique way to identify a host. Also called an Ethernet address. |
machine collating sequence	The sequence in which the computer orders characters. The machine collating sequence affects the outcome of sorts and other procedures that put lists in alphabetical order. Many computers use ASCII codes so their machine collating sequences correspond to the ordering of the ASCII codes for characters.
macro	A single instruction that a program replaces by several (usually more complex) instructions. The C compiler recognizes macros, which are defined using a #define instruction to the preprocessor.
magic number	A magic number, which occurs in the first 512 bytes of a binary file, is a 1-, 2-, or 4-byte numeric value or character string that uniquely identifies the type of file (much like a DOS 3-character filename extension). See **/usr/share/magic** and the **magic** man page for more information.
main memory	Random access memory (RAM), an integral part of the computer. Although disk storage is sometimes referred to as memory, it is never referred to as main memory.
major device number	A number assigned to a class of devices, such as terminals, printers, or disk drives. Using the ls utility with the –l option to list the contents of the **/dev** directory displays the major and minor device numbers of many devices (as major, minor).

MAN	Metropolitan area network. A network that connects computers and *LANs* (page 1172) at multiple sites in a small regional area, such as a city.
masquerade	To appear to come from one domain or IP address when actually coming from another. Said of a packet (iptables) or message (**sendmail**). See also *NAT* on page 1177.
MD5	Message Digest 5. A *one-way hash function* (page 1179). The *SHA1* (page 1187) algorithm has supplanted MD5 in many applications.
MDA	Mail delivery agent. One of the three components of a mail system; the other two are the *MTA* (page 1176) and *MUA* (page 1176). An MDA accepts inbound mail from an MTA and delivers it to a local user.
mebibyte	Mega binary byte. A unit of storage equal to 2^{20} bytes = 1,048,576 bytes = 1,024 kibibytes. Abbreviated as MiB. Contrast with *megabyte*.
megabyte	A unit of storage equal to 10^6 bytes. Sometimes used in place of *mebibyte*. Abbreviated as MB.
memory	See *RAM* on page 1184.
menu	A list from which the user might select an operation to be performed. This selection is often made with a mouse or other pointing device under a GUI but might also be controlled from the keyboard. Very convenient for beginners, menus show which commands are available and facilitate experimenting with a new program, often reducing the need for user documentation. Experienced users usually prefer keyboard commands, especially for frequently used operations, because they are faster to use.ᶠᵒᴸᴰᴼᶜ
merge	To combine two ordered lists so that the resulting list is still in order. The **sort** utility can merge files.
META key	On the keyboard, a key that is labeled META or ALT. Use this key as you would the SHIFT key. While holding it down, press another key. The **emacs** editor makes extensive use of the META key.
metacharacter	A character that has a special meaning to the shell or another program in a particular context. Metacharacters are used in the ambiguous file references recognized by the shell and in the regular expressions recognized by several utilities. You must quote a metacharacter if you want to use it without invoking its special meaning. See *regular character* (page 1185) and *special character* (page 1189).
metadata	Data about data. In data processing, metadata is definitional data that provides information about, or documentation of, other data managed within an application or environment.
	For example, metadata can document data about data elements or attributes (name, size, data type, and so on), records or *data structures* (page 1160) (length, fields, columns, and so on), and data itself (where it is located, how it is associated, who owns it, and so on). Metadata can include descriptive information about the context, quality and condition, or characteristics of the data.ᶠᵒᴸᴰᴼᶜ

metropolitan area network	See *MAN* on page 1175.
MIME	Multipurpose Internet Mail Extension. Originally used to describe how specific types of files that were attached to email were to be handled. Today MIME types describe how a file is to be opened or worked with, based on its contents, determined by its *magic number* (page 1174), and filename extension. An example of a MIME *type* is **image/jpeg**: The MIME *group* is **image** and the MIME *subtype* is **jpeg**. Many MIME groups exist, including application, audio, image, inode, message, text, and video.
minimize	See *iconify* on page 1169.
minor device number	A number assigned to a specific device within a class of devices. See *major device number* on page 1174.
modem	Modulator/demodulator. A peripheral device that modulates digital data into analog data for transmission over a voice-grade telephone line. Another modem demodulates the data at the other end.
module	See *loadable module* on page 1173.
mount	To make a filesystem accessible to system users. When a filesystem is not mounted, you cannot read from or write to files it contains.
mount point	A directory that you mount a local or remote filesystem on. See page 36.
mouse	A device you use to point to a particular location on a display screen, typically so you can choose a menu item, draw a line, or highlight some text. You control a pointer on the screen by sliding a mouse around on a flat surface; the position of the pointer moves relative to the movement of the mouse. You select items by pressing one or more buttons on the mouse.
mouse pointer	In a GUI, a marker that moves in correspondence with the mouse. It is usually a small black **x** with a white border or an arrow. Differs from the *cursor* (page 1160).
mouseover	The action of passing the mouse pointer over an object on the screen.
MTA	Mail transfer agent. One of the three components of a mail system; the other two are the *MDA* and *MUA*. An MTA accepts mail from users and MTAs.
MUA	Mail user agent. One of the three components of a mail system; the other two are the *MDA* (previous page) and *MTA*. An MUA is an end-user mail program such as KMail, mutt, or Outlook.
multiboot specification	Specifies an interface between a boot loader and an operating system. With compliant boot loaders and operating systems, any boot loader should be able to load any operating system. The object of this specification is to ensure that different operating systems will work on a single machine. For more information, go to odin-os.sourceforge.net/guides/multiboot.html.

multicast   A multicast packet has one source and multiple destinations. In multicast, source hosts register at a special address to transmit data. Destination hosts register at the same address to receive data. In contrast to *broadcast* (page 1154), which is LAN-based, multicast traffic is designed to work across routed networks on a subscription basis. Multicast reduces network traffic by transmitting a packet one time, with the router at the end of the path breaking it apart as needed for multiple recipients.

multitasking   A computer system that allows a user to run more than one job at a time. A multitasking system, such as Linux, allows you to run a job in the background while running a job in the foreground.

multiuser system   A computer system that can be used by more than one person at a time. Linux is a multiuser operating system. Contrast with *single-user system* (page 1188).

namespace   A set of names (identifiers) in which all names are unique.ᶠᴼᴸᴰᴼᶜ

NAT   Network Address Translation. A scheme that enables a LAN to use one set of IP addresses internally and a different set externally. The internal set is for LAN (private) use. The external set is typically used on the Internet and is Internet unique. NAT provides some privacy by hiding internal IP addresses and allows multiple internal addresses to connect to the Internet through a single external IP address. See also *masquerade* on page 1175.

NBT   NetBIOS over TCP/IP. A protocol that supports NetBIOS services in a TCP/IP environment. Also NetBT.

negative caching   Storing the knowledge that something does not exist. A cache normally stores information about something that exists. A negative cache stores the information that something, such as a record, does not exist.

NetBIOS   Network Basic Input/Output System. An *API* (page 1151) for writing network-aware applications.

netboot   To boot a computer over the network (as opposed to booting from a local disk).

netiquette   The conventions of etiquette—that is, polite behavior—recognized on Usenet and in mailing lists, such as not (cross-)posting to inappropriate groups and refraining from commercial advertising outside the business groups.

The most important rule of netiquette is "Think before you post." If what you intend to post will not make a positive contribution to the newsgroup and be of interest to several readers, do not post it. Personal messages to one or two individuals should not be posted to newsgroups; use private email instead.ᶠᴼᴸᴰᴼᶜ

network address   The network portion (**netid**) of an IP address. For a class A network, it is the first byte, or segment, of the IP address; for a class B network, it is the first two bytes; and for a class C network, it is the first three bytes. In each case the balance of the IP address is the host address (**hostid**). Assigned network addresses are globally unique within the Internet. Also *network number*.

Network Filesystem	See *NFS*.
Network Information Service	See *NIS*.
network mask	A bit mask used to identify which bits in an IP address correspond to the network address and subnet portions of the address. Called a network mask because the network portion of the address is determined by the number of bits that are set in the mask. The network mask has ones in positions corresponding to the network and subnet numbers and zeros in the host number positions. Also *subnet mask* or *mask*.
network number	See *network address*.
network segment	A part of an Ethernet or other network on which all message traffic is common to all nodes; that is, it is broadcast from one node on the segment and received by all others. This commonality normally occurs because the segment is a single continuous conductor. Communication between nodes on different segments is via one or more routers.^{FOLDOC}
network switch	A connecting device in networks. Switches are increasingly replacing shared media hubs in an effort to increase bandwidth. For example, a 16-port 10BaseT hub shares the total 10 megabits per second bandwidth with all 16 attached nodes. By replacing the hub with a switch, both sender and receiver can take advantage of the full 10 megabits per second capacity. Each port on the switch can give full bandwidth to a single server or client station or to a hub with several stations. Network switch refers to a device with intelligence. Contrast with *hub* (page 1169).
Network Time Protocol	See *NTP* on page 1179.
NFS	Network Filesystem. A remote filesystem designed by Sun Microsystems, available on computers from most UNIX system vendors.
NIC	Network interface card (or controller). An adapter circuit board installed in a computer to provide a physical connection to a network. Each NIC has a unique *MAC address* (page 1174).^{FOLDOC}
NIS	Network Information Service. A distributed service built on a shared database to manage system-independent information (such as usernames and passwords).
NIS domain name	A name that describes a group of systems that share a set of NIS files. Different from *domain name* (page 1162).
NNTP	Network News Transfer Protocol.

node	In a tree structure, the end of a branch that can support other branches. When the Linux filesystem hierarchy is conceptualized as a tree, directories are nodes. See *leaf* on page 1173.
nonprinting character	See *control character* on page 1158. Also *nonprintable character*.
nonvolatile storage	A storage device whose contents are preserved when its power is off. Also NVS and persistent storage. Some examples are CD-ROM, paper punch tape, hard disk, *ROM* (page 1186), *PROM* (page 1182), *EPROM* (page 1163), and *EEPROM* (page 1163). Contrast with *RAM* (page 1184).
NTP	Network Time Protocol. Built on top of TCP/IP, NTP maintains accurate local time by referring to known accurate clocks on the Internet.
null string	A string that could contain characters but does not. A string of zero length.
octal number	A base 8 number. Octal numbers are composed of the digits 0–7, inclusive. Refer to Table G-1 on page 1168.
one-way hash function	A one-way function that takes a variable-length message and produces a fixed-length hash. Given the hash, it is computationally infeasible to find a message with that hash; in fact, you cannot determine any usable information about a message with that hash. Also *message digest function*. See also *hash* (page 1167).
open source	A method and philosophy for software licensing and distribution designed to encourage use and improvement of software written by volunteers by ensuring that anyone can copy the source code and modify it freely.
	The term *open source* is now more widely used than the earlier term *free software* (promoted by the Free Software Foundation; www.fsf.org) but has broadly the same meaning—free of distribution restrictions, not necessarily free of charge.
OpenSSH	A free version of the SSH (secure shell) protocol suite that replaces TELNET, rlogin, and more with secure programs that encrypt all communication—even passwords—over a network.
operating system	A control program for a computer that allocates computer resources, schedules tasks, and provides the user with a way to access resources.
option	A command-line argument that modifies the effects of a command. Options are usually preceded by hyphens on the command line and traditionally have single-character names (such as **–h** or **–n**). Some commands allow you to group options following a single hyphen (for example, **–hn**). GNU utilities frequently have two arguments that do the same thing: a single-character argument and a longer, more descriptive argument that is preceded by two hyphens (such as **––show-all** and **––invert-match**).
ordinary file	A file that is used to store a program, text, or other user data. See *directory* (page 1161) and *device file* (page 1161).

output Information that a program sends to the terminal or another file. See *standard output* on page 1190.

P2P Peer-to-Peer. A network that does not divide nodes into clients and servers. Each computer on a P2P network can fulfill the roles of client and server. In the context of a file-sharing network, this ability means that once a node has downloaded (part of) a file, it can act as a server. BitTorrent implements a P2P network.

packet A unit of data sent across a network. *Packet* is a generic term used to describe a unit of data at any layer of the OSI protocol stack, but it is most correctly used to describe network or application layer data units ("application protocol data unit," APDU).ᶠᴼᴸᴰᴼᶜ See also *frame* (page 1165) and *datagram* (page 1160).

packet filtering A technique used to block network traffic based on specified criteria, such as the origin, destination, or type of each packet. See also *firewall* (page 1165).

packet sniffer A program or device that monitors packets on a network. See *sniff* on page 1189.

pager A utility that allows you to view a file one screen at a time (for example, less and more).

paging The process by which virtual memory is maintained by the operating system. The contents of process memory is moved (paged out) to the *swap space* (page 1191) as needed to make room for other processes.

PAM Linux-PAM or Linux-Pluggable Authentication Modules. These modules allow a system administrator to determine how various applications authenticate users.

parent process A process that forks other processes. See *process* (page 1182) and *child process* (page 1156).

partition A section of a (hard) disk that has a name so you can address it separately from other sections. A disk partition can hold a filesystem or another structure, such as the swap area. Under DOS and Windows, partitions (and sometimes whole disks) are labeled **C:**, **D:**, and so on. Also *disk partition* and *slice*.

passive FTP Allows FTP to work through a firewall by allowing the flow of data to be initiated and controlled by the client FTP program instead of the server. Also called PASV FTP because it uses the FTP PASV command.

passphrase A string of words and characters that you type in to authenticate yourself. A passphrase differs from a *password* only in length. A password is usually short—6 to 10 characters. A passphrase is usually much longer—up to 100 characters or more. The greater length makes a passphrase harder to guess or reproduce than a password and therefore more secure.ᶠᴼᴸᴰᴼᶜ

password To prevent unauthorized access to a user's account, an arbitrary string of characters chosen by the user or system administrator and used to authenticate the user when attempting to log in.ᶠᴼᴸᴰᴼᶜ See also *passphrase*.

PASV FTP See *passive FTP*.

pathname	A list of directories separated by slashes (/) and ending with the name of a file, which can be a directory. A pathname is used to trace a path through the file structure to locate or identify a file.
pathname, last element of a	The part of a pathname following the final /, or the whole filename if there is no /. A simple filename. Same as *basename* (page 1153).
pathname element	One of the filenames that forms a pathname.
peripheral device	See *device* on page 1161.
persistent	Data that is stored on nonvolatile media, such as a hard disk.
phish	An attempt to trick users into revealing or sharing private information, especially passwords or financial information. The most common form is email purporting to be from a bank or vendor that requests that a user fill out a form to "update" an account on a phoney Web site disguised to appear legitimate. Generally sent as *spam* (page 1189).
physical device	A tangible device, such as a disk drive, that is physically separate from other, similar devices.
PID	Process identification, usually followed by the word *number*. Linux assigns a unique PID number as each process is initiated.
pipe	A connection between programs such that standard output of one program is connected to standard input of the next. Also *pipeline*.
pixel	The smallest element of a picture, typically a single dot on a display screen.
plaintext	Text that is not encrypted. Also *cleartext*. Contrast with *ciphertext* (page 1157).
Pluggable Authentication Modules	See *PAM* on page 1180.
point-to-point link	A connection limited to two endpoints, such as the connection between a pair of modems.
port	A logical channel or channel endpoint in a communications system. The *TCP* (page 1192) and *UDP* (page 1194) transport layer protocols used on Ethernet use port numbers to distinguish between different logical channels on the same network interface on the same computer. The **/etc/services** file (see the beginning of this file for more information) or the *NIS* (page 1178) **services** database specifies a unique port number for each application program. The number links incoming data to the correct service (program). Standard, well-known ports are used by everyone: Port 80 is used for HTTP (Web) traffic. Some protocols, such as TELNET and HTTP (which is a special form of TELNET), have default ports specified as mentioned earlier but can use other ports as well.[FOLDOC]

port forwarding	The process by which a network *port* on one computer is transparently connected to a port on another computer. If port X is forwarded from system A to system B, any data sent to port X on system A is sent to system B automatically. The connection can be between different ports on the two systems. See also *tunneling* (page 1194).
portmapper	A server that converts TCP/IP port numbers into *RPC* (page 1186) program numbers. See "RPC Network Services" on page 398.
printable character	One of the graphic characters: a letter, number, or punctuation mark. Contrast with a nonprintable, or CONTROL, character. Also *printing character*.
private address space	*IANA* (page 1169) has reserved three blocks of IP addresses for private internets or LANs:

```
10.0.0.0 - 10.255.255.255
172.16.0.0 - 172.31.255.255
192.168.0.0 - 192.168.255.255
```

You can use these addresses without coordinating with anyone outside of your LAN (you do not have to register the system name or address). Systems using these IP addresses cannot communicate directly with hosts using the global address space but must go through a gateway. Because private addresses have no global meaning, routing information is not stored by DNSs and most ISPs reject privately addressed packets. Make sure that your router is set up not to forward these packets onto the Internet.

privileged port	A *port* (page 1181) with a number less than 1024. On Linux and other UNIX-like systems, only a process running with **root** privileges can bind to a privileged port. Any user on Windows 98 and earlier Windows systems can bind to any port. Also *reserved port*.
procedure	A sequence of instructions for performing a particular task. Most programming languages, including machine languages, enable a programmer to define procedures that allow the procedure code to be called from multiple places. Also *subroutine*.ᶠᴼᴸᴰᴼᶜ
process	The execution of a command by Linux. See "Processes" on page 316.
.profile file	A startup file in a user's home directory that the Bourne Again or Z Shell executes when you log in. The TC Shell executes **.login** instead. You can use the **.profile** file to run commands, set variables, and define functions.
program	A sequence of executable computer instructions contained in a file. Linux utilities, applications, and shell scripts are all programs. Whenever you run a command that is not built into a shell, you are executing a program.
PROM	Programmable readonly memory. A kind of nonvolatile storage. *ROM* (page 1186) that can be written to using a PROM programmer.
prompt	A cue from a program, usually displayed on the screen, indicating that it is waiting for input. The shell displays a prompt, as do some of the interactive utilities, such as

mail. By default the Bourne Again and Z Shells use a dollar sign ($) as a prompt, and the TC Shell uses a percent sign (%).

protocol
A set of formal rules describing how to transmit data, especially across a network. Low-level protocols define the electrical and physical standards, bit and byte ordering, and transmission, error detection, and correction of the bit stream. High-level protocols deal with data formatting, including message syntax, terminal-to-computer dialog, character sets, and sequencing of messages.FOLDOC

proxy
A service that is authorized to act for a system while not being part of that system. See also *proxy gateway* and *proxy server*.

proxy gateway
A computer that separates clients (such as browsers) from the Internet, working as a trusted agent that accesses the Internet on their behalf. A proxy gateway passes a request for data from an Internet service, such as HTTP from a browser/client, to a remote server. The data that the server returns goes back through the proxy gateway to the requesting service. A proxy gateway should be transparent to the user.

A proxy gateway often runs on a *firewall* (page 1165) system and acts as a barrier to malicious users. It hides the IP addresses of the local computers inside the firewall from Internet users outside the firewall.

You can configure browsers, such as Mozilla/Firefox and Netscape, to use a different proxy gateway or to use no proxy for each URL access method including FTP, netnews, SNMP, HTTPS, and HTTP. See also *proxy*.

proxy server
A *proxy gateway* that usually includes a *cache* (page 1155) that holds frequently used Web pages so that the next request for that page is available locally (and therefore more quickly). The terms proxy server and proxy gateway are frequently interchanged so that the use of cache does not rest exclusively with the proxy server. See also *proxy*.

Python
A simple, high-level, interpreted, object-oriented, interactive language that bridges the gap between C and shell programming. Suitable for rapid prototyping or as an extension language for C applications, Python supports packages, modules, classes, user-defined exceptions, a good C interface, and dynamic loading of C modules. It has no arbitrary restrictions. For more information, see www.python.org.FOLDOC

quote
When you quote a character, you take away any special meaning that it has in the current context. You can quote a character by preceding it with a backslash. When you are interacting with the shell, you can also quote a character by surrounding it with single quotation marks. For example, the command **echo *** or **echo '*'** displays *. The command **echo *** displays a list of the files in the working directory. See *ambiguous file reference* (page 1150), *metacharacter* (page 1175), *regular character* (page 1185), *regular expression* (page 1185), and *special character* (page 1189). See also *escape* on page 1163.

radio button
In a GUI, one of a group of buttons similar to those used to select the station on a car radio. Radio buttons within a group are mutually exclusive; only one button can be selected at a time.

RAID   Redundant array of inexpensive/independent disks. Two or more (hard) disk drives used in combination to improve fault tolerance and performance. RAID can be implemented in hardware or software.

RAM   Random access memory. A kind of volatile storage. A data storage device for which the order of access to different locations does not affect the speed of access. Contrast with a hard disk or tape drive, which provides quicker access to sequential data because accessing a nonsequential location requires physical movement of the storage medium and/or read/write head rather than just electronic switching. Contrast with *nonvolatile storage* (page 1179). Also *memory*.ᶠᵒᴸᴰᴼᶜ

RAM disk   *RAM* that is made to look like a floppy diskette or hard disk. A RAM disk is frequently used as part of the *boot* (page 1154) process.

RAS   Remote access server. In a network, a computer that provides access to remote users via analog modem or ISDN connections. RAS includes the dial-up protocols and access control (authentication). It might be a regular fileserver with remote access software or a proprietary system, such as Shiva's LANRover. The modems might be internal or external to the device.

RDF   Resource Description Framework. Being developed by W3C (the main standards body for the World Wide Web), a standard that specifies a mechanism for encoding and transferring *metadata* (page 1175). RDF does not specify what the metadata should or can be. It can integrate many kinds of applications and data, using XML as an interchange syntax. Examples of the data that can be integrated include library catalogs and worldwide directories; syndication and aggregation of news, software, and content; and collections of music and photographs. Go to www.w3.org/RDF for more information.

redirection   The process of directing standard input for a program to come from a file rather than from the keyboard. Also, directing standard output or standard error to go to a file rather than to the screen.

reentrant   Code that can have multiple simultaneous, interleaved, or nested invocations that do not interfere with one another. Noninterference is important for parallel processing, recursive programming, and interrupt handling.

    It is usually easy to arrange for multiple invocations (that is, calls to a subroutine) to share one copy of the code and any readonly data. For the code to be reentrant, however, each invocation must use its own copy of any modifiable data (or synchronized access to shared data). This goal is most often achieved by using a stack and allocating local variables in a new stack frame for each invocation. Alternatively, the caller might pass in a pointer to a block of memory that that invocation can use (usually for output), or the code might allocate some memory on a heap, especially if the data must survive after the routine returns.

    Reentrant code is often found in system software, such as operating systems and teleprocessing monitors. It is also a crucial component of multithreaded programs, where the term *thread-safe* is often used instead of reentrant.ᶠᵒᴸᴰᴼᶜ

regular character	A character that always represents itself in an ambiguous file reference or another type of regular expression. Contrast with *special character*.
regular expression	A string—composed of letters, numbers, and special symbols—that defines one or more strings. See Appendix A.
relative pathname	A pathname that starts from the working directory. Contrast with *absolute pathname* (page 1150).
remote access server	See *RAS* on page 1184.
remote filesystem	A filesystem on a remote computer that has been set up so that you can access (usually over a network) its files as though they were stored on your local computer's disks. An example of a remote filesystem is NFS.
remote procedure call	See *RPC* on page 1186.
resolver	The TCP/IP library software that formats requests to be sent to the *DNS* (page 1162) for hostname-to-Internet address conversion.^{FOLDOC}
Resource Description Framework	See *RDF* on page 1184.
restore	The process of turning an icon into a window. Contrast with *iconify* (page 1169).
return code	See *exit status* on page 1164.
RFC	Request for comments. Begun in 1969, one of a series of numbered Internet informational documents and standards widely followed by commercial software and freeware in the Internet and UNIX/Linux communities. Few RFCs are standards, but all Internet standards are recorded in RFCs. Perhaps the single most influential RFC has been RFC 822, the Internet electronic mail format standard.
	The RFCs are unusual in that they are floated by technical experts acting on their own initiative and reviewed by the Internet at large rather than being formally promulgated through an institution such as ANSI. For this reason they remain known as RFCs, even after they are adopted as standards. The RFC tradition of pragmatic, experience-driven, after-the-fact standard writing done by individuals or small working groups has important advantages over the more formal, committee-driven process typical of ANSI or ISO. For a complete list of RFCs, go to www.rfc-editor.org.^{FOLDOC}
roam	To move a computer between *wireless access points* (page 1197) on a wireless network without the user or applications being aware of the transition. Moving between access points typically results in some packet loss, although this loss is transparent to programs that use TCP.

ROM Readonly memory. A kind of nonvolatile storage. A data storage device that is manufactured with fixed contents. In general, ROM describes any storage system whose contents cannot be altered, such as a phonograph record or printed book. When used in reference to electronics and computers, ROM describes semiconductor integrated circuit memories, of which several types exist, and CD-ROM.

ROM is nonvolatile storage—it retains its contents even after power has been removed. ROM is often used to hold programs for embedded systems, as these usually have a fixed purpose. ROM is also used for storage of the *BIOS* (page 1153) in a computer. Contrast with *RAM* (page 1184).^{FOLDOC}

root directory The ancestor of all directories and the start of all absolute pathnames. The root directory has no name and is represented by / standing alone or at the left end of a pathname.

root filesystem The filesystem that is available when the system is brought up in single-user. This filesystem is always represented by /. You cannot unmount or mount the root filesystem. You can remount root to change its mount options.

root login Usually the username of *Superuser* (page 1191).

root (user) Another name for *Superuser* (page 1191).

root window Any place on the desktop not covered by a window, object, or panel.

rootkit Software that provides a user with **root** privileges while hiding its presence.

rotate When a file, such as a log file, gets indefinitely larger, you must keep it from taking up too much space on the disk. Because you might need to refer to the information in the log files in the near future, it is generally not a good idea to delete the contents of the file until it has aged. Instead you can periodically save the current log file under a new name and create a new, empty file as the current log file. You can keep a series of these files, renaming each as a new one is saved. You will then *rotate* the files. For example, you might remove **xyzlog.4**, **xyzlog.3**⇨**xyzlog.4**, **xyzlog.2**⇨**xyzlog.3**, **xyzlog.1**⇨ **xyzlog.2**, **xyzlog**⇨**xyzlog.1**, and create a new **xyzlog** file. By the time you remove **xyzlog.4**, it will not contain any information more recent than you want to remove.

router A device (often a computer) that is connected to more than one similar type of network to pass data between them. See *gateway* on page 1166.

RPC Remote procedure call. A call to a *procedure* (page 1182) that acts transparently across a network. The procedure itself is responsible for accessing and using the network. The RPC libraries make sure that network access is transparent to the application. RPC runs on top of TCP/IP or UDP/IP.

RSA A public key encryption (page 1127) technology that is based on the lack of an efficient way to factor very large numbers. Because of this lack, it takes an extraordinary amount of computer processing time and power to deduce an RSA key. The RSA algorithm is the de facto standard for data sent over the Internet.

run   To execute a program.

runlevel   Before the introduction of the systemd **init** daemon, runlevels specified the state of the system, including recovery (single-user) and multiuser. See Table 11-1 on page 448.

Samba   A free suite of programs that implement the Server Message Block (SMB) protocol. See *SMB* (page 1188).

schema   Within a GUI, a pattern that helps you see and interpret the information that is presented in a window, making it easier to understand new information that is presented using the same schema.

scroll   To move lines on a terminal or window up and down or left and right.

scrollbar   A *widget* (page 1197) found in graphical user interfaces that controls (scrolls) which part of a document is visible in the window. A window can have a horizontal scrollbar, a vertical scrollbar (more common), or both.FOLDOC

server   A powerful centralized computer (or program) designed to provide information to clients (smaller computers or programs) on request.

session   The lifetime of a process. For a desktop, it is the desktop session manager. For a character-based terminal, it is the user's login shell process. In KDE, it is launched by **kdeinit**. A session might also be the sequence of events between when you start using a program, such as an editor, and when you finish.

setgid   When you execute a file that has setgid (set group ID) permission, the process executing the file takes on the privileges of the group the file belongs to. The ls utility shows setgid permission as an **s** in the group's executable position. See also *setuid*.

setuid   When you execute a file that has setuid (set user ID) permission, the process executing the file takes on the privileges of the owner of the file. As an example, if you run a setuid program that removes all the files in a directory, you can remove files in any of the file owner's directories, even if you do not normally have permission to do so. When the program is owned by **root**, you can remove files in any directory that a user working with **root** privileges can remove files from. The ls utility shows setuid permission as an **s** in the owner's executable position. See also *setgid*.

sexillion   In the British system, 10^{36}. In the American system, this number is named *undecillion*. See also *large number* (page 1172).

SHA1   Secure Hash Algorithm 1. The SHA family is a set of cryptographic *hash* (page 1167) algorithms that were designed by the National Security Agency (NSA). The second member of this family is SHA1, a successor to *MD5* (page 1175). See also *cryptography* on page 1159.

SHA2   Secure Hash Algorithm 2. The third member of the SHA family (see *SHA1*), SHA2 is a set of four cryptographic hash functions named SHA-224, SHA-256, SHA-384, SHA-512 with digests that are 224, 256, 384, and 512 bits, respectively.

share	A filesystem hierarchy that is shared with another system using *SMB* (page 1188). Also *Windows share* (page 1197).
shared network topology	A network, such as Ethernet, in which each packet might be seen by systems other than its destination system. *Shared* means that the network bandwidth is shared by all users.
shell	A Linux system command processor. The three major shells are the *Bourne Again Shell* (page 1154), the *TC Shell* (page 1192), and the *Z Shell* (page 1198).
shell function	A series of commands that the shell stores for execution at a later time. Shell functions are like shell scripts but run more quickly because they are stored in the computer's main memory rather than in files. Also, a shell function is run in the environment of the shell that calls it (unlike a shell script, which is typically run in a subshell).
shell script	An ASCII file containing shell commands. Also shell program.
signal	A very brief message that the UNIX system can send to a process, apart from the process's standard input. Refer to "trap: Catches a Signal" on page 1025.
simple filename	A single filename containing no slashes (/). A simple filename is the simplest form of pathname. Also the last element of a pathname. Also *basename* (page 1153).
single-user system	A computer system that only one person can use at a time. Contrast with *multiuser system* (page 1177).
slider	A *widget* (page 1197) that allows a user to set a value by dragging an indicator along a line. Many sliders allow the user also to click on the line to move the indicator. Differs from a *scrollbar* (page 1187) in that moving the indicator does not change other parts of the display.
SMB	Server Message Block. Developed in the early 1980s by Intel, Microsoft, and IBM, SMB is a client/server protocol that is the native method of file and printer sharing for Windows. In addition, SMB can share serial ports and communications abstractions, such as named pipes and mail slots. SMB is similar to a remote procedure call (*RPC,* page 1186) that has been customized for filesystem access. Also *Microsoft Networking* or *CIFS* (page 1157).FOLDOC
SMP	Symmetric multiprocessing. Two or more similar processors connected via a high-bandwidth link and managed by one operating system, where each processor has equal access to I/O devices. The processors are treated more or less equally, with application programs able to run on any or all processors interchangeably, at the discretion of the operating system.FOLDOC
smiley	A character-based *glyph* (page 1166), typically used in email, that conveys an emotion. The characters :-) in a message portray a smiley face (look at it sideways). Because it can be difficult to tell when the writer of an electronic message is saying something in jest or in seriousness, email users often use :-) to indicate humor. The two original smileys, designed by Scott Fahlman, were :-) and :-(. Also *emoticon, smileys,* and *smilies.* For more information search on **smiley** on the Internet.

smilies	See *smiley*.
SMTP	Simple Mail Transfer Protocol. A protocol used to transfer electronic mail between computers. It is a server-to-server protocol, so other protocols are used to access the messages. The SMTP dialog usually happens in the background under the control of a message transport system such as **sendmail**.FOLDOC
snap (windows)	As you drag a window toward another window or edge of the workspace, it can move suddenly so that it is adjacent to the other window/edge. Thus the window *snaps* into position.
sneakernet	Using hand-carried magnetic media to transfer files between machines.
sniff	To monitor packets on a network. A system administrator can legitimately sniff packets and a malicious user can sniff packets to obtain information such as usernames and passwords. See also *packet sniffer* (page 1180).
SOCKS	A networking proxy protocol embodied in a SOCKS server, which performs the same functions as a *proxy gateway* (page 1183) or *proxy server* (page 1183). SOCKS works at the application level, requiring that an application be modified to work with the SOCKS protocol, whereas a *proxy* (page 1183) makes no demands on the application. SOCKSv4 does not support authentication or UDP proxy. SOCKSv5 supports a variety of authentication methods and UDP proxy.
sort	To put in a specified order, usually alphabetic or numeric.
SPACE character	A character that appears as the absence of a visible character. Even though you cannot see it, a SPACE is a printable character. It is represented by the ASCII code 32 (decimal). A SPACE character is considered a *blank* or *whitespace* (page 1196).
spam	Posting irrelevant or inappropriate messages to one or more Usenet newsgroups or mailing lists in deliberate or accidental violation of *netiquette* (page 1177). Also, sending large amounts of unsolicited email indiscriminately. This email usually promotes a product or service. Another common purpose of spam is to *phish* (page 1181). Spam is the electronic equivalent of junk mail. From the Monty Python "Spam" song.FOLDOC
sparse file	A file that is large but takes up little disk space. The data in a sparse file is not dense (thus its name). Examples of sparse files are core files and dbm files.
spawn	See *fork* on page 1165.
special character	A character that has a special meaning when it occurs in an ambiguous file reference or another type of regular expression, unless it is quoted. The special characters most commonly used with the shell are ✻ and ?. Also *metacharacter* (page 1175) and *wildcard*.
special file	See *device file* on page 1161.

spin box   In a GUI, a type of *text box* (page 1192) that holds a number you can change by typing over it or using the up and down arrows at the end of the box. Also *spinner*.

spinner   See *spin box*.

spoofing   See *IP spoofing* on page 1171.

spool   To place items in a queue, each waiting its turn for some action. Often used when speaking about printers. Also used to describe the queue.

SQL   Structured Query Language. A language that provides a user interface to relational database management systems (RDBMS). SQL, the de facto standard, is also an ISO and ANSI standard and is often embedded in other programming languages.^{FOLDOC}

square bracket A left square bracket ([) or a right square bracket (]). These special characters define character classes in ambiguous file references and other regular expressions.

standard error A file to which a program can send output. Usually only error messages are sent to this file. Unless you instruct the shell otherwise, it directs this output to the screen (that is, to the device file that represents the screen).

standard input A file from which a program can receive input. Unless you instruct the shell otherwise, it directs this input so that it comes from the keyboard (that is, from the device file that represents the keyboard).

standard output A file to which a program can send output. Unless you instruct the shell otherwise, it directs this output to the screen (that is, to the device file that represents the screen).

startup file A file that the login shell runs when you log in. The Bourne Again and Z Shells run **.profile**, and the TC Shell runs **.login**. The TC Shell also runs **.cshrc** whenever a new TC Shell or a subshell is invoked. The Z Shell runs an analogous file whose name is identified by the **ENV** variable.

status line   The bottom (usually the twenty-fourth) line of the terminal. The vim editor uses the status line to display information about what is happening during an editing session.

sticky bit   Originally, an access permission bit that caused an executable program to remain on the swap area of the disk. Today, Linux kernels do not use the sticky bit for this purpose but rather use it to control who can remove files from a directory. In this new capacity, the sticky bit is called the *restricted deletion flag*. If this bit is set on a directory, a file in the directory can be removed or renamed only by a user who is working with **root** privileges or by a user who has write permission for the directory *and* who owns the file or the directory.

streaming tape A tape that moves at a constant speed past the read/write heads rather than speeding up and slowing down, which can slow the process of writing to or reading from the tape. A proper blocking factor helps ensure that the tape device will be kept streaming.

streams   See *connection-oriented protocol* on page 1158.

string	A sequence of characters.
stylesheet	See *CSS* on page 1159.
subdirectory	A directory that is located within another directory. Every directory except the root directory is a subdirectory.
subnet	Subnetwork. A portion of a network, which might be a physically independent network segment, that shares a network address with other portions of the network and is distinguished by a subnet number. A subnet is to a network as a network is to an internet.FOLDOC
subnet address	The subnet portion of an IP address. In a subnetted network, the host portion of an IP address is split into a subnet portion and a host portion using a network mask (also subnet mask). See also *subnet number*.
subnet mask	See *network mask* on page 1178.
subnet number	The subnet portion of an IP address. In a subnetted network, the host portion of an IP address is split into a subnet portion and a host portion using a *network mask*. Also *subnet mask*. See also *subnet address*.
subpixel hinting	Similar to *anti-aliasing* (page 1151) but takes advantage of colors to do the anti-aliasing. Particularly useful on LCD screens.
subroutine	See *procedure* on page 1182.
subshell	A shell that is forked as a duplicate of its parent shell. When you run an executable file that contains a shell script by using its filename on the command line, the shell forks a subshell to run the script. Also, commands surrounded with parentheses are run in a subshell.
superblock	A block that contains control information for a filesystem. The superblock contains housekeeping information, such as the number of inodes in the filesystem and free list information.
superserver	The extended Internet services daemon.
Superuser	A user working with **root** privileges. This user has access to anything any other system user has access to and more. The system administrator must be able to become Superuser (work with **root** privileges) to establish new accounts, change passwords, and perform other administrative tasks. The username of Superuser is usually **root**. Also *root* or *root user*.
swap	The operating system moving a process from main memory to a disk, or vice versa. Swapping a process to the disk allows another process to begin or continue execution.
swap space	An area of a disk (that is, a swap file) used to store the portion of a process's memory that has been paged out. Under a virtual memory system, the amount of swap space—rather than the amount of physical memory—determines the maximum size of a single process and the maximum total size of all active processes. Also *swap area* or *swapping area*.FOLDOC

switch	See *network switch* on page 1178.
symbolic link	A directory entry that points to the pathname of another file. In most cases a symbolic link to a file can be used in the same ways a hard link can be used. Unlike a hard link, a symbolic link can span filesystems and can connect to a directory.
system administrator	The person responsible for the upkeep of the system. The system administrator has the ability to log in as **root** or use **sudo** to work with **root** privileges. See also *Superuser* on the previous page.
system console	See *console* on page 1158.
system mode	The designation for the state of the system while it is doing system work. Some examples are making system calls, running NFS and autofs, processing network traffic, and performing kernel operations on behalf of the system. Contrast with *user mode* (page 1195).
System V	One of the two major versions of the UNIX system.
TC Shell	tcsh. An enhanced but completely compatible version of the BSD UNIX C shell, csh.
TCP	Transmission Control Protocol. The most common transport layer protocol used on the Internet. This connection-oriented protocol is built on top of *IP* (page 1170) and is nearly always seen in the combination TCP/IP (TCP over *IP*). TCP adds reliable communication, sequencing, and flow control and provides full-duplex, process-to-process connections. *UDP* (page 1194), although connectionless, is the other protocol that runs on top of *IP*._{FOLDOC}
tera-	In the binary system, the prefix *tera-* multiplies by 2^{40} (1,099,511,627,776). Terabyte is a common use of this prefix. Abbreviated as *T*. See also *large number* on page 1172.
termcap	Terminal capability. On older systems, the **/etc/termcap** file contained a list of various types of terminals and their characteristics. *System V* replaced the function of this file with the *terminfo* system.
terminal	Differentiated from a *workstation* (page 1197) by its lack of intelligence, a terminal connects to a computer that runs Linux. A workstation runs Linux on itself.
terminfo	Terminal information. The **/usr/lib/terminfo** directory contains many subdirectories, each containing several files. Each of those files is named for and holds a summary of the functional characteristics of a particular terminal. Visually oriented textual programs, such as vim, use these files. An alternative to the **termcap** file.
text box	A GUI *widget* (page 1197) that allows a user to enter text.
theme	Defined as an implicit or recurrent idea, *theme* is used in a GUI to describe a look that is consistent for all elements of a desktop. Go to themes.freshmeat.net for examples.

thicknet   A type of coaxial cable (thick) used for an Ethernet network. Devices are attached to thicknet by tapping the cable at fixed points.

thinnet   A type of coaxial cable (thin) used for an Ethernet network. Thinnet cable is smaller in diameter and more flexible than *thicknet* cable. Each device is typically attached to two separate cable segments by using a T-shaped connector; one segment leads to the device ahead of it on the network and one to the device that follows it.

thread-safe   See *reentrant* on page 1184.

thumb   The movable button in the *scrollbar* (page 1187) that positions the image in the window. The size of the thumb reflects the amount of information in the buffer. Also *bubble*.

tick   A mark, usually in a *check box* (page 1156), that indicates a positive response. The mark can be a check mark (✔) or an **x**. Also *check mark* or *check*.

TIFF   Tagged Image File Format. A file format used for still-image bitmaps, stored in tagged fields. Application programs can use the tags to accept or ignore fields, depending on their capabilities.ᶠᴼᴸᴰᴼᶜ

tiled windows   An arrangement of windows such that no window overlaps another. The opposite of *cascading windows* (page 1155).

time to live   See *TTL* on the next page.

toggle   To switch between one of two positions. For example, the ftp **glob** command toggles the **glob** feature: Give the command once, and it turns the feature on or off; give the command again, and it sets the feature back to its original state.

token   A basic, grammatically indivisible unit of a language, such as a keyword, operator, or identifier.ᶠᴼᴸᴰᴼᶜ

token ring   A type of *LAN* (page 1172) in which computers are attached to a ring of cable. A token packet circulates continuously around the ring. A computer can transmit information only when it holds the token.

tooltip   A minicontext help system that a user activates by allowing the mouse pointer to *hover* (page 1168) over an object (such as those on a panel).

transient window   A dialog or other window that is displayed for only a short time.

Transmission Control Protocol   See *TCP* on page 1192.

Trojan horse   A program that does something destructive or disruptive to your system. Its action is not documented, and the system administrator would not approve of it if she were aware of it. See "Avoiding a Trojan Horse" on page 458.

The term *Trojan horse* was coined by MIT-hacker-turned-NSA-spook Dan Edwards. It refers to a malicious security-breaking program that is disguised as something benign, such as a directory lister, archive utility, game, or (in one notorious 1990 case on the Mac) a program to find and destroy viruses. Similar to *back door* (page 1152).ᶠᴼᴸᴰᴼᶜ

TTL   Time to live.

1. All DNS records specify how long they are good for—usually up to a week at most. This time is called the record's *time to live*. When a DNS server or an application stores this record in *cache* (page 1155), it decrements the TTL value and removes the record from cache when the value reaches zero. A DNS server passes a cached record to another server with the current (decremented) TTL guaranteeing the proper TTL, no matter how many servers the record passes through.

2. In the IP header, a field that indicates how many more hops the packet should be allowed to make before being discarded or returned.

TTY   Teletypewriter. The terminal device that UNIX was first run from. Today TTY refers to the screen (or window, in the case of a terminal emulator), keyboard, and mouse that are connected to a computer. This term appears in UNIX, and Linux has kept the term for the sake of consistency and tradition.

tunneling   Encapsulation of protocol A within packets carried by protocol B, such that A treats B as though it were a data link layer. Tunneling is used to transfer data between administrative domains that use a protocol not supported by the internet connecting those domains. It can also be used to encrypt data sent over a public internet, as when you use ssh to tunnel a protocol over the Internet.ᶠᴼᴸᴰᴼᶜ See also *VPN* (page 1196) and *port forwarding* (page 1182).

UDP   User Datagram Protocol. The Internet standard transport layer protocol that provides simple but unreliable datagram services. UDP is a *connectionless protocol* (page 1158) that, like *TCP* (page 1192), is layered on top of *IP* (page 1170).

Unlike *TCP*, UDP neither guarantees delivery nor requires a connection. As a result it is lightweight and efficient, but the application program must handle all error processing and retransmission. UDP is often used for sending time-sensitive data that is not particularly sensitive to minor loss, such as audio and video data.ᶠᴼᴸᴰᴼᶜ

UID   User ID. A number that the **passwd** database associates with a username.

undecillion   In the American system, 10^{36}. In the British system, this number is named *sexillion*. See also *large number* (page 1172).

unicast   A packet sent from one host to another host. Unicast means one source and one destination.

Unicode   A character encoding standard that was designed to cover all major modern written languages with each character having exactly one encoding and being represented by a fixed number of bits.

unmanaged window   See *ignored window* on page 1169.

URI   Universal Resource Identifier. The generic set of all names and addresses that are short strings referring to objects (typically on the Internet). The most common kinds of URIs are *URLs*._{FOLDOC}

URL   Uniform (was Universal) Resource Locator. A standard way of specifying the location of an object, typically a Web page, on the Internet. URLs are a subset of *URIs*.

usage message   A message displayed by a command when you call the command using incorrect command-line arguments.

User Datagram Protocol   See *UDP*.

User ID   See *UID*.

user interface   See *interface* on page 1170.

user mode   The designation for the state of the system while it is doing user work, such as running a user program (but not the system calls made by the program). Contrast with *system mode* (page 1192).

username   The name you enter in response to the **login:** prompt. Other users use your username when they send you mail or write to you. Each username has a corresponding user ID, which is the numeric identifier for the user. Both the username and the user ID are stored in the **passwd** database (**/etc/passwd** or the NIS equivalent). Also *login name*.

userspace   The part of memory (RAM) where applications reside. Code running in userspace cannot access hardware directly and cannot access memory allocated to other applications. Also *userland*. See the *KernelAnalysis-HOWTO*.

UTC   Coordinated Universal Time. UTC is the equivalent to the mean solar time at the prime meridian (0 degrees longitude). Also called Zulu time (Z stands for longitude zero) and GMT (Greenwich Mean Time).

UTF-8   An encoding that allows *Unicode* characters to be represented using sequences of 8-bit bytes.

utility   A program included as a standard part of Linux. You typically invoke a utility either by giving a command in response to a shell prompt or by calling it from within a shell script. Utilities are often referred to as commands. Contrast with *builtin (command)* (page 1155).

UUID
: Universally Unique Identifier. A 128-bit number that uniquely identifies an object on the Internet. Frequently used on Linux systems to identify an **ext2**, **ext3**, or **ext4** disk partition.

variable
: A name and an associated value. The shell allows you to create variables and use them in shell scripts. Also, the shell inherits several variables when it is invoked, and it maintains those and other variables while it is running. Some shell variables establish characteristics of the shell environment; others have values that reflect different aspects of your ongoing interaction with the shell.

viewport
: Same as *workspace* (page 1197).

virtual console
: Additional consoles, or displays, that you can view on the system, or physical, console.

virus
: A *cracker* (page 1159) program that searches out other programs and "infects" them by embedding a copy of itself in them, so that they become *Trojan horses* (page 1194). When these programs are executed, the embedded virus is executed as well, propagating the "infection," usually without the user's knowledge. By analogy with biological viruses.FOLDOC

VLAN
: Virtual LAN. A logical grouping of two or more nodes that are not necessarily on the same physical network segment but that share the same network number. A VLAN is often associated with switched Ethernet.FOLDOC

VPN
: Virtual private network. A private network that exists on a public network, such as the Internet. A VPN is a less expensive substitute for company-owned/leased lines and uses encryption to ensure privacy. A nice side effect is that you can send non-Internet protocols, such as AppleTalk, IPX, or *NetBIOS* (page 1177), over the VPN connection by *tunneling* (page 1194) them through the VPN IP stream.

W2K
: Windows 2000 Professional or Server.

W3C
: World Wide Web Consortium (www.w3.org).

WAN
: Wide area network. A network that interconnects *LANs* (page 1172) and *MANs* (page 1175), spanning a large geographic area (typically states or countries).

WAP
: Wireless access point. A bridge or router between wired and wireless networks. WAPs typically support some form of access control to prevent unauthorized clients from connecting to the network.

Web ring
: A collection of Web sites that provide information on a single topic or group of related topics. Each home page that is part of the Web ring has a series of links that let you go from site to site.

whitespace
: A collective name for SPACEs and/or TABs and occasionally NEWLINEs. Also *white space*.

wide area network
: See *WAN*.

widget	The basic objects of a graphical user interface. A button, *combo box* (page 1157), and *scrollbar* (page 1187) are examples of widgets.
wildcard	See *metacharacter* on page 1175.
Wi-Fi	Wireless Fidelity. A generic term that refers to any type of *802.11* (page 1150) wireless network.
window	On a display screen, a region that runs or is controlled by a particular program.
window manager	A program that controls how windows appear on a display screen and how you manipulate them.
Windows share	See *share* on page 1188.
WINS	Windows Internet Naming Service. The service responsible for mapping NetBIOS names to IP addresses. WINS has the same relationship to NetBIOS names that DNS has to Internet domain names.
WINS server	The program responsible for handling WINS requests. This program caches name information about hosts on a local network and resolves them to IP addresses.
wireless access point	See *WAP*.
word	A sequence of one or more nonblank characters separated from other words by TABs, SPACEs, or NEWLINEs. Used to refer to individual command-line arguments. In vim, a word is similar to a word in the English language—a string of one or more characters bounded by a punctuation mark, a numeral, a TAB, a SPACE, or a NEWLINE.
Work buffer	A location where vim stores text while it is being edited. The information in the Work buffer is not written to the file on the disk until you give the editor a command to write it.
working directory	The directory that you are associated with at any given time. The relative pathnames you use are *relative to* the working directory. Also *current directory*.
workspace	A subdivision of a *desktop* (page 1161) that occupies the entire display. See page 112.
workstation	A small computer, typically designed to fit in an office and be used by one person and usually equipped with a bit-mapped graphical display, keyboard, and mouse. Differentiated from a *terminal* (page 1192) by its intelligence. A workstation runs Linux on itself while a terminal connects to a computer that runs Linux.
worm	A program that propagates itself over a network, reproducing itself as it goes. Today the term has negative connotations, as it is assumed that only *crackers* (page 1159) write worms. Compare to *virus* (page 1196) and *Trojan horse* (page 1194). From **Tapeworm** in John Brunner's novel, *The Shockwave Rider*, Ballantine Books, 1990 (via XEROX PARC).^{FOLDOC}

WYSIWYG   What You See Is What You Get. A graphical application, such as a word processor, whose display is similar to its printed output.

X server   The X server is the part of the *X Window System* that runs the mouse, keyboard, and display. (The application program is the client.)

X terminal   A graphics terminal designed to run the X Window System.

X Window System   A design and set of tools for writing flexible, portable windowing applications, created jointly by researchers at MIT and several leading computer manufacturers.

XDMCP   X Display Manager Control Protocol. XDMCP allows the login server to accept requests from network displays. XDMCP is built into many X terminals.

xDSL   Different types of *DSL* (page 1163) are identified by a prefix, for example, ADSL, HDSL, SDSL, and VDSL.

Xinerama   An extension to X.org. Xinerama allows window managers and applications to use the two or more physical displays as one large virtual display. Refer to the Xinerama-HOWTO.

XML   Extensible Markup Language. A universal format for structured documents and data on the Web. Developed by *W3C* (page 1196), XML is a pared-down version of SGML. See www.w3.org/XML and www.w3.org/XML/1999/XML-in-10-points.

XSM   X Session Manager. This program allows you to create a session that includes certain applications. While the session is running, you can perform a *checkpoint* (saves the application state) or a *shutdown* (saves the state and exits from the session). When you log back in, you can load your session so that everything in your session is running just as it was when you logged off.

Z Shell   zsh. A *shell* (page 1188) that incorporates many of the features of the *Bourne Again Shell* (page 1154), *Korn Shell* (page 1172), and *TC Shell* (page 1192), as well as many original features.

Zulu time   See *UTC* on page 1195.

JumpStart Index

FILE TREE INDEX

A light page number such as 456 indicates a brief mention.

UTILITY INDEX

A light page number such as 456 indicates a brief mention. Page numbers followed by the letter t refer to tables.

Main Index

An italic page number such as *123* indicates a definition. A light page number such as 456 indicates a brief mention. Page numbers followed by the letter t refer to tables. Only variables that must always appear with a leading dollar sign are indexed with a leading dollar sign. Other variables are indexed without a leading dollar sign.

Symbols

^ in regular expressions 1108
^ quick substitution character 326
, (comma) operator 1037
; command separator 292
: (null) builtin 1018, 1027
:– substitutes default values for a variable 1017
:? displays an error message for a variable 1018
:= assigns default values for a variable 1017
! (NOT) Boolean operator 1040
!! re-executes the previous event 324
? in extended regular expressions 1112
? special character 245
. (dot) builtin 284, 1023
. directory 196, 515
. in regular expressions 1107
./ executes a file in the working directory 290, 309
.. directory 196, *515*
.jpg filename extension *1171*
` ...` *see* command, substitution
((...)) *see* arithmetic, evaluation

() command grouping 295
[] character class (regular expressions) 1107, *1156*
[] special characters 247
[...] *see* test utility
[[...]] builtin 1034
@ (origin, DNS) 869
@ in a network address 381
✻ in regular expressions 1108
✻ special character 246
/ (root) directory 36, 38, 192, 200
/ trailing within pathnames 36
/ within pathnames 36
\ escape character 146, 293, 303
\(in regular expressions 1110
\) in regular expressions 1110
& (AND) bitwise operator 1039
& background process 242, 318, *1153*
& command separator 293
& in replacement strings (regular expressions) 1111
&& (AND) Boolean operator 553, 1033, 1038–1039, 1040
# comment symbol 291, 980

C

X

DVD-ROM Warranty

Prentice Hall warrants the enclosed DVD-ROM to be free of defects in materials and faulty workmanship under normal use for a period of ninety days after purchase (when purchased new). If a defect is discovered in the DVD-ROM during this warranty period, a replacement DVD-ROM can be obtained at no charge by sending the defective DVD-ROM, postage prepaid, with proof of purchase to:

Disc Exchange
Prentice Hall
Pearson Technology Group
75 Arlington Street, Suite 300
Boston, MA 02116
Email: disc.exchange@pearson.com

Prentice Hall makes no warranty or representation, either expressed or implied, with respect to this software, its quality, performance, merchantability, or fitness for a particular purpose. In no event will Prentice Hall, its distributors, or dealers be liable for direct, indirect, special, incidental, or consequential damages arising out of the use or inability to use the software. The exclusion of implied warranties is not permitted in some states. Therefore, the above exclusion may not apply to you. This warranty provides you with specific legal rights. There may be other rights that you may have that vary from state to state. The contents of this DVD-ROM are intended for personal use only.

More information and updates are available at informit.com/ph

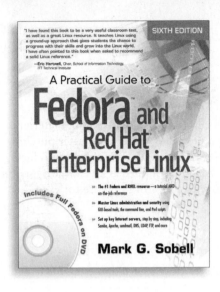

SIXTH EDITION

"I have found this book to be a very useful classroom text, as well as a great Linux resource. It teaches Linux using a ground-up approach that gives students the chance to progress with their skills and grow into the Linux world. I have often pointed to this book when asked to recommend a solid Linux reference."
—Eric Hartwell, Chair, School of Information Technology, ITT Technical Institute

A Practical Guide to

Fedora and Red Hat Enterprise Linux

» The #1 Fedora and RHEL resource—a tutorial AND on-the-job reference

» Master Linux administration and security using GUI-based tools, the command line, and Perl scripts

» Set up key Internet servers, step by step, including Samba, Apache, sendmail, DNS, LDAP, FTP, and more

Includes Full Fedora on DVD

Mark G. Sobell

FREE Online Edition

Your purchase of **A Practical Guide to Fedora™ and Red Hat® Enterprise Linux®, Sixth Edition,** includes access to a free online edition for 45 days through the Safari Books Online subscription service. Nearly every Prentice Hall book is available online through Safari Books Online, along with more than 5,000 other technical books and videos from publishers such as Addison-Wesley Professional, Cisco Press, Exam Cram, IBM Press, O'Reilly, Que, and Sams.

SAFARI BOOKS ONLINE allows you to search for a specific answer, cut and paste code, download chapters, and stay current with emerging technologies.

Activate your FREE Online Edition at
www.informit.com/safarifree

> **STEP 1:** Enter the coupon code: FCGAYYG.

> **STEP 2:** New Safari users, complete the brief registration form.
> Safari subscribers, just log in.

If you have difficulty registering on Safari or accessing the online edition,
please e-mail customer-service@safaribooksonline.com

Addison Wesley

Adobe Press

ALPHA

Cisco Press

FT Press
FINANCIAL TIMES

IBM Press

lynda.com

Microsoft Press

New Riders

O'REILLY

Peachpit Press

PRENTICE HALL

QUE

Redbooks

SAMS

SAS Publishing

Sun microsystems

WILEY